HUD's Affordable Housing Programs
Volume 1

Section 8 Occupancy Handbook

Housing Choice Voucher Program

Regulations and Comprehensive Index

2004 Edition

David Hoicka

Please Note: to be notified of updates, send an email with contact information to Books@HousingChoiceVoucher.info

- **Thank you for Cover Design to:**

Tchopshop Media, LLC
New Orleans, LA
www.tchopshop.com

- **Notes**:

The HUD Regulations, Forms, Handbooks, Guidebooks, and other documents referenced herein, are public documents published by HUD and the US Government Printing Office (GPO), and/or a local housing authority, respectively. These documents are generally available without cost by downloading from HUD's online internet document library at www.hudclips.org or www.hud.gov. Many are also available by calling HUD's clearinghouse. Some regulations are also available for free download from the GPO through www.access.gpo.gov. Housing Authority Plans such as Admin Plans and ACOPs are generally available through a local housing authority.

- **Disclaimers**:

This publication is authored by David Hoicka. All opinions, if there are any, in this publication are the sole opinions of the author, and not the opinions of the Housing Authority of New Orleans, HUD, NCHM, NAHRO, or any other entity.

Disclaimer of Warranty and Liability. The author and publisher, their dealers and distributors, make no representations or warranties with respect to the accuracy or completeness of the contents of this book and specifically disclaim any implied warranties of merchantability or fitness for a particular purpose. There are no warranties that extend beyond the descriptions contained here. This Handbook is sold "as is". No warranty may be created by any sales representatives or written sales materials. In no event shall the author, publisher, nor any dealers or distributors, be liable for any damages, direct, indirect, special, incidental, exemplary, or consequential damages arising out of use of this Handbook or use of the data contained herein, however caused, on any theory of liability, and whether or not the author has been advised of the possibility of such damage.

Legal Information Is Not Legal Advice. This Handbook provides information about the law designed to help users safely cope with their own legal needs. But legal information is not the same as legal advice -- the application of law to an individual's specific circumstances. Although the author goes to great lengths to make sure the information is accurate and useful, the author recommends you consult a lawyer if you want professional assurance that the enclosed information, and your interpretation of it, is appropriate to your particular situation.

Title: Section 8 Occupancy Handbook - Housing Choice
Voucher Program - Regulations and Comprehensive Index
Series: HUD's Affordable Housing Programs
Volume: Volume 1, 2004 Edition
Author: David Hoicka
Publisher: Aventine Press
ISBN: 1-59330-128-6

Table of Contents

1. Acknowledgments....4

2. Introduction....5

3. How to Use the Comprehensive Index....6

4. Statistics for Words appearing in the Comprehensive Index....6

5. Outline of Section 8 Housing Choice Voucher Occupancy Documents Indexed in this Handbook....7
   1) Section 8 Occupancy Forms
   2) HUD Section 8 Occupancy Manuals
   3) PIH Notices for Section 8 Occupancy
   4) Outline of Section 8 Administrative Plan ("Admin Plan")
   5) Note on Spelling in Source Documents

6. Code of Federal Regulations for the Section 8 HCV Program, Reprinted in this Handbook....11
   a) 24 CFR 5 General HUD Program Requirements
   b) 24 CFR 35 Lead-Based Paint in Leased Housing
   c) 24 CFR 982 Tenant-Based Assistance – Housing Choice Voucher Program

7. Comprehensive Index for the following HUD regulations....179
   a) HUD Regulations 24 CFR 5, 35, & 982
   b) HUD Forms
   c) HUD-7420.10G Housing Choice Voucher Program Guidebook
   d) PIH Notices
   e) Sample Administrative Plan

8. Useful Web Sites....569
   a) HUD – www.hud.gov, and HUDCLIPS – www.hudclips.org
   b) NAHRO – National Association of Housing and Redevelopment Officials – www.nahro.org
   c) PHADA – Public Housing Authorities Directors Association – www.phada.org
   d) NCHM – National Center for Housing Management – www.nchm.org

Acknowledgments

John Donne wrote, "No man is an island, entire of itself". Similarly, no book is an island, entire unto itself, but reflects the input and advice of many.

Thank you first to the many talented and hardworking people at the Housing Authority of New Orleans (HANO). There are so many, among whom are: Catherine Lamberg and Carmen Valenti, Lori Moon and Nadine Jarmon, Selarstean Mitchell, and Evelyn Stevens, Jacinta Hutchinson, Teresa Bonilla Schneider and Ken Cutno, and of course Bernice Campbell, Carole Williams, Terri Henderson, Rita Corass, Sharon Neely, Debra Thornton, Rhonda Broadway and Sandy Barnes, and Naomi Roberts, Djuana Glapion, Myrna Leufroy and Cristell Washington, and of course many more.

And at the National Center for Housing Management in Arlington VA, Mike DeGrandis, Mark Alper, John Zeichel, and the whole gang.

Introduction

The Section 8 Housing Choice Voucher Program ("HCVP") is HUD's largest national affordable housing program, serving more than 1.8 million families, and with a budget authority currently more than $13 billion annually. Housing Choice Vouchers are administered in all 50 states by more than 2600 Housing Authorities, non-profits, and governmental agencies.

The goal of this Handbook is to simplify Section 8 management, and save time for the busy Section 8 Administrator and Affordable Housing Professional. This Handbook's Comprehensive Index includes about 6,300 entries, and over 120,000 references, organizing access to the main sources of regulatory and management control of Section 8 HCVP Programs:

- Statutory and Federal Regulations, most notably 24 CFR 5 & 982,
- HUD Forms,
- HUD-7420.10G Guidebook,
- PIH Notices, and
- Administrative Plans for local agency rules and procedures.

All of these sources of regulation and management decisions are indexed.

The primary regulations, 24 CFRs 5, 35 & 982 (about 170 pages), are reprinted in the front portion of this Handbook, a few pages after this Introduction. The main HUD occupancy forms used by Section 8 Administrators (about 230 pages), PIH Notices (about 520 pages), and the HUD-7420.10G Guidebook (about 450) pages, are available for free from HUDCLIPS. All are completely indexed in this Handbook together with a typical Section 8 Admin Plan (about 140 pages), based on the Admin Plan used by the Housing Authority of New Orleans – for a total of about 1,500 pages indexed.

In this Comprehensive Index, the total number of times a word or phrase appears is on the first line of each index entry. Then the index references are listed individually for each regulatory source shown above.

The author welcomes suggestions and input to improve this Handbook, and for future Handbooks. For example, new words to add to the index, additional or changed forms, new regulations, or any other thoughts and suggestions the reader may have.

If you would like a Custom Index for your Admin Plan, or have other suggestions for indexing and facilitating HUD Affordable Housing, please contact the author (email below).

Please send all suggestions and comments to the author at the email below

David Hoicka
New Orleans, LA.
DavidHoicka@HousingChoiceVoucher.info

How to Use The Comprehensive Index

Following is a sample Index entry:

18 YEARS..31
24 CFR 5: .216; .230 (3); .609 (2); .611;
HUD-50058Instr: p2; p14; p15 (3); p17; p25 (2); p26; p27;
HUD-9886: p1 (2);
7420.10G Gbk: 5-15 Ex 5-2; 5-18 (2); 5-30 (2); 12 13 Ex 12-1;
PIH Notices: 01-15 Impr Integ Hbk (5);
Admin Plan: s2p1

- "31" refers to the number of times "18 years" appears in the texts indexed.
- References are organized according to type of source: 24 CFR (e.g. 24 CFR 5.230), HUD Forms, the HUD 7420.10G Guidebook, PIH Notices, and a typical Admin Plan.
- "(2)", "(3)", and such numbers underlined in the indices, means the indexed word or phrase occurs (2) or (3), (or more) times on that page.

Statistics for Words Appearing in the Index

Words indexed in Section 8 source documents	over 500,000
Pages indexed in source documents	about 1500
Index entry words & phrases in this Index	about 6,300
Total index references to source documents	over 120,000

Certain common words appear on nearly every page of the source documents, appearing at the frequency shown in the following table. Such common individual words were excluded from the printed index. However, where they form a part of an important phrase - e.g. in "family absence", "family breakup", "family characteristic", "family composition", "family income", "single family", "single family house", "working family", etc., these words are included in the indexed.

Common Word	Frequency		Common Word	Frequency
PHA	6,019		owner	2,288
family	5,359		HUD	2,199
program	3,095		rent	2,162
must	3,088		income	1,916
may	2,860		public	1,639
unit	2,745		families	1,569
assistance	2,665		voucher	1,545

HUD Documents Indexed

The following Section 8 Occupancy HUD forms, manuals and notices are indexed in this Handbook and Comprehensive Index. The originals of the HUD documents are available for free download from HUDCLIPS, www.hudclips.org.

1. Section 8 Occupancy Forms Indexed:

a) HUD-50058 Family Report (34 pages)
b) HUD-50058 Instruction Booklet (95 pages)
c) HUD-52517 Request for Tenancy Approval
d) HUD 52580 Inspection Checklist (7 pages)
e) HUD-52580-A Inspection Form (20 pages)
f) HUD-52641 Housing Assistance Payments Contract (HAP Contract)
g) HUD-52641-a Tenancy Addendum
h) HUD-52646 Voucher
i) HUD-52648 Section 8 Management Assessment Program (SEMAP) Certification
j) HUD-52665 Family Portability Information
k) HUD-52667 Allowances for Tenant-Furnished Utilities and Other Services
l) HUD-903 Housing Discrimination Complaint
m) HUD-903.1 Housing Discrimination Information Form
n) HUD-9886 Authorization for the Release of Information / Privacy Act Notice

2. HUD Section 8 Occupancy Manuals Indexed:

a) HUD-7420.10G Housing Choice Voucher Program Guidebook (about 450 pages) Not reproduced here; included in Comprehensive Index. Available for free download from HUDCLIPS.

3. PIH Notices Indexed for Section 8 Occupancy:

PIH #	Topic of PIH Notice Indexed	Applicability
03-23	FY2003 Omnibus Appropriations Act - HCVP	S8 SS8 Fin
03-20	HCVP Homeownership Reporting	S8
03-12	Rent Reasonableness	S8
03-11	Obtaining FBI Criminal Records	S8 PHOcc
03-05	Military in PersianGulf	S8 SS8 Multi PHOcc
02-27	SEMAP Guidance	S8 Fin
02-22	HCVP and LIHTC Rents	S8
02-21	Relocation Vouchers - Demo, Disposition, Conversion	S8 PHOcc Fin Mod
02-20	HCVP-Area Exception Payments	S8 Fin
02-15	HCVP and LIHTC Nondiscrimination	S8

02-14	HCVP-Voluntary Reduction in Baseline Units	S8 Fin
02-07	HCVP Admin Fees	S8 Fin
02-06	HCVP ACC Reserves	S8 Fin
02-03	HCVP and Assisted Living	S8
02-01	Section 504 and Assisted Housing - All	16
01-43	PIC and 50058 Reporting	S8 PHOcc Fin
01-41	HCVP Enhanced and Regular Vouchers for Conversions	S8 SS8 Multi Fin
01-40	Military - Operation Enduring Freedom and Assisted Housing	S8 SS8 Multi PHOcc
01-33	HCVP Conversion of Certificates to Vouchers	S8 Fin
01-29	Financial Mgt	S8 Mod Rehab SS8 Multi Fin
01-27	Immigration - Freely Assoc States and Assisted Housing	S8 SS8 Multi PHOcc
01-20	HCVP Relocation Vouchers - Demo, Disposition, Conversion	S8 PHOcc Fin Mod
01-15	Improving Income Integrity	S8 SS8 PHOcc
01-15 Impr Integ Hbk	Improving Income Integrity Guidebook	S8 SS8 PHOcc
01-11	Implementation of Revised 50058	S8 SS8 PHOcc Fin
01-10	HCVP Enhanced Vouchers for Term/Expir PBA & Mod Rehab	S8 SS8 Multi Fin
01-06	SEMAP Guidance	S8 SS8 Fin
01-02	HCVP and LIHTC Nondiscrimination	S8
01-01	HCVP FMRs and Payment Standards	S8 Fin
00-53	Implementation of Revised 50058	S8 SS8 Fin
00-49	HCVP and Lead-Based Paint	S8 SS8 Fin
00-46	HCVP Area Exception Payment Standards	S8 SS8 Fin
00-45	Section 504 and Assisted Housing - correction to 99-52	All
00-41	HCVP and Assisted Living	S8 SS8 Fin
00-34	SEMAP and Internet	S8 SS8 Fin
00-31	Renewal - Designation, Demo, Conversions, Homeownership - Special Application Center	All
00-28	HCVP Admin Fees	S8 Fin
00-27	HCVP Relocation Vouchers - Demo, Disposition, Conversion	S8 PHOcc Fin Mod
00-24	SEMAP Implementation Update	S8 SS8 Fin

00-23	Lead-Based Paint in Tenant-Based Assistance Programs	S8 SS8
00-14	Cancellation of Reports for Assisted Housing Programs	S8 SS8 Multi Fin
00-11	Cooperation Agreements for Economic Self-Sufficiency with TANF Agencies	S8 SS8 PHOcc Fin
00-09	HCVP Enhanced, Preservation and Regular Vouchers for Housing Conversion Actions	S8 SS8 Multi Fin
00-01	Census Taker Income Exclusion	S8 SS8 Multi PHOcc
99-52	Application of Section 504 to Assisted Housing	All
99-30	Renewal - Designation, Demo, Conversions, Homeownership - Special Application Center	All
99-11	Fire Safety in Assisted Housing	S8 SS8 Multi PHOcc
98-66	Census Taker Income Exclusion	S8 SS8 Multi PHOcc
96-65	Payment Requirements for Portability Vouchers	S8 Fin
95-48	ADA-and Section 504 and Assisted Housing	All
95-48 Tech Asst	ADA Title II Technical Assistance Manual	All

4. Outline of Section 8 Administrative Plan Indexed

The Section 8 Administrative Plan for the Housing Authority of New Orleans is included in the Index. This Admin Plan is similar to many other Admin Plans around the United States. Following are the Chapter Headings:

1. Statement of Policies and Objectives
2. Eligibility for Admission
3. Applying for Admission
4. Managing the Waiting List
5. Subsidy Standards
6. Total Tenant Payment
7. Verification Procedures
8. Voucher Issuance and Briefings
9. Approval of Tenancy and Contract Expiration
10. Housing Quality Standards and Inspections
11. Rent and Payment Standards
12. Re-Certifications
13. Program Moves and Portability
14. Contract Terminations
15. Denial or Termination of Assistance
16. Owner Prohibitions and Restrictions
17. Owner or Family Debts

18. Complaints and Appeals
19. Special Housing Types
20. Program Integrity
21. Section 8 Management Assessment Program
22. Homeownership
23. Moderate Rehabilitation
24. Project Based Assistance
25. Other Special Programs

5. Note on Spelling in Source Documents

The original source documents come with a wide variety of formats, spellings, and punctuations.

For consistency, spelling irregularities, hyphens, etc. in the original sources are retained as-is in the Index. Thus, e.g. the following words, all with about the same meaning, are indexed separately:

- "childcare",
- "child care", and
- "child-care"

For thoroughness, please check all word and punctuation forms, including apostrophes, hyphens, etc.

Custom Indices. If you would like a Custom Index for your Admin Plan, or have other suggestions for indexing Hud Affordable Housing, please contact the author David Hoicka at:

DavidHoicka@HousingChoiceVoucher.info.

Codes of Federal Regulations
Most Applicable to Section 8: 24 CFR 5 & 982

TITLE24--HOUSING AND URBAN DEVELOPMENT 18
PART 5--GENERAL HUD PROGRAM REQUIREMENTS; WAIVERS--Table of Contents} 18
[CITE: 24 CFR 5.100] 18
Subpart A--Generally Applicable Definitions and Federal Requirements; Waivers 18
Sec. 5.100 Definitions. 18
105 Other Federal requirements. 20
107 Audit requirements for non-profit organizations. 20
110 Waivers 20
Subpart B--Disclosure and Verification of Social Security Numbers and Employer Identification Numbers; Procedures for Obtaining Income Information 21
Sec. 5.210 Purpose, applicability, and Federal preemption. 21
Sec. 5.212 Compliance with the Privacy Act and other requirements. 21
Sec. 5.214 Definitions. 21
Disclosure and Verification of Social Security Numbers and Employer Identification Numbers for Applicants and Participants in Certain HUD Programs 23
Sec. 5.216 Disclosure and verification of Social Security and Employer Identification Numbers. ... 23
Sec. 5.218 Penalties for failing to disclose and verify Social Security and Employer Identification Numbers. 26
Procedures for Obtaining Income Information About Applicants and Participants 26
Sec. 5.230 Consent by assistance applicants and participants. 26
Sec. 5.232 Penalties for failing to sign consent forms. 27
Sec. 5.234 Requests for information from SWICAs and Federal agencies; restrictions on use. 27
Sec. 5.236 Procedures for termination, denial, suspension, or reduction of assistance based on information obtained from a SWICA or Federal agency. 28
Sec. 5.238 Criminal and civil penalties. 29
Sec. 5.240 Family disclosure of income information to the responsible entity and verification. 29
Subpart C--Pet Ownership for the Elderly or Persons With Disabilities 29
Sec. 5.300 Purpose. 29
Sec. 5.303 Exclusion for animals that assist persons with disabilities. 29
Sec. 5.306 Definitions. 30
Sec. 5.309 Prohibition against discrimination. 31
Sec. 5.312 Notice to tenants. 31
Sec. 5.315 Content of pet rules: General requirements. 31
318 Discretionary pet rules. 32
Sec. 5.321 Lease provisions. 35
Sec. 5.324 Implementation of lease provisions. 35
Sec. 5.327 Nuisance or threat to health or safety. 35
Pet Ownership Requirements for Housing Programs 35
Sec. 5.350 Mandatory pet rules for housing programs. 35
Sec. 5.353 Housing programs: Procedure for development of pet rules. 36
Sec. 5.356 Housing programs: Pet rule violation procedures. 37

Sec. 5.359 Housing programs: Rejection of units by applicants for tenancy. 38
Sec. 5.360 Housing programs: Additional lease provisions. 38
Sec. 5.363 Housing programs: Protection of the pet. 39
Pet Ownership Requirements for Public Housing Programs 39
Sec. 5.380 Public housing programs: Procedure for development of pet rules. 39
Subpart D--Definitions for Section 8 and Public Housing Assistance Under the United States Housing Act of 1937 40
Sec. 5.400 Applicability. 40
Sec. 5.403 Definitions. 40
Subpart E--Restrictions on Assistance to Noncitizens 41
Sec. 5.500 Applicability. 41
Sec. 5.502 Requirements concerning documents. 41
Sec. 5.504 Definitions. 42
Sec. 5.506 General provisions. 43
Sec. 5.508 Submission of evidence of citizenship or eligible immigration status. 43
Sec. 5.510 Documents of eligible immigration status. 46
Sec. 5.512 Verification of eligible immigration status. 46
Sec. 5.514 Delay, denial, reduction or termination of assistance. 47
Sec. 5.516 Availability of preservation assistance to mixed families and other families. 50
Sec. 5.518 Types of preservation assistance available to mixed families and other families. 51
Sec. 5.520 Proration of assistance. 53
Sec. 5.522 Prohibition of assistance to noncitizen students. 55
Sec. 5.524 Compliance with nondiscrimination requirements. 55
Sec. 5.526 Protection from liability for responsible entities and State and local government agencies and officials. 55
Sec. 5.528 Liability of ineligible tenants for reimbursement of benefits. 55
Subpart F--Section 8 and Public Housing, and Other HUD Assisted Housing Serving Persons with Disabilities: Family Income and Family Payment; Occupancy Requirements for Section 8 Project-Based Assistance 56
Sec. 5.601 Purpose and applicability. 56
Sec. 5.603 Definitions. 56
Family Income 59
Sec. 5.609 Annual income. 59
Sec. 5.611 Adjusted income. 61
Sec. 5.613 Public housing program and Section 8 tenant-based assistance program: PHA cooperation with welfare agency. 61
Sec. 5.615 Public housing program and Section 8 tenant-based assistance program: How welfare benefit reduction affects family income. 62
Sec. 5.617 Self-sufficiency incentives for persons with disabilities--Disallowance of increase in annual income. 63
Family Payment 65
Sec. 5.628 Total tenant payment. 65
Sec. 5.630 Minimum rent. 65
Sec. 5.632 Utility reimbursements. 66
Sec. 5.634 Tenant rent. 67

Section 8 Project-Based Assistance: Occupancy Requirements 67
Sec. 5.653 Section 8 project-based assistance programs: Admission--Income-eligibility and income-targeting. 67
Sec. 5.655 Section 8 project-based assistance programs: Owner preferences in selection for a project or unit. 68
Sec. 5.657 Section 8 project-based assistance programs: Reexamination of family income and composition. 69
Sec. 5.659 Family information and verification. 70
Sec. 5.661 Section 8 project-based assistance programs: Approval for police or other security personnel to live in project. 70
Subpart G--Physical Condition Standards and Inspection Requirements 72
Sec. 5.701 Applicability. 72
Sec. 5.703 Physical condition standards for HUD housing that is decent, safe, sanitary and in good repair (DSS/GR). 72
Sec. 5.705 Uniform physical inspection requirements. 73
Subpart H--Uniform Financial Reporting Standards 73
Sec. 5.801 Uniform financial reporting standards. 73
Subpart I--Preventing Crime in Federally Assisted Housing--Denying Admission and Terminating Tenancy for Criminal Activity or Alcohol Abuse 75
Sec. 5.850 Which subsidized housing is covered by this subpart? 75
Sec. 5.851 What authority do I have to screen applicants and to evict tenants? 76
Sec. 5.852 What discretion do I have in screening and eviction actions? 76
Sec. 5.853 Definitions. 76
Denying Admissions 76
Sec. 5.854 When must I prohibit admission of individuals who have engaged in drug-related criminal activity? 76
Sec. 5.855 When am I specifically authorized to prohibit admission of individuals who have engaged in criminal activity? 76
Sec. 5.856 When must I prohibit admission of sex offenders? 76
Sec. 5.857 When must I prohibit admission of alcohol abusers? 76
Terminating Tenancy 76
Sec. 5.858 What authority do I have to evict drug criminals? 76
Sec. 5.859 When am I specifically authorized to evict other criminals? 76
Sec. 5.860 When am I specifically authorized to evict alcohol abusers? 77
Sec. 5.861 What evidence of criminal activity must I have to evict? 77
Subpart J--Access to Criminal Records and Information 77
Sec. 5.901 To what criminal records and searches does this subpart apply? 77
Sec. 5.902 Definitions. 77
Sec. 5.903 What special authority is there to obtain access to criminal records? 78
Sec. 5.905 What special authority is there to obtain access to sex offender registration information? 81
PART 35--LEAD-BASED PAINT POISONING PREVENTION IN CERTAIN RESIDENTIAL STRUCTURES 83
[Cite 24 CFR 35] 83
Subpart M--Tenant-Based Rental Assistance 83
Sec. 35.1200 Purpose and applicability. 83

Sec. 35.1210 Notices and pamphlet. 84
Sec. 35.1215 Activities at initial and periodic inspection. 84
Sec. 35.1220 Ongoing lead-based paint maintenance activities. 84
Sec. 35.1225 Child with an environmental intervention blood lead level. 84
PART 982--SECTION 8 TENANT BASED ASSISTANCE: HOUSING CHOICE VOUCHER PROGRAM}
.... 86
.[CITE: 24 CFR 982] 86
Subpart A--General Information 89
Sec. 982.1 Programs: purpose and structure. 89
Sec. 982.2 Applicability. 90
Sec. 982.3 HUD. 90
Sec. 982.4 Definitions. 90
Sec. 982.5 Notices required by this part. 95
Subpart B--HUD Requirements and PHA Plan for Administration of Program 95
Sec. 982.51 PHA authority to administer program. 95
Sec. 982.52 HUD requirements. 95
Sec. 982.53 Equal opportunity requirements. 95
Sec. 982.54 Administrative plan. 96
Subpart C--Funding and PHA Application for Funding 97
Sec. 982.101 Allocation of funding. 97
Sec. 982.102 Allocation of budget authority for renewal of expiring consolidated ACC funding increments. 97
Sec. 982.103 PHA application for funding. 100
Sec. 982.104 HUD review of application. 100
Subpart D--Annual Contributions Contract and PHA Administration of Program 100
Sec. 982.151 Annual contributions contract. 101
Sec. 982.152 Administrative fee. 101
Sec. 982.153 PHA responsibilities. 102
Sec. 982.154 ACC reserve account. 102
Sec. 982.155 Administrative fee reserve. 102
Sec. 982.156 Depositary for program funds. 103
Sec. 982.157 Budget and expenditure. 103
Sec. 982.158 Program accounts and records. 103
Sec. 982.159 Audit requirements. 104
Sec. 982.160 HUD determination to administer a local program. 104
Sec. 982.161 Conflict of interest. 105
Sec. 982.162 Use of HUD-required contracts and other forms. 105
Sec. 982.163 Fraud recoveries. 105
Subpart E--Admission to Tenant-Based Program 105
Sec. 982.201 Eligibility and targeting. 105
Sec. 982.202 How applicants are selected: General requirements. 108
Sec. 982.203 Special admission (non-waiting list): Assistance targeted by HUD. 108
Sec. 982.204 Waiting list: Administration of waiting list. 109
Sec. 982.205 Waiting list: Different programs. 109
Sec. 982.206 Waiting list: Opening and closing; public notice. 110

Sec. 982.207 Waiting list: Local preferences in admission to program. 111
Subpart F [Reserved] 112
Subpart G--Leasing a Unit 112
Sec. 982.301 Information when family is selected. 112
Sec. 982.302 Issuance of voucher; Requesting PHA approval of assisted tenancy. 113
Sec. 982.303 Term of voucher. 113
Sec. 982.304 Illegal discrimination: PHA assistance to family. 114
Sec. 982.305 PHA approval of assisted tenancy. 114
Sec. 982.306 PHA disapproval of owner. 115
Sec. 982.307 Tenant screening. 116
Sec. 982.308 Lease and tenancy. 117
Sec. 982.309 Term of assisted tenancy. 118
Sec. 982.310 Owner termination of tenancy. 118
Sec. 982.311 When assistance is paid. 120
Sec. 982.312 Absence from unit. 121
Sec. 982.313 Security deposit: Amounts owed by tenant. 121
Sec. 982.314 Move with continued tenant-based assistance. 122
Sec. 982.315 Family break-up. 122
Sec. 982.316 Live-in aide. 122
Sec. 982.317 Lease-purchase agreements. 123
Subpart H--Where Family Can Live and Move 123
Sec. 982.351 Overview. 123
Sec. 982.352 Eligible housing. 123
Sec. 982.353 Where family can lease a unit with tenant-based assistance. 125
Sec. 982.355 Portability: Administration by receiving PHA. 125
Subpart I--Dwelling Unit: Housing Quality Standards, Subsidy Standards, Inspection and Maintenance 127
Sec. 982.401 Housing quality standards (HQS). 127
Sec. 982.402 Subsidy standards. 130
Sec. 982.403 Terminating HAP contract when unit is too small. 131
Sec. 982.404 Maintenance: Owner and family responsibility; PHA remedies. 132
Sec. 982.405 PHA initial and periodic unit inspection. 133
Sec. 982.406 Enforcement of HQS. 133
Subpart J--Housing Assistance Payments Contract and Owner Responsibility 133
Sec. 982.451 Housing assistance payments contract. 133
Sec. 982.452 Owner responsibilities. 134
Sec. 982.453 Owner breach of contract. 134
Sec. 982.454 Termination of HAP contract: Insufficient funding. 135
Sec. 982.455 Automatic termination of HAP contract. 135
Sec. 982.456 Third parties. 135
Subpart K--Rent and Housing Assistance Payment 135
Sec. 982.501 Overview. 135
Sec. 982.502 Conversion to voucher program. 136
Sec. 982.503 Voucher tenancy: Payment standard amount and schedule. 136
Sec. 982.504 Voucher tenancy: Payment standard for family in restructured subsidized multifamily project. 139

Sec. 982.505 Voucher tenancy: How to calculate housing assistance payment. 140
Sec. 982.506 Negotiating rent to owner. 141
Sec. 982.507 Rent to owner: Reasonable rent. 141
Sec. 982.508 Maximum family share at initial occupancy. 142
Sec. 982.509 Rent to owner: Effect of rent control. 142
Sec. 982.510 Other fees and charges. 142
Sec. 982.514 Distribution of housing assistance payment. 142
Sec. 982.515 Family share: Family responsibility. 142
Sec. 982.516 Family income and composition: Regular and interim examinations. 142
Sec. 982.517 Utility allowance schedule. 143
Sec. 982.518 Regular tenancy: How to calculate housing assistance payment. 145
Sec. 982.519 Regular tenancy: Annual adjustment of rent to owner. 145
Sec. 982.520 Regular tenancy: Special adjustment of rent to owner. 145
Sec. 982.521 Rent to owner in subsidized project. 146
Subpart L--Family Obligations; Denial and Termination of Assistance 146
Sec. 982.551 Obligations of participant. 146
Sec. 982.552 PHA denial or termination of assistance for family. 147
Sec. 982.553 Denial of admission and termination of assistance for criminals and alcohol abusers. 149
Sec. 982.554 Informal review for applicant. 151
Sec. 982.555 Informal hearing for participant. 152
Subpart M--Special Housing Types 154
Sec. 982.601 Overview. 154
Single Room Occupancy (SRO) 154
Sec. 982.602 SRO: Who may reside in an SRO? 154
Sec. 982.603 SRO: Lease and HAP contract. 154
Sec. 982.604 SRO: Voucher housing assistance payment. 155
Sec. 982.605 SRO: Housing quality standards. 155
Congregate Housing 156
Sec. 982.606 Congregate housing: Who may reside in congregate housing. 156
Sec. 982.607 Congregate housing: Lease and HAP contract. 156
Sec. 982.608 Congregate housing: Voucher housing assistance payment. 156
Sec. 982.609 Congregate housing: Housing quality standards. 156
Group Home 157
Sec. 982.610 Group home: Who may reside in a group home. 157
Sec. 982.611 Group home: Lease and HAP contract. 157
Sec. 982.612 Group home: State approval of group home. 157
Sec. 982.613 Group home: Rent and voucher housing assistance payment. 157
Sec. 982.614 Group home: Housing quality standards. 158
Shared Housing 159
Sec. 982.615 Shared housing: Occupancy. 159
Sec. 982.616 Shared housing: Lease and HAP contract. 159
Sec. 982.617 Shared housing: Rent and voucher housing assistance payment. 159
Sec. 982.618 Shared housing: Housing quality standards. 160
Cooperative 160
Sec. 982.619 Cooperative housing. 160

Manufactured Home 161
Sec. 982.620 Manufactured home: Applicability of requirements. 161
Sec. 982.621 Manufactured home: Housing quality standards. 162
Manufactured Home Space Rental 162
Sec. 982.622 Manufactured home space rental: Rent to owner. 162
Sec. 982.623 Manufactured home space rental: Housing assistance payment. 162
Sec. 982.624 Manufactured home space rental: Utility allowance schedule. 163
Homeownership Option 163
Sec. 982.625 Homeownership option: General. 163
Sec. 982.626 Homeownership option: Initial requirements. 165
Sec. 982.627 Homeownership option: Eligibility requirements for families. 165
Sec. 982.628 Homeownership option: Eligible units. 167
Sec. 982.629 Homeownership option: Additional PHA requirements for family search and purchase. 168
Sec. 982.630 Homeownership option: Homeownership counseling. 168
Sec. 982.631 Homeownership option: Home inspections, contract of sale, and PHA disapproval of seller. 169
Sec. 982.632 Homeownership option: Financing purchase of home; affordability of purchase. 169
Sec. 982.633 Homeownership option: Continued assistance requirements; Family obligations. 170
Sec. 982.634 Homeownership option: Maximum term of homeownership assistance. 171
Sec. 982.635 Homeownership option: Amount and distribution of monthly homeownership assistance payment. 172
Sec. 982.636 Homeownership option: Portability. 173
Sec. 982.637 Homeownership option: Move with continued tenant-based assistance. 174
Sec. 982.638 Homeownership option: Denial or termination of assistance for family. 174
Sec. 982.639 Homeownership option: Administrative fees. 175
Sec. 982.641 Homeownership option: Applicability of other requirements. 175
Sec. 982.642 Homeownership option: Pilot program for homeownership assistance for disabled families. 176
Sec. 982.643 Homeownership option: Downpayment assistance grants. 177

{[Code of Federal Regulations]
[Title 24, Volume 1]
[Revised as of April 1, 2003]
From the U.S. Government Printing Office
via GPO Access
[CITE: 24CFR5.100]

TITLE24--HOUSING AND URBAN DEVELOPMENT

PART 5--GENERAL HUD PROGRAM REQUIREMENTS; WAIVERS--Table of Contents}

[CITE: 24 CFR 5.100]

Subpart A--Generally Applicable Definitions and Federal Requirements; Waivers

Sec. 5.100 Definitions.

The following definitions apply to this part and also in other regulations, as noted:

1937 Act means the United States Housing Act of 1937 (42 U.S.C. 1437 et seq.)

ADA means the Americans with Disabilities Act of 1990 (42 U.S.C. 12101 et seq.).

ALJ means an administrative law judge appointed to HUD pursuant to 5 U.S.C. 3105 or detailed to HUD pursuant to 5 U.S.C. 3344.

Covered person, for purposes of 24 CFR 5, subpart I, and parts 966 and 982, means a tenant, any member of the tenant's household, a guest or another person under the tenant's control.

Department means the Department of Housing and Urban Development.

Drug means a controlled substance as defined in section 102 of the Controlled Substances Act (21 U.S.C. 802).

Drug-related criminal activity means the illegal manufacture, sale, distribution, or use of a drug, or the possession of a drug with intent to manufacture, sell, distribute or use the drug.

Elderly Person means an individual who is at least 62 years of age.

Fair Housing Act means title VIII of the Civil Rights Act of 1968, as amended by the Fair Housing Amendments Act of 1988 (42 U.S.C. 3601 et seq.).

Fair Market Rent (FMR) means the rent that would be required to be paid in the particular housing market area in order to obtain privately owned, decent, safe and sanitary rental housing of modest (non-luxury) nature with suitable amenities. This Fair Market Rent includes utilities (except telephone). Separate Fair Market Rents will be established by HUD for dwelling units of varying sizes (number of bedrooms) and will be published in the Federal Register in accordance with part 888 of this title.

Federally assisted housing (for purposes of subparts I and J of this part) means housing assisted under any of the following programs:

(1) Public housing;

(2) Housing receiving project-based or tenant-based assistance under Section 8 of the U.S. Housing Act of 1937 (42 U.S.C. 1437f);

(3) Housing that is assisted under section 202 of the Housing Act of 1959, as amended by section 801 of the National Affordable Housing Act (12 U.S.C. 1701q);

(4) Housing that is assisted under section 202 of the Housing Act of 1959, as such section existed before the enactment of the National Affordable Housing Act;

(5) Housing that is assisted under section 811 of the National Affordable Housing Act (42 U.S.C. 8013);

(6) Housing financed by a loan or mortgage insured under section 221(d)(3) of the National Housing Act (12 U.S.C. 1715l(d)(3)) that bears interest at a

rate determined under the proviso of section 221(d)(5) of such Act (12 U.S.C. 1715l(d)(5));

(7) Housing insured, assisted, or held by HUD or by a State or local agency under section 236 of the National Housing Act (12 U.S.C. 1715z- 1); or

(8) Housing assisted by the Rural Development Administration under section 514 or section 515 of the Housing Act of 1949 (42 U.S.C. 1483, 1484).

General Counsel means the General Counsel of HUD.

Grantee means the person or legal entity to which a grant is awarded and that is accountable for the use of the funds provided.

Guest, only for purposes of 24 CFR part 5, subparts A and I, and parts 882, 960, 966, and 982, means a person temporarily staying in the unit with the consent of a tenant or other member of the household who has express or implied authority to so consent on behalf of the tenant. The requirements of parts 966 and 982 apply to a guest as so defined.

Household, for purposes of 24 CFR part 5, subpart I, and parts, 960, 966, 882, and 982, means the family and PHA-approved live-in aide.

HUD means the same as Department.

MSA means a metropolitan statistical area.

NAHA means the Cranston-Gonzalez National Affordable Housing Act (42 U.S.C. 12701 et seq.).

NEPA means the National Environmental Policy Act of 1969 (42 U.S.C. 4321).

NOFA means Notice of Funding Availability.

OMB means the Office of Management and Budget.

Organizational Unit means the jurisdictional area of each Assistant Secretary, and each office head or field administrator reporting directly to the Secretary.

Other person under the tenant's control, for the purposes of the definition of covered person and for parts 5, 882, 966, and 982 means that the person, although not staying as a guest (as defined in this section) in the unit, is, or was at the time of the activity in question, on the premises (as premises is defined in this section) because of an invitation from the tenant or other member of the household who has express or implied authority to so consent on behalf of the tenant. Absent evidence to the contrary, a person temporarily and infrequently on the premises solely for legitimate commercial purposes is not under the tenant's control.

Premises, for purposes of 24 CFR part 5, subpart I, and parts 960 and 966, means the building or complex or development in which the public or assisted housing dwelling unit is located, including common areas and grounds.

Public housing means housing assisted under the 1937 Act, other than under Section 8. ``Public housing'' includes dwelling units in a mixed finance project that are assisted by a PHA with capital or operating assistance.

Public Housing Agency (PHA) means any State, county, municipality, or other governmental entity or public body, or agency or instrumentality of these entities, that is authorized to engage or assist in the development or operation of low-income housing under the 1937 Act.

Responsible entity means:

(1) For the public housing program, the Section 8 tenant-based assistance program (part 982 of this title), and the Section 8 project- based certificate or voucher programs (part 983 of this title), and the Section 8 moderate rehabilitation program (part 882 of this title), responsible entity means the PHA administering the program under an ACC with HUD;

(2) For all other Section 8 programs, responsible entity means the Section 8 project owner.

Section 8 means section 8 of the United States Housing Act of 1937 (42 U.S.C. 1437f).

Secretary means the Secretary of Housing and Urban Development.

URA means the Uniform Relocation Assistance and Real Property Acquisition Policies Act of 1970 (42 U.S.C. 4201-4655).

Violent criminal activity means any criminal activity that has as one of its elements the use, attempted use, or threatened use of physical force substantial enough to cause, or be reasonably likely to cause, serious bodily injury or property damage.
{61 FR 5202, Feb. 9, 1996, as amended at 63 FR 23853, Apr. 30, 1998; 65 FR 16715, Mar. 29, 2000; 66 FR 28791, May 24, 2001}

105 Other Federal requirements.

The following Federal requirements apply as noted in the respective program regulations:

(a) Nondiscrimination and equal opportunity. The Fair Housing Act (42 U.S.C. 3601-19) and implementing regulations at 24 CFR part 100 et seq.; Executive Order 11063, as amended by Executive Order 12259 (3 CFR, 1959-1963 Comp., p. 652 and 3 CFR, 1980 Comp., p. 307) (Equal Opportunity in Housing Programs) and implementing regulations at 24 CFR part 107; title VI of the Civil Rights Act of 1964 (42 U.S.C. 2000d-2000d-4) (Nondiscrimination in Federally Assisted Programs) and implementing regulations at 24 CFR part 1; the Age Discrimination Act of 1975 (42 U.S.C. 6101-6107) and implementing regulations at 24 CFR part 146; section 504 of the Rehabilitation Act of 1973 (29 U.S.C. 794) and implementing regulations at part 8 of this title; title II of the Americans with Disabilities Act, 42 U.S.C. 12101 et seq.; 24 CFR part 8; section 3 of the Housing and Urban Development Act of 1968 (12 U.S.C. 1701u) and implementing regulations at 24 CFR part 135; Executive Order 11246, as amended by Executive Orders 11375, 11478, 12086, and 12107 (3 CFR, 1964-1965 Comp., p. 339; 3 CFR, 1966-1970 Comp., p. 684; 3 CFR, 1966-1970 Comp., p. 803; 3 CFR, 1978 Comp., p. 230; and 3 CFR, 1978 Comp., p. 264, respectively) (Equal Employment Opportunity Programs) and implementing regulations at 41 CFR chapter 60; Executive Order 11625, as amended by Executive Order 12007 (3 CFR, 1971-1975 Comp., p. 616 and 3 CFR, 1977 Comp., p. 139) (Minority Business Enterprises); Executive Order 12432 (3 CFR, 1983 Comp., p. 198) (Minority Business Enterprise Development); and Executive Order 12138, as amended by Executive Order 12608 (3 CFR, 1977 Comp., p. 393 and 3 CFR, 1987 Comp., p. 245) (Women's Business Enterprise).

(b) Disclosure requirements. The disclosure requirements and prohibitions of 31 U.S.C. 1352 and implementing regulations at 24 CFR part 87; and the requirements for funding competitions established by the Department of Housing and Urban Development Reform Act of 1989 (42 U.S.C. 3531 et seq.).

(c) Debarred, suspended or ineligible contractors. The prohibitions at 24 CFR part 24 on the use of debarred, suspended or ineligible contractors.

(d) Drug-Free Workplace. The Drug-Free Workplace Act of 1988 (41 U.S.C. 701 et seq.) and HUD's implementing regulations at 24 CFR part 24.
{61 FR 5202, Feb. 9, 1996, as amended at 65 FR 16715, Mar. 29, 2000}

107 Audit requirements for non-profit organizations.

Non-profit organizations subject to regulations in the part 200 and part 800 series of title 24 of the CFR shall comply with the audit requirements of revised OMB Circular A-133, ``Audits of States, Local Governments, and Non-profit Organizations'' (see 24 CFR 84.26). For HUD programs, a non-profit organization is the mortgagor or owner (as these terms are defined in the regulations in the part 200 and part 800 series) and not a related or affiliated organization or entity.
{62 FR 61617, Nov. 18, 1997}

110 Waivers.

Upon determination of good cause, the Secretary may, subject to statutory limitations, waive any provision of this title

and delegate this authority in accordance with section 106 of the Department of Housing and Urban Development Reform Act of 1989 (42 U.S.C. 3535(q)).

Subpart B--Disclosure and Verification of Social Security Numbers and Employer Identification Numbers; Procedures for Obtaining Income Information

Sec. 5.210 Purpose, applicability, and Federal preemption.

Authority: 42 U.S.C. 3535(d), 3543, 3544, and 11901 et seq.

Source: 61 FR 11113, Mar. 18, 1996, unless otherwise noted.

(a) Purpose. This subpart B requires applicants for and participants in covered HUD programs to disclose, and submit documentation to verify, their Social Security Numbers (SSNs). This subpart B also enables HUD and PHAs to obtain income information about applicants and participants in the covered programs through computer matches with State Wage Information Collection Agencies (SWICAs) and Federal agencies, in order to verify an applicant's or participant's eligibility for or level of assistance. The purpose of this subpart B is to enable HUD to decrease the incidence of fraud, waste, and abuse in the covered programs.

(b) Applicability. (1) This subpart B applies to mortgage and loan insurance and coinsurance and housing assistance programs contained in chapter II, subchapter B, and chapters VIII and IX of this title.

(2) The information covered by consent forms described in this subpart involves income information from SWICAs, and wages, net earnings from self-employment, payments of retirement income, and unearned income as referenced at 26 U.S.C. 6103. In addition, consent forms may authorize the collection of other information from applicants and participants to determine eligibility or level of benefits.

(c) Federal preemption. This subpart B preempts any State law, including restrictions and penalties, that governs the collection and use of income information to the extent State law is inconsistent with this subpart.

{61 FR 11113, Mar. 18, 1996, as amended at 65 FR 16715, Mar. 29, 2000}

Sec. 5.212 Compliance with the Privacy Act and other requirements.

(a) Compliance with the Privacy Act. The collection, maintenance, use, and dissemination of SSNs, EINs, any information derived from SSNs and Employer Identification Numbers (EINs), and income information under this subpart shall be conducted, to the extent applicable, in compliance with the Privacy Act (5 U.S.C. 552a) and all other provisions of Federal, State, and local law.

(b) Privacy Act notice. All assistance applicants shall be provided with a Privacy Act notice at the time of application. All participants shall be provided with a Privacy Act notice at each annual income recertification.

Sec. 5.214 Definitions.

In addition to the definitions in Sec. 5.100, the following definitions apply to this subpart B:

Assistance applicant. Except as excluded pursuant to 42 U.S.C. 3543(b) and 3544(a)(2), this term means the following:

(1) For any program under 24 CFR parts 215, 221, 236, 290, or 891, or any program under Section 8 of the 1937 Act: A family or individual that seeks rental assistance under the program.

(2) For the public housing program: A family or individual that seeks admission to the program.

(3) For any program under 24 CFR part 235: A homeowner or cooperative member seeking homeownership assistance

(including where the individual seeks to assume an existing mortgage).

Computer match means the automated comparison of data bases containing records about individuals.

Computer matching agreement means the agreement that describes the responsibilities and obligations of the parties participating in a computer match.

Consent form means any consent form approved by HUD to be signed by assistance applicants and participants for the purpose of obtaining income information from employers and SWICAs; return information from the Social Security Administration (including wages, net earnings from self-employment, and payments of retirement income), as referenced at 26 U.S.C. 6103(l)(7)(A); and return information for unearned income from the Internal Revenue Service, as referenced at 26 U.S.C. 6103(l)(7)(B). The consent forms expire after a certain time and may authorize the collection of other information from assistance applicants or participants to determine eligibility or level of benefits as provided in Secs. 813.109, 913.109, and 950.315 of this title.

Employer Identification Number (EIN) means the nine-digit taxpayer identifying number that is assigned to an individual, trust, estate, partnership, association, company, or corporation pursuant to sections 6011(b), or corresponding provisions of prior law, or 6109 of the Internal Revenue Code.

Entity applicant. (1) Except as excluded pursuant to 42 U.S.C. 3543(b), 3544(a)(2), and paragraph (2) of this definition, this term means a partnership, corporation, or any other association or entity, other than an individual owner applicant, that seeks to participate as a private owner in any of the following:

(i) The project-based assistance programs under Section 8 of the 1937 Act;

(ii) The programs in 24 CFR parts 215, 221, or 236; or

(iii) The other mortgage and loan insurance programs in 24 CFR parts 201 through 267, except that the term ``entity applicant'' does not include a mortgagee or lender.

(2) The term does not include a public entity, such as a PHA, IHA, or State Housing Finance Agency.

Federal agency means a department of the executive branch of the Federal Government.

Income information means information relating to an individual's income, including:

(1) All employment income information known to current or previous employers or other income sources that HUD or the processing entity determines is necessary for purposes of determining an assistance applicant's or participant's eligibility for, or level of assistance in, a covered program;

(2) All information about wages, as defined in the State's unemployment compensation law, including any Social Security Number; name of the employee; quarterly wages of the employee; and the name, full address, telephone number, and, when known, Employer Identification Number of an employer reporting wages under a State unemployment compensation law;

(3) With respect to unemployment compensation:

(i) Whether an individual is receiving, has received, or has applied for unemployment compensation;

(ii) The amount of unemployment compensation the individual is receiving or is entitled to receive; and

(iii) The period with respect to which the individual actually received such compensation;

(4) Unearned IRS income and self-employment, wages and retirement income as described in the Internal Revenue Code, 26 U.S.C. 6103(l)(7); and

(5) Wage, social security (Title II), and supplemental security income (Title XVI) data obtaied from the Social Security Administration.

Individual owner applicant. Except as excluded pursuant to 42 U.S.C. 3543(b), 3544(a)(2), or paragraph (2) of this definition, this term means:

(1) An individual who seeks to participate as a private owner in any of:

(i) The project-based assistance programs under Section 8 of the 1937 Act; or

(ii) The programs in 24 CFR parts 215, 221, 235 (without homeownership assistance), or 236, including where the individual seeks to assume an existing mortgage; or

(2) An individual who:

(i) Either: (A) Applies for a mortgage or loan insured or coinsured under any of the programs referred to in paragraph (1)(iii) of the definition of ``entity applicant'' in this section; or

(B) Seeks to assume an existing mortgage or loan; and

(ii) Intends to hold the mortgaged property in his or her individual right.

IRS means the Internal Revenue Service.

Owner means the person or entity (or employee of an owner) that leases an assisted dwelling unit to an eligible family and includes, when applicable, a mortgagee.

Participant. Except as excluded pursuant to 42 U.S.C. 3543(b) and 3544(a)(2), this term has the following meaning:

(1) For any program under 24 CFR part 891, or Section 8 of the 1937 Act: A family receiving rental assistance under the program;

(2) For the public housing program: A family or individual that is assisted under the program;

(3) For 24 CFR parts 215, 221, 236, and 290: A tenant or qualified tenant under any of the programs; and

(4) For 24 CFR part 235: A homeowner or a cooperative member receiving homeownership assistance.

Processing entity means the person or entity that, under any of the programs covered under this subpart B, is responsible for making eligibility and related determinations and an income reexamination. (In the Section 8 and public housing programs, the ``processing entity'' is the ``responsible entity'' as defined in Sec. 5.100.)

Social Security Number (SSN) means the nine-digit number that is assigned to a person by the Social Security Administration and that identifies the record of the person's earnings reported to the Social Security Administration. The term does not include a number with a letter as a suffix that is used to identify an auxiliary beneficiary.

SSA means the Social Security Administration.

State Wage Information Collection Agency (SWICA) means the State agency, including any Indian tribal agency, receiving quarterly wage reports from employers in the State, or an alternative system that has been determined by the Secretary of Labor to be as effective and timely in providing employment-related income and eligibility information.

{61 FR 11113, Mar. 18, 1996, as amended at 63 FR 23853, Apr. 30, 1998; 65 FR 16715, Mar. 29, 2000}

Disclosure and Verification of Social Security Numbers and Employer Identification Numbers for Applicants and Participants in Certain HUD Programs

Sec. 5.216 Disclosure and verification of Social Security and Employer Identification Numbers.

(a) Disclosure: assistance applicants. Each assistance applicant must submit the following information to the processing entity when the assistant applicant's eligibility under the program involved is being determined:

(1)(i) The complete and accurate SSN assigned to the assistant applicant and to each member of the assistant applicant's household who is at least six years of age; and

(ii) The documentation referred to in paragraph (f)(1) of this section to verify each such SSN; or

(2) If the assistance applicant or any member of the assistance applicant's household who is at least six years of age has not been assigned an SSN, a certification executed by the individual involved that meets the requirements of paragraph (j) of this section.

(b) Disclosure: individual owner applicants. Each individual owner applicant must submit the following information to the processing entity when the individual owner applicant's eligibility under the program involved is being determined:

(1)(i) The complete and accurate SSNs assigned to the individual owner applicant and to each member of the individual owner applicant's household who will be obligated to pay the debt evidenced by the mortgage or loan documents; and

(ii) The documentation referred to in paragraph (f)(1) of this section to verify the SSNs; or

(2) If any person referred to in paragraph (b)(1)(i) of this section has not been assigned an SSN, a certification executed by the individual involved that meets the requirements of paragraph (j) of this section.

(c) Disclosure: certain officials of entity applicants. As explained more fully in HUD administrative instructions, each officer, director, principal stockholder, or other official of an entity applicant must submit the following information to the processing entity when the entity applicant's eligibility under the program involved is being determined:

(1) The complete and accurate SSN assigned to each such individual; and

(2) The documentation referred to in paragraph (f)(1) of this section to verify each SSN.

(d) Disclosure: participants--(1) Initial disclosure. Each participant whose initial determination of eligibility under the program involved was begun before November 6, 1989, must submit the following information to the processing entity at the next regularly scheduled income reexamination for the program involved:

(i)(A) The complete and accurate SSN assigned to the participant and to each member of the participant's family who is at least six years of age; and

(B) The documentation referred to in paragraph (f)(1) of this section to verify each such SSN; or

(ii) If the participant or any member of the participant's household who is at least six years of age has not been assigned an SSN, a certification executed by the individual(s) involved that meets the requirements of paragraph (j) of this section.

(2) Subsequent disclosure. Once a participant has disclosed and verified every SSN, or submitted any certification that an SSN has not been assigned, as provided by paragraph (a) of this section (for an assistance applicant) or paragraph (d)(1) (for a preexisting participant) of this section, the following rules apply:

(i) If the participant's household adds a new member who is at least six years of age, the participant must submit to the processing entity, at the next interim or regularly scheduled income reexamination that includes the new members:

(A) The complete and accurate SSNs assigned to each new member and the documentation referred to in paragraph (f)(1) of this section to verify the SSNs for each new member; or

(B) If the new member has not been assigned an SSN, a certification executed by the individual involved that meets the requirements of paragraph (j) of this section.

(ii) If the participant or any member of the participant's household who is at least six years of age obtains a previously undisclosed SSN, or has been assigned a new SSN, the participant must submit the following to the processing entity at the next regularly scheduled income reexamination:

(A) The complete and accurate SSN assigned to the participant or household member involved; and

(B) The documentation referred to in paragraph (f)(1) of this section to verify the SSN of each such individual.

(iii) Additional SSN disclosure and

verification requirements, including the nature of the disclosure and the verification required and the time and manner for making the disclosure and verification, may be specified in administrative instructions by:

(A) HUD; and

(B) In the case of the public housing program or the programs under parts 882 and 887 of this title, the PHA.

(e) Disclosure: entity applicants. Each entity applicant must submit the following information to the processing entity when the entity applicant's eligibility under the program involved is being determined:

(1) Any complete and accurate EIN assigned to the entity applicant; and

(2) The documentation referred to in paragraph (f)(2) of this section to verify the EIN.

(f) Required documentation--(1) Social Security Numbers. The documentation necessary to verify the SSN of an individual who is required to disclose his or her SSN under paragraphs (a) through (d) of this section is a valid SSN card issued by the SSA, or such other evidence of the SSN as HUD and, where applicable, the PHA may prescribe in administrative instructions.

(2) Employer Identification Numbers. The documentation necessary to verify any EIN of an entity applicant that is required to disclose its EIN under paragraph (e) of this section is the official, written communication from the IRS assigning the EIN to the entity applicant, or such other evidence of the EIN as HUD may prescribe in administrative instructions.

(g) Special documentation rules for assistance applicants and participants--(1) Certification of inability to meet documentation requirements. If an individual who is required to disclose his or her SSN under paragraph (a) (assistance applicants) of this section or paragraph (d) (participants) of this section is able to disclose the SSN, but cannot meet the documentation requirements of paragraph (f)(1) of this section, the assistance applicant or participant must submit to the processing entity the individual's SSN and a certification executed by the individual that the SSN submitted has been assigned to the individual, but that acceptable documentation to verify the SSN cannot be provided.

(2) Acceptance or certification by processing entity. Except as provided by paragraph (h) of this section, the processing entity must accept the certification referred to in paragraph (g)(1) of this section and continue to process the assistant applicant's or participant's eligibility to participate in the program involved.

(3) Effect on assistance applicants. If the processing entity determines that the assistance applicant is otherwise eligible to participate in the program, the assistance applicant may not become a participant in the program, unless it submits to the processing entity the documentation required under paragraph (f)(1) of this section within the time period specified in paragraph (g)(5) of this section. During such period, the assistance applicant will retain the position that it occupied in the program at the time the determination of eligibility was made, including its place on any waiting list maintained for the program, if applicable.

(4) Effect on participants. If the processing entity determines that the participant otherwise continues to be eligible to participate in the program, participation will continue, provided that the participant submits to the processing entity the documentation required under paragraph (f)(1) of this section within the time period specified in paragraph (g)(5) of this section.

(5) Time for submitting documentation. The time period referred to in paragraphs (g)(4) and (5) of this section is 60 calendar days from the date on which the certification referred to in paragraph (g)(1) of this section is executed, except that the processing entity may, in its discretion, extend this period for up to an additional 60 days if the individual is at least 62 years of age and is unable to submit the required documentation within the initial 60-day period.

(h) Rejection of documentation or certification. The processing entity may reject documentation referred to in paragraph

(f) of this section, or a certification provided under paragraphs (a)(2), (b)(2), (d), or (g)(1) of this section, only for such reasons as HUD and the PHA may prescribe in applicable administrative instructions.

(i) Information on SSNs and EINs. (1) Information regarding SSNs and SSN cards may be obtained by contacting the local SSA Office or consulting the SSA regulations at 20 CFR chapter III (see, particularly, part 422).

(2) Information regarding EINs may be obtained by contacting the local office of the IRS or consulting the appropriate regulations for the IRS.

(j) Form and manner of certifications. The certifications referred to in paragraphs (a)(2), (b)(2), (d), and (g)(1) of this section must be in the form and manner that HUD and the PHA prescribe in applicable administrative instructions. If an individual who is required to execute a certification is less than 18 years of age, the certification must be executed by his or her parent or guardian or, in accordance with administrative instructions, by the individual or another person.

(Approved by the Office of Management and Budget under control number 2502-0204)

Sec. 5.218 Penalties for failing to disclose and verify Social Security and Employer Identification Numbers.

(a) Denial of eligibility: assistance applicants and individual owner applicants. The processing entity must deny the eligibility of an assistance applicant or individual owner applicant in accordance with the provisions governing the program involved, if the assistance or individual owner applicant does not meet the applicable SSN disclosure, documentation and verification, and certification requirements specified in Sec. 5.216.

(b) Denial of eligibility: entity applicants. The processing entity must deny the eligibility of an entity applicant in accordance with the provisions governing the program involved; if:

(1) The entity applicant does not meet the applicable EIN disclosure and verification requirements specified in Sec. 5.216; or

(2) Any of the officials of the entity applicant referred to in Sec. 5.216(c) does not meet the applicable SSN disclosure, and documentation and verification requirements specified in Sec. 5.216.

(c) Termination of assistance or tenancy: participants. The processing entity must terminate the assistance or tenancy, or both, of a participant, in accordance with the provisions governing the program involved, if the participant does not meet the applicable SSN disclosure, documentation and verification, and certification requirements specified in Sec. 5.216.

(d) Cross reference. Individuals should consult the regulations and administrative instructions for the programs covered under this subpart B for further information on the use of SSNs and EINs in determinations regarding eligibility.

Procedures for Obtaining Income Information About Applicants and Participants

Sec. 5.230 Consent by assistance applicants and participants.

(a) Required consent by assistance applicants and participants. Each member of the family of an assistance applicant or participant who is at least 18 years of age, and each family head and spouse regardless of age, shall sign one or more consent forms.

(b) Consent authorization--(1) To whom and when. The assistance applicant shall submit the signed consent forms to the processing entity when eligibility under a covered program is being determined. A participant shall sign and submit consent forms at the next regularly scheduled income reexamination. Assistance applicants and participants shall be responsible for the signing and submitting of consent forms by each applicable family member.

(2) Subsequent consent forms--special

cases. Participants are required to sign and submit consent forms at the next interim or regularly scheduled income reexamination under the following circumstances:

(i) When any person 18 years or older becomes a member of the family;

(ii) When a member of the family turns 18 years of age; and

(iii) As required by HUD or the PHA in administrative instructions.

(c) Consent form--contents. The consent form required by this section shall contain, at a minimum, the following:

(1) A provision authorizing HUD and PHAs to obtain from SWICAs any information or materials necessary to complete or verify the application for participation and to maintain continued assistance under a covered program; and

(2) A provision authorizing HUD, PHAs, or the owner responsible for determining eligibility for or the level of assistance to verify with previous or current employers income information pertinent to the assistance applicant's or participant's eligibility for or level of assistance under a covered program;

(3) A provision authorizing HUD to request income return information from the IRS and the SSA for the sole purpose of verifying income information pertinent to the assistance applicant's or participant's eligibility or level of benefits; and

(4) A statement that the authorization to release the information requested by the consent form expires 15 months after the date the consent form is signed.

Sec. 5.232 Penalties for failing to sign consent forms.

(a) Denial or termination of benefits. In accordance with the provisions governing the program involved, if the assistance applicant or participant, or any member of the assistance applicant's or participant's family, does not sign and submit the consent form as required in Sec. 5.230, then:

(1) The processing entity shall deny assistance to and admission of an assistance applicant;

(2) Assistance to, and the tenancy of, a participant may be terminated.

(b) Cross references. Individuals should consult the regulations and administrative instructions for the programs covered under this subpart B for further information on the use of income information in determinations regarding eligibility.

Sec. 5.234 Requests for information from SWICAs and Federal agencies; restrictions on use.

(a) Information available from SWICAs and Federal agencies--to whom and what. Income information will generally be obtained through computer matching agreements between HUD and a SWICA or Federal agency, or between a PHA and a SWICA, as described in paragraph (c) of this section. Certification that the applicable assistance applicants and participants have signed appropriate consent forms and have received the necessary Privacy Act notice is required, as follows:

(1) When HUD requests the computer match, the processing entity shall certify to HUD; and

(2) When the PHA requests the computer match, the PHA shall certify to the SWICA.

(b) Restrictions on use of information. The restrictions of 42 U.S.C. 3544(c)(2)(A) apply to the use by HUD or a PHA of income information obtained from a SWICA. The restrictions of 42 U.S.C. 3544(c)(2)(A) and of 26 U.S.C. 6103(l)(7) apply to the use by HUD or a PHA of income information obtained from the IRS or SSA.

(c) Computer matching agreements. Computer matching agreements shall specify the purpose and the legal authority for the match, and shall include a description of the records to be matched, a statement regarding disposition of information generated through the match, a description of the administrative and technical safeguards to be used in protecting the information obtained through the match, a description of the use of records, the restrictions on duplication and

redisclosure, a certification, and the amount that will be charged for processing a request. (Approved by the Office of Management and Budget under control number 2508-0008)

Sec. 5.236 Procedures for termination, denial, suspension, or reduction of assistance based on information obtained from a SWICA or Federal agency.

(a) Termination, denial, suspension, or reduction of assistance. The provisions of 42 U.S.C. 3544(c)(2)(B) and (C) shall govern the termination, denial, suspension, or reduction of benefits for an assistance applicant or participant based on income information obtained from a SWICA or a Federal agency. Procedures necessary to comply with these provisions are provided in paragraph (b) of this section.

(b) Procedures for independent verification. (1) Any determination or redetermination of family income verified in accordance with this paragraph must be carried out in accordance with the requirements and procedures applicable to the individual covered program. Independent verification of information obtained from a SWICA or a Federal agency may be:

(i) By HUD;

(ii) In the case of the public housing program, by a PHA; or

(iii) In the case of any Section 8 program, by a PHA acting as contract administrator under an ACC.

(2) Upon receiving income information from a SWICA or a Federal agency, HUD or, when applicable, the PHA shall compare the information with the information about a family's income that was:

(i) Provided by the assistance applicant or participant to the PHA; or

(ii) Obtained by the owner (or mortgagee, as applicable) from the assistance applicant or participant or from his or her employer.

(3) When the income information reveals an employer or other income source that was not disclosed by the assistance applicant or participant, or when the income information differs substantially from the information received from the assistance applicant or participant or from his or her employer:

(i) HUD or, as applicable or directed by HUD, the PHA shall request the undisclosed employer or other income source to furnish any information necessary to establish an assistance applicant's or participant's eligibility for or level of assistance in a covered program. This information shall be furnished in writing, as directed to:

(A) HUD, with respect to programs under parts 215, 221, 235, 236, or 290 of this title;

(B) The responsible entity (as defined in Sec. 5.100) in the case of the public housing program or any Section 8 program.

(C) The owner or mortgagee, as applicable, with respect to the rent supplement, Section 221(d)(3) BMIR, Section 235 homeownership assistance, or Section 236 programs.

(ii) HUD or the PHA may verify the income information directly with an assistance applicant or participant. Such verification procedures shall not include any disclosure of income information prohibited under paragraph (b)(6) of this section.

(4) HUD and the PHA shall not be required to pursue these verification procedures when the sums of money at issue are too small to raise an inference of fraud or justify the expense of independent verification and the procedures related to termination, denial, suspension, or reduction of assistance.

(5) Based on the income information received from a SWICA or Federal agency, HUD or the PHA, as appropriate, may inform an owner (or mortgagee) that an assistance applicant's or participant's eligibility for or level of assistance is uncertain and needs to be verified. The owner (or mortgagee) shall then confirm the assistance applicant's or participant's income information by checking the accuracy of the information with the employer or other income source, or directly with the family.

(6) Nondisclosure of Income information. Neither HUD nor the PHA may disclose

income information obtained from a SWICA directly to an owner (unless a PHA is the owner). Disclosure of income information obtained from the SSA or IRS is restricted under 26 U.S.C. Sec. 6103(l)(7) and 42 U.S.C. 3544.

(c) Opportunity to contest. HUD, the PHA, or the owner (or mortgagee, as applicable) shall promptly notify any assistance applicant or participant in writing of any adverse findings made on the basis of the information verified in accordance with paragraph (b) of this section. The assistance applicant or participant may contest the findings in the same manner as applies to other information and findings relating to eligibility factors under the applicable program. Termination, denial, suspension, or reduction of assistance shall be carried out in accordance with requirements and procedures applicable to the individual covered program, and shall not occur until the expiration of any notice period provided by the statute or regulations governing the program.

{61 FR 11113, Mar. 18, 1996, as amended at 65 FR 16715, Mar. 29, 2000}

Sec. 5.238 Criminal and civil penalties.

Persons who violate the provisions of 42 U.S.C. 3544 or 26 U.S.C. 6103(l)(7) with respect to the use and disclosure of income information may be subject to civil or criminal penalties under 42 U.S.C. 3544(c)(3), 26 U.S.C. 7213(a), or 18 U.S.C. 1905.

Sec. 5.240 Family disclosure of income information to the responsible entity and verification.

(a) This section applies to families that reside in dwelling units with assistance under the public housing program, the Section 8 tenant- based assistance programs, or for which project-based assistance is provided under the Section 8, Section 202, or Section 811 program.

(b) The family must promptly furnish to the responsible entity any letter or other notice by HUD to a member of the family that provides information concerning the amount or verification of family income.

(c) The responsible entity must verify the accuracy of the income information received from the family, and change the amount of the total tenant payment, tenant rent or Section 8 housing assistance payment, or terminate assistance, as appropriate, based on such information.

{65 FR 16715, Mar. 29, 2000}

Subpart C--Pet Ownership for the Elderly or Persons With Disabilities

Sec. 5.300 Purpose.

Authority: 42 U.S.C. 1701r-1 and 3535(d).

General Requirements

(a) This subpart implements section 227 of the Housing and Urban- Rural Recovery Act of 1983 (12 U.S.C. 1701r-1) as it pertains to projects for the elderly or persons with disabilities under:

(1) The housing programs administered by the Assistant Secretary for Housing-Federal Housing Commissioner;

(2) Projects assisted under the programs contained in chapter VIII of this title 24; and

(3) The public housing program.

(b) [Reserved]

{61 FR 5202, Feb. 9, 1996, as amended at 65 FR 16715, Mar. 29, 2000}

Sec. 5.303 Exclusion for animals that assist persons with disabilities.

(a) This subpart C does not apply to animals that are used to assist persons with disabilities. Project owners and PHAs may not apply or enforce any pet rules developed under this subpart against individuals with animals that are used to assist persons with disabilities. This exclusion applies to animals that reside in projects for the elderly

or persons with disabilities, as well as to animals that visit these projects.

(1) A project owner may require resident animals to qualify for this exclusion. Project owners must grant this exclusion if:

(i) The tenant or prospective tenant certifies in writing that the tenant or a member of his or her family is a person with a disability;

(ii) The animal has been trained to assist persons with that specific disability; and

(iii) The animal actually assists the person with a disability.

(2) [Reserved]

(b) Nothing in this subpart C:

(1) Limits or impairs the rights of persons with disabilities;

(2) Authorizes project owners or PHAs to limit or impair the rights of persons with disabilities; or

(3) Affects any authority that project owners or PHAs may have to regulate animals that assist persons with disabilities, under Federal, State, or local law.

Sec. 5.306 Definitions.

Common household pet means:

(1) For purposes of Housing programs: A domesticated animal, such as a dog, cat, bird, rodent (including a rabbit), fish, or turtle, that is traditionally kept in the home for pleasure rather than for commercial purposes. Common household pet does not include reptiles (except turtles). If this definition conflicts with any applicable State or local law or regulation defining the pets that may be owned or kept in dwelling accommodations, the State or local law or regulation shall apply. This definition shall not include animals that are used to assist persons with disabilities.

(2) For purposes of Public Housing programs: PHAs may define the term ``common household pet'' under Sec. 5.318.

Elderly or disabled family means:

(1) For purposes of Housing programs: An elderly person, a person with a disability, or an elderly or disabled family for purposes of the program under which a project for the elderly or persons with disabilities is assisted or has its mortgage insured.

(2) For purposes of Public Housing programs: (i) An elderly person, a person with a disability, or an elderly or disabled family as defined in Sec. 5.403 in subpart A of this part.

(ii) [Reserved]

Housing programs means:

(1) The housing programs administered by the Assistant Secretary for Housing-Federal Housing Commissioner; and

(2) The programs contained in chapter VIII of this title 24 that assist rental projects that meet the definition of project for the elderly or persons with disabilities in this subpart C.

Project for the elderly or persons with disabilities means:

(1) For purposes of Housing programs: (i) A specific rental or cooperative multifamily property that, unless currently owned by HUD, is subject to a first mortgage, and:

(A) That is assisted under statutory authority identified by HUD through notice;

(B) That was designated for occupancy by elderly or disabled families when funds for the project were reserved, or when the commitment to insure the mortgage was issued or, of not then so designated, that is designated for such occupancy in an effective amendment to the regulatory agreement covering the project, made pursuant to the project owner's request, and that is assisted or insured under one of the programs identified by HUD through notice; or

(C) For which preference in tenant selection is given for all units in the project to elderly or disabled families and that is owned by HUD or assisted under one of the programs identified by HUD through notice.

(ii) This term does not include health and care facilities that have mortgage insurance under the National Housing Act. This term also does not include any of the project owner's other property that does not meet the criteria contained in any one of paragraphs (1)(i)(A) through (C) of this definition, even if the property is adjacent to or under joint

or common management with such specific property.

(2) For purposes of Public Housing programs: Any project assisted under title I of the United States Housing Act of 1937 (other than under section 8 or 17 of the Act), including any building within a mixed-use project, that was designated for occupancy by the elderly or persons with disabilities at its inception or, although not so designated, for which the PHA gives preference in tenant selection (with HUD approval) for all units in the project (or for a building within a mixed-use project) to elderly or disabled families. For purposes of this part, this term does not include projects assisted the Low-Rent Housing Homeownership Opportunity program or under title II of the United States Housing Act of 1937.

Project owner means an owner (including HUD, where HUD is the owner) or manager of a project for the elderly or persons with disabilities, or an agent authorized to act for an owner or manager of such housing.

Public Housing Agency (PHA) is defined in Sec. 5.100.

{61 FR 5202, Feb. 9, 1996, as amended at 65 FR 16715, Mar. 29, 2000}

Sec. 5.309 Prohibition against discrimination.

Except as otherwise specifically authorized under this subpart no project owner or PHA that owns or manages a project for the elderly or persons with disabilities may:

(a) As a condition of tenancy or otherwise, prohibit or prevent any tenant of such housing from owning common household pets or having such pets living in the tenant's dwelling unit; or

(b) Restrict or discriminate against any person in connection with admission to, or continued occupancy of, such housing by reason of the person's ownership of common household pets or the presence of such pets in the person's dwelling unit.

Sec. 5.312 Notice to tenants.

(a) During the development of pet rules as described in Secs. 5.353 or 5.380, the project owner or PHA shall serve written notice on all tenants of projects for the elderly or persons with disabilities in occupancy at the time of service, stating that:

(1) Tenants are permitted to own and keep common household pets in their dwelling units, in accordance with the pet rules (if any) promulgated under this subpart C;

(2) Animals that are used to assist persons with disabilities are excluded from the requirements of this subpart C, as provided in Sec. 5.303;

(3) Tenants may, at any time, request a copy of any current pet rule developed under this subpart C (as well as any current proposed rule or proposed amendment to an existing rule); and

(4) Tenants may request that their leases be amended under Sec. 5.321 to permit common household pets.

(b) The project owner or PHA shall provide to each applicant for tenancy when he or she is offered a dwelling unit in a project for the elderly or persons with disabilities, the written notice specified in paragraphs (a) (1), (2), and (3) of this section.

(c) If a PHA chooses not to promulgate pet rules, the notice shall be served within 60 days of the effective date of this part. PHAs shall serve notice under this section in accordance with their normal service of notice procedures.

Sec. 5.315 Content of pet rules: General requirements.

(a) Housing programs. The project owner shall prescribe reasonable rules to govern the keeping of common household pets. The pet rules must include the mandatory rules described in Sec. 5.350 and may, unless otherwise noted in this subpart C, include other discretionary provisions as provided in Sec. 5.318.

(b) Public Housing programs. (1) PHAs may choose not to promulgate rules

governing the keeping of common household pets or may include rules as provided in Sec. 5.318. PHAs may elect to include provisions based on those in Sec. 5.350. If they so choose, the PHAs may modify the provisions in Sec. 5.350 in any manner consistent with this subpart C.

(2) If PHAs choose to promulgate pet rules, tenants must be permitted to own and keep pets in their units in accordance with the terms and conditions of their leases, the provisions of this subpart C, and any applicable State or local law or regulation governing the owning or keeping of pets in dwelling accommodations.

(3) PHAs that choose not to promulgate pet rules, shall not impose, by lease modification or otherwise, any requirement that is inconsistent with the provisions of this subpart C.

(c) Use of discretion. (1) This subpart C does not define with specificity the limits of the project owners' or PHAs' discretion to promulgate pet rules. Where a project owner or PHA has discretion to prescribe pet rules under this subpart C, the pet rules should be:

(i) Reasonably related to furthering a legitimate interest of the project owner or PHA, such as the owner's or PHA's interest in providing a decent, safe, and sanitary living environment for existing and prospective tenants and in protecting and preserving the physical condition of the project and the owner's or PHA's financial interest in it; and

(ii) Drawn narrowly to achieve the owner's or PHA's legitimate interests, without imposing unnecessary burdens and restrictions on pet owners and prospective pet owners.

(2) Where a project owner or PHA has discretion to prescribe pet rules under this subpart C, the owner or PHA may vary the rules' content among projects and within individual projects, based on factors such as the size, type, location, and occupancy of the project or its units, provided that the applicable rules are reasonable and do not conflict with any applicable State or local law or regulation governing the owning or keeping of pets in dwelling accommodations.

(d) Conflict with State or local law. The pet rules adopted by the project owner or PHA shall not conflict with applicable State or local law or regulations. If such a conflict may exist, the State and local law or regulations shall apply.

318 Discretionary pet rules.

Pet rules promulgated by project owners and PHAs may include, but are not limited to, consideration of the following factors:

(a) Definitions of ``common household pet''--(1) For Public Housing programs. The pet rules established by a PHA may contain a reasonable definition of a common household pet.

(2) For Housing programs. Project owners wishing to define ``common household pet'' in their pet rules must use the Housing programs definition of the term in Sec. 5.306.

(b) Density of tenants and pets. (1)(i) The pet rules established under this section may take into account tenant and pet density. The pet rules may place reasonable limitations on the number of common household pets that may be allowed in each dwelling unit. In the case of group homes, the pet rules may place reasonable limitations on the number of common household pets that may be allowed in each home.

(ii) For Housing programs. Under these rules, project owners may limit the number of four-legged, warm-blooded pets to one pet in each dwelling unit or group home.

(iii) Other than the limitations described in this paragraph (b)(1), the pet rules may not limit the total number of pets allowed in the project.

(2) As used in paragraph (b)(1) of this section, the term ``group home'' means:

(i) For purposes of Housing programs. A small, communal living arrangement designed specifically for individuals who are chronically mentally ill, developmentally disabled, or physically disabled who require a planned program of continual supportive services or supervision (other than continual nursing, medical or psychiatric care).

(ii) For purposes of Public Housing programs. A dwelling or dwelling unit for the exclusive residential use of elderly persons or persons with disabilities who are not capable of living completely independently and who require a planned program of continual supportive services or supervision (other than continual nursing, medical or psychiatric care).

(c) Pet size and pet type. The pet rules may place reasonable limitations on the size, weight, and type of common household pets allowed in the project.

(d) Potential financial obligations of tenants--(1) Pet deposits. The pet rules may require tenants who own or keep pets in their units to pay a refundable pet deposit. In the case of project owners, this pet deposit shall be limited to those tenants who own or keep cats or dogs in their units. This deposit is in addition to any other financial obligation generally imposed on tenants of the project. The project owner or PHA may use the pet deposit only to pay reasonable expenses directly attributable to the presence of the pet in the project, including (but not limited to) the cost of repairs and replacements to, and fumigation of, the tenant's dwelling unit and, for project owners, the cost of animal care facilities under Sec. 5.363. The project owner or PHA shall refund the unused portion of the pet deposit to the tenant within a reasonable time after the tenant moves from the project or no longer owns or keeps a pet (or a cat or dog in the case of project owners) in the dwelling unit.

(2) Housing programs: Maximum pet deposit. (i) Pet deposits for the following tenants shall not exceed an amount periodically fixed by HUD through notice.

(A) Tenants whose rents are subsidized (including tenants of a HUD- owned project, whose rents were subsidized before HUD acquired it) under one of the programs identified by HUD through notice.

(B) Tenants who live in a project assisted (including tenants who live in a HUD-owned project that was assisted before HUD acquired it) under one of the programs identified by HUD through notice.

(C) For all other tenants of projects for the elderly or persons with disabilities, the pet deposit shall not exceed one month's rent at the time the pet is brought onto the premises.

(ii) In establishing the maximum amount of pet deposit under paragraph (d)(2)(i) of this section, HUD will consider factors such as:

(A) Projected, estimated expenses directly attributable to the presence of pets in the project;

(B) The ability of project owners to offset such expenses by use of security deposits or HUD-reimbursable expenses; and

(C) The low income status of tenants of projects for the elderly or persons with disabilities.

(iii) For pet deposits subject to paragraph (d)(2)(i)(A) of this section, the pet rules shall provide for gradual accumulation of the deposit by the pet owner through an initial payment not to exceed $50 when the pet is brought onto the premises, and subsequent monthly payments not to exceed $10 per month until the amount of the deposit is reached.

(iv) For pet deposits subject to paragraphs (d)(2)(i)(B) and (C) of this section, the pet rules may provide for gradual accumulation of the deposit by the pet owner.

(v) The project owner may (subject to the HUD-prescribed limits) increase the amount of the pet deposit by amending the house pet rules in accordance with Sec. 5.353.

(A) For pet deposits subject to paragraph (d)(2)(i)(A) of this section, the house pet rules shall provide for gradual accumulation of any such increase not to exceed $10 per month for all deposit amounts that are being accumulated.

(B) [Reserved]

(vi) Any pet deposit that is established within the parameters set forth by paragraph (d)(2) of this section shall be deemed reasonable for purposes of this subpart C.

(3) Public Housing programs: Maximum pet deposit. The maximum amount of pet deposit that may be charged by the PHA, on a per dwelling unit basis, shall not exceed the higher of the Total Tenant Payment

(as defined in 24 CFR 913.102) or such reasonable fixed amount as the PHA may require. The pet rules may permit gradual accumulation of the pet deposit by the pet owner.

(4) Housing programs: Waste removal charge. The pet rules may permit the project owner to impose a separate waste removal charge of up to five dollars ($5) per occurrence on pet owners that fail to remove pet waste in accordance with the prescribed pet rules. Any pet waste removal charge that is within this five dollar ($5) limitation shall be deemed to be a reasonable amount for the purposes of this subpart C.

(5) The pet deposit (for Housing and Public Housing programs) and waste removal charge (for Housing programs) are not part of the rent payable by the tenant. Except as provided in paragraph (d) of this section for Housing programs and, paragraph (d) of this section and 24 CFR 966.4(b) for Public Housing programs, project owners or PHAs may not prescribe pet rules that impose additional financial obligations on pet owners that are designed to compensate the project owner or PHA for costs associated with the presence of pets in the project, including (but not limited to) requiring pet owners:

(i) To obtain liability or other insurance to cover damage caused by the pet;

(ii) To agree to be strictly liable for all damages caused by the pet where this liability is not otherwise imposed by State or local law, or

(iii) To indemnify the project owner for pet-related litigation and attorney's fees.

(e) Standards of pet care. The pet rules may prescribe standards of pet care and handling, but must be limited to those necessary to protect the condition of the tenant's unit and the general condition of the project premises, or to protect the health or safety of present tenants, project employees, and the public. The pet rules may not require pet owners to have any pet's vocal cords removed. Permitted rules may:

(1) Bar pets from specified common areas (such as lobbies, laundry rooms, and social rooms), unless the exclusion will deny a pet reasonable ingress and egress to the project or building.

(2) Require the pet owner to control noise and odor caused by a pet.

(3) Housing programs: Project owners may also:

(i) Require pet owners to have their dogs and cats spayed or neutered; and

(ii) Limit the length of time that a pet may be left unattended in a dwelling unit.

(f) Pet licensing. The pet rules may require pet owners to license their pets in accordance with applicable State and local laws and regulations. (Failure of the pet rules to contain this requirement does not relieve the pet owner of responsibility for complying with applicable State and local pet licensing requirements.)

(g) Public Housing programs: Designated pet areas. (1) PHAs may designate buildings, floors of buildings, or sections of buildings as no-pet areas where pets generally may not be permitted. Similarly, the pet rules may designate buildings, floors of buildings, or sections of buildings for residency generally by pet-owning tenants. The PHA may direct such initial tenant moves as may be necessary to establish pet and no-pet areas. The PHA may not refuse to admit (or delay admission of) an applicant for tenancy on the grounds that the applicant's admission would violate a pet or no-pet area. The PHA may adjust the pet and no-pet areas or may direct such additional moves as may be necessary (or both) to accommodate such applicants for tenancy or to meet the changing needs of existing tenants.

(2) Project owners may not designate pet areas in buildings in their pet rules.

(h) Pets temporarily on the premises. The pet rules may exclude from the project pets not owned by a tenant that are to be kept temporarily on the project premises. For the purposes of paragraph (h) of this section, pets are to be kept ``temporarily'' if they are to be kept in the tenant's dwelling accommodations for a period of less than 14 consecutive days and nights. HUD, however, encourages project owners and PHAs to

permit the use of a visiting pet program sponsored by a humane society, or other nonprofit organization.

Sec. 5.321 Lease provisions.

(a) Lease provisions. (1) PHAs which have established pet rules and project owners shall ensure that the leases for all tenants of projects for the elderly or persons with disabilities:

(i) State that tenants are permitted to keep common household pets in their dwelling units (subject to the provisions of this subpart and the pet rules);

(ii) Shall incorporate by reference the pet rules promulgated by the project owner or PHA;

(iii) Shall provide that the tenant agrees to comply with these rules; and

(iv) Shall state that violation of these rules may be grounds for removal of the pet or termination of the pet owner's tenancy (or both), in accordance with the provisions of this subpart and applicable regulations and State or local law.

(2) [Reserved]

(b) Where a PHA has not established pet rules, the leases of all tenants of such projects shall not contain any provisions prohibiting the owning or keeping of common household pets, and shall state that owning and keeping of such pets will be subject to the general obligations imposed on the PHA and tenants in the lease and any applicable State or local law or regulation governing the owning or keeping of pets in dwelling accommodations.

Sec. 5.324 Implementation of lease provisions.

The lease for each tenant of a project for the elderly or persons with disabilities who is admitted on or after the date on which this subpart C is implemented shall contain the lease provisions described in Sec. 5.321 and, if applicable, Sec. 5.360. The lease for each tenant who occupies a unit in such a project under lease on the date of implementation of this part shall be amended to include the provisions described in Sec. 5.321 and, if applicable, Sec. 5.360:

(a) For Housing programs:

(1) Upon renewal of the lease and in accordance with any applicable regulation; and

(2) When a Housing program tenant registers a common household pet under Sec. 5.350

(b) For Public Housing programs:

(1) Upon annual reexamination of tenant income in accordance with any applicable regulation; and

(2) When a Public Housing program tenant wishes to own or keep a common household pet in his or her unit.

Sec. 5.327 Nuisance or threat to health or safety.

Nothing in this subpart C prohibits a project owner, PHA, or an appropriate community authority from requiring the removal of any pet from a project, if the pet's conduct or condition is duly determined to constitute, under the provisions of State or local law, a nuisance or a threat to the health or safety of other occupants of the project or of other persons in the community where the project is located.

Pet Ownership Requirements for Housing Programs

Sec. 5.350 Mandatory pet rules for housing programs.

Mandatory rules. The project owner must prescribe the following pet rules:

(a) Inoculations. The pet rules shall require pet owners to have their pets inoculated in accordance with State and local laws.

(b) Sanitary standards. (1) The pet rules shall prescribe sanitary standards to govern the disposal of pet waste. These rules may:

(i) Designate areas on the project premises for pet exercise and the deposit of pet waste;

(ii) Forbid pet owners from exercising their pets or permitting their pets to deposit waste on the project premises outside the designated areas;

(iii) Require pet owners to remove and properly dispose of all removable pet waste; and

(iv) Require pet owners to remove pets from the premises to permit the pet to exercise or deposit waste, if no area in the project is designated for such purposes.

(2) In the case of cats and other pets using litter boxes, the pet rules may require the pet owner to change the litter (but not more than twice each week), may require pet owners to separate pet waste from litter (but not more than once each day), and may prescribe methods for the disposal of pet waste and used litter.

(c) Pet restraint. The pet rules shall require that all cats and dogs be appropriately and effectively restrained and under the control of a responsible individual while on the common areas of the project.

(d) Registration. (1) The pet rules shall require pet owners to register their pets with the project owner. The pet owner must register the pet before it is brought onto the project premises, and must update the registration at least annually. The project owner may coordinate the annual update with the annual reexamination of tenant income, if applicable. The registration must include:

(i) A certificate signed by a licensed veterinarian or a State or local authority empowered to inoculate animals (or designated agent of such an authority) stating that the pet has received all inoculations required by applicable State and local law;

(ii) Information sufficient to identify the pet and to demonstrate that it is a common household pet; and

(iii) The name, address, and phone number of one or more responsible parties who will care for the pet if the pet owner dies, is incapacitated, or is otherwise unable to care for the pet.

(2) The project owner may require the pet owner to provide additional information necessary to ensure compliance with any discretionary rules prescribed under Sec. 5.318, and shall require the pet owner to sign a statement indicating that he or she has read the pet rules and agrees to comply with them.

(3) The pet rules shall permit the project owner to refuse to register a pet if:

(i) The pet is not a common household pet;

(ii) The keeping of the pet would violate any applicable house pet rule;

(iii) The pet owner fails to provide complete pet registration information or fails annually to update the pet registration; or

(iv) The project owner reasonably determines, based on the pet owner's habits and practices, that the pet owner will be unable to keep the pet in compliance with the pet rules and other lease obligations. The pet's temperament may be considered as a factor in determining the prospective pet owner's ability to comply with the pet rules and other lease obligations.

(4) The project owner may not refuse to register a pet based on a determination that the pet owner is financially unable to care for the pet or that the pet is inappropriate, based on the therapeutic value to the pet owner or the interests of the property or existing tenants.

(5) The pet rules shall require the project owner to notify the pet owner if the project owner refuses to register a pet. The notice shall state the basis for the project owner's action and shall be served on the pet owner in accordance with the requirements of Sec. 5.353(f)(1)(i) or (ii). The notice of refusal to register a pet may be combined with a notice of pet violation as required in Sec. 5.356.

Sec. 5.353 Housing programs: Procedure for development of pet rules.

(a) General. Project owners shall use the procedures specified in this section to promulgate the pet rules referred to in Secs. 5.318 and 5.350.

(b) Development and notice of proposed pet rules. Project owners shall develop proposed rules to govern the owning or keeping of common household pets in projects for the elderly or persons with disabilities. Notice of the proposed pet rules shall be served on each tenant of the project

as provided in paragraph (f) of this section. The notice shall:

(1) Include the text of the proposed rules;

(2) State that tenants or tenant representatives may submit written comments on the rules; and

(3) State that all comments must be submitted to the project owner no later than 30 days from the effective date of the notice of the proposed rules.

(4) The notice may also announce the date, time, and place for a meeting to discuss the proposed rules (as provided in paragraph (c) of this section).

(c) Tenant consultation. Tenants or tenant representatives may submit written comments on the proposed pet rules to the project owner by the date specified in the notice of proposed rules. In addition, the owner may schedule one or more meetings with tenants during the comment period to discuss the proposed rules. Tenants and tenant representatives may make oral comments on the proposed rules at these meetings. The project owner must consider comments made at these meetings only if they are summarized, reduced to writing, and submitted to the project owner before the end of the comment period.

(d) Development and notice of final pet rules. The project owner shall develop the final rules after reviewing tenants' written comments and written summaries of any owner-tenant meetings. The project owner may meet with tenants and tenant representatives to attempt to resolve issues raised by the comments. Subject to this subpart C, the content of the final pet rules, however, is within the sole discretion of the project owner. The project owner shall serve on each tenant of the project, a notice of the final pet rules as provided in paragraph (f) of this section. The notice must include the text of the final pet rules and must specify the effective date of the final pet rules.

(e) Amendment of pet rules. The project owner may amend the pet rules at any time by following the procedure for the development of pet rules specified in paragraphs (b) through (d) of this section.

(f) Service of notice. (1) The project owner must serve the notice required under this section by:

(i) Sending a letter by first class mail, properly stamped and addressed to the tenant at the dwelling unit, with a proper return address; or

(ii) Serving a copy of the notice on any adult answering the door at the tenant's leased dwelling unit, or if no adult responds, by placing the notice under or through the door, if possible, or else by attaching the notice to the door; or

(iii) For service of notice to tenants of a high-rise building, posting the notice in at least three conspicuous places within the building and maintaining the posted notices intact and in legible form for 30 days. For purposes of paragraph (f) of this section, a high-rise building is a structure that is equipped with an elevator and has a common lobby.

(2) For purposes of computing time periods following service of the notice, service is effective on the day that all notices are delivered or mailed, or in the case of service by posting, on the day that all notices are initially posted.

Sec. 5.356 Housing programs: Pet rule violation procedures.

(a) Notice of pet rule violation. If a project owner determines on the basis of objective facts, supported by written statements, that a pet owner has violated a rule governing the owning or keeping of pets; the project owner may serve a written notice of pet rule violation on the pet owner in accordance with Sec. 5.353(f)(1)(i) or (ii). The notice of pet rule violation must:

(1) Contain a brief statement of the factual basis for the determination and the pet rule or rules alleged to be violated;

(2) State that the pet owner has 10 days from the effective date of service of the notice to correct the violation (including, in appropriate circumstances, removal of the pet) or to make a written request for a meeting to discuss the violation;

(3) State that the pet owner is entitled to

be accompanied by another person of his or her choice at the meeting; and

(4) State that the pet owner's failure to correct the violation, to request a meeting, or to appear at a requested meeting may result in initiation of procedures to terminate the pet owner's tenancy.

(b)(1) Pet rule violation meeting. If the pet owner makes a timely request for a meeting to discuss an alleged pet rule violation, the project owner shall establish a mutually agreeable time and place for the meeting but no later than 15 days from the effective date of service of the notice of pet rule violation (unless the project owner agrees to a later date). At the pet rule violation meeting, the pet owner and project owner shall discuss any alleged pet rule violation and attempt to correct it. The project owner may, as a result of the meeting, give the pet owner additional time to correct the violation.

(2) Notice for pet removal. If the pet owner and project owner are unable to resolve the pet rule violation at the pet rule violation meeting, or if the project owner determines that the pet owner has failed to correct the pet rule violation within any additional time provided for this purpose under paragraph (b)(1) of this section, the project owner may serve a written notice on the pet owner in accordance with Sec. 5.353(f)(1) (i) or (ii) (or at the meeting, if appropriate), requiring the pet owner to remove the pet. The notice must:

(i) Contain a brief statement of the factual basis for the determination and the pet rule or rules that have been violated;

(ii) State that the pet owner must remove the pet within 10 days of the effective date of service of the notice of pet removal (or the meeting, if notice is served at the meeting); and

(iii) State that failure to remove the pet may result in initiation of procedures to terminate the pet owner's tenancy.

(c) Initiation of procedures to remove a pet or terminate the pet owner's tenancy. (1) The project owner may not initiate procedures to terminate a pet owner's tenancy based on a pet rule violation, unless:

(i) The pet owner has failed to remove the pet or correct a pet rule violation within the applicable time period specified in this section (including any additional time permitted by the owner); and

(ii) The pet rule violation is sufficient to begin procedures to terminate the pet owner's tenancy under the terms of the lease and applicable regulations.

(2) The project owner may initiate procedures to remove a pet under Sec. 5.327 at any time, in accordance with the provisions of applicable State or local law.

Sec. 5.359 Housing programs: Rejection of units by applicants for tenancy.

(a) An applicant for tenancy in a project for the elderly or persons with disabilities may reject a unit offered by a project owner if the unit is in close proximity to a dwelling unit in which an existing tenant of the project owns or keeps a common household pet. An applicant's rejection of a unit under this section shall not adversely affect his or her application for tenancy in the project, including (but not limited to) his or her position on the project waiting list or qualification for any tenant selection preference.

(b) Nothing in this subpart C imposes a duty on project owners to provide alternate dwelling units to existing or prospective tenants because of the proximity of common household pets to a particular unit or the presence of such pets in the project.

Sec. 5.360 Housing programs: Additional lease provisions.

(a) Inspections. In addition to other inspections permitted under the lease, the leases for all Housing program tenants of projects for the elderly or persons with disabilities may state that the project owner may, after reasonable notice to the tenant and during reasonable hours, enter and inspect the premises. The lease shall permit entry and inspection only if the project owner has received a signed, written complaint alleging

(or the project owner has reasonable grounds to believe) that the conduct or condition of a pet in the dwelling unit constitutes, under applicable State or local law, a nuisance or a threat to the health or safety of the occupants of the project or other persons in the community where the project is located.

(b) Emergencies. (1) If there is no State or local authority (or designated agent of such an authority) authorized under applicable State or local law to remove a pet that becomes vicious, displays symptoms of severe illness, or demonstrates other behavior that constitutes an immediate threat to the health or safety of the tenancy as a whole, the project owner may place a provision in tenant leases permitting the project owner to enter the premises (if necessary), remove the pet, and take such action with respect to the pet as may be permissible under State and local law, which may include placing it in a facility that will provide care and shelter for a period not to exceed 30 days.

(2) The lease shall permit the project owner to enter the premises and remove the pet or take such other permissible action only if the project owner requests the pet owner to remove the pet from the project immediately, and the pet owner refuses to do so, or if the project owner is unable to contact the pet owner to make a removal request. The lease may not contain a provision relieving the project owner from liability for wrongful removal of a pet. The cost of the animal care facility shall be paid as provided in Sec. 5.363.

(3) The project owner may place a provision in tenant leases permitting the project owner to enter the premises, remove the pet, and place the pet in a facility that will provide care and shelter, in accordance with the provisions of Sec. 5.363. The lease may not contain a provision relieving the project owner from liability for wrongful removal of a pet.

Sec. 5.363 Housing programs: Protection of the pet.

(a) If the health or safety of a pet is threatened by the death or incapacity of the pet owner, or by other factors that render the pet owner unable to care for the pet, the project owner may contact the responsible party or parties listed in the pet registration required under Sec. 5.350(d)(1)(iii).

(b) If the responsible party or parties are unwilling or unable to care for the pet, or the project owner, despite reasonable efforts, has been unable to contact the responsible party or parties, the project owner may contact the appropriate State or local authority (or designated agent of such an authority) and request the removal of the pet.

(c) If there is no State or local authority (or designated agent of such an authority) authorized to remove a pet under these circumstances and the project owner has placed a provision in the lease agreement (as described in Sec. 5.360(c)(2)), the project owner may enter the pet owner's unit, remove the pet, and place the pet in a facility that will provide care and shelter until the pet owner or a representative of the pet owner is able to assume responsibility for the pet, but not longer than 30 days.

(d) The cost of the animal care facility provided under this section shall be borne by the pet owner. If the pet owner (or the pet owner's estate) is unable or unwilling to pay, the cost of the animal care facility may be paid from the pet deposit, if imposed under the pet rules.

Pet Ownership Requirements for Public Housing Programs

Sec. 5.380 Public housing programs: Procedure for development of pet rules.

PHAs that choose to promulgate pet rules shall consult with tenants of projects for the elderly or persons with disabilities administered by them with respect to their promulgation and subsequent amendment. PHAs shall develop the specific procedures governing tenant consultation, but these procedures must be designed to give tenants (or, if appropriate, tenant councils) adequate opportunity to review and comment upon the

pet rules before they are issued for effect. PHAs are solely responsible for the content of final pet rules, but must give consideration to tenant comments. PHAs shall send to the responsible HUD field office, copies of the final (or amended) pet rules, as well as summaries or copies of all tenant comments received in the course of the tenant consultation.

Subpart D--Definitions for Section 8 and Public Housing Assistance Under the United States Housing Act of 1937

Sec. 5.400 Applicability.

Authority: 42 U.S.C. 1437a and 3535(d).

Source: 61 FR 5665, Feb. 13, 1996, unless otherwise noted.

This part applies to public housing and Section 8 programs.

{61 FR 5665, Feb. 13, 1996, as amended at 65 FR 16715, Mar. 29. 2000}

Sec. 5.403 Definitions.

Annual contributions contract (ACC) means the written contract between HUD and a PHA under which HUD agrees to provide funding for a program under the 1937 Act, and the PHA agrees to comply with HUD requirements for the program.

Applicant means a person or a family that has applied for housing assistance.

Disabled family means a family whose head, spouse, or sole member is a person with disabilities. It may include two or more persons with disabilities living together, or one or more persons with disabilities living with one or more live-in aides.

Displaced family means a family in which each member, or whose sole member, is a person displaced by governmental action, or a person whose dwelling has been extensively damaged or destroyed as a result of a disaster declared or otherwise formally recognized pursuant to Federal disaster relief laws.

Elderly family means a family whose head, spouse, or sole member is a person who is at least 62 years of age. It may include two or more persons who are at least 62 years of age living together, or one or more persons who are at least 62 years of age living with one or more live-in aides.

Family includes but is not limited to:

(1) A family with or without children (the temporary absence of a child from the home due to placement in foster care shall not be considered in determining family composition and family size);

(2) An elderly family;

(3) A near-elderly family;

(4) A disabled family;

(5) A displaced family;

(6) The remaining member of a tenant family; and

(7) A single person who is not an elderly or displaced person, or a person with disabilities, or the remaining member of a tenant family.

Live-in aide means a person who resides with one or more elderly persons, or near-elderly persons, or persons with disabilities, and who:

(1) Is determined to be essential to the care and well-being of the persons;

(2) Is not obligated for the support of the persons; and

(3) Would not be living in the unit except to provide the necessary supportive services.

Near-elderly family means a family whose head, spouse, or sole member is a person who is at least 50 years of age but below the age of 62; or two or more persons, who are at least 50 years of age but below the age of 62, living together; or one or more persons who are at least 50 years of age but below the age of 62 living with one or more live-in aides.

Person with disabilities:

(1) Means a person who:

(i) Has a disability, as defined in 42 U.S.C. 423;

(ii) Is determined, pursuant to HUD regulations, to have a physical, mental, or emotional impairment that:

(A) Is expected to be of long-continued and indefinite duration;

(B) Substantially impedes his or her ability

to live independently, and

(C) Is of such a nature that the ability to live independently could be improved by more suitable housing conditions; or

(iii) Has a developmental disability as defined in 42 U.S.C. 6001.

(2) Does not exclude persons who have the disease of acquired immunodeficiency syndrome or any conditions arising from the etiologic agent for acquired immunodeficiency syndrome;

(3) For purposes of qualifying for low-income housing, does not include a person whose disability is based solely on any drug or alcohol dependence; and

(4) Means ``individual with handicaps'', as defined in Sec. 8.3 of this title, for purposes of reasonable accommodation and program accessibility for persons with disabilities.

{61 FR 5665, Feb. 13, 1996, as amended at 63 FR 23853, Apr. 30, 1998; 65 FR 16715, Mar. 29, 2000}

Subpart E--Restrictions on Assistance to Noncitizens

Sec. 5.500 Applicability.

Authority: 42 U.S.C. 1436a and 3535(d).

(a) Covered programs/assistance. This subpart E implements Section 214 of the Housing and Community Development Act of 1980, as amended (42 U.S.C. 1436a). Section 214 prohibits HUD from making financial assistance available to persons who are not in eligible status with respect to citizenship or noncitizen immigration status. This subpart E is applicable to financial assistance provided under:

(1) Section 235 of the National Housing Act (12 U.S.C. 1715z) (the Section 235 Program);

(2) Section 236 of the National Housing Act (12 U.S.C. 1715z-1) (tenants paying below market rent only) (the Section 236 Program);

(3) Section 101 of the Housing and Urban Development Act of 1965 (12 U.S.C. 1701s) (the Rent Supplement Program); and

(4) The United States Housing Act of 1937 (42 U.S. C. 1437 et seq.) which covers:

(i) HUD's Public Housing Programs;

(ii) The Section 8 Housing Assistance Programs; and

(iii) The Housing Development Grant Programs (with respect to low income units only).

(b) Covered individuals and entities--(1) Covered individuals/ persons and families. The provisions of this subpart E apply to both applicants for assistance and persons already receiving assistance covered under this subpart E.

(2) Covered entities. The provisions of this subpart E apply to Public Housing Agencies (PHAs), project (or housing) owners, and mortgagees under the Section 235 Program. The term ``responsible entity'' is used in this subpart E to refer collectively to these entities, and is further defined in Sec. 5.504.

Sec. 5.502 Requirements concerning documents.

For any notice or document (decision, declaration, consent form, etc.) that this subpart E requires the responsible entity to provide to an individual, or requires the responsible entity to obtain the signature of an individual, the responsible entity, where feasible, must arrange for the notice or document to be provided to the individual in a language that is understood by the individual if the individual is not proficient in English. (See 24 CFR 8.6 of HUD's regulations for requirements concerning communications with persons with disabilities.)

Sec. 5.504 Definitions.

(a) The definitions 1937 Act, HUD, Public Housing Agency (PHA), and Section 8 are defined in subpart A of this part.

(b) As used in this subpart E:

Child means a member of the family other than the family head or spouse who is under 18 years of age.

Citizen means a citizen or national of the United States.

Evidence of citizenship or eligible status means the documents which must be submitted to evidence citizenship or eligible immigration status. (See Sec. 5.508(b).)

Family has the same meaning as provided in the program regulations of the relevant Section 214 covered program.

Head of household means the adult member of the family who is the head of the household for purposes of determining income eligibility and rent.

Housing covered programs means the following programs administered by the Assistant Secretary for Housing:

(1) Section 235 of the National Housing Act (12 U.S.C. 1715z) (the Section 235 Program);

(2) Section 236 of the National Housing Act (12 U.S.C. 1715z-1) (tenants paying below market rent only) (the Section 236 Program); and

(3) Section 101 of the Housing and Urban Development Act of 1965 (12 U.S.C. 1701s) (the Rent Supplement Program).

INS means the U.S. Immigration and Naturalization Service.

Mixed family means a family whose members include those with citizenship or eligible immigration status, and those without citizenship or eligible immigration status.

National means a person who owes permanent allegiance to the United States, for example, as a result of birth in a United States territory or possession.

Noncitizen means a person who is neither a citizen nor national of the United States.

Project owner means the person or entity that owns the housing project containing the assisted dwelling unit.

Public Housing covered programs means the public housing programs administered by the Assistant Secretary for Public and Indian Housing under title I of the 1937 Act. This definition does not encompass HUD's Indian Housing programs administered under title II of the 1937 Act. Further, this term does not include those programs providing assistance under section 8 of the 1937 Act. (See definition of ``Section 8 Covered Programs'' in this section.)

Responsible entity means the person or entity responsible for administering the restrictions on providing assistance to noncitizens with ineligible immigrations status. The entity responsible for administering the restrictions on providing assistance to noncitizens with ineligible immigration status under the various covered programs is as follows:

(1) For the Section 235 Program, the mortgagee.

(2) For Public Housing, the Section 8 Rental Certificate, the Section 8 Rental Voucher, and the Section 8 Moderate Rehabilitation programs, the PHA administering the program under an ACC with HUD.

(3) For all other Section 8 programs, the Section 236 Program, and the Rent Supplement Program, the owner.

Section 8 covered programs means all HUD programs which assist housing under Section 8 of the 1937 Act, including Section 8-assisted housing for which loans are made under section 202 of the Housing Act of 1959.

Section 214 means section 214 of the Housing and Community Development Act of 1980, as amended (42 U.S.C. 1436a).

Section 214 covered programs is the collective term for the HUD programs to which the restrictions imposed by Section 214 apply. These programs are set forth in Sec. 5.500.

Tenant means an individual or a family renting or occupying an assisted dwelling unit. For purposes of this subpart E, the term tenant will also be used to include a homebuyer, where appropriate.

Sec. 5.506 General provisions.

(a) Restrictions on assistance. Financial assistance under a Section 214 covered program is restricted to:

(1) Citizens; or

(2) Noncitizens who have eligible immigration status under one of the categories set forth in Section 214 (see 42 U.S.C. 1436a(a)).

(b) Family eligibility for assistance. (1) A family shall not be eligible for assistance unless every member of the family residing in the unit is determined to have eligible status, as described in paragraph (a) of this section, or unless the family meets the conditions set forth in paragraph (b)(2) of this section.

(2) Despite the ineligibility of one or more family members, a mixed family may be eligible for one of the three types of assistance provided in Secs. 5.516 and 5.518. A family without any eligible members and receiving assistance on June 19, 1995 may be eligible for temporary deferral of termination of assistance as provided in Secs. 5.516 and 5.518.

(c) Preferences. Citizens of the Republic of Marshall Islands, the Federated States of Micronesia, and the Republic of Palau who are eligible for assistance under paragraph (a)(2) of this section are entitled to receive local preferences for housing assistance, except that, within Guam, such citizens who have such local preference will not be entitled to housing assistance in preference to any United States citizen or national resident therein who is otherwise eligible for such assistance.

{61 FR 5202, Feb. 9, 1996, as amended at 67 FR 65273, Oct. 23, 2002}

Sec. 5.508 Submission of evidence of citizenship or eligible immigration status.

(a) General. Eligibility for assistance or continued assistance under a Section 214 covered program is contingent upon a family's submission to the responsible entity of the documents described in paragraph (b) of this section for each family member. If one or more family members do not have citizenship or eligible immigration status, the family members may exercise the election not to contend to have eligible immigration status as provided in paragraph (e) of this section, and the provisions of Secs. 5.516 and 5.518 shall apply.

(b) Evidence of citizenship or eligible immigration status. Each family member, regardless of age, must submit the following evidence to the responsible entity.

(1) For U.S. citizens or U.S. nationals, the evidence consists of a signed declaration of U.S. citizenship or U.S. nationality. The responsible entity may request verification of the declaration by requiring presentation of a United States passport or other appropriate documentation, as specified in HUD guidance.

(2) For noncitizens who are 62 years of age or older or who will be 62 years of age or older and receiving assistance under a Section 214 covered program on September 30, 1996 or applying for assistance on or after that date, the evidence consists of:

(i) A signed declaration of eligible immigration status; and

(ii) Proof of age document.

(3) For all other noncitizens, the evidence consists of:

(i) A signed declaration of eligible immigration status;

(ii) One of the INS documents referred to in Sec. 5.510; and

(iii) A signed verification consent form.

(c) Declaration. (1) For each family member who contends that he or she is a U.S. citizen or a noncitizen with eligible immigration status, the family must submit to the responsible entity a written declaration, signed under penalty of perjury, by which the family member declares whether he or she is a U.S. citizen or a noncitizen with eligible immigration status.

(i) For each adult, the declaration must be signed by the adult.

(ii) For each child, the declaration must be signed by an adult residing in the assisted dwelling unit who is responsible for the child.

(2) For Housing covered programs: The written declaration may be incorporated as part of the application for housing assistance or may constitute a separate document.

(d) Verification consent form--(1) Who signs. Each noncitizen who declares eligible immigration status (except certain noncitizens who are 62 years of age or older

as described in paragraph (b)(2) of this section) must sign a verification consent form as follows.

(i) For each adult, the form must be signed by the adult.

(ii) For each child, the form must be signed by an adult residing in the assisted dwelling unit who is responsible for the child.

(2) Notice of release of evidence by responsible entity. The verification consent form shall provide that evidence of eligible immigration status may be released by the responsible entity without responsibility for the further use or transmission of the evidence by the entity receiving it, to:

(i) HUD, as required by HUD; and

(ii) The INS for purposes of verification of the immigration status of the individual.

(3) Notice of release of evidence by HUD. The verification consent form also shall notify the individual of the possible release of evidence of eligible immigration status by HUD. Evidence of eligible immigration status shall only be released to the INS for purposes of establishing eligibility for financial assistance and not for any other purpose. HUD is not responsible for the further use or transmission of the evidence or other information by the INS.

(e) Individuals who do not contend that they have eligible status. If one or more members of a family elect not to contend that they have eligible immigration status, and other members of the family establish their citizenship or eligible immigration status, the family may be eligible for assistance under Secs. 5.516 and 5.518, or Sec. 5.520, despite the fact that no declaration or documentation of eligible status is submitted for one or more members of the family. The family, however, must identify in writing to the responsible entity, the family member (or members) who will elect not to contend that he or she has eligible immigration status.

(f) Notification of requirements of Section 214--(1) When notice is to be issued. Notification of the requirement to submit evidence of citizenship or eligible immigration status, as required by this section, or to elect not to contend that one has eligible status as provided by paragraph (e) of this section, shall be given by the responsible entity as follows:

(i) Applicant's notice. The notification described in paragraph (f)(1) of this section shall be given to each applicant at the time of application for assistance. Applicants whose applications are pending on June 19, 1995, shall be notified of the requirement to submit evidence of eligible status as soon as possible after June 19, 1995.

(ii) Notice to tenants. The notification described in paragraph (f)(1) of this section shall be given to each tenant at the time of, and together with, the responsible entity's notice of regular reexamination of income, but not later than one year following June 19, 1995.

(iii) Timing of mortgagor's notice. A mortgagor receiving Section 235 assistance must be provided the notification described in paragraph (f)(1) of this section and any additional requirements imposed under the Section 235 Program.

(2) Form and content of notice. The notice shall:

(i) State that financial assistance is contingent upon the submission and verification, as appropriate, of evidence of citizenship or eligible immigration status as required by paragraph (a) of this section;

(ii) Describe the type of evidence that must be submitted, and state the time period in which that evidence must be submitted (see paragraph (g) of this section concerning when evidence must be submitted); and

(iii) State that assistance will be prorated, denied or terminated, as appropriate, upon a final determination of ineligibility after all appeals have been exhausted (see Sec. 5.514 concerning INS appeal, and informal hearing process) or, if appeals are not pursued, at a time to be specified in accordance with HUD requirements. Tenants also shall be informed of how to obtain assistance under the preservation of families provisions of Secs. 5.516 and 5.518.

(g) When evidence of eligible status is required to be submitted. The responsible

entity shall require evidence of eligible status to be submitted at the times specified in paragraph (g) of this section, subject to any extension granted in accordance with paragraph (h) of this section.

(1) Applicants. For applicants, responsible entities must ensure that evidence of eligible status is submitted not later than the date the responsible entity anticipates or has knowledge that verification of other aspects of eligibility for assistance will occur (see Sec. 5.512(a)).

(2) Tenants. For tenants, evidence of eligible status is required to be submitted as follows:

(i) For financial assistance under a Section 214 covered program, with the exception of Section 235 assistance payments, the required evidence shall be submitted at the first regular reexamination after June 19, 1995, in accordance with program requirements.

(ii) For financial assistance in the form of Section 235 assistance payments, the mortgagor shall submit the required evidence in accordance with requirements imposed under the Section 235 Program.

(3) New occupants of assisted units. For any new occupant of an assisted unit (e.g., a new family member comes to reside in the assisted unit), the required evidence shall be submitted at the first interim or regular reexamination following the person's occupancy.

(4) Changing participation in a HUD program. Whenever a family applies for admission to a Section 214 covered program, evidence of eligible status is required to be submitted in accordance with the requirements of this subpart unless the family already has submitted the evidence to the responsible entity for a Section 214 covered program.

(5) One-time evidence requirement for continuous occupancy. For each family member, the family is required to submit evidence of eligible status only one time during continuously assisted occupancy under any Section 214 covered program.

(h) Extensions of time to submit evidence of eligible status--(1) When extension must be granted. The responsible entity shall extend the time, provided in paragraph (g) of this section, to submit evidence of eligible immigration status if the family member:

(i) Submits the declaration required under Sec. 5.508(a) certifying that any person for whom required evidence has not been submitted is a noncitizen with eligible immigration status; and

(ii) Certifies that the evidence needed to support a claim of eligible immigration status is temporarily unavailable, additional time is needed to obtain and submit the evidence, and prompt and diligent efforts will be undertaken to obtain the evidence.

(2) Thirty-day extension period. Any extension of time, if granted, shall not exceed thirty (30) days. The additional time provided should be sufficient to allow the individual the time to obtain the evidence needed. The responsible entity's determination of the length of the extension needed shall be based on the circumstances of the individual case.

(3) Grant or denial of extension to be in writing. The responsible entity's decision to grant or deny an extension as provided in paragraph (h)(1) of this section shall be issued to the family by written notice. If the extension is granted, the notice shall specify the extension period granted (which shall not exceed thirty (30) days). If the extension is denied, the notice shall explain the reasons for denial of the extension.

(i) Failure to submit evidence or to establish eligible status. If the family fails to submit required evidence of eligible immigration status within the time period specified in the notice, or any extension granted in accordance with paragraph (h) of this section, or if the evidence is timely submitted but fails to establish eligible immigration status, the responsible entity shall proceed to deny, prorate or terminate assistance, or provide continued assistance or temporary deferral of termination of assistance, as appropriate, in accordance with the provisions of Secs. 5.514, 5.516, and 5.518.

(ii) [Reserved]
{61 FR 13616, Mar. 27, 1996, as amended at 61 FR 60538, Nov. 29, 1996; 64 FR 25731, May 12, 1999}

Sec. 5.510 Documents of eligible immigration status.

(a) General. A responsible entity shall request and review original documents of eligible immigration status. The responsible entity shall retain photocopies of the documents for its own records and return the original documents to the family.

(b) Acceptable evidence of eligible immigration status. Acceptable evidence of eligible immigration status shall be the original of a document designated by INS as acceptable evidence of immigration status in one of the six categories mentioned in Sec. 5.506(a) for the specific immigration status claimed by the individual.
{61 FR 13616, Mar. 27, 1996, as amended at 61 FR 60539, Nov. 29, 1996; 64 FR 25731, May 12, 1999}

Sec. 5.512 Verification of eligible immigration status.

(a) General. Except as described in paragraph (b) of this section and Sec. 5.514, no individual or family applying for assistance may receive such assistance prior to the verification of the eligibility of at least the individual or one family member. Verification of eligibility consistent with Sec. 5.514 occurs when the individual or family members have submitted documentation to the responsible entity in accordance with Sec. 5.508.

(b) PHA election to provide assistance before verification. A PHA that is a responsible entity under this subpart may elect to provide assistance to a family before the verification of the eligibility of the individual or one family member.

(c) Primary verification--(1) Automated verification system. Primary verification of the immigration status of the person is conducted by the responsible entity through the INS automated system (INS Systematic Alien Verification for Entitlements (SAVE)). The INS SAVE system provides access to names, file numbers and admission numbers of noncitizens.

(2) Failure of primary verification to confirm eligible immigration status. If the INS SAVE system does not verify eligible immigration status, secondary verification must be performed.

(d) Secondary verification--(1) Manual search of INS records. Secondary verification is a manual search by the INS of its records to determine an individual's immigration status. The responsible entity must request secondary verification, within 10 days of receiving the results of the primary verification, if the primary verification system does not confirm eligible immigration status, or if the primary verification system verifies immigration status that is ineligible for assistance under a Section 214 covered program.

(2) Secondary verification initiated by responsible entity. Secondary verification is initiated by the responsible entity forwarding photocopies of the original INS documents required for the immigration status declared (front and back), attached to the INS document verification request form G-845S (Document Verification Request), or such other form specified by the INS to a designated INS office for review. (Form G-845S is available from the local INS Office.)

(3) Failure of secondary verification to confirm eligible immigration status. If the secondary verification does not confirm eligible immigration status, the responsible entity shall issue to the family the notice described in Sec. 5.514(d), which includes notification of the right to appeal to the INS of the INS finding on immigration status (see Sec. 5.514(d)(4)).

(e) Exemption from liability for INS verification. The responsible entity shall not be liable for any action, delay, or failure of the INS in conducting the automated or manual verification.
{61 FR 13616, Mar. 27, 1996, as amended at 61 FR 60539, Nov. 29, 1996; 64 FR 25731, May 12, 1999}

Sec. 5.514 Delay, denial, reduction or termination of assistance.

(a) General. Assistance to a family may not be delayed, denied, reduced or terminated because of the immigration status of a family member except as provided in this section.

(b) Restrictions on delay, denial, reduction or termination of assistance. (1) Restrictions on reduction, denial or termination of assistance for applicants and tenants. Assistance to an applicant or tenant shall not be delayed, denied, reduced, or terminated, on the basis of ineligible immigration status of a family member if:

(i) The primary and secondary verification of any immigration documents that were timely submitted has not been completed;

(ii) The family member for whom required evidence has not been submitted has moved from the assisted dwelling unit;

(iii) The family member who is determined not to be in an eligible immigration status following INS verification has moved from the assisted dwelling unit;

(iv) The INS appeals process under Sec. 5.514(e) has not been concluded;

(v) Assistance is prorated in accordance with Sec. 5.520; or

(vi) Assistance for a mixed family is continued in accordance with Secs. 5.516 and 5.518; or

(vii) Deferral of termination of assistance is granted in accordance with Secs. 5.516 and 5.518.

(2) Restrictions on delay, denial, reduction or termination of assistance pending fair hearing for tenants. In addition to the factors listed in paragraph (b)(1) of this section, assistance to a tenant cannot be delayed, denied, reduced or terminated until the completion of the informal hearing described in paragraph (f) of this section.

(c) Events causing denial or termination of assistance. (1) General. Assistance to an applicant shall be denied, and a tenant's assistance shall be terminated, in accordance with the procedures of this section, upon the occurrence of any of the following events:

(i) Evidence of citizenship (i.e., the declaration) and eligible immigration status is not submitted by the date specified in Sec. 5.508(g) or by the expiration of any extension granted in accordance with Sec. 5.508(h);

(ii) Evidence of citizenship and eligible immigration status is timely submitted, but INS primary and secondary verification does not verify eligible immigration status of a family member; and

(A) The family does not pursue INS appeal or informal hearing rights as provided in this section; or

(B) INS appeal and informal hearing rights are pursued, but the final appeal or hearing decisions are decided against the family member; or

(iii) The responsible entity determines that a family member has knowingly permitted another individual who is not eligible for assistance to reside (on a permanent basis) in the public or assisted housing unit of the family member. Such termination shall be for a period of not less than 24 months. This provision does not apply to a family if the ineligibility of the ineligible individual was considered in calculating any proration of assistance provided for the family.

(2) Termination of assisted occupancy. For termination of assisted occupancy, see paragraph (i) of this section.

(d) Notice of denial or termination of assistance. The notice of denial or termination of assistance shall advise the family:

(1) That financial assistance will be denied or terminated, and provide a brief explanation of the reasons for the proposed denial or termination of assistance;

(2) That the family may be eligible for proration of assistance as provided under Sec. 5.520;

(3) In the case of a tenant, the criteria and procedures for obtaining relief under the provisions for preservation of families in Secs. 5.514 and 5.518;

(4) That the family has a right to request an appeal to the INS of the results of secondary verification of immigration status and to submit additional documentation or a written explanation in support of the appeal in accordance with the procedures of paragraph (e) of this section;

(5) That the family has a right to request an informal hearing with the responsible entity either upon completion of the INS appeal or in lieu of the INS appeal as provided in paragraph (f) of this section;

(6) For applicants, the notice shall advise that assistance may not be delayed until the conclusion of the INS appeal process, but assistance may be delayed during the pendency of the informal hearing process.

(e) Appeal to the INS. (1) Submission of request for appeal. Upon receipt of notification by the responsible entity that INS secondary verification failed to confirm eligible immigration status, the responsible entity shall notify the family of the results of the INS verification, and the family shall have 30 days from the date of the responsible entity's notification, to request an appeal of the INS results. The request for appeal shall be made by the family communicating that request in writing directly to the INS. The family must provide the responsible entity with a copy of the written request for appeal and proof of mailing.

(2) Documentation to be submitted as part of appeal to INS. The family shall forward to the designated INS office any additional documentation or written explanation in support of the appeal. This material must include a copy of the INS document verification request form G-845S (used to process the secondary verification request) or such other form specified by the INS, and a cover letter indicating that the family is requesting an appeal of the INS immigration status verification results.

(3) Decision by INS--(i) When decision will be issued. The INS will issue to the family, with a copy to the responsible entity, a decision within 30 days of its receipt of documentation concerning the family's appeal of the verification of immigration status. If, for any reason, the INS is unable to issue a decision within the 30 day time period, the INS will inform the family and responsible entity of the reasons for the delay.

(ii) Notification of INS decision and of informal hearing procedures. When the responsible entity receives a copy of the INS decision, the responsible entity shall notify the family of its right to request an informal hearing on the responsible entity's ineligibility determination in accordance with the procedures of paragraph (f) of this section.

(4) No delay, denial, reduction, or termination of assistance until completion of INS appeal process; direct appeal to INS. Pending the completion of the INS appeal under this section, assistance may not be delayed, denied, reduced or terminated on the basis of immigration status.

(f) Informal hearing. (1) When request for hearing is to be made. After notification of the INS decision on appeal, or in lieu of request of appeal to the INS, the family may request that the responsible entity provide a hearing. This request must be made either within 30 days of receipt of the notice described in paragraph (d) of this section, or within 30 days of receipt of the INS appeal decision issued in accordance with paragraph (e) of this section.

(2) Informal hearing procedures--(i) Tenants assisted under a Section 8 covered program: For tenants assisted under a Section 8 covered program, the procedures for the hearing before the responsible entity are set forth in:

(A) For Section 8 Moderate Rehabilitation assistance: 24 CFR part 882;

(B) For Section 8 tenant-based assistance: 24 CFR part 982; or

(C) For Section 8 project-based certificate program: 24 CFR part 983.

(ii) Tenants assisted under any other Section 8 covered program or a Public Housing covered program: For tenants assisted under a Section 8 covered program not listed in paragraph (f)(3)(i) of this section or a Public Housing covered program,

the procedures for the hearing before the responsible entity are set forth in 24 CFR part 966.

(iii) Families under Housing covered programs and applicants for assistance under all covered programs. For all families under Housing covered programs (applicants as well as tenants already receiving assistance) and for applicants for assistance under all covered programs, the procedures for the informal hearing before the responsible entity are as follows:

(A) Hearing before an impartial individual. The family shall be provided a hearing before any person(s) designated by the responsible entity (including an officer or employee of the responsible entity), other than a person who made or approved the decision under review, and other than a person who is a subordinate of the person who made or approved the decision;

(B) Examination of evidence. The family shall be provided the opportunity to examine and copy at the individual's expense, at a reasonable time in advance of the hearing, any documents in the possession of the responsible entity pertaining to the family's eligibility status, or in the possession of the INS (as permitted by INS requirements), including any records and regulations that may be relevant to the hearing;

(C) Presentation of evidence and arguments in support of eligible status. The family shall be provided the opportunity to present evidence and arguments in support of eligible status. Evidence may be considered without regard to admissibility under the rules of evidence applicable to judicial proceedings;

(D) Controverting evidence of the responsible entity. The family shall be provided the opportunity to controvert evidence relied upon by the responsible entity and to confront and cross-examine all witnesses on whose testimony or information the responsible entity relies;

(E) Representation. The family shall be entitled to be represented by an attorney, or other designee, at the family's expense, and to have such person make statements on the family's behalf;

(F) Interpretive services. The family shall be entitled to arrange for an interpreter to attend the hearing, at the expense of the family, or responsible entity, as may be agreed upon by the two parties to the proceeding; and

(G) Hearing to be recorded. The family shall be entitled to have the hearing recorded by audiotape (a transcript of the hearing may, but is not required to, be provided by the responsible entity).

(3) Hearing decision. The responsible entity shall provide the family with a written final decision, based solely on the facts presented at the hearing, within 14 days of the date of the informal hearing. The decision shall state the basis for the decision.

(g) Judicial relief. A decision against a family member, issued in accordance with paragraphs (e) or (f) of this section, does not preclude the family from exercising the right, that may otherwise be available, to seek redress directly through judicial procedures.

(h) Retention of documents. The responsible entity shall retain for a minimum of 5 years the following documents that may have been submitted to the responsible entity by the family, or provided to the responsible entity as part of the INS appeal or the informal hearing process:

(1) The application for financial assistance;

(2) The form completed by the family for income reexamination;

(3) Photocopies of any original documents (front and back), including original INS documents;

(4) The signed verification consent form;

(5) The INS verification results;

(6) The request for an INS appeal;

(7) The final INS determination;

(8) The request for an informal hearing; and

(9) The final informal hearing decision.

(i) Termination of assisted occupancy. (1) Under Housing covered programs, and in the Section 8 covered programs other than the Section 8 Rental Certificate, Rental Voucher,

and Moderate Rehabilitation programs, assisted occupancy is terminated by:

(i) If permitted under the lease, the responsible entity notifying the tenant that because of the termination of assisted occupancy the tenant is required to pay the HUD-approved market rent for the dwelling unit.

(ii) The responsible entity and tenant entering into a new lease without financial assistance.

(iii) The responsible entity evicting the tenant. While the tenant continues in occupancy of the unit, the responsible entity may continue to receive assistance payments if action to terminate the tenancy under an assisted lease is promptly initiated and diligently pursued, in accordance with the terms of the lease, and if eviction of the tenant is undertaken by judicial action pursuant to State and local law. Action by the responsible entity to terminate the tenancy and to evict the tenant must be in accordance with applicable HUD regulations and other HUD requirements. For any jurisdiction, HUD may prescribe a maximum period during which assistance payments may be continued during eviction proceedings and may prescribe other standards of reasonable diligence for the prosecution of eviction proceedings.

(2) In the Section 8 Rental Certificate, Rental Voucher, and Moderate Rehabilitation programs, assisted occupancy is terminated by terminating assistance payments. (See provisions of this section concerning termination of assistance.) The PHA shall not make any additional assistance payments to the owner after the required procedures specified in this section have been completed. In addition, the PHA shall not approve a lease, enter into an assistance contract, or process a portability move for the family after those procedures have been completed.

{61 FR 13616, Mar. 27, 1996, as amended at 61 FR 60539, Nov. 29, 1996; 64 FR 25731, May 12, 1999}

Sec. 5.516 Availability of preservation assistance to mixed families and other families.

(a) Assistance available for tenant mixed families--(1) General. Preservation assistance is available to tenant mixed families, following completion of the appeals and informal hearing procedures provided in Sec. 5.514. There are three types of preservation assistance:

(i) Continued assistance (see paragraph (a) of Sec. 5.518);

(ii) Temporary deferral of termination of assistance (see paragraph (b) of Sec. 5.518); or

(iii) Prorated assistance (see Sec. 5.520, a mixed family must be provided prorated assistance if the family so requests).

(2) Availability of assistance--(i) For Housing covered programs: One of the three types of assistance described is available to tenant mixed families assisted under a National Housing Act or 1965 HUD Act covered program, depending upon the family's eligibility for such assistance. Continued assistance must be provided to a mixed family that meets the conditions for eligibility for continued assistance.

(ii) For Section 8 or Public Housing covered programs. One of the three types of assistance described may be available to tenant mixed families assisted under a Section 8 or Public Housing covered program.

(b) Assistance available for applicant mixed families. Prorated assistance is also available for mixed families applying for assistance as provided in Sec. 5.520.

(c) Assistance available to other families in occupancy. Temporary deferral of termination of assistance may be available to families receiving assistance under a Section 214 covered program on June 19, 1995, and who have no members with eligible immigration status, as set forth in paragraphs (c)(1) and (2) of this section.

(1) For Housing covered programs: Temporary deferral of termination of

assistance is available to families assisted under a Housing covered program.

(2) For Section 8 or Public Housing covered programs: The responsible entity may make temporary deferral of termination of assistance to families assisted under a Section 8 or Public Housing covered program.

(d) Section 8 covered programs: Discretion afforded to provide certain family preservation assistance--(1) Project owners. With respect to assistance under a Section 8 Act covered program administered by a project owner, HUD has the discretion to determine under what circumstances families are to be provided one of the two statutory forms of assistance for preservation of the family (continued assistance or temporary deferral of assistance). HUD is exercising its discretion by specifying the standards in this section under which a project owner must provide one of these two types of assistance to a family. However, project owners and PHAs must offer prorated assistance to eligible mixed families.

(2) PHAs. The PHA, rather than HUD, has the discretion to determine the circumstances under which a family will be offered one of the two statutory forms of assistance (continued assistance or temporary deferral of termination of assistance). The PHA must establish its own policy and criteria to follow in making its decision. In establishing the criteria for granting continued assistance or temporary deferral of termination of assistance, the PHA must incorporate the statutory criteria, which are set forth in paragraphs (a) and (b) of Sec. 5.518. However, the PHA must offer prorated assistance to eligible families.

{61 FR 13616, Mar. 27, 1996, as amended at 61 FR 60539, Nov. 29, 1996; 64 FR 25732, May 12, 1999}

Sec. 5.518 Types of preservation assistance available to mixed families and other families.

(a) Continued assistance. (1) General. A mixed family may receive continued housing assistance if all of the following conditions are met (a mixed family assisted under a Housing covered program must be provided continued assistance if the family meets the following conditions):

(i) The family was receiving assistance under a Section 214 covered program on June 19, 1995;

(ii) The family's head of household or spouse has eligible immigration status as described in Sec. 5.506; and

(iii) The family does not include any person (who does not have eligible immigration status) other than the head of household, any spouse of the head of household, any parents of the head of household, any parents of the spouse, or any children of the head of household or spouse.

(2) Proration of continued assistance. A family entitled to continued assistance before November 29, 1996 is entitled to continued assistance as described in paragraph (a) of this section. A family entitled to continued assistance after November 29, 1996 shall receive prorated assistance as described in Sec. 5.520.

(b) Temporary deferral of termination of assistance--(1) Eligibility for this type of assistance. If a mixed family qualifies for prorated assistance (and does not qualify for continued assistance), but decides not to accept prorated assistance, or if a family has no members with eligible immigration status, the family may be eligible for temporary deferral of termination of assistance if necessary to permit the family additional time for the orderly transition of those family members with ineligible status, and any other family members involved, to other affordable housing. Other affordable housing is used in the context of transition of an ineligible family from a rent level that reflects HUD assistance to a rent level that

is unassisted; the term refers to housing that is not substandard, that is of appropriate size for the family and that can be rented for an amount not exceeding the amount that the family pays for rent, including utilities, plus 25 percent.

(2) Housing covered programs: Conditions for granting temporary deferral of termination of assistance. The responsible entity shall grant a temporary deferral of termination of assistance to a mixed family if the family is assisted under a Housing covered program and one of the following conditions is met:

(i) The family demonstrates that reasonable efforts to find other affordable housing of appropriate size have been unsuccessful (for purposes of this section, reasonable efforts include seeking information from, and pursuing leads obtained from the State housing agency, the city government, local newspapers, rental agencies and the owner);

(ii) The vacancy rate for affordable housing of appropriate size is below five percent in the housing market for the area in which the project is located; or

(iii) The consolidated plan, as described in 24 CFR part 91 and if applicable to the covered program, indicates that the local jurisdiction's housing market lacks sufficient affordable housing opportunities for households having a size and income similar to the family seeking the deferral.

(3) Time limit on deferral period. If temporary deferral of termination of assistance is granted, the deferral period shall be for an initial period not to exceed six months. The initial period may be renewed for additional periods of six months, but the aggregate deferral period for deferrals provided after November 29, 1996 shall not exceed a period of eighteen months. The aggregate deferral period for deferrals granted prior to November 29, 1996 shall not exceed 3 years. These time periods do not apply to a family which includes a refugee under section 207 of the Immigration and Nationality Act or an individual seeking asylum under section 208 of that Act.

(4) Notification requirements for beginning of each deferral period. At the beginning of each deferral period, the responsible entity must inform the family of its ineligibility for financial assistance and offer the family information concerning, and referrals to assist in finding, other affordable housing.

(5) Determination of availability of affordable housing at end of each deferral period. (i) Before the end of each deferral period, the responsible entity must satisfy the applicable requirements of either paragraph (b)(5)(i)(A) or (B) of this section. Specifically, the responsible entity must:

(A) For Housing covered programs: Make a determination that one of the two conditions specified in paragraph (b)(2) of this section continues to be met (note: affordable housing will be determined to be available if the vacancy rate is five percent or greater), the owner's knowledge and the tenant's evidence indicate that other affordable housing is available; or

(B) For Section 8 or Public Housing covered programs: Make a determination of the availability of affordable housing of appropriate size based on evidence of conditions which when taken together will demonstrate an inadequate supply of affordable housing for the area in which the project is located, the consolidated plan (if applicable, as described in 24 CFR part 91), the responsible entity's own knowledge of the availability of affordable housing, and on evidence of the tenant family's efforts to locate such housing.

(ii) The responsible entity must also:

(A) Notify the tenant family in writing, at least 60 days in advance of the expiration of the deferral period, that termination will be deferred again (provided that the granting of another deferral will not result in aggregate deferral periods that exceeds the maximum deferral period). This time period does not apply to a family which includes a refugee under section 207 of the Immigration and Nationality Act or an individual seeking asylum under section 208 of that Act, and a determination was made that other affordable housing is not available; or

(B) Notify the tenant family in writing, at least 60 days in advance of the expiration of the deferral period, that termination of financial assistance will not be deferred because either granting another deferral will result in aggregate deferral periods that exceed the maximum deferral period (unless the family includes a refugee under section 207 of the Immigration and Nationality Act or an individual seeking asylum under section 208 of that Act), or a determination has been made that other affordable housing is available.

(c) Option to select proration of assistance at end of deferral period. A family who is eligible for, and receives temporary deferral of termination of assistance, may request, and the responsible entity shall provide proration of assistance at the end of the deferral period if the family has made a good faith effort during the deferral period to locate other affordable housing.

(d) Notification of decision on family preservation assistance. A responsible entity shall notify the family of its decision concerning the family's qualification for family preservation assistance. If the family is ineligible for family preservation assistance, the notification shall state the reasons, which must be based on relevant factors. For tenant families, the notice also shall inform the family of any applicable appeal rights.

{61 FR 13616, Mar. 27, 1996, as amended at 61 FR 60539, Nov. 29, 1996; 64 FR 25732, May 12, 1999}

Sec. 5.520 Proration of assistance.

(a) Applicability. This section applies to a mixed family other than a family receiving continued assistance, or other than a family who is eligible for and requests and receives temporary deferral of termination of assistance. An eligible mixed family who requests prorated assistance must be provided prorated assistance.

(b) Method of prorating assistance for Housing covered programs--(1) Proration under Rent Supplement Program. If the household participates in the Rent Supplement Program, the rent supplement paid on the household's behalf shall be the rent supplement the household would otherwise be entitled to, multiplied by a fraction, the denominator of which is the number of people in the household and the numerator of which is the number of eligible persons in the household;

(2) Proration under Section 235 Program. If the household participates in the Section 235 Program, the interest reduction payments paid on the household's behalf shall be the payments the household would otherwise be entitled to, multiplied by a fraction the denominator of which is the number of people in the household and the numerator of which is the number of eligible persons in the household;

(3) Proration under Section 236 Program without the benefit of additional assistance. If the household participates in the Section 236 Program without the benefit of any additional assistance, the household's rent shall be increased above the rent the household would otherwise pay by an amount equal to the difference between the market rate rent for the unit and the rent the household would otherwise pay multiplied by a fraction the denominator of which is the number of people in the household and the numerator of which is the number of ineligible persons in the household;

(4) Proration under Section 236 Program with the benefit of additional assistance. If the household participates in the Section 236 Program with the benefit of additional assistance under the rent supplement, rental assistance payment or Section 8 programs, the household's rent shall be increased above the rent the household would otherwise pay by:

(i) An amount equal to the difference between the market rate rent for the unit and the basic rent for the unit multiplied by a fraction, the denominator of which is the number of people in the household, and the numerator of which is the number of ineligible persons in the household, plus;

(ii) An amount equal to the rent supplement, housing assistance payment

or rental assistance payment the household would otherwise be entitled to multiplied by a fraction, the denominator of which is the number of people in the household and the numerator of which is the number of ineligible persons in the household.

(c) Method of prorating assistance for Section 8 covered programs-- (1) Section 8 assistance other than assistance provided for a tenancy under the Section 8 Rental Voucher Program or for an over-FMR tenancy in the Section 8 Rental Certificate Program. For Section 8 assistance other than assistance for a tenancy under the voucher program or an over-FMR tenancy under the certificate program, the PHA must prorate the family's assistance as follows:

(i) Step 1. Determine gross rent for the unit. (Gross rent is contract rent plus any allowance for tenant paid utilities).

(ii) Step 2. Determine total tenant payment in accordance with section 5.613(a). (Annual income includes income of all family members, including any family member who has not established eligible immigration status.)

(iii) Step 3. Subtract amount determined in paragraph (c)(1)(ii), (Step 2), from amount determined in paragraph (c)(1)(i), (Step 1).

(iv) Step 4. Multiply the amount determined in paragraph (c)(1)(iii), (Step 3) by a fraction for which:

(A) The numerator is the number of family members who have established eligible immigration status; and

(B) The denominator is the total number of family members.

(v) Prorated housing assistance. The amount determined in paragraph (c)(1)(iv), (Step 4) is the prorated housing assistance payment for a mixed family.

(vi) No effect on contract rent. Proration of the housing assistance payment does not affect contract rent to the owner. The family must pay as rent the portion of contract rent not covered by the prorated housing assistance payment.

(2) Assistance for a Section 8 voucher tenancy or over-FMR tenancy. For a tenancy under the voucher program or for an over-FMR tenancy under the certificate program, the PHA must prorate the family's assistance as follows:

(i) Step 1. Determine the amount of the pre-proration housing assistance payment. (Annual income includes income of all family members, including any family member who has not established eligible immigration status.)

(ii) Step 2. Multiply the amount determined in paragraph (c)(2)(i), (Step 1) by a fraction for which:

(A) The numerator is the number of family members who have established eligible immigration status; and

(B) The denominator is the total number of family members.

(iii) Prorated housing assistance. The amount determined in paragraph (c)(2)(ii), (Step 2) is the prorated housing assistance payment for a mixed family.

(iv) No effect on rent to owner. Proration of the housing assistance payment does not affect rent to owner. The family must pay the portion of rent to owner not covered by the prorated housing assistance payment.

(d) Method of prorating assistance for Public Housing covered programs. The PHA shall prorate the family's assistance by:

(1) Step 1. Determining total tenant payment in accordance with 24 CFR 913.107(a). (Annual income includes income of all family members, including any family member who has not established eligible immigration status.)

(2) Step 2. Subtracting the total tenant payment from a HUD-supplied ``public housing maximum rent'' applicable to the unit or the PHA. (This ``maximum rent'' shall be determined by HUD using the 95th percentile rent for the PHA.) The result is the maximum subsidy for which the family could qualify if all members were eligible (``family maximum subsidy'').

(3) Step 3. Dividing the family maximum subsidy by the number of persons in the family (all persons) to determine the maximum subsidy per each family member who has citizenship or eligible immigration status (``eligible family member''). The

subsidy per eligible family member is the ``member maximum subsidy''.

(4) Step 4. Multiplying the member maximum subsidy by the number of family members who have citizenship or eligible immigration status (``eligible family members'').

(5) Step 5. The product of steps 1 through 4, as set forth in paragraph (d)(2) of this section is the amount of subsidy for which the family is eligible (``eligible subsidy''). The family's rent is the ``public housing maximum rent'' minus the amount of the eligible subsidy.

{61 FR 5202, Feb. 9, 1996, as amended at 63 FR 23853, Apr. 30, 1998; 64 FR 13056, Mar. 16, 1999}

Sec. 5.522 Prohibition of assistance to noncitizen students.

(a) General. The provisions of Secs. 5.516 and 5.518 permitting continued assistance or temporary deferral of termination of assistance for certain families do not apply to any person who is determined to be a noncitizen student as in paragraph (c)(2)(A) of Section 214 (42 U.S.C. 1436a(c)(2)(A)). The family of a noncitizen student may be eligible for prorated assistance, as provided in paragraph (b)(2) of this section.

(b) Family of noncitizen students. (1) The prohibition on providing assistance to a noncitizen student as described in paragraph (a) of this section extends to the noncitizen spouse of the noncitizen student and minor children accompanying the student or following to join the student.

(2) The prohibition on providing assistance to a noncitizen student does not extend to the citizen spouse of the noncitizen student and the children of the citizen spouse and noncitizen student.

Sec. 5.524 Compliance with nondiscrimination requirements.

The responsible entity shall administer the restrictions on use of assisted housing by noncitizens with ineligible immigration status imposed by this part in conformity with all applicable nondiscrimination and equal opportunity requirements, including, but not limited to, title VI of the Civil Rights Act of 1964 (42 U.S.C. 2000d-2000d-5) and the implementing regulations in 24 CFR part 1, section 504 of the Rehabilitation Act of 1973 (29 U.S.C. 794) and the implementing regulations in 24 CFR part 8, the Fair Housing Act (42 U.S.C. 3601-3619) and the implementing regulations in 24 CFR part 100.

Sec. 5.526 Protection from liability for responsible entities and State and local government agencies and officials.

(a) Protection from liability for responsible entities. Responsible entities are protected from liability as set forth in Section 214(e) (42 U.S.C 1436a(e)).

(b) Protection from liability for State and local government agencies and officials. State and local government agencies and officials shall not be liable for the design or implementation of the verification system described in Sec. 5.512, as long as the implementation by the State and local government agency or official is in accordance with prescribed HUD rules and requirements.

{64 FR 25732, May 12, 1999}

Sec. 5.528 Liability of ineligible tenants for reimbursement of benefits.

Where a tenant has received the benefit of HUD financial assistance to which the tenant was not entitled because the tenant intentionally misrepresented eligible status, the ineligible tenant is responsible for reimbursing HUD for the assistance improperly paid. If the amount of the assistance is substantial, the responsible entity is encouraged to refer the case to the HUD Inspector General's office for further investigation. Possible criminal prosecution

may follow based on the False Statements Act (18 U.S.C. 1001 and 1010).

Subpart F--Section 8 and Public Housing, and Other HUD Assisted Housing Serving Persons with Disabilities: Family Income and Family Payment; Occupancy Requirements for Section 8 Project-Based Assistance

Sec. 5.601 Purpose and applicability.

Authority: 42 U.S.C. 1437a, 1437c, 1437d, 1437f, 1437n, and 3535(d).

Source: 61 FR 54498, Oct. 18, 1996, unless otherwise noted.

This subpart states HUD requirements on the following subjects:

(a) Determining annual and adjusted income of families who apply for or receive assistance in the Section 8 (tenant-based and project-based) and public housing programs;

(b) Determining payments by and utility reimbursements to families assisted in these programs;

(c) Additional occupancy requirements that apply to the Section 8 project-based assistance programs. These additional requirements concern:

(1) Income-eligibility and income-targeting when a Section 8 owner admits families to a Section 8 project or unit;

(2) Owner selection preferences; and

(3) Owner reexamination of family income and composition;

(d) Determining adjusted income, as provided in Sec. 5.611(a) and (b), for families who apply for or receive assistance under the following programs: HOME Investment Partnerships Program (24 CFR part 92); Rent Supplement Payments Program (24 CFR part 200, subpart W); Rental Assistance Payments Program (24 CFR part 236, subpart D); Housing Opportunities for Persons with AIDS (24 CFR part 574); Shelter Plus Care Program (24 CFR part 582); Supportive Housing Program (McKinney Act Homeless Assistance) (24 CFR part 583); Section 202 Supportive Housing Program for the Elderly (24 CFR 891, subpart B); Section 202 Direct Loans for Housing for the Elderly and Persons with Disabilities (24 CFR part 891, subpart E) and the Section 811 Supportive Housing for Persons with Disabilities (24 CFR part 891, subpart C). Unless specified in the regulations for each of the programs listed in paragraph (d) of this section or in another regulatory section of this part 5, subpart F, the regulations in part 5, subpart F, generally are not applicable to these programs; and

(e) Determining earned income disregard for persons with disabilities, as provided in Sec. 5.617, for the following programs: HOME Investment Partnerships Program (24 CFR part 92); Housing Opportunities for Persons with AIDS (24 CFR part 574); Supportive Housing Program (McKinney Act Homeless Assistance) (24 CFR part 583); and the Housing Choice Voucher Program (24 CFR part 982).

{66 FR 6222, Jan. 19, 2001}

Sec. 5.603 Definitions.

As used in this subpart:

(a) Terms found elsewhere in part 5--(1) Subpart A. The terms 1937 Act, elderly person, public housing, public housing agency (PHA), responsible entity and Section 8 are defined in Sec. 5.100.

(2) Subpart D. The terms ``disabled family'', ``elderly family'', ``family'', ``live-in aide'', and ``person with disabilities'' are defined in Sec. 5.403.

(b) The following terms shall have the meanings set forth below:

Adjusted income. See Sec. 5.611.

Annual income. See Sec. 5.609.

Child care expenses. Amounts anticipated to be paid by the family for the care of children under 13 years of age during the period for which annual income is computed, but only where such care is necessary to

enable a family member to actively seek employment, be gainfully employed, or to further his or her education and only to the extent such amounts are not reimbursed. The amount deducted shall reflect reasonable charges for child care. In the case of child care necessary to permit employment, the amount deducted shall not exceed the amount of employment income that is included in annual income.

Dependent. A member of the family (except foster children and foster adults) other than the family head or spouse, who is under 18 years of age, or is a person with a disability, or is a full-time student.

Disability assistance expenses. Reasonable expenses that are anticipated, during the period for which annual income is computed, for attendant care and auxiliary apparatus for a disabled family member and that are necessary to enable a family member (including the disabled member) to be employed, provided that the expenses are neither paid to a member of the family nor reimbursed by an outside source.

Economic self-sufficiency program. Any program designed to encourage, assist, train, or facilitate the economic independence of HUD-assisted families or to provide work for such families. These programs include programs for job training, employment counseling, work placement, basic skills training, education, English proficiency, workfare, financial or household management, apprenticeship, and any program necessary to ready a participant for work (including a substance abuse or mental health treatment program), or other work activities.

Extremely low income family. A family whose annual income does not exceed 30 percent of the median income for the area, as determined by HUD, with adjustments for smaller and larger families, except that HUD may establish income ceilings higher or lower than 30 percent of the median income for the area if HUD finds that such variations are necessary because of unusually high or low family incomes.

Full-time student. A person who is attending school or vocational training on a full-time basis.

Imputed welfare income. See Sec. 5.615.

Low income family. A family whose annual income does not exceed 80 percent of the median income for the area, as determined by HUD with adjustments for smaller and larger families, except that HUD may establish income ceilings higher or lower than 80 percent of the median income for the area on the basis of HUD's findings that such variations are necessary because of unusually high or low family incomes.

Medical expenses. Medical expenses, including medical insurance premiums, that are anticipated during the period for which annual income is computed, and that are not covered by insurance.

Monthly adjusted income. One twelfth of adjusted income.

Monthly income. One twelfth of annual income.

Net family assets. (1) Net cash value after deducting reasonable costs that would be incurred in disposing of real property, savings, stocks, bonds, and other forms of capital investment, excluding interests in Indian trust land and excluding equity accounts in HUD homeownership programs. The value of necessary items of personal property such as furniture and automobiles shall be excluded.

(2) In cases where a trust fund has been established and the trust is not revocable by, or under the control of, any member of the family or household, the value of the trust fund will not be considered an asset so long as the fund continues to be held in trust. Any income distributed from the trust fund shall be counted when determining annual income under Sec. 5.609.

(3) In determining net family assets, PHAs or owners, as applicable, shall include the value of any business or family assets disposed of by an applicant or tenant for less than fair market value (including a disposition in trust, but not in a foreclosure or bankruptcy sale) during the two years preceding the date of application for the

program or reexamination, as applicable, in excess of the consideration received therefor. In the case of a disposition as part of a separation or divorce settlement, the disposition will not be considered to be for less than fair market value if the applicant or tenant receives important consideration not measurable in dollar terms.

(4) For purposes of determining annual income under Sec. 5.609, the term ``net family assets'' does not include the value of a home currently being purchased with assistance under part 982, subpart M of this title. This exclusion is limited to the first 10 years after the purchase date of the home.

Owner has the meaning provided in the relevant program regulations. As used in this subpart, where appropriate, the term ``owner'' shall also include a ``borrower'' as defined in part 891 of this title.

Responsible entity. For Sec. 5.611, in addition to the definition of ``responsible entity'' in Sec. 5.100, and for Sec. 5.617, in addition to only that part of the definition of ``responsible entity'' in Sec. 5.100 which addresses the Section 8 program covered by Sec. 5.617 (public housing is not covered by Sec. 5.617), ``responsible entity'' means:

(1) For the HOME Investment Partnerships Program, the participating jurisdiction, as defined in 24 CFR 92.2;

(2) For the Rent Supplement Payments Program, the owner of the multifamily project;

(3) For the Rental Assistance Payments Program, the owner of the Section 236 project;

(4) For the Housing Opportunities for Persons with AIDS (HOPWA) program, the applicable ``State'' or ``unit of general local government'' or ``nonprofit organization'' as these terms are defined in 24 CFR 574.3, that administers the HOPWA Program;

(5) For the Shelter Plus Care Program, the ``Recipient'' as defined in 24 CFR 582.5;

(6) For the Supportive Housing Program, the ``recipient'' as defined in 24 CFR 583.5;

(7) For the Section 202 Supportive Housing Program for the Elderly, the ``Owner'' as defined in 24 CFR 891.205;

(8) For the Section 202 Direct Loans for Housing for the Elderly and Persons with Disabilities), the ``Borrower'' as defined in 24 CFR 891.505; and

(9) For the Section 811 Supportive Housing Program for Persons with Disabilities, the ``owner'' as defined in 24 CFR 891.305.

Tenant rent. The amount payable monthly by the family as rent to the unit owner (Section 8 owner or PHA in public housing). (This term is not used in the Section 8 voucher program.)

Total tenant payment. See Sec. 5.613.

Utility allowance. If the cost of utilities (except telephone) and other housing services for an assisted unit is not included in the tenant rent but is the responsibility of the family occupying the unit, an amount equal to the estimate made or approved by a PHA or HUD of the monthly cost of a reasonable consumption of such utilities and other services for the unit by an energy-conservative household of modest circumstances consistent with the requirements of a safe, sanitary, and healthful living environment.

Utility reimbursement. The amount, if any, by which the utility allowance for a unit, if applicable, exceeds the total tenant payment for the family occupying the unit. (This definition is not used in the Section 8 voucher program, or for a public housing family that is paying a flat rent.)

Very low income family. A family whose annual income does not exceed 50 percent of the median family income for the area, as determined by HUD with adjustments for smaller and larger families, except that HUD may establish income ceilings higher or lower than 50 percent of the median income for the area if HUD finds that such variations are necessary because of unusually high or low family incomes.

Welfare assistance. Welfare or other payments to families or individuals, based on need, that are made under programs funded, separately or jointly, by Federal, State or local governments (including assistance provided under the Temporary Assistance

for Needy Families (TANF) program, as that term is defined under the implementing regulations issued by the Department of Health and Human Services at 45 CFR 260.31).

Work activities. See definition at section 407(d) of the Social Security Act (42 U.S.C. 607(d)).

{61 FR 54498, Oct. 18, 1996, as amended at 65 FR 16716, Mar. 29, 2000; 65 FR 55161, Sept. 12, 2000; 66 FR 6223, Jan. 19, 2001; 67 FR 47432, July 18, 2002}

Family Income

Sec. 5.609 Annual income.

(a) Annual income means all amounts, monetary or not, which:

(1) Go to, or on behalf of, the family head or spouse (even if temporarily absent) or to any other family member; or

(2) Are anticipated to be received from a source outside the family during the 12-month period following admission or annual reexamination effective date; and

(3) Which are not specifically excluded in paragraph (c) of this section.

(4) Annual income also means amounts derived (during the 12-month period) from assets to which any member of the family has access.

(b) Annual income includes, but is not limited to:

(1) The full amount, before any payroll deductions, of wages and salaries, overtime pay, commissions, fees, tips and bonuses, and other compensation for personal services;

(2) The net income from the operation of a business or profession. Expenditures for business expansion or amortization of capital indebtedness shall not be used as deductions in determining net income. An allowance for depreciation of assets used in a business or profession may be deducted, based on straight line depreciation, as provided in Internal Revenue Service regulations. Any withdrawal of cash or assets from the operation of a business or profession will be included in income, except to the extent the withdrawal is reimbursement of cash or assets invested in the operation by the family;

(3) Interest, dividends, and other net income of any kind from real or personal property. Expenditures for amortization of capital indebtedness shall not be used as deductions in determining net income. An allowance for depreciation is permitted only as authorized in paragraph (b)(2) of this section. Any withdrawal of cash or assets from an investment will be included in income, except to the extent the withdrawal is reimbursement of cash or assets invested by the family. Where the family has net family assets in excess of $5,000, annual income shall include the greater of the actual income derived from all net family assets or a percentage of the value of such assets based on the current passbook savings rate, as determined by HUD;

(4) The full amount of periodic amounts received from Social Security, annuities, insurance policies, retirement funds, pensions, disability or death benefits, and other similar types of periodic receipts, including a lump-sum amount or prospective monthly amounts for the delayed start of a periodic amount (except as provided in paragraph (c)(14) of this section);

(5) Payments in lieu of earnings, such as unemployment and disability compensation, worker's compensation and severance pay (except as provided in paragraph (c)(3) of this section);

(6) Welfare assistance payments. (i) Welfare assistance payments made under the Temporary Assistance for Needy Families (TANF) program are included in annual income only to the extent such payments:

(A) Qualify as assistance under the TANF program definition at 45 CFR 260.31; and

(B) Are not otherwise excluded under paragraph (c) of this section.

(ii) If the welfare assistance payment includes an amount specifically designated for shelter and utilities that is subject to adjustment by the welfare assistance agency in accordance with the actual cost of shelter and utilities, the amount of welfare assistance income to be included as income shall consist of:

(A) The amount of the allowance or grant exclusive of the amount specifically designated for shelter or utilities; plus

(B) The maximum amount that the welfare assistance agency could in fact allow the family for shelter and utilities. If the family's welfare assistance is ratably reduced from the standard of need by applying a percentage, the amount calculated under this paragraph shall be the amount resulting from one application of the percentage.

(7) Periodic and determinable allowances, such as alimony and child support payments, and regular contributions or gifts received from organizations or from persons not residing in the dwelling;

(8) All regular pay, special pay and allowances of a member of the Armed Forces (except as provided in paragraph (c)(7) of this section).

(c) Annual income does not include the following:

(1) Income from employment of children (including foster children) under the age of 18 years;

(2) Payments received for the care of foster children or foster adults (usually persons with disabilities, unrelated to the tenant family, who are unable to live alone);

(3) Lump-sum additions to family assets, such as inheritances, insurance payments (including payments under health and accident insurance and worker's compensation), capital gains and settlement for personal or property losses (except as provided in paragraph (b)(5) of this section);

(4) Amounts received by the family that are specifically for, or in reimbursement of, the cost of medical expenses for any family member;

(5) Income of a live-in aide, as defined in Sec. 5.403;

(6) The full amount of student financial assistance paid directly to the student or to the educational institution;

(7) The special pay to a family member serving in the Armed Forces who is exposed to hostile fire;

(8)(i) Amounts received under training programs funded by HUD;

(ii) Amounts received by a person with a disability that are disregarded for a limited time for purposes of Supplemental Security Income eligibility and benefits because they are set aside for use under a Plan to Attain Self-Sufficiency (PASS);

(iii) Amounts received by a participant in other publicly assisted programs which are specifically for or in reimbursement of out-of-pocket expenses incurred (special equipment, clothing, transportation, child care, etc.) and which are made solely to allow participation in a specific program;

(iv) Amounts received under a resident service stipend. A resident service stipend is a modest amount (not to exceed $200 per month) received by a resident for performing a service for the PHA or owner, on a part-time basis, that enhances the quality of life in the development. Such services may include, but are not limited to, fire patrol, hall monitoring, lawn maintenance, resident initiatives coordination, and serving as a member of the PHA's governing board. No resident may receive more than one such stipend during the same period of time;

(v) Incremental earnings and benefits resulting to any family member from participation in qualifying State or local employment training programs (including training programs not affiliated with a local government) and training of a family member as resident management staff. Amounts excluded by this provision must be received under employment training programs with clearly defined goals and objectives, and are excluded only for the period during which the family member participates in the employment training program;

(9) Temporary, nonrecurring or sporadic income (including gifts);

(10) Reparation payments paid by a foreign government pursuant to claims filed under the laws of that government by persons who were persecuted during the Nazi era;

(11) Earnings in excess of $480 for each full-time student 18 years old or older (excluding the head of household and spouse);

(12) Adoption assistance payments in excess of $480 per adopted child;

(13) [Reserved]

(14) Deferred periodic amounts from supplemental security income and social security benefits that are received in a lump sum amount or in prospective monthly amounts.

(15) Amounts received by the family in the form of refunds or rebates under State or local law for property taxes paid on the dwelling unit;

(16) Amounts paid by a State agency to a family with a member who has a developmental disability and is living at home to offset the cost of services and equipment needed to keep the developmentally disabled family member at home; or

(17) Amounts specifically excluded by any other Federal statute from consideration as income for purposes of determining eligibility or benefits under a category of assistance programs that includes assistance under any program to which the exclusions set forth in 24 CFR 5.609(c) apply. A notice will be published in the Federal Register and distributed to PHAs and housing owners identifying the benefits that qualify for this exclusion. Updates will be published and distributed when necessary.

(d) Annualization of income. If it is not feasible to anticipate a level of income over a 12-month period (e.g., seasonal or cyclic income), or the PHA believes that past income is the best available indicator of expected future income, the PHA may annualize the income anticipated for a shorter period, subject to a redetermination at the end of the shorter period.

{61 FR 54498, Oct, 18, 1996, as amended at 65 FR 16716, Mar. 29, 2000; 67 FR 47432, July 18, 2002}

Sec. 5.611 Adjusted income.

Adjusted income means annual income (as determined by the responsible entity, defined in Sec. 5.100 and Sec. 5.603) of the members of the family residing or intending to reside in the dwelling unit, after making the following deductions:

(a) Mandatory deductions. In determining adjusted income, the responsible entity must deduct the following amounts from annual income:

(1) $480 for each dependent;

(2) $400 for any elderly family or disabled family;

(3) The sum of the following, to the extent the sum exceeds three percent of annual income:

(i) Unreimbursed medical expenses of any elderly family or disabled family; and

(ii) Unreimbursed reasonable attendant care and auxiliary apparatus expenses for each member of the family who is a person with disabilities, to the extent necessary to enable any member of the family (including the member who is a person with disabilities) to be employed. This deduction may not exceed the earned income received by family members who are 18 years of age or older and who are able to work because of such attendant care or auxiliary apparatus; and

(4) Any reasonable child care expenses necessary to enable a member of the family to be employed or to further his or her education.

(b) Additional deductions. (1) For public housing, a PHA may adopt additional deductions from annual income. The PHA must establish a written policy for such deductions.

(2) For the HUD programs listed in Sec. 5.601(d), the responsible entity shall calculate such other deductions as required and permitted by the applicable program regulations.

{66 FR 6223, Jan. 19, 2001}

Sec. 5.613 Public housing program and Section 8 tenant-based assistance program: PHA cooperation with welfare agency.

(a) This section applies to the public housing program and the Section 8 tenant-based assistance program.

(b) The PHA must make best efforts to enter into cooperation agreements with

welfare agencies under which such agencies agree:

(1) To target public assistance, benefits and services to families receiving assistance in the public housing program and the Section 8 tenant-based assistance program to achieve self-sufficiency;

(2) To provide written verification to the PHA concerning welfare benefits for families applying for or receiving assistance in these housing assistance programs.

{65 FR 16717, Mar. 29, 2000}

Sec. 5.615 Public housing program and Section 8 tenant-based assistance program: How welfare benefit reduction affects family income.

(a) Applicability. This section applies to covered families who reside in public housing (part 960 of this title) or receive Section 8 tenant-based assistance (part 982 of this title).

(b) Definitions. The following definitions apply for purposes of this section:

Covered families. Families who receive welfare assistance or other public assistance benefits (``welfare benefits'') from a State or other public agency (``welfare agency'') under a program for which Federal, State, or local law requires that a member of the family must participate in an economic self-sufficiency program as a condition for such assistance.

Economic self-sufficiency program. See definition at Sec. 5.603.

Imputed welfare income. The amount of annual income not actually received by a family, as a result of a specified welfare benefit reduction, that is nonetheless included in the family's annual income for purposes of determining rent.

Specified welfare benefit reduction.

(1) A reduction of welfare benefits by the welfare agency, in whole or in part, for a family member, as determined by the welfare agency, because of fraud by a family member in connection with the welfare program; or because of welfare agency sanction against a family member for noncompliance with a welfare agency requirement to participate in an economic self-sufficiency program.

(2) ``Specified welfare benefit reduction'' does not include a reduction or termination of welfare benefits by the welfare agency:

(i) at expiration of a lifetime or other time limit on the payment of welfare benefits;

(ii) because a family member is not able to obtain employment, even though the family member has complied with welfare agency economic self- sufficiency or work activities requirements; or

(iii) because a family member has not complied with other welfare agency requirements.

(c) Imputed welfare income.

(1) A family's annual income includes the amount of imputed welfare income (because of a specified welfare benefits reduction, as specified in notice to the PHA by the welfare agency), plus the total amount of other annual income as determined in accordance with Sec. 5.609.

(2) At the request of the PHA, the welfare agency will inform the PHA in writing of the amount and term of any specified welfare benefit reduction for a family member, and the reason for such reduction, and will also inform the PHA of any subsequent changes in the term or amount of such specified welfare benefit reduction. The PHA will use this information to determine the amount of imputed welfare income for a family.

(3) A family's annual income includes imputed welfare income in family annual income, as determined at the PHA's interim or regular reexamination of family income and composition, during the term of the welfare benefits reduction (as specified in information provided to the PHA by the welfare agency).

(4) The amount of the imputed welfare income is offset by the amount of additional income a family receives that commences after the time the sanction was imposed. When such additional income from other sources is at least equal to the imputed welfare income, the imputed welfare income is reduced to zero.

(5) The PHA may not include imputed welfare income in annual income if the family was not an assisted resident at the time of sanction.

(d) Review of PHA decision. (1) Public housing. If a public housing tenant claims that the PHA has not correctly calculated the amount of imputed welfare income in accordance with HUD requirements, and if the PHA denies the family's request to modify such amount, the PHA shall give the tenant written notice of such denial, with a brief explanation of the basis for the PHA determination of the amount of imputed welfare income. The PHA notice shall also state that if the tenant does not agree with the PHA determination, the tenant may request a grievance hearing in accordance with part 966, subpart B of this title to review the PHA determination. The tenant is not required to pay an escrow deposit pursuant to Sec. 966.55(e) for the portion of tenant rent attributable to the imputed welfare income in order to obtain a grievance hearing on the PHA determination.

(2) Section 8 participant. A participant in the Section 8 tenant- based assistance program may request an informal hearing, in accordance with Sec. 982.555 of this title, to review the PHA determination of the amount of imputed welfare income that must be included in the family's annual income in accordance with this section. If the family claims that such amount is not correctly calculated in accordance with HUD requirements, and if the PHA denies the family's request to modify such amount, the PHA shall give the family written notice of such denial, with a brief explanation of the basis for the PHA determination of the amount of imputed welfare income. Such notice shall also state that if the family does not agree with the PHA determination, the family may request an informal hearing on the determination under the PHA hearing procedure.

(e) PHA relation with welfare agency. (1) The PHA must ask welfare agencies to inform the PHA of any specified welfare benefits reduction for a family member, the reason for such reduction, the term of any such reduction, and any subsequent welfare agency determination affecting the amount or term of a specified welfare benefits reduction. If the welfare agency determines a specified welfare benefits reduction for a family member, and gives the PHA written notice of such reduction, the family's annual incomes shall include the imputed welfare income because of the specified welfare benefits reduction.

(2) The PHA is responsible for determining the amount of imputed welfare income that is included in the family's annual income as a result of a specified welfare benefits reduction as determined by the welfare agency, and specified in the notice by the welfare agency to the PHA. However, the PHA is not responsible for determining whether a reduction of welfare benefits by the welfare agency was correctly determined by the welfare agency in accordance with welfare program requirements and procedures, nor for providing the opportunity for review or hearing on such welfare agency determinations.

(3) Such welfare agency determinations are the responsibility of the welfare agency, and the family may seek appeal of such determinations through the welfare agency's normal due process procedures. The PHA shall be entitled to rely on the welfare agency notice to the PHA of the welfare agency's determination of a specified welfare benefits reduction.

{65 FR 16717, Mar. 29, 2000}

Sec. 5.617 Self-sufficiency incentives for persons with disabilities--Disallowance of increase in annual income.

(a) Applicable programs. The disallowance of increase in annual income provided by this section is applicable only to the following programs: HOME Investment Partnerships Program (24 CFR part 92); Housing Opportunities for Persons with AIDS (24 CFR part 574); Supportive Housing Program

(24 CFR part 583); and the Housing Choice Voucher Program (24 CFR part 982).

(b) Definitions. The following definitions apply for purposes of this section.

Disallowance. Exclusion from annual income.

Previously unemployed includes a person with disabilities who has earned, in the twelve months previous to employment, no more than would be received for 10 hours of work per week for 50 weeks at the established minimum wage.

Qualified family. A family residing in housing assisted under one of the programs listed in paragraph (a) of this section or receiving tenant-based rental assistance under one of the programs listed in paragraph (a) of this section.

(1) Whose annual income increases as a result of employment of a family member who is a person with disabilities and who was previously unemployed for one or more years prior to employment;

(2) Whose annual income increases as a result of increased earnings by a family member who is a person with disabilities during participation in any economic self-sufficiency or other job training program; or

(3) Whose annual income increases, as a result of new employment or increased earnings of a family member who is a person with disabilities, during or within six months after receiving assistance, benefits or services under any state program for temporary assistance for needy families funded under Part A of Title IV of the Social Security Act, as determined by the responsible entity in consultation with the local agencies administering temporary assistance for needy families (TANF) and Welfare-to-Work (WTW) programs. The TANF program is not limited to monthly income maintenance, but also includes such benefits and services as one-time payments, wage subsidies and transportation assistance--provided that the total amount over a six-month period is at least $500.

(c) Disallowance of increase in annual income--(1) Initial twelve month exclusion. During the cumulative twelve month period beginning on the date a member who is a person with disabilities of a qualified family is first employed or the family first experiences an increase in annual income attributable to employment, the responsible entity must exclude from annual income (as defined in the regulations governing the applicable program listed in paragraph (a) of this section) of a qualified family any increase in income of the family member who is a person with disabilities as a result of employment over prior income of that family member.

(2) Second twelve month exclusion and phase-in. During the second cumulative twelve month period after the date a member who is a person with disabilities of a qualified family is first employed or the family first experiences an increase in annual income attributable to employment, the responsible entity must exclude from annual income of a qualified family fifty percent of any increase in income of such family member as a result of employment over income of that family member prior to the beginning of such employment.

(3) Maximum four year disallowance. The disallowance of increased income of an individual family member who is a person with disabilities as provided in paragraph (c)(1) or (c)(2) is limited to a lifetime 48 month period. The disallowance only applies for a maximum of twelve months for disallowance under paragraph (c)(1) and a maximum of twelve months for disallowance under paragraph (c)(2), during the 48 month period starting from the initial exclusion under paragraph (c)(1) of this section.

(d) Inapplicability to admission. The disallowance of increases in income as a result of employment of persons with disabilities under this section does not apply for purposes of admission to the program (including the determination of income eligibility or any income targeting that may be applicable).

{66 FR 6223, Jan. 19, 2001, as amended at 67 FR 6820, Feb. 13, 2002}

Family Payment

Sec. 5.628 Total tenant payment.

(a) Determining total tenant payment (TTP). Total tenant payment is the highest of the following amounts, rounded to the nearest dollar:

(1) 30 percent of the family's monthly adjusted income;

(2) 10 percent of the family's monthly income;

(3) If the family is receiving payments for welfare assistance from a public agency and a part of those payments, adjusted in accordance with the family's actual housing costs, is specifically designated by such agency to meet the family's housing costs, the portion of those payments which is so designated; or

(4) The minimum rent, as determined in accordance with Sec. 5.630.

(b) Determining TTP if family's welfare assistance is ratably reduced. If the family's welfare assistance is ratably reduced from the standard of need by applying a percentage, the amount calculated under paragraph (a)(3) of this section is the amount resulting from one application of the percentage.

{65 FR 16718, Mar. 29, 2000}

Sec. 5.630 Minimum rent.

(a) Minimum rent. (1) The PHA must charge a family no less than a minimum monthly rent established by the responsible entity, except as described in paragraph (b) of this section.

(2) For the public housing program and the section 8 moderate rehabilitation, and certificate or voucher programs, the PHA may establish a minimum rent of up to $50.

(3) For other section 8 programs, the minimum rent is $25.

(b) Financial hardship exemption from minimum rent. (1) When is family exempt from minimum rent? The responsible entity must grant an exemption from payment of minimum rent if the family is unable to pay the minimum rent because of financial hardship, as described in the responsible entity's written policies. Financial hardship includes these situations:

(i) When the family has lost eligibility for or is awaiting an eligibility determination for a Federal, State, or local assistance program, including a family that includes a member who is a noncitizen lawfully admitted for permanent residence under the Immigration and Nationality Act who would be entitled to public benefits but for title IV of the Personal Responsibility and Work Opportunity Act of 1996;

(ii) When the family would be evicted because it is unable to pay the minimum rent;

(iii) When the income of the family has decreased because of changed circumstances, including loss of employment;

(iv) When a death has occurred in the family; and

(v) Other circumstances determined by the responsible entity or HUD.

(2) What happens if family requests a hardship exemption? (i) Public housing. (A) If a family requests a financial hardship exemption, the PHA must suspend the minimum rent requirement beginning the month following the family's request for a hardship exemption, and continuing until the PHA determines whether there is a qualifying financial hardship and whether it is temporary or long term.

(B) The PHA must promptly determine whether a qualifying hardship exists and whether it is temporary or long term.

(C) The PHA may not evict the family for nonpayment of minimum rent during the 90-day period beginning the month following the family's request for a hardship exemption.

(D) If the PHA determines that a qualifying financial hardship is temporary, the PHA must reinstate the minimum rent from the beginning of the suspension of the minimum rent. The PHA must offer the family a reasonable repayment agreement, on terms and conditions established by the PHA, for the amount of back minimum rent owed by the family.

(ii) All section 8 programs. (A) If a family requests a financial hardship exemption, the responsible entity must suspend the minimum rent requirement beginning the month following the family's request for a hardship exemption until the responsible entity determines whether there is a qualifying financial hardship, and whether such hardship is temporary or long term.

(B) The responsible entity must promptly determine whether a qualifying hardship exists and whether it is temporary or long term.

(C) If the responsible entity determines that a qualifying financial hardship is temporary, the PHA must not impose the minimum rent during the 90-day period beginning the month following the date of the family's request for a hardship exemption. At the end of the 90-day suspension period, the responsible entity must reinstate the minimum rent from the beginning of the suspension. The family must be offered a reasonable repayment agreement, on terms and conditions established by the responsible entity, for the amount of back rent owed by the family.

(iii) All programs. (A) If the responsible entity determines there is no qualifying financial hardship exemption, the responsible entity must reinstate the minimum rent, including back rent owed from the beginning of the suspension. The family must pay the back rent on terms and conditions established by the responsible entity.

(B) If the responsible entity determines a qualifying financial hardship is long term, the responsible entity must exempt the family from the minimum rent requirements so long as such hardship continues. Such exemption shall apply from the beginning of the month following the family's request for a hardship exemption until the end of the qualifying financial hardship.

(C) The financial hardship exemption only applies to payment of the minimum rent (as determined pursuant to Sec. 5.628(a)(4) and Sec. 5.630), and not to the other elements used to calculate the total tenant payment (as determined pursuant to Sec. 5.628(a)(1), (a)(2) and (a)(3)).

(3) Public housing: Grievance hearing concerning PHA denial of request for hardship exemption. If a public housing family requests a hearing under the PHA grievance procedure, to review the PHA's determination denying or limiting the family's claim to a financial hardship exemption, the family is not required to pay any escrow deposit in order to obtain a grievance hearing on such issues.

{65 FR 16718, Mar. 29, 2000}

Sec. 5.632 Utility reimbursements.

(a) Applicability. This section is applicable to:

(1) The Section 8 programs other than the Section 8 voucher program (for distribution of a voucher housing assistance payment that exceeds rent to owner, see Sec. 982.514(b) of this title);

(2) A public housing family paying an income-based rent (see Sec. 960.253 of this title). (Utility reimbursement is not paid for a public housing family that is paying a flat rent.)

(b) Payment of utility reimbursement. (1) The responsible entity pays a utility reimbursement if the utility allowance (for tenant-paid utilities) exceeds the amount of the total tenant payment.

(2) In the public housing program (where the family is paying an income-based rent), the Section 8 moderate rehabilitation program and the Section 8 certificate or voucher program, the PHA may pay the utility reimbursement either to the family or directly to the utility supplier to pay the utility bill on behalf of the family. If the PHA elects to pay the utility supplier, the PHA must notify the family of the amount paid to the utility supplier.

(3) In the other Section 8 programs, the owner must pay the utility reimbursement either:

(i) To the family, or

(ii) With consent of the family, to the utility supplier to pay the utility bill on behalf of the family.
{65 FR 16719, Mar. 29, 2000}

Sec. 5.634 Tenant rent.

(a) Section 8 programs. For Section 8 programs other than the Section 8 voucher program, tenant rent is total tenant payment minus any utility allowance.

(b) Public housing. See Sec. 960.253 of this title for the determination of tenant rent.
{65 FR 16719, Mar. 29, 2000}

Section 8 Project-Based Assistance: Occupancy Requirements

Sec. 5.653 Section 8 project-based assistance programs: Admission--Income-eligibility and income-targeting.

(a) Applicability. This section describes requirements concerning income-eligibility and income-targeting that apply to the Section 8 project-based assistance programs, except for the moderate rehabilitation and the project-based certificate or voucher programs.

(b) Who is eligible?

(1) Basic eligibility. An applicant must meet all eligibility requirements in order to receive housing assistance. At a minimum, the applicant must be a family, as defined in Sec. 5.403, and must be income-eligible, as described in this section. Such eligible applicants include single persons.

(2) Low income limit. No family other than a low income family is eligible for admission to the Section 8 project-based assistance programs. (This paragraph (b) does not apply to the Section 8 project- based voucher program under part 983 of this title.)

(c) Targeting to extremely low income families. For each project assisted under a contract for project-based assistance, of the dwelling units that become available for occupancy in any fiscal year that are assisted under the contract, not less than 40 percent shall be available for leasing only by families that are extremely low income families at the time of admission.

(d) Limitation on admission of non-very low income families.

(1) Admission to units available before October 1, 1981. Not more than 25 percent of the Section 8 project-based dwelling units that were available for occupancy under Section 8 Housing Assistance Payments Contracts effective before October 1, 1981 and that are leased on or after that date shall be available for leasing by low income families other than very low income families. HUD reserves the right to limit the admission of low income families other than very low income families to these units.

(2) Admission to units available on or after October 1, 1981. Not more than 15 percent of the Section 8 project-based dwelling units that initially become available for occupancy under Section 8 Housing Assistance Payments (HAP) Contracts on or after October 1, 1981 shall be available for leasing by low income families other than families that are very low income families at the time of admission to the Section 8 program. Except with the prior approval of HUD under paragraphs (d)(3) and (d)(4) of this section, the owner may only lease such units to very low income families.

(3) Request for exception. A request by an owner for approval of admission of low income families other than very low income families to section 8 project-based units must state the basis for requesting the exception and provide supporting data. Bases for exceptions that may be considered include the following:

(i) Need for admission of a broader range of tenants to preserve the financial or management viability of a project because there is an insufficient number of potential applicants who are very low income families;

(ii) Commitment of an owner to attaining occupancy by families with a broad range of incomes;

(iii) Project supervision by a State Housing Finance Agency having a policy of

occupancy by families with a broad range of incomes supported by evidence that the Agency is pursuing this goal throughout its assisted projects in the community, or a project with financing through Section 11(b) of the 1937 Act (42 U.S.C. 1437i) or under Section 103 of the Internal Revenue Code (26 U.S.C. 103); and

(iv) Low-income families that otherwise would be displaced from a Section 8 project.

(4) Action on request for exception. Whether to grant any request for exception is a matter committed by law to HUD's discretion, and no implication is intended to be created that HUD will seek to grant approvals up to the maximum limits permitted by statute, nor is any presumption of an entitlement to an exception created by the specification of certain grounds for exception that HUD may consider. HUD will review exceptions granted to owners at regular intervals. HUD may withdraw permission to exercise those exceptions for program applicants at any time that exceptions are not being used or after a periodic review, based on the findings of the review.

(e) Income used for eligibility and targeting. Family annual income (see Sec. 5.609) is used both for determination of income-eligibility and for income-targeting under this section.

(f) Reporting. The Section 8 owner must comply with HUD-prescribed reporting requirements, including income reporting requirements that will permit HUD to maintain the data necessary to monitor compliance with income-eligibility and income-targeting requirements.
{65 FR 16719, Mar. 29, 2000}

Sec. 5.655 Section 8 project-based assistance programs: Owner preferences in selection for a project or unit.

(a) Applicability. This section applies to the section 8 project- based assistance programs. The section describes requirements concerning the Section 8 owner's selection of residents to occupy a project or unit, except for the moderate rehabilitation and the project-based certificate or voucher programs.

(b) Selection. (1) Selection for owner's project or unit. Selection for occupancy of a project or unit is the function of the Section 8 owner. However, selection is subject to the income-eligibility and income-targeting requirements in Sec. 5.653.

(2) Tenant selection plan. The owner must adopt a written tenant selection plan in accordance with HUD requirements.

(3) Amount of income. The owner may not select a family for occupancy of a project or unit in an order different from the order on the owner's waiting list for the purpose of selecting a relatively higher income family. However, an owner may select a family for occupancy of a project or unit based on its income in order to satisfy the targeting requirements of Sec. 5.653(c).

(4) Selection for particular unit. In selecting a family to occupy a particular unit, the owner may match family characteristics with the type of unit available, for example, number of bedrooms. If a unit has special accessibility features for persons with disabilities, the owner must first offer the unit to families which include persons with disabilities who require such features (see Secs. 8.27 and 100.202 of this title).

(5) Housing assistance limitation for single persons. A single person who is not an elderly or displaced person, a person with disabilities, or the remaining member of a resident family may not be provided a housing unit with two or more bedrooms.

(c) Particular owner preferences. The owner must inform all applicants about available preferences and must give applicants an opportunity to show that they qualify for available preferences.

(1) Residency requirements or preferences. (i) Residency requirements are prohibited. Although the owner is not prohibited from adopting a residency preference, the owner may only adopt or implement residency preferences in accordance with non-discrimination and equal opportunity

requirements listed at Sec. 5.105(a).

(ii) A residency preference is a preference for admission of persons who reside in a specified geographic area (``residency preference area'').

(iii) An owner's residency preference must be approved by HUD in one of the following methods:

(A) Prior approval of the housing market area in the Affirmative Fair Housing Marketing plan (in accordance with Sec. 108.25 of this title) as a residency preference area;

(B) Prior approval of the residency preference area in the PHA plan of the jurisdiction in which the project is located;

(C) Modification of the Affirmative Fair Housing Marketing Plan, in accordance with Sec. 108.25 of this title,

(iv) Use of a residency preference may not have the purpose or effect of delaying or otherwise denying admission to a project or unit based on the race, color, ethnic origin, gender, religion, disability, or age of any member of an applicant family.

(v) A residency preference must not be based on how long an applicant has resided or worked in a residency preference area.

(vi) Applicants who are working or who have been notified that they are hired to work in a residency preference area must be treated as residents of the residency preference area. The owner may treat graduates of, or active participants in, education and training programs in a residency preference area as residents of the residency preference area if the education or training program is designed to prepare individuals for the job market.

(2) Preference for working families.
(i) The owner may adopt a preference for admission of working families (families where the head, spouse or sole member is employed). However, an applicant shall be given the benefit of the working family preference if the head and spouse, or sole member, is age 62 or older, or is a person with disabilities.

(ii) If the owner adopts a preference for admission of working families, the owner must not give a preference based on the amount of earned income.

(3) Preference for person with disabilities. The owner may adopt a preference for admission of families that include a person with disabilities. However, the owner may not adopt a preference for admission of persons with a specific disability.

(4) Preference for victims of domestic violence. The owner should consider whether to adopt a preference for admission of families that include victims of domestic violence.

(5) Preference for single persons who are elderly, displaced, homeless or persons with disabilities over other single persons. The owner may adopt a preference for admission of single persons who are age 62 or older, displaced, homeless, or persons with disabilities over other single persons.
{65 FR 16720, Mar. 29, 2000}

Sec. 5.657 Section 8 project-based assistance programs: Reexamination of family income and composition.

(a) Applicability. This section states requirements for reexamination of family income and composition in the Section 8 project- based assistance programs, except for the moderate rehabilitation and the project-based certificate or voucher programs.

(b) Regular reexamination. The owner must conduct a reexamination and redetermination of family income and composition at least annually.

(c) Interim reexaminations. A family may request an interim reexamination of family income because of any changes since the last examination. The owner must make the interim reexamination within a reasonable time after the family request. The owner may adopt policies prescribing when and under what conditions the family must report a change in family income or composition.
{65 FR 16720, Mar. 29, 2000}

Sec. 5.659 Family information and verification.

(a) Applicability. This section states requirements for reexamination of family income and composition in the Section 8 project- based assistance programs, except for the moderate rehabilitation program and the project-based certificate or voucher programs.

(b) Family obligation to supply information. (1) The family must supply any information that HUD or the owner determines is necessary in administration of the Section 8 program, including submission of required evidence of citizenship or eligible immigration status (as provided by part 5, subpart E of this title). ``Information'' includes any requested certification, release or other documentation.

(2) The family must supply any information requested by the owner or HUD for use in a regularly scheduled reexamination or an interim reexamination of family income and composition in accordance with HUD requirements.

(3) For requirements concerning the following, see part 5, subpart B of this title:

(i) Family verification and disclosure of social security numbers;

(ii) Family execution and submission of consent forms for obtaining wage and claim information from State Wage Information Collection Agencies (SWICAs).

(4) Any information supplied by the family must be true and complete.

(c) Family release and consent. (1) As a condition of admission to or continued occupancy of a unit with Section 8 assistance, the owner must require the family head, and such other family members as the owner designates, to execute a HUD-approved release and consent form (including any release and consent as required under Sec. 5.230 of this title) authorizing any depository or private source of income, or any Federal, State or local agency, to furnish or release to the owner or HUD such information as the owner or HUD determines to be necessary.

(2) The use or disclosure of information obtained from a family or from another source pursuant to this release and consent shall be limited to purposes directly connected with administration of the Section 8 program.

(d) Owner responsibility for verification. The owner must obtain and document in the family file third party verification of the following factors, or must document in the file why third party verification was not available:

(1) Reported family annual income;

(2) The value of assets;

(3) Expenses related to deductions from annual income; and

(4) Other factors that affect the determination of adjusted income.

{65 FR 16721, Mar. 29, 2000}

Sec. 5.661 Section 8 project-based assistance programs: Approval for police or other security personnel to live in project.

(a) Applicability. This section describes when a Section 8 owner may lease a Section 8 unit to police or other security personnel with continued Section 8 assistance for the unit. This section applies to the Section 8 project-based assistance programs.

(b) Terms. (1) Security personnel means:

(i) A police officer, or

(ii) A qualified security professional, with adequate training and experience to provide security services for project residents.

(2) Police officer means a person employed on a full-time basis as a duly licensed professional police officer by a Federal, State or local government or by any agency of these governments.

(3) Security includes the protection of project residents, including resident project management from criminal or other activity that is a threat to person or property, or that arouses fears of such threat.

(c) Owner application. (1) The owner may submit a written application to the contract administrator (PHA or HUD) for approval to lease an available unit in a

Section 8 project to security personnel who would not otherwise be eligible for Section 8 assistance, for the purpose of increasing security for Section 8 families residing in the project. (2) The owner's application must include the following information:

(i) A description of criminal activities in the project and the surrounding community, and the effect of criminal activity on the security of project residents.

(ii) Qualifications of security personnel who will reside in the project, and the period of residence by such personnel. How owner proposes to check backgrounds and qualifications of any security personnel who will reside in the project.

(iii) Full disclosure of any family relationship between the owner and any security personnel. For this purpose, ``owner'' includes a principal or other interested party.

(iv) How residence by security personnel in a project unit will increase security for Section 8 assisted families residing in the project.

(v) The amount payable monthly as rent to the unit owner by security personnel residing in the project (including a description of how this amount is determined), and the amount of any other compensation by the owner to such resident security personnel.

(vi) The terms of occupancy by such security personnel. The lease by owner to the approved security personnel may provide that occupancy of the unit is authorized only while the security personnel is satisfactorily performing any agreed responsibilities and functions for project security.

(vii) Other information as requested by the contract administrator.

(d) Action by contract administrator. (1) The contract administrator shall have discretion to approve or disapprove owner's application, and to impose conditions for approval of occupancy by security personnel in a section 8 project unit.

(2) Notice of approval by the contract administrator shall specify the term of such approved occupancy. Such approval may be withdrawn at the discretion of the contract administrator, for example, if the contract administrator determines that such occupancy is not providing adequate security benefits as proposed in the owner's application; or that security benefits from such occupancy are not a sufficient return for program costs.

(e) Housing assistance payment and rent. (1) During approved occupancy by security personnel as provided in this section, the amount of the monthly housing assistance payment to the owner shall be equal to the contract rent (as determined in accordance with the HAP contract and HUD requirements) minus the amount (as approved by the contract administrator) of rent payable monthly as rent to the unit owner by such security personnel. The owner shall bear the risk of collecting such rent from such security personnel, and the amount of the housing assistance payment shall not be increased because of non-payment by such security personnel. The owner shall not be entitled to receive any vacancy payment for the period following occupancy by such security personnel.

(2) In approving the amount of monthly rent payable by security personnel for occupancy of a contract unit, the contract administrator may consider whether security services to be performed are an adequate return for housing assistance payments on the unit, or whether the cost of security services should be borne by the owner from other project income.

{65 FR 16721, Mar. 29, 2000}

Effective Date Note: At 65 FR 16721, Mar. 29, 2000, Sec. 5.661 was added. This section contains information collection and recordkeeping requirements and will not become effective until approval has been given by the Office of Management and Budget.

Subpart G--Physical Condition Standards and Inspection Requirements

Sec. 5.701 Applicability.

Source: 63 FR 46577, Sept. 1, 1998, unless otherwise noted.

(a) This subpart applies to housing assisted under the HUD programs listed in 24 CFR 200.853(a).

(b) This subpart applies to housing with mortgages insured or held by HUD, or housing that is receiving assistance from HUD, under the programs listed in 24 CFR 200.853(b).

(c) This subpart also applies to Public Housing (housing receiving assistance under the U.S. Housing Act of 1937, other than under section 8 of the Act).

(d) For purposes of this subpart, the term ``HUD housing'' means the types of housing listed in paragraphs (a), (b), and (c) of this section.
{63 FR 46577, Sept. 1, 1998, as amended at 65 FR 77240, Dec. 8, 2000}

Sec. 5.703 Physical condition standards for HUD housing that is decent, safe, sanitary and in good repair (DSS/GR).

HUD housing must be decent, safe, sanitary and in good repair. Owners of housing described in Sec. 5.701(a), mortgagors of housing described in Sec. 5.701(b), and PHAs and other entities approved by HUD owning housing described in Sec. 5.701(c), must maintain such housing in a manner that meets the physical condition standards set forth in this section in order to be considered decent, safe, sanitary and in good repair. These standards address the major areas of the HUD housing: the site; the building exterior; the building systems; the dwelling units; the common areas; and health and safety considerations.

(a) Site. The site components, such as fencing and retaining walls, grounds, lighting, mailboxes/project signs, parking lots/driveways, play areas and equipment, refuse disposal, roads, storm drainage and walkways must be free of health and safety hazards and be in good repair. The site must not be subject to material adverse conditions, such as abandoned vehicles, dangerous walks or steps, poor drainage, septic tank back-ups, sewer hazards, excess accumulations of trash, vermin or rodent infestation or fire hazards.

(b) Building exterior. Each building on the site must be structurally sound, secure, habitable, and in good repair. Each building's doors, fire escapes, foundations, lighting, roofs, walls, and windows, where applicable, must be free of health and safety hazards, operable, and in good repair.

(c) Building systems. Each building's domestic water, electrical system, elevators, emergency power, fire protection, HVAC, and sanitary system must be free of health and safety hazards, functionally adequate, operable, and in good repair.

(d) Dwelling units. (1) Each dwelling unit within a building must be structurally sound, habitable, and in good repair. All areas and aspects of the dwelling unit (for example, the unit's bathroom, call-for-aid (if applicable), ceiling, doors, electrical systems, floors, hot water heater, HVAC (where individual units are provided), kitchen, lighting, outlets/switches, patio/porch/balcony, smoke detectors, stairs, walls, and windows) must be free of health and safety hazards, functionally adequate, operable, and in good repair.

(2) Where applicable, the dwelling unit must have hot and cold running water, including an adequate source of potable water (note for example that single room occupancy units need not contain water facilities).

(3) If the dwelling unit includes its own sanitary facility, it must be in proper operating condition, usable in privacy, and adequate for personal hygiene and the disposal of human waste.

(4) The dwelling unit must include at least one battery-operated or hard-wired smoke detector, in proper working condition, on

each level of the unit.

(e) Common areas. The common areas must be structurally sound, secure, and functionally adequate for the purposes intended. The basement/garage/carport, restrooms, closets, utility, mechanical, community rooms, day care, halls/corridors, stairs, kitchens, laundry rooms, office, porch, patio, balcony, and trash collection areas, if applicable, must be free of health and safety hazards, operable, and in good repair. All common area ceilings, doors, floors, HVAC, lighting, outlets/switches, smoke detectors, stairs, walls, and windows, to the extent applicable, must be free of health and safety hazards, operable, and in good repair. These standards for common areas apply, to a varying extent, to all HUD housing, but will be particularly relevant to congregate housing, independent group homes/ residences, and single room occupancy units, in which the individual dwelling units (sleeping areas) do not contain kitchen and/ or bathroom facilities.

(f) Health and safety concerns. All areas and components of the housing must be free of health and safety hazards. These areas include, but are not limited to, air quality, electrical hazards, elevators, emergency/fire exits, flammable materials, garbage and debris, handrail hazards, infestation, and lead-based paint. For example, the buildings must have fire exits that are not blocked and have hand rails that are undamaged and have no other observable deficiencies. The housing must have no evidence of infestation by rats, mice, or other vermin, or of garbage and debris. The housing must have no evidence of electrical hazards, natural hazards, or fire hazards. The dwelling units and common areas must have proper ventilation and be free of mold, odor (e.g., propane, natural gas, methane gas), or other observable deficiencies. The housing must comply with all requirements related to the evaluation and reduction of lead-based paint hazards and have available proper certifications of such (see 24 CFR part 35).

(g) Compliance with State and local codes. The physical condition standards in this section do not supersede or preempt State and local codes for building and maintenance with which HUD housing must comply. HUD housing must continue to adhere to these codes.

Sec. 5.705 Uniform physical inspection requirements.

Any entity responsible for conducting a physical inspection of HUD housing, to determine compliance with this subpart, must inspect such HUD housing annually in accordance with HUD-prescribed physical inspection procedures. The inspection must be conducted annually unless the program regulations governing the housing provide otherwise or unless HUD has provided otherwise by notice.
{65 FR 77240, Dec. 8, 2000}

Subpart H--Uniform Financial Reporting Standards

Sec. 5.801 Uniform financial reporting standards.

(a) Applicability. This subpart H implements uniform financial reporting standards for:

(1) Public housing agencies (PHAs) receiving assistance under sections 5, 9, or 14 of the 1937 Act (42 U.S.C. 1437c, 1437g, and 1437l) (Public Housing);

(2) PHAs as contract administrators for any Section 8 project-based or tenant-based housing assistance payments program, which includes assistance under the following programs:

(i) Section 8 project-based housing assistance payments programs, including, but not limited to, the Section 8 New Construction, Substantial Rehabilitation, Loan Management Set-Aside, Property Disposition, and Moderate Rehabilitation (including the Single Room Occupancy program for homeless individuals);

(ii) Section 8 Project-Based Certificate programs;

(iii) Any program providing Section 8 project-based renewal contracts; and

(iv) Section 8 tenant-based assistance under the Section 8 Certificate and Voucher program.

(3) Owners of housing assisted under any Section 8 project-based housing assistance payments program:

(i) Including, but not limited to, the Section 8 New Construction, Substantial Rehabilitation, Loan Management Set-Aside, and Property Disposition programs;

(ii) Excluding the Section 8 Moderate Rehabilitation Program (which includes the Single Room Occupancy program for homeless individuals) and the Section 8 Project-Based Certificate Program;

(4) Owners of multifamily projects receiving direct or indirect assistance from HUD, or with mortgages insured, coinsured, or held by HUD, including but not limited to housing under the following HUD programs:

(i) Section 202 Program of Supportive Housing for the Elderly;

(ii) Section 811 Program of Supportive Housing for Persons with Disabilities;

(iii) Section 202 loan program for projects for the elderly and handicapped (including 202/8 projects and 202/162 projects);

(iv) Section 207 of the National Housing Act (NHA) (12 U.S.C. 1701 et seq.) (Rental Housing Insurance);

(v) Section 213 of the NHA (Cooperative Housing Insurance);

(vi) Section 220 of the NHA (Rehabilitation and Neighborhood Conservation Housing Insurance);

(vii) Section 221(d) (3) and (5) of the NHA (Housing for Moderate Income and Displaced Families);

(viii) Section 221(d)(4) of the NHA (Housing for Moderate Income and Displaced Families);

(ix) Section 231 of the NHA (Housing for Elderly Persons);

(x) Section 232 of the NHA (Mortgage Insurance for Nursing Homes, Intermediate Care Facilities, Board and Care Homes);

(xi) Section 234(d) of the NHA (Rental) (Mortgage Insurance for Condominiums);

(xii) Section 236 of the NHA (Rental and Cooperative Housing for Lower Income Families);

(xiii) Section 241 of the NHA (Supplemental Loans for Multifamily Projects); and

(5) HUD-approved Title I and Title II nonsupervised lenders, nonsupervised mortgagees, and loan correspondents.

(b) Submission of financial information. Entities (or individuals) to which this subpart is applicable must provide to HUD, on an annual basis, such financial information as required by HUD. This financial information must be:

(1) Prepared in accordance with Generally Accepted Accounting Principles as further defined by HUD in supplementary guidance;

(2) Submitted electronically to HUD through the internet, or in such other electronic format designated by HUD, or in such non-electronic format as HUD may allow if the burden or cost of electronic reporting is determined by HUD to be excessive; and

(3) Submitted in such form and substance as prescribed by HUD.

(c) Annual financial report filing dates. (1) For entities listed in paragraphs (a)(1) and (2) of this section, the financial information to be submitted to HUD in accordance with paragraph (b) of this section, must be submitted to HUD annually, no later than 60 days after the end of the fiscal year of the reporting period, and as otherwise provided by law (for public housing agencies, see also 24 CFR 903.33).

(2) For entities listed in paragraphs (a)(3) and (4) of this section, the financial information to be submitted to HUD in accordance with paragraph (b) of this section, must be submitted to HUD annually, no later than 90 days after the end of the fiscal year of the reporting period, and as otherwise provided by law.

(3) For those entities listed in paragraph (a)(5) of this section, the financial information to be submitted to HUD in accordance with paragraph (b) of this section must be submitted to HUD annually,

no later than 90 days after the end of the fiscal year (or within an extended time if an extension is granted at the sole discretion of the Secretary). An extension request must be received no earlier than 45 days and no later than 15 days prior to the submission deadline.

(d) Reporting compliance dates. Entities (or individuals) that are subject to the reporting requirements in this section must commence compliance with these requirements as follows:

(1) For PHAs listed in paragraphs (a)(1) and (a)(2) of this section, the requirements of this section will begin with those PHAs with fiscal years ending September 30, 1999 and later. Unaudited financial statements will be required 60 days after the PHA's fiscal year end, and audited financial statements will then be required no later than 9 months after the PHA's fiscal year end, in accordance with the Single Audit Act and OMB Circular A-133 (See 24 CFR 84.26). A PHA with a fiscal year ending September 30, 1999 that elects to submit its unaudited financial report earlier than the due date of November 30, 1999 must submit its report as required in this section. On or after September 30, 1998, but prior to November 30, 1999 (except for a PHA with its fiscal year ending September 30, 1999), PHAs may submit their financial reports in accordance with this section.

(2) For entities listed in paragraphs (a)(3) and (a)(4) of this section, the requirements of this section will begin with those entities with fiscal years ending December 31, 1998 and later. Entities listed in paragraphs (a)(3) and (a)(4) of this section with fiscal years ending December 31, 1998 that elect to submit their reports earlier than the due date must submit their financial reports as required in this section. On or after September 30, 1998 but prior to January 1, 1999, these entities may submit their financial reports in accordance with this section.

(3) The requirements of this section apply to the entities listed in paragraph (a)(5) of this section with fiscal years ending on or after September 30, 2002. Audited financial statements submitted by lenders with fiscal years ending before September 30, 2002, may either be submitted in paper or electronically at the lenders' option. Audited financial statements submitted by lenders with fiscal years ending on or after September 30, 2002, must be submitted electronically.

(e) Limitation on changing fiscal years. To allow for a period of consistent assessment of the financial reports submitted to HUD under this subpart part, PHAs listed in paragraphs (a)(1) and (a)(2) of this section will not be allowed to change their fiscal years for their first three full fiscal years following October 1, 1998.

(f) Responsibility for submission of financial report. The responsibility for submission of the financial report due to HUD under this section rests with the individuals and entities listed in paragraph (a) of this section.

{63 FR 46591, Sept. 1, 1998, as amended at 64 FR 1505, Jan. 11, 1999; 64 FR 33755, June 24, 1999; 65 FR 16295, Mar. 27, 2000; 67 FR 53451, Aug. 15, 2002}

Subpart I--Preventing Crime in Federally Assisted Housing--Denying Admission and Terminating Tenancy for Criminal Activity or Alcohol Abuse

Sec. 5.850 Which subsidized housing is covered by this subpart?

Source: 66 FR 28792, May 24, 2001, unless otherwise noted. General

(a) If you are the owner of federally assisted housing, your federally assisted housing is covered, except as provided in paragraph (b) or (c) of this section.

(b) If you are operating public housing, this subpart does not apply, but similar provisions applicable to public housing units are found in parts 960 and 966 of this title. If you administer tenant-based assistance under

Section 8 or you are the owner of housing assisted with tenant-based assistance under Section 8, this subpart does not apply to you, but similar provisions that do apply are located in part 982 of this title.

(c) If you own or administer housing assisted by the Rural Housing Administration under section 514 or section 515 of the Housing Act of 1949, this subpart does not apply to you.

Sec. 5.851 What authority do I have to screen applicants and to evict tenants?

{This section does not apply to Public Housing or Section 8, per 25 CFR 5.850, and therefore is not reprinted here.}

Sec. 5.852 What discretion do I have in screening and eviction actions?

{This section does not apply to Public Housing or Section 8, per 25 CFR 5.850, and therefore is not reprinted here.}

Sec. 5.853 Definitions.

{This section does not apply to Public Housing or Section 8, per 25 CFR 5.850, and therefore is not reprinted here.}

Denying Admissions

{This section does not apply to Public Housing or Section 8, per 25 CFR 5.850, and therefore is not reprinted here.}

Sec. 5.854 When must I prohibit admission of individuals who have engaged in drug-related criminal activity?

{This section does not apply to Public Housing or Section 8, per 25 CFR 5.850, and therefore is not reprinted here.}

Sec. 5.855 When am I specifically authorized to prohibit admission of individuals who have engaged in criminal activity?

{This section does not apply to Public Housing or Section 8, per 25 CFR 5.850, and therefore is not reprinted here.}

Sec. 5.856 When must I prohibit admission of sex offenders?

{This section does not apply to Public Housing or Section 8, per 25 CFR 5.850, and therefore is not reprinted here.}

Sec. 5.857 When must I prohibit admission of alcohol abusers?

{This section does not apply to Public Housing or Section 8, per 25 CFR 5.850, and therefore is not reprinted here.}

Terminating Tenancy

{This section does not apply to Public Housing or Section 8, per 25 CFR 5.850, and therefore is not reprinted here.}

Sec. 5.858 What authority do I have to evict drug criminals?

{This section does not apply to Public Housing or Section 8, per 25 CFR 5.850, and therefore is not reprinted here.}

Sec. 5.859 When am I specifically authorized to evict other criminals?

(a) Threat to other residents. The lease must provide that the owner may terminate tenancy for any of the following types of criminal activity by a covered person:

(1) Any criminal activity that threatens the health, safety, or right to peaceful enjoyment of the premises by other residents (including property management staff residing on the premises); or

(2) Any criminal activity that threatens the health, safety, or right to peaceful enjoyment

of their residences by persons residing in the immediate vicinity of the premises.

(b) Fugitive felon or parole violator. The lease must provide that you may terminate the tenancy during the term of the lease if a tenant is:

(1) Fleeing to avoid prosecution, or custody or confinement after conviction, for a crime, or attempt to commit a crime, that is a felony under the laws of the place from which the individual flees, or that, in the case of the State of New Jersey, is a high misdemeanor; or

(2) Violating a condition of probation or parole imposed under Federal or State law.

Sec. 5.860 When am I specifically authorized to evict alcohol abusers?

{This section does not apply to Public Housing or Section 8, per 25 CFR 5.850, and therefore is not reprinted here.}

Sec. 5.861 What evidence of criminal activity must I have to evict?

{This section does not apply to Public Housing or Section 8, per 25 CFR 5.850, and therefore is not reprinted here.}

Subpart J--Access to Criminal Records and Information

Sec. 5.901 To what criminal records and searches does this subpart apply?

Source: 66 FR 28794, May 24, 2001, unless otherwise noted.

(a) General criminal records searches. This subpart applies to criminal conviction background checks by PHAs that administer the Section 8 and public housing programs when they obtain criminal conviction records, under the authority of section 6(q) of the 1937 Act (42 U.S.C. 1437d(q)), from a law enforcement agency to prevent admission of criminals to public housing and Section 8 housing and to assist in lease enforcement and eviction.

(b) Sex offender registration records searches. This subpart applies to PHAs that administer the Section 8 and public housing programs when they obtain sex offender registration information from State and local agencies, under the authority of 42 U.S.C. 13663, to prevent admission of dangerous sex offenders to federally assisted housing.

(c) Excluded records searches. The provisions of this subpart do not apply to criminal conviction information or sex offender information searches by a PHA or others of information from law enforcement agencies or other sources other than as provided under this subpart.

Sec. 5.902 Definitions.

(a) Terms found elsewhere. The following terms used in this subpart are defined in subpart A of this part: 1937 Act, drug, federally assisted housing, household, HUD, public housing, public housing agency (PHA), Section 8.

(b) Additional terms used in this subpart are as follows:

Adult. A person who is 18 years of age or older, or who has been convicted of a crime as an adult under any Federal, State, or tribal law.

Covered housing. Public housing, project-based assistance under section 8 (including new construction and substantial rehabilitation projects), and tenant-based assistance under section 8.

Law enforcement agency. The National Crime Information Center (NCIC), police departments and other law enforcement agencies that hold criminal conviction records.

Owner. The owner of federally assisted housing.

Responsible entity. For the public housing program, the Section 8 tenant-based assistance program (part 982 of this title), the Section 8 project-based certificate or project-based voucher program (part 983 of this title), and the Section 8 moderate rehabilitation program (part 882 of this title), responsible entity means the PHA

administering the program under an Annual Contributions Contract with HUD. For all other Section 8 programs, responsible entity means the Section 8 owner.

Sec. 5.903 What special authority is there to obtain access to criminal records?

(a) Authority. If you are a PHA that administers the Section 8 program and/or the public housing program, this section authorizes you to obtain criminal conviction records from a law enforcement agency, as defined in Sec. 5.902. You may use the criminal conviction records that you obtain from a law enforcement agency under the authority of this section to screen applicants for admission to covered housing programs and for lease enforcement or eviction of families residing in public housing or receiving Section 8 project-based assistance.

(b) Consent for release of criminal conviction records. (1) In order to obtain access to records under this section, as a responsible entity you must require every applicant family to submit a consent form signed by each adult household member.

(2) By execution of the consent form, an adult household member consents that:

(i) Any law enforcement agency may release criminal conviction records concerning the household member to a PHA in accordance with this section;

(ii) The PHA may receive the criminal conviction records from a law enforcement agency, and may use the records in accordance with this section.

(c) Procedure for PHA. (1) When the law enforcement agency receives your request, the law enforcement agency must promptly release to you a certified copy of any criminal conviction records concerning the household member in the possession or control of the law enforcement agency. NCIC records must be provided in accordance with NCIC procedures.

(2) The law enforcement agency may charge you a reasonable fee for releasing criminal conviction records.

(d) Owner access to criminal records--(1) General. (i) If an owner submits a request to the PHA for criminal records concerning an adult member of an applicant or resident household, in accordance with the provisions of paragraph (d) of this section, the PHA must request the criminal conviction records from the appropriate law enforcement agency or agencies, as determined by the PHA.

(ii) If the PHA receives criminal conviction records requested by an owner, the PHA must determine whether criminal action by a household member, as shown by such criminal conviction records, may be a basis for applicant screening, lease enforcement or eviction, as applicable in accordance with HUD regulations and the owner criteria.

(iii) The PHA must notify the owner whether the PHA has received criminal conviction records concerning the household member, and of its determination whether such criminal conviction records may be a basis for applicant screening, lease enforcement or eviction. However, except as provided in paragraph (e)(2)(ii) of this section, the PHA must not disclose the household member's criminal conviction record or the content of that record to the owner.

(2) Screening. If you are an owner of covered housing, you may request that the PHA in the jurisdiction of the property obtain criminal conviction records of an adult household member from a law enforcement agency on your behalf for the purpose of screening applicants.

(i) Your request must include a copy of the consent form, signed by the household member.

(ii) Your request must include your standards for prohibiting admission of drug criminals in accordance with Sec. 5.854, and for prohibiting admission of other criminals in accordance with Sec. 5.855.

(3) Eviction or lease enforcement. If you are an owner of a unit with Section 8 project-based assistance, you may request that the PHA in the location of the project obtain criminal conviction records of a

household member from an appropriate law enforcement agency on your behalf in connection with lease enforcement or eviction.

(i) Your request must include a copy of the consent form, signed by the household member.

(ii) If you intend to use the PHA determination regarding any such criminal conviction records in connection with eviction, your request must include your standards for evicting drug criminals in accordance with Sec. 5.857, and for evicting other criminals in accordance with Sec. 5.858.

(iii) If you intend to use the PHA determination regarding any such criminal conviction records for lease enforcement other than eviction, your request must include your standards for lease enforcement because of criminal activity by members of a household.

(4) Fees. If an owner requests a PHA to obtain criminal conviction records in accordance with this section, the PHA may charge the owner reasonable fees for making the request on behalf of the owner and for taking other actions for the owner. The PHA may require the owner to reimburse costs incurred by the PHA, including reimbursement of any fees charged to the PHA by the law enforcement agency, the PHA's own related staff and administrative costs. The owner may not pass along to the applicant or tenant the costs of a criminal records check.

(e) Permitted use and disclosure of criminal conviction records received by PHA--(1) Use of records. Criminal conviction records received by a PHA from a law enforcement agency in accordance with this section may only be used for the following purposes:

(i) Applicant screening. (A) PHA screening of applicants for admission to public housing (part 960 of this title);

(B) PHA screening of applicants for admission to the Housing Choice Voucher Program (section 8 tenant-based assistance) (part 982 of this title);

(C) PHA screening of applicants for admission to the Section 8 moderate rehabilitation program (part 882 of this title); or the Section 8 project-based certificate or project-based voucher program (part 983 of this title); or

(D) PHA screening concerning criminal conviction of applicants for admission to Section 8 project-based assistance, at the request of the owner. (For requirements governing use of criminal conviction records obtained by a PHA at the request of a Section 8 owner under this section, see paragraph (d) of this section.)

(ii) Lease enforcement and eviction. (A) PHA enforcement of public housing leases and PHA eviction of public housing residents;

(B) Enforcement of leases by a Section 8 project owner and eviction of residents by a Section 8 project owner. (However, criminal conviction records received by a PHA from a law enforcement agency under this section may not be used for lease enforcement or eviction of residents receiving Section 8 tenant-based assistance.)

(2) PHA disclosure of records. (i) A PHA may disclose the criminal conviction records which the PHA receives from a law enforcement agency only as follows:

(A) To officers or employees of the PHA, or to authorized representatives of the PHA who have a job-related need to have access to the information. For example, if the PHA is seeking to evict a public housing tenant on the basis of criminal activity as shown in criminal conviction records provided by a law enforcement agency, the records may be disclosed to PHA employees performing functions related to the eviction, or to a PHA hearing officer conducting an administrative grievance hearing concerning the proposed eviction.

(B) To the owner for use in connection with judicial eviction proceedings by the owner to the extent necessary in connection with a judicial eviction proceeding. For example, criminal conviction records may be included in pleadings or other papers filed in an eviction action, may be disclosed to

parties to the action or the court, and may be filed in court or offered as evidence.

(ii) This disclosure may be made only if the following conditions are satisfied:

(A) If the PHA has determined that criminal activity by the household member as shown by such records received from a law enforcement agency may be a basis for eviction from a Section 8 unit; and

(B) If the owner certifies in writing that it will use the criminal conviction records only for the purpose and only to the extent necessary to seek eviction in a judicial proceeding of a Section 8 tenant based on the criminal activity by the household member that is described in the criminal conviction records.

(iii) The PHA may rely on an owner's certification that the criminal record is necessary to proceed with a judicial eviction to evict the tenant based on criminal activity of the identified household member, as shown in the criminal conviction record.

(iv) Upon disclosure as necessary in connection with judicial eviction proceedings, the PHA is not responsible for controlling access to or knowledge of such records after such disclosure.

(f) Opportunity to dispute. If a PHA obtains criminal record information from a State or local agency under this section showing that a household member has been convicted of a crime relevant to applicant screening, lease enforcement or eviction, the PHA must notify the household of the proposed action to be based on the information and must provide the subject of the record and the applicant or tenant a copy of such information, and an opportunity to dispute the accuracy and relevance of the information. This opportunity must be provided before a denial of admission, eviction or lease enforcement action on the basis of such information.

(g) Records management. Consistent with the limitations on disclosure of records in paragraph (e) of this section, the PHA must establish and implement a system of records management that ensures that any criminal record received by the PHA from a law enforcement agency is:

(1) Maintained confidentially;

(2) Not misused or improperly disseminated; and

(3) Destroyed, once the purpose(s) for which the record was requested has been accomplished, including expiration of the period for filing a challenge to the PHA action without institution of a challenge or final disposition of any such litigation.

(h) Penalties for improper release of information--(1) Criminal penalty. Conviction for a misdemeanor and imposition of a penalty of not more than $5,000 is the potential for:

(i) Any person, including an officer, employee, or authorized representative of any PHA or of any project owner, who knowingly and willfully requests or obtains any information concerning an applicant for, or tenant of, covered housing assistance under the authority of this section under false pretenses; or

(ii) Any person, including an officer, employee, or authorized representative of any PHA or a project owner, who knowingly and willfully discloses any such information in any manner to any individual not entitled under any law to receive the information.

(2) Civil liability. (i) A PHA may be held liable to any applicant for, or tenant of, covered housing assistance affected by either of the following:

(A) A negligent or knowing disclosure of criminal records information obtained under the authority of this section about such person by an officer, employee, or authorized representative of the PHA if the disclosure is not authorized by this section; or

(B) Any other negligent or knowing action that is inconsistent with this section.

(ii) An applicant for, or tenant of, covered housing assistance may seek relief against a PHA in these circumstances by bringing a civil action for damages and such other relief as may be appropriate against the PHA responsible for such unauthorized action. The United States district court in which the affected applicant or tenant resides, in which the unauthorized action occurred, or in which

the officer, employee, or representative alleged to be responsible resides, has jurisdiction. Appropriate relief may include reasonable attorney's fees and other litigation costs.

Sec. 5.905 What special authority is there to obtain access to sex offender registration information?

(a) PHA obligation to obtain sex offender registration information. (1) A PHA that administers a Section 8 or public housing program under an Annual Contributions Contract with HUD must carry out background checks necessary to determine whether a member of a household applying for admission to any federally assisted housing program is subject to a lifetime sex offender registration requirement under a State sex offender registration program. This check must be carried out with respect to the State in which the housing is located and with respect to States where members of the applicant household are known to have resided.

(2) If the PHA requests such information from any State or local agency responsible for the collection or maintenance of such information, the State or local agency must promptly provide the PHA such information in its possession or control.

(3) The State or local agency may charge a reasonable fee for providing the information.

(b) Owner's request for sex offender registration information--(1) General. An owner of federally assisted housing that is located in the jurisdiction of a PHA that administers a Section 8 or public housing program under an Annual Contributions Contract with HUD may request that the PHA obtain information necessary to determine whether a household member is subject to a lifetime registration requirement under a State sex offender registration requirement.

(2) Procedure. If the request is made in accordance with the provisions of paragraph (b) of this section:

(i) The PHA must request the information from a State or local agency;

(ii) The State or local agency must promptly provide the PHA such information in its possession or control;

(iii) The PHA must determine whether such information may be a basis for applicant screening, lease enforcement or eviction, based on the criteria used by the owner as specified in the owner's request, and inform the owner of the determination.

(iv) The PHA must notify the owner of its determination whether sex offender registration information received by the PHA under this section concerning a household member may be a basis for applicant screening, lease enforcement or eviction in accordance with HUD requirements and the criteria used by the owner.

(3) Contents of request. As the owner, your request must specify whether you are asking the PHA to obtain the sex offender registration information concerning the household member for applicant screening, for lease enforcement, or for eviction and include the following information:

(i) Addresses or other information about where members of the household are known to have lived.

(ii) If you intend to use the PHA determination regarding any such sex offender registration information for applicant screening, your request must include your standards in accordance with Sec. 5.855(c) for prohibiting admission of persons subject to a lifetime sex offender registration requirement.

(iii) If you intend to use the PHA determination regarding any such sex offender registration information for eviction, your request must include your standards for evicting persons subject to a lifetime registration requirement in accordance with Sec. 5.858.

(iv) If you intend to use the PHA determination regarding any such sex offender registration information for lease enforcement other than eviction, your request must include your standards for lease enforcement because of criminal activity by

members of a household.

(4) PHA disclosure of records. The PHA must not disclose to the owner any sex offender registration information obtained by the PHA under this section.

(5) Fees. If an owner asks a PHA to obtain sex offender registration information concerning a household member in accordance with this section, the PHA may charge the owner reasonable fees for making the request on behalf of the owner and for taking other actions for the owner. The PHA may require the owner to reimburse costs incurred by the PHA, including reimbursement of any fees charged to the PHA by a State or local agency for releasing the information, the PHA's own related staff and administrative costs. The owner may not pass along to the applicant or tenant the costs of a sex offender registration records check.

(c) Records management. (1) The PHA must establish and implement a system of records management that ensures that any sex offender registration information record received by the PHA from a State or local agency under this section is:

(i) Maintained confidentially;

(ii) Not misused or improperly disseminated; and

(iii) Destroyed, once the purpose for which the record was requested has been accomplished, including expiration of the period for filing a challenge to the PHA action without institution of a challenge or final disposition of any such litigation.

(2) The records management requirements do not apply to information that is public information, or is obtained by a PHA other than under this section.

(d) Opportunity to dispute. If a PHA obtains sex offender registration information from a State or local agency under paragraph (a) of this section showing that a household member is subject to a lifetime sex offender registration requirement, the PHA must notify the household of the proposed action to be based on the information and must provide the subject of the record, and the applicant or tenant, with a copy of such information, and an opportunity to dispute the accuracy and relevance of the information. This opportunity must be provided before a denial of admission, eviction or lease enforcement action on the basis of such information.

{WAIS Document Retrieval [Code of Federal Regulations]
[Title 24, Volume 1]
[Revised as of April 1, 2003]
From the U.S. Government Printing Office via GPO Access
[CITE: 24CFR35]
[Page 303-348]
TITLE 24--HOUSING AND URBAN DEVELOPMENT

PART 35--LEAD-BASED PAINT POISONING PREVENTION IN CERTAIN RESIDENTIAL STRUCTURES

[Cite 24 CFR 35]

Subpart M--Tenant-Based Rental Assistance

35.1200 Purpose and applicability.
35.1205 Definitions and other general requirements.
35.1210 Notices and pamphlet.
35.1215 Activities at initial and periodic inspections.
35.1220 Ongoing lead-based paint maintenance activities.
35.1225 Child with an environmental intervention blood lead level.
Source: 64 FR 50216, Sept. 15, 1999, unless otherwise noted. }

Sec. 35.1200 Purpose and applicability.

(a) Purpose. The purpose of this subpart M is to establish procedures to eliminate as far as practicable lead-based paint hazards in housing occupied by families receiving tenant-based rental assistance. Such assistance includes tenant-based rental assistance under the Section 8 certificate program, the Section 8 voucher program, the HOME program, the Shelter Plus Care program, the Housing Opportunities for Persons With AIDS (HOPWA) program, and the Indian Housing Block Grant program. Tenant-based rental assistance means rental assistance that is not attached to the structure.

(b) Applicability. (1) This subpart applies only to dwelling units occupied or to be occupied by families or households that have one or more children of less than 6 years of age, common areas servicing such dwelling units, and exterior painted surfaces associated with such dwelling units or common areas. Common areas servicing a dwelling unit include those areas through which residents pass to gain access to the unit and other areas frequented by resident children of less than 6 years of age, including on-site play areas and child care facilities.

(2) For the purposes of the Section 8 tenant-based certificate program and the Section 8 voucher program:

(i) The requirements of this subpart are applicable where an initial or periodic inspection occurs on or after September 15, 2000; and

(ii) The PHA shall be the designated party.

(3) For the purposes of formula grants awarded under the Housing Opportunities for Persons with AIDS Program (HOPWA) (42 U.S.C. 12901 et seq.):

(i) The requirements of this subpart shall apply to activities for which program funds are first obligated on or after September 15, 2000; and

(ii) The grantee shall be the designated party.

(4) For the purposes of competitively awarded grants under the HOPWA Program and the Shelter Plus Care program (42 U.S.C. 11402-11407) tenant-based rental assistance component:

(i) The requirements of this subpart shall apply to grants awarded pursuant to Notices of Funding Availability published on or after September 15, 2000; and

(ii) The grantee shall be the designated party.

(5) For the purposes of the HOME program:

(i) The requirements of this subpart shall not apply to funds which are committed in

accordance with Sec. 92.2 of this title before September 15, 2000; and
(ii) The participating jurisdiction shall be the designated party.
(6) For the purposes of the Indian Housing Block Grant program:
(i) The requirements of this subpart shall apply to activities for which funds are first obligated on or after September 15, 2000; and
(ii) The IHBG recipient shall be the designated party.
(7) The housing agency, grantee, participating jurisdiction, or IHBG recipient may assign to a subrecipient or other entity the responsibilities of the designated party in this subpart.
[64 FR 50216, Sept. 15, 1999; 65 FR 3387, Jan. 21, 2000]
Sec. 35.1205 Definitions and other general requirements.
Definitions and other general requirements that apply to this subpart are found in subpart B of this part.

Sec. 35.1210 Notices and pamphlet.

(a) Notice. In cases where evaluation or paint stabilization is undertaken, the owner shall provide a notice to residents in accordance with Sec. 35.125. A visual assessment is not an evaluation. {[[Page 337]]}
(b) Lead hazard information pamphlet. The owner shall provide the lead hazard information pamphlet in accordance with Sec. 35.130.

Sec. 35.1215 Activities at initial and periodic inspection.

(a) (1) During the initial and periodic inspections, an inspector acting on behalf of the designated party and trained in visual assessment for deteriorated paint surfaces in accordance with procedures established by HUD shall conduct a visual assessment of all painted surfaces in order to identify any deteriorated paint.
(2) For tenant-based rental assistance provided under the HOME program, visual assessment shall be conducted as part of the initial and periodic inspections required under Sec. 92.209(i) of this title.
(b) The owner shall stabilize each deteriorated paint surface in accordance with Sec. 35.1330(a) and (b) before commencement of assisted occupancy. If assisted occupancy has commenced prior to a periodic inspection, such paint stabilization must be completed within 30 days of notification of the owner of the results of the visual assessment. Paint stabilization is considered complete when clearance is achieved in accordance with Sec. 35.1340.
(c) The owner shall provide a notice to occupants in accordance with Sec. 35.125(b)(1) and (c) describing the results of the clearance examination.

Sec. 35.1220 Ongoing lead-based paint maintenance activities.

The owner shall incorporate ongoing lead-based paint maintenance activities into regular building operations in accordance with Sec. 35.1355(a).

Sec. 35.1225 Child with an environmental intervention blood lead level.

(a) Within 15 days after being notified by a public health department or other medical health care provider that a child of less than 6 years of age living in an assisted dwelling unit has been identified as having an environmental intervention blood lead level, the designated party shall complete a risk assessment of the dwelling unit in which the child lived at the time the blood was last sampled and of the common areas servicing the dwelling unit. The risk assessment shall be conducted in accordance with Sec. 35.1320(b). When the risk assessment is complete, the designated party shall immediately provide the report of the risk assessment to the owner of the dwelling unit. If the child identified as having an environmental intervention blood lead

level is no longer living in the unit when the designated party receives notification from the public health department or other medical health care provider, but another household receiving tenant-based rental assistance is living in the unit or is planning to live there, the requirements of this section apply just as they do if the child still lives in the unit. If a public health department has already conducted an evaluation of the dwelling unit, or the designated party conducted a risk assessment of the unit and common areas servicing the unit between the date the child's blood was last sampled and the date when the designated party received the notification of the environmental intervention blood lead level, the requirements of this paragraph shall not apply.

(b) Verification. After receiving information from a source other than a public health department or other medical health care provider that a child of less than 6 years of age living in an assisted dwelling unit may have an environmental intervention blood lead level, the designated party shall immediately verify the information with a public health department or other medical health care provider. If that department or provider verifies that the child has an environmental intervention blood lead level, such verification shall constitute notification to the designated party as provided in paragraph (a) of this section, and the designated party shall take the action required in paragraphs (a) and (c) of this section.

(c) Hazard reduction. Within 30 days after receiving the risk assessment report from the designated party or the evaluation from the public health department, the owner shall complete the reduction of identified lead-based paint hazards in accordance with Sec. 35.1325 or Sec. 35.1330. Hazard reduction is considered complete when clearance is achieved in {[[Page 338]]} accordance with Sec. 35.1340 and the clearance report states that all lead-based paint hazards identified in the risk assessment have been treated with interim controls or abatement or when the public health department certifies that the lead-based paint hazard reduction is complete. If the owner does not complete the hazard reduction required by this section, the dwelling unit is in violation of Housing Quality Standards (HQS).

(d) Notice of evaluation and hazard reduction. The owner shall notify building residents of any evaluation or hazard reduction activities in accordance with Sec. 35.125.

(e) Reporting requirement. The designated party shall report the name and address of a child identified as having an environmental intervention blood lead level to the public health department within 5 working days of being so notified by any other medical health care professional.

(f) Data collection and record keeping responsibilities. At least quarterly, the designated party shall attempt to obtain from the public health department(s) with area(s) of jurisdiction similar to that of the designated party the names and/or addresses of children of less than 6 years of age with an identified environmental intervention blood lead level. At least quarterly, the designated party shall also report an updated list of the addresses of units receiving assistance under a tenant-based rental assistance program to the same public health department(s), except that the report(s) to the public health department(s) is not required if the health department states that it does not wish to receive such report. If it obtains names and addresses of environmental

intervention blood lead level children from the public health department(s), the designated party shall match information on cases of environmental intervention blood lead levels with the names and addresses of families receiving tenant-based rental assistance, unless the public health department performs such a matching procedure. If a match occurs, the designated party shall carry out the requirements of this section.

{Code of Federal Regulations
Title 24, Volume 4
Revised as of April 1, 2003
From the U.S. Government Printing Office via GPO Access
CITE: 24CFR982
Page 555-636
TITLE 24--HOUSING AND URBAN DEVELOPMENT

PART 982--SECTION 8 TENANT BASED ASSISTANCE: HOUSING CHOICE VOUCHER PROGRAM}

.[CITE: 24 CFR 982]

Subpart A--General Information

Sec.
982.1 Programs: Purpose and structure.
982.2 Applicability.
982.3 HUD.
982.4 Definitions.
982.5 Notices required by this part.

Subpart B--HUD Requirements and PHA Plan for Administration of Program

982.51 PHA authority to administer program.
982.52 HUD requirements.
982.53 Equal opportunity requirements.
982.54 Administrative plan.

Subpart C--Funding and PHA Application for Funding

982.101 Allocation of funding.
982.102 Allocation of budget authority for renewal of expiring CACC funding increments.
982.103 PHA application for funding.
982.104 HUD review of application.

Subpart D--Annual Contributions Contract and PHA Administration of Program

982.151 Annual contributions contract.
982.152 Administrative fee.
982.153 PHA responsibilities.
982.154 ACC reserve account.
982.155 Administrative fee reserve.
982.156 Depositary for program funds.
982.157 Budget and expenditure.
982.158 Program accounts and records.
982.159 Audit requirements.
982.160 HUD determination to administer a local program.
982.161 Conflict of interest.
982.162 Use of HUD-required contracts and other forms.
982.163 Fraud recoveries.

Subpart E--Admission to Tenant-Based Program

982.201 Eligibility and targeting.
982.202 How applicants are selected: General requirements.
982.203 Special admission (non-waiting list): Assistance targeted by HUD.
982.204 Waiting list: Administration of waiting list.
982.205 Waiting list: Different programs.
982.206 Waiting list: Opening and closing; public notice.
982.207 Waiting list: Local preferences in admission to program.

Subpart F {Reserved}

Subpart G--Leasing a Unit

982.301 Information when family is selected.
982.302 Issuance of certificate or voucher; Requesting PHA approval of assisted tenancy.
982.303 Term of voucher.
982.304 Illegal discrimination: PHA assistance to family.
982.305 PHA approval of assisted tenancy.
982.306 PHA disapproval of owner.
982.307 Tenant screening.
982.308 Lease and tenancy.
982.309 Term of assisted tenancy.
982.310 Owner termination of tenancy.
982.311 When assistance is paid.
982.312 Absence from unit.
982.313 Security deposit: Amounts owed by tenant.
982.314 Move with continued tenant-based assistance.
982.315 Family break-up.
982.316 Live-in aide.
982.317 Lease-purchase agreements.

Subpart H--Where Family Can Live and Move

982.351 Overview.
982.352 Eligible housing.
982.353 Where family can lease a unit with tenant-based assistance.
982.355 Portability: Administration by receiving PHA.

Subpart I--Dwelling Unit: Housing Quality Standards, Subsidy Standards, Inspection and Maintenance

982.401 Housing quality standards (HQS).
982.402 Subsidy standards.
982.403 Terminating HAP contract when unit is too small.
982.404 Maintenance: Owner and family responsibility; PHA remedies.
982.405 PHA initial and periodic unit inspection.
982.406 Enforcement of HQS.

Subpart J--Housing Assistance Payments Contract and Owner Responsibility

982.451 Housing assistance payments contract.
982.452 Owner responsibilities.
982.453 Owner breach of contract.
982.454 Termination of HAP contract: Insufficient funding.
982.455 Automatic termination of HAP contract.
982.456 Third parties.

Subpart K--Rent and Housing Assistance Payment

982.501 Overview.
982.502 Conversion to voucher program.
982.503 Voucher tenancy: Payment standard amount and schedule.
982.504 Voucher tenancy: Payment standard for family in restructured subsidized multifamily project.
982.505 Voucher tenancy: How to calculate housing assistance payment.
982.506 Negotiating rent to owner.
982.507 Rent to owner: Reasonable rent.
982.508 Maximum family share at initial occupancy.
982.509 Rent to owner: Effect of rent control.
982.510 Other fees and charges.
982.514 Distribution of housing assistance payment.
982.515 Family share: Family responsibility.
982.516 Family income and composition: Regular and interim examinations.
982.517 Utility allowance schedule.
982.518 Regular tenancy: How to calculate housing assistance payment.
982.519 Regular tenancy: Annual adjustment of rent to owner.
982.520 Regular tenancy: Special adjustment of rent to owner.
982.521 Rent to owner in subsidized project.

Subpart L--Family Obligations; Denial and Termination of Assistance

982.551 Obligations of participant.
982.552 PHA denial or termination of assistance for family.
982.553 Denial of admission and termination of assistance for criminals and alcohol abusers.
982.554 Informal review for applicant.
982.555 Informal hearing for participant.

Subpart M--Special Housing Types

982.601 Overview.

Single Room Occupancy (SRO)

982.602 SRO: Who may reside in an SRO?
982.603 SRO: Lease and HAP contract.
982.604 SRO: Voucher housing assistance payment.
982.605 SRO: Housing quality standards.

Congregate Housing

982.606 Congregate housing: Who may reside in congregate housing.
982.607 Congregate housing: Lease and HAP contract.
982.608 Congregate housing: Voucher housing assistance payment.
982.609 Congregate housing: Housing quality standards.

Group Home

982.610 Group home: Who may reside in a group home.
982.611 Group home: Lease and HAP contract.
982.612 Group home: State approval of group home.
982.613 Group home: Rent and voucher housing assistance payment.
982.614 Group home: Housing quality standards.

Shared Housing

982.615 Shared housing: Occupancy.
982.616 Shared housing: Lease and HAP contract.
982.617 Shared housing: Rent and voucher housing assistance payment.
982.618 Shared housing: Housing quality standards.

Cooperative

982.619 Cooperative housing.

Manufactured Home

982.620 Manufactured home: Applicability of requirements.
982.621 Manufactured home: Housing quality standards.

Manufactured Home Space Rental

982.622 Manufactured home space rental: Rent to owner.
982.623 Manufactured home space rental: Housing assistance payment.
982.624 Manufactured home space rental: Utility allowance schedule.

Homeownership Option

982.625 Homeownership option: General.
982.626 Homeownership option: Initial requirements.
982.627 Homeownership option: Eligibility requirements for families.
982.628 Homeownership option: Eligible units.
982.629 Homeownership option: Additional PHA requirements for family search and purchase.
982.630 Homeownership option: Homeownership counseling.
982.631 Homeownership option: Home inspections, contract of sale, and PHA disapproval of seller.
982.632 Homeownership option: Financing purchase of home; affordability of purchase.
982.633 Homeownership option: Continued assistance requirements; Family obligations.
982.634 Homeownership option: Maximum term of homeownership assistance.
982.635 Homeownership option: Amount and distribution of monthly homeownership assistance payment.
982.636 Homeownership option: Portability.
982.637 Homeownership option: Move with continued tenant-based assistance.
982.638 Homeownership option: Denial or termination of assistance for family.
982.639 Homeownership option: Administrative fees.
982.641 Homeownership option: Applicability of other requirements.
982.642 Homeownership option: Pilot program for homeownership assistance for disabled families.
982.643 Homeownership option: Downpayment assistance grants.

Authority: 42 U.S.C. 1437f and 3535(d).

Source: 59 FR 36682, July 18, 1994, unless otherwise noted.

Editorial Note: Nomenclature changes to part 982 appear at 64 FR 26640, May 14, 1999.

Subpart A--General Information

Source: 60 FR 34695, July 3, 1995, unless otherwise noted.

Sec. 982.1 Programs: purpose and structure.

(a) General description. (1) In the HUD Housing Choice Voucher Program (Voucher Program) and the HUD certificate program, HUD pays rental subsidies so eligible families can afford decent, safe and sanitary housing. Both programs are generally administered by State or local governmental entities called public housing agencies (PHAs). HUD provides housing assistance funds to the PHA. HUD also provides funds for PHA administration of the programs. PHAs are no longer allowed to enter into contracts for assistance in the certificate program.

(2) Families select and rent units that meet program housing quality standards. If the PHA approves a family's unit and tenancy, the PHA contracts with the owner to make rent subsidy payments on behalf of the family. A PHA may not approve a tenancy unless the rents is reasonable.

(3) In the certificate program, the rental subsidy is generally based on the actual rent of a unit leased by the assisted family. In the voucher program, the rental subsidy is determined by a formula.

(4)(i) In the certificate program, the subsidy for most families is the difference between the rent and 30 percent of adjusted monthly income.

(ii) In the voucher program, the subsidy is based on a local ``payment standard'' that reflects the cost to lease a unit in the local

housing market. If the rent is less than the payment standard, the family generally pays 30 percent of adjusted monthly income for rent. If the rent is more than the payment standard, the family pays a larger share of the rent.

(b) Tenant-based and project-based assistance. (1) Section 8 assistance may be ``tenant-based'' or ``project-based''. In project-
based programs, rental assistance is paid for families who live in specific housing developments or units. With tenant-based assistance, the assisted unit is selected by the family. The family may rent a unit anywhere in the United States in the jurisdiction of a PHA that runs a voucher program.

(2) To receive tenant-based assistance, the family selects a suitable unit. After approving the tenancy, the PHA enters into a contract to make rental subsidy payments to the owner to subsidize occupancy by the family. The PHA contract with the owner only covers a single unit and a specific assisted family. If the family moves out of the leased unit, the contract with the owner terminates. The family may move to another unit with continued assistance so long as the family is complying with program requirements.

{60 FR 34695, July 3, 1995, as amended at 64 FR 26640, May 14, 1999}

Sec. 982.2 Applicability.

(a) Part 982 is a unified statement of program requirements for the tenant-based housing assistance programs under Section 8 of the United States Housing Act of 1937 (42 U.S.C. 1437f). The tenant-based programs are the Section 8 tenant-based certificate program and the Section 8 voucher program.

(b) Unless specifically stated in this part, requirements for both tenant-based programs are the same.

{60 FR 34695, July 3, 1995, as amended at 64 FR 26640, May 14, 1999}

Sec. 982.3 HUD.

The HUD field offices have been delegated responsibility for day-to-day administration of the program by HUD. In exercising these functions, the field offices are subject to HUD regulations and other HUD requirements issued by HUD headquarters. Some functions are specifically reserved to HUD headquarters.

Sec. 982.4 Definitions.

(a) Definitions found elsewhere:

(1) General definitions. The terms 1937 Act, HUD, and MSA, are defined in 24 CFR part 5, subpart A.

(2) Terms found elsewhere. The following terms are defined in part 5, subpart A of this title: 1937 Act, covered person, drug, drug-related criminal activity, federally assisted housing, guest, household, HUD, MSA, other person under the tenant's control, public housing, Section 8, and violent criminal activity.

(3) Definitions concerning family income and rent. The terms ``adjusted income,'' ``annual income,'' ``extremely low income family,'' ``tenant rent,'' ``total tenant payment,'' ``utility allowance,'' ``utility reimbursement,'' and ``welfare assistance'' are defined in part 5, subpart F of this title. The definitions of ``tenant rent'' and ``utility reimbursement'' in part 5, subpart F of this title, apply to the certificate program, but do not apply to the tenant-based voucher program under part 982.

(b) In addition to the terms listed in paragraph (a) of this section, the following definitions apply:

Absorption. In portability (under subpart H of this part 982): the point at which a receiving PHA stops billing the initial PHA for assistance on behalf of a portability family. The receiving PPHA uses funds available under the receiving PHA consolidated ACC.

Administrative fee. Fee paid by HUD to the PHA for administration of the program. See Sec. 982.152.

Administrative fee reserve (formerly ``operating reserve''). Account established by PHA from excess administrative fee income. The administrative fee reserve must be used for housing purposes. See Sec. 982.155.

Administrative plan. The plan that describes PHA policies for administration of the tenant-based programs. See Sec. 982.54.

Admission. The point when the family becomes a participant in the program. The date used for this purpose is the effective date of the first HAP contract for a family (first day of initial lease term) in a tenant-based program.

Applicant (applicant family). A family that has applied for admission to a program but is not yet a participant in the program.

Budget authority. An amount authorized and appropriated by the Congress for payment to HAs under the program. For each funding increment in a PHA program, budget authority is the maximum amount that may be paid by HUD to the PHA over the ACC term of the funding increment.

Common space. In shared housing: Space available for use by the assisted family and other occupants of the unit.

Congregate housing. Housing for elderly persons or persons with disabilities that meets the HQS for congregate housing. A special housing type: see Sec. 982.606 to Sec. 982.609.

Continuously assisted. An applicant is continuously assisted under the 1937 Act if the family is already receiving assistance under any 1937 Act program when the family is admitted to the certificate or voucher program.

Cooperative. Housing owned by a corporation or association, and where a member of the corporation or association has the right to reside in a particular unit, and to participate in management of the housing.

Cooperative member. A family of which one or more members owns membership shares in a cooperative.

Domicile. The legal residence of the household head or spouse as determined in accordance with State and local law.

Downpayment assistance grant. A form of homeownership assistance in the homeownership option: A single downpayment assistance grant for the family. If a family receives a downpayment assistance grant, a PHA may not make monthly homeownership assistance payments for the family. A downpayment assistance grant is applied to the downpayment for purchase of the home or reasonable and customary closing costs required in connection with purchase of the home.

Fair market rent (FMR). The rent, including the cost of utilities (except telephone), as established by HUD for units of varying sizes (by number of bedrooms), that must be paid in the housing market area to rent privately owned, existing, decent, safe and sanitary rental housing of modest (non-luxury) nature with suitable amenities. See periodic publications in the Federal Register in accordance with 24 CFR part 888.

Family. A person or group of persons, as determined by the PHA, approved to reside in a unit with assistance under the program. See discussion of family composition at Sec. 982.201(c).

Family rent to owner. In the voucher program, the portion of rent to owner paid by the family. For calculation of family rent to owner, see Sec. 982.515(b).

Family self-sufficiency program (FSS program). The program established by a PHA in accordance with 24 CFR part 984 to promote self-
sufficiency of assisted families, including the coordination of supportive services (42 U.S.C. 1437u).

Family share. The portion of rent and utilities paid by the family. For calculation of family share, see Sec. 982.515(a).

Family unit size. The appropriate number of bedrooms for a family, as determined by the PHA under the PHA subsidy standards.

First-time homeowner. In the homeownership option: A family of which no member owned any present ownership interest in a residence of any family member during the three years before commencement

of homeownership assistance for the family. The term ``first-time homeowner'' includes a single parent or displaced homemaker (as those terms are defined in 12 U.S.C. 12713) who, while married, owned a home with his or her spouse, or resided in a home owned by his or her spouse.

Funding increment. Each commitment of budget authority by HUD to a PHA under the consolidated annual contributions contract for the PHA program.

Gross rent. The sum of the rent to owner plus any utility allowance.

Group home. A dwelling unit that is licensed by a State as a group home for the exclusive residential use of two to twelve persons who are elderly or persons with disabilities (including any live-in aide). A special housing type: see Sec. 982.610 to Sec. 982.614.

HAP contract. Housing assistance payments contract.

Home. In the homeownership option: A dwelling unit for which the PHA pays homeownership assistance.

Homeowner. In the homeownership option: A family of which one or more members owns title to the home.

Homeownership assistance. Assistance for a family under the homeownership option. There are two alternative and mutually exclusive forms of homeownership assistance by a PHA for a family: monthly homeownership assistance payments, or a single downpayment assistance grant. Either form of homeownership assistance may be paid to the family, or to a mortgage lender on behalf of the family.

Homeownership expenses. In the homeownership option: A family's allowable monthly expenses for the home, as determined by the PHA in accordance with HUD requirements (see Sec. 982.635).

Homeownership option. Assistance for a homeowner or cooperative member under Sec. 982.625 to Sec. 982.641. A special housing type.

Housing assistance payment. The monthly assistance payment by a PHA, which includes:

(1) A payment to the owner for rent to the owner under the family's lease; and

(2) An additional payment to the family if the total assistance payment exceeds the rent to owner.

Housing quality standards (HQS). The HUD minimum quality standards for housing assisted under the tenant-based programs. See Sec. 982.401.

Initial PHA. In portability, the term refers to both:

(1) a PHA that originally selected a family that later decides to move out of the jurisdiction of the selecting PHA; and

(2) a PHA that absorbed a family that later decides to move out of the jurisdiction of the absorbing PHA.

Initial payment standard. The payment standard at the beginning of the HAP contract term.

Initial rent to owner. The rent to owner at the beginning of the HAP contract term.

Interest in the home. In the homeownership option:

(1) In the case of assistance for a homeowner, ``interest in the home'' includes title to the home, any lease or other right to occupy the home, or any other present interest in the home.

(2) In the case of assistance for a cooperative member, ``interest in the home'' includes ownership of membership shares in the cooperative, any lease or other right to occupy the home, or any other present interest in the home.

Jurisdiction. The area in which the PHA has authority under State and local law to administer the program.

Lease. (1) A written agreement between an owner and a tenant for the leasing of a dwelling unit to the tenant. The lease establishes the conditions for occupancy of the dwelling unit by a family with housing assistance payments under a HAP contract between the owner and the PHA.

(2) In cooperative housing, a written agreement between a cooperative and a member of the cooperative. The agreement establishes the conditions for occupancy of the member's cooperative dwelling unit by

the member's family with housing assistance payments to the cooperative under a HAP contract between the cooperative and the PHA. For purposes of this part 982, the cooperative is the Section 8 ``owner'' of the unit, and the cooperative member is the Section 8 ``tenant.''

Manufactured home. A manufactured structure that is built on a permanent chassis, is designed for use as a principal place of residence, and meets the HQS. A special housing type: see Sec. 982.620 and Sec. 982.621.

Manufactured home space. In manufactured home space rental: A space leased by an owner to a family. A manufactured home owned and occupied by the family is located on the space. See Sec. 982.622 to Sec. 982.624.

Membership shares. In the homeownership option: shares in a cooperative. By owning such cooperative shares, the share-owner has the right to reside in a particular unit in the cooperative, and the right to participate in management of the housing.

Merger date. October 1, 1999.

Notice of Funding Availability (NOFA). For budget authority that HUD distributes by competitive process, the Federal Register document that invites applications for funding. This document explains how to apply for assistance and the criteria for awarding the funding.

Owner. Any person or entity with the legal right to lease or sublease a unit to a participant.

Participant (participant family). A family that has been admitted to the PHA program and is currently assisted in the program. The family becomes a participant on the effective date of the first HAP contract executed by the PHA for the family (first day of initial lease term).

Payment standard. The maximum monthly assistance payment for a family assisted in the voucher program (before deducting the total tenant payment by the family).

PHA plan. The annual plan and the 5-year plan as adopted by the PHA and approved by HUD in accordance with part 903 of this chapter.

Portability. Renting a dwelling unit with Section 8 tenant-based assistance outside the jurisdiction of the initial PHA.

Premises. The building or complex in which the dwelling unit is located, including common areas and grounds.

Present homeownership interest. In the homeownership option: ``Present ownership interest'' in a residence includes title, in whole or in part, to a residence, or ownership, in whole or in part, of membership shares in a cooperative. ``Present ownership interest'' in a residence does not include the right to purchase title to the residence under a lease-purchase agreement.

Private space. In shared housing: The portion of a contract unit that is for the exclusive use of an assisted family.

Program. The Section 8 tenant-based assistance program under this part.

Program receipts. HUD payments to the PHA under the consolidated ACC, and any other amounts received by the PHA in connection with the program.

Public housing agency (PHA). PHA includes both:

(1) Any State, county, municipality, or other governmental entity or public body which is authorized to administer the program (or an agency or instrumentality of such an entity), and

(2) Any of the following:

(i) A consortium of housing agencies, each of which meets the qualifications in paragraph (1) of this definition, that HUD determines has the capacity and capability to efficiently administer the program (in which case, HUD may enter into a consolidated ACC with any legal entity authorized to act as the legal representative of the consortium members);

(ii) Any other public or private non-profit entity that was administering a Section 8 tenant-based assistance program pursuant to a contract with the contract administrator of such program (HUD or a PHA) on October 21, 1998; or

(iii) For any area outside the jurisdiction of a PHA that is administering a tenant-based program, or where HUD determines that such PHA is not administering the program effectively, a private non-profit entity or a governmental entity or public body that would otherwise lack jurisdiction to administer the program in such area.

Reasonable rent. A rent to owner that is not more than rent charged:

(1) For comparable units in the private unassisted market; and

(2) For comparable unassisted units in the premises.

Receiving PHA. In portability: A PHA that receives a family selected for participation in the tenant-based program of another PHA. The receiving PHA issues a voucher and provides program assistance to the family.

Renewal units. The number of units, as determined by HUD, for which funding is reserved on HUD books for a PHA's program. This number is used is calculating renewal budget authority in accordance with Sec. 982.102.

Rent to owner. The total monthly rent payable to the owner under the lease for the unit. Rent to owner covers payment for any housing services, maintenance and utilities that the owner is required to provide and pay for.

Residency preference. A PHA preference for admission of families that reside anywhere in a specified area, including families with a member who works or has been hired to work in the area (``residency preference area'').

Residency preference area. The specified area where families must reside to qualify for a residency preference.

Shared housing. A unit occupied by two or more families. The unit consists of both common space for shared use by the occupants of the unit and separate private space for each assisted family. A special housing type: see Sec. 982.615 to Sec. 982.618.

Single room occupancy housing (SRO). A unit that contains no sanitary facilities or food preparation facilities, or contains either, but not both, types of facilities. A special housing type: see Sec. 982.602 to Sec. 982.605.

Special admission. Admission of an applicant that is not on the PHA waiting list or without considering the applicant's waiting list position.

Special housing types. See subpart M of this part 982. Subpart M of this part states the special regulatory requirements for: SRO housing, congregate housing, group home, shared housing, manufactured home (including manufactured home space rental), cooperative housing (rental assistance for cooperative member) and homeownership option (homeownership assistance for cooperative member or first-time homeowner).

Statement of homeowner obligations. In the homeownership option: The family's agreement to comply with program obligations.

Subsidy standards. Standards established by a PHA to determine the appropriate number of bedrooms and amount of subsidy for families of different sizes and compositions.

Suspension. Stopping the clock on the term of a family's voucher, for such period as determined by the PHA, from the time when the family submits a request for PHA approval of the tenancy, until the time when the PHA approves or denies the request.

Tenant. The person or persons (other than a live-in aide) who executes the lease as lessee of the dwelling unit.

Tenant rent. For a tenancy in the certificate program: The total tenant payment minus any utility allowance.

Utility reimbursement. In the voucher program, the portion of the housing assistance payment which exceeds the amount of the rent to owner. (See Sec. 982.514(b)). (For the certificate program, ``utility reimbursement'' is defined in part 5, subpart F of this title.)

Voucher holder. A family holding a voucher with an unexpired term (search time).

Voucher (rental voucher). A document

issued by a PHA to a family selected for admission to the voucher program. This document describes the program and the procedures for PHA approval of a unit selected by the family. The voucher also states obligations of the family under the program.

Waiting list admission. An admission from the PHA waiting list.

Welfare-to-work (WTW) families. Families assisted by a PHA with voucher funding awarded to the PHA under the HUD welfare-to-work voucher program (including any renewal of such WTW funding for the same purpose).

{63 FR 23857, Apr. 30, 1998; 63 FR 31625, June 10, 1998, as amended at 64 FR 26641, May 14, 1999; 64 FR 49658, Sept. 14, 1999; 64 FR 56887, 56911, Oct. 21, 1999; 65 FR 16821, Mar. 30, 2000; 65 FR 55161, Sept. 12, 2000; 66 FR 28804, May 24, 2001; 66 FR 33613, June 22, 2001; 67 FR 64492, Oct. 18, 2002}

Sec. 982.5 Notices required by this part.

Where part 982 requires any notice to be given by the PHA, the family or the owner, the notice must be in writing.

Subpart B--HUD Requirements and PHA Plan for Administration of Program

Source: 60 FR 34695, July 3, 1995, unless otherwise noted.

Sec. 982.51 PHA authority to administer program.

(a) The PHA must have authority to administer the program. The PHA must provide evidence, satisfactory to HUD, of its status as a PHA, of its authority to administer the program, and of the PHA jurisdiction.

(b) The evidence submitted by the PHA to HUD must include enabling legislation and a supporting legal opinion satisfactory to HUD. The PHA must submit additional evidence when there is a change that affects its status as a PHA, authority to administer the program, or the PHA jurisdiction.

{60 FR 34695, July 3, 1995, as amended at 64 FR 26641, May 14, 1999}

Sec. 982.52 HUD requirements.

(a) The PHA must comply with HUD regulations and other HUD requirements for the program. HUD requirements are issued by HUD headquarters, as regulations, Federal Register notices or other binding program directives.

(b) The PHA must comply with the consolidated ACC and the PHA's HUD-approved applications for program funding.

(Approved by the Office of Management and Budget under control number 2577-0169)
{60 FR 34695, July 3, 1995, as amended at 60 FR 45661, Sept. 1, 1995}

Sec. 982.53 Equal opportunity requirements.

(a) The tenant-based program requires compliance with all equal opportunity requirements imposed by contract or federal law, including the authorities cited at 24 CFR 5.105(a) and title II of the Americans with Disabilities Act, 42 U.S.C. 12101 et seq.

(b) Civil rights certification. The PHA must submit a signed certification to HUD that:

(1) The PHA will administer the program in conformity with the Fair Housing Act, Title VI of the Civil Rights Act of 1964, section 504 of the Rehabilitation Act of 1973, and Title II of the Americans with Disabilities Act.

(2) The PHA will affirmatively further fair housing in the administration of the program.

(c) Obligation to affirmatively further fair housing. The PHA shall affirmatively further fair housing as required by Sec. 903.7(o) of this title.

(d) State and local law. Nothing in part 982 is intended to pre-empt operation

of State and local laws that prohibit discrimination against a Section 8 voucher-holder because of status as a Section 8 voucher-
holder. However, such State and local laws shall not change or affect any requirement of this part, or any other HUD requirements for administration or operation of the program.

(Approved by the Office of Management and Budget under control number 2577-0169)
{60 FR 34695, July 3, 1995, as amended at 60 FR 45661, Sept. 1, 1995; 63 FR 23859, Apr. 30, 1998; 64 FR 26641, May 14, 1999; 64 FR 56911, Oct. 21, 1999}

Sec. 982.54 Administrative plan.

(a) The PHA must adopt a written administrative plan that establishes local policies for administration of the program in accordance with HUD requirements. The administrative plan and any revisions of the plan must be formally adopted by the PHA Board of Commissioners or other authorized PHA officials. The administrative plan states PHA policy on matters for which the PHA has discretion to establish local policies.

(b) The administrative plan must be in accordance with HUD regulations and requirements. The administrative plan is a supporting document to the PHA plan (part 903 of this title) and must be available for public review. The PHA must revise the administrative plan if needed to comply with HUD requirements.

(c) The PHA must administer the program in accordance with the PHA administrative plan.

(d) The PHA administrative plan must cover PHA policies on these subjects:

(1) Selection and admission of applicants from the PHA waiting list, including any PHA admission preferences, procedures for removing applicant names from the waiting list, and procedures for closing and reopening the PHA waiting list;

(2) Issuing or denying vouchers, including PHA policy governing the voucher term and any extensions or suspensions of the voucher term. ``Suspension'' means stopping the clock on the term of a family's voucher after the family submits a request for approval of the tenancy. If the PHA decides to allow extensions or suspensions of the voucher term, the PHA administrative plan must describe how the PHA determines whether to grant extensions or suspensions, and how the PHA determines the length of any extension or suspension;

(3) Any special rules for use of available funds when HUD provides funding to the PHA for a special purpose (e.g., desegregation), including funding for specified families or a specified category of families;

(4) Occupancy policies, including:

(i) Definition of what group of persons may qualify as a ``family'';

(ii) Definition of when a family is considered to be ``continuously assisted'';

(iii) Standards for denying admission or terminating assistance based on criminal activity or alcohol abuse in accordance with Sec. 982.553;

(5) Encouraging participation by owners of suitable units located outside areas of low income or minority concentration;

(6) Assisting a family that claims that illegal discrimination has prevented the family from leasing a suitable unit;

(7) Providing information about a family to prospective owners;

(8) Disapproval of owners;

(9) Subsidy standards;

(10) Family absence from the dwelling unit;

(11) How to determine who remains in the program if a family breaks up;

(12) Informal review procedures for applicants;

(13) Informal hearing procedures for participants;

(14) The process for establishing and revising voucher payment standards;

(15) The method of determining that rent to owner is a reasonable rent (initially and during the term of a HAP contract);

(16) Special policies concerning special housing types in the program (e.g., use of shared housing);

(17) Policies concerning payment by a family to the PHA of amounts the family owes the PHA;

(18) Interim redeterminations of family income and composition;

(19) Restrictions, if any, on the number of moves by a participant family (see Sec. 982.314(c)); and

(20) Restrictions, if any, on the number of moves by a participant family (see Sec. 982.314(c));

(21) Approval by the Board of Commissioners or other authorized officials to charge the administrative fee reserve;

(22) Procedural guidelines and performance standards for conducting required HQS inspections; and

(23) PHA screening of applicants for family behavior or suitability for tenancy.

(Approved by the Office of Management and Budget under control number 2577-0169) {60 FR 34695, July 3, 1995, as amended at 60 FR 45661, Sept. 1, 1995; 61 FR 27163, May 30, 1996; 63 FR 23859, Apr. 30, 1998; 64 FR 26641, May 14, 1999; 64 FR 49658, 64 FR Sept. 14, 1999; 56911, Oct. 21, 1999; 66 FR 28804, May 24, 2001}

Subpart C--Funding and PHA Application for Funding

Source: 60 FR 34695, July 3, 1995, unless otherwise noted.

Sec. 982.101 Allocation of funding.

(a) Allocation of funding. HUD allocates available budget authority for the tenant-based assistance program to HUD field offices.

(b) Section 213(d) allocation. (1) Section 213(d) of the HCD Act of 1974 (42 U.S.C. 1439) establishes requirements for allocation of assisted housing budget authority. Some budget authority is exempt by law from allocation under section 213(d). Unless exempted by law, budget authority for the tenant-based programs must be allocated in accordance with section 213(d).

(2) Budget authority subject to allocation under section 213(d) is allocated in accordance with 24 CFR part 791, subpart D. There are three categories of section 213(d) funding allocations under part 791 of this title:

(i) Funding retained in a headquarters reserve for purposes specified by law;

(ii) funding incapable of geographic formula allocation (e.g., for renewal of expiring funding increments); or

(iii) funding allocated by an objective fair share formula. Funding allocated by fair share formula is distributed by a competitive process.

(c) Competitive process. For budget authority that is distributed by competitive process, the Department solicits applications from HAs by publishing one or more notices of funding availability (NOFA) in the Federal Register. See 24 CFR part 12, subpart B; and 24 CFR 791.406. The NOFA explains how to apply for assistance, and specifies the criteria for awarding the assistance. The NOFA may identify any special program requirements for use of the funding.

{60 FR 34695, July 3, 1995, as amended at 64 FR 26642, May 14, 1999}

Sec. 982.102 Allocation of budget authority for renewal of expiring consolidated ACC funding increments.

(a) Applicability. This section applies to the renewal of consolidated ACC funding increments in the program (as described in Sec. 982.151(a)(2)) that expire after December 31, 1999 (including any assistance that the PHA has attached to units for project-based assistance under part 983 of this title). This section implements section 8(dd) of the 1937 Act (42 U.S.C. 1437f(dd)),

(b) Renewal Methodology. HUD will use the following methodology to determine the amount of budget authority to be allocated

to a PHA for the renewal of expiring consolidated ACC funding increments in the program, subject to the availability of appropriated funds. If the amount of appropriated funds is not sufficient to provide the full amount of renewal funding for PHAs, as calculated in accordance with this section, HUD may establish a procedure to adjust allocations for the shortfall in funding.

(c) Determining the amount of budget authority allocated for renewal of an expiring funding increment. Subject to availability of appropriated funds, as determined by HUD, the amount of budget authority allocated by HUD to a PHA for renewal of each program funding increment that expires during a calendar year will be equal to:

(1) Number of renewal units. The number of renewal units assigned to the funding increment (as determined by HUD pursuant to paragraph (d) of this section); multiplied by

(2) Adjusted annual per unit cost. The adjusted annual per unit cost (as determined by HUD pursuant to paragraph (e) of this section).

(d) Determining the number of renewal units.--(1) Number of renewal units. HUD will determine the total number of renewal units for a PHA's program as of the last day of the calendar year previous to the calendar year for which renewal funding is calculated. The number of renewal units for a PHA's program will be determined as follows:

(i) Step 1: Establishing the initial baseline. HUD will establish a baseline number of units (``baseline'') for each PHA program. The initial baseline equals the number of units reserved by HUD for the PHA program as of December 31, 1999.

(ii) Step 2: Establishing the adjusted baseline. The adjusted baseline equals the initial baseline with the following adjustments from the initial baseline as of the last day of the calendar year previous to the calendar year for which renewal funding is calculated:

(A) Additional units. HUD will add to the initial baseline any additional units reserved for the PHA after December 31, 1999.

(B) Units removed. HUD will subtract from the initial baseline any units de-reserved by HUD from the PHA program after December 31, 1999.

(iii) Step 3: Determining the number of renewal units. The number of renewal units equals the adjusted baseline minus the number of units supported by contract funding increments that expire after the end of the calendar year.

(2) Funding increments. HUD will assign all units reserved for a PHA program to one or more funding increment(s).

(3) Correction of errors. HUD may adjust the number of renewal units to correct errors.

(e) Determining the adjusted per unit cost. HUD will determine the PHA's adjusted per unit cost when HUD processes the allocation of renewal funding for an expiring contract funding increment. The adjusted per unit cost calculated will be determined as follows:

(1) Step 1: Determining monthly program expenditure.--(i) Use of most recent HUD-approved year end statement. HUD will determine the PHA's monthly per unit program expenditure for the PHA certificate and voucher programs (including project-based assistance under such programs) under the consolidated ACC with HUD using data from the PHA's most recent HUD-approved year end statement.

(ii) Monthly program expenditure. The monthly program expenditure equals:

(A) Total program expenditure. The PHA's total program expenditure (the total of housing assistance payments and administrative costs) for the PHA fiscal year covered by the approved year end statement; divided by

(B) Total unit months leased. The total of unit months leased for the PHA fiscal year covered by the approved year end statement.

(2) Step 2: Determining annual per unit cost. HUD will determine the PHA's annual per unit cost. The annual per unit cost equals the monthly program expenditures (as determined under paragraph (e)(1)(ii) of this section) multiplied by 12.

(3) Step 3: Determining adjusted annual per unit cost. (i) HUD will determine the PHA's adjusted annual per unit cost. The adjusted annual per unit cost equals the annual per unit cost (as determined under paragraph (e)(2) of this section) multiplied cumulatively by the applicable published Section 8 housing assistance payments program annual adjustment factors in effect during the period from the end of the PHA fiscal year covered by the approved year end statement to the time when HUD processes the allocation of renewal funding.

(ii) Use of annual adjustment factor applicable to PHA jurisdiction. For this purpose, HUD will use the annual adjustment factor from the notice published annually in the Federal Register pursuant to part 888 that is applicable to the jurisdiction of the PHA. For a PHA whose jurisdiction spans multiple annual adjustment factor areas, HUD will use the highest applicable annual adjustment factor.

(iii) Use of annual adjustment factors in effect subsequent to most recent Year End Statement. HUD will use the Annual Adjustment Factors in effect during the time period subsequent to the time covered by the most recent HUD approved Year End Statement and the time of the processing of the contract funding increment to be renewed.

(iii) Special circumstances. At its discretion, HUD may modify the adjusted annual per unit cost based on receipt of a modification request from a PHA. The modification request must demonstrate that because of special circumstances application of the annual adjustment factor will not provide an accurate adjusted annual per unit cost.

(4) Correction of errors. HUD may correct for errors in the adjusted per unit cost.

(f) consolidated ACC amendment to add renewal funding. HUD will reserve allocated renewal funding available to the PHA within a reasonable time prior to the expiration of the funding increment to be renewed and establish a new expiration date one-year from the date of such expiration.

(g) Modification of allocation of budget authority--(1) HUD authority to conform PHA program costs with PHA program finances through Federal Register notice. In the event that a PHA's costs incurred threaten to exceed budget authority and allowable reserves, HUD reserves the right, through Federal Register notice, to bring PHA program costs and the number of families served, in line with PHA program finances.

(2) HUD authority to limit increases of per unit cost through Federal Register notice. HUD may, by Federal Register notice, limit the amount or percentage of increases in the adjusted annual per unit cost to be used in calculating the allocation of budget authority.

(3) HUD authority to limit decreases to per unit costs through Federal Register notice. HUD may, by Federal Register notice, limit the amount or percentage of decreases in the adjusted annual per unit cost to be used in calculating the allocation of budget authority.

(4) Contents of Federal Register notice. If HUD publishes a Federal Register notice pursuant to paragraphs (g)(1), (g)(2) or (g)(3) of this section, it will describe the rationale, circumstances and procedures under which such modifications are implemented. Such circumstances and procedures shall, be consistent with the objective of enabling PHAs and HUD to meet program goals and requirements including but not limited to:

(i) Deconcentration of poverty and expanding housing opportunities;

(ii) Reasonable rent burden;

(iii) Income targeting;

(iv) Consistency with applicable consolidated plan(s);

(v) Rent reasonableness;

(vi) Program efficiency and economy;

(vii) Service to additional households within budgetary limitations; and

(viii) Service to the adjusted baseline number of families.

(5) Public consultation before issuance of Federal Register notice. HUD will design and undertake informal public consultation prior to issuing Federal Register notices pursuant to paragraphs (g)(1) or (g)(2) of this section.

(h) Ability to prorate and synchronize contract funding increments. Notwithstanding paragraphs (c) through (g) of this section, HUD may prorate the amount of budget authority allocated for the renewal of funding increments that expire on different dates throughout the calendar year. HUD may use such proration to synchronize the expiration dates of funding increments under the PHA's consolidated ACC.

(i) Reallocation of budget authority. If a PHA has performance deficiencies, such as a failure to adequately lease units, HUD may reallocate some of its budget authority to other PHAs. If HUD determines to reallocate budget authority, it will reduce the number of units reserved by HUD for the PHA program of the PHA whose budget authority is being reallocated and increase the number of units reserved by HUD for the PHAs whose programs are receiving the benefit of the reallocation, so that such PHAs can issue vouchers. HUD will publish a notice in the Federal Register that will describe the circumstances and procedures for reallocating budget authority pursuant to this paragraph.

{64 FR 56887, Oct. 21, 1999; 65 FR 16818, Mar. 30, 2000}

Sec. 982.103 PHA application for funding.

(a) a PHA must submit an application for program funding to HUD at the time and place and in the form required by HUD.

(b) For competitive funding under a NOFA, the application must be submitted by a PHA in accordance with the requirements of the NOFA.

(c) The application must include all information required by HUD. HUD requirements may be stated in the HUD-required form of application, the NOFA, or other HUD instructions.

(Approved by the Office of Management and Budget under control number 2577-0169) {60 FR 34695, July 3, 1995, as amended at 60 FR 45661, Sept. 1, 1995; 63 FR 23859, Apr. 30, 1998. Redesignated at 64 FR 56887, Oct. 21, 1999}

Sec. 982.104 HUD review of application.

(a) Competitive funding under NOFA. For competitive funding under a NOFA, HUD must evaluate an application on the basis of the selection criteria stated in the NOFA, and must consider the PHA's capacity and capability to administer the program.

(b) Approval or disapproval of PHA funding application. (1) HUD must notify the PHA of its approval or disapproval of the PHA funding application.

(2) When HUD approves an application, HUD must notify the PHA of the amount of approved funding.

(3) For budget authority that is distributed to PHAs by competitive process, documentation of the basis for provision or denial of assistance is available for public inspection in accordance with 24 CFR 12.14(b).

(c) PHA disqualification. HUD will not approve any PHA funding application (including an application for competitive funding under a NOFA) if HUD determines that the PHA is disbarred or otherwise disqualified from providing assistance under the program.

{60 FR 34695, July 3, 1995, as amended at 64 FR 26642, May 14, 1999. Redesignated at 64 FR 56887, Oct. 21, 1999}

Subpart D--Annual Contributions Contract and PHA Administration of Program

Source: 60 FR 34695, July 3, 1995, unless otherwise noted.

Sec. 982.151 Annual contributions contract.

(a) Nature of ACC. (1) An annual contributions contract (ACC) is a written contract between HUD and a PHA. Under the ACC, HUD agrees to make payments to the PHA, over a specified term, for housing assistance payments to owners and for the PHA administrative fee. The ACC specifies the maximum payment over the ACC term. The PHA agrees to administer the program in accordance with HUD regulations and requirements.

(2) HUD's commitment to make payments for each funding increment in the PHA program constitutes a separate ACC. However, commitments for all the funding increments in a PHA program are listed in one consolidated contractual document called the consolidated annual contributions contract (consolidated ACC). A single consolidated ACC covers funding for the PHA tenant-based assistance program.

(b) Budget authority. (1) Budget authority is the maximum amount that may be paid by HUD to a PHA over the ACC term of a funding increment. Before adding a funding increment to the consolidated ACC for a PHA program, HUD reserves budget authority from amounts authorized and appropriated by the Congress for the program.

(2) For each funding increment, the ACC specifies the term over which HUD will make payments for the PHA program, and the amount of available budget authority for each funding increment. The amount to be paid to the PHA during each PHA fiscal year (including payment from the ACC reserve account described in Sec. 982.154) must be approved by HUD.

(Approved by the Office of Management and Budget under control number 2577-0169) {60 FR 34695, July 3, 1995, as amended at 60 FR 45661, Sept. 1, 1995; 64 FR 26642, May 14, 1999}

Sec. 982.152 Administrative fee.

(a) Purposes of administrative fee. (1) HUD may approve administrative fees to the PHA for any of the following purposes:

(i) Ongoing administrative fee;

(ii) Costs to help families who experience difficulty finding or renting appropriate housing under the program;

(iii) The following types of extraordinary costs approved by HUD:

(A) Costs to cover necessary additional expenses incurred by the PHA to provide reasonable accommodation for persons with disabilities in accordance with part 8 of this title (e.g., additional counselling costs), where the PHA is unable to cover such additional expenses from ongoing administrative fee income or the PHA administrative fee reserve;

(B) Costs of audit by an independent public accountant;

(C) Other extraordinary costs determined necessary by HUD Headquarters;

(iv) Preliminary fee (in accordance with paragraph (c) of this section);

(v) Costs to coordinate supportive services for families participating in the family self-sufficiency (FSS) program.

(2) For each HA fiscal year, administrative fees are specified in the HA budget. The budget is submitted for HUD approval. Fees are paid in the amounts approved by HUD. Administrative fees may only be approved or paid from amounts appropriated by the Congress.

(3) HA administrative fees may only be used to cover costs incurred to perform HA administrative responsibilities for the program in accordance with HUD regulations and requirements.

(b) Ongoing administrative fee. (1) The PHA ongoing administrative fee is paid for each program unit under HAP contract on the first day of the month. The amount of the ongoing fee is determined by HUD in accordance with Section 8(q)(1) of the 1937 Act (42 U.S.C. 1437f(q)(1)).

(2) If appropriations are available, HUD may pay a higher ongoing administrative fee for a small program or a program operating

over a large geographic area. This higher fee level will not be approved unless the PHA demonstrates that it is efficiently administering its tenant-
based program, and that the higher ongoing administrative fee is reasonable and necessary for administration of the program in accordance with HUD requirements.

(3) HUD may pay a lower ongoing administrative fee for PHA-owned units.

(c) Preliminary fee. (1) If the PHA was not administering a program of Section 8 tenant-based assistance prior to the merger date, HUD will pay a one-time fee in the amount of $500 in the first year the PHA administers a program. The fee is paid for each new unit added to the PHA program by the initial funding increment under the consolidated ACC.

(2) The preliminary fee is used to cover expenses the PHA incurs to help families who inquire about or apply for the program, and to lease up new program units.

(d) Reducing PHA administrative fee. HUD may reduce or offset any administrative fee to the PHA, in the amount determined by HUD, if the PHA fails to perform PHA administrative responsibilities correctly or adequately under the program (for example, PHA failure to enforce HQS requirements; or to reimburse a receiving PHA promptly under portability procedures).

{60 FR 23695, July 3, 1995, as amended at 63 FR 23860, Apr. 30, 1998; 64 FR 26642, May 14, 1999}

Sec. 982.153 PHA responsibilities.

The PHA must comply with the consolidated ACC, the application, HUD regulations and other requirements, and the PHA administrative plan.

(Approved by the Office of Management and Budget under control number 2577-0169)
{60 FR 34695, July 3, 1995, as amended at 60 FR 45661, Sept. 1, 1995; 61 FR 13627, Mar. 27, 1996; 63 FR 23860, Apr. 30, 1998}

Sec. 982.154 ACC reserve account.

(a) HUD may establish and maintain an unfunded reserve account for the PHA program from available budget authority under the consolidated ACC. This reserve is called the ``ACC reserve account'' (formerly ``project reserve''). There is a single ACC reserve account for the PHA program.

(b) The amount in the ACC reserve account is determined by HUD. HUD may approve payments for the PHA program, in accordance with the PHA's HUD-approved budget, from available amounts in the ACC reserve account.

{64 FR 26642, May 14, 1999}

Sec. 982.155 Administrative fee reserve.

(a) The PHA must maintain an administrative fee reserve (formerly ``operating reserve'') for the program. There is a single administrative fee reserve for the PHA program. The PHA must credit to the administrative fee reserve the total of:

(1) The amount by which program administrative fees paid by HUD for a PHA fiscal year exceed the PHA program administrative expenses for the fiscal year; plus

(2) Interest earned on the administrative fee reserve.

(b)(1) The PHA must use funds in the administrative fee reserve to pay program administrative expenses in excess of administrative fees paid by HUD for a PHA fiscal year. If funds in the administrative fee reserve are not needed to cover PHA administrative expenses (to the end of the last expiring funding increment under the consolidated ACC), the PHA may use these funds for other housing purposes permitted by State and local law. However, HUD may prohibit use of the funds for certain purposes.

(2) The PHA Board of Commissioners or other authorized officials must establish the maximum amount that may be charged

against the administrative fee reserve without specific approval.

(3) If the PHA has not adequately administered any Section 8 program, HUD may prohibit use of funds in the administrative fee reserve, and may direct the PHA to use funds in the reserve to improve administration of the program or to reimburse ineligible expenses.

(Approved by the Office of Management and Budget under control number 2577-0169) {60 FR 34695, July 3, 1995, as amended at 60 FR 45661, Sept. 1, 1995; 64 FR 26642, May 14, 1999}

Sec. 982.156 Depositary for program funds.

(a) Unless otherwise required or permitted by HUD, all program receipts must be promptly deposited with a financial institution selected as depositary by the PHA in accordance with HUD requirements.

(b) The PHA may only withdraw deposited program receipts for use in connection with the program in accordance with HUD requirements.

(c) The PHA must enter into an agreement with the depositary in the form required by HUD.

(d)(1) If required under a written freeze notice from HUD to the depositary:

(i) The depositary may not permit any withdrawal by the PHA of funds held under the depositary agreement unless expressly authorized by written notice from HUD to the depositary; and

(ii) The depositary must permit withdrawals of such funds by HUD.

(2) HUD must send the PHA a copy of the freeze notice from HUD to the depositary.

(Approved by the Office of Management and Budget under control number 2577-0169) {60 FR 34695, July 3, 1995, as amended at 60 FR 45661, Sept. 1, 1995}

Sec. 982.157 Budget and expenditure.

(a) Budget submission. Each PHA fiscal year, the PHA must submit its proposed budget for the program to HUD for approval at such time and in such form as required by HUD.

(b) PHA use of program receipts. (1) Program receipts must be used in accordance with the PHA's HUD-approved budget. Such program receipts may only be used for:

(i) Housing assistance payments; and

(ii) PHA administrative fees.

(2) The PHA must maintain a system to ensure that the PHA will be able to make housing assistance payments for all participants within the amounts contracted under the consolidated ACC.

(c) Intellectual property rights. Program receipts may not be used to indemnify contractors or subcontractors of the PHA against costs associated with any judgment of infringement of intellectual property rights.

(Approved by the Office of Management and Budget under control number 2577-0169) {60 FR 34695, July 3, 1995, as amended at 60 FR 45661, Sept. 1, 1995; 64 FR 26642, May 14, 1999}

Sec. 982.158 Program accounts and records.

(a) The PHA must maintain complete and accurate accounts and other records for the program in accordance with HUD requirements, in a manner that permits a speedy and effective audit. The records must be in the form required by HUD, including requirements governing computerized or electronic forms of record-keeping. The PHA must comply with the financial reporting requirements in 24 CFR part 5, subpart H.

(b) The PHA must furnish to HUD accounts and other records, reports, documents and information, as required by HUD. For provisions on electronic transmission of required family data, see 24 CFR part 908.

(c) HUD and the Comptroller General of the United States shall have full and free access to all PHA offices and facilities, and to all accounts and other records of the PHA tPHAt are pertinent to administration of the program, including the right to examine or audit the records, and to make copies. The PHA must grant such access to computerized or other electronic records, and to any computers, equipment or facilities containing such records, and shall provide any information or assistance needed to access the records.

(d) The PHA must prepare a unit inspection report.

(e) During the term of each assisted lease, and for at least three years thereafter, the PHA must keep:

(1) A copy of the executed lease;

(2) The HAP contract; and

(3) The application from the family.

(f) The PHA must keep the following records for at least three years:

(1) Records that provide income, racial, ethnic, gender, and disability status data on program applicants and participants;

(2) An application from each ineligible family and notice that the applicant is not eligible;

(3) HUD-required reports;

(4) Unit inspection reports;

(5) Lead-based paint records as required by part 35, subpart B of this title.

(6) Accounts and other records supporting PHA budget and financial statements for the program;

(7) Records to document the basis for PHA determination that rent to owner is a reasonable rent (initially and during the term of a HAP contract); and

(8) Other records specified by HUD.

(Approved by the Office of Management and Budget under control number 2577-0169) {60 FR 34695, July 3, 1995, as amended at 60 FR 45661, Sept. 1, 1995; 61 FR 27163, May 30, 1996; 63 FR 23860, Apr. 30, 1998; 63 FR 46593, Sept. 1, 1998; 64 FR 50229, Sept. 15, 1999}

Sec. 982.159 Audit requirements.

(a) The PHA must engage and pay an independent public accountant to conduct audits in accordance with HUD requirements.

(b) The PHA is subject to the audit requirements in 24 CFR part 44.

(Approved by the Office of Management and Budget under control number 2577-0169) {60 FR 34695, July 3, 1995, as amended at 60 FR 45661, Sept. 1, 1995}

Sec. 982.160 HUD determination to administer a local program.

If the Assistant Secretary for Public and Indian Housing determines that there is no PHA organized, or that there is no PHA able and willing to implement the provisions of this part for an area, HUD (or an entity acting on behalf of HUD) may enter into HAP contracts with owners and perform the functions otherwise assigned to PHAs under this part with respect to the area.

(Approved by the Office of Management and Budget under control number 2577-0169) {60 FR 34695, July 3, 1995, as amended at 60 FR 45661, Sept. 1, 1995}

Sec. 982.161 Conflict of interest.

(a) Neither the PHA nor any of its contractors or subcontractors may enter into any contract or arrangement in connection with the tenant-
based programs in which any of the following classes of persons has any interest, direct or indirect, during tenure or for one year thereafter:

(1) Any present or former member or officer of the PHA (except a participant commissioner);

(2) Any employee of the PHA, or any contractor, subcontractor or agent of the

PHA, who formulates policy or who influences decisions with respect to the programs;

(3) Any public official, member of a governing body, or State or local legislator, who exercises functions or responsibilities with respect to the programs; or

(4) Any member of the Congress of the United States.

(b) Any member of the classes described in paragraph (a) of this section must disclose their interest or prospective interest to the PHA and HUD.

(c) The conflict of interest prohibition under this section may be waived by the HUD field office for good cause.

Sec. 982.162 Use of HUD-required contracts and other forms.

(a) The PHA must use program contracts and other forms required by HUD headquarters, including:

(1) The consolidated ACC between HUD and the PHA;

(2) The HAP contract between the PHA and the owner; and

(3) The tenancy addendum required by HUD (which is included both in the HAP contract and in the lease between the owner and the tenant).

(b) Required program contracts and other forms must be word-for-word in the form required by HUD headquarters. Any additions to or modifications of required program contracts or other forms must be approved by HUD headquarters.

{60 FR 34695, July 3, 1995, as amended at 64 FR 26642, May 14, 1999}

Sec. 982.163 Fraud recoveries.

Under 24 CFR part 792, the PHA may retain a portion of program fraud losses that the PHA recovers from a family or owner by litigation, court-order or a repayment agreement.

{60 FR 34695, July 3, 1995; 60 FR 43840, Aug. 23, 1995}

Subpart E--Admission to Tenant-Based Program

Sec. 982.201 Eligibility and targeting.

(a) When applicant is eligible: general. The PHA may only admit an eligible family to the program. To be eligible, the applicant must be a ``family'', must be income-eligible, and must be a citizen or a noncitizen who has eligible immigration status as determined in accordance with 24 CFR part 5.

(b) Income. (1) Income-eligibility. To be income-eligible, the applicant must be a family in any of the following categories:

(i) A ``very low income'' family;

(ii) A low-income family that is ``continuously assisted'' under the 1937 Housing Act;

(iii) A low-income family that meets additional eligibility criteria specified in the PHA administrative plan. Such additional PHA criteria must be consistent with the PHA plan and with the consolidated plans for local governments in the PHA jurisdiction;

(iv) A low-income family that qualifies for voucher assistance as a non-purchasing family residing in a HOPE 1 (HOPE for public housing homeownership) or HOPE 2 (HOPE for homeownership of multifamily units) project. (Section 8(o)(4)(D) of the 1937 Act (42 U.S.C. 1437f(o)(4)(D));

(v) A low-income or moderate-income family that is displaced as a result of the prepayment of the mortgage or voluntary termination of an insurance contract on

eligible low-income housing as defined in Sec. 248.101 of this title;

(vi) A low-income family that qualifies for voucher assistance as a non-purchasing family residing in a project subject to a resident homeownership program under Sec. 248.173 of this title.

(2) Income-targeting. (i) Not less than 75 percent of the families admitted to a PHA's tenant-based voucher program during the PHA fiscal year from the PHA waiting list shall be extremely low income families. Annual income of such families shall be verified within the period described in paragraph (e) of this section.

(ii) A PHA may admit a lower percent of extremely low income families during a PHA fiscal year (than otherwise required under paragraph (b)(2)(i) of this section) if HUD approves the use of such lower percent by the PHA, in accordance with the PHA plan, based on HUD's determination that the following circumstances necessitate use of such lower percent by the PHA:

(A) The PHA has opened its waiting list for a reasonable time for admission of extremely low income families residing in the same metropolitan statistical area (MSA) or non-metropolitan county, both inside and outside the PHA jurisdiction;

(B) The PHA has provided full public notice of such opening to such families, and has conducted outreach and marketing to such families, including outreach and marketing to extremely low income families on the Section 8 and public housing waiting lists of other PHAs with jurisdiction in the same MSA or non-metropolitan county;

(C) Notwithstanding such actions by the PHA (in accordance with paragraphs (b)(2)(ii)(A) and (B) of this section), there are not enough extremely low income families on the PHA's waiting list to fill available slots in the program during any fiscal year for which use of a lower percent is approved by HUD; and

(D) Admission of the additional very low income families other than extremely low income families to the PHA's tenant-based voucher program will substantially address worst case housing needs as determined by HUD.

(iii) If approved by HUD, the admission of a portion of very low income welfare-to-work (WTW) families that are not extremely low income families may be disregarded in determining compliance with the PHA's income-targeting obligations under paragraph (b)(2)(i) of this section. HUD will grant such approval only if and to the extent that the PHA has demonstrated to HUD's satisfaction that compliance with such targeting obligations with respect to such portion of WTW families would interfere with the objectives of the welfare-to-work voucher program. If HUD grants such approval, admission of that portion of WTW families is not counted in the base number of families admitted to a PHA's tenant-based voucher program during the fiscal year for purposes of income targeting.

(iv) Conversion of assistance for a participant in the PHA certificate program to assistance in the PHA voucher program does not count as an ``admission,'' and is not subject to targeting under paragraph (b)(2)(i) of this section.

(v) Admission of families as described in paragraphs (b)(1)(ii) or (b)(1)(v) of this section is not subject to targeting under paragraph (b)(2)(i) of this section.

(vi) If the jurisdictions of two or more PHAs that administer the tenant-based voucher program cover an identical geographic area, such PHAs may elect to be treated as a single PHA for purposes of targeting under paragraph (b)(2)(i) of this section. In such a case, the PHAs shall cooperate to assure that aggregate admissions by such PHAs comply with the targeting requirement. If such PHAs do not have a single fiscal year, HUD will determine which PHA's fiscal year is used for this purpose.

(vii) If a family initially leases a unit outside the PHA jurisdiction under portability procedures at admission to the voucher program on or after the merger date, such admission shall be counted against the targeting obligation of the initial PHA (unless the receiving PHA absorbs

the portable family into the receiving PHA voucher program from the point of admission).

(3) The annual income (gross income) of a participant family is used both for determination of income-eligibility under paragraph (b)(1) of this section and for targeting under paragraph (b)(2)(i) of this section. In determining annual income of a participant family which includes persons with disabilities, the determination must include the disallowance of increase in annual income as provided in 24 CFR 5.617, if applicable.

(4) The applicable income limit for issuance of a voucher when a family is selected for the program is the highest income limit (for the family size) for areas in the PHA jurisdiction. The applicable income limit for admission to the program is the income limit for the area where the family is initially assisted in the program. At admission, the family may only use the voucher to rent a unit in an area where the family is income eligible.

(c) Family composition. (1) A ``family'' may be a single person or a group of persons.

(2) A ``family'' includes a family with a child or children.

(3) A group of persons consisting of two or more elderly persons or disabled persons living together, or one or more elderly or disabled persons living with one or more live-in aides is a family. The PHA determines if any other group of persons qualifies as a ``family''.

(4) A single person family may be:

(i) An elderly person.

(ii) A displaced person.

(iii) A disabled person.

(iv) Any other single person.

(5) A child who is temporarily away from the home because of placement in foster care is considered a member of the family.

(d) Continuously assisted. (1) An applicant is continuously assisted under the 1937 Housing Act if the family is already receiving assistance under any 1937 Housing Act program when the family is admitted to the voucher program.

(2) The PHA must establish policies concerning whether and to what extent a brief interruption between assistance under one of these programs and admission to the voucher program will be considered to break continuity of assistance under the 1937 Housing Act.

(e) When PHA verifies that applicant is eligible. The PHA must receive information verifying that an applicant is eligible within the period of 60 days before the PHA issues a voucher to the applicant.

(f) Decision to deny assistance--(1) Notice to applicant. The PHA must give an applicant prompt written notice of a decision denying admission to the program (including a decision that the applicant is not eligible, or denying assistance for other reasons). The notice must give a brief statement of the reasons for the decision. The notice must also state that the applicant may request an informal review of the decision, and state how to arrange for the informal review.

(2) For description of the grounds for denying assistance because of action or inaction by the applicant, see Sec. 982.552(b) and (c) (requirement and authority to deny admission) and Sec. 982.553(a) (crime by family members).

{59 FR 36682, July 18, 1994, as amended at 60 FR 34717, July 3, 1995; 61 FR 13627, Mar. 27, 1996; 64 FR 26642, May 14, 1999; 64 FR 49658, Sept. 14, 1999; 64 FR 56911, Oct. 21, 1999; 66 FR 6226, Jan. 19, 2001; 66 FR 8174, Jan. 30, 2001; 67 FR 6820, Feb. 13, 2002}

Sec. 982.202 How applicants are selected: General requirements.

(a) Waiting list admissions and special admissions. The PHA may admit an applicant for participation in the program either:

(1) As a special admission (see Sec. 982.203).

(2) As a waiting list admission (see Sec. 982.204 through Sec. 982.210).

(b) Prohibited admission criteria--(1) Where family lives. Admission to the program may not be based on where the family lives before admission to the program. However, the PHA may target assistance for families who live in public housing or other federally assisted housing, or may adopt a residency preference (see Sec. 982.207).

(2) Where family will live. Admission to the program may not be based on where the family will live with assistance under the program.

(3) Family characteristics. The PHA preference system may provide a preference for admission of families with certain characteristics from the PHA waiting list. However, admission to the program may not be based on:

(i) Discrimination because members of the family are unwed parents, recipients of public assistance, or children born out of wedlock;

(ii) Discrimination because a family includes children (familial status discrimination);

(iii) Discrimination because of age, race, color, religion, sex, or national origin;

(iv) Discrimination because of disability; or

(v) Whether a family decides to participate in a family self-sufficiency program.

(c) Applicant status. An applicant does not have any right or entitlement to be listed on the PHA waiting list, to any particular position on the waiting list, or to admission to the programs. The preceding sentence does not affect or prejudice any right, independent of this rule, to bring a judicial action challenging an PHA violation of a constitutional or statutory requirement.

(d) Admission policy. The PHA must admit applicants for participation in accordance with HUD regulations and other requirements, and with PHA policies stated in the PHA administrative plan and the PHA plan. The PHA admission policy must state the system of admission preferences that the PHA uses to select applicants from the waiting list, including any residency preference or other local preference.

{59 FR 36682, July 18, 1994, as amended at 60 FR 34717, July 3, 1995; 61 FR 9048, Mar. 6, 1996; 61 FR 27163, May 30, 1996; 64 FR 26643, May 14, 1999; 65 FR 16821, Mar. 30, 2000}

Sec. 982.203 Special admission (non-waiting list): Assistance targeted by HUD.

(a) If HUD awards a PHA program funding that is targeted for families living in specified units:

(1) The PHA must use the assistance for the families living in these units.

(2) The PHA may admit a family that is not on the PHA waiting list, or without considering the family's waiting list position. The PHA must maintain records showing that the family was admitted with HUD-targeted assistance.

(b) The following are examples of types of program funding that may be targeted for a family living in a specified unit:

(1) A family displaced because of demolition or disposition of a public housing project;

(2) A family residing in a multifamily rental housing project when HUD sells, forecloses or demolishes the project;

(3) For housing covered by the Low Income Housing Preservation and Resident Homeownership Act of 1990 (41 U.S.C. 4101 et seq.):

(i) A non-purchasing family residing in a project subject to a homeownership program (under 24 CFR 248.173); or

(ii) A family displaced because of mortgage prepayment or voluntary termination of a mortgage insurance contract (as provided in 24 CFR 248.165);

(4) A family residing in a project covered by a project-based Section 8 HAP contract at or near the end of the HAP contract term; and

(5) A non-purchasing family residing in a HOPE 1 or HOPE 2 project.

{59 FR 36682, July 18, 1994, as amended at 64 FR 26643, May 14, 1999}

Sec. 982.204 Waiting list: Administration of waiting list.

(a) Admission from waiting list. Except for special admissions, participants must be selected from the PHA waiting list. The PHA must select participants from the waiting list in accordance with admission policies in the PHA administrative plan.

(b) Organization of waiting list. The PHA must maintain information that permits the PHA to select participants from the waiting list in accordance with the PHA admission policies. The waiting list must contain the following information for each applicant listed:

(1) Applicant name;

(2) Family unit size (number of bedrooms for which family qualifies under PHA occupancy standards);

(3) Date and time of application;

(4) Qualification for any local preference;

(5) Racial or ethnic designation of the head of household.

(c) Removing applicant names from the waiting list. (1) The PHA administrative plan must state PHA policy on when applicant names may be removed from the waiting list. The policy may provide that the PHA will remove names of applicants who do not respond to PHA requests for information or updates.

(2) An PHA decision to withdraw from the waiting list the name of an applicant family that includes a person with disabilities is subject to reasonable accommodation in accordance with 24 CFR part 8. If the applicant did not respond to the PHA request for information or updates because of the family member's disability, the PHA must reinstate the applicant in the family's former position on the waiting list.

(d) Family size. (1) The order of admission from the waiting list may not be based on family size, or on the family unit size for which the family qualifies under the PHA occupancy policy.

(2) If the PHA does not have sufficient funds to subsidize the family unit size of the family at the top of the waiting list, the PHA may not skip the top family to admit an applicant with a smaller family unit size. Instead, the family at the top of the waiting list will be admitted when sufficient funds are available.

(e) Funding for specified category of waiting list families. When HUD awards an PHA program funding for a specified category of families on the waiting list, the PHA must select applicant families in the specified category.

(f) Number of waiting lists. A PHA must use a single waiting list for admission to its Section 8 tenant-based assistance program. However, the PHA may use a separate single waiting list for such admissions for a county or municipality.

(Approved by the Office of Management and Budget under OMB control number 2577-0169)
{59 FR 36682, July 18, 1994, as amended at 60 FR 34717, July 3, 1995; 63 FR 23860, Apr. 30, 1998; 64 FR 26643, May 14, 1999; 65 FR 16821, Mar. 30, 2000}

Sec. 982.205 Waiting list: Different programs.

(a) Merger and cross-listing--(1) Merged waiting list. a PHA may merge the waiting list for tenant-based assistance with the PHA waiting list for admission to another assisted housing program, including a federal or local program. In admission from the merged

waiting list, admission for each federal program is subject to federal regulations and requirements for the particular program.

(2) Non-merged waiting list: Cross-listing. If the PHA decides not to merge the waiting list for tenant-based assistance with the waiting list for the PHA's public housing program, project-based voucher program or moderate rehabilitation program:

(i) If the PHA's waiting list for tenant-based assistance is open when an applicant is placed on the waiting list for the PHA's public housing program, project-based voucher program or moderate rehabilitation program, the PHA must offer to place the applicant on its waiting list for tenant-based assistance.

(ii) If the PHA's waiting list for its public housing program, project-based voucher program or moderate rehabilitation program is open when an applicant is placed on the waiting list for its tenant-based program, and if the other program includes units suitable for the applicant, the PHA must offer to place the applicant on its waiting list for the other program.

(b) Other housing assistance: Effect of application for, receipt or refusal.

(1) For purposes of this section, ``other housing subsidy'' means a housing subsidy other than assistance under the voucher program. Housing subsidy includes subsidy assistance under a federal housing program (including public housing), a State housing program, or a local housing program.

(2) The PHA may not take any of the following actions because an applicant has applied for, received, or refused other housing assistance:

(i) Refuse to list the applicant on the PHA waiting list for tenant-based assistance;

(ii) Deny any admission preference for which the applicant is currently qualified;

(iii) Change the applicant's place on the waiting list based on preference, date and time of application, or other factors affecting selection under the PHA selection policy; or

(iv) Remove the applicant from the waiting list.

{59 FR 36682, July 18, 1994, as amended at 61 FR 27163, May 30, 1996; 63 FR 23860, Apr. 30, 1998; 64 FR 26643, May 14, 1999; 65 FR 16821, Mar. 30, 2000}

Sec. 982.206 Waiting list: Opening and closing; public notice.

(a) Public notice. (1) When the PHA opens a waiting list, the PHA must give public notice that families may apply for tenant-based assistance. The public notice must state where and when to apply.

(2) The PHA must give the public notice by publication in a local newspaper of general circulation, and also by minority media and other suitable means. The notice must comply with HUD fair housing requirements.

(3) The public notice must state any limitations on who may apply for available slots in the program.

(b) Criteria defining what families may apply. (1) The PHA may adopt criteria defining what families may apply for assistance under a public notice.

(2) If the waiting list is open, the PHA must accept applications from families for whom the list is open unless there is good cause for not accepting the application (such as denial of assistance because of action or inaction by members of the family) for the grounds stated in Secs. 982.552 and 982.553.

(c) Closing waiting list. If the PHA determines that the existing waiting list contains an adequate pool for use of available program funding, the PHA may stop accepting new applications, or may accept only applications meeting criteria adopted by the PHA.

(Approved by the Office of Management and Budget under control number 2577-0169)
{59 FR 36682, July 18, 1994, as amended at 60 FR 34717, July 3, 1995; 60 FR 45661, Sept. 1, 1995; 63 FR 23860, Apr. 30, 1998; 64 FR 26643, May 14, 1999}

Sec. 982.207 Waiting list: Local preferences in admission to program.

(a) Establishment of PHA local preferences. (1) The PHA may establish a system of local preferences for selection of families admitted to the program. PHA selection preferences must be described in the PHA administrative plan.

(2) The PHA system of local preferences must be based on local housing needs and priorities, as determined by the PHA. In determining such needs and priorities, the PHA shall use generally accepted data sources. The PHA shall consider public comment on the proposed public housing agency plan (as received pursuant to Sec. 903.17 of this chapter) and on the consolidated plan for the relevant jurisdiction (as received pursuant to part 91 of this title).

(3) The PHA may limit the number of applicants that may qualify for any local preference.

(4) The PHA shall not deny a local preference, nor otherwise exclude or penalize a family in admission to the program, solely because the family resides in a public housing project. The PHA may establish a preference for families residing in public housing who are victims of a crime of violence (as defined in 18 U.S.C. 16).

(b) Particular local preferences. (1) Residency requirements or preferences. (i) Residency requirements are prohibited. Although a PHA is not prohibited from adopting a residency preference, the PHA may only adopt or implement residency preferences in accordance with non-discrimination and equal opportunity requirements listed at Sec. 5.105(a) of this title.

(ii) A residency preference is a preference for admission of persons who reside in a specified geographic area (``residency preference area''). A county or municipality may be used as a residency preference area. An area smaller than a county or municipality may not be used as a residency preference area.

(iii) Any PHA residency preferences must be included in the statement of PHA policies that govern eligibility, selection and admission to the program, which is included in the PHA annual plan (or supporting documents) pursuant to part 903 of this title. Such policies must specify that use of a residency preference will not have the purpose or effect of delaying or otherwise denying admission to the program based on the race, color, ethnic origin, gender, religion, disability, or age of any member of an applicant family.

(iv) A residency preference must not be based on how long an applicant has resided or worked in a residency preference area.

(v) Applicants who are working or who have been notified that they are hired to work in a residency preference area must be treated as residents of the residency preference area. The PHA may treat graduates of, or active participants in, education and training programs in a residency preference area as residents of the residency preference area if the education or training program is designed to prepare individuals for the job market.

(2) Preference for working families. The PHA may adopt a preference for admission of working families (families where the head, spouse or sole member is employed). However, an applicant shall be given the benefit of the working family preference if the head and spouse, or sole member is age 62 or older, or is a person with disabilities.

(3) Preference for person with disabilities. The PHA may adopt a preference for admission of families that include a person with disabilities. However, the PHA may not adopt a preference for admission of persons with a specific disability.

(4) Preference for victims of domestic violence. The PHA should consider whether to adopt a local preference for admission of families that include victims of domestic violence.

(5) Preference for single persons who are elderly, displaced, homeless, or persons with disabilities. The PHA may adopt a preference for admission of single persons who are age

62 or older, displaced, homeless, or persons with disabilities over other single persons.

(c) Selection among families with preference. The PHA system of preferences may use either of the following to select among applicants on the waiting list with the same preference status:

(1) Date and time of application; or

(2) A drawing or other random choice technique.

(d) Preference for higher-income families. The PHA must not select families for admission to the program in an order different from the order on the waiting list for the purpose of selecting higher income families for admission to the program.

(e) Verification of selection method. The method for selecting applicants from a preference category must leave a clear audit trail that can be used to verify that each applicant has been selected in accordance with the method specified in the administrative plan.

{64 FR 26643, May 14, 1999, as amended at 64 FR 56912, Oct. 21, 1999; 65 FR 16821, Mar. 30, 2000}

Subpart F [Reserved]

Subpart G--Leasing a Unit

Source: 60 FR 34695, July 3, 1995, unless otherwise noted.

Sec. 982.301 Information when family is selected.

(a) PHA briefing of family. (1) When the PHA selects a family to participate in a tenant-based program, the PHA must give the family an oral briefing. The briefing must include information on the following subjects:

(i) A description of how the program works;

(ii) Family and owner responsibilities; and

(iii) Where the family may lease a unit, including renting a dwelling unit inside or outside the PHA jurisdiction.

(2) For a family that qualifies to lease a unit outside the PHA jurisdiction under portability procedures, the briefing must include an explanation of how portability works. The PHA may not discourage the family from choosing to live anywhere in the PHA jurisdiction, or outside the PHA jurisdiction under portability procedures.

(3) If the family is currently living in a high poverty census tract in the PHA's jurisdiction, the briefing must also explain the advantages of moving to an area that does not have a high concentration of poor families.

(4) In briefing a family that includes any disabled person, the PHA must take appropriate steps to ensure effective communication in accordance with 24 CFR 8.6.

(5) In briefing a welfare-to-work family, the PHA must include specification of any local obligations of a welfare-to-work family and an explanation that failure to meet these obligations is grounds for PHA denial of admission or termination of assistance.

(b) Information packet. When a family is selected to participate in the program, the PHA must give the family a packet that includes information on the following subjects:

(1) The term of the voucher, and PHA policy on any extensions or suspensions of the term. If the PHA allows extensions, the packet must explain how the family can request an extension;

(2) How the PHA determines the amount of the housing assistance payment for a family, including:

(i) How the PHA determines the payment standard for a family; and

(ii) How the PHA determines the total tenant payment for a family.

(3) How the PHA determines the maximum rent for an assisted unit;

(4) Where the family may lease a unit. For a family that qualifies to lease a unit outside the PHA jurisdiction under portability procedures, the information packet must include an explanation of how portability works;

(5) The HUD-required ``tenancy addendum'' that must be included in the lease;

(6) The form that the family uses to request PHA approval of the assisted tenancy, and an explanation of how to request such approval;

(7) A statement of the PHA policy on providing information about a family to prospective owners;

(8) PHA subsidy standards, including when the PHA will consider granting exceptions to the standards;

(9) The HUD brochure on how to select a unit;

(10) Information on federal, State and local equal opportunity laws, and a copy of the housing discrimination complaint form;

(11) A list of landlords or other parties known to the PHA who may be willing to lease a unit to the family, or help the family find a unit;

(12) Notice that if the family includes a disabled person, the family may request a current listing of accessible units known to the PHA that may be available;

(13) Family obligations under the program;

(14) Family obligations under the program, including any obligations of a welfare-to-work family.

(15) PHA informal hearing procedures. This information must describe when the PHA is required to give a participant family the opportunity for an informal hearing, and how to request a hearing.

(Approved by the Office of Management and Budget under control number 2577-0169)
{60 FR 34695, July 3, 1995, as amended at 60 FR 45661, Sept. 1, 1995; 61 FR 27163, May 30, 1996; 64 FR 26644, May 14, 1999; 64 FR 50229, Sept. 15, 1999; 64 FR 56912, Oct. 21, 1999}

Sec. 982.302 Issuance of voucher; Requesting PHA approval of assisted tenancy.

(a) When a family is selected, or when a participant family wants to move to another unit, the PHA issues a voucher to the family. The family may search for a unit.

(b) If the family finds a unit, and the owner is willing to lease the unit under the program, the family may request PHA approval of the tenancy. The PHA has the discretion whether to permit the family to submit more than one request at a time.

(c) The family must submit to the PHA a request for approval of the tenancy and a copy of the lease, including the HUD-prescribed tenancy addendum. The request must be submitted during the term of the voucher.

(d) The PHA specifies the procedure for requesting approval of the tenancy. The family must submit the request for approval of the tenancy in the form and manner required by the PHA.

{64 FR 26644, May 14, 1999}

Sec. 982.303 Term of voucher.

(a) Initial term. The initial term of a voucher must be at least 60 calendar days. The initial term must be stated on the voucher.

(b) Extensions of term. (1) At its discretion, the PHA may grant a family one or more extensions of the initial voucher term in accordance with PHA policy as described in the PHA administrative plan. Any extension of the term is granted by PHA notice to the family.

(2) If the family needs and requests an extension of the initial voucher term as a reasonable accommodation, in accordance with part 8 of this title, to make the program accessible to a family member who is a person with disabilities, the PHA must extend the voucher term up to the term reasonably required for that purpose.

(c) Suspension of term. The PHA policy may or may not provide for suspension of the initial or any extended term of the voucher. At its discretion, and in accordance with PHA policy as described in the PHA administrative plan, the PHA may grant a

family a suspension of the voucher term if the family has submitted a request for approval of the tenancy during the term of the voucher. (Sec. 982.4 (definition of ``suspension''); Sec. 982.54(d)(2)) The PHA may grant a suspension for any part of the period after the family has submitted a request for approval of the tenancy up to the time when the PHA approves or denies the request.

(d) Progress report by family to the PHA. During the initial or any extended term of a voucher, the PHA may require the family to report progress in leasing a unit. Such reports may be required at such intervals or times as determined by the PHA.

(Approved by the Office of Management and Budget under control number 2577-0169)
{60 FR 34695, July 3, 1995, as amended at 60 FR 45661, Sept. 1, 1995; 63 FR 23860, Apr. 30, 1998; 64 FR 26644, May 14, 1999; 64 FR 56913, Oct. 21, 1999}

Sec. 982.304 Illegal discrimination: PHA assistance to family.

A family may claim that illegal discrimination because of race, color, religion, sex, national origin, age, familial status or disability prevents the family from finding or leasing a suitable unit with assistance under the program. The PHA must give the family information on how to fill out and file a housing discrimination complaint.

(Approved by the Office of Management and Budget under control number 2577-0169)
{60 FR 34695, July 3, 1995, as amended at 60 FR 45661, Sept. 1, 1995}

Sec. 982.305 PHA approval of assisted tenancy.

(a) Program requirements. The PHA may not give approval for the family of the assisted tenancy, or execute a HAP contract, until the PHA has determined that all the following meet program requirements:

(1) The unit is eligible;

(2) The unit has been inspected by the PHA and passes HQS;

(3) The lease includes the tenancy addendum;

(4) The rent to owner is reasonable; and

(5) At the time a family initially receives tenant-based assistance for occupancy of a dwelling unit, and where the gross rent of the unit exceeds the applicable payment standard for the family, the family share does not exceed 40 percent of the family's monthly adjusted income.

(b) Actions before lease term. (1) All of the following must always be completed before the beginning of the initial term of the lease for a unit:

(i) The PHA has inspected the unit and has determined that the unit satisfies the HQS;

(ii) The landlord and the tenant have executed the lease (including the HUD-prescribed tenancy addendum, and the lead-based paint disclosure information as required in Sec. 35.13(b) of this title); and

(2)(i) The PHA must inspect the unit, determine whether the unit satisfies the HQS, and notify the family and owner of the determination:

(A) In the case of a PHA with up to 1250 budgeted units in its tenant-based program, within fifteen days after the family and the owner submit a request for approval of the tenancy.

(B) In the case of a PHA with more than 1250 budgeted units in its tenant-based program, within a reasonable time after the family submits a request for approval of the tenancy. To the extent practicable, such inspection and determination must be completed within fifteen days after the family and the owner submit a request for approval of the tenancy.

(ii) The fifteen day clock (under paragraph (b)(2)(i)(A) or paragraph (b)(2)(i)(B) of this section) is suspended during any period when the unit is not available for inspection.

(3) In the case of a unit subject to a lease-purchase agreement, the PHA must provide written notice to the family of the environmental requirements that must be

met before commencing homeownership assistance for the family (see Sec. 982.626(c)).

(c) When HAP contract is executed. (1) The PHA must use best efforts to execute the HAP contract before the beginning of the lease term. The HAP contract must be executed no later than 60 calendar days from the beginning of the lease term.

(2) The PHA may not pay any housing assistance payment to the owner until the HAP contract has been executed.

(3) If the HAP contract is executed during the period of 60 calendar days from the beginning of the lease term, the PHA will pay housing assistance payments after execution of the HAP contract (in accordance with the terms of the HAP contract), to cover the portion of the lease term before execution of the HAP contract (a maximum of 60 days).

(4) Any HAP contract executed after the 60 day period is void, and the PHA may not pay any housing assistance payment to the owner.

(d) Notice to family and owner. After receiving the family's request for approval of the assisted tenancy, the PHA must promptly notify the family and owner whether the assisted tenancy is approved.

(e) Procedure after PHA approval. If the PHA has given approval for the family of the assisted tenancy, the owner and the PHA execute the HAP contract.

(Approved by the Office of Management and Budget under control number 2577-0169) {60 FR 34695, July 3, 1995, as amended at 60 FR 45661, Sept. 1, 1995; 64 FR 26644, May 14, 1999; 64 FR 56913, Oct. 21, 1999; 64 FR 59622, Nov. 3, 1999; 65 FR 16818, Mar. 30, 2000; 65 FR 55161, Sept. 12, 2000}

Sec. 982.306 PHA disapproval of owner.

(a) The PHA must not approve an assisted tenancy if the PHA has been informed (by HUD or otherwise) that the owner is debarred, suspended, or subject to a limited denial of participation under 24 CFR part 24.

(b) When directed by HUD, the PHA must not approve an assisted tenancy if:

(1) The federal government has instituted an administrative or judicial action against the owner for violation of the Fair Housing Act or other federal equal opportunity requirements, and such action is pending; or

(2) A court or administrative agency has determined that the owner violated the Fair Housing Act or other federal equal opportunity requirements.

(c) In its administrative discretion, the PHA may deny approval of an assisted tenancy for any of the following reasons:

(1) The owner has violated obligations under a HAP contract under Section 8 of the 1937 Act (42 U.S.C. 1437f);

(2) The owner has committed fraud, bribery or any other corrupt or criminal act in connection with any federal housing program;

(3) The owner has engaged in any drug-related criminal activity or any violent criminal activity;

(4) The owner has a history or practice of non-compliance with the HQS for units leased under the tenant-based programs, or with applicable housing standards for units leased with project-based Section 8 assistance or leased under any other federal housing program;

(5) The owner has a history or practice of failing to terminate tenancy of tenants of units assisted under Section 8 or any other federally assisted housing program for activity engaged in by the tenant, any member of the household, a guest or another person under the control of any member of the household that:

(i) Threatens the right to peaceful enjoyment of the premises by other residents;

(ii) Threatens the health or safety of other residents, of employees of the PHA, or of owner employees or other persons engaged in management of the housing;

(iii) Threatens the health or safety of, or the right to peaceful enjoyment of their residences, by persons residing in the immediate vicinity of the premises; or

(iv) Is drug-related criminal activity or violent criminal activity; or

(6) The owner has a history or practice of renting units that fail to meet State or local housing codes; or

(7) The owner has not paid State or local real estate taxes, fines or assessments.

(d) The PHA must not approve a unit if the owner is the parent, child, grandparent, grandchild, sister, or brother of any member of the family, unless the PHA determines that approving the unit would provide reasonable accommodation for a family member who is a person with disabilities. This restriction against PHA approval of a unit only applies at the time a family initially receives tenant-based assistance for occupancy of a particular unit, but does not apply to PHA approval of a new tenancy with continued tenant-based assistance in the same unit.

(e) Nothing in this rule is intended to give any owner any right to participate in the program.

(f) For purposes of this section, ``owner'' includes a principal or other interested party.

{60 FR 34695, July 3, 1995, as amended at 63 FR 27437, May 18, 1998; 64 FR 26644, May 14, 1999; 64 FR 56913, Oct. 21, 1999; 65 FR 16821, Mar. 30, 2000}

Sec. 982.307 Tenant screening.

(a) PHA option and owner responsibility. (1) The PHA has no liability or responsibility to the owner or other persons for the family's behavior or suitability for tenancy. However, the PHA may opt to screen applicants for family behavior or suitability for tenancy. The PHA must conduct any such screening of applicants in accordance with policies stated in the PHA administrative plan.

(2) The owner is responsible for screening and selection of the family to occupy the owner's unit. At or before PHA approval of the tenancy, the PHA must inform the owner that screening and selection for tenancy is the responsibility of the owner.

(3) The owner is responsible for screening of families on the basis of their tenancy histories. An owner may consider a family's background with respect to such factors as:

(i) Payment of rent and utility bills;

(ii) Caring for a unit and premises;

(iii) Respecting the rights of other residents to the peaceful enjoyment of their housing;

(iv) Drug-related criminal activity or other criminal activity that is a threat to the health, safety or property of others; and

(v) Compliance with other essential conditions of tenancy.

(b) PHA information about tenant. (1) The PHA must give the owner:

(i) The family's current and prior address (as shown in the PHA records); and

(ii) The name and address (if known to the PHA) of the landlord at the family's current and prior address.

(2) When a family wants to lease a dwelling unit, the PHA may offer the owner other information in the PHA possession, about the family, including information about the tenancy history of family members, or about drug-trafficking by family members.

(3) The PHA must give the family a statement of the PHA policy on providing information to owners. The statement must be included in the information packet that is given to a family selected to participate in the program. The PHA policy must provide that the PHA will give the same types of information to all families and to all owners.

(Approved by the Office of Management and Budget under control number 2577-0169)
{60 FR 34695, July 3, 1995, as amended at 60 FR 45661, Sept. 1, 1995; 61 FR 27163, May 30, 1996; 64 FR 26645, May 14, 1999; 64 FR 49658, Sept. 14, 1999}

Sec. 982.308 Lease and tenancy.

(a) Tenant's legal capacity. The tenant must have legal capacity to enter a lease under State and local law. ``Legal capacity'' means that the tenant is bound by the terms of the lease and may enforce the terms of the lease against the owner.

(b) Form of lease. (1) The tenant and the owner must enter a written lease for the unit.

The lease must be executed by the owner and the tenant.

(2) If the owner uses a standard lease form for rental to unassisted tenants in the locality or the premises, the lease must be in such standard form (plus the HUD-prescribed tenancy addendum). If the owner does not use a standard lease form for rental to unassisted tenants, the owner may use another form of lease, such as a PHA model lease (including the HUD-prescribed tenancy addendum). The HAP contract prescribed by HUD will contain the owner's certification that if the owner uses a standard lease form for rental to unassisted tenants, the lease is in such standard form.

(c) State and local law. The PHA may review the lease to determine if the lease complies with State and local law. The PHA may decline to approve the tenancy if the PHA determines that the lease does not comply with State or local law.

(d) Required information. The lease must specify all of the following:

(1) The names of the owner and the tenant;

(2) The unit rented (address, apartment number, and any other information needed to identify the contract unit);

(3) The term of the lease (initial term and any provisions for renewal);

(4) The amount of the monthly rent to owner; and

(5) A specification of what utilities and appliances are to be supplied by the owner, and what utilities and appliances are to be supplied by the family.

(e) Reasonable rent. The rent to owner must be reasonable (see Sec. 982.507).

(f) Tenancy addendum. (1) The HAP contract form required by HUD shall include an addendum (the ``tenancy addendum''), that sets forth:

(i) The tenancy requirements for the program (in accordance with this section and Secs. 982.309 and 982.310); and

(ii) The composition of the household as approved by the PHA (family members and any PHA-approved live-in aide).

(2) All provisions in the HUD-required tenancy addendum must be added word-for-word to the owner's standard form lease that is used by the owner for unassisted tenants. The tenant shall have the right to enforce the tenancy addendum against the owner, and the terms of the tenancy addendum shall prevail over any other provisions of the lease.

(g) Changes in lease or rent. (1) If the tenant and the owner agree to any changes in the lease, such changes must be in writing, and the owner must immediately give the PHA a copy of such changes. The lease, including any changes, must be in accordance with the requirements of this section.

(2) In the following cases, tenant-based assistance shall not be continued unless the PHA has approved a new tenancy in accordance with program requirements and has executed a new HAP contract with the owner:

(i) If there are any changes in lease requirements governing tenant or owner responsibilities for utilities or appliances;

(ii) If there are any changes in lease provisions governing the term of the lease;

(iii) If the family moves to a new unit, even if the unit is in the same building or complex.

(3) PHA approval of the tenancy, and execution of a new HAP contract, are not required for changes in the lease other than as specified in paragraph (g)(2) of this section.

(4) The owner must notify the PHA of any changes in the amount of the rent to owner at least sixty days before any such changes go into effect, and any such changes shall be subject to rent reasonableness requirements (see Sec. 982.503).

{64 FR 26645, May 14, 1999, as amended at 64 FR 56913, Oct. 21, 1999}

Sec. 982.309 Term of assisted tenancy.

(a) Initial term of lease. (1) Except as provided in paragraph (a)(2) of this section, the initial lease term must be for at least one year.

(2) The PHA may approve a shorter initial lease term if the PHA determines that:

(i) Such shorter term would improve housing opportunities for the tenant; and

(ii) Such shorter term is the prevailing local market practice.

(3) During the initial term of the lease, the owner may not raise the rent to owner.

(4) The PHA may execute the HAP contract even if there is less than one year remaining from the beginning of the initial lease term to the end of the last expiring funding increment under the consolidated ACC.

(b) Term of HAP contract. (1) The term of the HAP contract begins on the first day of the lease term and ends on the last day of the lease term.

(2) The HAP contract terminates if any of the following occurs:

(i) The lease is terminated by the owner or the tenant;

(ii) The PHA terminates the HAP contract; or

(iii) The PHA terminates assistance for the family.

(c) Family responsibility. (1) If the family terminates the lease on notice to the owner, the family must give the PHA a copy of the notice of termination at the same time. Failure to do this is a breach of family obligations under the program.

(2) The family must notify the PHA and the owner before the family moves out of the unit. Failure to do this is a breach of family obligations under the program.

{64 FR 26645, May 14, 1999}

Sec. 982.310 Owner termination of tenancy.

(a) Grounds. During the term of the lease, the owner may not terminate the tenancy except on the following grounds:

(1) Serious violation (including but not limited to failure to pay rent or other amounts due under the lease) or repeated violation of the terms and conditions of the lease;

(2) Violation of federal, State, or local law that imposes obligations on the tenant in connection with the occupancy or use of the premises; or

(3) Other good cause.

(b) Nonpayment by PHA: Not grounds for termination of tenancy. (1) The family is not responsible for payment of the portion of the rent to owner covered by the housing assistance payment under the HAP contract between the owner and the PHA.

(2) The PHA failure to pay the housing assistance payment to the owner is not a violation of the lease between the tenant and the owner. During the term of the lease the owner may not terminate the tenancy of the family for nonpayment of the PHA housing assistance payment.

(c) Criminal activity. (1) Evicting drug criminals due to drug crime on or near the premises. The lease must provide that drug-related criminal activity engaged in, on or near the premises by any tenant, household member, or guest, or such activity engaged in on the premises by any other person under the tenant's control, is grounds for the owner to terminate tenancy. In addition, the lease must provide that the owner may evict a family when the owner determines that a household member is illegally using a drug or when the owner determines that a pattern of illegal use of a drug interferes with the health, safety, or right to peaceful enjoyment of the premises by other residents.

(2) Evicting other criminals. (i) Threat to other residents. The lease must provide that the owner may terminate tenancy for any of the following types of criminal activity by a covered person:

(A) Any criminal activity that threatens the health, safety, or right to peaceful enjoyment of the premises by other residents (including property management staff residing on the premises);

(B) Any criminal activity that threatens the health, safety, or right to peaceful enjoyment of their residences by persons residing in the immediate vicinity of the premises; or

(C) Any violent criminal activity on or near the premises by a tenant, household member, or guest, or any such activity on the premises by any other person under the tenant's control.

(ii) Fugitive felon or parole violator. The lease must provide that the owner may terminate the tenancy if a tenant is:

(A) Fleeing to avoid prosecution, or custody or confinement after conviction, for a crime, or attempt to commit a crime, that is a felony under the laws of the place from which the individual flees, or that, in the case of the State of New Jersey, is a high misdemeanor; or

(B) Violating a condition of probation or parole imposed under Federal or State law.

(3) Evidence of criminal activity. The owner may terminate tenancy and evict by judicial action a family for criminal activity by a covered person in accordance with this section if the owner determines that the covered person has engaged in the criminal activity, regardless of whether the covered person has been arrested or convicted for such activity and without satisfying the standard of proof used for a criminal conviction. (See part 5, subpart J, of this title for provisions concerning access to criminal records.)

(d) Other good cause. (1) ``Other good cause'' for termination of tenancy by the owner may include, but is not limited to, any of the following examples:

(i) Failure by the family to accept the offer of a new lease or revision;

(ii) A family history of disturbance of neighbors or destruction of property, or of living or housekeeping habits resulting in damage to the unit or premises;

(iii) The owner's desire to use the unit for personal or family use, or for a purpose other than as a residential rental unit; or

(iv) A business or economic reason for termination of the tenancy (such as sale of the property, renovation of the unit, or desire to lease the unit at a higher rental).

(2) During the initial lease term, the owner may not terminate the tenancy for ``other good cause'', unless the owner is terminating the tenancy because of something the family did or failed to do. For example, during this period, the owner may not terminate the tenancy for ``other good cause'' based on any of the following grounds: failure by the family to accept the offer of a new lease or revision; the owner's desire to use the unit for personal or family use, or for a purpose other than as a residential rental unit; or a business or economic reason for termination of the tenancy (see paragraph (d)(1)(iv) of this section).

(e) Owner notice--(1) Notice of grounds.

(i) The owner must give the tenant a written notice that specifies the grounds for termination of tenancy during the term of the lease. The tenancy does not terminate before the owner has given this notice, and the notice must be given at or before commencement of the eviction action.

(ii) The notice of grounds may be included in, or may be combined with, any owner eviction notice to the tenant.

(2) Eviction notice. (i) Owner eviction notice means a notice to vacate, or a complaint or other initial pleading used under State or local law to commence an eviction action.

(ii) The owner must give the PHA a copy of any owner eviction notice to the tenant.

(f) Eviction by court action. The owner may only evict the tenant from the unit by instituting a court action.

(g) Regulations not applicable. 24 CFR part 247 (concerning evictions from certain subsidized and HUD-owned projects) does not apply to a tenancy assisted under this part 982.

(h) Termination of tenancy decisions.--(1) General. If the law and regulation permit the

owner to take an action but do not require action to be taken, the owner may take or not take the action in accordance with the owner's standards for eviction. The owner may consider all of the circumstances relevant to a particular eviction case, such as:

(i) The seriousness of the offending action;

(ii) The effect on the community of denial or termination or the failure of the owner to take such action;

(iii) The extent of participation by the leaseholder in the offending action;

(iv) The effect of denial of admission or termination of tenancy on household members not involved in the offending activity;

(v) The demand for assisted housing by families who will adhere to lease responsibilities;

(vi) The extent to which the leaseholder has shown personal responsibility and taken all reasonable steps to prevent or mitigate the offending action;

(vii) The effect of the owner's action on the integrity of the program.

(2) Exclusion of culpable household member. The owner may require a tenant to exclude a household member in order to continue to reside in the assisted unit, where that household member has participated in or been culpable for action or failure to act that warrants termination.

(3) Consideration of rehabilitation. In determining whether to terminate tenancy for illegal use of drugs or alcohol abuse by a household member who is no longer engaged in such behavior, the owner may consider whether such household member is participating in or has successfully completed a supervised drug or alcohol rehabilitation program, or has otherwise been rehabilitated successfully (42 U.S.C. 13661). For this purpose, the owner may require the tenant to submit evidence of the household member's current participation in, or successful completion of, a supervised drug or alcohol rehabilitation program or evidence of otherwise having been rehabilitated successfully.

(4) Nondiscrimination limitation. The owner's termination of assistance actions must be consistent with fair housing and equal opportunity provisions of Sec. 5.105 of this title.

(Approved by the Office of Management and Budget under control number 2577-0169) {60 FR 34695, July 3, 1995, as amended at 60 FR 45661, Sept. 1, 1995; 64 FR 26645, May 14, 1999; 64 FR 56913, Oct. 21, 1999; 66 FR 28804, May 24, 2001}

Sec. 982.311 When assistance is paid.

(a) Payments under HAP contract. Housing assistance payments are paid to the owner in accordance with the terms of the HAP contract. Housing assistance payments may only be paid to the owner during the lease term, and while the family is residing in the unit.

(b) Termination of payment: When owner terminates the lease. Housing assistance payments terminate when the lease is terminated by the owner in accordance with the lease. However, if the owner has commenced the process to evict the tenant, and if the family continues to reside in the unit, the PHA must continue to make housing assistance payments to the owner in accordance with the HAP contract until the owner has obtained a court judgment or other process allowing the owner to evict the tenant. The HA may continue such payments until the family moves from or is evicted from the unit.

(c) Termination of payment: Other reasons for termination. Housing assistance payments terminate if:

(1) The lease terminates;

(2) The HAP contract terminates; or

(3) The PHA terminates assistance for the family.

(d) Family move-out. (1) If the family moves out of the unit, the PHA may not make any housing assistance payment to the owner for any month after the month when the family moves out. The owner may keep the housing assistance payment for the

month when the family moves out of the unit.

(2) If a participant family moves from an assisted unit with continued tenant-based assistance, the term of the assisted lease for the new assisted unit may begin during the month the family moves out of the first assisted unit. Overlap of the last housing assistance payment (for the month when the family moves out of the old unit) and the first assistance payment for the new unit, is not considered to constitute a duplicative housing subsidy.

Sec. 982.312 Absence from unit.

(a) The family may be absent from the unit for brief periods. For longer absences, the PHA administrative plan establishes the PHA policy on how long the family may be absent from the assisted unit. However, the family may not be absent from the unit for a period of more than 180 consecutive calendar days in any circumstance, or for any reason. At its discretion, the PHA may allow absence for a lesser period in accordance with PHA policy.

(b) Housing assistance payments terminate if the family is absent for longer than the maximum period permitted. The term of the HAP contract and assisted lease also terminate.

(The owner must reimburse the PHA for any housing assistance payment for the period after the termination.)

(c) Absence means that no member of the family is residing in the unit.

(d)(1) The family must supply any information or certification requested by the PHA to verify that the family is residing in the unit, or relating to family absence from the unit. The family must cooperate with the PHA for this purpose. The family must promptly notify the PHA of absence from the unit, including any information requested on the purposes of family absences.

(2) The PHA may adopt appropriate techniques to verify family occupancy or absence, including letters to the family at the unit, phone calls, visits or questions to the landlord or neighbors.

(e) The PHA administrative plan must state the PHA policies on family absence from the dwelling unit. The PHA absence policy includes:

(1) How the PHA determines whether or when the family may be absent, and for how long. For example, the PHA may establish policies on absences because of vacation, hospitalization or imprisonment; and

(2) Any provision for resumption of assistance after an absence, including readmission or resumption of assistance to the family.

Sec. 982.313 Security deposit: Amounts owed by tenant.

(a) The owner may collect a security deposit from the tenant.

(b) The PHA may prohibit security deposits in excess of private market practice, or in excess of amounts charged by the owner to unassisted tenants.

(c) When the tenant moves out of the dwelling unit, the owner, subject to State or local law, may use the security deposit, including any interest on the deposit, in accordance with the lease, as reimbursement for any unpaid rent payable by the tenant, damages to the unit or for other amounts the tenant owes under the lease.

(d) The owner must give the tenant a written list of all items charged against the security deposit, and the amount of each item. After deducting the amount, if any, used to reimburse the owner, the owner must refund promptly the full amount of the unused balance to the tenant.

(e) If the security deposit is not sufficient to cover amounts the tenant owes under the lease, the owner may seek to collect the balance from the tenant.

Sec. 982.314 Move with continued tenant-based assistance.

(a) Applicability. This section states when a participant family may move to a new unit with continued tenant-based assistance:

(b) When family may move. A family may move to a new unit if:

(1) The assisted lease for the old unit has terminated. This includes a termination because:

(i) The PHA has terminated the HAP contract for the owner's breach; or

(ii) The lease has terminated by mutual agreement of the owner and the tenant.

(2) The owner has given the tenant a notice to vacate, or has commenced an action to evict the tenant, or has obtained a court judgment or other process allowing the owner to evict the tenant.

(3) The tenant has given notice of lease termination (if the tenant has a right to terminate the lease on notice to the owner, for owner breach or otherwise).

(c) How many moves. (1) A participant family may move one or more times with continued assistance under the program, either inside the PHA jurisdiction, or under the portability procedures. (See Sec. 982.353)

(2) The PHA may establish:

(i) Policies that prohibit any move by the family during the initial lease term; and

(ii) Policies that prohibit more than one move by the family during any one year period.

(3) The PHA policies may apply to moves within the PHA jurisdiction by a participant family, and to moves by a participant family outside the PHA jurisdiction under portability procedures.

(d) Notice that family wants to move. (1) If the family terminates the lease on notice to the owner, the family must give the PHA a copy of the notice at the same time.

(2) If the family wants to move to a new unit, the family must notify the PHA and the owner before moving from the old unit. If the family wants to move to a new unit that is located outside the initial PHA jurisdiction, the notice to the initial PHA must specify the area where the family wants to move. See portability procedures in subpart H of this part.

(e) When PHA may deny permission to move. (1) The PHA may deny permission to move if the PHA does not have sufficient funding for continued assistance.

(2) At any time, the PHA may deny permission to move in accordance with Sec. 982.552 (grounds for denial or termination of assistance).

{60 FR 34695, July 3, 1995, as amended at 64 FR 56913, Oct. 21, 1999}

Sec. 982.315 Family break-up.

(a) The PHA has discretion to determine which members of an assisted family continue to receive assistance in the program if the family breaks up. The PHA administrative plan must state PHA policies on how to decide who remains in the program if the family breaks up.

(b) The factors to be considered in making this decision under the PHA policy may include:

(1) Whether the assistance should remain with family members remaining in the original assisted unit.

(2) The interest of minor children or of ill, elderly or disabled family members.

(3) Whether family members are forced to leave the unit as a result or actual or threatened physical violence against family members by a spouse or other member of the household.

(4) Other factors specified by the PHA.

(c) If a court determines the disposition of property between members of the assisted family in a divorce or separation under a settlement or judicial decree, the PHA is bound by the court's determination of which family members continue to receive assistance in the program.

Sec. 982.316 Live-in aide.

(a) A family that consists of one or more elderly, near-elderly or disabled persons may request that the PHA approve a live-in aide to reside in the unit and provide necessary supportive services for a family member who is a person with disabilities. The PHA must approve a live-in aide if needed as a reasonable accommodation in accordance with 24 CFR part 8 to make the program accessible to and usable by the family member with a disability. (See Sec. 982.402(b)(6) concerning effect of live-in aide on family unit size.)

(b) At any time, the PHA may refuse to approve a particular person as a live-in aide, or may withdraw such approval, if:

(1) The person commits fraud, bribery or any other corrupt or criminal act in connection with any federal housing program;

(2) The person commits drug-related criminal activity or violent criminal activity; or

(3) The person currently owes rent or other amounts to the PHA or to another PHA in connection with Section 8 or public housing assistance under the 1937 Act.

{63 FR 23860, Apr. 30, 1998; 63 FR 31625, June 10, 1998}

Sec. 982.317 Lease-purchase agreements.

(a) A family leasing a unit with assistance under the program may enter into an agreement with an owner to purchase the unit. So long as the family is receiving such rental assistance, all requirements applicable to families otherwise leasing units under the tenant-based program apply. Any homeownership premium (e.g., increment of value attributable to the value of the lease-purchase right or agreement such as an extra monthly payment to accumulate a downpayment or reduce the purchase price) included in the rent to the owner that would result in a higher subsidy amount than would otherwise be paid by the PHA must be absorbed by the family.

(b) In determining whether the rent to owner for a unit subject to a lease-purchase agreement is a reasonable amount in accordance with Sec. 982.503, any homeownership premium paid by the family to the owner must be excluded when the PHA determines rent reasonableness.

{65 FR 55162, Sept. 12, 2000}

Subpart H--Where Family Can Live and Move

Source: 60 FR 34695, July 3, 1995, unless otherwise noted.

Sec. 982.351 Overview.

This subpart describes what kind of housing is eligible for leasing, and the areas where a family can live with tenant-based assistance. The subpart covers:

(a) Assistance for a family that rents a dwelling unit in the jurisdiction of the PHA that originally selected the family for tenant-based assistance.

(b) ``Portability'' assistance for a family PHA rents a unit outside the jurisdiction of the initial PHA.

Sec. 982.352 Eligible housing.

(a) Ineligible housing. The following types of housing may not be assisted by a PHA in the tenant-based programs:

(1) A public housing or Indian housing unit;

(2) A unit receiving project-based assistance under section 8 of the 1937 Act (42 U.S.C. 1437f);

(3) Nursing homes, board and care homes, or facilities providing continual psychiatric, medical, or nursing services;

(4) College or other school dormitories;

(5) Units on the grounds of penal, reformatory, medical, mental, and similar public or private institutions;

(6) A unit occupied by its owner or by a person with any interest in the unit.

(7) For provisions on PHA disapproval of an owner, see Sec. 982.306.

(b) PHA-owned housing. (1) A unit

that is owned by the PHA that administers the assistance under the consolidated ACC (including a unit owned by an entity substantially controlled by the PHA) may only be assisted under the tenant-based program if all the following conditions are satisfied:

(i) The PHA must inform the family, both orally and in writing, that the family has the right to select any eligible unit available for lease, and a PHA-owned unit is freely selected by the family, without PHA pressure or steering.

(ii) The unit is not ineligible housing.

(iii) During assisted occupancy, the family may not benefit from any form of housing subsidy that is prohibited under paragraph (c) of this section.

(iv)(A) The PHA must obtain the services of an independent entity to perform the following PHA functions as required under the program rule:

(1) To determine rent reasonableness in accordance with Sec. 982.507. The independent agency shall communicate the rent reasonableness determination to the family and the PHA.

(2) To assist the family negotiate the rent to owner in accordance with Sec. 982.506.

(3) To inspect the unit for compliance with the HQS in accordance with Sec. 982.305(a) and Sec. 982.405 (except that Sec. 982.405(e) is not applicable). The independent agency shall communicate the results of each such inspection to the family and the PHA.

(B) The independent agency used to perform these functions must be approved by HUD. The independent agency may be the unit of general local government for the PHA jurisdiction (unless the PHA is itself the unit of general local government or an agency of such government), or may be another HUD-approved independent agency.

(C) The PHA may compensate the independent agency from PHA ongoing administrative fee income for the services performed by the independent agency. The PHA may not use other program receipts to compensate the independent agency for such services. The PHA and the independent agency may not charge the family any fee or charge for the services provided by the independent agency.

(c) Prohibition against other housing subsidy. A family may not receive the benefit of tenant-based assistance while receiving the benefit of any of the following forms of other housing subsidy, for the same unit or for a different unit:

(1) Public or Indian housing assistance;

(2) Other Section 8 assistance (including other tenant-based assistance);

(3) Assistance under former Section 23 of the United States Housing Act of 1937 (before amendment by the Housing and Community Development Act of 1974);

(4) Section 101 rent supplements;

(5) Section 236 rental assistance payments;

(6) Tenant-based assistance under the HOME Program;

(7) Rental assistance payments under Section 521 of the Housing Act of 1949 (a program of the Rural Development Administration);

(8) Any local or State rent subsidy;

(9) Section 202 supportive housing for the elderly;

(10) Section 811 supportive housing for persons with disabilities;

(11) Section 202 projects for non-elderly persons with disabilities (Section 162 assistance); or

(12) Any other duplicative federal, State, or local housing subsidy, as determined by HUD. For this purpose, ``housing subsidy'' does not include the housing component of a welfare payment, a social security payment received by the family, or a rent reduction because of a tax credit.

(Approved by the Office of Management and Budget under control number 2577-0169)

{60 FR 34695, July 3, 1995, as amended at 60 FR 45661, Sept. 1, 1995; 63 FR 23860, Apr. 30, 1998; 64 FR 13057, Mar. 16, 1999; 64 FR 26645, May 14, 1999; 65 FR 55162, Sept. 12, 2000}

Sec. 982.353 Where family can lease a unit with tenant-based assistance.

(a) Assistance in the initial PHA jurisdiction. The family may receive tenant-based assistance to lease a unit located anywhere in the jurisdiction (as determined by State and local law) of the initial PHA. HUD may nevertheless restrict the family's right to lease such a unit anywhere in such jurisdiction if HUD determines that limitations on a family's opportunity to select among available units in that jurisdiction are appropriate to achieve desegregation goals in accordance with obligations generated by a court order or consent decree.

(b) Portability: Assistance outside the initial PHA jurisdiction. Subject to paragraph (c) of this section, and to Sec. 982.552 and Sec. 982.553, a voucher-holder or participant family has the right to receive tenant-based voucher assistance in accordance with requirements of this part to lease a unit outside the initial PHA jurisdiction, anywhere in the United States, in the jurisdiction of a PHA with a tenant-based program under this part. The initial PHA must not provide such portable assistance for a participant if the family has moved out of its assisted unit in violation of the lease.

(c) Nonresident applicants. (1) This paragraph (c) applies if neither the household head or spouse of an assisted family already had a ``domicile'' (legal residence) in the jurisdiction of the initial PHA at the time when the family first submitted an application for participation in the program to the initial PHA.

(2) The following apply during the 12 month period from the time when a family described in paragraph (c)(1) of this section is admitted to the program:

(i) The family may lease a unit anywhere in the jurisdiction of the initial PHA;

(ii) The family does not have any right to portability;

(iii) The initial PHA may choose to allow portability during this period.

(3) If both the initial PHA and a receiving PHA agree, the family may lease a unit outside the PHA jurisdiction under portability procedures.

(d) Income eligibility. (1) For admission to the program, a family must be income eligible in the area where the family initially leases a unit with assistance under the program.

(2) If a portable family is a participant in the initial PHA Section 8 tenant-based program (either the PHA voucher program or the PHA certificate program), income eligibility is not redetermined when the family moves to the receiving PHA program under portability procedures.

(3) Except as provided in paragraph (d)(2) of this section, a portable family must be income eligible for admission to the voucher program in the area where the family leases a unit under portability procedures.

(e) Leasing in-place. If the dwelling unit is approvable, a family may select the dwelling unit occupied by the family before selection for participation in the program.

(f) Freedom of choice. The PHA may not directly or indirectly reduce the family's opportunity to select among available units except as provided in paragraph (a) of this section, or elsewhere in this part 982 (e.g. prohibition on use of ineligible housing, housing not meeting HQS, or housing for which the rent to owner exceeds a reasonable rent).

{60 FR 34695, July 3, 1995, as amended at 61 FR 27163, May 30, 1996; 61 FR 42131, Aug. 13, 1996; 64 FR 26646, May 14, 1999}

Sec. 982.355 Portability: Administration by receiving PHA.

(a) When a family moves under portability (in accordance with Sec. 982.353(b)) to an area outside the initial PHA jurisdiction, another PHA (the ``receiving PHA'') must administer assistance for the family if a PHA with a tenant-based program has jurisdiction in the area where the unit is located.

(b) In the conditions described in paragraph (a) of this section, a PHA with jurisdiction in the area where the family wants to lease a unit must issue a voucher to the family. If there is more than one such PHA, the initial PHA may choose the receiving PHA.

(c) Portability procedures. (1) The receiving PHA does not redetermine elibilibility for a portable family that was already receiving assistance in the initial PHA Section 8 tenant-based program (either the PHA voucher program or certificate program). However, for a portable family that was not already receiving assistance in the PHA tenant-based program, the initial PHA must determine whether the family is eligible for admission to the receiving PHA voucher program.

(2) The initial PHA must advise the family how to contact and request assistance from the receiving PHA. The initial PHA must promptly notify the receiving PHA to expect the family.

(3) The family must promptly contact the receiving PHA, and comply with receiving PHA procedures for incoming portable families.

(4) The initial PHA must give the receiving PHA the most recent HUD Form 50058 (Family Report) for the family, and related verification information. If the receiving PHA opts to conduct a new reexamination, the receiving PHA may not delay issuing the family a voucher or otherwise delay approval of a unit unless the recertification is necessary to determine income eligibility.

(5) When the portable family requests assistance from the receiving PHA, the receiving PHA must promptly inform the initial PHA whether the receiving PHA will bill the initial PHA for assistance on behalf of the portable family, or will absorb the family into its own program.

(6) The receiving PHA must issue a voucher to the family. The term of the receiving PHA voucher may not expire before the expiration date of any initial PHA voucher. The receiving PHA must determine whether to extend the voucher term. The family must submit a request for approval of the tenancy to the receiving PHA during the term of the receiving PHA voucher.

(7) The receiving PHA must determine the family unit size for the portable family. The family unit size is determined in accordance with the subsidy standards of the receiving PHA.

(8) The receiving PHA must promptly notify the initial PHA if the family has leased an eligible unit under the program, or if the family fails to submit a request for approval of the tenancy for an eligible unit within the term of the voucher.

(9) To provide tenant-based assistance for portable families, the receiving PHA must perform all PHA program functions, such as reexaminations of family income and composition. At any time, either the initial PHA or the receiving PHA may make a determination to deny or terminate assistance to the family in accordance with Secs. 982.552 and 982.553.

(10) When the family has a right to lease a unit in the receiving PHA jurisdiction under portability procedures in accordance with Sec. 982.353(b), the receiving PHA must provide assistance for the family. Receiving PHA procedures and preferences for selection among eligible applicants do not apply, and the receiving PHA waiting list is not used. However, the receiving PHA may deny or terminate assistance for family action or inaction in accordance with Secs. 982.552 and 982.553.

(d) Absorption by the receiving PHA. (1) If funding is available under the consolidated ACC for the receiving PHA voucher program when the portable family is received, the receiving PHA may absorb the family into the receiving PHA voucher program. After absorption, the family is assisted with funds available under the consolidated ACC for the receiving PHA tenant-based program.

(2) HUD may require that the receiving PHA absorb all or a portion of the portable families.

(e) Portability Billing. (1) To cover assistance for a portable family, the receiving

PHA may bill the initial PHA for housing assistance payments and administrative fees. This paragraph (e) describes the billing procedure.

(2) The initial PHA must promptly reimburse the receiving PHA for the full amount of the housing assistance payments made by the receiving PHA for the portable family. The amount of the housing assistance payment for a portable family in the receiving PHA program is determined in the same manner as for other families in the receiving PHA program.

(3) The initial PHA must promptly reimburse the receiving PHA for 80 percent of the initial PHA on-going administrative fee for each unit month that the family receives assistance under the tenant-based programs from the receiving PHA. If both PHAs agree, the PHAs may negotiate a different amount of reimbursement.

(4) HUD may reduce the administrative fee to an initial or receiving PHA if the PHA does not comply with HUD portability requirements.

(5) In administration of portability, the initial PHA and the receiving PHA must comply with financial procedures required by HUD, including the use of HUD-required billing forms. The initial and receiving PHA must comply with billing and payment deadlines under the financial procedures.

(6) a PHA must manage the PHA tenant-based program in a manner that ensures that the PHA has the financial ability to provide assistance for families that move out of the PHA program under the portability procedures that have not been absorbed by the receiving PHA, as well as for families that remain in the PHA program.

(7) When a portable family moves out of the tenant-based program of a receiving PHA that has not absorbed the family, the PHA in the new jurisdiction to which the family moves becomes the receiving PHA, and the first receiving PHA is no longer required to provide assistance for the family.

(f) Portability funding. (1) HUD may transfer funds for assistance to portable families to the receiving PHA from funds available under the initial PHA ACC.

(2) HUD may provide additional funding (e.g., funds for incremental units) to the initial PHA for funds transferred to a receiving PHA for portability purposes.

(3) HUD may provide additional funding (e.g., funds for incremental units) to the receiving PHA for absorption of portable families.

(4) HUD may require the receiving PHA to absorb portable families.

{60 FR 34695, July 3, 1995, as amended at 61 FR 27163, May 30, 1996; 64 FR 26646, May 14, 1999; 64 FR 56914, Oct. 21, 1999}

Subpart I--Dwelling Unit: Housing Quality Standards, Subsidy Standards, Inspection and Maintenance

Source: 60 FR 34695, July 3, 1995, unless otherwise noted.

Sec. 982.401 Housing quality standards (HQS).

(a) Performance and acceptability requirements. (1) This section states the housing quality standards (HQS) for housing assisted in the programs.

(2)(i) The HQS consist of:

(A) Performance requirements; and

(B) Acceptability criteria or HUD approved variations in the acceptability criteria.

(ii) This section states performance and acceptability criteria for these key aspects of housing quality:

(A) Sanitary facilities;

(B) Food preparation and refuse disposal;

(C) Space and security;

(D) Thermal environment;

(E) Illumination and electricity;

(F) Structure and materials;

(G) Interior air quality;

(H) Water supply;

(I) Lead-based paint;

(J) Access;

(K) Site and neighborhood;

(L) Sanitary condition; and

(M) Smoke detectors.

(3) All program housing must meet the HQS performance requirements both at commencement of assisted occupancy, and throughout the assisted tenancy.

(4)(i) In addition to meeting HQS performance requirements, the housing must meet the acceptability criteria stated in this section, unless variations are approved by HUD.

(ii) HUD may approve acceptability criteria variations for the following purposes:

(A) Variations which apply standards in local housing codes or other codes adopted by the PHA; or

(B) Variations because of local climatic or geographic conditions.

(iii) Acceptability criteria variations may only be approved by HUD pursuant to paragraph (a)(4)(ii) of this section if such variations either:

(A) Meet or exceed the performance requirements; or

(B) Significantly expand affordable housing opportunities for families assisted under the program.

(iv) HUD will not approve any acceptability criteria variation if HUD believes that such variation is likely to adversely affect the health or safety of participant families, or severely restrict housing choice.

(b) Sanitary facilities--(1) Performance requirements. The dwelling unit must include sanitary facilities located in the unit. The sanitary facilities must be in proper operating condition, and adequate for personal cleanliness and the disposal of human waste. The sanitary facilities must be usable in privacy.

(2) Acceptability criteria. (i) The bathroom must be located in a separate private room and have a flush toilet in proper operating condition.

(ii) The dwelling unit must have a fixed basin in proper operating condition, with a sink trap and hot and cold running water.

(iii) The dwelling unit must have a shower or a tub in proper operating condition with hot and cold running water.

(iv) The facilities must utilize an approvable public or private disposal system (including a locally approvable septic system).

(c) Food preparation and refuse disposal--(1) Performance requirement. (i) The dwelling unit must have suitable space and equipment to store, prepare, and serve foods in a sanitary manner.

(ii) There must be adequate facilities and services for the sanitary disposal of food wastes and refuse, including facilities for temporary storage where necessary (e.g, garbage cans).

(2) Acceptability criteria. (i) The dwelling unit must have an oven, and a stove or range, and a refrigerator of appropriate size for the family. All of the equipment must be in proper operating condition. The equipment may be supplied by either the owner or the family. A microwave oven may be substituted for a tenant-supplied oven and stove or range. A microwave oven may be substituted for an owner-supplied oven and stove or range if the tenant agrees and microwave ovens are furnished instead of an oven and stove or range to both subsidized and unsubsidized tenants in the building or premises.

(ii) The dwelling unit must have a kitchen sink in proper operating condition, with a sink trap and hot and cold running water. The sink must drain into an approvable public or private system.

(iii) The dwelling unit must have space for the storage, preparation, and serving of food.

(iv) There must be facilities and services for the sanitary disposal of food waste and refuse, including temporary storage facilities where necessary (e.g., garbage cans).

(d) Space and security--(1) Performance requirement. The dwelling unit must provide adequate space and security for the family.

(2) Acceptability criteria. (i) At a minimum, the dwelling unit must have a living room, a kitchen area, and a bathroom.

(ii) The dwelling unit must have at least one bedroom or living/ sleeping room for each two persons. Children of opposite sex, other than very young children, may not be required to occupy the same bedroom or living/sleeping room.

(iii) Dwelling unit windows that are accessible from the outside, such as basement, first floor, and fire escape windows, must be lockable (such as window units with sash pins or sash locks, and combination windows with latches). Windows that are nailed shut are acceptable only if these windows are not needed for ventilation or as an alternate exit in case of fire.

(iv) The exterior doors of the dwelling unit must be lockable. Exterior doors are doors by which someone can enter or exit the dwelling unit.

(e) Thermal environment--(1) Performance requirement. The dwelling unit must have and be capable of maintaining a thermal environment healthy for the human body.

(2) Acceptability criteria. (i) There must be a safe system for heating the dwelling unit (and a safe cooling system, where present). The system must be in proper operating condition. The system must be able to provide adequate heat (and cooling, if applicable), either directly or indirectly, to each room, in order to assure a healthy living environment appropriate to the climate.

(ii) The dwelling unit must not contain unvented room heaters that burn gas, oil, or kerosene. Electric heaters are acceptable.

(f) Illumination and electricity--(1) Performance requirement. Each room must have adequate natural or artificial illumination to permit normal indoor activities and to support the health and safety of occupants. The dwelling unit must have sufficient electrical sources so occupants can use essential electrical appliances. The electrical fixtures and wiring must ensure safety from fire.

(2) Acceptability criteria. (i) There must be at least one window in the living room and in each sleeping room.

(ii) The kitchen area and the bathroom must have a permanent ceiling or wall light fixture in proper operating condition. The kitchen area must also have at least one electrical outlet in proper operating condition.

(iii) The living room and each bedroom must have at least two electrical outlets in proper operating condition. Permanent overhead or wall-mounted light fixtures may count as one of the required electrical outlets.

(g) Structure and materials--(1) Performance requirement. The dwelling unit must be structurally sound. The structure must not present any threat to the health and safety of the occupants and must protect the occupants from the environment.

(2) Acceptability criteria. (i) Ceilings, walls, and floors must not have any serious defects such as severe bulging or leaning, large holes, loose surface materials, severe buckling, missing parts, or other serious damage.

(ii) The roof must be structurally sound and weathertight.

(iii) The exterior wall structure and surface must not have any serious defects such as serious leaning, buckling, sagging, large holes, or defects that may result in air infiltration or vermin infestation.

(iv) The condition and equipment of interior and exterior stairs, halls, porches, walkways, etc., must not present a danger of tripping and falling. For example, broken or missing steps or loose boards are unacceptable.

(v) Elevators must be working and safe.

(h) Interior air quality--(1) Performance requirement. The dwelling unit must be free of pollutants in the air at levels that threaten the health of the occupants.

(2) Acceptability criteria. (i) The dwelling unit must be free from dangerous levels of air pollution from carbon monoxide, sewer gas, fuel gas, dust, and other harmful pollutants.

(ii) There must be adequate air circulation in the dwelling unit.

(iii) Bathroom areas must have one openable window or other adequate exhaust ventilation.

(iv) Any room used for sleeping must have at least one window. If the window is designed to be openable, the window must work.

(i) Water supply--(1) Performance requirement. The water supply must be free from contamination.

(2) Acceptability criteria. The dwelling unit must be served by an approvable public or private water supply that is sanitary and free from contamination.

(j) Lead-based paint performance requirement. The Lead-Based Paint Poisoning Prevention Act (42 U.S.C. 4821-4846), the Residential Lead-Based Paint Hazard Reduction Act of 1992 (42 U.S.C. 4851-4856), and implementing regulations at part 35, subparts A, B, M, and R of this title apply to units assisted under this part.

(k) Access performance requirement. The dwelling unit must be able to be used and maintained without unauthorized use of other private properties. The building must provide an alternate means of exit in case of fire (such as fire stairs or egress through windows).

(l) Site and Neighborhood--(1) Performance requirement. The site and neighborhood must be reasonably free from disturbing noises and reverberations and other dangers to the health, safety, and general welfare of the occupants.

(2) Acceptability criteria. The site and neighborhood may not be subject to serious adverse environmental conditions, natural or manmade, such as dangerous walks or steps; instability; flooding, poor drainage, septic tank back-ups or sewage hazards; mudslides; abnormal air pollution, smoke or dust; excessive noise, vibration or vehicular traffic; excessive accumulations of trash; vermin or rodent infestation; or fire hazards.

(m) Sanitary condition--(1) Performance requirement. The dwelling unit and its equipment must be in sanitary condition.

(2) Acceptability criteria. The dwelling unit and its equipment must be free of vermin and rodent infestation.

(n) Smoke detectors performance requirement--(1) Except as provided in paragraph (n)(2) of this section, each dwelling unit must have at least one battery-operated or hard-wired smoke detector, in proper operating condition, on each level of the dwelling unit, including basements but excepting crawl spaces and unfinished attics. Smoke detectors must be installed in accordance with and meet the requirements of the National Fire Protection Association Standard (NFPA) 74 (or its successor standards). If the dwelling unit is occupied by any hearing-impaired person, - smoke detectors must have an alarm system, designed for hearing-impaired persons as specified in NFPA 74 (or successor standards).

(2) For units assisted prior to April 24, 1993, owners who installed battery-operated or hard-wired smoke detectors prior to April 24, 1993 in compliance with HUD's smoke detector requirements, including the regulations published on July 30, 1992, (57 FR 33846), will not be required subsequently to comply with any additional requirements mandated by NFPA 74 (i.e., the owner would not be required to install a smoke detector in a basement not used for living purposes, nor would the owner be required to change the location of the smoke detectors that have already been installed on the other floors of the unit).

{60 FR 34695, July 3, 1995, as amended at 61 FR 27163, May 30, 1996; 63 FR 23861, Apr. 30, 1998; 64 FR 26646, May 14, 1999; 64 FR 49658, Sept. 14, 1999; 64 FR 50230, Sept. 15, 1999}

Sec. 982.402 Subsidy standards.

(a) Purpose. (1) The PHA must establish subsidy standards that determine the number of bedrooms needed for families of different sizes and compositions.

(2) For each family, the PHA determines the appropriate number of bedrooms under the PHA subsidy standards (family unit size).

(3) The family unit size number is entered on the voucher issued to the family. The

PHA issues the family a voucher for the family unit size when a family is selected for participation in the program.

(b) Determining family unit size. The following requirements apply when the PHA determines family unit size under the PHA subsidy standards:

(1) The subsidy standards must provide for the smallest number of bedrooms needed to house a family without overcrowding.

(2) The subsidy standards must be consistent with space requirements under the housing quality standards (See Sec. 982.401(d)).

(3) The subsidy standards must be applied consistently for all families of like size and composition.

(4) A child who is temporarily away from the home because of placement in foster care is considered a member of the family in determining the family unit size.

(5) A family that consists of a pregnant woman (with no other persons) must be treated as a two-person family.

(6) Any live-in aide (approved by the PHA to reside in the unit to care for a family member who is disabled or is at least 50 years of age) must be counted in determining the family unit size;

(7) Unless a live-in-aide resides with the family, the family unit size for any family consisting of a single person must be either a zero or one-bedroom unit, as determined under the PHA subsidy standards.

(8) In determining family unit size for a particular family, the PHA may grant an exception to its established subsidy standards if the PHA determines that the exception is justified by the age, sex, health, handicap, or relationship of family members or other personal circumstances. (For a single person other than a disabled or elderly person or remaining family member, such PHA exception may not override the limitation in paragraph (b)(7) of this section.)

(c) Effect of family unit size-maximum subsidy in voucher program. The family unit size as determined for a family under the PHA subsidy standard is used to determine the maximum rent subsidy for a family assisted in the voucher program. For a voucher tenancy, the PHA establishes payment standards by number of bedrooms. The payment standard for a family shall be the lower of:

(1) The payment standard amount for the family unit size; or

(2) The payment standard amount for the unit size of the unit rented by the family.

(3) Voucher program. For a voucher tenancy, the PHA establishes payment standards by number of bedrooms. The payment standards for the family must be the lower of:

(i) The payment standards for the family unit size; or

(ii) The payment standard for the unit size rented by the family.

(d) Size of unit occupied by family. (1) The family may lease an otherwise acceptable dwelling unit with fewer bedrooms than the family unit size. However, the dwelling unit must meet the applicable HQS space requirements.

(2) The family may lease an otherwise acceptable dwelling unit with more bedrooms than the family unit size.

{60 FR 34695, July 3, 1995, as amended at 63 FR 23861, Apr. 30, 1998; 64 FR 26646, May 14, 1999}

Sec. 982.403 Terminating HAP contract when unit is too small.

(a) Violation of HQS space standards. (1) If the PHA determines that a unit does not meet the HQS space standards because of an increase in family size or a change in family composition, the PHA must issue the family a new voucher, and the family and PHA must try to find an acceptable unit as soon as possible.

(2) If an acceptable unit is available for rental by the family, the PHA must terminate the HAP contract in accordance with its terms.

(b) Certificate program only--Subsidy too big for family size. (1) Paragraph (b) of this section applies to the tenant-based certificate program.

(2) The PHA must issue the family a new voucher, and the family and PHA must try to find an acceptable unit as soon as possible if:

(i) The family is residing in a dwelling unit with a larger number of bedrooms than appropriate for the family unit size under the PHA subsidy standards; and

(ii) The gross rent for the unit (sum of the contract rent plus any utility allowance for the unit size leased) exceeds the FMR/exception rent limit for the family unit size under the PHA subsidy standards.

(3) The PHA must notify the family that exceptions to the subsidy standards may be granted, and the circumstances in which the grant of an exception will be considered by the PHA.

(4) If an acceptable unit is available for rental by the family, the PHA must terminate the HAP contract in accordance with its terms.

(c) Termination. When the PHA terminates the HAP contract under paragraph (a) of this section:

(1) The PHA must notify the family and the owner of the termination; and

(2) The HAP contract terminates at the end of the calendar month that follows the calendar month in which the PHA gives such notice to the owner.

(3) The family may move to a new unit in accordance with Sec. 982.314.

(Approved by the Office of Management and Budget under control number 2577-0169) {60 FR 34695, July 3, 1995, as amended at 60 FR 45661, Sept. 1, 1995; 64 FR 26647, May 14, 1999}

Sec. 982.404 Maintenance: Owner and family responsibility; PHA remedies.

(a) Owner obligation. (1) The owner must maintain the unit in accordance with HQS.

(2) If the owner fails to maintain the dwelling unit in accordance with HQS, the PHA must take prompt and vigorous action to enforce the owner obligations. PHA remedies for such breach of the HQS include termination, suspension or reduction of housing assistance payments and termination of the HAP contract.

(3) The PHA must not make any housing assistance payments for a dwelling unit that fails to meet the HQS, unless the owner corrects the defect within the period specified by the PHA and the PHA verifies the correction. If a defect is life threatening, the owner must correct the defect within no more than 24 hours. For other defects, the owner must correct the defect within no more than 30 calendar days (or any PHA-approved extension).

(4) The owner is not responsible for a breach of the HQS that is not caused by the owner, and for which the family is responsible (as provided in Sec. 982.404(b) and Sec. 982.551(c)). (However, the PHA may terminate assistance to a family because of HQS breach caused by the family.)

(b) Family obligation. (1) The family is responsible for a breach of the HQS that is caused by any of the following:

(i) The family fails to pay for any utilities that the owner is not required to pay for, but which are to be paid by the tenant;

(ii) The family fails to provide and maintain any appliances that the owner is not required to provide, but which are to be provided by the tenant; or

(iii) Any member of the household or guest damages the dwelling unit or premises (damages beyond ordinary wear and tear).

(2) If an HQS breach caused by the family is life threatening, the family must correct the defect within no more than 24 hours. For other family-caused defects, the family must correct the defect within no more than 30 calendar days (or any PHA-approved extension).

(3) If the family has caused a breach of the HQS, the PHA must take prompt and vigorous action to enforce the family obligations. The PHA may terminate assistance for the family in accordance with Sec. 982.552.

(Approved by the Office of Management and Budget under control number 2577-0169)
{60 FR 34695, July 3, 1995, as amended at 60 FR 45661, Sept. 1, 1995}

Sec. 982.405 PHA initial and periodic unit inspection.

(a) The PHA must inspect the unit leased to a family prior to the initial term of the lease, at least annually during assisted occupancy, and at other times as needed, to determine if the unit meets the HQS. (See Sec. 982.305(b)(2) concerning timing of initial inspection by the PHA.)

(b) The PHA must conduct supervisory quality control HQS inspections.

(c) In scheduling inspections, the PHA must consider complaints and any other information brought to the attention of the PHA.

(d) The PHA must notify the owner of defects shown by the inspection.

(e) The PHA may not charge the family or owner for initial inspection or reinspection of the unit.

{60 FR 34695, July 3, 1995, as amended at 64 FR 26647, May 14, 1999; 64 FR 56914, Oct. 21, 1999}

Sec. 982.406 Enforcement of HQS.

Part 982 does not create any right of the family, or any party other tPHAn HUD or the PHA, to require enforcement of the HQS requirements by HUD or the PHA, or to assert any claim against HUD or the PHA, for damages, injunction or other relief, for alleged failure to enforce the HQS.

(Approved by the Office of Management and Budget under control number 2577-0169)
{60 FR 34695, July 3, 1995, as amended at 60 FR 45661, Sept. 1, 1995}

Subpart J--Housing Assistance Payments Contract and Owner Responsibility

Source: 60 FR 34695, July 3, 1995, unless otherwise noted.

Sec. 982.451 Housing assistance payments contract.

(a)(1) The HAP contract must be in the form required by HUD.

(2) The term of the HAP contract is the same as the term of the lease.

(b)(1) The amount of the monthly housing assistance payment by the PHA to the owner is determined by the PHA in accordance with HUD regulations and other requirements. The amount of the housing assistance payment is subject to change during the HAP contract term.

(2) The monthly housing assistance payment by the PHA is credited toward the monthly rent to owner under the family's lease.

(3) The total of rent paid by the tenant plus the PHA housing assistance payment to the owner may not be more than the rent to owner. The owner must immediately return any excess payment to the PHA.

(4)(i) The part of the rent to owner which is paid by the tenant may not be more than:

(A) The rent to owner; minus

(B) The PHA housing assistance payment to the owner.

(ii) The owner may not demand or accept any rent payment from the tenant in excess of this maximum, and must immediately return any excess rent payment to the tenant.

(iii) The family is not responsible for payment of the portion of rent to owner covered by the housing assistance payment under the HAP contract between the owner and the PHA. See Sec. 982.310(b).

(5)(i) The PHA must pay the housing assistance payment promptly when due to the owner in accordance with the HAP contract.

(ii)(A) The HAP contract shall provide for penalties against the PHA for late payment of housing assistance payments due to the owner if all the following circumstances apply:

(1) Such penalties are in accordance with generally accepted practices and law, as applicable in the local housing market, governing penalties for late payment of rent by a tenant;

(2) It is the owner's practice to charge such penalties for assisted and unassisted tenants; and

(3) The owner also charges such penalties against the tenant for late payment of family rent to owner.

(B) The PHA is not obligated to pay any late payment penalty if HUD determines that late payment by the PHA is due to factors beyond the PHA's control. The PHA may add HAP contract provisions which define when the housing assistance payment by the PHA is deemed received by the owner (e.g., upon mailing by the PHA or actual receipt by the owner).

(iii) The PHA may only use the following sources to pay a late payment penalty from program receipts under the consolidated ACC: administrative fee income for the program; or the administrative fee reserve for the program. The PHA may not use other program receipts for this purpose.

{60 FR 34695, July 3, 1995, as amended at 61 FR 27163, May 30, 1996; 63 FR 23861, Apr. 30, 1998; 64 FR 26647, May 14, 1999; 64 FR 56914, Oct. 21, 1999}

Sec. 982.452 Owner responsibilities.

(a) The owner is responsible for performing all of the owner's obligations under the HAP contract and the lease.

(b) The owner is responsible for:

(1) Performing all management and rental functions for the assisted unit, including selecting a voucher-holder to lease the unit, and deciding if the family is suitable for tenancy of the unit.

(2) Maintaining the unit in accordance with HQS, including performance of ordinary and extraordinary maintenance. For provisions on family maintenance responsibilities, see Sec. 982.404(a)(4).

(3) Complying with equal opportunity requirements.

(4) Preparing and furnishing to the PHA information required under the HAP contract.

(5) Collecting from the family:

(i) Any security deposit.

(ii) The tenant contribution (the part of rent to owner not covered by the housing assistance payment).

(iii) Any charges for unit damage by the family.

(6) Enforcing tenant obligations under the lease.

(7) Paying for utilities and services (unless paid by the family under the lease).

(c) For provisions on modifications to a dwelling unit occupied or to be occupied by a disabled person, see 24 CFR 100.203.

(Approved by the Office of Management and Budget under control number 2577-0169) {60 FR 34695, July 3, 1995, as amended at 60 FR 45661, Sept. 1, 1995; 63 FR 23861, Apr. 30, 1998; 64 FR 26647, May 14, 1999}

Sec. 982.453 Owner breach of contract.

(a) Any of the following actions by the owner (including a principal or other interested party) is a breach of the HAP contract by the owner:

(1) If the owner has violated any obligation under the HAP contract for the dwelling unit, including the owner's obligation to maintain the unit in accordance with the HQS.

(2) If the owner has violated any obligation under any other HAP contract under Section 8 of the 1937 Act (42 U.S.C. 1437f).

(3) If the owner has committed fraud, bribery or any other corrupt or criminal act in connection with any federal housing program.

(4) For projects with mortgages insured by HUD or loans made by HUD, if the owner

has failed to comply with the regulations for the applicable mortgage insurance or loan program, with the mortgage or mortgage note, or with the regulatory agreement; or if the owner has committed fraud, bribery or any other corrupt or criminal act in connection with the mortgage or loan.

(5) If the owner has engaged in drug-related criminal activity.

(6) If the owner has committed any violent criminal activity.

(b) The PHA rights and remedies against the owner under the HAP contract include recovery of overpayments, abatement or other reduction of housing assistance payments, termination of housing assistance payments, and termination of the HAP contract.

{60 FR 34695, July 3, 1995, as amended at 64 FR 26647, May 14, 1999; 64 FR 56914, Oct. 21, 1999; 65 FR 16821, Mar. 30, 2000}

Sec. 982.454 Termination of HAP contract: Insufficient funding.

The PHA may terminate the HAP contract if the PHA determines, in accordance with HUD requirements, that funding under the consolidated ACC is insufficient to support continued assistance for families in the program.

{60 FR 34695, July 3, 1995, as amended at 64 FR 26647, May 14, 1999}

Sec. 982.455 Automatic termination of HAP contract.

The HAP contract terminates automatically 180 calendar days after the last housing assistance payment to the owner.

{64 FR 26647, May 14, 1999}

Sec. 982.456 Third parties.

(a) Even if the family continues to occupy the unit, the PHA may exercise any rights and remedies against the owner under the HAP contract.

(b)(1) The family is not a party to or third party beneficiary of the HAP contract. Except as provided in paragraph (b)(2) of this section, the family may not exercise any right or remedy against the owner under the HAP contract.

(2) The tenant may exercise any right or remedy against the owner under the lease between the tenant and the owner, including enforcement of the owner's obligations under the tenancy addendum (which is included both in the HAP contract between the PHA and the owner; and in the lease between the tenant and the owner.)

(c) The HAP contract shall not be construed as creating any right of the family or other third party (other than HUD) to enforce any provision of the HAP contract, or to assert any claim against HUD, the PHA or the owner under the HAP contract.

{60 FR 34695, July 3, 1995, as amended at 64 FR 26647, May 14, 1999}

Subpart K--Rent and Housing Assistance Payment

Source: 63 FR 23861, Apr. 30, 1998, unless otherwise noted.

Sec. 982.501 Overview.

(a) This subpart describes program requirements concerning the housing assistance payment and rent to owner. These requirements apply to the Section 8 tenant-based program.

(b) There are two types of tenancies in the Section 8 tenant-based program:

(1) A tenancy under the voucher program.

(2) A tenancy under the certificate program (commenced before merger of the certificate and voucher programs on the merger date).

(c) Unless specifically stated, requirements of this part are the same for all tenancies. Sections 982.503, 982.504, and 982.505 only apply to a voucher tenancy. Sections 982.518, 982.519, and 982.520 only apply to a tenancy under the certificate program.

{64 FR 26647, May 14, 1999, as amended at 65 FR 42509, July 10, 2000}

Sec. 982.502 Conversion to voucher program.

(a) New HAP contracts. On and after the merger date, the PHA may only enter into a HAP contract for a tenancy under the voucher program, and may not enter into a new HAP contract for a tenancy under the certificate program.

(b) Over-FMR tenancy. If the PHA had entered into any HAP contract for an over-FMR tenancy under the certificate program prior to the merger date, on and after the merger date such tenancy shall be considered and treated as a tenancy under the voucher program, and shall be subject to the voucher program requirements under this part, including calculation of the voucher housing assistance payment in accordance with Sec. 982.505. However, Sec. 982.505(b)(2) shall not be applicable for calculation of the housing assistance payment prior to the effective date of the second regular reexamination of family income and compostion on or after the merger date.

(c) Voucher tenancy. If the PHA had entered into any HAP contract for a voucher tenancy prior to the merger date, on and after the merger date such tenancy shall continue to be considered and treated as a tenancy under the voucher program, and shall be subject to the voucher program requirements under this part, including calculation of the voucher housing assistance payment in accordance with Sec. 982.505. However, before the effective date of the second regular reexamination of family income and composition on or after the merger date, the payment standard for the family shall be the higher of:

(1) The initial payment standard for the family at the beginning of the HAP contract term; or

(2) The payment standard for the family as calculated in accordance with Sec. 982.505, except that Sec. 982.505(b)(2) shall not be applicable until the effective date of the second regular reexamination of family income and composition on or after the merger date.

(d) Regular certificate tenancy. The PHA must terminate program assistance under any outstanding HAP contract for a regular tenancy under the certificate program (entered prior to the merger date) at the effective date of the second regular reexamination of family income and composition on or after the merger date. Upon such termination of assistance, the HAP contract for such tenancy terminates automatically. The PHA must give at least 120 days written notice of such termination to the family and the owner, and the PHA must offer the family the opportunity for continued tenant-based assistance under the voucher program. The PHA may deny the family the opportunity for continued assistance in accordance with Secs. 982.552 and 982.553.

{64 FR 26648, May 14, 1999, as amended at 64 FR 56914, Oct. 21, 1999; 65 FR 16822, Mar. 30, 2000}

Sec. 982.503 Voucher tenancy: Payment standard amount and schedule.

(a) Payment standard schedule. (1) HUD publishes the fair market rents for each market area in the United States (see part 888 of this title). The PHA must adopt a payment standard schedule that establishes voucher payment standard amounts for each FMR area in the PHA jurisdiction. For each FMR area, the PHA must establish payment standard amounts for each ``unit size.'' Unit size is measured by number of bedrooms (zero-bedroom, one-bedroom, and so on).

(2) The payment standard amounts on the PHA schedule are used to calculate the monthly housing assistance payment for a family (Sec. 982.505).

(3) The PHA voucher payment standard schedule shall establish a single payment standard amount for each unit size. For each unit size, the PHA may establish a single payment standard amount for the whole FMR area, or may establish a separate payment standard amount for each designated part of the FMR area.

(b) Establishing payment standard amounts. (1)(i) The PHA may establish the payment standard amount for a unit size at any level between 90 percent and 110 percent of the published FMR for that unit size. HUD approval is not required to establish a payment standard amount in that range (``basic range'').

(ii) The PHA may establish a separate payment standard amount within the basic range for a designated part of an FMR area.

(2) The PHA must request HUD approval to establish a payment standard amount that is higher or lower than the basic range. HUD has sole discretion to grant or deny approval of a higher or lower payment standard amount. Paragraphs (c) and (e) of this section describe the requirements for approval of a higher payment standard amount (``exception payment standard amount'').

(c) HUD approval of exception payment standard amount. (1) HUD discretion. At HUD's sole discretion, HUD may approve a payment standard amount that is higher than the basic range for a designated part of the fair market rent area (called an ``exception area''). HUD may approve an exception payment standard amount in accordance with this paragraph (c) of this section for all units, or for all units of a given unit size, leased by program families in the exception area. Any PHA with jurisdiction in the exception area may use the HUD-approved exception payment standard amount.

(2) Above 110 percent of FMR to 120 percent of published FMR. (i) The HUD Field Office may approve an exception payment standard amount from above 110 percent of the published FMR to 120 percent of the published FMR (upper range) if the HUD Field Office determines that approval is justified by either the median rent method or the 40th or 50th percentile rent method as described in paragraph (c)(2)(i)(B) of this section (and that such approval is also supported by an appropriate program justification in accordance with paragraph (c)(4) of this section).

(A) Median rent method. In the median rent method, HUD determines the exception payment standard amount by multiplying the FMR times a fraction of which the numerator is the median gross rent of the exception area and the denominator is the median gross rent of the entire FMR area. In this method, HUD uses median gross rent data from the most recent decennial United States census, and the exception area may be any geographic entity within the FMR area (or any combination of such entities) for which median gross rent data is provided in decennial census products.

(B) 40th or 50th percentile rent method. In this method, HUD determines that the area exception payment standard amount equals either the 40th or 50th percentile of rents for standard quality rental housing in the exception area. HUD determines whether the 40th or 50th percentile rent applies in accordance with the methodology described in Sec. 888.113 of this title for determining FMRs. A PHA must present statistically representative rental housing survey data to justify HUD approval.

(ii) The HUD Field Office may approve an exception payment standard amount within the upper range if required as a reasonable accommodation for a family that includes a person with disabilities.

(3) Above 120 percent of FMR. (i) At the request of a PHA, the Assistant Secretary for Public and Indian Housing may approve an exception payment standard amount for the total area of a county, PHA jurisdiction, or place if the Assistant Secretary determines that:

(A) Such approval is necessary to prevent financial hardship for families;

(B) Such approval is supported by statistically representative rental housing survey data to justify HUD approval in accordance with the methodology described in Sec. 888.113 of this title; and

(C) Such approval is also supported by an appropriate program justification in accordance with paragraph (c)(4) of this section.

(ii) For purposes of paragraph (c)(3) of this section, the term ``place'' is an incorporated place or a U.S. Census designated place. An incorporated place is established by State law and includes cities, boroughs, towns, and villages. A U.S. Census designated place is the statistical counterpart of an incorporated place.

(4) Program justification. (i) HUD will only approve an exception payment standard amount (pursuant to paragraph (c)(2) or paragraph (c)(3) of this section) if HUD determines that approval of such higher amount is needed either:

(A) To help families find housing outside areas of high poverty, or

(B) Because voucher holders have trouble finding housing for lease under the program within the term of the voucher.

(ii) HUD will only approve an exception payment standard amount (pursuant to paragraph (c)(3) of this section) after six months from the date of HUD approval of an exception payment standard pursuant to paragraph (c)(2) of this section for the area.

(5) Population. The total population of HUD-approved exception areas in an FMR area may not include more than 50 percent of the population of the FMR area.

(6) Withdrawal or modification. At any time, HUD may withdraw or modify approval to use an exception payment standard amount.

(7) Transition: Area exception rents approved prior to merger date. Subject to paragraph (c)(6) of this section, the PHA may establish an exception payment standard amount up to the amount of a HUD-approved area exception rent in effect at the merger date.

(d) HUD approval of payment standard amount below the basic range. HUD may consider a PHA request for approval to establish a payment standard amount that is lower than the basic range. At HUD's sole discretion, HUD may approve PHA establishment of a payment standard lower than the basic range. In determining whether to approve the PHA request, HUD will consider appropriate factors, including rent burden of families assisted under the program. HUD will not approve a lower payment standard if the family share for more than 40 percent of participants in the PHA's voucher program exceeds 30 percent of adjusted monthly income. Such determination may be based on the most recent examinations of family income.

(e) HUD approval of success rate payment standard amounts. In order to increase the number of voucher holders who become participants, HUD may approve requests from PHAs whose FMRs are computed at the 40th percentile rent to establish higher, success rate payment standard amounts. A success rate payment standard amount is defined as any amount between 90 percent and 110 percent of the 50th percentile rent, calculated in accordance with the methodology described in Sec. 888.113 of this title.

(1) A PHA may obtain HUD Field Office approval of success rate payment standard amounts provided the PHA demonstrates to HUD that it meets the following criteria:

(i) Fewer than 75 percent of the families to whom the PHA issued rental vouchers during the most recent 6 month period for which there is success rate data available have become participants in the voucher program;

(ii) The PHA has established payment standard amounts for all unit sizes in the entire PHA jurisdiction within the FMR area at 110 percent of the published FMR for at least the 6 month period referenced in paragraph (e)(1)(i) of this section and up to the time the request is made to HUD; and

(iii) The PHA has a policy of granting automatic extensions of voucher terms to at least 90 days to provide a family who has

made sustained efforts to locate suitable housing with additional search time.

(2) In determining whether to approve the PHA request to establish success rate payment standard amounts, HUD will consider whether the PHA has a SEMAP overall performance rating of ``troubled''. If a PHA does not yet have a SEMAP rating, HUD will consider the PHA's SEMAP certification.

(3) HUD approval of success rate payment standard amounts shall be for all unit sizes in the FMR area. A PHA may opt to establish a success rate payment standard amount for one or more unit sizes in all or a designated part of the PHA jurisdiction within the FMR area.

(f) Payment standard protection for PHAs that meet deconcentration objectives. Paragraph (f) of this section applies only to a PHA with jurisdiction in an FMR area where the FMR had previously been set at the 50th percentile rent to provide a broad range of housing opportunities throughout a metropolitan area, pursuant to Sec. 888.113(c), but is now set at the 40th percentile rent.

(1) Such a PHA may obtain HUD Field Office approval of a payment standard amount based on the 50th percentile rent if the PHA scored the maximum number of points on the deconcentration bonus indicator in Sec. 985.3(h) in the prior year, or in two of the last three years.

(2) HUD approval of payment standard amounts based on the 50th percentile rent shall be for all unit sizes in the FMR area that had previously been set at the 50th percentile rent pursuant to Sec. 888.113(c). A PHA may opt to establish a payment standard amount based on the 50th percentile rent for one or more unit sizes in all or a designated part of the PHA jurisdiction within the FMR area.

(g) HUD review of PHA payment standard schedules. (1) HUD will monitor rent burdens of families assisted in a PHA's voucher program. HUD will review the PHA's payment standard for a particular unit size if HUD finds that 40 percent or more of such families occupying units of that unit size currently pay more than 30 percent of adjusted monthly income as the family share. Such determination may be based on the most recent examinations of family income.

(2) After such review, HUD may, at its discretion, require the PHA to modify payment standard amounts for any unit size on the PHA payment standard schedule. HUD may require the PHA to establish an increased payment standard amount within the basic range.

{64 FR 26648, May 14, 1999; 64 FR 49658, Sept. 14, 1999, as amended at 64 FR 56914, Oct. 21, 1999; 65 FR 16822, Mar. 30, 2000; 65 FR 58874, Oct. 2, 2000; 66 FR 30568, June 6, 2001; 67 FR 56688, Sept. 4, 2002}

Sec. 982.504 Voucher tenancy: Payment standard for family in restructured subsidized multifamily project.

(a) This section applies to tenant-based assistance under the voucher program if all the following conditions are applicable:

(1) Such tenant-based voucher assistance is provided to a family pursuant to Sec. 401.421 of this title when HUD has approved a restructuring plan, and the participating administrative entity has approved the use of tenant-based assistance to provide continued assistance for such families. Such tenant-based voucher assistance is provided for a family previously receiving project-based assistance in an eligible project (as defined in Sec. 401.2 of this title) at the time when the project-based assistance terminates.

(2) The family chooses to remain in the restructured project with tenant-based assistance under the program and leases a unit that does not exceed the family unit size;

(3) The lease for such assisted tenancy commences during the first year after the project-based assistance terminates.

(b) The initial payment standard for the family under such initial lease is the sum of the reasonable rent to owner for the unit plus the utility allowance for tenant-paid utilities.

(Determination of such initial payment standard for the family is not subject to paragraphs (c)(1) and (c)(2) of Sec. 982.505. Except for determination of the initial payment standard as specifically provided in paragraph (b) of this section, the payment standard and housing assistance payment for the family during the HAP contract term shall be determined in accordance with Sec. 982.505.)

{64 FR 26649, May 14, 1999}

Sec. 982.505 Voucher tenancy: How to calculate housing assistance payment.

(a) Use of payment standard. A payment standard is used to calculate the monthly housing assistance payment for a family. The ``payment standard'' is the maximum monthly subsidy payment.

(b) Amount of monthly housing assistance payment. The PHA shall pay a monthly housing assistance payment on behalf of the family that is equal to the lower of:

(1) The payment standard for the family minus the total tenant payment; or

(2) The gross rent minus the total tenant payment.

(c) Payment standard for family. (1) The payment standard for the family is the lower of:

(i) The payment standard amount for the family unit size; or

(ii) The payment standard amount for the size of the dwelling unit rented by the family.

(2) If the PHA has established a separate payment standard amount for a designated part of an FMR area in accordance with Sec. 982.503 (including an exception payment standard amount as determined in accordance with Sec. 982.503(b)(2) and Sec. 982.503(c)), and the dwelling unit is located in such designated part, the PHA must use the appropriate payment standard amount for such designated part to calculate the payment standard for the family. The payment standard for the family shall be calculated in accordance with this paragraph and paragraph (c)(1) of this section.

(3) Decrease in the payment standard amount during the HAP contract term. If the amount on the payment standard schedule is decreased during the term of the HAP contract, the lower payment standard amount generally must be used to calculate the monthly housing assistance payment for the family beginning at the effective date of the family's second regular reexamination following the effective date of the decrease in the payment standard amount. The PHA must determine the payment standard for the family as follows.

(i) Step 1: At the first regular reexamination following the decrease in the payment standard amount, the PHA shall determine the payment standard for the family in accordance with paragraphs (c)(1) and (c)(2) of this section (using the decreased payment standard amount).

(ii) Step 2 (first reexamination payment standard amount): The PHA shall compare the payment standard amount from step 1 to the payment standard amount last used to calculate the monthly housing assistance payment for the family. The payment standard amount used by the PHA to calculate the monthly housing assistance payment at the first regular reexamination following the decrease in the payment standard amount is the higher of these two payment standard amounts. The PHA shall advise the family that the application of the lower payment standard amount will be deferred until the second regular reexamination following the effective date of the decrease in the payment standard amount.

(iii) Step 3 (second reexamination payment standard amount): At the second regular reexamination following the decrease in the payment standard amount, the lower payment standard amount shall be used to calculate the monthly housing assistance payment for the family unless the PHA has subsequently increased the payment standard amount, in which case the payment standard amount is determined in accordance with paragraph (c)(4) of this section.

(4) Increase in the payment standard amount during the HAP contract term. If the payment standard amount is increased during the term of the HAP contract, the increased payment standard amount shall be used to calculate the monthly housing assistance payment for the family beginning at the effective date of the family's first regular reexamination on or after the effective date of the increase in the payment standard amount.

(5) Change in family unit size during the HAP contract term. Irrespective of any increase or decrease in the payment standard amount, if the family unit size increases or decreases during the HAP contract term, the new family unit size must be used to determine the payment standard amount for the family beginning at the family's first regular reexamination following the change in family unit size.

(d) PHA approval of higher payment standard for the family as a reasonable accommodation. If the family includes a person with disabilities and requires a higher payment standard for the family, as a reasonable accommodation for such person, in accordance with part 8 of this title, the PHA may establish a higher payment standard for the family within the basic range.

{64 FR 26649, May 14, 1999, as amended at 64 FR 56914, Oct. 21, 1999; 65 FR 16822, Mar. 30, 2000; 65 FR 42509, July 10, 2000; 66 FR 30568, June 6, 2001; 67 FR 56689, Sept. 4, 2002}

Sec. 982.506 Negotiating rent to owner.

The owner and the family negotiate the rent to owner. At the family's request, the PHA must help the family negotiate the rent to owner.

{63 FR 23861, Apr. 30, 1998. Redesignated at 64 FR 26648, May 14, 1999}

Sec. 982.507 Rent to owner: Reasonable rent.

(a) PHA determination. (1) The PHA may not approve a lease until the PHA determines that the initial rent to owner is a reasonable rent.

(2) The PHA must redetermine the reasonable rent:

(i) Before any increase in the rent to owner;

(ii) If there is a five percent decrease in the published FMR in effect 60 days before the contract anniversary (for the unit size rented by the family) as compared with the FMR in effect 1 year before the contract anniversary; or

(iii) If directed by HUD.

(3) The PHA may also redetermine the reasonable rent at any other time.

(4) At all times during the assisted tenancy, the rent to owner may not exceed the reasonable rent as most recently determined or redetermined by the PHA.

(b) Comparability. The PHA must determine whether the rent to owner is a reasonable rent in comparison to rent for other comparable unassisted units. To make this determination, the PHA must consider:

(1) The location, quality, size, unit type, and age of the contract unit; and

(2) Any amenities, housing services, maintenance and utilities to be provided by the owner in accordance with the lease.

(c) Owner certification of rents charged for other units. By accepting each monthly housing assistance payment from the PHA, the owner certifies that the rent to owner is not more than rent charged by the owner for comparable unassisted units in the premises. The owner must give the PHA information requested by the PHA on rents charged by the owner for other units in the premises or elsewhere.

{63 FR 23861, Apr. 30, 1998. Redesignated at 64 FR 26648, May 14, 1999}

Sec. 982.508 Maximum family share at initial occupancy.

At the time the PHA approves a tenancy for initial occupancy of a dwelling unit by a family with tenant-based assistance under the program, and where the gross rent of the unit exceeds the applicable payment standard for the family, the family share must not exceed 40 percent of the family's adjusted monthly income. The determination of adjusted monthly income must be based on verification information received by the PHA no earlier than 60 days before the PHA issues a voucher to the family.

{64 FR 59622, Nov. 3, 1999}

Sec. 982.509 Rent to owner: Effect of rent control.

In addition to the rent reasonableness limit under this subpart, the amount of rent to owner also may be subject to rent control limits under State or local law.

{63 FR 23861, Apr. 30, 1998. Redesignated and amended at 64 FR 26648, May 14, 1999}

Sec. 982.510 Other fees and charges.

(a) The cost of meals or supportive services may not be included in the rent to owner, and the value of meals or supportive services may not be included in the calculation of reasonable rent.

(b) The lease may not require the tenant or family members to pay charges for meals or supportive services. Non-payment of such charges is not grounds for termination of tenancy.

(c) The owner may not charge the tenant extra amounts for items customarily included in rent in the locality, or provided at no additional cost to unsubsidized tenants in the premises.

{63 FR 23861, Apr. 30, 1998. Redesignated at 64 FR 26648, May 14, 1999}

Sec. 982.514 Distribution of housing assistance payment.

The monthly housing assistance payment is distributed as follows:

(a) The PHA pays the owner the lesser of the housing assistance payment or the rent to owner.

(b) If the housing assistance payment exceeds the rent to owner, the PHA may pay the balance of the housing assistance payment (``utility reimbursement'') either to the family or directly to the utility supplier to pay the utility bill on behalf of the family. If the PHA elects to pay the utility supplier directly, the PHA must notify the family of the amount paid to the utility supplier.

{63 FR 23861, Apr. 30, 1998, as amended at 64 FR 56914, Oct. 21, 1999; 65 FR 16822, Mar. 30, 2000}

Sec. 982.515 Family share: Family responsibility.

(a) The family share is calculated by subtracting the amount of the housing assistance payment from the gross rent.

(b) The family rent to owner is calculated by subtracting the amount of the housing assistance payment to the owner from the rent to owner.

(c) The PHA may not use housing assistance payments or other program funds (including any administrative fee reserve) to pay any part of the family share, including the family rent to owner. Payment of the whole family share is the responsibility of the family.

{63 FR 23861, Apr. 30, 1998, as amended at 64 FR 56915, Oct. 21, 1999}

Sec. 982.516 Family income and composition: Regular and interim examinations.

(a) PHA responsibility for reexamination and verification. (1) The PHA must conduct a reexamination of family income and composition at least annually.

(2) The PHA must obtain and document in the tenant file third party verification of the following factors, or must document in the tenant file why third party verification was not available:

(i) Reported family annual income;

(ii) The value of assets;

(iii) Expenses related to deductions from annual income; and

(iv) Other factors that affect the determination of adjusted income.

(b) When PHA conducts interim reexamination. (1) At any time, the PHA may conduct an interim reexamination of family income and composition.

(2) At any time, the family may request an interim determination of family income or composition because of any changes since the last determination. The PHA must make the interim determination within a reasonable time after the family request.

(3) Interim examinations must be conducted in accordance with policies in the PHA administrative plan.

(c) Family reporting of change. The PHA must adopt policies prescribing when and under what conditions the family must report a change in family income or composition.

(d) Effective date of reexamination. (1) The PHA must adopt policies prescribing how to determine the effective date of a change in the housing assistance payment resulting from an interim redetermination.

(2) At the effective date of a regular or interim reexamination, the PHA must make appropriate adjustments in the housing assistance payment. (For a voucher tenancy, the housing assistance payment shall be calculated in accordance with Sec. 982.505. For a certificate tenancy, the housing assistance payment shall be calculated in accordance with Sec. 982.518.)

(e) Family member income. Family income must include income of all family members, including family members not related by blood or marriage. If any new family member is added, family income must include any income of the additional family member. The PHA must conduct a reexamination to determine such additional income, and must make appropriate adjustments in the housing assistance payment.

(f) Accuracy of family income data. The PHA must establish procedures that are appropriate and necessary to assure that income data provided by applicant or participant families is complete and accurate.

(g) Execution of release and consent. (1) As a condition of admission to or continued assistance under the program, the PHA shall require the family head, and such other family members as the PHA designates, to execute a HUD-approved release and consent form (including any release and consent as required under Sec. 5.230 of this title) authorizing any depository or private source of income, or any Federal, State or local agency, to furnish or release to the PHA or HUD such information as the PHA or HUD determines to be necessary.

(2) The PHA and HUD must limit the use or disclosure of information obtained from a family or from another source pursuant to this release and consent to purposes directly in connection with administration of the program.

(Information collection requirements contained in this section have been approved by the Office of Management and Budget under control number 2577-0169.)

{63 FR 23861, Apr. 30, 1998, as amended at 64 FR 13057, Mar. 16, 1999; 64 FR 26649, May 14, 1999; 64 FR 56915, Oct. 21, 1999; 65 FR 16822, Mar. 30, 2000}

Editorial Note: At 64 FR 26649, May 14, 1999, Sec. 982.516 was amended in paragraph (e) by removing the reference to ``and family unit size''; however paragraph (e) does not contain this phrase.

Sec. 982.517 Utility allowance schedule.

(a) Maintaining schedule. (1) The PHA must maintain a utility allowance schedule for all tenant-paid utilities (except telephone), for cost of tenant-supplied

refrigerators and ranges, and for other tenant-paid housing services (e.g., trash collection (disposal of waste and refuse)).

(2) The PHA must give HUD a copy of the utility allowance schedule. At HUD's request, the PHA also must provide any information or procedures used in preparation of the schedule.

(b) How allowances are determined. (1) The utility allowance schedule must be determined based on the typical cost of utilities and services paid by energy-conservative households that occupy housing of similar size and type in the same locality. In developing the schedule, the PHA must use normal patterns of consumption for the community as a whole and current utility rates.

(2)(i) a PHA's utility allowance schedule, and the utility allowance for an individual family, must include the utilities and services that are necessary in the locality to provide housing that complies with the housing quality standards. However, the PHA may not provide any allowance for non-essential utility costs, such as costs of cable or satellite television.

(ii) In the utility allowance schedule, the PHA must classify utilities and other housing services according to the following general categories: space heating; air conditioning; cooking; water heating; water; sewer; trash collection (disposal of waste and refuse); other electric; refrigerator (cost of tenant-supplied refrigerator); range (cost of tenant-supplied range); and other specified housing services. The PHA must provide a utility allowance for tenant-paid air-conditioning costs if the majority of housing units in the market provide centrally air-conditioned units or there is appropriate wiring for tenant-installed air conditioners.

(3) The cost of each utility and housing service category must be stated separately. For each of these categories, the utility allowance schedule must take into consideration unit size (by number of bedrooms), and unit types (e.g., apartment, row-house, town house, single-family detached, and manufactured housing) that are typical in the community.

(4) The utility allowance schedule must be prepared and submitted in accordance with HUD requirements on the form prescribed by HUD.

(c) Revisions of utility allowance schedule. (1) a PHA must review its schedule of utility allowances each year, and must revise its allowance for a utility category if there PHAs been a change of 10 percent or more in the utility rate since the last time the utility allowance schedule was revised. The PHA must maintain information supporting its annual review of utility allowances and any revisions made in its utility allowance schedule.

(2) At HUD's direction, the PHA must revise the utility allowance schedule to correct any errors, or as necessary to update the schedule.

(d) Use of utility allowance schedule. (1) The PHA must use the appropriate utility allowance for the size of dwelling unit actually leased by the family (rather than the family unit size as determined under the PHA subsidy standards).

(2) At reexamination, the PHA must use the PHA current utility allowance schedule.

(e) Higher utility allowance as reasonable accommodation for a person with disabilities. On request from a family that includes a person with disabilities, the PHA must approve a utility allowance which is higher than the applicable amount on the utility allowance schedule if a higher utility allowance is needed as a reasonable accommodation in accordance with 24 CFR part 8 to make the program accessible to and usable by the family member with a disability.

(Information collection requirements contained in this section have been approved by the Office of Management and Budget under control number 2577-0169.)

Sec. 982.518 Regular tenancy: How to calculate housing assistance payment.

The monthly housing assistance payment equals the gross rent, minus the higher of:

(a) The total tenant payment; or

(b) The minimum rent as required by law.

{63 FR 23861, Apr. 30, 1998. Redesignated at 64 FR 26648, May 14, 1999}

Sec. 982.519 Regular tenancy: Annual adjustment of rent to owner.

(a) When rent is adjusted. At each annual anniversary date of the HAP contract, the PHA must adjust the rent to owner at the request of the owner in accordance with this section.

(b) Amount of annual adjustment. (1) The adjusted rent to owner equals the lesser of:

(i) The pre-adjustment rent to owner multiplied by the applicable Section 8 annual adjustment factor, published by HUD in the Federal Register, that is in effect 60 days before the HAP contract anniversary;

(ii) The reasonable rent (as most recently determined or redetermined by the PHA in accordance with Sec. 982.503); or

(iii) The amount requested by the owner.

(2) In making the annual adjustment, the pre-adjustment rent to owner does not include any previously approved special adjustments.

(3) The rent to owner may be adjusted up or down in accordance with this section.

(4) Notwithstanding paragraph (b)(1) of this section, the rent to owner for a unit must not be increased at the annual anniversary date unless:

(i) The owner requests the adjustment by giving notice to the PHA; and

(ii) During the year before the annual anniversary date, the owner has complied with all requirements of the HAP contract, including compliance with the HQS.

(5) The rent to owner will only be increased for housing assistance payments covering months commencing on the later of:

(i) The first day of the first month commencing on or after the contract anniversary date; or

(ii) At least sixty days after the PHA receives the owner's request.

(6) To receive an increase resulting from the annual adjustment for an annual anniversary date, the owner must request the increase at least sixty days before the next annual anniversary date.

{63 FR 23861, Apr. 30, 1998, as amended at 64 FR 13057, Mar. 16, 1999. Redesignated at 64 FR 26648, May 14, 1999}

Sec. 982.520 Regular tenancy: Special adjustment of rent to owner.

(a) Substantial and general cost increases. (1) At HUD's sole discretion, HUD may approve a special adjustment of the rent to owner to reflect increases in the actual and necessary costs of owning and maintaining the unit because of substantial and general increases in:

(i) Real property taxes;

(ii) Special governmental assessments;

(iii) Utility rates; or

(iv) Costs of utilities not covered by regulated rates.

(2) An PHA may make a special adjustment of the rent to owner only if the adjustment has been approved by HUD. The owner does not have any right to receive a special adjustment.

(b) Reasonable rent. The adjusted rent may not exceed the reasonable rent. The owner may not receive a special adjustment if the adjusted rent would exceed the reasonable rent.

(c) Term of special adjustment. (1) The PHA may withdraw or limit the term of any special adjustment.

(2) If a special adjustment is approved to cover temporary or one-time costs, the special adjustment is only a temporary or one-time increase of the rent to owner.

{63 FR 23861, Apr. 30, 1998. Redesignated at 64 FR 26648, May 14, 1999}

Sec. 982.521 Rent to owner in subsidized project.

(a) Applicability to subsidized project. This section applies to a program tenancy in any of the following types of federally subsidized project:

(1) An insured or non-insured Section 236 project;

(2) A Section 202 project;

(3) A Section 221(d)(3) below market interest rate (BMIR) project; or

(4) A Section 515 project of the Rural Development Administration.

(b) How rent to owner is determined. The rent to owner is the subsidized rent as determined in accordance with requirements for the applicable federal program listed in paragraph (a) of this section. This determination is not subject to the prohibition against increasing the rent to owner during the initial lease term (see Sec. 982.309).

(c) Certificate tenancy--Rent adjustment. Rent to owner for a certificate tenancy is not subject to provisions governing annual adjustment (Sec. 982.519) or special adjustment (Sec. 982.520) of rent to owner.

{65 FR 16822, Mar. 30, 2000}

Subpart L--Family Obligations; Denial and Termination of Assistance

Source: 60 FR 34695, July 3, 1995, unless otherwise noted.

Sec. 982.551 Obligations of participant.

(a) Purpose. This section states the obligations of a participant family under the program.

(b) Supplying required information--(1) The family must supply any information that the PHA or HUD determines is necessary in the administration of the program, including submission of required evidence of citizenship or eligible immigration status (as provided by 24 CFR part 5). ``Information'' includes any requested certification, release or other documentation.

(2) The family must supply any information requested by the PHA or HUD for use in a regularly scheduled reexamination or interim reexamination of family income and composition in accordance with HUD requirements.

(3) The family must disclose and verify social security numbers (as provided by part 5, subpart B, of this title) and must sign and submit consent forms for obtaining information in accordance with part 5, subpart B, of this title.

(4) Any information supplied by the family must be true and complete.

(c) HQS breach caused by family. The family is responsible for an HQS breach caused by the family as described in Sec. 982.404(b).

(d) Allowing PHA inspection. The family must allow the PHA to inspect the unit at reasonable times and after reasonable notice.

(e) Violation of lease. The family may not commit any serious or repeated violation of the lease.

(f) Family notice of move or lease termination. The family must notify the PHA and the owner before the family moves out of the unit, or terminates the lease on notice to the owner. See Sec. 982.314(d).

(g) Owner eviction notice. The family must promptly give the PHA a copy of any owner eviction notice.

(h) Use and occupancy of unit.--(1) The family must use the assisted unit for residence by the family. The unit must be the family's only residence.

(2) The composition of the assisted family residing in the unit must be approved by the PHA. The family must promptly inform the PHA of the birth, adoption or court-awarded custody of a child. The family must request PHA approval to add any other family member as an occupant of the unit. No other person (i.e., nobody but members of the assisted family) may reside in the unit

(except for a foster child or live-in aide as provided in paragraph (h)(4) of this section).

(3) The family must promptly notify the PHA if any family member no longer resides in the unit.

(4) If the PHA has given approval, a foster child or a live-in-aide may reside in the unit. The PHA has the discretion to adopt reasonable policies concerning residence by a foster child or a live-in-aide, and defining when PHA consent may be given or denied.

(5) Members of the household may engage in legal profitmaking activities in the unit, but only if such activities are incidental to primary use of the unit for residence by members of the family.

(6) The family must not sublease or let the unit.

(7) The family must not assign the lease or transfer the unit.

(i) Absence from unit. The family must supply any information or certification requested by the PHA to verify that the family is living in the unit, or relating to family absence from the unit, including any PHA-requested information or certification on the purposes of family absences. The family must cooperate with the PHA for this purpose. The family must promptly notify the PHA of absence from the unit.

(j) Interest in unit. The family must not own or have any interest in the unit.

(k) Fraud and other program violation. The members of the family must not commit fraud, bribery or any other corrupt or criminal act in connection with the programs.

(l) Crime by household members. The members of the household may not engage in drug-related criminal activity or violent criminal activity or other criminal activity that threatens the health, safety or right to peaceful enjoyment of other residents and persons residing in the immediate vicinity of the premises (see Sec. 982.553).

(m) Alcohol abuse by household members. The members of the household must not abuse alcohol in a way that threatens the health, safety or right to peaceful enjoyment of other residents and persons residing in the immediate vicinity of the premises.

(n) Other housing assistance. An assisted family, or members of the family, may not receive Section 8 tenant-based assistance while receiving another housing subsidy, for the same unit or for a different unit, under any duplicative (as determined by HUD or in accordance with HUD requirements) federal, State or local housing assistance program.

(Approved by the Office of Management and Budget under control number 2577-0169)

{60 FR 34695, July 3, 1995, as amended at 60 FR 45661, Sept. 1, 1995; 61 FR 11119, Mar. 18, 1996; 61 FR 13627, Mar. 27, 1996; 61 FR 27163, May 30, 1996; 64 FR 26650, May 14, 1999; 66 FR 28805, May 24, 2001}

Sec. 982.552 PHA denial or termination of assistance for family.

(a) Action or inaction by family. (1) a PHA may deny assistance for an applicant or terminate assistance for a participant under the programs because of the family's action or failure to act as described in this section or Sec. 982.553. The provisions of this section do not affect denial or termination of assistance for grounds other than action or failure to act by the family.

(2) Denial of assistance for an applicant may include any or all of the following: denying listing on the PHA waiting list, denying or withdrawing a voucher, refusing to enter into a HAP contract or approve a lease, and refusing to process or provide assistance under portability procedures.

(3) Termination of assistance for a participant may include any or all of the following: refusing to enter into a HAP contract or approve a lease, terminating housing assistance payments under an outstanding HAP contract, and refusing to process or provide assistance under portability procedures.

(4) This section does not limit or affect exercise of the PHA rights and remedies against the owner under the HAP contract, including termination, suspension or

reduction of housing assistance payments, or termination of the HAP contract.

(b) Requirement to deny admission or terminate assistance. (1) For provisions on denial of admission and termination of assistance for illegal drug use, other criminal activity, and alcohol abuse that would threaten other residents, see Sec. 982.553.

(2) The PHA must terminate program assistance for a family evicted from housing assisted under the program for serious violation of the lease.

(3) The PHA must deny admission to the program for an applicant, or terminate program assistance for a participant, if any member of the family fails to sign and submit consent forms for obtaining information in accordance with part 5, subparts B and F of this title.

(4) The family must submit required evidence of citizenship or eligible immigration status. See part 5 of this title for a statement of circumstances in which the PHA must deny admission or terminate program assistance because a family member does not establish citizenship or eligible immigration status, and the applicable informal hearing procedures.

(c) Authority to deny admission or terminate assistance. (1) Grounds for denial or termination of assistance. The PHA may at any time deny program assistance for an applicant, or terminate program assistance for a participant, for any of the following grounds:

(i) If the family violates any family obligations under the program (see Sec. 982.551). See Sec. 982.553 concerning denial or termination of assistance for crime by family members.

(ii) If any member of the family has been evicted from federally assisted housing in the last five years;

(iii) If a PHA has ever terminated assistance under the program for any member of the family.

(iv) If any member of the family has committed fraud, bribery, or any other corrupt or criminal act in connection with any Federal housing program (see also Sec. 982.553(a)(1));

(v) If the family currently owes rent or other amounts to the PHA or to another PHA in connection with Section 8 or public housing assistance under the 1937 Act.

(vi) If the family has not reimbursed any PHA for amounts paid to an owner under a HAP contract for rent, damages to the unit, or other amounts owed by the family under the lease.

(vii) If the family breaches an agreement with the PHA to pay amounts owed to a PHA, or amounts paid to an owner by a PHA. (The PHA, at its discretion, may offer a family the opportunity to enter an agreement to pay amounts owed to a PHA or amounts paid to an owner by a PHA. The PHA may prescribe the terms of the agreement.)

(viii) If a family participating in the FSS program fails to comply, without good cause, with the family's FSS contract of participation.

(ix) If the family has engaged in or threatened abusive or violent behavior toward PHA personnel.

(x) If a welfare-to-work (WTW) family fails, willfully and persistently, to fulfill its obligations under the welfare-to-work voucher program.

(xi) If the family has been engaged in criminal activity or alcohol abuse as described in Sec. 982.553.

(2) Consideration of circumstances. In determining whether to deny or terminate assistance because of action or failure to act by members of the family:

(i) The PHA may consider all relevant circumstances such as the seriousness of the case, the extent of participation or culpability of individual family members, mitigating circumstances related to the disability of a family member, and the effects of denial or termination of assistance on other family members who were not involved in the action or failure.

(ii) The PHA may impose, as a condition of continued assistance for other family members, a requirement that other family

members who participated in or were culpable for the action or failure will not reside in the unit. The PHA may permit the other members of a participant family to continue receiving assistance.

(iii) In determining whether to deny admission or terminate assistance for illegal use of drugs or alcohol abuse by a household member who is no longer engaged in such behavior, the PHA consider whether such household member is participating in or has successfully completed a supervised drug or alcohol rehabilitation program, or has otherwise been rehabilitated successfully (42 U.S.C. 13661). For this purpose, the PHA may require the applicant or tenant to submit evidence of the household member's current participation in, or successful completion of, a supervised drug or alcohol rehabilitation program or evidence of otherwise having been rehabilitated successfully.

(iv) If the family includes a person with disabilities, the PHA decision concerning such action is subject to consideration of reasonable accommodation in accordance with part 8 of this title.

(v) Nondiscrimination limitation. The PHA's admission and eviction actions must be consistent with fair housing and equal opportunity provisions of Sec. 5.105 of this title.

(d) Information for family. The PHA must give the family a written description of:

(1) Family obligations under the program.

(2) The grounds on which the PHA may deny or terminate assistance because of family action or failure to act.

(3) The PHA informal hearing procedures.

(e) Applicant screening. The PHA may at any time deny program assistance for an applicant in accordance with the PHA policy, as stated in the PHA administrative plan, on screening of applicants for family behavior or suitability for tenancy.

(Approved by the Office of Management and Budget under control number 2577-0169) {60 FR 34695, July 3, 1995, as amended at 60 FR 45661, Sept. 1, 1995; 61 FR 13627, Mar. 27, 1996; 63 FR 23865, Apr. 30, 1998; 64 FR 26650, May 14, 1999; 64 FR 49659, Sept. 14, 1999; 64 FR 56915, Oct. 21, 1999; 65 FR 16823, Mar. 30, 2000; 66 FR 28805, May 24, 2001}

Sec. 982.553 Denial of admission and termination of assistance for criminals and alcohol abusers.

(a) Denial of admission. (1) Prohibiting admission of drug criminals.

(i) The PHA must prohibit admission to the program of an applicant for three years from the date of eviction if a household member has been evicted from federally assisted housing for drug-related criminal activity. However, the PHA may admit the household if the PHA determines:

(A) That the evicted household member who engaged in drug-related criminal activity has successfully completed a supervised drug rehabilitation program approved by the PHA; or

(B) That the circumstances leading to eviction no longer exist (for example, the criminal household member has died or is imprisoned).

(ii) The PHA must establish standards that prohibit admission if:

(A) The PHA determines that any household member is currently engaging in illegal use of a drug;

(B) The PHA determines that it has reasonable cause to believe that a household member's illegal drug use or a pattern of illegal drug use may threaten the health, safety, or right to peaceful enjoyment of the premises by other residents; or

(C) Any household member has ever been convicted of drug-related criminal activity for manufacture or production of methamphetamine on the premises of federally assisted housing.

(2) Prohibiting admission of other criminals--(i) Mandatory prohibition. The PHA must establish standards that prohibit admission to the program if any member of the household is subject to a lifetime registration requirement under a

State sex offender registration program. In this screening of applicants, the PHA must perform criminal history background checks necessary to determine whether any household member is subject to a lifetime sex offender registration requirement in the State where the housing is located and in other States where the household members are known to have resided.

(ii) Permissive prohibitions. (A) The PHA may prohibit admission of a household to the program if the PHA determines that any household member is currently engaged in, or has engaged in during a reasonable time before the admission:

(1) Drug-related criminal activity;

(2) Violent criminal activity;

(3) Other criminal activity which may threaten the health, safety, or right to peaceful enjoyment of the premises by other residents or persons residing in the immediate vicinity; or

(4) Other criminal activity which may threaten the health or safety of the owner, property management staff, or persons performing a contract administration function or responsibility on behalf of the PHA (including a PHA employee or a PHA contractor, subcontractor or agent).

(B) The PHA may establish a period before the admission decision during which an applicant must not to have engaged in the activities specified in paragraph (a)(2)(i) of this section (``reasonable time'').

(C) If the PHA previously denied admission to an applicant because a member of the household engaged in criminal activity, the PHA may reconsider the applicant if the PHA has sufficient evidence that the members of the household are not currently engaged in, and have not engaged in, such criminal activity during a reasonable period, as determined by the PHA, before the admission decision.

(1) The PHA would have ``sufficient evidence'' if the household member submitted a certification that she or he is not currently engaged in and has not engaged in such criminal activity during the specified period and provided supporting information from such sources as a probation officer, a landlord, neighbors, social service agency workers and criminal records, which the PHA verified.

(2) For purposes of this section, a household member is ``currently engaged in'' criminal activity if the person has engaged in the behavior recently enough to justify a reasonable belief that the behavior is current.

(3) Prohibiting admission of alcohol abusers. The PHA must establish standards that prohibit admission to the program if the PHA determines that it has reasonable cause to believe that a household member's abuse or pattern of abuse of alcohol may threaten the health, safety, or right to peaceful enjoyment of the premises by other residents.

(b) Terminating assistance--(1) Terminating assistance for drug criminals. (i) The PHA must establish standards that allow the PHA to terminate assistance for a family under the program if the PHA determines that:

(A) Any household member is currently engaged in any illegal use of a drug; or

(B) A pattern of illegal use of a drug by any household member interferes with the health, safety, or right to peaceful enjoyment of the premises by other residents.

(ii) The PHA must immediately terminate assistance for a family under the program if the PHA determines that any member of the household has ever been convicted of drug-related criminal activity for manufacture or production of methamphetamine on the premises of federally assisted housing.

(iii) The PHA must establish standards that allow the PHA to terminate assistance under the program for a family if the PHA determines that any family member has violated the family's obligation under Sec. 982.551 not to engage in any drug-related criminal activity.

(2) Terminating assistance for other criminals. The PHA must establish standards that allow the PHA to terminate assistance under the program for a family if the PHA determines that any household member has violated the family's obligation under Sec.

982.551 not to engage in violent criminal activity.

(3) Terminating assistance for alcohol abusers. The PHA must establish standards that allow termination of assistance for a family if the PHA determines that a household member's abuse or pattern of abuse of alcohol may threaten the health, safety, or right to peaceful enjoyment of the premises by other residents.

(c) Evidence of criminal activity. The PHA may terminate assistance for criminal activity by a household member as authorized in this section if the PHA determines, based on a preponderance of the evidence, that the household member has engaged in the activity, regardless of whether the household member has been arrested or convicted for such activity.

(d) Use of criminal record.--(1) Denial. If a PHA proposes to deny admission for criminal activity as shown by a criminal record, the PHA must provide the subject of the record and the applicant with a copy of the criminal record. The PHA must give the family an opportunity to dispute the accuracy and relevance of that record, in the informal review process in accordance with Sec. 982.554. (See part 5, subpart J for provision concerning access to criminal records.)

(2) Termination of assistance. If a PHA proposes to terminate assistance for criminal activity as shown by a criminal record, the PHA must notify the household of the proposed action to be based on the information and must provide the subject of the record and the tenant with a copy of the criminal record. The PHA must give the family an opportunity to dispute the accuracy and relevance of that record in accordance with Sec. 982.555.

(3) Cost of obtaining criminal record. The PHA may not pass along to the tenant the costs of a criminal records check.

{66 FR 28805, May 24, 2001}

Sec. 982.554 Informal review for applicant.

(a) Notice to applicant. The PHA must give an applicant for participation prompt notice of a decision denying assistance to the applicant. The notice must contain a brief statement of the reasons for the PHA decision. The notice must also state that the applicant may request an informal review of the decision and must describe how to obtain the informal review.

(b) Informal review process. The PHA must give an applicant an opportunity for an informal review of the PHA decision denying assistance to the applicant. The administrative plan must state the PHA procedures for conducting an informal review. The PHA review procedures must comply with the following:

(1) The review may be conducted by any person or persons designated by the PHA, other than a person who made or approved the decision under review or a subordinate of this person.

(2) The applicant must be given an opportunity to present written or oral objections to the PHA decision.

(3) The PHA must notify the applicant of the PHA final decision after the informal review, including a brief statement of the reasons for the final decision.

(c) When informal review is not required. The PHA is not required to provide the applicant an opportunity for an informal review for any of the following:

(1) Discretionary administrative determinations by the PHA.

(2) General policy issues or class grievances.

(3) A determination of the family unit size under the PHA subsidy standards.

(4) An PHA determination not to approve an extension or suspension of a voucher term.

(5) A PHA determination not to grant approval of the tenancy.

(6) An PHA determination that a unit selected by the applicant is not in compliance with HQS.

(7) An PHA determination that the unit is not in accordance with HQS because of the family size or composition.

(d) Restrictions on assistance for noncitizens. The informal hearing provisions for the denial of assistance on the basis of ineligible immigration status are contained in 24 CFR part 5.

(Approved by the Office of Management and Budget under control number 2577-0169) {60 FR 34695, July 3, 1995, as amended at 60 FR 45661, Sept. 1, 1995; 61 FR 13627, Mar. 27, 1996; 64 FR 26650, May 14, 1999}

Sec. 982.555 Informal hearing for participant.

(a) When hearing is required.--(1) a PHA must give a participant family an opportunity for an informal hearing to consider whether the following PHA decisions relating to the individual circumstances of a participant family are in accordance with the law, HUD regulations and PHA policies:

(i) A determination of the family's annual or adjusted income, and the use of such income to compute the housing assistance payment.

(ii) A determination of the appropriate utility allowance (if any) for tenant-paid utilities from the PHA utility allowance schedule.

(iii) A determination of the family unit size under the PHA subsidy standards.

(iv) A determination that a certificate program family is residing in a unit with a larger number of bedrooms than appropriate for the family unit size under the PHA subsidy standards, or the PHA determination to deny the family's request for an exception from the standards.

(v) A determination to terminate assistance for a participant family because of the family's action or failure to act (see Sec. 982.552).

(vi) A determination to terminate assistance because the participant family has been absent from the assisted unit for longer than the maximum period permitted under PHA policy and HUD rules.

(2) In the cases described in paragraphs (a)(1) (iv), (v) and (vi) of this section, the PHA must give the opportunity for an informal hearing before the PHA terminates housing assistance payments for the family under an outstanding HAP contract.

(b) When hearing is not required. The PHA is not required to provide a participant family an opportunity for an informal hearing for any of the following:

(1) Discretionary administrative determinations by the PHA.

(2) General policy issues or class grievances.

(3) Establishment of the PHA schedule of utility allowances for families in the program.

(4) a PHA determination not to approve an extension or suspension of a voucher term.

(5) a PHA determination not to approve a unit or tenancy.

(6) a PHA determination that an assisted unit is not in compliance with HQS. (However, the PHA must provide the opportunity for an informal hearing for a decision to terminate assistance for a breach of the HQS caused by the family as described in Sec. 982.551(c).)

(7) a PHA determination that the unit is not in accordance with HQS because of the family size.

(8) A determination by the PHA to exercise or not to exercise any right or remedy against the owner under a HAP contract.

(c) Notice to family. (1) In the cases described in paragraphs (a)(1) (i), (ii) and (iii) of this section, the PHA must notify the family that the family may ask for an explanation of the basis of the PHA determination, and that if the family does not agree with the determination, the family may request an informal hearing on the decision.

(2) In the cases described in paragraphs (a)(1) (iv), (v) and (vi) of this section, the PHA must give the family prompt written notice that the family may request a hearing. The notice must:

(i) Contain a brief statement of reasons for the decision,

(ii) State that if the family does not agree with the decision, the family may request an informal hearing on the decision, and

(iii) State the deadline for the family to request an informal hearing.

(d) Expeditious hearing process. Where a hearing for a participant family is required under this section, the PHA must proceed with the hearing in a reasonably expeditious manner upon the request of the family.

(e) Hearing procedures--(1) Administrative plan. The administrative plan must state the PHA procedures for conducting informal hearings for participants.

(2) Discovery--(i) By family. The family must be given the opportunity to examine before the PHA hearing any PHA documents that are directly relevant to the hearing. The family must be allowed to copy any such document at the family's expense. If the PHA does not make the document available for examination on request of the family, the PHA may not rely on the document at the hearing.

(ii) By PHA. The PHA hearing procedures may provide that the PHA must be given the opportunity to examine at PHA offices before the PHA hearing any family documents that are directly relevant to the hearing. The PHA must be allowed to copy any such document at the PHA's expense. If the family does not make the document available for examination on request of the PHA, the family may not rely on the document at the hearing.

(iii) Documents. The term ``documents'' includes records and regulations.

(3) Representation of family. At its own expense, the family may be represented by a lawyer or other representative.

(4) Hearing officer: Appointment and authority. (i) The hearing may be conducted by any person or persons designated by the PHA, other than a person who made or approved the decision under review or a subordinate of this person.

(ii) The person who conducts the hearing may regulate the conduct of the hearing in accordance with the PHA hearing procedures.

(5) Evidence. The PHA and the family must be given the opportunity to present evidence, and may question any witnesses. Evidence may be considered without regard to admissibility under the rules of evidence applicable to judicial proceedings.

(6) Issuance of decision. The person who conducts the hearing must issue a written decision, stating briefly the reasons for the decision. Factual determinations relating to the individual circumstances of the family shall be based on a preponderance of the evidence presented at the hearing. A copy of the hearing decision shall be furnished promptly to the family.

(f) Effect of decision. The PHA is not bound by a hearing decision:

(1) Concerning a matter for which the PHA is not required to provide an opportunity for an informal hearing under this section, or that otherwise exceeds the authority of the person conducting the hearing under the PHA hearing procedures.

(2) Contrary to HUD regulations or requirements, or otherwise contrary to federal, State, or local law.

(3) If the PHA determines that it is not bound by a hearing decision, the PHA must promptly notify the family of the determination, and of the reasons for the determination.

(g) Restrictions on assistance to noncitizens. The informal hearing provisions for the denial of assistance on the basis of ineligible immigration status are contained in 24 CFR part 5.

(Approved by the Office of Management and Budget under control number 2577-0169)
{60 FR 34695, July 3, 1995, as amended at 60 FR 45661, Sept. 1, 1995; 61 FR 13627, Mar. 27, 1996; 64 FR 26650, May 14, 1999; 65 FR 16823, Mar. 30, 2000}

Subpart M--Special Housing Types

Source: 63 FR 23865, Apr. 30, 1998, unless otherwise noted.

Sec. 982.601 Overview.

(a) Special housing types. This subpart describes program requirements for special housing types. The following are the special housing types:

(1) Single room occupancy (SRO) housing;

(2) Congregate housing;

(3) Group home;

(4) Shared housing;

(5) Manufactured home;

(6) Cooperative housing (excluding families that are not cooperative members); and

(7) Homeownership option.

(b) PHA choice to offer special housing type. (1) The PHA may permit a family to use any of the following special housing types in accordance with requirements of the program: single room occupancy (SRO) housing, congregate housing, group home, shared housing, manufactured home when the family owns the home and leases the manufactured home space, cooperative housing or homeownership option.

(2) In general, the PHA is not required to permit families (including families that move into the PHA program under portability procedures) to use any of these special housing types, and may limit the number of families using special housing types.

(3) The PHA must permit use of any special housing type if needed as a reasonable accommodation so that the program is readily accessible to and usable by persons with disabilities in accordance with 24 CFR part 8.

(4) For occupancy of a manufactured home, see Sec. 982.620(a).

(c) Program funding for special housing types. (1) HUD does not provide any additional or designated funding for special housing types, or for a specific special housing type (e.g, the homeownership option). Assistance for special housing types is paid from program funding available for the PHA's tenant-based program under the consolidated annual contributions contract.

(2) The PHA may not set aside program funding or program slots for special housing types or for a specific special housing type.

(d) Family choice of housing and housing type. The family chooses whether to use housing that qualifies as a special housing type under this subpart, or as any specific special housing type, or to use other eligible housing in accordance with requirements of the program. The PHA may not restrict the family's freedom to choose among available units in accordance with Sec. 982.353.

(e) Applicability of requirements. (1) Except as modified by this subpart, the requirements of other subparts of this part apply to the special housing types.

(2) Provisions in this subpart only apply to a specific special housing type. The housing type is noted in the title of each section.

(3) Housing must meet the requirements of this subpart for a single special housing type specified by the family. Such housing is not subject to requirements for other special housing types. A single unit cannot be designated as more than one special housing type.

{63 FR 23865, Apr. 30, 1998, as amended at 65 FR 55162, Sept. 12, 2000; 67 FR 64493, Oct. 18, 2002}

Single Room Occupancy (SRO)

Sec. 982.602 SRO: Who may reside in an SRO?

A single person may reside in an SRO housing unit.

{64 FR 26650, May 14, 1999}

Sec. 982.603 SRO: Lease and HAP contract.

For SRO housing, there is a separate lease and HAP contract for each assisted person.

Sec. 982.604 SRO: Voucher housing assistance payment.

(a) For a person residing in SRO housing, the payment standard is 75 percent of the zero-bedroom payment standard amount on the PHA payment standard schedule. For a person residing in SRO housing in an exception area, the payment standard is 75 percent of the HUD-approved zero-bedroom exception payment standard amount.

(b) The utility allowance for an assisted person residing in SRO housing is 75 percent of the zero bedroom utility allowance.

{64 FR 26650, May 14, 1999}

Sec. 982.605 SRO: Housing quality standards.

(a) HQS standards for SRO. The HQS in Sec. 982.401 apply to SRO housing. However, the standards in this section apply in place of Sec. 982.401(b) (sanitary facilities), Sec. 982.401(c) (food preparation and refuse disposal), and Sec. 982.401(d) (space and security). Since the SRO units will not house children, the housing quality standards in Sec. 982.401(j), concerning lead-based paint, do not apply to SRO housing.

(b) Performance requirements. (1) SRO housing is subject to the additional performance requirements in this paragraph (b).

(2) Sanitary facilities, and space and security characteristics must meet local code standards for SRO housing. In the absence of applicable local code standards for SRO housing, the following standards apply:

(i) Sanitary facilities. (A) At least one flush toilet that can be used in privacy, lavatory basin, and bathtub or shower, in proper operating condition, must be supplied for each six persons or fewer residing in the SRO housing.

(B) If SRO units are leased only to males, flush urinals may be substituted for not more than one-half the required number of flush toilets. However, there must be at least one flush toilet in the building.

(C) Every lavatory basin and bathtub or shower must be supplied at all times with an adequate quantity of hot and cold running water.

(D) All of these facilities must be in proper operating condition, and must be adequate for personal cleanliness and the disposal of human waste. The facilities must utilize an approvable public or private disposal system.

(E) Sanitary facilities must be reasonably accessible from a common hall or passageway to all persons sharing them. These facilities may not be located more than one floor above or below the SRO unit. Sanitary facilities may not be located below grade unless the SRO units are located on that level.

(ii) Space and security. (A) No more than one person may reside in an SRO unit.

(B) An SRO unit must contain at least one hundred ten square feet of floor space.

(C) An SRO unit must contain at least four square feet of closet space for each resident (with an unobstructed height of at least five feet). If there is less closet space, space equal to the amount of the deficiency must be subtracted from the area of the habitable room space when determining the amount of floor space in the SRO unit. The SRO unit must contain at least one hundred ten square feet of remaining floor space after subtracting the amount of the deficiency in minimum closet space.

(D) Exterior doors and windows accessible from outside an SRO unit must be lockable.

(3) Access. (i) Access doors to an SRO unit must have locks for privacy in proper operating condition.

(ii) An SRO unit must have immediate access to two or more approved means of exit, appropriately marked, leading to safe and open space at ground level, and any means of exit required by State and local law.

(iii) The resident must be able to access an SRO unit without passing through any other unit.

(4) Sprinkler system. A sprinkler system that protects all major spaces, hard wired smoke detectors, and such other fire and safety improvements as State or local law may require must be installed in each building. The term ``major spaces'' means hallways, large common areas, and other areas specified in local fire, building, or safety codes.

Congregate Housing

Sec. 982.606 Congregate housing: Who may reside in congregate housing.

(a) An elderly person or a person with disabilities may reside in a congregate housing unit.

(b)(1) If approved by the PHA, a family member or live-in aide may reside with the elderly person or person with disabilities.

(2) The PHA must approve a live-in aide if needed as a reasonable accommodation so that the program is readily accessible to and usable by persons with disabilities in accordance with 24 CFR part 8. See Sec. 982.316 concerning occupancy by a live-in aide.

Sec. 982.607 Congregate housing: Lease and HAP contract.

For congregate housing, there is a separate lease and HAP contract for each assisted family.

Sec. 982.608 Congregate housing: Voucher housing assistance payment.

(a) Unless there is a live-in aide:

(1) For a family residing in congregate housing, the payment standard is the zero-bedroom payment standard amount on the PHA payment standard schedule. For a family residing in congregate housing in an exception area, the payment standard is the HUD-approved zero-bedroom exception payment standard amount.

(2) However, if there are two or more rooms in the unit (not including kitchen or sanitary facilities), the payment standard for a family residing in congregate housing is the one-bedroom payment standard amount.

(b) If there is a live-in aide, the live-in aide must be counted in determining the family unit size.

{63 FR 23865, Apr. 30, 1998, as amended at 64 FR 26650, May 14, 1999}

Sec. 982.609 Congregate housing: Housing quality standards.

(a) HQS standards for congregate housing. The HQS in Sec. 982.401 apply to congregate housing. However, the standards in this section apply in place of Sec. 982.401(c) (food preparation and refuse disposal). Congregate housing is not subject to the HQS acceptability requirement in Sec. 982.401(d)(2)(i) that the dwelling unit must have a kitchen area.

(b) Food preparation and refuse disposal: Additional performance requirements. The following additional performance requirements apply to congregate housing:

(1) The unit must contain a refrigerator of appropriate size.

(2) There must be central kitchen and dining facilities on the premises. These facilities:

(i) Must be located within the premises, and accessible to the residents;

(ii) Must contain suitable space and equipment to store, prepare, and serve food in a sanitary manner;

(iii) Must be used to provide a food service that is provided for the residents, and that is not provided by the residents; and

(iv) Must be for the primary use of residents of the congregate units and be sufficient in size to accommodate the residents.

(3) There must be adequate facilities and services for the sanitary disposal of food

waste and refuse, including facilities for temporary storage where necessary.

Group Home

Sec. 982.610 Group home: Who may reside in a group home.

(a) An elderly person or a person with disabilities may reside in a State-approved group home.

(b)(1) If approved by the PHA, a live-in aide may reside with a person with disabilities.

(2) The PHA must approve a live-in aide if needed as a reasonable accommodation so that the program is readily accessible to and usable by persons with disabilities in accordance with 24 CFR part 8. See Sec. 982.316 concerning occupancy by a live-in aide.

(c) Except for a live-in aide, all residents of a group home, whether assisted or unassisted, must be elderly persons or persons with disabilities.

(d) Persons residing in a group home must not require continual medical or nursing care.

(e) Persons who are not assisted under the tenant-based program may reside in a group home.

(f) No more than 12 persons may reside in a group home. This limit covers all persons who reside in the unit, including assisted and unassisted residents and any live-in aide.

Sec. 982.611 Group home: Lease and HAP contract.

For assistance in a group home, there is a separate HAP contract and lease for each assisted person.

Sec. 982.612 Group home: State approval of group home.

A group home must be licensed, certified, or otherwise approved in writing by the State (e.g., Department of Human Resources, Mental Health, Retardation, or Social Services) as a group home for elderly persons or persons with disabilities.

Sec. 982.613 Group home: Rent and voucher housing assistance payment.

(a) Meaning of pro-rata portion. For a group home, the term ``pro-rata portion'' means the ratio derived by dividing the number of persons in the assisted household by the total number of residents (assisted and unassisted) residing in the group home. The number of persons in the assisted household equals one assisted person plus any PHA-approved live-in aide.

(b) Rent to owner: Reasonable rent limit. (1) The rent to owner for an assisted person may not exceed the pro-rata portion of the reasonable rent for the group home.

(2) The reasonable rent for a group home is determined in accordance with Sec. 982.507. In determining reasonable rent for the group home, the PHA must consider whether sanitary facilities, and facilities for food preparation and service, are common facilities or private facilities.

(c) Payment standard. (1) Family unit size. (i) Unless there is a live-in aide, the family unit size is zero or one bedroom.

(ii) If there is a live-in aide, the live-in aide must be counted in determining the family unit size.

(2) The payment standard for a person who resides in a group home is the lower of:

(i) The payment standard amount on the PHA payment standard schedule for the family unit size; or (ii) The pro-rata portion of the payment standard amount on the PHA payment standard schedule for the group home size.

(iii) If there is a live-in aide, the live-in aide must be counted in determining the family unit size.

(d) Utility allowance. The utility allowance for each assisted person residing in a group home is the pro-rata portion of the utility allowance for the group home unit size.

{63 FR 23865, Apr. 30, 1998, as amended at 64 FR 26651, May 14, 1999}

Sec. 982.614 Group home: Housing quality standards.

(a) Compliance with HQS. The PHA may not give approval to reside in a group home unless the unit, including the portion of the unit available for use by the assisted person under the lease, meets the housing quality standards.

(b) Applicable HQS standards. (1) The HQS in Sec. 982.401 apply to assistance in a group home. However, the standards in this section apply in place of Sec. 982.401(b) (sanitary facilities), Sec. 982.401(c) (food preparation and refuse disposal), Sec. 982.401(d) (space and security), Sec. 982.401(g) (structure and materials) and Sec. 982.401(l) (site and neighborhood).

(2) The entire unit must comply with the HQS.

(c) Additional performance requirements. The following additional performance requirements apply to a group home:

(1) Sanitary facilities. (i) There must be a bathroom in the unit. The unit must contain, and an assisted resident must have ready access to:

(A) A flush toilet that can be used in privacy;

(B) A fixed basin with hot and cold running water; and

(C) A shower or bathtub with hot and cold running water.

(ii) All of these facilities must be in proper operating condition, and must be adequate for personal cleanliness and the disposal of human waste. The facilities must utilize an approvable public or private disposal system.

(iii) The unit may contain private or common sanitary facilities. However, the facilities must be sufficient in number so that they need not be shared by more than four residents of the group home.

(iv) Sanitary facilities in the group home must be readily accessible to and usable by residents, including persons with disabilities.

(2) Food preparation and service. (i) The unit must contain a kitchen and a dining area. There must be adequate space to store, prepare, and serve foods in a sanitary manner.

(ii) Food preparation and service equipment must be in proper operating condition. The equipment must be adequate for the number of residents in the group home. The unit must contain the following equipment:

(A) A stove or range, and oven;

(B) A refrigerator; and

(C) A kitchen sink with hot and cold running water. The sink must drain into an approvable public or private disposal system.

(iii) There must be adequate facilities and services for the sanitary disposal of food waste and refuse, including facilities for temporary storage where necessary.

(iv) The unit may contain private or common facilities for food preparation and service.

(3) Space and security. (i) The unit must provide adequate space and security for the assisted person.

(ii) The unit must contain a living room, kitchen, dining area, bathroom, and other appropriate social, recreational or community space. The unit must contain at least one bedroom of appropriate size for each two persons.

(iii) Doors and windows that are accessible from outside the unit must be lockable.

(4) Structure and material. (i) The unit must be structurally sound to avoid any threat to the health and safety of the residents, and to protect the residents from the environment.

(ii) Ceilings, walls, and floors must not have any serious defects such as severe bulging or leaning, loose surface materials, severe buckling or noticeable movement under walking stress, missing parts or other significant damage. The roof structure must be firm, and the roof must be weathertight. The exterior or wall structure and exterior wall surface may not have any serious defects such as serious leaning, buckling, sagging, cracks or large holes, loose siding, or other serious damage. The condition and equipment of interior and exterior stairways, halls, porches, walkways, etc., must not present a danger of tripping or

falling. Elevators must be maintained in safe operating condition.

(iii) The group home must be accessible to and usable by a resident with disabilities.

(5) Site and neighborhood. The site and neighborhood must be reasonably free from disturbing noises and reverberations and other hazards to the health, safety, and general welfare of the residents. The site and neighborhood may not be subject to serious adverse environmental conditions, natural or manmade, such as dangerous walks or steps, instability, flooding, poor drainage, septic tank back-ups, sewage hazards or mud slides, abnormal air pollution, smoke or dust, excessive noise, vibrations or vehicular traffic, excessive accumulations of trash, vermin or rodent infestation, or fire hazards. The unit must be located in a residential setting.

Shared Housing

Sec. 982.615 Shared housing: Occupancy.

(a) Sharing a unit. An assisted family may reside in shared housing. In shared housing, an assisted family shares a unit with the other resident or residents of the unit. The unit may be a house or an apartment.

(b) Who may share a dwelling unit with assisted family? (1) If approved by the HA, a live-in aide may reside with the family to care for a person with disabilities. The PHA must approve a live-in aide if needed as a reasonable accommodation so that the program is readily accessible to and usable by persons with disabilities in accordance with 24 CFR part 8. See Sec. 982.316 concerning occupancy by a live-in aide.

(2) Other persons who are assisted under the tenant-based program, or other persons who are not assisted under the tenant-based program, may reside in a shared housing unit.

(3) The owner of a shared housing unit may reside in the unit. A resident owner may enter into a HAP contract with the PHA. However, housing assistance may not be paid on behalf of an owner. An assisted person may not be related by blood or marriage to a resident owner.

Sec. 982.616 Shared housing: Lease and HAP contract.

For assistance in a shared housing unit, there is a separate HAP contract and lease for each assisted family.

Sec. 982.617 Shared housing: Rent and voucher housing assistance payment.

(a) Meaning of pro-rata portion. For shared housing, the term ``pro-rata portion'' means the ratio derived by dividing the number of bedrooms in the private space available for occupancy by a family by the total number of bedrooms in the unit. For example, for a family entitled to occupy three bedrooms in a five bedroom unit, the ratio would be 3/5.

(b) Rent to owner: Reasonable rent. (1) The rent to owner for the family may not exceed the pro-rata portion of the reasonable rent for the shared housing dwelling unit.

(2) The reasonable rent is determined in accordance with Sec. 982.507.

(c) Payment standard. The payment standard for a family that resides in a shared housing is the lower of:

(1) The payment standard amount on the PHA payment standard schedule for the family unit size; or

(2) The pro-rata portion of the payment standard amount on the PHA payment standard schedule for the size of the shared housing unit.

(d) Utility allowance. The utility allowance for an assisted family residing in shared housing is the pro-rata portion of the utility allowance for the shared housing unit.

{63 FR 23865, Apr. 30, 1998, as amended by 64 FR 26651, May 14, 1999}

Sec. 982.618 Shared housing: Housing quality standards.

(a) Compliance with HQS. The PHA may not give approval to reside in shared housing unless the entire unit, including the portion of the unit available for use by the assisted family under its lease, meets the housing quality standards.

(b) Applicable HQS standards. The HQS in Sec. 982.401 apply to assistance in shared housing. However, the HQS standards in this section apply in place of Sec. 982.401(d) (space and security).

(c) Facilities available for family. The facilities available for the use of an assisted family in shared housing under the family's lease must include (whether in the family's private space or in the common space) a living room, sanitary facilities in accordance with Sec. 982.401(b), and food preparation and refuse disposal facilities in accordance with Sec. 982.401(c).

(d) Space and security: Performance requirements. (1) The entire unit must provide adequate space and security for all its residents (whether assisted or unassisted).

(2)(i) Each unit must contain private space for each assisted family, plus common space for shared use by the residents of the unit. Common space must be appropriate for shared use by the residents.

(ii) The private space for each assisted family must contain at least one bedroom for each two persons in the family. The number of bedrooms in the private space of an assisted family may not be less than the family unit size.

(iii) A zero or one bedroom unit may not be used for shared housing.

Cooperative

Sec. 982.619 Cooperative housing.

(a) Assistance in cooperative housing. This section applies to rental assistance for a cooperative member residing in cooperative housing. However, this section does not apply to:

(1) Assistance for a cooperative member under the homeownership option pursuant to Secs. 982.625 through 982.641; or

(2) Rental assistance for a family that leases a cooperative housing unit from a cooperative member (such rental assistance is not a special housing type, and is subject to requirements in other subparts of this part 982).

(b) Rent to owner. (1) The reasonable rent for a cooperative unit is determined in accordance with Sec. 982.507. For cooperative housing, the rent to owner is the monthly carrying charge under the occupancy agreement/lease between the member and the cooperative.

(2) The carrying charge consists of the amount assessed to the member by the cooperative for occupancy of the housing. The carrying charge includes the member's share of the cooperative debt service, operating expenses, and necessary payments to cooperative reserve funds. However, the carrying charge does not include down-payments or other payments to purchase the cooperative unit, or to amortize a loan to the family for this purpose.

(3) Gross rent is the carrying charge plus any utility allowance.

(4) For a regular tenancy under the certificate program, rent to owner is adjusted in accordance with Sec. 982.519 (annual adjustment) and Sec. 982.520 (special adjustments). For a cooperative, adjustments are applied to the carrying charge as determined in accordance with this section.

(5) The occupancy agreement/lease and other appropriate documents must provide that the monthly carrying charge is subject to Section 8 limitations on rent to owner.

(c) Housing assistance payment. The amount of the housing assistance payment is determined in accordance with subpart K of this part.

(d) Maintenance. (1) During the term of the HAP contract between the PHA and the cooperative, the dwelling unit and premises must be maintained in accordance with the HQS. If the dwelling unit and premises are not maintained in accordance with the HQS,

accordance with 24 CFR part 8. See Sec. 982.316 concerning occupancy by a live-in aide.

(2) If there is a live-in aide, the live-in aide must be counted in determining the family unit size.

Sec. 982.621 Manufactured home: Housing quality standards.

A manufactured home must meet all the HQS performance requirements and acceptability criteria in Sec. 982.401. A manufactured home also must meet the following requirements:

(a) Performance requirement. A manufactured home must be placed on the site in a stable manner, and must be free from hazards such as sliding or wind damage.

(b) Acceptability criteria. A manufactured home must be securely anchored by a tie-down device that distributes and transfers the loads imposed by the unit to appropriate ground anchors to resist wind overturning and sliding.

Manufactured Home Space Rental

Sec. 982.622 Manufactured home space rental: Rent to owner.

(a) What is included. (1) Rent to owner for rental of a manufactured home space includes payment for maintenance and services that the owner must provide to the tenant under the lease for the space.

(2) Rent to owner does not include the costs of utilities and trash collection for the manufactured home. However, the owner may charge the family a separate fee for the cost of utilities or trash collection provided by the owner.

(b) Reasonable rent. (1) During the assisted tenancy, the rent to owner for the manufactured home space may not exceed a reasonable rent as determined in accordance with this section. Section 982.503 is not applicable.

(2) The PHA may not approve a lease for a manufactured home space until the PHA determines that the initial rent to owner for the space is a reasonable rent. At least annually during the assisted tenancy, the PHA must redetermine that the current rent to owner is a reasonable rent.

(3) The PHA must determine whether the rent to owner for the manufactured home space is a reasonable rent in comparison to rent for other comparable manufactured home spaces. To make this determination, the PHA must consider the location and size of the space, and any services and maintenance to be provided by the owner in accordance with the lease (without a fee in addition to the rent).

(4) By accepting each monthly housing assistance payment from the PHA, the owner of the manufactured home space certifies that the rent to owner for the space is not more than rent charged by the owner for unassisted rental of comparable spaces in the same manufactured home park or elsewhere. The owner must give the PHA information, as requested by the PHA, on rents charged by the owner for other manufactured home spaces.

Sec. 982.623 Manufactured home space rental: Housing assistance payment.

(a) Housing assistance payment: For certificate tenancy. (1) During the term of a certificate tenancy (entered prior to the merger date), the amount of the monthly housing assistance payment equals the lesser of the amounts specified in paragraphs (b)(1)(i) or (b)(1)(ii) of this section:

(i) Manufactured home space cost minus the total tenant payment.

(ii) The rent to owner for the manufactured home space.

(2) ``Manufactured home space cost'' means the sum of:

(i) The amortization cost,

(ii) The utility allowance, and

(iii) The rent to owner for the manufactured home space.

(3) Amortization cost. (i) The amortization cost may include debt service to amortize cost (other than furniture costs) included in the purchase price of the manufactured home. The debt service includes the payment for principal and interest on the loan. The debt service amount must be reduced by 15 percent to exclude debt service to amortize the cost of furniture, unless the PHA determines that furniture was not included in the purchase price.

(ii) The amount of the amortization cost is the debt service established at time of application to a lender for financing purchase of the manufactured home if monthly payments are still being made. Any increase in debt service due to refinancing after purchase of the home is not included in amortization cost.

(iii) Debt service for set-up charges incurred by a family that relocates its home may be included in the monthly amortization payment made by the family. In addition, set-up charges incurred before the family became an assisted family may be included in the amortization cost if monthly payments are still being made to amortize such charges.

(b) Housing assistance payment for voucher tenancy. (1) There is a separate fair market rent for a manufactured home space. The FMR for a manufactured home space is determined in accordance with Sec. 888.113(e) of this title. The FMR for a manufactured home space is generally 40 percent of the published FMR for a two-bedroom unit.

(2) The payment standard shall be determined in accordance with Sec. 982.505.

(3) The PHA shall pay a monthly housing assistance payment on behalf of the family that is equal to the lower of:

(i) The payment standard minus the total tenant payment; or

(ii) The rent paid for rental of the real property on which the manufactured home owned by the family is located (``space rent'') minus the total tenant payment.

(4) The space rent is the sum of the following as determined by the PHA:

(i) Rent to owner for the manufactured home space;

(ii) Owner maintenance and management charges for the space;

(iii) The utility allowance for tenant-paid utilities.

{64 FR 26651, May 14, 1999; 64 FR 49659, Sept. 14, 1999; 64 FR 56915, Oct. 21, 1999}

Sec. 982.624 Manufactured home space rental: Utility allowance schedule.

The PHA must establish utility allowances for manufactured home space rental. For the first twelve months of the initial lease term only, the allowances must include a reasonable amount for utility hook-up charges payable by the family if the family actually incurs the expenses because of a move. Allowances for utility hook-up charges do not apply to a family that leases a manufactured home space in place. Utility allowances for manufactured home space must not cover costs payable by a family to cover the digging of a well or installation of a septic system.

Homeownership Option

Source: 65 FR 55163, Sept. 12, 2000, unless otherwise noted.

Sec. 982.625 Homeownership option: General.

(a) The homeownership option is used to assist a family residing in a home purchased and owned by one or more members of the family.

(b) A family assisted under the homeownership option may be a newly admitted or existing participant in the program.

(c) Forms of homeownership assistance. (1) A PHA may provide one of two forms of homeownership assistance for a family:

(i) Monthly homeownership assistance payments; or

the PHA may exercise all available remedies, regardless of whether the family or the cooperative is responsible for such breach of the HQS. PHA remedies for breach of the HQS include recovery of overpayments, abatement or other reduction of housing assistance payments, termination of housing assistance payments and termination of the HAP contract.

(2) The PHA may not make any housing assistance payments if the contract unit does not meet the HQS, unless any defect is corrected within the period specified by the PHA and the PHA verifies the correction. If a defect is life-threatening, the defect must be corrected within no more than 24 hours. For other defects, the defect must be corrected within the period specified by the PHA.

(3) The family is responsible for a breach of the HQS that is caused by any of the following:

(i) The family fails to perform any maintenance for which the family is responsible in accordance with the terms of the cooperative occupancy agreement between the cooperative member and the cooperative;

(ii) The family fails to pay for any utilities that the cooperative is not required to pay for, but which are to be paid by the cooperative member;

(iii) The family fails to provide and maintain any appliances that the cooperative is not required to provide, but which are to be provided by the cooperative member; or

(iv) Any member of the household or guest damages the dwelling unit or premises (damages beyond ordinary wear and tear).

(4) If the family has caused a breach of the HQS for which the family is responsible, the PHA must take prompt and vigorous action to enforce such family obligations. The PHA may terminate assistance for violation of family obligations in accordance with Sec. 982.552.

(5) Section 982.404 does not apply to assistance for cooperative housing under this section.

(e) Live-in aide. (1) If approved by the PHA, a live-in aide may reside with the family to care for a person with disabilities. The PHA must approve a live-in aide if needed as a reasonable accommodation so that the program is readily accessible to and usable by persons with disabilities in accordance with 24 CFR part 8. See Sec. 982.316 concerning occupancy by a live-in aide.

(2) If there is a live-in aide, the live-in aide must be counted in determining the family unit size.

{63 FR 23865, Apr. 30, 1998, as amended by 64 FR 26651, May 14, 1999; 65 FR 55162, Sept. 12, 2000}

Manufactured Home

Sec. 982.620 Manufactured home: Applicability of requirements.

(a) Assistance for resident of manufactured home. (1) A family may reside in a manufactured home with assistance under the program.

(2) The PHA must permit a family to lease a manufactured home and space with assistance under the program.

(3) The PHA may provide assistance for a family that owns the manufactured home and leases only the space. The PHA is not required to provide such assistance under the program.

(b) Applicability. (1) The HQS in Sec. 982.621 always apply when assistance is provided to a family occupying a manufactured home (under paragraph (a)(2) or (a)(3) of this section).

(2) Sections 982.622 to 982.624 only apply when assistance is provided to a manufactured home owner to lease a manufactured home space.

(c) Live-in aide. (1) If approved by the PHA, a live-in aide may reside with the family to care for a person with disabilities. The PHA must approve a live-in aide if needed as a reasonable accommodation so that the program is readily accessible to and usable by persons with disabilities in

(ii) A single downpayment assistance grant.

(2) Prohibition against combining forms of homeownership assistance. A family may only receive one form of homeownership assistance. Accordingly, a family that includes a person who was an adult member of a family that previously received either of the two forms of homeownership assistance may not receive the other form of homeownership assistance from any PHA.

(d) PHA choice to offer homeownership options. (1) The PHA may choose to offer either or both forms of homeownership assistance under this subpart, or choose not to offer either form of assistance. However, the PHA must offer either form of homeownership assistance if necessary as a reasonable accommodation for a person with disabilities in accordance with Sec. 982.601(b)(3).

(2) It is the sole responsibility of the PHA to determine whether it is reasonable to implement a homeownership program as a reasonable accommodation. The PHA will determine what is reasonable based on the specific circumstances and individual needs of the person with a disability. The PHA may determine that it is not reasonable to offer homeownership assistance as a reasonable accommodation in cases where the PHA has otherwise opted not to implement a homeownership program.

(e) Family choice. (1) The family chooses whether to participate in the homeownership option if offered by the PHA.

(2) If the PHA offers both forms of homeownership assistance, the family chooses which form of homeownership assistance to receive.

(f) The PHA must approve a live-in aide if needed as a reasonable accommodation so that the program is readily accessible to and useable by persons with disabilities in accordance with part 8 of this title. (See Sec. 982.316 concerning occupancy by a live-in aide.)

(g) The PHA must have the capacity to operate a successful Section 8 homeownership program. The PHA has the required capacity if it satisfies either paragraph (g)(1), (g)(2), or (g)(3) of this section.

(1) The PHA establishes a minimum homeowner downpayment requirement of at least 3 percent of the purchase price for participation in its Section 8 homeownership program, and requires that at least one percent of the purchase price come from the family's personal resources;

(2) The PHA requires that financing for purchase of a home under itsSection 8 homeownership program:

(i) Be provided, insured, or guaranteed by the state or Federal government;

(ii) Comply with secondary mortgage market underwriting requirements; or

(iii) Comply with generally accepted private sector underwriting standards; or

(3) The PHA otherwise demonstrates in its Annual Plan that it has the capacity, or will acquire the capacity, to successfully operate a Section 8 homeownership program.

(h) Recapture of homeownership assistance. A PHA shall not impose or enforce any requirement for the recapture of voucher homeownership assistance on the sale or refinancing of a home purchased with assistance under the homeownership option.

(i) Applicable requirements. The following specify what regulatory provisions (under the heading ``homeownership option'') are applicable to either or both forms of homeownership assistance (except as otherwise specifically provided):

(1) Common provisions. The following provisions apply to both forms of homeownership assistance:

(i) Section 982.625 (General);

(ii) Section 982.626 (Initial requirements);

(iii) Section 982.627 (Eligibility requirements for families);

(iv) Section 982.628 (Eligible units);

(v) Section 982.629 (Additional PHA requirements for family search and purchase);

(vi) Section 982.630 (Homeownership counseling);

(vii) Section 982.631 (Home inspections, contract of sale, and PHA disapproval of

seller);
(viii) Section 982.632 (Financing purchase of home; affordability of purchase);
(ix) Section 982.636 (Portability);
(x) Section 982.638 (Denial or termination of assistance for family); and
(xi) Section 982.641 (Applicability of other requirements).
(2) Monthly homeownership assistance payments. The following provisions only apply to homeownership assistance in the form of monthly homeownership assistance payments:
(i) Section 982.633 (Continued assistance requirements; family obligations);
(ii) Section 982.634 (Maximum term of homeownership assistance);
(iii) Section 982.635 (Amount and distribution of monthly homeownership assistance payment);
(iv) Section 982.637 (Move with continued tenant-based assistance); and
(v) Section 982.639 (Administrative fees).
(3) Downpayment assistance grant. The following provision only applies to homeownership assistance in the form of a downpayment assistance grant: Section 982.643 (Downpayment assistance grants).

{65 FR 55163, Sept. 12, 2000, as amended at 67 FR 64493, Oct. 18, 2002}

Sec. 982.626 Homeownership option: Initial requirements.

(a) List of initial requirements. Before commencing homeownership assistance for a family, the PHA must determine that all of the following initial requirements have been satisfied:
(1) The family is qualified to receive homeownership assistance (see Sec. 982.627);
(2) The unit is eligible (see Sec. 982.628); and
(3) The family has satisfactorily completed the PHA program of required pre-assistance homeownership counseling (see Sec. 982.630).
(b) Additional PHA requirements. Unless otherwise provided in this part, the PHA may limit homeownership assistance to families or purposes defined by the PHA, and may prescribe additional requirements for commencement of homeownership assistance for a family. Any such limits or additional requirements must be described in the PHA administrative plan.
(c) Environmental requirements. The PHA is responsible for complying with the authorities listed in Sec. 58.6 of this title requiring the purchaser to obtain and maintain flood insurance for units in special flood hazard areas, prohibiting assistance for acquiring units in the coastal barriers resource system, and requiring notification to the purchaser of units in airport runway clear zones and airfield clear zones.

Sec. 982.627 Homeownership option: Eligibility requirements for families.

(a) Determination whether family is qualified. The PHA may not provide homeownership assistance for a family unless the PHA determines that the family satisfies all of the following initial requirements at commencement of homeownership assistance for the family:
(1) The family has been admitted to the Section 8 Housing Choice Voucher program, in accordance with subpart E of this part.
(2) The family satisfies any first-time homeowner requirements (described in paragraph (b) of this section).
(3) The family satisfies the minimum income requirement (described in paragraph (c) of this section).
(4) The family satisfies the employment requirements (described in paragraph (d) of this section).
(5) The family has not defaulted on a mortgage securing debt to purchase a home under the homeownership option (see paragraph (e) of this section).
(6) Except for cooperative members who have acquired cooperative membership shares prior to commencement of homeownership assistance, no family member has a present ownership interest

in a residence at the commencement of homeownership assistance for the purchase of any home.

(7) Except for cooperative members who have acquired cooperative membership shares prior to the commencement of homeownership assistance, the family has entered a contract of sale in accordance with Sec. 982.631(c).

(8) The family also satisfies any other initial requirements established by the PHA (see Sec. 982.626(b)). Any such additional requirements must be described in the PHA administrative plan.

(b) First-time homeowner requirements. At commencement of homeownership assistance for the family, the family must be any of the following:

(1) A first-time homeowner (defined at Sec. 982.4);

(2) A cooperative member (defined at Sec. 982.4); or

(3) A family of which a family member is a person with disabilities, and use of the homeownership option is needed as a reasonable accommodation so that the program is readily accessible to and usable by such person, in accordance with part 8 of this title.

(c) Minimum income requirements. (1) At commencement of monthly homeownership assistance payments for the family, or at the time of a downpayment assistance grant for the family, the family must demonstrate that the annual income, as determined by the PHA in accordance with Sec. 5.609 of this title, of the adult family members who will own the home at commencement of homeownership assistance is not less than:

(i) In the case of a disabled family (as defined in Sec. 5.403(b) of this title), the monthly Federal Supplemental Security Income (SSI) benefit for an individual living alone (or paying his or her share of food and housing costs) multiplied by twelve; or

(ii) In the case of other families, the Federal minimum wage multiplied by 2,000 hours.

(2)(i) Except in the case of an elderly family or a disabled family (see the definitions of these terms at Sec. 5.403(b) of this title), the PHA shall not count any welfare assistance received by the family in determining annual income under this section.

(ii) The disregard of welfare assistance income under paragraph (c)(2)(i) of this section only affects the determination of minimum annual income used to determine if a family initially qualifies for commencement of homeownership assistance in accordance with this section, but does not affect:

(A) The determination of income-eligibility for admission to the voucher program;

(B) Calculation of the amount of the family's total tenant payment (gross family contribution); or

(C) Calculation of the amount of homeownership assistance payments on behalf of the family.

(iii) In the case of an elderly or disabled family, the PHA shall include welfare assistance for the adult family members who will own the home in determining if the family meets the minimum income requirement.

(3) A PHA may establish a minimum income standard that is higher than those described in paragraph (c)(1) of this section for either or both types of families. However, a family that meets the applicable HUD minimum income requirement described in paragraph (c)(1) of this section, but not the higher standard established by the PHA shall be considered to satisfy the minimum income requirement if:

(i) The family demonstrates that it has been pre-qualified or pre-approved for financing;

(ii) The pre-qualified or pre-approved financing meets any PHA established requirements under Sec. 982.632 for financing the purchase of the home (including qualifications of lenders and terms of financing); and

(iii) The pre-qualified or pre-approved financing amount is sufficient to purchase housing that meets HQS in the PHA's

jurisdiction.

(d) Employment requirements. (1) Except as provided in paragraph (d)(2) of this section, the family must demonstrate that one or more adult members of the family who will own the home at commencement of homeownership assistance:

(i) Is currently employed on a full-time basis (the term ``full-time employment'' means not less than an average of 30 hours per week); and

(ii) Has been continuously so employed during the year before commencement of homeownership assistance for the family.

(2) The PHA shall have discretion to determine whether and to what extent interruptions are considered to break continuity of employment during the year. The PHA may count successive employment during the year. The PHA may count self-employment in a business.

(3) The employment requirement does not apply to an elderly family or a disabled family (see the definitions of these terms at Sec. 5.403(b) of this title). Furthermore, if a family, other than an elderly family or a disabled family, includes a person with disabilities, the PHA shall grant an exemption from the employment requirement if the PHA determines that an exemption is needed as a reasonable accommodation so that the program is readily accessible to and usable by persons with disabilities in accordance with part 8 of this title.

(4) A PHA may not establish an employment requirement in addition to the employment standard established by this paragraph.

(e) Prohibition against assistance to family that has defaulted. The PHA shall not commence homeownership assistance for a family that includes an individual who was an adult member of a family at the time when such family received homeownership assistance and defaulted on a mortgage securing debt incurred to purchase the home.

{65 FR 55163, Sept. 12, 2000, as amended at 67 FR 64493, Oct. 18, 2002}

Sec. 982.628 Homeownership option: Eligible units.

(a) Initial requirements applicable to the unit. The PHA must determine that the unit satisfies all of the following requirements:

(1) The unit is eligible. (See Sec. 982.352. Paragraphs (a)(6), (a)(7) and (b) of Sec. 982.352 do not apply.)

(2) The unit is either under construction or already existing at the time the family enters into the contract of sale.

(3) The unit is either a one-unit property (including a manufactured home) or a single dwelling unit in a cooperative or condominium.

(4) The unit has been inspected by a PHA inspector and by an independent inspector designated by the family (see Sec. 982.631).

(5) The unit satisfies the HQS (see Sec. 982.401 and Sec. 982.631).

(b) Purchase of home where family will not own fee title to the real property. Homeownership assistance may be provided for the purchase of a home where the family will not own fee title to the real property on which the home is located, but only if:

(1) The home is located on a permanent foundation; and

(2) The family has the right to occupy the home site for at least forty years.

(c) PHA disapproval of seller. The PHA may not commence homeownership assistance for occupancy of a home if the PHA has been informed (by HUD or otherwise) that the seller of the home is debarred, suspended, or subject to a limited denial of participation under part 24 of this title.

(d) PHA-owned units. Homeownership assistance may be provided for the purchase of a unit that is owned by the PHA that administers the assistance under the consolidated ACC (including a unit owned by an entity substantially controlled by the PHA), only if all of the following conditions are satisfied:

(1) The PHA must inform the family, both orally and in writing, that the family has the right to purchase any eligible unit and a PHA-owned unit is freely selected by the

family without PHA pressure or steering;

(2) The unit is not ineligible housing;

(3) The PHA must obtain the services of an independent agency, in accordance with Sec. 982.352(b)(1)(iv)(B) and (C), to perform the following PHA functions:

(i) Inspection of the unit for compliance with the HQS, in accordance with Sec. 982.631(a);

(ii) Review of the independent inspection report, in accordance with Sec. 982.631(b)(4);

(iii) Review of the contract of sale, in accordance with Sec. 982.631(c); and

(iv) Determination of the reasonableness of the sales price and any PHA provided financing, in accordance with Sec. 982.632 and other supplementary guidance established by HUD.

{65 FR 55163, Sept. 12, 2000, as amended at 67 FR 64494, Oct. 18, 2002; 67 FR 65865, Oct. 28, 2002; 67 FR 67522, Nov. 6, 2002}

Sec. 982.629 Homeownership option: Additional PHA requirements for family search and purchase.

(a) The PHA may establish the maximum time for a family to locate a home, and to purchase the home.

(b) The PHA may require periodic family reports on the family's progress in finding and purchasing a home.

(c) If the family is unable to purchase a home within the maximum time established by the PHA, the PHA may issue the family a voucher to lease a unit or place the family's name on the waiting list for a voucher.

Sec. 982.630 Homeownership option: Homeownership counseling.

(a) Before commencement of homeownership assistance for a family, the family must attend and satisfactorily complete the pre-assistance homeownership and housing counseling program required by the PHA (pre-assistance counseling).

(b) Suggested topics for the PHA-required pre-assistance counseling program include:

(1) Home maintenance (including care of the grounds);

(2) Budgeting and money management;

(3) Credit counseling;

(4) How to negotiate the purchase price of a home;

(5) How to obtain homeownership financing and loan preapprovals, including a description of types of financing that may be available, and the pros and cons of different types of financing;

(6) How to find a home, including information about homeownership opportunities, schools, and transportation in the PHA jurisdiction;

(7) Advantages of purchasing a home in an area that does not have a high concentration of low-income families and how to locate homes in such areas;

(8) Information on fair housing, including fair housing lending and local fair housing enforcement agencies; and

(9) Information about the Real Estate Settlement Procedures Act (12 U.S.C. 2601 et seq.) (RESPA), state and Federal truth-in-lending laws, and how to identify and avoid loans with oppressive terms and conditions.

(c) The PHA may adapt the subjects covered in pre-assistance counseling (as listed in paragraph (b) of this section) to local circumstances and the needs of individual families.

(d) The PHA may also offer additional counseling after commencement of homeownership assistance (ongoing counseling). If the PHA offers a program of ongoing counseling for participants in the homeownership option, the PHA shall have discretion to determine whether the family is required to participate in the ongoing counseling.

(e) If the PHA is not using a HUD-approved housing counseling agency to provide the counseling for families

participating in the homeownership option, the PHA should ensure that its counseling program is consistent with the homeownership counseling provided under HUD's Housing Counseling program.

Sec. 982.631 Homeownership option: Home inspections, contract of sale, and PHA disapproval of seller.

(a) HQS inspection by PHA. The PHA may not commence monthly homeownership assistance payments or provide a downpayment assistance grant for the family until the PHA has inspected the unit and has determined that the unit passes HQS.

(b) Independent inspection. (1) The unit must also be inspected by an independent professional inspector selected by and paid by the family.

(2) The independent inspection must cover major building systems and components, including foundation and structure, housing interior and exterior, and the roofing, plumbing, electrical, and heating systems. The independent inspector must be qualified to report on property conditions, including major building systems and components.

(3) The PHA may not require the family to use an independent inspector selected by the PHA. The independent inspector may not be a PHA employee or contractor, or other person under control of the PHA. However, the PHA may establish standards for qualification of inspectors selected by families under the homeownership option.

(4) The independent inspector must provide a copy of the inspection report both to the family and to the PHA. The PHA may not commence monthly homeownership assistance payments, or provide a downpayment assistance grant for the family, until the PHA has reviewed the inspection report of the independent inspector. Even if the unit otherwise complies with the HQS (and may qualify for assistance under the PHA's tenant-based rental voucher program), the PHA shall have discretion to disapprove the unit for assistance under the homeownership option because of information in the inspection report.

(c) Contract of sale. (1) Before commencement of monthly homeownership assistance payments or receipt of a downpayment assistance grant, a member or members of the family must enter into a contract of sale with the seller of the unit to be acquired by the family. The family must give the PHA a copy of the contract of sale (see also Sec. 982.627(a)(7)).

(2) The contract of sale must:

(i) Specify the price and other terms of sale by the seller to the purchaser.

(ii) Provide that the purchaser will arrange for a pre-purchase inspection of the dwelling unit by an independent inspector selected by the purchaser.

(iii) Provide that the purchaser is not obligated to purchase the unit unless the inspection is satisfactory to the purchaser.

(iv) Provide that the purchaser is not obligated to pay for any necessary repairs.

(v) Contain a certification from the seller that the seller has not been debarred, suspended, or subject to a limited denial of participation under part 24 of this title.

(d) PHA disapproval of seller. In its administrative discretion, the PHA may deny approval of a seller for any reason provided for disapproval of an owner in Sec. 982.306(c).

{65 FR 55163, Sept. 12, 2000, as amended at 67 FR 64494, Oct. 18, 2002}

Sec. 982.632 Homeownership option: Financing purchase of home; affordability of purchase.

(a) The PHA may establish requirements for financing purchase of a home to be assisted under the homeownership option. Such PHA requirements may include requirements concerning qualification of lenders (for example, prohibition of seller financing or case-by-case approval of seller financing), or concerning terms of financing (for example, a prohibition of balloon

payment mortgages, establishment of a minimum homeowner equity requirement from personal resources, or provisions required to protect borrowers against high cost loans or predatory loans). A PHA may not require that families acquire financing from one or more specified lenders, thereby restricting the family's ability to secure favorable financing terms.

(b) If the purchase of the home is financed with FHA mortgage insurance, such financing is subject to FHA mortgage insurance requirements.

(c) The PHA may establish requirements or other restrictions concerning debt secured by the home.

(d) The PHA may review lender qualifications and the loan terms before authorizing homeownership assistance. The PHA may disapprove proposed financing, refinancing or other debt if the PHA determines that the debt is unaffordable, or if the PHA determines that the lender or the loan terms do not meet PHA qualifications. In making this determination, the PHA may take into account other family expenses, such as child care, unreimbursed medical expenses, homeownership expenses, and other family expenses as determined by the PHA.

(e) All PHA financing or affordability requirements must be described in the PHA administrative plan.

{65 FR 55163, Sept. 12, 2000, as amended at 66 FR 33613, June 22, 2001}

Sec. 982.633 Homeownership option: Continued assistance requirements; Family obligations.

(a) Occupancy of home. Homeownership assistance may only be paid while the family is residing in the home. If the family moves out of the home, the PHA may not continue homeownership assistance after the month when the family moves out. The family or lender is not required to refund to the PHA the homeownership assistance for the month when the family moves out.

(b) Family obligations. The family must comply with the following obligations.

(1) Ongoing counseling. To the extent required by the PHA, the family must attend and complete ongoing homeownership and housing counseling.

(2) Compliance with mortgage. The family must comply with the terms of any mortgage securing debt incurred to purchase the home (or any refinancing of such debt).

(3) Prohibition against conveyance or transfer of home. (i) So long as the family is receiving homeownership assistance, use and occupancy of the home is subject to Sec. 982.551(h) and (i).

(ii) The family may grant a mortgage on the home for debt incurred to finance purchase of the home or any refinancing of such debt.

(iii) Upon death of a family member who holds, in whole or in part, title to the home or ownership of cooperative membership shares for the home, homeownership assistance may continue pending settlement of the decedent's estate, notwithstanding transfer of title by operation of law to the decedent's executor or legal representative, so long as the home is solely occupied by remaining family members in accordance with Sec. 982.551(h).

(4) Supplying required information. (i) The family must supply required information to the PHA in accordance with Sec. 982.551(b).

(ii) In addition to other required information, the family must supply any information as required by the PHA or HUD concerning:

(A) Any mortgage or other debt incurred to purchase the home, and any refinancing of such debt (including information needed to determine whether the family has defaulted on the debt, and the nature of any such default), and information on any satisfaction or payment of the mortgage debt;

(B) Any sale or other transfer of any interest in the home; or

(C) The family's homeownership expenses.

(5) Notice of move-out. The family must notify the PHA before the family moves out of the home.

(6) Notice of mortgage default. The family must notify the PHA if the family defaults on a mortgage securing any debt incurred to purchase the home.

(7) Prohibition on ownership interest on second residence. During the time the family receives homeownership assistance under this subpart, no family member may have any ownership interest in any other residential property.

(8) Additional PHA requirements. The PHA may establish additional requirements for continuation of homeownership assistance for the family (for example, a requirement for post-purchase homeownership counseling or for periodic unit inspections while the family is receiving homeownership assistance). The family must comply with any such requirements.

(9) Other family obligations. The family must comply with the obligations of a participant family described in Sec. 982.551. However, the following provisions do not apply to assistance under the homeownership option: Sec. 982.551(c), (d), (e), (f), (g) and (j).

(c) Statement of homeowner obligations. Before commencement of homeownership assistance, the family must execute a statement of family obligations in the form prescribed by HUD. In the statement, the family agrees to comply with all family obligations under the homeownership option.

Sec. 982.634 Homeownership option: Maximum term of homeownership assistance.

(a) Maximum term of assistance. Except in the case of a family that qualifies as an elderly or disabled family (see paragraph (c) of this section), the family members described in paragraph (b) of this section shall not receive homeownership assistance for more than:

(1) Fifteen years, if the initial mortgage incurred to finance purchase of the home has a term of 20 years or longer; or

(2) Ten years, in all other cases.

(b) Applicability of maximum term. The maximum term described in paragraph (a) of this section applies to any member of the family who:

(1) Has an ownership interest in the unit during the time that homeownership payments are made; or

(2) Is the spouse of any member of the household who has an ownership interest in the unit during the time homeownership payments are made.

(c) Exception for elderly and disabled families. (1) As noted in paragraph (a) of this section, the maximum term of assistance does not apply to elderly and disabled families.

(2) In the case of an elderly family, the exception only applies if the family qualifies as an elderly family at the start of homeownership assistance. In the case of a disabled family, the exception applies if at any time during receipt of homeownership assistance the family qualifies as a disabled family.

(3) If, during the course of homeownership assistance, the family ceases to qualify as a disabled or elderly family, the maximum term becomes applicable from the date homeownership assistance commenced. However, such a family must be provided at least 6 months of homeownership assistance after the maximum term becomes applicable (provided the family is otherwise eligible to receive homeownership assistance in accordance with this part).

(d) Assistance for different homes or PHAs. If the family has received such assistance for different homes, or from different PHAs, the total of such assistance terms is subject to the maximum term described in paragraph (a) of this section.

Sec. 982.635 Homeownership option: Amount and distribution of monthly homeownership assistance payment.

(a) Amount of monthly homeownership assistance payment. While the family is residing in the home, the PHA shall pay a monthly homeownership assistance payment on behalf of the family that is equal to the lower of:

(1) The payment standard minus the total tenant payment; or

(2) The family's monthly homeownership expenses minus the total tenant payment.

(b) Payment standard for family. (1) The payment standard for a family is the lower of:

(i) The payment standard for the family unit size; or

(ii) The payment standard for the size of the home.

(2) If the home is located in an exception payment standard area, the PHA must use the appropriate payment standard for the exception payment standard area.

(3) The payment standard for a family is the greater of:

(i) The payment standard (as determined in accordance with paragraphs (b)(1) and (b)(2) of this section) at the commencement of homeownership assistance for occupancy of the home; or

(ii) The payment standard (as determined in accordance with paragraphs (b)(1) and (b)(2) of this section) at the most recent regular reexamination of family income and composition since the commencement of homeownership assistance for occupancy of the home.

(4) The PHA must use the same payment standard schedule, payment standard amounts, and subsidy standards pursuant to Secs. 982.402 and 982.503 for the homeownership option as for the rental voucher program.

(c) Determination of homeownership expenses. (1) The PHA shall adopt policies for determining the amount of homeownership expenses to be allowed by the PHA in accordance with HUD requirements.

(2) Homeownership expenses for a homeowner (other than a cooperative member) may only include amounts allowed by the PHA to cover:

(i) Principal and interest on initial mortgage debt, any refinancing of such debt, and any mortgage insurance premium incurred to finance purchase of the home;

(ii) Real estate taxes and public assessments on the home;

(iii) Home insurance;

(iv) The PHA allowance for maintenance expenses;

(v) The PHA allowance for costs of major repairs and replacements;

(vi) The PHA utility allowance for the home;

(vii) Principal and interest on mortgage debt incurred to finance costs for major repairs, replacements or improvements for the home. If a member of the family is a person with disabilities, such debt may include debt incurred by the family to finance costs needed to make the home accessible for such person, if the PHA determines that allowance of such costs as homeownership expenses is needed as a reasonable accommodation so that the homeownership option is readily accessible to and usable by such person, in accordance with part 8 of this title; and

(viii) Land lease payments (where a family does not own fee title to the real property on which the home is located; see Sec. 982.628(b)).

(3) Homeownership expenses for a cooperative member may only include amounts allowed by the PHA to cover:

(i) The cooperative charge under the cooperative occupancy agreement including payment for real estate taxes and public assessments on the home;

(ii) Principal and interest on initial debt incurred to finance purchase of cooperative membership shares and any refinancing of such debt;

(iii) Home insurance;

(iv) The PHA allowance for maintenance expenses;

(v) The PHA allowance for costs of major repairs and replacements;

(vi) The PHA utility allowance for the home; and

(vii) Principal and interest on debt incurred to finance major repairs, replacements or improvements for the home. If a member of the family is a person with disabilities, such debt may include debt incurred by the family to finance costs needed to make the home accessible for such person, if the PHA determines that allowance of such costs as homeownership expenses is needed as a reasonable accommodation so that the homeownership option is readily accessible to and usable by such person, in accordance with part 8 of this title.

(4) If the home is a cooperative or condominium unit, homeownership expenses may also include cooperative or condominium operating charges or maintenance fees assessed by the condominium or cooperative homeowner association.

(d) Payment to lender or family. The PHA must pay homeownership assistance payments either:

(1) Directly to the family or;

(2) At the discretion of the PHA, to a lender on behalf of the family. If the assistance payment exceeds the amount due to the lender, the PHA must pay the excess directly to the family.

(e) Automatic termination of homeownership assistance. Homeownership assistance for a family terminates automatically 180 calendar days after the last homeownership assistance payment on behalf of the family. However, a PHA has the discretion to grant relief from this requirement in those cases where automatic termination would result in extreme hardship for the family.

{65 FR 55163, Sept. 12, 2000, as amended at 67 FR 64494, Oct. 18, 2002}

Sec. 982.636 Homeownership option: Portability.

(a) General. A family may qualify to move outside the initial PHA jurisdiction with continued homeownership assistance under the voucher program in accordance with this section.

(b) Portability of homeownership assistance. Subject to Sec. 982.353(b) and (c), Sec. 982.552, and Sec. 982.553, a family determined eligible for homeownership assistance by the initial PHA may purchase a unit outside of the initial PHA's jurisdiction, if the receiving PHA is administering a voucher homeownership program and is accepting new homeownership families.

(c) Applicability of Housing Choice Voucher program portability procedures. In general, the portability procedures described in Secs. 982.353 and 982.355 apply to the homeownership option and the administrative responsibilities of the initial and receiving PHA are not altered except that some administrative functions (e.g, issuance of a voucher or execution of a tenancy addendum) do not apply to the homeownership option.

(d) Family and PHA responsibilities. The family must attend the briefing and counseling sessions required by the receiving PHA. The receiving PHA will determine whether the financing for, and the physical condition of the unit, are acceptable. The receiving PHA must promptly notify the initial PHA if the family has purchased an eligible unit under the program, or if the family is unable to purchase a home within the maximum time established by the PHA.

(e) Continued assistance under Sec. 982.637. Such continued assistance under portability procedures is subject to Sec. 982.637.

Sec. 982.637 Homeownership option: Move with continued tenant-based assistance.

(a) Move to new unit. (1) A family receiving homeownership assistance may move to a new unit with continued tenant-based assistance in accordance with this section. The family may move either with voucher rental assistance (in accordance with rental assistance program requirements) or with voucher homeownership assistance (in accordance with homeownership option program requirements).

(2) The PHA may not commence continued tenant-based assistance for occupancy of the new unit so long as any family member owns any title or other interest in the prior home.

(3) The PHA may establish policies that prohibit more than one move by the family during any one year period.

(b) Requirements for continuation of homeownership assistance. The PHA must determine that all initial requirements listed in Sec. 982.626 have been satisfied if a family that has received homeownership assistance wants to move to a new unit with continued homeownership assistance. However, the following requirements do not apply:

(1) The requirement for pre-assistance counseling (Sec. 982.630) is not applicable. However, the PHA may require that the family complete additional counseling (before or after moving to a new unit with continued assistance under the homeownership option).

(2) The requirement that a family must be a first-time homeowner (Sec. 982.627) is not applicable.

(c) When PHA may deny permission to move with continued assistance. The PHA may deny permission to move to a new unit with continued voucher assistance as follows:

(1) Lack of funding to provide continued assistance. The PHA may deny permission to move with continued rental or homeownership assistance if the PHA determines that it does not have sufficient funding to provide continued assistance.

(2) Termination or denial of assistance under Sec. 982.638. At any time, the PHA may deny permission to move with continued rental or homeownership assistance in accordance with Sec. 982.638.

Sec. 982.638 Homeownership option: Denial or termination of assistance for family.

(a) General. The PHA shall terminate homeownership assistance for the family, and shall deny voucher rental assistance for the family, in accordance with this section.

(b) Denial or termination of assistance under basic voucher program. At any time, the PHA may deny or terminate homeownership assistance in accordance with Sec. 982.552 (Grounds for denial or termination of assistance) or Sec. 982.553 (Crime by family members).

(c) Failure to comply with family obligations. The PHA may deny or terminate assistance for violation of participant obligations described in Sec. 982.551 or Sec. 982.633.

(d) Mortgage default. The PHA must terminate voucher homeownership assistance for any member of family receiving homeownership assistance that is dispossessed from the home pursuant to a judgment or order of foreclosure on any mortgage (whether FHA-insured or non-FHA) securing debt incurred to purchase the home, or any refinancing of such debt. The PHA, in its discretion, may permit the family to move to a new unit with continued voucher rental assistance. However, the PHA must deny such permission, if:

(1) The family defaulted on an FHA-insured mortgage; and

(2) The family fails to demonstrate that:

(i) The family has conveyed, or will convey, title to the home, as required by HUD, to HUD or HUD's designee; and

(ii) The family has moved, or will move, from the home within the period established or approved by HUD.

{65 FR 55163, Sept. 12, 2000, as amended at 66 FR 33613, June 22, 2001}

Sec. 982.639 Homeownership option: Administrative fees.

The ongoing administrative fee described in Sec. 982.152(b) is paid to the PHA for each month that homeownership assistance is paid by the PHA on behalf of the family.

Sec. 982.641 Homeownership option: Applicability of other requirements.

(a) General. The following types of provisions (located in other subparts of this part) do not apply to assistance under the homeownership option:

(1) Any provisions concerning the Section 8 owner or the HAP contract between the PHA and owner;

(2) Any provisions concerning the assisted tenancy or the lease between the family and the owner;

(3) Any provisions concerning PHA approval of the assisted tenancy;

(4) Any provisions concerning rent to owner or reasonable rent; and

(5) Any provisions concerning the issuance or term of voucher.

(b) Subpart G requirements. The following provisions of subpart G of this part do not apply to assistance under the homeownership option:

(1) Section 982.302 (Issuance of voucher; Requesting PHA approval of assisted tenancy);

(2) Section 982.303 (Term of voucher);

(3) Section 982.305 (PHA approval of assisted tenancy);

(4) Section 982.306 (PHA disapproval of owner) (except that a PHA may disapprove a seller for any reason described in paragraph (c), see Sec. 982.631(d)).

(5) Section 982.307 (Tenant screening);

(6) Section 982.308 (Lease and tenancy);

(7) Section 982.309 (Term of assisted tenancy);

(8) Section 982.310 (Owner termination of tenancy);

(9) Section 982.311 (When assistance is paid) (except that Sec. 982.311(c)(3) is applicable to assistance under the homeownership option);

(10) Section 982.313 (Security deposit: Amounts owed by tenant); and

(11) Section 982.314 (Move with continued tenant-based assistance).

(c) Subpart H requirements. The following provisions of subpart H of this part do not apply to assistance under the homeownership option:

(1) Section 982.352(a)(6) (Prohibition of owner-occupied assisted unit);

(2) Section 982.352(b) (PHA-owned housing); and

(3) Those provisions of Sec. 982.353(b)(1),(2), and (3) (Where family can lease a unit with tenant-based assistance) and Sec. 982.355 (Portability: Administration by receiving PHA) that are inapplicable per Sec. 982.636;

(d) Subpart I requirements. The following provisions of subpart I of this part do not apply to assistance under the homeownership option:

(1) Section 982.403 (Terminating HAP contract when unit is too small);

(2) Section 982.404 (Maintenance: Owner and family responsibility; PHA remedies); and

(3) Section 982.405 (PHA initial and periodic unit inspection).

(e) Subpart J requirements. The requirements of subpart J of this part (Housing Assistance Payments Contract and Owner Responsibility) (Secs. 982.451-456) do not apply to assistance under the homeownership option.

(f) Subpart K requirements. Except for those sections listed below, the requirements of subpart K of this part (Rent and Housing Assistance Payment) (Secs. 982.501-521) do not apply to assistance under the homeownership option:

(1) Section 982.503 (Voucher tenancy: Payment standard amount and schedule);

(2) Section 982.516 (Family income and composition: Regular and interim reexaminations); and

(3) Section 982.517 (Utility allowance schedule).

(g) Subpart L requirements. The following provisions of subpart L of this part do not apply to assistance under the homeownership option:

(1) Section 982.551(c) (HQS breach caused by family);

(2) Section 982.551(d) (Allowing PHA inspection);

(3) Section 982.551(e) (Violation of lease);

(4) Section 982.551(g) (Owner eviction notice); and

(5) Section 982.551(j) (Interest in unit).

(h) Subpart M requirements. The following provisions of subpart M of this part do not apply to assistance under the homeownership option:

(1) Sections 982.602-982.619; and

(2) Sections 982.622-982.624.

{65 FR 55163, Sept. 12, 2000, as amended at 67 FR 64494, Oct. 18, 2002}

Sec. 982.642 Homeownership option: Pilot program for homeownership assistance for disabled families.

(a) General. This section implements the pilot program authorized by section 302 of the American Homeownership and Economic Opportunity Act of 2000. Under the pilot program, a PHA may provide homeownership assistance to a disabled family residing in a home purchased and owned by one or more members of the family. A PHA that administers tenant-based assistance has the choice whether to offer homeownership assistance under the pilot program (whether or not the PHA has also decided to offer the homeownership option).

(b) Applicability of homeownership option requirements. Except as provided in this section, all of the regulations applicable to the homeownership option (as described in Secs. 982.625 through 982.641) are also applicable to the pilot program.

(c) Initial eligibility requirements. Before commencing homeownership assistance under the pilot program for a family, the PHA must determine that all of the following initial requirements have been satisfied:

(1) The family is a disabled family (as defined in Sec. 5.403 of this title);

(2) The family annual income does not exceed 99 percent of the median income for the area;

(3) The family is not a current homeowner;

(4) The family must close on the purchase of the home during the period starting on July 23, 2001 and ending on July 23, 2004; and

(5) The family meets the initial requirements described in Sec. 982.626; however, the following initial requirements do not apply to a family seeking to participate in the pilot program:

(i) The income eligibility requirements of Sec. 982.201(b)(1);

(ii) The first-time homeowner requirements of Sec. 982.627(b); and

(iii) The mortgage default requirements of Sec. 982.627(e), if the PHA determines that the default is due to catastrophic medical reasons or due to the impact of a federally declared major disaster or emergency.

(d) Amount and distribution of homeownership assistance payments.
(1) While the family is residing in the home, the PHA shall calculate a monthly homeownership assistance payment on behalf of the family in accordance with Sec. 982.635 and this section.

(2) A family that is a low income family (as defined at 24 CFR 5.603(b)) as determined by HUD shall receive the full amount of the monthly homeownership assistance payment calculated under Sec. 982.635.

(3) A family whose annual income is greater than the low income family ceiling

but does not exceed 89 percent of the median income for the area as determined by HUD shall receive a monthly homeownership assistance payment equal to 66 percent of the amount calculated under Sec. 982.635.

(4) A family whose annual income is greater than the 89 percent ceiling but does not exceed 99 percent of the median income for the area as determined by HUD shall receive a monthly homeownership assistance payment equal to 33 percent of the amount calculated under Sec. 982.635.

(5) A family whose annual income is greater than 99 percent of the median income for the area shall not receive homeownership assistance under the pilot program.

(e) Assistance payments to lender. The PHA must make homeownership assistance payments to a lender on behalf of the disabled family. If the assistance payment exceeds the amount due to the lender, the PHA must pay the excess directly to the family. The provisions of Sec. 982.635(d), which permit the PHA to make monthly homeownership assistance payments directly to the family, do not apply to the pilot program.

(f) Mortgage defaults. The requirements of Sec. 982.638(d) regarding mortgage defaults are applicable to the pilot program. However, notwithstanding Sec. 982.638(d), the PHA may, in its discretion, permit a family that has defaulted on its mortgage to move to a new unit with continued voucher homeownership assistance if the PHA determines that the default is due to catastrophic medical reasons or due to the impact of a federally declared major disaster or emergency. The requirements of Secs. 982.627(a)(5) and 982.627(e) do not apply to such a family.

{66 FR 33613, June 22, 2001}

Sec. 982.643 Homeownership option: Downpayment assistance grants.

(a) General. (1) A PHA may provide a single downpayment assistance grant for a participant that has received tenant-based or project-based rental assistance in the Housing Choice Voucher Program.

(2) The downpayment assistance grant must be applied toward the downpayment required in connection with the purchase of the home and/or reasonable and customary closing costs in connection with the purchase of the home.

(3) If the PHA permits the downpayment grant to be applied to closing costs, the PHA must define what fees and charges constitute reasonable and customary closing costs. However, if the purchase of a home is financed with FHA mortgage insurance, such financing is subject to FHA mortgage insurance requirements, including any requirements concerning closing costs (see Sec. 982.632(b) of this part regarding the applicability of FHA requirements to voucher homeownership assistance and Sec. 203.27 of this title regarding allowable fees, charges and discounts for FHA-insured mortgages).

(b) Maximum downpayment grant. A downpayment assistance grant may not exceed twelve times the difference between the payment standard and the total tenant payment.

(c) Payment of downpayment grant. The downpayment assistance grant shall be paid at the closing of the family's purchase of the home.

(d) Administrative fee. For each downpayment assistance grant made by the PHA, HUD will pay the PHA a one-time administrative fee in accordance with Sec. 982.152(a)(1)(iii).

(e) Return to tenant-based assistance. A family that has received a downpayment assistance grant may apply for and receive tenant-based rental assistance, in accordance with program requirements and PHA policies. However, the PHA may not commence tenant-based rental assistance for occupancy of the new unit so long as any member of the family owns any title or other interest in the home purchased with homeownership assistance. Further, eighteen

months must have passed since the family's receipt of the downpayment assistance grant.

(f) Implementation of downpayment assistance grants. A PHA may not offer downpayment assistance under this paragraph until HUD publishes a notice in the Federal Register.

{67 FR 64494, Oct. 18, 2002}

$0 11
7420.10G Gbk: 5-23; 6-7; 6-8; 18-9 (4);
PIH Notices: 03-23 (2); 02-21; 01-15 Impr Integ Hbk

$1 35
HUD-50058: p vii;
HUD-50058Instr: p35; p36; p37;
7420.10G Gbk: 5-17; 5-27 (2); 5-33 (2); 9-10 (5); 17-6 (2); 17-7 (2); 20-21 Ex 20-4; 20-22 Ex 20-5; 20-26 (2);
PIH Notices: 02-21 (9); 01-15 Impr Integ Hbk;
Admin Plan: s6p10; s24p1; s24p1

$10 16
24 CFR 5: .318 (2);
HUD-50058Instr: p35 (2);
7420.10G Gbk: 5-31; 18-6; 20-7 (2);
PIH Notices: 03-23 (7);
Admin Plan: s22p1

$100 58
HUD-50058Instr: p39 (4); p40; p41 (3); p43 (2); p45 (4); p49 (4); p51 (4); p52 (4); p54 (2); p69 (2);
7420.10G Gbk: 5-19 (2); 5-23 (3); 5-24; 6-6 (2); 8-16 (2); 20-26 (3); 20-27; 23-11 (3); 23-13 (2);
PIH Notices: 03-23; 02-27 (5); 01-10;
Admin Plan: s6p9; s17p3

$1000 1
HUD-50058Instr: p73

$100K 2
PIH Notices: 02-27; 02-27

$15 9
7420.10G Gbk: 5-17;
PIH Notices: 03-23 (7); 01-10

$2 33
HUD-50058Instr: p30 (3);
7420.10G Gbk: 5-31; 5-33 (5); 5-34 (7); 20-21 Ex 20-4; 23-16 Ex 23-2;
PIH Notices: 02-27 (2); 02-21 (11); 01-15 Impr Integ Hbk;
Admin Plan: s17p2

$200 21
24 CFR 5: .609;
HUD-50058Instr: p25; p37; p44 (2); p48; p49; p51 (4); p52 (2); p55 (2);
7420.10G Gbk: 5-15 Ex 5-2; 23-13 (2);
PIH Notices: 01-15 Impr Integ Hbk (2); 01-15 Impr Integ Hbk

$200 PER MONTH 5
24 CFR 5: .609;
HUD-50058Instr: p25;
7420.10G Gbk: 5-15 Ex 5-2;
PIH Notices: 01-15 Impr Integ Hbk; 01-15 Impr Integ Hbk

$25 26
24 CFR 5: .630;
HUD-50058: p vii;
HUD-50058Instr: p36; p39; p41; p43; p45; p49 (2); p51; p52;
HUD-52667: p i;
7420.10G Gbk: 6-1; 6-5; 6-6; 6-8 (2); 9-2 (2); 20-27;
PIH Notices: 02-27 (3); 01-15 Impr Integ Hbk (2);
Admin Plan: s6p4

$250 19
HUD-50058Instr: p44; p49; p52; p55;
7420.10G Gbk: 6-7 (3); 17-9 (2); 20-3;
PIH Notices: 02-07; 01-41 (4); 00-28; 00-09 (2); 00-09

$250K 1
PIH Notices: 02-27

$25K 1
PIH Notices: 02-27

$400 26
24 CFR 5: .611;
HUD-50058: p7; p vii;
HUD-50058Instr: p35 (3); p51 (2);
7420.10G Gbk: 5-28; 5-29; 17-6 (2); 17-8 (2); 20-9 (2); 20-19 Ex 20-3 (4); 23-13 (3);
PIH Notices: 01-15 Impr Integ Hbk (2);
Admin Plan: s6p1

$480 33
24 CFR 5: .609 (2); .611;
HUD-50058: p7; p vii;
HUD-50058Instr: p25 (2); p26; p27; p31; p36 (2);
7420.10G Gbk: 5-15 Ex 5-2 (2); 5-18 (5); 5-28; 5-29; 5-50 Ex 5-5; 9-2;
PIH Notices: 01-15 Impr Integ Hbk (7); 01-10;
Admin Plan: s6p1; s7p5

$5 35
24 CFR 5: .318 (2); .609;
HUD-50058: p6 (2);
HUD-50058Instr: p23 (3); p40; p68;
HUD-9886: p2;
7420.10G Gbk: 5-14 Ex 5-2; 5-23 (3); 5-24 (4); 5-27; 5-28; 9-9; 12-11; 20-9; 23-16 Ex 23-2 (2);
PIH Notices: 03-23 (2); 01-15 (3); 01-15 Impr Integ Hbk (2); 00-24B; 00-24B

$50 24
24 CFR 5: .318; .630;
HUD-50058: p viii;
HUD-50058Instr: p37;
7420.10G Gbk: 2-9; 5-5; 6-5 (2); 6-7; 6-8; 20-7 (2); 20-22 Ex 20-5; 20-24; 20-26 (6);
PIH Notices: 01-15 Impr Integ Hbk; 00-09;
Admin Plan: s11p1; s23p5

$500 42
24 CFR 5: .617;
24 CFR 982: .152;
HUD-50058Instr: p40 (2);
7420.10G Gbk: 5-5; 5-33; 6-4 (2); 6-5; 9-2 (4); 20-3 (2); 20-9 (2); 20-12 Ex 20-2 (2); 23-13 (4); 23-16 Ex 23-2;
PIH Notices: 02-07; 01-41 (2); 01-15 Impr Integ Hbk; 01-10 (5); 00-28; 00-09 (7);
Admin Plan: s6p2

$5000 1
Admin Plan: s21p4

$75 20
HUD-50058Instr: p37; p39 (2); p41 (2); p45 (2); p49 (2); p51 (2); p52 (2);
7420.10G Gbk: 6-8; 13-9; 20-4;
PIH Notices: 02-07 (2); 00-28; 00-28

$750 4
HUD-50058Instr: p37 (2);
7420.10G Gbk: 24-11;
PIH Notices: 02-21

0% 2
7420.10G Gbk: 2-13 Ex 2-1; 2-13 Ex 2-1

0 BEDROOM 1
PIH Notices: 01-41

1 YEAR 4
24 CFR 982: .507;
HUD-903: p2;
PIH Notices: 01-41; 00-09

10% 41
HUD-50058Instr: p66;
HUD-52580: p2 (3); p3 (3); p4 (2);
HUD-52580-A: p2 (2); p3; p5; p7; p9; p10; p11; p12; p17 (2);
HUD-52648: p1; p4;
7420.10G Gbk: 1-6 Ex 1-1 (2); 5-28; 6-1; 23-17 Ex 23-2; 24-6;
PIH Notices: 01-15 Impr Integ Hbk (2); 01-10; 00-45;
Admin Plan: s6p4; s6p13; s10p1; s10p2; s21p7 (2); s21p8 (2); s22p5

10 DAYS 20
24 CFR 5: .353 (2); .512;
7420.10G Gbk: 5-7; 5-9 Ex 5-1; 13-9;
Admin Plan: s3p1; s3p2; s4p2; s5p2; s6p4; s10p3; s18p2; s18p3; s18p4 (2); s18p6; s18p7; s20p7; s23p8

10 HOURS 4
24 CFR 5: .617;
HUD-50058Instr: p74;
PIH Notices: 01-15 Impr Integ Hbk;
Admin Plan: s6p2

10 MONTHS 1
7420.10G Gbk: 20-22

10 PERCENT 31
24 CFR 5: .628;
24 CFR 982: .517;
HUD-50058Instr: p37;
7420.10G Gbk: 2-13 Ex 2-1; 6-1; 6-10 Ex 6-2; 8-5; 10-18; 12-10 (2); 18-9 (2); 18-10; 19-3 (2); 24-6;
PIH Notices: 02-27; 01-41; 01-10 (3); 00-49; 00-28 (2); 00-24B (3); 00-09; 95-48; 95-48 Tech Asst;
Admin Plan: s21p4

10 YEARS 3
24 CFR 5: .603;
7420.10G Gbk: 5-38;
Admin Plan: s24p5

100% 9
7420.10G Gbk: 13-10; 20-16;
PIH Notices: 02-20;
Admin Plan: s4p2; s8p1 (2); s13p2; s20p2; s21p5

100 PERCENT 17

7420.10G Gbk: 7-3; 7-10; 19-2; 20-15; 20-16; 20-19 Ex 20-3; 20-20 (2); 24-1 (2); 24-6; 24-8;
PIH Notices: 01-01 (3); 95-48; 95-48 Tech Asst

1099 10
7420.10G Gbk: 5-12; 5-48 Ex 5-5; 11-19; 23-14;
PIH Notices: 01-15; 01-15 Impr Integ Hbk (3);
Admin Plan: s7p5; s7p8

10TH 1
PIH Notices: 02-06

110% 6
7420.10G Gbk: 1-6 Ex 1-1; 7-2 (2);
PIH Notices: 02-22;
Admin Plan: s11p3; s24p4

110 PERCENT 73
24 CFR 982: .503 (5);
HUD-52648: p2;
7420.10G Gbk: 2-3; 3-5; 7-1; 7-2 (5); 7-3; 7-4 (2); 7-6 (4); 7-9; 20-6 (2); 20-18; 24-11; 24-12;
PIH Notices: 02-22 (6); 02-20 (17); 02-07; 01-06 (2); 01-01 (5); 00-46 (14); 00-28

11063 2
24 CFR 5: .105;
7420.10G Gbk: 5-42

12% 4
7420.10G Gbk: 2-13 Ex 2-1; 19-7;
PIH Notices: 02-27;
Admin Plan: s20p1

12 CUMULATIVE MONTHS 1
Admin Plan: s6p2

12 MONTH 3
24 CFR 982: .353;
HUD-50058Instr: p33;
7420.10G Gbk: 5-23

12 MONTHS 80
HUD-50058Instr: p12 (3);
HUD-52648: p1; p2;
7420.10G Gbk: 4-6 (2); 5-17 (2); 5-24; 5-31; 5-32; 5-47 Ex 5-5 (2); 5-48 Ex 5-5 (3); 5-49 Ex 5-5 (3); 5-51 Ex 5-5 (2); 6-1; 10-21; 10-23; 10-35; 12-10; 12-13 Ex 12-1; 12-16 Ex 12-4; 13-9; 17-12; 18-4; 19-13; 20-7; 20-9; 23-6; 23-14; 23-16 Ex 23-2; 23-18; 24-1 (4); 24-2 (2); 24-6; 24-7 (2);
PIH Notices: 03-23 (2); 02-21; 02-07; 01-20 (4); 01-15 Impr Integ Hbk; 00-28; 00-24B (3);
Admin Plan: s6p1; s6p2; s6p3 (3); s7p4 (3); s7p5 (3); s7p6 (2); s7p7; s9p2; s15p3; s17p1; s21p4; s21p7

12 YEARS 1
7420.10G Gbk: 5-38

120% 2
PIH Notices: 02-20;
Admin Plan: s11p3

120 94
24 CFR 982: .502; .503 (3);
HUD-50058Instr: p66;
7420.10G Gbk: 5-23 (3); 5-24 (5); 7-4 (5); 20-10 (2); 21-20; 23-11 (2); 23-17 Ex 23-2; 24-1;
PIH Notices: 02-27; 02-20 (22); 01-41 (5); 01-33; 01-10; 01-06; 00-46 (21); 00-09 (5);
Admin Plan: s2p4; s2p5; s3p3; s6p7 (3); s7p1 (2); s7p8; s10p2; s11p3; s13p1

120 DAYS 30
24 CFR 982: .502;
7420.10G Gbk: 12-2; 12-4; 14-3; 23-6 (2); 24-5 (2); 24-6; 24-10;
PIH Notices: 01-41 (3); 01-33; 01-10; 00-09 (3);
Admin Plan: s2p4; s2p5; s3p3; s6p7 (3); s7p1 (2); s7p8; s10p2; s11p3; s13p1

120 PERCENT 51
24 CFR 982: .503 (3);
7420.10G Gbk: 7-4 (5);
PIH Notices: 02-20 (22); 00-46 (20); 00-46

1250 BUDGETED UNITS 2
24 CFR 982: .305; .305

13 YEARS 2
24 CFR 5: .603;
HUD-50058Instr: p70

14 CONSECUTIVE DAYS 1
24 CFR 5: .318

14 DAYS 1
24 CFR 5: .514

15 DAY 1
7420.10G Gbk: 24-13

15 DAYS 23
24 CFR 5: .353; .801;
24 CFR 35 SubM: .1225;
7420.10G Gbk: 10-20; 10-21 (2);

10-25 (2); 10-26; 19-11; 19-12; 21-9 (2); 24-13 (2);
PIH Notices: 02-07; 00-49; 00-28;
Admin Plan: s6p6; s6p8; s18p2; s18p5; s20p7

15 MONTHS....................................4
24 CFR 5: .230;
HUD-9886: p2;
7420.10G Gbk: 5-13; 12-3

15 PERCENT..................................21
24 CFR 5: .653;
24 CFR 982: .623;
HUD-50058Instr: p38;
7420.10G Gbk: 19-4;
PIH Notices: 02-21; 01-41 (3); 01-10 (9); 00-09 (3); 00-09

15-DAY...4
7420.10G Gbk: 8-17; 10-25 (2);
PIH Notices: 01-06

15TH...3
7420.10G Gbk: 10-25;
PIH Notices: 01-15;
Admin Plan: s11p1

1722..3
PIH Notices: 01-15 (2); 01-15

17-YEAR-OLD.................................1
PIH Notices: 01-15 Impr Integ Hbk

18 YEARS.......................................31
24 CFR 5: .216; .230 (3); .609 (2); .611;
HUD-50058Instr: p2; p14; p15 (3); p17; p25 (2); p26; p27;
HUD-9886: p1 (2);
7420.10G Gbk: 5-15 Ex 5-2; 5-18 (2); 5-30 (2); 12-13 Ex 12-1;
PIH Notices: 01-15 Impr Integ Hbk (5);
Admin Plan: s2p1

18 YEARS OLD 12
24 CFR 5: .609;
HUD-50058Instr: p17; p25 (4); p26 (2); p27 (2);
PIH Notices: 01-15 Impr Integ Hbk; 01-15 Impr Integ Hbk

180 CALENDAR DAYS 5
24 CFR 982: .455; .635;
HUD-52641: p3;
7420.10G Gbk: 11-5; 11-6

180 CONSECUTIVE CALENDAR DAYS..1
24 CFR 982: .312

180 CONSECUTIVE DAYS............5
PIH Notices: 03-05; 01-40;
Admin Plan: s6p5; s6p6; s6p6

180 DAYS.......................................18
HUD-50058Instr: p25;
7420.10G Gbk: 3-2; 3-4; 5-15 Ex 5-2; 15-5;
PIH Notices: 01-41 (2); 01-15 Impr Integ Hbk; 00-09 (2); 00-01; 98-66; 95-48; 95-48 Tech Asst;
Admin Plan: s8p5; s14p2; s15p1; s22p2

18-MONTH.......................................1
PIH Notices: 01-15

1937..133
24 CFR 5: .100 (6); .214 (4); .306 (2); .380; .403; .500; .504 (5); .603; .653; .701; .801;
24 CFR 982: .2; .4 (4); .102; .152; .201 (5); .306; .316; .352 (2); .453; .552;
HUD-50058: p i; p5; p v;
HUD-50058Instr: p5; p19 (2); p27; p70 (8); p71 (3); p73; p74 (2); p75 (4);
HUD-52641: p1; p10;
HUD-52641-A: p3;
7420.10G Gbk: 1-1 (3); 3-3; 4-20; 5-16 Ex 5-2;
PIH Notices: 03-11; 02-21 (3); 02-01 (2); 01-41 (9); 01-27; 01-20 (3); 01-15 Impr Integ Hbk; 01-10 (8); 01-02 (2); 00-27 (3); 00-23; 00-09 (11); 99-52;
Admin Plan: s1p1; s2p3; s2p4 (2); s2p6; s4p2; s15p2; s15p5; s16p1; s24p2 24 CFR 5 100; 24 CFR 982 352;
PIH Notices 01-27

1964..6
24 CFR 5: .105; .524;
24 CFR 982: .53;
HUD-50058: p i;
7420.10G Gbk: 3-8; 5-42

1965..17
24 CFR 5: .500; .504; .516;
HUD-50058Instr: p32 (2);
7420.10G Gbk: 1-2; 5-16 Ex 5-2;
PIH Notices: 01-41 (3); 01-27; 01-15 Impr Integ Hbk (2); 01-10; 00-09 (2); 00-09

1968..14
24 CFR 5: .100; .105;
HUD-903: p3;
7420.10G Gbk: 1-2 (2); 5-42 (2); 22-15;

PIH Notices: 02-01 (2); 00-45; 99-52 (2);
Admin Plan: s25p7

1969...1
24 CFR 5: .100

1970...1
24 CFR 5: .100

1971...2
7420.10G Gbk: 1-2;
PIH Notices: 00-23

1973...25
24 CFR 5: .105; .524;
24 CFR 982: .53;
7420.10G Gbk: 3-8; 5-16 Ex 5-2; 5-42; 5-44; 8-3;
PIH Notices: 02-01; 00-45; 99-52; 95-48 (8); 95-48 Tech Asst (5); 95-48 Tech Asst

1974...11
24 CFR 982: .101; .352;
HUD-50058Instr: p3; p71;
HUD-903: p3;
HUD-9886: p1;
7420.10G Gbk: 1-2; 1-3 (3);
Admin Plan: s1p1

1975...3
24 CFR 5: .105;
7420.10G Gbk: 5-42;
PIH Notices: 00-09

1977...6
24 CFR 5: .105 (2);
7420.10G Gbk: 5-16 Ex 5-2; 10-16;
PIH Notices: 95-48; 95-48 Tech Asst

1978...16
24 CFR 5: .105 (2);
HUD-52517: p2 (2); p13; p17;
7420.10G Gbk: 8-15; 10-11; 10-16; 10-17; 10-36 Ex 10-1;
PIH Notices: 01-41; 00-23 (2); 00-09;
Admin Plan: s23p1

1980...9
24 CFR 5: .105; .500; .504;
HUD-50058Instr: p30;
7420.10G Gbk: 1-2; 5-16 Ex 5-2; 5-42;
PIH Notices: 01-27; 01-15 Impr Integ Hbk

1981...7
24 CFR 5: .653 (4);
HUD-50058Instr: p14;
Admin Plan: s23p3; s23p3

1983...6
24 CFR 5: .105; .300;
7420.10G Gbk: 1-3;
PIH Notices: 01-41; 01-10; 00-09

1984...1
7420.10G Gbk: 1-4

1985...1
7420.10G Gbk: 5-16 Ex 5-2

1986...3
7420.10G Gbk: 22-16; 22-17;
PIH Notices: 02-22

1987...7
24 CFR 5: .105;
HUD-9886: p2;
7420.10G Gbk: 1-4;
PIH Notices: 01-41; 00-09; 95-48; 95-48 Tech Asst

1988...21
24 CFR 5: .100; .105;
HUD-50058Instr: p27;
HUD-903: p2; p3;
HUD-9886: p1;
PIH Notices: 02-01 (4); 01-41 (2); 00-45; 00-09 (2); 99-52 (4);
Admin Plan: s1p3; s20p3

1989...6
24 CFR 5: .105; .110; .216;
HUD-50058Instr: p32;
7420.10G Gbk: 5-16 Ex 5-2;
PIH Notices: 01-15 Impr Integ Hbk

1990...25
24 CFR 5: .100;
24 CFR 982: .203;
HUD-50058Instr: p70;
HUD-52648: p4;
7420.10G Gbk: 3-8; 4-22; 5-16 Ex 5-2 (2);
PIH Notices: 02-20 (4); 02-01 (3); 01-41; 00-46 (4); 00-45; 00-09; 99-52 (2); 99-52

1991...23
7420.10G Gbk: 5-16 Ex 5-2; 21-17 (5); 21-18 (3); 23-1;
PIH Notices: 02-01 (3); 01-41; 01-15 (2); 01-10; 00-09; 99-52 (3); 95-48; 95-48

1992...41
24 CFR 982: .401 (2);
HUD-50058Instr: p2;
HUD-52580-A: p8;
HUD-52648: p2;
HUD-9886: p1;
7420.10G Gbk: 10-11; 10-15; 22-17;
PIH Notices: 02-01 (3); 01-06 (2); 99-52 (3); 99-

11 (2); 95-48 (13); 95-48 Tech Asst (8); 95-48 Tech Asst

1993 ... 19
24 CFR 982: .401 (2);
HUD-52580-A: p8;
HUD-52648: p2;
HUD-9886: p1;
7420.10G Gbk: 23-1;
PIH Notices: 01-15 Impr Integ Hbk (3); 01-06 (2); 01-02; 95-48 (4); 95-48 Tech Asst (2);
Admin Plan: s25p4

1994 ... 20
HUD-50058Instr: 24 CFR 982; p3;
7420.10G Gbk: 1-4 (3); 21-17 (3); 21-18 (5);
PIH Notices: 02-01 (2); 99-52 (2); 99-11; 95-48; 95-48 Tech Asst

1995 ... 46
24 CFR 5: .506; .508 (4); .516; .518;
24 CFR 982: .5; .54; .104; .207; .317; .355; .406; .521;
HUD-50058Instr: p17;
7420.10G Gbk: 1-4 (3); 10-15; 14-5;
PIH Notices: 03-23; 03-20; 03-12; 03-11; 02-21; 01-10 (7); 99-11; 96-65; 95-48 (7); 95-48 Tech Asst (2); 95-48 Tech Asst

1996 ... 34
24 CFR 5: .210; .400; .508; .518 (4); .601; .630;
HUD-50058Instr: p17; p18 (3);
7420.10G Gbk: 2-13 Ex 2-1; 6-8;
PIH Notices: 02-01; 01-15 Impr Integ Hbk; 01-10 (10); 00-11 (2); 99-52; 96-65 (2); 95-48; 95-48

1997 ... 30
HUD-50058Instr: p14;
7420.10G Gbk: 18-9 (2); 20-8 Ex 20-1 (8); 21-19;
PIH Notices: 01-41 (2); 01-10 (5); 00-11A; 00-09 (8); 96-65

2 BEDROOMS ... 1
7420.10G Gbk: 17-8

2 MONTHS ... 6
Admin Plan: s21p7 (4); s21p8; s21p8

2 PERCENTAGE ... 2
7420.10G Gbk: 7-10; 7-10

2 WEEKS ... 1
PIH Notices: 03-11

2 YEARS ... 5
HUD-50058Instr: p22; p60;
7420.10G Gbk: 5-50 Ex 5-5;
PIH Notices: 01-41; 00-09

20 HOURS ... 1
7420.10G Gbk: 16-5

20 PERCENT ... 6
7420.10G Gbk: 4-2; 13-9; 20-6; 21-17; 24-15;
PIH Notices: 02-27

20 YEARS ... 1
24 CFR 982: .634

200 ... 38
24 CFR 5: .107 (2); .601; .701 (2);
HUD-903: p3;
7420.10G Gbk: 5-23 (2); 5-24; 10-31 (2); 19-7; 20-5; 20-8 Ex 20-1 (4); 21-6; 22-7 (2); 23-16 Ex 23-2 (2);
PIH Notices: 02-21 (6); 02-07; 01-27; 01-20 (4); 00-28; 95-48; 95-48 Tech Asst;
Admin Plan: s20p1

2000 ... 273
24 CFR 5: .661;
24 CFR 35 SubM: .1200 (6);
24 CFR 982: .624; .642;
HUD-50058: p1;
HUD-50058Instr: p14 (2); p16; p61;
7420.10G Gbk: 1-9 (2); 5-16 Ex 5-2; 5-22; 8-23; 10-15; 10-22; 10-31 (2); 10-32 (3); 18-9 (2); 20-8 Ex 20-1; 20-10 (2); 20-12 Ex 20-2 (3); 20-19 Ex 20-3 (3); 20-22; 22-7 (2);
PIH Notices: 02-27 (2); 02-22; 02-20 (2); 02-06; 02-01; 01-41 (2); 01-27 (5); 01-15 (2); 01-15 Impr Integ Hbk (9); 01-10 (17); 01-06 (27); 01-01 (5); 00-53 (6); 00-49; 00-46; 00-45 (2); 00-41 (2); 00-34 (17); 00-31 (2); 00-28 (3); 00-27 (18); 00-24 (15); 00-24A (6); 00-23 (5); 00-14; 00-11 (2); 00-09 (21); 00-01 (5); 99-52 (3); 99-30 (2); 99-11; 98-66 (4); 95-48 (21); 95-48 Tech Asst (19);
Admin Plan: s22p1

2001 ... 179

24 CFR 982: .642;
HUD-50058: p ii; p6; p xiii;
HUD-50058Instr: p i; p17; p21 (3); p30 (2); p32 (2); p42; p53; p78 (3);
HUD-52580: p1 (2); p2; p3; p4; p5; p6;
7420.10G Gbk: 1-1; 1-4; 14-1; 20-10 (2); 20-11 (2); 20-12 Ex 20-2 (4); 20-19 Ex 20-3 (3); 20-20; 20-21 Ex 20-4; 20-22 (2);
PIH Notices: 02-27 (3); 02-21; 02-20 (2); 02-14; 02-07 (2); 02-06; 02-03; 01-43 (3); 01-41 (4); 01-40; 01-33 (3); 01-27 (5); 01-20 (21); 01-15 (2); 01-15 Impr Integ Hbk (3); 01-11 (9); 01-10 (21); 01-06 (9); 01-02; 01-01 (5); 00-53 (17); 00-49; 00-46; 00-41; 00-34; 00-31 (2); 00-28; 00-27 (8); 00-24; 00-14; 00-11; 00-09; 00-01;
Admin Plan: s24p1

2002 79
24 CFR 5: .801 (3);
7420.10G Gbk: 20-12 Ex 20-2 (7); 20-19 Ex 20-3 (6); 20-22;
PIH Notices: 03-23 (20); 02-27 (8); 02-22; 02-21 (4); 02-20; 02-15 (2); 02-14; 02-07; 02-06 (2); 02-03; 02-01; 01-43 (2); 01-41; 01-40; 01-33; 01-27; 01-20 (7); 01-15; 01-10; 01-06 (2); 01-02;

2080 HOURS 2
7420.10G Gbk: 5-17; 24-7

24 HOUR 2
7420.10G Gbk: 2-11; 10-33

24 HOURS 26
24 CFR 982: .404 (2); .619;
HUD-52641: p3;
HUD-52648: p1;
7420.10G Gbk: 4-13; 10-27; 10-28; 10-29; 10-33; 24-12;
PIH Notices: 03-11; 00-49; 00-24B (2);
Admin Plan: s10p2 (5); s10p3; s10p4; s10p5; s18p5; s21p5; s21p5

24 MONTHS 4
24 CFR 5: .514;
HUD-50058Instr: p18;
7420.10G Gbk: 4-4; 5-8

24-HOUR 2
Admin Plan: s10p1; s10p1

25% 4
PIH Notices: 95-48; 95-48 Tech Asst;
Admin Plan: s24p2; s24p6

25 PERCENT 5
24 CFR 5: .518; .653;
7420.10G Gbk: 1-3; 7-3;
PIH Notices: 02-22

25 PERCENTAGE 1
7420.10G Gbk: 19-3

250 UNITMONTHS 1
7420.10G Gbk: 20-9

250 UNITS 9
7420.10G Gbk: 21-1; 21-11; 21-12 Ex 21-3;
PIH Notices: 02-27 (4); 02-01; 99-52

2ND 4
HUD-50058Instr: p47; p48;
7420.10G Gbk: 12-12 Ex 12-1; 19-13

3% 13
HUD-50058Instr: p22 (2); p23; p34;
7420.10G Gbk: 2-13 Ex 2-1; 5-30; 5-31; 5-32; 5-33 (2); 5-34;
PIH Notices: 01-15 Impr Integ Hbk;
Admin Plan: s22p3

3 BEDROOM 1
PIH Notices: 01-41

3 BEDROOMS 1
7420.10G Gbk: 17-8

3 MONTHS 15
7420.10G Gbk: 5-17;
PIH Notices: 03-23 (12); 02-27;
Admin Plan: s21p5

3 PERCENT 4
24 CFR 982: .625;
PIH Notices: 01-41; 01-15; 00-09

3 YEAR 1
HUD-50058Instr: p11

3 YEARS 7
24 CFR 5: .518;
HUD-50058Instr: p18;
PIH Notices: 03-11;
Admin Plan: s2p6; s15p3; s17p3; s17p3

30% 39
HUD-50058: p8; p viii; p xvii;
HUD-50058Instr: p37 (2); p62; p66 (3); p67;

7420.10G Gbk: 1-6 Ex 1-1 (2); 4-9; 6-1; 19-7; 23-11 (2); 23-12; 23-14; 23-16 Ex 23-2; 23-17 Ex 23-2 (4);
PIH Notices: 01-15 Impr Integ Hbk (2); 01-10 (9);
Admin Plan: s2p5; s6p4; s24p6; s24p6

30 CALENDAR DAYS 19
24 CFR 982: .404 (2);
HUD-52648: p1;
7420.10G Gbk: 1-11; 10-33;
PIH Notices: 02-27 (7); 01-06; 00-24B (2); 00-23 (2); 96-65;
Admin Plan: s21p5

30 DAY 1
24 CFR 5: .514

30 DAYS 38
24 CFR 5: .353 (2); .360; .363; .514 (4);
24 CFR 35 SubM: .1215; .1225;
HUD-50058Instr: p17;
7420.10G Gbk: 5-6; 5-11 (2); 9-2; 10-21 (2); 10-27; 10-34; 12-6 (2); 13-9; 16-3; 22-4;
PIH Notices: 03-23;
Admin Plan: s3p2 (2); s6p5; s6p6; s6p7; s10p3; s10p4; s10p5; s17p2; s18p4; s21p5; s23p4; s24p7

30 HOURS 1
24 CFR 982: .627

30 PERCENT 66
24 CFR 5: .603 (2); .628;
24 CFR 982: .1 (2); .503 (2);
HUD-50058Instr: p71 (2);
HUD-52646: p1;
7420.10G Gbk: 1-3; 1-4; 1-5; 4-19; 5-3; 6-1; 6-10 Ex 6-2; 7-3; 7-6; 8-5; 14-1; 14-4; 23-7; 23-11; 23-19 (6); 24-11;
PIH Notices: 02-20 (3); 01-41 (8); 01-10 (10); 00-46 (3); 00-24B (3); 00-09 (7);
Admin Plan: s4p2

30-45 DAYS...................................... 1
7420.10G Gbk: 11-9

30-DAY 6
7420.10G Gbk: 10-18; 10-29 (3); 10-34;
PIH Notices: 00-23

30-DAY NOTICE 2
7420.10G Gbk: 10-29; 10-29

30-DAYS.. 1
7420.10G Gbk: 10-28

30TH 2
Admin Plan: s21p2; s21p2

31 DAYS 1
7420.10G Gbk: 9-2

3BR 1
7420.10G Gbk: 17-9

3RD 1
Admin Plan: s21p4

4 BEDROOM 1
PIH Notices: 01-41

40% 6
7420.10G Gbk: 1-6 Ex 1-1; 6-2; 6-5;
PIH Notices: 00-45;
Admin Plan: s9p1; s11p1

40 DAYS 4
Admin Plan: s7p2 (3); s7p2

40 HOUR 1
7420.10G Gbk: 5-17

40 HOURS 1
7420.10G Gbk: 16-5

40 PERCENT 44
24 CFR 5: .653;
24 CFR 982: .305; .503 (2); .508; .623;
7420.10G Gbk: 6-2 (2); 6-6; 6-10 Ex 6-2 (3); 7-5; 7-9; 8-5; 8-16 (3); 14-4 (4); 17-12; 24-11 (2); 24-12 (2);
PIH Notices: 02-20 (3); 01-41 (3); 01-15; 00-46 (3); 00-24B; 00-09 (3); 95-48; 95-48 Tech Asst;
Admin Plan: s19p1

40TH 48
24 CFR 982: .503 (6);
7420.10G Gbk: 7-1; 7-2 (3); 7-3; 7-4 (3); 7-5 (5); 17-12;
PIH Notices: 02-20 (12); 01-01 (5); 00-46 (10);
Admin Plan: s11p3

40TH PERCENTILE 27
24 CFR 982: .503 (2);
7420.10G Gbk: 7-2 (2); 7-3; 7-4; 7-5 (2); 17-12;
PIH Notices: 02-20 (2); 01-01 (5); 00-46 (10);
Admin Plan: s11p3

45 CALENDAR DAY........................ 1
PIH Notices: 02-27

45 CALENDAR DAYS 4
7420.10G Gbk: 20-28; 20-29;

PIH Notices: 02-27; 01-06

4506 ... 2
PIH Notices: 01-15;
Admin Plan: s7p2

48 HOURS ... 2
Admin Plan: s10p2; s10p2

48 MONTH ... 6
24 CFR 5: .617 (2);
PIH Notices: 01-15 Impr Integ Hbk (3); 01-15 Impr Integ Hbk

5 BEDROOMS ... 1
HUD-52667: p i

5 DAYS ... 4
Admin Plan: s9p2; s10p2; s23p8; s23p8

5 MONTHS ... 1
7420.10G Gbk: 20-7

5 PERCENT ... 11
HUD-52648: p1;
7420.10G Gbk: 5-26; 24-6 (4);
PIH Notices: 02-21 (2); 01-20; 00-27;
Admin Plan: s21p3

5 PERCENTAGE ... 1
PIH Notices: 01-01

5 YEARS ... 5
24 CFR 5: .514;
HUD-50058: p xvii;
HUD-50058Instr: p61;
HUD-9886: p1; p1

50% ... 20
HUD-50058: p v;
HUD-50058Instr: p19;
HUD-52648: p4;
7420.10G Gbk: 20-14; 23-10 (2);
PIH Notices: 03-23 (2); 02-27; 02-01; 99-52; 95-48 (3); 95-48 Tech Asst (3);
Admin Plan: s2p4; s17p1; s24p6

50 PERCENT ... 52
24 CFR 5: .603 (2);
24 CFR 982: .503;
HUD-50058Instr: p76 (2);
7420.10G Gbk: 4-17; 5-2; 7-4; 19-8; 20-14 (2); 20-25 (3); 20-26 (2); 21-19; 23-6; 23-11; 24-6 (2);
PIH Notices: 02-22; 02-20 (9); 01-41 (2); 00-46 (9); 00-09 (3); 95-48 (3); 95-48 Tech Asst (3);
Admin Plan: s6p3

50 WEEKS ... 4
24 CFR 5: .617;
HUD-50058Instr: p74;
PIH Notices: 01-15 Impr Integ Hbk;
Admin Plan: s6p2

50 YEARS ... 5
24 CFR 5: .403 (3);
24 CFR 982: .402;
7420.10G Gbk: 5-41

50058 ... 69
24 CFR 982: .355;
HUD-50058Instr: p1; p2 (2); p5; p11 (3); p77;
7420.10G Gbk: 10-35; 13-9; 13-11 Ex 13-1; 13-12 Ex 13-2; 14-5;
PIH Notices: 03-20 (9); 02-27; 01-43 (6); 01-15; 01-11 (5); 00-53 (26); 00-24A;
Admin Plan: s2p2; s6p7; s6p13; s8p5; s13p2; s21p2

50TH PERCENTILE ... 82
24 CFR 982: .503 (10);
7420.10G Gbk: 7-1; 7-2 (4); 7-3 (12); 7-4 (2); 7-5 (7); 7-10 (3); 24-10; 24-12;
PIH Notices: 02-20 (16); 01-01 (24);
Admin Plan: s11p3

5-YEAR ... 2
24 CFR 982: .4;
7420.10G Gbk: 23-1

6 MONTH ... 7
24 CFR 982: .503 (2);
HUD-50058Instr: p18;
7420.10G Gbk: 13-11 Ex 13-1; 13-12 Ex 13-2;
PIH Notices: 02-20; 02-20

6 MONTHS ... 10
24 CFR 982: .634;
HUD-50058Instr: p18;
7420.10G Gbk: 5-49 Ex 5-5; 20-9;
PIH Notices: 02-27; 02-20 (2); 00-46 (2);
Admin Plan: s5p1

6 YEAR ... 1
7420.10G Gbk: 24-3

6 YEARS ... 9
24 CFR 35 SubM: .1200 (2); .1225 (3);
7420.10G Gbk: 10-12 (2); 10-17;
Admin Plan: s7p3

60% ... 3
7420.10G Gbk: 19-7; 24-4; 24-6

60 CALENDAR DAY ... 1
PIH Notices: 96-65

60 CALENDAR DAYS ... 14
24 CFR 5: .216;
24 CFR 982: .303; .305 (2);

7420.10G Gbk: 11-15;
PIH Notices: 02-27 (2); 01-41; 01-06 (3); 00-34; 00-09; 96-65

60 DAY 1
24 CFR 982: .305

60 DAYS 61
24 CFR 5: .216; .312; .518 (2); .801 (2);
24 CFR 982: .201; .305; .507; .508; .519;
HUD-52648: p1 (2);
7420.10G Gbk: 1-10; 4-19; 8-10; 8-11; 9-1 (2); 9-2; 9-12; 11-15; 11-16 Ex 11-1; 11-17; 12-8; 12-13 Ex 12-1 (2); 19-11; 24-5 (2); 24-6; 24-10 (3);
PIH Notices: 01-41 (11); 01-06; 00-24B (2); 00-09 (3);
Admin Plan: s2p5; s7p8; s8p5; s10p2; s11p2; s11p3; s21p3 (2); s24p2; s24p5

60 PERCENT 6
7420.10G Gbk: 1-11 (2); 21-19; 23-19 (2);
PIH Notices: 02-22

600 19
7420.10G Gbk: 5-17 (2); 5-33 (2); 5-34; 9-10; 10-31; 20-5 (2); 21-5; 21-6;
PIH Notices: 02-27 (5); 02-21; 01-15; 00-11

62 YEARS 18
24 CFR 5: .100; .216; .403 (3); .508 (3);
HUD-50058Instr: p17; p71 (2); p74;
7420.10G Gbk: 5-2; 5-9 Ex 5-1 (2); 5-29; 12-12 Ex 12-1;
Admin Plan: s7p8

70% 2
7420.10G Gbk: 24-4; 24-6

70 PERCENT 3
7420.10G Gbk: 7-3; 21-18; 23-19

72 HOURS 1
Admin Plan: s10p2

75 PERCENT 23
24 CFR 982: .201; .503; .604 (3);
7420.10G Gbk: 4-5; 4-19 (2); 5-3; 7-4; 7-10; 17-3 (2); 24-4; 24-7;
PIH Notices: 02-20; 01-41; 01-01 (3); 00-09;
Admin Plan: s19p1; s19p1

80% 24
HUD-50058Instr: p44; p48; p51; p54;
HUD-52648: p1 (3); p3;
7420.10G Gbk: 5-43; 13-10; 20-24 (3); 20-25 (4); 23-10; 23-11;
Admin Plan: s2p4; s13p2; s21p3; s21p4; s21p7

80 PERCENT 21
24 CFR 5: .603 (2);
24 CFR 982: .355;
HUD-50058Instr: p73 (2);
7420.10G Gbk: 4-14; 5-2; 13-5; 13-9; 20-24 (2); 20-25; 23-19 (2);
PIH Notices: 01-41 (3); 00-09 (3); 96-65

85 PERCENT 22
7420.10G Gbk: 19-1; 19-2 (3); 19-3 (3); 20-11;
PIH Notices: 01-06 (9); 00-53 (3); 00-28; 00-28

8821 2
PIH Notices: 01-15;
Admin Plan: s7p2

9 MONTHS 4
24 CFR 5: .801;
7420.10G Gbk: 5-17;
PIH Notices: 01-15; 01-06

90% 7
HUD-52648: p1;
7420.10G Gbk: 1-6 Ex 1-1; 7-2 (2);
PIH Notices: 02-20; 00-46;
Admin Plan: s21p4

90 CALENDAR DAYS 4
7420.10G Gbk: 20-28 (3);
PIH Notices: 02-27

90 DAYS 21
24 CFR 5: .801 (2);
24 CFR 982: .503;
7420.10G Gbk: 6-8; 7-4; 7-7; 20-7; 24-5; 24-6; 24-10;
PIH Notices: 02-27 (3); 02-20; 01-01 (3);
Admin Plan: s6p5; s10p2; s11p1; s22p3

90 PERCENT 52
24 CFR 982: .503 (2);
HUD-52648: p2;
7420.10G Gbk: 1-5; 1-11; 2-3; 7-1; 7-2 (5); 7-6 (4); 7-9; 12-11; 20-10 (6); 20-18; 20-19 Ex 20-3; 21-19 (2); 24-2 (2);
PIH Notices: 02-20 (7); 01-06 (2); 01-01 (2); 00-46 (6); 00-28 (4); 00-28

90-DAY 5
24 CFR 5: .630 (3);
7420.10G Gbk: 6-8; 24-5
90-DAY PERIOD 3
24 CFR 5: .630 (2);
7420.10G Gbk: 6-8
95% 9
7420.10G Gbk: 7-10 (2); 24-4; 24-6;
PIH Notices: 02-27 (2); 02-01; 99-52;
Admin Plan: s21p8
95 PERCENT 25
HUD-50058Instr: p40; p68;
7420.10G Gbk: 8-11; 8-22; 20-10; 20-11 (3); 24-2 (4); 24-16 (3);
PIH Notices: 02-07 (3); 01-41; 01-20 (4); 01-01; 00-09
95TH PERCENTILE 4
24 CFR 5: .520;
HUD-50058: p ix;
HUD-50058Instr: p40; p68
95TH PERCENTILE RENT 1
24 CFR 5: .520
98% 10
HUD-52648: p1 (4);
Admin Plan: s21p3 (2); s21p5; s21p6; s21p8; s21p8
98 PERCENT 6
7420.10G Gbk: 4-22; 8-11; 19-8; 24-2; 24-8; 24-16
AAF 10
7420.10G Gbk: 20-9 (5); 20-13;
PIH Notices: 03-23 (3);
Admin Plan: s23p6
ABANDONED 1
24 CFR 5: .703
ABANDONED VEHICLES 1
24 CFR 5: .703
ABANDONING 1
7420.10G Gbk: 5-5
ABATE 11
7420.10G Gbk: 10-27 (2); 10-28; 10-29; 10-33; 11-18; 22-15 (2);
PIH Notices: 00-49; 00-24B;
Admin Plan: s23p5
ABATED 10
HUD-52665: p3 (2);
7420.10G Gbk: 10-34; 10-46 Ex 10-8;
PIH Notices: 00-24B;
Admin Plan: s10p4; s10p5; s21p5 (2); s23p4
ABATEMENT 57
24 CFR 35 SubM: .1225;
24 CFR 982: .453; .619;
HUD-52641: p3; p4; p5;
7420.10G Gbk: 10-19; 10-21; 10-27; 10-28 (2); 10-29 (14); 10-33 (2); 10-34 (6); 10-37 Ex 10-2 (2); 10-40 Ex 10-4a; 10-41 Ex 10-4b; 10-45 Ex 10-7b; 10-46 Ex 10-8; 10-48 Ex 10-10; 19-13;
PIH Notices: 02-27; 00-23 (3);
Admin Plan: s10p2 (2); s10p3; s10p4 (8); s23p5
ABATEMENT OF RENT 1
7420.10G Gbk: 10-34
ABATEMENTS 6
7420.10G Gbk: 10-27; 10-30; 19-12; 19-13; 21-4;
Admin Plan: s17p1
ABILITIES 2
PIH Notices: 95-48; 95-48 Tech Asst
ABILITY 57
24 CFR 5: .318; .350; .403 (2);
24 CFR 982: .102; .355; .632;
HUD-50058: p i (2);
HUD-50058Instr: p15 (2); p62; p74 (2);
7420.10G Gbk: 4-7; 4-10; 6-2; 8-1; 8-2 (2); 8-9; 8-22; 11-4; 11-8; 14-5; 16-4; 19-6; 21-7; 22-8; 23-10; 23-18; 23-20; 24-13 (2); 24-15;
PIH Notices: 02-01 (2); 01-15 (2); 01-06 (2); 00-41; 99-52 (2); 95-48 (3); 95-48 Tech Asst (3);
Admin Plan: s9p2; s20p7; s21p5; s22p2; s25p2 (2); s25p6
ABILITY TO PAY 2
PIH Notices: 01-15;
Admin Plan: s25p6
ABNORMAL 5
24 CFR 982: .401; .614;
HUD-52580-A: p17;
7420.10G Gbk: 10-13; 17-5
ABNORMALLY 1
HUD-52580-A: p18
ABSENCE 56
24 CFR 5: .403;
24 CFR 982: Intro; .54; .312 (9); .551 (3); .605;
HUD-50058Instr: p72;
HUD-52580-A: p4; p6; p13 (2); p15;

7420.10G Gbk: 1-15 (2); 3-4 (3); 4-26 Ex 4-2; 15-5; 15-6 (4); 17-2; 18-6; 24-13;
PIH Notices: 03-05 (2); 01-40 (2); 95-48; 95-48 Tech Asst;
Admin Plan: s2p2; s6p1; s6p5; s6p6 (7); s6p7 (3); s7p8

ABSENCES......6
24 CFR 982: .312 (3); .551;
7420.10G Gbk: 5-36 Ex 5-4;
Admin Plan: s6p5

ABSENT......55
24 CFR 5: .100; .609;
24 CFR 982: .312 (5); .555;
HUD-50058: p v;
HUD-50058Instr: p17; p33; p36; p70;
HUD-52580-A: p6; p18;
7420.10G Gbk: 3-4 (4); 5-13; 5-18 (2); 5-36 Ex 5-4; 11-5; 15-5; 16-5;
PIH Notices: 03-05 (2); 01-40 (2); 01-15 Impr Integ Hbk;
Admin Plan: s5p1; s6p5 (7); s6p6 (13); s6p7; s7p8; s15p3

ABSENT FROM THE UNIT......8
24 CFR 982: .312 (2);
7420.10G Gbk: 3-4; 11-5;
Admin Plan: s6p6 (3); s6p6

ABSORB......33
24 CFR 982: .355 (4);
7420.10G Gbk: 2-9 (2); 13-4 (2); 13-5 (5); 13-6 (9); 13-7; 13-9; 13-11 Ex 13-1; 21-2; 21-8 (2); 23-18;
PIH Notices: 01-41; 01-10;
Admin Plan: s13p2; s13p2

ABSORBED......32
24 CFR 982: .4; .317; .355 (2);
HUD-50058: p10; p x; p11; p xi; p13; p xiii; p14; p xiv;
HUD-50058Instr: p42 (4); p46 (4); p53 (4); p56 (2); p73;
7420.10G Gbk: 13-6; 13-8 (2); 13-9; 20-25

ABSORBING......13
24 CFR 982: .4;
HUD-50058Instr: p73;
HUD-52665: p2;
7420.10G Gbk: 2-9 (2); 11-9; 13-4; 13-6 (3); 20-24;
PIH Notices: 01-41; 00-09

ABSORBS......16
24 CFR 982: .201;
HUD-50058Instr: p10; p42 (2); p46 (2); p53 (2); p56 (2);
7420.10G Gbk: 4-20; 13-7; 20-24; 21-2; 23-18; 23-18

ABSORPTION......7
24 CFR 982: .4; .355 (3);
HUD-50058Instr: p70; p71; p71

ABUSE......114
24 CFR 5: .210; .603;
24 CFR 982: .54; .310; .551 (2); .552 (3); .553 (4);
HUD-50058: p16;
HUD-50058Instr: p61; p71;
HUD-52580-A: p2;
HUD-52641: p9 (2);
HUD-52641-A: p2 (3);
7420.10G Gbk: 2-11; 3-3; 3-4; 11-10; 15-1; 15-2; 15-6; 15-7 (2); 20-6; 22-1 (6); 22-2 (2); 22-3 (4); 22-6; 22-8; 22-9 (3); 22-10 (7); 22-11 (5); 22-13; 22-14 (6); 22-15 (3); 22-16 (3); 22-17 (2); 22-18 (6);
PIH Notices: 03-11; 02-07; 01-15 Impr Integ Hbk; 00-28;
Admin Plan: s1p5; s6p3; s6p11; s7p7; s15p2 (4); s15p3; s16p2; s17p2; s20p1 (3); s20p2 (6); s20p3 (2); s20p4; s23p1; s23p2; s25p2; s25p3; s25p3

ABUSE OF ALCOHOL......7
HUD-52641: p9;
HUD-52641-A: p2 (2);
7420.10G Gbk: 4-15; 4-25 Ex 4-2; 15-2; 15-7

ABUSED......4
7420.10G Gbk: 22-11 (2); 22-14; 22-15

ABUSER......1
Admin Plan: s6p11

ABUSERS......4
24 CFR 982: Intro; .553 (2); .553

ABUSES......4
7420.10G Gbk: 22-1; 22-4 (2);
Admin Plan: s15p3

ABUSING......4
7420.10G Gbk: 15-7 (2); 22-9; 22-11

ABUSIVE......6
24 CFR 982: .552;

7420.10G Gbk: 15-6;
Admin Plan: s2p6; s15p2 (2); s15p5

ACC 220
24 CFR 5: .100; .236; .403; .504;
24 CFR 982: Intro; .4 (4); .52; .102 (6); .151 (12); .152; .153; .154 (5); .155; .157; .162; .309; .352; .355 (3); .451; .454; .628;
HUD-50058Instr: p1; p7; p70 (3);
7420.10G Gbk: 1-12; 8-11 (3); 8-17; 8-22; 19-8; 20-1 (2); 20-2; 20-5; 20-13 (6); 20-14 (13); 20-15 (12); 20-16 (9); 20-17 (2); 20-18; 20-19 Ex 20-3 (2); 20-22; 20-27; 20-28; 20-29; 21-1; 22-15; 22-18; 24-1 (3); 24-8; 24-15;
PIH Notices: 03-23 (22); 03-20; 02-27 (4); 02-21 (7); 02-07 (2); 02-06 (27); 01-41 (14); 01-20 (4); 01-06 (2); 00-49; 00-28 (2); 00-27; 00-09 (9);
Admin Plan: s14p2; s23p5 (2); s24p1; s24p5

ACC PROGRAM RESERVES..........1
PIH Notices: 00-49

ACC RESERVE ACCOUNT...........13
24 CFR 982: Intro; .151; .154 (4);
7420.10G Gbk: 20-14;
PIH Notices: 03-23 (2); 02-06 (3); 02-06

ACCEPT 62
24 CFR 5: .216; .518;
24 CFR 982: .206 (2); .310 (2); .451;
HUD-52641: p9;
HUD-52641-A: p2;
7420.10G Gbk: 4-1; 4-11; 5-12; 9-4; 9-14 Ex 9-1; 10-2; 10-6; 10-8; 10-26; 11-6; 15-2; 21-11; 22-18;
PIH Notices: 03-05; 02-27; 01-41 (2); 01-40; 01-27 (2); 01-15 Impr Integ Hbk; 01-06 (4); 00-53 (2); 00-34; 00-09 (2); 95-48 (6); 95-48 Tech Asst (6);
Admin Plan: s2p1; s3p1 (2); s20p7; s23p3; s23p4; s24p2; s25p1 (2); s25p3; s25p3

ACCEPTABILITY...........................57
24 CFR 982: .401 (18); .609; .621 (2);
7420.10G Gbk: 5-42; 10-1; 10-2 (7); 10-3 (3); 10-4 (3); 10-6; 10-7 (2); 10-8; 10-9 (3); 10-10; 10-11 (2); 10-12; 10-13 (3); 10-14 (2); 12-4; 17-10; 17-11;
PIH Notices: 02-27;
Admin Plan: s10p1

ACCEPTABLE..............................125
24 CFR 5: .216; .510 (3);
24 CFR 982: .401 (2); .402 (2); .403 (4); .636;
HUD-50058Instr: p18 (3);
HUD-52580-A: p1; p2 (2); p4 (2); p6; p15; p17 (3); p18;
7420.10G Gbk: 4-1; 5-10 Ex 5-1 (3); 5-17; 5-46 Ex 5-5; 5-47 Ex 5-5; 5-48 Ex 5-5; 5-49 Ex 5-5 (2); 5-50 Ex 5-5; 5-51 Ex 5-5; 5-52 Ex 5-5; 5-53 Ex 5-5; 7-1; 8-17 (2); 8-21; 10-5 (2); 10-6 (2); 10-7 (3); 10-8; 10-9; 10-13; 10-14 (2); 10-19; 10-31; 11-7; 12-4 (2); 13-2; 15-4; 19-2; 19-8; 22-3 (2); 22-5;
PIH Notices: 02-27; 02-20 (2); 01-41 (4); 01-15 (3); 01-15 Impr Integ Hbk (2); 01-06; 00-46 (2); 00-09 (2); 95-48 (6); 95-48 Tech Asst (6);
Admin Plan: s3p1; s7p1 (2); s7p4 (5); s7p5 (2); s7p6 (3); s7p7 (2); s8p1; s8p5; s9p2 (3); s9p4; s10p1; s15p6; s16p3 (2); s18p3; s22p3

ACCEPTABLE DOCUMENTATION5
24 CFR 5: .216;
HUD-50058Instr: p18 (2);
PIH Notices: 01-15;
Admin Plan: s16p3

ACCEPTABLE UNIT.....................10
24 CFR 982: .403 (4);
7420.10G Gbk: 8-17 (2); 15-4; 19-8;
PIH Notices: 01-41;
Admin Plan: s9p2

ACCEPTABLE UNITS 1
7420.10G Gbk: 7-1

ACCEPTANCE.................................9
24 CFR 5: .216;
PIH Notices: 02-27; 01-11;

01-02;
Admin Plan: s3p1 (2); s10p3; s24p5; s24p5

ACCEPTED....................................22
24 CFR 5: .801;
24 CFR 982: .207; .451; .625;
HUD-52641: p4;
7420.10G Gbk: 4-14 (2); 4-16; 5-46 Ex 5-5; 11-6; 14-5 (2); 20-29; 22-13;
PIH Notices: 02-01; 01-41; 01-15 Impr Integ Hbk; 01-06; 00-09; 99-52;
Admin Plan: s3p2; s4p2

ACCEPTING..................................21
24 CFR 982: .206 (2); .507; .622; .636;
7420.10G Gbk: 4-6; 4-11 (3); 8-13; 9-3; 10-17; 10-21; 15-3; 17-12; 21-3; 22-2;
PIH Notices: 02-01; 99-52;
Admin Plan: s11p2; s19p1

ACCEPTS..5
7420.10G Gbk: 11-18;
PIH Notices: 01-41; 01-15; 00-24B; 00-09

ACCESSIBILITY..........................204
24 CFR 5: .403; .655;
HUD-50058: p5 (2); p v (2);
HUD-50058Instr: p20 (4); p70; p74;
HUD-52580: p6;
HUD-52580-A: p19;
7420.10G Gbk: 4-9; 4-11; 5-25 Ex 5-3; 5-44 (2); 9-11; 9-19 Ex 9-4; 21-5; 21-6;
PIH Notices: 02-01 (40); 99-52 (38); 95-48 (55); 95-48 Tech Asst (45);
Admin Plan: s1p2; s1p3; s24p2

ACCESSIBILITY FEATURES 16
24 CFR 5: .655;
HUD-50058: p5 (2); p v (2);
HUD-50058Instr: p20 (4);
PIH Notices: 02-01 (3); 99-52 (3); 99-52

ACCESSIBLE 470
24 CFR 982: .301; .303; .316; .401; .517; .601; .605 (2); .606; .609; .610; .614 (3); .615; .619; .620; .625; .627 (2); .635 (4);
HUD-50058: p5; p v;
HUD-50058Instr: p20 (2); p70 (4);
HUD-52580: p6;
HUD-52580-A: p2 (2); p3; p5; p7; p9; p10; p11; p12; p14; p17; p19;
HUD-903-1: p2;
7420.10G Gbk: 1-7; 2-8; 2-13 Ex 2-1; 3-3 (2); 4-11 (4); 4-25 Ex 4-2; 5-25 Ex 5-3; 5-26; 5-42; 5-44 (4); 8-3 (2); 8-6; 8-9; 8-12; 9-5; 9-11 (2); 9-14 Ex 9-1 (2); 9-16 Ex 9-2 (2); 9-17 Ex 9-3; 10-6 (3); 17-2 (2); 17-3 (2); 17-4; 17-5; 18-8;
PIH Notices: 02-01 (72); 00-23; 99-52 (68); 95-48 (114); 95-48 Tech Asst (114);
Admin Plan: s1p3 (3); s1p4 (2); s1p5; s1p6; s3p2; s3p3; s6p8; s8p5; s19p1 (3); s23p2

ACCESSIBLE FEATURE.................2
PIH Notices: 02-01; 99-52

ACCESSIBLE FEATURES............17
7420.10G Gbk: 9-11;
PIH Notices: 02-01 (3); 99-52 (3); 95-48 (5); 95-48 Tech Asst (4); 95-48 Tech Asst

ACCESSIBLE FORMAT 1
Admin Plan: s3p2

ACCESSIBLE FORMATS................1
Admin Plan: s1p4

ACCESSIBLE ROUTE...................26
PIH Notices: 02-01 (3); 99-52 (3); 95-48 (10); 95-48 Tech Asst (9); 95-48 Tech Asst

ACCESSIBLE ROUTES...................4
PIH Notices: 95-48 (2); 95-48 Tech Asst; 95-48 Tech Asst

ACCESSIBLE UNIT.......................38
HUD-50058: p5; p v;
HUD-50058Instr: p20 (2);
7420.10G Gbk: 2-8; 4-25 Ex 4-2; 5-44 (2); 9-11;
PIH Notices: 02-01 (15); 99-52 (13); 99-52

ACCESSIBLE UNITS.....................31
24 CFR 982: .301;
HUD-50058Instr: p70;
7420.10G Gbk: 3-3; 5-44; 8-6; 9-14 Ex 9-1;
PIH Notices: 02-01 (12); 99-52 (12);
Admin Plan: s1p4

ACCIDENT 6
24 CFR 5: .609;
HUD-50058Instr: p31;
7420.10G Gbk: 5-15 Ex 5-2;

PIH Notices: 01-15 Impr Integ Hbk (2);
Admin Plan: s6p10
ACCIDENT INSURANCE 6
24 CFR 5: .609;
HUD-50058Instr: p31;
7420.10G Gbk: 5-15 Ex 5-2;
PIH Notices: 01-15 Impr Integ Hbk (2);
Admin Plan: s6p10
ACCIDENTAL 1
PIH Notices: 99-11
ACCOMMODATE 24
24 CFR 5: .318;
24 CFR 982: .609;
HUD-50058Instr: p35;
7420.10G Gbk: 4-11; 4-12; 4-13; 12-12 Ex 12-1; 22-8;
PIH Notices: 02-06; 02-01 (2); 01-11; 99-52 (2); 95-48 (3); 95-48 Tech Asst (3);
Admin Plan: s11p1; s21p8 (2); s25p8
ACCOMMODATES 1
7420.10G Gbk: 4-12
ACCOMMODATING 1
7420.10G Gbk: 4-12
ACCOMMODATION 126
24 CFR 5: .403;
24 CFR 982: .152; .204; .303; .306; .316; .503; .505 (2); .517 (2); .552; .601; .606; .610; .615; .619; .620; .625 (4); .627 (2); .635 (2);
HUD-50058Instr: p72; p74;
7420.10G Gbk: 18-9;
PIH Notices: 02-20; 02-01 (24); 00-46; 99-52 (23); 95-48 (12); 95-48 Tech Asst (12);
Admin Plan: s1p4 (4); s1p5 (7); s3p2; s3p3; s8p5; s10p3; s11p3; s13p1; s15p1; s16p2; s19p1 (3); s23p2; s25p3
ACCOMMODATIONS 46
24 CFR 5: .306; .315 (2); .318; .321;
HUD-50058Instr: p72;
HUD-903-1: p2;
7420.10G Gbk: 24-10;
PIH Notices: 02-01 (8); 99-52 (8); 95-48 (6); 95-48 Tech Asst (6);
Admin Plan: s1p3 (2); s1p4 (3); s8p1; s8p2; s23p2; s23p7; s25p3
ACCOUNT 213
24 CFR 5: .318;
24 CFR 982: Intro; .4; .151; .154 (5); .632;
HUD-50058: p i; p6; p16 (2); p17 (4); p xvii (3);
HUD-50058Instr: p ii; p22 (2); p60 (2); p61; p62 (12); p64; p65 (3); p66; p71 (2); p72 (3); p75;
HUD-52648: p3 (2);
7420.10G Gbk: 4-3; 4-5; 4-26 Ex 4-2 (3); 5-10 Ex 5-1; 5-24; 5-28; 5-44; 5-46 Ex 5-5; 5-48 Ex 5-5; 5-49 Ex 5-5; 8-10; 8-11; 9-10; 9-11; 10-8; 10-13; 10-24 (2); 10-33; 11-8; 12-16 Ex 12-4; 20-1; 20-2 (2); 20-7; 20-13 (3); 20-14 (4); 20-15 (10); 20-16 (2); 20-18; 20-19 Ex 20-3; 20-23 (5); 20-24 (2); 20-25 (6); 20-26 (6); 20-27 (4); 22-3; 23-1 (2); 23-10 (4); 23-12; 23-13 (2); 23-14 (14); 23-15 (3); 23-17 Ex 23-2; 23-18 (6); 23-19 (6); 24-1; 24-8;
PIH Notices: 03-23 (2); 02-27 (3); 02-06 (4); 02-01; 01-41; 01-15 (2); 01-15 Impr Integ Hbk (10); 01-06 (3); 00-24B; 00-11A; 99-52; 96-65; 95-48; 95-48 Tech Asst;
Admin Plan: s7p5 (2); s7p6; s11p1; s18p4; s21p2; s21p9 (2); s22p3 (2); s23p2; s25p4 (2); s25p5 (2); s25p5
ACCOUNT NUMBER 1
7420.10G Gbk: 4-26 Ex 4-2
ACCOUNT NUMBERS 1
7420.10G Gbk: 20-23
ACCOUNTABILITY......................... 4
7420.10G Gbk: 1-10; 13-7; 19-6;
PIH Notices: 02-27
ACCOUNTABLE 6
24 CFR 5: .100;
7420.10G Gbk: 12-8; 24-13;
PIH Notices: 02-27; 95-48; 95-48 Tech Asst
ACCOUNTANT 5
24 CFR 982: .152; .159;
7420.10G Gbk: 5-49 Ex 5-5; 20-2;
Admin Plan: s7p6

ACCOUNTANTS 1
7420.10G Gbk: 11-19
ACCOUNTANT'S............................. 2
7420.10G Gbk: 5-48 Ex 5-5;
Admin Plan: s7p5
ACCOUNTING 20
24 CFR 5: .801;
7420.10G Gbk: 11-7; 11-8; 20-23 (4); 20-24 (6); 20-25; 20-26; 20-29; 23-13;
PIH Notices: 01-15; 01-06; 00-14
ACCOUNTS 63
24 CFR 5: .603;
24 CFR 982: Intro; .158 (5);
HUD-50058: p6;
HUD-50058Instr: p22 (3); p28; p29; p60; p61 (2); p74;
HUD-52641: p5;
HUD-52648: p3;
7420.10G Gbk: 1-10; 1-11; 4-26 Ex 4-2 (3); 5-25 Ex 5-3 (3); 5-49 Ex 5-5 (2); 11-8; 11-13; 12-12 Ex 12-1; 12-13 Ex 12-1; 12-14 Ex 12-2; 20-13; 20-20; 20-23 (2); 20-24; 20-25 (3); 20-26 (2); 23-2; 23-4; 23-10; 23-13 (2); 23-14; 23-15; 23-18 (2); 24-1;
PIH Notices: 01-15 Impr Integ Hbk (4); 00-11 (3);
Admin Plan: s2p2; s21p1
ACCRUAL.. 2
PIH Notices: 03-23; 03-23
ACCUMULATE 1
24 CFR 982: .317
ACCUMULATED 6
24 CFR 5: .318;
7420.10G Gbk: 5-32; 6-8; 20-13; 24-13;
Admin Plan: s6p9
ACCUMULATION........................... 7
24 CFR 5: .318 (4);
HUD-52580-A: p17 (2); p18
ACCUMULATIONS 6
24 CFR 5: .703;
24 CFR 982: .401; .614;
7420.10G Gbk: 10-13 (2); 17-5
ACCURACY 36
24 CFR 5: .236; .240;
24 CFR 982: .516; .553 (2);
HUD-50058: p i;
HUD-50058Instr: p1;
HUD-52648: p3;
HUD-9886: p2;
7420.10G Gbk: 4-13; 4-18; 9-2; 10-36 Ex 10-1; 11-8; 15-7; 19-10 (2); 22-3; 22-5; 22-6 (2);
PIH Notices: 03-20 (3); 03-11; 02-27; 02-21; 01-41; 01-20; 01-15 (2); 00-53; 00-27; 00-09;
Admin Plan: s7p2; s11p1
ACCURATE 69
24 CFR 5: .216 (7);
24 CFR 982: .102; .158; .516;
HUD-52648: p3;
7420.10G Gbk: 4-10 (2); 4-15 (3); 4-23 Ex 4-1; 4-27 Ex 4-2; 5-13; 5-34 (2); 6-1; 8-11; 8-22; 8-23; 9-9; 10-36 Ex 10-1; 11-15; 12-16 Ex 12-4; 19-10; 20-1; 21-1; 22-5; 22-8; 24-8;
PIH Notices: 03-20 (2); 03-12; 01-15 (5); 01-15 Impr Integ Hbk (5); 01-06 (9); 01-01; 00-24 (2); 00-01; 98-66;
Admin Plan: s3p1; s4p1; s4p2; s6p1; s7p8 (2); s11p1
ACCURATE INFORMATION.......... 3
7420.10G Gbk: 5-34; 6-1; 22-5
ACCURATE RENT 3
PIH Notices: 01-15 Impr Integ Hbk (2); 01-15 Impr Integ Hbk
ACCURATELY................................ 20
7420.10G Gbk: 2-6; 4-16; 5-46 Ex 5-5; 5-48 Ex 5-5; 8-15; 8-23; 9-12; 10-35; 11-4; 11-9; 18-6; 19-6; 24-3;
PIH Notices: 03-23; 01-15 (3); 01-15 Impr Integ Hbk; 95-48; 95-48 Tech Asst
ACQUIRE... 2
24 CFR 982: .625; .632
ACQUIRED.................................... 14
24 CFR 5: .318 (2); .403 (2);
24 CFR 982: .627 (2); .631;
HUD-50058: p i;
HUD-50058Instr: p15; p74 (2);
Admin Plan: s22p1; s25p2; s25p2
ACQUIRED IMMUNODEFICIENCY SYNDROME 6
24 CFR 5: .403 (2);
HUD-50058Instr: p74 (2);
Admin Plan: s25p2; s25p2
ACQUIRING 5
24 CFR 982: .626;
PIH Notices: 95-48 (2); 95-

48 Tech Asst; 95-48 Tech Asst

ACQUISITION 6
24 CFR 5: .100;
PIH Notices: 95-48 (2); 95-48 Tech Asst (2);
Admin Plan: s25p7

ACTION 557
24 CFR 5: .350; .360 (2); .403; .512; .514 (3); .653; .661;
24 CFR 35 SubM: .1225;
24 CFR 982: .201; .202; .206; .306 (2); .310 (14); .314; .355; .404 (2); .552 (8); .553; .555; .619;
HUD-50058: p i (2); p2 (3); p ii (3); p3 (6); p iii; p4 (6); p iv; p5 (2); p v (6); p ix; p x; p xi; p xii; p xiii; p xiv; p xv; p16 (2); p xvi (2);
HUD-50058Instr: p ii (2); p1 (6); p2 (7); p9 (4); p10 (5); p11 (8); p12 (4); p14 (3); p15 (3); p19; p20 (6); p21 (5); p22; p39; p42 (2); p46 (2); p50; p53; p56; p58; p59 (10); p63; p72; p77 (5);
HUD-52641: p5; p6 (3); p9;
HUD-52641-A: p2;
HUD-52648: p1;
HUD-9886: p2;
7420.10G Gbk: 1-8 (2); 1-9 (3); 3-8; 4-10; 5-2; 5-7; 5-11; 5-38 (3); 8-18; 10-21; 10-23; 10-27; 10-33 (2); 10-34; 11-1; 11-12; 11-13 (3); 11-18 (2); 12-9; 12-15 Ex 12-3; 15-3; 15-5 (2); 15-6; 15-7; 15-8; 16-1 (2); 20-3 (3); 21-10; 22-1 (3); 22-4; 22-5; 22-9; 22-10; 22-11 (2); 22-14 (7); 22-15 (2); 22-16 (2); 22-18; 23-2; 23-3; 23-4 (6); 23-5; 23-6 (2);
PIH Notices: 03-11 (4); 03-05; 02-27 (73); 02-07 (4); 02-01 (6); 01-41 (56); 01-40; 01-10; 01-06 (11); 00-28 (2); 00-24 (3); 00-24A; 00-24B (3); 00-14; 00-09 (38); 99-52 (7); 99-11 (3); 96-65 (3); 95-48 (16); 95-48 Tech Asst (14);
Admin Plan: s1p6; s5p2; s5p3; s6p6; s6p9 (2); s7p2; s7p4; s7p5; s7p8; s9p2; s10p3; s10p5; s11p1 (2); s13p1; s13p2; s14p1 (2); s14p2; s15p1; s15p4 (2); s15p5 (3); s15p6; s16p1 (2); s18p1 (3); s18p3 (3); s18p4; s18p5 (2); s18p6 (2); s20p5 (2); s20p6 (2); s20p7 (5); s21p5 (2); s21p9 (3); s24p5; s25p4 (5); s25p6

ACTION PLAN 25
HUD-50058Instr: p72;
7420.10G Gbk: 3-8; 23-2; 23-3; 23-4 (6); 23-5; 23-6 (2);
PIH Notices: 02-01 (3); 99-52 (3);
Admin Plan: s21p9 (3); s25p4 (2); s25p4

ACTION PLAN ADDRESSES 1
Admin Plan: s25p4

ACTION PLAN AS 1
Admin Plan: s25p4

ACTION PLANS 4
PIH Notices: 02-01 (2); 99-52; 99-52

ACTIONS 195
24 CFR 982: .201; .205; .305; .310; .453; .552;
HUD-50058Instr: p62;
HUD-52641: p5;
HUD-52648: p2 (2);
7420.10G Gbk: 1-6 (2); 1-8 (3); 1-9 (5); 2-3 (2); 3-1; 3-5; 3-8; 4-8; 4-10 (2); 4-20; 5-44; 5-50 Ex 5-5; 8-3; 8-16; 10-26; 10-30; 11-9; 11-12; 11-17; 15-5; 16-1 (2); 19-2; 20-3 (3); 21-8; 21-10 (4); 22-1; 22-4; 22-5 (2); 22-10; 22-11; 22-14 (2); 22-15; 22-16; 22-18; 23-5;
PIH Notices: 03-23; 03-11; 03-05; 02-27 (6); 02-21 (2); 02-07 (4); 01-41 (39); 01-40; 01-20 (2); 01-10 (3); 01-01; 00-28 (3); 00-11; 00-11A; 00-09 (50); 95-48 (2); 95-48 Tech Asst (2);
Admin Plan: s9p3; s10p3; s11p1 (2); s15p4; s17p2; s18p2; s20p6 (2); s20p7; s21p6; s22p5; s23p3

ACTIVE DUTY 9
HUD-50058Instr: p26;

PIH Notices: 03-05 (4); 01-40 (3); 01-40

ACTIVITIES.................................343
24 CFR 5: .603 (2); .615; .661;
24 CFR 35 SubM: .1200 (2); .1215; .1220 (2); .1225;
24 CFR 982: .401; .551 (2); .553;
HUD-50058Instr: p15; p17; p71 (2); p73 (2); p75 (2);
HUD-52580-A: p2; p13; p17;
HUD-52641-A: p1;
7420.10G Gbk: 1-4; 1-15 (4); 1-16 Ex 1-3; 2-10; 2-11; 3-4; 3-6; 4-2; 4-4 (3); 4-5; 4-15; 4-22; 4-25 Ex 4-2; 5-14 Ex 5-2; 5-43; 5-44; 8-1 (2); 8-9; 8-11; 9-4; 10-8; 10-12; 10-15; 10-16; 10-17 (3); 10-18 (2); 10-19 (2); 10-21 (7); 10-22 (3); 10-37 Ex 10-2 (2); 10-38 Ex 10-3 (2); 11-4; 12-8; 13-7 (2); 13-8 (2); 14-1 (3); 15-3; 19-5; 19-11; 19-12; 20-5; 21-2 (4); 21-3 (4); 21-4; 21-7; 21-9; 21-11; 22-2; 22-17 (3); 23-1; 23-4; 23-5 (3); 23-6 (2); 23-8 Ex 23-1 (3); 23-14; 24-3; 24-4; 24-7 (2); 24-9; 24-12; 24-14; 24-15;
PIH Notices: 03-20; 02-27; 02-07; 02-06; 02-01 (25); 01-41; 01-15 (2); 00-41; 00-28; 00-24B; 00-11 (4); 00-11A (4); 00-09; 99-52 (24); 95-48 (70); 95-48 Tech Asst (66);
Admin Plan: s1p4; s1p6; s1p7; s6p12 (2); s6p13; s11p1 (3); s11p3; s13p1; s23p2; s24p6

ACTIVITY...................................229
24 CFR 5: .100 (4); .661 (2);
24 CFR 982: .4 (2); .54; .306 (5); .307 (2); .310 (13); .316 (2); .453 (2); .551 (3); .552 (2); .553 (20);
HUD-50058: p xvii;
HUD-50058Instr: p3 (2); p28; p62; p71;
HUD-52641: p6; p9;
HUD-52641-A: p2;
7420.10G Gbk: 2-9; 4-12; 5-34; 5-37 (3); 5-44; 8-8; 8-9; 8-19; 8-22; 8-23; 10-13; 10-17; 10-19 (2); 10-38 Ex 10-3 (3); 11-3; 11-7 (2); 12-2 (2); 12-9; 13-8; 15-2; 15-6; 20-23; 22-11; 22-16; 24-4; 24-6; 24-7; 24-14;
PIH Notices: 03-20; 03-11 (7); 02-06; 02-01 (5); 01-06; 00-14; 00-11A (4); 99-52 (5); 95-48 (33); 95-48 Tech Asst (33);
Admin Plan: s2p3 (2); s2p4; s2p6 (4); s2p7 (2); s6p6; s9p3 (2); s15p2 (3); s15p3 (5); s15p5 (2); s15p6 (2); s16p1 (2); s16p2 (3); s18p2; s18p3; s20p4 (2); s23p7 (2); s23p7

ACTUAL RECEIPT..........................4
24 CFR 982: .451;
HUD-52641: p1;
7420.10G Gbk: 11-7; 11-11

ACTUALLY...................................54
24 CFR 5: .214; .303; .615;
24 CFR 982: .517; .624;
HUD-50058: p xiv;
HUD-50058Instr: p16 (2); p57; p73;
HUD-9886: p2;
7420.10G Gbk: 1-4; 1-8; 5-21 (2); 5-23 (2); 9-12; 10-24; 12-7; 17-12; 18-2; 19-8; 20-2; 20-6; 22-17; 24-8 (2);
PIH Notices: 02-07 (2); 01-41 (2); 01-06; 00-28 (2); 00-09 (4); 95-48 (6); 95-48 Tech Asst (6);
Admin Plan: s6p12; s9p4; s19p1

ADAPT...1
24 CFR 982: .630

ADAPTABLE.................................10
PIH Notices: 02-01 (5); 99-52 (4); 99-52

ADAPTATIONS...............................2
7420.10G Gbk: 5-30;
Admin Plan: s10p3

ADAPTED.......................................4
7420.10G Gbk: 9-16 Ex 9-2; 11-8;
PIH Notices: 95-48; 95-48 Tech Asst

ADDED TO THE HOUSEHOLD.....3
HUD-52641: p2; 8;
HUD-52641-A: p1

ADDENDA.......................................1
7420.10G Gbk: 3-4

ADDENDUM..................................64
24 CFR 982: .162; .301; .302;

.305 (2); .308 (7); .456; .636;
HUD-50058: p2; p16 (3); p xvi (3); p xvii;
HUD-50058Instr: p ii; p1; p2 (3); p9; p11 (3); p13 (3); p59 (7); p60 (2); p77;
HUD-52648: p3; p4 (2);
7420.10G Gbk: 1-11;
PIH Notices: 01-41 (2); 01-06 (2); 00-24B; 00-09 (6);
Admin Plan: s8p2; s9p1; s9p2; s9p3 (2); s9p3

ADEQUATE POOL............................5
24 CFR 982: .206;
PIH Notices: 02-01; 99-52;
Admin Plan: s3p1; s4p1

ADEQUATE RETURN.....................1
24 CFR 5: .661

ADEQUATE SPACE.........................8
24 CFR 982: .401; .614 (2); .618;
HUD-52641: p4;
7420.10G Gbk: 10-6; 17-5; 17-8

ADJUST..23
24 CFR 5: .318;
24 CFR 982: .102 (2); .519;
HUD-50058: p viii;
HUD-50058Instr: p37;
7420.10G Gbk: 4-9; 6-8; 18-10; 20-17; 22-13;
PIH Notices: 03-23; 01-41; 01-15 Impr Integ Hbk; 00-24B (3); 00-09; 95-48; 95-48 Tech Asst;
Admin Plan: s7p5; s8p1; s24p5

ADJUSTED.................................237
24 CFR 5: .601 (2); .603 (3); .611 (3); .628 (2); .659;
24 CFR 982: .1 (2); .102 (17); .305; .503 (2); .508 (2); .516; .519 (3); .520 (2); .555; .619;
HUD-50058: p7; p vii; p8 (3); p viii (6); p13; p xiii (2); p15; p xv (2); p xvii;
HUD-50058Instr: p36 (2); p37 (10); p53 (2); p54; p58 (3); p62; p65 (3); p66 (6); p67; p70; p74 (2);
HUD-52648: p1 (4);
HUD-52667: p ii (2);
7420.10G Gbk: 5-20; 6-10 Ex 6-2 (2); 12-10; 18-1; 18-4 (2); 18-10; 20-8; 20-8 Ex 20-1 (4); 20-9; 20-10; 20-11 (3); 20-12 Ex 20-2 (2); 20-13 (3); 20-18; 20-19 Ex 20-3; 23-11; 23-17 Ex 23-2;
PIH Notices: 03-23 (4); 02-27 (3); 02-21 (3); 02-20 (3); 02-14 (2); 02-06; 02-01; 01-41 (15); 01-15 (5); 01-15 Impr Integ Hbk (12); 01-11; 01-10 (22); 01-06; 00-46 (3); 00-24B (7); 00-09 (13); 99-52;
Admin Plan: s5p2 (2); s6p1 (2); s9p1; s18p3; s21p1; s21p2; s21p4 (5); s21p6

ADJUSTED INCOME.....................76
24 CFR 5: .601 (2); .603 (2); .611 (3); .659;
24 CFR 982: .516; .555;
HUD-50058Instr: p65; p70;
HUD-52648: p1 (3);
7420.10G Gbk: 1-3 (2); 1-4; 1-6 Ex 1-1 (2); 1-10; 1-11; 4-15; 5-24; 5-28 (3); 5-31; 5-34 (2); 6-1; 8-16 (2); 12-4; 12-10; 12-11 (2); 16-2; 18-10; 22-3; 23-12; 23-14; 23-16 Ex 23-2 (2); 23-17 Ex 23-2 (4);
PIH Notices: 02-27 (3); 02-01; 01-15 (4); 01-15 Impr Integ Hbk (10); 01-06; 99-52;
Admin Plan: s6p1 (2); s18p3; s21p1; s21p2; s21p4 (2); s21p4

ADJUSTED INCOME LIMITATION 1
7420.10G Gbk: 24-12

ADJUSTING.....................................4
7420.10G Gbk: 3-3;
PIH Notices: 02-27; 01-10; 01-06

ADJUSTMENT...............................76
24 CFR 5: .609;
24 CFR 982: 24 CFR 982 (2); .102 (8); .519 (6); .520 (10); .521 (3); .619;
HUD-50058: p2; p xii;
HUD-50058Instr: p1; p9; p10; p11 (3); p50; p77;
HUD-52667: p ii;
7420.10G Gbk: 11-8; 12-2; 18-5 (2); 18-6 (2); 18-9 (2); 20-8 Ex 20-1;
PIH Notices: 03-23; 02-20; 01-15 Impr Integ Hbk (2); 01-10 (5); 01-06 (2); 00-46; 00-24B; 00-09 (2); 96-65; 95-48 (2); 95-48 Tech Asst (2);

Admin Plan: s6p9; s23p6 (2); s24p5; s24p5

ADJUSTMENTS.............................47
24 CFR 5: .603 (3);
24 CFR 982: .102; .516 (2); .519; .619 (2);
HUD-50058Instr: p1; p71; p73; p76;
HUD-52667: p i;
7420.10G Gbk: 5-14 Ex 5-2; 7-6; 9-4; 11-7; 11-8 (4); 11 9; 11-19; 18-4; 20-8 Ex 20-1 (2);
PIH Notices: 03-23; 02-20; 02-01; 01-27 (3); 01-15 Impr Integ Hbk; 01-10; 00-46; 00-24B; 00-09; 99-52;
Admin Plan: s11p1 (4); s23p6 (2); s24p5; s24p5

ADJUSTS...1
PIH Notices: 02-06

ADMINISTER................................95
24 CFR 5: .524;
24 CFR 982: 24 CFR 982 (2); .4 (4); .51 (4); .53; .54; .104; .151; .160; .201; .355;
HUD-50058Instr: p2 (2); p5; p73; p74;
HUD-52648: p2; p3 (3);
HUD-903-1: p6;
7420.10G Gbk: 2-9 (3); 4-12; 4-18; 5-36 Ex 5-4; 8-2; 13-5 (5); 13-6 (5); 13-7; 20-24; 21-1 (5); 21-2; 21-8 (3); 21-9; 23-2 (2); 23-18;
PIH Notices: 03-20 (2); 03-11; 02-06; 02-01; 01-41 (6); 01-15; 01-06 (4); 00-34; 00-24B (2); 00-09 (6); 99-52; 96-65; 95-48 (3); 95-48 Tech Asst;
Admin Plan: s1p1; s19p1; s22p2; s24p6

ADMINISTERED...........................45
24 CFR 5: .300; .306; .380; .504 (3); .516;
24 CFR 982: .1; .155;
HUD-50058Instr: p75;
HUD-52641: p1;
HUD-52648: p3 (2);
7420.10G Gbk: 1-2; 1-3; 2-1; 3-7 (2); 3-8 (2); 7-6; 13-6 (2); 22-18;
PIH Notices: 02-27 (2); 02-01 (2); 01-15; 01-10; 01-06 (7); 00-24B; 99-52 (2);
Admin Plan: s1p1; s4p2; s22p2; s25p1; s25p1

ADMINISTERING........................101
24 CFR 5: .100; .504 (3); .617;
24 CFR 982: .4 (3); .152 (2); .636;
HUD-50058: p16;
HUD-50058Instr: p59 (5);
HUD-52648: p1;
7420.10G Gbk: 1-9; 1-11; 1-12; 1-13; 2-9; 3-7; 4-20; 8-17; 11-3; 13-3; 13-4; 20-3; 20-5 (2); 20-24; 21-1; 21-9; 21-10 (2); 21-17 (2); 21-18; 22-3;
PIH Notices: 03-20; 03-12; 03-05; 02-27; 02-21; 02-20 (2); 02-15; 02-07 (6); 02-03; 01-43; 01-41 (5); 01-40; 01-33 (3); 01-20; 01-15 Impr Integ Hbk; 01-11; 01-10; 01-06; 01-02; 00-53; 00-49 (4); 00-46 (2); 00-41; 00-28 (7); 00-23 (2); 00-14 (2); 00-11; 00-11A; 00-09 (6); 96-65; 96-65

ADMINISTERS..............................23
24 CFR 5: .603;
24 CFR 982: .152; .352; .628; .642;
HUD-50058Instr: p7 (2);
7420.10G Gbk: 1-12 Ex 1-2; 1-13; 3-6; 10-30; 13-9;
PIH Notices: 02-27 (2); 02-07; 01-06 (2); 01-02; 00-28; 95-48; 95-48 Tech Asst;
Admin Plan: s25p6; s25p7

ADMINISTRATION....................140
24 CFR 5: .100; .214 (5); .659 (2);
24 CFR 982: 24 CFR 982 (4); .1; .3; .4 (2); .5; .53 (2); .54; .104; .152; .155; .158; .204; .352; .355 (2); .516; .521; .551; .553; .641;
HUD-50058: p i; p iii; p iv; p15; p xv (3);
HUD-50058Instr: p3; p16; p29; p43; p58 (4); p70 (2); p71; p75 (3);
HUD-9886: p1 (2);
7420.10G Gbk: 1-1 (2); 1-9 (2); 1-14; 1-15 (2); 1-16 Ex 1-3; 2-4; 2-13 Ex 2-1; 3-1; 3-2; 4-10; 5-12; 5-13; 5-34; 5-46 Ex 5-5 (2); 5-50 Ex 5-5; 8-1; 10-19;

12-13 Ex 12-1; 19-1; 21-1; 21-7; 21-8; 21-11; 21-13 (4); 21-16 Ex 21-6; 21-19; 21-20; 22-4 (2); 23-3; 23-5; 24-4;
PIH Notices: 02-27 (2); 02-22; 02-14; 02-07 (3); 01-41; 01-15; 01-15 Impr Integ Hbk (3); 01-06; 00-28 (3); 00-23; 00-11 (2); 00-11A; 00-09 (5); 99-11 (2); 96-65; 95-48 (6); 95-48 Tech Asst (4);
Admin Plan: s1p1; s2p5; s4p2; s7p7; s7p8; s23p7; s25p3

ADMINISTRATION'S......................3
7420.10G Gbk: 9-11;
PIH Notices: 03-20; 03-20

ADMINISTRATIVE......................461
24 CFR 5: .100; .216 (7); .218; .230; .232; .234;
24 CFR 982: 24 CFR 982 (4); .4 (5); .54 (11); .102; .151; .152 (18); .153; .155 (14); .157; .201; .202; .204 (2); .207 (2); .303 (2); .306 (3); .307; .312 (2); .315; .352; .355 (3); .451 (2); .504; .515; .516; .552; .554 (2); .555 (3); .625; .626; .627; .631; .632; .636 (2); .639 (2); .643 (2);
HUD-50058: p x; p xi; p xiii; p xiv;
HUD-50058Instr: p19; p42; p46; p53; p56; p70 (2);
HUD-52641: p6;
HUD-52648: p1 (3);
7420.10G Gbk: 1-1; 1-4; 1-13; 4-7; 4-11 (2); 4-18; 5-11; 5-44; 8-3; 8-18; 8-22; 11-1; 12-1; 12-9; 13-6; 16-2 (2); 20-2; 20-4; 20-5; 20-6 (2); 20-22 (6); 20-22 Ex 20-5 (4); 20-23; 20-27 (2); 21-1; 21-2; 21-3; 21-5; 21-6; 21-7; 21-9; 21-10; 21-12 Ex 21-2 (2); 21-12 Ex 21-3 (2); 21-15 Ex 21-5; 21-16 Ex 21-6 (2); 21-19; 22-4; 22-7; 22-10; 22-14; 22-15; 22-16; 22-17 (3); 23-2;
PIH Notices: 03-23 (73); 03-12; 03-11 (2); 03-05; 02-27 (4); 02-21 (4); 02-07 (24); 02-01 (11); 01-41 (10); 01-40; 01-20; 01-06 (2); 00-49 (10); 00-28 (26); 00-24B (7); 00-23 (2); 00-11A (2); 00-09 (8); 99-52 (9); 96-65 (10); 95-48 (16); 95-48 Tech Asst (16);
Admin Plan: s1p1; s1p2 (2); s1p3; s1p4; s1p5 (2); s1p6; s2p1; s2p7; s4p1 (2); s6p1; s10p1; s10p4; s13p2; s16p1 (2); s18p2; s18p4; s18p6; s20p7 (2); s21p3 (3); s23p1 (3); s24p7; s25p1; s25p4; s25p5; s25p6; s25p8

ADMINISTRATIVE AGENCY 5
24 CFR 982: .306;
HUD-52641: p6;
7420.10G Gbk: 8-18; 11-2;
Admin Plan: s16p1

ADMINISTRATIVE BURDEN 27
7420.10G Gbk: 4-11; 4-18; 5-44; 8-3;
PIH Notices: 02-01 (9); 01-41; 99-52 (9); 95-48; 95-48 Tech Asst;
Admin Plan: s1p3; s1p5

ADMINISTRATIVE BURDENS 8
PIH Notices: 95-48 (4); 95-48 Tech Asst (3); 95-48 Tech Asst

ADMINISTRATIVE ENTITY 2
24 CFR 982: .504;
PIH Notices: 01-41

ADMINISTRATIVE FEE................88
24 CFR 982: Intro; .4 (2); .151; .152 (11); .352; .355 (2); .451; .639; .643 (2);
HUD-50058: p x; p xi; p xiii; p xiv;
HUD-50058Instr: p42; p46; p53; p56; p70;
HUD-52665: p1;
7420.10G Gbk: 8-1; 10-31; 11-7; 13-5; 13-9 (3); 13-10; 15-4; 20-5 (3); 20-6 (4); 20-17; 20-24 (6); 20-25 (6); 20-28; 21-8; 22-18;
PIH Notices: 03-23 (7); 02-21; 02-07 (4); 00-28 (5); 96-65 (6);
Admin Plan: s13p2

ADMINISTRATIVE FEE PENALTY1
PIH Notices: 00-28

ADMINISTRATIVE FEE RESERVE47
24 CFR 982: Intro; .4 (2);

.54; .152; .155 (9); .451; .515;
7420.10G Gbk: 3-6 (2); 20-2; 20-6; 20-26; 20-27 (5); 23-2; 24-2;
PIH Notices: 03-23 (14); 02-07 (2); 00-28 (2); 96-65

ADMINISTRATIVE FEE RESERVE ACCOUNT 1
7420.10G Gbk: 20-2

ADMINISTRATIVE FEE RESERVES 11
7420.10G Gbk: 3-6; 11-7; 20-10; 20-26; 20-27; 22-12 (2); 24-15;
PIH Notices: 03-23 (2); 02-01

ADMINISTRATIVE FEES 131
24 CFR 982: Intro; .152 (4); .155 (2); .157; .355; .625; .639;
7420.10G Gbk: 13-9; 13-10; 19-2; 19-3 (2); 20-2 (2); 20-3; 20-5 (7); 20-6 (2); 20-16; 20-20; 20-21 Ex 20-4; 20-22 Ex 20-5; 20-27 (5); 20-28 (2); 20-29 (2); 21-2; 21-8; 21-9; 23-2; 24-7; 24-9;
PIH Notices: 03-23 (35); 02-21 (2); 02-07 (16); 02-01; 01-06; 00-49 (10); 00-28 (15); 00-24B; 00-23; 96-65; 96-65

ADMINISTRATIVE LAW JUDGE .. 1
24 CFR 5: .100

ADMINISTRATIVE PLAN 99
7420.10G Gbk: 1-14; 2-2; 2-3; 3-1 (11); 3-2 (9); 3-3 (5); 3-4 (7); 3-5 (8); 3-6 (5); 3-7 (2); 3-9 (4); 4-1 (2); 4-5; 4-7 (2); 4-8; 4-16 (2); 4-18 (2); 4-21 (2); 4-22 (2); 5-1; 5-2; 5-4; 5-27; 7-1; 8-12; 8-13 (2); 8-19; 8-20 (2); 10-2 (2); 10-30; 10-34; 11-4 (2); 11-5; 12-9; 15-5 (2); 16-3; 16-4 (3); 17-1; 18-1; 22-7; 23-10; 23-12; 23-18

ADMINISTRATIVE PLAN 163
24 CFR 982: .4; .54 (10); .153; .201; .202; .204 (2); .207 (2); .303 (2); .307; .312 (2); .315; .516; .552; .554; .555 (2); .626; .627; .632;
HUD-50058Instr: p19; p70;
HUD-52648: p1;
7420.10G Gbk: 1-14; 2-2; 2-3; 3-1 (10); 3-2 (9); 3-3 (5); 3-4 (7); 3-5 (8); 3-6 (5); 3-7 (2); 3-9 (4); 4-1 (2); 4-5; 4-7 (2); 4-8; 4-16 (2); 4-18 (2); 4-21; 4-22 (2); 5-1; 5-2; 5-4; 5-27; 7-1; 8-12; 8-13 (2); 8-19; 8-20 (2); 10-2; 10-30; 10-34; 11-4 (2); 11-5; 12-9; 15-5 (2); 16-3; 16-4 (3); 17-1; 18-1; 22-7; 23-10; 23-12; 23-18;
PIH Notices: 03-05; 02-27 (2); 02-21; 01-40; 01-20; 00-24B (5);
Admin Plan: s1p1; s1p2 (2); s1p4; s1p6; s2p1; s2p7; s4p1 (2); s6p1; s10p1; s10p4; s21p3 (3); s23p1; s24p7; s25p4; s25p5; s25p8

ADMINISTRATIVE PLAN A........... 1
7420.10G Gbk: 4-21

ADMINISTRATIVE PLAN ADDRESSES..................................... 1
Admin Plan: s23p1

ADMINISTRATIVE PLAN BASED 1
Admin Plan: s18p6
7420.10G Gbk: 6-7

ADMINISTRATIVE REMEDIES..... 4
7420.10G Gbk: 22-14;
PIH Notices: 95-48; 95-48 Tech Asst;
Admin Plan: s20p7

ADMINISTRATIVE RESERVE 2
7420.10G Gbk: 20-27;
PIH Notices: 03-23

ADMINISTRATIVE RESERVES 1
7420.10G Gbk: 20-27

ADMINISTRATOR......................... 21
24 CFR 5: .100; .236; .661 (9);
24 CFR 982: .4;
7420.10G Gbk: 21-16 Ex 21-6;
PIH Notices: 02-21 (2); 01-15; 96-65 (4); 96-65

ADMINISTRATORS....................... 19
24 CFR 5: .801;
7420.10G Gbk: 1-1;
PIH Notices: 02-03; 02-01; 01-27; 01-11; 01-06; 00-53; 00-45; 00-41; 00-28; 00-14; 00-01; 99-52; 99-11; 98-66; 96-65; 95-48; 95-48

ADMINISTRTAIVE 1
PIH Notices: 03-23

ADMISSION 366
24 CFR 5: .214; .232; .309; .318 (2); .508; .512; .609; .617 (2); .653 (9); .655 (8); .659;
24 CFR 982: .4 (8); .54 (3); .201 (13); .202 (12); .203; .204 (5); .205 (4); .207 (12); .301; .310; .353 (2); .355; .516; .552 (7); .553 (15); .627;
HUD-50058: p i; p2 (2); p ii; p5 (4); p v (4); p ix; p x; p xi; p xii; p xiii; p xiv; p xv;
HUD-50058Instr: p ii; p1; p9 (17); p10 (4); p11 (3); p12 (5); p19 (15); p33; p39; p42; p46; p47; p50; p56; p58; p70 (3); p75 (2); p76 (3); p77 (2);
HUD-52648: p1 (4);
7420.10G Gbk: 1-6 Ex 1-1; 1-13; 3-7; 4-8; 4-9 (3); 4-16; 4-17; 4-18 (4); 4-19 (4); 4-20 (3); 4-21; 4-22 (2); 4-25 Ex 4-2; 5-3 (2); 5-12; 5-13 (2); 5-38; 8-10; 12-4; 12-10; 13-3; 13-4; 13-8; 14-4; 14-5; 15-7; 15-8; 16-1; 19-2; 22-8 (3); 22-9; 24-4;
PIH Notices: 03-11 (10); 02-27; 02-01 (2); 01-41 (8); 01-27 (2); 01-15 (2); 01-15 Impr Integ Hbk (13); 01-10 (16); 01-01 (4); 00-24B (6); 00-11A; 00-09 (7); 99-52 (2); 95-48; 95-48 Tech Asst;
Admin Plan: s1p3; s2p1 (5); s2p4 (2); s2p5 (5); s2p6 (2); s2p7; s3p1; s4p1 (2); s6p1; s6p10; s7p2; s8p2; s8p4; s13p2; s15p3; s18p2; s20p6; s21p3 (2); s21p4; s21p6; s23p2 (2); s23p3; s23p4; s24p6; s24p6

ADMISSION PREFERENCE 2
24 CFR 982: .205;
7420.10G Gbk: 4-9

ADMISSION PREFERENCES 2
24 CFR 982: .54; .202

ADMISSION--INCOME-ELIGIBILITY 1
24 CFR 5: .653

ADMISSIONS 55
24 CFR 982: .201; .202 (2); .204 (2);
HUD-50058Instr: p4; p12;
HUD-52648: p1;
7420.10G Gbk: 1-4; 3-7; 4-10; 4-20 (2); 4-21 (4); 4-22 (3); 5-3; 5-53 Ex 5-5; 12-11; 12-13 Ex 12-1; 13-2; 13-7; 19-3; 19-4; 19-6; 22-6 (2); 22-7;
PIH Notices: 03-11 (2); 01-41; 01-15 (3); 01-01; 00-53; 00-11;
Admin Plan: s2p5; s4p1 (6); s4p2; s5p2; s13p2; s15p6; s20p6; s21p3; s24p6

ADMIT 21
24 CFR 5: .318;
24 CFR 982: .201 (2); .202 (2); .203; .204; .553;
7420.10G Gbk: 4-18; 4-19 (2); 4-20; 4-21; 20-15;
PIH Notices: 95-48 (2); 95-48 Tech Asst (2);
Admin Plan: s4p1; s23p3; s23p3

ADMITS 1
24 CFR 5: .601

ADMITTANCE 4
PIH Notices: 95-48 (2); 95-48 Tech Asst; 95-48 Tech Asst

ADMITTED.................................... 65
24 CFR 5: .324; .630;
24 CFR 982: .4 (2); .201 (3); .203; .204; .207; .353; .625; .627;
HUD-50058: p ii; p v;
HUD-50058Instr: p12 (2); p19 (3); p27; p71; p74;
HUD-52641: p6;
7420.10G Gbk: 4-5; 4-10; 4-16; 4-18; 4-19; 4-20 (2); 4-21; 5-3 (2); 5-5; 5-9 Ex 5-1 (2); 5-10 Ex 5-1 (2); 6-8; 19-10; 23-18 (3);
PIH Notices: 02-01 (2); 01-41 (2); 01-10 (2); 00-24B (4); 00-09 (2); 99-52 (2); 95-48; 95-48 Tech Asst;
Admin Plan: s2p4; s2p5; s4p1; s9p3; s23p3

ADMITTING.................................... 3
7420.10G Gbk: 4-9; 4-20; 4-21

ADOPT 84
24 CFR 5: .611; .655 (7); .657;

24 CFR 982: .54; .202; .206; .207 (6); .312; .503; .516 (2); .551; .635;
HUD-50058Instr: p34;
7420.10G Gbk: 3-1 (2); 3-2; 3-3; 3-4 (2); 3-9; 4-4; 4-16 (3); 4-17 (2); 4-19; 5-3 (2); 5-4; 5-40; 6-7; 7-2 (2); 7-4; 8-13; 8-19; 8-20; 11-3; 11-4; 15-6; 19-5; 21-7 (2); 23-6; 23-10 (3); 23-18; 24-11;
PIH Notices: 03-11 (2); 02-27; 02-20; 02-01 (2); 01-15; 01-15 Impr Integ Hbk (5); 00-46; 99-52 (2); 95-48 (3); 95-48 Tech Asst (3);
Admin Plan: s23p2

ADOPTED....................................35
24 CFR 5: .315; .609;
24 CFR 982: .4; .54; .206; .401;
HUD-50058Instr: p31;
HUD-52648: p2;
HUD-52667: p i;
7420.10G Gbk: 1-1; 2-2; 3-1 (2); 5-15 Ex 5-2; 5-39; 5-40; 7-9; 10-2 (2); 12-7;
PIH Notices: 02-20; 02-01; 01-15 Impr Integ Hbk; 01-06 (2); 00-24A; 99-52; 95-48; 95-48 Tech Asst;
Admin Plan: s5p3; s19p1; s21p3; s21p5; s21p7; s23p7

ADOPTED CHILD............................4
24 CFR 5: .609;
HUD-50058Instr: p31;
7420.10G Gbk: 5-15 Ex 5-2;
PIH Notices: 01-15 Impr Integ Hbk

ADOPTING......................................4
24 CFR 5: .655;
24 CFR 982: .207;
7420.10G Gbk: 7-4;
PIH Notices: 02-27

ADOPTION....................................17
24 CFR 5: .609;
24 CFR 982: .551;
HUD-50058Instr: p31;
HUD-52641: 8;
HUD-52641-A: p1;
HUD-52646: p2;
7420.10G Gbk: 1-15; 5-15 Ex 5-2;
PIH Notices: 01-15 Impr Integ Hbk (4);
Admin Plan: s5p2; s6p8 (2); s7p7; s11p2

ADOPTS...11
24 CFR 5: .655;
7420.10G Gbk: 3-4; 4-16; 5-40; 6-8; 10-2; 23-6;
PIH Notices: 95-48 (2); 95-48 Tech Asst; 95-48 Tech Asst

ADULT..78
24 CFR 5: .353 (2); .504; .508 (6);
24 CFR 982: .625; .627 (4);
HUD-50058: p i; p3 (2); p4 (2); p7;
HUD-50058Instr: p2 (3); p14 (4); p15 (4); p17; p29; p36 (2); p72; p73; p75;
HUD-9886: p1;
7420.10G Gbk: 5-9 Ex 5-1 (6); 5-13 (2); 5-35; 8-8 (2);
PIH Notices: 03-11 (4); 00-41; 00-11; 00-11A; 95-48; 95-48 Tech Asst;
Admin Plan: s2p2 (4); s3p2; s3p3; s6p2 (2); s6p7 (3); s6p10; s6p11 (3); s7p2; s7p3 (2); s7p8

ADULT FAMILY MEMBER.............4
HUD-50058Instr: p29;
Admin Plan: s6p2; s7p3; s7p3

ADULT FAMILY MEMBERS 4
24 CFR 982: .627 (2);
Admin Plan: s3p2; s7p2

ADULTS...53
24 CFR 5: .603; .609;
HUD-50058: p iii; p iv; p v; p ix; p x; p xi; p xii; p xiii; p xiv (2);
HUD-50058Instr: p14; p15; p17 (2); p22; p31; p34 (2); p36 (2); p40 (2); p44 (2); p48 (2); p51 (2); p54 (2); p57 (2); p68; p69; p71; p72 (2);
7420.10G Gbk: 4-23 Ex 4-1; 5-9 Ex 5-1; 5-15 Ex 5-2; 5-18; 8-8; 12-7;
PIH Notices: 01-15 Impr Integ Hbk (3);
Admin Plan: s1p6; s2p6; s5p1 (2); s7p7

ADVANCE NOTICE.........................4
7420.10G Gbk: 5-44; 12-2; 12-6; 12-8

ADVANCE NOTIFICATION.............2
7420.10G Gbk: 12-1; 12-6

ADVERSE......................................11
24 CFR 5: .236; .703;
24 CFR 982: .401; .614;
7420.10G Gbk: 1-9; 10-13; 17-

5;
PIH Notices: 01-41 (2); 00-09; 00-09

ADVERSE FINDINGS 1
24 CFR 5: .236

ADVERSELY 12
24 CFR 5: .359;
24 CFR 982: .401;
7420.10G Gbk: 5-22; 10-2;
PIH Notices: 01-41 (2); 00-53; 00-09 (2); 95-48; 95-48 Tech Asst;
Admin Plan: s10p1

ADVERTISE.................................. 12
HUD-903: p1;
HUD-903-1: p2;
7420.10G Gbk: 2-5 (2); 4-1; 9-5 (3); 24-12;
Admin Plan: s23p1; s23p3; s24p7

ADVERTISED................................. 2
7420.10G Gbk: 8-7;
Admin Plan: s24p2

ADVERTISEMENT 3
PIH Notices: 02-27 (2);
Admin Plan: s24p2

ADVERTISEMENTS 1
7420.10G Gbk: 2-5

ADVERTISING............................. 17
HUD-903: p2;
7420.10G Gbk: 2-5; 2-6; 4-1; 4-2 (3); 4-3 (4); 5-11; 9-5; 24-15;
PIH Notices: 02-01; 99-52;
Admin Plan: s1p6

ADVOCATE.................................... 7
PIH Notices: 02-01; 99-52;
Admin Plan: s1p3; s1p5; s3p3; s18p5; s18p6

ADVOCATES.................................. 4
PIH Notices: 02-01; 99-52 (2); 99-52

AFDC 1
HUD-50058Instr: p76

AFFECTED RESIDENTS................ 2
PIH Notices: 01-41; 00-09

AFFIDAVIT 9
7420.10G Gbk: 5-46 Ex 5-5; 5-47 Ex 5-5 (4); 5-49 Ex 5-5; 5-51 Ex 5-5 (2);
Admin Plan: s7p5

AFFIDAVITS................................... 1
7420.10G Gbk: 5-46 Ex 5-5

AFFIRMATIVE 3
24 CFR 5: .655 (2);
7420.10G Gbk: 5-45

AFFIRMATIVE FAIR HOUSING MARKETING PLAN 2
24 CFR 5: .655; .655

AFFIRMATIVELY 13
24 CFR 982: .53 (3);
7420.10G Gbk: 1-10; 3-8; 4-1; 7-1; 10-23;
PIH Notices: 02-21 (4); 01-06

AFFORDABLE HOUSING 38
24 CFR 5: .518 (14);
7420.10G Gbk: 1-1; 1-7; 2-1 (2); 2-8; 7-3; 7-5; 11-9;
PIH Notices: 02-01; 01-41 (3); 01-15 Impr Integ Hbk (2); 00-41; 00-09 (4); 99-52;
Admin Plan: s1p1; s1p2; s24p4; s25p2

AFFORDABLE HOUSING ACT...... 5
24 CFR 5: .100 (4);
PIH Notices: 01-27

AFFORDABLE HOUSING OPPORTUNITIES 2
24 CFR 5: .518;
24 CFR 982: .401

AFFORDABLE HOUSING PROGRAMS 1
Admin Plan: s25p7

AFRICA 3
HUD-50058Instr: p73;
HUD-903: p2; p2

AFRICAN 6
HUD-50058: p3; p4;
HUD-50058Instr: p15;
7420.10G Gbk: 2-13 Ex 2-1 (2); 4-23 Ex 4-1

AFRICAN AMERICAN 7
HUD-50058: p3; p4;
HUD-50058Instr: p15; p73;
7420.10G Gbk: 2-13 Ex 2-1 (2); 4-23 Ex 4-1

AFTER SCHOOL 1
PIH Notices: 01-15

AGE 215
24 CFR 5: .100; .105; .216 (8); .230 (3); .403 (9); .504; .508 (5); .603 (2); .609; .611; .655 (3);
24 CFR 35 SubM: .1200 (2); .1225 (3);
24 CFR 982: .202; .207 (3); .304; .402 (2); .507;
HUD-50058: p3 (6); p iii; p4 (6); p iv; p vii (4);
HUD-50058Instr: p2 (2); p14 (5); p15 (4); p16;

p17; p34; p35 (3); p36 (3); p70 (2); p71 (3); p74;
HUD-52580-A: p2 (2); p13 (3);
HUD-52641: p4; p5; p10;
HUD-52641-A: p3;
HUD-52646: p2;
HUD-52648: p1;
HUD-903-1: p2;
HUD-9886: p1 (2); p2 (4);
7420.10G Gbk: 4-16; 4-17 (2); 4-19; 4-25 Ex 4-2; 5-2; 5-9 Ex 5-1 (3); 5-12 (3); 5-18 (3); 5-28; 5-29 (4); 5-30 (2); 5-41 (2); 5-42 (3); 5-50 Ex 5-5; 8-14; 9-2; 9-12; 9-14 Ex 9-1; 9-15 Ex 9-2; 10-11; 10-12 (4); 10-16 (4); 10-17 (2); 10-20 (2); 10-22 (3); 11-13; 12-5 (2); 12-12 Ex 12-1; 12-16 Ex 12-4; 20-4 (2); 21-5; 21-8;
PIH Notices: 03-12 (2); 02-27; 02-07 (3); 01-41; 01-15; 01-15 Impr Integ Hbk (6); 00-49 (6); 00-24B; 00-23 (8); 95-48; 95-48 Tech Asst;
Admin Plan: s1p2; s2p1 (2); s2p2; s2p5; s5p1; s7p3; s7p8 (2); s9p1; s11p2; s11p1; s21p3; s22p1; s23p2; s23p4

AGE 12 1
7420.10G Gbk: 5-29

AGE 18 8
HUD-9886: p2 (2);
7420.10G Gbk: 5-13; 5-18; 5-43; 12-3;
Admin Plan: s11p1; s22p1

AGE 6 1
Admin Plan: s2p5

AGE 62 13
24 CFR 5: .655 (2);
24 CFR 982: .207 (2);
HUD-50058: p vii (2);
HUD-50058Instr: p34; p35 (3);
7420.10G Gbk: 4-16; 4-17; 4-17

AGE DISCRIMINATION 2
24 CFR 5: .105;
7420.10G Gbk: 5-42

AGE OF 18 ....
5
24 CFR 5: .609;
HUD-903-1: p2;
PIH Notices: 01-15 Impr Integ Hbk (2); 01-15 Impr Integ Hbk

AGE OF 62 3
24 CFR 5: .403 (2); .403

AGE SIX 25
HUD-50058Instr: p16;
HUD-52580-A: p2 (2); p13 (3);
7420.10G Gbk: 5-12 (3); 10-16 (4); 10-17; 10-20 (2); 10-22 (3); 20-4;
PIH Notices: 00-49 (2); 00-23;
Admin Plan: s2p1; s7p8

AGENCIES 273
24 CFR 5: .210 (2); .234; .500; .518; .526 (3); .613 (2); .615; .617; .659; .801 (2);
24 CFR 982: .1; .4; .630;
HUD-50058Instr: p1; p2; p3 (2); p5 (2); p7 (2); p25; p40; p68; p72;
HUD-52667: p i;
HUD-903: p2; p3;
HUD-903-1: p6;
HUD-9886: p1 (3); p2;
7420.10G Gbk: 1-1; 1-7; 2-8; 3-8; 4-3 (3); 5-12; 5-13 (2); 5-18; 5-22; 5-47 Ex 5-5; 8-8 (2); 10-31; 13-6 (2); 13-9; 18-4; 21-1 (2); 21-5; 21-11 (2); 22-16; 22-17; 23-4 (3); 23-6; 24-9; 24-10; 24-13 (2);
PIH Notices: 03-23 (5); 03-20 (2); 03-12 (2); 03-11 (8); 03-05 (2); 02-27 (2); 02-22 (2); 02-21 (3); 02-20 (2); 02-15; 02-14 (2); 02-07 (2); 02-06 (2); 02-03; 02-01 (5); 01-43; 01-41 (2); 01-40 (2); 01-33 (2); 01-27 (2); 01-20; 01-15 (8); 01-15 Impr Integ Hbk (8); 01-11; 01-10 (2); 01-06 (2); 01-02; 01-01; 00-53; 00-49 (2); 00-46 (2); 00-45; 00-41 (3); 00-34; 00-31; 00-28 (2); 00-27; 00-24; 00-24B; 00-23 (4); 00-14 (2); 00-11 (25); 00-11A (4); 00-09 (3); 00-01 (2); 99-52 (4); 99-30; 99-11 (2); 98-66 (2); 96-65 (2); 95-48 (22); 95-48 Tech Asst (18);
Admin Plan: s1p4; s1p6; s3p1; s4p2 (3); s7p2; s7p8; s17p1; s20p1 (2); s20p3 (2); s20p4 (2); s21p1; s22p2; s25p4;

s25p6

AGENCY 487
24 CFR 5: .100 (3); .214 (5); .234; .236 (5); .306; .504; .518; .526; .603; .609 (3); .613; .615 (22); .628 (2); .653 (2); .659; .661;
24 CFR 35 SubM: .1200;
24 CFR 982: .4 (2); .207; .306; .352 (11); .516; .553; .628; .630;
HUD-50058: p i (2); p2 (2); p ii (2); p viii (2); p16 (2); p17;
HUD-50058Instr: p ii; p3 (2); p7 (4); p25; p28 (4); p30; p37 (3); p43; p61 (3); p63 (3); p71 (2); p72 (4); p74 (4); p75 (4); p77;
HUD-52517: p1 (3); p15 (2); p17 (2); p18;
HUD-52641: p1; p2; p10;
HUD-52641-A: p3;
HUD-52646: p1 (7); p2 (3); p3 (2);
HUD-52667: p i;
HUD-903: p1; p2;
HUD-903-1: p3 (2); p5;
HUD-9886: p1 (2);
7420.10G Gbk: 1-7 (4); 2-7; 3-1; 3-6; 3-8 (2); 5-12; 5-14 Ex 5-2 (2); 5-15 Ex 5-2; 5-20 (3); 5-21 (2); 5-23 (2); 5-29; 5-46 Ex 5-5; 5-47 Ex 5-5 (3); 5-51 Ex 5-5; 5-52 Ex 5-5; 9-11; 10-3; 10-12; 10-20 (2); 10-30; 10-31 (5); 11-9; 13-1 (2); 13-3; 13-10; 15-10 Ex 15-2; 20-8 Ex 20-1; 20-14; 20-17; 21-1 (3); 21-14 Ex 21-4; 21-15 Ex 21-5; 22-11 (2); 22-16; 22-17; 22-18; 23-1; 23-9 (3); 23-18; 23-20; 24-2 (2); 24-3;
PIH Notices: 03-23; 03-20; 03-11 (10); 02-27 (7); 02-21 (2); 02-20; 02-14; 02-06; 02-01 (2); 01-43 (2); 01-41 (4); 01-20 (3); 01-15 (5); 01-15 Impr Integ Hbk (13); 01-11 (3); 01-06 (10); 01-02 (3); 01-01; 00-53 (4); 00-46; 00-45; 00-34 (2); 00-27 (2); 00-24 (2); 00-23 (5); 00-11 (10); 00-11A (51); 00-09 (4); 99-52 (2); 99-11 (2); 95-48 (28); 95-48 Tech Asst (28);
Admin Plan: s1p1; s1p2; s1p5; s2p7; s4p2 (3); s6p6; s6p7 (3); s6p9 (2); s6p12 (2); s6p13 (2); s7p3; s7p4 (3); s7p5; s7p7; s7p8; s8p4; s11p3; s16p1; s21p3 (6); s21p4 (3); s21p5 (3); s21p6 (3); s21p7 (4); s21p8 (3); s22p4; s24p1 (2); s25p1; s25p4; s25p7 (2); s25p7

AGENCY PLAN...............................7
24 CFR 982: .207;
PIH Notices: 02-01; 99-52;
Admin Plan: s1p2; s24p1 (2); s25p4

AGENCYS.......................................1
HUD-50058Instr: p71

AGENCY'S 16
24 CFR 5: .615 (2);
7420.10G Gbk: 3-1; 3-7; 4-19; 8-2; 8-7; 8-14; 13-4;
PIH Notices: 03-23; 01-06 (4);
Admin Plan: s21p8; s21p8

AGENT 43
24 CFR 5: .306; .350; .360; .363 (2); .403;
24 CFR 982: .161; .553;
HUD-50058: p i;
HUD-50058Instr: p15; p32 (2); p74;
HUD-52580: p1 (2); p6;
HUD-52580-A: p1 (3); p19;
HUD-52641: p6 (2);
HUD-903-1: p5;
7420.10G Gbk: 5-16 Ex 5-2; 8-19; 8-24 Ex 8-1; 10-17; 10-36 Ex 10-1 (2); 11-2; 11-3; 11-13; 11-16 Ex 11-1; 22-16;
PIH Notices: 03-11 (2); 01-15 Impr Integ Hbk (2);
Admin Plan: s7p6; s9p4; s16p1; s16p3; s25p2

AGENT ORANGE 5
HUD-50058Instr: p32 (2);
7420.10G Gbk: 5-16 Ex 5-2;
PIH Notices: 01-15 Impr Integ Hbk; 01-15 Impr Integ Hbk

AGENT-PRODUCT 1
7420.10G Gbk: 5-16 Ex 5-2

AGENTS..10
PIH Notices: 03-11; 02-27; 02-01 (2); 01-41; 01-15 Impr Integ Hbk; 00-09; 99-52 (2);
Admin Plan: s1p6

AGENT'S 2
7420.10G Gbk: 4-27 Ex 4-2; 10-36 Ex 10-1

AGGREGATE.................................12
24 CFR 5: .518 (4);
24 CFR 982: .201;
HUD-50058Instr: p18;
7420.10G Gbk: 4-20; 7-5; 11-8; 19-3 (2); 22-5

AGGREGATION...............................2
PIH Notices: 02-20; 00-46

AGREE..41
24 CFR 5: .318; .613; .615 (2);
24 CFR 982: .308; .353; .355; .555 (2);
HUD-52641: p7; p10;
HUD-52641-A: p3;
HUD-52665: p2;
7420.10G Gbk: 1-5; 2-9 (2); 4-16; 8-4; 8-6; 9-4; 11-18; 16-1; 21-8;
PIH Notices: 03-11; 02-01; 01-06; 00-11A (5); 99-52; 96-65 (2); 95-48; 95-48 Tech Asst;
Admin Plan: s2p3; s8p5; s18p1; s22p4; s22p4

AGREEABLE....................................1
24 CFR 5: .353

AGREED.......................................30
24 CFR 5: .514; .661;
HUD-50058Instr: p73;
HUD-52641: p3; 8; p9; p10 (2);
HUD-52641-A: p1; p2; p3 (2);
7420.10G Gbk: 2-9; 11-1; 11-12; 13-3; 13-9;
PIH Notices: 03-11 (4); 00-11A (3);
Admin Plan: s11p3 (2); s18p5; s24p5; s25p1; s25p3

AGREED-UPON..............................2
7420.10G Gbk: 2-9; 23-6

AGREEING.....................................5
7420.10G Gbk: 5-43; 23-15;
PIH Notices: 01-41; 00-09;
Admin Plan: s22p4

AGREEMENT...............................187
24 CFR 5: .214 (2); .306; .363; .630 (2);
24 CFR 982: .4 (5); .156 (2); .163; .305; .314; .317 (3); .453; .552 (3); .619 (3); .635;
HUD-50058: p2; p ii (2); p15 (2); p xv (4);
HUD-50058Instr: p9; p12 (3); p42; p56; p58 (7); p70; p73 (3); p74;
HUD-52641: p1; p5; p7 (2); p10 (2);
HUD-52641-A: p3 (2);
7420.10G Gbk: 1-9; 2-9; 2-10; 3-5; 5-7; 5-23; 5-37; 5-47 Ex 5-5; 8-10; 11-1; 11-9; 11-15; 11-18 (4); 13-9 (2); 14-2; 20-1; 20-23; 22-9; 22-13 (3); 22-14; 23-9;
PIH Notices: 02-27 (2); 02-01 (3); 01-41 (4); 01-20; 01-15; 01-06; 00-14; 00-11 (6); 00-11A (8); 00-09 (7); 99-52 (2); 95-48; 95-48 Tech Asst;
Admin Plan: s2p4; s5p3 (2); s6p7; s6p8 (2); s7p4; s7p5; s7p8; s8p3; s8p4; s8p5; s9p2; s9p3 (4); s11p1; s11p3; s11p2; s11p3; s13p1; s13p2; s16p2; s17p1 (9); s17p2 (6); s19p1; s20p7; s22p2 (2); s22p3 (4); s23p5 (3); s23p7; s24p2; s24p5 (4); s25p1; s25p3; s25p7; s25p7

AGREEMENT TO PAY.....................1
24 CFR 982: .552

AGREEMENTS..............................42
24 CFR 5: .234 (3); .613;
24 CFR 982: Intro; .317;
7420.10G Gbk: 1-8; 4-11; 5-22; 13-6 (3); 13-9; 15-1;
PIH Notices: 03-23; 02-27; 01-15; 01-15 Impr Integ Hbk (2); 00-11 (10); 00-11A (2);
Admin Plan: s6p7; s6p13; s7p7; s9p3 (4); s17p1 (2); s23p6; s24p1

AGREES...26
24 CFR 5: .321; .350; .353; .403 (2);
24 CFR 982: .151 (2); .401; .633;
HUD-50058Instr: p70 (2);
HUD-52580-A: p4;
HUD-52646: p1;
7420.10G Gbk: 10-4; 11-1; 11-3; 11-13; 12-6; 15-1; 20-1;
PIH Notices: 01-41 (2); 00-24B; 00-09 (2);
Admin Plan: s23p7

AIDS 47
24 CFR 5: .601 (2); .603;

.617;
24 CFR 35 SubM: .1200 (2);
HUD-50058: p i (2);
HUD-50058Instr: p15 (2); p74;
7420.10G Gbk: 5-11; 5-32; 5-43; 8-2;
PIH Notices: 95-48 (15); 95-48 Tech Asst (15);
Admin Plan: s8p1; s25p2

AIR CIRCULATION 3
24 CFR 982: .401;
7420.10G Gbk: 10-10; 10-10

AIR CONDITIONED 1
HUD-52667: p i

AIR CONDITIONER 1
7420.10G Gbk: 18-1

AIR CONDITIONERS 2
24 CFR 982: .517;
7420.10G Gbk: 18-1

AIR CONDITIONING 25
24 CFR 982: .517;
HUD-52517: p1;
HUD-52580-A: p15;
HUD-52641: p2;
HUD-52667: p1 (2); p i (2); p ii;
7420.10G Gbk: 6-9 Ex 6-1; 9-17 Ex 9-3 (2); 10-7 (2); 10-8; 10-10; 18-1 (2); 18-2 (2); 18-5; 18-8; 18-9 (2);
Admin Plan: s9p3

AIR INFILTRATION 3
24 CFR 982: .401;
HUD-52580-A: p2;
7420.10G Gbk: 10-9

AIR POLLUTION 8
24 CFR 982: .401 (2); .614;
HUD-52580-A: p17; p18;
7420.10G Gbk: 10-10; 10-13; 17-5

AIR QUALITY 8
24 CFR 5: .703;
24 CFR 982: .401;
HUD-52580: p5;
HUD-52580-A: p17 (2); p18;
7420.10G Gbk: 10-1; 10-10

AIR-CONDITIONED 1
24 CFR 982: .517

AIRFIELD 1
24 CFR 982: .626

AIRPORT ....
1
24 CFR 982: .626

ALASKA NATIVE CLAIMS 3
HUD-50058Instr: p30;
7420.10G Gbk: 5-16 Ex 5-2;
PIH Notices: 01-15 Impr Integ Hbk

ALCOHOL 46
24 CFR 5: .403;
24 CFR 982: Intro; .54; .310 (3); .551 (2); .552 (5); .553 (5);
HUD-50058: p16;
HUD-50058Instr: p61; p74;
HUD-52641: p9 (2);
HUD-52641-A: p2 (3);
7420.10G Gbk: 15-1; 15-2; 15-6; 15-7 (5);
PIH Notices: 03-11; 95-48 (2); 95-48 Tech Asst (2);
Admin Plan: s1p5 (3); s15p2; s15p3 (2); s15p3

ALCOHOL ABUSE 19
24 CFR 982: .54; .310; .551; .552 (3);
HUD-52641: p9 (2);
HUD-52641-A: p2 (2);
7420.10G Gbk: 15-1; 15-2; 15-6; 15-7 (2);
PIH Notices: 03-11;
Admin Plan: s1p5; s15p2; s15p3

ALCOHOL ABUSERS 4
24 CFR 982: Intro; .553 (2); .553

ALCOHOL REHABILITATION PROGRAM 5
24 CFR 982: .310 (2); .552 (2);
7420.10G Gbk: 15-7

ALCOHOLICS 1
Admin Plan: s1p5

ALCOHOLISM 7
7420.10G Gbk: 5-43;
PIH Notices: 95-48 (3); 95-48 Tech Asst (2); 95-48 Tech Asst

ALIEN 35
24 CFR 5: .512;
HUD-50058: p3 (6); p iii; p4 (6); p iv;
HUD-50058Instr: p15 (2); p16 (12);
7420.10G Gbk: 5-4 (2); 5-7; 5-10 Ex 5-1; 12-5;
PIH Notices: 01-27

ALIEN REGISTRATION 28
HUD-50058: p3 (6); p iii; p4 (6); p iv;
HUD-50058Instr: p15 (2); p16 (11);
7420.10G Gbk: 5-10 Ex 5-1

ALIEN STATUS 1
7420.10G Gbk: 12-5

ALIENS 1

7420.10G Gbk: 5-10 Ex 5-1

ALIMONY 15
24 CFR 5: .609;
7420.10G Gbk: 4-26 Ex 4-2 (2); 5-14 Ex 5-2; 5-23 (2); 5-47 Ex 5-5; 12-13 Ex 12-1;
PIH Notices: 01-15 Impr Integ Hbk (2);
Admin Plan: s6p9 (4); s7p4

ALJ 1
24 CFR 5: .100

ALL FAMILIES 31
24 CFR 5: .514;
24 CFR 982: .307; .402;
7420.10G Gbk: 3-4; 4-27 Ex 4-2; 5-39; 5-40 (2); 5-41; 8-7; 8-20; 12-10; 12-12 Ex 12-1; 22-4; 24-4;
PIH Notices: 01-41 (3); 01-15 Impr Integ Hbk; 00-24B; 00-11A (5); 00-09;
Admin Plan: s3p1; s6p4; s6p5; s18p1; s20p1

ALL FAMILY 1
Admin Plan: s20p2

ALL FAMILY MEMBERS 34
24 CFR 5: .520 (3);
24 CFR 982: .516;
HUD-50058: p ix; p x; p xi; p xii; p xiii; p xiv;
HUD-50058Instr: p10; p34; p40; p48; p51; p54; p57; p62; p69;
7420.10G Gbk: 5-5; 5-6 (2); 5-12; 5-31; 12-12 Ex 12-1; 12-14 Ex 12-2;
Admin Plan: s2p1; s2p5; s6p2; s7p3 (2); s7p7; s7p8; s18p8

ALL FAMILY OBLIGATIONS 2
24 CFR 982: .633;
Admin Plan: s25p5

ALLEGATION 10
7420.10G Gbk: 22-16;
Admin Plan: s20p1; s20p3 (5); s20p4 (2); s20p4

ALLEGATIONS 11
7420.10G Gbk: 22-11;
PIH Notices: 02-21; 01-20; 95-48; 95-48 Tech Asst;
Admin Plan: s20p3 (5); s20p4

ALLEGE 1
Admin Plan: s20p1

ALLEGED 25
24 CFR 5: .353 (3);
24 CFR 982: .406;
HUD-903-1: p3 (2); p5 (3);
7420.10G Gbk: 22-11 (2); 22-16 (2);
PIH Notices: 95-48 (6); 95-48 Tech Asst (5); 95-48 Tech Asst

ALLEGEDLY 1
7420.10G Gbk: 22-15

ALLEGIANCE 2
24 CFR 5: .504;
HUD-50058Instr: p74

ALLEGING 9
24 CFR 5: .360;
PIH Notices: 02-21 (2); 01-20 (2); 95-48 (2); 95-48 Tech Asst; 95-48 Tech Asst

ALLOCATE 6
HUD-50058Instr: p72;
7420.10G Gbk: 1-8; 1-13; 8-9; 12-8;
PIH Notices: 02-22

ALLOCATED 34
24 CFR 982: .101 (4); .102 (5);
7420.10G Gbk: 1-5 (2); 1-8; 8-8; 8-23; 20-6; 20-15 (2); 20-27; 24-16;
PIH Notices: 03-23 (3); 02-22 (4); 02-01; 99-52;
Admin Plan: s5p1 (2); s5p2 (3); s24p4

ALLOCATES 2
24 CFR 982: .101;
7420.10G Gbk: 1-7

ALLOCATING 3
7420.10G Gbk: 20-13; 21-4;
PIH Notices: 01-02

ALLOCATION 57
24 CFR 982: .101 (7); .102 (6);
7420.10G Gbk: 1-5; 1-8; 7-6; 8-10; 8-23 (3); 13-5; 20-13 (2); 20-14; 20-15; 24-15;
PIH Notices: 03-23 (2); 02-22; 02-07; 02-06; 02-01 (3); 01-41 (5); 01-15 Impr Integ Hbk; 01-10 (2); 00-09 (7); 99-52 (3);
Admin Plan: s25p1; s25p2; s25p8

ALLOCATION PLAN APPLICATIONS 2
PIH Notices: 02-01; 99-52

ALLOCATION PLANS 4
PIH Notices: 02-01 (2); 99-52; 99-52

ALLOCATIONS 27
24 CFR 982: .101; .102;
7420.10G Gbk: 1-6 (2); 1-7;

1-8 (2); 8-23; 21-5; 21-11 (5); 24-2; 24-7 (2); 24-16 (2);
PIH Notices: 02-22; 02-06 (4); 01-41; 01-06; 00-09

ALLOTMENT 2
7420.10G Gbk: 5-16 Ex 5-2;
PIH Notices: 01-15 Impr Integ Hbk

ALLOTTED...6
HUD-52665: p2;
7420.10G Gbk: 22-15; 24-7;
PIH Notices: 02-27;
Admin Plan: s22p2; s24p5

ALLOW 127
24 CFR 5: .508; .609 (2); .801 (2);
24 CFR 982: .54; .312; .353; .551; .553 (4);
HUD-50058Instr: p1; p14; p50 (2);
HUD-52580-A: p2 (2); p6; p13;
HUD-52646: p2;
HUD-52667: p i;
HUD-9886: p2;
7420.10G Gbk: 3-5; 4-8; 5-14 Ex 5-2; 5-15 Ex 5-2; 5-25 Ex 5-3; 5-30; 7-1; 7-6; 7-9; 8-4; 8-9 (2); 8-17 (2); 10-25; 10-29; 10-32; 10-34; 10-40 Ex 10-4a; 10-41 Ex 10-4b (2); 11-8; 12-1; 12-2; 12-4; 12-8; 13-2 (3); 14-1; 15-6; 15-7; 15-10 Ex 15-2; 17-1 (3); 17-10; 18-7; 22-2; 23-1; 23-7; 23-10; 23-15; 24-7; 24-10;
PIH Notices: 03-23; 03-20 (2); 03-11; 03-05; 02-27 (3); 02-06; 02-01 (4); 01-41; 01-40; 01-20; 01-15; 01-15 Impr Integ Hbk (6); 01-11; 01-06 (3); 00-41; 00-34; 00-27; 00-24B; 00-11; 99-52 (4); 99-11; 95-48 (5); 95-48 Tech Asst (5);
Admin Plan: s5p3; s6p1; s6p2; s7p1; s7p3; s9p1; s9p2; s10p2; s13p1; s15p6; s15p6

ALLOWABLE..................................35
24 CFR 982: .4; .102; .643;
HUD-50058: p6; p7;
HUD-50058Instr: p34 (2); p35;
7420.10G Gbk: 5-31 (2); 5-32 (2); 5-51 Ex 5-5; 6-10 Ex 6-2; 20-1;
PIH Notices: 01-15 (2); 01-15 Impr Integ Hbk (2); 00-09;
Admin Plan: s6p1 (4); s6p2 (2); s6p11 (5); s7p1; s7p6; s8p2; s23p6

ALLOWABLE DEDUCTION...........2
Admin Plan: s6p11; s6p11

ALLOWABLE DEDUCTIONS.........4
PIH Notices: 01-15; 01-15 Impr Integ Hbk;
Admin Plan: s6p1; s7p1

ALLOWABLE EXCLUSIONS 2
PIH Notices: 01-15; 01-15 Impr Integ Hbk

ALLOWABLE PROGRAM COSTS.1
7420.10G Gbk: 20-1

ALLOWANCE...............................388
24 CFR 5: .520; .603 (2); .609 (3); .632; .634;
24 CFR 982: .4 (3); .403; .504; .517 (23); .555 (2); .604 (2); .613 (3); .617 (3); .619; .623 (2); .624; .635 (8); .641;
HUD-50058: p7 (5); p vii (12); p9 (2); p ix (6); p10 (2); p x (4); p11 (2); p xi (5); p12 (2); p xii (5); p13; p xiii (2); p14 (3); p xiv (3); p15; p xv (3);
HUD-50058Instr: p25; p32; p34 (2); p35 (10); p36 (9); p39 (7); p40 (7); p41; p43 (9); p44 (9); p45; p47 (9); p48; p49 (9); p50 (4); p51 (5); p52 (8); p54 (5); p56 (6); p58 (6); p72; p76 (3);
HUD-52648: p1 (5); p i (8); p ii;
7420.10G Gbk: 1-2; 5-14 Ex 5-2 (3); 5-16 Ex 5-2; 5-29 (9); 5-30 (4); 5-31 (6); 5-32 (6); 5-33 (8); 5-34 (6); 5-47 Ex 5-5; 5-50 Ex 5-5; 5-52 Ex 5-5; 12-2; 12-11; 17-6; 17-12 (2); 18-1; 18-2 (2); 18-6 (3); 18-7; 18-8 (3); 18-9 (2); 19-10; 23-16 Ex 23-2 (3);
PIH Notices: 02-27; 02-20 (3); 01-41 (4); 01-15 Impr Integ Hbk (11); 01-10; 01-06; 00-46; 00-41; 00-24B (10); 00-09 (6);
Admin Plan: s5p3 (2); s6p1 (2); s6p11; s6p13 (9); s8p2; s11p1; s18p3; s19p1 (7); s21p1; s21p2; s21p4 (5); s21p8 (2); s23p3

ALLOWANCES 123

24 CFR 5: .609 (2); 24 CFR 982: .517 (3); .555; .624 (4); HUD-50058: p7; p vii (2); HUD-50058Instr: p26 (4); p32; p36 (4); HUD-52648: p1 (5); p i (17); p ii (7); 7420.10G Gbk: 1-2; 3-5; 4-15; 4-27 Ex 4-2; 5-14 Ex 5-2 (2); 5-16 Ex 5-2 (3); 5-23; 5-24; 5-34; 5-50 Ex 5-5; 11-15; 12-11; 12-16 Ex 12-4; 18-1 (3); 18-2 (5); 18-3 Ex 18-1; 18-4 (5); 18-5; 18-6; 18-7 (2); 18-8 (2); 18-9 (2); 18-10; 19-10 (2); 22-2; 22-3; 22-6; 23-12; PIH Notices: 02-27; 01-15 Impr Integ Hbk (6); 00-24B; Admin Plan: s3p3; s6p1; s6p5; s6p12; s6p13 (2); s7p3 (2); s8p3; s11p1; s11p2; s18p4; s19p1 (5); s21p4; s23p4

ALLOWANCE-TYPE 1

7420.10G Gbk: 1-2

ALLOWED 51

24 CFR 5: .318 (4); .801; 24 CFR 982: .1; .555 (2); .635 (3); HUD-52580-A: p13; 7420.10G Gbk: 1-2; 1-3; 1-4; 1-5; 3-2; 4-1; 4-11; 4-19; 5-37; 5-43; 6-3; 7-5; 8-5 (2); 10-23; 12-8 (2); 15-1; 16-4 (2); 20-19 Ex 20-3; 20-25; 21-7 (2); PIH Notices: 03-23; 02-01; 01-41; 00-24B; 99-52; 95-48; 95-48 Tech Asst; Admin Plan: s1p5; s3p3; s6p11 (2); s7p1; s7p2; s15p6; s18p5

ALLOWING 15

24 CFR 982: .311; .314; .551; .641; HUD-52580-A: p15; 7420.10G Gbk: 1-2; 1-15; 9-11; 12-10; 14-1; 20-4; 21-10; PIH Notices: 03-05; 01-40; Admin Plan: s14p2

ALLOWS 41

24 CFR 982: .301; HUD-50058: p ii; p v; HUD-50058Instr: p1; p10; p11; p17; p35; 7420.10G Gbk: 2-6; 4-14; 4-15; 5-21; 8-9; 8-14; 8-15; 9-9; 10-34; 12-1 (2); 12-2; 12-9; 13-1; 13-7; 15-4; 20-1; 20-19 Ex 20-3; 22-1; 22-3; 22-5; 23-12; 23-20; PIH Notices: 02-01; 01-06; 01-01; 00-53; 00-41; 99-52; 95-48; 95-48 Tech Asst; Admin Plan: s7p3; s9p2

ALONE 12

24 CFR 5: .609; 24 CFR 982: .627; HUD-50058Instr: p15; p31; p75 (2); 7420.10G Gbk: 5-15 Ex 5-2; PIH Notices: 03-23; 01-15 Impr Integ Hbk (2); 95-48; 95-48 Tech Asst

ALTER 4

PIH Notices: 02-01; 99-52; 95-48; 95-48 Tech Asst

ALTERATION 63

HUD-50058Instr: p70; 7420.10G Gbk: 5-44; PIH Notices: 02-01 (13); 99-52 (13); 95-48 (17); 95-48 Tech Asst (17); Admin Plan: s1p5

ALTERATIONS 108

PIH Notices: 02-01 (16); 99-52 (16); 95-48 (39); 95-48 Tech Asst (36); 95-48 Tech Asst

ALTERED 26

24 CFR 982: .636; 7420.10G Gbk: 5-6; PIH Notices: 02-01 (5); 01-15 Impr Integ Hbk; 99-52 (5); 95-48 (6); 95-48 Tech Asst (6); Admin Plan: s20p6

ALTERED DOCUMENTS 1

Admin Plan: s20p6

ALTERNATE 16

24 CFR 5: .359; 24 CFR 982: .401 (2); HUD-52580-A: p2; 7420.10G Gbk: 4-23 Ex 4-1; 10-12 (3); 12-4; 17-3; PIH Notices: 95-48 (2); 95-48 Tech Asst (2); Admin Plan: s1p3; s1p5

ALTERNATE EXIT 2

24 CFR 982: .401; HUD-52580-A: p2

ALTERNATIVE 51
24 CFR 5: .214;
24 CFR 982: .4;
HUD-52580-A: p17;
7420.10G Gbk: 1-8 (2); 4-11; 9-10; 11-2; 12-4 (2); 22-12; 22-13;
PIH Notices: 02-27; 02-01 (2); 01-15 Impr Integ Hbk; 01-11; 00-41; 99-52 (2); 95-48 (14); 95-48 Tech Asst (14);
Admin Plan: s1p3; s1p5; s23p4

ALTERNATIVE METHOD 1
7420.10G Gbk: 12-4

ALTERNATIVE METHODS 2
PIH Notices: 95-48; 95-48 Tech Asst

ALTERNATIVELY 7
HUD-50058Instr: p7;
7420.10G Gbk: 12-2;
PIH Notices: 02-27; 95-48 (2); 95-48 Tech Asst; 95-48 Tech Asst

ALTERNATIVES 18
7420.10G Gbk: 1-8; 11-3; 13-1; 22-12;
PIH Notices: 02-20; 02-01 (2); 00-46; 99-52 (2); 95-48 (3); 95-48 Tech Asst (3);
Admin Plan: s8p4; s19p1

AMEND 9
24 CFR 5: .353;
7420.10G Gbk: 6-7; 7-6; 23-2; 23-9;
PIH Notices: 00-49 (2); 00-09; 00-09

AMENDED 51
24 CFR 5: .100 (2); .105 (4); .312; .324; .380; .500; .504;
24 CFR 982: .516;
HUD-50058Instr: p3 (2);
HUD-9886: p1;
7420.10G Gbk: 3-8; 5-42; 5-44; 8-3; 10-11; 10-15 (2);
PIH Notices: 03-11; 02-22; 02-21 (3); 01-41 (2); 01-20 (3); 01-15 Impr Integ Hbk (7); 01-10 (3); 01-06; 00-27 (3); 95-48; 95-48 Tech Asst;
Admin Plan: s1p1; s23p5

AMENDING 2
24 CFR 5: .318;
Admin Plan: s25p4

AMENDMENT 23
24 CFR 5: .306; .312; .353; .380;
24 CFR 982: .102; .352;
7420.10G Gbk: 5-44; 22-11 (2);
PIH Notices: 02-07; 01-10; 01-06; 00-24A (4); 00-09 (2); 95-48; 95-48 Tech Asst;
Admin Plan: s23p1; s23p5; s23p5

AMENDMENTS 17
24 CFR 5: .100;
HUD-903: p2; p3;
HUD-9886: p1;
7420.10G Gbk: 5-43 (2); 20-17;
PIH Notices: 03-23 (2); 01-41; 01-10 (2); 00-24; 00-24A; 00-09;
Admin Plan: s1p3; s20p3

AMENDS 7
7420.10G Gbk: 3-1;
PIH Notices: 01-27; 01-01 (2); 00-24A; 00-09; 00-09

AMENITIES 41
24 CFR 5: .100;
24 CFR 982: .4; .507;
HUD-50058: p v (2);
HUD-50058Instr: p20 (3); p21 (5);
HUD-52580: p6;
HUD-52580-A: p19;
HUD-52641: p4;
HUD-52648: p1;
7420.10G Gbk: 8-14; 9-2; 9-5 (2); 9-8; 9-12; 9-13 Ex 9-1; 9-15 Ex 9-2; 9-17 Ex 9-3; 9-19 Ex 9-4; 10-28;
PIH Notices: 03-12 (2); 02-27; 02-22; 02-01; 01-27; 01-15 Impr Integ Hbk; 00-24B; 00-09; 99-52;
Admin Plan: s11p2; s21p3; s24p3

AMENITY 2
PIH Notices: 95-48; 95-48 Tech Asst

AMERICAN INDIAN 7
HUD-50058: p3; p4;
HUD-50058Instr: p15; p73;
HUD-903: p2;
7420.10G Gbk: 4-23 Ex 4-1; 4-25 Ex 4-2

AMERICORPS 1
7420.10G Gbk: 5-16 Ex 5-2

AMORTIZATION 36
24 CFR 5: .609 (2);
24 CFR 982: .623 (7);
HUD-50058: p13 (2); p xiii (4);

HUD-50058Instr: p25; p53 (7); p54 (2);
7420.10G Gbk: 5-14 Ex 5-2 (2); 5-19; 5-49 Ex 5-5 (2);
PIH Notices: 01-15 Impr Integ Hb k (4);
Admin Plan: s7p6; s7p6

AMORTIZE..8
24 CFR 982: .619; .623 (3);
HUD-50058: p xiii;
HUD-50058Instr: p53;
7420.10G Gbk: 17-10;
Admin Plan: s19p1

AMORTIZING..................................1
Admin Plan: s22p3

AMOUNT DUE...............................11
24 CFR 982: .635; .642;
HUD-52665: p3;
7420.10G Gbk: 6-8; 11-15; 22-12 (2); 22-13 (2); 22-15;
Admin Plan: s6p10

AMOUNT OWED...........................12
7420.10G Gbk: 22-12 (4); 22-13 (2); 23-10; 23-14 (3);
PIH Notices: 96-65;
Admin Plan: s18p6

AMOUNTS DUE.............................12
24 CFR 982: .310;
HUD-52641: p4 (2);
7420.10G Gbk: 5-47 Ex 5-5; 11-18 (2); 15-1; 22-15; 23-14 (3);
Admin Plan: s14p1

AMOUNTS OWED.........................14
24 CFR 982: .313; .552 (3); .641;
7420.10G Gbk: 5-37 (2); 22-13; 22-14;
PIH Notices: 01-15 Impr Integ Hbk;
Admin Plan: s15p2; s17p2; s20p5

ANALYZE.......................................22
HUD-50058Instr: p1 (2);
7420.10G Gbk: 4-2; 4-4; 4-6; 7-9; 19-4 (2); 19-10; 19-12; 20-20; 22-1; 22-6; 22-18; 24-3; 24-7 (2); 24-10;
PIH Notices: 03-20; 01-10; 95-48; 95-48 Tech Asst

ANALYZED......................................8
HUD-52648: p2;
7420.10G Gbk: 2-3 (2); 4-9; 21-18;
PIH Notices: 03-20;
Admin Plan: s21p6; s21p6

ANALYZER......................................2
PIH Notices: 00-23; 00-23

ANALYZING..................................11
HUD-50058Instr: p22;
7420.10G Gbk: 4-2; 4-9; 19-5; 19-6 (3); 19-8; 19-11; 19-12; 24-2

ANIMAL..11
24 CFR 5: .303 (2); .306; .318; .360; .363 (2);
PIH Notices: 02-01 (2); 99-52; 99-52

ANIMALS.......................................13
24 CFR 5: .303 (7); .306; .312; .350;
7420.10G Gbk: 5-43;
PIH Notices: 02-01; 99-52

ANNIVERSARY.............................45
24 CFR 982: .507 (2); .519 (7);
HUD-52648: p1 (2);
7420.10G Gbk: 1-6 Ex 1-1; 9-1 (3); 9-2 (4); 9-12; 12-1 (2); 13-6;
PIH Notices: 02-27; 00-24B (2);
Admin Plan: s5p3 (2); s8p3; s10p2 (4); s11p2; s11p3 (2); s11p1; s11p2 (2); s21p3 (3); s23p5 (2); s23p6

ANNIVERSARY DATE..................32
24 CFR 982: .519 (6);
7420.10G Gbk: 1-6 Ex 1-1; 9-1 (3); 9-2 (4); 12-1 (2); 13-6;
Admin Plan: s5p3 (2); s8p3; s10p2 (4); s11p3 (2); s11p1; s11p2 (2); s23p5 (2); s23p6

ANNUAL ADJUSTMENT.............24
24 CFR 982: .102 (8); .519 (5); .521; .619;
PIH Notices: 03-23; 01-10; 00-24B; 00-09;
Admin Plan: s23p6 (2); s24p5; s24p5

ANNUAL ADJUSTMENT FACTOR 24
24 CFR 982: .102 (5); .519;
7420.10G Gbk: 1-6 Ex 1-1; 14-3; 20-9; 20-12 Ex 20-2 (2); 20-17; 20-18; 20-19 Ex 20-3 (5);
PIH Notices: 03-23; 01-10; 00-09;
Admin Plan: s23p6; s24p5; s24p5

ANNUAL ADJUSTMENT FACTORS7
24 CFR 982: .102 (3);
7420.10G Gbk: 1-6 Ex 1-1; 20-

12 Ex 20-2; 20-19 Ex 20-3;
PIH Notices: 00-24B

ANNUAL BUDGET AUTHORITY 24
PIH Notices: 03-23 (4); 02-27; 02-21 (7); 02-07; 02-06 (10); 00-49

ANNUAL CONTRIBUTION............5
HUD-50058Instr: p7;
7420.10G Gbk: 20-2; 20-6; 20-18;
PIH Notices: 03-23

ANNUAL CONTRIBUTIONS...... 112
24 CFR 5: .403;
24 CFR 982: Intro; .4; .151 (3); .601;
HUD-50058Instr: p1; p70 (3);
7420.10G Gbk: 1-8; 1-12 Ex 1-2; 1-12; 3-7; 11-5; 20-1 (5); 20-2 (7); 20-6 (3); 20-7; 20-8 Ex 20-1; 20-9 (2); 20-12 Ex 20-2 (2); 20-13 (5); 20-16 (2); 20-17 (6); 20-18; 20-20; 20-22; 20-23; 20-24; 20-25 (4); 20-26 (4); 20-27 (4); 20-28 (7); 20-29 (5); 21-1;
PIH Notices: 03-23 (3); 03-20; 02-27 (3); 02-21 (3); 02-20 (2); 02-14 (2); 02-06 (2); 02-01; 01-41; 01-20 (2); 01-06; 00-46 (2); 00-28 (2); 00-27; 00-24B (2); 00-09; 99-52;
Admin Plan: s23p5; s24p1

ANNUAL CONTRIBUTIONS CONTRACT...................................34
24 CFR 5: .403;
24 CFR 982: Intro; .4; .151 (3); .601;
HUD-50058Instr: p1; p70 (3);
PIH Notices: 03-20; 02-27 (3); 02-21 (2); 02-20; 02-14 (2); 02-06 (2); 02-01; 01-41; 01-20 (2); 00-46; 00-28 (2); 00-27; 00-09; 99-52;
Admin Plan: s23p5; s24p1

ANNUAL CONTRIBUTIONS CONTRACTS...................................6
PIH Notices: 03-23 (3); 02-20; 00-46; 00-24B

ANNUAL INCOME.....................355
24 CFR 5: .212; .520 (3); .603 (11); .609 (7); .611 (4); .615 (9); .617 (10); .653; .659 (2);
24 CFR 982: .201 (4); .516 (2); .627 (3); .642 (4);
HUD-50058: p6 (4); p7 (2); p vii (4); p8 (2); p viii (3);
HUD-50058Instr: p24; p28 (2); p33 (6); p34 (5); p36 (5); p37 (6); p65 (5); p66 (7); p67; p70 (4); p71 (4); p73 (4); p74 (2); p76;
HUD-52665: p1;
7420.10G Gbk: 4-14; 4-15; 4-19; 4-26 Ex 4-2; 5-1; 5-3; 5-13 (7); 5-14 Ex 5-2; 5-17 (9); 5-18 (3); 5-19 (2); 5-20 (2); 5-21 (3); 5-22 (5); 5-23 (3); 5-24 (3); 5-25 Ex 5-3; 5-26 (2); 5-28 (2); 5-29; 5-31 (2); 5-32 (5); 5-33 (11); 5-34 (8); 5-35; 5-47 Ex 5-5; 12-4 (2); 12-10; 16-5 (2); 17-11; 22-3; 23-7 (2); 23-10; 23-11; 23-13; 23-16 Ex 23-2; 23-17 Ex 23-2 (6);
PIH Notices: 03-05; 01-41 (5); 01-40; 01-15 (6); 01-15 Impr Integ Hbk (51); 01-10 (18); 00-24B (7); 00-09 (7); 00-01 (3); 98-66;
Admin Plan: s2p4 (3); s6p1 (5); s6p2 (6); s6p3 (3); s6p4; s6p8 (2); s6p10 (3); s6p12 (2); s21p4 (2); s21p6

ANNUAL INCOMES........................1
7420.10G Gbk: 23-10

ANNUAL REVIEW..........................7
24 CFR 982: .517;
7420.10G Gbk: 7-6; 18-9; 18-10 (2); 24-11;
Admin Plan: s24p5

ANNUALIZATION..........................4
24 CFR 5: .609;
PIH Notices: 01-15 Impr Integ Hbk (2); 01-15 Impr Integ Hbk

ANNUALIZATION OF INCOME....4
24 CFR 5: .609;
PIH Notices: 01-15 Impr Integ Hbk (2); 01-15 Impr Integ Hbk

ANNUALIZE..................................3
24 CFR 5: .609;
7420.10G Gbk: 22-8;
PIH Notices: 01-15 Impr Integ Hbk

ANNUALIZED..................................1
7420.10G Gbk: 5-17

ANNUALIZING..............................2
7420.10G Gbk: 5-17; 5-17

ANNUALLY....................................90
24 CFR 5: .350 (2); .657; .705 (2); .801 (3);
24 CFR 982: .102; .405; .516; .622;
HUD-52648: p2;
7420.10G Gbk: 1-6 Ex 1-1; 2-3; 4-15; 5-2; 5-13 (2); 5-17; 5-18; 5-26; 7-6; 8-23; 10-1 (2); 10-24; 10-27; 10-30; 10-35; 10-40 Ex 10-4a; 11-8; 12-1; 17-12; 18-9; 19-12; 20-6; 20-9; 20-16; 20-28 (3); 20-29; 21-5; 21-8; 22-10; 23-14 (2);
PIH Notices: 03-23 (3); 02-27 (4); 02-07 (2); 02-06; 01-41; 01-15 (2); 01-15 Impr Integ Hbk (5); 01-06; 01-02; 00-28 (2); 00-24B (6); 00-09;
Admin Plan: s6p13; s10p1; s11p3; s11p1; s19p1 (3); s20p1; s20p3; s21p8; s23p6; s25p5

ANNUITIES.....................................6
24 CFR 5: .609;
HUD-50058Instr: p29;
7420.10G Gbk: 5-14 Ex 5-2; 12-13 Ex 12-1;
PIH Notices: 01-15 Impr Integ Hbk; 01-15 Impr Integ Hbk

ANNUITY...3
HUD-50058Instr: p71;
7420.10G Gbk: 4-26 Ex 4-2; 12-13 Ex 12-1

ANOTHER PHA.............................27
24 CFR 982: .4; .316; .355; .552;
HUD-50058Instr: p9; p59; p75;
HUD-52648: p3 (2);
7420.10G Gbk: 2-9; 5-37; 8-9; 9-4; 11-9; 15-5; 20-10; 21-1; 21-8;
PIH Notices: 02-27 (2); 01-41; 01-15; 00-09;
Admin Plan: s2p3; s2p6; s15p2; s15p5

ANOTHER PHA'S...........................4
HUD-50058Instr: p7 (2); p62; p63

ANTICIPATE......................................
12
24 CFR 5: .609;
HUD-50058Instr: p78;
7420.10G Gbk: 5-17; 5-31; 9-5;
PIH Notices: 02-06; 01-15; 01-15 Impr Integ Hbk; 95-48; 95-48 Tech Asst;
Admin Plan: s6p8; s7p5

ANTICIPATED...............................52
24 CFR 5: .603 (3); .609 (2);
HUD-50058: p6;
HUD-50058Instr: p22; p23; p33; p34; p70 (2); p71; p73;
HUD-52665: p1;
7420.10G Gbk: 5-13; 5-17 (4); 5-31 (2); 5-46 Ex 5-5; 5-47 Ex 5-5; 10-24 (2); 12-1; 12-13 Ex 12-1; 18-1; 20-2; 20-3; 20-20; 20-28; 24-8;
PIH Notices: 02-06; 01-41 (4); 01-15 (4); 01-15 Impr Integ Hbk (3); 00-24B (2);
Admin Plan: s6p1; s6p8; s7p4; s7p7

ANTICIPATED INCOME.................6
HUD-50058: p6;
HUD-50058Instr: p22; p23;
7420.10G Gbk: 5-17;
PIH Notices: 01-15; 01-15 Impr Integ Hbk

ANTICIPATED TO BE RECEIVED.5
24 CFR 5: .609;
HUD-50058Instr: p33; p70;
PIH Notices: 01-15 Impr Integ Hbk;
Admin Plan: s6p1

ANTICIPATED TOTAL INCOME....1
PIH Notices: 01-15

ANTICIPATES..................................6
24 CFR 5: .508;
7420.10G Gbk: 4-13; 4-21; 20-6; 20-13;
PIH Notices: 01-10

ANTIQUE CARS.............................1
7420.10G Gbk: 5-25 Ex 5-3

ANYWHERE..................................21
24 CFR 982: .1; .4; .301; .353 (4);
7420.10G Gbk: 2-2; 2-7; 6-7; 8-8; 13-1; 15-9 Ex 15-1 (4); 15-10 Ex 15-2; 18-9;
Admin Plan: s9p1; s10p5; s13p2

APARTMENT.................................38
24 CFR 982: .308; .517; .615;
HUD-50058Instr: p20 (2); p21; p71;
HUD-52517: p1 (4); p2; p4 (2); p15 (3);
HUD-52641: p1;
HUD-903-1: p4;

7420.10G Gbk: 2-13 Ex 2-1; 9-6; 9-9; 9-10 (3); 10-35; 10-37 Ex 10-2; 12-7; 17-9; 24-12;
PIH Notices: 03-12 (2); 02-01; 00-09; 99-52; 99-11;
Admin Plan: s1p6; s19p1

APARTMENTGUIDE 1
7420.10G Gbk: 9-5

APARTMENTS 11
HUD-52667: p i;
HUD-903-1: p2;
7420.10G Gbk: 9-5 (2); 9-10 (5); 18-2; 24-9

APPARENT 9
7420.10G Gbk: 4-8; 4-11;
PIH Notices: 02-27; 01-06 (2); 95-48; 95-48 Tech Asst;
Admin Plan: s1p4; s1p4

APPEAL....................................... 59
24 CFR 5: .508; .512; .514 (25); .518; .615;
7420.10G Gbk: 2-7; 5-8 (6); 5-10 Ex 5-1; 5-11 (4); 15-10 Ex 15-2;
PIH Notices: 02-27 (9); 00-24A;
Admin Plan: s18p7 (6); s18p8

APPEALED 1
PIH Notices: 02-27

APPEALING 1
7420.10G Gbk: 24-13

APPEALS 18
24 CFR 5: .508 (2); .514; .516;
7420.10G Gbk: 5-6; 5-7; 5-11;
PIH Notices: 02-27 (4); 00-24A; 00-11A (2);
Admin Plan: s15p6; s18p1; s18p7; s23p8

APPLIANCE 8
HUD-52580: p6;
HUD-52580-A: p19;
HUD-52667: p i;
7420.10G Gbk: 6-9 Ex 6-1; 10-28; 18-4;
Admin Plan: s6p13; s9p3

APPLIANCES 55
24 CFR 982: .308 (3); .401; .404; .619;
HUD-52517: p1 (4);
HUD-52580-A: p2; p4 (2);
HUD-52641: p1 (4); p2 (4); p4 (3); 8; p9 (2); p10;
HUD-52641-A: p1 (2); p2; p3;
HUD-52646: p2;
HUD-52667: p i; p ii;
7420.10G Gbk: 8-21 (2); 10-8; 10-9; 11-11 (2); 11-12 (3); 11-17; 18-8 (4);
Admin Plan: s9p2 (2); s9p3 (2); s10p1; s10p5

APPLICABILITY 78
24 CFR 5: .210 (2); .400; .500; .520; .601; .615; .632; .653; .655; .657; .659; .661; .701; .801;
24 CFR 35 SubM: .1200 (2);
24 CFR 982: 24 CFR 982 (3); .2; .102; .314; .521; .601; .620 (2); .625; .634; .636; .641; .642; .643;
7420.10G Gbk: 22-16;
PIH Notices: 03-20; 03-11; 02-27; 02-22; 02-20; 02-14; 02-07; 02-01 (3); 01-43; 01-41 (5); 01-33; 01-15; 01-11; 01-06 (2); 01-02; 01-01; 00-53; 00-49; 00-46; 00-34; 00-28; 00-24; 00-14; 00-09 (5); 00-01; 99-52 (3); 99-11; 95-48; 95-48 Tech Asst;
Admin Plan: s6p4; s19p1

APPLICABLE 436
24 CFR 5: 24 CFR 5; .212; .214; .216 (4); .218 (4); .230; .234; .236 (8); .306; .315 (4); .318 (2); .321 (2); .324 (4); .350 (3); .353 (3); .360 (2); .500; .514 (2); .518 (4); .520; .524; .601; .603 (4); .611; .617 (4); .632; .703 (5); .801;
24 CFR 35 SubM: .1200;
24 CFR 982: .102 (5); .201 (3); .305; .306; .310; .317; .352; .401; .402; .451; .453; .502 (2); .504; .508; .517; .519; .521; .552; .555; .605; .614; .618; .622; .625 (2); .627; .628; .634 (2); .637 (2); .641; .642 (3);
HUD-50058: p ii; p iii; p iv; p v (2); p14; p xiv (2); p17; p xvii;
HUD-50058Instr: p2 (3); p7 (2); p9; p10; p12; p16; p19; p20 (2); p27; p56 (3); p61 (2); p65; p66 (2); p70; p74; p76;
HUD-52580: p2 (3); p3 (3); p4 (2); p5 (3);
HUD-52580-A: p3; p5; p7; p9; p10; p11; p12; p14 (3); p17 (2); p18 (2);
HUD-52641: p4; p5 (2); p6;

p10;
HUD-52641-A: p3;
HUD-52646: p1 (2);
HUD-52648: p2 (4); p3;
HUD-52665: p2 (4); p3;
HUD-903: p1 (4);
7420.10G Gbk: 1-10; 1-14; 4-16; 4-27 Ex 4-2; 5-1; 5-3; 5-11; 5-47 Ex 5-5 (3); 5-48 Ex 5-5 (2); 5-50 Ex 5-5; 6-2; 6-5; 7-8; 7-9 (2); 8-4; 8-5; 8-6; 8-16; 8-19; 9-14 Ex 9-1; 9-16 Ex 9-2; 10-3; 10-5; 10-12; 11-3; 11-14; 11-18; 12-6; 13-2; 13-4 (4); 13-10; 16-5; 17-2; 17-3; 17-4 (2); 17-5; 17-7; 17-9 (2); 18-8; 20-1; 20-2; 20-6; 20-7; 20-10; 20-14; 20-27; 20-29; 23-11; 23-17 Ex 23-2 (3);
PIH Notices: 03-23 (2); 03-11 (2); 02-27 (5); 02-21 (4); 02-20 (3); 02-07; 02-06; 02-01 (8); 01-41 (24); 01-33; 01-27 (3); 01-20; 01-15; 01-15 Impr Integ Hbk (5); 01-10 (12); 01-06 (15); 00-49; 00-46 (3); 00-41; 00-28; 00-27; 00-24B (7); 00-23; 00-14; 00-11A; 00-09 (32); 99-52 (8); 95-48 (8); 95-48 Tech Asst (6);
Admin Plan: s1p2 (3); s1p3; s1p4; s2p1; s2p4; s2p5; s3p2; s6p1; s6p5; s9p1; s10p3 (2); s11p1; s18p1; s18p6; s20p8; s21p6; s21p7 (2); s22p2; s23p6; s24p3; s25p6

APPLICABLE-INCOME LIMIT 1
7420.10G Gbk: 13-3

APPLICANT 415
24 CFR 5: .214 (4); .216 (15); .218 (6); .230 (2); .232 (2); .236 (8); .312; .318; .359; .403; .508; .514 (2); .516; .603 (2); .653 (2); .655 (3);
24 CFR 982: Intro; .4 (4); .54; .158; .201 (12); .202 (3); .204 (9); .205 (9); .207 (4); .516; .552 (7); .553 (5); .554 (11);
HUD-50058Instr: p2; p22; p32 (2); p70 (2); p71; p75;
HUD-9886: p2 (2);
7420.10G Gbk: 1-7; 2-8; 3-4; 3-7; 3-8; 4-4 (2); 4-5 (4); 4-6; 4-7 (4); 4-8 (8); 4-9 (2); 4-10 (11); 4-12 (2); 4-13 (3); 4-17 (4); 4-18 (5); 4-25 Ex 4-2; 4-27 Ex 4-2; 5-1 (2); 5-4; 5-6; 5-7 (4); 5-13; 5-16 Ex 5-2; 5-25 Ex 5-3; 5-26 (4); 5-28; 5-29; 5-35 (3); 5-37; 5-46 Ex 5-5 (5); 5-47 Ex 5-5 (6); 5-48 Ex 5-5 (2); 5-49 Ex 5-5 (3); 5-50 Ex 5-5 (5); 5-51 Ex 5-5 (2); 5-52 Ex 5-5; 5-53 Ex 5-5; 6-1 (2); 7-4 (2); 7-10 (2); 8-10; 8-12; 8-23; 12-5; 13-4; 14-1; 16-1 (3); 16-2 (2); 16-3 (3); 17-1; 19-8; 21-2; 21-3; 21-4 (2); 21-8 (2); 21-10 (2); 21-11; 22-1; 22-14; 22-18; 24-3; 24-7;
PIH Notices: 03-11 (25); 02-21 (2); 02-01 (13); 01-20; 01-15 (6); 01-15 Impr Integ Hbk (3); 01-02 (2); 01-01 (11); 00-24B (2); 99-52 (13); 95-48 (2); 95-48 Tech Asst (2);
Admin Plan: s1p3 (3); s1p6; s2p1 (7); s2p3 (3); s2p4 (2); s2p5 (2); s2p6 (2); s2p7; s3p2 (3); s3p3 (2); s4p1 (2); s4p2 (2); s4p3; s5p2; s7p1 (3); s7p8 (3); s8p1 (2); s8p2; s8p4 (2); s9p3; s10p3; s13p2; s15p1; s15p2; s15p3 (3); s15p6; s18p1 (4); s18p2; s18p3 (3); s18p7 (3); s24p6 (2); s24p7 (2); s24p7

APPLICANT FAMILY 9
7420.10G Gbk: 4-6 (2); 4-9; 4-16 (2); 4-19; 5-4; 5-38; 5-41

APPLICANT FAMILY 19
24 CFR 5: .655;
24 CFR 982: .4; .204; .207;
7420.10G Gbk: 4-6 (2); 4-9; 4-16 (2); 4-19; 5-4; 5-38; 5-41;
PIH Notices: 03-11;
Admin Plan: s2p1; s2p3; s8p2; s18p7; s24p6

APPLICANT FAMILY'S 1
7420.10G Gbk: 5-35

APPLICANT INTERVIEWS 1

7420.10G Gbk: 4-13

APPLICANT SCREENING 8
24 CFR 982: .552;
7420.10G Gbk: 3-4; 3-7;
PIH Notices: 03-11 (4);
Admin Plan: s1p3

APPLICANT SELECTION 2
7420.10G Gbk: 13-4; 21-8

APPLICANT STATUS 4
24 CFR 982: .202;
7420.10G Gbk: 4-5; 4-7;
Admin Plan: s3p2

APPLICANTS 384
24 CFR 5: .210 (3); .212; .214 (3); .216 (7); .218 (4); .230 (3); .234; .318; .359; .500; .508 (3); .514 (5); .653 (3); .655 (3);
24 CFR 982: Intro; .54 (3); .158; .202 (3); .204; .207 (4); .307 (2); .353; .355; .552; .553;
HUD-50058Instr: p2 (2); p71 (2);
HUD-52648: p1 (2);
HUD-9886: p2;
7420.10G Gbk: 1-13; 1-14; 2-7 (2); 2-8; 2-9; 3-1; 3-2 (6); 3-3 (2); 3-5; 3-8; 3-9 (2); 4-1 (4); 4-4 (3); 4-5 (5); 4-6 (3); 4-7 (6); 4-9 (4); 4-10; 4-11; 4-12 (5); 4-13 (6); 4-14 (6); 4-15; 4-16 (5); 4-17 (2); 4-18 (6); 4-20 (2); 4-21; 4-22 (3); 4-27 Ex 4-2; 5-1; 5-3; 5-6; 5-8; 5-11; 5-12; 5-13 (3); 5-31; 5-34; 5-36 (2); 5-40 (2); 5-44; 5-47 Ex 5-5; 7-3; 8-2; 8-3; 8-12; 16-1; 16-3; 19-9 (5); 19-10 (2); 20-3; 20-17; 21-2; 21-4; 21-7; 21-8 (2); 21-10 (6); 21-11; 22-2 (2); 22-7; 22-18; 23-19 (2); 23-20; 24-3 (3); 24-4 (4); 24-6 (3); 24-7 (2); 24-14;
PIH Notices: 03-11 (12); 02-27; 02-21 (3); 02-01 (21); 01-41 (2); 01-27; 01-20 (2); 01-15 (5); 01-01 (8); 00-41; 00-24B (3); 99-52 (21); 95-48 (7); 95-48 Tech Asst (7);
Admin Plan: s1p3 (3); s1p4 (5); s1p5; s1p6 (2); s1p7; s2p3; s2p4 (2); s2p5 (3); s3p1 (3); s3p2 (7); s3p3 (2); s4p1 (2); s4p2 (3); s6p1; s7p1 (2); s7p4; s7p7; s8p1 (3); s8p2 (3); s8p3 (2); s8p4 (2); s9p3; s11p1; s11p3; s15p1; s15p3; s18p1 (2); s18p2; s18p3; s18p4; s18p7; s18p8; s20p2; s21p3; s22p2; s23p1; s23p2; s23p3 (4); s23p4 (2); s23p8; s24p6 (2); s25p3

APPLICANT'S 44
24 CFR 5: .210; .214; .216 (8); .230 (2); .232; .236 (3); .318; .359; .508;
24 CFR 982: .4; .205;
HUD-50058Instr: p75;
7420.10G Gbk: 4-5 (2); 4-7; 4-8; 4-9; 5-10 Ex 5-1; 5-25 Ex 5-3; 5-49 Ex 5-5; 5-50 Ex 5-5; 8-9; 19-10; 22-2;
PIH Notices: 03-11 (2); 95-48 (3); 95-48 Tech Asst (3);
Admin Plan: s1p4; s24p4

APPLICATION..............................365
24 CFR 5: .212; .230; .359; .508 (2); .514; .603; .609; .628; .661 (5);
24 CFR 982: 24 CFR 982 (3); .54; .102; .103 (5); .104 (7); .153; .158 (2); .204; .205 (2); .206; .207; .353; .505; .623;
HUD-50058Instr: p19 (2);
HUD-52580-A: p2; p13; p17;
HUD-52641: p4;
7420.10G Gbk: 1-1; 1-5 (3); 1-6; 1-16 Ex 1-3; 2-9; 2-11; 3-2; 4-1 (7); 4-2; 4-3; 4-4 (2); 4-5 (2); 4-7 (7); 4-8; 4-9; 4-10 (4); 4-11 (9); 4-12 (7); 4-13 (11); 4-14 (11); 4-15 (8); 4-16 (5); 4-17 (2); 4-25 Ex 4-2 (3); 5-6; 5-10 Ex 5-1 (4); 5-13; 5-14 Ex 5-2; 5-21; 5-33; 5-44 (2); 5-48 Ex 5-5; 5-50 Ex 5-5; 8-13; 10-18; 12-3; 12-16 Ex 12-4; 13-2 (4); 14-2; 14-3; 14-4; 19-6 (2); 20-2; 20-5; 21-3 (2); 21-7; 21-8 (3); 22-5; 22-8; 22-9; 22-11;
PIH Notices: 03-11; 02-27; 02-21 (25); 02-07; 02-01 (7); 01-41 (6); 01-

27; 01-20 (27); 01-15; 01-15 Impr Integ Hbk (3); 01-06; 00-31 (2); 00-28 (3); 00-27 (22); 00-24B (2); 00-11; 00-11A; 00-09 (9); 99-52 (9); 99-30 (3); 95-48 (14); 95-48 Tech Asst (14);

Admin Plan: s1p4 (2); s3p1 (5); s3p2 (7); s3p3 (5); s6p1; s6p4; s7p5; s23p2 (2); s23p3 (3); s24p3 (4); s24p4 (2); s24p5

APPLICATION FOR CONTINUED OCCUPANCY 2

7420.10G Gbk: 12-3; 12-16 Ex 12-4

APPLICATION FOR FUNDING......6

24 CFR 982: 24 CFR 982 (2); .54; .103;

Admin Plan: s23p2; s23p3

APPLICATIONS 144

24 CFR 5: .508;

24 CFR 982: .4; .52; .101; .206 (3);

7420.10G Gbk: 1-1; 1-5; 1-6; 1-14; 4-1; 4-3 (2); 4-4; 4-5; 4-6; 4-7; 4-10; 4-11 (5); 4-12 (9); 4-13 (10); 4-14 (2); 4-18; 5-44; 8-13; 10-25; 16-3; 19-10; 20-3; 21-3; 21-8; 21-11;

PIH Notices: 02-21 (17); 02-01 (3); 01-27; 01-20 (24); 00-45; 00-27 (22); 99-52 (3); 99-11; 95-48 (2); 95-48 Tech Asst (2);

Admin Plan: s2p1; s3p1 (6); s3p2 (3); s24p2 (2); s24p7

APPLICATION-TAKING 2

7420.10G Gbk: 4-12; 21-6

APPOINTMENT 41

24 CFR 982: .555;

7420.10G Gbk: 4-5; 4-12 (5); 10-23 (2); 10-40 Ex 10-4a (2); 10-41 Ex 10-4b; 12-2 (3); 12-12 Ex 12-1 (4); 12-13 Ex 12-1 (2); 12-14 Ex 12-2 (5); 21-10; 24-7;

Admin Plan: s3p3 (3); s7p5; s9p4; s11p1 (5); s15p6; s18p6; s20p4

APPOINTMENTS 17

7420.10G Gbk: 10-26; 12-2 (2); 24-7; 24-9;

Admin Plan: s1p4; s9p4; s11p1; s15p6 (8); s25p8

APPRAISALS 3

HUD-903-1: p2;

7420.10G Gbk: 5-49 Ex 5-5;

Admin Plan: s7p6

APPRAISER......................................1

Admin Plan: s24p4

APPRENTICESHIP..........................3

24 CFR 5: .603;

HUD-50058Instr: p71;

Admin Plan: s6p3

APPROPRIATE 374

24 CFR 5: .216; .234; .236; .240; .327; .353 (2); .363; .380; .504; .508 (4); .518 (4); .603;

24 CFR 982: .4 (2); .152; .301; .312; .353; .401 (2); .402; .403; .503 (3); .505; .516 (3); .517 (2); .555 (2); .609; .614 (2); .618; .619; .621; .635;

HUD-50058: p ii; p iii; p iv; p x; p xi; p xiii; p xiv; p xvi;

HUD-50058Instr: p1; p7 (3); p15; p42; p46; p53; p56; p59; p60; p61; p72; p75 (2);

HUD-52580: p1 (2); p8; p13; p15 (3);

HUD-52648: p1; p2;

HUD-52665: p1 (2);

HUD-52667: p i (3);

HUD-9886: p2 (3);

7420.10G Gbk: 1-1; 2-2; 2-3; 2-6; 3-3; 3-8; 4-12; 5-3; 5-4; 5-6 (2); 5-7; 5-21; 5-35; 5-41 (2); 5-44; 5-47 Ex 5-5; 5-48 Ex 5-5 (2); 5-49 Ex 5-5 (2); 5-50 Ex 5-5; 6-3; 6-8; 6-9 Ex 6-1; 7-6; 7-7 (2); 7-8; 7-9; 8-9 (2); 8-17; 9-7; 9-10; 9-11; 10-4; 10-7 (3); 10-12; 10-13; 10-21 (2); 10-22; 10-28; 10-30; 10-34; 10-37 Ex 10-2; 11-2; 12-5; 12-7 (3); 12-10; 12-11 (2); 13-5; 13-8; 15-6; 15-7; 15-10 Ex 15-2; 16-2; 17-3; 17-4; 17-5 (2); 17-11; 17-12; 18-10 (2); 19-8; 19-10; 19-11; 20-20; 21-1 (2); 21-2; 21-4; 21-8; 22-1 (2); 22-6; 22-13 (3); 22-15 (2); 22-16 (3); 22-18 (2); 23-3; 23-4; 23-5; 23-9; 23-10; 23-20; 24-

11;
PIH Notices: 03-23; 03-20; 03-12; 03-11; 03-05 (2); 02-27 (14); 02-21 (5); 02-20 (5); 02-14 (4); 02-01 (2); 01-41 (14); 01-40 (2); 01-20 (4); 01-15 (2); 01-15 Impr Integ Hbk (6); 01-06 (4); 00-46 (5); 00-27 (2); 00-11; 00-11A; 00-09 (13); 99-52 (2); 99-11 (4); 96-65 (3); 95-48 (21); 95-48 Tech Asst (21);
Admin Plan: s1p4; s2p3; s2p6; s2p7; s4p2; s5p2; s5p3; s6p6 (2); s6p7 (4); s7p2 (3); s7p8; s8p2; s9p4; s10p3; s10p5; s11p3 (2); s15p6; s16p3 (3); s17p2; s18p3; s19p1 (2); s20p3; s20p4; s20p5; s20p7; s21p4; s21p6; s22p4; s23p2; s23p4 (2); s24p1; s24p4; s24p5; s24p7

APPROPRIATE SIZE....................33
24 CFR 5: .518 (4);
24 CFR 982: .401; .609; .614;
7420.10G Gbk: 10-4; 12-5; 17-3; 17-5;
PIH Notices: 02-01; 01-41 (9); 01-15 Impr Integ Hbk; 00-09 (8); 99-52;
Admin Plan: s5p2; s5p3

APPROPRIATE SIZE UNIT..........18
7420.10G Gbk: 12-5;
PIH Notices: 01-41 (9); 01-15 Impr Integ Hbk; 00-09 (6); 00-09

APPROPRIATE SIZED....................3
PIH Notices: 01-41 (2); 00-09

APPROPRIATED..........................14
24 CFR 982: .4; .102 (3); .151; .152;
7420.10G Gbk: 1-7; 20-15; 24-1;
PIH Notices: 03-23 (4); 00-09

APPROPRIATELY.........................17
24 CFR 5: .350;
24 CFR 982: .605;
7420.10G Gbk: 17-2; 19-8; 22-7; 24-13;
PIH Notices: 03-11; 01-06; 99-11; 95-48 (3); 95-48 Tech Asst (3);
Admin Plan: s4p2; s21p5

APPROPRIATENESS......................4
PIH Notices: 02-21; 01-20; 00-27;
Admin Plan: s11p3

APPROPRIATES..............................3
7420.10G Gbk: 1-5; 1-12 Ex 1-2;
PIH Notices: 03-23

APPROPRIATION..........................10
PIH Notices: 03-23 (6); 02-06 (2); 00-09; 00-09

APPROPRIATIONS........................60
24 CFR 982: .152;
7420.10G Gbk: 1-9 (2);
PIH Notices: 03-23 (23); 02-21; 02-06 (2); 01-41 (10); 01-20; 01-10 (3); 00-41; 00-27 (2); 00-09 (13)

APPROVABLE..............................50
24 CFR 982: .353; .401 (4); .605; .614 (2);
HUD-52580: p5;
HUD-52580-A: p15; p16 (2); p17; p18;
HUD-52646: p1;
7420.10G Gbk: 8-10; 11-4; 17-5;
PIH Notices: 02-21 (6); 01-20 (12); 00-27 (12);
Admin Plan: s9p1; s9p2

APPROVAL.................................410
24 CFR 5: .306; .653 (2); .655 (2); .661 (6);
24 CFR 982: 24 CFR 982 (3); .4 (2); .54 (2); .104 (2); .152; .155; .157; .201 (2); .301 (2); .302 (5); .303 (2); .305 (8); .306 (3); .307; .308; .316; .355 (3); .503 (22); .505; .551 (2); .554; .612; .614; .618; .631; .632; .641 (3);
HUD-50058: p v; p17; p xvii;
HUD-50058Instr: p19 (2); p21; p63 (2); p75; p76;
HUD-52580: p1 (2); p2; p3; p4; p5;
HUD-52580-A: p1 (2); p3; p5; p7; p9; p10; p11; p12; p14; p16; p18;
HUD-52641: p6; p10;
HUD-52641-A: p3;
HUD-52646: p1; p2 (2);
HUD-52648: p1; p2 (2);
HUD-52665: p1; p2;
HUD-52667: p1 (2);
HUD-9886: p2;
7420.10G Gbk: 1-5; 1-15; 1-16 Ex 1-3; 2-3 (2); 3-1; 3-2; 3-6; 4-17; 4-19; 4-20; 5-39; 7-1; 7-

2; 7-3; 7-4 (7); 7-5 (3); 7-7; 7-9 (2); 7-10; 8-1; 8-6 (2); 8-11; 8-13; 8-15 (4); 8-18; 8-20; 10-2 (3); 10-24; 10-25 (2); 10-26 (6); 10-31; 11-1 (2); 11-4 (2); 11-14 (2); 13-5; 16-2; 17-1 (2); 17-3; 19-11; 19-13; 20-2; 20-5; 20-10; 21-4; 22-16; 23-2; 23-3; 23-4 (2); 24-7; 24-10; 24-11; 24-12;

PIH Notices: 03-12 (2); 02-27 (10); 02-21 (8); 02-20 (46); 02-14 (3); 02-07 (5); 02-06 (2); 01-41 (9); 01-20 (7); 01-06; 01-01 (15); 00-49 (3); 00-46 (39); 00-34; 00-28 (7); 00-27 (5); 00-11; 00-09 (10);

Admin Plan: s2p3 (2); s2p6; s5p2; s6p7 (2); s6p8 (4); s8p2; s8p3; s8p4; s8p5; s9p1 (4); s9p4; s10p1; s10p3; s11p2; s18p2; s21p6 (2); s22p1; s23p4; s23p6; s24p4; s25p5

APPROVALS....................................9

24 CFR 5: .653;

7420.10G Gbk: 10-24; 11-1 (2); 11-14; 11-18 (2);

PIH Notices: 01-01; 01-01

APPROVE....................................171

24 CFR 5: .514; .661;

24 CFR 982: .1; .104; .152; .154; .306 (3); .308; .309; .316 (3); .401 (2); .503 (12); .507; .517; .520; .552 (2); .554; .555 (2); .606; .610; .615; .619; .620; .622; .625;

HUD-52641: p1 (2);

7420.10G Gbk: 1-6 Ex 1-1; 3-5 (2); 3-6; 4-20; 5-35; 7-4 (2); 8-10; 8-12 (2); 8-18 (3); 8-19 (2); 8-22 (2); 9-1; 9-11; 10-2; 11-1; 11-2; 11-4; 11-17; 14-3; 15-3; 15-5; 16-2; 17-1 (2); 17-3; 17-4; 18-4; 18-8; 18-9; 20-3; 23-3 (2); 23-18;

PIH Notices: 03-11; 02-27 (2); 02-20 (23); 02-14; 02-07 (2); 02-06; 01-41 (6); 01-06; 01-01; 00-49 (2); 00-46 (21); 00-28; 00-24B; 00-09 (3);

Admin Plan: s2p3; s9p1; s9p3; s11p3; s15p1 (2); s16p3; s18p4 (2); s19p1 (10); s22p3

APPROVED..................................385

24 CFR 5: .214; .216; .234; .514 (2); .603; .655; .661 (4); .703;

24 CFR 982: .4 (2); .52 (2); .53; .54; .102 (4); .103; .104; .151 (2); .152 (4); .153; .155; .156; .157; .158; .159; .160; .162; .201 (2); .204; .206; .301; .303; .304; .305 (2); .307; .308 (2); .310; .352 (2); .401 (3); .402; .403; .404 (2); .406; .452; .503; .504 (2); .516; .517; .519; .520 (2); .551 (2); .552; .553; .554 (2); .555 (2); .605; .606; .610; .612; .615; .619; .620; .627; .638;

HUD-50058: p5; p v;

HUD-50058Instr: p19 (3); p43; p71 (2); p73 (2); p76;

HUD-52517: p2;

HUD-52580-A: p13;

HUD-52641: p1; p3; 8 (2); p10;

HUD-52641-A: p1 (2); p3;

HUD-52646: p1; p2 (4);

7420.10G Gbk: 1-5; 3-1; 3-5 (2); 4-16; 4-20; 5-18; 5-41; 6-3; 6-6; 7-2; 7-5; 7-9 (2); 8-1; 8-6 (2); 8-7; 8-10; 8-11; 8-12; 8-13; 8-16 (2); 8-17 (2); 8-18 (2); 8-21; 9-1; 9-4; 9-11 (2); 10-2; 10-3 (3); 10-5 (2); 10-11 (3); 10-17; 10-30; 10-33; 10-36 Ex 10-1; 10-43 Ex 10-6; 11-2; 11-11; 11-14 (2); 11-16 Ex 11-1 (2); 14-4; 16-3; 16-4; 17-2; 17-4; 17-7; 17-12; 19-3; 20-1; 20-3; 20-6; 20-7; 20-9; 20-10; 20-13 (3); 20-14 (2); 20-15 (3); 20-16; 20-18 (2); 20-26; 21-9 (2); 22-6; 23-18;

PIH Notices: 03-23 (8); 03-20; 03-12; 03-11 (10); 02-27 (11); 02-22 (3); 02-21 (7); 02-20 (27); 02-14 (3); 02-07 (4); 02-06 (5); 01-41 (4); 01-20 (5); 01-06 (7); 01-01 (3); 00-49 (2); 00-

46 (26); 00-41; 00-28 (3); 00-27 (4); 00-24B; 00-23; 00-09 (7);
Admin Plan: s2p6; s5p2; s6p13; s8p2 (2); s8p3; s8p5; s9p2; s9p3 (4); s9p4; s15p5; s15p6 (2); s16p3; s18p2; s18p6; s19p1 (7); s21p5; s21p6; s21p7 (2); s21p8 (2); s22p4; s23p3 (2); s23p5; s23p7; s23p8; s24p4; s24p5; s24p6; s24p7; s25p4; s25p5; s25p5

APPROVES....................................46
24 CFR 982: .1; .4; .104; .201; .303; .508;
HUD-50058Instr: p75;
HUD-52580-A: p17;
HUD-52646: p1; p2;
7420.10G Gbk: 1-16 Ex 1-3; 4-20; 8-5; 8-13; 8-18; 9-1; 13-5; 20-3; 20-5; 20-14;
PIH Notices: 02-07 (8); 01-41 (2); 01-06; 01-01 (2); 00-49 (2); 00-28 (6); 00-24B (2); 00-09 (2);
Admin Plan: s8p5

APPROVING..................................33
24 CFR 5: .661;
24 CFR 982: .1; .306;
HUD-52517: p2;
HUD-52641: p5; p6;
HUD-52646: p2;
7420.10G Gbk: 1-13; 8-1; 8-15; 8-17; 8-19; 11-2; 11-13; 14-4 (2); 20-10; 21-2; 22-2;
PIH Notices: 02-27 (2); 02-07; 01-41 (4); 01-06; 00-09 (5);
Admin Plan: s16p2

APRIL...50
24 CFR 982: .401 (2);
HUD-50058Instr: p11; p16; p30 (2); p32 (2);
HUD-52580-A: p8;
7420.10G Gbk: 19-9; 21-6; 24-3;
PIH Notices: 03-23 (10); 03-12; 03-11 (2); 02-21; 02-06; 01-15 Impr Integ Hbk (3); 01-11; 01-10; 01-06 (4); 00-53 (8); 00-24; 00-24A; 00-14 (2);

ARBITRARY....................................2
7420.10G Gbk: 9-9; 9-12

ARBITRATION................................1
Admin Plan: s18p6

ARBITRATORS................................1
Admin Plan: s18p6

ARCHITECTURAL BARRIERS....15
PIH Notices: 02-01 (3); 00-45; 99-52 (3); 95-48 (4); 95-48 Tech Asst (3); 95-48 Tech Asst

AREA OF OPERATION 1
PIH Notices: 02-27

AREAS OF HIGH POVERTY..........8
24 CFR 982: .503;
7420.10G Gbk: 2-4; 7-4;
PIH Notices: 02-20 (3); 00-46; 00-46

ARMED FORCES..........................17
24 CFR 5: .609 (2);
HUD-50058Instr: p26 (2);
7420.10G Gbk: 5-14 Ex 5-2; 5-15 Ex 5-2; 23-12;
PIH Notices: 03-05 (2); 01-40 (2); 01-15 Impr Integ Hbk (5); 01-15 Impr Integ Hbk

ARMY..1
PIH Notices: 01-15 Impr Integ Hbk

ARREST 3
Admin Plan: s2p6; s15p3; s15p4

ARRESTED.....................................9
24 CFR 982: .310; .553;
HUD-52641: p9;
HUD-52641-A: p2;
7420.10G Gbk: 4-25 Ex 4-2; 5-37; 15-2; 15-7;
Admin Plan: s2p6

ARRESTS..1
7420.10G Gbk: 4-15

ARRIVAL-DEPARTURE..................2
7420.10G Gbk: 5-10 Ex 5-1; 5-10 Ex 5-1

ARTICULATE..................................1
7420.10G Gbk: 3-1

ARTIFICIAL ILLUMINATION........3
24 CFR 982: .401;
HUD-52580-A: p8;
7420.10G Gbk: 10-8

AS APPROPRIATE........................26
24 CFR 5: .236; .240; .508 (3);
HUD-50058: p iii; p iv;
HUD-50058Instr: p15;
HUD-52580: p1 (2);
7420.10G Gbk: 5-6; 18-10;
PIH Notices: 02-27 (2); 02-21 (2); 01-20; 01-06; 00-27; 95-48 (2); 95-48 Tech Asst (2);
Admin Plan: s7p2 (2); s24p7

AS PAID 4
7420.10G Gbk: 1-6 Ex 1-1; 5-47 Ex 5-5; 5-53 Ex 5-5;
PIH Notices: 01-10
AS SOON AS POSSIBLE 10
24 CFR 5: .508;
24 CFR 982: .403 (2);
PIH Notices: 03-20; 01-41 (2); 01-27 (2); 01-06; 00-09
ASIA 2
HUD-50058Instr: p73;
HUD-903: p2
ASIAN 10
HUD-50058: p3; p4;
HUD-50058Instr: p15; p73;
HUD-903: p1; p2;
7420.10G Gbk: 2-13 Ex 2-1; 4-23 Ex 4-1; 4-25 Ex 4-2; 19-7
AS-PAID 13
7420.10G Gbk: 1-6 Ex 1-1; 5-20 (5); 5-21; 5-47 Ex 5-5; 6-1; 8-5;
PIH Notices: 01-41; 01-10; 01-10
ASSESS 20
HUD-50058Instr: p17;
HUD-52648: p1;
7420.10G Gbk: 1-10; 8-14; 10-2; 10-8; 19-1; 19-5 (2); 19-6; 19-7; 20-9; 20-16;
PIH Notices: 03-20; 02-27 (2); 96-65; 95-48; 95-48 Tech Asst;
Admin Plan: s18p5
ASSESSED 8
24 CFR 982: .619; .635;
HUD-50058Instr: p17;
7420.10G Gbk: 2-2;
PIH Notices: 95-48; 95-48 Tech Asst;
Admin Plan: s17p1; s19p1
ASSESSES... 6
7420.10G Gbk: 1-11; 2-2; 2-4;
PIH Notices: 03-23; 02-27; 02-27
ASSESSING 3
HUD-52580-A: p1;
7420.10G Gbk: 1-10;
PIH Notices: 02-27
ASSESSMENT ....
130
24 CFR 5: .801;
24 CFR 35 SubM: .1210; .1215 (4); .1225 (7);
HUD-50058Instr: p22;
HUD-52580-A: p2; p13; p17;
HUD-52648: p1; p3;
7420.10G Gbk: 1-1; 1-9; 2-2; 10-12 (3); 10-16; 10-17; 10-18 (2); 10-20 (5); 10-21 (6); 10-39 Ex 10-4 (6); 17-1; 18-9; 19-1; 19-2 (2); 19-3; 19-6; 20-4 (4); 20-10 (3); 20-29; 22-4; 22-7; 22-11; 22-14;
PIH Notices: 03-12; 02-27 (9); 02-21; 02-07 (3); 01-43 (3); 01-15; 01-15 Impr Integ Hbk; 01-11 (2); 01-06 (14); 00-53 (2); 00-49 (7); 00-34; 00-24; 00-24B (2); 99-11; 95-48 (4); 95-48 Tech Asst (4);
Admin Plan: s1p5; s7p6; s11p2; s21p1 (3); s21p9; s25p8
ASSESSMENTS.............................. 49
24 CFR 982: .306; .520; .635 (2);
HUD-50058: p14; p xiv;
HUD-50058Instr: p56 (3);
HUD-52641: p7;
7420.10G Gbk: 8-20; 10-20 (2); 10-22 (2); 11-4; 20-4 (2);
PIH Notices: 02-27 (4); 02-01 (5); 01-06 (10); 00-49 (4); 00-34; 00-23; 99-52 (5);
Admin Plan: s16p2
ASSESSOR....................................... 6
HUD-52580: p5 (2);
HUD-52580-A: p17 (2);
7420.10G Gbk: 10-20; 10-20
ASSESSORS 1
7420.10G Gbk: 10-22
ASSESSOR'S 1
Admin Plan: s11p2
ASSET 80
24 CFR 5: .603;
HUD-50058: p6 (13);
HUD-50058Instr: p22 (16); p23 (8); p24 (2); p25; p33;
7420.10G Gbk: 4-26 Ex 4-2; 5-23; 5-24 (2); 5-25 Ex 5-3 (4); 5-26 (3); 5-27 (9); 5-28 (5); 5-48 Ex 5-5; 5-49 Ex 5-5 (4); 5-50 Ex 5-5; 12-12 Ex 12-1; 17-11; 22-2;
PIH Notices: 00-11;
Admin Plan: s6p10; s7p6; s23p3
ASSET INCOME............................... 8
HUD-50058: p6 (3);
HUD-50058Instr: p23; p24 (2); p33;

7420.10G Gbk: 5-24

ASSETS....................................197
24 CFR 5: .603 (3); .609 (10); .659;
24 CFR 982: .516;
HUD-50058: p6 (8);
HUD-50058Instr: p ii; p22 (8); p23 (5); p24; p25 (3); p31; p33; p70; p74; p77;
7420.10G Gbk: 4-15; 4-26 Ex 4-2 (4); 4-27 Ex 4-2 (3); 5-14 Ex 5-2 (8); 5-15 Ex 5-2; 5-18 (3); 5-19 (3); 5-23; 5-24 (9); 5-25 Ex 5-3 (10); 5-26 (10); 5-27 (6); 5-28 (6); 5-34; 5-49 Ex 5-5 (5); 5-50 Ex 5-5 (4); 12-3; 12-4 (2); 12-5 (2); 12-11; 12-12 Ex 12-1 (2); 12-13 Ex 12-1; 12-14 Ex 12-2 (3); 12-16 Ex 12-4 (2); 20-30; 22-2; 22-3; 22-6; 22-8; 22-9; 23-5;
PIH Notices: 01-15; 01-15 Impr Integ Hbk (24); 00-24B (2);
Admin Plan: s3p3; s6p10 (11); s6p12; s7p1; s7p3 (3); s7p6 (8); s11p1; s20p5; s21p4

ASSET'S.......................................2
HUD-50058Instr: p22; p22

ASSIGN......................................34
24 CFR 35 SubM: .1200;
24 CFR 982: .102; .551;
HUD-52641: p6 (3); 8;
HUD-52641-A: p1;
HUD-52646: p2;
HUD-52648: p1;
7420.10G Gbk: 1-11; 5-36 Ex 5-4; 9-8 (2); 9-9; 11-15; 12-8; 21-5 (2); 21-6;
PIH Notices: 03-11 (2); 02-01; 01-06 (8); 00-09; 99-52;
Admin Plan: s8p5

ASSIGNED..................................85
24 CFR 5: .214 (2); .216 (14);
24 CFR 982: .102; .160;
HUD-50058Instr: p7 (2); p50; p75;
HUD-52641: p6 (3);
7420.10G Gbk: 1-11; 3-2; 5-7; 5-12 (2); 5-43; 8-1; 8-23; 10-28; 12-5; 19-2; 19-10; 20-14; 21-3; 21-5 (2);
PIH Notices: 03-23; 03-20; 03-12; 03-11 (3); 02-27 (8); 02-21; 01-15; 01-06 (12); 00-24; 95-48 (2); 95-48 Tech Asst (2);
Admin Plan: s3p2; s5p1; s9p4; s10p1; s13p1; s18p1 (3); s20p3 (2); s21p1

ASSIGNING.................................11
24 CFR 5: .216;
7420.10G Gbk: 1-15; 11-18; 21-6 (2); 23-6; 24-16;
PIH Notices: 01-06 (2); 00-24A;
Admin Plan: s23p7

ASSIGNMENT..............................16
HUD-52641: p6 (4);
7420.10G Gbk: 11-11; 19-4; 21-5;
PIH Notices: 03-11; 02-27; 02-21; 01-41; 01-06; 00-09; 95-48; 95-48 Tech Asst;
Admin Plan: s16p3

ASSIGNMENTS 9
7420.10G Gbk: 22-10 (2);
PIH Notices: 02-27; 02-21; 01-20; 01-06; 00-27; 95-48; 95-48 Tech Asst

ASSIGNS.......................................9
HUD-50058Instr: p7;
7420.10G Gbk: 9-11;
PIH Notices: 02-27 (3); 01-41; 01-06 (2); 00-09

ASSIST......................................176
24 CFR 5: .100; .303 (5); .306 (2); .312; .504; .518; .603;
24 CFR 982: .352; .625;
HUD-50058: p i;
HUD-50058Instr: p71; p72; p73; p75 (2);
HUD-52580-A: p17;
HUD-52641: p3; 8;
HUD-52641-A: p1;
HUD-9886: p2;
7420.10G Gbk: 1-6 (2); 1-7 (3); 1-8; 1-9 (2); 1-10; 2-8 (2); 2-10; 3-2; 3-3; 3-8; 4-3; 4-4; 4-13; 5-39; 5-43; 6-10 Ex 6-2; 8-2; 9-3; 10-13; 10-30; 11-13; 12-2; 19-3; 19-4; 21-5; 22-15 (2); 23-1 (2); 23-3 (4); 24-1; 24-14 (2);
PIH Notices: 03-23 (2); 03-20 (2); 03-12; 03-11; 02-27 (15); 02-21 (4); 02-20; 02-14; 02-07; 02-06; 02-01 (4); 01-41 (10); 01-20 (3); 01-15 (3); 01-15 Impr Integ Hbk; 01-10 (2); 00-46; 00-27; 00-11 (9); 00-11A (2); 00-09 (16); 99-52 (4); 95-48 (3); 95-48 Tech Asst (3);

Admin Plan: s1p1; s1p5; s1p6; s2p7; s5p3; s6p3; s8p1; s8p4; s18p3; s20p4; s20p7; s23p1; s24p6; s25p1; s25p4 (2); s25p6 (2); s25p7

ASSISTANCE APPLICANT 22
24 CFR 5: .214; .216 (7); .218; .230 (2); .232 (2); .236 (8);
HUD-50058Instr: p70

ASSISTANCE APPLICANTS 14
24 CFR 5: .212; .214 (2); .216 (4); .218; .230 (3); .234;
HUD-50058Instr: p71; p71

ASSISTANCE APPLICANT'S 8
24 CFR 5: .214; .216; .230 (2); .232; .236 (2); .236

ASSISTANCE EXPENSE 27
HUD-50058: p7 (3); p vii (5);
HUD-50058Instr: p34; p35 (9);
7420.10G Gbk: 5-30 (2); 5-33 (4); 5-34;
Admin Plan: s6p4; s6p4

ASSISTANCE EXPENSES 32
24 CFR 5: .603;
HUD-50058: p7 (2); p vii (5);
HUD-50058Instr: p34 (3); p35 (3); p71;
7420.10G Gbk: 5-29; 5-30; 5-31 (3); 5-32 (5); 5-33; 12-11;
PIH Notices: 01-15 Impr Integ Hbk;
Admin Plan: s6p2; s6p4; s7p3; s21p4

ASSISTANCE PAYMENT 47
HUD-52641: p1 (3); p2 (3); p3; p4 (8); 8 (7); p10;
HUD-52641-A: p1 (7); p3;
HUD-52646: p1 (5);
7420.10G Gbk: 1-12 Ex 1-2; 6-1; 11-5 (3); 11-6; 11-18; 13-5; 14-1; 15-4; 20-27

ASSISTANCE PAYMENT 287
24 CFR 5: .240; .520 (10); .632; .661 (3);
24 CFR 982: 24 CFR 982 (9); .4 (4); .301; .305 (2); .310 (3); .311 (4); .312; .355; .451 (8); .452; .455; .456; .501; .502 (3); .503; .504; .505 (9); .507; .514 (5); .515 (2); .516 (5); .518 (2); .555; .604; .608; .613; .617; .619 (2); .622; .623 (5); .635; .641; .642;
HUD-50058: p i; p x (8); p xi (11); p xii (7); p xiii (7); p xiv (4);
HUD-50058Instr: p3; p42; p43 (2); p44 (3); p45; p46; p48 (8); p49; p50 (2); p51 (4); p52 (2); p53; p54 (4); p55 (2); p56; p72 (3); p74; p76;
HUD-52641: p1 (3); p2 (3); p3; p4 (8); 8 (7); p10;
HUD-52641-A: p1 (7); p3;
HUD-52646: p1 (5);
HUD-52667: p i;
7420.10G Gbk: 1-12 Ex 1-2; 6-1; 11-5 (3); 11-6; 11-18; 13-5; 14-1; 15-4; 20-27;
PIH Notices: 03-12; 02-22; 02-20 (2); 01-41 (11); 01-10 (2); 00-49; 00-46 (2); 00-41 (3); 00-24B (2); 00-23; 00-14; 00-09 (15); 96-65;
Admin Plan: s6p5; s6p13; s8p2; s9p4; s10p4 (3); s11p2; s11p3; s13p2; s14p1; s14p2 (2); s15p1; s18p3; s19p1 (5); s22p3; s23p5

ASSISTANCE PAYMENTS 52
HUD-52641: p1 (2); p3 (6); p4 (11); p5 (4); p6; 8 (2); p10 (2);
HUD-52641-A: p1 (2); p3 (2);
HUD-52646: p1;
7420.10G Gbk: 5-15 Ex 5-2; 10-25; 10-34; 11-6; 11-8; 11-9 (2); 11-12; 11-18; 15-9 Ex 15-1; 20-2; 20-16; 20-23; 20-25; 20-26; 20-28 (2); 22-1; 22-13

ASSISTANCE PAYMENTS 162
24 CFR 5: .508 (2); .514 (4); .601; .603; .653 (2); .661; .801 (3);
24 CFR 982: 24 CFR 982 (2); .4 (3); .102 (2); .151; .157 (2); .305; .311 (5); .312; .352 (2); .355 (2); .404 (2); .406; .451 (2); .453 (2); .515; .519; .552 (2); .555; .619 (3); .641; .642;
HUD-50058Instr: p70 (2); p72; p73 (2);
HUD-52641: p1 (2); p3 (6); p4 (11); p5 (4); p6; 8 (2); p10 (2);
HUD-52641-A: p1 (2); p3 (2);

HUD-52646: p1 (2);
7420.10G Gbk: 10-25; 10-34; 11-6; 11-9 (2); 11-12; 11-18; 15-9 Ex 15-1; 20-2; 20-16; 20-23; 20-25; 20-26; 20-28 (2); 22-1; 22-13;
PIH Notices: 03-23; 03-05; 02-21; 01-41 (4); 01-40; 01-33; 01-06; 00-09 (11); 96-65 (3);
Admin Plan: s2p7; s6p1; s6p6; s8p3; s9p1; s9p2; s9p4; s10p1; s10p4; s11p1 (2); s14p1; s14p2; s15p1; s16p1; s16p3; s17p2; s20p5; s22p3; s22p5; s23p5; s23p7; s23p8; s24p1 (2); s24p5 (3); s24p6; s24p7

ASSISTANT 106
24 CFR 5: .100; .216 (4); .300; .306; .504 (2);
24 CFR 982: .160; .503 (2);
HUD-50058Instr: p75;
7420.10G Gbk: 5-17 (2); 7-4; 10-15; 21-11; 21-12 Ex 21-3; 21-14 Ex 21-4; 21-15 Ex 21-5; 21-16 Ex 21-6 (5);
PIH Notices: 03-23; 03-20; 03-12; 03-11 (2); 03-05; 02-27 (5); 02-22; 02-21 (2); 02-20 (7); 02-15; 02-14; 02-07; 02-06; 02-03; 02-01; 01-43; 01-41 (2); 01-40; 01-33; 01-27 (2); 01-20 (2); 01-15 (3); 01-11; 01-10; 01-06; 01-02; 01-01; 00-53; 00-49; 00-46 (7); 00-45; 00-41; 00-34; 00-31; 00-28; 00-27 (2); 00-24; 00-23; 00-14; 00-11; 00-09 (2); 00-01; 99-52; 99-30; 99-11; 98-66; 96-65; 95-48 (5); 95-48 Tech Asst (2); 95-48 Tech Asst

ASSISTED FAMILIES...................28
24 CFR 5: .661;
24 CFR 982: .4;
HUD-52648: p4;
7420.10G Gbk: 7-7; 10-16; 12-5; 19-1 (2); 20-8 Ex 20-1; 20-11; 22-4; 24-9;
PIH Notices: 02-20; 02-14; 02-06; 01-41; 01-06 (2); 00-46; 00-24B; 00-11; 00-09;
Admin Plan: s1p7; s6p3; s8p3 (2); s11p1; s20p2

ASSISTED FAMILIES'.....................1
7420.10G Gbk: 7-6

ASSISTED FAMILY 80
24 CFR 982: .1 (2); .4 (3); .315 (2); .353; .551 (3); .607; .615 (2); .616; .617; .618 (5); .623;
HUD-50058Instr: p74; p75;
HUD-52641: p1;
7420.10G Gbk: 3-4; 8-19; 10-17; 10-21 (2); 10-42 Ex 10-5; 11-2; 11-8; 12-1; 12-3; 12-5; 12-6; 12-10; 15-6; 17-7 (6); 17-8 (5); 17-9 (5); 22-2; 22-4;
PIH Notices: 03-05; 01-40; 00-49; 00-24B (2);
Admin Plan: s6p8; s6p11; s8p5; s9p2 (3); s10p4; s19p1 (5); s21p4; s21p6; s22p2 (2); s22p3; s22p4

ASSISTED FAMILY HEAD OF HOUSEHOLD 1
7420.10G Gbk: 12-3

ASSISTED FAMILY SHARES 1
24 CFR 982: .615

ASSISTED FAMILY'S......................4
PIH Notices: 01-41; 00-11; 00-09;
Admin Plan: s11p1

ASSISTED HOUSEHOLD 25
24 CFR 982: .613 (2);
HUD-50058Instr: p43; p44; p47 (2);
7420.10G Gbk: 5-7; 5-8; 5-22; 17-5; 17-6; 17-7;
Admin Plan: s2p2; s7p8; s8p4; s9p2; s10p3 (2); s10p4; s16p2; s19p1 (2); s22p3 (2); s22p3

ASSISTED HOUSEHOLD MEMBER 1
7420.10G Gbk: 5-7

ASSISTED HOUSEHOLDS 1
Admin Plan: s13p1

ASSISTED HOUSEHOLD'S............1
Admin Plan: s11p1

ASSISTED HOUSING....................86
24 CFR 5: .100 (2); .514; .524; .528;
24 CFR 982: .4; .101; .202; .310; .552; .553 (3);
HUD-50058Instr: p18; p25 (2); p26; p27; p72;
HUD-903-1: p5;
HUD-9886: p1 (4);

7420.10G Gbk: 1-3; 1-8; 1-9; 2-6; 5-35; 8-19; 10-15; 11-2; 11-3; 15-6; 19-3; 21-14 Ex 21-4;
PIH Notices: 03-11 (5); 02-20 (2); 02-07; 02-01; 01-41 (4); 01-40; 01-33; 01-27 (6); 01-15 (4); 01-15 Impr Integ Hbk (4); 00-49; 00-46 (2); 00-45; 00-41; 00-28; 00-23; 00-11 (4); 00-09 (3); 99-52; 99-11 (2); 95-48;
Admin Plan: s2p6; s23p1; s23p2

ASSISTED HOUSING PROGRAM . 5
24 CFR 982: .205; .306;
7420.10G Gbk: 2-1; 4-9;
Admin Plan: s16p2

ASSISTED HOUSING PROGRAMS 9
HUD-50058: p i;
HUD-9886: p1; p2;
7420.10G Gbk: 1-15;
PIH Notices: 01-15 Impr Integ Hbk; 00-14; 00-11; 00-01; 98-66

ASSISTED LIVING 14
PIH Notices: 02-03 (2); 00-41 (10);
Admin Plan: s9p2; s19p1

ASSISTED TENANT 1
7420.10G Gbk: 5-2

ASSISTING 27
24 CFR 982: .54;
HUD-903-1: p2;
7420.10G Gbk: 1-10; 1-13; 2-2; 3-3; 5-2; 5-20; 5-43; 24-9;
PIH Notices: 03-23; 02-27 (6); 02-21; 02-07 (2); 01-20; 00-28 (2); 00-11A; 95-48; 95-48 Tech Asst;
Admin Plan: s8p6

ASSISTIVE 18
PIH Notices: 02-01; 99-52; 95-48 (8); 95-48 Tech Asst (7); 95-48 Tech Asst

ASSISTIVE ANIMAL 2
PIH Notices: 02-01; 99-52

ASSISTS 5
24 CFR 5: .303;
HUD-50058Instr: p70;
7420.10G Gbk: 2-8;
PIH Notices: 01-15; 01-06

ASSOCIATED 59
24 CFR 5: .318;
24 CFR 35 SubM: .1200;
24 CFR 982: .157;
HUD-50058: p xiv; p xvi (2);
HUD-50058Instr: p56; p59; p60;
HUD-52517: p2;
HUD-52580-A: p13;
7420.10G Gbk: 4-13; 5-35; 5-43; 5-44; 10-12; 10-16; 10-17; 10-20; 24-2 (2); 24-15;
PIH Notices: 03-23 (2); 03-11; 02-21 (4); 02-20; 02-06; 01-41 (6); 01-27 (3); 01-15; 01-06 (3); 00-49 (2); 00-46; 00-28; 00-09 (7);
Admin Plan: s1p4; s7p3; s23p2; s24p4

ASSOCIATES 3
PIH Notices: 02-27; 02-01; 99-52

ASSOCIATION 34
24 CFR 5: .214 (2);
24 CFR 982: .4 (2); .401; .635;
HUD-50058: p xiv;
HUD-50058Instr: p56; p71 (2);
HUD-52580-A: p8;
HUD-903: p2;
7420.10G Gbk: 10-14; 17-9 (2); 22-10;
PIH Notices: 03-11; 01-27; 01-15 (2); 99-11 (3); 95-48 (5); 95-48 Tech Asst (5);
Admin Plan: s18p6

ASSOCIATIONS 9
7420.10G Gbk: 2-5 (3); 9-4; 21-4;
PIH Notices: 02-21; 01-20;
Admin Plan: s1p6; s11p2

ASSUME 20
24 CFR 5: .214 (3); .363;
HUD-50058Instr: p23;
HUD-52641: p6;
7420.10G Gbk: 5-26; 5-29; 10-43 Ex 10-6; 11-3; 12-14 Ex 12-2; 20-16 (3); 20-19 Ex 20-3; 24-1; 24-6;
PIH Notices: 01-41 (2); 00-09

ASSUMED 3
HUD-52667: p ii;
7420.10G Gbk: 12-6; 20-15

ASSUMES 1
7420.10G Gbk: 24-2

ASYLUM 10
24 CFR 5: .518 (3);
7420.10G Gbk: 5-10 Ex 5-1 (6); 5-10 Ex 5-1

AT RISK 5

7420.10G Gbk: 22-8; 22-10 (2);
PIH Notices: 00-41;
Admin Plan: s25p1

AT-RISK..1
7420.10G Gbk: 22-10

ATTACHMENT..............................79
HUD-50058: p iv;
HUD-50058Instr: p17;
HUD-903: p1; p2;
7420.10G Gbk: 10-19;
PIH Notices: 03-23 (6); 03-12; 02-27 (15); 02-20 (11); 01-41 (2); 01-10 (3); 01-01 (5); 00-46 (11); 00-34; 00-24 (4); 00-24A; 00-24B; 00-23; 00-11 (5); 00-11A (2); 00-09 (3); 95-48; 95-48

ATTACHMENTS 16
HUD-52665: p1 (2);
PIH Notices: 02-27 (2); 02-20 (3); 01-41; 01-01; 00-46 (2); 00-24 (4); 00-14

ATTACK...1
PIH Notices: 99-11

ATTEND SCHOOL 6
HUD-50058Instr: p61;
7420.10G Gbk: 23-9;
PIH Notices: 95-48; 95-48 Tech Asst;
Admin Plan: s6p2; s6p10

ATTENDANT CARE 14
24 CFR 5: .603; .611 (2);
HUD-50058Instr: p34; p71;
7420.10G Gbk: 5-30;
PIH Notices: 01-15 (2); 01-15 Impr Integ Hbk (3);
Admin Plan: s6p2; s7p3; s7p7

ATTENDING SCHOOL 5
24 CFR 5: .603;
HUD-50058Instr: p72;
7420.10G Gbk: 23-16 Ex 23-2;
Admin Plan: s3p2; s6p11

ATTIC 2
HUD-52580-A: p6; p8

ATTICS 2
24 CFR 982: .401;
7420.10G Gbk: 10-14

ATTORNEY....................................17
24 CFR 5: .514;
HUD-903: p2;
7420.10G Gbk: 5-47 Ex 5-5; 5-49 Ex 5-5;
PIH Notices: 95-48 (2); 95-48 Tech Asst (2);
Admin Plan: s6p9; s6p10 (3); s7p5; s7p6; s16p3; s18p3; s18p6

ATTORNEY FEES 3
Admin Plan: s6p10 (2); s6p10

ATTORNEY GENERAL 4
7420.10G Gbk: 5-9 Ex 5-1; 5-10 Ex 5-1 (2); 11-2

ATTORNEY GENERAL 8
7420.10G Gbk: 5-9 Ex 5-1; 5-10 Ex 5-1 (2); 11-2;
PIH Notices: 95-48 (2); 95-48 Tech Asst; 95-48 Tech Asst

ATTORNEY GENERAL'S'WITHHOLDING........1
7420.10G Gbk: 5-10 Ex 5-1

ATTORNEYS 2
7420.10G Gbk: 5-49 Ex 5-5; 16-4

ATTORNEY'S 12
24 CFR 5: .318;
PIH Notices: 95-48 (5); 95-48 Tech Asst (5);
Admin Plan: s6p10

ATTORNEY'S FEES......................11
24 CFR 5: .318;
PIH Notices: 95-48 (5); 95-48 Tech Asst (4); 95-48 Tech Asst

ATTRIBUTABLE 14
24 CFR 5: .318 (2); .615; .617 (2);
24 CFR 982: .317;
PIH Notices: 01-15 Impr Integ Hbk (4); 01-06; 95-48; 95-48 Tech Asst;
Admin Plan: s6p3

ATTRIBUTED.................................2
HUD-52648: p1;
7420.10G Gbk: 5-38

ATTRIBUTES..................................4
7420.10G Gbk: 12-11 (2);
PIH Notices: 00-24B;
Admin Plan: s21p4

AUDIT 91
24 CFR 5: .107 (2); .801;
24 CFR 982: Intro; .152; .158 (2); .159 (2); .207;
HUD-52641: p5;
7420.10G Gbk: 3-8 (3); 4-17; 4-18; 4-22; 12-2; 18-1; 20-2; 20-6 (6); 20-16 (2); 20-20; 20-21 Ex 20-4; 20-22 Ex 20-5 (2); 20-27 (2); 20-29 (2); 21-15 Ex 21-5; 22-17;
PIH Notices: 02-27 (6); 02-21 (2); 01-06 (21); 01-01; 00-24 (3); 00-24A (4); 00-24B (12); 95-48; 95-48 Tech Asst;

Admin Plan: s20p1; s21p9
AUDIT TRAIL 3
24 CFR 982: .207;
7420.10G Gbk: 4-18;
PIH Notices: 02-27
AUDITED 8
24 CFR 5: .801 (3);
HUD-52648: p1;
7420.10G Gbk: 5-48 Ex 5-5; 10-31;
PIH Notices: 01-06;
Admin Plan: s7p5
AUDITED FINANCIAL STATEMENTS 3
24 CFR 5: .801 (2); .801
AUDITING 1
7420.10G Gbk: 20-1
AUDITOR 12
HUD-52648: p1;
7420.10G Gbk: 9-10; 10-31; 20-29;
PIH Notices: 01-06 (4); 00-24; 00-24A; 00-24B;
Admin Plan: s21p9
AUDITORIUM 4
PIH Notices: 95-48 (2); 95-48 Tech Asst; 95-48 Tech Asst
AUDITORS 1
PIH Notices: 00-24
AUDITS 8
24 CFR 982: .159;
7420.10G Gbk: 4-22 (3); 20-2;
PIH Notices: 02-27 (2); 00-24A
AUGUST 46
HUD-50058Instr: p14;
7420.10G Gbk: 8-13; 10-29; 14-5; 19-2; 19-3; 24-5;
PIH Notices: 03-23 (3); 03-20 (2); 02-27; 02-21; 02-20; 01-33; 01-27 (2); 01-20 (4); 01-15 Impr Integ Hbk (2); 01-10; 01-06 (3); 00-34 (3); 00-31 (3); 00-28 (2); 00-27 (6); 00-24; 00-24A; 96-65; 96-65
AUTHENTICITY 1
Admin Plan: s20p2
AUTHORITATIVE 1
7420.10G Gbk: 5-50 Ex 5-5
AUTHORITIES 26
24 CFR 982: .53; .626;
HUD-50058Instr: p73 (2);
7420.10G Gbk: 9-3; 10-8; 21-18 (2);
PIH Notices: 03-11; 02-01 (2); 00-23; 00-11A; 99-52 (2); 96-65; 95-48 (6); 95-48 Tech Asst (2);
Admin Plan: s2p6; s25p6
AUTHORITY 249
24 CFR 5: .100 (2); .110; .210; .234; .300; .303; .306; .327; .350 (2); .360 (2); .363 (4); .400; .500; .601;
24 CFR 982: 24 CFR 982 (3); .4 (6); .51 (4); .101 (6); .102 (16); .104; .151 (4); .154; .201; .552; .555 (2);
HUD-50058: p i; p xv;
HUD-50058Instr: p3; p58; p73 (2); p74 (2);
HUD-52665: p1;
HUD-903: p3;
HUD-9886: p1 (2);
7420.10G Gbk: 3-1; 4-25 Ex 4-2; 5-49 Ex 5-5; 5-50 Ex 5-5; 7-9; 8-12; 8-13; 9-1; 10-8; 10-12; 10-15; 10-42 Ex 10-5; 12-7 (2); 12-16 Ex 12-4; 13-2; 13-3; 13-4; 13-6; 15-9 Ex 15-1 (2); 16-5; 18-9; 20-10; 20-11; 20-20; 20-21 Ex 20-4; 20-22; 20-22 Ex 20-5; 20-24; 22-4; 23-4 (2); 24-13;
PIH Notices: 03-23 (8); 03-11; 02-27; 02-21 (25); 02-20 (2); 02-14; 02-07 (2); 02-06 (14); 01-41 (9); 01-20 (8); 01-15 (6); 01-10; 01-06; 00-49; 00-46 (2); 00-28; 00-27; 00-09 (13); 99-11; 96-65; 95-48 (2); 95-48 Tech Asst (2);
Admin Plan: s1p1 (5); s1p2; s1p3 (3); s1p4 (2); s1p5; s1p6; s3p1 (2); s13p2 (2); s15p3 (2); s15p4; s18p7; s20p3; s21p3; s21p5 (2); s22p1; s24p1; s24p4; s25p1; s25p6; s25p7 (4); s25p8
AUTHORITY'S 4
7420.10G Gbk: 20-10; 21-6 Ex 21-1;
Admin Plan: s1p7; s21p5
AUTHORIY 1
PIH Notices: 01-41
AUTHORIZATION 26
24 CFR 5: .230;
HUD-50058Instr: p2 (3); p3;
HUD-9886: p1;

7420.10G Gbk: 5-10 Ex 5-1; 5-12; 5-13 (3); 5-35; 8-1; 8-10; 12-3; 20-14; 24-12;
PIH Notices: 99-11;
Admin Plan: s1p6; s7p1 (2); s7p2; s7p4; s20p3; s20p4; s22p4

AUTHORIZE.................................... 8
24 CFR 5: .210; .214;
HUD-50058Instr: p71;
PIH Notices: 03-11; 02-06; 01-15; 00-49;
Admin Plan: s25p5

AUTHORIZED.............................123
24 CFR 5: .100; .306; .309; .360; .363; .609; .661;
24 CFR 982: .4 (3); .54 (2); .151; .155; .156; .553; .642;
HUD-50058: p i;
HUD-50058Instr: p72; p73; p75;
HUD-52580: p1 (4);
HUD-52641: p3; p9;
HUD-52641-A: p2;
HUD-52665: p1;
HUD-52667: p i;
HUD-9886: p1;
7420.10G Gbk: 1-1; 1-3 (2); 1-4 (2); 3-6 (2); 4-10; 5-14 Ex 5-2; 5-20; 20-3; 20-5; 20-6; 20-8 Ex 20-1 (2); 20-18 (3); 20-20; 22-17; 24-1;
PIH Notices: 03-23 (29); 03-11 (8); 02-07 (3); 02-06; 01-41; 01-15 Impr Integ Hbk (4); 01-10; 00-28 (7); 00-24B; 00-23 (2); 00-14; 00-11A; 00-09; 99-11; 95-48 (2); 95-48 Tech Asst (2);
Admin Plan: s1p6; s5p3; s20p3; s23p2;

AUTHORIZES 11
24 CFR 5: .303;
HUD-9886: p1;
7420.10G Gbk: 5-13; 20-5;
PIH Notices: 03-23; 02-22; 02-06; 00-28 (3); 00-09

AUTHORIZING................................. 12
24 CFR 5: .230 (3); .659;
24 CFR 982: .516; .632;
HUD-9886: p1 (2);
7420.10G Gbk: 5-46 Ex 5-5; 5-47 Ex 5-5; 12-3;
PIH Notices: 01-15 Impr Integ Hbk

AUTOMATED................................56
24 CFR 5: .214; .512 (3);
7420.10G Gbk: 4-9; 4-22; 5-7 (2); 5-9 Ex 5-1; 5-46 Ex 5-5; 8-23; 9-3; 9-8; 10-24 (2); 11-7 (4); 11-8 (4); 11-9 (2); 11-10 (3); 11-19 (2); 12-8 (2); 19-1; 19-6 (3); 19-7; 21-3; 21-4; 21-5; 21-8; 22-6;
PIH Notices: 03-11 (3); 01-15 (3); 00-34 (2); 95-48 (2); 95-48 Tech Asst (2);
Admin Plan: s11p2; s11p1

AUTOMATIC 28
24 CFR 982: Intro; .455; .503; .635 (2);
7420.10G Gbk: 5-46 Ex 5-5 (2); 7-4; 15-3; 24-10 (2);
PIH Notices: 02-20; 01-06 (2); 01-01 (4); 00-11; 00-09; 99-11 (4); 95-48 (2); 95-48 Tech Asst; 95-48 Tech Asst

AUTOMATIC EXTENSIONS 8
24 CFR 982: .503;
7420.10G Gbk: 7-4; 24-10 (2);
PIH Notices: 02-20; 01-01 (2); 01-01

AUTOMATIC TERMINATION........ 2
24 CFR 982: .635;
7420.10G Gbk: 15-3

AUTOMATIC TERMINATION OF.. 4
24 CFR 982: Intro; .455; .635;
PIH Notices: 00-09

AUTOMATICALLY........................ 49
24 CFR 982: .455; .502; .635;
HUD-50058Instr: p47;
HUD-52641: p3 (4); p9 (2);
HUD-52641-A: p2 (2);
7420.10G Gbk: 4-13; 8-12; 11-4; 13-9; 14-1; 14-2; 15-3; 15-8; 23-9;
PIH Notices: 03-20; 03-11; 02-27 (2); 01-41 (2); 01-15; 01-06 (9); 00-24A; 00-09 (3);
Admin Plan: s2p3; s8p2 (2); s14p1; s14p2; s22p4; s23p4; s23p5

AUTOMATION................................. 5
7420.10G Gbk: 21-10;
PIH Notices: 00-34; 00-24; 00-24A; 00-24A

AUTOMOBILE 7
7420.10G Gbk: 23-15;
PIH Notices: 02-27 (2); 95-48 (2); 95-48 Tech Asst;

95-48 Tech Asst
AUTOMOBILES..............................3
24 CFR 5: .603;
HUD-50058Instr: p22; p74
AUXILIARY..................................56
24 CFR 5: .214; .603;
.611 (2);
HUD-50058Instr: p34; p71;
p75;
7420.10G Gbk: 5-30 (4); 5-
52 Ex 5-5;
PIH Notices: 01-15; 01-
15 Impr Integ Hbk (3);
95-48 (17); 95-
48 Tech Asst (17);
Admin Plan: s6p2; s7p3;
s7p7 (3); s7p7
AUXILIARY AID.............................8
PIH Notices: 95-48 (4); 95-
48 Tech Asst (3); 95-
48 Tech Asst
AUXILIARY AIDS..........................22
PIH Notices: 95-48 (11); 95-
48 Tech Asst (10); 95-
48 Tech Asst
AUXILIARY APPARATUS 20
24 CFR 5: .603; .611 (2);
HUD-50058Instr: p34; p71;
7420.10G Gbk: 5-30 (4); 5-
52 Ex 5-5;
PIH Notices: 01-15; 01-15 Impr
Integ Hbk (3);
Admin Plan: s6p2; s7p3;
s7p7 (3); s7p7
AUXILIARY BENEFICIARY...........2
24 CFR 5: .214;
HUD-50058Instr: p75
AVAILABILITY 96
24 CFR 5: .100; .516 (2);
.518 (3);
24 CFR 35 SubM: .1200;
24 CFR 982: .4; .101;
.102 (2);
7420.10G Gbk: 1-9 (2); 2-1;
2-5; 2-8; 3-7; 4-1; 4-
2; 4-11 (2); 4-12; 4-13;
4-15; 5-11; 7-6; 8-4 (2);
8-7; 8-14; 17-1; 20-14;
20-15;
PIH Notices: 03-23; 02-27 (2);
02-22; 02-21; 02-06; 02-
01 (5); 01-41 (7); 01-
20 (2); 01-15; 01-10 (2);
00-27 (4); 00-09 (8); 99-
52 (5); 95-48 (6); 95-
48 Tech Asst (6);
Admin Plan: s1p4; s1p5; s4p2;
s22p1; s23p4; s24p2 (3);
s24p5; s24p7; s25p4
AVAILABLE FOR OCCUPANCY....9
24 CFR 5: .653 (3);
24 CFR 982: .617;
7420.10G Gbk: 8-13; 17-8;
Admin Plan: s19p1; s23p3;
s23p3
AVERAGE INCOME 2
HUD-52667: p i;
7420.10G Gbk: 20-17
AVOID 50
24 CFR 982: .310; .614; .630;
HUD-52641: p9;
HUD-52641-A: p2;
7420.10G Gbk: 2-9 (4); 9-7;
11-4; 12-8; 13-2; 13-4;
15-2; 15-6; 15-7; 17-5;
19-11; 20-8 Ex 20-1; 21-8;
22-5; 22-7; 22-8; 23-5;
PIH Notices: 03-23; 03-11 (2);
02-06; 01-41 (2); 01-15;
01-15 Impr Integ Hbk; 00-
53; 00-41; 00-11A; 00-
09 (3); 99-11; 95-48 (3);
95-48 Tech Asst (3);
Admin Plan: s8p2; s17p1;
s18p4; s20p1
AVOIDED...2
7420.10G Gbk: 8-4; 11-8
AVOIDING......................................3
7420.10G Gbk: 2-1; 22-7;
Admin Plan: s5p1
AVOIDS...2
7420.10G Gbk: 9-5; 9-5
AWARD LETTER 3
7420.10G Gbk: 12-13 Ex 12-1 (2);
12-13 Ex 12-1
AWARD LETTERS 7
7420.10G Gbk: 5-46 Ex 5-5; 12-4;
PIH Notices: 01-15; 01-
15 Impr Integ Hbk (3); 01-
15 Impr Integ Hbk
AWAY AT SCHOOL.........................1
Admin Plan: s5p1
AWAY FROM HOME 5
HUD-50058Instr: p26;
7420.10G Gbk: 5-1;
Admin Plan: s2p2; s6p6; s6p7
AWAY IN THE MILITARY...............1
Admin Plan: s5p1
BACK RENT 3
24 CFR 5: .630 (2); .630
BACKGROUND 46
24 CFR 982: .307; .553;
HUD-50058: p5; p v;
HUD-50058Instr: p ii; p19;
p77;
7420.10G Gbk: 1-1 (2); 4-21;

8-20; 10-15; 13-3 (2); 21-4;
PIH Notices: 03-23; 03-20; 03-11; 02-27 (2); 02-14; 02-07; 02-06; 02-01; 01-41 (2); 01-33; 01-27; 01-15; 01-10; 01-02; 00-49; 00-28; 00-23; 00-14; 00-11 (2); 00-09 (2); 00-01; 99-52; 99-11; 98-66; 96-65; 95-48; 95-48

BACKGROUNDS 1
24 CFR 5: .661

BALANCE 70
24 CFR 982: .313 (2); .514;
HUD-50058: p17;
HUD-50058Instr: p51; p62;
HUD-52641: p10;
HUD-52641-A: p3;
7420.10G Gbk: 4-26 Ex 4-2; 5-25 Ex 5-3; 5-33; 5-49 Ex 5-5 (3); 8-4 (2); 10-35; 12-1; 12-13 Ex 12-1; 20-2; 20-6; 20-7; 20-27 (5); 20-30; 21-2; 22-17; 23-13; 23-14 (3);
PIH Notices: 03-23 (23); 03-05; 02-21; 01-40; 01-20; 01-15 Impr Integ Hbk (2); 01-06; 00-24B (2);
Admin Plan: s17p2 (3); s25p5

BALANCE SHEET 4
7420.10G Gbk: 20-29 (2); 20-30;
PIH Notices: 00-24B

BALANCES 17
HUD-52648: p3 (2);
7420.10G Gbk: 20-14; 23-12; 23-19 (7);
PIH Notices: 03-23; 02-27; 01-06 (2);
Admin Plan: s21p9; s21p9

BALCONIES 2
HUD-52580-A: p13;
7420.10G Gbk: 10-10

BALCONY 11
24 CFR 5: .703 (2);
HUD-52580: p6 (2);
HUD-52580-A: p13; p19 (2);
7420.10G Gbk: 9-13 Ex 9-1 (2); 9-15 Ex 9-2; 9-16 Ex 9-2

BALLOON PAYMENT 1
24 CFR 982: .632

BALLOON PAYMENTS 1
Admin Plan: s22p3

BANK 29
HUD-903: p1; p2;
HUD-903-1: p5 (2);
7420.10G Gbk: 4-26 Ex 4-2; 5-12; 5-46 Ex 5-5 (3); 5-48 Ex 5-5 (2); 11-19; 12-12 Ex 12-1; 12-13 Ex 12-1 (3); 12-14 Ex 12-2; 12-16 Ex 12-4 (2); 20-24;
PIH Notices: 01-15 Impr Integ Hbk (4); 95-48; 95-48 Tech Asst;
Admin Plan: s2p2; s7p5; s7p6

BANK ACCOUNT 1
7420.10G Gbk: 20-24

BANK ACCOUNTS 4
7420.10G Gbk: 12-12 Ex 12-1; 12-13 Ex 12-1; 12-14 Ex 12-2;
Admin Plan: s2p2

BANK STATEMENT 1
7420.10G Gbk: 12-16 Ex 12-4

BANK STATEMENTS 6
7420.10G Gbk: 5-12;
PIH Notices: 01-15 Impr Integ Hbk (3);
Admin Plan: s7p5; s7p6

BANK STATING 1
7420.10G Gbk: 12-13 Ex 12-1

BANKERS 2
7420.10G Gbk: 5-49 Ex 5-5;
PIH Notices: 03-11

BANKING 3
7420.10G Gbk: 11-7;
PIH Notices: 95-48; 95-48 Tech Asst

BANKRUPTCY 8
24 CFR 5: .603;
HUD-50058Instr: p22;
7420.10G Gbk: 5-12; 5-27;
PIH Notices: 01-15 Impr Integ Hbk (3);
Admin Plan: s6p10

BANKS 3
HUD-50058: p6;
HUD-50058Instr: p22; p22

BAPTISMAL 2
7420.10G Gbk: 5-50 Ex 5-5;
Admin Plan: s7p7

BAPTISMAL CERTIFICATE 2
7420.10G Gbk: 5-50 Ex 5-5;
Admin Plan: s7p7

BAR 6
24 CFR 5: .318;
PIH Notices: 95-48 (2); 95-48 Tech Asst (2);
Admin Plan: s18p6

BARRING 1
PIH Notices: 99-11

BASELINE.....................................76
24 CFR 982: .102 (11);
HUD-50058Instr: p1; p11;
7420.10G Gbk: 20-6 (2); 20-8 (3); 20-8 Ex 20-1 (9); 20-9; 20-10 (2); 20-11 (3); 20-12 Ex 20-2 (2); 20-13 (2); 20-19 Ex 20-3; 24-1; 24-16;
PIH Notices: 03-23 (17); 02-14 (14); 02-06 (2); 02-01; 99-52;
Admin Plan: s24p1

BASEMENT.....................................15
24 CFR 5: .703;
24 CFR 982: .401 (2);
HUD-52580-A: p1; p2; p8 (5); p13; p15 (3);
7420.10G Gbk: 10-6

BASEMENTS.....................................2
24 CFR 982: .401;
7420.10G Gbk: 10-14

BASES...4
24 CFR 5: .214; .653;
HUD-52580-A: p2; p17

BASIC RANGE..............................54
24 CFR 982: .503 (7); .505;
7420.10G Gbk: 2-3; 7-2 (6); 7-6 (2); 7-7; 7-9 (2);
PIH Notices: 02-20 (14); 01-06 (5); 01-01; 00-46 (13); 00-46

BASIC RENT...................................6
24 CFR 5: .520;
7420.10G Gbk: 9-11;
PIH Notices: 01-41 (2); 00-09; 00-09

BASIC SKILLS TRAINING.............3
24 CFR 5: .603;
HUD-50058Instr: p71;
Admin Plan: s6p3

BASIN...20
24 CFR 982: .401; .605 (2); .614;
HUD-52580: p2;
HUD-52580-A: p4; p6 (8); p7 (2);
7420.10G Gbk: 10-3 (2); 17-2; 17-4

BASIS..211
24 CFR 5: .236; .318; .350; .353 (3); .514 (4); .603 (2); .609; .615 (2); .653; .661; .801;
24 CFR 982: .104 (2); .158; .307; .554; .555 (2); .627;
HUD-50058: p xv;
HUD-50058Instr: p9; p12; p16; p25; p58; p72; p73; p74; p75;
HUD-52580-A: p8 (3);
HUD-52646: p2;
HUD-52667: p ii;
7420.10G Gbk: 3-6; 4-10; 4-12 (3); 5-1; 5-7; 5-11 (2); 5-15 Ex 5-2; 5-18; 5-22; 5-39; 5-42; 5-44; 8-3; 8-14; 9-3; 10-34; 11-8; 12-8; 12-9 (2); 13-9; 18-4 (2); 19-13; 20-9; 20-15 (3); 20-17; 20-29; 21-5; 22-5 (2); 22-7; 22-14; 22-17; 23-8 Ex 23-1; 23-19; 24-8; 24-12;
PIH Notices: 03-23 (4); 03-20; 03-11 (2); 03-05; 02-27; 02-21 (6); 02-20 (3); 02-06 (2); 02-01 (2); 01-41 (4); 01-40; 01-20 (6); 01-15 (2); 01-15 Impr Integ Hbk (2); 01-10; 01-02; 01-01; 00-46 (3); 00-27 (4); 00-24A (2); 00-24B; 00-09 (4); 99-52 (2); 99-11 (3); 96-65; 95-48 (20); 95-48 Tech Asst (18);
Admin Plan: s1p2; s1p5; s1p6; s2p1; s6p7; s6p8; s6p9 (2); s6p10; s8p1 (2); s8p3; s10p1; s11p1 (2); s11p3; s11p1; s18p3; s18p5; s18p7; s22p3 (4); s22p4; s24p2; s24p6; s25p7; s25p8

BATHING...1
Admin Plan: s19p1

BATHROOM...................................72
24 CFR 5: .703 (2);
24 CFR 982: .401 (4); .614 (2);
HUD-52580: p1; p2 (2);
HUD-52580-A: p1; p4; p6 (11); p7 (4); p8; p9; p10; p11; p12; p15; p17;
7420.10G Gbk: 9-9; 9-13 Ex 9-1; 9-16 Ex 9-2; 10-3 (2); 10-4 (5); 10-6; 10-8; 10-10 (3); 17-3; 17-4 (5); 17-5; 17-7;
PIH Notices: 02-01 (3); 99-52 (2); 95-48 (3); 95-48 Tech Asst (3);
Admin Plan: s19p1 (2); s24p3

BATHROOMS................................20
HUD-52580-A: p6;
7420.10G Gbk: 9-5; 9-13 Ex 9-1; 9-17 Ex 9-3; 9-19 Ex 9-4; 10-4; 17-4;

PIH Notices: 02-01 (4); 99-52 (3); 95-48 (2); 95-48 Tech Asst (2);
Admin Plan: s11p2; s19p1

BATHTUB 5
24 CFR 982: .605 (2); .614;
7420.10G Gbk: 17-2; 17-4

BATTERIES 8
7420.10G Gbk: 5-32; 10-14 (3);
PIH Notices: 99-11 (3); 99-11

BATTERY 5
PIH Notices: 99-11 (4); 99-11

BATTERYMARCH 1
PIH Notices: 99-11

BATTERY-OPERATED 7
24 CFR 5: .703;
24 CFR 982: .401 (2);
HUD-52580-A: p8 (2);
7420.10G Gbk: 10-14;
PIH Notices: 99-11

BEDROOM 100
24 CFR 982: .401 (3); .604 (2); .613; .614; .617; .618 (2);
HUD-52580: p1;
HUD-52580-A: p8 (3); p9; p10; p11; p12; p15;
HUD-52665: p1 (2); p2;
HUD-52667: p ii;
HUD-9886: p2;
7420.10G Gbk: 6-5 (5); 7-3 (3); 7-5; 9-3; 9-4; 9-13 Ex 9-1; 9-16 Ex 9-2; 10-6 (3); 10-11; 10-16; 12-7 (2); 17-3; 17-5; 17-8; 17-12; 18-4; 18-5; 18-6; 18-7; 20-17 (2); 20-19 Ex 20-3; 24-11;
PIH Notices: 02-20 (4); 02-01 (2); 01-41 (12); 00-46 (4); 00-27; 00-09 (2); 99-52 (2);
Admin Plan: s5p1 (6); s5p2; s9p1; s15p6; s19p1 (5); s22p2; s23p4; s24p3

BEDROOM SIZE 21
7420.10G Gbk: 7-1; 7-4; 7-6; 9-12; 9-14 Ex 9-1; 11-8; 17-10; 19-3; 19-6 (2); 19-7 (2); 19-10; 20-2; 20-3 (2); 22-12; 22-13 (2); 24-11; 24-11

BEDROOM SIZE 43
HUD-52665: p1 (2); p2 (2);
7420.10G Gbk: 7-1; 7-4; 7-6; 9-12; 9-14 Ex 9-1; 11-8; 17-10; 19-3; 19-6 (2); 19-7 (2); 19-10; 20-2; 20-3 (2); 22-12; 22-13 (2); 24-11 (2);
PIH Notices: 02-20 (3); 01-41 (6); 00-46 (3); 00-09 (2);
Admin Plan: s5p2; s9p1; s22p2; s23p4

BEDROOM SIZES 2
PIH Notices: 02-20; 00-46

BEDROOMS 94
24 CFR 5: .100; .655 (2);
24 CFR 982: .4 (3); .204; .402 (7); .403; .503; .517; .555; .617 (3); .618;
HUD-50058: p5; p v; p10; p x; p11; p xi; p13; p xiii;
HUD-50058Instr: p20 (4); p42 (2); p43 (2); p44 (2); p46 (2); p47 (4); p49 (2); p53 (2); p72; p75; p76;
HUD-52580: p1 (2); p15;
HUD-52667: p1; p i (2);
7420.10G Gbk: 4-25 Ex 4-2; 5-41; 6-6; 9-10; 9-13 Ex 9-1; 10-11; 12-7 (2); 17-4; 17-6; 17-7; 17-8 (4); 18-5;
PIH Notices: 02-20 (3); 00-46 (3); 95-48 (2); 95-48 Tech Asst (2);
Admin Plan: s5p1 (2); s5p3; s11p2; s19p1 (4); s23p3

BEGINNING 102
24 CFR 5: .518 (2); .617 (2); .630 (8);
24 CFR 982: .4 (2); .305 (4); .309; .502; .505 (3);
HUD-50058Instr: p14; p16 (2);
HUD-52517: p1;
HUD-52641: p2; p4; p9;
HUD-52641-A: p2;
HUD-52648: p1; p2;
HUD-52665: p3;
7420.10G Gbk: 3-5; 3-6; 5-17; 5-23; 5-24; 8-15; 8-16; 8-22; 10-33; 11-5; 11-15 (4); 11-16 Ex 11-1; 11-19 (2); 14-5; 20-7 (4); 20-9; 20-23; 20-27 (2); 20-28 (3); 21-5; 23-14; 24-3;
PIH Notices: 02-14; 01-41 (2); 01-15 Impr Integ Hbk (4); 01-10; 01-06 (2); 00-53; 00-24B (2); 00-11A; 00-09 (5); 99-52; 95-48 (2); 95-48 Tech Asst (2);
Admin Plan: s2p6; s6p2; s6p3 (4); s8p5; s9p3;

s10p1; s21p7; s21p8; s21p8

BEHAVIOR 43
24 CFR 5: .360;
24 CFR 982: .54; .307 (2); .310; .552 (3); .553 (2);
HUD-52517: p2;
HUD-52641: p3 (2);
7420.10G Gbk: 1-14; 3-3 (2); 5-38 (2); 5-40 (3); 8-21; 11-12 (2); 15-6; 15-7 (2); 21-10;
PIH Notices: 02-01; 99-52; 95-48; 95-48 Tech Asst;
Admin Plan: s2p6 (2); s8p2; s15p1 (2); s15p2 (2); s15p3 (2); s15p5; s20p3

BEHAVIORAL 1
PIH Notices: 00-23

BEHAVIORS 2
7420.10G Gbk: 5-40; 21-10

BELOW GRADE...............................2
24 CFR 982: .605;
7420.10G Gbk: 17-2

BENEFICIAL 2
7420.10G Gbk: 11-4; 24-14

BENEFICIARIES 6
PIH Notices: 95-48 (3); 95-48 Tech Asst (2); 95-48 Tech Asst

BENEFICIARY 5
24 CFR 5: .214;
24 CFR 982: .456;
HUD-50058Instr: p75;
HUD-52641: p5;
7420.10G Gbk: 11-13

BENEFIT 104
24 CFR 5: .520 (4); .528; .615 (6); .655;
24 CFR 982: .102; .207; .352 (3); .627;
HUD-50058Instr: p16 (2); p28; p29; p70; p71; p73; p75;
HUD-903: p1;
7420.10G Gbk: 4-4; 4-5; 4-13; 4-16; 4-17; 5-12 (2); 5-18; 5-21 (2); 5-23 (4); 5-24; 5-46 Ex 5-5 (2); 5-47 Ex 5-5 (3); 8-1 (2); 8-8; 9-4; 12-3; 20-25; 20-26; 22-11;
PIH Notices: 02-01; 01-41 (2); 01-15; 01-15 Impr Integ Hbk (5); 01-10; 00-11 (2); 00-11A; 00-09 (3); 99-52; 95-48 (10); 95-48 Tech Asst (10);
Admin Plan: s1p3; s1p4; s6p12; s6p13; s7p4 (2); s7p8; s8p1; s11p3; s18p1; s20p4; s25p2

BENEFIT AWARD LETTERS..........3
7420.10G Gbk: 5-12;
PIH Notices: 01-15 Impr Integ Hbk;
Admin Plan: s7p8

BENEFITED.....................................4
PIH Notices: 95-48 (2); 95-48 Tech Asst; 95-48 Tech Asst

BENEFITING 1
7420.10G Gbk: 2-1

BENEFITS.....................................238
24 CFR 5: .210; .214; .230; .232; .236; .528; .609 (6); .613 (2); .615 (13); .617 (2); .630; .661 (2);
HUD-50058: p6; p16; p xvi;
HUD-50058Instr: p3; p16 (2); p17; p27 (3); p28 (8); p29 (18); p31; p32; p60 (3); p71 (4); p75;
HUD-52641: p6 (2);
HUD-903: p2;
HUD-9886: p1 (9); p2;
7420.10G Gbk: 2-1 (2); 2-5; 2-7 (2); 4-3; 4-4; 4-26 Ex 4-2 (2); 5-14 Ex 5-2; 5-15 Ex 5-2 (3); 5-16 Ex 5-2 (2); 5-17; 5-21 (2); 5-23 (3); 5-24; 5-26; 5-46 Ex 5-5 (2); 5-47 Ex 5-5; 5-50 Ex 5-5 (5); 6-8; 8-2 (2); 8-9; 11-14; 12-9 (2); 12-13 Ex 12-1; 12-16 Ex 12-4; 19-13; 20-22 Ex 20-5; 20-26; 21-6; 22-1; 22-3; 22-14; 22-17; 23-3; 23-15 (3); 23-20;
PIH Notices: 02-27; 02-21 (2); 02-01; 01-20; 01-15 (8); 01-15 Impr Integ Hbk (19); 00-11 (2); 00-11A (5); 99-52; 95-48 (17); 95-48 Tech Asst (17);
Admin Plan: s1p3; s1p6; s6p2; s6p3; s6p12 (3); s6p13; s7p3 (2); s7p4; s7p5; s8p1; s8p3; s11p2; s11p3; s20p1 (2); s20p3; s25p7

BILINGUAL.......................................
3
7420.10G Gbk: 8-2 (2);
Admin Plan: s1p5

BILL...29
24 CFR 5: .632 (2);
24 CFR 982: .355 (2); .514;

HUD-50058: p i;
HUD-50058Instr: p7; p15;
7420.10G Gbk: 5-32; 13-4; 13-6 (3); 13-9 (3); 13-11 Ex 13-1; 20-24 (3); 20-25;
PIH Notices: 03-11; 01-15 Impr Integ Hbk; 96-65;
Admin Plan: s7p8; s10p5 (3); s25p2

BILLED....29
HUD-50058: p10 (2); p x; p11 (2); p xi; p13 (2); p xiii; p14 (2); p xiv;
HUD-50058Instr: p42 (3); p46 (3); p53 (3); p56 (3);
7420.10G Gbk: 10-8; 13-4; 20-25;
PIH Notices: 03-11; 01-06

BILLING....51
24 CFR 982: .4; .355 (4);
HUD-50058Instr: p70;
HUD-52665: p1 (2); p2 (6); p3 (7);
7420.10G Gbk: 13-4; 13-5; 13-6; 13-8 (2); 13-9 (4); 20-24; 21-8;
PIH Notices: 03-11 (2); 96-65 (15);
Admin Plan: s13p2; s13p2

BILLINGS....10
PIH Notices: 02-27 (8); 96-65; 96-65

BILLS....30
24 CFR 982: .307;
HUD-50058Instr: p10; p42; p46; p53; p56;
7420.10G Gbk: 4-27 Ex 4-2; 5-32; 5-51 Ex 5-5 (2); 13-5; 13-7; 13-9; 18-1;
PIH Notices: 01-15; 01-15 Impr Integ Hbk; 01-06; 95-48 (3); 95-48 Tech Asst (3);
Admin Plan: s2p6; s6p7; s6p8; s7p6; s7p7; s9p3; s16p3

BINDING....7
24 CFR 982: .52;
HUD-52641: p10;
HUD-52641-A: p3;
7420.10G Gbk: 11-15; 16-5;
PIH Notices: 99-11; 99-11

BIRD....
2
24 CFR 5: .306;
7420.10G Gbk: 9-7

BIRTH....44
24 CFR 5: .504;
24 CFR 982: .551;
HUD-50058: p3 (6); p iii; p4 (6); p iv;
HUD-50058Instr: p14 (2); p74;
HUD-52641: 8;
HUD-52641-A: p1;
HUD-52646: p2;
7420.10G Gbk: 1-15; 4-23 Ex 4-1 (2); 4-25 Ex 4-2; 5-50 Ex 5-5 (3); 12-13 Ex 12-1; 12-16 Ex 12-4;
PIH Notices: 03-11; 01-15 Impr Integ Hbk; 00-24B; 95-48; 95-48 Tech Asst;
Admin Plan: s2p2; s5p2; s6p8 (2); s7p7 (2); s11p2; s20p2

BIRTH CERTIFICATE....1
7420.10G Gbk: 5-50 Ex 5-5

BIRTH CERTIFICATES....4
7420.10G Gbk: 5-50 Ex 5-5; 12-13 Ex 12-1;
PIH Notices: 01-15 Impr Integ Hbk;
Admin Plan: s2p2

BIRTH DATE....1
7420.10G Gbk: 4-25 Ex 4-2

BLIND....7
HUD-50058Instr: p29;
7420.10G Gbk: 5-30; 5-50 Ex 5-5;
PIH Notices: 95-48 (2); 95-48 Tech Asst; 95-48 Tech Asst

BLOCK GRANT....13
24 CFR 35 SubM: .1200 (2);
HUD-50058Instr: p30;
7420.10G Gbk: 5-16 Ex 5-2; 24-15;
PIH Notices: 02-01 (3); 01-15 Impr Integ Hbk; 01-02; 99-52 (2); 99-52

BLOOD....45
24 CFR 35 SubM: .1225 (12);
24 CFR 982: .516; .615;
HUD-50058Instr: p71 (2);
7420.10G Gbk: 10-12; 10-16 (2); 10-20 (9); 10-22 (3); 17-7; 20-4;
PIH Notices: 02-07; 00-49 (2); 00-23 (6);
Admin Plan: s2p2; s19p1; s23p4

BLOOD-LEAD....
2
PIH Notices: 02-07; 00-49

BMIR....5
24 CFR 5: .236;
24 CFR 982: .521;
HUD-50058Instr: p43; p47;

HUD-52517: p1

BOARD 49
24 CFR 5: .609; .801;
24 CFR 982: .54 (2); .155; .352;
HUD-50058Instr: p25;
HUD-52648: p3;
7420.10G Gbk: 2-5; 3-1 (2); 3-2; 3-6; 3-8 (3); 3-9 (2); 5-15 Ex 5-2; 8-16; 20-10; 24-11; 24-14 (2);
PIH Notices: 02-27; 02-01 (2); 01-15 Impr Integ Hbk (6); 00-41; 99-52 (2); 95-48 (9); 95-48 Tech Asst (3);
Admin Plan: s24p2

BOARD MEMBERS 1
7420.10G Gbk: 3-9

BOARD OF COMMISSIONERS 9
24 CFR 982: .54 (2); .155;
HUD-52648: p3;
7420.10G Gbk: 2-5; 3-1; 3-2; 3-6; 24-11

BOARDERS 1
Admin Plan: s23p7

BOARDS 10
24 CFR 982: .401;
7420.10G Gbk: 3-8; 3-9; 9-6;
PIH Notices: 02-21; 01-20; 00-11 (2); 95-48; 95-48 Tech Asst

BODILY INJURY 2
24 CFR 5: .100;
Admin Plan: s15p3

BONA FIDE 1
7420.10G Gbk: 5-5

BOND 2
7420.10G Gbk: 5-49 Ex 5-5;
PIH Notices: 01-15 Impr Integ Hbk

BONDS 15
24 CFR 5: .603;
HUD-50058Instr: p22; p74;
7420.10G Gbk: 4-26 Ex 4-2; 4-27 Ex 4-2; 5-25 Ex 5-3; 5-27; 5-28; 5-48 Ex 5-5; 12-13 Ex 12-1; 12-16 Ex 12-4;
PIH Notices: 01-15 Impr Integ Hbk (2);
Admin Plan: s7p5; s7p6

BONUS 48
24 CFR 982: .503;
HUD-52648: p3 (2); p4 (6);
7420.10G Gbk: 1-10 (3); 1-11; 2-2; 2-4 (2); 7-10 (3);
PIH Notices: 02-27 (2); 02-20; 01-06 (17); 01-01; 00-24A (2); 00-24B (2);
Admin Plan: s7p4; s21p1; s21p2; s21p9

BONUSES 8
24 CFR 5: .609;
HUD-50058Instr: p27;
7420.10G Gbk: 5-14 Ex 5-2; 23-12;
PIH Notices: 01-15 Impr Integ Hbk (2);
Admin Plan: s6p8; s6p8

BOOKS OF ACCOUNT 3
7420.10G Gbk: 20-1; 20-2; 20-23

BOROUGHS 5
24 CFR 982: .503;
PIH Notices: 02-20 (2); 00-46; 00-46

BORROWERS 1
24 CFR 982: .632

BOTTLE GAS 14
HUD-52517: p1 (3);
HUD-52641: p2 (3);
HUD-52667: p1 (3); p i; p ii;
7420.10G Gbk: 18-8 (2); 18-8

BRAILLE 17
7420.10G Gbk: 4-11; 5-44; 8-3;
PIH Notices: 95-48 (7); 95-48 Tech Asst (6); 95-48 Tech Asst

BRAILLED 14
PIH Notices: 95-48 (7); 95-48 Tech Asst (6); 95-48 Tech Asst

BREACH 52
24 CFR 982: Intro; .309 (2); .314 (2); .404 (6); .453 (2); .551 (2); .555; .619 (4); .641;
HUD-52641: p3 (2); p4; p5 (7); p9 (2);
HUD-52641-A: p1; p2;
7420.10G Gbk: 1-14; 5-36 Ex 5-4; 11-5; 11-7; 11-11; 11-12; 11-17 (2); 11-18; 15-4; 15-5; 18-1; 20-14;
PIH Notices: 00-24B;
Admin Plan: s15p6 (2); s18p4

BRIBERY 27
24 CFR 982: .306; .316; .453 (2); .551; .552;
HUD-52641: p5 (2); p6;
HUD-52646: p2;
7420.10G Gbk: 1-15; 5-36 Ex 5-4; 5-37; 8-19; 11-3; 11-18 (2); 15-4 (2); 15-5; 22-14;
PIH Notices: 01-41;
Admin Plan: s2p3; s2p6; s15p2; s15p5; s16p1

BRIBES 1
7420.10G Gbk: 22-2
BRIBING 1
7420.10G Gbk: 22-2
BRIEFING 154
24 CFR 982: .301 (7); .636;
HUD-52648: p2;
7420.10G Gbk: 1-16 Ex 1-3; 2-2 (4); 2-3; 2-6 (2); 2-7 (2); 2-8; 5-45; 6-3; 6-9 Ex 6-1; 8-1 (8); 8-2 (10); 8-3 (10); 8-4; 8-5 (2); 8-6; 8-8 (9); 8-9 (8); 8-10; 8-11 (4); 8-20; 10-26; 11-15; 12-9; 13-1 (2); 13-7 (2); 13-10 (2); 19-9 (3); 20-3; 21-2 (2); 21-4 (2); 21-10; 21-11; 21-16 Ex 21-6; 22-9; 24-3; 24-7 (3); 24-8; 24-9;
PIH Notices: 01-41; 01-15; 00-09;
Admin Plan: s1p3 (2); s1p4; s1p7; s3p3; s5p2; s8p1 (7); s8p2 (11); s8p3 (3); s8p4; s9p3; s13p1 (2); s13p2; s15p3; s18p3; s20p2; s20p6; s23p4 (7); s24p7; s25p7; s25p8
BRIEFING PACKET 10
7420.10G Gbk: 3-4; 8-3; 8-5; 8-7 (2); 8-14; 13-1 (2); 13-10; 16-3
BRIEFING PACKET 19
7420.10G Gbk: 3-4; 8-3; 8-5; 8-7 (2); 8-14; 13-1 (2); 13-10; 16-3;
Admin Plan: s1p3; s1p7; s8p1; s8p2 (2); s8p3; s9p3; s13p1; s18p3
BRIEFING TOPICS 2
7420.10G Gbk: 8-3; 8-3
BRIEFINGS 39
7420.10G Gbk: 2-7 (4); 5-40; 8-1; 8-2; 8-8; 8-9 (5); 8-14; 13-2; 19-9 (3); 21-4; 21-7; 22-9; 24-4; 24-14 (3); 24-15;
PIH Notices: 00-09;
Admin Plan: s8p1 (5); s8p2 (3); s8p4 (2); s15p6; s25p7
BROAD RANGE 12
24 CFR 5: .653 (2);
24 CFR 982: .503;
7420.10G Gbk: 4-9; 7-3; 7-10;
PIH Notices: 02-20; 01-01 (3); 00-11;
Admin Plan: s1p7
BROAD RANGE OF INCOMES...... 2
24 CFR 5: .653; .653
BROCHURE..................................... 4
24 CFR 982: .301;
7420.10G Gbk: 2-6; 8-6;
Admin Plan: s8p2
BROCHURES 1
7420.10G Gbk: 8-7
BROKER 11
HUD-903: p1; p2;
HUD-903-1: p5;
7420.10G Gbk: 5-25 Ex 5-3; 5-28; 5-49 Ex 5-5;
PIH Notices: 01-15 Impr Integ Hbk;
Admin Plan: s7p6 (3); s7p6
BROKER FEES 1
7420.10G Gbk: 5-25 Ex 5-3
BROKERAGE 2
HUD-903: p2;
7420.10G Gbk: 5-11
BROKERS 2
7420.10G Gbk: 5-49 Ex 5-5; 5-49 Ex 5-5
BROKER'S 6
HUD-903: p1;
7420.10G Gbk: 5-27 (2); 5-48 Ex 5-5;
Admin Plan: s7p5; s7p5
BROTHER 12
24 CFR 982: .306;
HUD-52517: p2;
HUD-52641: p5; p6 (2);
HUD-52646: p2;
7420.10G Gbk: 8-15; 8-19; 11-2;
PIH Notices: 95-48; 95-48 Tech Asst;
Admin Plan: s16p2
BROTHERS..................................... 1
7420.10G Gbk: 12-7
BROTHER'S 1
HUD-50058Instr: p29
BUCKLING.................................... 11
24 CFR 982: .401 (2); .614 (2);
HUD-52580-A: p2 (3); p13 (2);
7420.10G Gbk: 10-9; 10-9
BUDGET 248
24 CFR 5: .100; .216; .234; .661;
24 CFR 982: 24 CFR 982 (2); .4 (5); .52; .53; .54; .101 (6); .102 (14); .103; .104; .151 (5); .152 (2); .153; .154 (2); .155; .156; .157 (5); .158 (2);

.159; .160; .204; .206; .301; .303; .304; .305; .307; .310; .352; .403; .404; .406; .452; .516; .517; .551; .552; .554; .555;
HUD-50058: p i;
HUD-50058Instr: p3; p15; p74;
HUD-52648: p2;
HUD-9886: p1;
7420.10G Gbk: 4-3 (2); 7-6; 18-4; 19-1; 20-2 (3); 20-5 (2); 20-6; 20-7 (11); 20-9; 20-10; 20-11 (5); 20-12 Ex 20-2 (3); 20-13 (2); 20-14 (4); 20-15; 20-16 (3); 20-18 (3); 20-20 (6); 20-22 (7); 20-22 Ex 20-5; 20-28 (3); 23-18; 24-2; 24-8;
PIH Notices: 03-23 (12); 03-20; 03-12; 03-11; 02-27 (2); 02-21 (26); 02-20; 02-14; 02-07 (2); 02-06 (21); 01-41 (9); 01-20 (7); 01-02; 00-49; 00-46; 00-28; 00-27; 00-24; 00-09 (7);
Admin Plan: s8p1; s9p1; s21p8; s21p8

BUDGET AUTHORITY 194
24 CFR 982: Intro; .4 (5); .101 (6); .102 (13); .104; .151 (4); .154;
7420.10G Gbk: 8-11 (2); 20-5; 20-6 (3); 20-7 (8); 20-9; 20-10 (11); 20-11 (15); 20-12 Ex 20-2 (4); 20-13 (7); 20-14 (3); 20-15 (8); 20-16 (9); 20-18; 20-19 Ex 20-3; 20-20 (8); 20-21 Ex 20-4; 20-22 (2); 20-27; 20-28; 24-2 (4); 24-8 (2);
PIH Notices: 03-23 (8); 02-27; 02-21 (24); 02-20; 02-07 (2); 02-06 (14); 01-41 (6); 01-20 (6); 00-49; 00-46; 00-28; 00-27; 00-09 (3); 00-09

BUDGETARY 1
24 CFR 982: .102

BUDGETED 12
24 CFR 982: .305 (2);
7420.10G Gbk: 8-4; 8-11; 8-17 (2); 10-25 (2); 20-16;
PIH Notices: 01-06;
Admin Plan: s9p1; s21p8

BUDGETING 10
24 CFR 982: .630;
7420.10G Gbk: 11-8; 20-2 (2); 20-13; 20-20; 20-22 (2);
Admin Plan: s8p3; s25p7

BUDGETS 8
7420.10G Gbk: 19-6; 20-20; 20-22 (2);
PIH Notices: 03-23 (2); 02-01; 99-52

BUILDING EXTERIOR 8
24 CFR 5: .703 (2);
HUD-52580: p5; p6;
HUD-52580-A: p1; p13; p14; p19

BUILDING SYSTEMS 6
24 CFR 5: .703 (2);
24 CFR 982: .631 (2);
HUD-50058Instr: p73;
Admin Plan: s22p3

BURDEN 53
24 CFR 5: .801;
24 CFR 982: .102; .503;
HUD-50058: p v;
HUD-52580: p1 (4);
HUD-52667: p i;
HUD-903: p1;
7420.10G Gbk: 4-11; 4-18; 5-44; 8-3;
PIH Notices: 02-20 (3); 02-01 (10); 01-41; 00-46 (3); 99-52 (10); 95-48 (3); 95-48 Tech Asst (3);
Admin Plan: s1p3; s1p5 (4); s6p7

BURDEN OF PROOF 1
Admin Plan: s6p7

BURDENED 1
PIH Notices: 01-27

BURDENS 24
24 CFR 5: .315;
24 CFR 982: .503;
7420.10G Gbk: 22-10;
PIH Notices: 02-20 (3); 01-10; 00-46 (3); 95-48 (7); 95-48 Tech Asst (6); 95-48 Tech Asst

BUS 5
7420.10G Gbk: 2-10; 2-13 Ex 2-1; 5-32;
PIH Notices: 95-48; 95-48 Tech Asst

BUS FARE 1
7420.10G Gbk: 5-32

BUSES 1
7420.10G Gbk: 4-3

BUSINESS 115
24 CFR 5: .105 (3); .603; .609 (4);
24 CFR 982: .310 (2); .627;

HUD-50058: p6;
HUD-50058Instr: p22; p25 (5); p71;
HUD-52641: p9;
HUD-52641-A: p2;
HUD-903: p1; p2;
7420.10G Gbk: 2-13 Ex 2-1; 4-1; 4-12 (2); 5-14 Ex 5-2 (4); 5-19 (13); 5-25 Ex 5-3 (2); 5-48 Ex 5-5 (3); 8-8; 10-34 (2); 11-7; 11-10; 11-19; 15-2; 15-3; 21-16 Ex 21-6; 23-12; 23-15; 24-7; 24-12 (2);
PIH Notices: 02-27 (8); 02-22; 01-41; 01-15 (5); 01-15 Impr Integ Hbk (11); 01-01; 00-24; 00-09; 95-48 (4); 95-48 Tech Asst (4);
Admin Plan: s1p6; s4p2 (2); s7p5 (5); s7p6; s15p6 (2); s17p1 (2); s18p2; s25p4

BUSINESS ASSETS 2
7420.10G Gbk: 5-25 Ex 5-3;
Admin Plan: s7p6

BUSINESS DAY 7
7420.10G Gbk: 4-1; 10-34 (2);
PIH Notices: 01-01;
Admin Plan: s17p1 (2); s18p2

BUSINESS DAYS 2
Admin Plan: s4p2; s4p2

BUSINESS EXPANSION 5
24 CFR 5: .609;
HUD-50058Instr: p25;
7420.10G Gbk: 5-14 Ex 5-2;
PIH Notices: 01-15 Impr Integ Hbk; 01-15 Impr Integ Hbk

BUSINESS EXPENSE 2
7420.10G Gbk: 5-19; 5-19

BUSINESS EXPENSES 5
7420.10G Gbk: 5-19 (4);
PIH Notices: 01-15

BUSINESS INCOME 4
PIH Notices: 01-15 (3); 01-15 Impr Integ Hbk

BUSINESS LOANS 1
7420.10G Gbk: 5-19

BUSINESSES 5
HUD-50058Instr: p61;
7420.10G Gbk: 23-4;
PIH Notices: 02-27 (2); 02-27

BUY 3
HUD-50058: p xvii;
HUD-50058Instr: p63;
HUD-903-1: p4

CABLE 3
24 CFR 982: .517;
7420.10G Gbk: 18-1;
Admin Plan: s6p13

CALCULATE 117
24 CFR 5: .611; .630;
24 CFR 982: 24 CFR 982 (2); .503; .505 (8); .518; .642;
HUD-50058: p iii; p iv; p ix;
HUD-50058Instr: p14; p22 (2); p23 (2); p35; p38; p39; p40 (2); p65; p68 (2); p72;
7420.10G Gbk: 5-17 (3); 5-20; 5-26 (2); 5-28; 6-1; 6-7 (2); 7-1; 7-7; 9-14 Ex 9-1; 9-15 Ex 9-2; 11-1; 17-5; 17-6; 17-8; 18-6; 18-7 (2); 18-8; 18-9 (4); 19-9 (2); 20-2; 20-3; 20-5; 20-6; 20-11 (3); 20-20; 20-21; 20-22; 20-28; 22-13; 24-4; 24-11;
PIH Notices: 03-23 (6); 02-20 (3); 02-07; 01-41 (9); 01-15 Impr Integ Hbk; 01-10 (2); 00-46 (3); 00-28; 00-24B; 00-09 (9);
Admin Plan: s5p3; s6p9; s6p11; s7p3; s8p2; s11p3; s19p1

CALCULATED 100
24 CFR 5: .609; .615 (2); .628;
24 CFR 982: .102 (4); .502; .503; .505; .515 (2); .516 (2); .642 (3);
HUD-50058: p6;
HUD-50058Instr: p22; p48; p65;
7420.10G Gbk: 5-5 (4); 5-14 Ex 5-2; 5-23 (3); 5-24 (2); 5-32 (2); 5-47 Ex 5-5; 6-1; 6-2 (2); 6-3; 6-4 (3); 6-5; 6-6 (2); 6-7 (2); 7-8; 8-2; 16-5 (2); 17-4; 17-5; 17-8; 18-6 (2); 18-9; 20-2 (2); 20-7 (2); 20-8 Ex 20-1 (2); 20-13; 23-11 (3); 23-13; 24-1; 24-6;
PIH Notices: 03-23 (9); 02-22; 02-20 (2); 01-41; 01-15; 01-15 Impr Integ Hbk (3); 00-46; 00-41; 00-09;
Admin Plan: s6p1 (2); s6p3 (2); s6p9; s6p10; s6p12; s11p1; s22p3; s22p5

CALCULATES 12

HUD-52648: p2;
7420.10G Gbk: 12-11; 20-15; 23-10;
PIH Notices: 01-41 (2); 01-10 (2); 00-09;
Admin Plan: s6p9; s21p4; s21p7

CALCULATING..............................92
24 CFR 5: .514;
24 CFR 982: .4; .102 (2);
HUD-50058Instr: p38; p78;
7420.10G Gbk: 1-13; 4-22; 4-25 Ex 4-2; 5-5; 5-17 (3); 5-21; 5-23; 5-26; 5-32; 5-34; 6-1 (2); 6-2 (2); 6-4; 6-5; 6-6 (2); 7-8; 8-5; 12-9; 13-7; 13-9; 17-1; 17-6; 17-9; 18-1; 18-2; 18-6 (2); 18-10; 20-6 (2); 20-7 (2); 20-8; 20-8 Ex 20-1 (2); 20-10; 20-11 (5); 20-12 Ex 20-2; 20-16; 20-19 Ex 20-3; 22-2; 23-7; 23-13; 24-2 (2); 24-6;
PIH Notices: 03-23 (2); 02-22; 02-21 (3); 01-41 (3); 01-20 (2); 01-15 (4); 01-15 Impr Integ Hbk (5); 01-10 (2); 00-09 (5); 00-01;
Admin Plan: s6p1 (2); s6p10

CALCULATION............................202
24 CFR 982: .4 (2); .502 (3); .510; .627 (2);
HUD-50058: p i; p v; p6 (2); p9 (3); p ix (2); p10 (2); p x; p11 (2); p xi; p12 (2); p13 (2); p xiii; p14 (2); p xiv (2);
HUD-50058Instr: p3; p22; p33; p35 (3); p37 (5); p39 (5); p40 (3); p41 (2); p43 (4); p44 (2); p45 (2); p48 (4); p49 (2); p51 (6); p52 (2); p54 (4); p55; p56; p57 (3); p68; p69 (3); p77; p78;
7420.10G Gbk: 1-4 (2); 4-20 (2); 5-5 (2); 5-13; 5-24 (3); 5-25 Ex 5-3; 5-26; 5-31 (2); 5-32 (2); 5-33; 5-36 Ex 5-4; 5-48 Ex 5-5; 6-1; 6-2; 6-8; 8-5; 12-3 (2); 12-4; 12-5 (4); 14-2; 16-2; 17-3; 17-4; 17-5; 17-8; 17-10; 17-11; 17-12; 19-4; 20-2; 20-4; 20-11; 20-19 Ex 20-3; 20-24; 20-27 (3); 20-28; 20-29 (2); 22-17; 23-11 (3); 23-12; 23-14 (2); 23-16 Ex 23-2 (3); 24-5; 24-7 (2);
PIH Notices: 03-23 (9); 02-21; 02-06; 01-41 (2); 01-20; 01-15 (3); 01-15 Impr Integ Hbk (2); 01-10 (7); 00-41; 00-09 (4);
Admin Plan: s3p3; s6p1 (2); s6p4; s6p5; s6p9 (5); s6p10; s6p12; s6p13 (2); s7p1; s7p5; s17p1

CALCULATION ERRORS...............1
7420.10G Gbk: 22-17

CALCULATIONS............................59
HUD-50058: p i; p6 (3);
HUD-50058Instr: p3 (2); p15; p22; p33 (2);
HUD-52648: p2;
7420.10G Gbk: 1-5; 1-9; 1-10; 5-18; 5-20; 5-34; 6-4; 8-5; 13-7; 14-1 (3); 14-2; 16-5; 19-10 (2); 20-7; 20-8 Ex 20-1; 22-6 (2); 22-14; 23-10;
PIH Notices: 03-23 (8); 02-27 (3); 01-20 (2); 01-15 (2); 01-06; 00-24A; 00-09; 00-01; 98-66;
Admin Plan: s21p1; s21p2; s21p7 (3); s21p7

CALENDAR MONTH......................2
24 CFR 982: .403; .403

CALENDAR MONTHS....................2
HUD-52641: p4;
7420.10G Gbk: 11-6

CALENDAR YEAR........................20
24 CFR 982: .102 (7);
HUD-50058Instr: p17;
7420.10G Gbk: 19-2; 20-8 Ex 20-1;
PIH Notices: 02-21 (5); 01-20 (3); 00-27; 00-27

CALL-FOR-AID................................1
24 CFR 5: .703

CANCEL...3
7420.10G Gbk: 10-26; 10-46 Ex 10-8; 22-15

CANCELED.....................................5
7420.10G Gbk: 10-41 Ex 10-4b;
PIH Notices: 01-15; 01-15 Impr Integ Hbk (2);
Admin Plan: s7p7

CANCELED CHECKS.....................4
PIH Notices: 01-15; 01-15 Impr Integ Hbk (2);
Admin Plan: s7p7

CANCELLATION.............................5
7420.10G Gbk: 10-26; 10-29;

12-13 Ex 12-1;
PIH Notices: 00-14; 00-14

CANCELLED....................................6
7420.10G Gbk: 5-51 Ex 5-5 (3); 5-52 Ex 5-5; 10-26;
PIH Notices: 01-15 Impr Integ Hbk

CANCELLED CHECKS...................5
7420.10G Gbk: 5-51 Ex 5-5 (3); 5-52 Ex 5-5;
PIH Notices: 01-15 Impr Integ Hbk

CAP...14
7420.10G Gbk: 5-33; 8-16;
PIH Notices: 03-23 (8); 02-27 (2);
Admin Plan: s6p4; s6p12

CAPACITIES....................................4
PIH Notices: 00-01; 98-66; 95-48; 95-48 Tech Asst

CAPACITY.....................................22
24 CFR 982: .4; .104; .308 (2); .625 (4);
HUD-52580-A: p2; p17;
HUD-52648: p3;
7420.10G Gbk: 8-21 (2); 10-2; 10-9; 10-11; 19-6;
PIH Notices: 02-27; 01-06 (2);
Admin Plan: s2p2; s8p1

CAPITAL..37
24 CFR 5: .100; .603; .609 (3);
HUD-50058Instr: p22; p25; p31; p74; p75;
7420.10G Gbk: 5-14 Ex 5-2 (2); 5-15 Ex 5-2; 5-19 (5); 5-25 Ex 5-3 (2);
PIH Notices: 02-21; 02-01 (5); 01-15 Impr Integ Hbk (6); 99-52 (4);
Admin Plan: s6p10

CAPITAL ASSETS............................2
7420.10G Gbk: 5-19; 5-19

CAPITAL FUND..............................7
PIH Notices: 02-21; 02-01 (3); 99-52 (2); 99-52

CAPITAL FUNDS............................2
PIH Notices: 02-01; 02-01

CAPITAL GAINS.............................7
24 CFR 5: .609;
HUD-50058Instr: p31;
7420.10G Gbk: 5-15 Ex 5-2; 5-25 Ex 5-3;
PIH Notices: 01-15 Impr Integ Hbk (2);
Admin Plan: s6p10

CAPITAL INVESTMENT.................3
24 CFR 5: .603;
HUD-50058Instr: p22; p74

CAPITAL INVESTMENTS..............1
7420.10G Gbk: 5-25 Ex 5-3

CAPPED..2
7420.10G Gbk: 5-33;
PIH Notices: 03-23

CAR..6
PIH Notices: 02-27 (2); 95-48 (2); 95-48 Tech Asst; 95-48 Tech Asst

CARBON MONOXIDE....................2
24 CFR 982: .401;
7420.10G Gbk: 10-10

CARD FILE.....................................1
7420.10G Gbk: 4-9

CARE ATTENDANT........................6
7420.10G Gbk: 4-27 Ex 4-2 (3); 5-30 (2); 5-51 Ex 5-5

CARE ATTENDANTS......................1
7420.10G Gbk: 5-30

CARE FACILITIES..........................6
24 CFR 5: .306;
PIH Notices: 00-41 (3); 95-48; 95-48 Tech Asst

CARPORT.......................................1
24 CFR 5: .703

CARS..1
7420.10G Gbk: 5-25 Ex 5-3

CASE BY CASE...............................7
7420.10G Gbk: 20-15;
PIH Notices: 02-06; 02-01; 99-52; 99-11 (2);
Admin Plan: s11p3

CASE BY CASE BASIS..................6
7420.10G Gbk: 20-15;
PIH Notices: 02-06; 02-01; 99-52; 99-11; 99-11

CASE-BY-CASE..............................6
24 CFR 982: .632;
PIH Notices: 01-41; 01-10; 00-09; 95-48; 95-48 Tech Asst

CASE-BY-CASE BASIS..................5
PIH Notices: 01-41; 01-10; 00-09; 95-48; 95-48 Tech Asst

CASELOAD....................................5
7420.10G Gbk: 22-10;
Admin Plan: s25p1 (2); s25p3; s25p3

CASELOADS....................................10
7420.10G Gbk: 21-5 (6); 21-17; 22-10 (2); 22-10

CASEWORKER............................10
7420.10G Gbk: 12-13 Ex 12-1;
Admin Plan: s2p3; s8p3;

s11p1 (2); s13p1; s18p1 (2); s20p3; s20p3

CASEWORKERS..............................2
Admin Plan: s20p3; s20p4

CASEWORKER'S 1
7420.10G Gbk: 12-13 Ex 12-1

CASH...82
24 CFR 5: .603; .609 (4);
HUD-50058: p6 (2);
HUD-50058Instr: p22 (2); p23; p25 (3); p28; p29; p71; p74;
7420.10G Gbk: 1-2; 4-26 Ex 4-2 (3); 5-14 Ex 5-2 (4); 5-18; 5-19 (2); 5-25 Ex 5-3 (2); 5-26 (3); 5-27 (7); 5-28 (5); 5-49 Ex 5-5 (6); 12-4; 12-16 Ex 12-4; 20-23; 20-24; 20-25 (2); 20-26; 23-14;
PIH Notices: 01-15; 01-15 Impr Integ Hbk (9); 00-24B; 00-11 (2); 95-48 (3); 95-48 Tech Asst (3);
Admin Plan: s6p9; s7p5; s7p6; s7p6

CASH CONTRIBUTIONS................1
PIH Notices: 01-15 Impr Integ Hbk

CASH GRANTS...............................2
PIH Notices: 95-48; 95-48 Tech Asst

CASH RECEIPTS 1
7420.10G Gbk: 20-23

CASH VALUE................................20
24 CFR 5: .603;
HUD-50058: p6 (2);
HUD-50058Instr: p22 (2); p23; p74;
7420.10G Gbk: 5-25 Ex 5-3 (2); 5-26 (2); 5-27 (3); 5-28; 5-49 Ex 5-5 (2); 12-4; 12-16 Ex 12-4;
Admin Plan: s7p6

CAT..2
24 CFR 5: .306; .318

CATEGORIES................................45
24 CFR 5: .506; .510;
24 CFR 982: .101; .201; .517 (2);
HUD-50058Instr: p73;
HUD-903: p2;
7420.10G Gbk: 1-6 (3); 3-2; 4-5; 4-23 Ex 4-1; 5-3 (2); 5-9 Ex 5-1; 5-10 Ex 5-1; 18-2; 18-6; 19-10; 23-20;
PIH Notices: 02-21 (3); 02-20 (2); 01-41 (2); 01-20 (3); 00-46 (2); 00-27 (3); 00-11; 00-09 (3); 95-48; 95-48 Tech Asst;
Admin Plan: s2p5; s16p1

CATEGORIZE..................................2
HUD-50058Instr: p15; p15

CATEGORIZED...............................1
HUD-50058Instr: p19

CATEGORIZES................................3
HUD-50058: p iii; p iv;
HUD-50058Instr: p14

CATEGORY....................................59
24 CFR 5: .609;
24 CFR 982: .54; .204 (3); .207; .517 (2);
HUD-50058: p16 (2); p xvi (2);
HUD-50058Instr: p27; p31; p59 (4); p63;
HUD-52580-A: p1;
7420.10G Gbk: 3-2; 4-4; 4-18; 4-21; 5-16 Ex 5-2; 7-6; 9-3; 9-4; 9-17 Ex 9-3; 9-19 Ex 9-4; 11-8; 18-2 (2); 18-5; 18-6; 20-8 Ex 20-1; 21-20; 22-5;
PIH Notices: 02-27; 02-21; 01-41 (2); 01-20 (2); 01-15 Impr Integ Hbk; 00-27 (2); 00-24B (3); 00-09 (2); 95-48 (3); 95-48 Tech Asst (3);
Admin Plan: s20p5

CATS...4
24 CFR 5: .318 (2); .350; .350

CAUSE 60
24 CFR 5: .100 (2); .110;
24 CFR 982: .161; .206; .310 (2); .552; .553 (2);
HUD-50058: p v;
HUD-50058Instr: p18; p72; p75;
HUD-52580-A: p1;
HUD-52641: p9;
HUD-52641-A: p2;
7420.10G Gbk: 9-8; 10-34; 10-40 Ex 10-4a; 12-10; 15-3; 18-1; 19-7; 19-8; 20-14; 20-17; 20-19 Ex 20-3; 22-5;
PIH Notices: 03-11; 02-27; 02-20; 02-06; 02-01; 01-41 (2); 00-46; 00-23; 99-52; 95-48 (2); 95-48 Tech Asst (2);
Admin Plan: s3p3; s9p2; s9p3; s10p3; s14p1; s14p2; s15p2 (2); s15p3 (3); s18p5 (2); s18p7; s23p6 (2); s23p6

CAUSED 33
24 CFR 5: .318 (3);
24 CFR 982: .404 (5); .551 (2);

.555; .619 (2); .641;
HUD-52580-A: p15;
HUD-52641: p9 (2);
HUD-52641-A: p1; p2;
7420.10G Gbk: 1-14; 2-1; 5-21; 5-23; 5-36 Ex 5-4; 5-38; 10-27;
PIH Notices: 03-20;
Admin Plan: s6p9; s10p4; s10p5 (2); s13p1; s21p5

CAUSES 20
HUD-52580-A: p16;
7420.10G Gbk: 6-6; 9-5; 11-1; 20-17; 22-5; 23-13; 24-2;
PIH Notices: 02-27 (3); 02-01; 01-15; 01-15 Impr Integ Hbk; 99-52; 95-48; 95-48 Tech Asst;
Admin Plan: s6p12; s11p2; s11p2

CAUSEWAY 1
HUD-903: p2

CDBG 1
7420.10G Gbk: 24-15

CEILING.. 66
24 CFR 5: .703;
24 CFR 982: .401; .642 (2);
HUD-50058: p9 (3); p ix (5);
HUD-50058Instr: p39 (12); p66; p68 (2);
HUD-52580: p1; p2 (2); p3 (3); p4 (2);
HUD-52580-A: p2 (4); p3 (2); p5 (2); p7 (2); p9 (2); p10 (2); p11 (2); p12 (2);
7420.10G Gbk: 1-3; 10-8; 10-10; 23-17 Ex 23-2;
PIH Notices: 02-22 (3); 01-15 Impr Integ Hbk (5);
Admin Plan: s10p4

CEILING RENT 25
HUD-50058: p9 (3); p ix (5);
HUD-50058Instr: p39 (12); p66; p68 (2);
7420.10G Gbk: 23-17 Ex 23-2;
PIH Notices: 01-15 Impr Integ Hbk

CEILING RENTS 3
PIH Notices: 01-15 Impr Integ Hbk (2); 01-15 Impr Integ Hbk

CEILINGS 14
24 CFR 5: .603 (3); .703;
24 CFR 982: .401; .614;
HUD-50058Instr: p71; p73; p76;
HUD-52580-A: p2 (2); p13; p17;
7420.10G Gbk: 10-9

CENSUS 184
24 CFR 982: .301; .503 (4);
HUD-50058Instr: p25;
HUD-52580: p1 (2);
HUD-52648: p3 (5); p4 (11);
7420.10G Gbk: 2-2; 2-4 (6); 2-7; 5-15 Ex 5-2; 5-50 Ex 5-5; 7-3 (4); 7-5 (3); 7-10 (4); 8-3; 8-9; 9-3 (5); 9-17 Ex 9-3; 9-19 Ex 9-4; 10-33; 10-35; 19-8;
PIH Notices: 02-27; 02-22 (17); 02-20 (30); 01-15 Impr Integ Hbk (3); 01-06 (10); 01-01 (2); 00-46 (30); 00-24B (5); 00-01 (10); 98-66 (10);
Admin Plan: s8p3 (3); s9p1; s11p2 (2); s21p9; s24p1; s24p4

CENSUS DATA 10
7420.10G Gbk: 7-5; 9-3 (2);
PIH Notices: 02-20 (3); 00-46 (3);
Admin Plan: s8p3

CENSUS EMPLOYEES.................... 5
HUD-50058Instr: p25;
7420.10G Gbk: 5-15 Ex 5-2;
PIH Notices: 01-15 Impr Integ Hbk; 00-01; 98-66

CENSUS RECORD 1
7420.10G Gbk: 5-50 Ex 5-5

CENSUS TAKER 2
PIH Notices: 00-01; 98-66

CENSUS TRACT 30
24 CFR 982: .301;
HUD-52580: p1 (2);
HUD-52648: p4;
7420.10G Gbk: 2-2; 2-7; 9-3; 9-17 Ex 9-3; 9-19 Ex 9-4; 10-33;
PIH Notices: 02-22 (14); 02-20; 00-46;
Admin Plan: s8p3; s9p1; s11p2; s24p4

CENSUS TRACTS 51
HUD-52648: p3 (5); p4 (8);
7420.10G Gbk: 2-4 (6); 7-3 (4); 7-5; 7-10 (4); 8-3; 8-9; 9-3;
PIH Notices: 02-20 (2); 01-06 (5); 01-01 (2); 00-46 (2); 00-24B (5);
Admin Plan: s8p3; s11p2; s21p9; s24p1

CENTRAL 41
24 CFR 982: .609;
HUD-50058Instr: p73;

HUD-52580-A: p15 (3);
HUD-52667: p ii;
HUD-903: p2;
7420.10G Gbk: 2-13 Ex 2-1; 7-5 (3); 8-8; 8-9; 9-13 Ex 9-1; 9-15 Ex 9-2; 9-17 Ex 9-3; 10-8 (2); 17-3 (2); 18-1;
PIH Notices: 03-23 (13); 00-53; 00-14; 00-11 (2); 95-48; 95-48 Tech Asst;
Admin Plan: s19p1

CENTRALIZED 3
7420.10G Gbk: 4-13 (2); 4-13

CENTRALLY 2
24 CFR 982: .517;
HUD-52667: p i

CEREBRAL PALSY 8
PIH Notices: 95-48 (4); 95-48 Tech Asst (3); 95-48 Tech Asst

CERTIFICATE 269
24 CFR 5: .100; .350; .504; .514 (3); .520 (3); .630; .632; .653; .655; .657; .659; .801 (3);
24 CFR 35 SubM: .1200 (2);
24 CFR 982: Intro; .1 (4); .2; .4 (4); .102; .201; .353; .355; .403 (2); .501 (3); .502 (4); .516; .521 (2); .555; .619; .623 (2);
HUD-50058: p10; p x; p13; p xiii;
HUD-50058Instr: p1 (2); p2; p5; p7; p9; p10 (2); p12 (2); p15; p42 (7); p53 (3); p61; p71; p72; p74;
HUD-52580-A: p15; p18;
HUD-52648: p2;
HUD-52665: p1 (9); p2 (4); p3;
HUD-52667: p i;
7420.10G Gbk: 1-1 (2); 1-3 (5); 1-4 (8); 1-5 (5); 4-25 Ex 4-2; 5-28; 5-29; 5-37 (2); 5-40; 5-50 Ex 5-5 (3); 10-10; 10-15; 14-1; 14-2; 14-3 (9); 14-4 (3); 20-8 Ex 20-1 (3); 21-17 (3); 21-18 (3); 21-19; 23-1 (3); 24-14;
PIH Notices: 02-21 (2); 01-43; 01-41 (7); 01-33 (5); 01-20 (3); 01-10 (22); 01-06 (5); 01-02 (3); 00-49 (4); 00-28 (3); 00-27 (2); 00-24B (8); 00-23 (2); 00-14 (2); 00-11; 00-09 (19); 99-52 (3); 96-65 (2);
Admin Plan: s3p1 (3); s7p7 (4); s15p6; s16p3; s20p2; s20p6; s21p5; s21p6 (4); s21p7; s24p5

CERTIFICATE OF DEPOSIT 1
7420.10G Gbk 5-28

CERTIFICATES 87
HUD-50058: p2; p10 (2); p x (4); p13; p xiii (3);
HUD-50058Instr: p ii (2); p1; p9; p10; p42 (4); p53 (2); p72 (3); p73; p76; p78 (2);
7420.10G Gbk: 1-1; 1-4; 1-5 (2); 1-6 Ex 1-1 (5); 2-11; 3-7; 4-26 Ex 4-2 (2); 5-25 Ex 5-3; 5-27; 5-48 Ex 5-5; 5-49 Ex 5-5; 5-50 Ex 5-5 (2); 12-13 Ex 12-1; 14-1 (3); 14-2 (2); 14-3; 14-5 (2); 24-15;
PIH Notices: 02-01 (3); 01-33; 01-15 Impr Integ Hbk (5); 01-10 (4); 01-06; 00-28; 00-14; 00-09 (2); 99-52 (5); 99-11 (2); 96-65;
Admin Plan: s2p2; s7p5; s7p6

CERTIFICATES OF DEPOSIT 9
7420.10G Gbk: 4-26 Ex 4-2 (2); 5-27; 5-48 Ex 5-5; 5-49 Ex 5-5;
PIH Notices: 01-15 Impr Integ Hbk (2);
Admin Plan: s7p5; s7p6

CERTIFICATION 311
24 CFR 5: .216 (14); .218 (2); .234 (2); .659;
24 CFR 982: .53 (2); .308; .312; .503; .507; .551 (3); .553; .631;
HUD-52517: p2 (2);
HUD-52580: p5 (4);
HUD-52580-A: p2; p13; p17 (5); p18 (2);
HUD-52641: p5;
HUD-52648: p1 (4); p3 (3); p4;
HUD-52665: p1 (2); p2 (2);
7420.10G Gbk: 1-10; 1-11 (2); 3-8 (2); 4-15; 4-27 Ex 4-2; 5-4; 5-12 (2); 5-22; 5-25 Ex 5-3; 5-27; 5-28; 5-31; 5-35; 5-45; 5-50 Ex 5-5 (2); 5-51 Ex 5-5; 5-52 Ex 5-5; 8-21; 9-3; 10-19 (2); 10-21 (2); 10-22 (2); 10-31; 10-36 Ex 10-

1; 10-37 Ex 10-2; 11-11; 11-12 (3); 11-19; 12-4; 12-5 (2); 12-11 (4); 12-13 Ex 12-1 (2); 13-10; 18-10; 19-5 (2); 19-13; 20-4; 20-5; 22-4; 23-3; 23-5 (2); 23-8 Ex 23-1 (2); 24-3;
PIH Notices: 02-27 (14); 02-21 (5); 02-20; 02-14; 01-41 (4); 01-15 (2); 01-15 Impr Integ Hbk (7); 01-06 (67); 01-01 (10); 00-49 (3); 00-34 (10); 00-24; 00-24A (5); 00-24B (3); 00-09 (4); 95-48 (5); 95-48 Tech Asst (5);
Admin Plan: s2p1; s2p5 (2); s6p1; s6p10 (3); s7p6 (3); s7p7 (5); s7p8 (3); s8p2; s15p6; s18p8 (2); s20p1; s20p2 (4); s20p6; s21p2 (4); s21p3 (2); s21p4 (2); s21p5 (2); s21p6 (2); s21p9; s23p4; s24p5 (3); s25p6

CERTIFICATIONS..........................57
24 CFR 5: .216 (2); .703;
HUD-52517: p2;
7420.10G Gbk: 5-28; 10-31; 10-34; 12-3; 22-8;
PIH Notices: 02-27 (7); 01-41 (6); 01-06 (12); 00-34 (11); 00-24 (3); 00-24B; 00-09 (6);
Admin Plan: s3p3; s7p6

CERTIFIED....................................47
24 CFR 982: .612;
HUD-52517: p2;
HUD-52580: p5 (2);
HUD-52580-A: p2 (2); p13 (2); p17 (4);
7420.10G Gbk: 4-7 (2); 8-15; 10-16; 10-19; 10-20 (2); 10-23; 10-31; 10-37 Ex 10-2 (5); 23-10;
PIH Notices: 01-15 Impr Integ Hbk; 01-06; 00-23; 95-48 (2); 95-48 Tech Asst (2);
Admin Plan: s6p7; s7p1; s7p7; s19p1; s20p6; s20p7; s22p2; s24p4; s25p1 (3); s25p3; s25p3

CERTIFIED COPY...........................1
Admin Plan: s7p7

CERTIFIED MAIL...........................2
7420.10G Gbk: 4-7;
Admin Plan: s20p7

CERTIFIES.....................................26
24 CFR 5: .303; .508;
24 CFR 35 SubM: .1225;
24 CFR 982: .507; .622;
HUD-52641: p3; p5; p6; 8;
HUD-52641-A: p1;
7420.10G Gbk: 5-6; 9-3; 10-21; 10-22; 10-37 Ex 10-2; 11-14; 17-12; 23-14;
PIH Notices: 01-06; 01-01 (3);
Admin Plan: s7p6; s10p1; s14p2; s19p1

CERTIFY.......................................48
24 CFR 5: .234 (2);
HUD-50058Instr: p72;
HUD-52517: p2;
HUD-52648: p3 (2);
HUD-52665: p1; p2;
7420.10G Gbk: 3-8 (2); 4-17; 4-23 Ex 4-1; 4-27 Ex 4-2; 5-6; 5-12; 5-13; 8-15 (3); 9-17 Ex 9-3; 9-19 Ex 9-4; 10-36 Ex 10-1; 12-5; 12-16 Ex 12-4; 18-9; 19-5; 22-2; 23-2; 23-14;
PIH Notices: 03-12; 02-27 (6); 02-01; 01-06 (3); 01-02; 01-01; 99-52;
Admin Plan: s1p4; s2p3; s2p6; s7p8; s16p2

CERTIFYING.................................15
24 CFR 5: .508;
HUD-52665: p1; p2;
7420.10G Gbk: 12-4; 20-3; 21-2; 22-2; 24-8; 24-9;
PIH Notices: 02-21; 01-41; 00-09;
Admin Plan: s7p5; s7p6; s11p2

CHANGE.....................................200
24 CFR 5: .240; .350; .657; .801;
24 CFR 982: .51; .53; .205; .401; .403; .451; .505 (2); .516 (3); .517;
HUD-50058: p2; p ii; p ix; p x; p xi; p xii; p xiii; p xiv; p xv;
HUD-50058Instr: p6 (3); p9 (2); p10; p11 (2); p12; p39; p42; p46; p50; p56; p58; p77;
HUD-52580-A: p1; p8;
HUD-52641: p2; p4 (2); p10 (2);
HUD-52641-A: p3 (2);
HUD-52646: p1 (2);
HUD-52665: p2 (2);
7420.10G Gbk: 1-5; 1-15; 2-4; 3-1; 3-5 (2); 4-5 (4); 4-9; 4-10 (2); 4-16 (2); 5-12; 5-17 (2); 5-38; 5-

51 Ex 5-5; 6-8; 7-7 (4); 7-8 (2); 8-23; 9-7; 10-2; 10-15; 11-5 (2); 11-6; 11-18 (3); 12-1; 12-2; 12-5; 12-6 (2); 12-9 (2); 12-10 (3); 13-6; 14-2; 15-4; 15-7; 16-2; 18-1 (2); 18-8 (2); 18-9; 18-10; 19-2; 20-3; 20-17; 20-27; 21-5; 21-10; 22-2; 22-6; 22-12 (6); 22-13; 23-9; 24-11;
PIH Notices: 02-27 (2); 02-06 (2); 01-41 (6); 01-27 (2); 01-15 Impr Integ Hbk (3); 01-10 (7); 01-06 (8); 00-34 (2); 00-24B (4); 00-09 (9); 95-48 (3); 95-48 Tech Asst (3);
Admin Plan: s1p4; s1p5; s5p2; s5p3; s6p4; s6p8; s7p2; s7p4; s7p8; s11p3 (3); s11p2 (3); s16p3; s21p4; s23p4 (2); s23p7

CHANGE IN CIRCUMSTANCES ... 1
7420.10G Gbk: 4-5

CHANGED ... 36
24 CFR 5: .630;
HUD-50058: p v;
HUD-50058Instr: p18 (2);
HUD-52665: p2;
7420.10G Gbk: 4-5; 4-22; 6-8; 8-10; 9-7; 10-40 Ex 10-4a; 12-7; 12-10; 21-8; 23-9; 23-10;
PIH Notices: 02-27 (2); 02-20 (2); 01-41; 01-15 Impr Integ Hbk (2); 01-06; 00-46 (2); 00-24A; 00-09; 95-48 (2); 95-48 Tech Asst (2);
Admin Plan: s6p4; s6p13; s13p1; s23p7

CHANGED CIRCUMSTANCES ... 5
24 CFR 5: .630;
7420.10G Gbk: 6-8;
PIH Notices: 01-15 Impr Integ Hbk (2);
Admin Plan: s6p4

CHANGES ... 253
24 CFR 5: .615; .657;
24 CFR 982: Intro; .308 (11); .516;
HUD-50058: p i;
HUD-50058Instr: p1; p3; p11 (4); p38 (2);
HUD-52641: p4; 8; p10 (10);
HUD-52641-A: p1; p3 (10);
HUD-52665: p2 (2);
7420.10G Gbk: 1-5; 2-1; 2-4; 3-1; 3-2; 4-7 (2); 4-10; 5-17; 5-36 Ex 5-4; 7-8; 8-7; 8-22; 9-7 (2); 9-8 (2); 10-24; 10-28; 11-5; 11-8 (4); 11-15 (2); 11-17 (7); 11-18; 12-1 (2); 12-5 (4); 12-7; 12-8 (2); 12-9 (6); 13-5; 13-8 (2); 16-3 (2); 18-4; 20-17 (5); 20-21; 20-28 (3); 21-7 (6); 22-2; 22-5; 22-7; 22-9; 22-10 (4); 22-11; 22-12; 23-4 (2); 23-12 (2); 24-3; 24-10 (2); 24-11; 24-12; 24-13; 24-14;
PIH Notices: 03-23 (5); 03-20; 03-11; 02-27; 02-20; 02-01 (3); 01-41 (6); 01-27; 01-15 (6); 01-15 Impr Integ Hbk (13); 01-11; 01-10 (3); 00-53 (3); 00-46; 00-24 (4); 00-09 (9); 99-52 (3); 95-48 (10); 95-48 Tech Asst (10);
Admin Plan: s1p2 (2); s2p7 (2); s3p2; s5p1; s5p2 (2); s6p5; s6p8 (3); s6p12; s6p13; s7p1; s7p4; s8p1; s8p3; s11p3 (2); s11p2 (7); s20p2; s20p5; s23p6; s25p4

CHARACTER ... 6
HUD-50058Instr: p20 (2);
PIH Notices: 95-48 (2); 95-48 Tech Asst; 95-48 Tech Asst

CHARACTERISTIC ... 6
HUD-50058Instr: p1;
7420.10G Gbk: 5-7;
PIH Notices: 01-15 Impr Integ Hbk; 00-28;
Admin Plan: s21p2; s21p2

CHARACTERISTICS ... 46
24 CFR 5: .655;
24 CFR 982: .202 (2); .605;
HUD-50058: p i (2);
HUD-50058Instr: p2; p14; p74;
HUD-52580: p6;
HUD-52580-A: p19;
7420.10G Gbk: 1-11; 2-3; 4-3; 4-9; 4-19; 4-21; 4-25 Ex 4-2; 9-14 Ex 9-1; 12-3; 12-5; 19-1 (2); 19-3 (3); 19-8 (2); 20-4; 23-4; 23-19;
PIH Notices: 01-41 (2); 01-15; 01-15 Impr Integ Hbk (2); 01-11; 01-06 (2); 00-53; 00-24; 00-14; 00-09; 95-48; 95-48 Tech Asst;

Admin Plan: s5p1

CHARACTERISTIC'S....................1
7420.10G Gbk: 13-8

CHARACTERIZE............................2
PIH Notices: 95-48; 95-48 Tech Asst

CHARACTERIZED.........................1
7420.10G Gbk: 10-18

CHARACTERS................................9
HUD-50058Instr: p16;
PIH Notices: 02-20 (2); 00-46 (2); 95-48 (2); 95-48 Tech Asst; 95-48 Tech Asst

CHARGE.......................................76
24 CFR 5: .318 (4); .630;
24 CFR 982: .54; .352 (2); .405; .451; .510; .619 (7); .622; .635;
HUD-50058: p15; p xv (4);
HUD-50058Instr: p40; p56; p58 (5); p68;
HUD-52641: 8;
HUD-52641-A: p1;
7420.10G Gbk: 6-8; 9-7 (2); 9-9; 9-12; 10-20; 10-31; 11-7 (2); 17-6; 17-10 (3); 17-11; 17-12 (2); 22-14; 22-16;
PIH Notices: 03-11 (3); 02-21 (3); 01-20 (3); 01-15 (2); 01-15 Impr Integ Hbk; 00-53 (2); 00-24B;
Admin Plan: s7p2; s18p5; s19p1 (5); s19p1

CHARGED....................................86
24 CFR 5: .234; .318;
24 CFR 982: .4; .155; .313 (2); .507 (3); .622 (2);
HUD-50058Instr: p72; p75;
HUD-52517: p2 (2);
HUD-52641: p1; p4 (2); p5; 8; p10 (2);
HUD-52641-A: p1; p2; p3;
7420.10G Gbk: 3-5; 3-6; 7-1; 8-4; 8-5 (2); 8-15; 8-16; 8-18 (2); 9-1 (2); 9-3 (3); 9-8; 9-12; 9-13 Ex 9-1 (2); 9-14 Ex 9-1; 9-16 Ex 9-2; 11-1; 11-11; 11-12; 11-13; 17-9 (2); 17-12; 21-4;
PIH Notices: 03-12 (6); 03-11; 02-27 (2); 02-22 (4); 02-21; 01-41; 01-20; 01-15 Impr Integ Hbk (2); 00-24B; 00-09;
Admin Plan: s8p4 (2); s9p1; s10p5; s11p1; s11p2 (2); s19p1; s21p3 (2); s24p4; s24p5

CHARGES......................................44
24 CFR 5: .603;
24 CFR 982: Intro; .451; .452; .510 (3); .623 (4); .624 (2); .635; .643 (2);
HUD-50058: p xiii (3); p xiv;
HUD-50058Instr: p36; p47; p53; p54 (2); p70;
HUD-52641: 8 (3);
HUD-52641-A: p1 (3);
7420.10G Gbk: 6-8; 8-4; 8-5; 11-14; 11-17; 17-12;
PIH Notices: 00-24B (2);
Admin Plan: s9p3; s19p1 (2); s19p1

CHART...29
HUD-50058Instr: p24; p25; p26; p27; p28; p33 (2); p77;
7420.10G Gbk: 1-1; 1-5; 20-24; 21-1 (2); 21-11 (2); 21-12 Ex 21-2; 21-12 Ex 21-3; 21-13 (3); 21-14 Ex 21-4; 21-15 Ex 21-5; 21-16 Ex 21-6 (2); 24-3; 24-4;
PIH Notices: 02-27 (2); 02-27

CHARTS..3
7420.10G Gbk: 4-26 Ex 4-2; 8-2; 21-1

CHECK..177
24 CFR 5: .661;
24 CFR 982: .553;
HUD-50058: p2 (2); p iii; p iv; p5; p x; p xi; p16 (6); p xvi (3); p17; p xvii;
HUD-50058Instr: p11; p13; p21; p41 (2); p42; p46; p59 (6); p60 (4); p63 (2);
HUD-52517: p2;
HUD-52580: p1; p6;
HUD-52580-A: p1 (3); p2 (3); p3; p4 (8); p5; p6 (5); p7; p8 (5); p9 (2); p10 (2); p11 (2); p12 (2); p13 (4); p14 (2); p15 (13); p16; p17 (6); p18 (2); p19;
HUD-52648: p1 (4); p2 (2); p3;
HUD-52665: p2 (2); p3;
HUD-903: p1 (5);
7420.10G Gbk: 4-23 Ex 4-1 (3); 4-25 Ex 4-2 (2); 5-46 Ex 5-5 (4); 5-47 Ex 5-5 (2); 5-49 Ex 5-5; 8-12; 9-14 Ex 9-1; 10-36 Ex 10-1 (2); 10-39 Ex 10-4; 11-1; 11-9 (6); 11-10; 12-13 Ex 12-1 (2);

12-16 Ex 12-4; 13-3 (2); 13-5; 13-7; 17-12; 19-5; 20-21 Ex 20-4; 22-6; 24-14;
PIH Notices: 03-11 (6); 02-20; 01-15; 01-15 Impr Integ Hbk; 00-46; 96-65;
Admin Plan: s2p6; s6p6; s7p4 (3); s7p6; s25p6; s25p6

CHECK RUN 7
7420.10G Gbk: 11-9 (6); 11-9

CHECK STUB....................................1
7420.10G Gbk: 5-46 Ex 5-5

CHECK STUBS 2
7420.10G Gbk: 12-13 Ex 12-1;
Admin Plan: s7p4

CHECKED.......................................12
HUD-50058: p5;
HUD-50058Instr: p21;
HUD-52580-A: p1; p8; p15;
HUD-52665: p3;
HUD-903: p1;
7420.10G Gbk: 10-10; 20-27;
PIH Notices: 01-15; 01-15 Impr Integ Hbk;
Admin Plan: s20p4

CHECKING......................................13
24 CFR 5: .236;
7420.10G Gbk: 4-23 Ex 4-1; 4-26 Ex 4-2 (3); 5-25 Ex 5-3; 5-49 Ex 5-5 (2); 12-13 Ex 12-1; 12-16 Ex 12-4;
PIH Notices: 01-15 Impr Integ Hbk (2);
Admin Plan: s7p6

CHECKING ACCOUNT..................4
7420.10G Gbk: 4-26 Ex 4-2; 12-16 Ex 12-4;
PIH Notices: 01-15 Impr Integ Hbk;
Admin Plan: s7p6

CHECKING ACCOUNTS 3
7420.10G Gbk: 5-25 Ex 5-3; 5-49 Ex 5-5;
PIH Notices: 01-15 Impr Integ Hbk

CHECKLIST....................................32
HUD-52580: p1 (11); p2; p6 (3); p8 (6); p13; p15;
7420.10G Gbk: 8-8; 9-10; 9-19 Ex 9-4; 10-1; 10-26; 10-27 (2);
PIH Notices: 01-15 Impr Integ Hbk; 01-06

CHECKLISTS 2
7420.10G Gbk: 10-3; 10-24

CHECK-OUT 10
PIH Notices: 95-48 (5); 95-48 Tech Asst (4); 95-48 Tech Asst

CHECK-RUNS 1
7420.10G Gbk: 11-10

CHECKS...48
24 CFR 982: .553;
HUD-52580-A: p1 (3);
7420.10G Gbk: 5-46 Ex 5-5 (3); 5-47 Ex 5-5; 5-48 Ex 5-5; 5-51 Ex 5-5 (3); 5-52 Ex 5-5; 11-7 (4); 11-8 (2); 11-9 (6); 11-10 (3); 20-23 (3); 20-26; 21-4; 21-5; 22-6; 24-12;
PIH Notices: 03-11 (3); 02-20; 01-15; 01-15 Impr Integ Hbk (5); 00-46;
Admin Plan: s7p7

CHECK-UPS 1
HUD-50058Instr: p61

CHEMICAL.......................................1
7420.10G Gbk: 10-19

CHILD 198
24 CFR 5: .403; .504; .508 (4); .603 (3); .609 (3); .611;
24 CFR 35 SubM: .1200; .1225 (8);
24 CFR 982: .201 (2); .306; .402; .551 (4); .632;
HUD-50058: p3; p4; p6; p7; p16;
HUD-50058Instr: p14 (3); p15 (5); p28 (3); p30 (5); p31; p32 (2); p36; p60 (3); p61 (3); p70 (4); p72 (3); p76;
HUD-52517: p2 (2); p13; p17;
HUD-52641: p5; p6 (2); 8;
HUD-52641-A: p1;
HUD-52646: p2 (3);
7420.10G Gbk: 1-7 (4); 1-15; 4-26 Ex 4-2 (2); 4-27 Ex 4-2; 5-1; 5-4; 5-9 Ex 5-1 (4); 5-14 Ex 5-2; 5-15 Ex 5-2; 5-16 Ex 5-2 (2); 5-19; 5-23 (2); 5-29; 5-30; 5-41; 5-47 Ex 5-5; 8-15; 8-19; 10-16; 10-20 (5); 10-22; 11-2; 12-13 Ex 12-1; 12-16 Ex 12-4; 16-5; 20-4 (3); 23-4;
PIH Notices: 02-07 (3); 02-01; 01-15 (2); 01-15 Impr Integ Hbk (19); 00-49 (7); 00-23 (4); 00-11; 00-11A; 99-52; 95-48 (2); 95-48 Tech Asst (2);
Admin Plan: s2p2; s5p1; s6p2; s6p4 (3); s6p6 (3); s6p8; s6p9 (5); s6p10; s6p11 (5);

s7p4; s7p6 (3); s8p6; s16p2; s21p4; s25p1 (2); s25p1

CHILD ABUSE 1
Admin Plan: s6p11

CHILD CARE................................ 29
7420.10G Gbk: 4-12; 4-13; 4-27 Ex 4-2 (2); 5-15 Ex 5-2; 5-16 Ex 5-2 (2); 5-28; 5-29 (7); 5-30 (3); 5-52 Ex 5-5; 8-8; 10-12; 10-16; 12-11; 12-13 Ex 12-1; 13-1; 23-4; 23-15; 23-16 Ex 23-2; 23-16 Ex 23-2

CHILD CARE................................ 71
24 CFR 5: .603 (3); .609; .611;
24 CFR 982: .632;
HUD-50058: p16;
HUD-50058Instr: p28 (3); p30 (2); p60 (3); p61 (3); p70 (3); p76;
7420.10G Gbk: 4-12; 4-13; 4-27 Ex 4-2 (2); 5-15 Ex 5-2; 5-16 Ex 5-2 (2); 5-28; 5-29 (7); 5-30 (3); 5-52 Ex 5-5; 8-8; 12-11; 12-13 Ex 12-1; 13-1; 23-4; 23-15; 23-16 Ex 23-2 (2);
PIH Notices: 02-01; 01-15 Impr Integ Hbk (8); 00-11; 00-11A; 99-52;
Admin Plan: s6p2; s6p4 (3); s6p10; s6p11; s7p6 (3); s21p4

CHILD CARE EXPENSES 9
24 CFR 5: .603; .611;
HUD-50058Instr: p70;
PIH Notices: 01-15 Impr Integ Hbk (3);
Admin Plan: s6p2; s6p10; s7p6

CHILD SUPPORT 25
24 CFR 5: .609;
HUD-50058: p6;
HUD-50058Instr: p30;
7420.10G Gbk: 4-26 Ex 4-2 (2); 5-14 Ex 5-2; 5-19; 5-23 (2); 5-29; 5-47 Ex 5-5; 12-13 Ex 12-1; 12-16 Ex 12-4; 16-5;
PIH Notices: 01-15 (2); 01-15 Impr Integ Hbk (3);
Admin Plan: s6p9 (5); s7p4

CHILDCARE................................. 41
HUD-50058: p7; p vii (2); p16; p xvi;
HUD-50058Instr: p36 (8);
7420.10G Gbk: 4-15; 23-5;
PIH Notices: 01-15 (9); 01-15 Impr Integ Hbk (2); 00-11 (2); 00-11A;
Admin Plan: s6p2; s6p10 (2); s6p11 (7); s7p3; s7p6

CHILD-CARE 1
7420.10G Gbk: 10-17

CHILDREN 229
24 CFR 5: .403; .518; .522 (2); .603 (2); .609 (3);
24 CFR 35 SubM: .1200 (2); .1225 (2);
24 CFR 982: .201; .202 (2); .315; .401 (2); .605;
HUD-50058: p iii; p iv; p v; p ix; p x; p xi; p xii; p xiii; p xiv (2); p16; p xvi;
HUD-50058Instr: p14; p17 (2); p22; p25 (4); p26 (2); p27 (2); p31; p34 (2); p36 (2); p40 (2); p44 (2); p48 (2); p51 (2); p54 (2); p57 (2); p60 (2); p61; p68; p69; p70; p71; p72 (4); p76;
HUD-52580: p1 (2); p2; p13 (2); p17;
HUD-52648: p3 (5); p4 (13);
HUD-903: p1 (2);
HUD-903-1: p2; p4 (2);
7420.10G Gbk: 1-7 (2); 2-1; 2-4 (6); 2-7; 3-4; 4-19 (2); 4-23 Ex 4-1; 5-1; 5-4 (2); 5-15 Ex 5-2; 5-19; 5-29; 5-42; 5-43; 5-52 Ex 5-5 (3); 7-9; 7-10 (4); 10-2 (2); 10-6 (2); 10-11; 10-12 (4); 10-15; 10-16 (3); 10-17 (2); 10-20 (2); 10-21; 10-22 (4); 10-23; 10-36 Ex 10-1; 23-6;
PIH Notices: 02-27; 01-15; 01-15 Impr Integ Hbk (7); 01-06 (7); 00-24B (7); 00-23 (11); 00-11; 99-11; 95-48 (6); 95-48 Tech Asst (6);
Admin Plan: s2p2 (2); s2p3 (2); s2p4 (3); s5p1; s6p2; s6p6 (4); s6p7 (3); s6p10; s7p6; s8p1; s8p5; s21p9; s23p4; s23p7; s25p1

CHILDREN'S.....................................
3
HUD-50058: p16;
PIH Notices: 95-48; 95-48 Tech Asst

CHILDS 1
7420.10G Gbk: 24-5

CHILD'S 10
24 CFR 35 SubM: .1225;
HUD-50058Instr: p29;
7420.10G Gbk: 5-30; 5-31; 10-20 (3); 10-22;
PIH Notices: 02-07;
Admin Plan: s2p2

CHRONIC 2
7420.10G Gbk: 20-9;
Admin Plan: s25p3

CHRONICALLY 1
24 CFR 5: .318

CHRONICALLY MENTALLY ILL .. 1
24 CFR 5: .318

CHRONOLOGICAL 2
7420.10G Gbk: 4-10; 4-10

CHRONOLOGICALLY 1
7420.10G Gbk: 1-1

CHURCH 4
7420.10G Gbk: 4-3; 8-9;
PIH Notices: 03-11;
Admin Plan: s7p7

CHURCHES 5
7420.10G Gbk: 4-3; 8-12; 9-6; 21-6;
Admin Plan: s3p1

CIAP 7
PIH Notices: 02-21; 02-01 (2); 01-20; 00-27; 99-52; 99-52

CIRCUMSTANCE 12
24 CFR 982: .312;
HUD-50058Instr: p9;
7420.10G Gbk: 23-14;
PIH Notices: 02-06; 01-41 (3); 01-06; 00-09 (3);
Admin Plan: s18p8

CIRCUMSTANCES 198
24 CFR 5: .230; .353; .363; .508; .516 (2); .603; .630 (2);
24 CFR 982: .102 (5); .201; .310; .402; .403; .451; .552 (4); .553; .555 (2); .625; .630;
HUD-50058Instr: p9 (4); p10; p76;
HUD-52580-A: p15;
HUD-903: p2 (2);
7420.10G Gbk: 1-6; 1-7 (2); 1-9; 1-11; 3-1; 3-2 (2); 3-5 (2); 3-6; 4-1 (2); 4-2; 4-5; 4-11; 4-17; 4-19; 5-1; 5-7; 5-17; 5-21; 5-34; 5-38 (3); 5-41; 6-8 (4); 8-12 (2); 10-27; 10-33; 11-3; 11-6 (2); 11-7; 12-1; 12-2; 12-5; 12-6; 12-9; 14-2; 14-5; 15-6; 16-1 (2); 16-2; 16-5; 19-7; 20-14; 20-15; 20-16; 20-25; 20-28 (3); 21-3; 21-8; 21-9 (2); 22-1 (5); 22-5; 22-12; 22-14 (4); 23-2 (2); 23-3; 23-7; 23-9; 23-13; 24-8;
PIH Notices: 03-11 (2); 03-05 (2); 02-27; 02-20 (2); 02-14; 02-06 (3); 02-01 (3); 01-41 (12); 01-40 (2); 01-15 Impr Integ Hbk (4); 01-06 (3); 00-46 (2); 00-24A; 00-24B; 00-09 (10); 99-52 (3); 95-48 (2); 95-48 Tech Asst (2);
Admin Plan: s2p1; s3p2; s5p2; s6p4 (3); s6p8; s6p9; s14p1; s15p4; s15p6; s18p6; s18p8 (2); s20p1 (2); s20p2; s20p3; s20p4; s20p6; s20p7 (2); s23p4; s24p1

CITIES 6
24 CFR 982: .503;
PIH Notices: 02-20 (2); 01-02; 00-46; 00-46

CITIZEN 35
24 CFR 5: .504 (3); .506; .508 (2); .522 (2);
24 CFR 982: .201;
HUD-50058: p3; p4;
HUD-50058Instr: p15 (2); p40; p44; p48; p51; p54; p57; p68 (2); p70 (2); p74;
7420.10G Gbk: 5-4 (3); 5-9 Ex 5-1;
PIH Notices: 01-27;
Admin Plan: s2p1; s2p5 (2); s6p11; s15p1; s18p7

CITIZENS 33
24 CFR 5: .506 (3); .508;
HUD-50058: p v (2);
HUD-50058Instr: p17 (2); p68;
7420.10G Gbk: 5-3; 5-4 (2); 5-5 (3); 6-6; 6-7 (2);
PIH Notices: 01-41; 01-27 (9); 00-41; 00-09 (2);
Admin Plan: s1p1; s6p12

CITIZEN'S 1
PIH Notices: 01-27

CITIZENSHIP 85
24 CFR 5: .500; .504 (4); .508 (7); .514 (2); .520 (2); .659;

24 CFR 982: .551; .552 (2);
HUD-50058: p3 (7); p iii; p4 (7); p iv;
HUD-50058Instr: p15 (4); p18 (4); p40; p44; p48; p51; p54; p57; p68; p71 (2); p73 (2);
HUD-52646: p2;
7420.10G Gbk: 1-14; 5-1 (2); 5-3; 5-4 (3); 5-6 (3); 5-8; 5-9 Ex 5-1 (2); 5-35; 12-5 (2); 13-3; 15-5; 19-4; 22-3;
PIH Notices: 01-27 (2); 01-15 Impr Integ Hbk;
Admin Plan: s2p1; s2p2; s2p5; s3p3; s7p3; s18p1

CITY 78
24 CFR 5: .518;
HUD-50058: p5 (2);
HUD-50058Instr: p20 (4);
HUD-52517: p1 (4); p15 (4); p17 (2);
HUD-52641: p2;
HUD-52667: p ii;
HUD-903: p1 (3); p3 (2); p4; p5;
7420.10G Gbk: 4-23 Ex 4-1; 4-25 Ex 4-2; 7-5; 10-10; 10-38 Ex 10-3 (2); 10-39 Ex 10-4 (2); 10-40 Ex 10-4a; 21-1;
PIH Notices: 02-27; 02-14; 01-06; 01-02; 01-01 (3); 95-48 (11); 95-48 Tech Asst (11);
Admin Plan: s1p1; s1p6; s3p1 (2); s6p13; s9p2; s10p3; s11p2 (2); s11p3; s25p7 (2); s25p7

CITY GOVERNMENT 1
24 CFR 5: .518

CIVIL ACTION 2
HUD-9886: p2;
PIH Notices: 03-11

CIVIL PENALTIES 2
24 CFR 5: .238;
HUD-52648: p3

CIVIL RIGHTS 50
24 CFR 5: .100; .105; .524;
24 CFR 982: .53 (2);
HUD-50058: p i;
HUD-903: p3;
7420.10G Gbk: 3-8 (2); 5-11; 5-42 (2); 22-15;
PIH Notices: 02-01 (2); 01-20 (2); 01-15; 01-02; 99-52 (2); 95-48 (16); 95-48 Tech Asst (12);
Admin Plan: s1p2

CLASS 25
24 CFR 5: .353;
24 CFR 982: .554; .555;
7420.10G Gbk: 4-7; 5-11; 16-2 (2); 23-8 Ex 23-1; 23-16 Ex 23-2;
PIH Notices: 02-01; 99-52; 95-48 (4); 95-48 Tech Asst (4);
Admin Plan: s6p13; s10p3; s18p2; s18p4; s23p6; s25p5

CLASSES 17
24 CFR 982: .161 (2);
HUD-50058Instr: p60; p61;
HUD-52641: p6;
7420.10G Gbk: 5-11; 23-8 Ex 23-1; 23-16 Ex 23-2 (2);
PIH Notices: 02-21 (2); 95-48 (3); 95-48 Tech Asst (2); 95-48 Tech Asst

CLASSIFICATION 1
PIH Notices: 02-06

CLASSIFICATIONS 2
PIH Notices: 95-48; 95-48 Tech Asst

CLASSIFIED 2
HUD-50058Instr: p9;
7420.10G Gbk: 18-2

CLASSIFY 4
24 CFR 982: .517;
HUD-50058Instr: p9 (2);
7420.10G Gbk: 18-2

CLEAN 9
7420.10G Gbk: 10-11;
PIH Notices: 02-01; 99-52; 95-48 (3); 95-48 Tech Asst (2); 95-48 Tech Asst

CLEANING 4
HUD-52580: p6;
HUD-52580-A: p19;
PIH Notices: 95-48; 95-48 Tech Asst

CLEANLINESS 6
24 CFR 982: .401; .605; .614;
HUD-52580: p6;
HUD-52580-A: p19;
7420.10G Gbk: 10-3

CLEANUP 1
PIH Notices: 00-49

CLEARANCE 71
24 CFR 35 SubM: .1215 (2); .1225 (2);
HUD-52580-A: p2 (2); p13; p17 (2);
7420.10G Gbk: 10-7; 10-8; 10-11; 10-16 (2); 10-17 (2);

10-18; 10-19 (5); 10-21 (3); 10-37 Ex 10-2 (4); 10-38 Ex 10-3 (5); 20-4 (7); 20-5;
PIH Notices: 02-07 (2); 00-49 (26); 00-49

CLEARANCE TEST......................14
7420.10G Gbk: 10-37 Ex 10-2; 20-4; 20-5;
PIH Notices: 02-07 (2); 00-49 (8); 00-49

CLEARANCE TESTING................18
HUD-52580-A: p2; p13; p17;
7420.10G Gbk: 10-38 Ex 10-3 (3); 20-4 (4);
PIH Notices: 00-49 (7); 00-49

CLEARANCE TESTS.......................7
7420.10G Gbk: 20-4 (2);
PIH Notices: 00-49 (4); 00-49

CLEARINGHOUSE..........................1
PIH Notices: 00-53

CLIENT..24
HUD-50058Instr: p3; p5;
7420.10G Gbk: 5-35 (3); 8-9; 21-2 (2); 21-3 (2); 21-5; 21-6; 21-7; 21-9 (4); 21-10; 21-16 Ex 21-6 (2); 22-9;
PIH Notices: 01-15 Impr Integ Hbk;
Admin Plan: s20p3; s25p7

CLIENTELE....................................2
7420.10G Gbk: 9-14 Ex 9-1; 21-9

CLIENTS.......................................13
7420.10G Gbk: 19-6; 21-1; 21-3; 21-5; 21-6 (2); 21-7; 21-8; 21-9;
PIH Notices: 00-11 (3);
Admin Plan: s23p2

CLIMATE...6
24 CFR 982: .401;
HUD-52580-A: p15 (2);
7420.10G Gbk: 10-7 (2); 10-13

CLINIC..2
7420.10G Gbk: 5-51 Ex 5-5;
Admin Plan: s7p7

CLOCK..10
24 CFR 982: .4; .54; .305;
HUD-50058Instr: p75;
7420.10G Gbk: 3-2; 8-13; 8-17; 10-25; 21-9;
Admin Plan: s8p5

CLOSE...23
24 CFR 5: .359;
24 CFR 982: .642;
HUD-52580-A: p2;
HUD-52667: p i;
HUD-903-1: p2;
7420.10G Gbk: 4-4; 4-7 (2); 10-33; 11-9; 11-15; 13-2; 14-4; 19-1; 21-6;
PIH Notices: 03-23; 01-06; 95-48; 95-48 Tech Asst;
Admin Plan: s17p1 (2); s18p2; s25p5

CLOSET...8
24 CFR 982: .605 (3);
HUD-52580-A: p15;
7420.10G Gbk: 17-2 (2);
PIH Notices: 02-01; 99-52

CLOSETS...2
24 CFR 5: .703;
HUD-52580-A: p15

CLOSING.......................................25
24 CFR 982: Intro; .4; .54; .206 (2); .643 (5);
7420.10G Gbk: 1-9; 3-2; 4-2; 4-4 (4); 4-5 (2); 5-49 Ex 5-5;
PIH Notices: 01-41; 00-09;
Admin Plan: s7p6; s22p3; s22p4

CLOTHING.....................................7
24 CFR 5: .609;
HUD-50058Instr: p28;
7420.10G Gbk: 5-15 Ex 5-2; 5-19;
PIH Notices: 01-15; 01-15 Impr Integ Hbk; 01-15 Impr Integ Hbk

COAL...12
HUD-52517: p1 (3);
HUD-52641: p2 (3);
HUD-52667: p1 (3);
7420.10G Gbk: 18-8 (2); 18-8

COALITION.....................................1
PIH Notices: 99-52

COASTAL BARRIER.......................1
Admin Plan: s24p2

COASTAL BARRIERS.....................1
24 CFR 982: .626

CODE..220
24 CFR 5: .214 (2); .653;
24 CFR 982: .605 (2);
HUD-50058: p2; p ii (7); p iii (6); p iv (6); p5 (3); p v (2); p6 (3); p10; p x; p11; p xi; p13; p xiii; p14; p xiv; p16 (3); p xvi (5);
HUD-50058Instr: p1 (2); p5 (2); p7 (13); p8 (3); p9 (2); p10 (3); p11 (2); p14; p15 (4); p16; p17 (2); p19 (5); p20 (7); p24 (4); p25; p26; p27; p28;

p29; p30; p31; p32; p33 (2); p36; p42 (2); p46 (2); p50 (3); p53 (2); p56 (2); p59 (4); p60 (5); p70;
HUD-52517: p1;
HUD-52580-A: p8 (4); p9 (5); p10 (5); p11 (5); p12 (5);
HUD-52641: p1; p3; p6; p7; p10;
HUD-52641-A: p3;
HUD-903: p1 (3);
HUD-903-1: p3; p4; p5;
HUD-9886: p1;
7420.10G Gbk: 1-14; 4-23 Ex 4-1; 4-25 Ex 4-2; 5-7 (2); 8-23; 10-2 (2); 10-3; 10-5; 10-8; 10-15 (2); 10-31; 10-33; 10-35; 10-47 Ex 10-9; 10-48 Ex 10-10; 17-2 (2); 22-6; 24-15;
PIH Notices: 02-27 (3); 02-22 (2); 01-41 (2); 01-15 Impr Integ Hbk (3); 01-06; 00-24; 00-24A; 00-23; 00-09 (2); 99-11 (2); 95-48; 95-48 Tech Asst;
Admin Plan: s4p2; s8p3; s11p2; s20p4; s24p4;
:
7420.10G Gbk: 10-8; 10-31

CODES 71
24 CFR 5: .703 (3);
24 CFR 982: .306; .401 (2); .605;
HUD-50058: p ii (2); p3; p iii (2); p4; p iv (2); p6; p16; p xvi;
HUD-50058Instr: p ii; p1 (2); p7 (4); p9; p13 (2); p14 (2); p15 (4); p17; p20; p40; p44; p48; p51; p54; p57; p63; p64; p68;
HUD-52580: p1;
HUD-52580-A: p8; p15 (3);
HUD-52641: p7;
7420.10G Gbk: 8-19; 10-2 (3); 10-7 (2); 10-14 (3); 10-25; 11-3; 17-2; 19-7;
PIH Notices: 02-01; 99-52; 99-11 (2);
Admin Plan: s11p2; s22p4; s24p5

COERCE 1
HUD-903-1: p2

COERCED 1
HUD-903: p1

COERCION 9
HUD-903: p2;
PIH Notices: 95-48 (4); 95-48 Tech Asst (3); 95-48 Tech Asst

COHEAD 4
HUD-50058Instr: p15; p34; p35; p36

CO-HEAD 49
HUD-50058: p3; p4; p7 (6); p vii (6);
HUD-50058Instr: p2; p14 (7); p15; p26; p35 (10); p36; p71;
7420.10G Gbk: 5-2 (2);
Admin Plan: s2p2 (4); s3p2; s7p3; s7p5; s8p5 (2); s11p1; s11p1

COIN COLLECTIONS 1
7420.10G Gbk: 5-25 Ex 5-3

COINSURANCE 1
24 CFR 5: .210

COINSURED 2
24 CFR 5: .214; .801

COLLABORATE 1
PIH Notices: 00-11

COLLABORATED 1
7420.10G Gbk: 9-4

COLLABORATING 1
PIH Notices: 02-27

COLLABORATION 3
PIH Notices: 00-11 (2); 00-11

COLLABORATIONS 1
Admin Plan: s1p1

COLLECT 42
24 CFR 982: .313 (2);
HUD-50058: p ii;
HUD-50058Instr: p1; p12; p13;
HUD-52580: p6 (2); p19;
HUD-52641: p10 (2);
HUD-52641-A: p2; p3;
7420.10G Gbk: 4-20; 5-13; 5-47 Ex 5-5 (2); 8-4 (2); 9-4 (2); 9-8 (4); 11-11; 14-5; 22-2; 22-8 (2); 22-11; 24-3;
PIH Notices: 03-11 (2); 00-53 (4); 00-11A;
Admin Plan: s6p11; s8p4; s17p1

COLLECTED 32
HUD-50058Instr: p1 (5);
HUD-903-1: p6;
HUD-9886: p2 (3);
7420.10G Gbk: 4-15 (2); 4-21 (2); 5-6; 5-13; 8-4; 9-3; 9-8 (2); 11-15; 12-3; 21-19; 22-5 (2); 22-13; 22-15 (2);

PIH Notices: 01-06; 00-24; 00-11;
Admin Plan: s10p5; s23p5

COLLECTIBLE................................1
Admin Plan: s17p3

COLLECTING...............................21
24 CFR 5: .661;
24 CFR 982: .452;
HUD-52641: p1; p10;
HUD-52641-A: p2;
7420.10G Gbk: 1-14; 9-8 (2); 10-16; 11-17; 19-5; 20-25; 22-2 (3); 22-13; 22-15 (2); 24-4;
PIH Notices: 02-27; 96-65

COLLECTION.............................102
24 CFR 5: .210 (3); .212; .214 (2); .659; .661; .703;
24 CFR 35 SubM: .1225;
24 CFR 982: .516; .517 (3); .622 (2);
HUD-50058: p i;
HUD-50058Instr: p2; p71 (2);
HUD-52580: p1 (21); p i (5);
HUD-903: p1 (3);
7420.10G Gbk: 1-2; 5-13; 9-7; 9-13 Ex 9-1; 10-22; 10-32; 20-25; 20-26; 20-29 (3); 22-3; 22-14; 22-17 (2); 24-5;
PIH Notices: 03-23 (4); 03-20 (3); 03-12 (3); 03-11 (3); 02-21 (3); 01-43; 01-15 (4); 01-15 Impr Integ Hbk; 01-06; 00-53 (3); 00-11A;
Admin Plan: s6p9 (4); s7p5; s17p1 (3); s19p1; s19p1

COLLECTION AGENCIES.............9
24 CFR 5: .210; .659;
HUD-9886: p1;
7420.10G Gbk: 5-13;
PIH Notices: 01-15 (3); 01-15 Impr Integ Hbk;
Admin Plan: s17p1

COLLECTION AGENCY................3
24 CFR 5: .214;
7420.10G Gbk: 22-17;
Admin Plan: s6p9

COLLECTION AGENCYS..............1
HUD-50058Instr: p71

COLLECTIONS..............................2
7420.10G Gbk: 5-25 Ex 5-3;
Admin Plan: s17p2

COLLECTIVE..................................1
24 CFR 5: .504

COLLECTIVELY...........................10
24 CFR 5: .500;
PIH Notices: 02-07; 01-41; 01-27 (2); 01-10; 00-49; 00-09 (2); 99-11

COLLECTOR...................................1
7420.10G Gbk: 9-13 Ex 9-1

COLLECTS......................................3
7420.10G Gbk: 4-14; 22-17; 24-4

COLLEGE......................................20
24 CFR 982: .352;
HUD-50058: p16;
HUD-50058Instr: p60; p61 (3);
7420.10G Gbk: 2-1; 8-16; 23-15;
PIH Notices: 95-48 (5); 95-48 Tech Asst (5);
Admin Plan: s6p7

COLOR..32
24 CFR 5: .655;
24 CFR 982: .202; .207; .304;
HUD-52580-A: p15;
HUD-52641: p5; p10;
HUD-52641-A: p3;
HUD-52646: p2;
HUD-903: p1 (2); p2 (3); p4;
7420.10G Gbk: 4-19; 5-11; 5-42 (3); 8-14; 11-13;
PIH Notices: 02-21; 01-15; 95-48 (3); 95-48 Tech Asst (3);
Admin Plan: s1p2; s23p2

COLORADO....................................3
HUD-50058Instr: p64;
HUD-903: p3;
PIH Notices: 03-11

COMBINATION.............................14
24 CFR 982: .401; .503;
HUD-50058: p5;
HUD-50058Instr: p21;
HUD-52667: p i;
7420.10G Gbk: 4-12; 10-6; 13-7; 18-6; 20-13; 21-10;
PIH Notices: 02-20; 00-46; 00-09

COMBINE.......................................7
7420.10G Gbk: 1-4 (3); 2-6; 21-5;
PIH Notices: 00-11; 00-11A

COMBINED..................................22
24 CFR 5: .350;
24 CFR 982: .310;
HUD-50058Instr: p2; p17;
HUD-52641: p9;
HUD-52641-A: p2;
PIH Notices: 02-22; 02-21 (2); 02-20; 01-20 (2); 01-06; 00-46; 00-11; 95-48; 95-48 Tech Asst;

Admin Plan: s6p4; s14p1; s15p4; s23p1; s25p3

COMBINING 1
24 CFR 982: .625

COMMENT 25
24 CFR 5: .353 (2); .380;
24 CFR 982: .207;
HUD-52580: p1; p2; p3; p4; p5;
HUD-52580-A: p6 (3);
7420.10G Gbk: 3-6; 3-7; 4-16 (4);
PIH Notices: 02-27; 01-06 (5); 01-06

COMMENT PERIOD 2
24 CFR 5: .353; .353

COMMERCIAL 17
24 CFR 5: .100; .306;
HUD-50058Instr: p71;
7420.10G Gbk: 4-3; 9-4; 10-13;
PIH Notices: 03-12; 95-48 (4); 95-48 Tech Asst (4);
Admin Plan: s15p3; s20p4

COMMISSION 23
HUD-50058Instr: p25; p30 (2); p32; p72 (2);
7420.10G Gbk: 5-16 Ex 5-2 (3);
PIH Notices: 01-15 (5); 01-15 Impr Integ Hbk (5); 95-48 (2); 95-48 Tech Asst; 95-48 Tech Asst

COMMISSIONER 11
24 CFR 5: .300; .306;
24 CFR 982: .161;
HUD-52641: p6 (2);
7420.10G Gbk: 8-19; 11-2; 16-4;
PIH Notices: 01-41; 01-27; 00-09

COMMISSIONERS 11
24 CFR 982: .54 (2); .155;
HUD-52648: p3;
7420.10G Gbk: 2-5; 3-1; 3-2; 3-6; 19-13 (2); 24-11

COMMISSIONS 10
24 CFR 5: .609;
HUD-50058Instr: p27;
HUD-52667: p i;
7420.10G Gbk: 5-14 Ex 5-2; 5-27; 18-4; 23-12;
PIH Notices: 01-15 Impr Integ Hbk (2); 01-15 Impr Integ Hbk

COMMON AREA 5
24 CFR 5: .703;
7420.10G Gbk: 5-43; 10-40 Ex 10-4a;
PIH Notices: 95-48; 95-48 Tech Asst

COMMON AREAS 49
24 CFR 5: .100; .318; .350; .703 (5);
24 CFR 35 SubM: .1200 (3); .1225 (2);
24 CFR 982: .4; .605;
HUD-50058Instr: p73 (2);
HUD-52517: p2 (3);
HUD-52580-A: p17;
HUD-52641: p10;
HUD-52641-A: p3;
7420.10G Gbk: 5-35; 5-43; 8-15; 10-12; 10-16 (2); 10-17; 10-20 (2); 10-37 Ex 10-2; 10-38 Ex 10-3; 10-39 Ex 10-4; 17-2;
PIH Notices: 02-01 (4); 01-15; 99-52 (4); 95-48; 95-48 Tech Asst;
Admin Plan: s20p2; s23p5

COMMON HALL 2
24 CFR 982: .605;
7420.10G Gbk: 17-2

COMMON HOUSEHOLD PET 8
24 CFR 5: .306 (2); .318; .324 (2); .350 (2); .359

COMMON HOUSEHOLD PETS ... 13
24 CFR 5: .309 (2); .312 (2); .315 (2); .318 (3); .321 (2); .353; .359

COMMON LOBBY 1
24 CFR 5: .353

COMMON SPACE 8
24 CFR 982: .4 (2); .618 (3);
HUD-50058Instr: p75;
7420.10G Gbk: 17-7;
Admin Plan: s19p1

COMMON USE 8
PIH Notices: 02-01 (2); 99-52 (2); 95-48 (2); 95-48 Tech Asst; 95-48 Tech Asst

COMMUNAL LIVING 1
24 CFR 5: .318

COMMUNICATION 79
24 CFR 5: .216;
24 CFR 982: .301;
7420.10G Gbk: 2-2; 2-5; 5-44 (2); 8-3 (2); 8-14; 13-8; 13-9; 22-9; 24-14;
PIH Notices: 02-01 (2); 01-41 (2); 00-09 (3); 99-52 (2); 95-48 (27); 95-48 Tech Asst (27);
Admin Plan: s1p3 (2); s25p8

COMMUNICATIONS 44
24 CFR 5: .502;

7420.10G Gbk: 2-6; 21-9; 21-16 Ex 21-6; 22-8 (2);
PIH Notices: 02-01; 99-52; 95-48 (18); 95-48 Tech Asst (17); 95-48 Tech Asst

COMMUNITIES 21
HUD-50058Instr: p5 (2);
HUD-52667: p i (4);
7420.10G Gbk: 2-1 (2); 9-3 (2); 9-4 (3); 9-5; 9-7; 13-4 (2);
PIH Notices: 00-41; 00-11;
Admin Plan: s1p1; s8p2

COMMUNITY..............................199
24 CFR 5: .327 (2); .360; .500; .504; .653; .661; .703;
24 CFR 982: .310; .352; .517 (2); .614;
HUD-50058: p3 (7); p iii (3); p4 (7); p iv (3); p16 (8); p17 (6); p28; p61 (3); p70; p71 (2); p72; p73; p75;
HUD-52667: p i;
HUD-903: p2;
HUD-9886: p1; p2;
7420.10G Gbk: 1-3 (3); 1-4; 2-4; 2-5 (2); 2-6; 2-11; 2-12 Ex 2-1; 2-13 Ex 2-1 (2); 3-6; 3-8 (2); 4-2 (3); 4-3 (4); 4-9; 5-2; 5-16 Ex 5-2; 5-40; 8-2; 8-4 (2); 8-9; 8-12; 9-3; 9-5; 9-6 (3); 9-11; 9-14 Ex 9-1; 9-17 Ex 9-3; 10-15; 10-20; 10-31; 11-15; 13-1; 13-3; 16-4; 17-4; 17-5; 18-2; 19-6; 19-8 (2); 20-1; 21-1; 21-4 (2); 21-6; 22-1; 22-10 (2); 22-18 (3); 23-4; 23-18 (3); 24-9; 24-12; 24-15;
PIH Notices: 02-22; 02-20 (2); 02-01 (5); 01-41 (2); 01-40; 01-27 (2); 01-15 (3); 01-15 Impr Integ Hbk; 01-10; 01-02 (3); 00-46 (2); 00-41; 00-11 (9); 00-11A (2); 00-09 (3); 99-52 (5); 95-48 (3); 95-48 Tech Asst (3);
Admin Plan: s1p1 (2); s1p4; s1p6 (2); s4p2; s6p2; s6p11; s8p3; s8p4; s11p3; s18p1; s20p1; s20p3; s23p1; s23p2; s25p1 (2); s25p7

COMMUNITY AGENCIES.............2
7420.10G Gbk: 4-3;
Admin Plan: s1p4

COMMUNITY AREA.......................3
7420.10G Gbk: 2-12 Ex 2-1; 2-13 Ex 2-1; 2-13 Ex 2-1

COMMUNITY BUILDERS.............6
PIH Notices: 01-40; 01-27; 01-10; 01-02; 00-11; 00-09

COMMUNITY BUILDINGS............2
PIH Notices: 02-01; 99-52

COMMUNITY COLLEGE 7
HUD-50058: p16;
HUD-50058Instr: p61 (2);
PIH Notices: 95-48 (2); 95-48 Tech Asst; 95-48 Tech Asst

COMMUNITY ORGANIZATIONS .4
7420.10G Gbk: 8-2; 8-12; 23-4;
Admin Plan: s23p2

COMMUNITY ROOM......................2
7420.10G Gbk: 9-14 Ex 9-1; 9-17 Ex 9-3

COMMUNITY ROOMS 2
24 CFR 5: .703;
7420.10G Gbk: 21-6

COMMUNITY SERVICE 47
HUD-50058: p3 (7); p iii (3); p4 (7); p iv (3);
HUD-50058Instr: p16 (7); p17 (6); p28; p70; p71; p75;
7420.10G Gbk: 3-8; 4-3; 5-16 Ex 5-2;
PIH Notices: 01-15 Impr Integ Hbk; 00-11 (4); 00-11A; 00-11A

COMMUNITY SERVICE AGENCIES 2
7420.10G Gbk: 4-3;
Admin Plan: s1p6

COMMUNITY SERVICES...............7
HUD-50058Instr: p72;
7420.10G Gbk: 3-8; 8-4;
PIH Notices: 95-48; 95-48 Tech Asst;
Admin Plan: s25p1; s25p1

COMMUNITY SPACE 3
24 CFR 982: .614;
7420.10G Gbk: 17-4; 17-5

COMMUNITY'S..............................1
7420.10G Gbk: 4-9

COMPANIES...................................... 13
HUD-52667: p ii;
7420.10G Gbk: 2-5; 8-7; 8-8; 8-12; 9-6; 10-25; 18-1; 18-4 (2);

PIH Notices: 95-48; 95-48 Tech Asst;
Admin Plan: s20p1

COMPANIONS 2
PIH Notices: 95-48; 95-48 Tech Asst

COMPANY 35
24 CFR 5: .214;
HUD-903: p1 (2);
HUD-903-1: p5;
7420.10G Gbk: 5-12; 5-25 Ex 5-3; 5-26 (3); 6-6; 9-6; 9-13 Ex 9-1; 12-16 Ex 12-4; 15-9 Ex 15-1;
PIH Notices: 03-11; 02-27 (2); 01-15 Impr Integ Hbk (2); 95-48 (6); 95-48 Tech Asst (6);
Admin Plan: s6p10; s7p7; s7p8; s7p8

COMPANY'S 1
7420.10G Gbk: 18-6

COMPARABILITY 22
24 CFR 982: .507;
7420.10G Gbk: 9-2 (2); 9-6; 9-10; 9-11; 9-12; 9-17 Ex 9-3; 9-19 Ex 9-4; 10-32;
PIH Notices: 03-12 (4); 02-22 (2); 01-41 (5);
Admin Plan: s24p5

COMPARABLE 105
24 CFR 982: .4 (2); .507 (2); .622 (2);
HUD-50058Instr: p27; p29; p75 (2);
HUD-52517: p2 (2);
HUD-52641: p1; p4 (2); p5; 8;
HUD-52641-A: p1 (2);
7420.10G Gbk: 5-39; 8-18 (2); 9-1; 9-2; 9-3; 9-4; 9-5; 9-8; 9-10 (5); 9-12; 9-17 Ex 9-3 (4); 9-19 Ex 9-4 (3); 11-12; 11-13; 17-7; 17-10; 17-11; 17-12 (2); 21-4; 21-19;
PIH Notices: 03-12 (7); 02-27 (2); 02-22 (4); 02-20; 02-01; 01-41 (6); 01-15; 01-15 Impr Integ Hbk (2); 00-46; 00-24B (2); 00-09 (7); 99-52; 95-48 (4); 95-48 Tech Asst (4);
Admin Plan: s11p1 (2); s11p2 (3); s11p3; s19p1 (2); s21p3; s24p4 (2); s24p5

COMPARABLES 4
7420.10G Gbk: 9-10 (2);

PIH Notices: 03-12;
Admin Plan: s11p3

COMPELLING 2
PIH Notices: 95-48; 95-48 Tech Asst

COMPENSATION 45
24 CFR 5: .214 (6); .609 (4); .661;
HUD-50058Instr: p25 (2); p27 (2); p31; p32 (2); p71;
HUD-9886: p1 (2);
7420.10G Gbk: 5-14 Ex 5-2; 5-16 Ex 5-2; 5-20; 23-12;
PIH Notices: 01-15 (2); 01-15 Impr Integ Hbk (11); 95-48; 95-48 Tech Asst;
Admin Plan: s6p10 (2); s7p4 (2); s20p3

COMPETITIVE FUNDING 4
24 CFR 982: .103; .104 (2); .104

COMPETITIVE PROCESS 5
24 CFR 982: .4; .101 (3); .104

COMPLAIN 2
HUD-903: p2; p2

COMPLAINANT 6
PIH Notices: 95-48 (3); 95-48 Tech Asst (2); 95-48 Tech Asst

COMPLAINANTS 6
PIH Notices: 95-48 (3); 95-48 Tech Asst (2); 95-48 Tech Asst

COMPLAINING 2
HUD-903: p1;
7420.10G Gbk: 18-1

COMPLAINT 116
24 CFR 5: .360;
24 CFR 982: .301; .304; .310;
HUD-52580-A: p1 (2);
HUD-52641: p5; p9;
HUD-52641-A: p2 (2);
HUD-903: p1 (9); p2 (5); p3 (6); p6;
7420.10G Gbk: 10-17; 10-21; 10-23; 10-24; 10-28 (5); 11-13; 15-3; 19-12; 21-4; 21-10; 22-15 (4); 22-18;
PIH Notices: 02-01; 99-52; 96-65; 95-48 (28); 95-48 Tech Asst (28);
Admin Plan: s1p3; s8p3; s10p2; s14p1; s18p1 (2); s18p1

COMPLAINTS 94
24 CFR 982: .405;
HUD-903: p1; p3;

HUD-903-1: p6;
7420.10G Gbk: 7-5; 10-2; 10-28 (2); 10-30 (3); 11-9; 22-18 (3); 24-12;
PIH Notices: 96-65; 95-48 (30); 95-48 Tech Asst (30);
Admin Plan: s15p5; s18p1 (11); s18p7; s20p1; s20p3 (2); s23p8

COMPLEMENT................................1
7420.10G Gbk: 23-20

COMPLETION................................76
24 CFR 5: .514 (4); .516;
24 CFR 982: .310; .552;
HUD-50058Instr: p3; p60; p62; p73;
7420.10G Gbk: 4-14 (2); 5-37; 10-19; 10-20; 10-21 (2); 10-26; 10-38 Ex 10-3 (2); 12-2 (2); 12-8; 15-7; 19-6; 19-12; 19-13 (3); 21-2; 21-3; 21-10; 22-6; 23-6; 23-7 (2); 23-8 Ex 23-1 (2); 23-14; 23-15;
PIH Notices: 03-20 (3); 02-27 (10); 02-01; 01-41; 01-06; 00-27; 00-09 (3); 99-52;
Admin Plan: s2p6; s3p2; s10p2; s11p2; s15p5; s20p2; s21p2; s21p8 (2); s22p2; s24p5 (2); s25p5; s25p5

COMPLEX......................................38
24 CFR 5: .100;
24 CFR 982: .4; .308;
HUD-52580-A: p15 (2);
HUD-52641: p10 (2);
HUD-52641-A: p3 (2);
7420.10G Gbk: 4-18 (3); 5-35; 8-5; 8-8; 9-6; 9-8; 10-23; 11-17; 21-3;
PIH Notices: 03-12 (4); 03-11; 02-21; 01-20; 95-48 (5); 95-48 Tech Asst (5);
Admin Plan: s25p3

COMPLIANCE............................259
24 CFR 5: .212 (3); .350 (2); .524; .653; .703; .705; .801 (2);
24 CFR 982: .53; .201 (2); .307; .352; .401; .519; .554; .555; .614; .618; .628; .633;
HUD-50058: p i;
HUD-50058Instr: p17 (2); p19 (2); p75;
HUD-52580-A: p8;
HUD-52641: p4; p5;
HUD-52648: p1;
7420.10G Gbk: 1-13 (2); 1-14; 2-3; 3-8; 4-11; 4-17; 4-18; 4-20 (2); 5-39; 5-45; 7-9; 8-20; 8-21; 10-1; 10-18 (2); 10-21 (3); 10-25; 10-26; 10-27 (3); 10-28; 10-29 (3); 10-30 (2); 10-31; 10-33 (2); 10-34 (4); 10-36 Ex 10-1; 10-37 Ex 10-2; 11-1 (2); 11-13; 11-15; 13-9; 15-9 Ex 15-1; 18-7; 19-3; 19-4; 19-7; 19-12 (2); 19-13; 20-28; 21-14 Ex 21-4; 22-7; 22-10; 22-18; 24-4; 24-14;
PIH Notices: 03-11; 02-27 (4); 02-21; 02-06; 02-01 (23); 01-20; 01-15; 01-15 Impr Integ Hbk; 01-06 (2); 00-53 (2); 00-49 (2); 00-24 (5); 00-24A (3); 00-24B (10); 00-23; 00-11; 00-11A (4); 99-52 (22); 99-11 (2); 95-48 (22); 95-48 Tech Asst (16);
Admin Plan: s1p1; s1p2; s1p3; s2p7; s8p3; s9p3; s9p4; s10p1; s10p2; s10p3; s10p4; s13p1; s14p2; s15p5; s15p6; s16p2; s18p2; s18p4; s19p1 (5); s20p1; s20p2 (2); s20p4; s21p1; s22p3; s22p4; s23p3; s23p5 (3); s24p4 (2); s24p6; s25p5; s25p6

COMPLIANCE AGREEMENTS......1
7420.10G Gbk: 4-11

COMPLIANCE EFFORTS...............2
PIH Notices: 02-01; 99-52

COMPLIANT...................................2
PIH Notices: 02-01; 99-52

COMPLIED....................................16
24 CFR 5: .615 (2);
24 CFR 982: .519;
HUD-52641: p4;
7420.10G Gbk: 5-21; 10-46 Ex 10-8; 15-10 Ex 15-2; 22-6; 23-18;
Admin Plan: s6p12 (3); s11p3; s20p5 (2); s25p6

COMPLY......................................202
24 CFR 5: .107; .236; .321; .350 (2); .403; .653; .703 (2);
24 CFR 982: .4; .52 (2); .54; .153; .158; .201; .206; .308; .355 (4); .401; .453; .552; .554; .614;

.625 (2); .633 (5); .638;
HUD-50058Instr: p16 (2); p70; p73 (2);
HUD-52580-A: p8;
HUD-52641: p3 (2); p5; p7; p9;
HUD-52641-A: p1;
7420.10G Gbk: 1-9; 3-9; 4-1; 4-14; 4-20; 5-11 (2); 5-14 Ex 5-2; 5-21; 5-42; 5-44; 10-19; 10-23 (3); 10-26 (2); 10-27; 10-28 (2); 10-29 (5); 10-34 (2); 11-4; 11-5; 11-12; 11-18 (2); 12-1; 12-3; 14-2; 14-5; 15-1; 15-4; 15-6; 15-10 Ex 15-2; 16-2 (2); 20-1; 21-1; 22-1; 22-9; 23-5; 23-6; 23-9; 23-10 (3); 24-15;
PIH Notices: 03-12 (2); 02-27; 02-21; 02-20; 02-01 (12); 01-41; 01-20; 01-15; 01-06 (3); 00-46; 00-45 (2); 00-11; 00-09; 99-52 (12); 99-11; 96-65 (2); 95-48 (22); 95-48 Tech Asst (18);
Admin Plan: s1p2; s6p8; s8p4; s10p3 (2); s11p3; s13p1; s16p2; s20p1; s20p6 (2); s22p4 (2); s22p5; s23p5; s23p7; s24p1 (2); s24p4

COMPLYING 19
24 CFR 5: .318;
24 CFR 982: .1; .452; .626;
7420.10G Gbk: 1-14 (3); 1-15; 3-2; 5-36 Ex 5-4; 11-17;
PIH Notices: 01-41; 00-09; 96-65; 95-48; 95-48 Tech Asst;
Admin Plan: s1p2; s8p1; s18p1

COMPOSITION 101
24 CFR 5: .403; .601; .615; .657 (4); .659 (2);
24 CFR 982: Intro; .4; .54; .201; .308; .355; .402; .403; .502 (3); .516 (5); .551 (2); .554; .635; .641;
HUD-50058Instr: p10; p12 (3); p72;
HUD-52641: 8;
HUD-52641-A: p1;
HUD-52646: p2;
7420.10G Gbk: 1-15; 3-5 (2); 4-7; 4-10; 4-25 Ex 4-2; 4-27 Ex 4-2; 5-36 Ex 5-4; 5-41 (2); 7-7; 7-8 (2); 8-21; 11-6; 11-14; 11-15; 12-1; 12-3; 12-5 (2); 12-7; 12-9; 12-16 Ex 12-4; 16-2; 20-4; 21-7; 22-10;
PIH Notices: 01-41; 01-33; 01-15 (2); 01-15 Impr Integ Hbk (7); 00-24B; 00-09 (2);
Admin Plan: s2p1; s3p3; s5p1; s5p2 (2); s5p3; s6p5; s6p8 (3); s7p1; s7p8; s8p1; s8p3; s11p1 (2); s11p2; s18p2; s22p4; s23p4; s24p6

COMPREHENSIVE 27
7420.10G Gbk: 3-6 (2); 4-2 (3); 4-13; 9-7; 11-9; 20-1; 22-8;
PIH Notices: 02-27 (5); 02-21 (2); 02-01 (2); 01-20 (2); 01-02; 00-27 (2); 99-52 (2);
Admin Plan: s25p3

COMPREHENSIVE IMPROVEMENT ASSISTANCE 3
PIH Notices: 02-21; 02-01; 99-52

COMPREHENSIVE PLANNING 1
7420.10G Gbk: 3-6

COMPTROLLER 3
24 CFR 982: .158;
PIH Notices: 95-48; 95-48 Tech Asst

COMPTROLLER GENERAL........... 2
HUD-52641: p5;
7420.10G Gbk: 11-13

COMPTROLLER GENERAL........... 3
24 CFR 982: .158;
HUD-52641: p5;
7420.10G Gbk: 11-13

COMPUTATION 3
7420.10G Gbk: 14-2;
Admin Plan: s1p3; s18p3

COMPUTE 20
24 CFR 982: .555;
HUD-50058Instr: p39; p40; p68;
HUD-52667: p1; p i;
7420.10G Gbk: 4-15; 5-33; 5-34; 5-49 Ex 5-5; 11-14; 18-7; 20-28 (2); 23-12;
PIH Notices: 02-27; 02-20; 00-46;
Admin Plan: s6p5; s6p8

COMPUTED ....
19
24 CFR 5: .603 (3);
24 CFR 982: .503;
HUD-50058Instr: p34; p70; p71; p73;

HUD-52667: p i (2);
7420.10G Gbk: 5-13; 5-32; 20-20;
PIH Notices: 02-20 (2); 01-06; 00-46;
Admin Plan: s7p5; s23p3

COMPUTER....................................67
24 CFR 5: .210; .214 (3); .234 (5);
HUD-50058Instr: p61;
HUD-9886: p1;
7420.10G Gbk: 2-6 (2); 4-13 (4); 10-23; 10-24; 10-25 (6); 11-7; 11-8 (2); 11-10; 12-2 (3); 12-13 Ex 12-1; 21-19; 22-6; 24-4;
PIH Notices: 01-15 (4); 00-34 (2); 95-48 (8); 95-48 Tech Asst (8);
Admin Plan: s3p2; s7p2 (3); s7p4 (2); s21p2 (2); s21p2

COMPUTER- 2
PIH Notices: 95-48; 95-48 Tech Asst

COMPUTER MATCH.......................4
24 CFR 5: .214 (2); .234; .234

COMPUTER MATCHES.................1
24 CFR 5: .210

COMPUTER MATCHING...............5
7420.10G Gbk: 5-13; 22-4 (3); 22-5

COMPUTER MATCHING.............13
24 CFR 5: .214; .234 (3);
HUD-9886: p1;
7420.10G Gbk: 5-13; 22-4 (3); 22-5;
Admin Plan: s7p2 (2); s7p2

COMPUTER REPORT......................2
Admin Plan: s7p4; s7p4

COMPUTER SKILLS......................1
HUD-50058Instr: p61

COMPUTER-ASSISTED.................4
PIH Notices: 95-48 (2); 95-48 Tech Asst; 95-48 Tech Asst

COMPUTER-BASED.......................3
7420.10G Gbk: 4-14;
PIH Notices: 00-24; 00-24

COMPUTER-GENERATED............3
7420.10G Gbk: 12-2;
Admin Plan: s7p4; s7p4

COMPUTERIZED.............................10
24 CFR 982: .158 (2);
HUD-52641: p5;
7420.10G Gbk: 10-22; 10-26; 11-13;
PIH Notices: 01-15;
Admin Plan: s3p1; s3p2; s21p2

COMPUTER-MATCHING...............1
7420.10G Gbk: 22-4

COMPUTERS...................................7
24 CFR 982: .158;
HUD-52641: p5;
7420.10G Gbk: 5-46 Ex 5-5; 10-9; 11-13;
PIH Notices: 95-48; 95-48 Tech Asst

COMPUTES.....................................5
7420.10G Gbk: 1-16 Ex 1-3;
PIH Notices: 02-20 (2); 00-46; 00-46

COMPUTING...................................6
24 CFR 5: .353;
HUD-52667: p ii;
7420.10G Gbk: 1-5; 5-20; 8-5;
Admin Plan: s6p10

CONCENTRATE..............................1
7420.10G Gbk: 12-9

CONCENTRATED...........................5
7420.10G Gbk: 7-5;
PIH Notices: 02-21 (3); 01-01

CONCENTRATION........................64
24 CFR 982: .54; .301; .630;
HUD-50058Instr: p5; p71;
HUD-52648: p2 (6);
7420.10G Gbk: 1-13; 2-1 (4); 2-2 (3); 2-3 (7); 2-4; 2-5; 2-6; 2-7 (2); 2-8; 2-10 (3); 2-11; 3-3 (2); 3-9; 4-12; 7-3; 7-7; 7-9; 8-3; 8-7; 8-9; 10-20; 13-1; 13-10 (2);
PIH Notices: 02-21 (2); 01-20 (2); 01-06 (2);
Admin Plan: s1p7; s8p1; s21p5 (2); s21p6 (3); s21p6

CONCENTRATIONS.......................7
7420.10G Gbk: 2-1; 2-11; 4-12; 7-1; 7-4; 13-1;
PIH Notices: 00-11

CONCERN.....................................11
24 CFR 5: .601;
7420.10G Gbk: 2-1; 4-12; 8-5; 19-7; 22-11;
PIH Notices: 01-06 (2); 00-23;
Admin Plan: s18p6; s18p6

CONCERNED................................10
HUD-52641: 8;
HUD-52641-A: p1;
7420.10G Gbk: 7-5; 9-8; 13-4; 19-11;
PIH Notices: 02-20; 01-15 Impr Integ Hbk; 00-46; 00-11A

CONCERNING 109
24 CFR 5: .240; .502 (2); .508 (2); .514 (2); .518 (2); .613; .630; .653; .655; .659;
24 CFR 982: .4; .54 (2); .201; .310 (2); .316; .405; .501; .551; .552 (2); .553; .555; .605; .606; .610; .615; .619; .620; .625; .632 (3); .633; .641 (5); .643;
HUD-52648: p4;
HUD-52665: p2;
HUD-9886: p1 (2); p2;
7420.10G Gbk: 5-36; 16-1; 16-5 (2); 20-16; 20-28; 20-29 (2); 20-30; 22-14;
PIH Notices: 03-23 (3); 03-20; 03-05; 02-27 (3); 02-22; 02-01; 01-41 (5); 01-40; 01-15; 01-15 Impr Integ Hbk (2); 01-06 (4); 01-01; 00-34 (3); 00-27; 00-24 (2); 00-24A; 00-24B; 00-09 (5); 00-01; 99-52; 98-66; 95-48 (4); 95-48 Tech Asst (2);
Admin Plan: s7p2; s21p9; s23p2

CONCERNS 19
24 CFR 5: .703;
HUD-52648: p1;
HUD-903-1: p3;
7420.10G Gbk: 2-6; 3-6; 8-9; 8-22; 15-9 Ex 15-1; 22-10; 22-11;
PIH Notices: 02-27 (2); 02-01; 01-41; 00-09; 99-52; 96-65; 95-48; 95-48 Tech Asst

CONDITION 229
24 CFR 5: .309; .315; .318 (2); .327; .360; .615; .659; .661; .703 (5);
24 CFR 982: .310; .401 (14); .516; .552; .605 (3); .614 (4); .636;
HUD-50058: p i;
HUD-50058Instr: p15; p71; p73 (2); p75;
HUD-52580: p1 (4); p2 (8); p3 (12); p4 (8); p5 (5); p6;
HUD-52580-A: p2 (9); p3 (4); p4 (6); p5 (4); p6 (6); p7 (4); p8 (2); p9 (4); p10 (4); p11 (4); p12 (4); p13 (6); p14 (5); p15 (2); p17; p19;
HUD-52641: p9; p10;
HUD-52641-A: p2; p3;
7420.10G Gbk: 4-7; 4-10; 5-12; 5-13; 5-37; 5-38; 5-43; 8-3; 8-17; 9-8; 10-1; 10-2 (2); 10-3 (4); 10-4 (2); 10-5 (2); 10-6; 10-7; 10-8 (3); 10-9; 10-10; 10-13 (2); 10-14 (3); 10-20; 10-22; 10-30; 12-3; 15-2; 15-6 (2); 15-7 (2); 17-2; 17-5; 22-14;
PIH Notices: 02-01 (3); 01-41 (4); 01-15 Impr Integ Hbk; 00-24B; 00-23; 00-09 (2); 99-52 (3); 95-48 (7); 95-48 Tech Asst (7);
Admin Plan: s6p7; s7p8

CONDITIONAL 1
7420.10G Gbk: 5-10 Ex 5-1

CONDITIONALLY 2
PIH Notices: 02-21; 02-21

CONDITIONED 6
HUD-52667: p i;
7420.10G Gbk: 5-43 (2);
PIH Notices: 01-41; 00-09; 00-09

CONDITIONERS 1
24 CFR 982: .517

CONDITIONING 9
24 CFR 982: .517 (2);
HUD-52580-A: p15;
HUD-52667: p1 (2); p i (2); p ii;
Admin Plan: s9p3

CONDITIONS 157
24 CFR 5: .315; .403 (2); .506; .516; .518 (6); .630 (3); .657; .661; .703;
24 CFR 982: .4 (2); .307; .310; .352; .355; .401 (2); .504; .516; .614; .628; .630; .631;
HUD-50058: p i;
HUD-50058Instr: p15 (2); p17; p70; p71; p73 (4); p74 (2);
HUD-52580: p5;
HUD-52580-A: p1 (3); p2; p15 (2); p16; p17 (4); p18 (2);
HUD-52646: p2;
HUD-52667: p i; p ii;
HUD-903: p1; p2 (2);
7420.10G Gbk: 5-39; 8-17; 8-20; 9-7; 10-2 (3); 10-4 (2); 10-6; 10-7 (2);

10-8; 10-13 (2); 10-18 (2); 10-19; 10-24; 10-29; 10-34; 10-44 Ex 10-7a; 10-45 Ex 10-7b; 15-1; 17-5; 18-1; 20-6 (2); 24-13 (2);
PIH Notices: 03-11; 02-27 (2); 02-20; 01-41 (9); 01-27; 01-15 Impr Integ Hbk; 01-10; 00-23; 00-11; 00-09 (13); 95-48 (9); 95-48 Tech Asst (9);
Admin Plan: s1p6; s2p7; s9p2 (2); s9p3; s13p1; s14p1; s23p2; s23p6; s23p8 (2); s25p2 (2); s25p4; s25p5

CONDUCT 170
24 CFR 5: .327; .360; .657;
24 CFR 35 SubM: .1215;
24 CFR 982: .159; .307; .355; .405; .516 (3); .555;
HUD-50058Instr: p9; p12 (3);
HUD-52580: p1 (2);
HUD-52641: p3;
HUD-52648: p1 (2); p2;
HUD-52667: p i;
HUD-903-1: p2;
7420.10G Gbk: 1-11; 2-4 (2); 2-7 (2); 2-9; 3-7; 4-2; 4-22; 5-7; 5-40 (2); 7-5; 8-1 (2); 9-2; 9-3 (2); 9-4 (4); 9-7; 10-1; 10-12; 10-17 (5); 10-21; 10-23 (2); 10-24 (2); 10-25 (3); 10-26; 10-28; 10-30 (3); 10-31; 10-33; 10-34; 10-35; 10-37 Ex 10-2 (2); 11-2; 11-12; 12-1; 12-2; 12-11; 13-8 (2); 16-1; 16-3; 16-4; 18-9; 18-10; 19-11 (2); 19-12; 20-4; 21-7; 22-10; 22-13; 23-12 (2); 24-14;
PIH Notices: 03-23; 03-20; 03-12; 03-11 (2); 02-27 (11); 02-21; 02-20 (2); 02-07 (2); 02-01 (3); 01-43; 01-41; 01-27 (3); 01-15 (2); 01-15 Impr Integ Hbk (8); 01-11; 01-10; 01-06 (3); 00-49 (4); 00-46 (2); 00-24B (2); 00-23; 00-09 (2); 99-52 (3); 99-11 (2); 95-48; 95-48 Tech Asst;
Admin Plan: s1p6; s8p1; s10p3; s11p2; s18p2; s20p4 (2); s22p3; s22p4; s23p4; s23p5; s24p2; s25p7

CONDUCTED 137
24 CFR 5: .212; .512; .705;
24 CFR 35 SubM: .1215; .1225 (3);
24 CFR 982: .201; .516; .554; .555;
HUD-50058Instr: p3; p9; p10 (2); p12 (3); p21;
7420.10G Gbk: 1-2 (2); 2-9; 4-19; 4-22; 5-9 Ex 5-1; 5-17 (2); 5-39; 9-3; 9-7; 9-9; 9-11; 10-12; 10-16; 10-18; 10-20; 10-22; 10-24; 10-27; 10-32; 10-34; 10-35 (2); 10-38 Ex 10-3; 10-45 Ex 10-7b; 14-2; 14-4; 15-5; 16-4; 18-10; 20-4; 20-8 Ex 20-1; 21-17 (3); 21-18 (4); 22-8;
PIH Notices: 03-11; 02-27; 02-07 (2); 02-01 (10); 01-41 (2); 01-15 (2); 00-49 (5); 00-09; 99-52 (10); 99-11 (3); 95-48 (6); 95-48 Tech Asst (6);
Admin Plan: s6p8; s7p3; s8p1 (4); s8p3 (2); s10p1 (2); s10p2 (2); s11p2 (6); s13p1; s18p2; s18p3; s18p6; s18p7; s20p2; s20p3; s23p5 (2); s23p8

CONDUCTING 84
24 CFR 5: .512; .705;
24 CFR 982: .54; .554; .555 (2);
HUD-52641: p5;
7420.10G Gbk: 1-13 (2); 2-10; 2-11 (2); 3-3; 3-4; 3-5 (2); 3-6; 4-1; 4-2 (3); 4-11; 4-13; 4-18; 5-7; 5-17; 5-39; 8-2 (3); 8-9 (2); 9-2; 9-3; 9-10; 10-19; 10-22 (2); 10-23; 10-27; 10-32; 11-13; 13-7; 13-8; 16-3; 16-5; 18-9; 19-10; 20-3; 20-4 (2); 21-4 (2); 22-9; 22-10; 24-8;
PIH Notices: 03-12; 02-27 (7); 02-01 (2); 01-41 (3); 01-06; 00-49 (2); 00-09 (3); 99-52 (2); 99-11 (2);
Admin Plan: s8p4; s11p1; s18p7; s20p3; s23p3

CONDUCTS 23
24 CFR 982: .516; .555 (2);
7420.10G Gbk: 4-14; 8-1; 9-5; 10-22; 10-27; 12-6; 16-4; 16-5; 20-2; 21-4 (2); 23-

12;
PIH Notices: 01-41 (2); 01-15 Impr Integ Hbk; 00-49; 00-09; 95-48; 95-48 Tech Asst;
Admin Plan: s20p4

CONFIDENCE 1
Admin Plan: s20p2

CONFIDENTIAL 5
HUD-50058: p i;
PIH Notices: 02-01; 99-52; 95-48; 95-48 Tech Asst

CONFIDENTIALITY 12
HUD-52648: p1 (2);
7420.10G Gbk: 4-10 (5);
PIH Notices: 01-15; 00-11; 95-48; 95-48 Tech Asst;
Admin Plan: s15p4

CONFIDENTIALLY 2
PIH Notices: 03-11;
Admin Plan: s15p4

CONFINED 8
7420.10G Gbk: 5-22 (2);
Admin Plan: s6p6; s6p8 (2); s6p9 (2); s17p3

CONFINEMENT 6
24 CFR 982: .310;
HUD-52641: p9;
HUD-52641-A: p2;
7420.10G Gbk: 15-2; 15-6;
PIH Notices: 03-11

CONFIRM 23
24 CFR 5: .236; .512 (4); .514;
7420.10G Gbk: 4-22; 5-11; 5-39; 5-46 Ex 5-5; 10-23;
PIH Notices: 02-01; 01-06 (5); 99-52;
Admin Plan: s6p7; s19p1; s20p2; s21p3; s21p3

CONFIRMATION 5
7420.10G Gbk: 10-34;
Admin Plan: s7p7 (2); s21p9; s22p2

CONFIRMATORY 16
7420.10G Gbk: 1-11;
PIH Notices: 02-27 (9); 01-06 (5); 01-01

CONFIRMED 9
HUD-50058Instr: p71;
7420.10G Gbk: 5-7; 5-39; 10-20; 20-4; 23-14;
PIH Notices: 01-11; 00-49;
Admin Plan: s1p5

CONFIRMING 4
PIH Notices: 01-15 Impr Integ Hbk; 01-06; 00-24B;
Admin Plan: s3p2

CONFIRMS 14
7420.10G Gbk: 22-6;
PIH Notices: 02-27; 00-41;
Admin Plan: s21p3 (2); s21p4 (3); s21p5 (2); s21p6; s21p7 (2); s21p7

CONFLICT 27
24 CFR 5: .315 (4);
24 CFR 982: Intro; .161 (2);
HUD-52641: 8; p10 (2);
HUD-52641-A: p1; p3 (2);
7420.10G Gbk: 11-14; 12-2;
PIH Notices: 02-01; 99-52; 95-48; 95-48 Tech Asst;
Admin Plan: s1p2; s9p3; s18p5; s18p6; s18p7; s20p1; s20p3; s20p7

CONFLICT OF INTEREST 9
HUD-52641: p6 (2);
7420.10G Gbk: 8-19; 11-2 (2); 11-3; 11-11; 11-14; 11-14

CONFLICT OF INTEREST 12
24 CFR 982: Intro; .161 (2);
HUD-52641: p6 (2);
7420.10G Gbk: 8-19; 11-2 (2); 11-3; 11-11; 11-14; 11-14

CONFLICTING 2
PIH Notices: 95-48; 95-48 Tech Asst

CONFLICTS 4
24 CFR 5: .306;
Admin Plan: s20p1; s20p4; s20p4

CONFLICTS OF INTEREST 4
7420.10G Gbk: 8-16; 8-19; 11-2; 11-14

CONFLICTS OF INTEREST 4
7420.10G Gbk: 8-16; 8-19; 11-2; 11-14

CONFORMING RULE 1
7420.10G Gbk: 1-4

CONFRONT 2
24 CFR 5: .514;
7420.10G Gbk: 22-11

CONGREGATE HOUSING 47
24 CFR 5: .703;
24 CFR 982: 24 CFR 982 (6); .4 (3); .601 (2); .605; .606 (3); .607 (2); .608 (4); .609 (5);
HUD-52641: p1;
7420.10G Gbk: 3-5; 10-1; 11-10; 17-3 (4); 17-4 (3);
Admin Plan: s19p1 (8); s19p1

CONGREGATE SHELTERS 3
HUD-50058Instr: p72;
Admin Plan: s23p2; s25p3

CONGRESS....................................32
24 CFR 982: .4; .151; .152; .161;
HUD-50058Instr: p1; p72;
HUD-52641: p6 (2);
7420.10G Gbk: 1-3; 1-4 (2); 1-5; 1-7; 1-12 Ex 1-2; 8-19 (2); 11-2; 23-19; 24-1 (3);
PIH Notices: 03-23 (2); 03-20; 01-20; 00-27 (2); 00-11 (4);
Admin Plan: s23p3

CONGRESS'....................................1
PIH Notices: 01-15 Impr Integ Hbk

CONGRESS-DOUGLAS.................1
7420.10G Gbk: 2-13 Ex 2-1

CONGRESSIONAL........................11
PIH Notices: 02-21 (4); 01-20 (3); 01-06; 00-27 (2); 00-27

CONGRESSPERSON......................1
7420.10G Gbk: 24-1

CONSECUTIVE DAYS...................9
24 CFR 5: .318;
7420.10G Gbk: 15-5;
PIH Notices: 03-05; 01-40;
Admin Plan: s6p5; s6p6 (3); s6p7

CONSECUTIVE MONTHS..............5
7420.10G Gbk: 23-7 (2); 23-9;
Admin Plan: s6p3; s6p6

CONSENT......................................93
24 CFR 5: .100 (3); .210 (2); .214 (3); .230 (13); .232 (2); .234; .502; .508 (5); .514; .632; .659 (5);
24 CFR 982: .353; .516 (4); .551 (2); .552;
HUD-50058Instr: p62; p71 (3);
HUD-52641: p6;
HUD-9886: p1 (11); p2 (6);
7420.10G Gbk: 5-46 Ex 5-5; 5-47 Ex 5-5; 5-48 Ex 5-5; 5-49 Ex 5-5 (2); 11-18; 23-9;
PIH Notices: 03-11 (4); 01-15 (3); 01-15 Impr Integ Hbk (5);
Admin Plan: s3p3; s7p2; s15p1; s15p3 (3); s22p4

CONSENT FORM..............................32
24 CFR 5: .214 (2); .230 (3); .232; .502; .508 (4); .514; .659;
24 CFR 982: .516;
HUD-50058Instr: p71 (2);
HUD-9886: p1 (8); p2 (3);
7420.10G Gbk: 5-4; 12-3;
PIH Notices: 03-11 (2); 01-15 Impr Integ Hbk

CONSENT FORM--CONTENTS.....1
24 CFR 5: .230

CONSENT FORMS.........................27
24 CFR 5: .210 (2); .214; .230 (5); .232; .234; .659;
24 CFR 982: .551; .552;
HUD-50058Instr: p71;
HUD-52646: p2;
7420.10G Gbk: 1-14; 5-35; 5-36 Ex 5-4; 15-5;
PIH Notices: 03-11 (2); 01-15 (2); 01-15 Impr Integ Hbk;
Admin Plan: s3p3; s7p2; s15p1

CONSENT FORMS--SPECIAL........1
24 CFR 5: .230

CONSENTS......................................1
Admin Plan: s3p3

CONSEQUENCE..............................1
PIH Notices: 01-06

CONSEQUENCES............................7
7420.10G Gbk: 24-13;
PIH Notices: 95-48; 95-48 Tech Asst;
Admin Plan: s7p2; s10p1; s10p5; s20p5

CONSEQUENTLY............................6
PIH Notices: 01-20; 01-06 (2); 00-27; 95-48; 95-48 Tech Asst

CONSERVATION..............................4
24 CFR 5: .801;
7420.10G Gbk: 10-8; 18-1; 18-1

CONSERVATIVELY.........................1
Admin Plan: s20p1

CONSIDER..................................147
24 CFR 5: .318; .353; .653; .655; .661;
24 CFR 982: .104; .207 (2); .301; .307; .310 (2); .405; .503 (4); .507; .552 (2); .555; .613; .622;
HUD-50058Instr: p9; p10; p24 (2); p34 (2); p36;
HUD-52580-A: p2;
HUD-52641: p4;
HUD-903: p2;
7420.10G Gbk: 2-2; 2-7 (2); 2-8; 2-9 (2); 2-10; 3-8; 4-4; 4-5 (2); 4-6 (4); 4-7; 4-10; 4-11 (2); 4-12 (2); 4-16 (2); 4-18;

5-38 (3); 5-39; 6-3; 7-6; 8-2; 8-3; 8-8; 8-11; 8-12 (2); 8-20; 9-2; 9-4; 9-7; 9-8; 10-5; 10-24 (2); 10-35; 11-4; 11-7 (3); 11-10; 12-5; 12-8; 12-9; 13-6; 15-6; 15-7; 16-3; 17-7; 17-9; 17-12; 18-1; 20-4; 22-1; 22-8; 22-14 (2); 22-15; 24-2; 24-7;
PIH Notices: 03-12 (5); 02-27; 02-20 (5); 02-01 (2); 01-41 (2); 01-27; 01-15 (4); 01-15 Impr Integ Hbk; 01-06 (2); 01-01; 00-46 (3); 00-24B; 00-09 (3); 99-52 (2); 95-48; 95-48 Tech Asst;
Admin Plan: s1p5; s5p2; s11p3; s15p3; s15p4; s16p2; s19p1 (2); s20p7; s25p5

CONSIDERABLE 4
HUD-52667: p ii;
7420.10G Gbk: 9-5; 9-9; 9-9

CONSIDERABLY 2
HUD-52667: p ii;
7420.10G Gbk: 21-5

CONSIDERATION..........................59
24 CFR 5: .318; .380; .603 (2); .609;
24 CFR 982: .310; .517; .552 (2);
HUD-50058Instr: p31;
HUD-52580: p6;
HUD-52580-A: p19;
HUD-52641: p5;
HUD-52648: p1;
7420.10G Gbk: 4-11; 4-12 (2); 5-5; 5-16 Ex 5-2; 5-38; 6-7; 8-7; 8-8; 9-12; 10-13; 11-4; 11-8; 15-6; 18-2; 20-19 Ex 20-3; 22-3; 22-7;
PIH Notices: 03-05; 02-27; 01-41 (3); 01-40; 01-20; 01-15 Impr Integ Hbk (2); 00-27; 00-09; 99-11; 95-48 (5); 95-48 Tech Asst (5);
Admin Plan: s5p1; s5p2; s8p2; s20p7; s24p4

CONSIDERATIONS ....
13
24 CFR 5: .703;
7420.10G Gbk: 4-20; 8-3; 8-9; 9-9; 21-5; 22-5; 22-14; 22-17;
PIH Notices: 02-01; 00-11; 00-11A; 99-52

CONSIDERED..............................189
24 CFR 5: .350; .403; .514 (2); .603 (2); .653; .703;
24 CFR 35 SubM: .1215; .1225;
24 CFR 982: .54; .201 (2); .311; .315; .402; .403; .502 (2); .555; .627 (2);
HUD-50058Instr: p15; p22 (2); p72 (2); p74;
HUD-52580-A: p6; p13; p17;
HUD-52648: p2;
HUD-52665: p1;
7420.10G Gbk: 3-3 (2); 3-4; 4-2; 4-6 (2); 4-11; 4-20; 5-1; 5-2; 5-23; 5-25 Ex 5-3; 5-27 (2); 5-41; 5-44 (3); 5-51 Ex 5-5; 5-52 Ex 5-5; 5-53 Ex 5-5; 8-22; 9-7; 10-2 (2); 10-6; 10-12; 10-13 (2); 10-19; 10-21; 10-33; 11-5; 13-9; 16-5; 17-7; 18-1; 18-6; 20-13; 20-24; 20-26; 21-4; 22-16; 23-2; 23-7; 23-14;
PIH Notices: 02-22 (2); 02-21; 02-20; 02-06; 02-01 (3); 01-41 (4); 01-27; 01-20 (4); 01-15; 01-15 Impr Integ Hbk; 00-46; 00-27 (3); 00-24B; 00-09 (4); 99-52 (3); 99-11; 96-65; 95-48 (7); 95-48 Tech Asst (7);
Admin Plan: s1p5 (2); s2p2 (2); s2p3; s2p4; s2p5; s2p7 (2); s6p6 (5); s6p7 (4); s6p8 (4); s6p9; s6p10 (3); s6p11 (2); s7p1; s7p5; s7p7 (3); s8p5; s8p6 (2); s9p2 (2); s10p1; s10p2; s10p3 (2); s10p5; s11p1; s11p3; s15p2; s15p4; s15p5; s15p6; s16p2; s16p3; s17p1; s18p6; s18p8 (2); s20p4; s20p6; s24p1 (2); s24p3; s24p5; s25p5; s25p5

CONSIDERING 14
24 CFR 982: .4; .203;
HUD-50058Instr: p75;
7420.10G Gbk: 2-7; 5-44; 9-7; 10-25; 11-8; 23-9; 24-10; 24-13;
PIH Notices: 01-15 Impr Integ Hbk; 01-06;
Admin Plan: s1p5

CONSIDERS 9
HUD-52648: p2;

7420.10G Gbk: 2-3;
PIH Notices: 03-12; 02-20; 01-10; 01-06; 00-46;
Admin Plan: s21p3; s21p6

CONSIST......................................13
24 CFR 5: .609;
24 CFR 982: .401;
7420.10G Gbk: 5-14 Ex 5-2; 10-12; 13-6;
PIH Notices: 02-20; 01-41; 01-15 Impr Integ Hbk (2); 00-46; 00-09;
Admin Plan: s2p4; s8p3

CONSISTED......................................1
PIH Notices: 01-10

CONSISTENCY..............................22
24 CFR 982: .102;
HUD-50058Instr: p1;
7420.10G Gbk: 2-10; 5-1; 9-4; 10-2; 10-34; 11-2; 21-13; 22-6; 22-7; 24-13 (3);
PIH Notices: 02-20; 00-46;
Admin Plan: s2p1; s10p1; s20p2; s21p4; s24p1; s24p1

CONSISTENT.................................56
24 CFR 5: .315; .512; .603; .801;
24 CFR 982: .102; .201; .310; .402; .552; .630;
HUD-50058Instr: p76;
HUD-52641: p3; p4;
7420.10G Gbk: 2-9; 2-10; 3-1; 4-1 (2); 4-16; 4-19; 5-35; 5-41; 8-1; 8-9; 9-11; 10-2; 10-14; 11-12 (2); 12-8; 15-10 Ex 15-2; 21-3; 22-1; 22-6; 22-10; 22-11; 23-15; 24-12;
PIH Notices: 03-12; 03-11; 02-27; 02-21; 01-41; 95-48 (2); 95-48 Tech Asst (2);
Admin Plan: s1p2; s3p1; s5p1; s6p1; s9p2; s9p3; s24p1 (2); s24p4

CONSISTENTLY............................15
24 CFR 982: .402;
7420.10G Gbk: 2-6; 2-9; 4-1; 4-16; 4-22; 5-11; 5-41; 9-4; 10-2; 11-15; 22-8; 22-11; 22-18;
Admin Plan: s1p6

CONSISTING....................................5
24 CFR 982: .201; .402;
7420.10G Gbk: 5-41;
PIH Notices: 02-01; 99-52

CONSISTS.......................................24
24 CFR 5: .508 (3);
24 CFR 982: .4; .316; .402; .619;
HUD-50058Instr: p40; p69; p75;
HUD-52641: p10;
HUD-52641-A: p3;
7420.10G Gbk: 3-6; 5-41; 10-1; 16-4; 17-4; 17-7 (2); 23-19;
PIH Notices: 00-09;
Admin Plan: s8p3; s19p1; s19p1

CONSOLIDATE................................3
7420.10G Gbk: 10-15; 20-9;
PIH Notices: 00-53

CONSOLIDATED............................44
24 CFR 5: .518 (2);
24 CFR 982: .4 (4); .52; .102 (7); .151 (5); .152; .153; .154; .155; .157; .162; .201; .207; .309; .352; .355 (2); .451; .454; .601; .628;
HUD-50058Instr: p70;
7420.10G Gbk: 20-13;
PIH Notices: 02-20; 02-14 (2); 00-46; 00-28; 00-09;
Admin Plan: s25p5

CONSOLIDATED ACC....................6
7420.10G Gbk: 1-14 (2); 8-22; 11-15; 13-6; 15-4

CONSOLIDATED ACC..................32
24 CFR 982: .4 (3); .52; .102 (6); .151 (3); .152; .153; .154; .155; .157; .162; .309; .352; .355 (2); .451; .454; .628;
7420.10G Gbk: 1-14 (2); 8-22; 11-15; 13-6; 15-4

CONSOLIDATED ANNUAL CONTRIBUTIONS CONTRACT...10
24 CFR 982: .4; .151; .601;
HUD-50058Instr: p70;
PIH Notices: 02-20; 02-14 (2); 00-46; 00-28; 00-09

CONSOLIDATED PLAN..................7
24 CFR 5: .518 (2);
24 CFR 982: .102; .207;
7420.10G Gbk: 4-16 (2); 4-16

CONSOLIDATED PLANS 1
24 CFR 982: .201

CONSOLIDATION...........................8
HUD-50058Instr: p5;
7420.10G Gbk: 1-8 (2); 20-9; 21-11;
PIH Notices: 02-21; 01-20;

00-27
CONSORTIUM 2
24 CFR 982: .4; .4
CONSPICUOUS 1
24 CFR 5: .353
CONSPICUOUSLY 1
Admin Plan: s20p2
CONSTITUTION 2
PIH Notices: 95-48; 95-48 Tech Asst
CONSTITUTIONAL 1
24 CFR 982: .202
CONSTRUCT 4
HUD-903-1: p2;
7420.10G Gbk: 4-14;
PIH Notices: 95-48; 95-48 Tech Asst
CONSTRUCTED 44
HUD-52580: p1 (2);
7420.10G Gbk: 1-3; 8-15; 9-14 Ex 9-1; 9-16 Ex 9-2;
PIH Notices: 02-22; 02-01 (10); 00-23 (3); 99-52 (10); 99-11 (2); 95-48 (7); 95-48 Tech Asst (4); 95-48 Tech Asst
CONSTRUCTING 2
PIH Notices: 95-48; 95-48 Tech Asst
CONSTRUCTION 124
24 CFR 5: .801 (2);
24 CFR 982: .628;
HUD-50058Instr: p70;
7420.10G Gbk: 8-16; 9-14 Ex 9-1; 9-16 Ex 9-2; 21-13; 23-8 Ex 23-1;
PIH Notices: 02-01 (19); 01-41 (3); 01-15 Impr Integ Hbk; 01-10; 00-24B; 00-11; 00-09; 99-52 (20); 99-11 (2); 95-48 (26); 95-48 Tech Asst (22);
Admin Plan: s22p3; s24p1 (2); s24p2; s24p3 (3); s24p4; s24p5 (9); s24p5
CONSULT 17
24 CFR 5: .218; .232; .380;
HUD-52667: p i;
7420.10G Gbk: 10-25; 23-4;
PIH Notices: 03-23; 02-27; 02-21; 01-20; 01-06 (2); 00-27; 95-48 (2); 95-48 Tech Asst; 95-48 Tech Asst
CONSULTANT 3
7420.10G Gbk: 10-31;
PIH Notices: 02-01; 99-52
CONSULTANTS 2
PIH Notices: 02-01; 99-52
CONSULTATION 23
24 CFR 5: .353; .380 (2); .617;
24 CFR 982: .102 (2);
HUD-50058Instr: p73;
7420.10G Gbk: 3-6; 10-14;
PIH Notices: 02-27; 02-01 (2); 01-15 Impr Integ Hbk (2); 00-53; 00-09; 99-52 (2); 99-11; 95-48 (2); 95-48 Tech Asst; 95-48 Tech Asst
CONSULTED 1
PIH Notices: 01-06
CONSULTING 4
24 CFR 5: .216 (2);
7420.10G Gbk: 21-20;
PIH Notices: 02-27
CONSULTS 2
PIH Notices: 95-48; 95-48 Tech Asst
CONSUMED 2
HUD-52667: p i;
7420.10G Gbk: 18-6
CONSUMER 3
PIH Notices: 01-15; 95-48; 95-48 Tech Asst
CONSUMING 1
7420.10G Gbk: 19-4
CONSUMPTION 36
24 CFR 5: .603;
24 CFR 982: .517;
HUD-50058Instr: p76;
HUD-52667: p i (5); p ii (7);
7420.10G Gbk: 6-3; 18-4 (8); 18-5 (5); 18-6 (3); 18-9 (2);
PIH Notices: 00-24B;
Admin Plan: s6p13
CONSUMPTIONS 3
HUD-52667: p ii (2); p ii
CONTAMINATED 1
PIH Notices: 00-23
CONTAMINATION 8
24 CFR 982: .401 (2);
HUD-52580-A: p15; p16;
7420.10G Gbk: 10-11 (2); 10-19; 10-21
CONTEST 4
24 CFR 5: .236 (2);
HUD-50058Instr: p15;
HUD-9886: p2
CONTEXT 6
24 CFR 5: .518;
PIH Notices: 95-48 (2); 95-48 Tech Asst (2);
Admin Plan: s1p2

CONTEXTUAL..................................2
PIH Notices: 95-48; 95-48 Tech Asst
CONTIGUOUS..................................3
HUD-52580-A: p8;
PIH Notices: 02-20; 00-46
CONTINUED ASSISTANCE 57
24 CFR 5: .230; .508 (2); .516 (6); .518 (7); .520; .522;
24 CFR 982: Intro; .1; .314 (2); .454; .502; .504; .516; .552; .625; .633; .636 (2); .637 (4);
HUD-50058Instr: p17 (2);
HUD-52641: p3;
7420.10G Gbk: 5-12; 5-13; 5-38; 11-5; 12-3; 12-6; 15-7 (2); 16-3; 20-8 Ex 20-1; 22-14;
PIH Notices: 02-06; 01-33; 01-15 Impr Integ Hbk; 00-11;
Admin Plan: s8p6; s13p1; s14p2; s23p5
CONTINUED OCCUPANCY 7
24 CFR 5: .309; .659;
7420.10G Gbk: 10-21; 12-3; 12-16 Ex 12-4;
PIH Notices: 00-24B;
Admin Plan: s20p5
CONTINUITY OF ASSISTANCE 1
24 CFR 982: .201
CONTINUOUSLY ASSISTED 26
24 CFR 5: .508;
24 CFR 982: .4 (2); .201 (2);
HUD-50058: p5; p v;
HUD-50058Instr: p12; p19 (3); p71 (2);
7420.10G Gbk: 3-3 (6); 4-20; 5-2; 12-5 (2);
Admin Plan: s2p4 (2); s4p2
CONTINUOUSLY ASSISTED FAMILY 1
Admin Plan: s24p6
CONTRACT ADMINISTRATION ... 6
24 CFR 982: .553;
7420.10G Gbk: 21-13 (2); 21-16 Ex 21-6; 21-19; 21-20
CONTRACT ADMINISTRATOR... 11
24 CFR 5: .236; .661 (9);
24 CFR 982: .4
CONTRACT ADMINISTRATORS .. 2
24 CFR 5: .801;
PIH Notices: 01-27
CONTRACT OF PARTICIPATION 91
24 CFR 982: .552;
HUD-50058: p17 (3); p xvii (4);
HUD-50058Instr: p59 (2); p60; p61 (5); p62 (5); p65 (6); p66 (8); p71 (5); p72; p73; p75;
7420.10G Gbk: 15-6; 23-1; 23-2; 23-5; 23-6 (3); 23-7 (3); 23-9 (4); 23-10; 23-11 (4); 23-12 (2); 23-13; 23-14; 23-15; 23-17 Ex 23-2 (13); 23-18 (6); 23-20 (2);
Admin Plan: s25p4 (2); s25p5
CONTRACT RENT.........................54
24 CFR 5: .520 (4); .661;
24 CFR 982: .403;
HUD-50058: p10; p x (5); p12; p xii (5);
HUD-50058Instr: p43 (7); p45 (2); p50; p51 (5); p52 (2); p72;
7420.10G Gbk: 8-18 (2); 9-17 Ex 9-3; 9-19 Ex 9-4; 11-8; 11-19; 15-9 Ex 15-1; 18-1 (2); 20-23; 23-13 (4);
PIH Notices: 00-24B;
Admin Plan: s23p6 (2); s24p3
CONTRACT UNIT..........................72
24 CFR 5: .661;
24 CFR 982: .4; .308; .507; .619;
HUD-50058: p xi;
HUD-50058Instr: p47; p74;
HUD-52641: p1; p2; p3 (12); p4 (6); p5 (7); p6 (2); 8 (5); p10 (5);
HUD-52641-A: p1 (5); p3 (6);
7420.10G Gbk: 9-2; 11-10; 11-11 (3); 11-12; 11-13 (2); 11-14; 15-4;
PIH Notices: 03-12; 00-09;
Admin Plan: s14p1; s23p7
CONTRACT UNIT MAINTENANCE1
7420.10G Gbk: 11-11
CONTRACT UNITS 4
7420.10G Gbk: 24-15;
PIH Notices: 03-23; 02-21; 02-21
CONTRACTED..............................20
24 CFR 982: .157;
7420.10G Gbk: 8-11 (2); 20-11; 20-12 Ex 20-2; 22-18; 24-1 (5); 24-2 (4); 24-8;
PIH Notices: 03-11; 02-07; 00-28; 00-23
CONTRACTING............................32
7420.10G Gbk: 4-6; 24-15;
PIH Notices: 03-11; 02-27 (19); 95-48 (5); 95-48 Tech Asst (4); 95-

48 Tech Asst
CONTRACTING OUT......................1
7420.10G Gbk: 4-6
CONTRACTOR..............................74
24 CFR 982: .161; .553; .631;
HUD-52641: p6;
7420.10G Gbk: 8-19; 11-2; 11-3; 11-9; 21-17; 21-19;
PIH Notices: 02-27 (62);
Admin Plan: s24p5; s24p5
CONTRACTORS............................38
24 CFR 5: .105 (2);
24 CFR 982: .157; .161;
HUD-52641: p6;
7420.10G Gbk: 11-14; 19-6;
PIH Notices: 03-11; 02-27 (23); 02-01 (2); 99-52 (2); 99-11; 95-48; 95-48 Tech Asst
CONTRACTOR'S.............................6
PIH Notices: 02-27 (5); 02-27
CONTRACTS.................................93
24 CFR 5: .653 (2); .801;
24 CFR 982: Intro; .1 (2); .160; .162 (4); .502;
HUD-50058Instr: p50;
HUD-52648: p2 (2);
7420.10G Gbk: 1-3; 1-5; 1-8 (2); 8-19; 8-20; 10-30; 11-1; 11-2 (3); 13-6; 14-2; 20-1; 20-13 (2); 21-1; 23-1; 23-2; 23-11;
PIH Notices: 03-23 (5); 03-11; 02-27 (5); 02-20; 02-14; 02-06; 02-01; 01-41 (9); 01-15; 01-10 (7); 01-06 (3); 00-46; 00-24B (5); 00-09 (8); 99-52;
Admin Plan: s2p4; s4p1; s10p1; s16p2; s20p8; s21p8; s24p1; s24p5
CONTRACT-SIGNING.....................1
Admin Plan: s9p4
CONTRACTUAL.............................7
24 CFR 982: .151;
7420.10G Gbk: 1-11; 8-10; 22-9;
PIH Notices: 02-27;
Admin Plan: s8p4; s15p3
CONTRARY....................................9
24 CFR 5: .100;
24 CFR 982: .555 (2);
7420.10G Gbk: 16-5 (3);
PIH Notices: 95-48; 95-48 Tech Asst;
Admin Plan: s15p3
CONTRARY TO HUD......................1
24 CFR 982: .555
CONTRIBUTE...............................14
HUD-50058Instr: p17;
7420.10G Gbk: 6-1 (3); 6-3 (2); 24-3; 24-13;
PIH Notices: 01-41; 01-10; 00-11; 00-09; 95-48; 95-48 Tech Asst
CONTRIBUTED...............................1
7420.10G Gbk: 5-18
CONTRIBUTES...............................5
HUD-50058: p xi; p xiv;
HUD-50058Instr: p24; p48; p57
CONTRIBUTING.............................4
7420.10G Gbk: 2-10; 6-2; 19-11;
PIH Notices: 03-20
CONTRIBUTION...........................42
24 CFR 982: .452; .627;
HUD-50058: p11; p xi (2); p xiv;
HUD-50058Instr: p7; p48 (2); p49 (6); p57;
7420.10G Gbk: 6-5; 20-17 (5); 20-19 Ex 20-3; 20-23; 21-7; 22-6;
PIH Notices: 03-23; 01-41; 00-11; 00-09 (7);
Admin Plan: s6p9; s6p12 (3); s25p4; s25p5
CONTRIBUTIONS.........................83
24 CFR 5: .403; .609;
24 CFR 982: 24 CFR 982 (2); .4; .104; .151 (3); .601;
HUD-50058Instr: p1; p30; p62; p70 (3);
7420.10G Gbk: 4-26 Ex 4-2; 5-14 Ex 5-2; 5-18 (3); 5-19; 5-25 Ex 5-3; 5-26; 5-27; 5-47 Ex 5-5 (2); 6-1; 19-3; 23-15;
PIH Notices: 03-23 (4); 03-20; 02-27 (3); 02-21 (9); 02-20 (2); 02-14 (2); 02-07; 02-06 (2); 02-01 (2); 01-41; 01-20 (2); 01-15 Impr Integ Hbk (3); 01-06; 00-46 (2); 00-28 (2); 00-27; 00-24B (2); 00-09; 99-52 (2);
Admin Plan: s6p8; s6p9 (3); s6p10 (2); s7p5; s23p5; s24p1; s25p5
CONTROL...................................155
24 CFR 5: .100 (3); .216; .234; .318; .350; .603;
24 CFR 982: .4; .52; .53; .54; .103; .151; .153; .155; .156; .157; .158; .159; .160; .204; .206; .301; .303; .304; .305;

.306; .307; .310 (3); .352; .403; .404; .405; .406; .451; .452; .509 (2); .516; .517; .551; .552; .554; .555; .631;
HUD-50058Instr: p14; p22;
HUD-52580: p1 (2); p14;
HUD-52641: p4; p6; 8; p10;
HUD-52641-A: p1; p3;
HUD-52646: p1 (9);
HUD-52667: p i;
7420.10G Gbk: 8-1; 8-9; 8-19; 9-2 (4); 10-8; 10-15; 10-19 (2); 10-21; 10-33; 10-47 Ex 10-9; 11-3; 11-7; 15-2; 19-12 (2); 20-1; 20-17; 20-22; 21-2; 21-3; 21-8; 21-16 Ex 21-6; 22-6; 23-7;
PIH Notices: 03-23 (2); 03-20 (2); 03-12 (2); 03-11 (3); 02-27 (9); 02-21 (2); 02-01; 01-15 (4); 01-15 Impr Integ Hbk (2); 01-06; 00-24B (5); 00-23; 99-52; 95-48 (4); 95-48 Tech Asst (4);
Admin Plan: s10p1; s11p2; s15p3 (3); s16p2; s20p1; s20p2; s21p1; s21p2; s21p4 (2); s21p5 (2); s24p3

CONTROLLED 38
24 CFR 5: .100 (2);
24 CFR 982: .352; .628;
7420.10G Gbk: 4-15; 4-25 Ex 4-2; 5-25 Ex 5-3; 5-37 (3); 5-43; 8-17; 9-2; 10-30; 22-17;
PIH Notices: 01-15; 95-48 (9); 95-48 Tech Asst (9);
Admin Plan: s15p2 (2); s15p3; s15p3

CONTROLLED SUBSTANCE 10
24 CFR 5: .100;
7420.10G Gbk: 4-25 Ex 4-2; 5-37 (2); 5-43;
PIH Notices: 95-48; 95-48 Tech Asst;
Admin Plan: s15p2; s15p3; s15p3

CONTROLLED SUBSTANCES 16
24 CFR 5: .100;
7420.10G Gbk: 4-15; 5-37;
PIH Notices: 95-48 (6); 95-48 Tech Asst (6);
Admin Plan: s15p2

CONTROLLING 3
7420.10G Gbk: 1-12; 1-12 Ex 1-2; 22-17

CONTROLS 32
24 CFR 35 SubM: .1225;
HUD-50058Instr: p1;
7420.10G Gbk: 10-21; 11-9; 19-6; 20-2;
PIH Notices: 02-01; 99-52; 95-48 (12); 95-48 Tech Asst (11); 95-48 Tech Asst

CONTROL'S 1
7420.10G Gbk: 10-18

CONTROVERT 1
24 CFR 5: .514

CONTROVERT EVIDENCE 1
24 CFR 5: .514

CONTROVERTING 1
24 CFR 5: .514

CONVERSATIONS 2
7420.10G Gbk: 15-6; 19-3

CONVERSELY 4
PIH Notices: 02-27; 00-11; 95-48; 95-48 Tech Asst

CONVERSION 245
24 CFR 982: Intro; .201; .502;
HUD-50058Instr: p9; p10; p11;
7420.10G Gbk: 1-1; 1-5 (3); 1-6 (2); 1-8 (3); 1-9 (4); 14-1 (3); 14-3 (2); 14-4 (4); 14-5 (2); 20-3 (9); 20-6; 20-8 Ex 20-1 (2); 20-29; 23-2;
PIH Notices: 02-21 (6); 02-07 (7); 01-41 (71); 01-33 (2); 01-20 (6); 01-10 (30); 00-28 (4); 00-27 (6); 00-09 (67);
Admin Plan: s23p5; s23p5

CONVERSION FEE 6
7420.10G Gbk: 20-3 (3); 20-6;
PIH Notices: 02-07; 00-28

CONVERSION FEES 3
7420.10G Gbk: 20-3;
PIH Notices: 02-07; 00-28

CONVERSIONS 6
7420.10G Gbk: 14-4; 23-2;
PIH Notices: 01-41; 01-33; 00-31; 99-30

CONVERT 31
HUD-50058Instr: p7 (3); p9;
7420.10G Gbk: 1-2; 1-5; 5-17 (2); 5-26; 5-27 (3); 5-28 (3); 5-49 Ex 5-5 (2); 14-1; 14-2; 14-4;
PIH Notices: 01-10 (2); 00-09 (3);
Admin Plan: s4p1; s22p2 (2);

s22p4; s23p5; s24p6

CONVERTED....35
HUD-50058: p xiii;
HUD-50058Instr: p1; p9; p10; p53;
7420.10G Gbk: 1-2; 5-28; 5-49 Ex 5-5; 6-1; 14-1; 14-2; 14-3; 23-13;
PIH Notices: 02-01; 01-41 (5); 01-33; 01-10 (9); 01-06 (2); 00-09; 99-52;
Admin Plan: s7p6; s23p5

CONVERTING....5
7420.10G Gbk: 19-4;
PIH Notices: 01-10 (3); 01-10

CONVEYANCE....1
24 CFR 982: .633

CONVICTED....14
24 CFR 982: .310; .553 (3);
HUD-52641: p9;
HUD-52641-A: p2;
7420.10G Gbk: 5-35; 5-37; 15-2; 15-6; 15-7;
PIH Notices: 03-11;
Admin Plan: s2p6; s15p1

CONVICTION....12
24 CFR 982: .310 (2);
HUD-52641: p9;
HUD-52641-A: p2;
HUD-52648: p3;
7420.10G Gbk: 15-2; 15-6;
PIH Notices: 03-11 (3);
Admin Plan: s2p6; s15p3

COOKING....22
24 CFR 982: .517;
HUD-52517: p1;
HUD-52641: p2;
HUD-52667: p1 (2); p i (3); p ii (2);
7420.10G Gbk: 6-9 Ex 6-1; 9-14 Ex 9-1; 9-15 Ex 9-2; 18-2 (2); 18-5 (2); 18-6 (3); 18-7; 18-8

COOLING....19
24 CFR 982: .401 (2);
HUD-52580: p5;
HUD-52580-A: p15 (5); p16 (3);
HUD-52667: p i (2); p ii;
7420.10G Gbk: 10-7; 10-8 (2); 18-4; 18-4

COOPERATE....11
24 CFR 982: .201; .312; .551;
HUD-52641: p5;
7420.10G Gbk: 4-20; 5-12; 11-13; 13-7; 21-10;
Admin Plan: s7p2; s20p7

COOPERATING....3
7420.10G Gbk: 2-9 (2);
Admin Plan: s23p7

COOPERATION....28
24 CFR 5: .613 (2);
7420.10G Gbk: 5-22; 10-44 Ex 10-7a; 10-45 Ex 10-7b; 23-3 (5);
PIH Notices: 01-15; 01-15 Impr Integ Hbk; 00-11 (12); 00-11A (3);
Admin Plan: s25p6

COOPERATION AGREEMENT....6
PIH Notices: 00-11 (4); 00-11A; 00-11A

COOPERATION AGREEMENTS..11
24 CFR 5: .613;
7420.10G Gbk: 5-22;
PIH Notices: 01-15 Impr Integ Hbk; 00-11 (7); 00-11A

COOPERATIVE....119
24 CFR 5: .214 (2); .306; .801 (2);
24 CFR 982: 24 CFR 982 (2); .4 (21); .601 (3); .618; .619 (25); .627 (5); .628; .633; .635 (8);
HUD-50058Instr: p56 (4); p71; p73 (6);
HUD-52580: p1 (2);
HUD-52646: p2;
7420.10G Gbk: 2-1; 2-9; 5-36 Ex 5-4; 8-17; 11-8; 13-6 (2); 17-10 (3);
PIH Notices: 00-11 (2); 00-11A;
Admin Plan: s9p2; s19p1 (17); s22p1; s22p3

COOPERATIVE AGREEMENT....1
7420.10G Gbk: 2-9

COOPERATIVE AGREEMENTS....4
7420.10G Gbk: 13-6;
PIH Notices: 00-11 (2); 00-11A

COOPERATIVE HOUSING....10
HUD-52641: p1;
7420.10G Gbk: 3-5; 11-10; 17-9 (3); 17-10 (3); 17-10

COOPERATIVE HOUSING....32
24 CFR 5: .801 (2);
24 CFR 982: Intro; .4 (2); .601 (2); .619 (6);
HUD-50058Instr: p73;
HUD-52641: p1;
7420.10G Gbk: 3-5; 11-10; 17-9 (3); 17-10 (4);
Admin Plan: s9p2; s19p1 (6); s19p1

COOPERATIVE MEMBER....17
24 CFR 5: .214 (2);
24 CFR 982: .4 (6); .619 (6);

.627; .635; .635
COOPERATIVE MEMBERS............4
24 CFR 982: .601; .627 (2);
Admin Plan: s22p1
COOPERATIVE MEMBER'S 1
Admin Plan: s19p1
COOPERATIVE MEMBERSHIP SHARES 4
24 CFR 982: .627 (2); .633;
.635
COOPERATIVES 3
7420.10G Gbk: 5-25 Ex 5-3; 8-17;
Admin Plan: s19p1
COORDINATE 17
24 CFR 5: .350;
24 CFR 982: .152;
HUD-50058Instr: p72;
7420.10G Gbk: 10-23; 21-4;
PIH Notices: 02-20; 00-46;
00-11; 00-11A (2); 99-11;
95-48; 95-48 Tech Asst;
Admin Plan: s9p4; s13p1;
s22p2; s25p3
COORDINATED 8
7420.10G Gbk: 1-7; 23-5 (2);
PIH Notices: 01-15; 00-11;
00-11A; 99-11;
Admin Plan: s10p3
COORDINATES................................2
PIH Notices: 01-41; 01-41
COORDINATING 11
7420.10G Gbk: 22-18; 23-1; 23-3 (2);
PIH Notices: 00-11 (2); 00-11A (2);
Admin Plan: s11p1; s25p4;
s25p4
COORDINATION 29
24 CFR 5: .609;
24 CFR 982: .4;
7420.10G Gbk: 5-15 Ex 5-2; 16-4; 19-12; 21-5; 21-8;
23-5; 23-19;
PIH Notices: 02-27; 01-15 (3);
01-15 Impr Integ Hbk (2); 00-11 (4); 00-11A (3); 99-11 (2); 95-48 (2); 95-48 Tech Asst (2);
Admin Plan: s10p1
COORDINATOR............................22
7420.10G Gbk: 5-40; 21-15 Ex 21-5; 21-16 Ex 21-6; 23-3;
PIH Notices: 02-27 (4); 02-21; 02-01 (2); 01-20; 01-06 (3); 00-27; 99-52 (2);
95-48; 95-48 Tech Asst;
Admin Plan: s25p6; s25p6
COORDINATORS...........................31
PIH Notices: 03-23; 03-11; 02-27 (10); 02-21; 02-06;
02-01 (2); 01-41; 01-20;
01-10; 00-45 (2); 00-31;
00-27; 00-09; 00-01; 99-52 (2); 99-30; 99-11 (2);
98-66
COP...7
Admin Plan: s25p4 (3);
s25p5 (3); s25p5
COPIED 3
7420.10G Gbk: 12-4;
PIH Notices: 01-06;
Admin Plan: s7p1
COPIES..53
24 CFR 5: .380 (2);
24 CFR 982: .158;
HUD-50058: p1;
HUD-52641: p5;
HUD-52646: p2 (3);
HUD-52665: p1;
HUD-52667: p ii;
7420.10G Gbk: 5-44; 5-46 Ex 5-5; 5-47 Ex 5-5; 5-48 Ex 5-5 (3); 5-49 Ex 5-5 (3); 5-51 Ex 5-5 (3); 5-52 Ex 5-5 (2); 10-36 Ex 10-1; 12-4;
13-3 (2); 13-8; 18-4; 22-9;
PIH Notices: 02-27 (3); 02-20;
02-01; 01-41 (2); 01-15;
01-15 Impr Integ Hbk (2); 00-46; 00-09 (2); 99-52; 95-48 (2);
Admin Plan: s7p6 (2); s7p7;
s18p5 (2); s22p3
COPY...208
24 CFR 5: .312; .353;
.514 (5);
24 CFR 982: .156; .158;
.301; .302; .308;
.309; .310; .314; .517;
.551; .553 (2); .555 (3);
.631 (2);
HUD-50058: p7 (5); p vii (5);
p9; p ix; p10 (2);
p x (2); p11 (3); p xi;
p12 (2); p xii; p13;
p xiii; p14 (2); p xiv;
p15;
HUD-50058Instr: p2; p3; p34;
p35 (5); p39; p43 (2);
p44 (2); p48 (4); p49;
p50 (2); p52; p54 (2);
p57 (3); p58; p68;
HUD-52641: p7; 8; p9; p10;
HUD-52641-A: p1; p2; p3;
HUD-52646: p1; p2 (4);
HUD-52648: p4;

HUD-52665: p1 (2); p2 (2);
HUD-52667: p ii;
HUD-903: p1;
7420.10G Gbk: 1-15; 3-1; 5-11 (3); 5-47 Ex 5-5 (2); 5-49 Ex 5-5 (2); 8-6; 8-10; 8-15; 10-17 (2); 10-19; 11-18 (2); 11-19 (3); 12-13 Ex 12-1; 13-3; 13-9; 15-1; 15-3; 15-7 (2); 16-4 (2); 16-5; 18-4; 22-9; 22-16;
PIH Notices: 03-11 (3); 02-27 (6); 02-21 (6); 02-14 (2); 02-07 (2); 02-01; 01-41 (3); 01-27; 01-20 (6); 01-06 (2); 00-28; 00-27 (7); 00-09 (2); 96-65 (2); 95-48 (3); 95-48 Tech Asst (3);
Admin Plan: s7p4 (4); s7p5; s7p6; s7p7 (2); s18p2; s18p3 (2); s18p5 (4); s18p6; s18p7 (2); s20p1; s20p6 (2); s22p3 (2); s23p5; s23p6

CORPORATION 14
24 CFR 5: .214 (2);
24 CFR 982: .4 (2);
HUD-50058Instr: p71 (2);
7420.10G Gbk: 17-9 (2); 21-20;
PIH Notices: 00-11A; 95-48; 95-48 Tech Asst;
Admin Plan: s19p1; s25p7

CORPORATIONS 17
7420.10G Gbk: 21-1;
PIH Notices: 03-11; 03-05; 02-01 (3); 01-40; 01-27; 01-15; 00-45; 00-11; 00-01; 99-52 (3); 99-11; 98-66

CORRECT 107
24 CFR 5: .353 (6);
24 CFR 982: .102 (2); .404 (4); .517;
HUD-50058: p ii;
HUD-50058Instr: p1 (2); p11 (2); p33 (2);
HUD-52580: p5;
HUD-52580-A: p17; p18 (2);
HUD-52641: p3 (2);
HUD-52648: p2;
HUD-52665: p1; p2;
HUD-903: p1 (2);
7420.10G Gbk: 1-10 (2); 1-11 (2); 8-18; 10-17; 10-22; 10-27 (2); 10-28 (3); 10-29 (2); 10-34 (2); 10-35; 10-40 Ex 10-4a; 10-42 Ex 10-5; 10-45 Ex 10-7b; 10-46 Ex 10-8; 11-9 (2); 12-4; 12-5; 15-7; 16-1; 16-5; 18-4; 18-9; 18-10; 19-2; 19-4 (3); 19-10; 19-12; 22-5; 22-6 (3); 22-11; 22-14; 22-15; 24-9;
PIH Notices: 02-27 (8); 01-15 (2); 01-06 (9); 00-24B (5);
Admin Plan: s6p1; s6p4; s10p3 (2); s15p6; s21p4; s21p7

CORRECTED................................. 47
24 CFR 982: .619 (3);
HUD-50058: p ii;
HUD-50058Instr: p11 (3); p12 (2);
HUD-52580-A: p2; p13; p17;
HUD-52648: p1 (3);
7420.10G Gbk: 10-18; 10-27 (2); 10-28; 10-33 (4); 10-34;
PIH Notices: 03-20; 02-21; 01-20 (5); 01-06 (3); 00-45; 00-27 (3);
Admin Plan: s10p4 (3); s20p5; s21p5 (4); s21p5

CORRECTING................................. 7
7420.10G Gbk: 10-28; 22-5 (2);
PIH Notices: 03-20; 02-27 (2); 02-27

CORRECTION 69
24 CFR 982: .102 (2); .404; .619;
HUD-50058: p2 (7); p ii (3);
HUD-50058Instr: p1; p6 (2); p11 (8); p12 (3); p21;
HUD-52641: p3;
HUD-52648: p1;
7420.10G Gbk: 10-18; 10-21 (2); 10-23 (3); 10-29; 10-30; 10-33; 10-34; 11-18;
PIH Notices: 02-27 (2); 02-21; 01-20; 01-06 (7); 00-45 (3); 00-27; 00-24A; 00-24B (5);
Admin Plan: s10p5; s21p5 (2); s22p3;
:
PIH Notices: 95-48 (2); 95-48 Tech Asst (2);
Admin Plan: s7p8

CORRECTIONS............................ 19
HUD-50058Instr: p1;
7420.10G Gbk: 10-21; 10-22 (2); 10-27; 10-29; 10-33; 10-34 (2); 10-44 Ex 10-7a; 11-12; 22-5;
PIH Notices: 03-20; 00-53; 00-24A; 00-09; 99-11;

Admin Plan: s10p5; s10p5
CORRECTIVE 77
7420.10G Gbk: 22-16;
PIH Notices: 02-27 (67); 02-07; 01-06 (3); 00-28; 00-24 (2); 96-65;
Admin Plan: s23p3
CORRECTIVE ACTION 9
HUD-52641: p5;
7420.10G Gbk: 1-11; 10-37 Ex 10-2; 20-6; 22-1; 22-5; 22-11 (2); 22-14
CORRECTIVE ACTION 23
HUD-52641: p5;
7420.10G Gbk: 10-37 Ex 10-2; 20-6; 22-1; 22-5; 22-11 (2); 22-14;
PIH Notices: 02-27 (10); 01-06; 00-28; 00-24 (2); 96-65
CORRECTIVE ACTION PLAN 42
7420.10G Gbk: 1-11;
PIH Notices: 02-27 (39); 01-06; 01-06
CORRECTIVE ACTION PLAN ACTIVITIES 1
PIH Notices: 02-27
CORRECTIVE ACTION PLANS ... 12
PIH Notices: 02-27 (11); 02-27
CORRECTIVE ACTIONS 5
PIH Notices: 02-27 (4);
Admin Plan: s23p3
CORRECTLY 17
24 CFR 5: .615 (3);
24 CFR 982: .152;
HUD-52648: p2;
7420.10G Gbk: 5-26; 9-12; 12-10; 18-2; 19-6; 19-10; 19-12;
PIH Notices: 01-15;
Admin Plan: s20p2; s21p4; s21p6; s21p7
CORRECTS 8
24 CFR 982: .404;
HUD-52641: p3;
7420.10G Gbk: 1-16 Ex 1-3; 11-12;
PIH Notices: 00-45; 00-24A; 95-48; 95-48 Tech Asst
CORRIDORS 8
24 CFR 5: .703;
HUD-52580: p1;
HUD-52580-A: p8 (2); p9; p10; p11; p12
CORROBORATING 1
Admin Plan: s20p3
CORRUPT 27
24 CFR 982: .306; .316; .453 (2); .551; .552;
HUD-52641: p5 (2); p6;
HUD-52646: p2;
7420.10G Gbk: 1-15; 5-36 Ex 5-4; 5-37; 8-19; 11-3; 11-18 (2); 15-4 (2); 15-5; 22-14;
PIH Notices: 01-41;
Admin Plan: s2p3; s2p6; s15p2; s15p5; s16p1
COST 350
24 CFR 5: .318 (2); .360; .363 (2); .603 (2); .609 (3); .661; .801;
24 CFR 982: .1; .4; .102 (18); .510 (2); .517 (5); .520; .553; .622; .623 (9); .632;
HUD-50058: p7; p viii; p10; p11; p13; p xiii (2); p14; p xiv (2); p15 (3); p xv (5);
HUD-50058Instr: p10; p22 (2); p28; p30; p32; p36 (3); p37; p42; p46; p53 (3); p56 (3); p58 (9); p76 (2);
HUD-52641: 8 (2);
HUD-52641-A: p1 (3); p i (6);
HUD-903: p2;
7420.10G Gbk: 1-4; 1-10; 2-8; 4-4; 4-12; 4-27 Ex 4-2 (2); 5-3; 5-14 Ex 5-2; 5-15 Ex 5-2 (2); 5-16 Ex 5-2; 5-19; 5-30; 5-44; 6-3 (2); 6-4; 6-9 Ex 6-1; 8-3; 8-4; 10-1; 10-8; 10-19 (2); 10-23; 10-24; 10-25; 11-7 (3); 12-9; 13-6; 17-11; 18-1 (2); 18-2 (2); 18-4 (2); 18-6 (5); 18-7 (4); 20-3 (3); 20-6; 20-8; 20-9 (4); 20-11 (2); 20-12 Ex 20-2 (3); 20-13 (2); 20-14; 20-16 (2); 20-17; 20-18 (16); 20-19 Ex 20-3 (11); 20-20 (5); 20-21 Ex 20-4 (3); 20-21 (5); 20-22 (2); 20-22 Ex 20-5; 20-25 (2); 20-26; 21-7; 21-9 (2); 21-10 (3); 22-3; 22-18; 24-7; 24-8; 24-9 (2); 24-15;
PIH Notices: 03-23 (15); 03-11 (2); 02-27 (9); 02-22; 02-21; 02-20 (3); 02-06 (4); 02-01 (5); 01-41 (5); 01-20; 01-15 (4); 01-15 Impr Integ Hbk (7); 01-10 (2); 00-46 (2); 00-41; 00-27 (2); 00-24B (2); 00-23 (5); 00-09 (10); 99-

52 (5); 96-65; 95-48 (8); 95-48 Tech Asst (8);
Admin Plan: s6p13 (2); s10p5; s11p1; s19p1 (2); s21p1; s25p6

COST OF UTILITIES 21
24 CFR 5: .603;
24 CFR 982: .4; .517; .622;
HUD-50058Instr: p76;
HUD-52667: p i (2);
7420.10G Gbk: 6-3; 10-8; 17-11; 18-4 (2);
PIH Notices: 02-22; 02-20; 00-46; 00-24B (2);
Admin Plan: s6p13 (2); s19p1; s19p1

COSTS 292
24 CFR 5: .318; .603; .628 (2); .661;
24 CFR 982: .4; .102 (5); .152 (8); .157; .517 (3); .520 (3); .553; .622; .623; .624; .627; .635 (7); .643 (4);
HUD-50058: p7; p xiv;
HUD-50058Instr: p28; p36 (3); p37; p56; p74;
HUD-52667: p i (5);
7420.10G Gbk: 2-6; 2-7 (2); 2-8; 4-4; 5-16 Ex 5-2; 5-25 Ex 5-3; 5-27 (3); 5-28 (4); 5-30 (3); 5-49 Ex 5-5 (3); 5-51 Ex 5-5 (2); 5-52 Ex 5-5 (3); 6-1 (5); 6-2; 6-3 (3); 8-1; 8-4; 8-15; 9-7; 9-8 (2); 11-9; 12-9; 17-4; 17-12; 18-1 (4); 18-2; 18-4 (2); 18-5 (2); 18-9; 19-9; 19-11; 20-1; 20-2 (3); 20-3 (2); 20-4 (2); 20-5 (2); 20-6 (5); 20-13 (3); 20-14; 20-15; 20-17; 20-18 (2); 20-21 Ex 20-4; 20-22; 20-22 Ex 20-5 (2); 20-23; 20-26; 20-27 (2); 20-29; 21-8; 21-10; 22-3; 22-17 (5); 23-2; 23-15; 23-16 Ex 23-2 (2); 24-9 (2); 24-12;
PIH Notices: 03-23 (37); 03-11 (4); 02-27 (13); 02-21 (2); 02-20 (3); 02-07 (7); 02-06 (3); 02-01; 01-41 (7); 01-15; 01-15 Impr Integ Hbk (7); 01-10; 00-49 (8); 00-46 (2); 00-28 (7); 00-24B; 00-23 (2); 00-11; 00-09 (10); 99-52; 95-48; 95-48 Tech Asst;
Admin Plan: s1p4; s6p2; s6p11; s6p13; s7p3; s7p7; s19p1; s22p2 (3); s22p3; s23p6; s24p3

COUNSEL 4
24 CFR 5: .100 (2);
Admin Plan: s18p5; s18p6

COUNSELED.................................. 1
7420.10G Gbk: 18-1

COUNSELING 91
24 CFR 5: .603;
24 CFR 982: Intro; .625; .626; .630 (15); .633 (3); .636; .637 (2);
HUD-50058: p16;
HUD-50058Instr: p13; p28; p61; p71;
7420.10G Gbk: 2-2; 2-11 (3); 8-14; 20-3; 20-5 (3); 20-6; 21-10 (2); 21-11; 23-15; 24-9 (3); 24-14;
PIH Notices: 02-21 (2); 02-07 (5); 02-01; 01-20; 00-28 (4); 00-11; 00-11A; 99-52;
Admin Plan: s6p3; s8p3; s8p4 (4); s20p2 (2); s20p6; s22p1; s22p2 (2); s22p4 (2); s25p2; s25p4; s25p5; s25p6 (3); s25p7 (6); s25p7

COUNSELING FEE......................... 2
7420.10G Gbk: 20-6;
PIH Notices: 02-07

COUNSELING FEES....................... 6
7420.10G Gbk: 20-5 (2);
PIH Notices: 02-07 (2); 00-28; 00-28

COUNSELLING.............................. 1
24 CFR 982: .152

COUNSELOR 1
7420.10G Gbk: 5-53 Ex 5-5

COUNSELORS 1
7420.10G Gbk: 21-16 Ex 21-6

COUNT.. 47
24 CFR 982: .201; .401; .627 (3);
HUD-50058: p v; p7; p xvi;
HUD-50058Instr: p17 (2); p24; p36; p60;
HUD-52580-A: p1 (2); p2 (2); p6;
HUD-52648: p2;
7420.10G Gbk: 5-18 (5); 5-21; 5-23; 5-26 (2); 5-50 Ex 5-5; 10-8; 21-18;
PIH Notices: 02-14; 02-01; 01-01 (5); 00-01; 99-52; 98-66;

Admin Plan: s6p5; s6p10 (2); s23p5; s24p3; s24p3

COUNTED 60
24 CFR 5: .603;
24 CFR 982: .201 (2); .402; .608; .613 (2); .619; .620;
HUD-50058Instr: p19;
7420.10G Gbk: 4-20 (3); 4-22; 5-18 (6); 5-19 (2); 5-21; 5-22; 5-23 (2); 5-27; 5-29; 5-31; 5-41; 5-47 Ex 5-5; 5-49 Ex 5-5; 12-13 Ex 12-1; 17-5; 17-11; 24-1; 24-4; 24-5;
PIH Notices: 03-05; 01-41; 01-40; 01-15; 01-01 (5); 00-09;
Admin Plan: s2p3; s6p1; s6p5 (2); s6p9 (4); s6p10; s7p5 (2); s19p1

COUNTER....................................15
HUD-52580: p6;
HUD-52580-A: p19;
PIH Notices: 95-48 (6); 95-48 Tech Asst (6);
Admin Plan: s19p1

COUNTERPART 5
24 CFR 982: .503;
PIH Notices: 02-20 (2); 00-46; 00-46

COUNTERPARTS............................2
PIH Notices: 02-21; 01-20

COUNTERS 16
PIH Notices: 95-48 (8); 95-48 Tech Asst (7); 95-48 Tech Asst

COUNTER-TOP...............................3
HUD-52580: p6;
HUD-52580-A: p19;
7420.10G Gbk: 10-5

COUNTIES......................................3
7420.10G Gbk: 20-5;
PIH Notices: 02-07; 00-28

COUNTING...................................11
HUD-50058: p16; p xvi;
HUD-50058Instr: p59; p60 (2);
7420.10G Gbk: 5-27; 20-8 Ex 20-1;
PIH Notices: 95-48 (2); 95-48 Tech Asst; 95-48 Tech Asst

COUNTRY.....................................12
HUD-52580-A: p15;
7420.10G Gbk: 5-5 (3); 5-7; 9-5 (2); 10-20; 13-3; 19-5; 19-6;
PIH Notices: 02-14

COUNTS 2
7420.10G Gbk: 13-7;
PIH Notices: 01-06

COUNTY.......................................59
24 CFR 5: .100;
24 CFR 982: .4; .201 (2); .204; .207 (2); .503;
HUD-50058Instr: p72; p74;
HUD-52580: p1 (3); p17 (2);
HUD-903: p1 (3);
7420.10G Gbk: 4-8; 4-17 (2); 4-19 (2); 5-20; 21-1; 21-8;
PIH Notices: 03-11; 02-20 (6); 01-06; 01-02; 01-01 (3); 00-46 (6); 00-11 (2); 95-48 (6); 95-48 Tech Asst (6);
Admin Plan: s18p6

COUNTY-OWNED 2
PIH Notices: 95-48; 95-48 Tech Asst

COUNTY-RUN.................................2
PIH Notices: 95-48; 95-48 Tech Asst

COUNTY'S 2
PIH Notices: 02-20; 00-46

COUNTY-SPONSORED..................6
PIH Notices: 95-48 (3); 95-48 Tech Asst (2); 95-48 Tech Asst

COURT 67
24 CFR 982: .306; .310 (2); .311; .314; .315; .353;
HUD-50058Instr: p30 (2);
HUD-52641: p6;
HUD-903: p2 (3);
7420.10G Gbk: 4-11; 5-10 Ex 5-1 (2); 5-12; 5-16 Ex 5-2; 5-47 Ex 5-5 (3); 8-13; 8-18; 11-2; 12-13 Ex 12-1; 15-4; 21-9; 22-16;
PIH Notices: 01-15 Impr Integ Hbk (3); 95-48 (7); 95-48 Tech Asst (7);
Admin Plan: s2p3 (2); s6p7 (2); s6p8; s6p9 (2); s7p4; s7p7; s7p8; s8p5; s8p6; s9p2; s10p5; s14p2; s15p4; s15p5 (2); s16p1; s17p2; s20p4; s25p1

COURT ACTION 7
HUD-52641: p9 (3);
HUD-52641-A: p2 (3);
7420.10G Gbk: 15-3

COURT ACTION 12
24 CFR 982: .310 (2);
HUD-52641: p9 (3);
HUD-52641-A: p2 (3);

7420.10G Gbk: 15-3;
Admin Plan: s9p2; s15p5; s15p5

COURT AWARDED CUSTODY 1
Admin Plan: s6p8

COURT DECISION 3
7420.10G Gbk: 5-10 Ex 5-1 (2);
Admin Plan: s2p3

COURT DECISIONS 2
7420.10G Gbk: 8-13; 21-9

COURT ORDER 5
24 CFR 982: .353;
HUD-50058Instr: p30;
7420.10G Gbk: 12-13 Ex 12-1;
Admin Plan: s6p7; s6p7

COURT ORDERS 1
7420.10G Gbk: 4-11

COURT RECORDS 3
7420.10G Gbk: 5-12;
PIH Notices: 01-15 Impr Integ Hbk;
Admin Plan: s15p4

COURT TRUSTEE 1
Admin Plan: s7p4

COURT-AWARDED 5
24 CFR 982: .551;
Admin Plan: s5p2; s6p7; s6p8; s11p2

COURT-AWARDED CUSTODY 9
24 CFR 982: .551;
HUD-52641: 8;
HUD-52641-A: p1;
HUD-52646: p2;
7420.10G Gbk: 1-15;
Admin Plan: s5p2; s6p7; s6p8; s11p2

COURTESY 4
Admin Plan: s1p6; s10p2 (2); s20p4

COURTHOUSE 6
HUD-903: p3;
PIH Notices: 95-48 (2); 95-48 Tech Asst (2);
Admin Plan: s20p4

COURT-ORDER 1
24 CFR 982: .163

COURT-ORDERED 3
7420.10G Gbk: 5-23; 22-17;
Admin Plan: s7p7

COURTROOM 8
PIH Notices: 95-48 (4); 95-48 Tech Asst (3); 95-48 Tech Asst

COURTS 6
HUD-903: p2;
7420.10G Gbk: 5-47 Ex 5-5;
PIH Notices: 95-48 (2); 95-48 Tech Asst; 95-48 Tech Asst

COURT'S 1
24 CFR 982: .315

COVER LETTER 6
24 CFR 5: .514;
7420.10G Gbk: 5-11;
PIH Notices: 02-21 (2); 01-20; 00-27

COVERED HOUSING 7
PIH Notices: 01-41 (3); 00-09 (3); 00-09

COVERED INDIVIDUAL 5
HUD-52641: p6 (4); p6

COVERED INDIVIDUALS 2
24 CFR 5: .500; .500

COVERED PERSON 8
24 CFR 5: .100 (2);
24 CFR 982: .4; .310 (4);
Admin Plan: s15p3

COVERED PROGRAM 33
24 CFR 5: .214; .230 (3); .236 (3); .504; .506; .508 (6); .512; .514 (6); .516 (6); .518 (4);
HUD-50058Instr: p17

COVERED PROGRAMS 26
24 CFR 5: .210 (2); .500; .504 (5); .508; .514 (6); .516 (5); .518 (3); .520;
PIH Notices: 02-01; 99-52

CR 7
HUD-50058: p9 (2); p10 (2); p11; p12; p12

CRANSTON-GONZALES 1
PIH Notices: 01-27

CRAWL SPACES 2
24 CFR 982: .401;
HUD-52580-A: p8

CREDIBLE 3
Admin Plan: s15p4 (2); s15p4

CREDIBLE EVIDENCE 3
Admin Plan: s15p4 (2); s15p4

CREDIT 159
24 CFR 982: .155; .352; .630;
HUD-50058: p9 (2); p ix (2); p10 (2); p x (2); p11; p xi; p12 (2); p xii (2); p16; p xvi; p17;
HUD-50058Instr: p ii; p32; p39 (3); p40; p41 (2); p43 (3); p44; p45 (2); p49 (3); p51 (3); p52 (3); p60; p62; p64; p65 (8); p66; p67; p72;
7420.10G Gbk: 2-11; 5-24 (2); 14-1; 19-10; 20-24 (2);

20-25 (3); 20-26 (5); 22-10; 23-6; 23-10 (2); 23-11 (8); 23-12 (5); 23-13; 23-14 (2); 23-16 Ex 23-2 (6); 23-17 Ex 23-2 (3); 24-9 (4); 24-14;
PIH Notices: 03-11; 02-22 (19); 02-15; 01-15 (10); 01-15 Impr Integ Hbk (2); 01-02 (7);
Admin Plan: s2p2; s7p5 (2); s8p3; s17p1; s20p1; s20p3 (2); s20p4 (3); s22p2; s24p4

CREDIT COUNSELING....................3
24 CFR 982: .630;
7420.10G Gbk: 24-9; 24-14

CREDIT DATABASE........................1
PIH Notices: 01-15

CREDIT HISTORY...........................2
PIH Notices: 01-15;
Admin Plan: s2p2

CREDIT REPORT.............................3
7420.10G Gbk: 22-10;
Admin Plan: s7p5; s7p5

CREDIT REPORTS...........................4
7420.10G Gbk: 24-9;
PIH Notices: 01-15 (2); 01-15

CREDITED.....................................21
24 CFR 982: .451;
HUD-50058: p xvii;
HUD-50058Instr: p62 (2); p72;
HUD-52641: p4; 8;
HUD-52641-A: p1;
7420.10G Gbk: 5-48 Ex 5-5; 11-5; 20-2; 20-25; 20-26 (2); 23-1; 23-14 (3);
PIH Notices: 01-10;
Admin Plan: s7p5; s25p5

CREDITOR..1
Admin Plan: s20p4

CREDITS..9
HUD-50058Instr: p28; p60;
7420.10G Gbk: 5-53 Ex 5-5; 20-26; 23-7; 23-14;
PIH Notices: 02-22; 01-15 Impr Integ Hbk;
Admin Plan: s7p5

CREED 1
Admin Plan: s1p2

CRIME OF VIOLENCE....................2
24 CFR 982: .207;
7420.10G Gbk: 4-17

CRIME VICTIM COMPENSATION 3
HUD-50058Instr: p32;
7420.10G Gbk: 5-16 Ex 5-2;
PIH Notices: 01-15 Impr Integ Hbk

CRIMINAL....................................188
24 CFR 5: .100 (3); .238 (2); .528; .661 (3);
24 CFR 982: .4 (2); .54; .306 (5); .307 (2); .310 (11); .316 (3); .453 (4); .551 (4); .552 (3); .553 (29);
HUD-52641: p5 (2); p6;
HUD-52646: p2;
HUD-52648: p3;
HUD-9886: p2;
7420.10G Gbk: 1-15; 2-5; 5-36 Ex 5-4 (2); 5-37; 8-19; 11-3; 11-18 (2); 13-3 (2); 15-4 (2); 15-5; 15-7 (2); 22-14; 22-15; 22-16; 22-17;
PIH Notices: 03-11 (42); 01-41;
Admin Plan: s2p3 (3); s2p6 (6); s2p7 (2); s6p6; s9p3 (2); s11p1; s15p2 (4); s15p3 (4); s15p4 (3); s15p5 (3); s16p1 (2); s16p2 (2); s17p2; s18p2 (3); s18p3 (3); s20p7 (3); s23p7 (2); s23p7

CRIMINAL ACTIVITIES 1
24 CFR 5: .661

CRIMINAL ACTIVITY 151
24 CFR 5: .100 (3); .661;
24 CFR 982: .4 (2); .54; .306 (4); .307 (2); .310 (9); .316 (2); .453 (2); .551 (3); .552 (2); .553 (18);
HUD-52641: p5 (2); p6 (2); p7 (2); p9 (9);
HUD-52641-A: p2 (12);
7420.10G Gbk: 1-15 (2); 3-4 (2); 4-15; 5-1 (2); 5-36 Ex 5-4; 5-37 (2); 5-39 (2); 8-19 (2); 8-20 (4); 11-3 (2); 11-4 (2); 15-1; 15-2 (7); 15-4; 15-6 (4); 15-7 (4); 21-4; 24-14;
PIH Notices: 03-11 (5);
Admin Plan: s2p3 (2); s2p6 (4); s2p7 (2); s6p6; s9p3 (2); s15p2 (3); s15p3 (4); s15p5 (2); s16p1 (2); s16p2 (2); s18p2; s18p3; s23p7 (2); s23p7

CRIMINAL BACKGROUND CHECK 2
7420.10G Gbk: 13-3; 13-3

CRIMINAL CONDUCT...................1
PIH Notices: 03-11

CRIMINAL HISTORY....................19

24 CFR 982: .553;
PIH Notices: 03-11 (17);
Admin Plan: s2p6

CRIMINAL INTENT........................2
Admin Plan: s20p7; s20p7

CRIMINAL PROSECUTION 4
24 CFR 5: .528;
7420.10G Gbk: 22-16;
Admin Plan: s17p2; s20p7

CRIMINAL RECORD....................20
24 CFR 982: .553 (6);
7420.10G Gbk: 15-7 (2);
PIH Notices: 03-11 (6);
Admin Plan: s11p1; s15p4;
s18p2 (2); s18p3; s18p3

CRIMINAL RECORDS 15
24 CFR 982: .310; .553 (3);
7420.10G Gbk: 2-5;
PIH Notices: 03-11 (9);
Admin Plan: s15p4

CRIMINALS 7
24 CFR 982: Intro; .310 (2);
.553 (3); .553

CRISIS 2
HUD-50058Instr: p28;
7420.10G Gbk: 23-15

CRITERIA...................................167
24 CFR 5: .306; .514;
.516 (3);
24 CFR 982: .4; .101;
.104; .201 (2); .206 (3);
.401 (17); .503; .621 (2);
HUD-50058Instr: p13; p16 (2);
p17 (2); p19 (2);
HUD-52580-A: p4;
HUD-52648: p1; p4 (3);
7420.10G Gbk: 1-5; 1-7 (2);
2-9; 3-2; 3-8; 4-5; 4-16; 4-21; 4-22; 5-1 (2);
5-35; 7-3; 10-1 (2); 10-2 (6); 10-3 (2); 10-4;
10-6; 10-7; 10-8; 10-9 (2); 10-10; 10-11 (2);
10-12; 10-13 (2); 10-14 (2); 17-10; 17-11; 20-11; 23-20 (5);
PIH Notices: 03-12 (5); 03-11; 02-27 (4); 02-21; 02-20; 02-06; 01-41; 01-15 Impr Integ Hbk; 01-06;
01-01; 00-09 (2); 95-48 (6); 95-48 Tech Asst (6);
Admin Plan: s2p1 (4); s2p4;
s2p5 (3); s2p7; s3p3;
s5p3; s6p7; s9p1; s9p2;
s10p1; s14p1; s15p5;
s16p1; s20p1; s20p6;
s20p7; s21p3; s21p4;
s22p1 (2); s23p2 (2);
s23p3 (5); s24p1; s24p2;
s24p3 (4); s24p4 (4);
s24p6 (2); s24p6

CRITERION 1
Admin Plan: s21p3

CROSS REFERENCE......................6
24 CFR 5: .218;
PIH Notices: 02-01; 01-43;
01-11; 00-53; 00-45

CROSS REFERENCED 1
PIH Notices: 00-23

CROSS REFERENCES..................36
24 CFR 5: .232;
PIH Notices: 03-23; 03-20;
03-12; 03-11; 02-27; 02-21; 02-20; 02-15; 02-14;
02-07; 02-06; 02-03; 01-41; 01-33; 01-20; 01-10;
01-06; 01-02; 01-01; 00-49; 00-46; 00-41; 00-34;
00-31; 00-28; 00-27; 00-24; 00-23; 00-14; 00-09;
00-01; 98-66; 96-65; 95-48; 95-48

CROSS-EXAMINE 1
24 CFR 5: .514

CROSS-LISTING 1
24 CFR 982: .205

CULPABILITY................................4
24 CFR 982: .552;
7420.10G Gbk: 5-38; 22-14;
Admin Plan: s15p4

CULPABLE 5
24 CFR 982: .310 (2); .552;
7420.10G Gbk: 5-38; 22-14

CULTURAL.....................................7
HUD-50058Instr: p73;
HUD-903: p2;
7420.10G Gbk: 4-3;
PIH Notices: 95-48 (2); 95-48 Tech Asst; 95-48 Tech Asst

CULTURE 2
HUD-50058Instr: p73;
HUD-903: p2

CUMULATIVE...............................18
24 CFR 5: .617 (2);
HUD-50058: p17; p xvii;
HUD-50058Instr: p62 (2);
PIH Notices: 02-21 (2); 01-15 Impr Integ Hbk (4); 01-01;
Admin Plan: s6p2 (2); s6p3 (2);
s6p3

CUMULATIVE MONTHS.................
1
Admin Plan: s6p2

CUMULATIVELY...........................2
24 CFR 982: .102;

7420.10G Gbk: 19-13
CURRENT INCOME........................2
7420.10G Gbk: 5-17; 5-17
CURRENT LISTING........................2
24 CFR 982: .301;
7420.10G Gbk: 8-6
CURRENT LISTING OF ACCESSIBLE UNITS........................1
24 CFR 982: .301
CURRENT PARTICIPANT...............2
7420.10G Gbk: 14-2;
Admin Plan: s22p2
CURRENT PARTICIPANTS.............2
7420.10G Gbk: 4-3; 7-6
CURRENT PARTICIPATION...........3
24 CFR 982: .310; .552;
7420.10G Gbk: 15-7
CURRENT PER-UNIT COST...........5
7420.10G Gbk: 20-18 (4); 20-20
CURRENTLY ENGAGED IN..........7
24 CFR 982: .553 (4);
PIH Notices: 03-11; 95-48; 95-48 Tech Asst
CURRENTLY ENGAGING IN.........2
24 CFR 982: .553;
Admin Plan: s15p2
CUSTODY........................24
24 CFR 982: .310; .551;
HUD-52641: p9;
HUD-52641-A: p2;
7420.10G Gbk: 1-7; 5-43; 15-2; 15-6;
PIH Notices: 03-11; 01-15 Impr Integ Hbk (2);
Admin Plan: s2p4 (3); s5p2; s6p7 (2); s6p8 (3); s7p7; s8p5 (2); s11p2
CUSTODY AGREEMENTS.............1
Admin Plan: s7p7
CUSTOM........................2
PIH Notices: 95-48; 95-48 Tech Asst
CUSTOMARILY........................6
24 CFR 982: .510;
HUD-52641: 8;
HUD-52641-A: p1;
PIH Notices: 95-48; 95-48 Tech Asst;
Admin Plan: s15p2
CUSTOMARILY INCLUDED IN RENT 1
24 CFR 982: .510
CUSTOMARY........................3
24 CFR 982: .4; .643; .643
CUSTOMER........................12
7420.10G Gbk: 4-12 (3); 10-23; 11-15; 19-6; 19-11; 21-6; 21-9;
PIH Notices: 02-27; 01-27; 01-15
CUSTOMERS........................2
7420.10G Gbk: 19-6;
Admin Plan: s18p3
CUSTOMIZED........................2
7420.10G Gbk: 12-2; 19-4
CUT-OFF........................6
7420.10G Gbk: 11-9 (3);
PIH Notices: 02-27 (2); 02-27
CUT-OFF DATE........................6
7420.10G Gbk: 11-9 (3);
PIH Notices: 02-27 (2); 02-27
CYCLIC........................2
24 CFR 5: .609;
PIH Notices: 01-15 Impr Integ Hbk
DAMAGE........................42
24 CFR 5: .100; .318;
24 CFR 982: .310; .401; .452; .614 (2); .621;
HUD-52580-A: p1; p2; p13 (3); p15;
HUD-52641: p9;
HUD-52641-A: p2 (4);
HUD-52665: p3 (2);
7420.10G Gbk: 1-14; 5-38; 10-9; 10-28; 11-17; 15-3 (3); 17-10; 17-11; 24-9;
PIH Notices: 00-24B; 00-23; 95-48; 95-48 Tech Asst;
Admin Plan: s9p3; s10p4 (2); s10p5; s15p3; s19p1
DAMAGED........................11
24 CFR 5: .403;
HUD-52580-A: p2 (4); p17;
7420.10G Gbk: 5-2; 10-2; 10-4; 10-7; 10-18
DAMAGES........................25
24 CFR 5: .318;
24 CFR 982: .313; .404 (2); .406; .552; .619 (2);
HUD-52641: p5; p9; p10;
HUD-52641-A: p2; p3;
HUD-9886: p2;
7420.10G Gbk: 5-37; 8-4; 11-18; 14-5 (2); 15-5;
Admin Plan: s8p4; s13p1; s15p2; s23p8; s23p8
DANGER........................
11
24 CFR 982: .401; .614;
HUD-50058Instr: p72; p73;
HUD-52580-A: p2;
7420.10G Gbk: 1-7; 9-9; 10-

9 (2); 11-16 Ex 11-1;
Admin Plan: s10p4

DANGEROUS.................................11
24 CFR 5: .703;
24 CFR 982: .401 (2); .614;
HUD-52580-A: p17;
7420.10G Gbk: 10-10; 10-13; 17-5; 20-17; 20-22;
PIH Notices: 99-11

DANGEROUSLY.............................1
HUD-52580-A: p2

DANGERS...2
24 CFR 982: .401;
7420.10G Gbk: 10-13

DATA BASE......................................3
7420.10G Gbk: 9-10;
PIH Notices: 01-06; 01-06

DATA BASED...................................1
PIH Notices: 01-15 Impr Integ Hbk

DATA BASES...................................1
24 CFR 5: .214

DATA ENTRY................................13
HUD-50058Instr: p3;
7420.10G Gbk: 4-13; 10-25; 11-9; 11-16 Ex 11-1 (2); 19-10; 21-14 Ex 21-4; 22-6;
PIH Notices: 02-20; 00-53 (2); 00-46

DATA REPORTING.........................1
PIH Notices: 01-15 Impr Integ Hbk

DATA SOURCES............................12
24 CFR 982: .207;
HUD-52580: p1 (4);
HUD-52667: p i;
HUD-903: p1;
7420.10G Gbk: 4-16;
PIH Notices: 02-20 (2); 00-46; 00-46

DATABASE....................................58
HUD-50058Instr: p1; p11 (3); p74;
7420.10G Gbk: 2-7; 2-10; 4-9; 4-13; 9-3 (5); 9-4; 9-6; 9-7 (6); 9-8 (5); 9-10 (4); 9-11 (3); 9-12; 12-3; 21-4 (4); 24-11;
PIH Notices: 03-11 (3); 02-27 (2); 02-20; 01-15 (5); 00-46;
Admin Plan: s8p4; s11p2 (3); s21p2

DATABASE-MATCHING 2
PIH Notices: 02-20; 00-46

DATABASES....................................7
7420.10G Gbk: 2-6 (2); 9-3; 9-4; 9-11; 19-6;
PIH Notices: 01-15

DAUGHTER.....................................7
7420.10G Gbk: 5-19; 5-27; 17-8; 17-9 (2);
PIH Notices: 01-15 Impr Integ Hbk;
Admin Plan: s2p4

DAY CARE.....................................11
24 CFR 5: .703;
HUD-50058: p17;
HUD-50058Instr: p63;
7420.10G Gbk: 2-7; 8-7; 9-17 Ex 9-3; 23-16 Ex 23-2;
PIH Notices: 95-48 (2); 95-48 Tech Asst; 95-48 Tech Asst

DAY CARE FACILITIES.................1
HUD-50058Instr: p63

DEADLINE....................................54
24 CFR 5: .801;
24 CFR 982: .555;
HUD-52641: p5;
7420.10G Gbk: 1-5; 4-7 (5); 4-12; 4-13; 5-8; 8-13; 10-22; 10-26; 10-28; 10-34; 11-15; 11-16 Ex 11-1; 11-18; 13-9; 13-11 Ex 13-1; 13-12 Ex 13-2; 16-1; 20-29; 21-2 (2); 24-10;
PIH Notices: 01-20 (11); 01-06; 00-53; 00-27 (8);
Admin Plan: s3p1 (2); s15p6; s18p6; s24p2

DEADLINES..................................20
24 CFR 982: .355;
7420.10G Gbk: 10-30; 12-8; 13-7; 19-13; 21-3 (2); 22-5; 23-7;
PIH Notices: 02-27 (3); 01-41; 00-09; 96-65 (3);
Admin Plan: s15p6 (2); s15p6

DEADLINES FOR...........................3
7420.10G Gbk: 10-30; 22-5;
PIH Notices: 96-65

DEATH 17
24 CFR 5: .363; .609; .630;
24 CFR 982: .633;
HUD-50058: p v;
HUD-50058Instr: p18; p29;
7420.10G Gbk: 5-14 Ex 5-2; 6-8; 8-12;
PIH Notices: 01-15 Impr Integ Hbk (3); 95-48; 95-48 Tech Asst;
Admin Plan: s6p4; s16p3

DEATH BENEFIT............................1
HUD-50058Instr: p29

DEATH BENEFITS..........................4
24 CFR 5: .609;

7420.10G Gbk: 5-14 Ex 5-2;
PIH Notices: 01-15 Impr Integ Hbk; 01-15 Impr Integ Hbk

DEATHS 1
7420.10G Gbk: 12-16 Ex 12-4

DEBARMENT 2
7420.10G Gbk: 11-1;
Admin Plan: s24p6

DEBARMENTS 2
PIH Notices: 01-41; 00-09

DEBARRED 11
24 CFR 5: .105 (2);
24 CFR 982: .306; .628; .631;
HUD-52641: p6;
7420.10G Gbk: 8-18; 11-1;
PIH Notices: 01-41 (2); 00-09

DEBIT 8
7420.10G Gbk: 20-24; 20-25 (4); 20-26 (2); 20-26

DEBRIS 9
24 CFR 5: .703 (2);
HUD-52580: p5;
HUD-52580-A: p17 (3); p18 (2);
7420.10G Gbk: 10-13

DEBT 68
24 CFR 5: .216;
24 CFR 982: .619; .623 (7); .627 (2); .632 (3); .633 (9); .635 (10); .638 (2);
HUD-50058: p12; p xii (2); p14; p xiv (2); p15; p xv;
HUD-50058Instr: p50 (3); p56 (4); p58 (2);
7420.10G Gbk: 17-10; 22-13 (4); 22-14;
Admin Plan: s2p6; s17p1 (5); s17p3; s19p1; s22p4; s22p4

DEBT SERVICE 20
24 CFR 982: .619; .623 (7);
HUD-50058: p12; p xii (2); p15; p xv;
HUD-50058Instr: p50 (3); p58 (2);
7420.10G Gbk: 17-10;
Admin Plan: s19p1

DEBTOR 4
Admin Plan: s17p3 (3); s17p3

DEBTS 12
Admin Plan: s17p1 (4); s17p2 (3); s17p3 (3); s25p5; s25p6

DECEASED 1
Admin Plan: s17p3

DECEDENT'S 2
24 CFR 982: .633; .633

DECEIVE 2
7420.10G Gbk: 22-1;
Admin Plan: s17p2

DECEMBER 61
24 CFR 5: .801 (2);
24 CFR 982: .102 (4);
7420.10G Gbk: 5-23 (2); 5-24; 10-16; 10-32 (3); 19-2 (2); 19-3; 20-8; 20-8 Ex 20-1 (4); 20-9; 20-10; 20-12 Ex 20-2 (6); 20-22; 24-16;
PIH Notices: 03-23 (2); 02-27 (4); 02-21 (2); 02-01; 01-43 (4); 01-11; 01-10 (4); 01-06; 01-01; 00-53 (3); 00-45; 00-24; 99-52 (3); 98-66; 98-66

DECENNIAL 6
24 CFR 982: .503 (2);
PIH Notices: 02-20 (2); 00-46; 00-46

DECISION 182
24 CFR 5: .502; .508; .514 (16); .516; .518 (2); .615;
24 CFR 982: .201 (5); .204; .315; .552; .553 (2); .554 (8); .555 (13);
HUD-52580: p1 (5); p3; p5; p7; p9; p10; p11; p12; p14; p16; p17; p18;
7420.10G Gbk: 4-1; 4-6; 4-19; 5-1; 5-8; 5-10 Ex 5-1 (2); 5-11; 5-38 (3); 8-20 (2); 9-3 (2); 11-3; 12-15 Ex 12-3; 13-5; 13-6 (4); 13-7; 15-6; 15-7; 15-10 Ex 15-2 (2); 16-1 (5); 16-2; 16-3 (6); 16-4 (2); 16-5 (7); 17-1; 20-14; 22-11; 22-14; 23-10; 24-8;
PIH Notices: 03-23; 03-11; 02-21 (2); 01-41 (4); 01-20 (2); 01-10 (3); 00-27; 00-09 (2); 95-48 (4); 95-48 Tech Asst (4);
Admin Plan: s1p5 (2); s2p1; s2p3; s3p1; s3p3; s6p5; s8p4; s18p1 (3); s18p2 (3); s18p3 (10); s18p6 (7); s18p7 (3); s24p6

DECISIONMAKING 2
PIH Notices: 95-48; 95-48 Tech Asst

DECISION-MAKING 2

7420.10G Gbk: 10-12; 16-1

DECISIONS....................................45
24 CFR 5: .514;
24 CFR 982: .161; .310; .555;
HUD-52580: p6;
HUD-52580-A: p19;
HUD-52641: p6;
7420.10G Gbk: 1-13; 3-1; 8-13; 8-19; 8-22; 9-11; 10-2; 11-2; 13-2; 13-6; 13-8; 15-6; 16-1 (5); 16-2; 16-4 (3); 16-5 (3); 19-1; 21-1; 21-9; 22-5; 24-2;
PIH Notices: 01-41 (2); 00-11; 95-48; 95-48 Tech Asst;
Admin Plan: s8p3; s18p2; s18p3; s18p6

DECLARATION..............................28
24 CFR 5: .502; .508 (11); .514;
7420.10G Gbk: 5-4 (3); 5-6; 5-8; 5-9 Ex 5-1 (7); 5-35;
Admin Plan: s2p1; s20p6

DECLARATIONS 2
7420.10G Gbk: 5-9 Ex 5-1;
Admin Plan: s3p3

DECLARE..3
HUD-903: p1;
7420.10G Gbk: 15-5; 23-9

DECLARED 7
24 CFR 5: .403; .512;
24 CFR 982: .642 (2);
HUD-50058Instr: p14; p62;
7420.10G Gbk: 5-2

DECLARES.......................................3
24 CFR 5: .508 (2);
HUD-903: p2

DECONCENTRATING.....................1
Admin Plan: s24p1

DECONCENTRATION...................49
24 CFR 982: .102; .503 (2);
HUD-52648: p3 (2); p4 (2);
7420.10G Gbk: 1-10 (2); 1-11; 2-1; 2-2 (4); 2-4; 7-3; 7-10 (3); 8-7; 20-5;
PIH Notices: 02-27 (2); 02-21 (2); 02-20 (2); 01-06 (12); 01-01; 00-24A (2); 00-24B; 00-11 (2);
Admin Plan: s21p1; s21p9; s24p1

DE-CONCENTRATION ....
3
PIH Notices: 02-27;
Admin Plan: s21p2; s21p9

DECONCENTRATION BONUS....30
24 CFR 982: .503;
HUD-52648: p3 (2); p4;
7420.10G Gbk: 1-10 (2); 1-11; 2-4; 7-10 (2);
PIH Notices: 02-27 (2); 02-20; 01-06 (12); 01-01; 00-24A (2); 00-24B;
Admin Plan: s21p1

DECONCENTRATION BONUS INDICATOR..................................15
24 CFR 982: .503;
HUD-52648: p3 (2); p4;
7420.10G Gbk: 1-10 (2); 1-11; 2-4;
PIH Notices: 02-20; 01-06 (3); 01-01; 00-24A; 00-24B

DECONCENTRATION OF POVERTY
3
24 CFR 982: .102;
PIH Notices: 00-11;
Admin Plan: s24p1

DECREASE IN INCOME.................7
PIH Notices: 01-15 Impr Integ Hbk; 01-10 (3); 00-11A; 00-09;
Admin Plan: s11p2

DEDUCT 17
24 CFR 5: .611;
HUD-50058: p vii (3); p xiii; p xv;
HUD-50058Instr: p33; p34 (2); p35; p54; p58;
HUD-52641: p4;
7420.10G Gbk: 5-19; 11-18; 22-17;
PIH Notices: 01-15 Impr Integ Hbk

DEDUCTION 34
24 CFR 5: .611;
HUD-50058: p7; p vii (2); p13; p xiii (2);
HUD-50058Instr: p34 (3); p53 (2); p54;
7420.10G Gbk: 5-14 Ex 5-2; 5-30 (2); 5-31 (2); 5-50 Ex 5-5; 5-51 Ex 5-5; 12-13 Ex 12-1; 20-26;
PIH Notices: 01-15 (6); 01-15 Impr Integ Hbk;
Admin Plan: s6p11 (4); s6p11

DEDUCTIONS............................107
24 CFR 5: .609 (3); .611 (6); .659;
24 CFR 982: .516;
HUD-50058: p7 (2); p vii;
HUD-50058Instr: p24; p25; p34 (7); p36; p70; p77;
7420.10G Gbk: 4-27 Ex 4-2; 5-14 Ex 5-2 (2); 5-28; 5-34; 5-46 Ex 5-5; 12-4; 12-5; 12-11; 12-16 Ex 12-4; 23-12; 23-14;

PIH Notices: 02-01; 01-15 (8); 01-15 Impr Integ Hbk (42); 00-24B (2); 99-52;
Admin Plan: s3p3; s6p1 (4); s6p4 (2); s6p11; s6p12; s7p1; s7p3; s11p1; s11p2; s20p2; s21p4

DEED..3
7420.10G Gbk: 5-49 Ex 5-5;
Admin Plan: s16p3; s16p3

DEFECT..15
24 CFR 982: .404 (6); .619 (4);
HUD-52641: p3 (4);
7420.10G Gbk: 10-18

DEFECTIVE..7
7420.10G Gbk: 10-15; 10-18;
PIH Notices: 00-23 (4); 00-23

DEFECTS..67
24 CFR 982: .401 (3); .404 (2); .405; .614 (2); .619;
HUD-52580-A: p2 (6); p3 (3); p4 (8); p5 (3); p6 (5); p7 (3); p9 (3); p10 (3); p11 (3); p12 (3); p13 (8);
HUD-52641: p3 (2);
7420.10G Gbk: 10-9 (3); 10-10; 10-18;
PIH Notices: 00-24B;
Admin Plan: s21p5; s21p5

DEFER..2
PIH Notices: 02-21;
Admin Plan: s18p7

DEFERRAL..50
24 CFR 5: .506; .508; .514; .516 (7); .518 (26); .520; .522;
HUD-50058Instr: p18 (4);
7420.10G Gbk: 4-15; 5-8 (2);
PIH Notices: 02-21;
Admin Plan: s18p7 (2); s18p8; s25p5

DEFERRAL PERIOD..15
24 CFR 5: .518 (14); .518

DEFERRAL PERIODS..2
24 CFR 5: .518; .518

DEFERRALS..4
24 CFR 5: .518 (2);
HUD-50058Instr: p18; p18

DEFERRED..12
24 CFR 5: .518 (2); .609;
24 CFR 982: .505;
HUD-50058Instr: p29 (2);
7420.10G Gbk: 5-15 Ex 5-2; 5-23;
PIH Notices: 01-15 Impr Integ Hbk (3);
Admin Plan: s6p9

DEFERS..2
7420.10G Gbk: 4-14; 4-15

DEFICIENCIES..96
24 CFR 5: .703 (2);
24 CFR 982: .102;
HUD-52648: p1 (4);
7420.10G Gbk: 1-10; 1-11 (2); 10-27 (2); 10-28 (5); 10-29 (3); 10-33 (6); 10-34 (2); 10-40 Ex 10-4a; 10-42 Ex 10-5; 10-44 Ex 10-7a; 10-45 Ex 10-7b; 10-46 Ex 10-8; 11-9; 11-12 (2); 22-5; 22-15 (2); 24-3;
PIH Notices: 03-20; 02-27 (21); 02-21 (3); 01-41; 01-20 (3); 01-06 (5); 00-27 (2); 00-24B (8); 00-09;
Admin Plan: s10p3; s10p4; s10p5; s21p1; s21p5 (4); s22p3; s24p5; s24p5

DEFICIENCY..26
24 CFR 982: .605 (2);
HUD-50058: p i;
HUD-50058Instr: p15;
7420.10G Gbk: 1-11; 10-29 (3); 10-33 (2); 10-34; 10-45 Ex 10-7b; 11-9; 11-10; 17-2; 22-6;
PIH Notices: 02-27; 02-21; 01-20 (2); 01-06 (5); 00-24

DEFICIENT..5
HUD-52648: p1; p3;
PIH Notices: 02-27 (2);
Admin Plan: s3p2

DEGREE..20
HUD-50058Instr: p18; p61 (2);
HUD-52667: p ii (3);
7420.10G Gbk: 5-29; 8-11; 20-1; 20-16; 21-13; 22-3; 23-1; 23-16 Ex 23-2;
PIH Notices: 02-27; 95-48 (2); 95-48 Tech Asst (2);
Admin Plan: s24p4

DEGREE DAYS..3
7420.10G Gbk: 18-4 (2); 18-4

DEGREE DAYS..6
HUD-52667: p ii (3);
7420.10G Gbk: 18-4 (2); 18-4

DEGREE-GRANTING..1
HUD-50058Instr: p15

DEGREES..4
7420.10G Gbk: 10-19; 18-4;
Admin Plan: s10p4; s10p4

DELAY..32
24 CFR 5: .318; .512; .514 (5);
24 CFR 982: .355 (2);
HUD-903: p3;

HUD-9886: p2;
7420.10G Gbk: 5-7 (3); 8-10; 11-9; 11-16 Ex 11-1; 12-8; 13-7 (2); 16-3; 19-9; 21-10;
PIH Notices: 01-10; 01-06; 00-34;
Admin Plan: s11p2 (3); s15p1; s24p3; s25p1

DELAYED 29
24 CFR 5: .514 (6); .609;
HUD-52641: p4;
7420.10G Gbk: 5-6; 5-8 (2); 5-11; 5-14 Ex 5-2; 5-23 (2); 5-24; 10-18; 11-7; 12-8;
PIH Notices: 03-05; 01-40; 01-15 Impr Integ Hbk (2); 01-11 (2); 00-23;
Admin Plan: s11p1; s18p7; s18p7

DELAYED START 4
24 CFR 5: .609;
7420.10G Gbk: 5-14 Ex 5-2;
PIH Notices: 01-15 Impr Integ Hbk; 01-15 Impr Integ Hbk

DELAYING 2
24 CFR 5: .655;
24 CFR 982: .207

DELAYS 12
7420.10G Gbk: 4-5 (2); 4-14; 5-23; 8-8; 10-29; 21-8;
PIH Notices: 02-27 (2); 95-48; 95-48 Tech Asst;
Admin Plan: s6p9

DELEGATE 2
24 CFR 5: .110;
HUD-52641: p6

DELEGATED 2
24 CFR 982: .3;
HUD-50058Instr: p74

DELINQUENT 5
PIH Notices: 96-65 (4);
Admin Plan: s22p4

DEMOGRAPHIC 7
HUD-50058: p i;
7420.10G Gbk: 12-3; 19-1; 19-3 (2);
PIH Notices: 01-15;
Admin Plan: s1p7

DEMOGRAPHICS 9
7420.10G Gbk: 2-6; 17-1; 19-7; 19-8 (5); 23-4

DEMOLISHED 16
PIH Notices: 02-21 (6); 01-20 (6); 00-27 (3); 00-27

DEMOLISHES 3
24 CFR 982: .203;
7420.10G Gbk: 4-21;
Admin Plan: s4p1

DEMOLISHING 3
PIH Notices: 02-21; 01-20; 00-27

DEMOLITION 46
24 CFR 982: .203;
HUD-52648: p2;
7420.10G Gbk: 1-8 (2); 4-21; 20-5; 21-11; 23-2;
PIH Notices: 02-21 (12); 02-07; 02-01; 01-20 (11); 01-06; 00-28; 00-27 (10);
Admin Plan: s4p1

DEMONSTRATE 46
24 CFR 5: .350; .518;
24 CFR 982: .102; .627 (2); .638;
7420.10G Gbk: 1-8; 2-2; 2-3 (3); 2-5; 5-37; 7-4; 12-5; 19-3; 19-12; 23-18;
PIH Notices: 02-27; 02-01; 01-15; 99-52; 96-65 (2); 95-48 (9); 95-48 Tech Asst (9);
Admin Plan: s2p6; s20p6; s21p7; s25p6

DEMONSTRATED 4
24 CFR 982: .201;
HUD-50058Instr: p19;
7420.10G Gbk: 4-20; 8-12

DEMONSTRATES 16
24 CFR 5: .360; .518;
24 CFR 982: .152; .503; .625; .627;
7420.10G Gbk: 4-6; 22-14; 24-11;
PIH Notices: 02-20 (2); 00-46;
Admin Plan: s21p3; s21p7; s24p4; s25p6

DEMONSTRATING 3
7420.10G Gbk: 7-5; 23-14;
PIH Notices: 01-01

DEMONSTRATION 16
7420.10G Gbk: 1-2 (4); 1-4; 2-1;
PIH Notices: 03-23; 02-27 (2); 01-06 (4); 00-53;
Admin Plan: s25p6; s25p6

DEMONSTRATIONS 2
PIH Notices: 01-06; 01-06

DEN 6
HUD-52580: p1;
HUD-52580-A: p8; p9; p10; p11; p12

DENIAL....................................127
24 CFR 5: .218 (2); .232; .236 (5); .508 (2); .514 (9); .615 (2); .630;
24 CFR 982: 24 CFR 982 (4); .104; .206; .301; .306; .310 (2); .314; .521; .552 (7); .553 (3); .554; .555; .625; .628; .631; .637; .638 (3);
HUD-50058Instr: p2 (2); p3;
HUD-9886: p1 (2);
7420.10G Gbk: 3-2 (2); 5-6; 5-7; 5-35 (2); 5-38 (3); 10-2; 16-2 (2); 16-3 (2); 22-14;
PIH Notices: 03-11; 02-27; 01-41 (3); 00-09 (2); 95-48 (4); 95-48 Tech Asst (4);
Admin Plan: s2p1 (5); s2p5 (5); s2p6; s3p1; s3p3 (2); s7p2; s10p3; s15p1 (8); s15p2 (3); s15p3; s15p5; s15p6 (2); s16p1; s18p1; s18p2; s23p7; s23p8; s25p5 (2); s25p5

DENIAL OF ADMISSION.............11
24 CFR 982: Intro; .301; .310; .552; .553 (2);
Admin Plan: s2p1 (2); s2p5; s2p6; s7p2

DENIAL OF ASSISTANCE............15
24 CFR 982: .104; .206; .552; .554; .555; .637;
7420.10G Gbk: 3-5; 5-1 (2); 5-35 (2); 5-36;
Admin Plan: s2p5; s15p1; s18p2

DENIAL OF ELIGIBILITY.............4
24 CFR 5: .218 (2);
HUD-9886: p1; p1

DENIAL OF PARTICIPATION.......14
24 CFR 982: .306; .628; .631;
HUD-52641: p6;
7420.10G Gbk: 8-18; 11-1;
PIH Notices: 01-41 (2); 00-09; 95-48 (2); 95-48 Tech Asst (2);
Admin Plan: s16p1

DENIAL OF PLACEMENT.............3
Admin Plan: s2p1; s2p5; s3p1

DENIED..
59
24 CFR 5: .508 (2); .514 (6);
24 CFR 982: .551; .553;
HUD-50058Instr: p3;
HUD-52641: p4;
HUD-903-1: p1; p4 (4);
7420.10G Gbk: 5-6 (4); 5-8 (2); 5-11; 5-35 (2); 5-38; 10-26; 10-42 Ex 10-5; 11-2; 11-7; 24-11;
PIH Notices: 03-11; 95-48 (3); 95-48 Tech Asst (3);
Admin Plan: s1p3; s1p5; s2p3; s2p4; s2p5; s2p7; s3p3; s8p2; s8p5 (3); s18p1 (2); s18p7 (2); s18p8 (3); s23p4; s25p5

DENOMINATOR............................15
24 CFR 5: .520 (7);
24 CFR 982: .503;
PIH Notices: 02-20; 01-06 (5); 00-46

DENSITY...2
24 CFR 5: .318; .318

DENTAL...1
7420.10G Gbk: 5-32

DENTED..4
HUD-52580-A: p4 (3); p4

DENTIST...2
7420.10G Gbk: 5-51 Ex 5-5;
Admin Plan: s7p7

DENTISTRY....................................4
PIH Notices: 95-48 (2); 95-48 Tech Asst; 95-48 Tech Asst

DEPARTMENT OF JUSTICE.........34
HUD-903: p3;
HUD-903-1: p6;
PIH Notices: 02-21; 02-01; 01-20; 99-52; 95-48 (16); 95-48 Tech Asst (11); 95-48 Tech Asst

DEPARTMENT OF SOCIAL SERVICES..1
Admin Plan: s11p3

DEPENDENT.................................28
24 CFR 5: .603; .611;
HUD-50058: p7 (2); p vii (4);
HUD-50058Instr: p14; p36 (7); p71; p76;
7420.10G Gbk: 5-18; 5-28; 5-29 (2); 5-50 Ex 5-5; 23-1;
PIH Notices: 01-15 Impr Integ Hbk (2);
Admin Plan: s2p2; s6p1

DEPENDENT ALLOWANCE 7
HUD-50058: p7; p vii;
HUD-50058Instr: p36 (3);
7420.10G Gbk: 5-29;
Admin Plan: s6p1

DEPENDENTS...............................23
HUD-50058: p7; p vii (2);
HUD-50058Instr: p36 (6);
7420.10G Gbk: 4-15; 5-14 Ex 5-2; 5-18 (4); 23-16 Ex 23-2;

PIH Notices: 03-05 (2); 01-40 (2); 01-15 Impr Integ Hbk (2); 01-15 Impr Integ Hbk

DEPLETE 1
7420.10G Gbk: 20-17

DEPLETED 10
7420.10G Gbk: 20-14; 20-15 (5); 20-16; 23-15;
PIH Notices: 03-23; 02-06

DEPOSIT 64
24 CFR 5: .318 (18); .350 (3); .363; .615; .630;
24 CFR 982: Intro; .313 (6); .452; .641;
HUD-52641: p10;
HUD-52641-A: p3;
7420.10G Gbk: 4-26 Ex 4-2 (2); 5-27; 5-28; 5-46 Ex 5-5 (3); 5-48 Ex 5-5; 5-49 Ex 5-5 (2); 20-23; 23-13;
PIH Notices: 01-15 Impr Integ Hbk (4);
Admin Plan: s7p5; s7p6; s8p4 (4); s10p5 (2); s11p1; s22p3; s23p5 (2); s25p5

DEPOSITARY 12
24 CFR 982: Intro; .156 (9);
7420.10G Gbk: 20-1; 20-23

DEPOSITED...................................... 7
24 CFR 982: .156 (2);
HUD-50058Instr: p71;
7420.10G Gbk: 20-1; 23-1; 23-13;
PIH Notices: 01-15 Impr Integ Hbk

DEPOSITING.................................... 1
PIH Notices: 01-15 Impr Integ Hbk

DEPOSITORY.................................. 6
24 CFR 5: .659;
24 CFR 982: .516;
7420.10G Gbk: 20-24; 23-13;
PIH Notices: 01-15; 01-15 Impr Integ Hbk

DEPOSITS...................................... 18
24 CFR 5: .318 (6);
24 CFR 982: .313;
7420.10G Gbk: 2-11; 8-15; 20-23; 20-24 (2); 23-10; 23-13; 24-9;
PIH Notices: 00-11;
Admin Plan: s8p3; s8p4

DEPRECIATION............................ 21
24 CFR 5: .609 (3);
HUD-50058Instr: p25 (2);
7420.10G Gbk: 5-14 Ex 5-2 (3); 5-19 (2); 5-48 Ex 5-5 (2);
PIH Notices: 01-15 Impr Integ Hbk (6);
Admin Plan: s7p5 (2); s7p5

DESEGREGATION........................... 3
24 CFR 982: .54; .353;
7420.10G Gbk: 2-1

DESERT STORM 1
HUD-50058Instr: p26

DESIGN.. 73
24 CFR 5: .526;
24 CFR 982: .102;
HUD-50058Instr: p70;
HUD-52667: p ii (2);
HUD-903-1: p2;
7420.10G Gbk: 4-1; 4-2; 9-3; 21-1; 21-2 (3); 22-10; 23-3;
PIH Notices: 02-01 (20); 99-52 (22); 99-11; 95-48 (9); 95-48 Tech Asst (5);
Admin Plan: s24p5

DESIGNATE................................... 12
24 CFR 5: .318 (3); .350;
7420.10G Gbk: 23-15;
PIH Notices: 02-01; 99-52; 95-48 (2); 95-48 Tech Asst (2);
Admin Plan: s10p1

DESIGNATED.............................. 206
24 CFR 5: .306 (5); .318; .350 (3); .360; .363 (2); .510; .512; .514 (2); .609 (2); .628 (2); .801;
24 CFR 35 SubM: .1200 (6); .1215; .1225 (15);
24 CFR 982: .503 (7); .505 (3); .554; .555; .601 (2); .628;
HUD-50058: p i; p ii; p v (2);
HUD-50058Instr: p8; p14; p18; p20; p37; p72;
HUD-52580-A: p15;
HUD-52648: p2;
7420.10G Gbk: 1-7; 1-8 (2); 4-12; 5-14 Ex 5-2 (2); 5-20; 6-10 Ex 6-2; 7-4; 7-6; 10-18; 16-3; 16-4; 20-14 (2); 23-9;
PIH Notices: 02-27 (11); 02-22 (2); 02-21; 02-20 (14); 02-01 (3); 01-41; 01-15 Impr Integ Hbk (4); 01-11 (2); 00-53 (3); 00-49; 00-46 (12); 00-45; 00-01 (2); 99-52 (3); 99-11 (2); 98-66 (2); 95-48 (17); 95-48 Tech Asst (17);
Admin Plan: s1p7; s2p2 (2); s3p1; s3p2; s4p1;

s4p2 (4); s8p5; s9p1; s11p1; s18p5; s19p1 (2); s20p4; s22p1; s22p2; s22p4; s24p1; s24p1

DESIGNATED FAMILIES 1
7420.10G Gbk: 1-7

DESIGNATED HOUSING............. 16
7420.10G Gbk: 1-8;
PIH Notices: 02-01 (3); 01-11; 00-53 (2); 00-01 (2); 99-52 (3); 99-11 (2); 98-66; 98-66

DESIGNATES 8
24 CFR 5: .659;
24 CFR 982: .516;
HUD-50058: p viii;
HUD-50058Instr: p37;
PIH Notices: 01-15 Impr Integ Hbk; 95-48; 95-48 Tech Asst;
Admin Plan: s16p3

DESIGNATING................................ 5
7420.10G Gbk: 1-8;
PIH Notices: 95-48 (2); 95-48 Tech Asst; 95-48 Tech Asst

DESIGNATION 17
24 CFR 982: .204;
7420.10G Gbk: 1-8; 4-7; 4-8; 4-14;
PIH Notices: 02-27; 00-31; 99-30; 95-48 (3); 95-48 Tech Asst (3);
Admin Plan: s4p1; s5p2; s16p3

DESIGNATIONS.............................. 8
PIH Notices: 02-27 (4); 95-48 (2); 95-48 Tech Asst; 95-48 Tech Asst

DESIGNED.................................... 97
24 CFR 5: .318 (2); .380; .603; .655;
24 CFR 982: .4; .207; .401 (2);
HUD-50058Instr: p1; p28 (3); p61 (2); p71; p72 (3); p73;
HUD-52580: p6;
HUD-52580-A: p2; p8 (2); p19;
HUD-52667: p ii (2);
7420.10G Gbk: 1-4; 1-9; 1-10; 2-8; 4-13; 4-17; 5-38; 5-43; 9-1; 9-4; 9-8; 9-9; 9-16 Ex 9-2; 10-6; 10-10 (2); 10-14; 17-10; 20-21; 21-1; 22-8; 23-14; 23-15;
PIH Notices: 03-11; 02-01 (3); 01-41 (3); 01-15 Impr Integ Hbk; 00-41; 00-11A (2); 00-09; 99-52 (3); 99-11; 95-48 (8); 95-48 Tech Asst (8);
Admin Plan: s1p4; s1p6 (2); s6p3; s7p1; s8p1; s8p4 (2); s9p1; s19p1; s23p1; s23p2 (3); s25p2

DESIGNEE 6
24 CFR 5: .514;
24 CFR 982: .638;
PIH Notices: 95-48; 95-48 Tech Asst;
Admin Plan: s1p5; s3p3

DESIGNING.................................... 4
7420.10G Gbk: 9-4; 20-1; 21-9; 22-10

DESIGNS... 2
PIH Notices: 02-01; 99-52

DESTROY 8
PIH Notices: 95-48 (4); 95-48 Tech Asst (3); 95-48 Tech Asst

DESTROYED................................... 8
24 CFR 5: .403;
7420.10G Gbk: 5-2;
PIH Notices: 03-11 (3); 95-48; 95-48 Tech Asst;
Admin Plan: s15p4

DESTROYING 3
7420.10G Gbk: 15-3;
PIH Notices: 95-48; 95-48 Tech Asst

DESTROYING PROPERTY 1
7420.10G Gbk: 15-3

DESTRUCTION 5
24 CFR 982: .310;
HUD-52641: p9;
HUD-52641-A: p2;
7420.10G Gbk: 5-38; 5-38

DESTRUCTION OF PROPERTY..... 3
24 CFR 982: .310;
HUD-52641: p9;
HUD-52641-A: p2

DETERIORATED........................... 92
24 CFR 35 SubM: .1215 (3);
HUD-52580: p2 (6); p3 (6); p4 (4); p5 (3);
HUD-52580-A: p2 (6); p3 (2); p5 (2); p6; p7 (2); p9 (2); p10 (2); p11 (2); p12 (2); p13 (4); p14 (2); p17 (6); p18 (2);
7420.10G Gbk: 10-12 (2); 10-16; 10-17 (4); 10-18 (10); 10-19; 10-21 (3); 10-22; 20-4;
PIH Notices: 02-07 (2); 00-49 (4); 00-23 (5);
Admin Plan: s23p1

DETERIORATION..........................13
HUD-52580-A: p2 (4); p3; p4; p5; p7; p9; p10; p11; p12; p13

DETERMINABLE 5
24 CFR 5: .609;
HUD-50058Instr: p22;
7420.10G Gbk: 5-14 Ex 5-2;
PIH Notices: 01-15 Impr Integ Hbk; 01-15 Impr Integ Hbk

DETERMINATION.......................312
24 CFR 5: .110; .216 (2); .236; .350; .353 (2); .508 (2); .514 (2); .518 (5); .615 (10); .617; .630 (2); .634; .653; .659;
24 CFR 982: Intro; .158; .160; .201 (3); .305 (2); .315; .352; .355; .503 (2); .504 (2); .507 (2); .508; .516 (4); .521; .554 (5); .555 (16); .622; .627 (3); .628; .632; .635;
HUD-50058Instr: p24 (2); p33; p65;
HUD-52517: p2;
HUD-52580-A: p4 (2); p5 (3); p6;
HUD-52646: p2;
HUD-52648: p1 (3);
7420.10G Gbk: 1-10; 1-11; 1-16 Ex 1-3 (3); 3-5; 3-7; 4-6 (2); 4-10; 4-14; 4-17; 4-18; 4-19; 5-6 (2); 5-22; 5-34; 5-37; 5-41; 6-1; 6-8; 7-7; 8-17 (2); 8-18; 9-1; 9-2; 9-3; 9-4; 9-8; 9-9; 9-10; 9-11; 10-2; 10-30; 10-32; 10-33; 11-18 (2); 12-5; 12-10; 12-11; 14-4; 16-1; 16-2 (7); 16-3 (3); 18-10; 20-8; 20-8 Ex 20-1; 20-9; 20-19 Ex 20-3; 20-24; 20-27; 20-29; 21-4; 21-8; 21-10; 22-3; 22-6; 22-11; 22-18; 23-6; 23-17 Ex 23-2;
PIH Notices: 03-12 (8); 02-27 (7); 02-21; 02-20 (5); 02-01; 01-41 (13); 01-27; 01-15 (6); 01-15 Impr Integ Hbk (10); 01-06 (2); 00-46 (5); 00-24A; 00-24B (5); 00-11A; 00-09 (8); 00-01; 99-11; 95-48 (5); 95-48 Tech Asst (5);
Admin Plan: s1p6; s2p3; s2p6 (6); s2p7; s3p2; s3p3 (2); s5p1 (2); s6p1; s6p4; s6p6; s6p7; s6p11; s7p3; s8p5 (2); s10p2; s10p4; s11p1 (2); s15p5; s17p3; s18p2 (4); s18p3 (2); s18p4 (7); s18p5; s18p7 (2); s18p8; s20p3; s20p6; s20p7; s21p4; s22p2; s23p3; s24p4; s24p5; s24p7; s25p4; s25p6

DETERMINATIONS.......................58
24 CFR 5: .214; .218; .232; .615 (3);
24 CFR 982: .554; .555 (2);
HUD-9886: p2;
7420.10G Gbk: 2-9; 4-1; 4-5; 4-22; 5-13; 6-8; 9-1; 9-2; 9-11 (2); 16-2 (3); 16-3; 16-5; 21-3; 21-4 (3); 21-11; 22-2; 24-4;
PIH Notices: 03-12 (3); 02-27 (2); 01-15 (5); 01-15 Impr Integ Hbk; 00-09; 00-01; 98-66;
Admin Plan: s6p2; s11p2; s18p2 (2); s18p3 (2); s18p4 (3); s18p6; s18p8; s21p4

DETERMINING UNIT SIZE............2
Admin Plan: s5p1; s23p3

DETRIMENTAL...............................1
7420.10G Gbk: 3-3

DETRIMENTALLY..........................1
7420.10G Gbk: 20-25

DEVELOP 61
24 CFR 5: .353 (2); .380;
7420.10G Gbk: 1-13; 2-6 (2); 2-11; 3-1; 3-6; 4-1; 4-2; 4-3; 8-5; 10-15; 10-22 (2); 10-30; 12-8 (2); 12-9 (2); 12-10; 18-4; 19-6; 19-7; 19-8; 20-1; 21-2; 21-11; 23-1; 23-4; 24-2; 24-12; 24-15;
PIH Notices: 03-11; 02-27 (8); 02-01; 01-15; 00-53; 00-11A; 99-52; 95-48 (3); 95-48 Tech Asst (3);
Admin Plan: s1p6; s6p1; s6p13; s13p1; s22p2; s25p2; s25p3

DEVELOPED................................34
24 CFR 5: .303; .312;
HUD-50058Instr: p72;
7420.10G Gbk: 1-2; 2-5; 8-23; 12-3 (2); 13-9; 21-1; 24-15;
PIH Notices: 03-11; 02-27;

02-06; 01-15; 00-53 (4); 00-24B; 00-11; 00-11A (6); 99-11 (2); 95-48; 95-48 Tech Asst;
Admin Plan: s4p2; s22p2; s25p5

DEVELOPING 29
24 CFR 982: .517;
HUD-52667: p i;
7420.10G Gbk: 2-10; 4-3; 4-4; 4-11; 5-39; 9-3 (2); 11-4; 19-5; 20-4; 22-10; 23-4; 23-20; 24-3;
PIH Notices: 03-12; 02-27 (8); 02-01; 00-24; 00-24B; 99-52

DEVELOPMENT 264
24 CFR 5: 24 CFR 5; .100 (5); .105 (3); .110; .312; .353 (4); .380; .500 (3); .504 (2); .609;
24 CFR 982: .352 (2); .521;
HUD-50058: p1; p i; p ii; p16;
HUD-50058Instr: p i; p3; p5; p7 (2); p13; p25; p28; p30; p43; p61 (2); p71; p72 (2); p73; p75;
HUD-52517: p1 (4); 8; p10;
HUD-52641-A: p1; p3;
HUD-52648: p1 (4); p2 (3); p3 (8);
HUD-903-1: p1 (2); p2;
7420.10G Gbk: 1-3 (2); 1-4; 1-8; 3-1; 3-8 (3); 4-16; 4-21; 5-15 Ex 5-2; 5-16 Ex 5-2; 5-42; 9-5 (2); 9-6 (2); 9-11; 10-15; 10-31; 21-1; 21-2; 23-1; 23-3; 23-5; 23-15; 24-15 (2);
PIH Notices: 03-23; 03-20; 03-12; 03-11; 03-05; 02-27 (6); 02-22 (3); 02-21 (6); 02-20; 02-15; 02-14; 02-07; 02-06; 02-03; 02-01 (9); 01-43; 01-41 (5); 01-40; 01-33; 01-27 (3); 01-20 (6); 01-15 (3); 01-15 Impr Integ Hbk (6); 01-11; 01-10 (3); 01-06 (2); 01-02 (3); 01-01 (2); 00-53 (10); 00-49; 00-46; 00-45; 00-41 (2); 00-34; 00-31; 00-28; 00-27 (7); 00-24 (2); 00-24B; 00-23; 00-14; 00-11; 00-11A; 00-09 (7); 00-01; 99-52 (11); 99-30; 99-11 (2); 98-66; 96-65 (2); 95-48 (10); 95-48 Tech Asst (6);
Admin Plan: s1p1 (2); s8p3; s8p4; s9p2; s20p1; s21p1; s22p1; s23p1; s24p1; s24p2; s25p1 (2); s25p2 (2); s25p3; s25p4; s25p6; s25p7

DEVELOPMENTAL 13
24 CFR 5: .403; .609;
HUD-50058: p i (2);
HUD-50058Instr: p15 (2); p28; p74;
PIH Notices: 01-15 Impr Integ Hbk (2);
Admin Plan: s7p8; s25p2; s25p2

DEVELOPMENTAL DISABILITIES 4
HUD-50058: p i;
HUD-50058Instr: p15;
Admin Plan: s7p8; s25p2

DEVELOPMENTAL DISABILITY .. 9
24 CFR 5: .403; .609;
HUD-50058: p i;
HUD-50058Instr: p15; p28; p74;
PIH Notices: 01-15 Impr Integ Hbk (2);
Admin Plan: s25p2

DEVELOPMENTALLY 8
24 CFR 5: .318; .609;
HUD-50058Instr: p28;
7420.10G Gbk: 5-15 Ex 5-2 (2);
PIH Notices: 01-15 Impr Integ Hbk (2); 01-15 Impr Integ Hbk

DEVELOPMENTALLY DISABLED 1
24 CFR 5: .318

DEVELOPMENTS 22
24 CFR 982: .1;
7420.10G Gbk: 1-2; 9-4; 9-5; 9-6 (2); 9-7; 9-8;
PIH Notices: 02-15; 02-01 (3); 01-02 (4); 00-53; 00-11; 99-52 (3); 99-11

DEVELOPMENT'S 2
PIH Notices: 00-09;
Admin Plan: s1p1

DEVELOPS 2
7420.10G Gbk: 19-2;
Admin Plan: s24p4

DEVIATE 1
7420.10G Gbk: 8-11

DEVIATION 1
PIH Notices: 01-06

DEVIATIONS 1
7420.10G Gbk: 4-19

DIAGNOSE 1
7420.10G Gbk: 19-4
DIAGNOSED 3
PIH Notices: 95-48; 95-48 Tech Asst;
Admin Plan: s13p1
DIAGNOSTICIAN 1
Admin Plan: s7p8
DIED 2
24 CFR 982: .553;
7420.10G Gbk: 24-3
DIFFERENT GENERATIONS 1
Admin Plan: s5p1
DIFFICULT 17
7420.10G Gbk: 2-10 (2); 4-5; 4-18; 8-13; 9-6; 9-7; 10-5; 10-8; 16-4; 21-1; 21-2; 21-3; 21-5; 21-6; 24-3;
PIH Notices: 01-15 Impr Integ Hbk
DIFFICULTIES 19
HUD-52648: p2 (2);
7420.10G Gbk: 1-7; 2-3 (2); 7-7; 7-9; 8-4; 13-1; 17-1;
PIH Notices: 01-06 (3); 96-65 (2); 95-48; 95-48 Tech Asst;
Admin Plan: s21p6; s21p6
DIFFICULTY.................................. 26
24 CFR 982: .152;
HUD-52580-A: p8;
7420.10G Gbk: 4-13; 4-21; 7-5; 8-7; 9-6; 9-7 (2); 12-2; 21-13; 21-19; 24-11; 24-12;
PIH Notices: 02-20; 01-15 Impr Integ Hbk; 01-10; 01-06; 01-01 (2); 00-46; 96-65; 95-48 (2); 95-48 Tech Asst; 95-48 Tech Asst
DILAPIDATED 1
HUD-52580-A: p17
DILIGENT 2
24 CFR 5: .508;
7420.10G Gbk: 5-6
DILIGENTLY 2
24 CFR 5: .514;
7420.10G Gbk: 10-30
DINING AREA.................................. 12
24 CFR 982: .614 (2);
HUD-52580: p1;
HUD-52580-A: p8; p9; p10; p11; p12;
7420.10G Gbk: 17-3; 17-4; 17-5; 17-5
DINING AREAS 4
PIH Notices: 95-48 (2); 95-48 Tech Asst; 95-48 Tech Asst
DINING ROOM 7
HUD-52580: p1;
HUD-52580-A: p8; p9; p10; p11; p12; p15
DIRECT COST 1
7420.10G Gbk: 20-26
DIRECT COSTS............................... 3
7420.10G Gbk: 20-26;
PIH Notices: 02-27; 02-27
DIRECT DEPOSIT 1
Admin Plan: s11p1
DIRECT LOAN 2
7420.10G Gbk: 9-11;
PIH Notices: 01-27
DIRECT LOANS.............................. 2
24 CFR 5: .601; .603
DIRECTLY ASSISTED 1
PIH Notices: 01-15 Impr Integ Hbk
DIRECTLY PAYING........................ 1
7420.10G Gbk: 6-6
DIRECTLY TO 26
24 CFR 5: .100; .236; .514; .609; .632;
24 CFR 982: .514; .635 (2); .642 (2);
HUD-50058Instr: p31;
HUD-903: p2;
PIH Notices: 03-11 (2); 02-27; 01-41; 01-15 (4); 01-15 Impr Integ Hbk (4);
Admin Plan: s22p3; s22p3
DIRECTOR...................................... 66
24 CFR 5: .216;
HUD-52648: p3;
7420.10G Gbk: 5-10 Ex 5-1; 21-11; 21-12 Ex 21-3 (2); 21-13; 21-14 Ex 21-4; 21-15 Ex 21-5; 21-16 Ex 21-6 (3); 21-20;
PIH Notices: 03-11; 02-27 (6); 02-21 (3); 02-20 (5); 02-14 (4); 02-01; 01-41; 01-27; 01-20; 01-15; 01-06 (6); 01-01 (3); 00-46 (5); 00-45; 00-27; 00-11A; 99-52; 99-11; 96-65 (6); 95-48; 95-48 Tech Asst;
Admin Plan: s20p5; s25p6
DIRECTORATE 2
PIH Notices: 95-48; 95-48 Tech Asst
DIRECTORIES................................. 2
PIH Notices: 95-48; 95-

48 Tech Asst
DIRECTORS 95
7420.10G Gbk: 21-13;
PIH Notices: 03-23 (2); 03-20 (3); 03-12; 03-11 (2); 03-05 (3); 02-27 (13); 02-22; 02-21; 02-20 (2); 02-15 (2); 02-14 (3); 02-07 (2); 02-06; 02-03; 02-01 (3); 01-43; 01-41 (3); 01-40 (2); 01-33; 01-27 (2); 01-20; 01-15; 01-11; 01-10; 01-06 (2); 01-02; 01-01 (2); 00-53; 00-49; 00-46 (2); 00-45 (2); 00-41; 00-34 (2); 00-31; 00-28; 00-27; 00-24 (2); 00-23; 00-14; 00-11; 00-09 (5); 00-01; 99-52 (2); 99-30; 99-11 (2); 98-66; 96-65; 95-48 (5); 95-48
DIRECTORY.....................................1
7420.10G Gbk: 9-11
DISABILITIES..............................598
24 CFR 5: .100; .105; .240; .300; .303 (7); .306 (6); .309; .312 (3); .318 (3); .321; .324; .353; .359; .360; .380; .403 (7); .502; .528; .601 (3); .603 (2); .609; .611 (2); .617 (9); .655 (8); .801;
24 CFR 982: .4 (2); .53 (2); .152; .201; .204; .207 (5); .303; .306; .316; .352 (2); .503; .505; .517 (2); .552; .601; .606 (3); .610 (4); .612; .614 (2); .615 (2); .619 (2); .620 (2); .625 (2); .627 (3); .635 (2);
HUD-50058: p i (3);
HUD-50058Instr: p3; p15 (2); p17; p25 (2); p26; p27; p31; p43; p47 (2); p70; p71 (3); p72 (2); p73; p74 (2); p75;
HUD-52517: p2;
HUD-52641: p1; p5; p6; p10;
HUD-52641-A: p3;
HUD-52646: p2;
7420.10G Gbk: 1-7 (2); 1-8 (2); 1-13; 2-2; 2-8; 3-3; 3-5; 3-8; 4-1; 4-2 (3); 4-6; 4-9; 4-11; 4-15; 4-16; 4-17 (3); 4-18; 4-25 Ex 4-2; 4-27 Ex 4-2; 5-2 (4); 5-15 Ex 5-2 (2); 5-16 Ex 5-2; 5-29 (2); 5-30 (2); 5-42; 5-43 (3); 5-44 (6); 7-9; 8-3; 8-6; 8-12; 8-15; 8-19; 10-16; 11-13; 12-2; 12-3; 12-12 Ex 12-1; 12-13 Ex 12-1; 13-9; 14-4; 15-6; 17-1; 17-3 (4); 17-4 (5); 17-5; 17-6 (2); 17-7 (2); 20-4; 21-9; 22-14; 23-6; 24-10;
PIH Notices: 02-20; 02-07; 02-01 (55); 01-15 (2); 01-15 Impr Integ Hbk (5); 00-46; 00-45; 99-52 (53); 95-48 (106); 95-48 Tech Asst (97);
Admin Plan: s1p3 (5); s1p4 (4); s2p3; s6p2 (7); s6p3 (7); s6p11; s7p7 (3); s7p8; s11p3; s18p8; s19p1 (10); s25p2 (10); s25p2
DISABILITIES--DISALLOWANCE 1
24 CFR 5: .617
DISABILITY 449
24 CFR 5: .303 (3); .306 (2); .403 (3); .603 (2); .609 (4); .655 (2);
24 CFR 982: .158; .202; .204; .207 (2); .304; .316; .517; .552; .625;
HUD-50058: p i (2); p3 (6); p iii; p4 (6); p iv; p v (2); p7 (13); p vii (29);
HUD-50058Instr: p3 (2); p5; p15 (7); p20 (3); p21 (3); p28; p29; p34 (15); p35 (33); p36 (4); p71 (2); p74 (4);
HUD-52580: p6 (2);
HUD-52580-A: p19 (2);
HUD-52641: p5; p10;
HUD-52641-A: p3;
HUD-52646: p2 (3); p4;
7420.10G Gbk: 1-7 (2); 4-6 (2); 4-13 (2); 4-15; 4-17; 4-19; 4-23 Ex 4-1; 5-14 Ex 5-2; 5-28; 5-29; 5-30 (4); 5-31 (4); 5-32 (7); 5-33 (17); 5-34 (6); 5-42; 5-43 (5); 5-44 (3); 5-46 Ex 5-5; 5-50 Ex 5-5 (3); 5-51 Ex 5-5; 5-52 Ex 5-5; 8-3 (2); 8-14; 11-13; 12-3 (2); 12-11; 15-6; 18-8; 18-9; 22-14;
PIH Notices: 02-21; 02-07; 02-01 (23); 01-20; 01-15 (4); 01-15 Impr Integ Hbk (8); 01-06; 00-28; 99-52 (26); 95-48 (50); 95-

48 Tech Asst (48);
Admin Plan: s1p2; s1p4 (3); s1p5 (5); s3p3 (2); s5p2; s6p2; s6p4 (3); s7p3 (2); s7p4; s7p7; s7p8 (3); s8p5; s10p3; s13p1; s15p1 (2); s16p2; s18p8; s19p1; s21p4; s23p2; s25p2; s25p2

DISABILITY BENEFITS..................2
7420.10G Gbk: 5-50 Ex 5-5;
PIH Notices: 01-15

DISABILITY COMPENSATION 3
24 CFR 5: .609;
PIH Notices: 01-15 Impr Integ Hbk; 01-15 Impr Integ Hbk

DISABILITY INCOME 2
7420.10G Gbk: 5-46 Ex 5-5;
Admin Plan: s7p4

DISABILITY STATUS......................5
24 CFR 982: .158;
HUD-50058Instr: p15 (2);
7420.10G Gbk: 5-50 Ex 5-5; 12-3

DISABLE...1
PIH Notices: 99-11

DISABLED....................................193
24 CFR 5: .306 (6); .318 (2); .403 (2); .603 (2); .609; .611 (2);
24 CFR 982: Intro; .201 (3); .301 (2); .315; .316; .402 (2); .452; .627 (5); .634 (6); .642 (4);
HUD-50058: p7 (5); p vii (5); p xi;
HUD-50058Instr: p15 (2); p28; p29 (3); p34 (2); p35 (11); p36 (2); p42; p44; p46 (5); p71 (3); p72; p74;
HUD-52580: p6;
HUD-52580-A: p19;
7420.10G Gbk: 1-7 (2); 1-8 (5); 3-4; 4-3; 4-11 (2); 5-2; 5-15 Ex 5-2 (2); 5-18; 5-25 Ex 5-3; 5-28; 5-29 (4); 5-30 (2); 5-31 (6); 5-32; 5-41 (3); 5-43 (2); 5-50 Ex 5-5 (3); 5-51 Ex 5-5 (2); 5-52 Ex 5-5 (2); 9-14 Ex 9-1 (2); 9-16 Ex 9-2; 11-2; 20-4; 21-11;
PIH Notices: 02-07; 02-01 (5); 01-41; 01-15; 01-15 Impr Integ Hbk (8); 01-06; 00-28 (2); 00-14; 00-11; 00-09; 99-52 (5); 99-11; 95-48; 95-48 Tech Asst;
Admin Plan: s1p5 (2); s2p2; s6p1 (3); s6p2 (5); s6p3; s6p4; s6p11; s7p3 (2); s8p1; s8p2; s22p1 (2); s23p2; s24p2; s24p4; s25p2 (4); s25p2

DISABLED FAMILIES...................12
24 CFR 5: .306 (3);
24 CFR 982: .634 (2); .642;
7420.10G Gbk: 1-7 (2);
Admin Plan: s6p2; s6p4; s24p2; s25p2

DISABLED FAMILY 45
24 CFR 5: .306 (3); .403 (2); .611 (2);
24 CFR 982: .627 (5); .634 (3); .642 (3);
HUD-50058Instr: p71; p72;
7420.10G Gbk: 5-2; 5-28; 5-29 (2); 5-32;
PIH Notices: 02-01 (2); 01-41; 01-15; 01-15 Impr Integ Hbk (4); 00-09; 99-52 (2);
Admin Plan: s6p2 (4); s22p1; s25p2 (3); s25p2

DISABLED FAMILY MEMBER......7
24 CFR 5: .603;
HUD-50058: p xi;
HUD-50058Instr: p34; p46; p71;
7420.10G Gbk: 11-2;
PIH Notices: 01-15 Impr Integ Hbk

DISABLED FAMILY MEMBERS....4
24 CFR 982: .315;
7420.10G Gbk: 5-29; 5-50 Ex 5-5; 5-51 Ex 5-5

DISABLED FAMILY MEMBER'S ..1
Admin Plan: s6p3

DISABLING.....................................3
PIH Notices: 95-48; 95-48 Tech Asst;
Admin Plan: s1p5

DISALLOW.......................................1
7420.10G Gbk: 17-1

DISALLOWANCE 50
24 CFR 5: .617 (9);
24 CFR 982: .201;
HUD-50058: p6;
HUD-50058Instr: p25 (2); p26; p27; p71;
7420.10G Gbk: 5-16 Ex 5-2 (2);
PIH Notices: 01-15 (5); 01-15 Impr Integ Hbk (14); 00-11; 00-11A;
Admin Plan: s6p2; s6p3 (8); s6p4; s6p4

DISALLOWED 4

PIH Notices: 03-23; 02-07; 01-15 Impr Integ Hbk; 00-28

DISAPPROVAL..............................30
24 CFR 982: 24 CFR 982 (2); .54; .104 (2); .306; .352; .625; .628; .631 (3); .641;
HUD-52646: p1; p2;
7420.10G Gbk: 1-5; 3-4; 8-18 (2); 10-19; 11-1; 11-14;
PIH Notices: 02-20 (2); 02-14; 00-46 (2);
Admin Plan: s9p1; s16p1; s16p1

DISAPPROVE................................15
24 CFR 5: .661;
24 CFR 982: .631; .632; .641;
7420.10G Gbk: 3-4; 8-19; 8-20; 11-4;
PIH Notices: 01-41 (4); 01-01; 00-09;
Admin Plan: s16p1

DISAPPROVED...............................3
HUD-52646: p2;
7420.10G Gbk: 3-4; 8-18

DISAPPROVES................................1
PIH Notices: 02-14

DISAPPROVING.............................4
7420.10G Gbk: 8-19; 11-3; 11-4; 11-4

DISASTER......................................6
24 CFR 5: .403 (2);
24 CFR 982: .642 (2);
7420.10G Gbk: 5-2; 5-2

DISBURSED...................................7
HUD-50058: p17;
HUD-50058Instr: p62 (2);
7420.10G Gbk: 20-26; 23-15 (2);
Admin Plan: s25p5

DISBURSEMENT............................8
7420.10G Gbk: 23-14 (2); 23-15 (2);
Admin Plan: s25p5 (3); s25p6

DISBURSEMENTS.........................13
HUD-50058: p xvii;
HUD-50058Instr: p62;
7420.10G Gbk: 11-8; 20-23;
PIH Notices: 03-23 (3); 02-06;
Admin Plan: s25p5 (2); s25p6 (2); s25p6

DISBURSES......................................
1
7420.10G Gbk: 1-12 Ex 1-2

DISCIPLINARY ACTION................1
Admin Plan: s1p6

DISCLOSE.....................................28
24 CFR 5: .210; .216 (4); .218; .236;
24 CFR 982: .161; .551;
HUD-52641: p6;
HUD-52646: p2;
HUD-9886: p1;
7420.10G Gbk: 5-12 (2); 5-34; 10-17 (2); 10-26; 10-36 Ex 10-1; 22-4 (3); 22-9;
PIH Notices: 01-15;
Admin Plan: s2p5; s7p2; s7p8; s16p2

DISCLOSED....................................9
24 CFR 5: .216; .236;
HUD-903: p3;
HUD-903-1: p6;
HUD-9886: p2;
7420.10G Gbk: 5-12;
PIH Notices: 03-11;
Admin Plan: s20p3; s20p3

DISCLOSES.....................................2
HUD-9886: p2;
7420.10G Gbk: 22-4

DISCLOSING..................................2
7420.10G Gbk: 20-28;
Admin Plan: s7p2

DISCLOSURE................................53
24 CFR 5: .105 (2); .214; .216 (11); .218 (4); .236 (2); .238; .240; .659 (2); .661;
24 CFR 982: .305; .516;
HUD-52517: p2 (2);
HUD-903: p3;
HUD-9886: p2 (2);
7420.10G Gbk: 5-12 (2); 5-36 Ex 5-4; 8-15; 10-15; 10-17 (4); 10-36 Ex 10-1 (2); 11-3; 13-3; 22-4;
PIH Notices: 01-15; 01-15 Impr Integ Hbk (2); 00-23;
Admin Plan: s1p6; s8p2; s8p3

DISCLOSURES................................3
HUD-9886: p1; p2;
PIH Notices: 03-11

DISCONTINUE...............................3
HUD-50058Instr: p10;
PIH Notices: 96-65;
Admin Plan: s8p2

DISCONTINUED.............................3
HUD-50058: p v;
HUD-50058Instr: p18;
Admin Plan: s1p5

DISCOUNT.....................................1
7420.10G Gbk: 4-3

DISCOUNTS....................................2
24 CFR 982: .643;
7420.10G Gbk: 9-7

DISCOURAGE....8
24 CFR 982: .301;
7420.10G Gbk: 2-2; 2-7; 2-9; 8-3; 23-10;
PIH Notices: 00-11; 96-65

DISCOURAGED....1
PIH Notices: 01-15 Impr Integ Hbk

DISCOURAGES....1
7420.10G Gbk: 4-21

DISCOURAGING....1
PIH Notices: 00-11A

DISCOVER....2
7420.10G Gbk: 8-4; 22-13

DISCOVERED....2
7420.10G Gbk: 10-28; 20-25

DISCOVERS....1
Admin Plan: s20p1

DISCOVERY....2
24 CFR 982: .555
7420.10G Gbk: 22-12

DISCREPANCIES....17
7420.10G Gbk: 12-5; 19-4 (4); 19-10 (2); 20-23; 22-4 (6); 22-5; 22-14;
PIH Notices: 01-15

DISCREPANCY....19
7420.10G Gbk: 19-4; 19-9; 19-13; 22-4 (3); 22-5;
PIH Notices: 03-20 (2);
Admin Plan: s7p2 (7); s7p3 (2); s7p3

DISCREPANT....1
Admin Plan: s20p1

DISCRETION....97
24 CFR 5: .216; .315 (4); .353; .516 (4); .653; .661 (2); .801;
24 CFR 982: .54; .102; .302; .303 (2); .306; .312; .315; .503 (5); .520; .551; .552; .627; .630; .631 (2); .635 (2); .638; .642;
HUD-52646: p2;
7420.10G Gbk: 3-1 (2); 3-2 (5); 3-4 (2); 4-4; 5-1; 5-3; 5-9 Ex 5-1; 5-10 Ex 5-1; 5-38 (2); 8-13; 8-15 (2); 8-19; 11-11; 12-10 (2); 15-6; 20-1; 20-17; 21-7 (2); 22-10; 22-13; 22-14; 22-15; 23-5; 24-11;
PIH Notices: 03-11; 02-20 (4); 01-15 Impr Integ Hbk; 01-06 (3); 00-46 (4); 00-11; 96-65 (2);
Admin Plan: s6p1; s8p5; s13p1; s15p4 (2); s16p1; s22p3; s25p5

DISCRETIONARY....16
24 CFR 5: .315; .318; .350;
24 CFR 982: .554; .555;
7420.10G Gbk: 5-2; 8-12; 11-4; 13-2; 16-2 (2); 21-7 (2); 22-7;
Admin Plan: s18p2; s18p4

DISCRIMINATE....27
24 CFR 5: .309;
HUD-52641: p5; p10;
HUD-52641-A: p3;
HUD-903: p1 (3);
7420.10G Gbk: 5-43 (2); 11-13; 23-6;
PIH Notices: 95-48 (8); 95-48 Tech Asst (7); 95-48 Tech Asst

DISCRIMINATED....14
HUD-52646: p2;
HUD-903: p1; p2;
HUD-903-1: p4 (2); p5;
7420.10G Gbk: 4-27 Ex 4-2; 5-43; 8-14; 22-15;
PIH Notices: 95-48 (2); 95-48 Tech Asst; 95-48 Tech Asst

DISCRIMINATES....1
PIH Notices: 01-15

DISCRIMINATING....7
HUD-903: p2;
PIH Notices: 02-01; 99-52; 95-48 (2); 95-48 Tech Asst; 95-48 Tech Asst

DISCRIMINATION....151
24 CFR 5: .105; .309;
24 CFR 982: .53; .54; .202 (5); .207; .301; .304 (3);
HUD-50058Instr: p3;
HUD-52641: p5; p10;
HUD-52641-A: p3;
HUD-52646: p2;
HUD-903: p1; p2 (5); p3 (3);
HUD-903-1: p1 (2); p2; p3 (4); p5 (4); p6 (3);
7420.10G Gbk: 3-3 (2); 5-11 (4); 5-42 (5); 5-44; 5-45; 8-3; 11-11; 11-13; 11-14; 13-2; 19-7; 22-15;
PIH Notices: 02-21 (4); 02-15; 01-20 (3); 01-02 (6); 95-48 (36); 95-48 Tech Asst (34);
Admin Plan: s1p2; s1p3 (2); s8p3; s24p6

DISCRIMINATORY....12
HUD-903: p1; p2 (4);
PIH Notices: 95-48 (3); 95-

48 Tech Asst (3);
Admin Plan: s1p2
DISINCENTIVES.............................1
PIH Notices: 01-15 Impr Integ Hbk
DISORDER 3
PIH Notices: 95-48; 95-48 Tech Asst;
Admin Plan: s25p3
DISORDERS 11
PIH Notices: 95-48 (5); 95-48 Tech Asst (5);
Admin Plan: s25p2
DISPARATE 1
Admin Plan: s1p3
DISPARATE TREATMENT.............1
Admin Plan: s1p3
DISPLACE 3
PIH Notices: 95-48; 95-48 Tech Asst;
Admin Plan: s24p3
DISPLACED 33
24 CFR 5: .403 (4); .653; .655 (3); .801 (2);
24 CFR 982: .4; .201 (2); .203 (2); .207 (2);
HUD-50058Instr: p19; p72 (2); p75;
7420.10G Gbk: 1-8; 4-17 (2); 4-20; 4-21; 4-22; 5-2 (2); 5-3;
Admin Plan: s2p2; s2p4; s2p4
DISPLACED FAMILIES 2
24 CFR 5: .801; .801
DISPLACED FAMILY 1
7420.10G Gbk: 5-2
DISPLACED FAMILY 4
24 CFR 5: .403 (2);
HUD-50058Instr: p72;
7420.10G Gbk: 5-2
DISPLACED PERSON 7
24 CFR 5: .403; .655;
24 CFR 982: .201;
HUD-50058Instr: p72; p75;
7420.10G Gbk: 5-2;
Admin Plan: s2p2
DISPLACEMENT 9
7420.10G Gbk: 1-8; 5-50 Ex 5-5 (2);
PIH Notices: 01-41 (2); 00-09 (2);
Admin Plan: s24p2; s24p3
DISPOSABLE ....
1
7420.10G Gbk: 5-19
DISPOSAL......................................44
24 CFR 5: .350 (2); .703 (2);
24 CFR 982: .401 (5); .517 (2); .605 (3); .609 (3); .614 (5); .618;
HUD-52580: p5; p6;
HUD-52580-A: p15; p16; p17; p18 (2); p19;
7420.10G Gbk: 5-27; 9-13 Ex 9-1; 9-15 Ex 9-2; 9-17 Ex 9-3; 10-1; 10-3 (3); 10-4; 10-5; 17-3; 17-5; 17-7
DISPOSAL OF WASTE 2
24 CFR 982: .517; .517
DISPOSE 2
24 CFR 5: .350;
7420.10G Gbk: 5-28
DISPOSED 38
24 CFR 5: .603;
7420.10G Gbk: 4-27 Ex 4-2; 5-25 Ex 5-3; 5-27 (11); 5-28; 5-50 Ex 5-5 (5);
PIH Notices: 02-21 (2); 01-20 (2); 01-15 Impr Integ Hbk; 00-27;
Admin Plan: s6p10 (6); s7p3; s7p6 (4); s7p6
DISPOSES 1
HUD-50058Instr: p22
DISPOSING......................................2
24 CFR 5: .603;
HUD-50058Instr: p74
DISPOSITION................................58
24 CFR 5: .234; .603 (3); .801 (2);
24 CFR 982: .203; .315;
HUD-50058Instr: p22; p30;
HUD-52648: p2;
7420.10G Gbk: 1-8 (2); 1-9; 4-21; 5-16 Ex 5-2; 5-50 Ex 5-5; 8-16; 20-3; 21-11; 23-2;
PIH Notices: 03-11; 02-21 (7); 02-07; 01-41 (3); 01-20 (7); 01-15 Impr Integ Hbk (2); 01-10; 01-06; 00-28; 00-27 (7); 00-09 (3);
Admin Plan: s2p6; s4p1; s7p6
DISPOSITIONS................................1
Admin Plan: s20p6
DISPOSSESSED 1
24 CFR 982: .638
DISQUALIFICATION 1
24 CFR 982: .104
DISQUALIFIED................................3
24 CFR 982: .104;
PIH Notices: 02-21; 01-20
DISRUPTING...................................1
7420.10G Gbk: 4-6

DISRUPTION 1
PIH Notices: 01-41
DISSEMINATED 2
PIH Notices: 03-11;
Admin Plan: s15p4
DISSEMINATING 1
PIH Notices: 99-11
DISSEMINATION 2
24 CFR 5: .212;
PIH Notices: 03-11
DISTRESSED 5
HUD-50058Instr: p72 (2);
PIH Notices: 02-21; 01-20; 00-27
DISTRICT DIRECTOR 1
7420.10G Gbk: 5-10 Ex 5-1
DISTURB 2
PIH Notices: 95-48; 95-48 Tech Asst
DISTURBANCE 3
24 CFR 982: .310;
HUD-52641: p9;
HUD-52641-A: p2
DISTURBING 4
24 CFR 982: .401; .614;
7420.10G Gbk: 10-13; 15-2
DIVESTITURE 1
7420.10G Gbk: 11-3
DIVIDEND 2
7420.10G Gbk: 5-28; 5-48 Ex 5-5
DIVIDENDS 9
24 CFR 5: .609;
HUD-9886: p1 (2);
7420.10G Gbk: 4-26 Ex 4-2; 5-14 Ex 5-2; 5-24;
PIH Notices: 01-15 Impr Integ Hbk (2);
Admin Plan: s7p5
DIVORCE 19
24 CFR 5: .603;
24 CFR 982: .315;
7420.10G Gbk: 5-12; 5-23; 5-27; 5-47 Ex 5-5; 5-50 Ex 5-5;
PIH Notices: 01-15 Impr Integ Hbk (2);
Admin Plan: s2p3; s6p10; s6p11; s7p4; s7p5; s7p7 (2); s7p8; s8p5; s20p4
DIVORCE SETTLEMENT 1
24 CFR 5: .603
DIVORCED 3
HUD-50058Instr: p29 (2);
7420.10G Gbk: 5-19
DOCTOR 8
7420.10G Gbk: 5-51 Ex 5-5 (2); 5-52 Ex 5-5;
PIH Notices: 01-15 Impr Integ Hbk;
Admin Plan: s2p3; s5p2; s6p11; s7p7
DOCTOR COSTS 1
Admin Plan: s6p11
DOCTORS 1
7420.10G Gbk: 5-31
DOCUMENT PACKAGE 2
PIH Notices: 03-23; 02-27
DOCUMENTATION 190
24 CFR 5: .210; .216 (19); .218 (3); .508 (2); .512; .514 (4); .659;
24 CFR 982: .104; .551;
HUD-50058Instr: p5; p15; p18 (6);
HUD-52648: p2 (3);
HUD-52667: p ii (2);
7420.10G Gbk: 2-3 (3); 4-10 (3); 4-22; 5-1; 5-4 (3); 5-6 (7); 5-8 (2); 5-9 Ex 5-1 (2); 5-10 Ex 5-1 (2); 5-11 (2); 5-23; 5-28; 5-35; 5-46 Ex 5-5; 6-8; 7-7 (2); 9-3; 9-7; 9-10; 9-12 (2); 12-2; 12-5 (4); 13-2 (2); 15-5; 15-6; 15-7 (2); 18-4 (2); 19-1; 19-5; 20-8 Ex 20-1; 20-14 (2); 22-2; 22-13; 22-14;
PIH Notices: 03-12; 02-27 (5); 02-20 (6); 02-01; 01-41 (3); 01-15 (6); 01-15 Impr Integ Hbk (2); 01-06 (3); 00-46 (6); 00-24; 00-24B (2); 00-09 (2); 99-52; 95-48 (3); 95-48 Tech Asst (3);
Admin Plan: s2p2; s2p3 (2); s2p4; s6p4; s6p7; s6p9; s6p11; s7p6 (2); s7p8 (4); s9p4; s11p2; s11p1 (2); s15p4; s15p6; s16p3 (5); s17p1 (2); s18p3; s18p7; s18p8 (2); s19p1; s20p1 (2); s20p3; s21p2; s21p6; s25p5 (2); s25p6
DOCUMENTED 56
HUD-52648: p1 (2);
7420.10G Gbk: 1-9; 4-7; 4-22; 5-46 Ex 5-5; 5-47 Ex 5-5 (4); 5-48 Ex 5-5; 5-49 Ex 5-5 (2); 5-50 Ex 5-5; 5-51 Ex 5-5 (2);

5-52 Ex 5-5 (2); 5-53 Ex 5-5 (2); 6-7; 9-1; 9-11 (2); 12-4; 12-16 Ex 12-4; 19-10; 22-3; 22-11; 24-10;
PIH Notices: 03-12; 02-27; 02-20; 01-41; 01-15 Impr Integ Hbk; 00-46; 00-24B (4); 00-09;
Admin Plan: s2p2; s6p11; s7p1; s7p3 (2); s8p5; s10p5; s18p1; s20p3; s20p5 (2); s21p3 (2); s21p4; s24p4

DOCUMENTING........................20
7420.10G Gbk: 2-10; 3-9; 5-35; 5-50 Ex 5-5; 9-3; 9-8; 10-33; 10-47 Ex 10-9; 20-3; 22-13 (2);
PIH Notices: 02-20 (2); 00-46 (2); 00-24B (4);
Admin Plan: s21p3

DOG........................2
24 CFR 5: .306; .318

DOGS........................3
24 CFR 5: .318 (2); .350

DOJ........................6
PIH Notices: 95-48 (5); 95-48

DOLLAR........................72
24 CFR 5: .318; .603; .628;
HUD-50058: p i (2); p6 (4); p vii; p ix; p xvii (3);
HUD-50058Instr: p3 (2); p22 (4); p23; p28; p33; p34; p37; p39; p62 (3); p68;
HUD-52667: p1; p i; p ii;
7420.10G Gbk: 18-4; 18-6 (2); 21-7; 22-3; 22-17; 22-18;
PIH Notices: 02-27; 02-22; 02-21; 02-20 (3); 01-41 (8); 01-20; 01-15 Impr Integ Hbk (2); 01-10 (5); 00-46 (3); 00-09 (6); 00-09

DOLLAR AMOUNT........................32
HUD-50058: p ix; p xvii (2);
HUD-50058Instr: p28; p39; p62 (2); p68;
PIH Notices: 02-22; 02-21; 01-41 (8); 01-20; 01-15 Impr Integ Hbk; 01-10 (5); 00-09 (6); 00-09

DOLLAR AMOUNTS........................12
HUD-50058: p i; p6; p vii;
HUD-50058Instr: p3; p33; p34;
7420.10G Gbk: 22-3;
PIH Notices: 02-20 (2); 01-15 Impr Integ Hbk; 00-46; 00-46

DOLLARS........................15
24 CFR 5: .318;
HUD-50058: p6 (2); p vii;
HUD-50058Instr: p28; p33 (2); p35;
7420.10G Gbk: 9-9 (3); 19-10; 24-11;
PIH Notices: 01-15 Impr Integ Hbk;
Admin Plan: s20p1

DOMESTIC........................26
24 CFR 5: .655 (2); .703;
24 CFR 982: .207 (2);
HUD-50058Instr: p27;
HUD-52667: p ii (5);
7420.10G Gbk: 2-11; 3-3; 3-4; 4-16; 4-17; 5-16 Ex 5-2; 18-5 (4); 18-6 (4);
PIH Notices: 01-15 Impr Integ Hbk

DOMESTIC ABUSE........................2
7420.10G Gbk: 3-3; 3-4

DOMESTIC VIOLENCE........................7
24 CFR 5: .655 (2);
24 CFR 982: .207 (2);
7420.10G Gbk: 2-11; 4-16; 4-17

DOMESTIC VOLUNTEER SERVICES ACT........................3
HUD-50058Instr: p27;
7420.10G Gbk: 5-16 Ex 5-2;
PIH Notices: 01-15 Impr Integ Hbk

DOMESTICATED........................1
24 CFR 5: .306

DOMESTICATED ANIMAL........................1
24 CFR 5: .306

DOMICILE........................2
24 CFR 982: .4;
7420.10G Gbk: 13-2

DONATIONS........................2
PIH Notices: 02-01; 99-52

DOOR........................33
24 CFR 5: .353 (3);
HUD-52580: p6;
HUD-52580-A: p2 (2); p4 (2); p17 (3); p19;
7420.10G Gbk: 10-3; 10-5 (2); 10-6 (3); 10-7; 10-11; 10-12;
PIH Notices: 95-48 (6); 95-48 Tech Asst (5); 95-48 Tech Asst

DOORS........................60
24 CFR 5: .703 (3);
24 CFR 982: .401 (3); .605 (2); .614;
HUD-52580: p6 (4);

HUD-52580-A: p2 (4); p3; p4; p5; p7; p9; p10; p11; p12; p13; p14; p17; p19 (4);
7420.10G Gbk: 10-2; 10-6 (2); 10-8; 17-2 (2);
PIH Notices: 02-01; 00-23; 99-52; 99-11 (5); 95-48 (7); 95-48 Tech Asst (6); 95-48 Tech Asst

DOORWAY....................................1
HUD-52580-A: p17

DOORWAYS....................................2
PIH Notices: 02-01; 99-52

DOUBLE....................................10
HUD-50058Instr: p24; p35;
HUD-52580: p6 (3);
HUD-52580-A: p19 (3);
7420.10G Gbk: 20-8 Ex 20-1; 20-21 Ex 20-4

DOUBLE-CHECK....................................3
7420.10G Gbk: 20-21 (2);
PIH Notices: 01-06

DOUBLE-COUNTED....................................1
PIH Notices: 01-06

DOUBLE-COUNTING....................................5
PIH Notices: 01-06 (4); 01-06

DOUBLED....................................1
HUD-50058Instr: p35

DOWNPAYMENT ASSISTANCE..24
24 CFR 982: Intro; .4 (5); .625 (4); .627; .631 (3); .643 (9); .643

DOWN-PAYMENTS....................................3
24 CFR 982: .619;
7420.10G Gbk: 17-10;
Admin Plan: s19p1

DRAIN....................................15
24 CFR 982: .401; .614;
HUD-52580-A: p4 (3); p6 (5); p15;
7420.10G Gbk: 10-3; 10-5 (2); 17-5

DRAINAGE....................................7
24 CFR 5: .703 (2);
24 CFR 982: .401; .614;
HUD-52580-A: p17;
7420.10G Gbk: 10-13; 17-5

DRIVER'S LICENSE....................................6
7420.10G Gbk: 5-12; 5-50 Ex 5-5;
PIH Notices: 01-15 Impr Integ Hbk; 95-48; 95-48 Tech Asst;
Admin Plan: s7p8

DRIVEWAY....................................2
HUD-52580: p6;
HUD-52580-A: p19

DRIVEWAYS....................................1
24 CFR 5: .703

DROP....................................3
7420.10G Gbk: 2-1; 9-7;
PIH Notices: 00-53

DROP OUT....................................1
7420.10G Gbk: 2-1

DROPOUT....................................1
7420.10G Gbk: 7-7

DROPOUTS....................................1
PIH Notices: 01-15 Impr Integ Hbk

DROP-OUTS....................................1
7420.10G Gbk: 21-8

DROPPED....................................1
7420.10G Gbk: 4-4

DROPPINGS....................................2
HUD-52580-A: p17;
7420.10G Gbk: 10-14

DRUG....................................93
24 CFR 5: .100 (4); .403;
24 CFR 982: .4; .310 (6); .552 (3); .553 (8);
HUD-50058: p16;
HUD-50058Instr: p13; p61; p74;
7420.10G Gbk: 2-11; 3-4; 8-20; 10-13; 15-2; 15-7 (4); 21-4;
PIH Notices: 03-11 (4); 02-01 (2); 99-52 (2); 95-48 (17); 95-48 Tech Asst (17);
Admin Plan: s1p5 (5); s2p6; s15p2 (5); s15p3 (2); s15p4

DRUG ABUSE....................................3
HUD-50058: p16;
HUD-50058Instr: p61;
7420.10G Gbk: 2-11

DRUG CRIME....................................1
24 CFR 982: .310

DRUG CRIMINALS....................................3
24 CFR 982: .310; .553; .553

DRUG RAIDS....................................1
Admin Plan: s15p4

DRUG USER....................................1
Admin Plan: s1p5

DRUG USERS....................................3
PIH Notices: 95-48; 95-48 Tech Asst;
Admin Plan: s1p5

DRUG-FREE....................................2
24 CFR 5: .105; .105

DRUGRELATED....................................1
HUD-50058Instr: p61

DRUG-RELATED....................................50

24 CFR 5: .100;
24 CFR 982: .4; .306 (2); .307; .310; .316; .453; .551; .553 (6);
HUD-52641: p5; p6; p7; p9;
HUD-52641-A: p2 (2);
7420.10G Gbk: 1-15; 5-1 (2); 5-36 Ex 5-4; 5-37 (2); 5-39; 8-19; 8-20 (2); 11-3; 11-4; 15-2; 15-6 (2);
PIH Notices: 03-11;
Admin Plan: s2p3; s2p6 (3); s2p7; s6p6; s9p3; s15p2 (2); s15p5; s16p1; s16p2; s23p7

DRUGS 50
24 CFR 982: .310; .552;
7420.10G Gbk: 5-37; 15-7; 24-14;
PIH Notices: 01-15 Impr Integ Hbk; 95-48 (22); 95-48 Tech Asst (21); 95-48 Tech Asst

DRUG-TRAFFICKING 4
24 CFR 982: .307;
7420.10G Gbk: 2-7; 5-39; 15-4

DRYER 6
HUD-52580-A: p8;
HUD-52667: p ii;
7420.10G Gbk: 9-13 Ex 9-1; 9-15 Ex 9-2; 9-17 Ex 9-3; 9-17 Ex 9-3

DSS 1
24 CFR 5: .703

DUE DATE 6
24 CFR 5: .801 (2);
7420.10G Gbk: 12-14 Ex 12-2;
PIH Notices: 96-65;
Admin Plan: s17p1; s17p1

DUE DATE 1
7420.10G Gbk: 12-12 Ex 12-1

DUE PROCESS 1
24 CFR 5: .615

DUPLICATE 2
HUD-50058Instr: p11;
7420.10G Gbk: 11-8

DUPLICATED 1
PIH Notices: 00-11A

DUPLICATES 1
Admin Plan: s3p1

DUPLICATING 1
PIH Notices: 02-27

DUPLICATION 5
24 CFR 5: .234;
7420.10G Gbk: 23-5;
PIH Notices: 01-15; 00-53; 00-11A

DUPLICATIVE 7
24 CFR 982: .311; .352; .551;
7420.10G Gbk: 5-36 Ex 5-4; 8-22; 11-5;
PIH Notices: 00-11

DURATION 17
24 CFR 5: .403;
HUD-50058: p i;
HUD-50058Instr: p15; p74;
7420.10G Gbk: 4-10; 7-8;
PIH Notices: 95-48 (4); 95-48 Tech Asst (4);
Admin Plan: s6p5; s20p7; s25p2

DURATIONAL 1
Admin Plan: s6p12

DUST 11
24 CFR 982: .401 (2); .614;
HUD-52580-A: p18;
7420.10G Gbk: 10-10; 10-13; 10-20; 10-21; 10-36 Ex 10-1; 17-5;
PIH Notices: 00-23

DUST-LEAD 2
7420.10G Gbk: 10-38 Ex 10-3; 10-39 Ex 10-4

DWELLING UNIT 189
24 CFR 5: .100; .214; .309 (2); .312; .318 (7); .353 (2); .359; .360; .504 (2); .508 (2); .514 (3); .609; .611; .703 (5);
24 CFR 35 SubM: .1200; .1225 (7);
24 CFR 982: .4 (8); .54; .301; .305; .307; .312; .313; .351; .353 (2); .401 (28); .402 (3); .403; .404 (3); .452; .453; .505 (2); .508; .517; .609; .615; .617; .619 (3); .628; .631;
HUD-50058: p i;
HUD-50058Instr: p9 (3); p10; p31; p70 (2); p72; p73 (3); p74 (3); p75 (2); p76;
HUD-52580-A: p8; p17;
HUD-52667: p ii (2);
7420.10G Gbk: 3-4; 5-9 Ex 5-1; 5-15 Ex 5-2; 5-28; 8-17; 10-3 (2); 10-4 (4); 10-5 (2); 10-6 (4); 10-7 (3); 10-8; 10-9; 10-10 (3); 10-11; 10-12 (3); 10-13 (2); 10-14 (2); 10-

20 (2); 10-37 Ex 10-2; 10-43 Ex 10-6; 18-4; 18-5;
PIH Notices: 02-01 (5); 01-41 (2); 01-15 Impr Integ Hbk (3); 00-24B; 00-23; 00-09 (2); 99-52 (5);
Admin Plan: s5p3; s19p1; s23p6 (2); s23p7

DWELLING UNIT SIZE 2
7420.10G Gbk: 20-23;
PIH Notices: 00-24B

DWELLING UNITS........................ 42
24 CFR 5: .100 (2); .240; .312; .321; .359; .653 (3); .703 (4);
24 CFR 35 SubM: .1200 (3);
HUD-50058Instr: p75;
7420.10G Gbk: 10-1; 10-11; 10-37 Ex 10-2;
PIH Notices: 02-22 (2); 02-01 (6); 01-41; 01-10; 00-11 (2); 00-09; 99-52 (6); 99-11; 95-48; 95-48 Tech Asst

EARLY.. 29
HUD-50058Instr: p42; p78;
7420.10G Gbk: 4-12 (2); 8-9; 9-8; 11-9; 11-10; 13-3; 14-4; 21-2; 23-15 (4); 24-12;
PIH Notices: 02-14 (3); 01-41; 01-15 Impr Integ Hbk; 01-06 (4); 01-01; 00-09 (2); 99-52

EARNED INCOME DISALLOWANCE 12
HUD-50058Instr: p25 (2); p26; p27;
7420.10G Gbk: 5-16 Ex 5-2;
PIH Notices: 01-15 (2); 01-15 Impr Integ Hbk;
Admin Plan: s6p3 (2); s6p4; s6p4

EARNED INCOME TAX.................. 7
HUD-50058: p16; p xvi;
HUD-50058Instr: p28; p32; p60;
PIH Notices: 01-15 Impr Integ Hbk; 01-15 Impr Integ Hbk

EARNED INCOME TAX CREDIT .. 5
HUD-50058: p16; p xvi;
HUD-50058Instr: p32; p60;
PIH Notices: 01-15 Impr Integ Hbk

EARNED INCOME TAX CREDITS 2
HUD-50058Instr: p28;
PIH Notices: 01-15 Impr Integ Hbk

ECONOMIC 70
24 CFR 5: .603 (2); .615 (4); .617;
24 CFR 982: .310 (2); .642;
HUD-50058Instr: p13; p71 (4); p72; p75;
7420.10G Gbk: 4-9; 5-14 Ex 5-2; 5-21 (2); 5-22; 23-1 (2); 23-19; 24-12;
PIH Notices: 02-20 (2); 02-01; 01-15 Impr Integ Hbk (3); 01-10; 01-01; 00-46 (2); 00-11 (11); 00-11A (6); 99-52; 95-48 (2); 95-48 Tech Asst (2);
Admin Plan: s6p2; s6p3 (3); s6p12 (2); s6p13; s11p3 (3); s24p1; s25p3

ECONOMIC INDEPENDENCE....... 8
24 CFR 5: .603;
HUD-50058Instr: p71; p72;
7420.10G Gbk: 23-1 (2);
PIH Notices: 00-11;
Admin Plan: s6p3; s25p3

ECONOMIC REASON 5
24 CFR 982: .310 (2);
HUD-52641: p9;
HUD-52641-A: p2;
7420.10G Gbk: 15-2

ECONOMIC REASONS 1
7420.10G Gbk: 15-3

ECONOMIC SELF-SUFFICIENCY38
24 CFR 5: .603; .615 (3); .617;
HUD-50058Instr: p71 (2); p75;
7420.10G Gbk: 5-14 Ex 5-2; 5-21 (2); 5-22; 23-19;
PIH Notices: 01-15 Impr Integ Hbk (2); 00-11 (9); 00-11A (6);
Admin Plan: s6p2; s6p3 (2); s6p12 (2); s6p13; s11p3; s11p3

ECONOMICALLY 7
HUD-50058Instr: p75;
PIH Notices: 02-27 (2); 01-15 Impr Integ Hbk; 00-11A (2);
Admin Plan: s25p5

ECONOMIES 1
7420.10G Gbk: 21-18

ECONOMIST 23
PIH Notices: 02-20 (11); 01-41; 00-46 (10); 00-46

ECONOMISTS 10
PIH Notices: 02-20 (5); 00-46 (4); 00-46

ECONOMY 2

24 CFR 982: .102;
7420.10G Gbk: 13-6

EDUCATE 8
7420.10G Gbk: 2-5; 2-7; 22-9; 22-10; 24-14;
PIH Notices: 01-15 (2);
Admin Plan: s20p1

EDUCATING.................................... 1
7420.10G Gbk: 24-13

EDUCATION.................................. 64
24 CFR 5: .603 (2); .611; .655 (2);
24 CFR 982: .207 (2);
HUD-50058: p vii; p16 (2);
HUD-50058Instr: p32; p36 (2); p60 (2); p61 (2); p70; p71;
7420.10G Gbk: 5-16 Ex 5-2; 5-29; 5-52 Ex 5-5 (2); 10-35; 23-1 (2); 23-4; 23-5; 23-9; 24-14;
PIH Notices: 01-15; 01-15 Impr Integ Hbk (7); 00-11; 99-11 (2); 95-48 (7); 95-48 Tech Asst (7);
Admin Plan: s6p3; s7p3; s20p2; s22p1; s25p4 (3); s25p5; s25p6

EDUCATION COSTS 1
PIH Notices: 01-15 Impr Integ Hbk

EDUCATIONAL 24
24 CFR 5: .609;
HUD-50058Instr: p15 (2); p31;
7420.10G Gbk: 2-11; 5-15 Ex 5-2; 5-20 (2); 5-53 Ex 5-5; 23-6 (2);
PIH Notices: 02-01; 01-15 Impr Integ Hbk (4); 00-11; 99-52;
Admin Plan: s1p1; s7p5; s8p4; s25p5 (2); s25p7

EDUCATIONAL PROGRAM........... 1
7420.10G Gbk: 23-6

EDUCATION-RELATED................. 1
PIH Notices: 01-15 Impr Integ Hbk

EFFECTIVE DATE 288
24 CFR 5: .312; .353 (5); .609; .661;
24 CFR 982: .4 (2); .502 (4); .505 (5); .516 (3);
HUD-50058: p i (2); p2 (2); p ii (3); p3 (6); p iii; p4 (6); p iv; p5 (2); p v (6); p16 (2); p xvi (2); p xvii;
HUD-50058Instr: p ii; p11 (6); p12 (6); p14 (3); p15 (3); p18; p19; p20 (6); p21 (3); p22; p33; p38 (2); p59 (7); p61; p63; p65 (6); p66 (7); p70 (2); p71; p74;
HUD-52665: p2; p3;
7420.10G Gbk: 5-9 Ex 5-1; 5-13; 7-6; 7-8 (2); 9-2 (2); 10-35 (2); 11-16 Ex 11-1; 12-1 (3); 12-2 (2); 12-3; 12-4; 12-6 (4); 12-7 (2); 12-10; 14-1; 15-4; 15-7; 15-9 Ex 15-1; 15-10 Ex 15-2; 19-6; 19-11 (4); 19-12; 19-13; 22-12 (2); 23-11 (4); 23-13; 23-17 Ex 23-2 (11); 23-18;
PIH Notices: 03-12; 02-20; 02-14; 02-07; 01-41 (32); 01-33; 01-20 (2); 01-15 Impr Integ Hbk; 01-10 (18); 01-01 (2); 00-53; 00-49; 00-46; 00-34; 00-28; 00-24 (2); 00-24A; 00-24B; 00-14; 00-09 (31); 95-48; 95-48 Tech Asst;
Admin Plan: s2p7; s7p4; s7p6 (2); s9p4 (2); s11p2 (3); s14p1; s15p4; s18p1

EFFECTIVE DATES......................... 9
7420.10G Gbk: 2-10; 5-46 Ex 5-5; 12-1; 12-9;
PIH Notices: 02-14; 01-41; 01-11; 00-53; 00-09

EFFICIENCIES 2
HUD-50058Instr: p5;
PIH Notices: 00-11

EFFICIENCY.................................. 16
24 CFR 982: .102;
HUD-50058Instr: p20 (2); p42; p46;
HUD-52580-A: p2; p4;
7420.10G Gbk: 13-4; 19-11; 21-10 (2); 21-18 (3); 22-3;
PIH Notices: 00-11

EFFICIENT.................................... 22
7420.10G Gbk: 4-12; 4-16; 8-9; 8-11; 8-23; 10-23; 10-24; 11-7; 21-4; 21-6; 21-10; 24-12;
PIH Notices: 01-15 (2); 01-15 Impr Integ Hbk; 00-11A (2); 95-48; 95-48 Tech Asst;
Admin Plan: s1p1; s9p1; s10p1

EFFICIENT ALLOCATION 1
PIH Notices: 01-15 Impr Integ Hbk

EFFICIENTLY................................ 11
24 CFR 982: .4; .152;
7420.10G Gbk: 2-9; 8-2; 10-

23; 11-4; 11-9; 22-3; 22-11; 22-18;
PIH Notices: 01-15 Impr Integ Hbk

EGRESS..14
24 CFR 5: .318;
24 CFR 982: .401;
7420.10G Gbk: 10-17;
PIH Notices: 02-01; 99-52; 99-11 (3); 95-48 (3); 95-48 Tech Asst (2); 95-48 Tech Asst

EIGHT HOURS PER MONTH.........1
PIH Notices: 00-11

EIGHTEEN.......................................2
24 CFR 5: .518;
24 CFR 982: .643

EIGHTEEN MONTHS......................2
24 CFR 5: .518;
24 CFR 982: .643

EIN...8
24 CFR 5: .214; .216 (6); .218

ELDERLY.....................................192
24 CFR 5: .100; .240; .300; .303; .306 (13); .309; .312 (2); .318 (3); .321; .324; .353; .359; .360; .380; .403 (4); .601 (2); .603 (3); .611 (2); .655 (2); .801 (3);
24 CFR 982: .4 (2); .201 (3); .207; .315; .316; .352; .402; .606 (2); .610 (2); .612; .627 (4); .634 (6);
HUD-50058: p7 (3); p vii (3);
HUD-50058Instr: p15; p35 (9); p36; p42; p43; p44; p46; p47 (2); p71 (2); p72 (3); p73; p75;
HUD-52580-A: p2; p13; p17;
7420.10G Gbk: 1-7; 1-8 (4); 3-4; 4-2 (4); 4-3; 4-9; 4-11 (3); 4-15; 4-18; 4-27 Ex 4-2; 5-2 (2); 5-19; 5-28; 5-29 (4); 5-31 (4); 5-32; 5-33 (2); 5-34; 5-41 (2); 5-43 (2); 5-50 Ex 5-5 (3); 5-51 Ex 5-5; 9-14 Ex 9-1; 10-16; 12-2; 12-3; 12-7 (2); 17-3 (3); 17-4 (3); 24-10;
PIH Notices: 02-01; 01-41; 01-15 (2); 01-15 Impr Integ Hbk (4); 00-41; 00-14; 00-11; 00-09; 99-11 (2);
Admin Plan: s2p2; s2p3; s2p5; s6p1; s6p2; s6p11; s7p3; s7p8; s8p2; s19p1 (6); s22p1 (2); s24p2; s24p4; s25p2

ELDERLY / DISABLED...................2
Admin Plan: s6p1; s6p2

ELDERLY FAMILIES.......................5
7420.10G Gbk: 4-2 (2); 4-9; 4-15; 4-27 Ex 4-2

ELDERLY FAMILY........................22
24 CFR 5: .403 (2); .611 (2);
24 CFR 982: .627 (3); .634 (3);
HUD-50058Instr: p71; p72;
7420.10G Gbk: 5-2; 5-28; 5-32; 5-33 (2); 5-34;
PIH Notices: 01-15 Impr Integ Hbk (3); 01-15 Impr Integ Hbk

ELDERLY HOUSEHOLDS.............1
7420.10G Gbk: 1-8

ELDERLY HOUSING CHOICE VOUCHER.......................................1
7420.10G Gbk: 5-19

ELDERLY PERSON.......................22
24 CFR 5: .100; .306 (2); .603;
24 CFR 982: .201; .402; .606 (2); .610;
HUD-50058Instr: p43; p47 (2); p71; p75;
7420.10G Gbk: 5-41; 17-3; 24-10;
Admin Plan: s2p2; s2p3; s19p1 (2); s19p1

ELDERLY PERSONS....................18
24 CFR 5: .318; .403; .801;
24 CFR 982: .4; .201; .610; .612;
HUD-50058Instr: p73;
7420.10G Gbk: 17-3 (2); 17-4 (3);
PIH Notices: 00-11; 99-11;
Admin Plan: s2p5; s19p1; s19p1

ELECT..23
24 CFR 5: .315; .508 (3); .512; .801;
24 CFR 982: .201;
HUD-52665: p2;
7420.10G Gbk: 1-6 Ex 1-1; 3-2; 4-16; 4-20; 5-5; 5-6; 6-6;
PIH Notices: 02-27 (2); 01-41 (2); 00-09;
Admin Plan: s9p2 (2); s23p5

ELECTED..2
HUD-50058Instr: p15;
PIH Notices: 00-09

ELECTING.......................................1

7420.10G Gbk: 13-2

ELECTION 3
24 CFR 5: .508; .512;
7420.10G Gbk: 23-5

ELECTRIC 39
24 CFR 982: .401; .517;
HUD-52517: p1 (3);
HUD-52580-A: p2 (2); p6 (3); p15 (2);
HUD-52641: p2 (3);
HUD-52667: p1 (5); p i (2); p ii;
7420.10G Gbk: 6-6; 6-9 Ex 6-1; 9-14 Ex 9-1 (2); 9-15 Ex 9-2 (2); 10-7 (3); 10-9; 18-4; 18-6 (2); 18-8 (2); 18-8

ELECTRIC HEATERS 2
24 CFR 982: .401;
7420.10G Gbk: 10-7

ELECTRICAL 61
24 CFR 5: .703 (4);
24 CFR 982: .401 (6); .631;
HUD-52580: p1; p2 (2); p3 (3); p4 (3);
HUD-52580-A: p2 (2); p3 (2); p5 (2); p6 (2); p7 (2); p9 (2); p10 (2); p11 (2); p12 (2); p13; p14 (2); p17;
HUD-52667: p i; p ii;
7420.10G Gbk: 10-5 (2); 10-8 (7); 10-9; 10-19;
PIH Notices: 95-48 (2); 95-48 Tech Asst (2);
Admin Plan: s10p4; s22p3

ELECTRICAL APPLIANCES 4
24 CFR 982: .401;
HUD-52580-A: p2;
HUD-52667: p ii;
7420.10G Gbk: 10-8

ELECTRICAL FIXTURES 2
24 CFR 982: .401;
7420.10G Gbk: 10-8

ELECTRICAL OUTLET 4
24 CFR 982: .401;
7420.10G Gbk: 10-8;
PIH Notices: 95-48; 95-48 Tech Asst

ELECTRICAL OUTLETS 7
24 CFR 982: .401 (2);
7420.10G Gbk: 10-8 (2); 10-19;
PIH Notices: 95-48; 95-48 Tech Asst

ELECTRICITY 37
24 CFR 982: .401;
HUD-52580: p1; p2 (2); p3 (3); p4 (2);
HUD-52580-A: p2 (2); p3; p4 (3); p5; p6; p7; p8 (2); p9; p10; p11; p12;
HUD-52667: p i (3); p ii;
7420.10G Gbk: 10-1; 10-4; 10-8; 17-6 (2); 18-5; 18-6 (2); 18-6

ELECTRONIC 24
24 CFR 5: .801 (2);
24 CFR 982: .158 (3);
7420.10G Gbk: 11-7; 12-10; 19-2;
PIH Notices: 02-21 (2); 01-20 (2); 01-15; 01-06 (2); 00-34; 00-27 (3); 00-09 (2);
Admin Plan: s1p6; s21p8; s21p8

ELECTRONIC MEDIA 1
Admin Plan: s1p6

ELECTRONIC RECORDS 3
24 CFR 982: .158;
HUD-52641: p5;
7420.10G Gbk: 11-13

ELECTRONIC TRANSMISSION 2
24 CFR 982: .158;
7420.10G Gbk: 19-2

ELECTRONICALLY 28
24 CFR 5: .801 (3);
HUD-50058Instr: p1; p2 (3);
7420.10G Gbk: 1-11; 3-6; 4-9; 11-16 Ex 11-1; 12-3; 13-4; 13-7; 19-2; 20-29;
PIH Notices: 03-23; 03-11; 02-27; 01-15 (2); 01-06; 00-34; 00-24B;
Admin Plan: s7p1; s7p4 (2); s21p2

ELECTS 18
24 CFR 5: .632; .801;
24 CFR 982: .514;
HUD-50058Instr: p72; p73;
7420.10G Gbk: 1-9 (2); 5-26; 8-22; 13-4; 17-1; 23-2;
PIH Notices: 01-41; 01-15 Impr Integ Hbk; 00-09; 95-48; 95-48 Tech Asst;
Admin Plan: s6p10

ELEMENT 9
7420.10G Gbk: 1-7; 24-10;
PIH Notices: 02-01; 01-15 Impr Integ Hbk; 99-52; 95-48 (2); 95-48 Tech Asst; 95-48 Tech Asst

ELEMENTARY 4
PIH Notices: 95-48 (2); 95-48 Tech Asst; 95-48 Tech Asst

ELEMENTS....................................32
24 CFR 5: .100; .630;
7420.10G Gbk: 3-1; 3-3; 3-7 (2); 5-18; 9-9; 9-12; 10-9; 19-12; 22-5;
PIH Notices: 02-27 (2); 02-01 (4); 00-11A; 99-52 (4); 95-48 (3); 95-48 Tech Asst (3);
Admin Plan: s2p3; s15p3; s15p3

ELEVATED.......................................8
HUD-50058Instr: p71;
PIH Notices: 00-23 (5); 95-48; 95-48 Tech Asst

ELEVATED BLOOD LEAD LEVEL 4
HUD-50058Instr: p71;
PIH Notices: 00-23 (2); 00-23

ELEVATOR 54
24 CFR 5: .353;
HUD-50058: p5;
HUD-50058Instr: p21 (2);
HUD-52517: p1;
HUD-52580-A: p17;
7420.10G Gbk: 9-13 Ex 9-1 (3); 9-15 Ex 9-2 (3); 10-10 (2);
PIH Notices: 02-01 (3); 99-52 (3); 95-48 (19); 95-48 Tech Asst (14); 95-48 Tech Asst

ELEVATORS 32
24 CFR 5: .703 (2);
24 CFR 982: .401; .614;
HUD-50058Instr: p21;
HUD-52580: p5;
HUD-52580-A: p17 (2); p18 (2);
7420.10G Gbk: 10-9; 17-5;
PIH Notices: 02-01; 99-52; 95-48 (9); 95-48 Tech Asst (8); 95-48 Tech Asst

ELIGIBILITY 368
24 CFR 5: .210 (2); .214 (4); .216 (7); .218 (5); .230 (4); .232; .236 (3); .504; .506; .508 (3); .512 (3); .514; .516 (2); .518; .609 (2); .617; .630 (2); .653 (3);
24 CFR 982: 24 CFR 982 (2); .201 (2); .207; .353 (2); .355; .625; .627; .642 (2);
HUD-50058: p5; p v;
HUD-50058Instr: p2 (2); p15 (2); p17; p18 (2); p19; p24 (2); p29; p31; p37 (2); p38 (3); p71; p72; p76;
HUD-9886: p1 (5); p2 (4);
7420.10G Gbk: 1-1; 1-7 (2); 1-13; 1-16 Ex 1-3; 3-4; 3-7 (2); 3-8; 4-1; 4-5 (2); 4-6 (2); 4-7; 4-14; 4-17; 4-18 (2); 4-23 Ex 4-1; 5-1 (6); 5-2 (2); 5-3 (5); 5-5 (2); 5-6; 5-9 Ex 5-1; 5-13 (3); 5-15 Ex 5-2; 5-16 Ex 5-2; 5-34 (2); 5-35 (2); 5-41; 5-44; 5-50 Ex 5-5; 6-7; 6-8 (2); 8-1; 8-10; 12-1; 12-3; 12-5 (2); 13-2 (3); 13-3 (2); 13-7; 14-5; 16-1; 19-1; 19-9; 19-10; 20-3; 21-2; 21-3; 21-4 (2); 21-10 (3); 21-11 (2); 22-2; 22-3; 22-5; 22-8 (2); 23-6; 23-20; 24-8;
PIH Notices: 02-21; 01-41 (38); 01-27 (5); 01-20; 01-15; 01-15 Impr Integ Hbk (3); 01-10 (5); 01-02 (3); 01-01; 00-41; 00-27; 00-24B (10); 00-11 (2); 00-11A (3); 00-09 (42); 00-01; 98-66; 95-48 (12); 95-48 Tech Asst (12);
Admin Plan: s1p3 (2); s1p5; s2p1 (7); s2p3; s2p6 (7); s2p7 (2); s3p1; s3p2 (2); s3p3 (5); s6p4 (2); s7p1; s7p3; s7p8; s8p1 (3); s15p6; s18p3; s20p3; s22p1 (2); s23p2 (2); s23p3 (3); s23p7; s24p2; s24p4

ELIGIBILITY DETERMINATION 20
24 CFR 5: .630;
7420.10G Gbk: 1-16 Ex 1-3; 4-6 (2); 4-18; 5-6; 6-8; 12-5; 21-10;
PIH Notices: 01-41;
Admin Plan: s2p6 (6); s3p2; s6p4; s20p3; s23p3

ELIGIBILITY DETERMINATIONS 2
PIH Notices: 00-01; 98-66

ELIGIBILITY REQUIREMENT.......2
PIH Notices: 95-48; 95-48 Tech Asst

ELIGIBILITY REQUIREMENTS ..22
24 CFR 5: .653;
24 CFR 982: Intro; .625; .627; .642 (2);
7420.10G Gbk: 1-7; 5-1; 23-20;
PIH Notices: 95-48 (6); 95-48 Tech Asst (6);

Admin Plan: s23p2

ELIGIBLE FAMILY 17
24 CFR 5: .214;
24 CFR 982: .201;
HUD-50058Instr: p74;
7420.10G Gbk: 4-2; 13-1; 20-4 (2); 23-2;
PIH Notices: 01-41 (3); 01-27; 01-10; 00-11A; 00-09 (2);
Admin Plan: s25p1

ELIGIBLE FAMILY MEMBER........ 1
24 CFR 5: .520

ELIGIBLE FAMILY MEMBERS 8
HUD-50058Instr: p40; p44; p48; p51; p54; p57; p68;
Admin Plan: s18p7

ELIGIBLE HOUSEHOLD 1
7420.10G Gbk: 5-16 Ex 5-2

ELIGIBLE HOUSEHOLD MEMBERS 2
Admin Plan: s6p12; s6p12

ELIGIBLE HOUSING....................... 6
24 CFR 982: Intro; .352; .601;
Admin Plan: s9p1; s19p1; s24p1

ELIGIBLE IMMIGRANT 12
HUD-50058Instr: p18 (4);
Admin Plan: s2p1; s2p5 (2); s6p11; s7p3; s15p1; s18p1; s18p7

ELIGIBLE IMMIGRANTS............... 5
HUD-50058Instr: p68;
7420.10G Gbk: 5-3; 6-7;
Admin Plan: s2p5; s6p12

ELIGIBLE IMMIGRATION STATUS 105
24 CFR 5: .504 (3); .506; .508 (22); .510 (4); .512 (6); .514 (5); .516; .518 (3); .520 (7); .659;
24 CFR 982: .201; .551; .552 (2);
HUD-50058: p v;
HUD-50058Instr: p17 (3); p71; p73 (2);
HUD-52646: p2;
7420.10G Gbk: 1-14; 5-1; 5-3 (2); 5-4 (5); 5-5 (4); 5-6 (2); 5-7 (2); 5-8; 5-9 Ex 5-1 (8); 5-10 Ex 5-1 (2); 5-11; 5-36 Ex 5-4; 6-6 (2); 6-7; 12-5 (2); 15-8;
PIH Notices: 01-15 Impr Integ Hbk;
Admin Plan: s2p1; s2p5; s18p8

ELIGIBLE NONCITIZEN 11
HUD-50058: p3; p4;
HUD-50058Instr: p15; p40; p44; p48; p51; p54; p57; p68;
7420.10G Gbk: 15-5

ELIGIBLE POPULATION................ 5
7420.10G Gbk: 1-5; 4-2 (2); 4-4; 19-8

ELIGIBLE SUBSIDY...................... 16
24 CFR 5: .520;
HUD-50058: p9; p ix;
HUD-50058Instr: p40 (3); p68; p69 (7);
7420.10G Gbk: 5-5; 6-7

EMAIL 9
PIH Notices: 02-27; 01-41 (3); 01-27 (2); 01-06; 01-01; 00-09

E-MAIL.. 2
PIH Notices: 02-27; 01-41

EMANCIPATED............................... 3
HUD-50058Instr: p14;
Admin Plan: s2p1; s8p6

EMANCIPATED MINOR 3
HUD-50058Instr: p14;
Admin Plan: s2p1; s8p6

EMERGENCIES............................... 4
24 CFR 5: .360;
PIH Notices: 99-11;
Admin Plan: s15p6; s21p5

EMERGENCY 104
24 CFR 5: .703 (2);
24 CFR 982: .642 (2);
HUD-52580-A: p17;
7420.10G Gbk: 5-10 Ex 5-1; 8-12; 10-12 (2); 10-13; 10-27; 10-28; 10-33 (2); 10-34; 10-48 Ex 10-10 (2); 23-15;
PIH Notices: 01-41 (3); 00-09; 99-11 (9); 95-48 (31); 95-48 Tech Asst (31);
Admin Plan: s10p1; s10p2; s10p3 (2); s10p4 (3); s10p5 (2); s23p2; s25p5

EMERGENCY EXIT........................ 3
HUD-52580-A: p17;
7420.10G Gbk: 10-12; 10-13

EMERGENCY EXITS 1
PIH Notices: 99-11

EMERGENCY POWER.................... 1
24 CFR 5: .703

EMOTIONAL ILLNESS 3
7420.10G Gbk: 5-43;
PIH Notices: 95-48; 95-48 Tech Asst

EMOTIONAL IMPAIRMENT..........5
24 CFR 5: .403;
HUD-50058: p i;
HUD-50058Instr: p15; p74;
Admin Plan: s25p2

EMPLOY..........4
7420.10G Gbk: 10-19; 21-8;
PIH Notices: 95-48; 95-48 Tech Asst

EMPLOYED..........55
24 CFR 5: .603 (2); .611 (2); .617 (2); .655; .661;
24 CFR 982: .207; .627 (2);
HUD-50058: p16;
HUD-50058Instr: p28 (2); p34; p36; p60 (2); p70; p71; p74 (2);
7420.10G Gbk: 4-16; 4-17; 5-26 (2); 5-30; 5-52 Ex 5-5; 21-17; 23-12; 23-15; 23-18;
PIH Notices: 01-15 (4); 01-15 Impr Integ Hbk (8); 00-23; 00-11;
Admin Plan: s6p3; s6p10; s7p3 (2); s7p7 (3); s11p1; s18p6

EMPLOYEE..........51
24 CFR 5: .214 (3); .514;
24 CFR 982: .161; .553; .631;
HUD-50058Instr: p28; p29; p71; p74;
HUD-52641: p6;
HUD-9886: p2 (2);
7420.10G Gbk: 4-12; 5-26; 8-19; 10-24; 11-2; 11-3 (3); 11-8; 12-8; 21-1; 21-2; 21-3 (2); 22-10; 22-11 (2); 22-14 (2); 22-15 (5); 23-15;
PIH Notices: 03-11; 95-48 (5); 95-48 Tech Asst (5);
Admin Plan: s6p10

EMPLOYEES..........102
24 CFR 5: .318;
24 CFR 982: .306 (2);
HUD-50058Instr: p25;
HUD-52641: p6; p7 (2);
HUD-9886: p1;
7420.10G Gbk: 3-6; 5-15 Ex 5-2; 8-20 (2); 10-24; 11-3 (2); 11-13; 21-2 (5); 21-3; 22-1; 22-2; 22-6; 22-9 (2); 22-11; 22-15; 22-18;
PIH Notices: 02-01; 01-15 (2); 01-15 Impr Integ Hbk; 00-01 (2); 99-52; 98-66 (2); 95-48 (31); 95-48 Tech Asst (29);
Admin Plan: s1p1; s16p2; s18p1

EMPLOYEE'S..........5
7420.10G Gbk: 22-10;
PIH Notices: 01-15 Impr Integ Hbk; 95-48; 95-48 Tech Asst;
Admin Plan: s7p4

EMPLOYER..........39
24 CFR 5: .110; .212; .214 (4); .216 (2); .218; .236 (5);
HUD-50058: p16;
HUD-50058Instr: p60 (3); p61 (2); p63; p74;
7420.10G Gbk: 5-12; 5-46 Ex 5-5 (3); 5-52 Ex 5-5; 12-13 Ex 12-1; 22-11;
PIH Notices: 01-15 (2); 01-15 Impr Integ Hbk (2);
Admin Plan: s6p8; s7p3; s7p4; s7p7 (2); s7p8

EMPLOYERS..........22
24 CFR 5: .214 (3); .230;
HUD-50058Instr: p28; p71;
HUD-9886: p1 (3);
7420.10G Gbk: 4-3 (2); 5-13; 5-49 Ex 5-5; 12-3; 23-15;
PIH Notices: 01-15; 95-48 (2); 95-48 Tech Asst (2);
Admin Plan: s20p4; s20p4

EMPLOYER'S..........3
7420.10G Gbk: 12-16 Ex 12-4;
PIH Notices: 01-15; 01-15 Impr Integ Hbk

EMPLOYER-SPONSORED..........2
PIH Notices: 95-48; 95-48 Tech Asst

EMPLOYING..........1
7420.10G Gbk: 10-19

EMPLOYMENT..........285
24 CFR 5: .105; .214; .603 (4); .609 (4); .615; .617 (10); .630;
24 CFR 982: .627 (8);
HUD-50058: p vii; p16 (4); p xvi (2); p17;
HUD-50058Instr: p25 (5); p26; p27 (4); p28; p36 (2); p60 (6); p61 (2); p63; p70 (3); p71 (2); p74;
HUD-9886: p1 (2);
7420.10G Gbk: 2-1; 2-6; 2-11; 5-10 Ex 5-1; 5-15 Ex 5-2 (5); 5-17; 5-20 (5); 5-21; 5-22 (3); 5-26 (2); 5-46 Ex 5-5 (3); 5-49 Ex 5-5; 5-51 Ex 5-5; 5-52 Ex 5-5 (4); 6-8; 8-7; 8-12; 11-3;

12-13 Ex 12-1; 23-1; 23-4; 23-5; 23-7 (2); 23-8 Ex 23-1 (3); 23-9 (5); 23-13 (2); 23-16 Ex 23-2; 23-20 (2);
PIH Notices: 02-01 (2); 01-15 (12); 01-15 Impr Integ Hbk (33); 00-24B; 00-11 (2); 00-11A (7); 00-01 (4); 99-52 (2); 98-66 (4); 95-48 (30); 95-48 Tech Asst (30);
Admin Plan: s1p2; s6p2 (4); s6p3 (8); s6p4 (3); s6p10 (3); s6p12; s7p3; s7p4 (3); s7p7; s11p3; s20p3; s20p6; s22p1; s25p4 (7); s25p6

EMPLOYMENT AUTHORIZATION 1
7420.10G Gbk: 5-10 Ex 5-1

EMPLOYMENT COUNSELING 3
24 CFR 5: .603;
HUD-50058Instr: p71;
Admin Plan: s6p3

EMPLOYMENT INCOME 9
24 CFR 5: .214; .603;
HUD-50058Instr: p70;
7420.10G Gbk: 5-46 Ex 5-5; 23-13 (2);
PIH Notices: 01-15 Impr Integ Hbk;
Admin Plan: s6p4; s7p3

EMPLOYMENT SUITABILITY 1
HUD-9886: p1

EMPLOYMENT TRAINING............ 2
HUD-50058Instr: p27;
PIH Notices: 01-15 Impr Integ Hbk

EMPLOYMENT TRAINING PROGRAM.. 6
24 CFR 5: .609;
7420.10G Gbk: 5-15 Ex 5-2; 5-20 (2);
PIH Notices: 01-15 Impr Integ Hbk; 01-15 Impr Integ Hbk

EMPLOYMENT TRAINING PROGRAMS 15
24 CFR 5: .609 (2);
HUD-50058Instr: p27;
7420.10G Gbk: 5-15 Ex 5-2 (2); 5-20 (2);
PIH Notices: 01-15 (3); 01-15 Impr Integ Hbk (4); 01-15 Impr Integ Hbk

EMPLOYMENT-RELATED 4
24 CFR 5: .214;
HUD-50058Instr: p28;
PIH Notices: 00-11; 00-11A

EMPLOYS 8
PIH Notices: 95-48 (4); 95-48 Tech Asst (3); 95-48 Tech Asst

ENABLE.. 55
24 CFR 5: .210; .603 (2); .611 (2);
HUD-50058Instr: p34; p70; p71; p72;
7420.10G Gbk: 4-6; 5-27; 5-29 (3); 5-30 (3); 7-9; 8-14; 13-5; 18-1; 19-9; 20-9; 20-22; 21-1; 22-6; 24-4;
PIH Notices: 03-23; 02-20 (2); 02-06; 02-01; 01-15 (2); 01-15 Impr Integ Hbk (3); 01-06; 00-46 (2); 00-28 (2); 00-11; 99-52; 95-48; 95-48 Tech Asst;
Admin Plan: s1p3; s6p2; s6p10; s7p7; s8p2 (2); s23p6; s25p2; s25p3

ENABLED 7
7420.10G Gbk: 5-29; 5-34; 5-52 Ex 5-5;
PIH Notices: 01-01 (2);
Admin Plan: s6p11; s6p11

ENABLES.. 16
24 CFR 5: .210;
7420.10G Gbk: 1-7; 2-4; 2-6; 4-21; 5-33 (2); 5-34; 9-7; 11-16 Ex 11-1; 19-6 (2); 21-2;
PIH Notices: 03-11; 95-48; 95-48 Tech Asst

ENABLING 2
24 CFR 982: .51; .102

ENDORSEMENT 4
7420.10G Gbk: 5-38; 11-1;
PIH Notices: 01-41; 00-09

ENERGY 13
HUD-50058Instr: p32;
HUD-52667: p i; p ii;
7420.10G Gbk: 5-16 Ex 5-2; 10-8; 18-1 (2);
PIH Notices: 01-15 Impr Integ Hbk; 95-48 (2); 95-48 Tech Asst (2);
Admin Plan: s6p13

ENERGY AUDIT 1
7420.10G Gbk: 18-1

ENERGY CONSERVATION............. 2
7420.10G Gbk: 10-8; 18-1

ENERGY-CONSERVATIVE 5
24 CFR 5: .603;
24 CFR 982: .517;
HUD-50058Instr: p76;
HUD-52667: p i;

Admin Plan: s6p13

ENERGY-CONSERVING.................1
7420.10G Gbk: 18-1

ENFORCE.......................................30
24 CFR 5: .303;
24 CFR 982: .152; .308 (2); .404 (2); .406; .456; .619; .625;
HUD-52641: p5; p6; 8;
HUD-52641-A: p1 (2);
HUD-903: p2;
7420.10G Gbk: 4-16; 8-21 (2); 10-33; 11-4; 11-13 (2); 11-14; 12-8; 12-10;
PIH Notices: 00-24B (2);
Admin Plan: s21p5; s21p5

ENFORCED......................................6
7420.10G Gbk: 10-2 (3); 19-12;
PIH Notices: 95-48; 95-48 Tech Asst

ENFORCEMENT..........................118
24 CFR 982: Intro; .406 (2); .456; .630;
HUD-52648: p1;
HUD-903: p2 (3); p3 (7);
HUD-9886: p1;
7420.10G Gbk: 1-9 (3); 1-10; 1-11; 5-22; 5-23; 10-8; 10-23; 10-30; 10-31 (2); 10-32; 10-33; 10-34; 19-12; 19-13; 20-3; 22-7;
PIH Notices: 03-11 (22); 02-27 (2); 02-07; 02-01 (2); 01-41 (14); 01-06; 00-28; 00-24B (2); 00-09 (13); 99-52 (2); 95-48 (7); 95-48 Tech Asst (7);
Admin Plan: s6p9 (2); s7p5 (2); s10p1; s21p1; s21p2; s21p5

ENGLISH.......................................15
24 CFR 5: .502; .603;
HUD-50058Instr: p71;
7420.10G Gbk: 5-11; 8-2; 21-9;
PIH Notices: 00-11; 95-48 (2); 95-48 Tech Asst (2);
Admin Plan: s1p5 (2); s6p3; s8p1

ENGLISH PROFICIENCY...............3
24 CFR 5: .603;
HUD-50058Instr: p71;
Admin Plan: s6p3

ENTIRE AGREEMENT....................5
HUD-52641: p7 (2);
7420.10G Gbk: 11-11; 11-14; 11-14

ENTITLE..1
PIH Notices: 03-11

ENTITLED.....................................78
24 CFR 5: .214; .353; .506 (2); .514 (3); .518 (3); .520 (3); .528; .615; .630; .661;
24 CFR 982: .617;
HUD-50058Instr: p17; p29;
HUD-52641: p4;
7420.10G Gbk: 5-30; 6-8; 10-29; 11-5; 11-18; 14-5; 16-5; 20-3; 20-6; 20-7; 20-24; 22-1; 22-11; 22-12 (3); 22-13 (3);
PIH Notices: 02-01; 01-15; 01-15 Impr Integ Hbk (2); 00-28; 99-52; 95-48 (9); 95-48 Tech Asst (5);
Admin Plan: s2p3; s2p4; s2p5; s4p2; s6p4; s6p11; s8p5 (2); s8p6; s10p2; s17p2; s18p1; s18p8 (2); s19p1; s20p1; s23p7; s23p8

ENTITLEMENT...............................7
24 CFR 5: .653;
24 CFR 982: .202;
7420.10G Gbk: 4-26 Ex 4-2 (2); 5-50 Ex 5-5;
PIH Notices: 01-15 Impr Integ Hbk;
Admin Plan: s20p1

ENTITLEMENTS.............................3
24 CFR 5: .512;
7420.10G Gbk: 5-7; 5-20

ENTITY APPLICANT.......................9
24 CFR 5: .214; .216 (5); .218 (2); .218

ENTITY APPLICANTS....................3
24 CFR 5: .216 (2); .218

ENTRANCE..................................48
HUD-50058: p2; p ii;
HUD-50058Instr: p8 (4);
HUD-52580: p1;
HUD-52580-A: p8 (3); p9; p10; p11; p12;
PIH Notices: 02-01; 99-52; 95-48 (15); 95-48 Tech Asst (15);
Admin Plan: s10p3; s10p4

ENTRANCES................................14
PIH Notices: 95-48 (7); 95-48 Tech Asst (6); 95-48 Tech Asst

ENTRY...57
24 CFR 5: .360;
HUD-50058: p i;
HUD-50058Instr: p3 (2);
HUD-52580-A: p8; p13 (2);
7420.10G Gbk: 4-13; 4-14; 5-

10 Ex 5-1; 10-25; 10-34 (2); 10-40 Ex 10-4a; 10-41 Ex 10-4b (2); 11-9; 11-16 Ex 11-1 (2); 19-10; 20-24; 20-25 (4); 21-14 Ex 21-4; 22-6;
PIH Notices: 02-27; 02-20; 01-06 (5); 00-53 (3); 00-46; 95-48 (2); 95-48 Tech Asst (2);
Admin Plan: s3p1 (10); s3p2 (4); s3p2

ENVELOPE......3
7420.10G Gbk: 4-7; 24-14;
Admin Plan: s4p3

ENVIRONMENT......25
24 CFR 5: .315; .603;
24 CFR 982: .401 (4); .614;
HUD-50058Instr: p76;
HUD-52580-A: p15 (2);
7420.10G Gbk: 2-5; 10-1; 10-7 (4); 10-9; 21-3;
PIH Notices: 00-53; 00-23; 95-48 (2); 95-48 Tech Asst (2);
Admin Plan: s8p1

ENVIRONMENTAL......38
24 CFR 5: .100;
24 CFR 35 SubM: .1225 (10);
24 CFR 982: .305; .401; .614; .626;
7420.10G Gbk: 10-12; 10-13; 10-16 (2); 10-20 (6); 10-22 (3);
PIH Notices: 02-07; 02-01; 00-49; 00-23; 99-52; 95-48 (2); 95-48 Tech Asst (2);
Admin Plan: s24p2

ENVIRONMENTS......2
7420.10G Gbk: 21-1;
PIH Notices: 00-11

EPILEPSY......4
PIH Notices: 95-48 (2); 95-48 Tech Asst; 95-48 Tech Asst

EPITHETS......1
Admin Plan: s15p2

EQUAL ACCESS......3
PIH Notices: 95-48; 95-48 Tech Asst;
Admin Plan: s1p5

EQUAL HOUSING OPPORTUNITIES 1
Admin Plan: s1p3

EQUAL HOUSING OPPORTUNITY 1
7420.10G Gbk: 4-2

EQUAL OPPORTUNITY......80
24 CFR 5: .105 (2); .524; .655;
24 CFR 982: Intro; .53 (2); .207; .301; .306 (2); .310; .452; .552;
HUD-52641: p5 (2); p6 (2); p10;
HUD-52641-A: p3;
HUD-903: p1 (2); p3;
HUD-903-1: p1;
7420.10G Gbk: 1-14 (2); 4-17; 4-27 Ex 4-2; 5-42 (2); 5-43; 5-44; 5-45; 8-6; 8-14; 8-18 (2); 11-1; 11-2; 11-13; 11-17; 22-15;
PIH Notices: 02-21; 02-01 (4); 01-20; 01-15; 99-52 (4); 95-48 (11); 95-48 Tech Asst (9);
Admin Plan: s1p2 (2); s1p4; s3p1; s16p1 (2); s24p2

EQUALLY RESPONSIBLE......2
HUD-50058Instr: p14;
Admin Plan: s2p2

EQUIPMENT......83
24 CFR 5: .609 (2); .703;
24 CFR 982: .158; .401 (6); .609; .614 (4);
HUD-50058Instr: p28;
HUD-52580: p5 (2);
HUD-52580-A: p15 (5); p16 (3);
HUD-52641: p5;
HUD-52667: p i; p ii;
7420.10G Gbk: 4-27 Ex 4-2 (2); 5-15 Ex 5-2 (2); 5-19; 5-30; 10-4; 10-5 (4); 10-6 (2); 10-7; 10-8 (3); 10-9 (2); 10-11 (2); 10-13 (2); 11-13; 17-2; 18-7; 20-23;
PIH Notices: 02-27 (2); 02-01; 01-15; 01-15 Impr Integ Hbk (5); 99-52; 99-11; 95-48 (8); 95-48 Tech Asst (7); 95-48 Tech Asst

EQUITABLE......3
7420.10G Gbk: 5-34;
PIH Notices: 95-48; 95-48 Tech Asst

EQUITY......13
24 CFR 5: .603;
24 CFR 982: .632;
HUD-50058Instr: p22; p74;
7420.10G Gbk: 5-25 Ex 5-3 (3); 5-26 (5); 17-11

ERRONEOUS......4
HUD-50058Instr: p11 (2);
7420.10G Gbk: 22-3;
PIH Notices: 01-06

ERRONEOUSLY......11

PIH Notices: 01-06 (7); 95-48 (2); 95-48 Tech Asst; 95-48 Tech Asst

ERROR...41
HUD-50058: p ii;
HUD-50058Instr: p1 (2); p11 (2);
7420.10G Gbk: 11-10; 19-2; 19-4; 22-1 (2); 22-3; 22-5 (5); 22-6; 22-8 (3); 22-10; 22-12 (8); 22-13 (2);
PIH Notices: 02-27 (2); 01-15 (6); 01-06;
Admin Plan: s17p2

ERROR-PRONE...............................1
7420.10G Gbk: 22-10

ERRORS.......................................70
24 CFR 982: .102 (4); .517;
HUD-50058Instr: p11;
7420.10G Gbk: 4-22; 5-34 (2); 11-9; 16-1; 18-4; 19-2; 19-4 (5); 19-10 (4); 19-12; 20-6; 22-1 (5); 22-2 (3); 22-3 (6); 22-5 (5); 22-6; 22-7 (3); 22-8; 22-9; 22-11; 22-12; 22-13; 22-14; 22-17 (2); 22-18 (4);
PIH Notices: 03-20 (2); 02-07; 01-41; 01-15 (3); 01-06; 00-28; 00-09;
Admin Plan: s5p2

ESCROW.....................................122
24 CFR 5: .615; .630;
HUD-50058: p xvii;
HUD-50058Instr: p ii; p62; p64; p65 (7); p66; p67; p71; p72;
HUD-52648: p3 (3);
7420.10G Gbk: 1-10; 1-11; 23-1 (2); 23-2; 23-4; 23-7 (2); 23-10 (6); 23-11 (7); 23-12 (8); 23-13 (8); 23-14 (11); 23-15 (8); 23-16 Ex 23-2 (6); 23-17 Ex 23-2 (3); 23-18 (5); 23-19 (7);
PIH Notices: 02-27 (2); 02-01; 01-15 Impr Integ Hbk; 01-06 (2); 00-11; 99-52;
Admin Plan: s18p4; s21p1; s21p2; s21p9 (2); s25p4 (4); s25p5 (7); s25p6

ESCROW DEPOSIT.........................3
24 CFR 5: .615; .630;
7420.10G Gbk: 23-13

ESSENTIAL..................................70
24 CFR 5: .403;
24 CFR 982: .307; .401;
HUD-50058: p17;
HUD-50058Instr: p7; p15; p62 (2); p73;
7420.10G Gbk: 4-8; 5-3; 5-34 (2); 5-39; 8-20; 10-8; 10-35; 13-8; 15-1; 15-7; 19-2; 19-10; 19-13; 24-4; 24-13 (2);
PIH Notices: 02-27; 02-01 (4); 00-53 (2); 00-09; 99-52 (4); 99-11 (2); 95-48 (13); 95-48 Tech Asst (13);
Admin Plan: s1p5; s2p3; s2p7; s9p3

ESSENTIAL OBLIGATIONS..........2
PIH Notices: 02-01; 99-52

ESSENTIALLY 3
HUD-52667: p i;
7420.10G Gbk: 11-3;
PIH Notices: 01-41

ESTATE...58
24 CFR 5: .214; .363;
24 CFR 982: .306; .630; .633; .635 (2);
HUD-50058Instr: p56;
HUD-52667: p i;
HUD-903: p2;
HUD-903-1: p5;
7420.10G Gbk: 4-26 Ex 4-2; 5-12; 5-25 Ex 5-3; 5-26; 5-27; 5-28 (2); 5-49 Ex 5-5 (2); 8-12; 9-6; 18-4; 20-29; 22-4; 24-9; 24-11; 24-14 (2);
PIH Notices: 02-21; 02-20 (2); 02-07 (2); 01-33; 01-20; 01-15 Impr Integ Hbk (2); 01-10; 01-06; 01-02; 01-01 (2); 00-49; 00-46 (2); 00-41; 00-28 (2);
Admin Plan: s1p6 (2); s7p6 (3); s11p2; s16p2; s16p3; s20p4

ESTATE-RELATED 1
7420.10G Gbk: 5-11

ETHNIC...14
24 CFR 5: .655;
24 CFR 982: .158; .204; .207;
HUD-50058Instr: p73;
HUD-903: p2;
7420.10G Gbk: 2-13 Ex 2-1; 4-3; 4-8; 4-9; 4-14; 23-4;
Admin Plan: s1p2; s4p1

ETHNIC ORIGIN............................3
24 CFR 5: .655;
24 CFR 982: .207;
Admin Plan: s1p2

ETHNICITY 28

HUD-50058: p3 (7); p iii; p4 (7); p iv;
HUD-50058Instr: p15; p16;
7420.10G Gbk: 4-15; 4-23 Ex 4-1; 4-25 Ex 4-2; 19-3; 19-6 (2); 19-7 (3);
PIH Notices: 01-02

ETIOLOGIC AGENT 5
24 CFR 5: .403;
HUD-50058: p i;
HUD-50058Instr: p15; p74;
Admin Plan: s25p2

EVALUATE 11
24 CFR 982: .104;
7420.10G Gbk: 1-10; 5-1; 12-8; 22-1;
PIH Notices: 03-12; 02-27; 01-43;
Admin Plan: s2p1; s6p5; s20p6

EVALUATED 10
HUD-52580-A: p15;
7420.10G Gbk: 5-38; 9-12; 12-5; 23-19;
PIH Notices: 02-27;
Admin Plan: s20p3 (2); s20p6; s21p2

EVALUATES 4
HUD-50058Instr: p2;
7420.10G Gbk: 9-12 (2);
Admin Plan: s1p7

EVALUATING 5
HUD-52580-A: p17;
7420.10G Gbk: 4-4; 9-3; 9-4;
Admin Plan: s21p1

EVALUATION 38
24 CFR 5: .703;
24 CFR 35 SubM: .1210 (2); .1225 (4);
7420.10G Gbk: 1-2; 9-10; 10-15; 10-20 (2); 10-37 Ex 10-2; 22-15;
PIH Notices: 02-27 (4); 02-20; 02-07; 00-49; 00-46; 95-48 (6); 95-48 Tech Asst (4);
Admin Plan: s20p5; s20p6; s24p2; s24p3; s24p4; s24p4

EVALUATIONS 4
7420.10G Gbk: 3-9; 4-11; 9-11; 19-12

EVICT 21
24 CFR 5: .514; .630;
24 CFR 982: .310 (3); .311 (2); .314 (2);
HUD-52641: p9 (2);
HUD-52641-A: p2 (2);
7420.10G Gbk: 8-19; 11-3; 15-3; 15-4;
PIH Notices: 03-11 (2);
Admin Plan: s13p1; s14p2

EVICTED 20
24 CFR 5: .630;
24 CFR 982: .311; .552 (2); .553 (2);
7420.10G Gbk: 4-25 Ex 4-2; 5-1; 5-37; 5-38 (2); 6-8; 15-5; 15-6;
PIH Notices: 03-11;
Admin Plan: s2p6 (2); s6p4; s15p2; s15p5

EVICTING 3
24 CFR 5: .514;
24 CFR 982: .310; .310

EVICTION 64
24 CFR 5: .514 (3);
24 CFR 982: .310 (9); .551 (2); .552; .553 (2); .641;
HUD-52641: p9 (5);
HUD-52641-A: p2 (6);
7420.10G Gbk: 1-15; 5-1 (2); 5-36 Ex 5-4; 10-27 (2); 15-3 (5); 15-4;
PIH Notices: 03-11 (9); 00-41;
Admin Plan: s2p6; s9p3 (2); s14p1 (4); s14p2 (2); s15p5 (3); s23p6

EVICTION NOTICE 21
24 CFR 982: .310 (4); .551 (2); .641;
HUD-52641: p9 (3);
HUD-52641-A: p2 (4);
7420.10G Gbk: 1-15; 5-36 Ex 5-4; 15-3 (3);
Admin Plan: s14p1; s14p1

EVICTIONS 5
24 CFR 982: .310;
7420.10G Gbk: 4-15;
PIH Notices: 03-11 (2);
Admin Plan: s14p1

EVICTS 1
7420.10G Gbk: 15-3

EVIDENCE 187
24 CFR 5: .100; .216 (2); .504 (2); .508 (40); .510 (3); .514 (10); .518 (3); .653; .659; .703 (2);
24 CFR 982: .51 (3); .310 (3); .551; .552 (3); .553 (3); .555 (5);
HUD-50058Instr: p71 (2);
HUD-52580: p5;
HUD-52580-A: p2; p13 (2); p15 (2); p17 (3); p18;
HUD-52646: p2;
HUD-52648: p1; p3;
7420.10G Gbk: 1-14; 5-4; 5-6 (3); 5-9 Ex 5-1 (4); 5-

10 Ex 5-1 (2); 5-37 (2); 5-38; 5-50 Ex 5-5; 5-52 Ex 5-5; 7-3; 8-10; 9-12; 10-14; 12-5 (2); 15-7; 16-5 (6); 19-5; 20-6; 22-11; 22-14 (2); 22-16; 24-11;
PIH Notices: 02-07; 01-15 Impr Integ Hbk (3); 00-28 (2); 00-24B; 95-48 (4); 95-48 Tech Asst (4);
Admin Plan: s2p2 (3); s7p8 (2); s15p3; s15p4 (13); s16p3; s18p3; s18p5 (5); s18p6 (4); s20p4 (2); s20p7 (2); s24p3 (3); s24p3

EXAMINATION 36
24 CFR 5: .514; .657;
24 CFR 35 SubM: .1215;
24 CFR 982: .555 (2);
HUD-50058Instr: p2;
HUD-52665: p1;
7420.10G Gbk: 5-50 Ex 5-5; 10-16; 10-19 (2); 10-21; 10-37 Ex 10-2; 22-9;
PIH Notices: 02-22; 01-41 (2); 01-15; 00-49 (3); 00-09 (5); 95-48 (5); 95-48 Tech Asst (4); 95-48 Tech Asst

EXAMINATIONS 28
24 CFR 982: Intro; .503 (2); .516 (2);
7420.10G Gbk: 10-19 (2); 10-37 Ex 10-2;
PIH Notices: 02-20 (3); 01-15; 00-46 (3); 95-48 (6); 95-48 Tech Asst (6);
Admin Plan: s11p1

EXAMINE 20
24 CFR 5: .514;
24 CFR 982: .158; .555 (2);
HUD-52641: p5;
7420.10G Gbk: 9-12; 10-9; 16-4 (2); 22-6;
PIH Notices: 03-23; 03-20; 02-27; 02-06; 95-48; 95-48 Tech Asst;
Admin Plan: s18p5; s18p6; s25p1; s25p3

EXAMINED 4
HUD-52667: p i;
7420.10G Gbk: 3-8;
PIH Notices: 95-48; 95-48 Tech Asst

EXCEEDS THE AUTHORITY 2
24 CFR 982: .555;
7420.10G Gbk: 16-5

EXCEPTION AREAS 23
24 CFR 982: .503;
7420.10G Gbk: 7-4 (4);
PIH Notices: 02-20 (9); 00-46 (8); 00-46

EXCEPTION PAYMENT STANDARD 148
24 CFR 982: .503 (13); .505; .604; .608; .635 (2);
HUD-52648: p2;
PIH Notices: 02-22 (6); 02-20 (61); 01-06 (3); 00-46 (58);
Admin Plan: s24p4

EXCEPTIONAL 12
HUD-52580: p6 (4);
HUD-52580-A: p19 (4);
7420.10G Gbk: 20-15;
PIH Notices: 02-06; 95-48; 95-48 Tech Asst

EXCEPTION-CENSUS 2
PIH Notices: 02-20; 00-46

EXCEPTIONS 77
24 CFR 5: .653 (4);
24 CFR 982: .301; .403;
7420.10G Gbk: 3-4; 7-4; 7-5; 7-9; 8-6; 14-2; 17-7; 20-13; 23-2;
PIH Notices: 03-05; 02-20 (21); 02-01 (2); 01-41 (2); 01-40; 01-20; 01-06; 00-46 (21); 00-09 (2); 99-52 (2); 99-11; 95-48; 95-48 Tech Asst;
Admin Plan: s3p2; s5p2 (2); s6p5; s10p3

EXCESS 82
24 CFR 5: .603; .609 (3); .703;
24 CFR 982: .4; .155; .313 (2); .451 (3); .635; .642;
HUD-50058Instr: p25 (2); p26; p27; p31;
HUD-52641: p1 (2); p4; p10 (2);
HUD-52641-A: p2 (2);
7420.10G Gbk: 2-9; 5-14 Ex 5-2; 5-15 Ex 5-2 (2); 6-10 Ex 6-2; 11-6 (3); 11-11 (2); 12-10; 20-1 (3); 20-8 Ex 20-1 (2); 20-13 (4); 20-14; 20-16 (2); 20-22 Ex 20-5; 20-27; 20-30; 22-2 (2); 23-10;
PIH Notices: 03-23 (12); 02-06; 01-15; 01-15 Impr Integ Hbk (8); 95-48; 95-48 Tech Asst;
Admin Plan: s2p4; s10p5; s23p6

EXCESS PAYMENT 2
24 CFR 982: .451;
7420.10G Gbk: 11-6
EXCESS PAYMENTS 2
7420.10G Gbk: 20-1; 20-1
EXCESS RENT 3
HUD-52641: 8;
HUD-52641-A: p1;
7420.10G Gbk: 11-6
EXCESS RENT PAYMENT 4
24 CFR 982: .451;
HUD-52641: 8;
HUD-52641-A: p1;
7420.10G Gbk: 11-6
EXCESS RENTAL 2
7420.10G Gbk: 22-4; 22-4
EXCESS RENTAL 2
7420.10G Gbk: 22-4; 22-4
EXCESSIVE 23
24 CFR 5: .801;
24 CFR 982: .401 (2); .614 (2);
HUD-50058Instr: p71 (2);
HUD-52580-A: p17;
7420.10G Gbk: 2-1; 4-12; 7-7; 10-9; 10-13 (2); 17-5 (2); 20-13; 20-16; 20-17;
PIH Notices: 03-12; 01-15 Impr Integ Hbk; 95-48; 95-48 Tech Asst
EXCESSIVELY 1
7420.10G Gbk: 7-7
EXCLUDE 41
24 CFR 5: .318; .403; .617 (2);
24 CFR 982: .207; .310; .623;
HUD-50058Instr: p24; p26; p33;
HUD-52648: p2;
7420.10G Gbk: 4-16; 5-11; 5-18; 5-20 (3); 5-26; 10-24;
PIH Notices: 01-15 Impr Integ Hbk (4); 01-06 (2); 00-11; 00-01; 98-66 (2); 95-48 (4); 95-48 Tech Asst (4);
Admin Plan: s6p3 (2); s23p5; s25p2
EXCLUDED 77
24 CFR 5: .214 (4); .312; .603; .609 (5);
24 CFR 982: .317;
HUD-50058: p6;
HUD-50058Instr: p3; p26; p31; p33 (2); p70; p74;
7420.10G Gbk: 5-13; 5-15 Ex 5-2 (2); 5-16 Ex 5-2; 5-20; 5-23; 5-47 Ex 5-5; 20-10; 21-13; 21-18; 21-20; 24-2 (2);
PIH Notices: 03-05; 02-21 (3); 01-40; 01-20; 01-15 (2); 01-15 Impr Integ Hbk (10); 01-06 (4); 00-01; 98-66; 95-48 (5); 95-48 Tech Asst (5);
Admin Plan: s1p3; s1p5; s2p3; s6p1 (3); s6p2; s6p3; s6p10; s7p3
EXCLUDED INCOME 1
PIH Notices: 01-15
EXCLUDES 7
HUD-50058: p xiii;
HUD-50058Instr: p3; p15; p54;
7420.10G Gbk: 24-16;
PIH Notices: 01-15; 01-15
EXCLUDING 31
24 CFR 5: .603 (2); .609; .801;
24 CFR 982: .601;
HUD-50058Instr: p25 (2); p26; p27; p74 (2);
7420.10G Gbk: 5-15 Ex 5-2; 5-53 Ex 5-5; 10-11; 10-14; 21-20; 23-1; 24-7;
PIH Notices: 02-27; 02-20; 02-06; 01-15 Impr Integ Hbk (2); 01-06; 01-01; 00-46; 00-23; 95-48; 95-48 Tech Asst;
Admin Plan: s18p5; s21p6
EXCLUSION 64
24 CFR 5: .303 (4); .318; .603; .609; .617 (4);
24 CFR 982: .310;
HUD-50058: p6;
HUD-50058Instr: p24; p25; p27 (2); p71;
HUD-52641: p5;
7420.10G Gbk: 5-16 Ex 5-2 (4); 11-11; 11-13;
PIH Notices: 01-15 (6); 01-15 Impr Integ Hbk (12); 00-01 (5); 98-66 (4); 95-48; 95-48 Tech Asst;
Admin Plan: s6p2 (2); s6p3 (7); s6p4
EXCLUSION FROM 3
24 CFR 5: .617;
HUD-50058Instr: p71;
PIH Notices: 01-15 Impr Integ Hbk
EXCLUSIONARY 2
PIH Notices: 95-48; 95-48 Tech Asst
EXCLUSIONS 76
24 CFR 5: .609;
HUD-50058: p6 (5);

HUD-50058Instr: p24 (3); p25 (2); p26 (2); p27 (2); p28 (3); p29 (2); p30 (2); p31 (3); p32 (2); p33 (10); p34; p35;
7420.10G Gbk: 5-14 Ex 5-2; 5-24; 5-25 Ex 5-3;
PIH Notices: 01-15 (6); 01-15 Impr Integ Hbk (21); 00-11; 95-48 (2); 95-48 Tech Asst (2);
Admin Plan: s6p3; s6p4

EXCLUSIVE 16
24 CFR 5: .318; .609;
24 CFR 982: .4 (3);
HUD-50058Instr: p72; p74;
HUD-52580-A: p6 (2); p7;
7420.10G Gbk: 5-14 Ex 5-2; 10-3; 17-1;
PIH Notices: 01-15 Impr Integ Hbk (2);
Admin Plan: s19p1

EXCLUSIVE USE 5
24 CFR 982: .4;
HUD-50058Instr: p74;
HUD-52580-A: p6;
7420.10G Gbk: 10-3; 17-1

EXCLUSIVELY 2
PIH Notices: 95-48; 95-48 Tech Asst

EXECUTE 66
24 CFR 5: .216; .659;
24 CFR 982: .305 (3); .309; .516; .633;
HUD-52646: p2 (3);
7420.10G Gbk: 1-11; 1-16 Ex 1-3 (2); 5-12; 5-45; 6-8; 8-18 (2); 8-20; 8-21; 8-22 (2); 9-1; 10-43 Ex 10-6; 11-1; 11-2; 11-3; 11-4; 11-9; 11-15 (5); 11-17; 14-2; 14-3; 21-7; 24-3 (2); 24-6; 24-8;
PIH Notices: 01-41 (3); 01-15 Impr Integ Hbk; 00-23; 00-09 (10);
Admin Plan: s7p5; s9p2; s9p3; s20p7; s22p4; s23p5; s24p5; s25p4

EXECUTED 88
24 CFR 5: .216 (7);
24 CFR 982: .4; .158; .305 (6); .308 (2);
HUD-50058Instr: p10; p59 (4); p74;
HUD-52641: p1; p7; p10;
HUD-52641-A: p3;
HUD-52646: p2 (8); p3;
7420.10G Gbk: 8-11; 8-16; 10-17 (2); 10-19; 11-4; 11-15 (3); 11-16 Ex 11-1; 11-18; 12-6; 13-7; 13-12 Ex 13-2; 14-3; 14-4; 19-6; 19-11 (2); 19-12; 20-23; 23-6; 23-18 (2); 24-5;
PIH Notices: 03-23; 03-11; 01-41 (5); 00-14; 00-09 (5);
Admin Plan: s2p7; s9p3; s9p4; s11p1; s11p3; s16p3; s19p1 (2); s23p5; s24p5 (2); s25p4; s25p7; s25p7

EXECUTES 10
24 CFR 982: .4;
HUD-50058Instr: p75;
HUD-52648: p2;
7420.10G Gbk: 5-3; 11-15; 22-14;
PIH Notices: 01-41 (2); 00-09; 00-09

EXECUTING.................................... 6
7420.10G Gbk: 8-15; 11-1; 11-4; 13-4; 20-1;
PIH Notices: 00-09

EXECUTION.................................. 74
24 CFR 5: .659;
24 CFR 982: .305 (2); .308; .516; .636;
HUD-52580: p5;
HUD-52580-A: p17;
HUD-52641: p6; p10;
HUD-52641-A: p3;
HUD-52665: p2 (2);
7420.10G Gbk: 8-11; 8-15; 10-1; 10-17 (2); 10-22; 10-25; 10-26 (2); 10-35; 11-1; 11-4; 11-9 (3); 11-14 (2); 11-15 (5); 11-16 Ex 11-1 (2); 11-17; 11-19; 13-9; 14-1; 14-2 (2); 14-3; 19-6; 19-8; 19-11 (2); 20-3; 22-9; 22-11; 23-6; 23-7; 23-9; 23-12;
PIH Notices: 01-41 (3); 01-15 Impr Integ Hbk; 00-09 (3);
Admin Plan: s2p7; s9p1; s9p4 (2); s16p3 (2); s17p1; s21p8; s23p6; s24p2; s24p5; s24p5

EXECUTIVE 33
24 CFR 5: .105 (9); .214;
HUD-50058Instr: p3; p5;
HUD-52648: p3;
7420.10G Gbk: 13-9; 19-13; 20-10; 23-4;
PIH Notices: 02-27 (2); 02-21 (3); 02-14; 01-20; 01-

06 (4); 00-11A; 95-48 (2); 95-48 Tech Asst; 95-48 Tech Asst

EXECUTIVE DIRECTOR 9
HUD-52648: p3;
PIH Notices: 02-21 (2); 02-14; 01-06 (4); 00-11A

EXECUTIVE ORDER 1
7420.10G Gbk: 5-42

EXECUTIVE ORDER 9
24 CFR 5: .105 (8);
7420.10G Gbk: 5-42

EXECUTIVE ORDERS 4
HUD-52641: p5; p10;
HUD-52641-A: p3;
7420.10G Gbk: 5-42

EXECUTIVE ORDERS 7
24 CFR 5: .105;
HUD-52641: p5; p10;
HUD-52641-A: p3;
7420.10G Gbk: 5-42;
PIH Notices: 02-21; 01-20

EXECUTOR 2
24 CFR 982: .633;
Admin Plan: s16p3

EX-EMPLOYERS 2
Admin Plan: s20p4; s20p4

EXEMPT.. 21
24 CFR 5: .630 (2);
24 CFR 982: .101;
HUD-50058: p3; p4;
HUD-50058Instr: p16; p17; p75;
HUD-903: p2;
7420.10G Gbk: 5-43; 9-2; 10-16 (2);
PIH Notices: 02-27; 01-06; 00-11 (4); 00-11A;
Admin Plan: s6p5

EXEMPTED 4
24 CFR 982: .101;
HUD-50058Instr: p17;
PIH Notices: 02-27; 02-27

EXEMPTION 56
24 CFR 5: .512; .630 (15);
24 CFR 982: .627 (2);
HUD-50058: p8; p viii (2);
HUD-50058Instr: p16; p17; p37 (2); p38 (3);
7420.10G Gbk: 3-6 (2); 4-20 (2); 5-43; 16-2; 23-3;
PIH Notices: 02-01; 99-52; 95-48 (9); 95-48 Tech Asst (7);
Admin Plan: s6p5 (2); s11p2

EXEMPTIONS 6
HUD-50058Instr: p16;
7420.10G Gbk: 6-8 (2);
PIH Notices: 01-15; 00-11; 00-11A

EXEMPTS 1
PIH Notices: 02-27

EXERCISE 46
24 CFR 5: .350 (2); .508; .653;
24 CFR 982: .456 (3); .552; .555 (2); .619;
HUD-50058Instr: p73;
HUD-52641: p3 (2); p5 (5); p6;
7420.10G Gbk: 5-10 Ex 5-1; 5-11; 7-7; 10-15; 10-35; 11-18; 13-2; 14-4; 16-2 (2); 20-15; 21-7; 21-8;
PIH Notices: 02-06; 01-41 (2); 00-09; 95-48 (4); 95-48 Tech Asst (2);
Admin Plan: s13p2; s18p4; s18p4

EXERCISED.................................... 4
HUD-50058Instr: p62; p63;
PIH Notices: 95-48; 95-48 Tech Asst

EXERCISES 8
24 CFR 982: .161;
HUD-50058Instr: p9 (3);
HUD-52641: p6;
7420.10G Gbk: 8-19; 11-2;
PIH Notices: 01-41

EXHAUST 11
24 CFR 982: .401;
HUD-52580-A: p6; p15; p18;
7420.10G Gbk: 10-19 (3); 12-13 Ex 12-1; 20-20;
PIH Notices: 95-48; 95-48 Tech Asst

EXHAUST VENTILATION............. 1
24 CFR 982: .401

EXHAUSTED.................................. 2
24 CFR 5: .508;
7420.10G Gbk: 5-33

EXHAUSTING................................ 2
PIH Notices: 02-27; 02-06

EXHAUSTION................................ 2
PIH Notices: 95-48; 95-48 Tech Asst

EXHAUSTS..................................... 1
7420.10G Gbk: 10-7

EXISTING 134
24 CFR 5: .214 (3); .312; .315; .318; .350; .359 (2);
24 CFR 982: .4; .206; .625; .628;
HUD-50058: p xvii;
HUD-50058Instr: p62;

HUD-52580: p1 (2); p17;
HUD-52648: p1 (2);
HUD-52667: p i (2);
HUD-903: p1;
7420.10G Gbk: 1-2 (3); 1-3 (4); 1-4; 3-8; 4-14; 4-21; 9-3 (4); 9-4; 9-7; 9-8; 10-2; 10-3; 11-2; 11-7; 19-10; 19-12; 20-3; 20-16; 21-2 (3); 23-4; 23-18;
PIH Notices: 03-23 (2); 03-20; 02-27 (3); 02-22; 02-20; 02-14; 02-06; 02-01 (8); 01-41 (4); 00-53; 00-46; 00-09 (9); 99-52 (8); 99-11 (2); 95-48 (15); 95-48 Tech Asst (15);
Admin Plan: s1p6; s22p2; s23p1; s24p1 (2); s25p1; s25p3

EXISTING HOUSING 8
HUD-50058: p xvii;
HUD-50058Instr: p62;
HUD-52667: p i;
7420.10G Gbk: 1-2; 11-2;
PIH Notices: 02-01; 99-52;
Admin Plan: s24p1

EXIT 57
24 CFR 982: .401 (3); .605 (2);
HUD-50058: p16 (2); p17 (5); p xvii;
HUD-50058Instr: p13 (3); p59 (4); p61; p62 (4); p63 (2);
HUD-52580-A: p2; p17 (4); p18;
7420.10G Gbk: 10-12 (5); 10-13; 17-2 (2); 19-2;
PIH Notices: 02-27 (2); 95-48 (6); 95-48 Tech Asst (6);
Admin Plan: s10p4

EXITED 1
HUD-50058Instr: p63

EXITING 3
HUD-50058Instr: p62;
Admin Plan: s24p7; s25p6

EXITS 10
24 CFR 5: .703 (2);
HUD-50058Instr: p10; p11; p59;
HUD-52580: p5;
HUD-52580-A: p17; p18;
7420.10G Gbk: 19-4;
PIH Notices: 99-11

EXPANDING HOUSING OPPORTUNITIES 21
24 CFR 982: .102;
HUD-52648: p2;
7420.10G Gbk: 1-10; 2-1; 2-2; 3-9; 7-7 (2); 8-7; 19-5;
PIH Notices: 02-27 (2); 02-21 (3); 01-20; 01-06 (3);
Admin Plan: s21p2; s21p5

EXPANDING HOUSING OPPORTUNITY 1
Admin Plan: s21p1

EXPEDITE 1
Admin Plan: s18p3

EXPEDITED 2
7420.10G Gbk: 4-12;
PIH Notices: 03-11

EXPEDITIOUS 3
24 CFR 982: .555 (2);
7420.10G Gbk: 16-1

EXPEDITIOUS HEARING 1
24 CFR 982: .555

EXPEDITIOUSLY 12
PIH Notices: 95-48 (7); 95-48 Tech Asst (4); 95-48 Tech Asst

EXPENSE 103
24 CFR 5: .236; .514 (3);
24 CFR 982: .555 (3);
HUD-50058: p7 (4); p vii (7); p14; p xiv (3);
HUD-50058Instr: p34 (2); p35 (12); p36; p56; p57 (3);
7420.10G Gbk: 5-19 (2); 5-26; 5-27 (2); 5-28 (2); 5-29 (2); 5-30 (4); 5-33 (4); 5-34; 5-35; 5-43; 5-48 Ex 5-5; 5-51 Ex 5-5; 5-52 Ex 5-5; 8-4 (2); 12-3; 16-4 (2); 16-5; 17-4; 18-6 (2); 20-21 Ex 20-4 (2); 20-23 (2); 20-25; 21-6 (2);
PIH Notices: 02-01; 01-15; 01-15 Impr Integ Hbk; 99-52; 95-48; 95-48 Tech Asst;
Admin Plan: s6p4 (2); s6p11 (4); s7p3; s7p5; s7p6; s7p7; s18p3; s18p5 (4); s22p3; s24p3

EXPENSES 279
24 CFR 5: .318 (4); .603 (6); .609 (2); .611 (3); .659;
24 CFR 982: .4 (2); .152 (3); .155 (4); .516; .619; .624; .632 (4); .633; .635 (10);
HUD-50058: p7 (5); p vii (18);
HUD-50058Instr: p25; p27; p28; p30 (2); p34 (11); p35 (14); p36 (3); p70; p71 (3); p73 (2); p76 (2);

HUD-52648: p1;
7420.10G Gbk: 2-11; 4-27 Ex 4-2 (2); 5-15 Ex 5-2; 5-19 (5); 5-27; 5-29 (5); 5-30 (3); 5-31 (9); 5-32 (7); 5-33 (3); 5-34 (2); 5-48 Ex 5-5; 5-51 Ex 5-5 (3); 5-52 Ex 5-5 (2); 12-3; 12-4; 12-9; 12-11 (2); 17-10; 18-1 (2); 20-2; 20-3; 20-6; 20-20 (2); 20-22 (2); 20-22 Ex 20-5 (3); 20-27 (2); 22-3; 22-17; 23-15 (2); 23-18; 24-8;
PIH Notices: 03-23 (11); 03-20; 02-21 (2); 02-07 (2); 01-15 (14); 01-15 Impr Integ Hbk (23); 00-28 (3); 00-24B (2); 00-11 (2); 00-09 (2); 95-48 (3); 95-48 Tech Asst (3);
Admin Plan: s6p1 (3); s6p2 (3); s6p4; s6p8; s6p9 (2); s6p10 (2); s6p11 (7); s7p3 (2); s7p6 (2); s7p7 (4); s19p1 (2); s21p4 (2); s25p5

EXPERT..5
HUD-52580-A: p2;
PIH Notices: 02-01; 99-52; 95-48; 95-48 Tech Asst

EXPERTISE......................................2
7420.10G Gbk: 21-3;
PIH Notices: 02-27

EXPERTS 4
7420.10G Gbk: 9-9 (2);
PIH Notices: 02-01; 99-52

EXPIRATION...............................113
24 CFR 5: .236; .514; .518 (2); .615;
24 CFR 982: .102 (4); .355;
HUD-50058: p2; p xvii;
HUD-50058Instr: p1; p10 (2); p11; p17; p38; p61; p62; p77;
HUD-52646: p1 (2); p2;
HUD-52665: p1 (3);
7420.10G Gbk: 1-8; 1-9; 8-10; 8-12; 8-13 (4); 8-14 (5); 8-15; 10-29; 10-33; 11-5; 13-4; 13-5 (2); 19-2; 21-9 (3); 23-2; 23-3; 23-7; 23-9; 23-11; 23-18; 24-5; 24-10;
PIH Notices: 03-23; 03-11 (2); 02-14 (3); 01-41 (15); 01-10 (16); 01-01 (2); 00-11A; 00-09 (9);
Admin Plan: s6p3; s6p12; s8p5; s11p1; s11p3

EXPIRATIONS...............................17
7420.10G Gbk: 1-8; 8-11; 20-13;
PIH Notices: 03-23 (2); 02-07; 01-41; 01-10 (8); 01-01; 01-01

EXPIRE..16
24 CFR 5: .214;
24 CFR 982: .102 (3); .355;
HUD-50058Instr: p71;
HUD-52646: p2 (2);
HUD-52665: p1;
7420.10G Gbk: 7-7; 13-5; 13-7; 20-7; 20-9; 20-13;
PIH Notices: 03-11

EXPIRED.......................................24
HUD-50058: p17;
HUD-50058Instr: p62 (2);
7420.10G Gbk: 5-21; 7-7; 8-10; 8-23; 24-4;
PIH Notices: 03-23 (2); 02-20; 02-15; 02-03 (2); 02-01; 01-43; 01-10; 01-01; 00-46; 00-31; 00-11; 99-30;
Admin Plan: s3p2; s8p5

EXPIRES 80
24 CFR 5: .230;
24 CFR 982: .102;
HUD-50058Instr: p10; p11;
HUD-52646: p1 (3);
HUD-52665: p3;
HUD-9886: p2;
7420.10G Gbk: 1-16 Ex 1-3; 7-3; 8-13; 11-4; 13-2; 13-7; 13-8; 13-11 Ex 13-1; 13-12 Ex 13-2 (2); 14-2; 19-9; 20-7;
PIH Notices: 03-23; 03-20 (2); 03-12; 03-11; 03-05; 02-27; 02-22; 02-21; 02-20; 02-15; 02-14 (2); 02-07; 02-06; 02-01; 01-43; 01-41 (3); 01-40; 01-33; 01-27; 01-20; 01-15; 01-11; 01-10; 01-06; 01-02; 01-01 (3); 00-53; 00-49; 00-46; 00-45; 00-41; 00-34 (2); 00-31; 00-28; 00-27; 00-24; 00-23; 00-14; 00-09 (4); 00-01; 99-52; 99-30; 99-11; 98-66; 96-65; 95-48 (2);
Admin Plan: s22p2

EXPIRING.....................................72
24 CFR 982: Intro; .101; .102 (4); .155; .309;
HUD-50058Instr: p38;
7420.10G Gbk: 1-9 (3); 20-7 (3); 20-9; 20-13;
PIH Notices: 03-23 (14); 02-21;

02-14 (8); 01-41 (19); 01-06; 00-09 (11); 00-09

EXPIRING CONTRACT FUNDING INCREMENT 1
24 CFR 982: .102

EXPIRING FUNDING INCREMENT2
7420.10G Gbk: 8-22; 11-15

EXPIRING FUNDING INCREMENT6
24 CFR 982: .102; .155; .309;
7420.10G Gbk: 8-22; 11-15;
PIH Notices: 03-23

EXPIRING FUNDING INCREMENTS 1
24 CFR 982: .101

EXPLANATION 51
24 CFR 5: .514 (3); .615 (2);
24 CFR 982: .301 (4); .555;
HUD-50058: p6;
HUD-52580-A: p1; p4; p6;
HUD-52648: p2;
7420.10G Gbk: 2-2; 2-3; 2-7; 4-3; 5-1; 5-8; 5-35; 8-3; 8-4; 8-5; 8-6 (3); 8-7; 8-8; 8-15; 10-3; 11-3 (2); 12-5; 13-10; 19-9 (2); 20-21;
PIH Notices: 03-23; 02-14; 00-24;
Admin Plan: s2p1; s8p2 (2); s18p3 (2); s20p2; s20p3; s21p6; s23p4

EXPLANATIONS 5
HUD-52580-A: p8; p13;
7420.10G Gbk: 2-5; 20-23; 24-14

EXPLETIVES 1
Admin Plan: s15p2

EXPRESS 7
24 CFR 5: .100 (2);
7420.10G Gbk: 16-5;
PIH Notices: 00-27;
Admin Plan: s3p1; s15p3; s15p3

EX-SPOUSE 2
7420.10G Gbk: 5-47 Ex 5-5; 5-47 Ex 5-5

EXTEND 24
24 CFR 5: .216; .508; .522;
24 CFR 982: .303; .355;
HUD-50058Instr: p28; p61;
7420.10G Gbk: 8-12; 10-27 (2); 10-29; 16-2 (2); 16-3; 23-7; 23-9; 23-15;
PIH Notices: 01-41 (2); 01-20; 00-09;
Admin Plan: s8p5; s10p4; s18p2

EXTENDED 29
24 CFR 5: .801;
24 CFR 982: .303 (2);
HUD-50058: p17; p xvii;
HUD-50058Instr: p61 (2); p62 (2);
HUD-52580-A: p13; p17;
HUD-52646: p1; p2;
7420.10G Gbk: 8-13; 8-23; 19-3; 21-9 (2); 24-10 (3);
PIH Notices: 01-10; 01-02 (2); 00-28; 95-48; 95-48 Tech Asst;
Admin Plan: s8p5; s18p7

EXTENDS 16
24 CFR 5: .522;
PIH Notices: 01-41; 00-31; 00-28; 00-09 (2); 95-48 (6); 95-48 Tech Asst (3); 95-48 Tech Asst

EXTENSION 94
24 CFR 5: .508 (12); .514; .801 (2);
24 CFR 982: .54; .301; .303 (2); .404 (2); .554; .555;
HUD-52580-A: p2;
HUD-52641: 8; p9 (2);
HUD-52641-A: p1; p2 (2);
HUD-52646: p1 (2); p2 (3);
HUD-52648: p1;
7420.10G Gbk: 1-16 Ex 1-3; 3-2 (2); 3-3; 5-6 (5); 5-8; 8-5; 8-11; 8-12 (6); 8-13; 8-14; 8-23; 10-21 (2); 10-33; 12-14 Ex 12-2; 12-15 Ex 12-3; 13-5; 13-7; 13-12 Ex 13-2; 15-2; 19-9 (2); 23-7 (3); 24-10;
PIH Notices: 02-27; 01-41; 01-20; 00-31; 00-24B (2); 00-09; 00-01; 98-66; 95-48; 95-48 Tech Asst;
Admin Plan: s7p8; s8p4; s8p5 (3); s9p2; s18p4; s21p5 (2); s24p5; s24p5

EXTENSION OF TIME 2
24 CFR 5: .508;
7420.10G Gbk: 10-33

EXTENSIONS 62
24 CFR 5: .508;
24 CFR 982: .54 (3); .301 (2); .303 (2); .503;
HUD-50058Instr: p11; p62;
HUD-52641: p3;
HUD-52646: p2;
7420.10G Gbk: 3-7; 5-44; 7-4; 8-5; 8-11; 8-12 (7); 8-23; 10-34 (4); 11-4; 13-4; 13-5 (2); 13-7; 15-1;

15-5; 21-9; 24-7; 24-10 (4);
PIH Notices: 02-20 (2); 02-01; 01-20 (2); 01-01 (3); 00-46; 00-09 (2); 99-52;
Admin Plan: s8p2; s8p5 (3); s9p2; s22p2; s24p5

EXTENSIONS OF TIME 1
24 CFR 5: .508

EXTENSIVE..................................... 8
7420.10G Gbk: 1-2;
PIH Notices: 03-12; 00-53; 99-11; 95-48 (2); 95-48 Tech Asst; 95-48 Tech Asst

EXTENSIVELY................................ 5
24 CFR 5: .403;
7420.10G Gbk: 5-2;
PIH Notices: 01-41; 00-09; 00-09

EXTENT 98
24 CFR 5: .210; .212; .603; .609 (3); .611 (2); .703 (2);
24 CFR 982: .201 (2); .305; .310 (2); .552; .627; .633;
HUD-50058Instr: p19; p38; p70;
HUD-52580-A: p6 (2);
HUD-52667: p i;
7420.10G Gbk: 1-4; 4-6 (2); 4-18; 4-20; 5-14 Ex 5-2 (2); 5-30; 5-38; 7-6; 8-2; 11-10; 18-10; 21-5; 22-3; 22-5; 22-11; 22-14 (2); 22-18; 23-10; 23-19;
PIH Notices: 03-23 (2); 03-20; 03-12; 03-11; 02-27 (2); 02-21; 02-01 (5); 01-41 (2); 01-20; 01-15 (2); 01-15 Impr Integ Hbk (7); 01-06 (2); 00-27 (2); 00-09 (3); 99-52 (5); 99-11; 95-48 (5); 95-48 Tech Asst (5);
Admin Plan: s7p7; s15p4; s21p9; s24p5

EXTENUATING............................... 1
PIH Notices: 03-11

EXTENUATING CIRCUMSTANCES3
7420.10G Gbk: 8-12 (2); 24-10

EXTERIOR.................................... 65
24 CFR 5: .703 (2);
24 CFR 35 SubM: .1200;
24 CFR 982: .401 (4); .605; .614 (3); .631;
HUD-52517: p2 (2);
HUD-52580: p5 (4); p6;
HUD-52580-A: p1; p4; p13 (7); p14 (6); p19;
7420.10G Gbk: 8-15; 10-2; 10-6; 10-9 (2); 10-12; 10-16; 10-17; 10-18 (4); 10-20; 10-21 (2); 10-37 Ex 10-2; 17-2; 18-2;
PIH Notices: 00-49 (2); 00-23 (3); 95-48 (3); 95-48 Tech Asst (3);
Admin Plan: s22p3

EXTERIOR DOORS 5
24 CFR 982: .401 (2); .605;
7420.10G Gbk: 10-6; 17-2

EXTRA AMOUNTS 3
24 CFR 982: .510;
HUD-52641: 8;
HUD-52641-A: p1

EXTREMELY LOW 1
7420.10G Gbk: 24-11

EXTREMELY LOW INCOME 14
24 CFR 5: .603; .653 (2);
24 CFR 982: .201 (7);
HUD-50058Instr: p19; p71;
7420.10G Gbk: 24-4;
Admin Plan: s4p2

EXTREMELY LOW INCOME FAMILIES 10
24 CFR 5: .653 (2);
24 CFR 982: .201 (7);
HUD-50058Instr: p19

EXTREMELY LOW INCOME FAMILY 2
24 CFR 5: .603;
HUD-50058Instr: p71

EXTREMELY LOW-INCOME....... 18
7420.10G Gbk: 3-7; 4-5 (3); 4-8; 4-9; 4-19 (4); 4-20; 4-21 (5); 5-3; 13-7

EYEGLASSES 3
7420.10G Gbk: 5-32;
PIH Notices: 95-48; 95-48 Tech Asst

FACE-TO-FACE............................... 1
7420.10G Gbk: 22-8

FACILITATE 20
24 CFR 5: .603;
HUD-50058Instr: p71;
PIH Notices: 03-11; 02-27; 02-21; 01-20; 01-15 Impr Integ Hbk; 00-11; 00-11A (2); 00-09; 95-48 (3); 95-48 Tech Asst (3);
Admin Plan: s1p1; s6p3; s23p5

FACILITATES 1
7420.10G Gbk: 19-12

FACILITATING................................ 2

PIH Notices: 00-11; 00-11

FACILITATION 8
PIH Notices: 95-48 (4); 95-48 Tech Asst (3); 95-48 Tech Asst

FACILITIES 261
24 CFR 5: .306; .318; .703 (2); .801;
24 CFR 35 SubM: .1200;
24 CFR 982: .4 (3); .158 (2); .352; .401 (9); .605 (8); .608; .609 (4); .613 (4); .614 (10); .618 (4);
HUD-50058Instr: p42; p46; p63; p75 (3);
HUD-52580: p6;
HUD-52580-A: p4; p6 (6); p15; p17 (4); p18; p19;
HUD-52641: p5;
HUD-903: p1;
7420.10G Gbk: 5-31; 8-7; 8-16; 9-8; 9-14 Ex 9-1 (2); 9-16 Ex 9-2 (2); 9-17 Ex 9-3; 9-19 Ex 9-4; 10-1; 10-3 (6); 10-4 (4); 10-5 (5); 10-12; 10-13; 10-16; 10-17; 10-40 Ex 10-4a; 11-13; 17-1 (2); 17-2 (4); 17-3 (2); 17-4; 17-5; 17-7 (8); 20-2;
PIH Notices: 02-27 (2); 02-03; 02-01 (9); 00-41 (12); 99-52 (9); 99-11 (2); 95-48 (44); 95-48 Tech Asst (42);
Admin Plan: s1p3 (3); s9p2 (2); s19p1 (5); s23p2 (3); s24p2

FACILITY 83
24 CFR 5: .360 (3); .363 (3); .703;
HUD-50058Instr: p70 (4);
HUD-52580-A: p4 (2); p6; p15; p17;
7420.10G Gbk: 9-17 Ex 9-3; 17-1; 17-2 (3); 17-3; 17-4 (3);
PIH Notices: 02-01 (11); 00-41 (2); 99-52 (11); 99-11 (2); 95-48 (13); 95-48 Tech Asst (13);
Admin Plan: s1p3; s6p5; s7p8; s19p1 (2); s19p1

FACSIMILE 3
7420.10G Gbk: 10-26; 13-3;
Admin Plan: s7p1

FACT SHEET 1
PIH Notices: 00-09

FACT SHEETS 1
Admin Plan: s1p6

FACT-FINDING 1
Admin Plan: s15p4

FAIL 122
24 CFR 5: .318;
24 CFR 982: .306;
HUD-50058Instr: p2; p21;
HUD-52580: p1 (2); p2; p3; p4; p5; p7 (2);
HUD-52580-A: p1 (5); p2; p3 (3); p4 (5); p5 (3); p6 (2); p7 (3); p8; p9 (3); p10 (3); p11 (3); p12 (3); p14 (3); p15; p16 (3); p17; p18 (3); p20 (2);
HUD-52641: p7;
HUD-903-1: p2;
7420.10G Gbk: 3-5; 5-35; 8-3; 8-8; 10-23 (4); 10-24 (2); 10-25; 10-26; 10-27 (4); 10-28 (2); 10-30; 10-33 (2); 10-34; 10-40 Ex 10-4a; 11-4; 12-12 Ex 12-1; 19-2 (2); 19-3; 19-9; 19-11; 20-17; 21-10; 22-1 (2); 22-9; 23-10; 24-3; 24-6; 24-12;
PIH Notices: 02-01 (2); 01-15 Impr Integ Hbk; 00-28; 00-24B; 00-09; 99-52 (2); 99-11; 96-65; 95-48; 95-48 Tech Asst;
Admin Plan: s3p3; s4p2; s7p8; s8p2 (2); s10p3 (2); s18p8; s23p4

FAIL TO RESPOND 1
Admin Plan: s4p2

FAILED 57
24 CFR 5: .353 (2); .514;
24 CFR 982: .310; .453;
HUD-50058: p v;
HUD-50058Instr: p21 (2); p62;
HUD-52641: p5; p9;
HUD-52641-A: p2;
HUD-52648: p1;
HUD-52665: p2;
7420.10G Gbk: 4-6; 5-14 Ex 5-2; 10-21; 10-26 (2); 10-28; 10-32; 10-33 (2); 10-34; 10-41 Ex 10-4b; 12-10 (2); 12-14 Ex 12-2; 13-7; 15-2; 15-3; 15-9 Ex 15-1; 15-10 Ex 15-2; 19-12; 20-11; 21-4; 22-6; 22-7;
PIH Notices: 02-27 (5); 01-20 (2); 01-06; 00-49; 00-24B (4);
Admin Plan: s10p1; s10p2; s14p1; s16p2; s21p9; s23p5

FAILING....................................14
24 CFR 5: .218; .232;
24 CFR 982: .306;
HUD-52641: p6;
7420.10G Gbk: 5-34; 10-13; 19-8; 22-2 (2); 24-2;
PIH Notices: 96-65;
Admin Plan: s10p1; s15p6; s16p2

FAILS....................................79
24 CFR 5: .350 (2); .508 (2);
24 CFR 982: .152; .355; .404 (4); .552 (3); .619 (3); .638;
HUD-50058Instr: p2; p10;
HUD-52580-A: p1;
HUD-52641: p3;
HUD-903: p2;
7420.10G Gbk: 3-5; 4-5; 5-9 Ex 5-1; 5-46 Ex 5-5; 8-4; 8-20; 10-33; 10-34; 11-12; 13-9; 15-1; 15-5 (2); 15-6 (2); 20-10; 21-9 (2); 22-15 (2); 23-9; 23-12; 23-18 (2); 24-2 (2); 24-3;
PIH Notices: 01-41; 01-06 (2); 01-01; 00-49 (3); 00-09 (2);
Admin Plan: s4p2; s7p2 (2); s7p3 (4); s9p4 (2); s10p3 (2); s15p1; s15p2; s15p6; s18p8; s20p5; s20p6 (2); s23p5 (2); s24p5

FAILURE....................................167
24 CFR 5: .318; .353 (2); .508; .512 (3);
24 CFR 982: .102; .152; .301; .309 (2); .310 (6); .406; .552 (6); .555; .638;
HUD-50058Instr: p2; p59; p73;
HUD-52641: p6 (2); 8; p9 (2);
HUD-52641-A: p1 (2); p2;
HUD-903: p3;
HUD-9886: p1 (2); p2;
7420.10G Gbk: 1-9; 4-10; 5-7 (2); 5-11; 5-21 (2); 5-34; 5-38 (5); 10-14; 10-19; 10-21 (2); 10-23; 10-27 (2); 10-28 (3); 10-29 (3); 10-33; 10-34 (3); 10-40 Ex 10-4a; 10-41 Ex 10-4b; 10-44 Ex 10-7a; 10-45 Ex 10-7b; 11-4; 11-13; 11-18; 12-1; 12-3; 12-9; 12-10; 15-1 (2); 15-2; 15-4; 15-5 (2); 15-6; 15-8 (2); 15-9 Ex 15-1; 15-10 Ex 15-2; 18-1 (2); 19-9; 19-10; 19-11; 20-6 (2); 22-2 (3); 22-14 (3); 23-5; 23-9 (2); 23-10 (2); 24-1; 24-3;
PIH Notices: 02-27 (4); 02-07; 01-41 (2); 01-15; 01-06 (2); 00-49; 00-28; 00-24B; 00-11; 00-09 (2); 99-11; 96-65;
Admin Plan: s2p3; s2p5; s3p3 (4); s6p10; s6p12; s8p2; s10p3; s10p4; s10p5 (2); s11p2; s13p1; s14p1; s15p1; s15p4; s15p5; s15p6 (2); s16p2; s17p2; s18p5; s18p8 (2); s20p5; s22p5; s23p4; s23p6; s23p7 (2); s24p6; s25p5; s25p5

FAILURE TO ACT....................................11
24 CFR 982: .310; .552 (4); .555;
HUD-52641: p6 (2);
Admin Plan: s15p1; s15p4; s15p5

FAILURE TO REPORT....................................2
Admin Plan: s17p2; s20p5

FAILURE TO SIGN....................................3
HUD-9886: p1 (2);
Admin Plan: s3p3

FAILURES....................................7
7420.10G Gbk: 19-11; 21-9;
PIH Notices: 02-27; 95-48 (2); 95-48 Tech Asst; 95-48 Tech Asst

FAIR....................................186
24 CFR 5: .100 (5); .105; .514; .524; .603 (2); .655 (2);
24 CFR 982: .4; .53 (4); .101 (2); .206; .306 (2); .310; .503 (2); .552; .623; .630 (3);
HUD-50058: p i (2); p xvii;
HUD-50058Instr: p3; p22; p39; p62;
HUD-52667: p i (2);
HUD-903: p1 (3); p2 (11); p3 (12);
HUD-903-1: p1 (2); p2 (2); p3 (2); p4; p5; p6 (2);
7420.10G Gbk: 1-5 (2); 2-5; 4-1; 4-7; 5-34; 22-1; 22-11; 23-8 Ex 23-1;
PIH Notices: 02-27; 02-22 (2); 02-21 (15); 02-20 (3); 02-01 (14); 01-20 (5); 01-15 (3); 01-15 Impr Integ Hbk; 01-06; 01-02; 01-01; 00-46 (4); 00-45 (2); 00-24B (2); 00-09 (2); 99-52 (13); 95-48 (5); 95-

48 Tech Asst;
Admin Plan: s1p1; s1p2; s1p3 (2); s2p7 (2); s3p1; s5p1; s6p10 (5); s7p3; s7p6 (3); s8p3; s9p3; s11p3 (2); s16p1 (2); s23p4; s24p4; s24p6

FAIR HOUSING..............................94
24 CFR 5: .100;
24 CFR 982: .53 (3); .206; .310; .552; .630 (3);
HUD-903: p1 (3); p2 (7); p3 (12);
HUD-903-1: p1 (2); p2; p3 (2); p4; p5; p6 (2);
7420.10G Gbk: 1-10; 1-14 (2); 3-8; 4-2; 4-6; 4-11; 4-27 Ex 4-2; 5-11 (2); 5-45; 7-1; 8-4; 8-8; 8-14 (2); 19-8; 22-15 (2);
PIH Notices: 02-21 (8); 02-01 (3); 01-20 (3); 01-15; 01-06; 99-52 (3); 95-48 (3); 95-48 Tech Asst;
Admin Plan: s1p1; s1p2; s1p3 (2); s2p7 (2); s5p1; s8p3; s9p3; s23p4; s24p6

FAIR HOUSING ACT.....................45
24 CFR 5: .100; .105; .524;
24 CFR 982: .53; .306 (2);
HUD-50058: p i;
HUD-903: p2 (5);
PIH Notices: 02-21 (3); 02-01 (10); 01-20 (2); 01-15; 01-02; 00-45 (2); 99-52 (10); 95-48 (2);
Admin Plan: s16p1; s16p1

FAIR MARKET RENT...................31
24 CFR 5: .100 (2);
24 CFR 982: .4; .503; .623;
HUD-50058: p i; p xvii;
HUD-50058Instr: p3; p39; p62;
HUD-52667: p i;
7420.10G Gbk: 1-3; 1-4; 2-2; 7-1; 10-2; 14-1; 20-18; 24-10;
PIH Notices: 02-27; 02-22; 02-20 (3); 00-46 (2); 00-24B (2); 00-09 (2);
Admin Plan: s24p4

FAIR MARKET RENTS...................9
24 CFR 5: .100;
24 CFR 982: .503;
HUD-52667: p i;
7420.10G Gbk: 1-6 Ex 1-1;
PIH Notices: 02-22; 01-01; 00-46;
Admin Plan: s11p3; s11p3

FAIR SHARE....................................4
24 CFR 982: .101 (2);
7420.10G Gbk: 1-5; 1-5

FAIR SHARE FORMULA................3
24 CFR 982: .101 (2);
7420.10G Gbk: 1-5

FAIRLY..5
7420.10G Gbk: 4-1; 22-3; 22-18;
PIH Notices: 01-06; 01-06

FALL...16
7420.10G Gbk: 1-6; 4-21; 5-2; 21-2; 21-3; 21-10; 24-8; 24-10;
PIH Notices: 01-41 (2); 01-15 Impr Integ Hbk; 00-24 (2); 00-09 (2);
Admin Plan: s2p5

FALSE...19
24 CFR 5: .528;
HUD-52648: p3;
HUD-9886: p2;
7420.10G Gbk: 4-4; 4-23 Ex 4-1; 4-27 Ex 4-2 (2); 11-18; 12-16 Ex 12-4 (2); 22-1; 22-5 (2);
Admin Plan: s17p2; s20p3; s20p6 (2); s20p7; s20p7

FALSE NAME..................................1
Admin Plan: s20p6

FALSE STATEMENT........................2
7420.10G Gbk: 22-1;
Admin Plan: s17p2

FALSE STATEMENTS 8
24 CFR 5: .528;
7420.10G Gbk: 4-27 Ex 4-2 (2); 11-18; 12-16 Ex 12-4 (2);
Admin Plan: s20p7; s20p7

FALSE STATEMENTS ACT............1
24 CFR 5: .528

FALSELY..2
HUD-903: p1; p2

FALSIFY..2
7420.10G Gbk: 22-2;
Admin Plan: s20p1

FAMILIAL......................................13
24 CFR 982: .202; .304;
HUD-903: p1; p2 (3); p4;
PIH Notices: 01-15; 95-48; 95-48 Tech Asst;
Admin Plan: s1p2; s7p3; s7p7

FAMILIAL STATUS 17
24 CFR 982: .202; .304;
HUD-52641: p5; p10;
HUD-52641-A: p3;
HUD-52646: p2;
HUD-903: p1; p2 (3); p4;
7420.10G Gbk: 5-11; 5-42 (2); 8-14; 11-13;

PIH Notices: 01-15

FAMILIAR 16
7420.10G Gbk: 13-4; 21-6;
PIH Notices: 01-06; 00-24; 99-11 (3); 95-48 (4); 95-48 Tech Asst (4);
Admin Plan: s18p6

FAMILIARIZE 2
PIH Notices: 95-48; 95-48

FAMILY ABSENCE 2
HUD-52646: p2;
7420.10G Gbk: 16-5

FAMILY ABSENCE 11
24 CFR 982: .54; .312 (2); .551;
HUD-52646: p2;
7420.10G Gbk: 16-5;
PIH Notices: 03-05 (2); 01-40 (2);
Admin Plan: s6p6

FAMILY ABSENCES 3
24 CFR 982: .312; .551;
7420.10G Gbk: 5-36 Ex 5-4

FAMILY ASSET 2
HUD-50058Instr: p22;
7420.10G Gbk: 17-11

FAMILY ASSETS 11
24 CFR 5: .603; .609;
HUD-50058Instr: p31;
7420.10G Gbk: 5-15 Ex 5-2; 5-24; 5-27;
PIH Notices: 01-15 Impr Integ Hbk (3);
Admin Plan: s6p10; s7p6

FAMILY BEHAVIOR 11
24 CFR 982: .54; .307; .552;
7420.10G Gbk: 1-14; 3-3; 5-38 (2); 5-40; 8-21; 11-12;
Admin Plan: s2p6

FAMILY BREAKS UP 7
24 CFR 982: .54; .315 (2);
HUD-52641: p4;
7420.10G Gbk: 3-4; 11-5; 15-4

FAMILY BREAK-UP 1
24 CFR 982: .315

FAMILY CHARACTERISTICS........4
24 CFR 5: .655;
24 CFR 982: .202;
7420.10G Gbk: 19-3;
Admin Plan: s5p1

FAMILY COMPOSITION...............47
24 CFR 5: .403;
24 CFR 982: .4; .201; .403;
HUD-50058Instr: p10; p12; p72;
HUD-52641: p4;
7420.10G Gbk: 4-5; 4-15; 5-12; 5-36 Ex 5-4; 5-50 Ex 5-5; 11-5; 12-5 (2); 12-9; 12-12 Ex 12-1; 12-16 Ex 12-4; 14-2; 15-4; 22-2 (2); 22-9 (2); 22-10 (3);
PIH Notices: 01-15; 01-15 Impr Integ Hbk (2); 00-09;
Admin Plan: s2p1; s3p3; s5p2 (2); s5p3; s6p5; s6p8 (2); s7p1; s7p8; s8p1; s8p3; s11p1; s22p4; s23p4

FAMILY DAMAGE 2
HUD-52641: p9;
HUD-52641-A: p2

FAMILY DEBTS 2
Admin Plan: s17p1; s17p1

FAMILY EXPENSES 2
24 CFR 982: .632; .632

FAMILY HEAD...............................15
24 CFR 5: .230; .504; .603; .609; .659;
24 CFR 982: .516;
HUD-50058Instr: p33; p70 (2); p71;
7420.10G Gbk: 5-13; 12-16 Ex 12-4; 23-7;
PIH Notices: 01-15 Impr Integ Hbk; 01-15 Impr Integ Hbk

FAMILY HOUSEHOLD MEMBER . 1
Admin Plan: s22p1

FAMILY INCOME 114
24 CFR 5: .236; .240; .528; .601; .603 (2); .615 (2); .657 (5); .659 (2);
24 CFR 982: Intro; .4; .54; .355; .502 (4); .503 (2); .516 (8); .551; .635; .641;
HUD-50058: p vii;
HUD-50058Instr: p9 (2); p34; p35; p38; p76;
HUD-52646: p2 (2);
7420.10G Gbk: 1-13; 1-14; 3-5; 4-23 Ex 4-1; 5-30; 12-1; 12-9; 12-11; 16-5; 19-10; 20-3; 20-17; 23-11; 24-3;
PIH Notices: 03-05 (2); 02-20 (3); 01-41 (10); 01-40 (2); 01-33; 01-15 (3); 01-15 Impr Integ Hbk (11); 01-10 (5); 00-46 (3); 00-24B; 00-09 (8);
Admin Plan: s6p1; s7p2; s7p5 (2); s21p4; s23p7

FAMILY INCOMES 6

24 CFR 5: .603 (3); HUD-50058Instr: p71; p73; p76

FAMILY INFORMATION 19
24 CFR 5: .518; .659;
24 CFR 982: .304;
HUD-52646: p2;
7420.10G Gbk: 3-3; 4-10; 12-1; 12-3; 12-5; 13-1; 22-6; 23-19;
PIH Notices: 02-27; 01-15 Impr Integ Hbk;
Admin Plan: s1p6 (4); s21p2

FAMILY IS RESPONSIBLE 19
24 CFR 982: .404 (2); .551; .619 (3);
HUD-52641: p3; 8;
HUD-52641-A: p1 (2);
7420.10G Gbk: 8-4; 11-6; 12-10;
PIH Notices: 01-41; 00-24B; 00-09;
Admin Plan: s10p5 (2); s14p1

FAMILY MEMBER....................... 339
24 CFR 5: .230; .508 (8); .512 (2); .514 (9); .520 (4); .603 (2); .609 (6); .615 (9); .617 (8);
24 CFR 982: .4; .303; .306; .316 (2); .402 (2); .516 (3); .517; .551 (2); .552 (2); .553; .606; .627 (2); .633 (2); .637;
HUD-50058: p iii (2); p iv (3); p6 (8); p7 (2); p vii;
HUD-50058Instr: p9; p15 (4); p16 (3); p18 (2); p22 (6); p24 (5); p25; p26 (2); p27; p29 (3); p30; p33 (3); p34 (3); p36; p62; p70 (2); p71; p73 (4); p75 (3);
HUD-52517: p2;
HUD-52641: p1; p5; p6 (3); p10;
HUD-52641-A: p3;
HUD-52646: p2 (6);
7420.10G Gbk: 1-15; 2-8; 4-25 Ex 4-2; 5-2; 5-7 (2); 5-9 Ex 5-1 (2); 5-12 (4); 5-13; 5-15 Ex 5-2 (5); 5-18 (2); 5-20; 5-22; 5-29 (6); 5-30 (6); 5-33 (2); 5-34; 5-35 (2); 5-37 (7); 5-41 (2); 5-53 Ex 5-5; 7-9; 8-8; 8-19; 11-3; 11-13; 12-5 (3); 14-4; 15-5 (2); 15-6 (3); 15-7; 16-5; 18-8; 18-9; 22-14 (2); 23-1; 23-6 (2); 23-7; 23-10; 23-12 (3); 23-14 (2); 23-15;
PIH Notices: 03-05; 02-01 (4); 01-40; 01-15 (2); 01-15 Impr Integ Hbk (33); 00-11A; 99-52 (5); 95-48 (2); 95-48 Tech Asst (2);
Admin Plan: s2p2; s2p3; s2p5; s2p6 (3); s5p1; s5p2; s6p2 (5); s6p3 (8); s6p5 (2); s6p6 (5); s6p8 (3); s6p9 (2); s6p11; s6p12 (4); s7p3 (2); s7p7; s7p8 (6); s8p5 (2); s11p2 (2); s16p2; s18p7; s18p8; s19p1; s20p4; s22p1 (2); s22p4; s23p7

FAMILY MEMBERS 186
24 CFR 5: .506; .508 (2); .512; .518 (2); .520 (5); .611; .659;
24 CFR 982: .201; .307 (2); .308; .315 (4); .402; .510; .516 (2); .552 (5); .627 (2); .633; .634; .638;
HUD-50058: p iii; p iv; p v (2); p6; p vii; p ix (3); p x (3); p xi (3); p xii (3); p xiii (3); p xiv (4); p xvi (2); p17; p xvii;
HUD-50058Instr: p2; p14; p16; p17; p18 (2); p24; p26; p29 (2); p34; p36; p39; p40 (5); p44 (7); p48 (7); p51 (7); p54 (7); p57 (5); p60; p61; p62 (2); p68 (2); p69 (2); p72;
HUD-52641: p4; 8;
HUD-52641-A: p1;
7420.10G Gbk: 3-4 (3); 4-19; 5-4; 5-5; 5-6; 5-12; 5-18 (3); 5-37; 5-38 (4); 5-39 (2); 5-41; 8-8; 13-1; 15-4; 15-6 (2); 18-1; 22-8; 22-14 (4); 23-1; 23-7; 23-9; 23-14;
PIH Notices: 01-15 Impr Integ Hbk (7); 00-24B; 00-23;
Admin Plan: s2p2; s3p2; s5p1 (2); s5p2; s6p1 (2); s7p2 (2); s7p8; s15p5 (3); s16p2; s20p4; s23p7

FAMILY MEMBER'S 9
24 CFR 982: .204;
HUD-50058Instr: p15 (2); p18 (2); p25;
7420.10G Gbk: 4-6;
PIH Notices: 01-15; 01-

15 Impr Integ Hbk
FAMILY MEMBERSHIP..................2
PIH Notices: 01-15 Impr Integ Hbk; 01-15 Impr Integ Hbk
FAMILY OBLIGATION..................17
24 CFR 5: .659;
24 CFR 982: .404;
7420.10G Gbk: 12-3;
PIH Notices: 01-15 Impr Integ Hbk;
Admin Plan: s1p5; s2p6; s6p8; s7p2; s15p2; s15p4 (2); s15p5; s15p6 (2); s18p4; s20p6; s20p6
FAMILY OBLIGATIONS................54
24 CFR 982: Intro; .301 (2); .309 (2); .404; .552 (2); .619 (2); .625; .633 (4); .638;
HUD-52648: p1;
7420.10G Gbk: 1-12 Ex 1-2; 1-15; 5-36 Ex 5-4 (2); 8-6 (2); 8-8; 8-10 (2); 8-11 (2); 10-33; 11-15 (2); 15-1; 15-5; 15-8;
PIH Notices: 00-24B (2);
Admin Plan: s2p2; s6p8; s10p3; s13p2; s15p1; s15p3; s15p4; s15p5; s15p6; s20p1; s20p6; s21p5 (2); s22p2; s22p4 (2); s23p4; s25p5
FAMILY OCCUPANCY...................2
24 CFR 982: .312;
7420.10G Gbk: 15-6
FAMILY PARTICIPATED.................1
HUD-50058Instr: p2
FAMILY PARTICIPATES................15
HUD-50058: p ii (2); p ix; p xvi (2);
HUD-50058Instr: p2 (2); p7; p13; p39; p42; p59 (3); p59
FAMILY PARTICIPATING..............4
24 CFR 982: .552;
7420.10G Gbk: 1-1; 23-18;
PIH Notices: 02-22
FAMILY PRESERVATION...............4
24 CFR 5: .516; .518 (2); .518
FAMILY RENT...............................25
24 CFR 982: .4 (2); .451; .515 (2);
HUD-50058Instr: p72;
HUD-52648: p2;
7420.10G Gbk: 1-6 Ex 1-1; 5-34 (2); 6-6 (6); 11-6; 11-7; 11-14; 11-17; 21-7; 23-13;
PIH Notices: 01-41; 01-15 Impr Integ Hbk; 01-15 Impr Integ Hbk
FAMILY RENT BURDEN................1
7420.10G Gbk: 19-4
FAMILY RENTING..........................2
24 CFR 5: .504;
HUD-50058Instr: p75
FAMILY SELF SUFFICIENCY......10
HUD-50058: p17;
HUD-50058Instr: p59; p61;
PIH Notices: 02-27; 02-01 (3); 99-52 (2); 99-52
FAMILY SELF-SUFFICIENCY......47
24 CFR 982: .4; .152;
HUD-50058: p i; p ii; p16; p xvi (3); p xvii;
HUD-50058Instr: p ii; p2; p3; p4; p10; p13; p59; p72;
HUD-52648: p2; p3;
7420.10G Gbk: 1-9; 1-10; 4-16; 4-19; 21-5; 21-11; 21-13; 23-1 (2); 23-7; 23-8 Ex 23-1; 23-17 Ex 23-2; 23-18;
PIH Notices: 01-06 (4); 00-24A; 00-24B; 00-11; 00-11A (2);
Admin Plan: s8p3; s21p9; s22p2 (2); s25p3; s25p3
FAMILY SHARE.............................99
24 CFR 982: 24 CFR 982 (2); .4 (2); .305; .503 (2); .508 (2); .515 (4);
HUD-50058: p11; p14 (2);
HUD-50058Instr: p48; p57 (3); p72;
7420.10G Gbk: 1-3; 1-5; 1-6 Ex 1-1; 1-13; 1-14; 5-5 (2); 5-21; 6-2; 6-5 (10); 6-6 (5); 6-7 (2); 8-6; 8-16 (2); 11-6 (3); 11-15; 12-2; 12-6; 12-10 (2); 14-4; 16-3; 22-2;
PIH Notices: 02-20 (3); 01-41 (8); 01-10 (19); 00-46 (3); 00-09 (4); 00-09
FAMILY SHARES............................5
HUD-50058Instr: p43; p44; p47 (2); p49
FAMILY TYPE.................................2
7420.10G Gbk: 5-50 Ex 5-5;
Admin Plan: s4p2
FAMILY TYPES...............................1
Admin Plan: s4p2
FAMILY UNIFICATION................11
HUD-50058Instr: p13; p72;
7420.10G Gbk: 1-7 (2); 4-1; 21-8; 21-11;

Admin Plan: s4p2; s25p1 (2); s25p1
FAMILY UNIT....................................3
PIH Notices: 00-09;
Admin Plan: s2p3; s8p5
FAMILY UNIT SIZE.......................98
24 CFR 982: .4; .204 (4); .316; .355 (2); .402 (14); .403 (2); .504; .505 (5); .516 .517; .554; .555 (2); .608; .613 (5); .617; .618; .619; .620; .635;
HUD-50058Instr: p47 (4); p57; p72;
7420.10G Gbk: 2-9; 4-8; 4-14; 4-15; 4-18 (3); 5-41 (5); 6-6 (2); 7-8; 14-2; 17-5 (2); 17-6 (3); 17-8 (4); 18-2; 23-7; 23-12;
PIH Notices: 01-41 (3); 00-09 (6);
Admin Plan: s5p1; s5p3 (2); s8p6; s18p2; s18p3; s19p1 (3); s19p1
FAMILY UNIT SIZE-MAXIMUM ... 1
24 CFR 982: .402
FAMILY-CAUSED...........................3
24 CFR 982: .404;
PIH Notices: 00-24B;
Admin Plan: s21p5
FAMILY-SELF-SUFFICIENCY........1
Admin Plan: s21p1
FAMILY-SUPPLIED........................1
Admin Plan: s10p5
FAN..3
HUD-52580-A: p6; p15;
7420.10G Gbk: 10-10
FARM 3
HUD-50058Instr: p22 (2);
Admin Plan: s7p5
FARMING 3
7420.10G Gbk: 5-25 Ex 5-3;
PIH Notices: 95-48; 95-48 Tech Asst
FAST FOOD 1
PIH Notices: 01-15 Impr Integ Hbk
FATHER...1
HUD-50058Instr: p14
FATHER'S 1
HUD-50058Instr: p29
FAX..23
HUD-903: p2 (3); p3 (8);
7420.10G Gbk: 4-13 (3); 10-33; 10-34; 12-13 Ex 12-1 (2); 13-4; 13-11 Ex 13-1;
PIH Notices: 03-11 (2); 02-27
FAXED 1
PIH Notices: 00-27
FEAR 3
7420.10G Gbk: 5-10 Ex 5-1;
PIH Notices: 02-01; 99-52
FEARS 1
24 CFR 5: .661
FEASIBILITY 1
7420.10G Gbk: 1-2
FEASIBLE.....................................21
24 CFR 5: .502; .609;
7420.10G Gbk: 5-11; 21-3; 23-2;
PIH Notices: 02-01 (4); 01-15 Impr Integ Hbk; 99-52 (4); 95-48 (3); 95-48 Tech Asst (3);
Admin Plan: s1p5
FEBRUARY...................................34
7420.10G Gbk: 19-2; 19-3; 20-10;
PIH Notices: 03-23 (5); 02-21 (2); 02-03; 01-41 (2); 01-33; 01-20; 01-10 (3); 01-06 (2); 00-28; 00-27 (2); 00-09 (9); 99-11; 99-11
FEDERAL EMERGENCY MANAGEMENT AGENCY 1
PIH Notices: 99-11
FEDERAL FINANCIAL ASSISTANCE 39
HUD-50058Instr: p3;
7420.10G Gbk: 5-44; 20-29;
PIH Notices: 02-01 (7); 99-52 (9); 95-48 (11); 95-48 Tech Asst (8); 95-48 Tech Asst
FEDERAL REGISTER...................87
24 CFR 5: .100; .609;
24 CFR 982: .4 (2); .52; .101; .102 (12); .519; .643;
HUD-50058Instr: p5 (2); p30 (2); p32 (2);
HUD-52641: p10;
HUD-52641-A: p3;
7420.10G Gbk: 5-10 Ex 5-1; 5-13; 5-16 Ex 5-2; 10-38 Ex 10-3; 10-39 Ex 10-4; 13-9; 20-4; 20-5; 20-6; 20-9; 20-11; 20-24 (2);
PIH Notices: 03-23 (5); 03-12; 02-21; 02-20 (3); 02-14 (2); 02-07 (3); 02-06 (2); 02-01 (3); 01-20; 01-15; 01-15 Impr Integ Hbk (4); 01-

06; 01-01; 00-49 (2); 00-46 (2); 00-34; 00-28 (2); 00-27; 00-24 (2); 00-24A (4); 00-11; 99-52 (2); 99-52

FEDERALLY ASSISTED HOUSING21
24 CFR 5: .100;
24 CFR 982: .4; .202; .306; .552; .553 (3);
HUD-52641: p6;
7420.10G Gbk: 4-15; 4-19; 5-43; 15-6;
PIH Notices: 03-11; 01-27 (4); 00-23;
Admin Plan: s2p6; s16p2

FEE 262
24 CFR 982: 24 CFR 982 (2); .4 (5); .54; .151; .152 (19); .155 (9); .352 (2); .355 (2); .451 (2); .515; .622 (2); .628 (2); .635; .639; .643 (2);
HUD-50058: p x; p xi; p xiii; p xiv;
HUD-50058Instr: p42; p46; p53; p56; p70 (2);
HUD-52665: p1; p3 (2);
HUD-903: p2;
7420.10G Gbk: 2-9 (2); 5-27; 5-53 Ex 5-5; 9-4; 10-31; 13-9 (4); 17-11; 20-3 (13); 20-4 (6); 20-5; 20-6 (7); 20-22; 20-22 Ex 20-5; 20-24; 20-28; 21-8; 24-14;
PIH Notices: 03-23 (32); 03-11 (8); 02-27; 02-21 (6); 02-07 (23); 02-01; 01-41 (18); 01-15; 01-15 Impr Integ Hbk; 01-10; 00-49 (4); 00-28 (22); 00-09 (23); 96-65 (7);
Admin Plan: s11p2; s13p2; s19p1; s22p3

FEE RESERVE....................4
PIH Notices: 03-23 (3); 03-23

FEED....................2
HUD-52580-A: p15;
7420.10G Gbk: 24-15

FEEDBACK 4
7420.10G Gbk: 9-11; 10-33; 19-10; 19-12

FEE-FOR-SERVICE....................1
PIH Notices: 01-15

FEEL....................6
7420.10G Gbk: 2-10; 2-11; 21-3;
PIH Notices: 95-48; 95-48 Tech Asst;
Admin Plan: s2p7

FEELINGS....................1
7420.10G Gbk: 10-8

FEELS....................1
Admin Plan: s1p5

FEES 219
24 CFR 5: .318; .609;
24 CFR 982: 24 CFR 982 (2); .152 (5); .155 (2); .157; .355; .510; .625; .635; .639; .643 (2);
HUD-50058Instr: p27; p54;
HUD-52641: 8;
HUD-52641-A: p1;
7420.10G Gbk: 2-11; 5-14 Ex 5-2; 5-25 Ex 5-3; 5-27; 5-28; 11-14; 13-9; 13-10; 20-2 (2); 20-3 (8); 20-4 (3); 20-5 (2); 20-6 (2); 20-16 (2); 20-20 (2); 20-21 Ex 20-4; 20-22 Ex 20-5; 20-27 (3); 20-28; 20-29 (3); 22-17 (3); 23-12; 24-2; 24-15;
PIH Notices: 03-23 (54); 03-11 (4); 02-21 (3); 02-07 (25); 02-01; 01-15 Impr Integ Hbk (2); 01-06; 00-49 (12); 00-41 (2); 00-28 (24); 00-24B; 00-23; 96-65 (3); 95-48 (7); 95-48 Tech Asst (7);
Admin Plan: s6p10 (3); s11p1; s11p1

FEET....................48
24 CFR 982: .605 (4);
HUD-52580: p2 (3); p3 (3); p4 (2); p5;
HUD-52580-A: p3; p5; p7; p9; p10; p11; p12;
7420.10G Gbk: 9-13 Ex 9-1; 9-19 Ex 9-4; 10-6; 10-18 (2); 17-2 (4);
PIH Notices: 00-49 (2); 00-23 (3); 95-48 (8); 95-48 Tech Asst (5); 95-48 Tech Asst

FELON....................1
24 CFR 982: .310

FELONS 1
PIH Notices: 03-11

FELONY....................8
24 CFR 982: .310;
HUD-52641: p9;
HUD-52641-A: p2;
7420.10G Gbk: 15-2 (2); 15-6 (2);
PIH Notices: 03-11

FEMALE....................6

HUD-50058Instr: p14;
HUD-903: p1 (3);
7420.10G Gbk: 4-23 Ex 4-1; 4-23 Ex 4-1

FHA......10
24 CFR 982: .632 (2); .643 (3);
7420.10G Gbk: 9-11;
PIH Notices: 02-01 (2); 99-52;
Admin Plan: s4p1

FIFTEEN......15
24 CFR 982: .305 (3); .634;
7420.10G Gbk: 10-19;
PIH Notices: 02-27 (2);
Admin Plan: s4p2 (2); s10p3; s21p3; s21p4; s21p8; s22p3; s22p4

FIFTEEN DAY......1
24 CFR 982: .305

FIFTEEN DAYS......2
24 CFR 982: .305; .305

FIFTEEN YEAR......1
Admin Plan: s22p3

FIFTEEN YEARS......2
24 CFR 982: .634;
Admin Plan: s22p4

FIFTEEN-YEAR......2
7420.10G Gbk: 1-8;
Admin Plan: s22p4

FIFTY PERCENT......6
24 CFR 5: .617;
7420.10G Gbk: 22-17;
PIH Notices: 03-23; 01-15 Impr Integ Hbk (2); 00-11A

FIGHTING......5
PIH Notices: 99-11 (4); 99-11

FILE CABINET......1
Admin Plan: s20p4

FILE CABINETS......2
PIH Notices: 95-48; 95-48 Tech Asst

FILE DATA......3
Admin Plan: s20p1; s20p3; s20p4

FILE DOCUMENTATION......6
7420.10G Gbk: 5-46 Ex 5-5; 7-7;
PIH Notices: 02-27 (2);
Admin Plan: s19p1; s20p3

FILE DOCUMENTS......3
7420.10G Gbk: 22-6;
Admin Plan: s20p2; s20p2

FINAL DECISION......8
24 CFR 5: .514;
24 CFR 982: .554 (2);
7420.10G Gbk: 16-3 (2);
PIH Notices: 03-11;
Admin Plan: s18p3; s18p7

FINAL DISPOSITION......1
PIH Notices: 03-11

FINANCE......47
24 CFR 5: .100; .214; .653;
24 CFR 982: .633; .634; .635 (6);
HUD-50058Instr: p56; p75;
7420.10G Gbk: 21-12 Ex 21-2; 21-12 Ex 21-3; 21-16 Ex 21-6; 21-17; 21-18;
PIH Notices: 02-27; 02-21 (6); 02-14 (6); 02-06; 02-01; 01-41 (3); 01-20 (3); 01-10 (2); 00-27 (3); 95-48; 95-48 Tech Asst;
Admin Plan: s17p3

FINANCED......4
24 CFR 5: .100;
24 CFR 982: .632; .643;
7420.10G Gbk: 2-11

FINANCES......3
24 CFR 982: .102 (2);
7420.10G Gbk: 20-1

FINANCIAL......343
24 CFR 5: .315; .318 (3); .500 (2); .506; .508 (4); .514 (3); .518 (2); .528; .603; .609; .630 (14); .653; .705; .801 (20);
24 CFR 982: .156; .158 (2); .355 (3); .503;
HUD-50058: p v; p viii (2);
HUD-50058Instr: p3; p17; p28 (2); p30; p31; p37 (2); p38 (3); p71;
HUD-9886: p1 (3); p2;
7420.10G Gbk: 1-1; 1-9; 2-11; 3-7; 4-6; 4-7; 4-11; 5-6; 5-8; 5-9 Ex 5-1; 5-15 Ex 5-2; 5-20 (3); 5-44 (2); 5-48 Ex 5-5 (2); 5-49 Ex 5-5; 6-8 (2); 7-4; 8-3; 8-4; 8-15; 20-1 (8); 20-2 (3); 20-3 (2); 20-5 (2); 20-6 (2); 20-16; 20-23; 20-26; 20-28 (5); 20-29 (5); 20-30 (3); 21-14 Ex 21-4; 21-15 Ex 21-5; 21-19; 23-20; 24-8; 24-10;
PIH Notices: 03-23 (3); 02-27; 02-22; 02-21 (2); 02-20 (4); 02-14 (3); 02-07 (14); 02-06 (4); 02-01 (18); 01-41 (3); 01-27 (3); 01-20 (5); 01-15 Impr Integ Hbk (11); 01-06 (5); 00-53 (2); 00-49 (2); 00-46 (4); 00-

28 (13); 00-27 (5); 00-24B (2); 00-11 (2); 00-09 (4); 99-52 (18); 96-65 (2); 95-48 (19); 95-48 Tech Asst (17);
Admin Plan: s1p3; s1p5 (3); s6p3; s6p4 (4); s6p5; s7p5 (6); s7p6 (5); s20p4 (2); s22p2 (3); s24p4; s25p5 (3); s25p7

FINANCIAL ASSISTANCE 78
24 CFR 5: .500 (2); .506; .508 (4); .514 (3); .518 (2); .528; .609;
HUD-50058: p v;
HUD-50058Instr: p3; p17; p28; p31;
7420.10G Gbk: 2-11; 5-6; 5-8; 5-9 Ex 5-1; 5-15 Ex 5-2; 5-20 (2); 5-44; 8-4; 8-15; 20-29;
PIH Notices: 02-01 (8); 01-27 (3); 01-15 Impr Integ Hbk (3); 99-52 (9); 95-48 (13); 95-48 Tech Asst (11);
Admin Plan: s6p4

FINANCIAL DATA 3
7420.10G Gbk: 20-29 (2); 20-29

FINANCIAL HARDSHIP 33
24 CFR 5: .630 (8);
24 CFR 982: .503;
HUD-50058: p viii;
HUD-50058Instr: p37; p38;
7420.10G Gbk: 6-8 (2); 7-4;
PIH Notices: 02-20 (3); 01-15 Impr Integ Hbk (7); 00-46 (3);
Admin Plan: s1p5; s6p4 (3); s6p5

FINANCIAL HARDSHIP EXEMPTION 10
24 CFR 5: .630 (6);
HUD-50058: p viii;
HUD-50058Instr: p37; p38; p38

FINANCIAL HARDSHIPS 2
PIH Notices: 02-20; 00-46

FINANCIAL INFORMATION 6
24 CFR 5: .801 (5); .801

FINANCIAL INSTITUTION 13
24 CFR 982: .156;
7420.10G Gbk: 5-48 Ex 5-5; 5-49 Ex 5-5 (2); 20-1;
Admin Plan: s7p5 (2); s7p6 (3); s22p2 (2); s22p2

FINANCIAL INSTITUTIONS 6
HUD-9886: p1 (3);
7420.10G Gbk: 5-49 Ex 5-5;
PIH Notices: 02-22;
Admin Plan: s25p5

FINANCIAL MANAGEMENT 76
7420.10G Gbk: 1-1; 20-1 (6); 20-2; 20-3 (2); 20-5 (2); 20-6 (2); 20-16; 20-28 (4); 20-29; 21-15 Ex 21-5;
PIH Notices: 03-23 (3); 02-21 (2); 02-14 (3); 02-07 (13); 02-06 (3); 01-41 (2); 01-20 (5); 00-49 (2); 00-28 (13); 00-27 (5); 00-09 (3);
Admin Plan: s25p7

FINANCIAL MANAGEMENT CONTROLS 1
7420.10G Gbk: 20-2

FINANCIAL OBLIGATION 1
24 CFR 5: .318

FINANCIAL OBLIGATIONS 2
24 CFR 5: .318; .318

FINANCIAL RECORD 1
7420.10G Gbk: 20-1

FINANCIAL REPORT 4
24 CFR 5: .801 (3); .801

FINANCIAL REPORTING 5
24 CFR 5: .705; .801 (2);
24 CFR 982: .158;
PIH Notices: 00-24B

FINANCIAL REPORTS 8
24 CFR 5: .801 (4);
7420.10G Gbk: 20-2; 20-30 (2); 20-30

FINANCIAL STABILITY 1
7420.10G Gbk: 24-8

FINANCIAL STATEMENT 8
7420.10G Gbk: 5-48 Ex 5-5 (2); 20-26;
PIH Notices: 01-15 Impr Integ Hbk; 00-53 (2);
Admin Plan: s7p5; s7p5

FINDING 42
24 CFR 5: .512; .518;
24 CFR 982: .152; .304; .503; .629;
HUD-52648: p2;
7420.10G Gbk: 1-13; 2-3; 2-8; 2-10; 6-10 Ex 6-2; 7-1; 7-3; 7-4; 7-5; 7-7; 7-9; 8-12; 8-13; 11-4; 21-9; 24-4; 24-13;
PIH Notices: 02-20 (4); 02-06; 02-01; 01-15 Impr Integ Hbk; 01-01 (3); 00-46 (4); 00-11; 99-52;
Admin Plan: s21p6; s23p7

FINDINGS....................................35
24 CFR 5: .236 (3); .603; .653;
HUD-50058Instr: p73;
7420.10G Gbk: 3-8; 5-11; 10-39 Ex 10-4; 22-11; 22-16;
PIH Notices: 02-27 (6); 02-21 (4); 02-01; 01-20 (4); 01-06; 99-52; 95-48; 95-48 Tech Asst;
Admin Plan: s18p3; s18p6; s20p5 (2); s20p7

FINED...1
HUD-9886: p2

FINES 5
24 CFR 982: .306;
HUD-52641: p7;
7420.10G Gbk: 8-20; 11-4;
Admin Plan: s16p2

FINGERPRINT...............................37
PIH Notices: 03-11 (36); 03-11

FINGERPRINTING 1
PIH Notices: 03-11

FINGERPRINTS 7
PIH Notices: 03-11 (6); 03-11

FIRE...131
24 CFR 5: .609 (2); .703 (6);
24 CFR 982: .401 (7); .605 (2); .614;
HUD-50058Instr: p26;
HUD-52580: p5;
HUD-52580-A: p2 (2); p8; p15; p17 (6); p18;
7420.10G Gbk: 5-15 Ex 5-2 (2); 10-6 (3); 10-7 (2); 10-8 (2); 10-12 (6); 10-13; 10-14 (4); 17-2 (4); 17-5; 23-12;
PIH Notices: 03-05; 01-40; 01-15 Impr Integ Hbk (4); 99-11 (54); 95-48 (6); 95-48 Tech Asst (6);
Admin Plan: s6p5; s10p4

FIRE ESCAPE 5
24 CFR 982: .401;
HUD-52580-A: p2; p17;
7420.10G Gbk: 10-6; 10-6

FIRE ESCAPES................................2
24 CFR 5: .703;
7420.10G Gbk: 10-6

FIRE EXIT.......................................2
HUD-52580-A: p17; p18

FIRE EXITS.....................................3
24 CFR 5: .703 (2);
HUD-52580: p5

FIRE EXTINGUISHERS 1
PIH Notices: 99-11

FIRE HAZARD 3
7420.10G Gbk: 10-7; 10-8; 10-8

FIRE HAZARDS..............................7
24 CFR 5: .703 (2);
24 CFR 982: .401; .614;
HUD-52580-A: p17;
7420.10G Gbk: 10-13; 17-5

FIRE PATROL 4
24 CFR 5: .609;
7420.10G Gbk: 5-15 Ex 5-2;
PIH Notices: 01-15 Impr Integ Hbk; 01-15 Impr Integ Hbk

FIRE PROTECTION.........................8
24 CFR 5: .703;
24 CFR 982: .401;
HUD-52580-A: p8;
7420.10G Gbk: 10-14;
PIH Notices: 99-11 (3); 99-11

FIRST CLASS MAIL 4
24 CFR 5: .353;
7420.10G Gbk: 4-7;
Admin Plan: s6p13; s10p3

FIRST DAY....................................28
24 CFR 982: .4 (2); .152; .309; .519;
HUD-50058Instr: p70; p71; p74;
HUD-52641: p2; p3;
7420.10G Gbk: 11-1; 12-6 (2); 12-10 (2); 20-5 (2); 20-7 (4); 24-1;
PIH Notices: 03-23; 00-09;
Admin Plan: s6p5; s11p1; s11p2; s13p2

FIRST DAY OF THE MONTH 11
24 CFR 982: .152;
HUD-50058Instr: p71;
7420.10G Gbk: 12-6 (2); 12-10 (2); 24-1;
Admin Plan: s6p5; s11p1; s11p2; s13p2

FIRST FLOOR................................12
24 CFR 982: .401;
HUD-52580-A: p2; p17;
7420.10G Gbk: 10-6;
PIH Notices: 02-01; 99-52; 95-48 (3); 95-48 Tech Asst (2); 95-48 Tech Asst

FIRST JOB.......................................1
7420.10G Gbk: 23-1

FIRST OFFER 1
24 CFR 5: .655

FIRST-TIME HOMEOWNER 8
24 CFR 982: .4 (2); .627 (3); .637; .642;
PIH Notices: 03-20

FISCAL....................................191
24 CFR 5: .653; .801 (16);
24 CFR 982: .102 (3); .151; .152; .155 (3); .157; .201 (6);
HUD-50058Instr: p16 (2); p17; p19;
HUD-52648: p1 (3); p3; p4;
PIH Notices: 03-23 (26); 02-27 (7); 02-21 (15); 02-14 (4); 02-07 (4); 02-06 (8); 01-41; 01-20 (4); 01-10 (4); 01-06 (32); 01-01 (4); 00-49 (2); 00-34 (11); 00-28 (5); 00-27; 00-24 (2); 00-24B (3); 00-09 (3); 99-52;
Admin Plan: s4p2; s8p1 (2); s21p2; s21p4; s21p8 (6); s21p9; s25p5

FISCAL YEAR..............................197
24 CFR 5: .653; .801 (3);
24 CFR 982: .102 (3); .151; .152; .155 (3); .157; .201 (6);
HUD-50058Instr: p17; p19;
HUD-52648: p1 (3); p3; p4;
7420.10G Gbk: 1-7; 1-10 (2); 2-4 (5); 3-6 (2); 3-7; 3-8; 4-19 (2); 4-20 (6); 5-3; 7-10 (4); 9-12 (2); 10-32 (3); 10-33; 19-13; 20-1; 20-2; 20-4; 20-5 (2); 20-6 (4); 20-7 (7); 20-8 Ex 20-1; 20-9 (4); 20-10; 20-12 Ex 20-2; 20-13; 20-14; 20-19 Ex 20-3 (2); 20-27 (3); 20-28 (4); 20-29 (3); 24-1 (2); 24-2; 24-16;
PIH Notices: 03-23 (22); 02-27 (2); 02-21 (8); 02-14 (4); 02-07 (4); 02-06 (8); 01-41; 01-20; 01-06 (18); 01-01 (4); 00-49 (2); 00-28 (5); 00-27; 00-24B (3); 00-09 (2);
Admin Plan: s4p2; s8p1 (2); s21p2; s21p4; s21p8 (6); s21p9; s25p5

FISCAL YEAR END..........................
29
24 CFR 5: .801 (2);
PIH Notices: 03-23 (3); 02-27 (2); 02-21; 01-06 (12); 00-34 (8); 00-24

FISCAL YEAR ENDED...................9
7420.10G Gbk: 20-12 Ex 20-2;
PIH Notices: 02-21 (6); 01-20; 01-20

FISCAL YEAR ENDING.................4
24 CFR 5: .801 (2);
PIH Notices: 02-27; 02-27

FISCAL YEAR ENDS.......................4
7420.10G Gbk: 10-32; 20-10; 20-12 Ex 20-2;
PIH Notices: 01-06

FISCAL YEAR-END.........................1
PIH Notices: 00-09

FISCAL YEARS...............................6
7420.10G Gbk: 2-4; 7-10; 20-3; 20-9 (2); 20-21 Ex 20-4

FISCAL YEARS.............................30
24 CFR 5: .801 (9);
HUD-50058Instr: p16 (2);
7420.10G Gbk: 2-4; 7-10; 20-3; 20-9 (2); 20-21 Ex 20-4;
PIH Notices: 03-23; 02-27; 01-20; 01-10 (4); 01-06; 00-34 (3); 00-24; 99-52

FISH..1
24 CFR 5: .306

FIVE MONTHS................................1
7420.10G Gbk: 19-3

FIVE PERCENT.............................23
24 CFR 5: .518 (2);
24 CFR 982: .507;
7420.10G Gbk: 3-5; 3-9; 4-2; 7-3; 9-1 (2); 9-2 (3); 9-12; 12-10; 20-6; 20-28;
PIH Notices: 03-23; 00-24B; 95-48 (2); 95-48 Tech Asst (2);
Admin Plan: s11p2

FIVE PERCENTAGE.......................1
7420.10G Gbk: 7-10

FIVE WORKING DAYS..................1
Admin Plan: s23p6

FIVE YEAR.....................................5
7420.10G Gbk: 3-7; 3-8;
PIH Notices: 02-21; 01-20; 00-27

FIVE YEARS...................................6
24 CFR 982: .552;
7420.10G Gbk: 15-6; 16-3; 23-7;
Admin Plan: s24p2; s24p5

FLAMMABLE 1
24 CFR 5: .703

FLAT RENT.................................100
24 CFR 5: .603; .632;
HUD-50058: p2 (3); p ii (3); p9; p ix (4);
HUD-50058Instr: p ii; p9; p10 (10); p11 (2); p12 (17); p39 (7); p41 (2); p67; p68 (13); p69 (11);

p77; p78;
PIH Notices: 01-15 Impr Integ Hbk (19); 01-15 Impr Integ Hbk

FLAT RENT CALCULATION..........5
HUD-50058: p9; p ix;
HUD-50058Instr: p39 (2); p68

FLAT RENTS 9
HUD-50058Instr: p1;
PIH Notices: 01-15; 01-15 Impr Integ Hbk (6); 01-15 Impr Integ Hbk

FLOOD 4
24 CFR 982: .626 (2);
Admin Plan: s24p2; s24p2

FLOOD HAZARD.............................1
24 CFR 982: .626

FLOOD HAZARDS 1
Admin Plan: s24p2

FLOODING.....................................7
24 CFR 982: .401; .614;
HUD-52580-A: p13; p17;
7420.10G Gbk: 10-13; 17-5;
Admin Plan: s10p4

FLOOR 128
24 CFR 982: .401; .605 (4);
HUD-52580: p1; p2 (2); p3 (3); p4 (2);
HUD-52580-A: p2 (8); p3 (2); p5 (2); p6 (3); p7 (2); p8 (3); p9 (4); p10 (4); p11 (4); p12 (4); p13; p15; p17 (2);
HUD-903: p3 (3);
7420.10G Gbk: 9-5; 10-6; 10-9; 10-12; 17-2 (3);
PIH Notices: 02-01 (9); 00-45 (3); 00-23 (2); 99-52 (7); 95-48 (23); 95-48 Tech Asst (20); 95-48 Tech Asst

FLOORING.....................................1
7420.10G Gbk: 10-10

FLOORS 20
24 CFR 5: .318 (2); .703 (2);
24 CFR 982: .401 (2); .614;
HUD-52580: p6 (2);
HUD-52580-A: p2 (2); p8; p13; p17; p19 (2);
7420.10G Gbk: 10-9;
PIH Notices: 99-11; 95-48; 95-48 Tech Asst

FLUCTUATE...................................1
7420.10G Gbk: 18-4

FLUCTUATES 1
7420.10G Gbk: 24-12

FLUSH TOILET 10
24 CFR 982: .401; .605 (2); .614;
HUD-52580: p2;
HUD-52580-A: p6; p7;
7420.10G Gbk: 10-3; 17-2; 17-4

FLUSH TOILETS.............................1
24 CFR 982: .605

FMR...394
24 CFR 5: .100;
24 CFR 982: .4; .403; .503 (24); .505; .507 (2); .623 (3);
HUD-50058: p i; p xvii;
HUD-50058Instr: p3; p39; p62;
HUD-52580: p1 (3); p2 (14); p3;
7420.10G Gbk: 1-6 Ex 1-1 (2); 1-10; 2-2; 2-3; 2-4; 3-5 (2); 3-9; 7-1 (3); 7-2 (12); 7-3 (10); 7-4 (7); 7-5 (6); 7-6 (9); 7-9 (2); 7-10 (2); 9-1 (5); 9-2 (8); 9-4; 9-12; 9-19 Ex 9-4; 17-12 (4); 19-11; 20-18; 20-19 Ex 20-3 (2); 23-7; 23-12; 23-14; 24-10 (2); 24-11 (2); 24-12 (2);
PIH Notices: 02-27; 02-22 (6); 02-20 (91); 01-06 (21); 01-01 (28); 00-46 (78); 00-24A; 00-24B (3);
Admin Plan: s11p2; s11p3 (4); s19p1 (4); s21p3 (2); s21p6 (2); s21p7 (2); s21p7

FOLLOW-UP.................................27
7420.10G Gbk: 2-6 (3); 2-11; 4-13; 9-5 (2); 9-6; 9-7; 9-8 (2); 10-23; 10-35; 19-13; 21-11; 22-15; 24-7;
PIH Notices: 02-27 (4); 99-11;
Admin Plan: s20p1 (3); s20p3; s20p3

FOOD..72
24 CFR 982: .4; .401 (5); .605; .609 (5); .613; .614 (5); .618; .627;
HUD-50058: p16; p xvi;
HUD-50058Instr: p28 (2); p42; p46; p60; p75; p76 (2);
HUD-52580: p2;
HUD-52580-A: p4 (5); p5 (3); p18;
7420.10G Gbk: 5-16 Ex 5-2; 10-1; 10-4 (2); 10-5 (6); 17-1; 17-3 (3); 17-4; 17-5 (3); 17-7 (2); 17-9; 23-15;
PIH Notices: 01-15; 01-15 Impr Integ Hbk (2); 95-

48 (3); 95-48 Tech Asst (3);
Admin Plan: s19p1

FOOD PREPARATION 27
24 CFR 982: .4; .401 (2); .605; .609 (2); .613; .614 (4); .618;
HUD-50058Instr: p42; p46; p75;
HUD-52580-A: p4;
7420.10G Gbk: 10-1; 10-4; 10-5; 17-1; 17-3; 17-5 (2); 17-7 (2); 17-9;
Admin Plan: s19p1

FOOD STAMP..................................2
7420.10G Gbk: 5-16 Ex 5-2;
PIH Notices: 01-15 Impr Integ Hbk

FOOD STAMPS 9
HUD-50058: p16; p xvi;
HUD-50058Instr: p28; p60; p76;
7420.10G Gbk: 23-15;
PIH Notices: 01-15; 95-48; 95-48 Tech Asst

FOODS 2
24 CFR 982: .401; .614

FOR PROFIT 5
HUD-50058: p16;
HUD-50058Instr: p61 (2);
Admin Plan: s23p2; s25p7

FORBEARANCE 15
HUD-50058Instr: p2;
7420.10G Gbk: 19-2 (6); 19-3 (3);
PIH Notices: 01-06 (2); 00-53 (2); 00-28

FORBID..1
24 CFR 5: .350

FORECLOSURE 7
24 CFR 5: .603;
24 CFR 982: .638;
HUD-50058Instr: p22;
7420.10G Gbk: 5-27;
PIH Notices: 01-41; 01-15 Impr Integ Hbk;
Admin Plan: s6p10

FOREIGN 6
24 CFR 5: .609;
HUD-50058Instr: p31;
7420.10G Gbk: 5-15 Ex 5-2;
PIH Notices: 01-15 Impr Integ Hbk (2); 01-15 Impr Integ Hbk

FOREIGN GOVERNMENT 6
24 CFR 5: .609;
HUD-50058Instr: p31;
7420.10G Gbk: 5-15 Ex 5-2;
PIH Notices: 01-15 Impr Integ Hbk (2); 01-15 Impr Integ Hbk

FORFEIT 2
7420.10G Gbk: 23-18;
PIH Notices: 02-14

FORFEITED......................................1
7420.10G Gbk: 23-18

FORFEITURE 4
7420.10G Gbk: 23-18;
Admin Plan: s18p4; s25p2; s25p3

FORGED 2
7420.10G Gbk: 5-6;
Admin Plan: s20p6

FORGETTING 2
7420.10G Gbk: 22-2; 22-8

FORM 1040 8
7420.10G Gbk: 5-46 Ex 5-5; 5-48 Ex 5-5; 5-51 Ex 5-5;
PIH Notices: 01-15; 01-15 Impr Integ Hbk (2);
Admin Plan: s7p5; s7p6

FORM 1099 10
7420.10G Gbk: 5-12; 5-48 Ex 5-5; 11-19; 23-14;
PIH Notices: 01-15; 01-15 Impr Integ Hbk (3);
Admin Plan: s7p5; s7p8

FORM 4506 1
PIH Notices: 01-15

FORM 8821 1
PIH Notices: 01-15

FORMAL...14
HUD-50058: p16; p xvi;
HUD-50058Instr: p22; p60 (3);
7420.10G Gbk: 2-9; 3-1; 3-2; 9-5; 22-8; 22-13; 22-15;
Admin Plan: s3p2

FORMALIZE....................................2
7420.10G Gbk: 22-7;
PIH Notices: 01-15

FORMALIZES 1
7420.10G Gbk: 10-2

FORMALLY 14
24 CFR 5: .403;
24 CFR 982: .54;
7420.10G Gbk: 1-4; 3-1; 3-4; 5-2; 6-7; 23-10; 24-11;
PIH Notices: 02-27; 95-48; 95-48 Tech Asst;
Admin Plan: s20p1; s21p3

FORMAT 50
24 CFR 5: .801 (2);
HUD-50058: p i;
HUD-50058Instr: p3; p11; p12 (4); p14; p16 (2); p21 (3); p50 (2);
HUD-52667: p i;

7420.10G Gbk: 4-8; 4-10; 4-14; 9-10; 9-19 Ex 9-4; 13-4; 19-2;
PIH Notices: 03-23; 02-27; 02-21 (2); 02-20; 01-01 (3); 00-53 (2); 00-46; 95-48 (3); 95-48 Tech Asst (3);
Admin Plan: s1p3; s3p2; s7p8; s16p3; s17p1; s24p5; s25p4; s25p6

FORMATS....................................13
7420.10G Gbk: 19-6 (3);
PIH Notices: 95-48 (4); 95-48 Tech Asst (4);
Admin Plan: s1p3; s1p4

FORM--CONTENTS.........................1
24 CFR 5: .230

FORMED...1
7420.10G Gbk: 3-8

FORMER..26
24 CFR 982: .161; .204; .352;
HUD-50058: p5; p v;
HUD-50058Instr: p10; p18 (3);
HUD-52641: p6;
HUD-9886: p1;
7420.10G Gbk: 5-19; 5-22; 8-19; 11-2; 11-18 (2); 20-17; 22-4;
PIH Notices: 01-10; 00-09 (2); 95-48; 95-48 Tech Asst;
Admin Plan: s1p5; s9p3

FORMERLY....................................9
24 CFR 982: .4; .154; .155;
HUD-50058Instr: p27;
PIH Notices: 01-41; 00-09; 95-48; 95-48 Tech Asst;
Admin Plan: s7p8

FORMS--SPECIAL...........................1
24 CFR 5: .230

FORMULA....................................31
24 CFR 35 SubM: .1200;
24 CFR 982: .1; .101 (3);
HUD-50058Instr: p1;
7420.10G Gbk: 1-5; 4-1; 6-1; 6-7; 7-6; 14-2; 14-3; 14-5; 20-11; 20-18; 20-19 Ex 20-3;
PIH Notices: 03-23 (2); 02-22; 02-06 (2); 02-01; 01-41 (3); 01-10 (2); 00-09; 99-52;
Admin Plan: s6p1

FORMULAS....................................4
7420.10G Gbk: 8-5 (2); 14-2; 23-10

FORMULATES 4
24 CFR 982: .161;
HUD-52641: p6;
7420.10G Gbk: 8-19; 11-2

FORMULATING...............................1
PIH Notices: 00-11

FOR-PROFIT....................................1
HUD-50058Instr: p75

FORTY YEARS................................1
24 CFR 982: .628

FORWARDING ADDRESS 1
Admin Plan: s4p3

FOSTER..91
24 CFR 5: .403; .603 (2); .609 (3);
24 CFR 982: .201; .402; .551 (3);
HUD-50058: p3 (2); p iii (2); p4 (2); p iv (2); p v; p7; p ix; p x; p xi; p xii; p xiii; p xiv (2);
HUD-50058Instr: p14 (4); p15 (5); p17; p22; p25 (2); p26; p27; p31 (2); p34 (2); p36 (2); p40 (2); p44 (2); p48 (2); p51 (2); p54 (2); p57 (2); p68; p69; p71 (2); p72 (3);
7420.10G Gbk: 1-7; 5-1; 5-15 Ex 5-2; 5-18 (2); 5-41; 22-10;
PIH Notices: 01-15 Impr Integ Hbk (7); 00-11; 95-48; 95-48 Tech Asst;
Admin Plan: s2p2 (3); s5p1; s6p6; s6p6

FOSTER ADULT..............................3
HUD-50058: p3; p4;
HUD-50058Instr: p15

FOSTER ADULTS 11
24 CFR 5: .603; .609;
HUD-50058: p iii; p iv;
HUD-50058Instr: p15; p31; p71;
7420.10G Gbk: 5-15 Ex 5-2; 5-18;
PIH Notices: 01-15 Impr Integ Hbk; 01-15 Impr Integ Hbk

FOSTER CHILD 15
24 CFR 982: .551 (3);
HUD-50058: p3; p4; p7;
HUD-50058Instr: p14 (3); p15 (3); p36;
7420.10G Gbk: 5-18; 5-29

FOSTER CHILDREN 52
24 CFR 5: .603; .609 (2);
HUD-50058: p iii; p iv; p v;

p ix; p x; p xi; p xii; p xiii; p xiv (2);
HUD-50058Instr: p14; p17; p22; p25 (2); p26; p27; p31; p34 (2); p36; p40 (2); p44 (2); p48 (2); p51 (2); p54 (2); p57 (2); p68; p69; p71; p72 (2);
7420.10G Gbk: 5-15 Ex 5-2 (2); 5-18; 5-29; 5-53 Ex 5-5;
PIH Notices: 01-15 Impr Integ Hbk (5);
Admin Plan: s5p1

FOSTER CHILD'S 1
Admin Plan: s2p2

FOUNDATION 15
24 CFR 982: .628; .631;
HUD-52580: p5;
HUD-52580-A: p13; p14 (2);
7420.10G Gbk: 4-4; 10-9; 19-6;
PIH Notices: 95-48 (2); 95-48 Tech Asst (2);
Admin Plan: s19p1; s22p3

FOUNDATIONS 3
24 CFR 5: .703;
HUD-52580-A: p13; p13

FOUR MONTHS 4
HUD-50058Instr: p28;
7420.10G Gbk: 20-9; 20-11; 23-15

FOUR YEAR 5
24 CFR 5: .617;
7420.10G Gbk: 5-16 Ex 5-2;
PIH Notices: 01-15 Impr Integ Hbk (2);
Admin Plan: s6p3

FOUR YEAR DISALLOWANCE 5
24 CFR 5: .617;
7420.10G Gbk: 5-16 Ex 5-2;
PIH Notices: 01-15 Impr Integ Hbk (2);
Admin Plan: s6p3

FOUR-LEGGED 1
24 CFR 5: .318

FOURTEEN 4
Admin Plan: s6p7 (2); s18p7; s18p7

FOURTEEN DAYS 2
Admin Plan: s18p7; s18p7

FRACTION 10
24 CFR 5: .520 (7);
24 CFR 982: .503;
PIH Notices: 02-20; 00-46

FRAIL ELDERLY 1
PIH Notices: 00-41

FRAUD 120
24 CFR 5: .210; .236; .615;
24 CFR 982: .163 (2); .306; .316; .453 (2); .551 (2); .552;
HUD-50058: p i;
HUD-50058Instr: p1; p28; p75;
HUD-52641: p5 (2); p6;
HUD-52646: p2;
7420.10G Gbk: 1-15; 5-14 Ex 5-2; 5-21 (3); 5-36 Ex 5-4; 5-37; 8-8; 8-19; 11-3; 11-10; 11-18 (2); 12-9; 15-4; 15-5; 20-25 (7); 20-26 (2); 22-1 (8); 22-2 (2); 22-3 (4); 22-6; 22-8; 22-10; 22-14 (3); 22-16 (3); 22-17 (5); 22-18 (3);
PIH Notices: 01-41; 01-15; 01-15 Impr Integ Hbk (2); 01-06; 00-28; 00-11 (4); 00-11A (4);
Admin Plan: s2p3; s2p6; s6p12; s6p13; s7p3; s11p2; s15p2; s15p5; s16p1; s16p2 (2); s17p1; s17p2 (4); s18p8 (2); s20p1 (3); s20p2 (5); s20p3; s20p4; s20p5; s20p8

FRAUDULENT 5
7420.10G Gbk: 19-1; 22-11; 22-16; 22-17; 23-15

FRAUDULENT ACTIVITIES 1
7420.10G Gbk: 22-17

FRAUDULENT ACTIVITY 2
7420.10G Gbk: 22-11; 22-16

FRAUDULENTLY 1
7420.10G Gbk: 23-13

FREE 122
24 CFR 5: .703 (8);
24 CFR 982: .158; .401 (6); .614; .621;
HUD-52517: p2 (4); p3 (3); p4 (2); p5;
HUD-52580-A: p2; p3 (6); p5 (6); p7 (6); p9 (6); p10 (6); p11 (6); p12 (6); p13 (2); p14 (8); p16 (3); p17; p18 (6);
HUD-52641: p5;
HUD-52667: p ii;
7420.10G Gbk: 7-3; 8-15; 10-4 (2); 10-5; 10-8; 10-9; 10-10 (2); 10-11 (4); 10-13 (3); 10-20; 10-37 Ex 10-2; 11-13; 13-6; 17-5; 17-10; 17-11; 21-7;

PIH Notices: 01-27; 01-15; 01-15 Impr Integ Hbk; 00-53 (2);
Admin Plan: s19p1

FREED 2
7420.10G Gbk: 5-32; 5-33

FREELY 7
24 CFR 982: .352; .628;
7420.10G Gbk: 8-17;
PIH Notices: 01-27 (3); 01-27

FREEZE 3
24 CFR 982: .156 (2);
PIH Notices: 96-65

FRIDAY 6
HUD-50058Instr: p3;
7420.10G Gbk: 10-40 Ex 10-4a; 10-41 Ex 10-4b; 10-42 Ex 10-5; 10-46 Ex 10-8

FRIEND 9
7420.10G Gbk: 24-5;
PIH Notices: 02-01; 01-15 Impr Integ Hbk; 99-52; 95-48 (2); 95-48 Tech Asst (2);
Admin Plan: s1p3

FRIENDS 8
7420.10G Gbk: 4-3; 4-27 Ex 4-2;
PIH Notices: 02-01; 99-52; 95-48 (2); 95-48 Tech Asst; 95-48 Tech Asst

FROZEN 2
7420.10G Gbk: 20-10; 24-2

FSS 473
24 CFR 982: .4; .152; .552 (2);
HUD-50058: p i; p2 (2); p16 (5); p xvi (5); p17 (12); p xvii (14);
HUD-50058Instr: p ii (2); p2 (8); p3; p9 (4); p10 (2); p11 (4); p13 (11); p59 (23); p60; p61 (9); p62 (22); p64; p65 (13); p66 (9); p71 (6); p72 (11); p73 (4); p75 (5); p77 (2);
HUD-52648: p2 (5); p3 (8);
7420.10G Gbk: 1-9; 1-10; 1-11; 1-13; 3-8 (3); 15-6; 19-2; 19-4; 21-16 Ex 21-6 (2); 21-19; 21-20; 23-1 (11); 23-2 (9); 23-3 (10); 23-4 (11); 23-5 (17); 23-6 (13); 23-7 (5); 23-8 Ex 23-1 (2); 23-9 (4); 23-10 (14); 23-11 (4); 23-12 (3); 23-13 (7); 23-14 (5); 23-15 (3); 23-16 Ex 23-2 (2); 23-17 Ex 23-2 (17); 23-18 (17); 23-19 (25); 23-20 (4);
PIH Notices: 02-27 (8); 02-01 (2); 01-06 (30); 00-24A (2); 00-24B (2); 00-11; 00-11A; 99-52 (2);
Admin Plan: s18p4; s21p1; s21p2; s21p9 (10); s22p2; s25p3; s25p4 (15); s25p5 (2); s25p6; s25p6

FSS CONTRACT OF PARTICIPATION 37
24 CFR 982: .552;
HUD-50058: p xvii (4);
HUD-50058Instr: p59; p61 (3); p62; p65 (4); p66 (7); p71;
7420.10G Gbk: 23-1; 23-6; 23-9; 23-17 Ex 23-2 (11); 23-20

FUEL GAS 3
24 CFR 982: .401;
HUD-52580-A: p18;
7420.10G Gbk: 10-10

FUGITIVE 2
24 CFR 982: .310;
PIH Notices: 03-11

FUGITIVE FELON 1
24 CFR 982: .310

FUGITIVE FELONS 1
PIH Notices: 03-11

FULL AMOUNT 34
24 CFR 5: .609 (3);
24 CFR 982: .102; .313; .355; .642;
HUD-50058Instr: p26 (2); p31;
HUD-52641: p10;
HUD-52641-A: p3;
7420.10G Gbk: 5-14 Ex 5-2 (2); 5-15 Ex 5-2; 6-6; 8-4; 13-9; 15-10 Ex 15-2; 20-22; 22-13; 22-15; 23-10; 23-12;
PIH Notices: 01-15 Impr Integ Hbk (6); 96-65 (2);
Admin Plan: s6p9; s10p5

FULL APPLICATION 15
7420.10G Gbk: 4-13 (2); 4-14 (2); 4-15 (6); 4-16; 4-25 Ex 4-2;
Admin Plan: s3p2; s3p3; s23p3

FULL TIME EMPLOYMENT 1
Admin Plan: s22p1

FULL TIME STUDENT 2
HUD-50058Instr: p36;
Admin Plan: s7p5

FULL TIME STUDENTS 2

Admin Plan: s7p5; s7p5

FULL UTILIZATION........................6
7420.10G Gbk: 4-9; 20-20;
PIH Notices: 03-23 (2); 02-06;
Admin Plan: s3p2

FULL-TIME EMPLOYMENT..........3
7420.10G Gbk: 5-17; 23-8 Ex 23-1; 23-8 Ex 23-1

FULL-TIME STUDENT 25
24 CFR 5: .603 (2); .609;
HUD-50058: p3; p4; p7;
HUD-50058Instr: p14 (2); p15; p25 (2); p26; p27; p36; p71; p72;
7420.10G Gbk: 5-15 Ex 5-2; 5-18 (2); 5-29 (2); 5-53 Ex 5-5;
PIH Notices: 01-15 Impr Integ Hbk (2);
Admin Plan: s7p5

FULL-TIME STUDENT STATUS....7
7420.10G Gbk: 5-53 Ex 5-5; 12-13 Ex 12-1; 22-3;
Admin Plan: s3p3; s6p6; s7p3; s7p5

FULL-TIME STUDENTS.................7
HUD-50058: p vii;
HUD-50058Instr: p36;
7420.10G Gbk: 5-18 (2);
PIH Notices: 01-15 Impr Integ Hbk (2);
Admin Plan: s6p1

FUMES 1
Admin Plan: s10p4

FUMIGATION.................................1
24 CFR 5: .318

FUND..67
24 CFR 5: .603 (4);
HUD-50058Instr: p32 (2);
7420.10G Gbk: 1-7; 5-16 Ex 5-2 (2); 5-26 (2); 9-4; 20-30;
PIH Notices: 03-23 (22); 02-21 (6); 02-06; 02-01 (4); 01-41; 01-20 (4); 01-15 Impr Integ Hbk (3); 00-27 (6); 00-09; 99-52 (4); 95-48; 95-48 Tech Asst

FUNDAMENTAL...............................
23
7420.10G Gbk: 1-4; 5-44;
PIH Notices: 02-01 (4); 99-52 (4); 95-48 (6); 95-48 Tech Asst (6);
Admin Plan: s1p5

FUNDAMENTAL ALTERATION ..20
7420.10G Gbk: 5-44;
PIH Notices: 02-01 (4); 99-52 (4); 95-48 (5); 95-48 Tech Asst (5);
Admin Plan: s1p5

FUNDAMENTALLY.........................2
PIH Notices: 95-48; 95-48 Tech Asst

FUNDAMENTALLY ALTER 2
PIH Notices: 95-48; 95-48 Tech Asst

FUNDED 85
24 CFR 5: .603; .609; .617;
HUD-50058Instr: p1; p17 (2); p27 (2); p28; p32 (2); p76;
HUD-52648: p2 (2);
7420.10G Gbk: 5-15 Ex 5-2; 5-16 Ex 5-2 (3); 5-20; 17-1; 20-17; 20-19 Ex 20-3 (2); 23-4; 23-20 (3);
PIH Notices: 03-23 (3); 02-21 (5); 02-14; 02-01 (8); 01-20 (4); 01-15; 01-15 Impr Integ Hbk (6); 01-06 (6); 00-27 (5); 00-11A (2); 99-52 (8); 95-48 (4); 95-48 Tech Asst (2);
Admin Plan: s1p1; s25p4; s25p6

FUNDING.....................................552
24 CFR 5: .100; .105; .403;
24 CFR 35 SubM: .1200;
24 CFR 982: 24 CFR 982 (5); .4 (9); .52; .54 (3); .101 (10); .102 (23); .103 (3); .104 (7); .151 (7); .152; .155; .203 (2); .204 (2); .206; .309; .314; .355 (4); .454 (2); .601 (4); .637 (2);
HUD-50058: p xii;
HUD-50058Instr: p13 (2); p50 (4); p70; p72; p76 (2);
HUD-52648: p2;
7420.10G Gbk: 1-1; 1-5 (7); 1-6 (3); 1-7 (6); 1-8 (9); 1-12 Ex 1-2 (3); 1-12 (2); 2-7; 3-2 (3); 4-2; 7-6; 8-22; 17-1; 19-1; 19-6; 20-2 (2); 20-3; 20-6 (2); 20-7 (5); 20-8; 20-8 Ex 20-1 (2); 20-9 (5); 20-11 (2); 20-12 Ex 20-2 (3); 20-13 (6); 20-14 (2); 20-15; 20-16 (6); 20-18 (6); 20-19 Ex 20-3 (4); 20-20 (3); 20-21 Ex 20-4 (2); 20-21 (2); 20-26; 20-27; 21-8 (2); 21-9; 23-1; 23-2 (4); 23-

3 (2); 23-19 (3); 23-20 (4); 24-1 (4); 24-2 (2); 24-7; 24-11;
PIH Notices: 03-23 (48); 02-27 (4); 02-21 (34); 02-20 (2); 02-14 (3); 02-07 (4); 02-06 (16); 02-01 (7); 01-41 (37); 01-20 (38); 01-10 (6); 01-06 (4); 00-53; 00-49; 00-46 (2); 00-28 (2); 00-27 (27); 00-11; 00-09 (39); 99-52 (7); 95-48 (7); 95-48 Tech Asst (7);
Admin Plan: s4p1 (2); s4p2 (4); s8p1; s13p2; s14p2; s19p1; s21p9; s23p2 (2); s23p3; s24p1 (4); s24p3; s24p5; s25p1 (3); s25p2; s25p4; s25p6; s25p8

FUNDING DECISIONS....................1
7420.10G Gbk: 19-1

FUNDING INCREMENT...............13
7420.10G Gbk: 13-9; 20-5; 20-7 (2); 20-8; 20-9 (4); 20-12 Ex 20-2 (2); 20-13; 24-2

FUNDING INCREMENT...............51
24 CFR 982: .4 (3); .102 (6); .151 (5); .152; .155; .309;
HUD-50058: p xii;
HUD-50058Instr: p50 (2);
7420.10G Gbk: 13-9; 20-5; 20-7 (2); 20-8; 20-9 (4); 20-12 Ex 20-2 (2); 20-13; 24-2;
PIH Notices: 03-23 (2); 02-21 (4); 02-07 (2); 01-41 (2); 01-20 (2); 00-28 (2); 00-27; 00-09 (2); 00-09

FUNDING INCREMENTS.............18
7420.10G Gbk: 20-6 (2); 20-7 (11); 20-9 (4); 20-9

FUNDING INCREMENTS.............37
24 CFR 982: Intro; .101; .102 (8); .151;
7420.10G Gbk: 20-6 (2); 20-7 (10); 20-9 (5);
PIH Notices: 03-23; 02-21 (5); 01-41; 01-06;
Admin Plan: s24p1

FUNDS...290
24 CFR 5: .100; .306; .609;
24 CFR 35 SubM: .1200 (3);
24 CFR 982: Intro; .1 (2); .4; .54; .102 (3); .155 (6); .156 (3); .204 (2); .355 (6); .515; .619;
HUD-50058: p xvii;
HUD-50058Instr: p7 (2); p22; p30 (5); p62 (2); p70; p71; p75;
HUD-52641: p10;
HUD-52641-A: p3;
HUD-9886: p2 (2);
7420.10G Gbk: 1-5 (2); 1-12 Ex 1-2; 1-13; 2-11; 3-6; 3-7 (2); 4-4; 4-6; 4-18 (2); 5-14 Ex 5-2; 5-16 Ex 5-2 (3); 5-25 Ex 5-3 (3); 5-26 (2); 5-44; 7-10; 8-10 (3); 8-11 (2); 8-14; 9-1; 10-19 (2); 12-13 Ex 12-1; 13-6 (3); 15-4; 17-10; 20-1; 20-2 (2); 20-5; 20-6; 20-13; 20-14 (2); 20-15 (2); 20-16 (2); 20-18; 20-19 Ex 20-3; 20-25; 20-26 (4); 20-27; 20-28 (2); 21-16 Ex 21-6; 23-1; 23-2; 23-13 (4); 23-14 (3); 23-15 (8); 23-18 (2); 24-1 (5); 24-2 (4); 24-8; 24-9 (8); 24-15;
PIH Notices: 03-23 (29); 02-27 (3); 02-21 (3); 02-07 (2); 02-06 (10); 02-01 (11); 01-41; 01-20 (5); 01-15 Impr Integ Hbk (7); 01-10 (3); 01-02 (3); 00-28 (2); 00-27 (3); 00-24B (2); 00-11 (10); 00-09 (5); 99-52 (11); 95-48 (3); 95-48 Tech Asst (3);
Admin Plan: s4p1; s6p10 (3); s8p1; s9p1; s11p2 (2); s17p2; s19p1; s22p2; s22p3; s25p5 (8); s25p6 (3); s25p6

FUP..11
HUD-50058Instr: p13; p72;
7420.10G Gbk: 1-7 (2); 21-16 Ex 21-6;
Admin Plan: s25p1 (5); s25p2

FURNITURE.................................22
24 CFR 5: .603;
24 CFR 982: .623 (3);
HUD-50058: p13; p xiii (2);
HUD-50058Instr: p22; p53 (6); p74;
HUD-52580-A: p17;
HUD-52641: 8 (2);
HUD-52641-A: p1 (2);
PIH Notices: 95-48; 95-48 Tech Asst

FYE..32
PIH Notices: 03-23 (8); 02-

27 (9); 01-06 (13); 00-24A; 00-24A

G-845S 6
24 CFR 5: .512 (2); .514;
7420.10G Gbk: 5-7; 5-9 Ex 5-1; 5-11

GAAP 3
7420.10G Gbk: 20-29 (2); 20-29

GAAP-BASED 1
7420.10G Gbk: 20-29

GALLON 1
7420.10G Gbk: 18-9

GARAGE 9
24 CFR 5: .703;
HUD-52580: p6;
HUD-52580-A: p8; p17; p19;
7420.10G Gbk: 9-14 Ex 9-1; 9-16 Ex 9-2; 9-17 Ex 9-3;
Admin Plan: s9p3

GARAGES 10
HUD-52580-A: p13;
7420.10G Gbk: 10-16; 10-17;
PIH Notices: 00-23; 95-48 (3); 95-48 Tech Asst (2); 95-48 Tech Asst

GARBAGE 18
24 CFR 5: .703 (2);
24 CFR 982: .401 (2);
HUD-52580: p5; p6;
HUD-52580-A: p17 (3); p18 (2); p19;
7420.10G Gbk: 9-13 Ex 9-1; 9-14 Ex 9-1; 9-15 Ex 9-2 (2); 9-17 Ex 9-3; 10-13

GARBAGE CANS 2
24 CFR 982: .401; .401

GARDEN 18
HUD-52517: p1 (2);
HUD-52667: p i;
7420.10G Gbk: 9-9; 9-10 (8); 9-13 Ex 9-1; 9-15 Ex 9-2; 18-2; 24-11 (2);
PIH Notices: 99-52

GAS 55
24 CFR 5: .703 (2);
24 CFR 982: .401 (3);
HUD-52580-A: p4 (5); p15 (4); p18 (2);
HUD-52667: p1 (6); p i (5); p ii (3);
7420.10G Gbk: 6-9 Ex 6-1; 9-14 Ex 9-1; 9-15 Ex 9-2; 10-5 (3); 10-7 (3); 10-10 (3); 10-11; 18-4; 18-5; 18-6 (4); 18-7 (2);
PIH Notices: 01-15; 01-15 Impr Integ Hbk;
Admin Plan: s10p4; s25p6

GED 5
HUD-50058: p16;
HUD-50058Instr: p60 (3);
7420.10G Gbk: 23-8 Ex 23-1

GEMS 1
7420.10G Gbk: 5-25 Ex 5-3

GENDER 8
24 CFR 5: .655;
24 CFR 982: .158; .207;
HUD-50058: p iii; p iv;
HUD-50058Instr: p14;
PIH Notices: 95-48; 95-48 Tech Asst

GENERAL ASSISTANCE 4
HUD-50058: p6; p16;
HUD-50058Instr: p76;
Admin Plan: s7p4

GENERAL ASSISTANCE PAYMENTS 1
HUD-50058Instr: p28

GENERAL CIRCULATION 5
24 CFR 982: .206;
7420.10G Gbk: 4-1;
Admin Plan: s1p6; s4p2; s24p2

GENERAL COUNSEL 2
24 CFR 5: .100; .100

GENERAL FUND 5
7420.10G Gbk: 20-23; 20-26 (3); 20-26

GENERAL FUNDAMENTAL ALTERATION 2
PIH Notices: 95-48; 95-48 Tech Asst

GENERAL FUNDS 2
7420.10G Gbk: 20-26; 20-27

GENERAL LEDGER 7
7420.10G Gbk: 20-20; 20-23 (5); 20-23

GENERALIST 6
7420.10G Gbk: 21-2 (4); 21-3; 21-3

GENERALISTS 1
7420.10G Gbk: 21-2

GENERALLY ACCEPTED 9
24 CFR 5: .801;
24 CFR 982: .207; .451; .625;
HUD-52641: p4;
7420.10G Gbk: 4-16; 11-6; 20-29;
PIH Notices: 01-06

GENERALLY ACCEPTED ACCOUNTING PRINCIPLES 2
24 CFR 5: .801;
7420.10G Gbk: 20-29

GEOGRAPHIC 43

24 CFR 5: .655;
24 CFR 982: .101; .152; .201; .207; .401; .503;
HUD-52648: p4;
HUD-52667: p ii (3);
7420.10G Gbk: 4-12; 4-17; 4-20; 9-10 (4); 10-2; 20-5 (2); 21-5 (3); 21-6 (4);
PIH Notices: 02-22; 02-20 (2); 02-07 (3); 01-06 (3); 00-46 (2); 00-28 (3);
Admin Plan: s13p1

GEOGRAPHIC AREA 20
24 CFR 5: .655;
24 CFR 982: .152; .201; .207;
HUD-52667: p ii (2);
7420.10G Gbk: 4-12; 4-17; 4-20; 9-10 (2); 20-5 (2); 21-5; 21-6;
PIH Notices: 02-22; 02-20; 02-07; 00-46; 00-28

GEOGRAPHIC AREAS 2
HUD-52667: p ii;
7420.10G Gbk: 21-6

GEOGRAPHICAL 2
7420.10G Gbk: 8-9; 24-11

GEOGRAPHICALLY 1
7420.10G Gbk: 9-7

GEOGRAPHY 2
PIH Notices: 02-20; 00-46

GERMANY 1
PIH Notices: 01-15 Impr Integ Hbk

GIFT 3
7420.10G Gbk: 24-14; 24-15;
Admin Plan: s6p9

GIFTS 25
24 CFR 5: .609 (2);
HUD-50058Instr: p31;
7420.10G Gbk: 5-14 Ex 5-2; 5-15 Ex 5-2; 5-18 (2); 5-19 (2); 5-47 Ex 5-5 (4);
PIH Notices: 01-15 Impr Integ Hbk (5);
Admin Plan: s6p8; s6p9 (2); s7p5 (3); s7p5

GLASS 4
HUD-52580: p6;
HUD-52580-A: p19;
7420.10G Gbk: 10-4;
Admin Plan: s10p4

GOAL 31
24 CFR 5: .653;
7420.10G Gbk: 2-1; 4-2; 4-5; 5-20; 8-14; 10-1; 11-9; 23-6; 23-7; 23-8 Ex 23-1 (5); 24-2; 24-6 (2);
PIH Notices: 03-20; 02-27; 01-15 Impr Integ Hbk; 95-48 (3); 95-48 Tech Asst (3);
Admin Plan: s21p1; s25p5 (2); s25p6

GOALS 51
24 CFR 5: .609;
24 CFR 982: .102; .353;
7420.10G Gbk: 1-13; 3-6; 3-7; 4-4; 4-12; 5-15 Ex 5-2; 5-20; 8-23; 12-8; 19-2; 19-6 (3); 19-7; 21-2; 21-7; 22-7; 23-1 (5); 23-6; 23-7; 23-9 (3); 23-15; 23-20;
PIH Notices: 01-15 Impr Integ Hbk (3); 00-11; 00-11A (2); 95-48; 95-48 Tech Asst;
Admin Plan: s1p1 (2); s1p2; s8p1; s21p1; s22p2; s25p4; s25p5 (2); s25p6; s25p7

GOOD CAUSE 40
24 CFR 5: .110;
24 CFR 982: .161; .206; .310 (2); .552;
HUD-52641: p6; p9 (5);
HUD-52641-A: p2 (5);
7420.10G Gbk: 8-19; 11-2; 15-1; 15-2 (3); 15-3 (2); 15-6; 16-3; 23-7 (2); 23-10; 23-18;
PIH Notices: 01-41; 95-48; 95-48 Tech Asst;
Admin Plan: s14p1; s18p5 (2); s18p7; s23p6; s23p6

GOOD FAITH 15
24 CFR 5: .518;
HUD-50058Instr: p47;
7420.10G Gbk: 5-22;
PIH Notices: 02-01; 01-41 (3); 00-53; 00-09 (4); 99-52; 95-48; 95-48 Tech Asst

GOOD FAITH EFFORT 7
24 CFR 5: .518;
HUD-50058Instr: p47;
PIH Notices: 01-41 (2); 00-53; 00-09; 00-09

GOOD FAITH EFFORTS 5
7420.10G Gbk: 5-22;
PIH Notices: 02-01; 99-52; 95-48; 95-48 Tech Asst

GOOD REPAIR 11
24 CFR 5: .703 (10); .703

GOOD STANDING 2
7420.10G Gbk: 8-15; 11-4

GOOD-FAITH 1
7420.10G Gbk: 23-9

GOVERN 11

24 CFR 5: .236; .315; .350; .353;
24 CFR 982: .207;
7420.10G Gbk: 3-1; 3-7;
PIH Notices: 01-15 Impr Integ Hbk; 95-48; 95-48 Tech Asst;
Admin Plan: s6p11

GOVERNED....................................1
7420.10G Gbk: 13-7

GOVERNING.................................57
24 CFR 5: .218 (3); .232; .236; .315 (3); .321; .353; .380; .609; .617; .705;
24 CFR 982: .54; .158; .161; .308 (2); .451; .521;
HUD-50058Instr: p25; p71;
HUD-52641: p4; p10 (2);
HUD-52641-A: p3 (2);
7420.10G Gbk: 1-15; 3-2; 3-7; 5-15 Ex 5-2; 8-4; 11-6; 11-17 (2); 12-8; 20-10; 22-7;
PIH Notices: 02-14; 01-15 Impr Integ Hbk (6); 00-24B; 00-09; 95-48; 95-48 Tech Asst;
Admin Plan: s1p2; s8p4; s23p8; s25p4 (3); s25p6

GOVERNING BOARD..................10
24 CFR 5: .609;
HUD-50058Instr: p25;
7420.10G Gbk: 5-15 Ex 5-2; 20-10;
PIH Notices: 01-15 Impr Integ Hbk (5); 01-15 Impr Integ Hbk

GOVERNING BODY........................9
24 CFR 982: .161;
HUD-52641: p6;
7420.10G Gbk: 3-1; 3-2; 8-19; 11-2; 11-3; 24-11;
Admin Plan: s25p4

GOVERNMENT...........................130
24 CFR 5: 24 CFR 5; .214; .518; .526 (4); .603 .609 (3); .661;
24 CFR 982: .306; .352 (3); .625;
HUD-50058Instr: p5; p15; p25 (3); p28 (2); p31 (2); p73; p74;
HUD-52641: p6;
HUD-903: p2;
HUD-9886: p1;
7420.10G Gbk: 1-2 (2); 2-6; 4-16; 5-12; 5-15 Ex 5-2 (3); 8-18; 9-1; 9-11 (2); 10-31 (3); 11-1; 11-8 (2); 11-9; 20-10; 21-1 (2); 21-12 Ex 21-2; 21-12 Ex 21-3; 23-3 (5); 23-4 (2); 24-15;
PIH Notices: 03-11; 02-27 (9); 02-01; 01-27; 01-15; 01-15 Impr Integ Hbk (11); 01-06; 01-02; 00-11; 99-52; 95-48 (19); 95-48 Tech Asst (17);
Admin Plan: s7p7; s7p8; s18p6; s25p7

GOVERNMENTAL.........................15
24 CFR 5: .100; .403;
24 CFR 982: .1; .4 (2); .520;
HUD-50058Instr: p72; p74 (2);
7420.10G Gbk: 5-2; 5-50 Ex 5-5; 24-9;
PIH Notices: 01-15; 00-11; 00-11A

GOVERNMENTAL ACTION...........2
24 CFR 5: .403;
7420.10G Gbk: 5-2

GOVERNMENTS 33
24 CFR 5: .107; .603; .661;
24 CFR 982: .201;
HUD-50058Instr: p74; p76;
7420.10G Gbk: 1-3; 9-3; 9-4;
PIH Notices: 02-01; 01-27; 01-15 (2); 01-02; 99-52; 95-48 (12); 95-48 Tech Asst (5); 95-48 Tech Asst

GOVERNMENT'S............................4
HUD-50058: p i;
HUD-9886: p2;
7420.10G Gbk: 1-3;
Admin Plan: s23p1

GOVERNMENTWIDE.....................2
PIH Notices: 95-48; 95-48 Tech Asst

GOVERNS...3
24 CFR 5: .210;
7420.10G Gbk: 11-15;
Admin Plan: s1p2

GR...1
24 CFR 5: .703

GRAB BARS....................................2
PIH Notices: 02-01; 99-52

GRADUATE.....................................3
HUD-50058Instr: p60;
7420.10G Gbk: 23-2; 23-15

GRADUATED..................................1
7420.10G Gbk: 23-1

GRADUATES...................................5
24 CFR 5: .655;
24 CFR 982: .207;
7420.10G Gbk: 4-17; 23-2; 24-

9

GRAND RIVER BAND....................3
HUD-50058Instr: p30;
7420.10G Gbk: 5-16 Ex 5-2;
PIH Notices: 01-15 Impr Integ Hbk

GRANDCHILD..............................10
24 CFR 982: .306;
HUD-52517: p2;
HUD-52641: p5; p6 (2);
HUD-52646: p2;
7420.10G Gbk: 8-15; 8-19; 11-2;
Admin Plan: s16p2

GRANDPARENT............................10
24 CFR 982: .306;
HUD-52517: p2;
HUD-52641: p5; p6 (2);
HUD-52646: p2;
7420.10G Gbk: 8-15; 8-19; 11-2;
Admin Plan: s16p2

GRANT.......................................114
24 CFR 5: .100; .303; .500; .508 (2); .518; .609; .630; .653 (2);
24 CFR 35 SubM: .1200 (2);
24 CFR 982: .4 (5); .54; .158; .201; .303 (3); .402; .403; .503; .554; .625 (3); .627 (2); .631 (3); .633; .635; .643 (10);
HUD-50058Instr: p19; p30; p37;
HUD-52641: p5;
HUD-52646: p2;
7420.10G Gbk: 1-16 Ex 1-3; 5-14 Ex 5-2; 5-16 Ex 5-2; 5-20; 5-21 (4); 5-22 (2); 5-41; 6-8; 8-12 (3); 10-2; 10-34 (2); 11-13; 16-2; 20-15; 21-9; 23-3; 23-7; 23-8 Ex 23-1; 23-16 Ex 23-2 (2); 24-9 (2); 24-15 (2);
PIH Notices: 03-11; 02-21 (2); 02-06; 02-01 (6); 01-20; 01-15; 01-15 Impr Integ Hbk (4); 01-02; 00-27; 99-52 (5); 95-48; 95-48 Tech Asst;
Admin Plan: s6p5; s7p4; s7p8; s18p2; s25p6; s25p6

GRANTS.......................................29
24 CFR 35 SubM: .1200 (3);
24 CFR 982: .201; .625; .643 (2);
HUD-50058Instr: p19; p75;
HUD-52646: p2;
7420.10G Gbk: 2-11; 5-20; 8-11; 8-12; 10-21; 21-14 Ex 21-4; 24-9; 24-15;
PIH Notices: 02-01 (2); 01-20; 00-28; 00-24A; 99-52 (2); 95-48; 95-48 Tech Asst;
Admin Plan: s4p2; s7p5

GRIEVANCE..................................20
24 CFR 5: .615 (2); .630 (3);
HUD-9886: p1;
PIH Notices: 95-48 (7); 95-48 Tech Asst (6); 95-48 Tech Asst

GRIEVANCE PROCEDURE............7
24 CFR 5: .630;
PIH Notices: 95-48 (3); 95-48 Tech Asst (2); 95-48 Tech Asst

GRIEVANCE PROCEDURES..........8
HUD-9886: p1;
7420.10G Gbk: 23-10;
PIH Notices: 95-48 (3); 95-48 Tech Asst (2); 95-48 Tech Asst

GRIEVANCES.................................6
24 CFR 982: .554; .555;
7420.10G Gbk: 16-2 (2);
Admin Plan: s18p2; s18p4

GRIEVE...1
7420.10G Gbk: 23-10

GROCERIES...................................1
7420.10G Gbk: 5-19

GROCERY......................................2
7420.10G Gbk: 2-13 Ex 2-1; 9-6

GROCERY STORES.......................1
7420.10G Gbk: 9-6

GROSS FAMILY.............................6
24 CFR 982: .627;
HUD-50058: p15; p xv;
HUD-50058Instr: p58 (2); p58

GROSS PAY....................................2
7420.10G Gbk: 5-46 Ex 5-5;
Admin Plan: s7p4

GROSS RENT...............................281
24 CFR 5: .520 (2);
24 CFR 982: .4; .305; .403; .503 (4); .505; .508; .515; .518; .619;
HUD-50058: p10 (2); p x (4); p11 (2); p xi (5); p12; p xii (2); p13 (2); p xiii (5);
HUD-50058Instr: p42; p43 (2); p44 (3); p46; p47 (5); p48 (5); p51 (3); p52 (2); p54 (4); p55 (2); p72;
HUD-52646: p1 (2);
HUD-52667: p i;
7420.10G Gbk: 1-3; 1-6 Ex 1-

1 (6); 5-5 (4); 6-2 (3); 6-3 (2); 6-4 (12); 6-5 (11); 6-6 (2); 6-7 (5); 6-9 Ex 6-1; 6-10 Ex 6-2 (3); 7-1; 7-5 (2); 7-6; 7-8 (5); 8-6 (3); 8-16 (3); 9-14 Ex 9-1; 9-15 Ex 9-2; 9-17 Ex 9-3; 9-19 Ex 9-4; 11-6; 12-10; 12-11; 14-4; 17-3; 17-4; 17-6 (3); 17-7; 17-8; 17-9 (4); 17-11; 18-1; 18-9; 18-10; 20-2 (2);
PIH Notices: 02-22 (3); 02-20 (13); 01-41 (27); 01-10 (25); 00-46 (13); 00-41; 00-24B (4); 00-09 (31);
Admin Plan: s5p3; s19p1; s21p4; s23p3; s23p7

GROSS RENT INCREASE............... 1
PIH Notices: 01-10

GROSS RENTS............................... 12
HUD-52667: p i;
7420.10G Gbk: 6-3; 7-3; 9-4; 9-10; 18-7; 24-11;
PIH Notices: 01-10; 01-01;
Admin Plan: s21p6 (2); s21p7

GROUND 36
24 CFR 982: .605; .621;
HUD-52580-A: p2; p13 (3); p17 (2);
7420.10G Gbk: 10-6 (3); 10-10; 17-2; 17-11; 17-12;
PIH Notices: 02-01 (6); 00-45 (2); 00-23 (2); 99-52 (4); 95-48 (3); 95-48 Tech Asst (3);
Admin Plan: s19p1

GROUND FLOOR 18
PIH Notices: 02-01 (6); 00-45 (2); 99-52 (4); 95-48 (3); 95-48 Tech Asst (2); 95-48 Tech Asst

GROUND LEVEL............................. 2
24 CFR 982: .605;
7420.10G Gbk: 17-2

GROUNDING 1
7420.10G Gbk: 10-8

GROUNDS..................................... 78
24 CFR 5: .100; .318; .321; .360; .653; .703;
24 CFR 982: .4; .201; .206; .301; .310 (8); .314; .352; .510; .552 (4); .630; .638;
HUD-50058Instr: p2;
HUD-52580: p6;
HUD-52580-A: p19;
HUD-52641: p3; p9 (3); p10;
HUD-52641-A: p2 (3); p3;
7420.10G Gbk: 5-35; 8-6; 8-13; 8-17; 9-14 Ex 9-1; 12-1; 12-16 Ex 12-4; 15-2; 15-8;
PIH Notices: 01-41 (3); 01-33; 01-02; 00-41; 00-09; 95-48 (5); 95-48 Tech Asst (5);
Admin Plan: s2p5; s14p1 (2); s14p2; s15p1 (2); s15p2; s15p3; s15p4; s16p2; s23p6; s24p2; s24p6

GROUNDS FOR DENIAL................ 6
24 CFR 982: .314; .552; .638;
Admin Plan: s2p5; s15p2; s15p3

GROUNDS FOR DENIAL OF ASSISTANCE.................................... 1
7420.10G Gbk: 5-35

GROUNDS FOR DENIAL OF ELIGIBILITY................................... 1
HUD-50058Instr: p2

GROUNDS FOR TERMINATION ... 8
7420.10G Gbk: 4-27 Ex 4-2; 8-8; 12-16 Ex 12-4; 23-9;
PIH Notices: 00-41;
Admin Plan: s14p2; s15p1; s15p4

GROUNDS FOR TERMINATION OF TENANCY....................................... 10
24 CFR 982: .310 (2); .510;
HUD-52641: 8; p9;
HUD-52641-A: p1; p2;
7420.10G Gbk: 15-2;
Admin Plan: s14p1; s16p2

GROUP HOME 109
24 CFR 5: .318;
24 CFR 982: 24 CFR 982 (8); .4 (3); .601 (2); .609; .610 (7); .611 (2); .612 (4); .613 (10); .614 (8);
HUD-50058: p10; p11;
HUD-50058Instr: p42 (2); p43 (3); p44 (3); p46 (2); p47 (7); p72 (2);
HUD-52641: p1;
7420.10G Gbk: 17-4 (7); 17-5 (4); 17-6 (10); 17-7 (4);
Admin Plan: s19p1 (15); s19p1

GROUP HOMES 18
24 CFR 5: .318; .703;
7420.10G Gbk: 3-5; 11-10; 17-4 (4); 17-5 (4); 17-7;
PIH Notices: 00-41;
Admin Plan: s9p2; s19p1 (2); s19p1

GROUP RESIDENCE 2

HUD-52580: p1;
HUD-52580-A: p1

GROUP RESIDENCES....................1
7420.10G Gbk: 10-1

GUAM..8
24 CFR 5: .506;
HUD-50058Instr: p64;
PIH Notices: 01-27 (5); 01-27

GUARANTEE................................7
7420.10G Gbk: 5-40; 8-8; 10-34;
PIH Notices: 01-41; 00-09; 95-48; 95-48 Tech Asst

GUARANTEED..............................2
24 CFR 982: .625;
7420.10G Gbk: 24-9

GUEST...25
24 CFR 5: .100 (4);
24 CFR 982: .4; .306; .310 (2); .404; .619;
HUD-52641: p6; p9 (2);
HUD-52641-A: p2 (3);
7420.10G Gbk: 2-5; 8-19; 11-3; 15-2;
Admin Plan: s10p5; s15p3 (3); s16p2

GUIDANCE................................114
24 CFR 5: .508; .801;
24 CFR 982: .628;
HUD-50058Instr: p13; p24; p33 (2); p38;
7420.10G Gbk: 1-13; 1-15; 5-1; 5-26; 9-11; 10-1; 10-2; 10-3; 10-12; 10-32; 12-9; 20-1; 21-1 (3); 21-3; 22-8;
PIH Notices: 03-12 (3); 03-11; 03-05; 02-27 (5); 02-21; 02-06; 02-01 (2); 01-41 (10); 01-40; 01-27 (4); 01-20; 01-15; 01-15 Impr Integ Hbk; 01-06 (9); 01-01 (2); 00-53; 00-34 (2); 00-27; 00-24 (7); 00-24A (3); 00-11 (5); 00-09 (12); 99-52 (2); 95-48 (6); 95-48 Tech Asst (4);
Admin Plan: s8p1; s23p1; s24p1

GUIDE..22
HUD-50058Instr: p1 (2); p5 (2);
7420.10G Gbk: 1-1; 19-4; 20-23; 20-29 (2);
PIH Notices: 01-41; 01-11; 01-06 (4); 00-24; 00-09; 99-11 (3);
Admin Plan: s7p5; s17p1

GUIDEBOOK...............................22
HUD-50058Instr: p40; p68;
7420.10G Gbk: 1-1 (9); 1-15; 10-15; 10-30; 11-11 (2); 14-4;
PIH Notices: 01-41; 01-15 (3); 01-15 Impr Integ Hbk

GUIDELINE...................................3
Admin Plan: s6p11 (2); s6p11

GUIDELINES..............................45
24 CFR 982: .54;
7420.10G Gbk: 3-2 (2); 3-6 (2); 5-1; 5-2; 6-10 Ex 6-2; 10-32; 12-15 Ex 12-3;
PIH Notices: 03-23; 03-20; 02-21; 02-07; 02-01 (6); 99-52 (6); 95-48 (4); 95-48 Tech Asst (2);
Admin Plan: s1p2; s5p1 (2); s5p2 (4); s6p11; s10p1; s17p1; s17p2 (2); s23p6

GUIDES...3
7420.10G Gbk: 20-1;
PIH Notices: 95-48; 95-48 Tech Asst

HABITABLE..................................4
24 CFR 5: .703 (2);
24 CFR 982: .605;
7420.10G Gbk: 17-2

HABITS...3
24 CFR 5: .350;
24 CFR 982: .310;
Admin Plan: s10p5

HALFWAY HOUSES......................2
PIH Notices: 95-48; 95-48 Tech Asst

HALL...8
24 CFR 5: .609;
24 CFR 982: .605;
HUD-52580-A: p2; p8;
7420.10G Gbk: 5-15 Ex 5-2; 17-2;
PIH Notices: 01-15 Impr Integ Hbk; 01-15 Impr Integ Hbk

HALL MONITORING.....................4
24 CFR 5: .609;
7420.10G Gbk: 5-15 Ex 5-2;
PIH Notices: 01-15 Impr Integ Hbk; 01-15 Impr Integ Hbk

HALLS...28
24 CFR 5: .703;
24 CFR 982: .401; .614;
HUD-52580: p1 (2); p3; p4; p5;
HUD-52580-A: p8 (4); p9 (3); p10 (3); p11 (3); p12 (3); p17; p18 (2);
7420.10G Gbk: 10-9

HALLWAY..9
HUD-52580-A: p6; p15;
PIH Notices: 99-11; 95-48 (3); 95-48 Tech Asst (2); 95-48 Tech Asst

HALLWAYS.....................................6
24 CFR 982: .605;
7420.10G Gbk: 10-6; 10-17; 17-2;
PIH Notices: 95-48; 95-48 Tech Asst

HAND RAILS..................................1
24 CFR 5: .703

HANDICAP....................................15
24 CFR 982: .402;
HUD-903: p1 (2); p2 (3);
7420.10G Gbk: 5-11 (3); 5-41; 5-42;
PIH Notices: 95-48; 95-48 Tech Asst;
Admin Plan: s1p2; s1p2

HANDICAPPED...............................9
24 CFR 5: .801;
HUD-50058: p v;
HUD-50058Instr: p20;
HUD-52580-A: p2; p13; p17;
PIH Notices: 01-15 Impr Integ Hbk; 95-48; 95-48 Tech Asst

HANDICAPS....................................5
24 CFR 5: .403
HUD-50058Instr: p70; p74;
PIH Notices: 02-01; 99-52

HANDRAIL......................................3
24 CFR 5: .703;
HUD-52580-A: p13; p17

HANDRAILS...................................1
7420.10G Gbk: 10-10

HAPPY...3
7420.10G Gbk: 9-7; 9-11; 24-14

HAPS..6
PIH Notices: 03-23; 00-24B (4); 00-24B

HAPS\UAPS....................................1
7420.10G Gbk: 20-21 Ex 20-4

HARASS...
1
HUD-903-1: p2

HARASSED.....................................1
HUD-903-1: p4

HARASSES......................................2
PIH Notices: 95-48; 95-48 Tech Asst

HARASSMENT...............................1
Admin Plan: s1p3

HARD COPY....................................3
PIH Notices: 03-11;
Admin Plan: s7p4; s7p4

HARDSHIP.....................................94
24 CFR 5: .630 (25);
24 CFR 982: .503; .635;
HUD-50058: p8; p viii (3);
HUD-50058Instr: p37 (4); p38 (4);
7420.10G Gbk: 3-6; 4-12; 6-8 (8); 7-4; 11-3; 16-2; 22-3;
PIH Notices: 02-20 (3); 01-41 (3); 01-15 Impr Integ Hbk (8); 00-46 (3); 00-09 (3); 95-48 (5); 95-48 Tech Asst (5);
Admin Plan: s1p5; s3p2; s6p4 (4); s6p5 (4); s6p5

HARDSHIP EXEMPTION..............13
24 CFR 5: .630 (7);
HUD-50058: p8; p viii;
HUD-50058Instr: p37; p38;
7420.10G Gbk: 3-6; 16-2

HARDSHIPS.....................................3
PIH Notices: 02-20; 00-46;
Admin Plan: s6p5

HARD-TO-HOUSE........................22
HUD-52665: p3;
7420.10G Gbk: 13-9; 13-10; 20-2; 20-4 (5); 20-6; 20-16; 20-22 Ex 20-5;
PIH Notices: 02-07 (5); 00-28 (4); 00-28

HARDWARE....................................8
HUD-52580-A: p4;
7420.10G Gbk: 4-13; 10-2; 10-25; 11-7;
PIH Notices: 01-11; 95-48; 95-48 Tech Asst

HARD-WIRED...............................13
24 CFR 5: .703;
24 CFR 982: .401 (2);
HUD-52580-A: p8 (2);
7420.10G Gbk: 10-14; 17-2;
PIH Notices: 99-11 (5); 99-11

HARMFUL POLLUTANTS.............2
24 CFR 982: .401;
7420.10G Gbk: 10-10

HAZARD..56
24 CFR 35 SubM: .1210 (2); .1225 (6);
24 CFR 982: .401; .626;
HUD-52517: p2 (2); p6; p13 (2); p14; p17; p18;
HUD-52580-A: p15
7420.10G Gbk: 10-2; 10-4; 10-5; 10-7; 10-8 (2); 10-10; 10-11; 10-12; 10-15; 10-17 (2); 10-18; 10-19; 10-

21 (10); 10-37 Ex 10-2 (2); 10-38 Ex 10-3 (5); 20-4 (2);
PIH Notices: 02-07; 02-01; 00-49 (2); 99-52

HAZARDOUS 44
HUD-52580: p4;
HUD-52580-A: p2 (3); p3 (3); p4; p5 (3); p7 (3); p9 (3); p10 (3); p11 (3); p12 (3); p13 (5); p14 (3);
7420.10G Gbk: 10-5; 10-8; 10-19;
PIH Notices: 95-48 (3); 95-48 Tech Asst (3);
Admin Plan: s6p5

HAZARDOUS DUTY PAY 1
Admin Plan: s6p5

HAZARDS 129
24 CFR 5: .703 (15);
24 CFR 35 SubM: .1200; .1225 (2);
24 CFR 982: .401 (2); .614 (3); .621;
HUD-52517: p2;
HUD-52580: p1; p2 (2); p3 (3); p4 (3); p5 (3);
HUD-52580-A: p2; p3 (2); p5 (2); p6 (2); p7 (2); p9 (2); p10 (2); p11 (2); p12 (2); p13 (2); p14 (7); p15; p17 (8); p18 (5);
HUD-52665: p1;
7420.10G Gbk: 10-2 (3); 10-4 (2); 10-5; 10-9; 10-11 (2); 10-12; 10-13 (2); 10-15 (3); 10-17 (3); 10-20 (2); 10-21 (2); 10-22; 10-23; 10-36 Ex 10-1 (8); 10-37 Ex 10-2; 10-39 Ex 10-4 (4); 17-5 (3); 17-10; 17-11;
PIH Notices: 00-23 (7);
Admin Plan: s19p1; s24p2

HEAD 232
24 CFR 5: .100; .230; .403 (3); .504 (3); .518 (5); .603; .609 (2); .655 (2); .659;
24 CFR 982: .4; .204; .207 (2); .353; .516;
HUD-50058: p i (2); p ii (5); p3 (2); p iii (3); p4; p iv; p5 (2); p v (2); p7 (6); p vii (6); p16 (4); p xvi (4);
HUD-50058Instr: p2; p6 (5); p10; p14 (7); p15 (2); p16 (2); p17 (3); p18 (6); p25 (2); p26 (4); p27; p33; p34; p35 (13); p36 (2); p60 (18); p65; p70 (2); p71 (3); p72 (3); p73 (2);
HUD-52580: p6;
HUD-52580-A: p19;
HUD-52665: p1 (2); p2 (2);
7420.10G Gbk: 4-16 (2); 4-17 (2); 4-25 Ex 4-2 (3); 4-27 Ex 4-2; 5-2 (2); 5-13; 5-14 Ex 5-2; 5-29 (2); 5-31 (2); 5-32; 5-53 Ex 5-5; 12-13 Ex 12-1; 12-16 Ex 12-4 (4); 23-6 (2); 23-7 (2); 23-9 (4); 23-14 (2); 23-17 Ex 23-2; 23-18;
PIH Notices: 02-22; 01-15 Impr Integ Hbk (5); 00-24B; 95-48 (2); 95-48 Tech Asst (2);
Admin Plan: s2p1; s2p2 (6); s3p2; s4p1; s6p1 (2); s6p5 (2); s6p6; s6p8; s6p13; s7p2; s7p3 (3); s7p5; s8p5 (2); s11p1 (3); s20p4 (2); s22p1; s25p2; s25p4 (4); s25p5 (2); s25p6

HEAD OF HOUSEHOLD 113
24 CFR 5: .504; .518 (5); .609;
24 CFR 982: .204;
HUD-50058: p i (2); p ii (3); p3; p iii (2); p iv; p5; p v; p7; p vii (2); p16 (3); p xvi (3);
HUD-50058Instr: p2; p6 (3); p10; p14 (6); p16; p17 (2); p18 (4); p25 (2); p26 (2); p27; p34; p35 (4); p36 (2); p60 (13); p72;
HUD-52665: p1 (2); p2 (2);
7420.10G Gbk: 4-7; 4-8; 4-14; 4-23 Ex 4-1 (2); 4-25 Ex 4-2 (4); 5-15 Ex 5-2; 5-18 (2); 5-30; 8-8; 12-3 (2); 13-2; 23-6; 23-15;
PIH Notices: 01-15 Impr Integ Hbk (2); 00-24B;
Admin Plan: s2p2 (3); s4p1; s6p5; s6p6; s6p8; s7p2; s7p3; s8p5; s11p1 (2); s20p4 (2); s25p5

HEAD OF HOUSEHOLD'S 16
HUD-50058: p ii (2); p5; p v; p16; p xvi;
HUD-50058Instr: p6 (2); p18 (2); p26; p60 (4); p60

HEADED 3

HUD-52580-A: p1 (2); p1

HEADING 6
24 CFR 982: .625;
HUD-50058: p ii (2); p6;
PIH Notices: 95-48; 95-48 Tech Asst

HEADINGS 2
PIH Notices: 95-48; 95-48 Tech Asst

HEADQUARTERS..........................87
24 CFR 982: .3 (2); .52; .101; .152; .162 (3);
HUD-50058Instr: p3; p4;
HUD-52641: p10;
HUD-52641-A: p3;
7420.10G Gbk: 19-3; 20-5; 20-6;
PIH Notices: 02-27 (15); 02-21 (3); 02-20 (6); 02-14; 02-07 (4); 01-41 (6); 01-20 (3); 01-06 (7); 01-01 (2); 00-46 (6); 00-28 (4); 00-27 (4); 00-24B (2); 00-09 (8); 00-09

HEADS 1
7420.10G Gbk: 5-18

HEADS OF HOUSEHOLD..............1
7420.10G Gbk: 5-18

HEALTH.......................................227
24 CFR 5: .306; .318; .327 (2); .360 (2); .363; .603 (2); .609; .703 (9);
24 CFR 35 SubM: .1225 (19);
24 CFR 982: .306 (2); .307; .310 (3); .401 (5); .402; .551 (2); .553 (6); .612; .614 (2);
HUD-50058: p16 (3);
HUD-50058Instr: p31; p60 (3); p61 (2); p71; p76;
HUD-52580: p5;
HUD-52580-A: p1; p8; p15; p17 (6); p18 (2);
HUD-52641: p7 (2); p9 (3);
HUD-52641-A: p2 (5);
7420.10G Gbk: 5-15 Ex 5-2; 5-16 Ex 5-2; 5-31 (2); 5-41; 5-51 Ex 5-5; 8-8; 8-20 (3); 10-1; 10-2; 10-3; 10-5; 10-7; 10-8 (3); 10-9; 10-10 (2); 10-11; 10-13 (2); 10-16 (2); 10-19; 10-20 (13); 10-21; 10-22 (7); 10-31; 10-36 Ex 10-1; 11-3; 11-4 (2); 15-2 (3); 15-7; 17-5 (2); 20-4 (2); 23-15;
PIH Notices: 03-11; 02-07 (2); 02-01; 01-15; 01-15 Impr Integ Hbk (3); 00-49 (6); 00-23 (4); 99-52; 95-48 (18); 95-48 Tech Asst (18);
Admin Plan: s2p7; s5p2 (2); s6p3; s6p10; s7p7; s9p3; s10p3; s15p2 (2); s15p3; s16p2 (2); s18p5; s25p3; s25p3

HEALTH CARE 19
24 CFR 35 SubM: .1225 (5);
HUD-50058Instr: p76;
7420.10G Gbk: 5-31; 10-16; 10-20 (3); 20-4; 23-15;
PIH Notices: 01-15 Impr Integ Hbk; 00-49; 95-48 (2); 95-48 Tech Asst; 95-48 Tech Asst

HEALTH DEPARTMENT...............12
24 CFR 35 SubM: .1225;
7420.10G Gbk: 10-5; 10-16; 10-20 (2); 10-22 (2); 10-31; 20-4;
PIH Notices: 02-07; 00-49; 00-49

HEALTH DEPARTMENTS 1
PIH Notices: 00-23

HEALTH INSURANCE....................3
HUD-50058: p16;
HUD-50058Instr: p60; p60

HEALTHFUL 2
24 CFR 5: .603;
HUD-50058Instr: p76

HEALTHFUL LIVING ENVIRONMENT 2
24 CFR 5: .603;
HUD-50058Instr: p76

HEALTH-RELATED.........................4
PIH Notices: 95-48 (2); 95-48 Tech Asst; 95-48 Tech Asst

HEALTHY 9
24 CFR 982: .401 (2);
HUD-52580-A: p15 (2);
7420.10G Gbk: 10-7 (3); 10-18;
PIH Notices: 00-11

HEARING.....................................292
24 CFR 5: .508; .514 (30); .516; .615 (6); .630 (3);
24 CFR 982: Intro; .54; .301 (3); .401 .552 (2); .554; .555 (36);
HUD-50058Instr: p18;
HUD-52580-A: p9; p10; p11; p12;
HUD-903: p3;
HUD-9886: p1;
7420.10G Gbk: 3-7 (3); 3-8; 4-11; 5-32; 5-44 (2); 8-3; 12-3; 12-15 Ex 12-3 (2);

15-6; 15-7 (2); 15-8; 15-10 Ex 15-2; 16-1 (5); 16-3; 16-4 (7); 16-5 (6); 23-5;
PIH Notices: 02-01 (9); 99-52 (9); 95-48 (32); 95-48 Tech Asst (32);
Admin Plan: s1p3; s1p5; s2p5; s2p7; s8p5 (2); s10p5; s11p1 (2); s15p4 (2); s15p6; s18p1 (2); s18p3 (6); s18p4 (10); s18p5 (13); s18p6 (18); s18p7 (11); s18p8 (7); s20p6; s20p6

HEARING AID....................................2
PIH Notices: 95-48; 95-48 Tech Asst

HEARING AIDS 5
7420.10G Gbk: 5-32;
PIH Notices: 95-48 (2); 95-48 Tech Asst; 95-48 Tech Asst

HEARING IMPAIRED....................10
HUD-52580-A: p9; p10; p11; p12;
HUD-903: p3;
7420.10G Gbk: 4-11; 5-44 (2);
PIH Notices: 02-01; 99-52

HEARING IMPAIRMENT................2
PIH Notices: 95-48; 95-48 Tech Asst

HEARING IMPAIRMENTS 27
PIH Notices: 02-01 (2); 99-52 (2); 95-48 (11); 95-48 Tech Asst (11);
Admin Plan: s1p3

HEARING OFFICER......................16
24 CFR 982: .555;
7420.10G Gbk: 16-4 (4); 16-5 (5);
Admin Plan: s18p5; s18p6 (4); s18p7

HEARING OFFICERS......................9
7420.10G Gbk: 16-4 (6); 16-5 (2);
Admin Plan: s18p6

HEARING OFFICER'S 1
Admin Plan: s18p7

HEARING-IMPAIRED 5
24 CFR 982: .401;
HUD-52580-A: p8 (2);
7420.10G Gbk: 10-14; 10-14

HEARINGS 16
24 CFR 982: .555;
7420.10G Gbk: 1-13; 3-8 (2); 5-6; 16-1; 16-3; 16-4;
PIH Notices: 95-48; 95-48 Tech Asst;
Admin Plan: s8p3; s15p1; s18p1; s18p4; s23p8; s23p8

HEAT 40
24 CFR 982: .401;
HUD-52580: p6;
HUD-52580-A: p4; p15 (18); p16; p19;
HUD-52667: p ii;
7420.10G Gbk: 6-3; 6-9 Ex 6-1; 9-14 Ex 9-1; 9-15 Ex 9-2; 10-5; 10-7 (7); 10-8 (2); 10-19;
Admin Plan: s10p4

HEATED 3
HUD-52580-A: p15 (2); p15

HEATER 11
24 CFR 5: .703;
HUD-52580: p5;
HUD-52580-A: p15 (7); p16; p16

HEATERS.......................................12
24 CFR 982: .401 (2);
HUD-52580-A: p15 (6); p16;
7420.10G Gbk: 10-7 (2); 10-7

HEATING 82
24 CFR 982: .401; .517 (2); .631;
HUD-52517: p1;
HUD-52580: p5 (3);
HUD-52580-A: p1; p6; p15 (20); p16 (5);
HUD-52641: p2;
HUD-52667: p1 (4); p i (8); p ii (8);
7420.10G Gbk: 10-7 (6); 10-8 (3); 10-40 Ex 10-4a; 18-2 (2); 18-4 (3); 18-5 (3); 18-6 (3); 18-7 (2); 18-8; 18-9;
Admin Plan: s22p3

HEATING SYSTEM 15
HUD-52580-A: p15 (11);
HUD-52667: p ii;
7420.10G Gbk: 10-7; 10-8; 10-8

HEATING SYSTEMS 3
24 CFR 982: .631;
HUD-52580-A: p15;
Admin Plan: s22p3

HIGH MISDEMEANOR...................4
24 CFR 982: .310;
HUD-52641: p9;
HUD-52641-A: p2;
7420.10G Gbk: 15-6

HIGH POVERTY 19
24 CFR 982: .301; .503;
7420.10G Gbk: 2-2 (2); 2-4;

7-4;
PIH Notices: 02-20 (7); 00-46 (5); 00-46
HIGH POVERTY CENSUS TRACT 2
24 CFR 982: .301;
7420.10G Gbk: 2-2
HIGH RISE....4
HUD-50058: p5;
HUD-52580: p1 (2);
HUD-52667: p i
HIGH SCHOOL....10
HUD-50058: p16;
HUD-50058Instr: p60 (3); p61 (2);
7420.10G Gbk: 23-1;
PIH Notices: 95-48; 95-48 Tech Asst;
Admin Plan: s7p3
HIGH SCHOOL-EQUIVALENCY...1
HUD-50058Instr: p60
HIGH STANDARD....1
Admin Plan: s20p4
HIGHER EDUCATION....6
HUD-50058Instr: p32;
7420.10G Gbk: 5-16 Ex 5-2; 23-1;
PIH Notices: 01-15 Impr Integ Hbk; 95-48; 95-48 Tech Asst
HIGHER RENT....9
HUD-52641: p9;
HUD-52641-A: p2;
7420.10G Gbk: 7-3; 7-9; 9-9 (3); 9-11; 9-11
HIGHER RENTAL....1
24 CFR 982: .310
HIGHER STANDARD....4
24 CFR 982: .627;
7420.10G Gbk: 7-7; 10-2; 10-2
HIGHER SUBSIDY....1
24 CFR 982: .317
HIGH-POVERTY....7
7420.10G Gbk: 2-2 (2); 2-7 (2); 8-3 (2); 8-9
HIGH-RISE....12
24 CFR 5: .353 (2);
HUD-50058Instr: p21;
HUD-52517: p1;
7420.10G Gbk: 9-13 Ex 9-1; 9-15 Ex 9-2; 18-2;
PIH Notices: 99-11 (4);
Admin Plan: s9p2
HIGHWAY....2
PIH Notices: 95-48; 95-48 Tech Asst
HIGHWAYS....6
PIH Notices: 95-48 (3); 95-48 Tech Asst (2); 95-48 Tech Asst
HISPANIC....13
HUD-50058: p3 (2); p4 (2);
HUD-50058Instr: p16 (2); p73;
HUD-903: p1; p2 (2);
7420.10G Gbk: 2-13 Ex 2-1; 4-23 Ex 4-1; 4-25 Ex 4-2; 19-7
HISPANIC'S....1
7420.10G Gbk: 2-13 Ex 2-1
HISTORIC....101
7420.10G Gbk: 2-13 Ex 2-1 (2);
PIH Notices: 02-20; 00-46; 00-11; 95-48 (47); 95-48 Tech Asst (47);
Admin Plan: s10p3; s24p4
HISTORIC PRESERVATION....25
PIH Notices: 95-48 (12); 95-48 Tech Asst (12);
Admin Plan: s10p3
HISTORIC PROPERTIES....15
PIH Notices: 95-48 (7); 95-48 Tech Asst (7);
Admin Plan: s24p4
HISTORIC PROPERTY....6
PIH Notices: 95-48 (3); 95-48 Tech Asst (2); 95-48 Tech Asst
HISTORICAL....19
HUD-50058: p2;
HUD-50058Instr: p1 (2); p10; p11 (4); p77;
7420.10G Gbk: 1-1; 19-3; 19-8; 20-8; 20-18 (5); 24-3
HISTORICAL FUNDING....1
7420.10G Gbk: 20-18
HISTORICAL PER UNIT COST....2
7420.10G Gbk: 20-8; 20-18
HISTORIES....11
24 CFR 982: .307;
7420.10G Gbk: 5-39; 5-40 (2);
PIH Notices: 95-48 (3); 95-48 Tech Asst (3);
Admin Plan: s2p6
HISTORY....61
24 CFR 982: .306 (3); .307; .310; .553;
HUD-52641: p6 (2); p7;
7420.10G Gbk: 1-1 (2); 2-11; 3-4 (2); 4-10; 5-17; 5-39; 5-40; 8-19; 10-42 Ex 10-5; 11-3; 11-8 (2); 22-9; 23-6;
PIH Notices: 03-11 (17); 01-41 (2); 01-15; 00-09; 95-48 (2); 95-48 Tech Asst (2);
Admin Plan: s2p2; s2p6;

s9p3 (2); s15p5; s15p6; s16p1; s16p2; s20p7; s22p1; s25p7

HIV 13
HUD-903-1: p2;
7420.10G Gbk: 5-11;
PIH Notices: 95-48 (5); 95-48 Tech Asst (5);
Admin Plan: s25p2

HOLIDAY 3
7420.10G Gbk: 5-52 Ex 5-5; 10-34;
Admin Plan: s17p1

HOLIDAYS 3
HUD-50058Instr: p3;
7420.10G Gbk: 10-33;
Admin Plan: s18p5

HOME 438
24 CFR 5: .306; .318 (2); .403; .601 (2); .603 (3); .609 (2); .617;
24 CFR 35 SubM: .1200 (2); .1215;
24 CFR 982: 24 CFR 982 (17); .4 (22); .201; .352; .402; .601 (7); .609; .610 (7); .611 (2); .612 (4); .613 (10); .614 (8); .619; .620 (8); .621 (6); .622 (10); .623 (14); .624 (4); .625 (5); .627 (7); .628 (8); .629 (4); .630 (4); .631; .632 (4); .633 (15); .634; .635 (18); .636; .637; .638 (4); .642 (3); .643 (5);
HUD-50058: p5; p v; p10 (2); p x; p11 (2); p13; p xiii (3); p14; p xiv (3); p xvii;
HUD-50058Instr: p ii (2); p17; p26 (2); p28 (2); p32; p36; p42 (3); p43 (3); p44 (3); p46 (6); p47 (8); p53 (3); p56 (4); p63; p71; p72 (4); p73 (4); p78 (3);
HUD-52517: p1 (2); p5;
HUD-52580-A: p1; p14 (2);
HUD-903: p1;
HUD-903-1: p5 (2);
7420.10G Gbk: 4-11 (2); 4-13 (2); 4-25 Ex 4-2; 5-1; 5-3; 5-15 Ex 5-2 (2); 5-16 Ex 5-2; 5-22; 5-27 (2); 5-41; 5-49 Ex 5-5; 8-9; 9-5; 9-6; 9-9; 9-10; 10-17; 10-36 Ex 10-1; 12-3; 12-16 Ex 12-4; 13-2; 17-10; 17-11 (2); 19-4; 23-15;
PIH Notices: 02-20 (8); 02-15; 02-01; 01-15 Impr Integ Hbk (8); 01-02 (7); 00-46 (8); 00-41; 99-52 (2); 95-48 (3); 95-48 Tech Asst (3);
Admin Plan: s2p2 (2); s2p4; s6p5; s6p6 (5); s6p7 (2); s6p8 (2); s9p2 (2); s19p1 (43); s22p2; s22p3 (6); s22p4 (3); s22p4

HOME ENERGY ASSISTANCE 3
HUD-50058Instr: p32;
7420.10G Gbk: 5-16 Ex 5-2;
PIH Notices: 01-15 Impr Integ Hbk

HOME INSURANCE 2
24 CFR 982: .635; .635

HOME MAINTENANCE 1
24 CFR 982: .630

HOME PROGRAM 5
24 CFR 35 SubM: .1200 (2); .1215;
24 CFR 982: .352;
7420.10G Gbk: 24-15

HOME PROGRAM FUNDS 2
PIH Notices: 02-01; 99-52

HOME PROGRAMS 1
PIH Notices: 01-02

HOME VISITS 5
7420.10G Gbk: 4-11; 4-13 (2);
PIH Notices: 95-48; 95-48 Tech Asst

HOME-ASSISTED 1
PIH Notices: 01-02

HOMEBUYER 9
24 CFR 5: .504;
HUD-50058Instr: p58; p74;
Admin Plan: s22p1; s22p2 (4); s22p2

HOMEBUYERS 2
Admin Plan: s25p7; s25p7

HOMEBUYER'S 2
HUD-50058: p xv;
HUD-50058Instr: p58

HOMELESS 45
24 CFR 5: .601 (2); .655 (2); .801 (2);
24 CFR 982: .207 (2);
HUD-50058: p5; p v; p12 (2); p xii (2);
HUD-50058Instr: p19 (4); p50 (4); p72 (3); p73;
HUD-9886: p1;
7420.10G Gbk: 4-3; 4-4; 4-17;
PIH Notices: 95-48 (2); 95-48 Tech Asst (2);

Admin Plan: s20p3; s23p1 (2); s23p2 (3); s23p3; s25p2; s25p3 (2); s25p3

HOMELESS ASSISTANCE.............4
24 CFR 5: .601 (2);
HUD-9886: p1;
Admin Plan: s20p3

HOMELESS FAMILIES 1
7420.10G Gbk: 4-4

HOMELESS FAMILY.......................2
HUD-50058Instr: p72; p72

HOMELESS SHELTERS.................4
PIH Notices: 95-48 (2); 95-48 Tech Asst; 95-48 Tech Asst

HOMEMAKER.................................1
24 CFR 982: .4

HOMEOWNER...............................26
24 CFR 5: .214 (2);
24 CFR 982: .4 (6); .625; .627 (3); .632; .633; .635 (2); .637; .642 (2);
HUD-50058: p xiv;
HUD-50058Instr: p57; p72;
PIH Notices: 03-20;
Admin Plan: s22p1 (2); s22p2

HOMEOWNER OBLIGATIONS......2
24 CFR 982: .4; .633

HOMEOWNERS..............................6
HUD-50058: p xiv;
7420.10G Gbk: 1-2; 9-1;
PIH Notices: 03-20 (2); 03-20

HOMEOWNERSHIP....................382
24 CFR 5: .214 (3); .236; .306; .603;
24 CFR 982: 24 CFR 982 (23); .4 (23); .201 (3); .203 (2); .305; .317 (2); .601 (3); .619; .624; .625 (35); .626 (6); .627 (17); .628 (4); .629; .630 (10); .631 (6); .632 (4); .633 (15); .634 (11); .635 (21); .636 (8); .637 (10); .638 (5); .639 (2); .641 (10); .642 (18); .643 (3);
HUD-50058: p i; p5 (2); p v (2); p14 (3); p xiv (12); p16; p17 (2); p xvii (2);
HUD-50058Instr: p ii; p1; p3; p13; p19; p21 (2); p22; p56 (9); p57 (12); p61 (2); p62 (2); p63; p74; p75; p78;
7420.10G Gbk: 1-2; 3-5; 3-8 (2); 4-22 (2); 5-3; 11-10;
PIH Notices: 03-20 (26); 02-01 (4); 01-41; 01-10; 00-31; 00-09; 99-52 (3); 99-30;
Admin Plan: s2p4; s8p3; s9p2; s22p1 (8); s22p2 (9); s22p4 (2); s22p5

HOMEOWNERSHIP EXPENSE......8
HUD-50058: p14; p xiv (3);
HUD-50058Instr: p56; p57 (2); p57

HOMEOWNERSHIP EXPENSES..12
24 CFR 982: .4; .632; .633; .635 (8);
PIH Notices: 03-20

HOMEOWNERSHIP INTEREST.....1
24 CFR 982: .4

HOMEOWNERSHIP OPTION.....100
24 CFR 982: 24 CFR 982 (19); .4 (12); .601 (3); .619; .624; .625 (5); .626; .627 (3); .628; .629; .630 (3); .631 (3); .632 (2); .633 (3); .634; .635 (4); .636 (3); .637 (3); .638; .639; .641 (10); .642 (4); .643;
HUD-52641: p1;
7420.10G Gbk: 3-8 (3);
PIH Notices: 03-20 (9); 03-20

HOMEOWNERSHIP-COUNSELING1
Admin Plan: s22p2

HOMES 45
24 CFR 5: .318; .703; .801 (2);
24 CFR 982: .352 (2); .630; .634 (2);
HUD-50058Instr: p5 (2); p61;
HUD-52580-A: p13 (3); p14;
HUD-52667: p i;
HUD-903-1: p2;
7420.10G Gbk: 3-5; 8-16 (2); 9-5; 9-8; 9-10 (4); 10-18;
PIH Notices: 00-41 (4); 00-23; 00-11; 95-48; 95-48 Tech Asst;
Admin Plan: s9p2 (3); s19p1 (4); s22p3; s24p2

HOME'S 6
HUD-50058: p xiii (2);
HUD-50058Instr: p53 (3); p53

HOMESTEAD..................................1
Admin Plan: s11p2

HOOK-UP...6
24 CFR 982: .624;
7420.10G Gbk: 10-8; 17-12 (2);

Admin Plan: s19p1; s19p1

HOPE 73
24 CFR 982: .201 (4); .203 (2);
HUD-50058: p i;
HUD-50058Instr: p3 (2); p13; p19 (2); p72 (2);
7420.10G Gbk: 4-4; 4-22 (2); 5-3 (2); 20-5;
PIH Notices: 02-21 (5); 02-07; 02-01 (16); 01-20 (4); 00-28; 00-27 (4); 99-52 (16); 99-11; 95-48; 95-48 Tech Asst;
Admin Plan: s22p2 (2); s25p7

HOPE VI 52
HUD-50058Instr: p72 (2);
7420.10G Gbk: 20-5;
PIH Notices: 02-21 (5); 02-07; 02-01 (16); 01-20 (4); 00-28; 00-27 (4); 99-52 (16);
Admin Plan: s22p2; s22p2

HOPWA 5
24 CFR 5: .603 (2);
24 CFR 35 SubM: .1200 (2); .1200

HOSPITAL 15
7420.10G Gbk: 5-22; 5-51 Ex 5-5; 23-16 Ex 23-2;
PIH Notices: 95-48 (4); 95-48 Tech Asst (4);
Admin Plan: s6p5; s6p8; s6p11; s7p7

HOSPITALIZATION 2
24 CFR 982: .312;
7420.10G Gbk: 4-13

HOSPITALS 5
7420.10G Gbk: 4-3; 8-7;
PIH Notices: 00-41; 95-48; 95-48 Tech Asst

HOSTILE FIRE 9
24 CFR 5: .609;
HUD-50058Instr: p26;
7420.10G Gbk: 5-15 Ex 5-2; 23-12;
PIH Notices: 03-05; 01-40; 01-15 Impr Integ Hbk (2);
Admin Plan: s6p5

HOT WATER 22
HUD-52580-A: p4 (3); p6; p15;
HUD-52667: p ii (3);
7420.10G Gbk: 6-3; 9-14 Ex 9-1; 9-15 Ex 9-2; 10-3; 10-4; 10-5; 18-5 (3); 18-6 (4);
Admin Plan: s10p4

HOT WATER HEATER 1
24 CFR 5: .703

HOTEL 4
PIH Notices: 02-27 (2); 95-48; 95-48 Tech Asst

HOTELS 5
HUD-50058Instr: p72;
PIH Notices: 95-48; 95-48 Tech Asst;
Admin Plan: s23p2; s25p3

HOTLINE 22
HUD-50058: p i; p ii; p x; p xi; p xiii; p xiv; p xvi;
HUD-50058Instr: p3 (3); p42; p46; p53; p56; p59;
HUD-903: p3;
7420.10G Gbk: 19-2; 22-18;
PIH Notices: 00-53 (3);
Admin Plan: s3p1

HOUSE 59
24 CFR 5: .318 (2); .350;
24 CFR 982: .402; .517; .605; .615;
HUD-50058: p11; p xi (2);
HUD-50058Instr: p46 (7);
HUD-52517: p1 (10); p2;
7420.10G Gbk: 5-3; 5-19; 5-30; 5-41; 7-9; 8-10 (2); 9-13 Ex 9-1; 9-15 Ex 9-2; 9-16 Ex 9-2; 20-3;
PIH Notices: 02-21 (3); 02-01; 01-15 Impr Integ Hbk; 00-01; 99-52; 99-11; 95-48 (4); 95-48 Tech Asst (4);
Admin Plan: s2p6; s9p3; s19p1; s22p4

HOUSE RULES 1
Admin Plan: s9p3

HOUSED 8
7420.10G Gbk: 1-8; 4-2; 20-4; 20-6;
PIH Notices: 02-07 (2); 00-28; 00-28

HOUSEHOLD COMPLETED 6
HUD-50058: p16; p xvi;
HUD-50058Instr: p60 (3); p60

HOUSEHOLD COMPOSITION 16
7420.10G Gbk: 1-15; 3-5 (2); 4-7; 4-25 Ex 4-2; 4-27 Ex 4-2; 5-36 Ex 5-4; 12-3; 12-5; 12-16 Ex 12-4; 21-7; 22-10;
Admin Plan: s6p8; s11p1; s11p2; s24p6

HOUSEHOLD HEAD 3
24 CFR 982: .4; .353;
7420.10G Gbk: 5-29

HOUSEHOLD INCOME 7
HUD-50058: p6;
HUD-50058Instr: p23;
7420.10G Gbk: 5-20; 6-7;

Admin Plan: s4p1; s6p6; s22p1

HOUSEHOLD MANAGEMENT 3
24 CFR 5: .603;
HUD-50058Instr: p71;
Admin Plan: s6p3

HOUSEHOLD MEMBER............ 117
24 CFR 5: .216;
24 CFR 982: .310 (8); .552 (2); .553 (15);
HUD-50058: p iii (11); p iv (12);
HUD-50058Instr: p14 (9); p15 (3); p16 (2); p17;
HUD-52641: p9 (3);
HUD-52641-A: p2 (4);
7420.10G Gbk: 4-27 Ex 4-2 (2); 5-4 (2); 5-34; 5-36 Ex 5-4; 5-43; 5-51 Ex 5-5; 5-52 Ex 5-5 (2); 6-8; 12-9; 15-2 (5); 15-6; 15-7 (5);
PIH Notices: 03-11 (3);
Admin Plan: s2p2 (4); s2p3; s6p7; s6p8; s6p11; s7p8; s8p5 (2); s10p5; s13p1; s15p2; s15p3 (4); s20p6; s22p1

HOUSEHOLD MEMBERS 42
24 CFR 982: .310; .551 (2); .553;
HUD-50058: p iii (2); p iv (2);
HUD-50058Instr: p2; p14 (3); p17 (2); p36 (2); p72 (2);
HUD-52641: p1 (2); 8;
HUD-52641-A: p1;
HUD-9886: p2 (2);
7420.10G Gbk: 4-26 Ex 4-2; 5-4; 5-41; 6-7 (2); 11-11; 12-3;
Admin Plan: s2p2; s5p2 (2); s6p1; s6p8; s6p11 (2); s6p12 (2); s11p1; s22p1

HOUSEHOLD MEMBER'S 15
24 CFR 982: .310; .552; .553 (3);
HUD-50058: p iii (3); p iv (3);
HUD-50058Instr: p15; p16;
PIH Notices: 03-11;
Admin Plan: s15p2

HOUSEHOLD PET 8
24 CFR 5: .306 (2); .318; .324 (2); .350 (2); .359

HOUSEHOLD PETS......................13
24 CFR 5: .309 (2); .312 (2); .315 (2); .318 (3); .321 (2); .353; .359

HOUSEHOLDS..............................68
24 CFR 5: .518;
24 CFR 35 SubM: .1200;
24 CFR 982: .102; .517;
HUD-50058Instr: p1; p10; p61; p72;
HUD-52667: p i;
7420.10G Gbk: 1-2; 1-8; 1-12; 2-13 Ex 2-1; 4-9; 5-3; 5-6; 5-31 (3); 5-32; 5-43; 7-1; 12-13 Ex 12-1; 14-1; 14-2; 17-1 (6); 18-1; 19-3; 19-4; 19-7 (3); 19-8; 19-10 (2); 22-4; 23-11;
PIH Notices: 03-23 (3); 02-22; 01-15 (4);
Admin Plan: s1p6; s1p7; s2p3; s4p1; s4p2; s6p11; s6p13; s7p3; s8p4; s8p5; s9p1; s11p1; s13p1; s19p1; s22p2; s22p3; s24p2; s25p7

HOUSEHOLD'S.............................30
24 CFR 5: .520 (4);
HUD-50058: p ii (2); p5; p v; p vii; p16; p xvi;
HUD-50058Instr: p6 (2); p18 (2); p26; p36; p60 (5);
HUD-9886: p1;
7420.10G Gbk: 5-1; 12-3; 17-5; 23-6;
Admin Plan: s2p1; s11p1; s15p5

HOUSEKEEPING 4
24 CFR 982: .310;
PIH Notices: 00-41;
Admin Plan: s8p3; s25p7

HOUSEKEEPING HABITS.............4
HUD-52641: p9;
HUD-52641-A: p2;
7420.10G Gbk: 15-3; 15-3

HOUSEKEEPING HABITS.............5
24 CFR 982: .310;
HUD-52641: p9;
HUD-52641-A: p2;
7420.10G Gbk: 15-3; 15-3

HOUSES 5
HUD-52667: p i;
HUD-903: p2;
7420.10G Gbk: 18-2;
PIH Notices: 95-48; 95-48 Tech Asst

HOUSING ACT............................106
24 CFR 5: .100 (8); .306 (3); .380; .500 (3); .504 (3); .516; .701; .801;
24 CFR 982: .2; .201 (4); .352 (2);
HUD-50058: p i; p5; p v;
HUD-50058Instr: p5; p19 (2); p70 (2); p75 (2);
HUD-52580: p1 (3); p10;

HUD-52641-A: p3;
HUD-52665: p1;
HUD-52667: p i;
7420.10G Gbk: 1-1 (2); 1-2 (2); 1-3; 3-3; 4-20;
PIH Notices: 03-11; 02-22; 02-21 (4); 02-01 (2); 01-41 (8); 01-27 (3); 01-20 (3); 01-15 Impr Integ Hbk; 01-10 (8); 01-02 (2); 00-27 (3); 00-23; 00-09 (10); 99-52 (2);
Admin Plan: s1p1; s2p4 (2); s4p2; s24p2

HOUSING ASSISTANCE PAYMENTS CONTRACT 29
24 CFR 982: Intro; .4; .451; .641;
HUD-50058Instr: p70; p72;
PIH Notices: 01-41; 00-09 (6);
Admin Plan: s2p7; s8p3; s9p1; s9p2; s9p4; s10p1; s10p4; s11p1; s16p1; s16p3; s23p5; s23p8; s24p1; s24p5 (2); s24p7

HOUSING ASSISTANCE PAYMENTS CONTRACTS 2
24 CFR 5: .653;
Admin Plan: s24p1

HOUSING CHOICE VOUCHER . 383
24 CFR 5: .601; .617;
24 CFR 982: .1; .627; .636; .643;
HUD-50058Instr: p1; p9; p10; p73;
HUD-52517: p2;
HUD-52580: p1 (2); p2; p13; p17;
7420.10G Gbk: 1-5 (2); 1-6 (2); 1-7 (6); 1-8 (5); 1-9; 2-1 (3); 2-3; 2-4 (6); 2-11 (3); 3-2; 3-3 (2); 4-2; 4-8 (3); 4-9 (2); 4-14; 4-18; 4-19; 5-19; 5-22; 5-37; 5-40; 5-41 (2); 5-42 (2); 6-1; 6-2 (2); 6-6 (2); 8-1 (2); 8-3; 8-10; 8-11; 8-13 (4); 8-17 (3); 8-19; 8-20; 10-15; 12-1; 12-12 Ex 12-1; 12-15 Ex 12-3; 13-1; 13-2; 13-5 (6); 13-7 (3); 13-8; 13-9; 14-1 (2); 14-2 (6); 14-3 (4); 14-4 (2); 14-5; 15-8; 18-7; 19-3; 21-1; 21-4; 21-5; 21-7; 21-10; 21-13 (2); 22-4 (3); 22-13; 22-15 (2); 23-1 (2); 23-2; 23-3 (2); 23-5; 23-9 (2); 23-10 (2); 23-11 (2); 23-12; 23-18 (2); 23-19; 23-20;
PIH Notices: 03-23 (5); 03-20 (5); 03-12 (2); 03-11; 03-05; 02-27 (14); 02-22 (5); 02-21 (8); 02-20 (10); 02-14 (3); 02-07 (9); 02-06 (5); 02-01 (12); 01-43; 01-41 (37); 01-40 (2); 01-33 (4); 01-27 (3); 01-20 (6); 01-15 (2); 01-10 (7); 01-02 (2); 01-01 (3); 00-49 (7); 00-46 (10); 00-41 (3); 00-28 (7); 00-27 (5); 00-23 (2); 00-14; 00-09 (14); 99-52 (2);
Admin Plan: s3p1; s3p2; s4p2; s6p2; s8p2 (3); s8p4; s8p5; s9p2; s10p3; s13p2; s15p3; s19p1 (3); s22p1; s22p2; s22p3; s22p4; s22p5; s23p1; s23p5; s23p8; s24p1 (2); s24p5; s24p6 (2); s24p7; s25p1; s25p2; s25p3; s25p4; s25p5; s25p5

HOUSING CHOICE VOUCHER HOLDER 1
7420.10G Gbk: 2-6

HOUSING CHOICE VOUCHER HOLDER-OWNER 1
7420.10G Gbk: 2-11

HOUSING CHOICE VOUCHER HOLDERS 11
7420.10G Gbk: 1-15; 2-3 (3); 2-6; 2-8; 2-10 (2); 3-7; 8-22; 13-10

HOUSING CHOICE VOUCHER ISSUANCE 4
7420.10G Gbk: 6-1; 8-1; 8-22; 8-22

HOUSING CHOICE VOUCHER PROGRAM 293
HUD-52517: p1 (3); 8; p10 (2);
HUD-52641-A: p1; p3 (2);
HUD-52646: p1 (5); p2 (3);
7420.10G Gbk: 1-1; 1-4 (2); 1-5 (6); 1-7; 1-9; 1-10 (2); 1-11 (2); 1-12 (2); 1-12 Ex 1-2; 1-13; 1-14; 2-1 (4); 2-3; 2-5; 2-6 (2); 2-7; 2-10; 3-1 (6); 3-3 (2); 3-4; 3-5 (2); 3-6 (2); 3-7 (4); 3-8 (4); 3-9 (3); 4-1; 4-2 (2); 4-4; 4-5; 4-8 (3);

4-9 (2); 4-11; 4-14; 4-18; 4-19; 4-20 (2); 4-23 Ex 4-1 (2); 4-25 Ex 4-2; 5-1 (2); 5-2; 5-3; 5-4; 5-12; 5-13; 5-19; 5-22; 5-23; 5-35; 5-36 Ex 5-4; 5-38 (2); 5-40; 5-42; 5-44 (2); 5-45; 6-2; 6-10 Ex 6-2; 7-5; 7-6; 7-7 (2); 7-8; 7-9; 8-1 (4); 8-2 (4); 8-3; 8-4 (3); 8-5; 8-6; 8-7 (2); 8-8; 8-11; 8-16; 8-17; 8-19; 8-21 (2); 8-22; 8-23; 9-1; 9-6 (2); 10-1; 10-11; 10-15; 10-30; 10-37 Ex 10-2; 10-40 Ex 10-4a; 10-41 Ex 10-4b; 10-42 Ex 10-5; 10-43 Ex 10-6; 11-1 (2); 11-2 (3); 11-3 (6); 11-4; 11-9 (2); 11-10 (2); 11-11 (2); 11-15; 11-18 (2); 12-2; 12-12 Ex 12-1; 12-14 Ex 12-2; 12-15 Ex 12-3; 13-1; 13-2; 13-3 (3); 13-5; 13-9; 14-1 (4); 14-3 (3); 14-4 (4); 14-5; 15-1 (2); 15-5 (3); 15-8; 15-10 Ex 15-2; 16-1; 16-4; 17-1 (2); 17-3; 17-4 (2); 17-7 (2); 17-10 (2); 17-11; 17-12; 18-1 (2); 18-8; 19-2; 19-8; 20-1 (3); 20-3 (2); 20-5; 20-6 (3); 20-13 (2); 20-17; 20-18; 20-20; 20-21 Ex 20-4; 20-22; 20-23 (2); 20-26 (2); 20-27; 20-28; 20-29; 20-30; 21-1 (2); 21-3; 21-4; 21-5; 21-6 Ex 21-1; 21-7; 21-8; 21-11 (2); 21-12 Ex 21-2; 21-12 Ex 21-3; 21-13 (4); 21-14 Ex 21-4 (2); 21-15 Ex 21-5 (3); 21-16 Ex 21-6; 22-3; 22-7; 22-14; 22-16; 22-17 (2); 23-1 (2); 23-3 (2); 23-5 (3); 23-10; 23-11; 23-12; 23-18; 23-20; 24-1; 24-8; 24-12; 24-14 (2); 24-14

HOUSING CHOICE VOUCHER PROGRAM FUNDING.................... 1
7420.10G Gbk: 4-21

HOUSING CHOICE VOUCHER PROGRAM FUNDS......................... 2
7420.10G Gbk: 22-1; 22-16

HOUSING CHOICE VOUCHER PROGRAM MOVES........................ 1
7420.10G Gbk: 3-3

HOUSING CHOICE VOUCHER PROGRAMS 8
7420.10G Gbk: 3-7; 4-13; 19-5; 21-1 (2); 21-2; 21-11; 21-17

HOUSING CHOICE VOUCHER-HOLDERS 1
PIH Notices: 01-02

HOUSING CHOICE VOUCHERS . 91
7420.10G Gbk: 1-1 (2); 1-5 (3); 1-6 Ex 1-1 (2); 1-7 (5); 1-8 (4); 1-9 (2); 2-5; 2-9; 3-7; 8-22; 9-14 Ex 9-1; 12-1; 14-1 (2); 14-2; 14-4; 14-5; 20-3; 23-1; 23-19; 24-4;
PIH Notices: 03-05; 02-27; 02-22; 02-21 (8); 02-15; 02-03; 01-41 (8); 01-20 (9); 01-15; 01-10; 01-02 (2); 00-41 (4); 00-28 (2); 00-27 (7); 00-23; 00-14; 00-09 (6);
Admin Plan: s22p1; s25p2; s25p8

HOUSING CODE............................. 1
7420.10G Gbk: 22-6

HOUSING CODES 6
24 CFR 982: .306; .401;
HUD-52641: p7;
7420.10G Gbk: 8-19; 10-2; 11-3

HOUSING DISCRIMINATION COMPLAINT 12
24 CFR 982: .301; .304;
HUD-52646: p2;
HUD-903: p1;
7420.10G Gbk: 3-3; 5-42; 5-45; 8-6; 8-14 (3);
Admin Plan: s8p3

HOUSING DISCRIMINATION COMPLAINTS................................. 2
HUD-903: p3;
HUD-903-1: p6

HOUSING DISCRIMINATION INFORMATION FORM.................... 1
HUD-903-1: p3

HOUSING INTERIOR...................... 2
24 CFR 982: .631;
Admin Plan: s22p3

HOUSING MARKET...................... 28
24 CFR 5: .100; .518 (2); .655;
24 CFR 982: .1; .4; .451;
HUD-52641: p4;

7420.10G Gbk: 4-2; 8-4; 8-7 (3); 8-12 (3); 9-12; 13-2; 19-11; 20-15; 21-9; 24-2 (2); 24-10; 24-12; 24-15;
PIH Notices: 02-22;
Admin Plan: s25p6

HOUSING MARKETS 7
7420.10G Gbk: 2-11; 9-10; 11-4; 13-6; 24-8; 24-9; 24-10

HOUSING NEEDS.......................... 21
24 CFR 982: .201; .207;
HUD-50058: p i;
7420.10G Gbk: 3-1; 3-7 (2); 4-9 (2); 4-15; 4-16 (2); 4-20; 4-25 Ex 4-2; 5-3; 21-8; 24-3;
PIH Notices: 02-21; 02-01 (2); 00-27; 99-52

HOUSING OPPORTUNITIES........ 64
24 CFR 5: .601 (2); .603; .617;
24 CFR 35 SubM: .1200 (2);
24 CFR 982: .102; .309; .503;
HUD-52641: p1;
HUD-52648: p2 (2);
7420.10G Gbk: 1-7; 1-10; 2-1 (3); 2-2; 2-3; 2-7; 3-9; 4-13; 7-3; 7-7 (3); 7-10; 8-4; 8-7 (2); 8-22; 13-1 (2); 13-10 (2); 19-5;
PIH Notices: 02-27 (2); 02-21 (3); 02-20 (2); 01-41 (2); 01-20; 01-06 (3); 01-01 (4); 00-46; 00-09 (2);
Admin Plan: s1p3; s1p7; s9p2; s21p2; s21p5; s25p2 (2); s25p2

HOUSING OPPORTUNITY 4
7420.10G Gbk: 4-2; 8-7;
Admin Plan: s8p3; s21p1

HOUSING PROGRAM................... 43
24 CFR 5: .324; .360;
24 CFR 982: .205 (3); .306 (2); .316; .453; .552;
HUD-50058Instr: p9; p10;
HUD-52641: p6 (2);
7420.10G Gbk: 1-2; 3-3; 5-37; 8-19 (2); 11-3 (2); 11-18; 15-5; 15-9 Ex 15-1; 15-10 Ex 15-2; 22-14;
PIH Notices: 02-27; 01-41 (3); 00-11A; 00-09;
Admin Plan: s1p2; s1p3; s1p4; s1p5; s2p3; s2p6; s3p3; s15p2; s15p5; s16p1; s16p1

HOUSING PROGRAM REQUIREMENTS............................. 1
PIH Notices: 00-11A

HOUSING PROGRAMS 41
24 CFR 5: .105; .300; .306 (5); .315; .318 (9); .324; .327; .350; .353 (2); .359; .360; .363; .504;
HUD-50058Instr: p1 (2); p5; p12; p24; p74;
7420.10G Gbk: 1-1; 15-4; 19-3;
PIH Notices: 01-27; 00-24B; 99-11;
Admin Plan: s1p2; s1p3; s10p1

HOUSING QUALITY STANDARD 2
HUD-52580-A: p1;
7420.10G Gbk: 10-37 Ex 10-2

HOUSING QUALITY STANDARDS 111
24 CFR 35 SubM: .1225;
24 CFR 982: 24 CFR 982 (7); .1; .4; .355; .401 (2); .402; .517; .605 (2); .609; .614 (2); .618 (2); .621;
HUD-50058: p i; p v (2); p xiv;
HUD-50058Instr: p3; p21; p56; p72; p73 (3);
HUD-52580: p1; p6;
HUD-52580-A: p1 (3); p19;
HUD-52641: p3; p10;
HUD-52641-A: p3;
HUD-52646: p2;
7420.10G Gbk: 1-13; 5-41; 8-7; 8-17; 10-1 (3); 10-15; 15-9 Ex 15-1; 16-2 (3); 17-1; 17-2; 17-3 (2); 17-5; 20-6;
PIH Notices: 02-27 (2); 02-07; 01-41 (8); 00-49; 00-41; 00-24B (4); 00-23; 00-09 (7);
Admin Plan: s5p1; s5p3 (2); s6p13; s9p3; s9p4; s10p1 (2); s10p3; s10p4; s15p6; s19p1 (7); s21p4; s22p3; s23p5 (2); s24p1; s24p5

HOUSING RESOURCE.................... 1
PIH Notices: 01-15

HOUSING RESOURCES 4
PIH Notices: 03-05; 01-40; 01-15 Impr Integ Hbk;
Admin Plan: s20p1

HOUSING SEARCH....................... 33
HUD-50058: p17;

HUD-50058Instr: p63;
7420.10G Gbk: 1-16 Ex 1-3; 2-1; 2-6; 2-10; 3-3; 8-1 (5); 8-3; 8-4; 8-5; 8-13 (2); 8-14 (2); 8-22; 8-24 Ex 8-1; 13-7 (2); 20-17; 22-9; 24-9;
PIH Notices: 00-09 (2);
Admin Plan: s8p2; s8p3 (2); s8p4; s8p4

HOUSING SERVICE 6
24 CFR 982: .517;
7420.10G Gbk: 8-16 (2); 18-2;
PIH Notices: 02-27;
Admin Plan: s8p4

HOUSING SERVICES 30
24 CFR 5: .603;
24 CFR 982: .4; .507; .517 (3);
HUD-50058Instr: p75; p76;
HUD-52641: p3; p4; 8; p9 (2);
HUD-52641-A: p1; p2 (2);
HUD-52648: p1;
7420.10G Gbk: 9-2; 9-12; 11-12; 18-1; 18-2 (2);
PIH Notices: 03-12 (3); 02-27; 01-15 Impr Integ Hbk; 00-24B;
Admin Plan: s21p3

HQS 489
24 CFR 35 SubM: .1225;
24 CFR 982: 24 CFR 982 (2); .4 (3); .54; .152; .305 (3); .306; .352; .353; .401 (5); .402; .403 (2); .404 (9); .405 (2); .406 (3); .452; .453; .519; .551 (2); .554 (2); .555 (3); .605 (2); .609 (3); .614 (4); .618 (4); .619 (7); .620; .621; .627; .628 (2); .631 (3); .641;
HUD-50058: p i; p2; p5 (2); p v (4); p14; p xiv; p17;
HUD-50058Instr: p1 (2); p3; p10 (3); p11 (2); p21 (12); p56 (2); p63 (2); p72; p73 (2); p77;
HUD-52580: p5 (3);
HUD-52580-A: p17 (3);
HUD-52641: p3 (8); p4 (2); p5 (2); p6; 8; p9 (3); p10;
HUD-52641-A: p1 (3); p2; p3;
HUD-52646: p2;
HUD-52648: p1 (8); p2 (3);
7420.10G Gbk: 1-10 (4); 1-11; 1-14 (2); 1-16 Ex 1-3 (3); 2-9; 2-10; 3-6 (2); 5-36 Ex 5-4 (2); 5-41; 5-42; 8-3 (2); 8-8; 8-15; 8-16; 8-17 (4); 8-19; 9-5; 9-16 Ex 9-2; 10-1 (6); 10-2 (5); 10-3; 10-4; 10-8; 10-18; 10-19; 10-21 (2); 10-22; 10-23 (6); 10-24 (2); 10-25 (2); 10-26 (6); 10-27 (7); 10-28 (8); 10-29 (6); 10-30 (5); 10-31 (6); 10-32 (6); 10-33 (7); 10-34 (4); 10-35 (2); 10-37 Ex 10-2 (2); 10-42 Ex 10-5; 10-43 Ex 10-6 (3); 10-44 Ex 10-7a (3); 10-45 Ex 10-7b (3); 10-46 Ex 10-8; 11-1; 11-3; 11-4; 11-5 (2); 11-9 (2); 11-11; 11-12 (7); 11-17 (2); 11-19 (3); 12-1; 13-8; 15-4 (2); 17-1 (2); 17-2; 17-3; 17-4 (2); 17-7 (2); 17-10 (6); 17-11 (2); 18-1 (2); 18-7; 19-4; 19-11 (4); 19-12 (5); 19-13; 21-4; 21-8; 21-9; 21-10 (3); 22-2 (3); 22-6 (2); 22-7 (2); 22-9; 22-10; 22-13; 22-15; 24-12; 24-13 (2); 24-14; 24-15 (2);
PIH Notices: 02-27 (7); 02-07; 01-41 (7); 01-06 (11); 00-49 (2); 00-24 (2); 00-24A (3); 00-24B (20); 00-23 (8); 00-09 (6);
Admin Plan: s5p3 (2); s8p2; s10p1 (8); s10p2; s10p3 (6); s10p4 (2); s10p5 (2); s11p1; s13p1; s16p1; s18p1 (2); s18p2 (2); s18p4 (3); s19p1; s21p1 (3); s21p2 (3); s21p4; s21p5 (5); s21p7 (2); s21p8 (5); s22p3; s22p4; s23p5 (3); s24p1 (2); s24p6; s24p7

HQS ENFORCEMENT 16
HUD-52648: p1;
7420.10G Gbk: 1-10; 1-11; 10-23; 10-31; 10-32; 10-33; 10-34; 19-13; 22-7;
PIH Notices: 02-27; 01-06; 00-24B;
Admin Plan: s21p1; s21p2; s21p5

HQS INSPECTION 62
24 CFR 982: .631;
HUD-50058: p2; p5 (2);

p v (2); p14;
HUD-50058Instr: p1 (2); p10 (3); p11 (2); p21 (11); p56; p77;
HUD-52648: p2;
7420.10G Gbk: 1-16 Ex 1-3 (2); 10-23; 10-25; 10-26; 10-35; 10-44 Ex 10-7a; 11-9; 11-19; 19-11 (2); 19-12; 21-8; 21-10; 22-10; 24-12; 24-13;
PIH Notices: 01-41; 01-06 (5); 00-24; 00-24A; 00-23; 00-09;
Admin Plan: s10p1; s10p2; s11p1; s21p7; s21p8 (2); s22p3

HQS INSPECTIONS....................50
24 CFR 982: .54; .405;
HUD-52648: p1 (3); p2 (2);
7420.10G Gbk: 1-10 (2); 3-6 (2); 5-36 Ex 5-4; 10-23; 10-30; 10-31 (3); 10-32 (2); 11-19 (2); 12-1; 13-8; 19-4; 19-12; 21-9; 21-10; 22-9;
PIH Notices: 02-27; 01-06 (4); 00-49; 00-24; 00-24A (2); 00-24B (5); 00-09;
Admin Plan: s21p1; s21p5; s21p7; s21p8 (3); s23p5

HQS QUALITY CONTROL..............6
HUD-52648: p1;
PIH Notices: 02-27; 01-06;
Admin Plan: s21p1; s21p2; s21p4

HUD APPROVAL..........................83
24 CFR 5: .306;
24 CFR 982: .152; .503 (10);
HUD-52648: p2;
7420.10G Gbk: 2-3 (2); 3-1; 4-17; 4-19; 4-20; 7-1; 7-2; 7-3; 7-4 (5); 7-5 (3); 7-7; 7-10; 10-2 (2); 10-24; 10-31; 17-1; 20-10; 22-16; 23-2; 23-4; 24-10;
PIH Notices: 02-27; 02-21; 02-20 (13); 02-14 (2); 02-06 (2); 01-20; 01-01 (8); 00-46 (10); 00-27; 00-11;
Admin Plan: s21p6

HUD APPROVED.........................25
24 CFR 982: .102; .401;
HUD-50058: p5; p v;
HUD-50058Instr: p19;
7420.10G Gbk: 7-2; 9-4; 9-11;
PIH Notices: 02-27 (7); 02-22 (2); 02-14; 02-06 (2);
Admin Plan: s8p2 (2); s8p3; s23p3; s25p4

HUD APPROVES...........................4
24 CFR 982: .104; .201;
7420.10G Gbk: 4-20;
PIH Notices: 01-01

HUD DISCRETION........................3
24 CFR 982: .503;
PIH Notices: 02-20; 00-46

HUD FIELD OFFICE..................222
24 CFR 5: .380;
24 CFR 982: .161; .503 (5);
HUD-50058: p ii; p6; p x; p xi; p xiii; p xiv; p xvi;
HUD-50058Instr: p4; p22; p42; p46; p53; p56; p59;
HUD-52580-A: p13;
HUD-52641: p6;
HUD-52646: p2;
HUD-52667: p ii;
7420.10G Gbk: 1-11; 5-20; 5-46 Ex 5-5; 8-14; 8-19; 11-2; 11-3; 13-4; 18-4; 19-2; 22-15; 23-2; 23-3;
PIH Notices: 03-12; 02-27 (2); 02-21 (10); 02-20 (16); 02-07; 01-41 (3); 01-20 (20); 01-15 (2); 01-10 (2); 01-06 (82); 01-01 (6); 00-53; 00-46 (13); 00-28; 00-27 (19); 00-14; 00-09 (3);
Admin Plan: s24p6

HUD FIELD OFFICES..................39
24 CFR 982: .3; .101;
HUD-50058Instr: p3;
7420.10G Gbk: 23-3;
PIH Notices: 02-27 (3); 02-21 (5); 02-01; 01-20 (4); 01-15; 01-06 (13); 01-01; 00-34; 00-27 (4); 00-14; 99-52

HUD FIELD OFFICE'S...................5
PIH Notices: 02-21; 01-20 (2); 00-27; 00-27

HUD FINANCIAL MANAGEMENT CENTER...6
7420.10G Gbk: 20-3; 20-28 (4); 20-29

HUD HEADQUARTERS...............23
24 CFR 982: .3 (2); .52; .152; .162 (3);
HUD-50058Instr: p3; p4;
HUD-52641: p10;
HUD-52641-A: p3;
7420.10G Gbk: 20-5; 20-6;
PIH Notices: 02-27 (2); 01-41 (4); 00-24B (2); 00-09; 00-09

HUD HOUSING 9
24 CFR 5: .703 (6); .705;
7420.10G Gbk: 10-1;
PIH Notices: 00-24B
HUD INSPECTOR GENERAL'S 1
24 CFR 5: .528
HUD REQUIREMENTS 68
24 CFR 5: .403; .508; .514; .601; .615 (2); .655; .659; .661;
24 CFR 982: .3; .4; .52 (3); .53; .54 (2); .103; .152; .156 (2); .158; .159; .454; .517; .551 (2); .635;
HUD-50058Instr: p70;
HUD-52641: p2; p3 (2); p4 (5); p7; 8 (3); p9 (2); p10 (4);
HUD-52641-A: p1 (3); p2 (2); p3 (4);
7420.10G Gbk: 9-11; 11-12; 11-14; 14-1; 15-1; 19-11; 23-9;
PIH Notices: 01-15 Impr Integ Hbk; 00-24B;
Admin Plan: s1p2; s20p1; s24p6
HUD-185 1
PIH Notices: 02-21
HUD-50058 127
HUD-50058: p1 (2); p i; p ii (2); p iii; p6 (5);
HUD-50058Instr: p i; p1 (11); p2 (8); p3 (2); p5 (4); p7; p11 (2); p16; p59 (2); p65 (4); p66 (3); p69;
HUD-52665: p1 (4); p2 (5); p3 (2);
7420.10G Gbk: 1-11; 12-3 (2); 12-5; 12-10; 13-3; 13-4; 13-7; 13-8 (2); 19-2 (2); 19-3 (2); 19-4 (2); 19-5; 20-6;
PIH Notices: 01-11 (11); 01-06 (5); 01-01 (3); 00-53 (24); 00-28; 00-24; 00-24B;
Admin Plan: s21p7
HUD-50059S 7
PIH Notices: 01-41 (3); 00-09 (3); 00-09
HUD-51234 1
HUD-50058Instr: p39
HUD-52515 8
PIH Notices: 02-21; 01-41 (2); 01-20; 00-27 (2); 00-09; 00-09
HUD-52517 6
7420.10G Gbk: 8-15 (2);
PIH Notices: 03-12 (3); 03-12
HUD-52580 10
HUD-52580: p1 (2); p2; p3; p4; p5; p6;
7420.10G Gbk: 10-1; 10-3; 10-26
HUD-52580-A 21
HUD-52580-A: p1; p2; p3; p4; p5; p6; p7; p8; p9; p10; p11; p12; p13; p14; p15; p16; p17; p18; p19; p20;
7420.10G Gbk: 10-3
HUD-52595 2
7420.10G Gbk: 20-29;
PIH Notices: 00-24B
HUD-52636 1
PIH Notices: 01-10
HUD-52641 4
7420.10G Gbk: 8-7; 11-10; 11-11;
PIH Notices: 00-09
HUD-52646 2
7420.10G Gbk: 1-15; 8-10
HUD-52648 4
7420.10G Gbk: 1-10;
PIH Notices: 01-06; 00-24B; 00-24B
HUD-52650 1
7420.10G Gbk: 23-6
HUD-52652 2
HUD-50058Instr: p65; p65
HUD-52663 4
7420.10G Gbk: 20-28 (3); 20-29
HUD-52665 11
HUD-52665: p3;
7420.10G Gbk: 13-3 (2); 13-4 (2); 13-5; 13-7 (2); 13-8 (2);
PIH Notices: 96-65
HUD-52667 11
HUD-52667: p1; p i (5); p ii (2);
7420.10G Gbk: 18-2 (2); 18-3 Ex 18-1
HUD-52672 10
7420.10G Gbk: 20-2 (2); 20-3; 20-4; 20-5; 20-28 (4); 20-28
HUD52673 1
7420.10G Gbk: 20-21 Ex 20-4
HUD-52673 10
7420.10G Gbk: 20-2; 20-6 (2); 20-7; 20-28 (5); 20-29

HUD-52681 26
7420.10G Gbk: 20-4; 20-5; 20-8 Ex 20-1; 20-12 Ex 20-2; 20-18; 20-21 Ex 20-4 (2); 20-26; 20-28; 20-29 (5); 24-2; 24-15;
PIH Notices: 02-21 (5); 01-20 (2); 01-06; 00-24B; 00-09

HUD-52681B 5
PIH Notices: 03-23 (4); 03-23

HUD-52683 5
PIH Notices: 00-14 (4); 00-14

HUD-52685 4
PIH Notices: 00-14 (3); 00-14

HUD-52860 4
PIH Notices: 02-21 (2); 01-20; 00-27

HUD-903 4
7420.10G Gbk: 5-45; 8-6; 8-14; 22-15

HUD-9886 6
HUD-50058Instr: p2; p3 (2);
7420.10G Gbk: 5-13; 12-3;
PIH Notices: 01-15 Impr Integ Hbk

HUD-APPROVED 64
24 CFR 5: .514; .659; .801;
24 CFR 982: .102 (2); .154; .157; .352; .503 (3); .516; .604; .608; .630;
HUD-52648: p2;
7420.10G Gbk: 1-14; 7-4 (2); 10-2; 20-1; 20-9;
PIH Notices: 03-23; 02-27 (3); 02-22 (3); 02-21 (7); 02-20 (5); 01-20 (5); 01-06 (8); 00-46 (5); 00-27 (3);
Admin Plan: s21p7; s21p9

HUD-ASSISTED 6
24 CFR 5: .603;
HUD-50058Instr: p71;
HUD-9886: p2;
7420.10G Gbk: 5-3;
PIH Notices: 99-11;
Admin Plan: s20p1

HUD-DESIGNATED 1
7420.10G Gbk: 1-5

HUD-DETERMINED 1
7420.10G Gbk: 5-26

HUD-ESTABLISHED 1
7420.10G Gbk: 1-3

HUD-INSURED 4
7420.10G Gbk: 1-6; 1-9 (2); 11-18

HUD-OWNED 2
24 CFR 5: .318;
24 CFR 982: .310

HUD-OWNER 1
7420.10G Gbk: 23-2

HUD-PHA 1
7420.10G Gbk: 20-29

HUD-PRESCRIBED 13
24 CFR 5: .318; .653; .705;
24 CFR 982: .302; .305; .308 (2);
HUD-52646: p2;
7420.10G Gbk: 8-15; 8-16; 8-21;
PIH Notices: 01-41;
Admin Plan: s9p3

HUD-PUBLISHED 5
PIH Notices: 01-06 (3); 01-01; 01-01

HUD-REIMBURSABLE 1
24 CFR 5: .318

HUD-REQUIRED 12
24 CFR 982: Intro; .103; .158; .162; .301; .308; .355;
HUD-52641: p10;
HUD-52641-A: p3;
7420.10G Gbk: 1-1; 20-28;
PIH Notices: 00-23

HUD-SUPPLIED 1
24 CFR 5: .520

HUD-TARGETED 2
24 CFR 982: .203;
7420.10G Gbk: 4-22

HUMAN BEINGS 3
HUD-50058Instr: p72;
Admin Plan: s23p2; s25p3

HUMAN WASTE 5
24 CFR 5: .703;
24 CFR 982: .401; .605; .614;
7420.10G Gbk: 10-3

HVAC 3
24 CFR 5: .703 (2); .703

HYGIENE 1
24 CFR 5: .703

I-551 1
7420.10G Gbk: 5-10 Ex 5-1

I-688 1
7420.10G Gbk: 5-10 Ex 5-1

I-688B 1
7420.10G Gbk: 5-10 Ex 5-1

I-94 2
7420.10G Gbk: 5-10 Ex 5-1; 5-10 Ex 5-1

IDENTIFICATION NUMBER 41
24 CFR 5: .214 (2);
HUD-50058: p i; p ii; p x (3); p xi (3); p xii;

p xiii (3); p xiv (2); p xvi;
HUD-50058Instr: p3; p42 (3); p43; p46 (3); p47; p50; p53 (4); p56 (3); p59 (2); p76;
7420.10G Gbk: 11-19 (2);
Admin Plan: s9p1; s11p1

IDENTITY.......................................6
7420.10G Gbk: 22-16;
PIH Notices: 95-48; 95-48 Tech Asst;
Admin Plan: s7p7 (2); s7p7

ILL.......................................5
24 CFR 5: .318;
24 CFR 982: .315;
PIH Notices: 95-48; 95-48 Tech Asst;
Admin Plan: s23p2

ILLEGAL.......................................69
24 CFR 5: .100;
24 CFR 982: .54; .304 (2); .310 (2); .552 (2); .553 (5);
HUD-52646: p2;
7420.10G Gbk: 3-3 (2); 4-18; 4-25 Ex 4-2; 5-37 (2); 5-42; 5-43; 15-7; 22-2; 22-9;
PIH Notices: 03-11 (3); 95-48 (17); 95-48 Tech Asst (17);
Admin Plan: s9p3; s15p2 (4); s15p3; s20p6

ILLEGAL ACTION.......................................1
Admin Plan: s20p6

ILLEGAL ACTIVITIES.......................................1
7420.10G Gbk: 22-2

ILLEGAL DRUG.......................................9
24 CFR 982: .552; .553 (2);
7420.10G Gbk: 15-7;
PIH Notices: 03-11 (3);
Admin Plan: s15p2; s15p2

ILLEGAL DRUGS.......................................4
PIH Notices: 95-48 (2); 95-48 Tech Asst; 95-48 Tech Asst

ILLEGALLY.......................................12
24 CFR 982: .310;
7420.10G Gbk: 22-11; 22-15;
PIH Notices: 95-48 (4); 95-48 Tech Asst (4);
Admin Plan: s15p3

ILLNESS.......................................10
24 CFR 5: .360;
7420.10G Gbk: 4-13; 5-43; 8-12; 23-7;
PIH Notices: 95-48 (2); 95-48 Tech Asst (2);
Admin Plan: s25p3

ILLNESSES.......................................1
HUD-903-1: p2

ILLUMINATION.......................................22
24 CFR 982: .401 (3);
HUD-52580: p3 (3); p4 (2);
HUD-52580-A: p8 (2); p9 (2); p10 (2); p11 (2); p12 (2);
7420.10G Gbk: 10-1; 10-4; 10-8; 10-8

IMMEDIATE.......................................26
24 CFR 5: .360;
24 CFR 982: .306; .310; .551 (2); .553; .605;
HUD-52580-A: p18;
HUD-52641: p6 (2);
7420.10G Gbk: 2-6; 14-1; 14-2; 17-2; 21-7; 22-11 (2); 22-14;
PIH Notices: 03-23 (2); 95-48 (2); 95-48 Tech Asst (2);
Admin Plan: s16p2; s16p2

IMMEDIATE FAMILY MEMBERS.1
Admin Plan: s16p2

IMMEDIATE VICINITY.......................................12
24 CFR 982: .306; .310; .551 (2); .553;
HUD-52641: p7; p9;
HUD-52641-A: p2 (3);
7420.10G Gbk: 15-2;
Admin Plan: s16p2

IMMEDIATELY.......................................57
24 CFR 5: .360;
24 CFR 35 SubM: .1225 (2);
24 CFR 982: .308; .451 (2); .553;
HUD-50058Instr: p19;
HUD-52641: 8; p10;
HUD-52641-A: p1; p3;
7420.10G Gbk: 1-5; 2-6; 4-7; 5-23; 8-9; 8-11; 10-20; 11-6 (2); 13-5; 15-6; 22-12 (4); 22-13 (2); 22-15 (4); 24-13;
PIH Notices: 03-20 (2); 03-11; 02-21 (2); 01-41 (5); 01-20 (2); 01-15 Impr Integ Hbk; 00-27 (2); 00-09 (5);
Admin Plan: s22p4 (2); s24p7

IMMIGRANT.......................................16
HUD-50058Instr: p18 (4);
7420.10G Gbk: 5-3; 5-9 Ex 5-1;
Admin Plan: s2p1; s2p5 (3); s6p11; s7p3; s15p1; s18p1; s18p7; s18p7

IMMIGRANTS.......................................4
HUD-50058Instr: p68 (2);
Admin Plan: s2p5; s6p12

IMMIGRATION 107
24 CFR 5: .500; .504 (5); .506; .508 (23); .510 (6); .512 (11); .514 (12); .516; .518 (6); .520 (7); .524; .630; .659;
24 CFR 982: .201; .551; .552 (2); .554; .555;
HUD-50058: p v;
HUD-50058Instr: p3; p17 (3); p71; p73 (3);
7420.10G Gbk: 5-3 (2); 5-6; 5-8 (2); 16-3 (3);
PIH Notices: 01-27; 01-15 Impr Integ Hbk;
Admin Plan: s2p1; s2p5 (2); s3p3; s18p7; s18p8

IMMIGRATION STATUS 22
24 CFR 5: .500; .508; .510 (2); .512 (5); .514 (5);
7420.10G Gbk: 5-6; 5-8 (2); 16-3 (2);
Admin Plan: s2p5; s3p3; s18p7

IMMIGRATIONS 1
24 CFR 5: .504

IMMUNODEFICIENCY 6
24 CFR 5: .403 (2);
HUD-50058Instr: p74 (2);
Admin Plan: s25p2; s25p2

IMPAIR 1
24 CFR 5: .303

IMPAIRED 23
24 CFR 982: .401;
HUD-52580-A: p9; p10; p11; p12;
HUD-903: p3;
7420.10G Gbk: 4-11; 5-44 (3); 8-3;
PIH Notices: 02-01 (2); 99-52 (2); 95-48 (4); 95-48 Tech Asst (3); 95-48 Tech Asst

IMPAIRMENT 95
24 CFR 5: .403;
HUD-50058: p i;
HUD-50058Instr: p15; p29; p74;
7420.10G Gbk: 5-37 (2); 5-43; 5-44;
PIH Notices: 95-48 (41); 95-48 Tech Asst (41);
Admin Plan: s1p4 (3); s25p2

IMPAIRMENTS 109
7420.10G Gbk: 4-11; 5-43 (3); 5-44 (2);
PIH Notices: 02-01 (7); 99-52 (7); 95-48 (44); 95-48 Tech Asst (44);
Admin Plan: s1p3

IMPAIRS 1
24 CFR 5: .303

IMPARTIAL 5
24 CFR 5: .514;
7420.10G Gbk: 16-4 (2);
PIH Notices: 95-48; 95-48 Tech Asst

IMPARTIALITY 1
7420.10G Gbk: 16-4

IMPARTIALLY 3
7420.10G Gbk: 24-13;
PIH Notices: 95-48; 95-48 Tech Asst

IMPLEMENT 42
24 CFR 5: .655;
24 CFR 982: .160; .207; .625 (2);
HUD-50058Instr: p17;
7420.10G Gbk: 1-13; 3-8; 3-9; 4-21 (2); 9-11; 10-15; 12-8; 16-3; 22-3;
PIH Notices: 03-11; 02-27 (5); 01-41; 01-15; 01-11 (2); 00-53 (4); 00-11 (2); 00-11A (6); 00-09 (2);
Admin Plan: s1p6; s23p2

IMPLEMENTATION 68
24 CFR 5: .324 (2); .526 (2);
24 CFR 982: .643;
HUD-50058Instr: p78;
HUD-52641: p6 (2);
7420.10G Gbk: 2-1; 3-1; 4-4; 4-14; 4-16; 5-11; 14-1; 22-4; 23-3; 23-5 (3);
PIH Notices: 03-23; 03-20; 03-12; 02-27 (8); 02-01; 01-43; 01-27 (5); 01-15 Impr Integ Hbk; 01-11 (5); 01-06; 01-01 (2); 00-53 (8); 00-31; 00-24 (2); 00-11; 99-52; 99-30; 99-11 (2); 95-48 (2); 95-48 Tech Asst (2);
Admin Plan: s25p4

IMPLEMENTED 35
24 CFR 5: .324;
24 CFR 982: .102;
HUD-50058Instr: p17; p42; p78;
HUD-52641: p7;
7420.10G Gbk: 1-2; 2-2; 10-15; 11-9; 11-14; 22-5;
PIH Notices: 03-23; 02-27 (2); 02-01; 01-15 (3); 01-06; 00-24; 00-11A; 99-52; 95-48 (4); 95-48 Tech Asst (4);
Admin Plan: s1p1; s21p1; s21p3; s21p5

IMPLEMENTING 60
24 CFR 5: .105 (9); .524 (3); .603;
24 CFR 982: .401;
7420.10G Gbk: 3-9; 4-13; 5-11; 10-11; 11-13; 11-14; 20-11; 22-4; 22-5; 23-4; 24-14;
PIH Notices: 03-20; 02-27 (3); 02-06; 02-01 (8); 00-34; 00-11; 99-52 (8); 95-48 (9); 95-48 Tech Asst (2); 95-48 Tech Asst

IMPLEMENTS 13
24 CFR 5: .300; .500; .801;
24 CFR 982: .102; .642;
HUD-52648: p1;
7420.10G Gbk: 9-12;
PIH Notices: 03-23; 01-41; 01-01; 00-53; 95-48; 95-48

IMPLIED AUTHORITY 4
24 CFR 5: .100 (2);
Admin Plan: s15p3; s15p3

IMPOSE 29
24 CFR 5: .315; .318 (2); .630; .661;
24 CFR 982: .552; .625;
HUD-903-1: p2;
7420.10G Gbk: 5-38; 13-9; 20-6; 22-14;
PIH Notices: 00-28; 96-65 (3); 95-48 (6); 95-48 Tech Asst (6);
Admin Plan: s6p5

IMPOSED 32
24 CFR 5: .318 (2); .321; .363; .504; .508 (2); .524; .615;
24 CFR 982: .53; .310; .621;
HUD-50058Instr: p75;
HUD-52580-A: p13;
7420.10G Gbk: 1-3; 5-22; 11-6; 15-6; 17-11; 17-12;
PIH Notices: 00-28; 96-65 (2); 95-48 (2); 95-48 Tech Asst (2);
Admin Plan: s6p5 (2); s6p12; s15p6; s19p1

IMPOSES 5
24 CFR 5: .359;
24 CFR 982: .310;
HUD-52641: p9;
HUD-52641-A: p2;
7420.10G Gbk: 20-28

IMPRISONED 3
24 CFR 982: .553;
HUD-50058Instr: p72;
Admin Plan: s23p3

IMPRISONMENT 1
24 CFR 982: .312

IMPROPER 15
HUD-52580-A: p2; p15 (3);
HUD-9886: p1; p2 (2);
7420.10G Gbk: 10-7; 10-8 (2);
PIH Notices: 01-41; 00-09; 95-48; 95-48 Tech Asst;
Admin Plan: s1p6

IMPROPERLY 3
24 CFR 5: .528;
PIH Notices: 03-11;
Admin Plan: s15p4

IMPROVE 47
24 CFR 982: .155; .309;
HUD-50058Instr: p70;
HUD-52641: p1;
7420.10G Gbk: 2-1; 2-4; 2-5 (2); 4-4; 8-1; 8-11; 8-14; 8-22; 11-9; 12-8; 19-2; 19-5; 19-6; 19-10 (2); 19-11 (2); 21-10 (2); 22-8; 24-3; 24-6; 24-9 (2); 24-10;
PIH Notices: 02-27 (3); 02-01; 01-41; 01-15 (3); 00-53 (2); 00-11 (2); 00-09; 99-52; 99-11;
Admin Plan: s9p2; s21p9

IMPROVED 21
24 CFR 5: .403;
HUD-50058: p i;
HUD-50058Instr: p15; p74;
7420.10G Gbk: 2-7; 4-4; 11-8; 19-5; 19-11; 20-11; 21-3; 21-9; 21-10;
PIH Notices: 02-27; 02-21; 01-20; 01-06; 95-48; 95-48 Tech Asst;
Admin Plan: s18p3; s25p2

IMPROVEMENT 22
7420.10G Gbk: 7-9; 19-3; 19-13; 21-10;
PIH Notices: 02-27 (8); 02-21; 02-01; 01-20; 00-27; 00-11 (2); 99-52;
Admin Plan: s1p1; s21p9; s25p7

IMPROVEMENTS 21
24 CFR 982: .605; .635 (2);
HUD-50058: p14; p xiv;
HUD-50058Instr: p56 (2); p72 (2); p73 (2);
7420.10G Gbk: 5-19; 8-22; 10-28 (2); 19-6;
PIH Notices: 02-27 (4); 99-11

IMPROVES 1
7420.10G Gbk: 24-2

IMPROVING..................................27
7420.10G Gbk: 1-10; 2-1; 2-11; 7-4; 8-11; 8-14; 19-2; 21-4; 21-10 (2); 24-8 (2); 24-9; 24-10; 24-13;
PIH Notices: 02-27; 01-15 (9); 01-15 Impr Integ Hbk;
Admin Plan: s21p1

IMPUTED......................................51
24 CFR 5: .603; .615 (16);
HUD-50058: p6 (3);
HUD-50058Instr: p22 (2); p23 (7); p28; p73;
7420.10G Gbk: 5-21 (2); 5-22 (8); 5-24; 5-26 (2); 5-28;
PIH Notices: 01-15;
Admin Plan: s6p12 (3); s6p13; s6p13

IMPUTED ASSET INCOME............5
HUD-50058: p6;
HUD-50058Instr: p23 (3); p23

IMPUTED INCOME.........................8
HUD-50058: p6;
HUD-50058Instr: p23 (3);
7420.10G Gbk: 5-24; 5-26; 5-28;
PIH Notices: 01-15

IMPUTED WELFARE INCOME...35
24 CFR 5: .603; .615 (16);
HUD-50058: p6;
HUD-50058Instr: p28; p73;
7420.10G Gbk: 5-21 (2); 5-22 (8);
Admin Plan: s6p12 (3); s6p13; s6p13

IN TRUST.......................................10
24 CFR 5: .603 (2);
HUD-50058Instr: p22; p30 (2);
7420.10G Gbk: 5-16 Ex 5-2 (2);
PIH Notices: 01-15 Impr Integ Hbk (2); 01-15 Impr Integ Hbk

IN WRITING.................................80
24 CFR 5: .236 (2); .303; .508 (2); .514; .518 (2); .615;
24 CFR 982: .5; .308; .352; .612; .628;
HUD-50058Instr: p2;
HUD-52641: p7 (2); p10 (2);
HUD-52641-A: p3 (2);
HUD-52646: p2 (5);
7420.10G Gbk: 1-11; 4-7; 4-11; 4-14 (2); 5-6; 5-11; 5-40; 8-17; 10-27; 11-14; 11-18 (2); 12-2; 12-6; 12-10; 15-10 Ex 15-2; 22-11;
PIH Notices: 03-11; 02-27; 02-21; 02-07; 01-27; 01-20; 01-06 (2); 00-28 (2); 00-27; 95-48; 95-48 Tech Asst;
Admin Plan: s2p7; s3p2 (2); s3p3 (2); s5p2; s6p4; s6p8; s7p2; s7p8; s9p3; s11p3; s18p1 (2); s18p2; s18p3 (2); s18p6; s19p1; s23p3; s23p7; s24p6; s25p6

INACTION......................................9
24 CFR 982: .201; .206; .355; .552;
Admin Plan: s18p1 (3); s18p6; s20p6

INADVERTENT...............................1
7420.10G Gbk: 5-11

INADVERTENTLY..........................2
7420.10G Gbk: 22-8;
PIH Notices: 99-11

INAPPROPRIATE............................5
24 CFR 5: .350;
HUD-52580-A: p15;
7420.10G Gbk: 16-5; 19-10;
Admin Plan: s1p6

INAPPROPRIATELY.......................2
7420.10G Gbk: 9-1; 9-8

INCAPACITATED...........................1
24 CFR 5: .350

INCENTIVE..................................18
HUD-52648: p2;
7420.10G Gbk: 2-11; 11-9; 14-1 (4); 23-1; 24-15;
PIH Notices: 02-22; 01-10 (6); 01-06; 01-06

INCENTIVES................................10
24 CFR 5: .617;
7420.10G Gbk: 23-4 (2); 24-14; 24-15;
PIH Notices: 01-15 Impr Integ Hbk; 00-11 (3); 00-11A

INCIDENTAL..................................5
24 CFR 982: .551;
HUD-50058Instr: p28;
HUD-52641: 8;
HUD-52641-A: p1;
7420.10G Gbk: 1-15

INCLUSION...................................6
HUD-50058Instr: p1;
7420.10G Gbk: 10-26; 10-43 Ex 10-6; 23-9;
PIH Notices: 00-27;
Admin Plan: s22p2

INCLUSIONS..................................6
7420.10G Gbk: 5-13; 5-14 Ex 5-

2 (2); 5-15 Ex 5-2; 5-24; 5-25 Ex 5-3
INCLUSIVE 1
HUD-52580-A: p15
INCOME CEILINGS........................... 6
24 CFR 5: .603 (3);
HUD-50058Instr: p71; p73; p76
INCOME DEDUCTIONS 4
HUD-50058Instr: p24;
PIH Notices: 01-15 Impr Integ Hbk (2); 01-15 Impr Integ Hbk
INCOME DISCREPANCY 5
7420.10G Gbk: 22-4 (2);
Admin Plan: s7p2 (2); s7p2
INCOME EXCLUDED 3
HUD-50058: p6;
HUD-50058Instr: p33;
Admin Plan: s6p2
INCOME EXCLUSION 5
HUD-50058: p6;
PIH Notices: 01-15; 00-01; 98-66;
Admin Plan: s6p2
INCOME EXCLUSIONS................ 27
HUD-50058: p6 (3);
HUD-50058Instr: p24 (2); p25; p26; p27; p28; p29; p30; p31; p32; p33 (4); p34;
7420.10G Gbk: 5-14 Ex 5-2 (3); 5-15 Ex 5-2;
PIH Notices: 01-15 Impr Integ Hbk (4); 01-15 Impr Integ Hbk
INCOME FAMILY 1
24 CFR 5: .655
INCOME FROM ASSET 1
7420.10G Gbk: 5-49 Ex 5-5
INCOME FROM ASSETS 18
HUD-50058: p6;
HUD-50058Instr: p23 (2);
7420.10G Gbk: 4-26 Ex 4-2; 5-18 (3); 5-24 (4); 5-26 (6);
PIH Notices: 01-15 Impr Integ Hbk
INCOME LIMIT.............................. 13
24 CFR 982: .201 (4);
7420.10G Gbk: 5-1; 5-2; 5-3 (3); 5-35; 13-4;
Admin Plan: s2p4; s2p4
INCOME LIMITATIONS.................. 2
Admin Plan: s2p4; s23p3
INCOME LIMITS 4
Admin Plan: s2p1; s2p5; s6p1; s13p2
INCOME MATCHING...................... 2
HUD-50058: p i;
7420.10G Gbk: 22-4
INCOME MIX 1
Admin Plan: s24p2
INCOME TARGETING 29
24 CFR 5: .617;
24 CFR 982: .102; .201;
HUD-50058: p5; p v;
HUD-50058Instr: p19 (4);
7420.10G Gbk: 4-5 (2); 4-8; 4-19 (2); 4-21 (2); 13-7 (2);
PIH Notices: 01-41 (3); 01-15 Impr Integ Hbk; 00-09 (3);
Admin Plan: s3p2; s4p1; s4p2; s4p2
INCOME-BASED 18
24 CFR 5: .632 (2);
HUD-50058Instr: p12; p78;
PIH Notices: 01-15 Impr Integ Hbk (13); 01-15 Impr Integ Hbk
INCOME-BASED RENT 14
24 CFR 5: .632 (2);
HUD-50058Instr: p78;
PIH Notices: 01-15 Impr Integ Hbk (10); 01-15 Impr Integ Hbk
INCOME-BASED RENTS................ 1
PIH Notices: 01-15 Impr Integ Hbk
INCOME-DEDUCTIONS 1
PIH Notices: 01-15
INCOME-ELIGIBILITY 8
24 CFR 5: .601; .653 (3); .655;
24 CFR 982: .201 (2); .627
INCOME-ELIGIBLE 13
24 CFR 5: .653;
24 CFR 982: .201 (2);
HUD-52665: p1;
PIH Notices: 01-41 (5); 00-09 (2);
Admin Plan: s2p4; s20p1
INCOME-LIMIT 1
7420.10G Gbk: 5-2
INCOMES 17
24 CFR 5: .603 (3); .615; .653 (2);
HUD-50058Instr: p71; p73; p76;
7420.10G Gbk: 3-3; 4-9; 4-19; 4-20; 5-2; 5-3;
PIH Notices: 00-11;
Admin Plan: s24p6
INCOME-TARGETING................. 24
24 CFR 5: .601; .653 (4); .655;
24 CFR 982: .201 (2);
HUD-50058Instr: p19;
7420.10G Gbk: 4-9; 4-14; 4-19; 4-20 (9); 4-21 (2);

4-21

INCOMPLETE INFORMATION...... 1
PIH Notices: 01-15 Impr Integ Hbk

INCONCLUSIVE............................ 62
HUD-52580: p1 (4); p3 (3); p4 (4); p5 (3); p6 (3); p7 (3); p8; p9 (3); p10 (3); p11 (3); p12 (3); p14 (3); p15 (4); p16 (3); p17; p18 (3);
HUD-52580-A: p2
7420.10G Gbk: 10-23 (3); 10-26 (2); 10-27 (3); 10-28 (3); 10-30;
PIH Notices: 03-11 (2);
Admin Plan: s20p5

INCORPORATE................................ 7
24 CFR 5: .321; .516;
24 CFR 35 SubM: .1220;
7420.10G Gbk: 4-4; 10-15;
PIH Notices: 02-01; 99-52

INCORPORATED........................... 27
24 CFR 5: .508;
24 CFR 982: .503 (3);
HUD-50058Instr: p73;
7420.10G Gbk: 10-37 Ex 10-2; 18-1;
PIH Notices: 02-20 (8); 02-01; 00-46 (8); 00-23; 99-52;
Admin Plan: s25p4

INCORPORATED PLACE 19
24 CFR 982: .503 (3);
PIH Notices: 02-20 (8); 00-46 (7); 00-46

INCORPORATES............................ 10
HUD-50058Instr: p1; p65;
PIH Notices: 02-01; 01-06; 01-01; 99-52; 95-48; 95-48 Tech Asst;
Admin Plan: s1p6; s25p4

INCORPORATING 2
7420.10G Gbk: 20-11;
PIH Notices: 02-27

INCORPORATION 1
PIH Notices: 02-27

INCORRECT.................................. 16
7420.10G Gbk: 5-34; 22-1; 22-2 (2); 22-6; 22-13; 22-17;
PIH Notices: 01-41; 01-15; 01-15 Impr Integ Hbk; 01-06; 00-09;
Admin Plan: s7p3; s21p7 (2); s21p7

INCORRECT RENT......................... 1
PIH Notices: 01-15 Impr Integ Hbk

INCORRECTLY............................... 9
7420.10G Gbk: 4-13; 16-5; 22-1; 22-2 (2); 22-11 (2); 22-12; 22-12

INCREASE IN EXPENSES............. 1
PIH Notices: 01-15 Impr Integ Hbk

INCREASE SECURITY.................... 1
24 CFR 5: .661

INCREMENT 53
24 CFR 982: .4 (3); .102 (7); .151 (5); .152; .155; .309; .317;
HUD-50058: p xii;
HUD-50058Instr: p50 (3);
7420.10G Gbk: 8-23; 20-11; 22-7 (3);
PIH Notices: 03-23 (2); 02-21 (6); 02-14 (2); 02-07 (2); 01-41 (2); 01-20 (2); 00-28 (2); 00-27 (3); 00-09 (3); 00-09

INCREMENTAL 15
24 CFR 5: .609;
24 CFR 982: .355 (2);
HUD-50058Instr: p27; p28;
7420.10G Gbk: 5-15 Ex 5-2; 5-20; 20-8 Ex 20-1;
PIH Notices: 01-15; 01-15 Impr Integ Hbk (3);
Admin Plan: s6p3 (2); s6p3

INCREMENTAL EARNINGS 9
24 CFR 5: .609;
HUD-50058Instr: p27; p28;
7420.10G Gbk: 5-15 Ex 5-2; 5-20;
PIH Notices: 01-15; 01-15 Impr Integ Hbk (2); 01-15 Impr Integ Hbk

INCREMENTS............................... 33
24 CFR 982: Intro; .101; .102 (8); .151;
7420.10G Gbk: 4-1; 8-22; 19-7;
PIH Notices: 03-23 (2); 02-21 (7); 02-20; 02-14 (5); 01-41; 01-06; 00-46;
Admin Plan: s24p1

INDEFINITE 14
24 CFR 5: .403;
HUD-50058: p i;
HUD-50058Instr: p15; p74;
PIH Notices: 03-05; 02-27 (3); 02-21; 02-20; 02-15;
Admin Plan: s6p7; s9p2; s25p2

INDEFINITE DURATION 5
24 CFR 5: .403;
HUD-50058: p i;
HUD-50058Instr: p15; p74;
Admin Plan: s25p2

INDEFINITELY............................... 2

PIH Notices: 02-15;
Admin Plan: s17p3
INDEMNIFY 2
24 CFR 5: .318;
24 CFR 982: .157
INDEPENDENCE 17
24 CFR 5: .603;
HUD-50058Instr: p71; p72;
7420.10G Gbk: 23-1 (3); 23-8 Ex 23-1; 23-9;
PIH Notices: 00-11; 95-48 (3); 95-48 Tech Asst (3);
Admin Plan: s6p3; s25p3
INDEPENDENT 64
24 CFR 5: .236 (3); .703;
24 CFR 982: .152; .159; .202; .352 (11); .628 (3); .631 (9);
HUD-50058Instr: p73;
HUD-52580: p1 (4);
7420.10G Gbk: 4-22; 10-30 (2); 10-31 (5); 11-19; 12-11 (2); 20-2; 21-1;
PIH Notices: 02-27 (4); 01-06 (2); 00-41 (2); 00-24; 00-24A;
Admin Plan: s7p1 (2); s20p1; s21p9; s22p3; s23p2
INDEPENDENT AUDIT 5
7420.10G Gbk: 4-22;
PIH Notices: 02-27 (2); 01-06; 00-24A
INDEPENDENT AUDITOR 5
HUD-52648: p1;
7420.10G Gbk: 10-31;
PIH Notices: 01-06; 00-24;
Admin Plan: s21p9
INDEPENDENT VERIFICATION ... 6
24 CFR 5: .236 (3);
HUD-9886: p1;
7420.10G Gbk: 12-11;
Admin Plan: s20p1
INDEPENDENTLY 21
24 CFR 5: .318; .403 (2);
HUD-50058: p i;
HUD-50058Instr: p15; p74 (2);
HUD-9886: p2;
7420.10G Gbk: 1-11; 5-39; 8-11; 22-3;
PIH Notices: 01-41; 01-06; 00-41;
Admin Plan: s7p7; s20p1; s20p3 (2); s20p6; s25p2
INDEPENDENTLY VERIFIABLE... 3
Admin Plan: s20p1; s20p3; s20p3
INDEPENDENTLY VERIFIED 1
Admin Plan: s20p6
INDEPENDENTLY VERIFY 1
7420.10G Gbk: 22-3
INDEPENDENTLY VERIFYING 1
HUD-9886: p2
INDIAN 312
24 CFR 5: .214; .504 (2); .603;
24 CFR 35 SubM: .1200 (2);
24 CFR 982: .160; .352 (2); .503;
HUD-50058: p1 (2); p i (2); p2 (5); p ii (4); p3; p4; p5 (3); p v (3); p6; p7; p vii; p9 (2); p ix (5); p15; p xv (3);
HUD-50058Instr: p i; p ii (2); p1; p3; p5; p7 (5); p8 (4); p9 (3); p10; p11; p12; p15; p20 (3); p22; p24; p30 (8); p32; p36; p39 (3); p40 (4); p58 (5); p68 (4); p69 (5); p70; p71 (2); p73 (4); p74 (4); p75 (3); p78 (3);
HUD-52580: p1 (6); p2 (2);
7420.10G Gbk: 4-23 Ex 4-1; 4-25 Ex 4-2 (2); 5-16 Ex 5-2 (6); 5-25 Ex 5-3; 7-4; 8-16; 19-3;
PIH Notices: 03-23 (2); 03-20 (2); 03-12 (2); 03-11; 03-05 (2); 02-27 (4); 02-22 (2); 02-21 (2); 02-20 (5); 02-15 (2); 02-14 (2); 02-07 (2); 02-06 (2); 02-03 (2); 02-01 (17); 01-43 (4); 01-41 (2); 01-40 (2); 01-33 (2); 01-27 (2); 01-20 (2); 01-15 (3); 01-15 Impr Integ Hbk (9); 01-11 (5); 01-10 (2); 01-06 (3); 01-02 (2); 01-01 (2); 00-53 (6); 00-49 (2); 00-46 (5); 00-45 (3); 00-41 (2); 00-34 (3); 00-31 (2); 00-28 (2); 00-27 (2); 00-24 (2); 00-23 (2); 00-14 (2); 00-11 (2); 00-09 (3); 00-01 (3); 99-52 (17); 99-30 (2); 99-11 (9); 98-66 (2); 96-65 (3); 95-48 (7); 95-48
INDIAN TRUST LAND 3
24 CFR 5: .603;
HUD-50058Instr: p22; p74
INDICATOR 1 8
7420.10G Gbk: 1-10; 4-18; 4-22 (4);

Admin Plan: s21p2; s21p3

INDICATOR 10 2
7420.10G Gbk: 1-10;
Admin Plan: s21p2

INDICATOR 11 6
7420.10G Gbk: 1-10; 10-31; 10-35; 11-19 (2);
Admin Plan: s21p2

INDICATOR 12 9
7420.10G Gbk: 1-10; 10-31; 10-35;
PIH Notices: 01-06 (5);
Admin Plan: s21p2

INDICATOR 14 14
7420.10G Gbk: 23-19;
PIH Notices: 01-06 (12);
Admin Plan: s21p2

INDICATOR 15 9
PIH Notices: 01-06 (8);
Admin Plan: s21p2

INDICATOR 2 7
7420.10G Gbk: 1-10; 9-12 (2); 10-31; 10-32;
Admin Plan: s21p2; s21p3

INDICATOR 3 7
7420.10G Gbk: 1-10; 12-10; 12-11; 18-10; 19-10;
Admin Plan: s21p2; s21p4

INDICATOR 4 3
7420.10G Gbk: 1-10; 18-10;
Admin Plan: s21p2

INDICATOR 5 5
7420.10G Gbk: 1-10; 10-31; 10-32 (2);
Admin Plan: s21p2

INDICATOR 6 5
7420.10G Gbk: 1-10; 10-31; 10-32; 10-33;
Admin Plan: s21p2

INDICATOR 7 16
7420.10G Gbk: 1-10; 2-2; 2-3 (2); 2-4; 7-7; 7-9; 8-7; 13-10;
PIH Notices: 01-06 (6);
Admin Plan: s21p2

INDICATOR 8 15
7420.10G Gbk: 1-10; 7-9;
PIH Notices: 01-06 (12);
Admin Plan: s21p2

INDICATOR 9 3
7420.10G Gbk: 1-10; 12-10;
Admin Plan: s21p2

INDIRECT 6
24 CFR 5: .801;
24 CFR 982: .161;
HUD-52580-A: p15;
HUD-52641: p6;
PIH Notices: 02-27;
Admin Plan: s20p4

INDIRECT COSTS 1
PIH Notices: 02-27

INDIRECTLY 8
24 CFR 982: .353; .401;
HUD-52580-A: p15; p16;
7420.10G Gbk: 10-7; 10-31;
PIH Notices: 95-48; 95-48 Tech Asst

INDIVIDUAL METER 1
Admin Plan: s6p13

INDIVIDUAL RETIREMENT ACCOUNTS 1
HUD-50058Instr: p29

INDIVIDUAL SAVINGS ACCOUNT1
HUD-50058: p i

INDIVIDUAL SAVINGS ACCOUNTS 4
HUD-50058: p6;
PIH Notices: 01-15 Impr Integ Hbk (2); 00-11

INDIVIDUALIZED 4
PIH Notices: 95-48 (2); 95-48 Tech Asst; 95-48 Tech Asst

INDIVIDUALIZED ASSESSMENT 2
PIH Notices: 95-48; 95-48 Tech Asst

INDIVIDUALLY 8
7420.10G Gbk: 5-3; 8-8;
PIH Notices: 03-12; 95-48; 95-48 Tech Asst;
Admin Plan: s2p5; s6p13; s6p13

INDIVIDUALLY METERED 2
Admin Plan: s6p13; s6p13

INELIGIBILITY 12
24 CFR 5: .506; .508; .514 (2); .518;
7420.10G Gbk: 4-10; 4-11; 5-4; 5-6; 16-3;
Admin Plan: s18p1; s18p7

INELIGIBLE EXPENSES 1
24 CFR 982: .155

INELIGIBLE FAMILIES 4
7420.10G Gbk: 4-15;
PIH Notices: 01-41; 00-09;
Admin Plan: s2p7

INELIGIBLE FAMILY 2
24 CFR 5: .518;
24 CFR 982: .158

INELIGIBLE FAMILY MEMBERS . 5
HUD-50058Instr: p44; p48; p51; p54; p57

INFANTS 1
HUD-50058Instr: p16
INFERENCE 1
24 CFR 5: .236
INFESTATION 24
24 CFR 5: .703 (3);
24 CFR 982: .401 (3); .614;
HUD-52580: p5;
HUD-52580-A: p17 (2); p18 (2);
7420.10G Gbk: 10-9; 10-13 (4); 10-14 (4); 17-5;
Admin Plan: s10p5; s10p5
INFLAMMATORY 1
Admin Plan: s20p4
INFLUENCE 1
7420.10G Gbk: 5-38
INFLUENCES 4
24 CFR 982: .161;
HUD-52641: p6;
7420.10G Gbk: 8-19; 11-2
INFORM 78
24 CFR 5: .236; .514; .518 (2); .615 (3); .655;
24 CFR 982: .307; .352; .355; .551; .628;
HUD-52641: 8;
HUD-52641-A: p1;
7420.10G Gbk: 2-2; 2-5; 4-3; 4-7; 4-11; 4-14; 5-6; 5-11; 5-39; 5-40 (2); 8-2 (2); 8-4; 8-6; 8-11; 8-20; 10-22; 10-26; 12-3; 12-6; 12-12 Ex 12-1; 13-1; 13-5; 13-6; 14-3 (2); 16-5; 20-14 (2); 21-10; 22-2; 22-9 (2); 22-12; 22-15; 24-14;
PIH Notices: 02-27 (2); 02-21; 02-20; 02-01; 01-41; 01-15 (2); 01-15 Impr Integ Hbk (2); 00-46; 00-41; 00-23; 99-52; 96-65; 95-48; 95-48 Tech Asst;
Admin Plan: s1p6; s2p6; s3p2 (2); s5p2; s6p8; s6p13; s9p3; s23p1
INFORMAL 95
24 CFR 5: .508; .514 (14); .516; .615 (2);
24 CFR 982: 24 CFR 982 (2); .54 (2); .102; .201 (2); .301 (2); .552 (2); .553; .554 (10); .555 (11);
HUD-9886: p1;
7420.10G Gbk: 22-7;
PIH Notices: 02-01 (2); 01-41; 00-09; 99-52 (2); 95-48; 95-48 Tech Asst;
Admin Plan: s1p5; s2p4; s2p7 (2); s3p2; s3p3; s8p3; s10p5; s11p1; s15p1; s15p4 (2); s18p1 (4); s18p2 (5); s18p3 (3); s18p4 (3); s18p6; s18p7 (2); s18p8; s20p6; s23p8; s23p8
INFORMAL HEARING 96
24 CFR 5: .508; .514 (14); .516; .615 (2);
24 CFR 982: Intro; .54; .301 (2); .552 (2); .554; .555 (10);
HUD-9886: p1;
7420.10G Gbk: 3-5 (2); 5-6; 5-8 (3); 5-22; 6-8; 8-6; 12-6 (2); 12-10; 12-15 Ex 12-3 (2); 13-8 (2); 15-8; 15-10 Ex 15-2; 16-1 (6); 16-2 (2); 16-3 (5); 16-4 (3); 16-5 (5); 22-17; 23-10;
PIH Notices: 02-01; 99-52;
Admin Plan: s1p5; s2p7; s10p5; s11p1; s15p4 (2); s18p1 (2); s18p3 (3); s18p4 (2); s18p6; s18p7 (2); s20p6
INFORMAL HEARING PANEL 1
7420.10G Gbk: 16-4
INFORMAL HEARING PROCEDURES 8
24 CFR 5: .514; .516;
24 CFR 982: .54; .301; .552 (2);
HUD-9886: p1;
Admin Plan: s18p3
INFORMAL HEARINGS 10
24 CFR 982: .555;
7420.10G Gbk: 16-3 (3); 16-4; 22-18;
Admin Plan: s8p3; s15p1; s18p4; s23p8
INFORMAL REVIEW 48
24 CFR 982: Intro; .54; .201 (2); .553; .554 (9);
7420.10G Gbk: 3-5 (2); 3-8; 4-11; 4-14; 16-1 (10); 16-2; 16-3 (4);
PIH Notices: 02-01; 01-41; 00-09; 99-52;
Admin Plan: s2p4; s2p7; s3p2; s3p3; s18p1; s18p2 (4); s18p8
INFORMAL REVIEWS 8
7420.10G Gbk: 1-13; 3-8; 16-1; 16-3 (2);
Admin Plan: s18p1; s18p2; s23p8

INFORMALLY 1
Admin Plan: s20p1
INFORMATION PACKET 24
24 CFR 982: .301 (2); .307;
HUD-52648: p2 (2);
7420.10G Gbk: 2-2; 2-3 (2); 2-6 (2); 2-8; 5-39; 5-40 (2); 5-45; 8-2 (3); 8-5; 8-7; 8-11; 8-20;
Admin Plan: s21p6; s21p6
INFORMATION PACKETS 2
7420.10G Gbk: 2-2; 2-8
INFORMATIONAL 6
7420.10G Gbk: 5-44;
PIH Notices: 00-09;
Admin Plan: s1p4; s3p2; s11p3; s17p1
INFORMATIVE 4
7420.10G Gbk: 24-11;
PIH Notices: 95-48; 95-48 Tech Asst;
Admin Plan: s8p1
INFORMED 30
24 CFR 5: .508;
24 CFR 982: .306; .628;
7420.10G Gbk: 2-4; 5-40; 5-45; 8-4; 8-8; 8-18 (2); 9-4; 9-12; 10-36 Ex 10-1; 13-5; 13-8 (2); 16-4; 22-5; 22-9; 22-11;
PIH Notices: 03-23 (2); 01-41; 01-15 Impr Integ Hbk (2); 95-48; 95-48 Tech Asst;
Admin Plan: s1p7; s15p5; s18p8
INFORMING 15
7420.10G Gbk: 1-5; 1-15; 2-1; 4-2; 5-8; 13-3; 13-4; 15-1; 22-9;
PIH Notices: 01-41 (2); 01-06;
Admin Plan: s8p4; s10p4; s18p4
INFRINGEMENT 1
24 CFR 982: .157
INGRESS 3
24 CFR 5: .318;
PIH Notices: 02-01; 99-52
INHERITANCE 1
PIH Notices: 01-15 Impr Integ Hbk
INHERITANCES 9
24 CFR 5: .609;
HUD-50058Instr: p31;
7420.10G Gbk: 5-15 Ex 5-2; 5-23; 5-25 Ex 5-3; 12-13 Ex 12-1;
PIH Notices: 01-15 Impr Integ Hbk (2);
Admin Plan: s6p10
INITIAL APPLICANT 1
Admin Plan: s8p1
INITIAL APPLICATION 4
7420.10G Gbk: 4-17 (2); 21-8;
Admin Plan: s3p1
INITIAL BASELINE 11
24 CFR 982: .102 (6);
7420.10G Gbk: 20-8; 20-8 Ex 20-1 (3); 20-8 Ex 20-1
INITIAL INTAKE 1
7420.10G Gbk: 21-5
INITIAL INTERVIEW 2
7420.10G Gbk: 19-6; 19-7
INITIAL NOTICE 1
7420.10G Gbk: 12-3
INITIAL OCCUPANCY 9
24 CFR 982: Intro; .508 (2);
7420.10G Gbk: 14-1; 14-4;
PIH Notices: 00-49; 00-24B;
Admin Plan: s10p1; s24p7
INITIAL PAYMENT STANDARD 6
24 CFR 982: .4; .502; .504 (3);
PIH Notices: 00-09
INITIAL PHA 164
24 CFR 982: .4 (3); .201; .314 (2); .351; .353 (11); .355 (19); .636 (3);
HUD-50058: p i; p x; p xi; p xiii; p xiv;
HUD-50058Instr: p7 (2); p9; p10; p13; p42 (2); p46 (2); p53 (2); p56 (2); p70; p73; p74;
HUD-52648: p3 (2);
7420.10G Gbk: 2-9; 4-20; 9-5; 13-1; 13-2 (4); 13-3 (10); 13-4 (7); 13-5 (5); 13-6 (4); 13-7 (6); 13-8 (15); 13-9 (13); 13-12 Ex 13-2 (2); 20-24 (9); 20-25 (4); 21-8 (3); 23-18 (5);
PIH Notices: 02-27; 01-06; 01-01 (6);
Admin Plan: s13p2; s13p2
INITIAL PHAS 1
Admin Plan: s21p9
INITIAL PHA'S 33
24 CFR 982: .636;
HUD-50058: p x (2); p xi (2); p xiii (2); p xiv (2);
HUD-50058Instr: p42 (3); p46 (3); p53 (3); p56 (3);
7420.10G Gbk: 13-4; 13-5 (2); 13-7 (2); 13-8; 13-10; 20-24 (4); 23-18
INITIAL PLEADING 5

24 CFR 982: .310;
HUD-52641: p9;
HUD-52641-A: p2;
7420.10G Gbk: 15-3;
Admin Plan: s14p1

INITIAL RENT TO OWNER..........13
24 CFR 982: .4; .507; .622;
HUD-52641: p1; p2 (2); 8;
HUD-52641-A: p1;
PIH Notices: 01-41; 00-09;
Admin Plan: s11p1; s19p1; s19p1

INITIAL TERM..............................28
24 CFR 982: .303 (3); .305; .308; .309 (2); .405;
HUD-52641: p3; 8 (2); p9;
HUD-52641-A: p1 (2); p2 (2);
7420.10G Gbk: 8-12; 8-21; 15-1 (3); 23-7;
Admin Plan: s8p5 (2); s9p2 (3); s9p3

INJUNCTIVE RELIEF......................2
HUD-52641: p5;
7420.10G Gbk: 11-18

INJURED...3
HUD-52641: p6;
7420.10G Gbk: 11-13;
Admin Plan: s10p4

INJURY...8
24 CFR 5: .100;
HUD-52641: p6;
PIH Notices: 99-11; 95-48 (2); 95-48 Tech Asst (2);
Admin Plan: s15p3

INOCULATIONS..............................2
24 CFR 5: .350; .350

IN-PERSON....................................14
7420.10G Gbk: 4-11; 5-46 Ex 5-5; 5-47 Ex 5-5; 5-48 Ex 5-5; 5-49 Ex 5-5 (2); 5-50 Ex 5-5; 5-51 Ex 5-5 (2); 5-52 Ex 5-5 (2); 5-53 Ex 5-5 (2); 12-2

IN-PLACE...9
24 CFR 982: .353;
HUD-50058Instr: p42; p46;
7420.10G Gbk: 14-1; 14-4;
PIH Notices: 01-41; 01-01; 00-09; 00-09

INS...115
24 CFR 5: .504; .508 (5); .510; .512 (15); .514 (37);
HUD-50058Instr: p3; p15 (3); p16; p18 (2); p73;
7420.10G Gbk: 5-3; 5-4; 5-7 (8); 5-8 (7); 5-9 Ex 5-1 (8); 5-10 Ex 5-1 (6); 5-11 (7); 12-5; 13-3; 16-3;
Admin Plan: s18p7 (6); s18p7

INS SAVE...3
24 CFR 5: .512 (2);
Admin Plan: s18p7

INSPECT..35
24 CFR 5: .360; .705;
24 CFR 982: .305; .352; .405; .551;
HUD-52580-A: p2; p13; p17;
HUD-52641: p3;
HUD-52646: p2 (2);
7420.10G Gbk: 1-15; 2-6; 8-16; 10-25; 10-40 Ex 10-4a; 10-42 Ex 10-5; 11-12; 19-5; 20-2; 24-9;
PIH Notices: 01-41; 00-24B (2); 00-23 (3); 00-09 (2);
Admin Plan: s10p1 (2); s10p2; s15p6; s15p6

INSPECTED...................................33
24 CFR 982: .305 (2); .628; .631 (2);
HUD-52580: p1 (2); p7;
HUD-52580-A: p1 (3); p20;
HUD-52646: p2;
7420.10G Gbk: 8-15; 10-23; 10-27; 10-30; 10-35 (2); 10-37 Ex 10-2; 10-40 Ex 10-4a; 11-1; 15-10 Ex 15-2; 21-6;
PIH Notices: 01-41; 00-24B; 00-09; 99-11 (2);
Admin Plan: s9p3; s10p2; s21p5; s21p5

INSPECTING...................................7
7420.10G Gbk: 10-8; 10-31; 21-2;
PIH Notices: 00-23 (2); 00-09;
Admin Plan: s23p4

INSPECTION...............................403
24 CFR 5: .360; .661; .705 (4);
24 CFR 35 SubM: .1200; .1215 (2);
24 CFR 982: 24 CFR 982 (2); .104; .158 (2); .305 (2); .352; .355; .405 (4); .551; .628 (2); .631 (8); .641 (2);
HUD-50058: p2; p5 (2); p v (4); p14; p xiv;
HUD-50058Instr: p1 (2); p10 (3); p11 (2); p21 (13); p56 (2); p77;
HUD-52517: p1; p2;
HUD-52580: p1 (5); p7 (3);
HUD-52580-A: p1 (8); p2; p6; p13 (2); p15 (7); p17 (4); p18; p20 (3);
HUD-52641: p3;

HUD-52648: p1 (2); p2 (2);
7420.10G Gbk: 1-16 Ex 1-3 (2); 2-9; 8-15; 8-17; 9-8 (5); 9-11; 9-15 Ex 9-2 (2); 10-1 (3); 10-2 (2); 10-3 (2); 10-8; 10-10; 10-14; 10-15; 10-16; 10-17; 10-18; 10-22 (4); 10-23 (6); 10-24 (2); 10-25 (15); 10-26 (12); 10-27 (13); 10-28 (3); 10-30 (3); 10-31 (4); 10-32 (3); 10-33 (9); 10-34 (3); 10-35 (11); 10-40 Ex 10-4a (6); 10-41 Ex 10-4b (5); 10-42 Ex 10-5; 10-43 Ex 10-6 (2); 10-44 Ex 10-7a; 10-45 Ex 10-7b; 10-46 Ex 10-8; 10-47 Ex 10-9 (2); 10-48 Ex 10-10 (4); 11-9 (2); 11-16 Ex 11-1; 11-19; 13-7; 19-6 (2); 19-9; 19-11 (12); 19-12 (7); 19-13; 20-4; 20-24; 21-4 (3); 21-5 (2); 21-6; 21-8; 21-9; 21-10 (3); 21-11; 21-16 Ex 21-6 (3); 22-6; 22-7; 22-9; 22-10; 24-12 (2); 24-13 (7); 24-15 (2);
PIH Notices: 01-41 (2); 01-06 (5); 00-24; 00-24A; 00-24B (6); 00-23 (11); 00-09; 99-11 (3); 95-48 (2); 95-48 Tech Asst (2);
Admin Plan: s1p7; s9p4 (2); s10p1 (10); s10p2 (11); s10p3 (10); s10p4; s11p1; s20p2; s21p4; s21p5 (3); s21p7; s21p8 (5); s22p3 (5); s23p5 (2); s23p7; s23p8 (5); s24p5; s24p6

INSPECTION-RELATED 1
7420.10G Gbk: 10-30

INSPECTIONS 238
24 CFR 5: .360 (2);
24 CFR 35 SubM: .1215 (2);
24 CFR 982: Intro; .54; .405 (2); .625; .631; .633;
HUD-52580-A: p15;
HUD-52648: p1 (4); p2 (2);
7420.10G Gbk: 1-1; 1-10 (3); 2-9 (2); 2-10 (2); 3-6 (2); 5-36 Ex 5-4; 8-3; 9-5; 10-1 (2); 10-8; 10-12; 10-16; 10-17; 10-20; 10-22; 10-23 (20); 10-24 (15); 10-25; 10-26; 10-28 (4); 10-30 (9); 10-31 (6); 10-32 (6); 10-33 (2); 10-34 (2); 10-35 (7); 10-40 Ex 10-4a; 10-43 Ex 10-6; 10-47 Ex 10-9 (2); 11-19 (2); 12-1; 13-8; 15-9 Ex 15-1; 19-4; 19-11; 19-12 (7); 19-13 (3); 20-3; 21-4 (6); 21-5 (4); 21-6 (2); 21-7; 21-9 (2); 21-10 (4); 21-11; 21-14 Ex 21-4; 21-16 Ex 21-6; 22-9; 24-7; 24-12; 24-13 (2);
PIH Notices: 02-27 (11); 02-07; 01-41 (2); 01-06 (5); 00-49 (3); 00-24; 00-24A (2); 00-24B (7); 00-23 (2); 00-09 (3); 99-11 (6);
Admin Plan: s1p6; s9p1; s10p1 (6); s10p2; s10p3 (5); s10p4; s15p6; s19p1 (2); s21p1 (2); s21p2; s21p4; s21p5; s21p7; s21p8 (5); s23p5 (4); s24p5

INSPECTIONS-INCREASING 1
7420.10G Gbk: 21-10

INSPECTOR 74
24 CFR 5: .528;
24 CFR 35 SubM: .1215;
24 CFR 982: .628 (2); .631 (7);
HUD-50058: p v;
HUD-50058Instr: p21 (3);
HUD-52517: p2;
HUD-52580: p1; p5 (2); p7;
HUD-52580-A: p1; p2; p13; p17 (4); p20;
7420.10G Gbk: 8-15; 9-8; 9-16 Ex 9-2; 10-2 (2); 10-12; 10-18 (2); 10-21; 10-24 (2); 10-27 (2); 10-28 (3); 10-33 (3); 10-35; 10-37 Ex 10-2 (3); 10-41 Ex 10-4b; 10-47 Ex 10-9; 21-4; 21-6 (2); 21-10; 21-11; 21-12 Ex 21-3; 21-15 Ex 21-5 (2); 21-16 Ex 21-6; 24-13;
PIH Notices: 02-27 (2); 01-15; 00-23 (2);
Admin Plan: s17p2; s20p3 (2); s20p4; s20p7; s20p7

INSPECTOR GENERAL 8
7420.10G Gbk: 5-6;
PIH Notices: 01-15;
Admin Plan: s17p2; s20p3 (2); s20p4; s20p7; s20p7

INSPECTOR GENERAL'S 1
24 CFR 5: .528

INSPECTORS 27
24 CFR 982: .631;
HUD-52648: p1;

7420.10G Gbk: 9-11; 10-18; 10-32 (2); 10-33 10-34 (2); 19-12; 21-4 (3); 21-5 (2); 21-6 (2); 21-13; 21-14 Ex 21-4 (2); 21-15 Ex 21-5; 21-16 Ex 21-6 (3); 24-13;
PIH Notices: 00-09;
Admin Plan: s21p4; s21p5

INSPECTOR'S 9
7420.10G Gbk: 9-15 Ex 9-2; 10-33 (2); 10-37 Ex 10-2; 22-6 (2); 24-13 (2); 24-13

INSPECTS 6
HUD-52648: p2;
PIH Notices: 01-41 (2); 00-09 (2);
Admin Plan: s21p8

INSTABILITY 4
24 CFR 982: .401; .614;
7420.10G Gbk: 10-13; 17-5

INSTITUTION 32
24 CFR 5: .609;
24 CFR 982: .156;
HUD-50058Instr: p15 (3); p31; p72;
HUD-903-1: p5;
7420.10G Gbk: 5-15 Ex 5-2; 5-20; 5-29 (2); 5-53 Ex 5-5; 11-7; 20-24;
PIH Notices: 03-11; 01-15 Impr Integ Hbk (3);
Admin Plan: s7p5 (3); s7p6 (3); s17p3; s22p2 (3); s23p2; s25p3; s25p5

INSTITUTIONALIZATION 1
PIH Notices: 00-41

INSTITUTIONALIZED......................
3
HUD-50058Instr: p72;
Admin Plan: s23p2; s25p3

INSTITUTIONS 17
24 CFR 982: .352;
HUD-9886: p1 (3);
7420.10G Gbk: 8-17; 23-4;
PIH Notices: 02-22; 95-48 (4); 95-48 Tech Asst (4);
Admin Plan: s24p2; s25p5

INSTRUCT 4
HUD-50058: p ii;
HUD-50058Instr: p13;
7420.10G Gbk: 5-45; 10-26

INSTRUCTED..............................11
HUD-50058: p2;
HUD-50058Instr: p13;
7420.10G Gbk: 5-11;
PIH Notices: 03-12; 01-11; 01-06; 00-34; 95-48 (2); 95-48 Tech Asst; 95-48 Tech Asst

INSTRUCTION 25
HUD-50058: p1 (2); p i; p ii; p v; p6 (4); p9; p ix; p11;
HUD-50058Instr: p i; p1 (2); p3 (2); p47;
HUD-52580-A: p15;
7420.10G Gbk: 10-2; 10-19;
PIH Notices: 01-01; 00-34; 95-48; 95-48 Tech Asst

INSTRUCTIONS..............................91
24 CFR 5: .216 (7); .218; .230; .232;
24 CFR 982: .103;
HUD-50058: p1; p ii;
HUD-50058Instr: p13; p14; p65; p68;
HUD-52580: p1 (8); p4 (2);
HUD-52665: p1 (2); p2 (2);
HUD-52667: p1; p i (2);
HUD-903: p1 (2);
HUD-903-1: p3;
7420.10G Gbk: 3-7; 8-2; 11-11; 12-3 (2); 19-4; 20-14; 22-11;
PIH Notices: 03-11 (3); 02-27 (3); 02-22; 02-20 (6); 02-14; 02-07; 01-41 (2); 01-15; 01-10; 01-06 (2); 01-01 (2); 00-53 (2); 00-49; 00-46 (6); 00-34 (2); 00-28; 00-27; 00-24; 00-09 (2); 95-48 (2); 95-48 Tech Asst (2);
Admin Plan: s6p1; s8p3; s20p6

INSTRUCTIVE 4
HUD-52580-A: p15;
7420.10G Gbk: 10-7;
Admin Plan: s20p2; s20p2

INSTRUMENTALITIES 3
HUD-50058Instr: p25;
PIH Notices: 02-01; 99-52

INSTRUMENTALITY 6
24 CFR 5: .100;
24 CFR 982: .4;
HUD-50058Instr: p72; p75;
PIH Notices: 95-48; 95-48 Tech Asst

INSUFFICIENT APPLICANTS........1
Admin Plan: s1p6

INSULT..............................1
Admin Plan: s15p2

INSULTING..............................1
Admin Plan: s15p2

INSURANCE..............................132
24 CFR 5: .210; .214; .306;

.318; .603 (2); .609 (3); .801 (5);
24 CFR 982: .201; .203; .453; .626; .632 (2); .635 (3); .643 (2);
HUD-50058: p vii; p xiv (2); p16;
HUD-50058Instr: p5 (3); p13; p19; p29 (4); p31 (2); p35; p38; p56 (2); p60 (2); p73 (2);
HUD-52641: p5;
HUD-903-1: p2;
7420.10G Gbk: 4-20; 4-22; 4-27 Ex 4-2; 5-3; 5-12 (2); 5-14 Ex 5-2; 5-15 Ex 5-2 (2); 5-23; 5-25 Ex 5-3 (2); 5-31 (2); 5-46 Ex 5-5; 5-51 Ex 5-5 (2); 12-16 Ex 12-4; 15-4; 23-2;
PIH Notices: 02-21; 01-41 (14); 01-20; 01-15; 01-15 Impr Integ Hbk (15); 01-10 (2); 00-27; 00-09 (10); 95-48; 95-48 Tech Asst;
Admin Plan: s2p2; s2p4; s6p10 (2); s6p11; s7p6; s7p7 (3); s7p8 (2); s16p3; s22p2; s24p2; s25p6

INSURANCE POLICIES 6
24 CFR 5: .609;
7420.10G Gbk: 5-14 Ex 5-2;
PIH Notices: 01-15 Impr Integ Hbk (3);
Admin Plan: s2p2

INSURANCE POLICY 1
7420.10G Gbk: 12-16 Ex 12-4

INSURANCE PREMIUMS 2
PIH Notices: 01-15;
Admin Plan: s6p11

INSURE 6
24 CFR 5: .306;
7420.10G Gbk: 3-1; 5-32; 10-14; 19-1;
Admin Plan: s21p5

INSURED 19
24 CFR 5: .100 (2); .214; .306 (2); .701; .801;
24 CFR 982: .453; .521; .625; .638;
HUD-52517: p1;
HUD-52641: p5;
7420.10G Gbk: 15-4;
PIH Notices: 01-41; 00-09;
Admin Plan: s4p1; s16p2; s24p4

INSURMOUNTABLE 3
7420.10G Gbk: 24-2;
PIH Notices: 95-48; 95-48 Tech Asst

INTAKE 28
7420.10G Gbk: 4-12; 4-13; 19-12; 20-3; 21-2 (2); 21-4 (2); 21-5 (2); 21-8; 21-13 (3); 21-14 Ex 21-4; 21-15 Ex 21-5 (2); 21-16 Ex 21-6 (4); 21-19;
PIH Notices: 01-15 (2); 00-11 (2); 00-11A;
Admin Plan: s3p1

INTEGRATED 12
7420.10G Gbk: 5-44;
PIH Notices: 00-34; 95-48 (5); 95-48 Tech Asst (4); 95-48 Tech Asst

INTEGRATED SETTING 7
7420.10G Gbk: 5-44;
PIH Notices: 95-48 (3); 95-48 Tech Asst (2); 95-48 Tech Asst

INTELLECTUAL PROPERTY 2
24 CFR 982: .157; .157

INTENTION 4
7420.10G Gbk: 5-5; 13-3; 15-1;
Admin Plan: s23p7

INTENTIONAL 13
7420.10G Gbk: 20-6; 22-1 (4); 22-5; 22-9; 22-14; 22-16 (2);
PIH Notices: 00-28;
Admin Plan: s20p5; s20p6

INTENTIONALLY 9
24 CFR 5: .528;
7420.10G Gbk: 11-7; 22-1; 22-2 (4); 22-10; 22-14

INTEREST 180
24 CFR 5: .100; .315 (3); .520; .609;
24 CFR 982: .4 (5); .155; .161 (5); .313; .315; .352; .521; .551 (2); .623; .627; .633 (3); .634 (2); .635 (4); .637; .641; .643;
HUD-50058: p i; p6 (3); p xiii; p14; p xiv (2);
HUD-50058Instr: p22 (4); p23 (3); p43; p53; p56 (4); p71;
HUD-52641: p5; p6 (3); p10;
HUD-52641-A: p3;
HUD-52646: p2;
HUD-9886: p1 (2); p2;
7420.10G Gbk: 1-15; 2-7; 3-4; 4-2; 4-4; 4-7; 4-26 Ex 4-2 (2); 5-10 Ex 5-1; 5-14 Ex 5-2; 5-19; 5-24; 5-25 Ex 5-3; 5-26 (4); 5-28;

5-36 Ex 5-4; 5-48 Ex 5-5 (3); 5-49 Ex 5-5 (5); 8-4; 8-7; 8-8; 8-17; 8-18; 8-19 (2); 11-2 (2); 11-13; 12-13 Ex 12-1; 13-3 (2); 20-2; 20-26 (11); 20-27 (9); 23-3 (2); 23-6 (2); 23-14 (3); 24-12 (2); 24-13;
PIH Notices: 02-27 (2); 02-21; 02-01; 01-41; 01-15 Impr Integ Hbk (8); 00-11A; 00-09; 00-01; 99-52; 99-11; 98-66; 95-48; 95-48 Tech Asst;
Admin Plan: s3p1; s3p2; s4p2; s7p5; s7p6 (5); s8p4; s19p1 (2); s22p1; s22p2; s22p4; s23p1; s24p3; s25p5; s25p8

INTEREST BEARING....................1
PIH Notices: 01-15 Impr Integ Hbk

INTEREST EARNED 15
24 CFR 982: .155;
7420.10G Gbk: 20-2; 20-26 (5); 20-27 (5); 23-14;
PIH Notices: 02-21; 01-15 Impr Integ Hbk

INTEREST EARNINGS 3
7420.10G Gbk: 20-26 (2); 20-26

INTEREST IN THE HOME..............6
24 CFR 982: .4 (3); .633; .643;
Admin Plan: s22p4

INTEREST REDUCTION.................1
24 CFR 5: .520

INTEREST-BEARING......................2
7420.10G Gbk: 23-13;
PIH Notices: 00-11

INTERESTED PARTIES..................6
HUD-50058Instr: p1;
7420.10G Gbk: 3-1; 4-12;
PIH Notices: 01-02;
Admin Plan: s17p1; s24p2

INTERESTED PARTY...................11
24 CFR 5: .661;
24 CFR 982: .306; .453;
HUD-52517: p2;
HUD-52641: p5 (2); p6 (2);
7420.10G Gbk: 8-18; 11-1; 11-17

INTERFERE......................................7
24 CFR 982: .201;
HUD-50058Instr: p19;
HUD-903-1: p2;
7420.10G Gbk: 4-20;
PIH Notices: 02-01; 99-52;
Admin Plan: s15p3

INTERFERED 1
HUD-903: p1

INTERFERENCE.............................3
HUD-903: p2;
PIH Notices: 95-48; 95-48 Tech Asst

INTERFERES.................................10
24 CFR 982: .310; .553;
PIH Notices: 03-11; 95-48 (3); 95-48 Tech Asst (3);
Admin Plan: s15p2

INTERIM......................................136
24 CFR 5: .216; .230; .508; .615; .657 (3); .659;
24 CFR 35 SubM: .1225;
24 CFR 982: Intro; .54; .516 (8); .551; .641;
HUD-50058: p2; p ix; p x; p xi; p xii; p xiii; p xiv; p xv;
HUD-50058Instr: p2; p9; p10; p11; p12; p33; p37; p39; p42; p46; p50; p53; p56; p58; p65; p77;
HUD-52665: p1; p2;
7420.10G Gbk: 1-4 (2); 5-6; 5-23; 5-46 Ex 5-5; 10-21; 11-15; 12-9 (3); 13-8 (2); 21-4; 22-9 (3); 22-10; 23-6 (2); 23-7; 23-8 Ex 23-1 (4); 23-9; 23-15; 23-17 Ex 23-2;
PIH Notices: 02-27; 01-41; 01-27 (6); 01-15 (4); 01-15 Impr Integ Hbk (7); 01-11; 01-10 (2); 01-01 (4); 00-53 (2); 00-24A (2); 00-24B; 00-09; 95-48 (2); 95-48 Tech Asst (2);
Admin Plan: s6p8 (2); s6p9 (2); s6p10; s7p2; s11p1 (3); s11p2 (6); s20p1; s20p6; s22p4; s25p4; s25p5 (7)

INTERIM CHANGE 2
7420.10G Gbk: 3-5; 22-6

INTERIM CHANGES.......................5
7420.10G Gbk: 3-5; 12-1; 12-9; 21-5; 22-9

INTERIM DISBURSEMENT 5
7420.10G Gbk: 23-15 (2);
Admin Plan: s25p5 (2); s25p6

INTERIM RECERTIFICATION 1
7420.10G Gbk: 22-10

INTERIM RE-CERTIFICATION......8
Admin Plan: s6p8; s7p2; s11p2 (5); s22p4

INTERIM RECERTIFICATIONS.....1

7420.10G Gbk: 22-9

INTERIM RE-CERTIFICATIONS.... 1
Admin Plan: s11p2

INTERIM REDETERMINATION 4
24 CFR 982: .516;
HUD-52665: p1;
PIH Notices: 01-41; 00-09

INTERIM RE-DETERMINATION... 1
Admin Plan: s20p1

INTERIM REDETERMINATIONS .. 1
24 CFR 982: .54

INTERIM REEXAM 1
HUD-50058Instr: p77

INTERIM REEXAMINATION....... 59
24 CFR 5: .657 (2); .659;
24 CFR 982: .516 (3); .551;
HUD-50058: p2; p ix; p x; p xi; p xii; p xiii; p xiv; p xv;
HUD-50058Instr: p2; p9; p10; p11; p12; p33; p37; p39; p42; p46; p50; p53; p56; p58;
HUD-52646: p2;
7420.10G Gbk: 5-17 (3); 5-23 (2); 5-24 (2); 12-6; 12-9 (5); 12-10 (2); 19-2; 21-7 (2); 23-6; 23-12 (2); 23-16 Ex 23-2;
PIH Notices: 01-15 (2); 01-15 Impr Integ Hbk (3); 00-24B;
Admin Plan: s6p8

INTERIM RE-EXAMINATION 2
PIH Notices: 01-27; 01-27

INTERIM REEXAMINATIONS..... 15
24 CFR 5: .657;
24 CFR 982: .641;
7420.10G Gbk: 1-14; 3-5; 7-8; 12-9; 21-2; 21-7; 23-12 (3);
PIH Notices: 01-15; 01-15 Impr Integ Hbk (2); 01-15 Impr Integ Hbk

INTERIM RE-EXAMINATIONS 3
PIH Notices: 01-27 (2); 01-27

INTERIM REGULATION................ 1
PIH Notices: 01-27

INTERIM RENT 1
Admin Plan: s11p1

INTERIM REPORT.......................... 2
PIH Notices: 01-15; 01-15 Impr Integ Hbk

INTERIM REPORTING................. 12
7420.10G Gbk: 11-15; 12-9 (3); 12-10 (2); 22-10 (3);
PIH Notices: 01-11;
Admin Plan: s6p9; s11p1

INTERIM-COMPLETED................. 1
7420.10G Gbk: 5-47 Ex 5-5

INTERIOR 63
24 CFR 982: .401 (3); .614; .631;
HUD-50058Instr: p30;
HUD-52580: p5 (3);
HUD-52580-A: p2 (2); p4 (2); p13 (2); p14; p17 (5); p18 (5);
7420.10G Gbk: 5-43 (2); 10-1; 10-7; 10-9; 10-10 (2); 10-16; 10-17; 10-18 (4);
PIH Notices: 02-01; 01-15 Impr Integ Hbk; 00-49 (2); 99-52; 95-48 (9); 95-48 Tech Asst (9);
Admin Plan: s22p3

INTERIOR AIR QUALITY.............. 6
24 CFR 982: .401;
HUD-52580: p5;
HUD-52580-A: p17; p18;
7420.10G Gbk: 10-1; 10-10

INTERMEDIATE CARE.................. 1
Admin Plan: s24p2

INTERMEDIATE CARE FACILITIES 2
24 CFR 5: .801;
PIH Notices: 00-41

INTERNAL FILE REVIEW.............. 2
Admin Plan: s20p1; s20p3

INTERNAL FINANCIAL REPORTS2
7420.10G Gbk: 20-30; 20-30

INTERNET 49
24 CFR 5: .801;
HUD-50058Instr: p5 (7);
7420.10G Gbk: 4-11; 4-19; 5-2; 9-5 (4); 9-6 (2); 9-7 (2); 19-3 (2);
PIH Notices: 02-01 (2); 01-15 (4); 01-15 Impr Integ Hbk (2); 01-06 (2); 01-02; 00-53 (3); 00-34 (9); 00-24 (2); 00-24A; 99-52; 99-52

INTERPRET 10
7420.10G Gbk: 10-3;
PIH Notices: 02-01; 99-52; 95-48 (3); 95-48 Tech Asst (3);
Admin Plan: s1p3

INTERPRETATION 9
HUD-52641: p7;
7420.10G Gbk: 11-11; 11-14; 22-10;
PIH Notices: 03-12; 02-01; 99-52;

Admin Plan: s1p3; s6p1
INTERPRETED.................................7
HUD-52641: p7;
7420.10G Gbk: 4-13; 11-14; 22-8; 22-10;
PIH Notices: 95-48; 95-48 Tech Asst
INTERPRETER...............................49
24 CFR 5: .514;
7420.10G Gbk: 4-11; 5-44; 8-2; 8-3;
PIH Notices: 95-48 (22); 95-48 Tech Asst (21); 95-48 Tech Asst
INTERPRETERS.............................15
7420.10G Gbk: 8-3;
PIH Notices: 95-48 (7); 95-48 Tech Asst (6); 95-48 Tech Asst
INTERPRETING.............................10
7420.10G Gbk: 10-1;
PIH Notices: 00-09; 95-48 (4); 95-48 Tech Asst (3); 95-48 Tech Asst
INTERPRETIVE...............................1
24 CFR 5: .514
INTERRUPTED................................2
HUD-50058Instr: p10; p10
INTERRUPTION...............................4
24 CFR 982: .201;
HUD-50058Instr: p9 (2);
7420.10G Gbk: 18-1
INTERRUPTIONS............................3
24 CFR 982: .627;
PIH Notices: 95-48; 95-48 Tech Asst
INTERVENE....................................1
7420.10G Gbk: 2-5
INTERVIEW...................................41
7420.10G Gbk: 4-16; 9-9; 12-2 (2); 12-3; 19-6; 19-7 (3); 19-10; 19-13 (3); 21-4; 21-8; 21-16 Ex 21-6 (2); 21-19 (2); 22-2; 22-9; 22-11; 24-3 (2);
PIH Notices: 00-24B;
Admin Plan: s3p2 (5); s3p3 (3); s6p6; s8p3; s11p1 (4); s20p2; s20p2
INTERVIEWED................................4
7420.10G Gbk: 24-3; 24-4; 24-6;
Admin Plan: s20p4
INTERVIEWING..............................2
7420.10G Gbk: 9-9; 24-7
INTERVIEWS.................................20
7420.10G Gbk: 4-11; 4-13; 9-9 (2); 12-3; 21-8; 21-10 (2); 21-20; 22-8; 23-6; 24-4; 24-7 (2);
PIH Notices: 01-15 Impr Integ Hbk; 00-09;
Admin Plan: s20p4 (3); s25p4
INTIMIDATE...................................2
HUD-903-1: p2;
Admin Plan: s15p2
INTIMIDATED.................................1
HUD-903: p1
INTIMIDATION................................3
HUD-903: p2;
PIH Notices: 95-48; 95-48 Tech Asst
INTRODUCTION............................12
HUD-50058Instr: p ii; p1;
7420.10G Gbk: 1-1; 8-1; 8-10; 10-31 (2);
PIH Notices: 02-27 (2); 00-53; 95-48; 95-48 Tech Asst
INVEST...1
7420.10G Gbk: 21-2
INVESTED.....................................12
24 CFR 5: .609 (2);
HUD-50058Instr: p25;
7420.10G Gbk: 5-14 Ex 5-2 (2); 5-19; 20-1; 24-13;
PIH Notices: 01-15 Impr Integ Hbk (3); 01-15 Impr Integ Hbk
INVESTIGATE................................15
HUD-903: p2; p3;
HUD-903-1: p6;
7420.10G Gbk: 10-28; 10-30; 19-7;
PIH Notices: 95-48 (4); 95-48 Tech Asst (4);
Admin Plan: s20p1
INVESTIGATING.............................1
7420.10G Gbk: 22-18
INVESTIGATION............................26
24 CFR 5: .528;
7420.10G Gbk: 5-6; 10-20 (2); 22-16 (2); 22-17;
PIH Notices: 03-11 (2); 02-01; 99-52; 95-48 (3); 95-48 Tech Asst (3);
Admin Plan: s16p1; s20p1 (3); s20p3; s20p4 (3); s20p4
INVESTIGATIONS............................6
HUD-52641: p5;
7420.10G Gbk: 10-20; 11-13; 22-18 (2);
PIH Notices: 03-11
INVESTIGATIVE..............................2
Admin Plan: s20p5; s20p5

INVESTIGATORS 2
HUD-9886: p2;
Admin Plan: s20p4
INVESTMENT...............................33
24 CFR 5: .601 (2); .603 (2); .609; .617;
HUD-50058Instr: p22; p27; p62; p74;
7420.10G Gbk: 5-14 Ex 5-2; 5-16 Ex 5-2 (2); 5-25 Ex 5-3 (3); 11-3 (2); 11-9; 21-2; 21-10; 21-19; 23-14 (2); 24-7; 24-8;
PIH Notices: 01-15 Impr Integ Hbk (3); 00-11 (3);
Admin Plan: s7p6
INVESTMENTS...............................7
7420.10G Gbk: 5-25 Ex 5-3; 20-26 (4); 20-27; 21-2
INVESTORS....................................1
Admin Plan: s24p3
INVITATION.................................10
24 CFR 5: .100;
7420.10G Gbk: 4-5 (2);
PIH Notices: 01-41 (3); 00-09 (3);
Admin Plan: s15p3
INVITE 4
7420.10G Gbk: 2-5; 3-7; 11-15;
PIH Notices: 99-11
INVITED 12
7420.10G Gbk: 1-6; 1-8; 8-1; 21-19; 24-3 (2); 24-4;
PIH Notices: 99-11; 95-48 (2); 95-48 Tech Asst; 95-48 Tech Asst
INVITEES..1
7420.10G Gbk: 21-19
INVITES 1
24 CFR 982: .4
INVOLUNTARILY 3
7420.10G Gbk: 4-17;
PIH Notices: 02-14;
Admin Plan: s8p5
INVOLUNTARILY DISPLACED 1
7420.10G Gbk: 4-17
INVOLUNTARY..............................2
7420.10G Gbk: 20-9; 23-7
INVOLVE......................................14
7420.10G Gbk: 8-2; 10-20; 21-8; 21-11; 22-5;
PIH Notices: 03-11; 99-52 (2); 95-48 (3); 95-48 Tech Asst (2); 95-48 Tech Asst
INVOLVED 71
24 CFR 5: .216 (12); .218 (3); .232; .518;
24 CFR 982: .310; .552;
HUD-903: p1 (2); p3;
HUD-903-1: p6;
7420.10G Gbk: 5-38; 9-7; 9-11; 13-9; 20-1; 20-3; 21-11; 21-13 (3); 21-17 (3); 21-18; 21-19 (2); 22-11; 22-14; 23-15;
PIH Notices: 02-21; 02-01; 01-20; 00-27; 00-11; 00-09; 99-52; 99-11 (2); 95-48 (7); 95-48 Tech Asst (7);
Admin Plan: s10p2; s15p3; s15p5; s16p2; s20p4; s20p7
INVOLVEMENT...........................10
7420.10G Gbk: 1-2 (2); 13-9 (2); 15-6; 21-4;
PIH Notices: 02-27 (2); 00-11;
Admin Plan: s8p3
INVOLVES....................................12
24 CFR 5: .210;
7420.10G Gbk: 9-1; 11-3 (4); 19-5; 22-1; 22-4;
PIH Notices: 03-11; 01-15 Impr Integ Hbk;
Admin Plan: s18p6
INVOLVING 18
HUD-50058Instr: p73 (2);
7420.10G Gbk: 10-22; 11-3; 22-2;
PIH Notices: 03-05; 01-41; 01-40; 00-09; 95-48 (3); 95-48 Tech Asst (3);
Admin Plan: s20p4; s20p6; s20p6
IPA...3
PIH Notices: 02-27 (2); 02-21
IRA...2
7420.10G Gbk: 5-25 Ex 5-3;
PIH Notices: 01-15 Impr Integ Hbk
IRREGULAR..................................2
7420.10G Gbk: 12-1;
Admin Plan: s7p5
IRREGULAR INCOME...................1
7420.10G Gbk: 12-1
IRREGULARITIES..........................2
7420.10G Gbk: 22-1; 22-3
IRREGULARITY............................1
7420.10G Gbk: 22-3
IRS 48
24 CFR 5: .214 (2); .216 (3); .230; .234; .236;
HUD-50058Instr: p25; p73;
7420.10G Gbk: 5-12; 5-13 (2); 5-48 Ex 5-5 (3); 5-51 Ex 5-5;

11-19 (6); 19-1; 22-4 (3); 23-14 (2);
PIH Notices: 01-15 (5); 01-15 Impr Integ Hbk (3);
Admin Plan: s6p11; s7p2 (2); s7p3; s7p5 (3); s7p6 (2); s7p8; s24p4

ISA 2
HUD-50058: p i; p6

ISSUANCE 83
24 CFR 982: Intro; .102; .201; .302; .555; .636; .641 (2);
HUD-50058: p2;
HUD-50058Instr: p1; p10 (2); p11; p77;
HUD-52646: p1 (2);
7420.10G Gbk: 1-16 Ex 1-3; 3-2; 4-14; 4-15; 4-19; 5-10 Ex 5-1; 8-1 (2); 8-8; 8-22; 11-8; 19-6; 19-7; 21-10; 22-9; 24-6; 24-7;
PIH Notices: 03-11 (2); 02-06; 02-01; 01-41 (4); 01-20; 01-10; 01-01 (2); 00-34; 00-27 (2); 00-09 (3); 99-52;
Admin Plan: s1p6; s2p3; s2p4; s2p7; s3p3 (2); s4p2; s5p2 (2); s7p1 (3); s8p1 (3); s8p3; s8p4; s8p5; s10p3; s13p1 (2); s15p6 (2); s17p2; s18p2; s18p3; s18p4; s20p2; s22p2 (2); s23p4

JANUARY 88
24 CFR 5: .801;
HUD-50058Instr: p16; p32;
HUD-52517: p2 (2); p13; p17;
7420.10G Gbk: 5-16 Ex 5-2 (2); 5-17; 10-16; 10-32; 20-7; 20-9; 20-12 Ex 20-2;
PIH Notices: 03-23 (5); 03-05; 02-21 (2); 02-15; 02-03 (2); 02-01 (5); 01-41; 01-15 Impr Integ Hbk (2); 01-10 (5); 01-06 (7); 01-02 (2); 01-01 (3); 00-28; 00-23 (2); 00-09; 00-01 (2); 99-52 (4); 95-48 (16); 95-48 Tech Asst (10);
Admin Plan: s24p1

JAPAN 1
HUD-903: p2

JOB READINESS 1
7420.10G Gbk: 23-1

JOB TRAINING 16
24 CFR 5: .603;
HUD-50058: p16;
HUD-50058Instr: p27; p61 (2); p71;
7420.10G Gbk: 5-16 Ex 5-2 (2); 23-6; 23-15;
PIH Notices: 02-01; 00-11A; 99-52;
Admin Plan: s6p3; s25p4; s25p4

JOB TRAINING PARTNERSHIP 1
HUD-50058Instr: p27

JOB TRAINING PROGRAM 5
24 CFR 5: .617;
PIH Notices: 01-15 Impr Integ Hbk; 00-11A;
Admin Plan: s6p2; s6p3

JOB TRAINING PROGRAMS 2
7420.10G Gbk: 23-4; 23-5

JOINING THE FAMILY 1
Admin Plan: s2p5

JOINT CUSTODY 3
Admin Plan: s2p4 (2); s6p8

JOINT CUSTODY AGREEMENT ... 1
Admin Plan: s2p4

JOURNAL VOUCHERS 2
7420.10G Gbk: 20-23; 20-23

JTPA 2
HUD-50058Instr: p27;
7420.10G Gbk: 23-5

JUDGE 3
24 CFR 5: .100;
7420.10G Gbk: 8-11; 10-2

JUDGEMENT 8
HUD-50058Instr: p30;
7420.10G Gbk: 9-12 (2); 10-2 (2); 22-17;
PIH Notices: 01-15 Impr Integ Hbk; 01-15 Impr Integ Hbk

JUDGES 1
PIH Notices: 01-41

JUDGING 1
7420.10G Gbk: 19-1

JUDGMENT 24
24 CFR 982: .157; .311; .314; .638;
HUD-50058Instr: p30 (2);
7420.10G Gbk: 5-12; 5-16 Ex 5-2; 5-38; 9-8; 10-2 (2); 15-4; 20-25; 22-17 (4); 24-14;
PIH Notices: 01-15 Impr Integ Hbk; 95-48; 95-48 Tech Asst;
Admin Plan: s14p2; s17p3

JUDGMENTS 2
PIH Notices: 02-01;

Admin Plan: s20p4

JUDICIAL....................................17
24 CFR 5: .514 (4);
24 CFR 982: .202; .306; .310; .315; .555;
7420.10G Gbk: 15-10 Ex 15-2; 16-5;
PIH Notices: 03-11; 01-41;
Admin Plan: s16p1; s18p6; s23p6; s23p6

JUDICIAL ACTION..........................8
24 CFR 5: .514;
24 CFR 982: .202; .306; .310;
HUD-52641: p6;
7420.10G Gbk: 8-18; 11-1;
Admin Plan: s16p1

JUDICIAL DECREE.........................1
24 CFR 982: .315

JUDICIAL EVICTION......................1
PIH Notices: 03-11

JUDICIAL ORDER...........................2
HUD-52641: p5;
7420.10G Gbk: 11-18

JUDICIAL PROCEDURES...............1
24 CFR 5: .514

JUDICIAL PROCEEDING 1
Admin Plan: s23p6

JUDICIAL PROCEEDINGS 5
24 CFR 5: .514;
24 CFR 982: .555;
7420.10G Gbk: 15-10 Ex 15-2; 16-5;
Admin Plan: s18p6

JUDICIAL RELIEF 1
24 CFR 5: .514

JUDICIAL REMEDY........................1
PIH Notices: 01-41

JUDICIOUSLY..................................
1
Admin Plan: s20p1

JULY 80
24 CFR 982: 24 CFR 982 (2); .5; .54; .104; .207; .317; .355; .401; .406; .521; .642 (2);
HUD-50058Instr: p16;
HUD-52580-A: p8;
7420.10G Gbk: 1-4 (3); 5-16 Ex 5-2; 8-14; 10-29 (8); 20-9; 20-12 Ex 20-2 (2); 21-6; 24-3; 24-5 (5);
PIH Notices: 02-27 (2); 02-21; 01-20 (4); 01-10 (5); 01-06; 00-34 (2); 00-31; 00-27; 00-24 (2); 00-11A; 00-01; 99-30 (3); 98-66; 96-65; 95-48 (11); 95-48 Tech Asst (4); 95-48 Tech Asst

JUNE..97
24 CFR 5: .506; .508 (4); .516; .518;
HUD-50058Instr: p i; p3; p17;
7420.10G Gbk: 1-4; 8-13 (2); 8-14 (2); 10-29 (6); 14-4; 19-2 (2); 19-3 (3); 19-9; 20-10; 20-12 Ex 20-2 (2); 20-20; 20-21 Ex 20-4; 21-6; 24-3; 24-5 (10);
PIH Notices: 03-23 (7); 02-27; 02-21 (4); 02-15; 02-14 (2); 02-07; 02-01 (4); 01-20 (2); 01-11 (3); 01-10 (2); 00-53 (2); 00-34 (6); 00-24 (5); 00-24A (2); 00-23; 00-09 (5); 99-52 (3); 99-52

JURISDICTION 351
24 CFR 5: .514; .603; .655;
24 CFR 35 SubM: .1200 (2); .1225;
24 CFR 982: .1; .4 (6); .51 (2); .102 (3); .201 (5); .207; .301 (6); .314 (4); .351 (2); .352; .353 (10); .355 (5); .503 (7); .627; .630; .636 (2);
HUD-50058: p i; p ix; p10; p x; p11; p xi; p13; p xiii; p14; p xiv;
HUD-50058Instr: p9 (4); p10 (2); p28; p40; p42 (3); p46 (3); p53 (2); p56 (3); p59 (3); p60; p62; p63; p65 (2); p66; p68; p73 (3); p74;
HUD-52648: p2 (6); p3;
HUD-52665: p1 (2); p2 (2); p3 (2);
HUD-903: p1 (2);
7420.10G Gbk: 2-1; 2-2 (6); 2-3 (4); 2-6 (2); 2-7 (5); 2-8; 2-9; 2-10; 3-7; 4-16; 4-17; 4-19 (2); 4-20; 5-3 (4); 7-1 (3); 7-4 (2); 7-5 (3); 7-7 (2); 7-10 (3); 8-3; 8-4 (2); 8-7 (2); 8-8; 8-9; 8-14; 9-1; 9-4 (3); 9-5; 9-6; 9-8; 10-7; 10-11; 10-22; 13-1 (4); 13-2 (9); 13-3 (5); 13-4 (3); 13-5 (2); 13-7 (4); 13-8 (6); 13-10 (2); 18-7; 20-9; 20-24 (5); 21-5 (2); 21-7 (2); 21-8; 23-17 Ex 23-2 (2); 23-18 (4);
PIH Notices: 03-11; 02-27;

02-20 (16); 02-14; 02-01 (2); 01-41 (2); 01-27 (3); 01-06 (23); 01-02 (2); 01-01 (14); 00-46 (12); 00-24B (3); 00-09; 99-52 (2); 99-11 (2); 95-48 (5); 95-48 Tech Asst (5);
Admin Plan: s1p1 (2); s1p5; s1p7 (3); s2p5; s9p1; s13p1 (4); s13p2 (3); s18p6; s21p5; s21p6 (2); s21p6

JURISDICTIONAL 4
24 CFR 5: .100;
PIH Notices: 01-06 (2);
Admin Plan: s20p4

JURISDICTIONS 29
24 CFR 982: .201;
7420.10G Gbk: 2-4; 2-6; 2-9 (2); 2-10; 3-8; 4-8; 4-20; 7-7; 8-7 (2); 9-4 (2); 13-1 (3); 13-4; 13-6; 13-8; 13-10; 21-6;
PIH Notices: 02-27 (2); 02-07; 01-06 (3); 00-28

JURISDICTION'S 2
24 CFR 5: .518;
PIH Notices: 02-21

JUSTIFICATION 27
24 CFR 982: .503 (3);
7420.10G Gbk: 11-2; 20-6; 20-14 (3);
PIH Notices: 02-27 (3); 02-20 (5); 02-07; 00-46 (5); 00-28; 00-09 (2);
Admin Plan: s5p2; s25p6

JUSTIFICATIONS 3
7420.10G Gbk: 20-3;
PIH Notices: 95-48; 95-48 Tech Asst

JUSTIFIED 10
24 CFR 982: .402; .503;
HUD-903: p2;
7420.10G Gbk: 5-41; 9-11;
PIH Notices: 02-20 (2); 00-46 (2); 00-09

JUSTIFY 18
24 CFR 5: .236;
24 CFR 982: .503 (2); .553;
7420.10G Gbk: 4-18; 9-9; 9-11;
PIH Notices: 03-12; 02-20 (4); 00-46 (4); 95-48; 95-48 Tech Asst

JUVENILE 1
Admin Plan: s25p1

JUVENILE COURT 1
Admin Plan: s25p1

KEOGH 2
7420.10G Gbk: 4-26 Ex 4-2; 5-25 Ex 5-3

KEROSENE 3
24 CFR 982: .401;
HUD-52580-A: p15;
7420.10G Gbk: 10-7

KEY 47
24 CFR 982: .401;
7420.10G Gbk: 1-1 (3); 1-3; 1-4; 1-10; 1-11; 1-15 (2); 1-16 Ex 1-3; 4-13; 5-25 Ex 5-3; 8-5; 8-23 (2); 9-4; 9-12; 19-1; 19-4 (3); 19-5; 19-6; 19-8 (3); 19-9; 19-10 (3); 19-11; 19-13; 20-1; 20-2; 20-22; 21-2; 22-8 (2);
PIH Notices: 02-27 (3); 02-01; 00-24B (2); 99-52; 99-11

KICKBACKS 1
7420.10G Gbk: 22-2

KITCHEN 54
24 CFR 5: .703 (2);
24 CFR 982: .401 (4); .608; .609 (2); .614 (3);
HUD-52580: p2 (2); p6;
HUD-52580-A: p1; p4 (8); p5 (5); p6 (2); p15 (2); p19;
7420.10G Gbk: 10-2; 10-5; 10-6 (2); 10-7; 10-8 (2); 17-3 (2); 17-4 (4); 17-5 (3);
Admin Plan: s19p1 (3); s19p1

KITCHENS 5
24 CFR 5: .703;
PIH Notices: 02-01; 99-52; 95-48; 95-48 Tech Asst

KNOWLEDGE ....
41
24 CFR 5: .508; .518 (2);
HUD-52641: p5;
HUD-52648: p3 (2);
7420.10G Gbk: 4-27 Ex 4-2; 8-8; 9-3; 9-9; 9-10; 9-12; 10-17; 10-36 Ex 10-1 (2); 11-13; 12-16 Ex 12-4; 16-4 (2); 21-3; 22-11; 22-13; 22-16; 24-10; 24-13;
PIH Notices: 01-41; 01-06 (3); 00-09; 95-48 (2); 95-48 Tech Asst (2);
Admin Plan: s8p1; s15p3; s20p1; s20p4; s20p6 (2); s20p6

KNOWLEDGEABLE 8
7420.10G Gbk: 2-5; 2-6; 19-5;

PIH Notices: 01-15;
Admin Plan: s2p3; s6p11; s7p7; s20p7

LAB...2
PIH Notices: 00-23; 00-23

LABORATORY.................................1
PIH Notices: 01-15 Impr Integ Hbk

LABORATORY REPORTS...............1
PIH Notices: 01-15 Impr Integ Hbk

LANDLORD...................................73
24 CFR 982: .305; .307; .312; .553;
HUD-52646: p2;
HUD-903-1: p5;
7420.10G Gbk: 1-12 Ex 1-2; 4-25 Ex 4-2 (2); 5-39; 5-40 (6); 8-20; 13-8; 21-4 (4); 22-9 (2); 22-11; 22-12 (3); 22-18; 23-13 (2); 24-12 (2); 24-13 (5); 24-14 (8); 24-15 (5);
PIH Notices: 00-24B; 95-48; 95-48 Tech Asst;
Admin Plan: s1p6; s6p7; s8p3 (3); s8p4 (2); s9p1; s9p3 (2); s10p2 (2); s10p3 (2); s10p4; s11p1; s20p8; s25p6; s25p7

LANDLORDS 51
24 CFR 982: .301;
7420.10G Gbk: 2-1; 21-4 (2); 22-10; 22-18; 24-9 (6); 24-12 (3); 24-13 (3); 24-14 (12); 24-15 (4);
PIH Notices: 02-27; 02-21; 01-41; 01-20; 00-09;
Admin Plan: s1p6 (4); s1p7; s8p4 (3); s9p3; s16p3; s21p5; s25p8

LANDLORD'S...................................
7
7420.10G Gbk: 5-40; 24-12; 24-13 (4); 24-13

LANDSCAPER.................................1
PIH Notices: 01-15 Impr Integ Hbk

LANDSCAPER'S.............................2
PIH Notices: 01-15; 01-15 Impr Integ Hbk

LANGUAGE..................................67
24 CFR 5: .502;
HUD-52641: p1 (3); 8;
HUD-52641-A: p1;
7420.10G Gbk: 4-3; 4-4; 5-7; 5-11; 8-2 (2); 9-3; 10-29 (2); 10-33; 11-11 (2); 11-12; 22-8; 23-9;
PIH Notices: 02-06; 02-01 (2); 00-24A; 00-11; 99-52 (2); 95-48 (15); 95-48 Tech Asst (15);
Admin Plan: s1p3 (2); s1p5 (2); s7p8; s8p1; s15p2; s20p4; s20p4

LANGUAGES..................................3
7420.10G Gbk: 4-14; 8-2;
Admin Plan: s1p5

LARGE FAMILIES...........................5
7420.10G Gbk: 20-4; 24-10;
PIH Notices: 02-07; 00-28;
Admin Plan: s24p4

LARGER FAMILIES........................6
24 CFR 5: .603 (3);
HUD-50058Instr: p71; p73; p76

LARGER UNIT.................................5
7420.10G Gbk: 22-12 (2);
PIH Notices: 02-01; 99-52;
Admin Plan: s5p2

LARGER UNIT SIZES 1
PIH Notices: 00-27

LAST DAY.......................................8
24 CFR 982: .102 (2); .309;
HUD-52641: p3;
7420.10G Gbk: 11-9; 15-4;
PIH Notices: 01-11;
Admin Plan: s23p4

LATE..37
24 CFR 982: .451 (6);
7420.10G Gbk: 8-4; 10-15; 11-9; 11-10; 15-1; 19-4 (6); 19-13; 22-2;
PIH Notices: 03-05; 02-27; 01-40; 01-15 Impr Integ Hbk; 01-06; 96-65;
Admin Plan: s11p1 (3); s11p2 (3); s17p1; s17p2; s21p8 (3); s22p4

LATE PAYMENT 23
24 CFR 982: .451 (6);
HUD-52641: p4 (4);
7420.10G Gbk: 11-6 (2); 11-7 (5); 11-9; 24-12;
PIH Notices: 03-05; 01-40;
Admin Plan: s11p2; s11p2

LATE PAYMENT PENALTY 3
24 CFR 982: .451 (2);
Admin Plan: s11p2

LATE PAYMENTS...........................3
7420.10G Gbk: 11-6;
Admin Plan: s17p1; s22p4

LATINO...10
HUD-50058: p3 (2); p4 (2);
HUD-50058Instr: p16 (2);
7420.10G Gbk: 4-23 Ex 4-1 (2); 4-25 Ex 4-2; 4-25 Ex 4-2

LAUNDROMATS 2
7420.10G Gbk: 4-3; 9-6
LAUNDRY 6
24 CFR 5: .318; .703;
7420.10G Gbk: 9-14 Ex 9-1; 9-16 Ex 9-2; 9-17 Ex 9-3;
PIH Notices: 00-41
LAUNDRY FACILITIES 2
7420.10G Gbk: 9-14 Ex 9-1; 9-16 Ex 9-2
LAUNDRY FACILITY...................... 1
7420.10G Gbk: 9-17 Ex 9-3
LAUNDRY ROOMS 2
24 CFR 5: .318; .703
LAVATORY 14
24 CFR 982: .605 (2);
HUD-52580: p2; p6 (2); p7; p19;
7420.10G Gbk: 10-3 (4); 10-4 (2); 17-2
LAW ENFORCEMENT 12
HUD-9886: p1;
7420.10G Gbk: 22-16;
PIH Notices: 03-11 (8); 95-48; 95-48 Tech Asst
LAWN 10
24 CFR 5: .609;
HUD-52580: p6;
HUD-52580-A: p19;
HUD-52667: p i; p ii;
7420.10G Gbk: 5-15 Ex 5-2; 18-5;
PIH Notices: 01-15 Impr Integ Hbk (2);
Admin Plan: s10p5
LAWN MAINTENANCE 4
24 CFR 5: .609;
7420.10G Gbk: 5-15 Ex 5-2;
PIH Notices: 01-15 Impr Integ Hbk; 01-15 Impr Integ Hbk
LAWNS.. 1
7420.10G Gbk: 9-6
LAYOFF 4
PIH Notices: 95-48 (2); 95-48 Tech Asst; 95-48 Tech Asst
LAYOUT 1
PIH Notices: 99-11
LEAD BASED.................................. 9
7420.10G Gbk: 10-19;
PIH Notices: 02-07 (2); 02-01; 00-49; 99-52;
Admin Plan: s1p2; s8p2; s8p3
LEAD-BASED PAINT 174
24 CFR 5: .703 (2);
24 CFR 35 SubM: .1200; .1220 (2); .1225 (3);
24 CFR 982: .158; .305; .401 (3); .605;
HUD-52517: p2 (8); p3 (3); p4 (2); p5 (7);
HUD-52580-A: p2 (6); p3; p5; p7; p9; p10; p11; p12; p13 (5); p14; p17 (12); p18 (4);
7420.10G Gbk: 8-15 (2); 10-1; 10-11 (3); 10-12; 10-15 (6); 10-16 (4); 10-17 (4); 10-18; 10-19; 10-20 (2); 10-21 (3); 10-22 (4); 10-36 Ex 10-1 (14); 10-37 Ex 10-2 (12); 10-38 Ex 10-3 (2); 10-39 Ex 10-4 (4); 10-42 Ex 10-5; 17-2; 17-3; 17-5; 20-4 (4);
PIH Notices: 02-07 (2); 00-49 (5); 00-23 (24);
Admin Plan: s8p2; s23p4
LEAD-SAFE..................................... 2
7420.10G Gbk: 10-18; 10-18
LEASE COMPLIANCE 2
Admin Plan: s1p3; s8p3
LEASE ENFORCEMENT............... 10
PIH Notices: 03-11 (8); 02-01; 99-52
LEASE RATE 2
7420.10G Gbk: 20-10; 20-10
LEASE REQUIREMENTS 7
24 CFR 982: .308;
HUD-52641: p10;
HUD-52641-A: p3;
7420.10G Gbk: 11-17;
PIH Notices: 01-41; 00-09;
Admin Plan: s9p1
LEASE REQUIRING 2
PIH Notices: 02-01; 99-52
LEASE TERM 82
24 CFR 982: .4 (2); .305 (5); .309 (5); .310; .311; .314; .521; .624;
HUD-50058Instr: p70; p74;
HUD-52641: p1 (6); p2 (5); p3 (2); 8; p9 (3);
HUD-52641-A: p1; p2 (3);
7420.10G Gbk: 1-14; 8-16; 8-22 (4); 11-1; 11-4; 11-5 (2); 11-11; 11-15 (4); 11-19; 15-2 (4); 15-3 (2); 17-12; 20-23; 21-10;
PIH Notices: 01-41 (6); 00-24B; 00-09 (8);
Admin Plan: s9p3; s19p1
LEASE TERMINATES 7
24 CFR 982: .311;
HUD-50058Instr: p11;
HUD-52641: p9 (2);

HUD-52641-A: p2 (2); 7420.10G Gbk: 8-22

LEASE TERMINATION....................3
24 CFR 982: .314; .551; 7420.10G Gbk: 13-3

LEASE VIOLATION.........................3
PIH Notices: 01-41; 99-11; Admin Plan: s10p5

LEASE VIOLATIONS 6
7420.10G Gbk: 5-40; 8-8; 15-7 (2); Admin Plan: s15p5; s15p5

LEASED HOUSING 2
7420.10G Gbk: 1-2; 8-16

LEASED HOUSING 1
7420.10G Gbk: 8-16

LEASED-UP......................................1
7420.10G Gbk: 21-11

LEASEHOLDER...............................2
24 CFR 982: .310; .310

LEASEHOLDERS.............................1
7420.10G Gbk: 4-14

LEASE-PURCHASE.........................6
24 CFR 982: Intro; .4; .305; .317 (2); .317

LEASES..79
24 CFR 5: .214; .312; .315; .321 (2); .360 (3);
24 CFR 982: .201; .353 (2); .504; .601; .619; .620; .624;
HUD-50058Instr: p42; p46 (3); p74;
HUD-52641: p1 (2); p10;
HUD-52641-A: p3;
7420.10G Gbk: 1-14; 3-4; 4-20; 6-5; 7-1; 8-19; 11-2 (2); 11-10; 13-2 (2); 13-5; 13-7; 13-8 (2); 13-9; 14-4; 17-10 (2); 17-11; 17-12; 19-8 (2); 19-9; 20-17; 24-3 (3); 24-4; 24-5 (2); 24-6 (4); 24-8; 24-13;
PIH Notices: 01-41 (3); 01-15 Impr Integ Hbk (2); 01-01; 00-24B (2); 00-14; 00-09 (3);
Admin Plan: s7p6; s9p2 (2); s19p1; s19p1

LEASE-SANCTION.........................1
PIH Notices: 02-07

LEASEUP 1
7420.10G Gbk: 20-10

LEASE-UP....................................104
HUD-52648: p2;
7420.10G Gbk: 1-10; 2-10; 8-11 (3); 8-23; 13-8; 19-8 (3); 19-9; 19-12; 20-10 (2); 20-11 (5); 20-15; 21-2; 21-5; 21-10; 21-11; 21-16 Ex 21-6; 21-19; 24-2 (2); 24-15;
PIH Notices: 03-23 (3); 02-21 (18); 02-07; 02-06 (6); 01-20 (5); 01-06 (28); 01-01 (3); 00-34; 00-28 (2); 00-24A;
Admin Plan: s13p1; s14p1; s21p1; s21p2; s21p3; s21p8

LEASE-UPS 1
PIH Notices: 02-06

LEASING 245
24 CFR 5: .653 (3);
24 CFR 982: .4; .54; .303; .304; .317 (2); .351; .353;
HUD-50058Instr: p1; p70; p73;
HUD-52517: p2;
HUD-52641: p3; 8 (2);
HUD-52641-A: p1 (3); p2;
HUD-52648: p1;
HUD-52667: p i (2);
7420.10G Gbk: 1-1; 1-4; 2-2; 2-8 (2); 2-9; 2-10; 2-11 (3); 3-3; 4-1 (2); 4-5 (2); 4-6; 4-11; 4-12; 4-18; 6-5; 7-1; 7-7; 7-9; 8-1 (7); 8-2; 8-3; 8-4; 8-5; 8-8 (2); 8-9 (7); 8-10; 8-11; 8-13; 8-14 (3); 8-17; 8-18; 8-22 (5); 8-23 (2); 10-24; 10-26; 11-1; 11-4; 11-8; 11-10; 11-11; 11-16 Ex 11-1; 13-6 (3); 13-7 (2); 13-8; 13-12 Ex 13-2; 14-1; 14-4; 17-10; 17-11 (2); 18-4; 18-7; 19-10; 19-11 (6); 19-12 (3); 20-2; 20-3; 20-8 Ex 20-1 (2); 20-9; 20-15 (3); 20-16 (2); 20-17 (2); 20-19 Ex 20-3 (2); 20-20 (12); 20-21 Ex 20-4; 20-22 (2); 21-2 (3); 21-6; 21-9; 21-14 Ex 21-4; 21-16 Ex 21-6 (2); 21-19; 22-9; 24-2 (2); 24-3 (2); 24-4; 24-6; 24-7 (7); 24-8 (3); 24-10 (2);
PIH Notices: 03-23 (31); 02-27; 02-21; 02-20; 02-14; 02-06 (11); 01-41 (3); 01-20; 01-02; 01-01 (12); 00-46; 00-24B (3); 00-09 (2); 99-11;
Admin Plan: s9p3; s19p1;

s21p3
LEAVE..43
24 CFR 982: .207; .315;
HUD-50058: p i; p ii; p iii; p iv; p v; p6; p17;
HUD-50058Instr: p7 (2); p12; p13; p14; p15; p19; p20 (2); p24; p42; p46; p53; p56; p61; p62;
HUD-903: p1;
HUD-903-1: p3;
7420.10G Gbk: 4-18; 4-26 Ex 4-2 (2); 5-30; 7-2; 10-11; 22-13; 22-15; 24-3; 24-7; 24-8 (2);
PIH Notices: 02-27; 95-48; 95-48 Tech Asst;
Admin Plan: s23p7
LEAVES..9
7420.10G Gbk: 23-2; 23-9;
PIH Notices: 03-05; 01-41; 01-40; 00-09;
Admin Plan: s6p5; s8p5; s23p5
LEDGER..13
7420.10G Gbk: 20-20; 20-23 (10); 23-13; 23-14
LEDGERS..3
7420.10G Gbk: 20-23 (2); 20-23
LEGAL ASSISTANCE......................1
7420.10G Gbk: 8-8
LEGAL CAPACITY..........................5
24 CFR 982: .308 (2);
7420.10G Gbk: 8-21 (2);
Admin Plan: s2p2
LEGAL COUNSEL...........................2
Admin Plan: s18p5; s18p6
LEGAL FEES....................................3
7420.10G Gbk: 5-28; 22-17; 22-17
LEGAL PROFITMAKING ACTIVITIES.....................................2
24 CFR 982: .551;
HUD-52641: 8
LEGAL PROFIT-MAKING ACTIVITIES.....................................1
7420.10G Gbk: 1-15
LEGAL REPRESENTATIVE............2
24 CFR 982: .4; .633
LEGAL SEPARATION.....................3
Admin Plan: s2p3; s7p8; s8p5
LEGISLATION...............................13
24 CFR 982: .51;
HUD-50058Instr: p5;
7420.10G Gbk: 1-3; 1-4 (3); 1-13;
PIH Notices: 02-01; 01-15 Impr Integ Hbk (2); 99-52; 95-48; 95-48 Tech Asst
LEGISLATIVE.................................3
PIH Notices: 01-06; 95-48; 95-48 Tech Asst
LEGISLATOR..................................4
24 CFR 982: .161;
HUD-52641: p6;
7420.10G Gbk: 8-19; 11-2
LEGITIMATE...................................9
24 CFR 5: .100; .315 (2);
7420.10G Gbk: 22-9;
PIH Notices: 02-06; 96-65; 95-48; 95-48 Tech Asst;
Admin Plan: s15p3
LENDING INSTITUTION................1
HUD-903-1: p5
LENGTH OF TIME...........................9
24 CFR 5: .318;
7420.10G Gbk: 3-4; 4-17; 19-7; 23-6;
PIH Notices: 00-11A;
Admin Plan: s6p12; s15p5; s17p1
LESS THAN FAIR MARKET VALUE 24
24 CFR 5: .603 (2);
HUD-50058Instr: p22;
7420.10G Gbk: 4-27 Ex 4-2; 5-25 Ex 5-3; 5-27 (7); 5-28; 5-50 Ex 5-5 (2);
PIH Notices: 01-15 Impr Integ Hbk;
Admin Plan: s6p10 (4); s7p3; s7p6 (2); s7p6
LETTER...170
24 CFR 5: .214; .240; .353; .514;
HUD-50058: p iii (2); p iv (2); p6;
HUD-50058Instr: p7; p16 (2); p24; p75;
7420.10G Gbk: 4-7 (3); 5-10 Ex 5-1 (2); 5-11; 5-12; 5-47 Ex 5-5; 10-23; 10-40 Ex 10-4a (2); 10-41 Ex 10-4b (2); 10-42 Ex 10-5; 10-43 Ex 10-6 (2); 10-44 Ex 10-7a; 10-45 Ex 10-7b; 10-46 Ex 10-8; 12-2; 12-12 Ex 12-1 (2); 12-13 Ex 12-1 (8); 12-14 Ex 12-2 (3); 12-15 Ex 12-3; 15-7 (2); 15-10 Ex 15-2 (2); 19-13 (3); 20-2; 20-5; 21-5; 22-4 (7); 22-5; 22-10;
PIH Notices: 02-27; 02-21 (14); 02-14; 02-07 (2); 02-06; 02-01 (4); 01-41 (5); 01-

20 (13); 01-15 (3); 01-15 Impr Integ Hbk (3); 01-06 (6); 00-28 (4); 00-27 (9); 00-09 (5); 99-52 (4); 96-65 (3); 95-48 (2); 95-48 Tech Asst (2);
Admin Plan: s4p3 (2); s7p2 (7); s7p3 (4); s7p4; s7p6; s18p4 (2); s18p7 (2); s23p6; s25p7

LETTERS 46
24 CFR 982: .312;
HUD-50058Instr: p7;
HUD-52667: p ii;
7420.10G Gbk: 1-1; 5-12; 5-46 Ex 5-5 (2); 5-47 Ex 5-5; 5-49 Ex 5-5; 10-23; 10-25; 10-33; 10-34; 12-3; 12-4; 12-13 Ex 12-1; 18-4;
PIH Notices: 02-27; 02-20; 01-15; 01-15 Impr Integ Hbk (8); 01-06 (4); 00-46; 95-48 (3); 95-48 Tech Asst (3);
Admin Plan: s1p4 (2); s6p6; s7p2; s7p4; s7p6; s7p8

LEVEL OF SERVICES 1
Admin Plan: s1p3

LIABILITIES.................................... 1
7420.10G Gbk: 20-30

LIABILITY..................................... 24
24 CFR 5: .318 (2); .360 (2); .512; .526 (4); .528;
24 CFR 982: .307;
HUD-50058Instr: p32;
HUD-52641: p3; p6;
HUD-52646: p1;
7420.10G Gbk: 5-16 Ex 5-2; 5-40; 20-25; 20-26; 23-14; 24-10 (2);
PIH Notices: 01-15 Impr Integ Hbk;
Admin Plan: s15p4

LICENSE 26
24 CFR 5: .318;
HUD-50058Instr: p61;
7420.10G Gbk: 5-12; 5-50 Ex 5-5; 9-3 (3);
PIH Notices: 01-15 Impr Integ Hbk (2); 95-48 (8); 95-48 Tech Asst (8);
Admin Plan: s7p8

LICENSED 15
24 CFR 5: .350; .661;
24 CFR 982: .4; .612;
HUD-50058Instr: p72; p74;
7420.10G Gbk: 9-6; 10-19;
PIH Notices: 95-48 (2); 95-48 Tech Asst (2);
Admin Plan: s7p6; s7p8; s19p1

LICENSEE....................................... 2
PIH Notices: 95-48; 95-48 Tech Asst

LICENSEES 3
7420.10G Gbk: 9-3;
PIH Notices: 95-48; 95-48 Tech Asst

LICENSES....................................... 4
PIH Notices: 95-48 (2); 95-48 Tech Asst; 95-48 Tech Asst

LICENSING 39
24 CFR 5: .318 (2);
HUD-50058Instr: p75;
HUD-52580-A: p17;
7420.10G Gbk: 9-3 (2);
PIH Notices: 95-48 (16); 95-48 Tech Asst (16);
Admin Plan: s19p1

LICENSING REQUIREMENTS....... 5
HUD-50058Instr: p75;
PIH Notices: 95-48 (2); 95-48 Tech Asst; 95-48 Tech Asst

LIFE INSURANCE 1
HUD-50058Instr: p29

LIFE THREATENING 8
24 CFR 982: .404 (2);
HUD-52641: p3;
7420.10G Gbk: 10-28; 10-29;
PIH Notices: 00-24B (2);
Admin Plan: s21p5

LIFE-THREATENING...................... 5
24 CFR 982: .619;
HUD-52648: p1;
7420.10G Gbk: 10-27; 10-33;
PIH Notices: 00-09

LIFETIME 13
24 CFR 5: .615; .617;
24 CFR 982: .553 (2);
7420.10G Gbk: 5-21;
PIH Notices: 03-11; 01-15 Impr Integ Hbk (2); 00-11A;
Admin Plan: s6p3; s6p12; s11p3; s15p2

LIFETIME REGISTRATION............ 3
24 CFR 982: .553;
PIH Notices: 03-11;
Admin Plan: s15p2

LIFETIME SEX OFFENDER 1
24 CFR 982: .553

LIFETIME TIME LIMIT.................. 2
Admin Plan: s6p12; s11p3

LIGHT FIXTURE............................ 14
24 CFR 982: .401;
HUD-52580-A: p2 (3); p3; p4; p5; p6; p7; p8; p9;

p10; p11; p12

LIGHT FIXTURES 4
24 CFR 982: .401;
HUD-52580-A: p2;
7420.10G Gbk: 10-8; 10-9

LIGHTING 11
24 CFR 5: .703 (4);
HUD-52580-A: p18;
HUD-52667: p i; p ii;
7420.10G Gbk: 18-5; 18-6;
PIH Notices: 99-11; 99-11

LIHTC 18
PIH Notices: 02-22 (14); 02-15;
01-02 (2); 01-02

LIMIT 108
24 CFR 5: .303; .318 (3);
.518; .615; .653 (2);
24 CFR 982: .102 (4); .201 (4);
.207; .403; .509; .516;
.520; .552; .601; .610;
.613; .626;
HUD-50058: p5; p v;
HUD-50058Instr: p19 (4);
p65 (3); p66 (3); p67;
HUD-52641: p4;
HUD-52667: p ii;
7420.10G Gbk: 1-6 Ex 1-1; 1-10;
2-2; 4-3; 4-6; 4-12 (2);
4-13; 4-16; 5-21; 5-43;
6-3; 7-2; 8-5; 8-8; 8-12; 10-2; 10-35; 11-4;
13-3; 14-4 (2); 17-2; 23-18; 24-10 (3);
PIH Notices: 03-11; 03-05;
02-27; 01-40; 00-24B; 00-11A; 00-09; 95-48 (11);
95-48 Tech Asst (11);
Admin Plan: s2p4 (2);
s6p12 (2); s11p1; s11p3;
s18p2; s18p3; s19p1;
s21p6; s21p7

LIMITATION 43
24 CFR 5: .318; .653; .655;
.801;
24 CFR 982: .310; .402; .552;
7420.10G Gbk: 1-4; 4-1; 8-18;
17-1; 22-2; 24-12 (2);
PIH Notices: 02-20 (3); 01-41; 01-15 Impr Integ Hbk;
00-46 (3); 00-09 (2); 95-48 (8); 95-48 Tech Asst (8);
Admin Plan: s5p3; s15p6;
s24p2

LIMITATION ON ADMISSION 1
24 CFR 5: .653

LIMITATIONS 38
24 CFR 5: .110; .318 (4);
24 CFR 982: .102; .206; .353;
.619;
7420.10G Gbk: 19-11;
PIH Notices: 03-11; 00-11 (2); 95-48 (8); 95-48 Tech Asst (8);
Admin Plan: s1p5; s2p4; s3p1;
s8p1; s13p1 (2); s13p2;
s19p1; s23p3

LIMITED 158
24 CFR 5: .318 (5); .359;
.403; .524; .603;
.609 (3); .617 (2); .659;
.703; .801 (3);
24 CFR 982: .102; .306;
.310 (2); .628; .631;
HUD-50058Instr: p22; p29 (2);
p72;
HUD-52580-A: p4 (2);
HUD-52641: p6;
HUD-9886: p1 (3);
7420.10G Gbk: 1-6 Ex 1-1; 4-1;
5-3; 5-15 Ex 5-2 (2); 5-32;
6-2; 8-7; 8-8; 8-9 (2);
8-18; 8-21 (2); 9-1; 9-2; 9-14 Ex 9-1; 10-19 (2);
11-1; 11-10; 16-4; 17-2;
20-5; 20-6; 20-13; 20-16;
21-3; 21-17; 22-3; 22-4;
22-7 (2); 23-11; 24-12;
PIH Notices: 03-23; 03-11;
03-05; 02-27 (9); 02-22;
02-01 (2); 01-41 (4); 01-40; 01-15 Impr Integ Hbk (10); 01-10; 01-06 (2); 00-11A (3); 00-09 (5); 99-52 (2); 98-66; 95-48 (15);
95-48 Tech Asst (15);
Admin Plan: s1p4 (2); s1p6;
s2p2; s6p3; s6p11; s8p1;
s14p1; s16p1; s17p1;
s20p2; s20p4; s22p1;
s25p4

LIMITED CIRCUMSTANCES......... 2
7420.10G Gbk: 20-16;
PIH Notices: 01-41

LIMITED DENIAL OF PARTICIPATION............................... 7
24 CFR 982: .306; .628; .631;
PIH Notices: 01-41 (2); 00-09;
Admin Plan: s16p1

LIMITING 7
24 CFR 5: .630;
7420.10G Gbk: 5-11; 15-5; 21-6; 21-9;
PIH Notices: 95-48; 95-48 Tech Asst

LIMITS 54
24 CFR 5: .303; .315; .318;
.653;
24 CFR 982: .509; .626;

7420.10G Gbk: 3-8; 4-12; 4-13; 4-14; 5-3 (2); 5-11; 5-44; 8-11; 9-2; 9-12; 10-14; 11-14; 16-4; 18-7; 21-3;
PIH Notices: 00-11; 95-48 (11); 95-48 Tech Asst (11);
Admin Plan: s1p4; s2p1; s2p4 (2); s2p5; s3p2; s6p1; s13p2; s21p7

LIQUIDATED....................................1
Admin Plan: s7p6

LIQUIDATION..................................1
7420.10G Gbk: 5-49 Ex 5-5

LIST..326
24 CFR 5: .216; .359; .655;
24 CFR 35 SubM: .1225;
24 CFR 982: 24 CFR 982 (6); .4 (4); .54 (3); .201 (3); .202 (6); .203 (3); .204 (19); .205 (18); .206 (6); .207 (3); .301; .313; .355; .552; .626; .629;
HUD-50058: p5; p v; p6; p ix;
HUD-50058Instr: p7; p14 (3); p19 (4); p22; p40 (2); p60; p68 (2); p75 (2); p76 (2);
HUD-52580: p6;
HUD-52580-A: p19;
HUD-52641: p10;
HUD-52641-A: p3;
HUD-52648: p1 (5); p2 (4);
HUD-903: p1;
7420.10G Gbk: 2-3 (5); 2-6; 2-8 (2); 2-9; 3-7; 3-8; 4-6 (3); 4-8; 4-11; 4-14; 4-22; 4-25 Ex 4-2; 4-26 Ex 4-2; 4-27 Ex 4-2 (4); 5-16 Ex 5-2; 5-43; 6-9 Ex 6-1; 8-4; 8-6; 8-7 (7); 8-8; 8-10; 9-3 (2); 9-6; 9-19 Ex 9-4 (4); 10-22; 10-23; 10-28; 10-36 Ex 10-1; 10-38 Ex 10-3; 10-39 Ex 10-4; 10-43 Ex 10-6; 10-44 Ex 10-7a; 10-45 Ex 10-7b; 12-16 Ex 12-4 (3); 13-1; 13-10; 19-7; 20-7; 21-10; 22-4 (2); 24-4; 24-9;
PIH Notices: 03-11 (2); 02-27 (12); 02-20 (4); 02-06; 02-01 (4); 01-41 (7); 01-27 (3); 01-15 (2); 01-06; 01-02 (2); 01-01 (3); 00-46 (4); 00-34; 00-24B (12); 00-11; 00-09 (6); 99-52 (4); 95-48; 95-48 Tech Asst;
Admin Plan: s1p6; s1p7 (2); s2p1 (5); s2p3 (3); s2p5; s3p1 (3); s3p2 (6); s4p1 (10); s4p2 (5); s5p1; s7p2; s7p4; s15p1; s18p2; s18p8; s21p1; s21p2; s21p3 (4); s21p5; s21p6 (4); s23p1 (3); s23p3 (3); s23p5; s24p6 (6); s24p7; s25p1 (2); s25p3 (2); s25p3

LISTED..143
24 CFR 5: .363; .514 (2); .601; .611; .617 (3); .655; .701 (3); .801 (9);
24 CFR 982: .4; .151; .202; .204; .207; .521; .626; .630; .637; .641;
HUD-50058: p iii; p iv; p6 (8); p vii (2); p viii; p x; p xi; p xiii;
HUD-50058Instr: p14 (2); p16; p17; p22 (7); p23 (2); p33 (2); p34; p36; p38; p42; p46; p53; p61; p69;
HUD-52580: p6;
HUD-52580-A: p19;
HUD-52646: p2;
HUD-52667: p ii (3);
HUD-903: p2 (2);
HUD-903-1: p4;
HUD-9886: p1; p2;
7420.10G Gbk: 2-4; 3-7; 4-25 Ex 4-2 (2); 5-2; 5-10 Ex 5-1; 5-36; 6-6 (2); 8-11; 8-17; 8-19; 9-5; 9-6; 10-4; 10-9; 10-34; 10-36 Ex 10-1; 10-38 Ex 10-3; 11-3; 12-12 Ex 12-1; 20-6; 21-3; 23-7;
PIH Notices: 03-12; 03-11 (3); 02-27 (4); 02-21; 02-20; 02-07; 01-20; 01-15; 01-15 Impr Integ Hbk; 01-10; 00-46; 00-28 (2); 00-27; 95-48 (4); 95-48 Tech Asst (4);
Admin Plan: s2p2 (2); s4p1; s5p3; s7p8; s8p5; s15p2; s15p5; s20p2; s20p4; s23p7

LISTEN...2
PIH Notices: 95-48; 95-48 Tech Asst

LISTENING....................................18
PIH Notices: 95-48 (9); 95-48 Tech Asst (8); 95-

48 Tech Asst

LISTING 44
24 CFR 982: .301; .552;
HUD-50058: p ii;
HUD-903: p2;
7420.10G Gbk: 1-1; 3-7; 5-35; 5-48 Ex 5-5; 8-6; 9-5; 9-7 (2); 19-4; 21-3;
PIH Notices: 03-11; 02-27 (10); 02-20; 01-15 (2); 01-02 (2); 00-46; 95-48 (5); 95-48 Tech Asst (5);
Admin Plan: s1p7; s11p1; s18p2

LISTING OF ACCESSIBLE UNITS 1
24 CFR 982: .301

LISTINGS 14
HUD-903-1: p3;
7420.10G Gbk: 2-7; 8-12; 8-15; 9-3; 9-5 (4); 9-6; 9-7 (2); 9-8;
PIH Notices: 02-27

LISTS 21
24 CFR 982: .201; .204;
HUD-50058Instr: p23; p24;
7420.10G Gbk: 2-8; 3-7 (2); 8-11; 9-6 (2); 23-6; 23-7; 24-9;
PIH Notices: 02-27 (2); 02-21; 01-20; 01-15 (2); 01-06;
Admin Plan: s1p7

LITERACY 1
PIH Notices: 00-11

LITIGATION 34
24 CFR 5: .318;
24 CFR 982: .163;
HUD-50058Instr: p32;
7420.10G Gbk: 5-16 Ex 5-2; 20-5; 20-10 (2); 20-11; 22-16 (2); 22-17 (2); 24-2; 24-16;
PIH Notices: 03-11; 02-27; 02-21 (6); 02-07; 02-06; 01-06; 00-28; 95-48 (4); 95-48 Tech Asst (3); 95-48 Tech Asst

LITTER 4
24 CFR 5: .350 (3); .350

LITTER BOXES 1
24 CFR 5: .350

LIVE ALONE 7
24 CFR 5: .609;
HUD-50058Instr: p15; p31; p75;
7420.10G Gbk: 5-15 Ex 5-2;
PIH Notices: 01-15 Impr Integ Hbk; 01-15 Impr Integ Hbk

LIVE INDEPENDENTLY 8
24 CFR 5: .403 (2);
HUD-50058: p i;
HUD-50058Instr: p15; p74 (2);
PIH Notices: 00-41;
Admin Plan: s25p2

LIVE TOGETHER 1
7420.10G Gbk: 5-3

LIVE-IN 135
24 CFR 5: .100; .403 (4); .609;
24 CFR 982: Intro; .4 (2); .201; .308; .316 (5); .402; .551; .606 (3); .608 (3); .610 (5); .613 (6); .615 (3); .619 (6); .620 (6); .625 (2);
HUD-50058: p3; p iii; p4; p iv; p v; p7; p ix; p x; p xi; p xii; p xiii; p xiv (2);
HUD-50058Instr: p14 (2); p15 (4); p16; p17 (3); p22; p27; p34 (2); p36; p40 (2); p43; p44 (2); p47 (2); p48 (2); p51 (2); p54 (2); p57 (2); p68; p69; p71; p72 (3); p73; p75;
7420.10G Gbk: 5-32;
PIH Notices: 01-15 Impr Integ Hbk (2);
Admin Plan: s2p2 (4); s2p3 (8); s5p1 (2); s8p6; s19p1 (13); s25p2

LIVE-IN AID 1
Admin Plan: s2p2

LIVE-IN AIDE 105
24 CFR 5: .100; .403; .609;
24 CFR 982: Intro; .4 (2); .308; .316 (5); .402; .551; .606 (3); .608 (3); .610 (5); .613 (6); .615 (3); .619 (6); .620 (6); .625 (2);
HUD-50058: p3; p4; p7;
HUD-50058Instr: p14; p15 (4); p27; p36; p43; p47 (2); p72; p73; p75;
HUD-52641: p1; p10 (2);
HUD-52641-A: p3 (2);
7420.10G Gbk: 5-15 Ex 5-2; 5-29; 5-41; 17-3 (2); 17-4 (2); 17-5 (2); 17-6 (2); 17-7 (2);
PIH Notices: 01-15 Impr Integ Hbk (2);
Admin Plan: s2p2 (2); s2p3 (5); s5p1; s19p1 (12); s19p1

LIVE-IN AIDES 47
24 CFR 5: .403 (3);
24 CFR 982: .201;
HUD-50058: p iii; p iv; p v; p ix; p x; p xi; p xii; p xiii; p xiv (2);
HUD-50058Instr: p14; p16; p17 (3); p22; p34 (2); p40 (2); p44 (2); p48 (2); p51 (2); p54 (2); p57 (2); p68; p69; p71; p72 (2);
7420.10G Gbk: 5-2 (2); 17-4 (2);
Admin Plan: s2p3 (3); s25p2

LIVE-IN ATTENDANT 1
Admin Plan: s8p6

LIVE-IN ATTENDANTS 2
Admin Plan: s2p2; s5p1

LIVE-IN-AIDE 12
24 CFR 982: .402; .551 (2);
HUD-50058Instr: p44;
7420.10G Gbk: 5-18; 5-41;
PIH Notices: 02-01 (3); 99-52 (2); 99-52

LIVE-IN-AIDES 2
PIH Notices: 02-01; 99-52

LIVES ALONE 1
HUD-50058Instr: p75

LIVING 244
24 CFR 5: .309; .315; .318 (2); .403 (7); .603; .609;
24 CFR 35 SubM: .1225 (4);
24 CFR 982: .201 (2); .203 (3); .301; .310; .401 (7); .551; .614; .618; .627;
HUD-50058Instr: p15; p20; p28; p65 (2); p66; p71 (2); p72 (2); p73; p76 (2);
HUD-52580: p1 (3); p2; p3; p4 (2); p6 (2);
HUD-52580-A: p1 (4); p2 (3); p3 (3); p4; p6; p8 (10); p9 (2); p10 (2); p11 (2); p12 (2); p13 (6); p14; p15 (9); p16; p19 (2);
HUD-52641: p9;
HUD-52641-A: p2 (2);
7420.10G Gbk: 1-3; 1-7; 1-8 (3); 2-2 (2); 2-6; 2-7; 3-4; 4-13; 4-17 (2); 4-21; 4-22 (2); 4-25 Ex 4-2 (2); 4-26 Ex 4-2; 5-2 (2); 5-14 Ex 5-2; 5-15 Ex 5-2; 5-21; 5-29; 5-38; 5-42 (2); 8-3; 8-9; 8-10; 8-17; 10-6 (4); 10-7 (3); 10-8 (2); 10-11; 10-13; 10-20; 11-4; 12-16 Ex 12-4; 13-2; 15-3; 17-1; 17-3 (3); 17-4 (4); 17-5 (2); 17-7; 17-8; 17-9; 21-7; 22-11; 23-17 Ex 23-2 (2);
PIH Notices: 03-11; 03-05; 02-21 (2); 02-03 (2); 02-01 (2); 01-41; 01-40; 01-20 (2); 01-15 Impr Integ Hbk (3); 00-41 (11); 00-27; 00-23 (2); 00-11 (6); 00-11A (9); 99-52 (2); 95-48; 95-48 Tech Asst;
Admin Plan: s2p2; s2p3; s2p4; s5p1; s5p3 (4); s6p7; s6p13; s8p5; s9p2; s10p5; s15p6; s19p1 (5); s23p2 (2); s25p2

LIVING ENVIRONMENT 7
24 CFR 5: .315; .603;
24 CFR 982: .401;
HUD-50058Instr: p76;
HUD-52580-A: p15;
7420.10G Gbk: 10-7; 10-7

LIVING ROOM 37
24 CFR 982: .401 (3); .614; .618;
HUD-52580: p1 (3); p2; p6;
HUD-52580-A: p1 (2); p2 (3); p3 (3); p4; p6 p8; p9; p10; p11; p12; p15 (2); p19;
7420.10G Gbk: 5-42; 10-6 (2); 10-8 (2); 17-3; 17-4; 17-5; 17-7;
Admin Plan: s5p3; s5p3

LIVING TOGETHER........................8
24 CFR 5: .403 (3);
24 CFR 982: .201;
HUD-50058Instr: p71;
7420.10G Gbk: 5-2;
Admin Plan: s2p4; s25p2

LOAD-BEARING 8
PIH Notices: 02-01 (3); 99-52 (3); 95-48; 95-48 Tech Asst

LOAN 39
24 CFR 5: .100; .210; .214 (3); .216; .801 (4);
24 CFR 982: .453 (2); .619; .623; .630; .632 (2);
HUD-50058Instr: p50 (2);
HUD-52641: p5 (2);
HUD-903: p2 (3); p4 (2);
7420.10G Gbk: 5-26; 5-48 Ex 5-5; 8-16; 9-11; 11-18; 15-4; 17-10;
PIH Notices: 01-41; 01-27;

01-10; 00-09;
Admin Plan: s7p5; s19p1

LOAN APPLICATION........................2
7420.10G Gbk: 5-48 Ex 5-5;
Admin Plan: s7p5

LOAN INSURANCE..........................2
24 CFR 5: .210; .214

LOAN MANAGEMENT...................6
24 CFR 5: .801 (2);
7420.10G Gbk: 8-16;
PIH Notices: 01-41; 01-10; 00-09

LOAN MANAGEMENT SET-ASIDE2
24 CFR 5: .801; .801

LOANS 20
24 CFR 5: .504; .601; .603; .801;
24 CFR 982: .453; .630; .632 (2);
HUD-52641: p5;
HUD-903-1: p2;
7420.10G Gbk: 2-11; 5-19; 5-25 Ex 5-3; 5-26; 5-27; 8-15; 11-18; 15-4;
Admin Plan: s16p2; s25p5

LOBBIES..1
24 CFR 5: .318

LOBBY 1
24 CFR 5: .353

LOCAL AGENCIES........................10
24 CFR 5: .617;
HUD-52667: p i;
HUD-9886: p2;
7420.10G Gbk: 18-4;
PIH Notices: 01-15 Impr Integ Hbk; 00-11 (2); 95-48; 95-48 Tech Asst;
Admin Plan: s7p2

LOCAL AGENCY...........................16
24 CFR 5: .100; .659;
24 CFR 982: .516;
HUD-52580-A: p18;
HUD-903: p2;
7420.10G Gbk: 3-1; 5-12; 10-3; 22-11;
PIH Notices: 01-15; 01-15 Impr Integ Hbk (3); 00-23 (2);
Admin Plan: s7p8

LOCAL GOVERNMENT 44
24 CFR 5: .526 (4); .603 .609; .661;
24 CFR 982: .352 (2);
HUD-50058Instr: p28 (2); p74;
7420.10G Gbk: 2-6; 4-16; 5-15 Ex 5-2; 10-31 (2); 11-8; 21-1; 23-3 (2); 23-4; 24-15;
PIH Notices: 01-15 Impr Integ Hbk (2); 95-48 (10); 95-48 Tech Asst (9); 95-48 Tech Asst

LOCAL GOVERNMENTAL 2
24 CFR 982: .1;
PIH Notices: 00-11

LOCAL GOVERNMENTS 29
24 CFR 5: .107; .603;
24 CFR 982: .201;
HUD-50058Instr: p76;
7420.10G Gbk: 1-3; 9-3; 9-4;
PIH Notices: 02-01; 01-15 (2); 99-52; 95-48 (12); 95-48 Tech Asst (5); 95-48 Tech Asst

LOCAL GOVERNMENT'S..............1
Admin Plan: s23p1

LOCAL HEALTH DEPARTMENT ..7
7420.10G Gbk: 10-5; 10-16; 10-20; 20-4;
PIH Notices: 02-07; 00-49; 00-49

LOCAL HOUSING NEEDS 4
24 CFR 982: .207;
7420.10G Gbk: 4-16 (2); 5-3

LOCAL LAW...................................94
24 CFR 5: .212; .303; .306 (2); .315 (5); .318; .321 (2); .327; .350; .353; .360 (3); .514; .609; .615;
24 CFR 982: .4 (2); .53; .155; .308 (4); .310 (2); .313; .353; .509; .555; .605 (2);
HUD-50058Instr: p27; p31; p71; p73; p75;
HUD-52641: p3; p9 (2); p10;
HUD-52641-A: p2 (2); p3;
7420.10G Gbk: 4-24 Ex 4-1; 4-25 Ex 4-2; 5-15 Ex 5-2; 5-20; 8-21 (2); 10-2; 10-19; 11-3; 11-12; 15-1; 15-3 (2); 16-5; 17-2 (2); 22-15; 22-16;
PIH Notices: 01-41 (4); 01-15 Impr Integ Hbk (2); 01-10 (3); 00-23; 00-09 (3); 95-48 (4); 95-48 Tech Asst (4);
Admin Plan: s2p2; s8p4; s9p2; s14p1; s23p6; s23p6

LOCAL LAW ENFORCEMENT......5
PIH Notices: 03-11 (4); 03-11

LOCAL LAWS 16
24 CFR 5: .318; .350;
24 CFR 982: .53 (2);
HUD-903: p2;

7420.10G Gbk: 1-14; 8-4; 8-20; 11-2; 17-2;
PIH Notices: 02-27 (2); 02-01; 99-52;
Admin Plan: s15p6; s18p7

LOCAL NEWSPAPER......................5
24 CFR 982: .206;
7420.10G Gbk: 4-1; 4-3; 4-11; 4-14

LOCAL NEWSPAPERS....................5
24 CFR 5: .518;
7420.10G Gbk: 4-3 (3); 9-5

LOCAL PREFERENCE..................15
24 CFR 5: .506;
24 CFR 982: .202; .204; .207 (3);
HUD-52665: p2;
7420.10G Gbk: 4-4; 4-8; 4-14; 4-16 (4); 4-18

LOCAL PREFERENCES................15
24 CFR 5: .506;
24 CFR 982: Intro; .207 (5);
7420.10G Gbk: 4-2; 4-5; 4-16 (2); 4-17; 4-18 (2);
PIH Notices: 02-27

LOCAL RESIDENCY PREFERENCE 1
7420.10G Gbk: 4-19

LOCAL SITUATIONS......................1
7420.10G Gbk: 13-6

LOCAL-ASSISTED..........................1
7420.10G Gbk: 21-5

LOCALITIES..................................9
7420.10G Gbk: 5-20 (3); 5-47 Ex 5-5; 9-2; 9-3 (3); 14-2

LOCALITY....................................30
24 CFR 982: .308; .510; .517 (2);
HUD-50058: p6;
HUD-50058Instr: p22 (2);
HUD-52641: p3; 8;
HUD-52641-A: p1 (2); p i (2);
7420.10G Gbk: 1-7; 4-17; 5-27; 5-28; 8-21; 18-1; 18-4 (3); 18-7; 18-9 (3);
PIH Notices: 02-01; 99-52; 99-11;
Admin Plan: s6p2

LOCALLY.......................................6
24 CFR 982: .401;
7420.10G Gbk: 1-3; 9-5; 10-3;
PIH Notices: 00-53; 00-24B

LOCATION..................................113
24 CFR 5: .315;
24 CFR 982: .401; .507; .622;
HUD-50058: p ii;
HUD-50058Instr: p7; p19;
HUD-52580: p3 (3); p4 (2);
HUD-52580-A: p8 (4); p9; p10; p11; p12; p15; p17;
HUD-52641: p4;
HUD-52648: p1;
7420.10G Gbk: 2-1; 2-6; 4-11; 4-12; 8-3; 8-8; 8-9 (2); 9-2; 9-3 (3); 9-4; 9-5; 9-8; 9-9 (2); 9-10 (3); 9-12; 9-13 Ex 9-1 (2); 9-14 Ex 9-1 (2); 9-15 Ex 9-2; 9-16 Ex 9-2 (3); 9-19 Ex 9-4; 10-4; 10-6; 10-7; 10-9; 10-14 (2); 10-20; 10-33; 10-38 Ex 10-3; 10-39 Ex 10-4; 12-2; 13-1 (3); 15-1; 17-12;
PIH Notices: 03-12 (3); 02-01 (2); 01-41; 01-15 Impr Integ Hbk; 00-53; 00-24B; 00-11 (2); 00-09; 99-52 (2); 95-48 (9); 95-48 Tech Asst (9);
Admin Plan: s1p6; s3p1; s8p3; s9p1; s11p2; s13p1; s13p2; s18p4; s19p1; s21p3; s23p2

LOCATIONS..................................40
7420.10G Gbk: 1-2; 2-3; 4-12 (2); 8-7; 9-6; 10-7; 10-17; 10-38 Ex 10-3 (5); 10-39 Ex 10-4 (3); 13-6 (3); 21-5; 21-6; 24-9;
PIH Notices: 02-01 (2); 00-11; 99-52 (2); 99-11; 95-48 (5); 95-48 Tech Asst (5);
Admin Plan: s1p3; s3p1

LOCK...5
HUD-52580-A: p2 (2); p17;
7420.10G Gbk: 10-3; 10-6

LOCKABLE...................................... 16
24 CFR 982: .401 (2); .605; .614;
HUD-52580-A: p2; p3; p5; p7; p9; p10; p11; p12; p14;
7420.10G Gbk: 10-6 (2); 17-2

LOCKED..3
HUD-50058: p i;
PIH Notices: 99-11;
Admin Plan: s20p4

LOCKING...1
7420.10G Gbk: 10-6

LOCK-OUTS....................................1
PIH Notices: 99-11

LOCKS..8
24 CFR 982: .401; .605;

7420.10G Gbk: 10-2; 10-6 (3); 10-7; 17-2

LODGERS 1
Admin Plan: s23p7

LOG 28
7420.10G Gbk: 10-34; 10-48 Ex 10-10; 11-15 (2); 11-16 Ex 11-1; 13-4 (3); 13-7 (5); 13-11 Ex 13-1; 13-12 Ex 13-2; 19-7; 19-8 (2); 19-9; 19-11; 19-12 (3); 19-13 (4); 24-12

LOGISTICS 2
PIH Notices: 02-27; 02-27

LOGO 1
7420.10G Gbk: 4-2

LONG TERM 16
24 CFR 5: .630 (5);
7420.10G Gbk: 3-6; 4-13; 6-8; 20-15; 20-16; 20-22 (2);
PIH Notices: 02-06;
Admin Plan: s6p5 (2); s24p5

LONG-TERM 5
7420.10G Gbk: 3-1;
PIH Notices: 95-48; 95-48 Tech Asst;
Admin Plan: s6p5; s6p5

LOOSE BOARDS 1
24 CFR 982: .401

LOSS OF EARNINGS 1
PIH Notices: 01-15 Impr Integ Hbk

LOTTERIES 1
7420.10G Gbk: 5-14 Ex 5-2

LOTTERY 36
7420.10G Gbk: 4-6; 4-8 (2); 4-11; 4-12; 4-13 (2); 4-14 (5); 5-25 Ex 5-3; 23-6;
PIH Notices: 01-41;
Admin Plan: s3p1 (13); s3p2 (7); s3p2

LOTTERY WINNINGS 1
7420.10G Gbk: 5-25 Ex 5-3

LOW CONCENTRATION 1
7420.10G Gbk: 7-5

LOW CONCENTRATIONS 3
7420.10G Gbk: 2-1; 7-6; 7-6

LOW INCOME 37
24 CFR 5: .318; .500; .653 (11);
24 CFR 982: .54; .201 (2); .203;
HUD-50058Instr: p19;
7420.10G Gbk: 1-2; 1-3; 4-22;
PIH Notices: 02-21 (2); 01-41 (3); 01-20; 01-02 (2); 00-24B; 00-23; 00-09 (3);
Admin Plan: s1p1; s4p2; s24p4

LOW INCOME HOUSING TAX CREDIT 2
PIH Notices: 01-02;
Admin Plan: s24p4

LOW POVERTY 40
HUD-52648: p3 (5); p4 (9);
7420.10G Gbk: 2-4; 2-6; 7-9; 7-10 (2); 21-16 Ex 21-6;
PIH Notices: 02-27; 01-06 (5); 00-24B (5);
Admin Plan: s1p6; s8p3; s8p4 (3); s11p3; s25p6 (2); s25p8

LOWER INCOME 2
24 CFR 5: .801;
Admin Plan: s23p1

LOWER INCOME FAMILIES 2
24 CFR 5: .801;
Admin Plan: s23p1

LOWER PERCENT 5
24 CFR 982: .201 (4);
HUD-52648: p2

LOWER PERCENTAGE 4
7420.10G Gbk: 4-19 (3); 4-20

LOWER-INCOME 3
HUD-50058Instr: p65 (2); p65

LOW-INCOME 133
24 CFR 5: .100; .403; .653;
24 CFR 982: .201 (6); .630;
HUD-50058: p5; p v;
HUD-50058Instr: p19 (8); p32; p61; p66 (3); p67; p72; p73; p74; p75;
7420.10G Gbk: 1-1; 1-2; 3-3 (3); 3-7; 4-16; 4-20 (2); 5-3 (3); 5-16 Ex 5-2; 7-3; 8-7; 10-1; 11-9; 19-8 (3); 23-10 (2); 23-11 (2); 23-19;
PIH Notices: 03-20; 02-22 (7); 02-15; 02-01 (3); 01-41 (16); 01-15 Impr Integ Hbk; 01-02 (6); 00-53; 00-11 (5); 00-11A (2); 00-09 (12); 00-01 (2); 99-52 (3); 98-66 (2);
Admin Plan: s1p1; s1p2; s2p4 (7); s4p2; s19p1 (2); s23p1; s23p3 (2); s25p4

LOW-POVERTY 14
7420.10G Gbk: 2-1; 2-4 (5); 2-8 (2); 2-11; 7-10 (2); 8-4; 8-9;
Admin Plan: s21p9

LUMP 12
24 CFR 5: .609;
HUD-50058Instr: p29 (2);

PIH Notices: 01-15 Impr Integ Hbk (2);
Admin Plan: s6p9; s6p10 (5); s17p1

LUMP SUM 25
24 CFR 5: .609;
HUD-50058Instr: p29 (2);
7420.10G Gbk: 5-23 (10); 5-24; 5-25 Ex 5-3; 5-26;
PIH Notices: 01-15 Impr Integ Hbk (2);
Admin Plan: s6p9; s6p10 (5); s17p1

LUMP-SUM 21
24 CFR 5: .609 (2);
HUD-50058Instr: p29; p31;
7420.10G Gbk: 5-14 Ex 5-2; 5-15 Ex 5-2 (2); 22-13;
PIH Notices: 01-15 Impr Integ Hbk (6);
Admin Plan: s6p9 (3); s6p10 (3); s6p10

MACHINE 7
7420.10G Gbk: 13-3; 24-13 (2);
PIH Notices: 01-15; 01-15 Impr Integ Hbk; 95-48; 95-48 Tech Asst

MACHINES 12
7420.10G Gbk: 4-11; 5-44 (2); 8-3;
PIH Notices: 95-48 (4); 95-48 Tech Asst (3); 95-48 Tech Asst

MACHINE-SANDING 1
7420.10G Gbk: 10-19

MAIL 50
24 CFR 5: .353;
HUD-50058: p v;
HUD-50058Instr: p20 (8);
HUD-52641: p2 (3);
HUD-903-1: p3;
7420.10G Gbk: 2-5; 4-7 (2); 4-13 (2); 4-14; 4-15; 5-35; 10-33 (2); 10-34; 11-9; 12-2 (3); 12-15 Ex 12-3; 21-17; 21-18;
PIH Notices: 03-11; 02-21; 01-20; 00-27 (3); 00-09 (2);
Admin Plan: s3p2 (2); s3p3; s6p13; s7p1; s7p2; s10p3; s11p1; s20p1; s20p7

MAILBOX 2
HUD-50058Instr: p13;
PIH Notices: 02-21

MAILBOXES 1
24 CFR 5: .703

MAILED 15
24 CFR 5: .353;
HUD-52665: p2;
HUD-903: p1;
HUD-903-1: p3;
7420.10G Gbk: 4-13; 11-9; 11-16 Ex 11-1 (2); 12-2;
PIH Notices: 02-14;
Admin Plan: s3p1; s4p2; s11p1; s11p2; s20p4

MAIL-IN 3
7420.10G Gbk: 4-3; 4-11; 4-13

MAILING 24
24 CFR 5: .514;
24 CFR 982: .451;
HUD-50058: p5 (2); p v (2);
HUD-50058Instr: p20 (5);
HUD-52641: p1;
7420.10G Gbk: 4-7; 4-23 Ex 4-1; 11-7; 11-11;
PIH Notices: 03-11 (2);
Admin Plan: s3p1 (4); s4p2; s18p7

MAILING ADDRESS 11
HUD-50058: p5 (2); p v (2);
HUD-50058Instr: p20 (5);
7420.10G Gbk: 4-23 Ex 4-1;
PIH Notices: 03-11

MAILINGS 2
7420.10G Gbk: 10-22; 22-9

MAILS 1
7420.10G Gbk: 12-3

MAINE INDIAN CLAIMS 3
HUD-50058Instr: p30;
7420.10G Gbk: 5-16 Ex 5-2;
PIH Notices: 01-15 Impr Integ Hbk

MAINSTREAM 14
7420.10G Gbk: 1-7; 1-8; 21-11;
PIH Notices: 01-06; 95-48; 95-48 Tech Asst;
Admin Plan: s4p2; s25p2 (6); s25p3

MAINSTREAMING 2
PIH Notices: 95-48; 95-48 Tech Asst

MAINTAIN 128
24 CFR 5: .230; .653; .703;
24 CFR 982: .154; .155; .157; .158; .203; .204; .404 (3); .453; .517 (2); .619; .626;
HUD-52580-A: p4;
HUD-52641: p3 (2); p5; 8; p9;
HUD-52641-A: p1; p2 (2);
HUD-52667: p ii;
7420.10G Gbk: 2-10; 3-1; 4-1; 4-6; 4-7 (2); 4-10; 4-18; 4-22 (2); 5-7; 8-7; 8-11;

8-22; 9-3; 10-5 (2); 10-33; 11-12; 11-17; 11-19; 12-2; 15-9 Ex 15-1; 18-1; 18-4 (2); 18-9; 20-13; 20-15; 20-19 Ex 20-3;
7420.10G Fbk: 20-23;
7420.10G Gbk: 20-24; 21-2; 21-19; 22-1; 22-3; 22-9; 22-13; 22-17; 23-7; 23-8 Ex 23-1 (3); 23-9; 23-18; 23-20; 24-2 (2); 24-3; 24-6; 24-8; 24-10; 24-11; 24-12;
PIH Notices: 03-23; 03-11; 02-27; 02-06 (4); 02-01 (2); 01-41; 01-15 Impr Integ Hbk (2); 00-24B (3); 99-52 (2); 95-48 (3); 95-48 Tech Asst (3);
Admin Plan: s1p1; s1p6 (2); s1p7; s3p1; s4p1 (2); s6p4; s7p1; s7p5; s8p1; s10p1; s10p5 (2); s11p1; s19p1 (2); s20p2 (2); s20p4; s22p4 (2); s24p6; s25p4

MAINTAINED 39
24 CFR 5: .216;
24 CFR 982: .401; .614; .619 (2);
HUD-52665: p1 (2);
7420.10G Gbk: 3-8; 4-10; 4-18; 5-9 Ex 5-1; 7-4; 9-11; 9-14 Ex 9-1; 9-16 Ex 9-2; 10-37 Ex 10-2; 12-5; 13-4; 13-7; 19-12; 20-1; 20-2; 20-23 (2);
PIH Notices: 03-23; 03-11 (2); 02-01; 99-52; 99-11 (2); 95-48 (2); 95-48 Tech Asst (2);
Admin Plan: s4p3; s15p4; s20p1; s22p1

MAINTAINING 56
24 CFR 5: .353;
24 CFR 982: .401; .452; .517; .520;
HUD-52580: p1 (2); p15;
HUD-52641: p5;
HUD-52648: p1 (2);
HUD-52667: p i;
HUD-903: p1;
7420.10G Gbk: 1-13; 1-14; 2-6; 4-1; 4-4; 4-7; 4-8; 4-10; 8-11; 8-22; 9-3; 9-9; 9-11; 10-5; 10-7; 11-17; 18-1; 19-7; 19-8; 20-2; 20-14; 21-2; 21-4; 21-8; 22-18; 23-18; 23-20; 24-3 (3); 24-9; 24-12 (2); 24-14;
PIH Notices: 02-27 (2); 02-01; 01-15; 01-15 Impr Integ Hbk; 00-53; 99-52;
Admin Plan: s1p1; s4p1

MAINTAINS 14
HUD-50058Instr: p73;
HUD-52580-A: p5;
HUD-52648: p1;
HUD-903: p2;
7420.10G Gbk: 4-8; 11-12; 13-3; 21-4; 24-3; 24-10;
PIH Notices: 01-02;
Admin Plan: s11p2; s11p1; s21p4

MAINTENANCE 130
24 CFR 5: .212; .609; .617; .703;
24 CFR 35 SubM: .1220 (2);
24 CFR 982: 24 CFR 982 (2); .4; .355; .404; .452 (2); .507; .619 (2); .622 (2); .623; .630; .635 (3); .641;
HUD-50058: p xiii; p14; p xiv;
HUD-50058Instr: p47; p54; p56 (3); p73 (2); p75;
HUD-52580: p6;
HUD-52580-A: p1; p15; p19;
HUD-52641: p3; p4; 8 (4);
HUD-52641-A: p1 (5);
7420.10G Gbk: 1-2 (2); 1-14 (2); 4-10; 4-13; 5-15 Ex 5-2; 5-46 Ex 5-5; 9-2; 9-12; 9-14 Ex 9-1 (4); 9-16 Ex 9-2 (4); 9-17 Ex 9-3; 9-19 Ex 9-4; 10-12; 10-14; 10-17 (2); 10-21; 10-37 Ex 10-2; 11-7; 11-11; 11-12; 11-14; 11-17; 17-11 (2); 17-12 (2); 21-2; 23-14; 24-14;
PIH Notices: 03-12 (2); 02-27; 02-01; 01-15; 01-15 Impr Integ Hbk (5); 00-24B; 00-11; 99-52; 99-11 (3); 95-48 (6); 95-48 Tech Asst (6);
Admin Plan: s7p6; s7p7 (2); s8p4; s19p1 (3); s21p3; s22p2; s22p3 (2); s22p4; s24p3; s25p6

MAJOR LIFE ACTIVITIES 21
7420.10G Gbk: 5-43; 5-44;
PIH Notices: 95-48 (9); 95-48 Tech Asst (9);
Admin Plan: s1p4

MAJOR LIFE ACTIVITY 42
PIH Notices: 95-48 (21); 95-48 Tech Asst (20); 95-

48 Tech Asst

MAJOR RECONSTRUCTION 1
PIH Notices: 02-21

MAJOR REPAIR 2
HUD-50058: p14;
HUD-50058Instr: p56

MAJOR REPAIRS 5
24 CFR 982: .635 (4);
HUD-50058Instr: p56

MALE 4
HUD-50058Instr: p14;
HUD-903: p1;
7420.10G Gbk: 4-23 Ex 4-1; 4-23 Ex 4-1

MALES 1
24 CFR 982: .605

MANAGE 14
24 CFR 982: .355;
7420.10G Gbk: 2-1; 4-14; 10-31; 19-13; 20-2; 20-15; 20-17; 21-3 (3);
PIH Notices: 02-27; 02-06; 02-06

MANAGED 10
7420.10G Gbk: 1-1; 1-2; 10-36 Ex 10-1; 19-1 (2); 19-9;
PIH Notices: 03-11; 02-20; 02-06; 00-46

MANAGEMENT 314
24 CFR 5: .100; .216; .234; .306; .603; .609; .653; .661 (2); .801 (2);
24 CFR 982: .4 (2); .52; .53; .54; .103; .151; .153; .155; .156; .157; .158; .159; .160; .204; .206; .301; .303; .304; .305; .306; .307; .310 (2); .352; .403; .404; .406; .452 (2); .516; .517; .551; .552; .553; .554; .555; .623; .630;
HUD-50058: p i; p xiii;
HUD-50058Instr: p3; p5; p15; p28; p47; p54; p71 (2); p72; p74;
HUD-52641: p6 (2);
HUD-52648: p1 (2); p3;
HUD-52667: p i;
7420.10G Gbk: 1-1 (2); 1-2; 1-9; 1-10; 2-5; 2-13 Ex 2-1; 3-1; 3-7 (2); 4-4; 4-8 (2); 4-10; 4-22; 5-15 Ex 5-2; 5-20; 5-38; 8-16; 9-5; 9-6; 9-12; 9-14 Ex 9-1 (3); 9-16 Ex 9-2 (3); 9-17 Ex 9-3; 9-19 Ex 9-4; 10-26; 10-35; 11-17; 13-9; 15-9 Ex 15-1; 17-12; 18-4; 19-1; 19-4 (4); 19-5; 19-6; 19-7; 19-8; 19-10; 19-13 (2); 20-1 (7); 20-2 (2); 20-3 (2); 20-5 (2); 20-6 (2); 20-16; 20-28 (4); 20-29; 21-2; 21-3; 21-4; 21-5; 21-7; 21-11; 21-13; 21-14 Ex 21-4; 21-15 Ex 21-5; 21-16 Ex 21-6; 21-17; 21-18; 21-19; 22-5; 22-6; 22-7; 22-8 (2); 23-15; 24-3; 24-8;
PIH Notices: 03-23 (4); 03-20 (2); 03-12 (2); 03-11 (4); 03-05; 02-27 (14); 02-22; 02-21 (5); 02-14 (3); 02-07 (15); 02-06 (5); 02-01 (3); 01-41 (4); 01-40; 01-27; 01-20 (6); 01-15 (2); 01-15 Impr Integ Hbk (2); 01-10; 01-06; 00-49 (2); 00-45; 00-34 (2); 00-28 (15); 00-27 (5); 00-24 (2); 00-24A; 00-24B; 00-11 (3); 00-11A; 00-09 (5); 00-01; 99-52 (3); 99-11 (5); 98-66; 95-48 (2); 95-48 Tech Asst (2);
Admin Plan: s1p1; s1p6; s3p1; s6p3; s16p1; s16p2; s16p3; s19p1; s20p2 (3); s20p3; s20p4; s21p1 (4); s21p2 (2); s21p9; s24p3; s24p4; s24p7; s25p2 (2); s25p7

MANAGEMENT AGENT 2
Admin Plan: s16p1; s16p3

MANAGEMENT AGENTS 1
Admin Plan: s1p6

MANAGEMENT OF THE HOUSING 2
HUD-52641: p7;
7420.10G Gbk: 17-9

MANAGEMENT OF THE HOUSING 7
24 CFR 982: .4 (2); .306;
HUD-50058Instr: p71;
HUD-52641: p7;
7420.10G Gbk: 17-9;
Admin Plan: s16p2

MANAGEMENT OF THE HOUSING CHOICE VOUCHER PROGRAM....1
7420.10G Gbk: 3-7

MANAGEMENT OFFICE 1
7420.10G Gbk: 9-5

MANAGEMENT OFFICES 1

Admin Plan: s3p1

MANAGEMENT RESPONSIBILITIES 2
PIH Notices: 01-41; 00-09

MANAGER....................................38
24 CFR 5: .306 (2);
HUD-52580-A: p2; p4 (2); p6 (3); p15 (5); p17;
HUD-903: p1;
7420.10G Gbk: 9-7; 9-13 Ex 9-1; 9-14 Ex 9-1; 9-16 Ex 9-2; 19-7; 19-9; 21-11; 21-13; 21-15 Ex 21-5 (2); 21-16 Ex 21-6 (7); 23-1;
PIH Notices: 01-15; 95-48 (2); 95-48 Tech Asst; 95-48 Tech Asst

MANAGERIAL................................3
7420.10G Gbk: 1-9;
PIH Notices: 01-41; 00-09

MANAGERS.................................23
7420.10G Gbk: 2-5; 9-4; 9-11 (2); 19-1 (2); 19-7 (2); 19-13 (2); 21-13; 21-20; 22-2; 22-6; 22-10; 24-7; 24-8;
PIH Notices: 02-21; 01-27; 01-20; 00-11;
Admin Plan: s8p2; s18p6

MANDATE.......................................6
7420.10G Gbk: 4-14; 19-2;
PIH Notices: 95-48 (2); 95-48 Tech Asst; 95-48 Tech Asst

MANDATED....................................9
24 CFR 982: .401;
HUD-50058Instr: p15;
HUD-52580-A: p8;
7420.10G Gbk: 21-7; 23-2;
PIH Notices: 01-15 Impr Integ Hbk (2); 95-48; 95-48 Tech Asst

MANDATES....................................3
PIH Notices: 00-11; 95-48; 95-48 Tech Asst

MANDATORY...............................72
24 CFR 5: .315; .350 (2); .611;
24 CFR 982: .553;
HUD-50058Instr: p2;
HUD-52648: p1; p2 (3);
7420.10G Gbk: 4-11; 5-28; 7-10 (2); 10-2; 23-2; 23-19 (7);
PIH Notices: 02-27; 02-21 (5); 01-20 (5); 01-15 Impr Integ Hbk (3); 01-10; 01-06 (11); 01-01; 00-27 (5); 00-24A (2); 00-11; 00-09; 96-65;
Admin Plan: s2p5; s8p1; s8p3; s13p1; s15p1; s15p2; s15p3; s20p2; s21p9 (2); s25p4; s25p4

MANDATORY DEDUCTIONS........4
24 CFR 5: .611;
7420.10G Gbk: 5-28;
PIH Notices: 01-15 Impr Integ Hbk; 01-15 Impr Integ Hbk

MANIFESTATION............................2
PIH Notices: 02-01; 99-52

MANIFESTLY..................................2
PIH Notices: 95-48; 95-48 Tech Asst

MANIFESTS....................................1
Admin Plan: s7p5

MANMADE.....................................3
24 CFR 982: .401; .614;
7420.10G Gbk: 10-13

MANUAL.......................................78
24 CFR 5: .512 (3);
HUD-50058: p i;
HUD-50058Instr: p3;
HUD-52580-A: p6; p15 (2);
7420.10G Gbk: 3-2; 5-7 (2); 8-23; 10-1; 10-3; 10-26; 11-7 (4); 11-8; 11-9; 11-10 (2); 11-19 (2); 12-2; 12-8 (2); 19-7; 19-8; 21-8; 22-6;
PIH Notices: 01-15; 01-06 (2); 00-53; 95-48 (23); 95-48 Tech Asst (17);
Admin Plan: s18p7; s20p2

MANUAL VERIFICATION.............2
24 CFR 5: .512;
7420.10G Gbk: 5-7

MANUALLY..................................20
7420.10G Gbk: 10-23; 11-9; 11-16 Ex 11-1; 13-4; 13-7; 19-6; 19-12; 21-3;
PIH Notices: 02-20; 01-15; 01-06 (8); 00-46; 00-24A

MANUALS......................................7
7420.10G Gbk: 3-7;
PIH Notices: 95-48 (3); 95-48 Tech Asst (2); 95-48 Tech Asst

MANUFACTURE............................7
24 CFR 5: .100 (2);
24 CFR 982: .553 (2);
7420.10G Gbk: 15-6;
Admin Plan: s15p2; s15p3

MANUFACTURED......................150
24 CFR 982: 24 CFR 982 (7); .4 (7); .517; .601 (4);

.619; .620 (8); .621 (6); .622 (10); .623 (11); .624 (4); .628;
HUD-50058: p5; p10; p x; p11; p13; p xiii (5);
HUD-50058Instr: p ii (2); p42; p46 (3); p47; p53 (7); p73 (5); p78 (3);
HUD-52580: p1; p5;
HUD-52580-A: p1; p13 (3); p14 (3);
HUD-52667: p i;
7420.10G Gbk: 3-5; 17-10; 17-11;
PIH Notices: 02-20 (8); 00-46 (8);
Admin Plan: s9p2 (2); s19p1 (26); s19p1

MANUFACTURED HOME............49
HUD-52517: p1 (5);
HUD-52646: p2 (2);
7420.10G Gbk: 8-17 (3); 11-10 (4); 17-10 (9); 17-11 (14); 17-12 (11); 17-12

MANUFACTURED HOME..........179
24 CFR 982: 24 CFR 982 (7); .4 (6); .601 (4); .619; .620 (8); .621 (6); .622 (10); .623 (11); .624 (4); .628;
HUD-50058: p5; p10; p x; p11; p13; p xiii (3);
HUD-50058Instr: p ii (2); p42; p46 (3); p47; p53 (3); p73 (4); p78 (3);
HUD-52517: p1 (2); p5;
HUD-52580-A: p1; p14 (2);
HUD-52641: p1 (4);
HUD-52646: p2 (2);
7420.10G Gbk: 8-17 (3); 11-10 (4); 17-10 (9); 17-11 (14); 17-12 (12);
PIH Notices: 02-20 (8); 00-46 (8);
Admin Plan: s19p1 (25); s19p1

MANUFACTURED HOMES 15
HUD-52580-A: p13 (3); p14;
HUD-52667: p i;
7420.10G Gbk: 5-25 Ex 5-3; 10-1; 10-10; 17-1; 17-10 (2); 18-2;
Admin Plan: s9p2 (2); s19p1

MANUFACTURED HOME'S..........6
HUD-50058: p xiii (2);
HUD-50058Instr: p53 (3); p53

MANUFACTURED HOUSING 3
24 CFR 982: .517;
7420.10G Gbk: 3-5; 17-11

MANUFACTURER'S.......................1
7420.10G Gbk: 10-19

MANUFACTURING........................2
7420.10G Gbk: 5-35;
Admin Plan: s15p1

MAP...3
7420.10G Gbk: 2-6; 8-7;
PIH Notices: 02-27

MAPLES'...3
7420.10G Gbk: 12-7 (2); 12-7

MAPPING 2
PIH Notices: 02-20; 00-46

MAPS..18
HUD-52648: p2 (2);
7420.10G Gbk: 2-3 (2); 2-6 (5); 2-8 (3); 8-2; 8-7 (2); 13-1; 13-10;
Admin Plan: s21p6

MARCH..62
HUD-50058Instr: p11;
7420.10G Gbk: 19-9; 20-22; 24-3;
PIH Notices: 03-23 (5); 02-27; 02-21; 02-07 (2); 02-06 (2); 02-01 (3); 01-27 (4); 01-15 (2); 01-15 Impr Integ Hbk (8); 01-11 (2); 01-10 (5); 01-06; 00-53 (7); 00-24 (3); 00-24A; 00-11; 00-09 (2); 00-01; 99-52 (3); 98-66;

MARGINAL....................................2
7420.10G Gbk: 2-1; 21-10

MARGINALLY 1
Admin Plan: s23p1

MARITAL..3
7420.10G Gbk: 23-6;
Admin Plan: s1p2; s7p3

MARITAL STATUS ....
3
7420.10G Gbk: 23-6;
Admin Plan: s1p2; s7p3

MARKET.....................................221
24 CFR 5: .100 (4); .500; .504; .514; .518 (2); .520 (2); .603 (2); .655 (2);
24 CFR 982: .1; .4 (3); .207; .309; .313; .451; .503 (3); .517; .521; .623; .625;
HUD-50058: p i; p xvii;
HUD-50058Instr: p3; p22; p39; p43; p62; p75;
HUD-52641: p1; p4;
HUD-52667: p i (3);
7420.10G Gbk: 1-7 (2); 2-9; 2-10; 3-3; 4-2 (2); 4-17;

4-21; 5-25 Ex 5-3 (2); 5-26 (3); 5-27 (5); 5-28 (2); 5-38 (2); 5-49 Ex 5-5; 7-2 (2); 7-5; 7-7; 8-4; 8-5; 8-7 (4); 8-12 (3); 8-22 (2); 9-1 (3); 9-3 (5); 9-4 (4); 9-5 (2); 9-6; 9-7 (2); 9-8 (6); 9-9 (5); 9-11 (2); 9-12; 9-14 Ex 9-1; 9-16 Ex 9-2; 10-2; 10-24; 11-6; 13-2; 17-1; 19-11 (3); 20-15; 21-4; 21-9; 21-16 Ex 21-6 (2); 22-6; 23-9; 24-2 (3); 24-10; 24-11 (3); 24-12 (4); 24-15 (2);
PIH Notices: 03-12; 02-27 (4); 02-22 (5); 02-20 (5); 01-41 (6); 01-15 Impr Integ Hbk (7); 01-10; 01-01 (2); 00-46 (6); 00-24B (4); 00-09 (9);
Admin Plan: s6p10 (6); s7p3; s7p6 (5); s8p4 (2); s11p1; s11p2 (3); s11p3 (2); s23p5; s23p7; s24p4 (3); s24p5 (2); s25p6

MARKET ANALYSIS....................... 3
PIH Notices: 02-20; 01-01; 00-46

MARKET ANALYST....................... 6
7420.10G Gbk: 9-11; 9-14 Ex 9-1; 9-16 Ex 9-2; 21-4; 21-16 Ex 21-6; 21-16 Ex 21-6

MARKET RENT 37
24 CFR 5: .100 (2); .500; .504; .514;
24 CFR 982: .4; .503; .623;
HUD-50058: p i; p xvii;
HUD-50058Instr: p3; p39; p62;
HUD-52667: p i;
7420.10G Gbk: 9-4; 9-5; 9-11;
PIH Notices: 02-27; 02-22; 02-20 (3); 01-41; 01-15 Impr Integ Hbk (2); 01-10; 00-46 (2); 00-24B (2); 00-09 (4);
Admin Plan: s23p5; s23p7; s24p4

MARKET RENTS 10
24 CFR 5: .100;
24 CFR 982: .503;
HUD-52667: p i;
7420.10G Gbk: 24-11; 24-12;
PIH Notices: 02-22; 01-01; 00-46;
Admin Plan: s11p3; s11p3

MARKET VALUE.......................... 31
24 CFR 5: .603 (2);
HUD-50058Instr: p22;
7420.10G Gbk: 5-25 Ex 5-3; 5-26 (3); 5-27 (5); 5-28 (2); 5-49 Ex 5-5; 9-8;
PIH Notices: 01-15 Impr Integ Hbk (3);
Admin Plan: s6p10 (6); s7p3; s7p6 (4); s7p6

MARKETABILITY 2
PIH Notices: 02-01; 99-52

MARKETABLE 2
PIH Notices: 02-01; 99-52

MARKET-DRIVEN........................... 1
Admin Plan: s1p2

MARKETED 2
7420.10G Gbk: 10-23; 19-8

MARKETING................................. 17
24 CFR 5: .655 (2);
24 CFR 982: .201 (2);
7420.10G Gbk: 2-11; 4-19 (2); 5-40; 21-13; 21-15 Ex 21-5; 22-9; 22-10;
Admin Plan: s1p4; s1p6; s8p4; s21p2; s21p2

MARKET-ORIENTED...................... 1
7420.10G Gbk: 24-12

MARKETPLACE 5
7420.10G Gbk: 9-1 (2); 9-9 (2); 9-9

MARKET-RATE............................... 2
7420.10G Gbk: 9-13 Ex 9-1; 9-13 Ex 9-1

MARKETS 19
7420.10G Gbk: 2-10; 2-11; 8-7 (2); 9-4; 9-7 (3); 9-8; 9-9; 9-10; 11-4; 13-6; 24-8; 24-9 (2); 24-10;
PIH Notices: 01-41; 00-09

MARRIAGE 16
24 CFR 982: .516; .615;
HUD-50058: p v;
HUD-50058Instr: p14; p18;
7420.10G Gbk: 5-12; 5-50 Ex 5-5; 17-7; 23-12;
PIH Notices: 01-15 Impr Integ Hbk (2);
Admin Plan: s2p2; s7p7 (2); s19p1; s20p4

MARRIAGES.................................... 1
7420.10G Gbk: 12-16 Ex 12-4

MARRIED 1
24 CFR 982: .4

MARSHALL ISLANDS.................... 4
24 CFR 5: .506;
HUD-50058Instr: p64;
PIH Notices: 01-27; 01-27

MATERIAL FACT.............................2
Admin Plan: s20p5; s20p6
MATERIAL FACTOR.......................1
Admin Plan: s1p5
MATERIAL FACTS 2
Admin Plan: s20p1; s20p6
MATERIAL WEAKNESS.................1
PIH Notices: 01-15 Impr Integ Hbk
MAXIMUM.................................281
24 CFR 5: .318 (4); .514; .518 (2); .520 (8); .609; .617 (3); .653;
24 CFR 982: 24 CFR 982 (2); .4 (2); .151 (2); .155; .301; .305; .312; .402; .451; .503; .505; .508; .555; .625; .629 (2); .634 (8); .636; .643;
HUD-50058: p7; p vii (4); p9 (2); p ix (6); p xi; p15; p xv (4);
HUD-50058Instr: p34 (3); p35 (2); p37; p40 (13); p58 (5); p68 (12); p69 (7); p74;
HUD-52646: p1;
7420.10G Gbk: 3-4; 3-6; 5-14 Ex 5-2; 5-16 Ex 5-2; 5-18; 5-21 (3); 5-34; 5-42 (2); 5-47 Ex 5-5 (4); 6-1 (2); 6-2 (14); 6-3 (7); 6-4 (2); 6-5 (3); 6-6 (4); 6-10 Ex 6-2 (6); 7-5; 8-5 (6); 8-6; 8-11; 8-16 (2); 11-5; 11-6; 11-15; 12-11; 14-4 (4); 15-5; 20-6 (2); 24-1;
PIH Notices: 03-23 (2); 03-11; 02-27 (3); 02-22 (2); 02-21 (3); 02-20 (5); 02-07 (2); 02-06; 02-01 (5); 01-41 (4); 01-20 (2); 01-15 Impr Integ Hbk (8); 00-46; 00-28; 00-24B; 00-09 (5); 99-52 (5); 95-48 (6); 95-48 Tech Asst (6);
Admin Plan: s5p2; s5p3 (3); s6p3 (3); s6p11; s8p1; s8p2; s8p4; s11p1; s11p3; s17p1 (2); s21p3; s21p4 (2); s21p5 (2); s21p6 (2); s21p7 (2); s21p8; s23p5; s24p1; s24p4; s24p4
MAXIMUM NUMBER....................5
24 CFR 982: .503;
7420.10G Gbk: 24-1;
PIH Notices: 02-21; 02-20;
Admin Plan: s5p2
MAXIMUM PERIOD PERMITTED 3
24 CFR 982: .312; .555;
7420.10G Gbk: 11-5
MAXIMUM RENT 35
24 CFR 5: .520; .520
24 CFR 982: .301; .402;
HUD-50058: p9; p ix (4);
HUD-50058Instr: p40 (9); p68 (9); p69 (5);
7420.10G Gbk: 8-6;
PIH Notices: 01-41; 00-09
MCKINLEY.......................................1
Admin Plan: s20p3
MCKINNEY ACT 2
24 CFR 5: .601; .601
MEALS...11
24 CFR 982: .510 (3);
HUD-52580-A: p4;
HUD-52641: 8 (2);
HUD-52641-A: p1 (2);
PIH Notices: 00-41 (2); 00-41
MEANINGFUL 1
PIH Notices: 01-15 Impr Integ Hbk
MECHANICAL................................6
24 CFR 5: .703;
7420.10G Gbk: 10-7;
PIH Notices: 95-48 (2); 95-48 Tech Asst; 95-48 Tech Asst
MEDIA...9
24 CFR 982: .206;
7420.10G Gbk: 4-1; 8-2; 19-3; 22-10;
PIH Notices: 03-20;
Admin Plan: s1p6 (2); s1p6
MEDIAN...92
24 CFR 5: .603 (6);
24 CFR 982: .503 (7); .642 (4);
HUD-50058: p v;
HUD-50058Instr: p19; p71 (2); p73 (2); p76 (2);
7420.10G Gbk: 2-13 Ex 2-1 (2); 4-9; 4-19; 5-2 (2); 5-3; 7-4; 7-5 (7); 21-19; 23-10 (2); 23-11 (2);
PIH Notices: 02-22; 02-20 (14); 01-41 (5); 00-46 (14); 00-09 (6);
Admin Plan: s2p4 (2); s2p5; s4p2; s11p3; s24p6; s24p6
MEDIAN FAMILY INCOME 2
24 CFR 5: .603;
HUD-50058Instr: p76
MEDIAN INCOME........................41
24 CFR 5: .603 (5);
24 CFR 982: .642 (4);
HUD-50058: p v;
HUD-50058Instr: p19; p71 (2); p73 (2); p76;

7420.10G Gbk: 4-9; 4-19; 5-2 (2); 5-3; 23-10 (2); 23-11;
PIH Notices: 01-41 (5); 00-09 (6);
Admin Plan: s2p4 (2); s2p5; s4p2; s24p6; s24p6

MEDIAN RENT 15
24 CFR 982: .503 (3);
7420.10G Gbk: 7-4; 7-5 (3);
PIH Notices: 02-20 (4); 00-46 (3); 00-46

MEDIAN RENTS 2
7420.10G Gbk: 2-13 Ex 2-1; 7-5

MEDIATION 1
Admin Plan: s18p6

MEDIATORS 1
Admin Plan: s18p6

MEDICAID 8
HUD-50058: p16; p xvi;
HUD-50058Instr: p60; p76;
7420.10G Gbk: 5-12;
PIH Notices: 01-15; 00-41;
Admin Plan: s7p8

MEDICAID-ELIGIBLE 1
PIH Notices: 00-41

MEDICAL 196
24 CFR 5: .318 (2); .603 (3); .609; .611;
24 CFR 35 SubM: .1225 (5);
24 CFR 982: .352 (2); .610; .632; .642 (2);
HUD-50058: p6; p7 (4); p vii (14);
HUD-50058Instr: p28 (2); p30 (4); p34 (6); p35 (17); p36; p73 (3);
7420.10G Gbk: 4-26 Ex 4-2; 4-27 Ex 4-2 (2); 5-12; 5-31 (3); 5-32 (3); 5-51 Ex 5-5 (4); 5-52 Ex 5-5; 5-53 Ex 5-5; 8-16; 8-17; 10-16; 10-20 (5); 12-3; 12-11; 12-13 Ex 12-1 (2); 17-4; 20-4;
PIH Notices: 02-07; 02-01 (2); 01-15 (7); 01-15 Impr Integ Hbk (14); 00-49 (3); 00-41 (2); 99-52 (2); 95-48 (19); 95-48 Tech Asst (19);
Admin Plan: s5p1; s5p2; s6p2; s6p5; s6p6; s6p9 (2); s6p11 (6); s7p3; s7p7 (3); s7p8 (2); s15p6; s19p1; s21p4; s24p2 (2); s25p3 (2); s25p3

MEDICAL EQUIPMENT 1
PIH Notices: 01-15 Impr Integ Hbk

MEDICAL EXPENSE 17
HUD-50058: p7; p vii;
HUD-50058Instr: p35 (3);
7420.10G Gbk: 5-31 (2); 5-32 (2); 5-33 (4); 5-34 (2);
PIH Notices: 01-15;
Admin Plan: s6p11

MEDICAL EXPENSES 71
24 CFR 5: .603 (2); .609; .611;
24 CFR 982: .632;
HUD-50058: p7; p vii (6);
HUD-50058Instr: p30 (2); p35 (6); p73 (2);
7420.10G Gbk: 4-15; 4-27 Ex 4-2; 5-15 Ex 5-2; 5-28; 5-31 (4); 5-32 (8); 5-33 (7); 5-34 (2); 5-51 Ex 5-5 (4);
PIH Notices: 01-15 (4); 01-15 Impr Integ Hbk (7);
Admin Plan: s6p2; s6p9 (2); s6p11 (4); s7p3; s7p7

MEDICAL FACILITY 2
PIH Notices: 95-48; 95-48 Tech Asst

MEDICAL INSURANCE 8
HUD-50058: p vii;
HUD-50058Instr: p35;
7420.10G Gbk: 4-27 Ex 4-2; 5-12;
PIH Notices: 01-15 Impr Integ Hbk (2);
Admin Plan: s7p8; s7p8

MEDICAL RECORDS 2
PIH Notices: 02-01; 99-52

MEDICARE 6
7420.10G Gbk: 4-27 Ex 4-2; 5-12; 5-46 Ex 5-5 (2);
Admin Plan: s7p7; s7p8

MEDICARE PREMIUM 1
7420.10G Gbk: 5-46 Ex 5-5

MEDICARE PREMIUMS 1
Admin Plan: s7p7

MEDICATION 7
PIH Notices: 00-41; 95-48 (3); 95-48 Tech Asst (2); 95-48 Tech Asst

MEDICATIONS 1
7420.10G Gbk: 12-13 Ex 12-1

MEDICINE 5
7420.10G Gbk: 10-4;
PIH Notices: 95-48 (2); 95-48 Tech Asst; 95-48 Tech Asst

MEDICINES 4
7420.10G Gbk: 5-32;
Admin Plan: s6p11 (2); s6p11

MEETING 89

24 CFR 5: .353 (14);
24 CFR 982: .206; .353; .401;
HUD-50058: p3 (6); p4 (6);
HUD-50058Instr: p16 (3); p17; p76 (2);
7420.10G Gbk: 1-7; 2-11; 4-16; 4-21; 5-40; 7-7; 8-22 (2); 11-16 Ex 11-1; 21-3; 21-4; 21-8; 22-2; 22-9; 23-15; 24-13;
PIH Notices: 03-20; 02-27 (3); 02-21; 02-06; 02-01; 01-20 (2); 00-27; 00-11A; 99-52; 95-48 (10); 95-48 Tech Asst (10);
Admin Plan: s7p2; s7p3 (4); s24p4

MEETING FACILITIES 2
PIH Notices: 95-48; 95-48 Tech Asst

MEETINGS 26
24 CFR 5: .353 (4);
7420.10G Gbk: 2-4; 2-5; 8-9; 10-22; 10-26; 21-4; 22-10; 24-14 (3);
PIH Notices: 02-27 (2); 02-01; 00-09; 99-52; 95-48 (2); 95-48 Tech Asst (2);
Admin Plan: s8p4; s18p1; s25p7

MEMBER OF THE FAMILY..........20
HUD-52517: p2;
HUD-52641: p5; p6; p10;
HUD-52641-A: p3;
HUD-52646: p2;
7420.10G Gbk: 3-4; 5-1; 5-9 Ex 5-1; 5-25 Ex 5-3; 5-37 (2); 5-41; 8-15; 11-13; 15-2; 15-5; 15-6 (2); 23-7

MEMBER OF THE FAMILY..........76
24 CFR 5: .230 (3); .240; .504 (2); .506; .603 (3); .609; .611 (3); .615;
24 CFR 982: .201; .306; .312; .402; .552 (4); .634; .635 (2); .643;
HUD-50058Instr: p22; p34; p70 (2); p71 (3); p72;
HUD-52517: p2;
HUD-52641: p5; p6; p10;
HUD-52641-A: p3;
HUD-52646: p2;
7420.10G Gbk: 3-4; 5-1; 5-9 Ex 5-1; 5-25 Ex 5-3; 5-37 (2); 5-41; 8-15; 11-13; 15-2; 15-5; 15-6 (2); 23-7;
PIH Notices: 03-05; 01-40; 01-15 (2); 01-15 Impr Integ Hbk (5); 00-11; 00-11A;
Admin Plan: s2p2; s2p5; s2p6 (2); s7p3; s8p6; s15p1 (2); s15p2; s15p2

MEMBER OF THE FAMILY'S 1
Admin Plan: s15p2

MEMBER OF THE HOUSEHOLD 53
24 CFR 5: .100 (2);
24 CFR 982: .306 (2); .315; .404; .553 (3); .619; .634;
HUD-50058: p i;
HUD-50058Instr: p14 (2); p15 (4);
HUD-52641: p6 (2); p9 (4);
HUD-52641-A: p2 (4);
7420.10G Gbk: 5-13; 8-19 (2); 11-3 (2); 12-3; 15-6;
PIH Notices: 02-01; 99-52;
Admin Plan: s2p2; s6p6 (2); s6p7 (2); s6p8; s6p11; s7p8; s8p5; s8p6; s15p2; s15p3 (2); s16p2 (2); s16p2

MEMBERSHIP................................16
24 CFR 982: .4 (4); .627 (2); .633; .635;
HUD-903: p2;
7420.10G Gbk: 23-3; 23-4;
PIH Notices: 01-15 Impr Integ Hbk (2);
Admin Plan: s22p1; s25p4; s25p4

MEMBERSHIP SHARES 5
24 CFR 982: .4 (4);
Admin Plan: s22p1

MEMBERSHIPS 1
PIH Notices: 01-15 Impr Integ Hbk

MEMORANDUM OF UNDERSTANDING.......................... 7
7420.10G Gbk: 1-7 (2);
PIH Notices: 03-11; 01-15 (2);
Admin Plan: s25p1; s25p7

MEN...1
7420.10G Gbk: 17-2

MENTAL 67
24 CFR 5: .403; .603;
24 CFR 982: .352; .612;
HUD-50058: p i;
HUD-50058Instr: p15; p71; p74;
HUD-903: p1;
HUD-903-1: p2;
7420.10G Gbk: 5-43; 5-44; 8-17;
PIH Notices: 95-48 (23); 95-48 Tech Asst (23);

Admin Plan: s1p4; s1p5; s6p3; s23p2; s24p2; s25p2; s25p3; s25p3
MENTAL HEALTH............................6
24 CFR 5: .603;
24 CFR 982: .612;
HUD-50058Instr: p71;
PIH Notices: 95-48; 95-48 Tech Asst;
Admin Plan: s6p3
MENTAL IMPAIRMENT 20
7420.10G Gbk: 5-44;
PIH Notices: 95-48 (9); 95-48 Tech Asst (9);
Admin Plan: s1p4
MENTAL IMPAIRMENTS 9
7420.10G Gbk: 5-43;
PIH Notices: 95-48 (4); 95-48 Tech Asst (3); 95-48 Tech Asst
MENTAL RETARDATION...............2
PIH Notices: 95-48; 95-48 Tech Asst
MENTALLY 6
24 CFR 5: .318;
PIH Notices: 95-48 (2); 95-48 Tech Asst (2);
Admin Plan: s23p2
MENTALLY ILL 4
24 CFR 5: .318;
PIH Notices: 95-48; 95-48 Tech Asst;
Admin Plan: s23p2
MENTALLY RETARDED 2
PIH Notices: 95-48; 95-48 Tech Asst
MERGE...6
24 CFR 982: .205 (2);
HUD-50058Instr: p5;
7420.10G Gbk: 1-4; 4-9; 4-9
MERGED..3
24 CFR 982: .205 (2);
HUD-50058Instr: p73
MERGER..43
24 CFR 982: .4; .152; .201; .205; .501 (2); .502 (10); .503 (2); .623;
HUD-50058Instr: p73 (2);
7420.10G Gbk: 1-4 (3); 11-2; 14-1; 14-2; 14-3; 14-4 (2);
PIH Notices: 02-20 (2); 01-33 (2); 01-06 (3); 00-46 (2); 00-24;
MERGER DATE.............................35
24 CFR 982: .4; .152; .201; .501; .502 (10); .503 (2); .623;
HUD-50058Instr: p73;
7420.10G Gbk: 1-4; 14-1 (2); 14-2 (3); 14-3 (3); 14-5;
PIH Notices: 02-20 (2); 01-33 (2); 01-06; 00-46; 00-46
METER 1
Admin Plan: s6p13
METERED...2
Admin Plan: s6p13; s6p13
METHAMPHETAMINE...................5
24 CFR 982: .553 (2);
7420.10G Gbk: 5-35; 15-6;
PIH Notices: 03-11
METHANE GAS 1
24 CFR 5: .703
METHOD 136
24 CFR 5: .520 (3);
24 CFR 982: .54; .207 (3); .503 (7);
HUD-50058Instr: p38;
HUD-52648: p1 (3);
7420.10G Gbk: 3-2; 3-4; 3-5; 4-1; 4-4; 4-11 (3); 4-12 (5); 4-13; 4-14 (2); 4-16; 4-18 (2); 5-9 Ex 5-1; 5-17 (2); 7-4 (2); 7-5 (4); 8-9; 8-14 (2); 8-15 (2); 8-23; 9-12; 10-21; 10-24; 12-4; 21-6; 23-5; 23-6;
PIH Notices: 03-23 (3); 02-27 (10); 02-20 (10); 02-01; 01-41 (3); 01-15 (2); 01-15 Impr Integ Hbk (4); 01-06; 00-46 (10); 00-24B (2); 00-09 (3); 99-52; 99-11; 95-48 (7); 95-48 Tech Asst (7);
Admin Plan: s6p9; s7p1 (4); s8p2; s11p2; s17p1; s21p3 (3); s21p3
METHODOLOGIES 1
PIH Notices: 02-27
METHODOLOGY..........................34
24 CFR 982: .102 (2); .503 (3);
7420.10G Gbk: 5-40; 19-7; 19-8; 20-13 (2);
PIH Notices: 02-27 (3); 02-21 (7); 02-20 (4); 01-41; 01-20 (2); 00-46 (3); 00-27;
Admin Plan: s6p9 (2); s6p10
METHODS 98
24 CFR 5: .350; .655;
7420.10G Gbk: 2-1; 3-9; 5-17 (3); 7-5 (2); 10-15; 10-19 (2); 10-21; 10-22; 10-23; 10-26; 10-30; 10-35; 12-4 (2); 12-8; 19-8 (2); 19-9; 19-10 (2);

19-11; 21-1; 21-6; 22-1; 22-3;
PIH Notices: 02-27 (5); 02-20; 02-01 (4); 01-15 (4); 01-15 Impr Integ Hbk; 00-46; 00-11A; 99-52 (4); 95-48 (15); 95-48 Tech Asst (15);
Admin Plan: s6p1; s7p1 (3); s7p4 (5); s7p5 (2); s7p6 (2); s7p7; s17p1; s20p2

METROPOLITAN STATISTICAL AREA...5
24 CFR 5: .100;
24 CFR 982: .201;
HUD-50058Instr: p74;
7420.10G Gbk: 4-19;
PIH Notices: 01-06

MICE...5
24 CFR 5: .703;
HUD-52580-A: p17; p18;
7420.10G Gbk: 10-13; 10-14

MICRONESIA..................................4
24 CFR 5: .506;
HUD-50058Instr: p64;
PIH Notices: 01-27; 01-27

MICROWAVE 22
24 CFR 982: .401 (3);
HUD-52517: p1;
HUD-52580: p6 (2);
HUD-52580-A: p4 (3); p5 (2); p19 (2);
HUD-52641: p2;
HUD-52667: p1 (2);
7420.10G Gbk: 10-4 (3); 10-6; 18-8;
Admin Plan: s19p1

MICROWAVES 2
HUD-52580-A: p5;
7420.10G Gbk: 10-6

MID-MONTH....................................1
Admin Plan: s11p1

MILEAGE..1
7420.10G Gbk: 5-32

MILITARY......................................30
HUD-50058: p6;
HUD-50058Instr: p26 (4); p27;
HUD-903: p1;
7420.10G Gbk: 4-26 Ex 4-2;
PIH Notices: 03-05 (8); 01-41 (2); 01-40 (7);
Admin Plan: s5p1; s6p5 (3); s7p7

MILITARY PAY................................7
HUD-50058: p6;
HUD-50058Instr: p26 (3); p27;
Admin Plan: s6p5; s6p5

MILITARY PERSONNEL.................3
PIH Notices: 03-05 (2); 01-40

MINIMUM 328
24 CFR 5: .230; .514; .617; .628; .630 (21); .653;
24 CFR 982: .4; .401; .518; .605; .625; .627 (8); .632;
HUD-50058: p8 (3); p viii (4);
HUD-50058Instr: p2 (3); p37 (10); p38 (6); p59; p72 (2); p73 (2); p74;
HUD-52580-A: p1 (2); p6; p8;
HUD-52641: p10;
HUD-52641-A: p3;
HUD-52648: p1;
7420.10G Gbk: 2-10 (2); 3-3; 3-8 (2); 5-12; 5-27; 5-42; 6-1 (3); 6-3; 6-7; 8-3; 8-5; 8-14; 10-1; 10-2 (3); 10-6; 10-14; 10-31 (3); 10-34; 12-2; 16-3; 19-2 (5); 19-3; 19-6; 19-7; 19-10 (2); 20-23; 22-7 (2); 22-9 (3); 22-11; 22-16; 23-1 (2); 23-2 (6); 23-3 (2); 23-9; 23-18; 24-10;
PIH Notices: 02-27; 02-20 (3); 02-14; 02-01 (2); 01-41 (39); 01-15 Impr Integ Hbk (6); 01-10 (27); 01-06 (2); 00-53; 00-46 (3); 00-28 (4); 00-09 (36); 99-52 (2); 99-11 (2); 95-48 (4); 95-48 Tech Asst (4);
Admin Plan: s1p4; s1p7; s2p2; s3p1; s4p2; s5p1 (2); s5p2; s6p2 (3); s6p4 (12); s6p5 (12); s6p8 (2); s9p2; s10p1 (3); s10p3; s11p2; s11p1; s22p1; s22p2; s22p3; s24p1; s24p3; s24p4; s24p7; s25p4; s25p5

MINIMUM INCOME.......................8
24 CFR 982: .627 (6);
Admin Plan: s6p8; s6p8

MINIMUM RENT.........................187
24 CFR 5: .628; .630 (20);
24 CFR 982: .518;
HUD-50058: p8 (3); p viii (4);
HUD-50058Instr: p37 (10); p38 (5);
7420.10G Gbk: 1-6 Ex 1-1 (2); 3-6 (2); 3-7; 6-1 (2); 6-5; 6-7 (5); 6-8 (9); 6-10 Ex 6-2; 8-5 (2); 16-2;

PIH Notices: 01-41 (35); 01-15 Impr Integ Hbk (4); 01-10 (25); 00-09 (31);
Admin Plan: s6p4 (11); s6p5 (10); s6p5

MINIMUM RENT CALCULATION 2
PIH Notices: 00-09;
Admin Plan: s6p5

MINIMUM RENT CHANGES 7
HUD-50058Instr: p38;
PIH Notices: 01-41 (2); 01-10 (2); 00-09; 00-09

MINIMUM RENT POLICY..............2
7420.10G Gbk: 6-7; 6-8

MINIMUM RENTS............................1
Admin Plan: s6p4

MINIMUM WAGE............................7
24 CFR 5: .617;
24 CFR 982: .627;
HUD-50058Instr: p74;
PIH Notices: 01-15 Impr Integ Hbk;
Admin Plan: s6p2 (2); s6p2

MINOR..43
24 CFR 5: .522;
24 CFR 982: .315;
HUD-50058: p ii;
HUD-50058Instr: p14;
HUD-52580-A: p2 (2); p4 (4); p6 (3);
7420.10G Gbk: 3-4; 5-4 (2); 5-12; 5-29; 9-14 Ex 9-1; 9-16 Ex 9-2; 10-4 (2); 10-10; 22-18;
PIH Notices: 02-27; 02-20 (2); 01-15 Impr Integ Hbk; 00-46 (2); 00-24; 95-48 (2); 95-48 Tech Asst (2);
Admin Plan: s2p1; s6p8 (2); s8p5 (2); s8p6 (2); s8p6

MINOR CHILD................................2
7420.10G Gbk: 5-4;
Admin Plan: s8p6

MINOR CHILDREN.........................5
24 CFR 5: .522;
24 CFR 982: .315;
7420.10G Gbk: 3-4; 5-4;
Admin Plan: s8p5

MINORITIES 1
7420.10G Gbk: 4-2

MINORITY.....................................73
24 CFR 5: .105 (2);
24 CFR 982: .54; .206;
HUD-50058Instr: p73;
HUD-52648: p2 (7);
7420.10G Gbk: 1-13; 2-1 (4); 2-2 (2); 2-3 (7); 2-4; 2-5; 2-6; 2-7; 2-8; 2-10 (3); 2-11; 3-3 (2); 3-9; 4-1; 4-2; 4-3 (3); 4-7; 7-1; 7-5; 7-6 (2); 7-7; 7-9; 8-7; 13-1 (2); 13-10 (2); 23-4; 23-6;
PIH Notices: 02-21 (2); 01-20 (2); 01-06 (2);
Admin Plan: s1p6; s1p7; s8p1; s21p5 (2); s21p6 (4); s21p6

MINORITY CONCENTRATION ...49
24 CFR 982: .54;
HUD-52648: p2 (6);
7420.10G Gbk: 1-13; 2-1 (3); 2-2 (2); 2-3 (7); 2-4; 2-5; 2-6; 2-7; 2-8; 2-10; 2-11; 3-3 (2); 3-9; 7-7; 7-9; 8-7; 13-1; 13-10 (2);
PIH Notices: 02-21; 01-20 (2); 01-06 (2);
Admin Plan: s1p7; s8p1; s21p5 (2); s21p6 (3); s21p6

MINORS...20
HUD-50058: p xi;
HUD-50058Instr: p16; p46 (4);
7420.10G Gbk: 5-18 (2); 5-23; 5-24; 13-9; 20-4 (2); 23-16 Ex 23-2 (2);
PIH Notices: 02-07; 00-28;
Admin Plan: s6p1; s6p7; s7p7

MIRROR...2
7420.10G Gbk: 19-8; 19-8

MIRRORS 3
HUD-52580: p6;
HUD-52580-A: p19;
7420.10G Gbk: 10-4

MISCALCULATING 1
7420.10G Gbk: 22-2

MISCALCULATION 1
PIH Notices: 01-15

MISDEMEANOR.............................2
24 CFR 982: .310;
HUD-9886: p2

MISLEAD...2
7420.10G Gbk: 22-1;
Admin Plan: s17p2

MISREPORTED...............................5
HUD-50058: p ii;
HUD-50058Instr: p12 (2);
7420.10G Gbk: 5-6;
Admin Plan: s20p4

MISREPORTING 6
7420.10G Gbk: 8-8; 22-1 (3); 22-9; 22-16

MISREPRESENT 2
Admin Plan: s2p6; s20p5

MISREPRESENTATION 9
7420.10G Gbk: 4-23 Ex 4-1; 22-2; 22-9; 22-12; 22-16;
Admin Plan: s11p2; s20p6; s20p7; s20p8
MISREPRESENTATIONS 5
Admin Plan: s17p2; s20p6 (3); s20p7
MISREPRESENTED 2
24 CFR 5: .528;
7420.10G Gbk: 22-14
MISREPRESENTING 3
7420.10G Gbk: 22-2 (2); 22-10
MISREPRESENTS 1
Admin Plan: s20p6
MISSING STEPS 3
24 CFR 982: .401;
HUD-52580-A: p13; p18
MISSION 10
7420.10G Gbk: 3-1 (2); 3-6 (2); 3-7 (2);
PIH Notices: 00-11;
Admin Plan: s1p1 (2); s1p1
MISSION STATEMENT 3
7420.10G Gbk: 3-1 (2);
Admin Plan: s1p1
MISTAKENLY 2
7420.10G Gbk: 16-5; 22-13
MISTAKES 7
7420.10G Gbk: 19-10;
PIH Notices: 02-07; 01-15 (3); 01-15 Impr Integ Hbk; 00-28
MITIGATE 3
24 CFR 982: .310;
PIH Notices: 95-48; 95-48 Tech Asst
MITIGATED 2
PIH Notices: 95-48; 95-48 Tech Asst
MITIGATING 13
24 CFR 982: .552;
7420.10G Gbk: 15-6; 22-1; 22-14;
PIH Notices: 02-01; 99-52; 96-65; 95-48; 95-48 Tech Asst;
Admin Plan: s18p8 (2); s20p7; s20p7
MITIGATING CIRCUMSTANCE 1
Admin Plan: s18p8
MITIGATING CIRCUMSTANCES .. 8
24 CFR 982: .552;
7420.10G Gbk: 15-6; 22-1; 22-14;
PIH Notices: 02-01; 99-52;
Admin Plan: s18p8; s20p7
MITIGATING EVIDENCE 1
Admin Plan: s20p7
MIXED FAMILIES 16
24 CFR 5: .516 (7); .518;
HUD-50058Instr: p18; p68;
7420.10G Gbk: 5-5 (3);
PIH Notices: 01-27;
Admin Plan: s2p5; s6p11
MIXED FAMILY 119
24 CFR 5: .504; .506; .514; .516 (2); .518 (4); .520 (4);
HUD-50058: p i; p9 (2); p ix (2); p10 (2); p x (3); p11 (2); p xi (4); p12 (2); p xii (4); p13 (2); p xiii; p14; p xiv;
HUD-50058Instr: p ii; p3; p17; p39 (4); p40 (7); p41; p44 (7); p45 (5); p48 (2); p49 (11); p51; p52 (11); p54 (2); p55 (2); p57 (2); p67; p68 (7); p69 (7); p73;
7420.10G Gbk: 5-5 (2); 5-8;
PIH Notices: 01-27;
Admin Plan: s6p12
MIXED FAMILY'S 3
HUD-50058Instr: p39; p69; p69
MIXED-USE 2
24 CFR 5: .306; .306
MOBILE 5
HUD-903-1: p5;
7420.10G Gbk: 3-5; 21-7;
Admin Plan: s9p2; s9p2
MOBILITY 49
7420.10G Gbk: 1-2; 2-1 (3); 2-7 (3); 2-9; 19-4; 21-13 (2); 21-16 Ex 21-6 (2);
PIH Notices: 02-01 (2); 99-52 (2); 99-11; 95-48 (10); 95-48 Tech Asst (10);
Admin Plan: s1p1; s1p7; s8p3 (4); s8p4 (3); s25p6; s25p7
MOBILITY IMPAIRMENT 4
PIH Notices: 95-48 (2); 95-48 Tech Asst; 95-48 Tech Asst
MOBILITY IMPAIRMENTS 16
PIH Notices: 02-01; 99-52; 95-48 (7); 95-48 Tech Asst (6); 95-48 Tech Asst
MOBILITY PROBLEMS 1
PIH Notices: 99-11
MODEL LEASE 3
24 CFR 982: .308;
7420.10G Gbk: 8-21; 8-21

MODERATE REHABILITATION..54
24 CFR 5: .514; .630; .653; .655; .657; .801;
HUD-50058: p12; p xii (2);
HUD-50058Instr: p ii; p7; p50 (2); p73 (2);
7420.10G Gbk: 1-8 (2); 3-7; 5-37; 8-16; 19-3; 20-5; 20-13 (3); 20-23; 21-19; 21-20; 23-3;
PIH Notices: 03-23; 02-14; 02-07; 02-01; 01-41 (3); 01-15; 01-10 (3); 00-09 (3); 99-52; 99-11;
Admin Plan: s23p1 (2); s23p2; s23p3 (2); s23p5 (3); s23p5

MODERATE REHABILITATION PROGRAM....................................34
24 CFR 5: .100; .632; .659; .801;
24 CFR 982: .205 (3);
7420.10G Gbk: 1-1; 4-9; 10-15; 21-17; 23-3;
PIH Notices: 03-23 (2); 02-01 (2); 01-41; 01-27 (2); 01-10; 00-14 (2); 00-09; 99-52 (2);
Admin Plan: s23p1 (7); s23p4; s23p6

MODERATE REHABILITATION PROGRAMS 11
24 CFR 5: .504; .514 (2);
HUD-50058Instr: p9; p74;
7420.10G Gbk: 4-8 (2);
PIH Notices: 03-05; 01-40; 01-15; 00-14

MODERATE REHABILITATIONS..1
Admin Plan: s23p1

MODERNIZATION 22
PIH Notices: 02-01 (9); 00-11; 99-52 (11); 99-11

MODERNIZED 6
PIH Notices: 02-01 (3); 99-52 (2); 99-52

MODIFIABLE..................................1
PIH Notices: 02-27

MODIFICATION............................44
24 CFR 5: .315; .655;
24 CFR 982: .102 (3); .503;
HUD-52641: p1;
PIH Notices: 02-27 (4); 02-20; 02-01 (7); 01-06 (11); 00-46; 99-52 (7); 95-48 (3); 95-48 Tech Asst (2); 95-48 Tech Asst

MODIFICATION REQUEST...........2
24 CFR 982: .102; .102

MODIFICATIONS 62
24 CFR 982: .102; .162; .452;
HUD-52580-A: p4; p6; p8;
HUD-903-1: p2;
7420.10G Gbk: 5-43; 14-5; 23-9;
PIH Notices: 02-27; 02-20; 02-01 (4); 01-20; 00-46; 00-24B; 99-52 (4); 95-48 (20); 95-48 Tech Asst (16);
Admin Plan: s1p4; s10p3; s10p3

MODIFIED.....................................25
24 CFR 982: .601;
HUD-50058: p ii;
HUD-50058Instr: p6 (2);
7420.10G Gbk: 1-11; 4-7; 11-10; 23-9; 23-18;
PIH Notices: 02-27; 02-01; 01-15; 01-06 (4); 99-52; 95-48 (4); 95-48 Tech Asst (3); 95-48 Tech Asst

MODIFIES.......................................3
HUD-50058: p ii;
HUD-50058Instr: p6;
PIH Notices: 01-06

MODIFY...54
24 CFR 5: .315; .615 (2);
24 CFR 982: .102; .503 (2);
HUD-52665: p2;
7420.10G Gbk: 4-4; 14-5; 23-9 (2); 23-10;
PIH Notices: 02-27 (6); 02-20 (7); 02-01 (3); 01-41; 01-06 (10); 00-46 (7); 00-24A (2); 00-09; 99-52 (3); 95-48; 95-48 Tech Asst

MODIFYING....................................6
PIH Notices: 02-27 (2); 02-01; 99-52; 95-48; 95-48 Tech Asst

MOLD..1
24 CFR 5: .703

MONDAY...4
HUD-50058Instr: p3;
7420.10G Gbk: 10-40 Ex 10-4a; 10-41 Ex 10-4b; 10-46 Ex 10-8

MONETARY..................................16
24 CFR 5: .609;
HUD-50058: p i (2);
HUD-50058Instr: p3 (2); p33; p70;
7420.10G Gbk: 1-9; 5-13; 5-18; 22-11; 22-16;
PIH Notices: 01-41; 01-15 Impr Integ Hbk; 00-09;
Admin Plan: s6p1

MONEY MANAGEMENT 1
24 CFR 982: .630
MONEY MARKET 1
7420.10G Gbk: 5-25 Ex 5-3
MONITOR 69
24 CFR 5: .653;
24 CFR 982: .503;
HUD-50058: p i;
HUD-50058Instr: p1;
7420.10G Gbk: 1-13; 4-4 (3); 4-18; 4-20; 4-21 (4); 8-11; 8-22; 10-25; 10-26; 10-30; 10-34 (2); 11-15 (3); 11-16 Ex 11-1; 12-2; 19-1; 19-6; 19-8; 19-9 (2); 19-10; 19-11; 19-12; 19-13 (3); 20-1; 20-13; 20-15; 20-16; 20-17; 20-18; 20-20; 21-3; 22-7 (2); 22-10 (2); 24-10;
PIH Notices: 02-27 (7); 02-20 (3); 00-46 (3);
Admin Plan: s10p1 (2); s20p1; s20p4; s23p2; s23p3
MONITORED 6
7420.10G Gbk: 4-22; 9-11; 10-35; 11-10; 21-8;
Admin Plan: s8p1
MONITORING 73
24 CFR 5: .609;
HUD-50058: p i;
HUD-9886: p2;
7420.10G Gbk: 4-22 (2); 5-15 Ex 5-2; 8-22; 8-23 (2); 9-11; 10-30; 10-33; 11-7 (2); 11-8; 12-1 (2); 12-2; 13-4; 13-7 (2); 13-9; 19-1 (4); 19-5 (3); 19-7; 19-9; 19-11; 19-13 (2); 20-2; 20-7; 20-13 (2); 20-16; 20-20; 20-22; 21-3 (4); 21-5; 21-9; 21-10; 22-10; 22-18 (2); 24-3; 24-4; 24-8; 24-10;
PIH Notices: 02-27 (7); 02-20; 01-15 Impr Integ Hbk (2); 00-46; 00-41; 00-24;
Admin Plan: s11p1; s21p2; s23p2 (2); s25p4
MONITORS 3
7420.10G Gbk: 10-35; 11-9; 11-16 Ex 11-1
MONTH 294
24 CFR 5: .318 (2); .609; .617 (6); .630 (5);
24 CFR 982: .152; .311 (5); .353; .355; .403 (2); .503 (2); .519; .633 (2); .639;
HUD-50058: p ii; p iii; p iv; p8; p10; p11; p13; p14;
HUD-50058Instr: p9; p10; p11; p12; p17 (3); p18; p21; p25; p33; p37 (2); p39 (2); p40; p42; p43; p45; p46; p49; p51; p52; p53; p54; p56; p70; p71 (2);
HUD-52641: p2; p4 (5); 8;
HUD-52641-A: p1 (2);
HUD-52665: p2;
HUD-52667: p1; p i;
7420.10G Gbk: 5-15 Ex 5-2; 5-17 (3); 5-19 (4); 5-23; 5-24 (2); 6-8; 8-22; 9-7; 10-23; 10-24; 10-25 (3); 10-27; 10-29 (2); 10-33; 10-34; 11-1; 11-5 (6); 11-7 (4); 11-8; 11-9 (4); 11-19; 12-1 (2); 12-6 (3); 12-10 (2); 12-12 Ex 12-1; 15-4 (2); 16-4; 18-4 (2); 19-2; 19-8; 19-9; 19-13; 20-3; 20-5 (5); 20-7 (2); 20-9 (3); 20-19 Ex 20-3 (2); 20-20 (2); 20-21 Ex 20-4 (2); 20-21; 21-5 (5); 22-7; 22-12; 22-13; 23-7; 24-1 (2); 24-2; 24-3 (4); 24-6; 24-7 (3); 24-12;
PIH Notices: 03-23 (21); 03-11; 02-27 (3); 02-21 (2); 02-20 (2); 02-06 (17); 01-41 (2); 01-33; 01-15 (8); 01-15 Impr Integ Hbk (15); 01-06 (2); 01-01 (9); 00-34; 00-28; 00-24B; 00-11; 00-09; 96-65 (3);
Admin Plan: s6p5 (2); s6p7; s6p13; s10p4; s11p1 (10); s11p2 (5); s13p2; s14p1 (3); s14p2 (2); s21p5 (2); s23p4; s23p4
MONTH-BY-MONTH 3
7420.10G Gbk: 19-8;
PIH Notices: 02-21; 01-20
MONTHLY 520
24 CFR 5: .318; .603 (4); .609 (2); .617; .628 (2); .630; .661 (4);
24 CFR 982: .1 (2); .4 (6); .102 (5); .305; .308; .317; .451 (3); .503 (3); .505 (9); .507; .508 (2); .514; .518; .619 (2); .622; .623 (5); .625 (4); .627 (2); .631 (3); .635 (4); .642 (5);
HUD-50058: p2; p8 (3); p viii (9); p ix (2);

p x (5); p xi (5); p xii (6); p13; p xiii (8); p14 (5); p xiv (4); p15 (3); p xv (8); p17; p xvii;
HUD-50058Instr: p2; p12; p16 (2); p29 (2); p37 (13); p39; p40; p42; p43 (3); p44; p46; p47 (2); p49; p50 (4); p51; p52; p53 (8); p54 (4); p56 (9); p57; p58 (11); p62 (2); p65; p66 (4); p72; p74 (3); p75 (2); p76;
HUD-52641: p1 (2); p2; p4 (4); 8 (3); p10;
HUD-52641-A: p1 (3); p3;
HUD-52646: p1 (4); p2; p3 (4);
HUD-52667: p1; p i; p ii;
7420.10G Gbk: 1-6 Ex 1-1; 4-15; 4-17; 4-21; 4-27 Ex 4-2; 5-15 Ex 5-2; 5-17; 5-23 (4); 5-24 (5); 5-32 (2); 5-46 Ex 5-5; 5-49 Ex 5-5; 6-1 (6); 6-2 (3); 6-3; 6-5; 6-6; 6-10 Ex 6-2 (4); 7-5; 7-7; 8-2 (2); 8-5 (3); 8-21; 9-3; 9-6; 10-26; 10-34; 10-35 (2); 11-1; 11-5 (3); 11-6; 11-8 (2); 11-9; 11-11; 11-19 (3); 12-2; 12-8; 12-13 Ex 12-1; 13-2; 13-7 (2); 13-9; 14-4 (3); 17-4; 17-10 (2); 17-12; 18-5 (2); 18-6 (3); 19-2; 19-5 (2); 19-13 (4); 20-6; 20-9; 20-17; 20-20 (5); 20-21 Ex 20-4 (4); 20-21 (2); 20-22; 20-23 (4); 20-30 (2); 21-2; 21-5 (3); 21-6 Ex 21-1 (3); 22-5; 22-7; 22-13; 23-7; 23-8 Ex 23-1; 23-11 (5); 23-14; 23-17 Ex 23-2 (5); 24-3; 24-6; 24-9; 24-11; 24-12;
PIH Notices: 03-23 (6); 03-20; 02-27 (14); 02-22; 02-20 (5); 02-07 (2); 01-41 (17); 01-15 Impr Integ Hbk (11); 01-10 (26); 01-06; 00-53; 00-46 (5); 00-28 (3); 00-24B (8); 00-11A; 00-09 (15);
Admin Plan: s6p3; s6p4; s7p6; s7p7; s8p1; s9p1; s10p1; s11p2; s19p1 (4); s22p3 (2); s24p3; s24p6; s25p5

MONTHLY ADJUSTED 4
HUD-50058Instr: p65; p66 (2); p66

MONTHLY ADJUSTED FAMILY INCOME 1
HUD-52646: p1

MONTHLY AMOUNT 13
HUD-50058: p2; p x; p xi; p xiii (2); p xiv;
HUD-50058Instr: p12; p42; p46; p53 (2); p56;
7420.10G Gbk: 20-20

MONTHLY AMOUNT DUE 1
HUD-52665: p2

MONTHLY AMOUNTS 8
24 CFR 5: .609 (2);
HUD-50058Instr: p29 (2);
PIH Notices: 01-15 Impr Integ Hbk (3); 01-15 Impr Integ Hbk

MONTHLY INCOME 70
24 CFR 5: .603; .617; .628;
24 CFR 982: .1 (2); .503 (2); .508 (2);
HUD-50058: p8 (3); p viii (7); p15; p xv (2);
HUD-50058Instr: p37 (12); p58 (3); p74;
7420.10G Gbk: 4-17; 6-10 Ex 6-2 (3); 8-5;
PIH Notices: 02-20 (3); 01-41 (6); 01-15 Impr Integ Hbk; 01-10 (3); 00-46 (3); 00-24B (2); 00-09 (7);
Admin Plan: s6p3; s6p4

MONTHLY PAYMENT..................... 8
24 CFR 982: .317;
HUD-50058: p15; p xv (2);
HUD-50058Instr: p58 (3);
7420.10G Gbk: 5-32

MONTHLY PAYMENT SCHEDULE2
HUD-50058: p xv;
HUD-50058Instr: p58

MONTHLY PAYMENTS 8
24 CFR 5: .318;
24 CFR 982: .623 (2);
HUD-52646: p1;
7420.10G Gbk: 5-15 Ex 5-2; 5-32; 21-2;
Admin Plan: s7p7

MONTHLY-ADJUSTED.................. 3
Admin Plan: s6p4; s11p1; s17p1

MONTHLY-ADJUSTED INCOME .. 4
7420.10G Gbk: 8-16;
Admin Plan: s6p4; s11p1; s17p1

MONTHS..................................... 222

24 CFR 5: .230; .514; .518 (3); .617 (4); .801;
24 CFR 982: .102 (2); .503; .519; .624; .634; .643;
HUD-50058Instr: p9; p10; p12 (3); p18 (3); p28; p71; p74;
HUD-52580-A: p8; p15 (3);
HUD-52641: p4;
HUD-52648: p1; p2;
HUD-52665: p1;
HUD-9886: p2;
7420.10G Gbk: 5-17; 5-23; 5-27; 10-20; 10-24; 11-6; 12-1; 12-10; 19-8; 19-13; 20-7; 22-13; 23-7 (2); 23-9; 24-3; 24-8 (2);
PIH Notices: 03-23 (68); 03-05; 02-27 (2); 02-21 (3); 02-20 (3); 02-14; 02-07; 02-06 (2); 01-41 (4); 01-40; 01-20 (4); 01-15 (2); 01-15 Impr Integ Hbk (8); 01-10 (2); 01-06; 01-01; 00-53; 00-46 (3); 00-28; 00-24B (3); 00-11A; 00-09 (5); 00-01 (2); 98-66 (2);
Admin Plan: s5p1; s6p1; s6p2 (3); s6p3 (4); s6p6 (2); s6p7 (2); s6p8 (2); s6p9; s7p4 (3); s7p5 (5); s7p6 (2); s7p7; s9p2; s15p3; s17p1; s19p1; s21p4; s21p5; s21p7 (5); s21p8 (5); s22p2; s25p5

MONTH'S 2
24 CFR 5: .318;
Admin Plan: s23p5

MONTHS'.. 2
PIH Notices: 03-23; 03-23

MORTGAGE 167
24 CFR 5: .100; .210; .214 (5); .216; .306 (4); .801 (2);
24 CFR 982: .4; .201; .203 (2); .453 (4); .625; .627 (2); .632 (2); .633 (7); .634; .635 (3); .638 (3); .642 (4); .643 (2);
HUD-50058: p xiv (2);
HUD-50058Instr: p13 (2); p19 (2); p38 (2); p56 (2);
HUD-52641: p5 (4);
HUD-903-1: p2 (3); p4;
7420.10G Gbk: 1-6; 1-9 (4); 4-20; 4-22 (2); 5-3 (2); 5-26 (2); 9-8; 11-18 (3); 15-4; 20-3; 23-2 (2); 24-12;
PIH Notices: 01-41 (34); 01-15 Impr Integ Hbk; 01-10 (3); 00-28; 00-09 (27);
Admin Plan: s2p4 (2); s4p2; s16p2; s22p1; s22p2; s22p3 (3); s22p4 (5); s24p4

MORTGAGE DEFAULT.................. 3
24 CFR 982: .633; .638; .642

MORTGAGE DEFAULTS 2
24 CFR 982: .642; .642

MORTGAGE INSURANCE 42
24 CFR 5: .306; .801 (2);
24 CFR 982: .203; .453; .632 (2); .643 (2);
HUD-50058Instr: p13; p19; p38;
HUD-52641: p5;
7420.10G Gbk: 4-22; 5-3; 15-4; 23-2;
PIH Notices: 01-41 (13); 01-10 (2); 00-09 (9);
Admin Plan: s2p4

MORTGAGE PREPAYMENT 3
24 CFR 982: .203;
7420.10G Gbk: 4-22;
Admin Plan: s4p2

MORTGAGED 1
24 CFR 5: .214

MORTGAGEE.................................. 9
24 CFR 5: .214 (2); .236 (5); .504;
HUD-50058Instr: p74

MORTGAGEE-IN-POSSESSION 3
7420.10G Gbk: 1-9;
PIH Notices: 01-41; 00-09

MORTGAGEES 2
24 CFR 5: .500; .801

MORTGAGES 12
24 CFR 5: .701; .801;
24 CFR 982: .453; .632; .643;
HUD-52641: p5;
HUD-52648: p2;
7420.10G Gbk: 11-18; 15-4;
PIH Notices: 01-06;
Admin Plan: s7p6; s16p2

MORTGAGOR 7
24 CFR 5: .107; .508 (2);
PIH Notices: 01-41 (2); 00-09; 00-09

MORTGAGORS............................... 1
24 CFR 5: .703

MORTGAGOR'S 1
24 CFR 5: .508

MOTELS... 2

PIH Notices: 95-48; 95-48 Tech Asst

MOTHER....7
HUD-50058Instr: p14;
7420.10G Gbk: 5-30; 17-8; 17-9 (2);
PIH Notices: 01-15 Impr Integ Hbk;
Admin Plan: s2p4

MOTHER'S....2
HUD-50058Instr: p29;
7420.10G Gbk: 5-19

MOTOR VEHICLE....6
PIH Notices: 95-48 (3); 95-48 Tech Asst (2); 95-48 Tech Asst

MOUSE....2
7420.10G Gbk: 10-14; 10-14

MOVE....238
24 CFR 5: .514;
24 CFR 982: 24 CFR 982 (3); .1; .4 (2); .302; .314 (14); .317; .355; .403; .551; .601; .624; .625; .636; .637 (10); .638 (2); .641; .642;
HUD-50058: p10; p x; p11; p xi; p13; p xiii; p14; p xiv; p17;
HUD-50058Instr: p9 (2); p10 (4); p42 (2); p46 (2); p53 (2); p56 (2); p60; p62; p63 (7); p73 (2);
HUD-52641: p10;
HUD-52641-A: p2;
7420.10G Gbk: 1-5; 1-7; 1-8; 2-1; 2-3; 2-7 (5); 2-8; 2-11; 3-4; 3-6; 4-5; 4-25 Ex 4-2; 5-40; 7-1; 7-3; 7-7; 8-9; 8-10; 8-20; 9-5; 10-29 (2); 11-4; 11-8; 11-14; 12-1; 12-5; 12-7 (2); 13-1 (2); 13-2 (4); 13-3 (3); 13-8; 13-10; 14-3 (2); 14-4; 16-3 (2); 17-12; 19-11; 20-4 (2); 21-3; 21-4 (3); 21-5; 21-7; 21-10; 22-11; 22-12 (2); 22-13 (2); 23-3; 23-18 (3); 24-13;
PIH Notices: 03-05; 02-20; 02-01 (2); 01-41 (21); 01-40; 01-15 Impr Integ Hbk; 01-06; 01-01; 00-46; 00-24B; 00-11 (4); 00-09 (14); 99-52 (2);
Admin Plan: s6p6; s6p8; s7p1; s8p3 (3); s10p2; s10p4; s13p1 (11); s14p1; s14p2 (2); s15p5 (3); s17p2 (2); s19p1; s22p2; s23p4 (2); s23p5; s23p7; s23p8; s24p6 (2); s25p6

MOVE IN....6
24 CFR 982: .314;
7420.10G Gbk: 24-13;
PIH Notices: 01-41; 00-09;
Admin Plan: s6p8; s23p7

MOVE INTO....16
24 CFR 982: .601;
HUD-50058: p10; p11; p13; p14;
HUD-50058Instr: p9; p10; p42; p46 (2); p53; p56;
7420.10G Gbk: 2-1; 11-4;
PIH Notices: 03-05; 01-40

MOVE OUT....15
24 CFR 982: .4 (2); .355;
HUD-50058Instr: p10; p73 (2);
HUD-52641: p10;
HUD-52641-A: p2;
7420.10G Gbk: 11-14; 13-2; 23-18;
Admin Plan: s6p6; s10p2; s23p5; s23p8

MOVE OUTSIDE....3
24 CFR 982: .636;
PIH Notices: 01-41; 00-09

MOVE-IN....23
HUD-50058: p2; p x; p xi; p xiii; p xiv;
HUD-50058Instr: p9 (5); p11; p12; p42 (2); p46 (2); p53; p56; p77;
HUD-52665: p2;
7420.10G Gbk: 19-2;
PIH Notices: 00-24B;
Admin Plan: s6p8

MOVEOUT....1
HUD-50058Instr: p77

MOVE-OUT....17
24 CFR 982: .311; .633;
HUD-50058: p2; p17 (2);
HUD-50058Instr: p10 (3); p11; p62 (2); p63 (2);
HUD-52665: p1;
7420.10G Gbk: 13-8; 14-5; 19-2

MOVES....108
24 CFR 5: .318 (3);
24 CFR 982: .1; .54 (2); .308; .309; .311 (7); .313; .314 (3); .353; .355 (3); .551; .633 (4);
HUD-50058Instr: p9 (2); p10 (2); p13; p19 (2); p42; p59;
HUD-52641: p3; p10;
HUD-52641-A: p3;

7420.10G Gbk: 1-6 Ex 1-1; 2-1; 2-7 (2); 2-9; 2-10; 3-6; 5-7; 6-2; 7-8; 11-5; 11-17; 12-5; 12-7; 13-2 (2); 13-4; 14-1; 14-2 (2); 14-3 (2); 15-3; 15-4; 19-12; 20-4; 20-24 (3); 21-4; 21-5 (4); 21-7 (2); 21-16 Ex 21-6; 22-15; 23-9;
PIH Notices: 01-41 (6); 01-15 Impr Integ Hbk; 01-10; 01-01 (2); 00-24B (2); 00-09 (6);
Admin Plan: s8p3; s13p1 (7); s15p5; s23p6; s25p7

MOVES OUT 28
24 CFR 982: .1; .309; .311 (5); .313; .355; .551; .633 (4);
HUD-52641: p4; p10 (2);
HUD-52641-A: p2; p3;
7420.10G Gbk: 8-4; 8-22; 11-1; 11-5 (2); 14-5;
PIH Notices: 01-15 Impr Integ Hbk; 00-24B; 00-24B

MOVING 96
24 CFR 982: .301; .314; .637;
HUD-50058: p10; p x; p11; p xi (2); p14; p xiv; p17; p xvii (2);
HUD-50058Instr: p9; p10; p13; p42 (2); p46 (6); p56 (2); p62; p63;
HUD-52665: p1; p2 (2);
7420.10G Gbk: 1-15; 2-1 (3); 2-2 (2); 2-7 (5); 2-9 (3); 2-11; 5-40; 7-10 (2); 8-3 (2); 8-4; 8-15; 11-4; 13-1 (3); 13-3; 13-5; 13-6; 13-7 (2); 14-4; 21-10; 23-18; 24-4; 24-9 (2);
PIH Notices: 03-23 (4); 02-21 (2); 01-41 (3); 01-20; 01-15 Impr Integ Hbk (2); 01-06 (3); 00-53 (2); 00-11; 00-09 (4); 95-48; 95-48 Tech Asst;
Admin Plan: s6p6; s8p1; s8p3; s13p1

MOVING COSTS.............................5
7420.10G Gbk: 2-7; 8-4; 8-15; 24-9; 24-9

MOVING INTO..............................14
HUD-50058: p x; p xi; p xiv;
HUD-50058Instr: p42; p46; p56;
HUD-52665: p2 (2);
7420.10G Gbk: 2-9 (2); 11-4; 13-5; 13-7; 13-7

MOVING OUT.................................9
HUD-52646: p2;
HUD-52665: p1;
7420.10G Gbk: 5-36 Ex 5-4; 7-7 (2); 13-2;
PIH Notices: 01-15 Impr Integ Hbk;
Admin Plan: s6p6; s13p1

MOVING OUTSIDE.........................1
Admin Plan: s8p1

MSA..11
24 CFR 5: .100;
24 CFR 982: .4 (2); .201 (2);
HUD-50058Instr: p74;
7420.10G Gbk: 4-19 (2); 7-5;
PIH Notices: 02-20; 00-46

MTCS...238
HUD-50058: p1; p i (4); p ii; p x; p xi; p xiii; p xiv; p xvi;
HUD-50058Instr: p ii; p1 (4); p2 (5); p3 (3); p4; p5 (9); p7 (2); p10 (2); p11 (4); p13; p42; p46; p53; p56; p59; p69; p70 (2); p71; p72; p73; p74 (3); p75;
7420.10G Gbk: 1-11; 4-21; 10-32; 10-35 (4); 12-3; 12-10; 13-8 (3); 14-5 (2); 19-1 (8); 19-2 (9); 19-3 (5); 19-4 (10); 19-5 (8); 19-6 (3); 19-8 (2); 19-10 (2); 19-13 (4); 22-4; 22-6; 23-19 (5);
PIH Notices: 02-27; 01-15 (5); 01-15 Impr Integ Hbk (2); 01-11 (3); 01-06 (49); 01-01 (4); 00-53 (17); 00-28; 00-24 (6); 00-24A (3); 00-14;
Admin Plan: s21p2 (5); s21p6; s21p7 (4); s21p8 (3); s21p9 (2); s21p9

MULTIFAMILY..............................84
24 CFR 5: .306; .603; .801 (2);
24 CFR 982: Intro; .201; .203; .504;
HUD-50058: p i;
HUD-50058Instr: p1; p2; p13 (2); p19; p21; p47 (2); p74;
HUD-52648: p2;
7420.10G Gbk: 1-8; 1-9; 1-11; 2-1; 4-21; 5-3; 5-27; 10-38 Ex 10-3; 12-3; 13-8; 19-1 (2); 23-19;
PIH Notices: 03-12 (3); 02-

07; 02-01 (5); 01-41 (12); 01-27; 01-15; 01-11; 01-10 (2); 01-06; 00-53; 00-28; 00-24; 00-14; 00-09 (8); 99-52 (5); 99-11 (2); 95-48 (2);
Admin Plan: s4p1;

MULTIPLY 36
24 CFR 5: .520 (2);
HUD-50058: p vii (2); p viii (2); p ix; p x; p xi; p xii; p xiii; p xiv; p xv;
HUD-50058Instr: p23 (2); p34; p36; p37 (2); p40; p44; p48; p51; p53; p54; p57; p58; p69;
HUD-52667: p i;
7420.10G Gbk: 5-5; 5-17 (5); 6-7

MUNICIPAL.................................... 12
PIH Notices: 95-48 (6); 95-48 Tech Asst (5); 95-48 Tech Asst

MUNICIPALITY 10
24 CFR 5: .100;
24 CFR 982: .4; .204; .207 (2);
HUD-50058Instr: p72; p74;
7420.10G Gbk: 4-8; 4-17; 4-17

MUTUAL AGREEMENT 2
24 CFR 982: .314;
7420.10G Gbk: 23-9

MUTUAL AGREEMENTS 1
7420.10G Gbk: 13-9

MUTUALLY AGREE 1
7420.10G Gbk: 2-9

MUTUALLY AGREEABLE 1
24 CFR 5: .353

MUTUALLY AGREED..................... 1
Admin Plan: s11p3

NAILED SHUT 6
24 CFR 982: .401;
HUD-52580-A: p2 (2); p17;
7420.10G Gbk: 10-6; 10-10

NATION... 3
HUD-50058Instr: p30;
7420.10G Gbk: 5-16 Ex 5-2;
PIH Notices: 01-15 Impr Integ Hbk

NATIONAL 91
24 CFR 5: .100 (7); .306; .500 (2); .504 (5); .506; .516; .801;
24 CFR 982: .202; .304; .401;
HUD-50058Instr: p15; p18; p26; p70; p72 (2); p74 (3);
HUD-52580-A: p8;
HUD-52667: p i;
HUD-903: p1 (2); p2 (4); p4;
7420.10G Gbk: 2-1; 4-27 Ex 4-2; 5-9 Ex 5-1; 5-10 Ex 5-1; 5-16 Ex 5-2; 9-12; 10-14; 18-4 (3); 18-5;
PIH Notices: 03-11 (5); 02-27; 02-22; 02-21; 02-20; 01-27 (2); 01-15 (2); 00-46; 99-11 (4); 95-48 (9); 95-48 Tech Asst (9);
Admin Plan: s1p2; s19p1; s23p2 (2); s24p2

NATIONAL AFFORDABLE HOUSING ACT.. 5
24 CFR 5: .100 (4);
PIH Notices: 01-27

NATIONAL FIRE PROTECTION ASSOCIATION 6
24 CFR 982: .401;
HUD-52580-A: p8;
7420.10G Gbk: 10-14;
PIH Notices: 99-11 (2); 99-11

NATIONAL HOUSING ACT.......... 10
24 CFR 5: .100 (2); .306; .500 (2); .504 (2); .516; .801;
PIH Notices: 01-27

NATIONAL ORIGIN 22
24 CFR 982: .202; .304;
HUD-52641: p5; p10;
HUD-52641-A: p3;
HUD-52646: p2;
HUD-903: p1 (2); p2 (3); p4;
7420.10G Gbk: 4-19; 5-11; 5-42 (3); 8-14; 11-13;
PIH Notices: 02-21; 01-15;
Admin Plan: s23p2

NATIONALITY.................................. 5
24 CFR 5: .508; .518 (3); .630

NATIONALS 3
24 CFR 5: .508;
HUD-50058: p v;
HUD-50058Instr: p17

NATION'S 1
PIH Notices: 00-11

NATIONWIDE 1
7420.10G Gbk: 22-4

NATIVE AMERICAN 28
HUD-50058Instr: p74;
7420.10G Gbk: 2-13 Ex 2-1;
PIH Notices: 02-03; 02-01 (4); 01-27; 01-11; 00-53; 00-45; 00-41; 00-28; 00-14; 00-01 (3); 99-52 (4); 99-11; 98-66; 96-65 (3); 95-48; 95-48

NATIVE AMERICANS....................2
HUD-50058Instr: p74;
PIH Notices: 02-01
NATURAL GAS.............................19
24 CFR 5: .703;
HUD-52517: p1 (3);
HUD-52641: p2 (3);
HUD-52667: p1 (3); p i (2); p ii;
7420.10G Gbk: 18-4; 18-5; 18-8 (3);
Admin Plan: s10p4
NATURALIZATION SERVICE........5
24 CFR 5: .504;
HUD-50058Instr: p3; p73;
7420.10G Gbk: 5-3; 16-3
NAVY..1
PIH Notices: 01-15 Impr Integ Hbk
NAZI..5
24 CFR 5: .609;
HUD-50058Instr: p31;
7420.10G Gbk: 5-15 Ex 5-2;
PIH Notices: 01-15 Impr Integ Hbk; 01-15 Impr Integ Hbk
NEAR-ELDERLY..............................7
24 CFR 5: .403 (3);
24 CFR 982: .316;
HUD-50058Instr: p72; p73;
Admin Plan: s2p3
NECESSARY................................326
24 CFR 5: .214; .216 (2); .230; .234; .236 (2); .318 (3); .350; .360; .403; .518; .603 (8); .609; .611 (2); .653; .659 (2);
24 CFR 982: .152 (3); .316; .355; .401 (2); .503; .516 (2); .517 (2); .520; .551; .553; .609; .614; .619; .625; .631;
HUD-50058Instr: p7 (2); p13; p15 (2); p22; p34; p36; p70 (2); p71 (3); p73 (2); p74; p76;
HUD-52580-A: p1 (3); p3; p5 (2); p7 (2); p9 (2); p10 (2); p11 (2); p12 (2); p14 (2); p15; p16; p18;
HUD-52641: p3; p10;
HUD-52641-A: p3;
HUD-52646: p2 (2);
HUD-52667: p i;
7420.10G Gbk: 1-8; 1-14; 2-3; 4-15 (2); 4-18; 4-20; 4-27 Ex 4-2; 5-13; 5-16 Ex 5-2; 5-22; 5-25 Ex 5-3; 5-29 (2); 5-30; 5-36 Ex 5-4; 5-43 (2); 5-51 Ex 5-5; 5-52 Ex 5-5 (3); 7-3; 7-4; 8-10; 8-11; 8-22; 9-4; 9-8; 9-12; 10-1; 10-2; 10-5; 10-17; 10-22; 10-26; 10-27; 10-30; 10-40 Ex 10-4a; 10-48 Ex 10-10; 11-9; 11-12; 11-19; 12-16 Ex 12-4; 13-6; 13-8; 14-2; 15-9 Ex 15-1; 17-10; 18-1 (2); 18-4; 18-9; 19-4; 20-7; 20-8 Ex 20-1; 20-19 Ex 20-3; 20-28; 21-2; 21-3 (2); 21-4; 21-6; 21-7; 21-8; 21-10 (2); 21-11; 22-4; 22-5; 22-9; 22-17 (2); 23-9 (5); 24-7; 24-10;
PIH Notices: 03-23 (2); 03-12; 03-11 (3); 02-27 (5); 02-21; 02-20 (3); 02-06; 02-01 (9); 01-41 (4); 01-20; 01-15 (4); 01-15 Impr Integ Hbk (8); 01-11; 01-10 (2); 01-06 (5); 01-01; 00-53; 00-46 (3); 00-34 (2); 00-27; 00-24B (3); 00-11; 00-11A (2); 00-09 (8); 99-52 (9); 99-11; 96-65; 95-48 (25); 95-48 Tech Asst (25);
Admin Plan: s3p1; s3p3; s5p2; s6p2; s6p3; s6p4; s6p13; s7p6; s7p7; s8p1; s11p1 (2); s19p1; s20p1; s21p6; s21p9; s23p5; s24p3; s24p4; s24p5; s25p4
NEED..214
24 CFR 5: .603; .609; .628; .653; .703;
24 CFR 982: .614;
HUD-50058: p16; p xvi;
HUD-50058Instr: p1; p28; p60 (2); p61 (13); p76;
HUD-52580-A: p1; p6;
HUD-903-1: p3;
HUD-9886: p1;
7420.10G Gbk: 1-2; 1-8; 2-1; 3-3; 4-1; 4-2 (6); 4-3; 4-6 (3); 4-8; 4-14; 4-17; 4-20; 4-21; 4-25 Ex 4-2; 5-6; 5-12; 5-14 Ex 5-2; 5-22; 5-28; 6-3; 7-1; 7-5; 7-7; 9-4; 9-10 (2); 10-2; 10-22; 10-24; 10-33; 10-46 Ex 10-8; 12-10; 13-1 (2); 13-2 (3); 13-5 (2); 17-1; 18-4; 19-5; 19-9 (2); 19-11 (2); 19-12;

19-13; 20-14; 20-17 (2); 20-19 Ex 20-3; 20-20 (2); 20-21; 21-2; 21-6 (2); 21-10; 22-5; 22-8; 23-7; 23-20; 24-1 (3); 24-3 (2); 24-4; 24-6 (2); 24-12 (2);
PIH Notices: 03-23 (3); 03-20 (2); 03-12; 03-11 (2); 03-05; 02-27 (24); 02-21; 02-20 (2); 02-06; 02-01 (9); 01-40; 01-15 (5); 01-15 Impr Integ Hbk (2); 01-06 (6); 00-46 (2); 00-41; 00-11A; 99-52 (9); 99-11; 95-48 (11); 95-48 Tech Asst (9);
Admin Plan: s1p3; s1p5; s1p6; s3p1; s4p2; s8p1; s11p2; s18p4; s19p1; s20p1

NEEDED......................................202
24 CFR 5: .508 (4); .609;
24 CFR 982: .54; .155; .158; .308; .316; .401; .402 (2); .405; .503; .517; .601; .606; .610; .615; .619; .620; .625; .627 (2); .633; .635 (4);
HUD-50058Instr: p28; p61; p63 (7);
HUD-52580: p1 (2); p2; p15;
HUD-52641: p3 (2); p5; p9;
HUD-52641-A: p1 (3);
HUD-52667: p i;
HUD-903: p1;
7420.10G Gbk: 1-8; 2-9; 2-11; 3-4; 3-5; 4-1; 4-4; 4-7; 4-14; 4-21; 5-15 Ex 5-2; 5-41 (3); 7-3; 7-4; 7-6 (2); 7-7 (2); 8-1; 8-6; 8-12; 8-15; 9-6; 9-8 (3); 9-10; 9-14 Ex 9-1 (2); 9-16 Ex 9-2 (2); 10-22; 10-24; 10-43 Ex 10-6; 11-12; 11-16 Ex 11-1; 17-1; 17-3; 17-4; 18-8; 18-9; 19-7; 19-8; 19-9; 19-13; 20-2; 20-20; 20-23 (2); 20-27; 20-29; 21-5; 21-19; 23-10; 23-15; 24-4; 24-7 (2); 24-8;
PIH Notices: 03-23 (5); 02-27 (15); 02-21 (3); 02-20 (4); 02-01 (5); 01-41; 01-20 (3); 01-15 (2); 01-15 Impr Integ Hbk (2); 01-06 (4); 00-46 (4); 00-27; 00-11 (2); 00-09 (2); 00-01; 99-52 (6); 99-11 (2); 98-66; 95-48 (3); 95-48 Tech Asst (3);
Admin Plan: s1p6; s2p1; s2p3; s3p3; s6p2; s7p2; s7p3; s8p2 (2); s11p3; s15p4; s15p6; s19p1 (3); s25p4 (2); s25p5; s25p6; s25p8

NEEDIEST 1
7420.10G Gbk: 5-2

NEEDING......................................13
7420.10G Gbk: 2-5; 10-41 Ex 10-4b; 10-44 Ex 10-7a; 19-13; 24-10;
PIH Notices: 02-01 (4); 99-52 (3); 99-52

NEEDS...191
24 CFR 5: .236; .318;
24 CFR 982: .201; .207 (2); .303; .625; .630;
HUD-50058: p i; p16; p xvi (3); p17;
HUD-50058Instr: p16 (2); p28 (3); p60; p61 (3); p63 (3); p72;
HUD-52580: p6 (4);
HUD-52580-A: p4 (2); p19 (4);
HUD-52641: p1;
7420.10G Gbk: 2-8; 3-1 (2); 3-6; 3-7 (4); 4-1; 4-2 (2); 4-4; 4-8; 4-9 (2); 4-11; 4-12; 4-13; 4-15; 4-16 (3); 4-17; 4-18; 4-20; 4-25 Ex 4-2; 5-3; 5-6; 5-21 (2); 7-9; 8-1 (2); 8-8 (2); 8-9 (2); 8-17; 9-5; 10-5 (2); 10-11; 10-43 Ex 10-6; 10-45 Ex 10-7b; 11-7; 12-5; 12-6; 12-12 Ex 12-1; 13-7; 13-8 (2); 17-1; 19-5; 19-6; 19-10 (2); 19-11; 19-12 (2); 19-13; 20-1 (2); 20-6; 20-17 (2); 21-8 (3); 21-9; 23-4; 23-5 (2); 23-13; 23-14; 23-15 (3); 23-20; 24-3 (2); 24-4; 24-7; 24-9; 24-13 (2);
PIH Notices: 03-23 (7); 03-20 (2); 03-05; 02-27 (4); 02-21 (2); 02-20; 02-06; 02-01 (11); 01-40; 01-20 (2); 01-15; 01-10; 00-46; 00-27 (2); 00-24B (2); 00-11 (2); 00-11A; 00-09; 99-52 (9); 95-48 (3); 95-48 Tech Asst (3);
Admin Plan: s1p1; s1p3; s1p5; s2p2; s3p2; s8p1 (2); s17p1; s19p1; s25p8

NEEDS ASSESSMENTS 10
PIH Notices: 02-01 (5); 99-52 (4); 99-52

NEEDY 17
24 CFR 5: .603; .609; .617 (2);
HUD-50058: p i;
HUD-50058Instr: p3; p28;
7420.10G Gbk: 4-1; 12-4; 22-4; 24-9;
PIH Notices: 01-15 Impr Integ Hbk (3); 00-11 (2); 00-11A

NEEDY FAMILIES 17
24 CFR 5: .603; .609; .617 (2);
HUD-50058: p i;
HUD-50058Instr: p3; p28;
7420.10G Gbk: 4-1; 12-4; 22-4; 24-9;
PIH Notices: 01-15 Impr Integ Hbk (3); 00-11 (2); 00-11A

NEGATIVE 71
HUD-50058: p7 (3); p vii (3); p9 (2); p10 (3); p x; p11 (2); p xi; p12 (4); p xii (2);
HUD-50058Instr: p3 (2); p35 (6); p39 (2); p41 (2); p43 (2); p45 (4); p49 (6); p51 (4); p52 (4); p54; p65; p66 (2); p68 (2); p69 (3);
7420.10G Gbk: 4-10; 20-13; 22-8; 23-10; 23-17 Ex 23-2 (3); 24-9;
PIH Notices: 00-23

NEGLIGENT 1
HUD-9886: p2

NEGOTIATE 13
24 CFR 982: .352; .355; .506 (2); .630;
HUD-52580-A: p1;
7420.10G Gbk: 8-3;
PIH Notices: 95-48; 95-48 Tech Asst;
Admin Plan: s1p4; s9p2; s11p3; s25p5

NEGOTIATED 3
PIH Notices: 02-27 (2); 02-06

NEGOTIATING 5
24 CFR 982: Intro; .506;
7420.10G Gbk: 2-11; 21-4;
Admin Plan: s8p4

NEGOTIATIONS 3
7420.10G Gbk: 8-18;
Admin Plan: s10p2; s25p8

NEIGHBOR 1
PIH Notices: 99-11

NEIGHBORHOOD 56
24 CFR 5: .801;
24 CFR 982: .401 (3); .614 (4);
HUD-52580: p1; p5;
HUD-52580-A: p1; p17; p18 (2);
7420.10G Gbk: 2-6 (3); 2-7 (3); 2-8; 2-10; 4-3; 8-14; 9-3; 9-4; 9-6; 9-10; 9-14 Ex 9-1 (2); 9-16 Ex 9-2; 9-17 Ex 9-3; 9-19 Ex 9-4; 10-1; 10-13 (6); 10-33; 10-47 Ex 10-9; 17-5 (2); 17-9; 22-10; 24-11;
PIH Notices: 02-01; 00-01; 99-52; 98-66;
Admin Plan: s15p5; s23p1; s24p1; s24p3; s25p7

NEIGHBORHOODS 47
HUD-52648: p1;
HUD-903-1: p2;
7420.10G Gbk: 1-2; 2-1 (7); 2-2 (3); 2-6; 2-7 (4); 2-8 (2); 2-13 Ex 2-1; 7-1; 7-3; 7-5; 8-4; 8-12; 8-14; 10-32; 13-1 (2); 13-10; 21-6; 21-10; 24-9;
PIH Notices: 02-21 (4); 02-01; 01-20 (3); 99-52;
Admin Plan: s1p7; s21p5; s25p6; s25p6

NEIGHBORING 21
HUD-52648: p2 (2);
HUD-52667: p i (2);
7420.10G Gbk: 2-1; 2-3; 2-6; 2-8 (2); 8-7; 10-31; 11-3 (2); 13-1; 13-4; 13-10; 18-4; 23-4;
PIH Notices: 01-41; 00-09;
Admin Plan: s21p6

NEIGHBORS 20
24 CFR 982: .310; .312; .553;
HUD-52641: p9;
HUD-52641-A: p2;
7420.10G Gbk: 2-10; 4-3; 11-4; 15-2; 15-6;
PIH Notices: 02-01 (2); 99-52 (2);
Admin Plan: s6p6; s6p7; s8p3; s15p4; s20p4; s20p4

NEIGHBORS' 3
7420.10G Gbk: 8-20 (2); 11-4

NET CASH VALUE 2
24 CFR 5: .603;
HUD-50058Instr: p74

NET FAMILY 2
HUD-50058: p xv;
HUD-50058Instr: p58

NET FAMILY ASSETS 16
24 CFR 5: .603 (2); .609 (2);

HUD-50058Instr: p74;
7420.10G Gbk: 4-27 Ex 4-2; 5-14 Ex 5-2 (2); 5-24; 5-49 Ex 5-5; 12-16 Ex 12-4;
PIH Notices: 01-15 Impr Integ Hbk (4); 01-15 Impr Integ Hbk

NET INCOME 25
24 CFR 5: .609 (4);
HUD-50058Instr: p25 (2);
7420.10G Gbk: 5-14 Ex 5-2 (4); 5-19 (2); 5-48 Ex 5-5; 23-12;
PIH Notices: 01-15 Impr Integ Hbk (8);
Admin Plan: s7p5 (2); s7p6

NEUTERED 1
24 CFR 5: .318

NEW CONSTRUCTION 66
24 CFR 5: .801 (2);
7420.10G Gbk: 8-16; 21-13;
PIH Notices: 02-01 (6); 01-41; 01-10; 00-09; 99-52 (6); 95-48 (19); 95-48 Tech Asst (17);
Admin Plan: s22p3; s24p1 (2); s24p3 (2); s24p4; s24p5 (4); s24p5

NEW EMPLOYEES 1
7420.10G Gbk: 22-6

NEW EMPLOYMENT 3
24 CFR 5: .617;
PIH Notices: 01-15 Impr Integ Hbk;
Admin Plan: s6p2

NEW EMPLOYMENT INCOME 2
7420.10G Gbk: 5-22; 5-22

NEW HEAD OF HOUSEHOLD 2
HUD-50058: p5;
HUD-50058Instr: p18

NEW OWNER 21
HUD-52641: p6 (9); p7 (2);
7420.10G Gbk: 1-9; 11-18 (6);
PIH Notices: 01-41; 00-09;
Admin Plan: s16p3

NEW OWNERS 5
7420.10G Gbk: 2-5; 2-6; 2-11; 9-6; 11-15

NEW OWNERSHIP 2
PIH Notices: 01-41; 00-09

NEW PROJECT BASED 1
Admin Plan: s24p1

NEW TENANCY 6
24 CFR 982: .306; .308;
HUD-52641: p10;
HUD-52641-A: p3;
7420.10G Gbk: 11-17;
Admin Plan: s15p5

NEWSPAPER 19
24 CFR 982: .206;
7420.10G Gbk: 2-5; 4-1; 4-3; 4-11; 4-14; 8-12; 8-24 Ex 8-1; 9-5 (2); 9-6 (3); 9-7; 9-8; 23-8 Ex 23-1;
Admin Plan: s1p6; s7p5; s24p2

NEWSPAPER QUOTATIONS 1
Admin Plan: s7p5

NEWSPAPERS 11
24 CFR 5: .518;
7420.10G Gbk: 4-3 (4); 9-5; 9-6 (2);
Admin Plan: s1p6; s4p2; s11p2

NFPA 24
24 CFR 982: .401 (3);
HUD-52580-A: p8 (3); p9; p10; p11; p12;
7420.10G Gbk: 10-14 (3);
PIH Notices: 99-11 (10); 99-11

NIGHTTIME RESIDENCE 6
HUD-50058Instr: p72 (2);
Admin Plan: s23p2 (2); s25p3; s25p3

NINE MONTHS 1
7420.10G Gbk: 5-17

NO HEAT 2
HUD-52580-A: p15;
Admin Plan: s10p4

NO INCOME 6
7420.10G Gbk: 4-26 Ex 4-2; 5-25 Ex 5-3; 12-13 Ex 12-1; 21-7; 23-14;
Admin Plan: s7p5

NO LONGER EXIST ....
2
24 CFR 982: .553;
PIH Notices: 03-11

NOFA 24
24 CFR 5: .100;
24 CFR 982: .4; .101 (3); .103 (3); .104 (4);
7420.10G Gbk: 1-5 (4); 1-6; 23-3;
PIH Notices: 02-01; 99-52 (4); 99-52

NOISE 5
24 CFR 5: .318;
24 CFR 982: .401; .614;
7420.10G Gbk: 10-13; 17-5

NOISES 3
24 CFR 982: .401; .614;
7420.10G Gbk: 10-13

NON-ACCESSIBLE 5
PIH Notices: 02-01 (2); 99-

52 (2); 99-52
NON-ACCESSIBLE UNIT 5
PIH Notices: 02-01 (2); 99-52 (2); 99-52
NON-CASH 2
7420.10G Gbk: 5-18;
Admin Plan: s6p9
NONCITIZEN 59
24 CFR 5: .500; .504; .508 (4); .522 (10); .630;
24 CFR 982: .201;
HUD-50058: p3 (2); p iii; p4 (2); p iv; p ix; p x; p xi; p xii; p xiii; p xiv (2);
HUD-50058Instr: p15 (2); p16; p18; p40 (3); p44 (3); p48 (3); p51 (3); p54 (3); p57 (3); p68; p69; p74;
7420.10G Gbk: 6-7; 6-8; 15-5
NON-CITIZEN 20
7420.10G Gbk: 5-4 (5); 5-5; 5-9 Ex 5-1 (4); 5-10 Ex 5-1 (5); 5-35;
Admin Plan: s2p3; s2p5 (2); s2p7
NON-CITIZEN RULE 4
7420.10G Gbk: 5-4; 5-9 Ex 5-1; 5-10 Ex 5-1;
Admin Plan: s2p3
NONCITIZEN STUDENT 7
24 CFR 5: .522 (6); .522
NONCITIZEN STUDENTS 2
24 CFR 5: .522; .522
NONCITIZENS 36
24 CFR 5: .403; .504 (2); .506; .508 (3); .512; .524;
24 CFR 982: .554; .555;
HUD-50058: p i; p5; p v (3); p ix; p x; p xi; p xii; p xiii; p xiv;
HUD-50058Instr: p3; p17 (3); p39; p40 (2); p44; p48; p51; p54; p57; p68; p68
NON-CITIZENS 10
7420.10G Gbk: 5-3; 5-4; 5-9 Ex 5-1; 5-10 Ex 5-1; 5-11 (2); 16-1 (2);
Admin Plan: s18p7; s18p8
NONCOMPLIANCE 26
24 CFR 5: .615;
HUD-50058Instr: p28; p75;
7420.10G Gbk: 5-21 (2); 8-21; 11-18;
PIH Notices: 02-27 (2); 02-21; 02-01; 01-20; 01-15 Impr Integ Hbk; 00-11 (2); 00-11A (5); 99-52;
Admin Plan: s6p12; s6p13; s7p3 (2); s11p3
NON-COMPLIANCE 29
24 CFR 982: .306;
HUD-52641: p6 (2);
7420.10G Gbk: 8-19; 10-29; 10-30; 11-3; 19-8; 23-10;
PIH Notices: 02-27 (2); 02-01 (2); 01-41 (3); 00-09; 99-52 (2);
Admin Plan: s10p1; s10p3; s15p6; s16p1; s20p1; s20p2; s20p5 (3); s20p5
NONDISCLOSURE 1
24 CFR 5: .236
NONDISCRIMINATION 27
24 CFR 5: .105 (2); .524 (2);
24 CFR 982: .310; .552;
HUD-50058Instr: p2;
PIH Notices: 02-15; 02-01; 01-15; 01-02; 99-52; 95-48 (7); 95-48 Tech Asst (5);
Admin Plan: s1p2 (2); s1p2
NON-DISCRIMINATION 18
24 CFR 5: .655;
7420.10G Gbk: 4-1; 4-2; 4-17; 5-42 (2);
PIH Notices: 02-21; 02-01 (5); 99-52 (5);
Admin Plan: s1p2
NONDISCRIMINATORY 6
PIH Notices: 02-01; 99-52; 95-48 (2); 95-48 Tech Asst; 95-48 Tech Asst
NON-EARNED 1
7420.10G Gbk: 5-18
NON-EARNED INCOME ....
1
7420.10G Gbk: 5-18
NON-ELDERLY 9
24 CFR 982: .352;
HUD-50058Instr: p74;
7420.10G Gbk: 1-7; 1-8 (5); 1-8
NON-ELDERLY DISABLED 1
HUD-50058Instr: p74
NON-ELECTRONIC 1
24 CFR 5: .801
NON-ENGLISH 3
7420.10G Gbk: 4-2;
Admin Plan: s1p5; s1p5
NON-EXERCISE 1
HUD-52641: p5
NON-INVOLVED 1
7420.10G Gbk: 15-6

NON-LIQUID ASSETS....................1
7420.10G Gbk: 5-49 Ex 5-5
NON-MINORITY.............................5
7420.10G Gbk: 23-4; 23-6;
PIH Notices: 02-21 (2); 02-21
NONPAYMENT 10
24 CFR 5: .630;
24 CFR 982: .310 (2);
HUD-52641: 8 (2);
HUD-52641-A: p1 (2);
PIH Notices: 00-41;
Admin Plan: s9p3; s15p5
NON-PAYMENT..............................2
24 CFR 5: .661;
24 CFR 982: .510
NON-PREFERENCE 1
7420.10G Gbk: 4-5
NONPRESCRIPTION.......................1
Admin Plan: s6p11
NON-PRESCRIPTION 1
7420.10G Gbk: 5-32
NONRECURRENT 1
HUD-50058Instr: p28
NONRECURRING............................8
24 CFR 5: .609;
HUD-50058Instr: p31;
7420.10G Gbk: 5-15 Ex 5-2; 23-15;
PIH Notices: 01-15 Impr Integ Hbk (2); 00-01; 98-66
NON-RENEWAL..............................7
7420.10G Gbk: 23-2;
PIH Notices: 02-06; 01-41 (2); 01-10; 00-09; 00-09
NONRESIDENT...............................1
24 CFR 982: .353
NON-RESIDENT 1
7420.10G Gbk: 13-2
NO-PET AREA................................1
24 CFR 5: .318
NO-PET AREAS 3
24 CFR 5: .318 (2); .318
NORMAL WEAR AND TEAR.........2
HUD-52641: p9;
HUD-52641-A: p2
NOT APPLICABLE 59
24 CFR 982: .310; .352; .622; .637 (2);
HUD-52580: p2 (3); p3 (3); p4 (2); p5 (2);
HUD-52580-A: p3; p5; p7; p9; p10; p11; p12; p14 (3); p17; p18 (2);
HUD-52648: p2 (2); p3;
HUD-903: p1;
7420.10G Gbk: 5-47 Ex 5-5; 5-48 Ex 5-5 (2);
PIH Notices: 02-21; 01-41 (2); 01-20; 01-06 (10); 00-27; 00-24B (6); 00-09 (2); 00-09
NOT CAUSE 2
PIH Notices: 02-01; 99-52
NOT CAUSED 2
24 CFR 982: .404;
HUD-52641: p3
NOT CHARGE OR ACCEPT 2
HUD-52641: 8;
HUD-52641-A: p1
NOT CONSTITUTE..........................4
HUD-52580-A: p8;
PIH Notices: 95-48; 95-48 Tech Asst;
Admin Plan: s8p4
NOT EXCEED...............................122
24 CFR 5: .318 (3); .508 (2); .518 (2); .603 (4); .611;
24 CFR 982: .305; .504; .507; .508; .520; .613; .617; .622; .642 (3); .643;
HUD-50058: p vii; p11 (2); p xi;
HUD-50058Instr: p18 (2); p25; p35; p36 (3); p48 (4); p70; p71; p73; p76;
HUD-52641: p4; p5; 8; p10;
HUD-52641-A: p1; p3;
HUD-52648: p2;
7420.10G Gbk: 5-1; 5-15 Ex 5-2; 5-29; 5-30; 6-2; 7-9; 8-16; 9-2; 11-12; 11-13; 17-7 (2); 17-9 (2); 17-12; 20-2 (2); 20-14; 20-18; 20-28; 23-11; 24-8;
PIH Notices: 03-23 (3); 03-05; 02-27 (2); 02-22 (2); 02-20; 01-41 (7); 01-40; 01-15; 01-15 Impr Integ Hbk (4); 01-06; 00-46; 00-24B; 00-09 (9); 00-01; 98-66;
Admin Plan: s2p4; s4p2; s6p4; s6p11; s8p4; s9p1 (2); s11p2; s19p1 (4); s21p7; s24p4
NOT EXCEEDING 11
24 CFR 5: .518;
7420.10G Gbk: 12-10; 20-14; 20-20;
PIH Notices: 02-27 (2); 02-20 (2); 01-15 Impr Integ Hbk; 00-46; 00-46
NOT FOR PROFIT............................2
Admin Plan: s23p2; s25p7
NOT LISTED....................................3

24 CFR 5: .514;
7420.10G Gbk: 4-25 Ex 4-2; 4-25 Ex 4-2

NOT RESPONSIBLE......................21
24 CFR 5: .508; .615;
24 CFR 982: .310; .404; .451;
HUD-52641: p3; 8; p9 (2);
HUD-52641-A: p1 (2); p2;
7420.10G Gbk: 6-6; 11-6 (2); 11-12; 11-13; 22-12;
PIH Notices: 00-24B; 00-23; 00-23

NOT RESTRICT...............................1
24 CFR 982: .601

NOT SUFFICIENT...........................9
24 CFR 982: .102; .313;
HUD-52641: p3; p10;
HUD-52641-A: p3;
7420.10G Gbk: 5-47 Ex 5-5; 8-4; 11-5;
Admin Plan: s7p6

NOT TERMINATE..........................16
24 CFR 982: .310 (5);
HUD-52641: 8;
HUD-52641-A: p1;
7420.10G Gbk: 10-27; 11-4; 15-1; 15-2; 15-3; 22-15; 23-10;
PIH Notices: 01-41;
Admin Plan: s14p1

NOTARIZED..................................18
7420.10G Gbk: 5-46 Ex 5-5 (2); 5-47 Ex 5-5 (4); 5-49 Ex 5-5; 5-51 Ex 5-5 (2); 12-4; 12-13 Ex 12-1; 22-4;
PIH Notices: 01-15;
Admin Plan: s7p4; s7p5 (2); s7p6; s16p3

NOTARIZED STATEMENT.............. 11
7420.10G Gbk: 5-46 Ex 5-5; 5-47 Ex 5-5 (4); 5-49 Ex 5-5; 5-51 Ex 5-5 (2); 12-4; 22-4;
Admin Plan: s7p5

NOTARIZED STATEMENTS...........2
7420.10G Gbk: 5-46 Ex 5-5;
PIH Notices: 01-15

NOT-FOR-PROFIT 1
HUD-50058Instr: p75

NOT-HISPANIC 2
7420.10G Gbk: 4-23 Ex 4-1; 4-25 Ex 4-2

NOTICE OF ACTION.......................1
Admin Plan: s7p4

NOTICE OF FUNDING...................4
24 CFR 5: .100;
24 CFR 982: .4;
PIH Notices: 02-01; 99-52

NOTICE OF FUNDING AVAILABILITY 6
24 CFR 5: .100;
24 CFR 982: .4;
7420.10G Gbk: 1-5; 23-3;
PIH Notices: 02-01; 99-52

NOTICE OF TERMINATION 10
24 CFR 982: .309;
7420.10G Gbk: 10-29; 10-30; 15-1; 15-7; 15-10 Ex 15-2;
Admin Plan: s11p1; s15p4; s15p6; s23p6

NOTICE PERIOD 1
24 CFR 5: .236

NOTICE TO VACATE 6
24 CFR 982: .310; .314;
HUD-52641: p9;
HUD-52641-A: p2;
Admin Plan: s13p1; s14p1

NOTICEABLE 1
24 CFR 982: .614

NOTICEABLY 1
HUD-52580-A: p15

NOTICED...1
PIH Notices: 01-06

NOTICES OF FUNDING AVAILABILITY 3
24 CFR 35 SubM: .1200;
24 CFR 982: .101;
PIH Notices: 00-27

NOTIFICATION...........................146
24 CFR 5: .508 (5); .512; .514 (4); .518 (3);
24 CFR 35 SubM: .1215; .1225 (3);
24 CFR 982: .626;
7420.10G Gbk: 1-11; 2-9 (2); 4-7 (2); 5-6; 5-8; 5-11; 5-36 Ex 5-4; 5-46 Ex 5-5; 5-47 Ex 5-5; 8-18; 10-15; 10-17; 10-18; 10-20 (3); 10-21; 10-22; 10-28; 10-29; 10-30; 12-1; 12-2 (3); 12-3; 12-6 (2); 12-10 (2); 15-3; 15-6; 15-7; 15-8; 20-2; 20-9; 21-9;
PIH Notices: 02-27 (11); 02-21 (8); 02-06 (2); 01-20 (10); 01-06 (9); 00-49 (2); 00-27 (9); 00-23; 00-11A; 00-01; 98-66; 96-65; 95-48; 95-48 Tech Asst;
Admin Plan: s3p2; s3p3 (3); s4p2; s6p4 (2); s6p7; s7p2 (2); s7p4; s8p1;

s8p2; s10p2 (2); s10p4; s11p1; s14p2 (2); s15p5; s18p2; s18p4 (2); s20p5; s20p7; s23p3; s23p4; s24p2; s24p3; s24p7; s25p1

NOTIFICATIONS..............................8
7420.10G Gbk: 2-9; 10-28; 19-2; 19-4;
PIH Notices: 02-01; 01-06; 99-52;
Admin Plan: s23p2

NOTIFIED......................................54
24 CFR 5: .508; .655;
24 CFR 35 SubM: .1225 (2);
24 CFR 982: .207;
HUD-52517: p2;
HUD-52641: p5; p6;
HUD-52646: p2;
HUD-52665: p3;
7420.10G Gbk: 4-14; 4-17; 4-19; 5-22; 10-25; 10-28; 10-29; 10-34; 10-37 Ex 10-2; 10-41 Ex 10-4b; 10-42 Ex 10-5; 10-43 Ex 10-6; 12-2; 12-10; 13-7;
PIH Notices: 03-23 (3); 02-27 (3); 02-21; 02-14; 01-27; 01-20; 00-49; 00-27;
Admin Plan: s2p5; s2p7; s3p2 (2); s3p3; s7p2; s9p2; s9p4; s10p3 (2); s10p4; s11p1; s18p1; s18p3; s18p6; s23p3; s23p4

NOTIFIES......................................11
HUD-52641: p9;
HUD-52641-A: p2;
7420.10G Gbk: 1-5; 10-21; 11-14; 21-4;
PIH Notices: 00-24B; 00-09;
Admin Plan: s15p5; s18p7; s23p7

NOTIFY.......................................153
24 CFR 5: .236; .350; .508; .514 (2); .518 (3); .632;
24 CFR 35 SubM: .1225;
24 CFR 982: .104 (2); .305 (2); .308; .309; .312; .314; .355 (2); .403 (2); .405; .514; .551 (3); .553; .554; .555 (2); .633 (2); .636;
HUD-52517: p2;
HUD-52641: p3; p4; p5; p10 (2);
HUD-52641-A: p2; p3;
HUD-52646: p2 (6);
7420.10G Gbk: 1-11; 4-2; 4-7; 4-14; 5-6; 5-9 Ex 5-1; 5-11; 5-46 Ex 5-5; 8-17; 8-18 (2); 10-17; 10-18; 10-20 (2); 10-21 (2); 10-22; 10-27 (2); 10-34; 10-40 Ex 10-4a; 10-43 Ex 10-6; 11-5; 11-12; 11-17; 11-18; 12-6; 13-8; 15-1; 15-4; 16-3; 16-5; 22-2; 22-13; 22-15;
PIH Notices: 03-11 (2); 02-27 (5); 02-21 (5); 02-20 (4); 02-14 (2); 02-07; 01-27 (3); 01-20 (5); 01-15 (4); 01-15 Impr Integ Hbk; 01-06 (3); 00-49 (3); 00-46 (4); 00-28; 00-27 (5); 00-24; 95-48 (2);
Admin Plan: s3p2; s4p2; s6p4; s6p6 (2); s7p2 (2); s11p3; s13p2; s18p4; s20p7 (2); s22p4 (2); s23p8; s24p5; s24p6; s24p7

NOTIFYING....................................10
24 CFR 5: .514;
7420.10G Gbk: 1-15 (2); 8-7; 10-19; 10-22; 10-27;
Admin Plan: s7p3; s11p1; s15p6

NOVEMBER..................................46
24 CFR 5: .216; .518 (4); .801 (2);
HUD-50058Instr: p18 (2);
7420.10G Gbk: 5-23 (2); 5-24; 9-2;
PIH Notices: 03-23 (2); 02-22 (2); 02-21; 02-14; 02-06; 01-41 (2); 01-40 (2); 01-27 (6); 01-10 (9); 01-06 (3); 01-01; 00-09 (2);
Admin Plan: s21p2

NUISANCE......................................3
24 CFR 5: .327 (2); .360

NUMBER OF BEDROOMS...........87
24 CFR 5: .100; .655;
24 CFR 982: .4 (3); .204; .402 (5); .403; .503; .517; .555; .617 (2); .618;
HUD-50058: p5; p v; p10; p x; p11; p xi; p13; p xiii;
HUD-50058Instr: p20 (4); p42 (2); p43 (2); p44 (2); p46 (2); p47 (4); p49 (2); p53 (2); p72; p75; p76;
HUD-52517: p1 (6); p i;
7420.10G Gbk: 3-4; 4-8; 5-41 (4); 8-15; 8-17; 9-5; 9-9 (2); 9-10 (3); 9-17 Ex 9-3; 9-19 Ex 9-4; 10-

24; 17-8 (3); 18-2;
PIH Notices: 02-20 (2); 00-46 (2);
Admin Plan: s5p1; s11p2; s19p1 (3); s23p3

NUMBER OF MOVES 2
24 CFR 982: .54; .54

NUMERATOR................................ 10
24 CFR 5: .520 (7);
24 CFR 982: .503;
PIH Notices: 02-20; 00-46

NURSING....................................... 31
24 CFR 5: .318 (2); .801;
24 CFR 982: .352 (2); .610;
7420.10G Gbk: 5-22; 8-16 (2); 12-16 Ex 12-4; 17-4; 23-16 Ex 23-2;
PIH Notices: 00-41 (4); 95-48 (4); 95-48 Tech Asst (4);
Admin Plan: s6p5; s6p6; s6p8 (2); s19p1; s24p2; s24p2

NURSING HOME............................. 8
7420.10G Gbk: 5-22; 12-16 Ex 12-4;
PIH Notices: 95-48; 95-48 Tech Asst;
Admin Plan: s6p5; s6p6; s6p8; s6p8

NURSING HOMES.......................... 7
24 CFR 5: .801;
24 CFR 982: .352;
7420.10G Gbk: 8-16;
PIH Notices: 00-41; 95-48; 95-48 Tech Asst;
Admin Plan: s24p2

NURSING SERVICES 4
24 CFR 982: .352;
7420.10G Gbk: 8-16;
PIH Notices: 00-41;
Admin Plan: s24p2

OBJECT.. 4
PIH Notices: 95-48 (2); 95-48 Tech Asst; 95-48 Tech Asst

OBJECTIONS 4
24 CFR 982: .554;
7420.10G Gbk: 16-3;
Admin Plan: s18p3; s18p5

OBJECTIVE 29
24 CFR 5: .353;
24 CFR 982: .101; .102;
HUD-50058Instr: p75;
HUD-52667: p i;
7420.10G Gbk: 2-1; 4-2; 7-1; 9-8; 22-6 (4); 23-1; 23-6;
PIH Notices: 03-20; 02-27; 00-24B (5); 95-48; 95-48 Tech Asst;
Admin Plan: s4p1; s18p4; s20p2; s21p4; s25p4

OBJECTIVE EVIDENCE 2
PIH Notices: 95-48; 95-48 Tech Asst

OBJECTIVELY 1
Admin Plan: s21p1

OBJECTIVES.................................. 43
24 CFR 5: .609;
24 CFR 982: .201; .503;
HUD-50058Instr: p19;
7420.10G Gbk: 2-2 (4); 3-6; 3-7; 4-1; 4-2; 4-4 (3); 4-9; 4-12; 4-20; 5-15 Ex 5-2; 5-20; 7-7; 8-2 (2); 11-9; 22-7; 23-1; 23-9;
PIH Notices: 02-27 (4); 02-20; 01-15 Impr Integ Hbk (3); 00-24B;
Admin Plan: s1p1; s1p2; s8p1; s9p1; s22p2; s23p1; s25p7

OBJECTIVITY 2
7420.10G Gbk: 5-1;
Admin Plan: s2p1

OBJECTS... 4
PIH Notices: 95-48 (2); 95-48 Tech Asst; 95-48 Tech Asst

OBLIGATION 74
24 CFR 5: .318; .659;
24 CFR 982: .53; .201; .404 (2); .453 (3); .553 (2);
HUD-50058Instr: p75;
HUD-52641: p5 (3);
HUD-52646: p1;
7420.10G Gbk: 3-8; 4-20; 5-12; 8-10; 11-17; 11-18; 12-3; 13-2; 17-1; 23-2; 23-12;
PIH Notices: 03-23 (3); 02-21; 02-01; 01-15 Impr Integ Hbk; 01-06 (3); 00-24B; 99-52; 95-48 (9); 95-48 Tech Asst (9);
Admin Plan: s1p5; s2p6; s6p1; s6p8; s7p2; s15p2 (2); s15p4 (2); s15p5; s15p6 (2); s18p4; s20p5 (2); s20p6 (2); s25p4

OBLIGATIONS............................ 168
24 CFR 5: .214; .318 (2); .321; .350 (2);
24 CFR 982: 24 CFR 982 (3); .4 (3); .201 (2); .301 (5); .306; .309 (2); .310; .353; .404 (2); .452 (2); .456; .521; .551 (2);

.552 (3); .619 (2); .625; .633 (8); .638 (2);
HUD-50058: p17 (3); p xvii;
HUD-50058Instr: p19 (2); p59; p62 (4); p63 (2); p76;
HUD-52641: p6; p9;
HUD-52641-A: p2 (2);
HUD-52648: p1;
7420.10G Gbk: 1-9; 1-12 Ex 1-2 (4); 1-15; 4-12; 4-20; 5-36; 5-36 Ex 5-4 (2); 8-6 (3); 8-8; 8-10 (2); 8-11 (4); 8-19; 10-33; 10-36 Ex 10-1; 11-3; 11-15 (2); 11-17; 15-1 (2); 15-5; 15-6; 15-8; 18-1; 22-9 (2); 23-2; 23-6 (2); 23-7; 23-10; 23-12; 23-14 (2); 23-18 (3); 24-13 (2);
PIH Notices: 02-01; 01-41 (3); 01-02; 00-24B (2); 00-09 (2); 99-52; 95-48 (8); 95-48 Tech Asst (8);
Admin Plan: s2p2; s6p8; s10p3; s13p2; s15p1; s15p3 (3); s15p4; s15p5; s15p6 (2); s16p1; s20p1; s20p6; s21p5 (2); s22p2; s22p4 (2); s22p5; s23p4; s23p5; s23p7; s25p5; s25p5

OBSOLETE....................................38
HUD-50058: p6; p xiii;
HUD-50058Instr: p53;
HUD-52580: p1; p2; p3; p4; p5; p6; p7;
HUD-52580-A: p1; p2; p3; p4; p5; p6; p7; p8; p9; p10; p11; p12; p13; p14; p15; p16; p17; p18; p19; p20;
HUD-52667: p1; p i; p ii;
PIH Notices: 02-22; 02-21; 01-20; 00-27; 00-23

OBSOLETE PROJECTS..................3
PIH Notices: 02-21; 01-20; 00-27

OCCUPANCIES...............................2
PIH Notices: 95-48; 95-48 Tech Asst

OCCUPANCY 245
24 CFR 5: .306 (3); .309; .312; .315; .508 (3); .514 (7); .516; .528; .601; .634; .653 (5); .655 (3); .659; .661 (9); .703 (2); .801 (2);
24 CFR 35 SubM: .1215 (2);
24 CFR 982: 24 CFR 982 (3); .1; .4 (3); .54; .204 (2); .305; .306; .310; .312; .352; .401; .405; .508 (2); .551; .601 (4); .606; .610; .615 (2); .617; .619 (5); .620; .625; .628; .633 (2); .635 (3); .637; .643;
HUD-50058: p i; p v; p xii (2); p xiv; p xv;
HUD-50058Instr: p3; p4; p9 (4); p18; p20 (2); p39; p42; p46; p50; p56; p58 (2); p73 (3); p74; p75;
HUD-52580: p1 (2);
HUD-52641: p3 (2); 8; p9;
HUD-52641-A: p1; p2;
HUD-903: p1; p2;
7420.10G Gbk: 1-8; 3-2; 3-3; 3-4; 4-1; 4-8; 4-18; 4-25 Ex 4-2; 5-6; 5-42; 5-43; 6-6 (2); 8-11; 8-13 (2); 8-19; 9-9 (2); 9-11; 9-14 Ex 9-1; 10-2; 10-17; 10-21; 11-2; 12-3; 12-5 (3); 12-16 Ex 12-4; 13-9; 14-1; 14-4; 15-1; 15-6; 15-10 Ex 15-2; 17-2; 17-3; 17-4 (2); 17-7; 17-8; 17-9; 17-10; 17-11; 20-3; 20-24; 21-4 (3); 21-5 (5); 21-10; 22-6;
PIH Notices: 02-07; 02-01 (4); 01-41; 01-27 (2); 01-15 (9); 01-15 Impr Integ Hbk (11); 00-49 (2); 00-24B (2); 00-23; 00-11; 00-09; 99-52 (4); 99-11; 95-48 (2);
Admin Plan: s5p3 (2); s9p2; s10p1; s10p5; s13p1; s19p1 (5); s20p2; s20p5; s23p1; s23p3 (2); s24p3; s24p5; s24p6; s24p7; s24p7

OCCUPANCY AGREEMENT........11
24 CFR 982: .619 (3); .635;
HUD-50058: p xv;
HUD-50058Instr: p9; p56; p58 (2); p74;
Admin Plan: s19p1

OCCUPANCY POLICIES.................4
24 CFR 982: .54;
7420.10G Gbk: 3-2;
PIH Notices: 01-15; 01-15 Impr Integ Hbk

OCCUPANCY POLICY....................2
24 CFR 982: .204;
7420.10G Gbk: 4-18

OCCUPANCY SPECIALIST............4
7420.10G Gbk: 21-4 (3); 21-5

OCCUPANCY SPECIALISTS..........5
7420.10G Gbk: 9-11; 21-5 (2);
PIH Notices: 01-15; 01-15

OCCUPANCY STAFF.......................2
7420.10G Gbk: 21-5;
Admin Plan: s20p2

OCCUPANCY STANDARDS...........4
24 CFR 982: .204;
7420.10G Gbk: 4-8;
PIH Notices: 02-01; 99-52

OCCUPANT...................................20
24 CFR 5: .508;
24 CFR 982: .551;
HUD-52580-A: p18;
HUD-52646: p2;
7420.10G Gbk: 17-1 (2); 17-2 (2); 17-3; 17-4; 17-5; 17-6 (2);
PIH Notices: 02-01 (2); 99-52 (2); 99-11 (2);
Admin Plan: s6p8

OCCUPANTS.................................38
24 CFR 5: .327; .360; .508;
24 CFR 35 SubM: .1215;
24 CFR 982: .4 (2); .401 (6);
HUD-50058Instr: p43; p44; p47 (2); p75;
HUD-52580-A: p6 (2);
7420.10G Gbk: 10-3; 10-4 (2); 10-8 (2); 10-9 (2); 10-10 10-13; 10-15; 10-17; 10-19 (2); 10-21; 10-37 Ex 10-2 (2); 17-7;
PIH Notices: 02-01; 99-52;
Admin Plan: s5p3

OCCUPANT'S....................................
4
7420.10G Gbk: 10-17; 10-21;
PIH Notices: 95-48; 95-48 Tech Asst

OCTOBER...................................107
24 CFR 5: .653 (4); .801;
24 CFR 982: .4 (2);
HUD-50058Instr: p16; p27; p48 (2); p73;
7420.10G Gbk: 1-1; 1-4 (3); 1-5 (2); 5-23; 7-2 (2); 9-2; 10-7; 14-1 (4); 14-3; 14-5; 20-8 Ex 20-1 (8); 20-11 (2); 20-12 Ex 20-2; 22-16; 22-17 (2); 23-1 (2); 23-2;
PIH Notices: 03-23 (6); 02-27; 02-21 (2); 02-20 (3); 02-07 (2); 01-41 (2); 01-33; 01-20 (2); 01-15 Impr Integ Hbk (2); 01-10 (4); 01-06 (3); 01-01 (3); 00-49 (2); 00-46; 00-41; 00-34; 00-28 (2); 00-27 (2); 00-24A; 00-11; 00-09 (11); 99-11 (2);
Admin Plan: s21p1; s21p2; s22p1;

OFFENSIVE......................................2
PIH Notices: 95-48; 95-48 Tech Asst

OFFER OF A NEW LEASE..............5
24 CFR 982: .310 (2);
HUD-52641: p9;
HUD-52641-A: p2;
7420.10G Gbk: 15-3

OFFICE SPACE.................................1
7420.10G Gbk: 21-6

OFFICER..48
24 CFR 5: .216; .514; .661 (3);
24 CFR 982: .161; .553; .555;
HUD-50058Instr: p74 (4); p75;
HUD-52641: p6;
HUD-9886: p2;
7420.10G Gbk: 2-5; 5-10 Ex 5-1 (2); 8-19; 11-2; 11-3; 12-13 Ex 12-1; 16-5; 20-10; 21-14 Ex 21-4 (2); 23-4;
PIH Notices: 03-11; 02-27 (6); 02-14; 01-15; 95-48 (2); 95-48 Tech Asst (2);
Admin Plan: s7p7; s18p3; s18p5; s18p6 (4); s18p7

OFFICERS......................................10
HUD-50058Instr: p39; p50; p74;
7420.10G Gbk: 16-4;
PIH Notices: 03-11; 02-27; 01-15; 01-11; 00-53;
Admin Plan: s18p6

OFFICER'S 1
Admin Plan: s18p7

OFFICES 123
24 CFR 982: .3 (2); .101; .158; .555;
HUD-50058Instr: p3;
HUD-903: p2;
7420.10G Gbk: 1-8; 2-11; 4-3 (2); 4-11; 9-6; 10-8; 16-4; 20-2; 21-5; 21-6 (2); 23-3;
PIH Notices: 02-27 (12); 02-21 (7); 02-03; 02-01 (6); 01-41; 01-20 (5); 01-15; 01-15 Impr Integ Hbk (2); 01-06 (24); 01-02; 01-01; 00-53; 00-45; 00-34 (4); 00-27 (6); 00-24 (2); 00-24A (4); 00-14; 00-11;

00-09 (3); 99-52 (6); 99-11; 96-65 (3); 95-48; 95-48 Tech Asst;
Admin Plan: s1p3 (2); s1p5; s3p1 (2); s3p3; s11p2

OFFICIAL......26
24 CFR 5: .216 (2); .526;
24 CFR 982: .161;
HUD-50058Instr: p15; p61; p70;
HUD-52646: p1 (3); p2;
7420.10G Gbk: 3-1; 4-24 Ex 4-1; 4-25 Ex 4-2; 5-18; 5-50 Ex 5-5; 12-3;
PIH Notices: 01-15 Impr Integ Hbk; 01-06; 00-11A; 95-48 (2); 95-48 Tech Asst (2);
Admin Plan: s7p5; s15p6

OFFICIALLY......1
PIH Notices: 00-24

OFFICIALS......23
24 CFR 5: .216; .218; .526 (3);
24 CFR 982: .54 (2); .155;
7420.10G Gbk: 3-6; 10-12; 10-14; 23-3 (2);
PIH Notices: 99-11 (9); 99-11

OFF-SITE......2
7420.10G Gbk: 4-13; 22-7

OIL......29
24 CFR 982: .401;
HUD-52517: p1 (3);
HUD-52580-A: p15 (2);
HUD-52641: p2 (3);
HUD-52667: p1 (3); p i; p ii (2);
7420.10G Gbk: 9-14 Ex 9-1; 9-15 Ex 9-2; 10-7 (4); 18-4; 18-5; 18-8 (3); 18-9 (2); 18-9

OLDER AMERICANS ACT......3
HUD-50058Instr: p32;
7420.10G Gbk: 5-16 Ex 5-2;
PIH Notices: 01-15 Impr Integ Hbk

OMISSION......13
7420.10G Gbk: 22-1 (3); 22-3; 22-12 (6);
Admin Plan: s11p2; s17p2; s20p6

OMISSIONS......22
7420.10G Gbk: 1-9; 11-9; 22-1 (4); 22-2 (2); 22-3 (3); 22-5 (2); 22-6; 22-7 (2); 22-9; 22-11; 22-18;
PIH Notices: 01-41; 01-15 Impr Integ Hbk; 00-09

ONE HALF......1
7420.10G Gbk: 17-2

ONE MONTH......25
HUD-50058Instr: p9; p10;
7420.10G Gbk: 20-3; 22-13;
PIH Notices: 03-23 (7); 02-06 (13); 02-06

ONE MONTH'S......2
24 CFR 5: .318;
Admin Plan: s23p5

ONE MONTH'S RENT......1
24 CFR 5: .318

ONE UNIT......10
HUD-50058Instr: p9;
7420.10G Gbk: 13-2; 20-3; 24-1 (2); 24-2 (2);
PIH Notices: 02-01; 99-52; 99-52

ONE WEEK......1
Admin Plan: s7p3

ONE YEAR......51
24 CFR 5: .508;
24 CFR 982: .161; .309 (2); .314; .637;
HUD-50058Instr: p47;
HUD-52641: p1; p6;
HUD-52648: p2;
HUD-903-1: p3 (2);
7420.10G Gbk: 5-37; 8-19; 8-22 (2); 9-1; 9-2; 11-2; 11-15; 20-6; 20-7; 24-2 (3); 24-12;
PIH Notices: 02-27; 02-22; 01-41 (3); 01-06; 00-09 (7); 95-48 (2); 95-48 Tech Asst (2);
Admin Plan: s2p2; s8p3; s13p2; s17p1; s22p1; s24p6; s25p5; s25p6

ONE-BEDROOM......9
24 CFR 982: .402; .503; .608;
7420.10G Gbk: 2-13 Ex 2-1; 5-3; 5-41 (2); 12-7; 12-7

ONE-FOR-ONE......4
PIH Notices: 01-41 (3); 00-09

ONE-FOR-ONE REPLACEMENT...4
PIH Notices: 01-41 (3); 00-09

ONE-FOURTH......1
7420.10G Gbk: 2-13 Ex 2-1

ONE-HALF......2
24 CFR 982: .605;
PIH Notices: 01-15 Impr Integ Hbk

ONE-SIXTH......2
7420.10G Gbk: 20-13; 20-15

ONE-TIME......8
24 CFR 5: .508; .617;
24 CFR 982: .152; .520; .643;

7420.10G Gbk: 20-3;
PIH Notices: 01-15 Impr Integ Hbk;
Admin Plan: s6p3

ONE-TIME COSTS..........................1
7420.10G Gbk: 20-3

ONE-UNIT..1
24 CFR 982: .628

ONE-YEAR.......................................4
24 CFR 982: .102;
7420.10G Gbk: 20-7;
PIH Notices: 01-20; 00-27

ON-HAND...1
7420.10G Gbk: 20-1

ONLY RESIDENCE..........................8
24 CFR 982: .551;
HUD-52641: p5; 8;
HUD-52641-A: p1;
HUD-52646: p2;
7420.10G Gbk: 1-15; 5-36 Ex 5-4; 11-13

ON-SITE...58
24 CFR 35 SubM: .1200;
7420.10G Gbk: 1-11; 4-12; 9-5; 9-14 Ex 9-1; 9-16 Ex 9-2; 9-17 Ex 9-3 (2); 10-20;
PIH Notices: 02-27 (43); 01-15 Impr Integ Hbk; 01-06 (2); 00-24; 00-11A; 00-11A

OPEN..38
24 CFR 982: .205 (2); .206 (2); .605;
HUD-52580-A: p2; p15 (3); p17;
7420.10G Gbk: 4-1 (4); 4-8 (2); 4-11 (2); 5-44; 10-5; 10-10; 10-19; 17-2; 23-1 (2);
PIH Notices: 02-27 (2); 01-27; 95-48 (5); 95-48 Tech Asst (4); 95-48 Tech Asst

OPEN SPACE...................................2
24 CFR 982: .605;
7420.10G Gbk: 17-2

OPERATE.......................................45
24 CFR 982: .625 (2);
HUD-52648: p2;
7420.10G Gbk: 1-1; 2-3; 2-6; 3-1; 3-7; 3-8; 4-13; 4-20; 8-1; 9-6; 10-10; 11-9; 21-1 (2); 21-3; 23-2 (2); 23-3 (2);
PIH Notices: 02-20; 02-01 (2); 01-15; 01-11; 01-06; 00-53 (2); 00-46; 00-24B; 99-52 (2); 95-48 (5); 95-48 Tech Asst (5);
Admin Plan: s21p6

OPERATED...................................20
HUD-50058Instr: p9; p72;
7420.10G Gbk: 5-20; 5-43 (2); 10-19;
PIH Notices: 01-15; 01-06 (2); 99-11 (3); 95-48 (3); 95-48 Tech Asst (3);
Admin Plan: s23p2; s25p7

OPERATES.......................................7
HUD-52580-A: p15;
7420.10G Gbk: 3-1;
PIH Notices: 95-48 (2); 95-48 Tech Asst (2);
Admin Plan: s13p2

OPERATING.................................112
24 CFR 5: .100; .703;
24 CFR 982: .152; .401 (11); .605 (3); .614 (3); .619; .635;
HUD-50058Instr: p5; p71; p75;
HUD-52580-A: p6 (2);
HUD-52648: p3 (3); p4 (10);
7420.10G Gbk: 3-2; 4-8; 10-3 (4); 10-5 (2); 10-7 (2); 10-8 (4); 10-14 (2); 10-19; 13-1; 13-4; 17-2; 17-10; 20-2 (2); 20-27 (2); 20-29 (3); 21-1; 21-18; 22-5 (2); 22-7;
PIH Notices: 02-27; 02-14; 02-01 (3); 01-06 (13); 00-24B (5); 00-11; 99-52 (3); 99-11; 95-48 (3); 95-48 Tech Asst (3);
Admin Plan: s7p6; s19p1; s21p8; s21p9; s25p6

OPERATING RESERVE..................1
7420.10G Gbk: 20-29

OPERATING RESERVES................2
PIH Notices: 02-01; 99-52

OPERATING STATEMENT.............9
7420.10G Gbk: 20-8 Ex 20-1; 20-26; 20-27; 20-28; 20-29; 20-30;
PIH Notices: 01-06; 00-24B;
Admin Plan: s21p8

OPERATION..................................84
24 CFR 5: .100; .609 (3);
24 CFR 982: .53 (2); .633;
HUD-50058Instr: p25 (4); p56; p60; p72; p73 (2); p75;
7420.10G Gbk: 2-10; 3-1; 3-6; 3-7; 5-14 Ex 5-2 (3); 5-19; 5-25 Ex 5-3; 9-12; 10-6; 19-3; 21-19; 23-3; 23-4; 23-10; 23-12; 23-13;
PIH Notices: 02-27; 01-40 (9); 01-15 Impr Integ Hbk (6);

01-06 (3); 00-53; 99-11 (4); 95-48 (10); 95-48 Tech Asst (10);
Admin Plan: s1p2; s2p2; s25p4 (2); s25p4

OPERATION OF LAW 3
24 CFR 982: .633;
7420.10G Gbk: 23-10;
Admin Plan: s2p2

OPERATIONAL 7
7420.10G Gbk: 3-6;
PIH Notices: 02-27; 99-11 (3);
Admin Plan: s21p9; s23p1

OPERATIONS 47
24 CFR 35 SubM: .1220;
7420.10G Gbk: 1-10; 1-15; 2-4; 9-1; 10-37 Ex 10-2; 13-4; 19-1; 19-3; 19-6 (2); 20-10; 21-13; 21-20; 22-3;
PIH Notices: 03-20; 02-27 (8); 02-22; 02-06; 02-01; 01-06 (7); 00-01; 99-52; 98-66; 96-65; 95-48 (4); 95-48 Tech Asst (4);
Admin Plan: s9p1

OPERATOR......................................2
PIH Notices: 95-48; 95-48 Tech Asst

OPERATORS...................................7
7420.10G Gbk: 2-13 Ex 2-1;
PIH Notices: 02-01; 99-52; 95-48 (2); 95-48 Tech Asst; 95-48 Tech Asst

OPERATOR'S 2
PIH Notices: 95-48; 95-48 Tech Asst

OPPORTUNITY TO EXPLAIN.......... 2
Admin Plan: s2p1; s20p7

OPPOSITE SEX 3
24 CFR 982: .401;
7420.10G Gbk: 10-6;
Admin Plan: s5p1

OPT 14
24 CFR 982: .307; .503 (2);
7420.10G Gbk: 3-3; 4-14 (2); 4-15; 8-21; 11-3; 11-15; 23-10;
PIH Notices: 02-20 (2);
Admin Plan: s8p3

OPT OUT...2
7420.10G Gbk: 1-9; 1-9

OPTING OUT...................................1
PIH Notices: 01-41

OPTION.......................................154
24 CFR 5: .518; .801;
24 CFR 982: 24 CFR 982 (19); .4 (12); .307; .601 (3); .619; .624; .625 (5); .626; .627 (3); .628; .629; .630 (3); .631 (3); .632 (2); .633 (3); .634; .635 (4); .636 (3); .637 (3); .638; .639; .641 (10); .642 (4); .643;
HUD-50058Instr: p12; p58; p74;
7420.10G Gbk: 1-9; 3-5; 4-12 (2); 5-23; 5-24 (2); 6-1; 7-7; 11-8; 11-10; 12-2; 13-5; 14-1; 14-2; 17-1; 21-7; 22-13; 23-2 (2); 23-15; 23-18; 24-14;
PIH Notices: 03-20 (16); 02-22; 01-41; 01-15 Impr Integ Hbk (5); 01-10; 00-53 (2); 00-24B; 00-09; 95-48 (2); 95-48 Tech Asst (2);
Admin Plan: s9p2; s9p3; s13p2; s18p3; s18p7; s22p1; s24p1

OPTIONAL.....................................38
HUD-50058: p16;
HUD-50058Instr: p34; p60; p77 (16);
HUD-52580: p6 (3); p7;
HUD-52580-A: p19 (3); p20;
HUD-52648: p3;
7420.10G Gbk: 2-4; 7-10; 10-48 Ex 10-10; 23-5; 23-14; 23-16 Ex 23-2 (2);
PIH Notices: 00-11; 95-48; 95-48 Tech Asst

OPTIONS..21
24 CFR 982: .625;
HUD-50058Instr: p16;
7420.10G Gbk: 1-4; 4-12; 6-1; 7-2; 8-23; 9-4; 10-3; 10-20; 11-8; 17-1; 19-5; 21-7;
PIH Notices: 03-11; 02-01; 01-15 Impr Integ Hbk (2); 00-53; 99-52;
Admin Plan: s23p4

OPT-OUT..44
7420.10G Gbk: 21-16 Ex 21-6; 23-2;
PIH Notices: 01-41 (20); 01-10 (6); 00-09 (14);
Admin Plan: s4p1; s4p2

OPT-OUTS......................................31
HUD-50058Instr: p38;
7420.10G Gbk: 1-9; 20-3; 21-5; 21-13;

PIH Notices: 02-07; 01-41 (13); 00-28; 00-09 (10); 00-09

ORAL..30
24 CFR 5: .353;
24 CFR 982: .301; .554;
7420.10G Gbk: 2-9; 5-35; 5-46 Ex 5-5 (2); 5-47 Ex 5-5; 5-48 Ex 5-5; 5-49 Ex 5-5; 5-50 Ex 5-5; 5-51 Ex 5-5; 5-52 Ex 5-5; 5-53 Ex 5-5; 10-2; 12-4; 13-1; 16-3; 22-3; 22-9;
PIH Notices: 95-48 (2); 95-48 Tech Asst (2);
Admin Plan: s7p1; s7p5; s15p2 (2); s18p3; s18p5

ORAL BRIEFING 1
24 CFR 982: .301

ORAL COMMENTS 1
24 CFR 5: .353

ORALLY..8
24 CFR 982: .352; .628;
7420.10G Gbk: 4-7; 8-1; 8-17;
PIH Notices: 02-01; 99-52;
Admin Plan: s1p3

ORDER..258
24 CFR 5: .100; .105 (8); .210; .615; .630; .653; .655 (3); .703;
24 CFR 35 SubM: .1215;
24 CFR 982: .204; .207 (2); .310; .353; .401; .503; .638;
HUD-50058Instr: p1; p22; p30;
HUD-52580-A: p2;
HUD-52641: p5;
HUD-52646: p2;
HUD-52648: p1;
HUD-52665: p2;
HUD-9886: p1 (2);
7420.10G Gbk: 2-3; 2-5; 4-4; 4-5; 4-6; 4-8; 4-10; 4-12; 4-16; 4-18 (4); 4-20; 4-21 (2); 4-22; 5-17; 5-23; 5-26; 5-28; 5-49 Ex 5-5; 8-2; 8-7; 8-11; 9-4; 9-6; 9-8 (2); 9-12; 10-2; 10-7; 10-10; 10-24; 10-32; 10-34 (2); 10-43 Ex 10-6; 11-5; 11-15; 11-18; 12-4; 12-12 Ex 12-1; 12-13 Ex 12-1; 13-6; 19-10 (2); 19-11; 19-13; 20-1; 20-3; 20-9; 20-20 (3); 20-22 (2); 21-2; 21-8 (2); 22-8; 22-14; 23-5;
PIH Notices: 03-23 (4); 03-20; 03-12; 03-11 (5); 02-27 (20); 02-21 (2); 02-20; 02-06; 02-01 (4); 01-43; 01-41 (12); 01-20; 01-15 (2); 01-11; 01-10 (5); 01-06; 00-53; 00-41; 00-34; 00-27; 00-11; 00-11A (4); 00-09 (17); 99-52 (3); 99-11; 95-48 (10); 95-48 Tech Asst (10);
Admin Plan: s2p5; s3p2; s4p2; s6p1; s6p6; s6p7 (2); s6p9; s7p1; s7p4 (5); s7p5 (2); s7p6 (2); s7p7; s7p8 (2); s8p1 (2); s10p1; s15p1; s15p6; s16p1; s17p1; s18p3; s18p6; s19p1; s20p1 (2); s20p2; s20p3 (2); s20p4; s20p8; s21p3; s22p4; s23p3; s24p4; s25p1 (2); s25p3 (2); s25p7

ORDER OF PROTECTION..............1
Admin Plan: s7p8

ORDERED...2
7420.10G Gbk: 4-13;
Admin Plan: s18p6

ORDERLY 1
24 CFR 5: .518

ORDERLY TRANSITION 1
24 CFR 5: .518

ORDERS..9
24 CFR 5: .105;
7420.10G Gbk: 4-11; 4-13; 21-8;
PIH Notices: 02-27 (3); 02-21; 01-20

ORGANIZATION...........................47
24 CFR 5: .107 (2); .318; .603;
24 CFR 982: .204;
HUD-50058: p16;
HUD-50058Instr: p61 (5); p75;
HUD-903: p1 (4);
HUD-903-1: p5;
7420.10G Gbk: 1-1; 2-8; 3-7; 9-4; 10-38 Ex 10-3 (2); 10-39 Ex 10-4 (2); 11-7 (2); 21-1; 21-11 (2); 21-12 Ex 21-2 (2); 21-12 Ex 21-3 (2); 21-13 (3); 21-14 Ex 21-4; 21-15 Ex 21-5; 21-16 Ex 21-6; 21-19; 22-15; 23-4;
PIH Notices: 01-06; 00-11A;
Admin Plan: s3p1; s6p8; s25p7

ORGANIZATIONAL 9
24 CFR 5: .100;
7420.10G Gbk: 21-1 (5); 21-11 (2);
PIH Notices: 00-09

ORGANIZATIONAL STRUCTURE 3

7420.10G Gbk: 21-1 (2); 21-11

ORGANIZATIONAL STRUCTURES2
7420.10G Gbk: 21-11;
PIH Notices: 00-09

ORGANIZATIONAL UNIT............. 1
24 CFR 5: .100

ORGANIZATIONS......................... 51
24 CFR 5: .107 (2); .609;
HUD-52648: p2 (2);
7420.10G Gbk: 1-1; 1-7; 2-2; 2-3 (2); 2-8; 4-3; 4-4; 4-26 Ex 4-2; 8-2; 8-7; 8-8 (2); 8-12; 21-1; 21-2; 21-3 (2); 21-4; 21-11; 23-2; 23-4 (4); 24-11; 24-14;
PIH Notices: 02-21; 02-01; 01-20; 01-15 (2); 01-15 Impr Integ Hbk (2); 00-11 (2); 99-52; 95-48 (2); 95-48 Tech Asst (2);
Admin Plan: s21p6 (2); s23p2 (2); s25p2

ORGANIZE....................................... 2
7420.10G Gbk: 4-18; 21-13

ORGANIZED................................... 5
24 CFR 982: .160;
HUD-50058Instr: p71;
7420.10G Gbk: 4-10; 12-3;
PIH Notices: 00-11

ORGANIZING................................. 2
7420.10G Gbk: 19-13; 21-1

ORIENTATION................................ 9
7420.10G Gbk: 11-15; 23-6;
PIH Notices: 95-48; 95-48 Tech Asst;
Admin Plan: s1p2; s3p3; s20p2 (2); s20p2

ORIENTATION SESSIONS............. 3
7420.10G Gbk: 23-6;
Admin Plan: s20p2; s20p2

ORIGINAL...................................... 68
24 CFR 5: .510 (3); .512; .514 (2);
24 CFR 982: .315;
HUD-50058Instr: p62; p73 (2);
HUD-903: p1; p2 (3);
7420.10G Gbk: 4-7 (2); 5-7; 5-9 Ex 5-1 (2); 5-12; 5-13; 5-47 Ex 5-5; 10-17; 10-29; 10-33 (2); 10-34; 10-47 Ex 10-9 (2); 11-15 (2); 11-19 (2); 12-4; 12-12 Ex 12-1; 12-13 Ex 12-1 (2); 12-14 Ex 12-2; 13-8 (2); 14-4; 18-9; 22-6; 23-15;
PIH Notices: 02-21 (2); 02-01; 01-20 (2); 01-15 Impr Integ Hbk (5); 01-06 (2); 00-24A; 99-52; 95-48; 95-48 Tech Asst;
Admin Plan: s2p2; s3p3; s4p2; s6p7; s7p3; s18p2; s23p6; s24p6

ORIGINAL SIGNATURES............... 1
7420.10G Gbk: 11-15

ORIGINALLY................................. 12
24 CFR 982: .4; .351;
HUD-50058: p v;
HUD-50058Instr: p11; p18; p73;
7420.10G Gbk: 10-15; 23-13;
PIH Notices: 02-01; 01-10; 99-52;
Admin Plan: s25p7

ORIGINALS..................................... 1
7420.10G Gbk: 11-15

OSHA.. 1
7420.10G Gbk: 10-19

OTHER ELECTRIC........................ 10
24 CFR 982: .517;
HUD-52517: p1;
HUD-52641: p2;
HUD-52667: p1 (2);
7420.10G Gbk: 6-3; 18-2 (2); 18-7; 18-8

OTHER FEES.................................. 5
24 CFR 982: Intro; .510;
HUD-52641: 8;
HUD-52641-A: p1;
7420.10G Gbk: 11-14

OTHER GOOD CAUSE..................... 6
24 CFR 982: .310 (2);
PIH Notices: 01-41;
Admin Plan: s14p1; s23p6; s23p6

OTHER PERSON UNDER THE TENANT'S CONTROL.................... 5
24 CFR 5: .100;
24 CFR 982: .4; .310 (2);
Admin Plan: s15p3

OTHER RESIDENT.......................... 1
24 CFR 982: .615

OTHER RESIDENTIAL................... 1
24 CFR 982: .633

OTHER RESIDENTS...................... 38
24 CFR 982: .306 (2); .307; .310 (3); .551 (2); .552; .553 (5);
HUD-52641: p6; p7; p9 (2);
HUD-52641-A: p2 (4);
7420.10G Gbk: 3-3; 8-20 (2); 11-3; 15-2; 15-7; 17-4;

17-5; 17-7;
PIH Notices: 03-11;
Admin Plan: s2p7; s9p3; s15p2; s15p3; s16p2; s16p2

OTTAWA INDIANS 3
HUD-50058Instr: p30;
7420.10G Gbk: 5-16 Ex 5-2;
PIH Notices: 01-15 Impr Integ Hbk

OUT OF POCKET 4
PIH Notices: 01-15; 00-09;
Admin Plan: s6p9; s6p9

OUT OF POCKET EXPENSES 1
PIH Notices: 01-15

OUT OF STATE 1
Admin Plan: s3p2

OUT OF WEDLOCK 2
24 CFR 982: .202;
7420.10G Gbk: 4-19

OUTLET 12
24 CFR 982: .401;
HUD-52580-A: p3; p4; p5; p8; p9; p10; p11; p12;
7420.10G Gbk: 10-8;
PIH Notices: 95-48; 95-48 Tech Asst

OUTLETS 29
24 CFR 5: .703 (2);
24 CFR 982: .401 (2);
HUD-52580-A: p2 (7); p3; p6; p9; p10; p11; p12;
7420.10G Gbk: 10-8 (2); 10-9 (5); 10-19;
PIH Notices: 02-01; 99-52; 95-48; 95-48 Tech Asst

OUT-OF-POCKET 14
24 CFR 5: .609;
HUD-50058Instr: p27;
7420.10G Gbk: 5-15 Ex 5-2; 20-3;
PIH Notices: 01-41; 01-15; 01-15 Impr Integ Hbk (3); 01-10; 00-28; 00-09 (2); 00-09

OUT-OF-POCKET EXPENSES 9
24 CFR 5: .609;
HUD-50058Instr: p27;
7420.10G Gbk: 5-15 Ex 5-2; 20-3;
PIH Notices: 01-15; 01-15 Impr Integ Hbk (3); 00-28

OUT-OF-STATE 1
7420.10G Gbk: 4-13

OUTREACH 78
24 CFR 982: .201 (2);
7420.10G Gbk: 1-1; 1-13; 2-1; 2-4; 3-3; 4-1 (2); 4-2 (18); 4-3 (10); 4-4 (11); 4-9; 4-12; 4-19 (2); 5-40; 5-44 (2); 19-7; 19-8 (2); 21-4 (3); 23-4 (2); 23-6; 24-12; 24-14;
PIH Notices: 02-01; 99-52;
Admin Plan: s1p6 (2); s1p7; s8p3; s8p4 (2); s23p1; s23p2 (2); s23p2

OUTREACH EFFORT 6
7420.10G Gbk: 4-2 (2); 4-3 (2); 4-4; 4-4

OUTREACH EFFORTS 13
7420.10G Gbk: 4-2 (2); 4-4 (4); 5-44; 19-8; 23-4 (2);
PIH Notices: 02-01; 99-52;
Admin Plan: s23p2

OUTSIDE SOURCE 6
24 CFR 5: .603;
HUD-50058Instr: p34; p71;
7420.10G Gbk: 5-31; 10-20;
Admin Plan: s6p9

OUTSTANDING 20
24 CFR 982: .502; .552; .555;
7420.10G Gbk: 4-27 Ex 4-2; 5-51 Ex 5-5 (2); 8-10; 15-5;
PIH Notices: 02-01; 01-33; 01-27; 01-01 (2); 99-52; 96-65 (2);
Admin Plan: s2p6; s15p1 (2); s25p6

OUTSTANDING DEBT 1
Admin Plan: s2p6

OUTSTANDING DEBTS 1
Admin Plan: s25p6

OVEN 36
24 CFR 982: .401 (6); .614;
HUD-52580: p2; p6 (2);
HUD-52580-A: p4 (10); p5 (5); p19 (2);
7420.10G Gbk: 10-4 (4); 10-5; 10-6 (3); 17-5

OVENS 4
24 CFR 982: .401;
HUD-52580-A: p4 (2);
7420.10G Gbk: 10-4

OVER HOUSE 2
PIH Notices: 02-01; 99-52

OVER INCOME 4
24 CFR 5: .617;
PIH Notices: 01-15 Impr Integ Hbk (2);
Admin Plan: s6p3

OVERALL 79
24 CFR 982: .503;
HUD-52580: p6;
HUD-52580-A: p1; p19;

HUD-52648: p1; p4;
7420.10G Gbk: 1-11 (5); 2-4; 4-7; 7-5; 9-3; 9-4; 9-16 Ex 9-2; 19-10; 20-14; 21-1; 21-3; 21-9 (2); 21-10; 21-17; 21-18; 22-5; 22-7; 24-16;
PIH Notices: 03-23; 03-12; 02-27 (13); 02-20; 02-06; 01-06 (25); 01-01; 00-24; 00-24A; 99-11;
Admin Plan: s19p1; s21p1; s21p9; s23p1

OVERCOME.................................6
7420.10G Gbk: 2-1; 2-6; 24-2;
PIH Notices: 02-21; 02-01; 99-52

OVERCOMING.................................1
PIH Notices: 00-11

OVER-COUNTING.................................1
PIH Notices: 00-53

OVERCROWDED.................................4
7420.10G Gbk: 8-10;
PIH Notices: 01-41;
Admin Plan: s23p4; s23p7

OVERCROWDING.................................4
24 CFR 982: .402;
7420.10G Gbk: 5-41;
Admin Plan: s5p1; s24p7

OVERDUE.................................7
7420.10G Gbk: 12-10 (3);
Admin Plan: s21p7 (3); s21p7

OVER-FAIR.................................1
PIH Notices: 01-10

OVER-FMR.................................
9
24 CFR 5: .520 (4);
24 CFR 982: .502 (2);
7420.10G Gbk: 1-5; 14-2;
Admin Plan: s21p6

OVERHAUL.................................2
HUD-50058Instr: p35;
PIH Notices: 00-11

OVERHEAD.................................7
24 CFR 982: .401;
7420.10G Gbk: 10-8; 21-18; 21-19;
PIH Notices: 02-27; 95-48; 95-48 Tech Asst

OVERHOUSED.................................2
HUD-50058Instr: p47;
7420.10G Gbk: 8-10

OVER-HOUSED.................................3
PIH Notices: 01-41 (2); 01-41

OVERINCOME.................................1
7420.10G Gbk: 3-3

OVER-INCOME.................................2
HUD-50058Instr: p39; p74

OVER-INCOME FAMILIES.................................1
HUD-50058Instr: p39

OVER-INCOME FAMILY.................................1
HUD-50058Instr: p74

OVERISSUANCE.................................1
7420.10G Gbk: 8-11

OVER-ISSUANCE.................................8
7420.10G Gbk: 20-15; 24-8 (2);
PIH Notices: 02-06 (4); 02-06

OVERISSUE.................................1
7420.10G Gbk: 8-11

OVER-ISSUED.................................2
Admin Plan: s8p1; s8p1

OVERISSUING.................................3
7420.10G Gbk: 8-11 (2); 8-11

OVER-ISSUING.................................2
7420.10G Gbk: 24-8; 24-9

OVERLAP.................................6
24 CFR 982: .311;
7420.10G Gbk: 9-6;
PIH Notices: 02-01; 00-11; 00-11A; 99-52

OVERLAPPING.................................4
7420.10G Gbk: 2-9; 2-10; 9-4; 9-4

OVERLAPS.................................1
7420.10G Gbk: 9-4

OVER-LEASED.................................7
7420.10G Gbk: 24-8 (4);
PIH Notices: 03-23 (2);
Admin Plan: s8p1

OVER-LEASING.................................
16
7420.10G Gbk: 20-16; 20-17; 20-22;
PIH Notices: 03-23 (12);
Admin Plan: s8p1

OVERLOADED.................................2
HUD-52580-A: p2;
7420.10G Gbk: 10-9

OVERLOADING.................................1
7420.10G Gbk: 10-9

OVERLY.................................3
7420.10G Gbk: 2-11;
PIH Notices: 95-48; 95-48 Tech Asst

OVERNIGHT.................................2
7420.10G Gbk: 10-33;
PIH Notices: 02-27

OVERPAID.................................6
7420.10G Gbk: 9-9; 9-12; 22-12;
Admin Plan: s17p1; s20p5;

s20p8
OVERPAY 1
7420.10G Gbk: 9-1
OVERPAYMENT 13
HUD-52641: p4 (2);
HUD-52665: p2;
7420.10G Gbk: 9-10; 11-18 (2); 20-25; 20-27; 20-29;
PIH Notices: 03-11; 01-15;
Admin Plan: s20p5; s20p6
OVERPAYMENTS 12
24 CFR 982: .453; .619;
HUD-52641: p3; p4; p5;
7420.10G Gbk: 11-12; 22-13 (3); 22-18;
Admin Plan: s20p8; s20p8
OVER-REQUISITIONED................. 2
7420.10G Gbk: 20-26; 20-27
OVERREQUISITIONING 1
7420.10G Gbk: 20-28
OVERRIDE 10
24 CFR 982: .402;
7420.10G Gbk: 5-41;
PIH Notices: 02-01; 01-06 (6); 99-52
OVERRIDES 1
PIH Notices: 01-06
OVERSEE... 3
PIH Notices: 01-06; 95-48; 95-48 Tech Asst
OVERSIGHT 7
7420.10G Gbk: 20-24;
PIH Notices: 02-27 (2); 01-41; 01-06; 00-53; 00-09
OVER-SIMPLIFIED ....
1
7420.10G Gbk: 20-19 Ex 20-3
OVERSIZED 24
HUD-50058Instr: p47 (2);
PIH Notices: 01-41 (9); 00-09 (12); 00-09
OVER-SIZED 2
PIH Notices: 01-41; 00-09
OVERSPENDING 1
7420.10G Gbk: 20-13
OVER-SPENDING 2
7420.10G Gbk: 20-2; 20-2
OVERSTATED 2
PIH Notices: 01-06; 01-06
OVERTIME 11
24 CFR 5: .609;
7420.10G Gbk: 5-14 Ex 5-2; 5-17; 23-12;
PIH Notices: 01-15; 01-15 Impr Integ Hbk (3);
Admin Plan: s6p8 (2); s7p4
OVER-TIME...................................... 1
PIH Notices: 00-09
OVERTIME PAY 6
24 CFR 5: .609;
7420.10G Gbk: 5-14 Ex 5-2; 23-12;
PIH Notices: 01-15 Impr Integ Hbk (2); 01-15 Impr Integ Hbk
OVERTURNING 5
24 CFR 982: .621;
HUD-52580-A: p13;
7420.10G Gbk: 17-11; 17-12;
Admin Plan: s19p1
OVERVIEW 38
24 CFR 982: 24 CFR 982 (3); .351; .501; .601;
7420.10G Gbk: 2-1; 3-1; 4-1; 5-1; 5-13; 5-42; 6-1; 7-1; 8-1; 8-3; 9-1; 10-1; 10-23; 11-1; 12-1; 13-1; 14-1; 15-1 (2); 16-1; 17-1; 18-1; 19-1 (2); 20-1; 21-1; 22-1; 23-1; 24-1;
PIH Notices: 03-11; 02-20; 00-46
OWE 5
7420.10G Gbk: 3-5;
Admin Plan: s15p5; s17p1; s17p2; s17p2
OWED... 43
24 CFR 5: .630 (3);
24 CFR 982: Intro; .313; .552 (3); .641;
HUD-50058Instr: p72;
7420.10G Gbk: 3-5; 5-37 (2); 14-5; 20-26; 22-12 (5); 22-13 (4); 22-14; 23-10; 23-14 (3);
PIH Notices: 01-15 Impr Integ Hbk; 96-65;
Admin Plan: s2p6; s15p2; s17p1; s17p2 (2); s17p3; s18p6 (2); s20p5 (3); s20p6
OWES 27
24 CFR 5: .504;
24 CFR 982: .54; .313 (2); .316; .552;
HUD-50058Instr: p74;
HUD-52641: p10 (2);
HUD-52641-A: p3 (2);
7420.10G Gbk: 5-37; 8-4 (2); 15-5; 21-3; 22-13; 23-14;
PIH Notices: 01-41; 00-09;
Admin Plan: s2p3; s6p9; s13p2; s15p2; s17p1; s17p2; s20p5
OWES RENT 5

24 CFR 982: .316; .552;
7420.10G Gbk: 5-37;
Admin Plan: s2p3; s15p2

OWING...1
7420.10G Gbk: 23-5

OWN...113
24 CFR 5: .312; .315; .318 (2); .324; .510; .516; .518; .703;
24 CFR 982: .355; .551; .555; .627 (3); .628 (2); .635;
HUD-50058: p6; p11; p xvi;
HUD-50058Instr: p16 (2); p25; p42; p46 (3); p53; p56;
HUD-52517: p2;
HUD-52580-A: p15;
HUD-52641: p5;
HUD-52646: p2 (2);
HUD-903: p1;
7420.10G Gbk: 1-3; 1-10 (2); 1-14; 2-3; 2-9; 2-11; 4-26 Ex 4-2; 5-9 Ex 5-1; 5-30; 5-36 Ex 5-4; 5-39; 5-43; 8-1; 8-2; 8-5; 9-3; 9-4; 10-23; 10-40 Ex 10-4a; 10-41 Ex 10-4b; 10-42 Ex 10-5 (2); 10-43 Ex 10-6; 10-45 Ex 10-7b; 10-46 Ex 10-8; 11-13; 12-9 (2); 13-5 (2); 13-6 (2); 13-7 (2); 16-5; 17-11 (2); 18-7; 19-7; 19-13; 20-24; 21-4; 21-6; 21-8 (2); 21-12 Ex 21-2; 21-12 Ex 21-3;
PIH Notices: 03-11 (4); 02-01; 01-41 (2); 01-15; 01-06; 00-53; 00-24B (2); 00-11; 00-09 (2); 99-52; 95-48 (3); 95-48 Tech Asst (3);
Admin Plan: s2p4; s6p13; s13p1; s18p3; s18p5; s22p3; s22p3

OWNED..56
24 CFR 5: .100; .306 (3); .318 (2);
24 CFR 982: .4 (6); .352 (2); .623; .625; .628 (2); .642;
HUD-50058Instr: p22; p71; p73;
HUD-52646: p2;
7420.10G Gbk: 1-1; 1-2 (3); 1-3 (2); 2-13 Ex 2-1; 3-4; 3-5; 4-27 Ex 4-2; 5-25 Ex 5-3; 5-26 (2); 8-17; 10-30 (2); 10-31; 13-10; 15-5; 17-9; 20-5; 22-17;
PIH Notices: 02-22; 02-01; 99-52; 95-48 (2); 95-48 Tech Asst (2);
Admin Plan: s7p6; s9p2; s19p1; s24p4

OWNER APPLICANT.......................6
24 CFR 5: .214 (2); .216 (2); .218; .218

OWNER APPLICANTS....................2
24 CFR 5: .216; .218

OWNER APPLICANT'S 2
24 CFR 5: .216; .216

OWNER OBLIGATION....................1
24 CFR 982: .404

OWNER OBLIGATIONS 1
24 CFR 982: .404

OWNER-ADMINISTERED.............1
PIH Notices: 01-15

OWNER-CAUSED............................1
7420.10G Gbk: 10-14

OWNER-FAMILY.............................1
7420.10G Gbk: 11-2

OWNER-OCCUPIED........................2
24 CFR 982: .641;
7420.10G Gbk: 5-25 Ex 5-3

OWNER-ORIENTED........................1
7420.10G Gbk: 24-12

OWNER-PROVIDED 1
7420.10G Gbk: 18-7

OWNERSHIP..................................43
24 CFR 5: .240; .309; .327; .363;
24 CFR 982: .4 (5); .627; .633 (3); .634 (2);
HUD-50058Instr: p71;
7420.10G Gbk: 5-3; 5-36 Ex 5-4; 10-35; 11-8; 11-18 (4); 21-3 (3);
PIH Notices: 01-41; 00-09; 99-52;
Admin Plan: s2p4; s9p4 (2); s16p2; s16p3 (5); s19p1 (2); s22p1; s22p3

OWNER-SUPPLIED........................4
24 CFR 982: .401;
HUD-52580-A: p4; p5;
7420.10G Gbk: 10-4

OWNER-TENANT............................1
24 CFR 5: .353

OWNING..11
24 CFR 5: .309; .315 (2); .321 (3); .353 (2); .703;
24 CFR 982: .4; .520

OWNS..29
24 CFR 5: .309; .318; .359; .504;
24 CFR 982: .4 (2); .601; .620; .637; .643;
HUD-50058: p xiv;

HUD-50058Instr: p46; p57; p72; p74;
HUD-52580: p6;
HUD-52580-A: p19;
HUD-52641: p1;
7420.10G Gbk: 5-19; 11-10; 17-10; 17-11;
PIH Notices: 95-48 (2); 95-48 Tech Asst (2);
Admin Plan: s9p2 (2); s19p1

PACKET 28
24 CFR 982: .301 (4); .307;
HUD-52648: p2 (2);
7420.10G Gbk: 2-8; 8-3 (2); 8-7 (3); 13-8 (2);
Admin Plan: s1p3; s1p7; s8p1; s8p2 (3); s8p3; s9p3; s13p1; s14p2; s18p3; s21p6; s21p6

PACKETS 1
7420.10G Gbk: 2-8

PAIN..2
PIH Notices: 95-48; 95-48 Tech Asst

PAINT 320
24 CFR 5: .703 (2);
24 CFR 35 SubM: .1200; .1210; .1215 (5); .1220 (2); .1225 (3);
24 CFR 982: .158; .305; .401 (4); .605;
HUD-52517: p2 (11); p3 (6); p4 (4); p5 (10);
HUD-52580-A: p2 (20); p3 (2); p5 (2); p7 (2); p9 (2); p10 (2); p11 (2); p12 (2); p13 (11); p14 (2); p17 (19); p18 (6);
7420.10G Gbk: 5-19 (5); 8-15 (2); 10-1; 10-10; 10-11 (3); 10-12 (2); 10-15 (8); 10-16 (7); 10-17 (9); 10-18 (18); 10-19 (6); 10-20 (4); 10-21 (10); 10-22 (5); 10-23; 10-36 Ex 10-1 (17); 10-37 Ex 10-2 (15); 10-38 Ex 10-3 (3); 10-39 Ex 10-4 (6); 10-42 Ex 10-5; 17-2; 17-3; 17-5; 20-3; 20-4 (6);
PIH Notices: 02-07 (8); 02-01; 00-49 (12); 00-23 (35); 99-52;
Admin Plan: s1p2; s8p2 (2); s8p3; s23p4

PAINTED.......................................42
24 CFR 35 SubM: .1200; .1215;
HUD-52517: p2 (5); p3 (3); p4 (2); p5;
HUD-52580-A: p2 (5); p3; p5; p7; p9; p10; p11; p12; p13 (3); p14; p17 (5);
7420.10G Gbk: 10-10; 10-12 (2); 10-17; 10-18; 10-37 Ex 10-2;
PIH Notices: 00-23; 00-23

PAINTER...2
7420.10G Gbk: 5-19; 5-19

PAINTING..1
PIH Notices: 99-11

PALAU...4
24 CFR 5: .506;
HUD-50058Instr: p64;
PIH Notices: 01-27; 01-27

PAPER 22
24 CFR 5: .801;
HUD-50058: p iv;
HUD-50058Instr: p17;
HUD-52580-A: p2; p15;
7420.10G Gbk: 10-24; 19-6; 21-4;
PIH Notices: 03-11; 01-15 (3); 01-06 (6); 00-34 (3); 00-34

PAPERS 7
7420.10G Gbk: 4-3 (2);
PIH Notices: 01-15 Impr Integ Hbk;
Admin Plan: s7p7 (2); s15p5; s15p5

PAPERWORK 16
7420.10G Gbk: 8-11; 11-10; 13-8;
PIH Notices: 03-23 (2); 03-20 (2); 03-12 (2); 03-11 (2); 02-21 (2); 02-01; 99-52;
Admin Plan: s1p3

PARENT 21
24 CFR 5: .216;
24 CFR 982: .4; .306;
HUD-50058Instr: p30 (2);
HUD-52517: p2;
HUD-52641: p5; p6 (2);
HUD-52646: p2;
7420.10G Gbk: 5-4; 5-12; 8-15; 8-19; 11-2; 21-12 Ex 21-2; 21-12 Ex 21-3; 21-19;
Admin Plan: s2p4; s6p7; s16p2

PARENTAL 1
HUD-50058Instr: p14

PARENTING 1
Admin Plan: s8p3

PARENTS 8
24 CFR 5: .518 (2);
24 CFR 982: .202;
HUD-50058Instr: p17;
7420.10G Gbk: 4-19; 8-14;

PIH Notices: 95-48; 95-48 Tech Asst

PARENT'S..1
HUD-50058Instr: p29

PARISH..3
Admin Plan: s1p1; s25p1; s25p7

PARKING LOT 2
PIH Notices: 95-48; 95-48 Tech Asst

PARKING LOTS 7
24 CFR 5: .703;
PIH Notices: 95-48 (3); 95-48 Tech Asst (2); 95-48 Tech Asst

PARKING SPACES..........................2
PIH Notices: 95-48; 95-48 Tech Asst

PAROLE 8
24 CFR 982: .310 (2);
HUD-52641: p9;
HUD-52641-A: p2;
7420.10G Gbk: 5-10 Ex 5-1; 15-2; 15-6;
PIH Notices: 03-11

PAROLE VIOLATOR 1
24 CFR 982: .310

PAROLE VIOLATORS 1
PIH Notices: 03-11

PAROLED 1
7420.10G Gbk: 5-10 Ex 5-1

PARTIAL MONTH...........................2
HUD-52641: p4;
7420.10G Gbk: 11-5

PARTICIPANT....................................254
24 CFR 5: .214; .216 (13); .218 (2); .230 (2); .232 (2); .236 (8); .603; .609; .615 (2);
24 CFR 982: 24 CFR 982 (2); .4 (6); .54 (2); .161; .201 (3); .301; .302; .311; .314 (4); .353 (3); .401; .516; .551 (2); .552 (5); .555 (7); .625; .633; .638; .643;
HUD-50058Instr: p2; p10; p13; p62; p70; p71; p74 (4);
HUD-52641: p6;
HUD-52646: p1 (4);
HUD-9886: p2 (2);
7420.10G Gbk: 1-12 Ex 1-2; 2-7 (3); 2-11; 3-8; 4-10; 4-16; 4-22; 5-4; 5-8; 5-15 Ex 5-2; 5-19; 5-21; 5-26 (2); 5-35; 6-1 (3); 8-1; 8-4; 8-15; 8-19; 8-22; 9-12; 10-2; 11-1; 11-2; 11-5; 12-2; 12-3 (3); 12-6; 12-12 Ex 12-1 (3); 12-13 Ex 12-1; 12-14 Ex 12-2; 13-2 (2); 13-4; 13-7; 13-11 Ex 13-1; 13-12 Ex 13-2; 14-1 (2); 14-2 (2); 15-4; 16-1 (3); 16-2; 17-1 (2); 19-1; 19-10 (2); 19-12; 20-24; 21-2; 21-5; 21-7; 22-1; 22-2; 22-4; 22-9 (3); 22-10; 22-11; 22-13; 22-14; 22-18; 23-8 Ex 23-1; 23-20; 24-11;
PIH Notices: 03-20; 02-27; 02-20; 02-01; 01-41 (2); 01-15 Impr Integ Hbk (2); 01-10; 00-46; 00-11; 00-11A (5); 00-09 (2); 99-52;
Admin Plan: s1p1; s1p4; s1p6; s2p3; s2p7; s6p3; s6p13; s7p1 (3); s7p2; s7p8 (3); s8p2; s8p3; s8p5; s9p3; s13p2; s15p1; s15p2 (2); s15p3 (2); s15p6; s17p1; s18p3; s18p4 (2); s18p7 (4); s20p2 (5); s20p3; s20p4; s20p6 (13); s20p7 (4); s22p2 (3); s25p5 (2); s25p6

PARTICIPANT FAMILY.................35
24 CFR 982: .4; .54 (2); .201 (2); .301; .302; .311; .314 (4); .353; .551; .552; .555 (6); .633;
HUD-50058Instr: p74;
7420.10G Gbk: 5-38; 13-2; 13-3 (2); 14-3; 14-4; 16-3; 21-7; 22-14;
Admin Plan: s2p3; s13p2; s15p2

PARTICIPANT FAMILY'S 1
7420.10G Gbk: 5-13

PARTICIPANTS 260
24 CFR 5: .210 (3); .212; .214 (3); .216 (2); .218 (2); .230 (4); .234; .655;
24 CFR 982: .54; .157; .158; .204 (3); .207; .503 (3); .555; .630;
HUD-50058: p i
HUD-50058Instr: p2 (2); p34; p60 (4); p61 (4); p71 (2); p74; p76;
HUD-52648: p3;
HUD-9886: p2;
7420.10G Gbk: 1-2; 1-4; 1-13;

1-15; 2-2 (2); 2-4; 2-5; 2-6; 2-7 (2); 2-8; 2-9; 2-10 (2); 3-3 (2); 3-4; 3-5; 3-6 (2); 3-8 (4); 4-2; 4-3 (2); 4-4; 4-17; 4-18 (2); 5-11; 5-12; 5-13 (2); 5-16 Ex 5-2; 5-19; 5-20; 5-31; 5-34 (2); 7-1; 7-3 (2); 7-6; 8-1; 8-2 (2); 8-7; 8-14; 8-20; 9-1; 9-4; 10-1; 10-16; 12-2 (2); 12-9; 12-10; 14-1 (3); 14-2; 14-5; 16-1; 16-2; 16-3; 16-4; 17-1; 17-7; 18-1; 19-1; 19-3; 19-8 (2); 19-12; 20-2; 20-3; 20-4; 20-13; 20-17; 21-5; 21-6; 21-7; 21-11; 22-2; 22-4 (2); 22-9; 22-10; 22-15; 22-18 (2); 23-1; 23-3; 23-4; 23-5 (3); 23-10 (3); 23-11; 23-19 (2); 23-20; 24-2 (2); 24-4 (2); 24-6; 24-7; 24-8; 24-11 (2);

PIH Notices: 03-20 (2); 02-20 (8); 02-01; 01-41; 01-27 (2); 01-10; 01-06 (2); 01-01 (2); 00-53; 00-46 (6); 00-41; 00-24B; 00-11 (2); 00-11A (2); 00-09; 99-52; 95-48 (5); 95-48 Tech Asst (5);

Admin Plan: s1p3; s1p4 (2); s1p5; s1p6; s1p7; s7p1 (2); s7p4; s8p2 (7); s8p3 (2); s8p4; s11p1; s11p3; s11p1; s11p2 (2); s15p1; s15p3 (3); s17p3; s18p3 (2); s18p4 (2); s18p7; s18p8 (2); s19p1; s20p1 (2); s20p2; s21p9; s22p1; s22p2; s23p1; s23p7; s23p8; s24p3; s24p6; s25p4; s25p6 (2); s25p7 (2); s25p7

PARTICIPANT'S 25

24 CFR 5: .210; .214; .216 (5); .230 (2); .232; .236 (3);

HUD-50058: p xvi;

HUD-50058Instr: p61;

7420.10G Gbk: 5-19; 22-9; 22-16; 23-9; 23-13;

Admin Plan: s15p3; s20p3 (2); s20p4; s20p6

PARTIES 55

24 CFR 5: .214; .350; .363 (3); .514;

24 CFR 982: Intro; .301; .456;

HUD-50058Instr: p1; p28;

7420.10G Gbk: 1-11 (2); 2-3; 2-11; 8-18; 8-19; 9-4; 10-36 Ex 10-1; 11-2 (2); 12-3 (2); 12-8; 19-3; 22-11 (3); 23-8 Ex 23-1 (3); 23-15;

PIH Notices: 02-21; 01-41; 01-20; 01-02; 00-24B; 00-11; 00-11A (4); 00-09 (2); 95-48 (2); 95-48 Tech Asst (2);

Admin Plan: s1p7; s14p1; s16p3; s17p1; s21p5; s24p2; s24p3

PARTNER 14

HUD-50058Instr: p14;

7420.10G Gbk: 9-4; 21-11;

PIH Notices: 02-27 (2);

Admin Plan: s4p2 (5); s8p4; s22p2; s25p2; s25p7

PARTNERED 1

Admin Plan: s25p7

PARTNERS 9

7420.10G Gbk: 24-9 (2); 24-12;

PIH Notices: 01-15; 00-11 (3);

Admin Plan: s25p7; s25p7

PARTNERSHIP 8

24 CFR 5: .214 (2);

HUD-50058Instr: p27;

7420.10G Gbk: 3-8; 4-4; 5-16 Ex 5-2 (2);

PIH Notices: 01-15 Impr Integ Hbk

PARTNERSHIPS 10

24 CFR 5: .601 (2); .603; .617;

7420.10G Gbk: 4-4; 24-9;

PIH Notices: 02-01; 01-15; 00-11; 99-52

PART-TIME EMPLOYEES 4

PIH Notices: 95-48 (2); 95-48 Tech Asst; 95-48 Tech Asst

PARTY 110

24 CFR 5: .363 (3); .659 (2); .661;

24 CFR 35 SubM: .1200 (6); .1215; .1225 (15);

24 CFR 982: .306; .406; .453; .456 (3); .516 (2);

HUD-52641: p5;

HUD-52646: p1 (4);

7420.10G Gbk: 5-48 Ex 5-5; 5-49 Ex 5-5; 8-18; 10-16; 10-18; 10-33; 10-34; 11-1; 11-13; 22-16 (2); 23-6;

PIH Notices: 03-11; 02-27; 02-01; 01-15 (5); 01-15 Impr Integ Hbk (2); 00-49; 00-41; 00-24B (4); 00-

11A (6); 99-52; 95-48 (7); 95-48 Tech Asst (7);
Admin Plan: s1p5; s7p1 (5); s7p3; s7p6; s8p4; s10p2; s15p5; s16p1; s18p5; s18p6 (3); s21p4 (2); s24p3; s25p7

PASS 90
24 CFR 5: .609;
24 CFR 35 SubM: .1200;
24 CFR 982: .553;
HUD-50058Instr: p29;
HUD-52580: p1 (2); p2; p3; p4; p5; p7 (2);
HUD-52580-A: p1 (3); p2 (4); p3 (2); p4 (3); p5 (2); p6 (4); p7 (2); p8 (2); p9 (2); p10 (2); p11 (2); p12 (2); p13 (2); p14 (2); p15 (3); p16 (2); p18 (2); p20 (2);
7420.10G Gbk: 5-15 Ex 5-2; 5-20; 10-7; 10-12; 10-16; 10-23 (2); 10-25; 10-26 (2); 10-27 (2); 10-35 (2); 11-9 (3); 11-19; 12-13 Ex 12-1; 19-11 (3); 19-12; 21-10; 24-13;
PIH Notices: 03-11; 02-01; 01-15 Impr Integ Hbk; 00-53; 00-49; 99-52; 95-48; 95-48 Tech Asst;
Admin Plan: s10p1; s10p4

PASSAGE 2
HUD-52580-A: p17;
7420.10G Gbk: 10-12

PASSAGEWAY 4
24 CFR 982: .605;
7420.10G Gbk: 17-2;
PIH Notices: 95-48; 95-48 Tech Asst

PASSAGEWAYS 2
PIH Notices: 95-48; 95-48 Tech Asst

PASSBOOK.................................... 25
24 CFR 5: .609;
HUD-50058: p6 (5);
HUD-50058Instr: p22 (9); p23 (3);
7420.10G Gbk: 5-14 Ex 5-2; 5-24; 5-26 (2); 5-28;
PIH Notices: 01-15 Impr Integ Hbk; 01-15 Impr Integ Hbk

PASSBOOK SAVINGS RATE 5
24 CFR 5: .609;
7420.10G Gbk: 5-14 Ex 5-2; 5-24;
PIH Notices: 01-15 Impr Integ Hbk; 01-15 Impr Integ Hbk

PASSBOOKS..................................... 5
7420.10G Gbk: 5-48 Ex 5-5; 5-49 Ex 5-5;
PIH Notices: 01-15 Impr Integ Hbk;
Admin Plan: s7p5; s7p6

PASSPORT 3
24 CFR 5: .508;
7420.10G Gbk: 5-4;
Admin Plan: s7p7

PAST DUE.. 2
PIH Notices: 96-65; 96-65

PAST PERFORMANCE.................... 1
PIH Notices: 02-27

PATIO... 10
24 CFR 5: .703 (2);
HUD-52580: p6 (2);
HUD-52580-A: p19 (2);
7420.10G Gbk: 9-13 Ex 9-1 (2); 9-15 Ex 9-2; 9-16 Ex 9-2

PATTERN 17
24 CFR 982: .310; .553 (4);
HUD-903: p3;
HUD-903-1: p6;
7420.10G Gbk: 15-7; 22-1; 22-15;
PIH Notices: 02-21; 01-20;
Admin Plan: s15p2; s15p3 (3); s17p2

PATTERNS 6
24 CFR 982: .517;
HUD-52667: p i;
7420.10G Gbk: 2-10; 3-3; 15-7; 24-3

PAY STUBS...................................... 3
7420.10G Gbk: 5-51 Ex 5-5;
PIH Notices: 01-15; 01-15 Impr Integ Hbk

PAY THE UTILITY SUPPLIER DIRECTLY 1
24 CFR 982: .514

PAYCHECK STUBS 1
7420.10G Gbk: 5-46 Ex 5-5

PAYMENT AGREEMENT.............. 12
Admin Plan: s17p1 (6); s17p2 (5); s17p2

PAYMENT AGREEMENTS 3
PIH Notices: 01-15 Impr Integ Hbk;
Admin Plan: s17p1; s17p1

PAYMENT SCHEDULE 2
7420.10G Gbk: 5-47 Ex 5-5;
PIH Notices: 03-23

PAYMENT SCHEDULE CONTAINS1

7420.10G Gbk: 7-9

PAYMENT SCHEDULES.................2
Admin Plan: s7p4; s7p5

PAYMENT STANDARD...............526
24 CFR 982: Intro; .1 (2); .4 (3); .301; .305; .402 (2); .502 (3); .503 (10); .504 (5); .505 (13); .508; .604 (3); .608 (4); .613 (4); .617 (4); .623 (2); .635 (12); .643;
HUD-50058: p11; p xi (2); p14; p xiv (3); p17;
HUD-50058Instr: p47 (9); p57 (4); p63; p74;
HUD-52580: p1 (5);
HUD-52646: p1 (3);
HUD-52648: p2 (2);
7420.10G Gbk: 1-6 Ex 1-1 (6); 1-9; 2-3; 3-3; 5-44; 6-1; 6-2 (6); 6-4 (4); 6-5 (10); 6-6; 6-7; 6-10 Ex 6-2 (5); 7-1 (4); 7-2 (5); 7-3; 7-4; 7-5 (2); 7-6 (6); 7-7 (6); 7-8 (16); 7-9 (3); 7-10; 8-5 (2); 8-6 (5); 8-16 (3); 8-17 (3); 9-1 (2); 9-4 (3); 9-19 Ex 9-4; 11-1; 11-6; 12-5; 12-6 (3); 12-7 (14); 13-3; 14-1; 14-2 (2); 14-4; 17-1; 17-3 (3); 17-4 (5); 17-5 (4); 17-6 (12); 17-8 (13); 17-9 (2); 17-10 (5); 17-11 (5); 17-12 (3); 20-2 (2); 20-17 (2); 20-18 (3); 20-19 Ex 20-3 (5); 20-22; 22-6; 22-12; 22-13; 23-13; 24-10 (5); 24-11 (9); 24-12 (3); 24-15;
PIH Notices: 03-23; 02-27; 02-22 (4); 02-20 (25); 02-06; 01-41 (27); 01-10 (18); 01-06 (23); 01-01 (6); 00-46 (24); 00-41; 00-24A (3); 00-24B (3); 00-09 (47);
Admin Plan: s5p3; s9p1; s11p1; s11p3 (4); s19p1 (15); s21p6; s22p2; s24p4

PAYMENT STANDARD AMOUNT207
24 CFR 982: Intro; .402 (2); .503 (30); .505 (28); .604 (2); .608 (3); .613 (2); .617 (2); .641;
7420.10G Gbk: 3-5; 6-4; 6-6; 6-7; 7-1 (3); 7-2; 7-3; 7-7 (6); 7-8 (5); 7-9 (4); 7-10 (2); 12-7; 17-3 (2); 20-18;
PIH Notices: 02-22 (4); 02-20 (50); 01-06 (3); 01-01 (3); 00-46 (40);
Admin Plan: s5p3 (2); s19p1 (3); s19p1

PAYMENT STANDARD AMOUNTS 164
24 CFR 982: .503 (12); .505; .635;
HUD-52648: p2;
7420.10G Gbk: 3-5 (2); 7-1 (4); 7-2 (10); 7-3 (4); 7-4 (14); 7-5 (2); 7-6 (7); 7-7 (3); 7-9 (2); 7-10;
PIH Notices: 02-27; 02-22; 02-20 (37); 01-06 (8); 01-01 (27); 00-46 (25); 00-46

PAYMENT STANDARDS 107
24 CFR 982: .54; .402 (4);
HUD-52648: p2 (3);
7420.10G Gbk: 1-6 Ex 1-1 (2); 1-10; 1-11; 2-3 (2); 2-9 (2); 3-5; 3-7; 7-1 (2); 7-3 (2); 7-5 (3); 7-6 (8); 7-7; 7-8; 7-9 (3); 8-6; 9-4; 12-8; 13-4; 13-5 (2); 14-2 (5); 18-7; 19-5; 20-17 (3); 24-10; 24-11; 24-12 (2); 24-15;
PIH Notices: 02-27; 02-20 (8); 02-01; 01-06 (6); 01-01 (11); 00-46 (9);
Admin Plan: s5p2; s5p3; s8p2; s11p1 (3); s11p3 (2); s19p1; s21p1; s21p2; s21p6

PAYMENTS..................................432
24 CFR 5: .210; .214; .318; .508 (2); .514 (4); .520 (2); .601 (3); .603 (3); .609 (10); .617; .628 (3); .653 (2); .661; .801 (3);
24 CFR 982: 24 CFR 982 (2); .1 (2); .4 (6); .102 (2); .151 (4); .154; .157 (2); .305; .311 (7); .312; .352 (2); .355 (2); .404 (2); .406; .451 (2); .453 (2); .515; .519; .552 (2); .555; .619 (5); .623 (2); .625 (3); .627 (2); .631 (3); .634 (2); .635 (2); .641; .642 (4);
HUD-50058: p iii; p iv; p ix; p xii; p xv;
HUD-50058Instr: p14; p27 (2);

p28 (5); p30 (4); p31 (5); p32 (6); p50; p58; p70 (2); p71 (3); p72 (2); p73 (2); p76;
HUD-52641: p2; p5; p6;
HUD-52646: p1 (2);
HUD-52665: p3;
HUD-9886: p1;
7420.10G Gbk: 1-3 (2); 1-6 Ex 1-1; 1-16 Ex 1-3; 2-6 (2); 2-9 (2); 2-10; 3-5; 5-14 Ex 5-2 (3); 5-15 Ex 5-2 (6); 5-16 Ex 5-2 (11); 5-18 (3); 5-19; 5-23 (7); 5-24; 5-26; 5-29; 5-30 (4); 5-32; 5-46 Ex 5-5; 5-47 Ex 5-5 (5); 5-51 Ex 5-5 (4); 5-52 Ex 5-5 (2); 6-1; 7-8; 10-25; 10-27; 10-28 (2); 10-29 (4); 10-40 Ex 10-4a; 10-41 Ex 10-4b; 10-46 Ex 10-8; 11-1; 11-5 (2); 11-8; 11-13; 11-14; 11-16 Ex 11-1; 13-8; 15-4; 15-9 Ex 15-1; 17-10 (2); 19-10; 20-1 (4); 20-17; 20-20; 20-23; 20-27; 20-29; 21-2; 22-2 (3); 22-3; 22-6 (2); 22-9; 22-13; 22-15 (3); 22-17; 23-14 (2); 23-15; 24-12 (2);
PIH Notices: 03-23 (3); 03-05; 02-27; 02-21; 02-20 (4); 01-41 (8); 01-40; 01-33; 01-15 (3); 01-15 Impr Integ Hbk (34); 01-06; 00-49; 00-46 (3); 00-09 (15); 96-65 (8);
Admin Plan: s1p1; s2p7; s6p1; s6p3; s6p6; s6p9 (5); s6p10 (4); s6p13; s7p4 (3); s7p5 (2); s7p6 (2); s7p7 (3); s7p8; s8p3; s8p4 (2); s9p1; s9p2; s9p3; s9p4; s10p1; s10p4 (2); s11p1 (9); s13p1; s14p1 (2); s14p2; s15p1; s16p1; s16p3; s17p1 (2); s17p2 (3); s19p1 (2); s20p5; s20p8; s21p7; s22p3 (3); s22p4 (2); s22p5; s23p5; s23p7; s23p8 (2); s24p1 (2); s24p5 (3); s24p6 (2); s24p7; s25p5

PAYROLL DEDUCTIONS 5
24 CFR 5: .609;
7420.10G Gbk: 5-14 Ex 5-2; 23-12;
PIH Notices: 01-15 Impr Integ Hbk; 01-15 Impr Integ Hbk

PAYSTUBS..4
7420.10G Gbk: 5-46 Ex 5-5;
PIH Notices: 01-15 Impr Integ Hbk (2); 01-15 Impr Integ Hbk

PEACEFUL ENJOYMENT 40
24 CFR 982: .306 (2); .307; .310 (3); .551 (2); .553 (5);
HUD-52641: p6; p7; p9 (3);
HUD-52641-A: p2 (5);
7420.10G Gbk: 5-39; 8-20 (3); 11-3; 11-4; 15-2 (3); 15-7;
PIH Notices: 03-11;
Admin Plan: s2p7; s15p2 (2); s15p3; s16p2; s16p2

PEDESTRIAN 6
PIH Notices: 95-48 (3); 95-48 Tech Asst (2); 95-48 Tech Asst

PENAL...3
24 CFR 982: .352;
7420.10G Gbk: 8-17;
Admin Plan: s24p2

PENALIZE 3
24 CFR 982: .207;
7420.10G Gbk: 4-16; 10-34

PENALIZED.....................................1
7420.10G Gbk: 24-1

PENALTIES....................................38
24 CFR 5: .210; .218; .232; .238 (2);
24 CFR 982: .451 (5);
HUD-52641: p4 (2);
HUD-52648: p3;
HUD-9886: p1; p2 (2);
7420.10G Gbk: 5-28; 5-49 Ex 5-5 (2); 11-6 (5); 11-7 (2); 11-9; 20-6 (2);
PIH Notices: 01-15 Impr Integ Hbk; 96-65 (4);
Admin Plan: s11p2; s16p1; s16p2; s20p2

PENALTY.......................................22
24 CFR 5: .508;
24 CFR 982: .451 (2);
HUD-52641: p4 (2);
HUD-903: p1; p3;
HUD-9886: p2;
7420.10G Gbk: 5-9 Ex 5-1 (2); 5-25 Ex 5-3; 5-28; 11-7 (3); 20-10;
PIH Notices: 00-28 (2); 96-65 (2);
Admin Plan: s11p2; s16p2

PENSION..15
HUD-50058: p6;
HUD-50058Instr: p29; p71;
7420.10G Gbk: 4-26 Ex 4-2; 5-25 Ex 5-3; 5-26 (4); 5-46 Ex 5-5; 5-49 Ex 5-5; 12-13 Ex 12-1; 12-16 Ex 12-4;
PIH Notices: 01-15 Impr Integ Hbk;
Admin Plan: s6p10

PENSION FUNDS 4
7420.10G Gbk: 5-25 Ex 5-3; 5-26 (2);
Admin Plan: s6p10

PENSIONS 11
24 CFR 5: .609;
HUD-50058: p6;
HUD-50058Instr: p29 (3);
7420.10G Gbk: 4-27 Ex 4-2; 5-14 Ex 5-2; 5-46 Ex 5-5;
PIH Notices: 01-15 Impr Integ Hbk (2);
Admin Plan: s7p4

PERCENTAGE.............................187
24 CFR 5: .609 (3); .628 (2);
24 CFR 982: .102 (2);
HUD-50058: p8; p viii (2); p10; p x (2); p11; p xi (2); p12; p xii (2); p13; p xiii (2); p14; p xiv (2); p xv (2);
HUD-50058Instr: p18; p34; p37 (4); p44 (5); p48 (5); p51 (5); p54 (5); p57 (5); p58 (2);
HUD-52648: p3 (2); p4 (2);
7420.10G Gbk: 2-4 (2); 2-13 Ex 2-1; 4-19 (3); 4-20; 4-21 (2); 5-5; 5-14 Ex 5-2 (3); 5-21 (2); 5-24; 5-28 (3); 6-7; 6-10 Ex 6-2; 7-5; 7-6; 7-10 (4); 11-7; 13-7; 19-3 (2); 19-7; 19-8; 19-9 (6); 19-10; 19-11 (2); 19-12; 20-6; 20-10 (3); 20-11; 20-17; 23-6;
PIH Notices: 02-27 (2); 02-21 (2); 02-20 (10); 02-07; 02-01; 01-41 (9); 01-15 Impr Integ Hbk (7); 01-10 (6); 01-06 (4); 01-01; 00-46 (10); 00-28; 00-11; 00-09 (9); 99-52; 95-48 (3); 95-48 Tech Asst (3);
Admin Plan: s19p1; s21p9

PERCENTAGES...............................5
7420.10G Gbk: 19-6;
PIH Notices: 02-21 (2); 02-20; 00-46

PERCENTILE..............................113
24 CFR 5: .520;
24 CFR 982: .503 (12);
HUD-50058: p ix;
HUD-50058Instr: p40; p68;
7420.10G Gbk: 7-1; 7-2 (6); 7-3 (13); 7-4 (3); 7-5 (9); 7-10 (3); 17-12; 24-10; 24-12;
PIH Notices: 02-20 (18); 01-01 (29); 00-46 (10);
Admin Plan: s11p3; s11p3

PERFORMANCE STANDARD 4
7420.10G Gbk: 5-7;
PIH Notices: 01-01 (2); 01-01

PERFORMANCE STANDARDS 5
24 CFR 982: .54;
7420.10G Gbk: 3-6; 9-11;
PIH Notices: 01-06; 01-06

PERIOD** 1
PIH Notices: 01-01

PERIOD..410
24 CFR 5: .214; .216 (6); .236; .318; .353 (3); .360; .508 (4); .514 (3); .518 (19); .603 (3); .609 (7); .617 (5); .630 (3); .661 (2); .801 (3);
24 CFR 982: .4; .102 (2); .201 (2); .303; .305 (3); .310; .312 (4); .314; .353 (2); .404; .503 (2); .553 (3); .555; .619 (2); .637; .638; .642;
HUD-50058: p6 (2); p vii; p17; p xvii;
HUD-50058Instr: p17; p18 (2); p22; p24; p27; p33 (2); p34; p36; p61; p62; p70 (3); p71; p73; p75;
HUD-52580: p5;
HUD-52580-A: p4; p5; p15; p17 (2);
HUD-52641: p3 (2);
HUD-52646: p2;
HUD-52648: p1;
HUD-52665: p2;
HUD-52667: p i;
HUD-9886: p1 (2);
7420.10G Gbk: 1-2; 1-7; 2-2; 3-4; 3-6; 4-1 (2); 4-2; 4-4 (2); 4-6; 4-7; 4-12; 4-13 (2); 4-14; 4-26 Ex 4-2; 5-6 (2); 5-13; 5-15 Ex 5-2 (2); 5-18; 5-20; 5-23 (3); 5-46 Ex 5-5 (4); 5-50 Ex 5-5; 6-8 (3); 7-4; 8-11 (2); 8-12 (2); 8-17; 9-7; 10-18; 10-24; 10-25;

10-26; 10-27; 10-28; 10-29; 10-33; 10-34; 10-35; 10-40 Ex 10-4a; 11-5 (2); 11-10; 11-15; 12-1; 12-3; 12-6 (2); 14-1 (5); 14-3; 14-4; 15-5; 15-10 Ex 15-2; 16-3; 18-4; 19-2 (2); 19-3 (3); 19-7; 20-3; 20-6; 20-18; 20-28; 21-5; 22-7 (2); 22-11; 22-12; 22-13 (2); 22-15; 22-16; 23-1; 23-2; 23-3; 23-9; 23-14 (4); 24-3; 24-4 (3); 24-15;
PIH Notices: 03-23 (4); 03-11 (2); 03-05 (2); 02-27 (11); 02-21 (6); 02-20 (3); 01-43; 01-41 (8); 01-40 (2); 01-20; 01-15 Impr Integ Hbk (25); 01-10 (2); 01-06; 01-01 (6); 00-46; 00-28; 00-27; 00-24B (5); 00-23; 00-11; 00-11A (5); 00-09 (7); 96-65; 95-48 (8); 95-48 Tech Asst (8);
Admin Plan: s2p6 (2); s2p7; s3p2; s3p3; s5p2 (2); s6p2 (2); s6p3 (10); s6p5 (3); s6p6 (2); s6p7 (2); s6p10 (2); s7p5; s8p1; s8p3; s8p4 (2); s8p5 (3); s9p2 (2); s10p4 (4); s10p5; s13p2 (2); s16p2; s18p7; s20p6; s21p2 (2); s21p5 (2); s21p9; s22p1 (2); s22p2; s24p5 (5); s25p4; s25p5 (2); s25p6

PERIODIC 55
24 CFR 5: .609 (5); .653;
24 CFR 35 SubM: .1200; .1215 (4);
24 CFR 982: Intro; .4; .405; .629; .633; .641;
HUD-50058Instr: p29 (3); p32;
HUD-52580-A: p15;
7420.10G Gbk: 2-4; 5-14 Ex 5-2 (4); 5-15 Ex 5-2; 5-17; 5-23 (2); 5-26; 5-32; 5-52 Ex 5-5; 8-14; 9-4; 9-11; 11-8; 21-4; 21-6;
PIH Notices: 01-15 Impr Integ Hbk (9); 95-48; 95-48 Tech Asst;
Admin Plan: s1p6; s3p1; s6p9; s6p9

PERIODIC PAYMENT.......................1
7420.10G Gbk: 5-14 Ex 5-2

PERIODIC PAYMENTS 9
HUD-50058Instr: p32;
7420.10G Gbk: 5-14 Ex 5-2; 5-15 Ex 5-2; 5-23 (2); 5-26; 5-52 Ex 5-5;
Admin Plan: s6p9; s6p9

PERIODIC RECEIPTS.......................4
24 CFR 5: .609;
7420.10G Gbk: 5-14 Ex 5-2;
PIH Notices: 01-15 Impr Integ Hbk; 01-15 Impr Integ Hbk

PERIODICALLY..............................19
24 CFR 5: .318;
7420.10G Gbk: 1-5; 1-6; 1-7; 3-6; 4-1; 4-9; 9-4; 9-7; 20-1; 20-2; 20-5; 20-23; 23-14; 24-7;
PIH Notices: 99-11;
Admin Plan: s1p7; s4p2; s25p1

PERIODS...20
24 CFR 5: .353; .518 (4);
24 CFR 982: .312;
HUD-50058Instr: p18;
7420.10G Gbk: 3-4; 4-1; 5-52 Ex 5-5; 24-5; 24-10; 24-12;
PIH Notices: 01-15 Impr Integ Hbk; 01-06; 95-48 (2); 95-48 Tech Asst (2);
Admin Plan: s7p6

PERJURY...2
24 CFR 5: .508;
HUD-903: p1

PERMANENT 45
24 CFR 5: .504; .514; .630;
24 CFR 982: .4; .401 (2); .628;
HUD-50058Instr: p5; p61; p73; p74;
HUD-52580-A: p2; p4; p6; p8;
7420.10G Gbk: 4-10; 5-9 Ex 5-1 (2); 5-10 Ex 5-1 (2); 5-22; 6-7; 6-8; 10-7; 10-8 (2); 12-16 Ex 12-4; 17-10;
PIH Notices: 03-11; 01-10; 00-23; 00-09; 95-48 (4); 95-48 Tech Asst (4);
Admin Plan: s6p7 (2); s7p8; s19p1; s25p3

PERMANENTLY 34
HUD-52580-A: p2; p4; p5; p6; p7 (2); p8 (2); p9; p10; p11; p12; p15;
7420.10G Gbk: 10-6;
PIH Notices: 95-48; 95-48 Tech Asst;

Admin Plan: s6p5 (3); s6p6 (9); s6p7; s6p8 (2); s7p8; s9p3; s24p3

PERMANENTLY ABSENT............12
Admin Plan: s6p5 (3); s6p6 (7); s6p7; s7p8

PERMANENTLY CONFINED.........3
Admin Plan: s6p6; s6p8; s6p8

PERMISSIVE DEDUCTIONS..........5
PIH Notices: 01-15 Impr Integ Hbk (4); 01-15 Impr Integ Hbk

PERMIT..71
24 CFR 5: .312; .318 (3); .350 (2); .360 (2); .518; .603; .653;
24 CFR 982: .156 (2); .302; .310; .401; .552; .601 (3); .620; .638; .642 (2);
HUD-50058Instr: p13; p70;
HUD-52646: p2;
7420.10G Gbk: 4-27 Ex 4-2; 5-3; 5-38; 5-43; 8-13; 8-15; 10-8; 12-7; 14-4; 14-5; 15-6 (3); 19-3; 20-15; 21-7; 22-2; 22-14; 22-17; 24-10;
PIH Notices: 03-23 (2); 02-27 (3); 02-01 (3); 01-41; 00-09; 99-52 (3);
Admin Plan: s1p3; s5p3; s6p4; s7p7; s10p3; s13p1; s13p2; s19p1 (2); s24p5; s25p5

PERMITS..28
24 CFR 982: .158; .204; .643;
HUD-50058Instr: p18;
7420.10G Gbk: 3-5; 5-43; 19-5 (2);
PIH Notices: 03-05; 02-27; 02-20 (2); 02-01; 01-41; 01-40; 00-46 (2); 00-09; 99-52; 95-48 (5); 95-48 Tech Asst (3);
Admin Plan: s4p1

PERMITTED.................................87
24 CFR 5: .312; .315; .318 (2); .321; .353; .360; .514 (3); .609; .611; .653;
24 CFR 982: .155; .156; .312; .555;
HUD-52641: p1;
HUD-9886: p2;
7420.10G Gbk: 1-4; 3-4 (2); 4-17; 5-4; 5-8; 5-14 Ex 5-2; 5-31; 5-46 Ex 5-5; 8-22; 10-7; 10-15; 10-19; 11-5; 14-3; 14-4; 14-5; 20-2; 20-4; 20-14; 20-15; 20-16; 20-18; 21-7; 23-6; 24-8; 24-10;
PIH Notices: 03-23 (4); 01-41; 01-27 (2); 01-15 Impr Integ Hbk (2); 00-23; 99-11; 95-48 (13); 95-48 Tech Asst (13);
Admin Plan: s6p8; s6p11; s8p1; s13p1

PERMITTING................................13
24 CFR 5: .350; .360 (2); .522;
7420.10G Gbk: 5-3; 5-30; 5-34; 5-36 Ex 5-4; 24-10;
PIH Notices: 01-41; 00-09;
Admin Plan: s22p4; s23p7

PERSON UNDER THE CONTROL.5
24 CFR 982: .306;
HUD-52641: p6;
7420.10G Gbk: 8-19; 11-3;
Admin Plan: s16p2

PERSON WITH DISABILITIES..119
24 CFR 5: .403 (3); .611 (2); .617 (8); .655 (4);
24 CFR 982: .204; .207 (3); .303; .306; .316; .503; .505; .517 (2); .552; .606 (2); .610 (2); .615; .619; .620; .625; .627 (2); .635 (2);
HUD-50058: p i;
HUD-50058Instr: p15; p43; p47 (2); p71; p72; p74; p75;
HUD-52517: p2;
HUD-52641: p1; p5; p6; p10;
HUD-52641-A: p3;
HUD-52646: p2;
7420.10G Gbk: 3-5; 4-6; 4-16; 4-17 (3); 4-25 Ex 4-2; 5-2 (2); 5-15 Ex 5-2; 5-29 (2); 5-30 (2); 5-44; 8-6; 8-12; 8-15; 8-19; 12-3; 12-12 Ex 12-1; 12-13 Ex 12-1; 13-9; 15-6; 17-3; 17-4; 17-6 (2); 17-7 (2); 20-4; 22-14; 24-10;
PIH Notices: 02-20; 01-15 Impr Integ Hbk (2); 00-46;
Admin Plan: s2p3; s6p2 (5); s6p3 (7); s6p11; s7p7 (2); s11p3; s19p1 (4); s25p2 (3); s25p2

PERSONAL....................................75
24 CFR 5: .603; .609 (3); .630; .703;
24 CFR 982: .310 (3); .401;

.402; .605; .614; .625; .632;
HUD-50058Instr: p22; p27; p28; p31; p74;
7420.10G Gbk: 2-5 (3); 4-10; 5-7; 5-14 Ex 5-2 (2); 5-15 Ex 5-2; 5-25 Ex 5-3 (3); 5-37; 5-41; 6-8; 10-3; 10-8; 10-11 (2); 10-33; 12-5; 15-2; 15-3 (2); 18-1; 18-7; 23-12;
PIH Notices: 01-15 Impr Integ Hbk (6); 00-41; 00-11; 95-48 (8); 95-48 Tech Asst (8);
Admin Plan: s1p6; s6p10; s7p6; s20p6; s25p7

PERSONAL CARE 2
HUD-50058Instr: p28;
PIH Notices: 00-41

PERSONAL CLEANLINESS 4
24 CFR 982: .401; .605; .614;
7420.10G Gbk: 10-3

PERSONAL DECLARATION 1
Admin Plan: s20p6

PERSONAL OR FAMILY USE 2
HUD-52641: p9;
HUD-52641-A: p2

PERSONAL PROPERTY 10
24 CFR 5: .603; .609;
HUD-50058Instr: p22; p74;
7420.10G Gbk: 5-14 Ex 5-2; 5-25 Ex 5-3 (2);
PIH Notices: 01-15 Impr Integ Hbk (2);
Admin Plan: s7p6

PERSONAL RESPONSIBILITY 4
24 CFR 5: .630;
24 CFR 982: .310;
7420.10G Gbk: 6-8;
PIH Notices: 00-11

PERSONAL SERVICES 14
24 CFR 5: .609;
HUD-50058Instr: p27;
7420.10G Gbk: 5-14 Ex 5-2; 23-12;
PIH Notices: 01-15 Impr Integ Hbk (2); 95-48 (4); 95-48 Tech Asst (3); 95-48 Tech Asst

PERSONALITY 2
PIH Notices: 95-48; 95-48 Tech Asst

PERSONNEL.................................. 62
24 CFR 5: .661 (21);
24 CFR 982: .552;
HUD-50058Instr: p50; p74; p75;
HUD-903: p1;
7420.10G Gbk: 10-1; 15-6; 21-12 Ex 21-2; 21-12 Ex 21-3; 21-15 Ex 21-5; 21-16 Ex 21-6; 21-17; 21-18; 22-15;
PIH Notices: 03-11 (2); 03-05 (2); 02-27 (4); 02-01; 01-40; 01-06 (2); 00-23; 99-52; 99-11 (4); 95-48; 95-48 Tech Asst;
Admin Plan: s1p1; s2p6; s7p7; s15p2 (2); s15p5; s20p2

PERTINENT 21
24 CFR 5: .230 (2);
24 CFR 982: .158;
HUD-52641: p5; p6;
7420.10G Gbk: 3-1; 5-13; 11-13; 12-3; 19-11;
PIH Notices: 02-27 (2); 02-01; 00-11A; 99-52;
Admin Plan: s3p1; s3p3; s18p5 (3); s20p2

PER-UNIT COST 29
7420.10G Gbk: 20-12 Ex 20-2 (3); 20-18 (14); 20-19 Ex 20-3 (6); 20-20 (2); 20-22 (2);
PIH Notices: 03-23; 03-23

PER-UNIT COSTS 3
7420.10G Gbk: 20-18;
PIH Notices: 03-23; 02-06

PER-UNIT MONTH.......................... 1
7420.10G Gbk: 20-3

PET 267
24 CFR 5: .303; .306 (2); .312 (4); .315 (11); .318 (80); .321 (6); .324 (2); .327 (2); .350 (59); .353 (58); .359; .360 (13); .363 (21); .380 (5);
PIH Notices: 02-01; 99-52

PET CARE....................................... 2
24 CFR 5: .318; .318

PET DEPOSIT 14
24 CFR 5: .318 (13); .363

PET DEPOSITS................................ 5
24 CFR 5: .318 (4); .318

PET EXERCISE 1
24 CFR 5: .350

PET LICENSING 1
24 CFR 5: .318

PET POLICIES................................. 2
PIH Notices: 02-01; 99-52

PET REGISTRATION....................... 3
24 CFR 5: .350 (2); .363

PET REMOVAL 2
24 CFR 5: .353; .353
PET RESTRAINT 1
24 CFR 5: .350
PET RULE 19
24 CFR 5: .312; .350;
.353 (16); .353
PET RULE VIOLATION 15
24 CFR 5: .353 (14); .353
PET RULES 73
24 CFR 5: .303; .312 (3);
.315 (9); .318 (25);
.321 (4); .350 (12);
.353 (13); .363; .380 (4);
.380
PET SIZE 1
24 CFR 5: .318
PET VIOLATION 1
24 CFR 5: .350
PET WASTE 6
24 CFR 5: .318; .350 (4); .350
PETS 46
24 CFR 5: .306; .309 (4);
.312 (2); .315 (5);
.318 (15); .321 (4);
.350 (6); .353 (2);
.359 (2);
7420.10G Gbk: 5-43;
PIH Notices: 02-01 (2); 99-52;
99-52
PETS TEMPORARILY 1
24 CFR 5: .318
PHA CONTRACTOR 1
24 CFR 982: .553
PHA EMPLOYEE ....
5
24 CFR 982: .553; .631;
7420.10G Gbk: 11-3; 22-11;
22-14
PHA EMPLOYEES 7
7420.10G Gbk: 3-6; 8-20; 11-3;
22-1; 22-2; 22-11;
PIH Notices: 01-15
PHA OBLIGATIONS 2
7420.10G Gbk: 1-12 Ex 1-2; 1-
12 Ex 1-2
PHA PERSONNEL 4
24 CFR 982: .552;
7420.10G Gbk: 15-6;
Admin Plan: s15p2; s15p5
PHA PLAN 34
24 CFR 5: .655;
24 CFR 982: Intro; .4; .5;
.54; .201 (2); .202;
7420.10G Gbk: 3-1 (6); 3-6 (5);
3-7 (2); 3-8 (4); 3-9; 4-
14; 4-16 (2); 4-19;
PIH Notices: 02-01; 01-15;
01-15 Impr Integ Hbk; 99-52
PHA-APPROVED 13
24 CFR 5: .100;
24 CFR 982: .308; .404; .613;
HUD-52641: p1; 8; p10;
HUD-52641-A: p1; p3;
HUD-52648: p1;
PIH Notices: 00-24B (2);
Admin Plan: s19p1
PHA-OWNED 8
24 CFR 982: .152; .352 (2);
.628 (2); .641;
7420.10G Gbk: 8-17; 10-30
PHARMACIST 2
7420.10G Gbk: 5-51 Ex 5-5;
Admin Plan: s7p7
PHARMACISTS 1
PIH Notices: 01-15
PHARMACY 5
7420.10G Gbk: 4-27 Ex 4-2; 12-
13 Ex 12-1;
PIH Notices: 01-15; 95-48;
95-48 Tech Asst
PHASED IN 1
7420.10G Gbk: 20-19 Ex 20-3
PHASE-IN 10
24 CFR 5: .617;
7420.10G Gbk: 5-16 Ex 5-2;
PIH Notices: 01-
15 Impr Integ Hbk (2); 00-
11A;
Admin Plan: s6p2; s6p3 (3);
s6p4
PHONE CALL ....
1
7420.10G Gbk: 22-11
PHONE CALLS 6
24 CFR 982: .312;
7420.10G Gbk: 4-13; 9-6; 10-
33; 22-18; 24-7
PHONE NUMBER 9
24 CFR 5: .350;
HUD-52580: p1 (2); p2;
HUD-903: p1;
7420.10G Gbk: 4-7; 10-17; 10-
21; 12-13 Ex 12-1
PHONE NUMBERS 2
7420.10G Gbk: 4-27 Ex 4-2; 10-26
PHOTOGRAPHS 2
7420.10G Gbk: 4-3; 9-5
PHYSICAL 102
24 CFR 5: .100; .315; .403;
.703 (3); .705 (3);
24 CFR 982: .315; .636;
HUD-50058: p i;

HUD-50058Instr: p15; p70; p72; p74;
HUD-52665: p1 (2);
HUD-903-1: p2;
7420.10G Gbk: 4-3; 5-43; 5-44; 10-18;
PIH Notices: 02-01 (2); 01-41 (2); 00-41; 00-09; 99-52 (2); 95-48 (31); 95-48 Tech Asst (31);
Admin Plan: s1p4; s1p5; s15p2 (3); s15p3 (2); s23p2; s25p2

PHYSICAL ABUSE 2
Admin Plan: s15p2; s15p2

PHYSICAL ALTERATION 2
PIH Notices: 02-01; 99-52

PHYSICAL CONDITION 6
24 CFR 5: .315; .703 (3);
24 CFR 982: .636;
PIH Notices: 01-41

PHYSICAL FEATURES 2
PIH Notices: 02-01; 99-52

PHYSICAL FORCE 3
24 CFR 5: .100;
Admin Plan: s15p3; s15p3

PHYSICAL IMPAIRMENT 2
PIH Notices: 95-48; 95-48 Tech Asst

PHYSICAL IMPAIRMENTS 10
PIH Notices: 95-48 (5); 95-48 Tech Asst (4); 95-48 Tech Asst

PHYSICAL VIOLENCE 1
24 CFR 982: .315

PHYSICALLY 8
24 CFR 5: .318;
HUD-50058Instr: p20 (3);
PIH Notices: 01-41; 95-48; 95-48 Tech Asst;
Admin Plan: s8p2

PHYSICIAN 5
7420.10G Gbk: 5-32; 5-50 Ex 5-5;
PIH Notices: 95-48; 95-48 Tech Asst;
Admin Plan: s7p8

PHYSICIANS 2
PIH Notices: 01-15; 01-15 Impr Integ Hbk

PHYSIOLOGICAL 2
PIH Notices: 95-48; 95-48 Tech Asst

PIC 142
HUD-50058: p1; p i; p ii; p x; p xi; p xiii; p xiv; p xvi;
HUD-50058Instr: p1; p7; p8 (6); p42; p46; p53; p56; p59; p74;
PIH Notices: 03-20 (11); 02-27 (9); 01-43 (6); 01-11 (3); 01-06 (63); 00-53 (26); 00-34; 00-24

PILOT 12
24 CFR 982: Intro; .642 (10);
HUD-52580-A: p4

PILOT PROGRAM 11
24 CFR 982: Intro; .642 (9); .642

PLACEMENT 46
24 CFR 5: .403; .603;
24 CFR 982: .201; .402;
HUD-50058: p16;
HUD-50058Instr: p61 (2); p71; p72;
7420.10G Gbk: 4-7; 4-8; 4-14; 5-1; 5-41; 9-10; 10-29 (2); 12-16 Ex 12-4; 23-1; 23-8 Ex 23-1 (2);
PIH Notices: 00-11 (2); 00-11A (2); 95-48; 95-48 Tech Asst;
Admin Plan: s1p7; s2p1 (4); s2p2; s2p3 (2); s2p5; s3p1 (2); s6p3; s6p6 (2); s10p5; s15p1; s18p8; s25p1; s25p7

PLAN TO ATTAIN SELF-SUFFICIENCY 3
24 CFR 5: .609;
HUD-50058Instr: p29;
PIH Notices: 01-15 Impr Integ Hbk

PLAUSIBLE 1
Admin Plan: s20p3

PLAY AREAS 5
24 CFR 5: .703;
24 CFR 35 SubM: .1200;
HUD-52580-A: p13;
7420.10G Gbk: 10-12; 10-16

PLAYGROUND 3
7420.10G Gbk: 9-14 Ex 9-1; 9-16 Ex 9-2; 9-17 Ex 9-3

PLAYGROUNDS 3
7420.10G Gbk: 10-17;
PIH Notices: 02-01; 99-52

PLEASURE 1
24 CFR 5: .306

PLUMBING 17
24 CFR 982: .631;
HUD-52580: p5 (2);
HUD-52580-A: p1; p6; p15 (2); p16 (4);
7420.10G Gbk: 10-4 (2); 10-7;

10-11;
Admin Plan: s10p4; s22p3

PMSA....2
PIH Notices: 02-20; 00-46

PO BOX....1
HUD-50058Instr: p20

POISON....3
HUD-52580-A: p17;
PIH Notices: 95-48; 95-48 Tech Asst

POISONED....1
7420.10G Gbk: 10-12

POISONING....7
24 CFR 982: .401;
7420.10G Gbk: 10-11; 10-15 (2); 10-36 Ex 10-1;
PIH Notices: 00-23; 00-23

POLICE....29
24 CFR 5: .661 (5);
HUD-50058Instr: p39; p50; p74 (5); p75;
7420.10G Gbk: 2-5; 22-11;
PIH Notices: 03-11 (2); 95-48 (4); 95-48 Tech Asst (4);
Admin Plan: s15p4; s15p5; s20p3; s20p4

POLICE OFFICER....8
24 CFR 5: .661 (3);
HUD-50058Instr: p74 (3); p75;
7420.10G Gbk: 2-5

POLICE OFFICERS....3
HUD-50058Instr: p39; p50; p74

POLICE RECORDS....1
Admin Plan: s20p4

POLICIES....321
24 CFR 5: .100; .609; .630; .657;
24 CFR 982: .4; .54 (6); .201; .202; .204 (2); .207 (2); .307; .312 (2); .314 (3); .315; .516 (3); .551; .555; .635; .637; .643;
HUD-50058Instr: p29; p38; p70;
HUD-52646: p2;
HUD-52648: p1 (3); p2;
7420.10G Gbk: 1-13; 1-15; 2-2; 2-3; 2-10; 3-1 (6); 3-2 (6); 3-3 (3); 3-4 (2); 3-5 (3); 3-7 (5); 3-8; 3-9 (7); 4-1 (2); 4-18 (2); 4-22 (6); 5-2; 5-3; 5-4; 5-12; 5-14 Ex 5-2; 5-25 Ex 5-3; 5-36; 5-43; 8-5; 8-12; 10-32; 11-4 (4); 11-9; 12-8; 12-9 (3); 13-1; 13-3; 13-4 (6); 13-5 (3); 13-7 (3); 15-5; 15-6 (2); 15-7; 16-1; 17-1; 18-1; 19-6; 21-1 (2); 21-3; 21-5; 21-7 (7); 21-9; 21-17; 22-1; 22-5; 22-7 (2); 22-8; 22-15; 22-18; 23-4; 23-5 (4); 23-10 (3); 23-18; 23-19;
PIH Notices: 03-23; 03-11 (2); 03-05; 02-27 (2); 02-21 (2); 02-01 (5); 01-41 (3); 01-40; 01-20 (2); 01-15 (5); 01-15 Impr Integ Hbk (16); 00-53; 00-24B (6); 00-09 (3); 99-52 (5); 95-48 (37); 95-48 Tech Asst (37);
Admin Plan: s1p1; s1p2 (2); s2p2; s3p1; s4p1 (2); s6p1; s8p1; s8p2; s9p1; s10p1; s13p1 (2); s14p1; s15p1; s17p1; s18p1; s18p2; s18p4; s20p1; s21p3 (4); s23p1 (3); s24p6; s24p7 (2); s25p4

POLICY....280
24 CFR 5: .100; .516; .611; .653;
24 CFR 982: .54 (2); .161; .202 (2); .204 (3); .205; .301 (2); .303 (3); .307 (2); .312 (3); .315; .503; .552; .554; .555 (2);
HUD-50058: p i;
HUD-50058Instr: p3; p5; p14; p34;
HUD-52641: p6;
HUD-52646: p1;
HUD-52648: p2 (3);
7420.10G Gbk: 1-13; 2-2; 2-3 (2); 2-9; 3-1 (7); 3-3 (2); 3-4 (11); 3-5 (4); 3-6 (2); 3-7; 4-5; 4-7 (3); 4-8; 4-9; 4-15; 4-18 (2); 4-21 (2); 4-22 (3); 4-27 Ex 4-2; 5-3 (2); 5-4 (2); 5-35 (2); 5-36 Ex 5-4; 5-39 (4); 5-40 (5); 6-7 (3); 6-8; 7-4; 8-5 (3); 8-6; 8-7; 8-8; 8-12; 8-13 (4); 8-19 (3); 8-20 (3); 8-22; 10-2; 10-26; 10-27; 10-34; 11-2; 11-3; 11-4 (4); 11-15; 12-1; 12-9 (5); 12-10 (3); 12-16 Ex 12-4; 13-7; 15-4; 15-5 (2); 15-6; 15-10 Ex 15-2; 16-2 (2); 16-4; 16-5 (2); 19-10 (3);

20-15; 20-23; 21-7 (3); 21-8; 21-9; 22-1; 22-8; 22-10; 23-4; 23-5; 23-10 (3); 23-12 (4); 23-18; 24-10;
PIH Notices: 03-23 (2); 02-27 (8); 02-20 (2); 02-06 (5); 02-01 (3); 01-41 (9); 01-15; 01-15 Impr Integ Hbk (10); 01-06 (2); 01-01 (12); 00-46; 00-09 (5); 99-52 (3); 96-65 (3); 95-48 (3); 95-48 Tech Asst (3);
Admin Plan: s1p1; s1p2; s1p4 (2); s2p1; s3p1; s6p5; s6p6; s7p2; s8p2 (2); s9p3; s11p1; s13p2; s16p1; s17p1; s18p1; s18p2; s18p4; s20p2; s20p5; s20p7; s21p5; s21p6; s23p1 (2); s23p8

POLICY A....................................2
7420.10G Gbk: 5-3; 12-9

POLITICAL....................................2
HUD-50058Instr: p71;
7420.10G Gbk: 5-10 Ex 5-1

POLLUTANT....................................1
7420.10G Gbk: 10-10

POLLUTANTS....................................5
24 CFR 982: .401 (2);
HUD-52580-A: p18;
7420.10G Gbk: 10-10; 10-10

POOL....................................16
24 CFR 982: .206;
7420.10G Gbk: 4-13 (2); 4-14; 9-16 Ex 9-2; 9-17 Ex 9-3; 11-9; 20-24;
PIH Notices: 02-27; 02-22; 02-01; 99-52;
Admin Plan: s3p1; s3p2 (2); s4p1

POOLS....................................2
PIH Notices: 95-48; 95-48 Tech Asst

POOR....................................22
24 CFR 5: .703;
24 CFR 982: .301; .401; .614;
HUD-52580-A: p17;
7420.10G Gbk: 4-2; 4-12; 5-40 (2); 7-1; 7-5; 7-6; 10-13; 17-5; 21-7; 21-9; 21-10 (2); 22-15;
PIH Notices: 95-48; 95-48 Tech Asst;
Admin Plan: s25p5

POOR DRAINAGE....................................5
24 CFR 5: .703;
24 CFR 982: .401; .614;
7420.10G Gbk: 10-13; 17-5

PORCH....................................12
24 CFR 5: .703 (2);
HUD-52580: p6 (2);
HUD-52580-A: p2; p8 (2); p13; p17; p19 (2);
7420.10G Gbk: 10-6

PORCHES....................................12
24 CFR 982: .401; .614;
HUD-52580: p5;
HUD-52580-A: p13 (3); p14 (2);
7420.10G Gbk: 10-6; 10-9; 10-10;
PIH Notices: 00-23

PORTABILITY....................................261
24 CFR 5: .514;
24 CFR 982: 24 CFR 982 (2); .4 (5); .152; .201; .301 (5); .314 (3); .353 (6); .355 (10); .552 (2); .601; .625; .636 (5); .641;
HUD-50058: p i; p2 (2); p10; p x (2); p11; p xi (2); p13; p xiii (2); p14; p xiv (2); p17 (2);
HUD-50058Instr: p7 (2); p8; p9 (11); p10 (6); p11 (2); p12; p13; p42 (5); p46 (5); p53 (3); p56 (3); p62 (2); p63 (2); p70 (2); p73; p74; p75; p77 (2);
HUD-52648: p2 (2); p3 (4);
HUD-52665: p1 (3); p2 (2);
7420.10G Gbk: 2-1; 2-2 (2); 2-3 (3); 2-7 (6); 2-8 (2); 2-9 (12); 2-10; 4-20; 5-3; 5-35; 7-7 (2); 8-3 (3); 8-6; 8-7; 9-5; 13-1 (12); 13-2 (9); 13-3 (7); 13-4 (3); 13-5 (2); 13-6 (3); 13-7 (2); 13-8 (2); 13-9 (3); 13-10 (2); 13-11 Ex 13-1 (2); 13-12 Ex 13-2 (2); 15-5; 19-2 (2); 19-4; 20-24 (4); 21-7; 21-8 (3); 21-16 Ex 21-6 (3); 23-18;
PIH Notices: 02-27; 01-41; 01-01 (5); 00-24B (2); 00-09; 96-65 (7);
Admin Plan: s2p5; s8p2 (2); s13p1 (4); s13p2 (5); s15p1 (2); s18p2; s21p6 (2); s25p6

PORTABILITY BILLING....................................5
24 CFR 982: .355;
7420.10G Gbk: 13-9;
PIH Notices: 96-65 (2); 96-65

PORTABLE 63
24 CFR 982: .201; .353 (3); .355 (16);
HUD-52580-A: p4 (3); p6; p15 (3);
7420.10G Gbk: 2-9; 4-20; 10-5; 10-7; 13-1; 13-2; 13-3; 13-4 (2); 13-5 (3); 13-6 (4); 13-8; 13-9 (3); 20-24 (3); 20-25; 23-5 (2); 23-19;
PIH Notices: 96-65 (4); 95-48 (2); 95-48 Tech Asst (2);
Admin Plan: s13p2

POSITION 26
24 CFR 5: .216; .359;
24 CFR 982: .4; .202; .203; .204;
HUD-50058Instr: p14; p19; p61; p75;
7420.10G Gbk: 4-12; 9-11 (2); 11-3; 11-4; 21-2; 21-4 (2); 22-2;
PIH Notices: 01-41; 00-09; 95-48; 95-48 Tech Asst;
Admin Plan: s23p1; s25p1; s25p3

POSITIONS 11
7420.10G Gbk: 9-11; 21-2; 21-3 (3); 21-13 (2);
PIH Notices: 00-11A (2); 00-01; 98-66

POSITIVE....................................45
HUD-50058: p7; p9 (2); p10 (2); p11; p12 (2);
HUD-50058Instr: p34; p35; p39 (2); p40 (2); p43 (2); p44 (2); p49 (2); p51 (2); p52 (2); p68; p69 (2);
HUD-52580: p6 (2);
HUD-52580-A: p19 (2);
7420.10G Gbk: 2-1; 2-5 (3); 4-6 (2); 5-38; 20-13; 22-5 (3); 22-18;
PIH Notices: 03-11;
Admin Plan: s1p1

POSSESS 6
HUD-50058Instr: p18;
7420.10G Gbk: 5-37;
PIH Notices: 95-48 (2); 95-48 Tech Asst; 95-48 Tech Asst

POSSESSES 4
7420.10G Gbk: 5-39; 15-7;
PIH Notices: 95-48; 95-48 Tech Asst

POSSESSION 15
24 CFR 5: .100; .504; .514 (2);
24 CFR 982: .307;
HUD-50058Instr: p74;
7420.10G Gbk: 3-4; 5-37 (3); 11-15;
PIH Notices: 95-48; 95-48 Tech Asst;
Admin Plan: s15p2; s18p5

POSSESSIONS....................................1
PIH Notices: 01-27

POST OFFICE 8
HUD-50058Instr: p19; p20 (2);
7420.10G Gbk: 4-5;
Admin Plan: s3p1 (2); s4p3; s6p6

POSTAL RECORDS 1
Admin Plan: s20p4

POSTED NOTICE....................................1
Admin Plan: s10p3

POSTED NOTICES 1
24 CFR 5: .353

POSTERS 5
7420.10G Gbk: 2-5; 22-10;
PIH Notices: 95-48; 95-48 Tech Asst;
Admin Plan: s1p3

POSTMARKED 2
7420.10G Gbk: 4-14;
Admin Plan: s3p1

POTABLE WATER....................................1
24 CFR 5: .703

POVERTY 116
24 CFR 982: .102; .301; .503;
HUD-50058Instr: p5;
HUD-52648: p2 (6); p3 (5); p4 (12);
7420.10G Gbk: 1-13; 2-1 (4); 2-2 (4); 2-3 (7); 2-4; 2-5; 2-7; 2-8; 2-10 (3); 2-11; 3-3 (2); 3-9; 7-4; 7-6; 7-7; 13-1 (2); 13-10 (2);
PIH Notices: 02-27; 02-22; 02-20 (7); 01-06 (7); 00-46 (7); 00-24B (5); 00-11 (2); 95-48; 95-48 Tech Asst;
Admin Plan: s1p6; s1p7; s8p1; s8p3 (3); s8p4 (3); s11p3; s21p5 (2); s21p6 (5); s24p1 (3); s25p6 (2); s25p8

POVERTY RATE 4
HUD-52648: p4 (3);
PIH Notices: 02-22

POVERTY RATES 1
Admin Plan: s24p1

PRACTICABLE....................................2
24 CFR 35 SubM: .1200;
24 CFR 982: .305

PRACTICAL 10
7420.10G Gbk: 8-9; 8-15;
PIH Notices: 03-12; 02-01 (2); 01-10 (2); 99-52 (2);
Admin Plan: s8p4

PRACTICE 47
24 CFR 982: .306 (3); .309; .313; .451;
HUD-52580-A: p2; p13; p17; p18 (2);
HUD-52641: p1; p6 (2); p7;
HUD-903: p3;
HUD-903-1: p6;
7420.10G Gbk: 2-9; 5-40; 8-2; 8-13; 8-19; 8-22; 10-2 (2); 10-5; 11-3; 11-7; 23-10; 24-8; 24-13; 24-14;
PIH Notices: 03-23; 02-27; 02-21; 02-06; 01-41 (3); 01-20; 01-15; 00-09 (2);
Admin Plan: s1p4; s10p5; s16p1; s16p2

PRACTICES 105
24 CFR 5: .350;
24 CFR 982: .451;
HUD-50058Instr: p15;
HUD-52580-A: p17 (2);
HUD-52641: p4;
7420.10G Gbk: 1-1; 2-3; 2-8; 2-10 (2); 5-38; 10-17; 10-18 (2); 10-22; 11-6; 13-7; 18-1; 24-12 (2);
PIH Notices: 02-27 (7); 02-21; 02-01 (2); 01-20; 01-15 (3); 00-49 (2); 00-11A; 00-09; 99-52 (2); 95-48 (30); 95-48 Tech Asst (30);
Admin Plan: s1p4; s8p2; s8p4; s20p2

PREAPPLICATION 3
7420.10G Gbk: 4-13; 4-20; 4-24 Ex 4-1

PRE-APPLICATION 9
7420.10G Gbk: 4-13; 4-14 (4); 4-15 (2); 4-20; 4-23 Ex 4-1

PRE-APPLICATIONS 1
7420.10G Gbk: 4-14

PREAPPROVALS 1
24 CFR 982: .630

PRE-APPROVED 3
24 CFR 982: .627 (2);
7420.10G Gbk: 8-7

PRECEDENCE 2
Admin Plan: s1p2; s9p2

PRECEDENT 2
PIH Notices: 02-01; 99-52

PREDATORY 1
24 CFR 982: .632

PREDATORY LOANS 1
24 CFR 982: .632

PREEMPTION 2
24 CFR 5: .210; .210

PREFERENCE 164
24 CFR 5: .306 (2); .359; .506 (2); .655 (26);
24 CFR 982: .4 (5); .202 (5); .204; .205 (2); .207 (30);
HUD-50058: p17; p xvii;
HUD-50058Instr: p62 (2);
HUD-52665: p2;
7420.10G Gbk: 4-4; 4-5 (2); 4-7; 4-8; 4-9 (2); 4-10; 4-14; 4-16 (13); 4-17 (8); 4-18 (10); 4-19 (2); 5-35; 10-2 (2); 10-3; 10-4 (2); 10-6; 10-7; 10-8; 10-9; 10-10; 10-11 (2); 10-12; 10-13 (2); 10-14; 10-15 (2); 12-3; 17-1; 19-7; 19-10; 21-8 (2); 22-3; 23-5 (2); 23-6 (4); 23-19;
PIH Notices: 02-27; 02-21 (2); 02-01; 01-27; 01-20 (2); 99-52;
Admin Plan: s3p1; s18p1

PREFERENCE STATUS 5
24 CFR 982: .207;
7420.10G Gbk: 4-5; 4-10; 4-16; 22-3

PREFERENCES 58
24 CFR 5: .506 (2); .601; .655 (6);
24 CFR 982: Intro; .54; .202; .207 (10); .355;
7420.10G Gbk: 1-7; 3-2 (2); 3-7; 3-8 (2); 4-2; 4-5; 4-15; 4-16 (6); 4-17 (2); 4-18 (7); 5-3; 5-50 Ex 5-5; 20-17; 21-8 (5); 23-6;
PIH Notices: 02-27; 01-27

PREGNANCY 1
PIH Notices: 01-15 Impr Integ Hbk

PREGNANT 9
24 CFR 982: .402;
HUD-903: p1 (2);
7420.10G Gbk: 5-41; 5-42; 5-43; 10-36 Ex 10-1;
PIH Notices: 01-15 Impr Integ Hbk;
Admin Plan: s5p1

PREGNANT WOMAN 2
24 CFR 982: .402;
7420.10G Gbk: 5-41

PREGNANT WOMEN 2

7420.10G Gbk: 5-42; 10-36 Ex 10-1

PREJUDICE 1
24 CFR 982: .202

PRELIMINARY.............................. 43
24 CFR 982: .152 (3);
7420.10G Gbk: 4-7; 4-14; 4-15 (2); 13-9; 20-2; 20-3 (9); 20-6; 20-20; 20-27; 20-28; 20-29; 21-3;
PIH Notices: 02-07 (4); 01-06 (8); 00-28 (4);
Admin Plan: s20p3 (2); s20p3

PRELIMINARY ELIGIBILITY DETERMINATIONS......................... 1
7420.10G Gbk: 21-3

PRELIMINARY FEE 15
24 CFR 982: .152 (3);
7420.10G Gbk: 13-9; 20-3 (5); 20-6; 20-28;
PIH Notices: 02-07 (2); 00-28; 00-28

PRELIMINARY FEES 9
7420.10G Gbk: 20-2; 20-3 (3); 20-20; 20-27; 20-29;
PIH Notices: 02-07; 00-28

PREMISES 167
24 CFR 5: .100 (4); .318 (5); .350 (4); .360 (4);
24 CFR 982: .4 (2); .306 (2); .307; .308; .310 (11); .401; .404; .507 (2); .510; .551 (2); .553 (7); .609 (2); .619 (3);
HUD-50058Instr: p75;
HUD-52517: p2;
HUD-52580-A: p4;
HUD-52641: p3 (3); p4 (2); p5 (4); p6 (3); p7; 8 (3); p9 (8); p10;
HUD-52641-A: p1 (3); p2 (8); p3;
HUD-52646: p2 (4);
7420.10G Gbk: 5-35; 5-39; 5-43; 8-18; 8-20 (2); 9-1 (2); 9-3 (2); 10-4; 10-6; 11-3; 11-11; 11-12 (4); 11-13 (4); 15-1; 15-2 (5); 15-3 (2); 15-6; 15-7; 17-3;
PIH Notices: 03-12; 03-11; 02-27; 02-01 (9); 01-41; 00-09; 99-52 (9);
Admin Plan: s2p6; s9p2; s10p1; s10p5 (2); s11p2 (2); s15p2; s15p3 (3); s16p2 (2); s23p7

PREMIUM.. 9
24 CFR 982: .317 (2); .635;
HUD-50058: p xiv;
HUD-50058Instr: p56;
7420.10G Gbk: 4-27 Ex 4-2 (2); 5-46 Ex 5-5; 5-51 Ex 5-5

PREPAYMENT............................. 104
24 CFR 982: .201; .203;
HUD-50058Instr: p19; p38 (2);
7420.10G Gbk: 4-20; 4-22; 5-3; 20-3; 23-2;
PIH Notices: 01-41 (42); 01-10; 00-28; 00-09 (48);
Admin Plan: s2p4; s4p2

PREPONDERANCE 9
24 CFR 982: .553; .555;
7420.10G Gbk: 5-37; 16-5; 22-14; 22-16;
Admin Plan: s15p4 (2); s18p6

PREPONDERANCE OF THE EVIDENCE...................................... 4
24 CFR 982: .553; .555;
7420.10G Gbk: 16-5;
Admin Plan: s18p6

PRE-PURCHASE 1
24 CFR 982: .631

PRE-QUALIFIED............................. 4
24 CFR 982: .627 (3);
Admin Plan: s22p2

PRESCRIBED 35
24 CFR 5: .318; .350; .526; .801;
24 CFR 982: .308; .517; .633;
HUD-52641: p1; p5; p10 (2);
HUD-52641-A: p3 (2);
HUD-52646: p1;
7420.10G Gbk: 5-32; 8-21; 10-17; 10-33 (2); 11-1; 11-11; 15-5; 20-19 Ex 20-3; 23-17 Ex 23-2;
PIH Notices: 03-12; 00-24B; 95-48; 95-48 Tech Asst;
Admin Plan: s7p2; s8p4; s9p2; s24p3; s24p5; s25p4; s25p6

PRESCRIPTION 7
7420.10G Gbk: 5-32;
PIH Notices: 01-15 Impr Integ Hbk; 95-48 (2); 95-48 Tech Asst (2);
Admin Plan: s6p11

PRESCRIPTION DRUGS 1
PIH Notices: 01-15 Impr Integ Hbk

PRESERVATION 160
24 CFR 5: .508; .514; .516 (5); .518 (4);
24 CFR 982: .203;
HUD-50058Instr: p13; p38;
7420.10G Gbk: 4-22; 5-8; 21-5;

PIH Notices: 02-07; 01-41 (39); 01-10 (2); 01-06; 00-09 (70); 95-48 (14); 95-48 Tech Asst (14);
Admin Plan: s4p2; s10p3
PRESERVATION OF FAMILIES......3
24 CFR 5: .508; .514;
7420.10G Gbk: 5-8
PRESERVATION VOUCHER.........12
PIH Notices: 00-09 (11); 00-09
PRESERVATION VOUCHERS 7
PIH Notices: 00-09 (6); 00-09
PRESERVE...4
24 CFR 5: .653;
7420.10G Gbk: 1-2; 15-1;
Admin Plan: s23p1
PRESERVED....................................2
PIH Notices: 01-41; 00-09
PRESERVES.....................................1
Admin Plan: s24p4
PRESERVING 5
24 CFR 5: .315;
PIH Notices: 01-41; 00-41; 00-09; 00-09
PRESUMPTION...............................1
24 CFR 5: .653
PREVIOUS LANDLORD.................1
7420.10G Gbk: 4-25 Ex 4-2
PRIMARY.......................................76
24 CFR 5: .512 (6); .514 (2);
24 CFR 982: .551; .609;
HUD-50058: p2; p ii; p17 (2);
HUD-50058Instr: p5; p11 (2); p16; p17 (2); p63; p72 (3);
HUD-52580-A: p15 (2);
7420.10G Gbk: 1-2; 2-1; 4-5; 5-7 (2); 5-8 (2); 5-9 Ex 5-1; 8-2; 8-15; 10-7; 18-7; 19-1; 19-4; 21-5;
PIH Notices: 03-20 (3); 01-41 (2); 00-09 (2); 99-11; 95-48 (10); 95-48 Tech Asst (10);
Admin Plan: s3p1; s20p2; s23p2; s25p1 (3); s25p3
PRIMARY CARE.............................1
HUD-50058Instr: p16
PRIMARY CAREGIVERS................2
HUD-50058Instr: p17; p17
PRIMARY PURPOSE.......................3
PIH Notices: 95-48; 95-48 Tech Asst;
Admin Plan: s3p1
PRIMARY USE 5
24 CFR 982: .551; .609;
HUD-52641: 8;
HUD-52641-A: p1;
7420.10G Gbk: 1-15
PRIMARY VERIFICATION 8
24 CFR 5: .512 (5);
7420.10G Gbk: 5-7 (2); 5-9 Ex 5-1
PRINCIPAL 73
24 CFR 5: .216; .661;
24 CFR 982: .4; .306; .453; .623; .635 (4);
HUD-50058: p xiii; p14; p xiv (2);
HUD-50058Instr: p53; p56 (4); p73;
HUD-52517: p2;
HUD-52641: p5 (2); p6 (2);
HUD-52648: p3 (3); p4 (10);
7420.10G Gbk: 5-49 Ex 5-5; 8-18; 11-1; 11-17; 17-10; 22-16 (2);
PIH Notices: 02-21; 01-15 Impr Integ Hbk; 01-06 (11); 00-24B (4); 00-11; 95-48; 95-48 Tech Asst;
Admin Plan: s7p6; s16p1; s19p1; s21p9; s22p2; s22p4; s24p3; s25p4
PRINCIPAL STOCKHOLDER.........1
24 CFR 5: .216
PRINCIPALS.....................................2
PIH Notices: 01-06;
Admin Plan: s24p3
PRIOR APPROVAL 7
24 CFR 5: .653; .655 (2);
PIH Notices: 01-41; 00-09;
Admin Plan: s6p7; s6p8
PRIOR ARRANGEMENTS..............1
Admin Plan: s11p1
PRIOR INCOME...............................4
24 CFR 5: .617;
PIH Notices: 01-15 Impr Integ Hbk (2);
Admin Plan: s6p3
PRIOR WRITTEN APPROVAL........5
HUD-52641: p2; 8;
HUD-52641-A: p1;
Admin Plan: s6p8; s6p8
PRIOR WRITTEN CONSENT 1
HUD-52641: p6
PRIORITIES.....................................7
24 CFR 982: .207 (2);
7420.10G Gbk: 4-16 (3); 19-1;
PIH Notices: 03-20
PRIORITIZE.....................................3
PIH Notices: 02-20; 01-10; 00-46
PRIORITY 22

7420.10G Gbk: 13-7; 19-13; 20-11; 22-1;
PIH Notices: 03-12; 02-21; 02-20; 02-14; 01-20; 00-46; 95-48 (5); 95-48 Tech Asst (5);
Admin Plan: s11p1; s24p4

PRIVACY 43
24 CFR 5: .212 (6); .234; .703;
24 CFR 982: .401; .605 (2); .614;
HUD-50058: p i;
HUD-50058Instr: p2 (6); p3 (3);
HUD-52580-A: p6;
HUD-52665: p1 (2);
HUD-903: p3;
HUD-9886: p1 (3);
7420.10G Gbk: 8-9; 10-3 (2); 17-2 (2); 17-4;
PIH Notices: 03-11; 01-15; 01-15 Impr Integ Hbk; 00-24B; 00-11A;
Admin Plan: s1p6 (2); s7p2

PRIVACY ACT 31
24 CFR 5: .212 (6); .234;
HUD-50058: p i;
HUD-50058Instr: p2 (6); p3 (3);
HUD-52665: p1 (2);
HUD-903: p3;
HUD-9886: p1 (2);
7420.10G Gbk: 5-13 (3); 12-3;
PIH Notices: 01-15; 01-15 Impr Integ Hbk; 00-24B;
Admin Plan: s1p6; s7p2

PRIVACY LAW 1
HUD-9886: p1

PRIVACY RIGHTS 1
Admin Plan: s1p6

PRIVATE MARKET 9
24 CFR 982: .313;
7420.10G Gbk: 1-7 (2); 8-5; 9-1; 10-24;
PIH Notices: 02-22;
Admin Plan: s8p4; s24p4

PRIVATE MARKET PRACTICE 4
24 CFR 982: .313;
HUD-52641: p1; p10;
HUD-52641-A: p2

PRIVATE MARKET PRACTICES ... 1
7420.10G Gbk: 11-11

PRIVATE MARKET RENTAL 1
7420.10G Gbk: 5-38

PRIVATE RENTAL MARKET 4
7420.10G Gbk: 5-38; 19-11; 22-6;
PIH Notices: 00-24B

PRIVATE SPACE 20
24 CFR 982: .4 (2); .617; .618 (4);
HUD-50058Instr: p43; p44; p47 (2); p49; p74; p75;
7420.10G Gbk: 17-7; 17-8 (3);
Admin Plan: s19p1; s19p1

PRIVILEGES 2
PIH Notices: 95-48; 95-48 Tech Asst

PROBATION 7
24 CFR 982: .310; .553;
HUD-52641: p9;
HUD-52641-A: p2;
7420.10G Gbk: 15-2; 15-6; 22-15

PROBATION OFFICER 1
24 CFR 982: .553

PROCEDURAL 5
24 CFR 982: .54;
7420.10G Gbk: 3-6;
Admin Plan: s20p5 (2); s20p5

PROCEDURAL GUIDELINES 2
24 CFR 982: .54;
7420.10G Gbk: 3-6

PROCEDURE 54
24 CFR 5: .353 (2); .380; .615; .630;
24 CFR 35 SubM: .1225;
24 CFR 982: .102; .302; .305; .355;
7420.10G Gbk: 4-7 (3); 4-14; 4-21; 8-15; 10-25; 10-26 (3); 10-27; 10-30 (2); 10-32; 10-33; 10-34; 22-6; 22-8 (2); 22-9;
PIH Notices: 03-23 (2); 01-15; 00-24B; 00-11 (2); 00-09 (2); 95-48 (4); 95-48 Tech Asst (4);
Admin Plan: s4p1; s15p6; s18p1; s18p2; s20p5 (3); s20p5

PROCEDURES 339
24 CFR 5: .110; .218; .236 (8); .312; .353 (8); .380 (2); .514 (11); .516; .615 (2); .705;
24 CFR 35 SubM: .1200; .1215;
24 CFR 982: .4; .54 (4); .102 (3); .152; .201; .301 (4); .314 (3); .353 (3); .355 (7); .516; .517; .552 (4); .554 (2); .555 (4); .601; .630; .636 (3);
HUD-50058Instr: p65; p76;
HUD-52665: p1 (3);
7420.10G Gbk: 1-5; 2-9; 2-10;

3-2 (4); 3-3 (2); 3-5 (6); 3-6; 3-8 (2); 3-9 (2); 4-3; 4-4; 4-7 (4); 4-9; 4-14; 4-17; 4-20; 4-21; 4-22 (2); 4-24 Ex 4-1; 4-25 Ex 4-2; 5-1; 5-2; 5-7; 5-8; 5-11; 5-34; 5-45; 7-1; 8-5; 9-11; 9-12; 10-2; 10-15; 10-18; 10-22; 10-23 (3); 10-27; 10-29; 10-32; 10-34 (2); 10-35 (3); 10-43 Ex 10-6; 11-9; 11-16 Ex 11-1; 12-1 (2); 12-2 (3); 12-4; 12-5 (2); 12-8 (2); 13-1 (2); 13-2 (2); 13-4 (4); 13-7 (2); 13-9; 15-5; 15-8; 16-3 (2); 16-4; 16-5; 19-6 (2); 19-11; 19-12; 20-14; 21-7; 22-1; 22-2; 22-5 (3); 22-6 (2); 22-7 (6); 22-8 (3); 22-10; 22-18; 23-4; 23-5 (2); 23-6; 23-10; 23-20; 24-13; 24-14;

PIH Notices: 03-23 (2); 03-20; 03-12 (3); 03-11 (4); 02-27 (9); 02-22; 02-21; 02-14 (4); 02-06 (2); 02-01 (2); 01-41 (4); 01-20; 01-15 (3); 01-10; 00-53; 00-34; 00-27; 00-24B (8); 00-23 (2); 00-09 (2); 99-52 (2); 99-11 (6); 96-65 (4); 95-48 (13); 95-48 Tech Asst (13);

Admin Plan: s3p1; s3p3; s5p1; s6p4; s6p7; s7p1 (2); s7p3; s8p1; s8p2; s10p1; s10p4 (2); s11p1; s13p1; s13p2; s14p1; s15p1 (3); s15p6; s18p1 (3); s18p2 (2); s18p3 (3); s18p4; s18p5; s19p1 (2); s20p5; s23p2 (3); s25p4

PROCEED 9

24 CFR 5: .508;

24 CFR 982: .555;

HUD-52580-A: p6;

7420.10G Gbk: 10-20; 16-1;

PIH Notices: 01-06;

Admin Plan: s18p4; s18p7; s24p5

PROCEEDED 1

PIH Notices: 03-11

PROCEEDING 10

24 CFR 5: .514;

7420.10G Gbk: 5-48 Ex 5-5; 22-17;

PIH Notices: 03-11; 95-48 (2); 95-48 Tech Asst (2);

Admin Plan: s23p6; s23p6

PROCEEDINGS 21

24 CFR 5: .514 (3);

24 CFR 982: .555;

7420.10G Gbk: 15-10 Ex 15-2; 16-5;

PIH Notices: 03-11; 95-48 (6); 95-48 Tech Asst (6);

Admin Plan: s7p3; s18p6

PROCEEDS 13

7420.10G Gbk: 1-1; 5-23; 5-49 Ex 5-5; 22-17 (3);

PIH Notices: 02-21; 01-20; 00-27;

Admin Plan: s6p10; s7p6; s10p4; s22p5

PROCEEED 1

HUD-52580-A: p1

PROCESS 342

24 CFR 5: .216; .508; .514 (7); .615;

24 CFR 982: .4; .54; .101 (3); .104; .311 (2); .314; .552 (2); .553; .554; .555;

HUD-50058Instr: p16; p17; p18;

HUD-903: p3;

HUD-903-1: p6;

7420.10G Gbk: 1-1; 1-5; 3-3; 3-5; 3-6; 3-9; 4-1 (2); 4-5; 4-7; 4-11 (4); 4-12 (4); 4-14 (3); 4-15; 4-20; 4-22 (2); 5-7 (2); 5-8 (3); 5-11 (2); 5-12; 5-24; 5-35; 5-44 (2); 6-1; 6-8; 8-1 (3); 8-2; 8-3; 8-6; 8-9 (2); 8-14 (2); 8-18; 8-22; 8-23; 9-8; 9-9; 9-10; 9-11; 9-12 (2); 10-25 (3); 10-26 (2); 10-27 (2); 10-30; 10-31; 10-35 (3); 10-43 Ex 10-6; 11-7 (5); 11-9; 11-10; 11-14; 11-16 Ex 11-1; 12-1; 12-2 (2); 12-5; 12-8 (3); 12-9; 13-3; 15-3; 15-4; 15-5; 16-1; 16-3 (2); 16-4; 18-9; 19-7; 19-9; 19-11; 19-13 (3); 20-2 (3); 20-7; 20-8 Ex 20-1; 20-9; 20-11 (3); 20-27; 20-29; 21-7 (2); 21-8; 21-10 (3); 21-19; 22-3; 22-8; 22-9; 22-10; 22-11 (3); 22-12 (3); 23-17 Ex 23-2; 24-7 (4); 24-8; 24-13;

PIH Notices: 03-23; 03-20;

03-11 (4); 02-27 (12); 02-14; 02-06 (2); 02-01 (5); 01-43 (2); 01-41 (18); 01-20; 01-15 (7); 01-11; 01-10 (8); 01-06 (2); 00-34; 00-24; 00-11 (2); 00-11A (10); 00-09 (24); 99-52 (5); 96-65; 95-48 (12); 95-48 Tech Asst (12);
Admin Plan: s1p4; s3p1 (2); s3p2 (2); s3p3 (2); s4p1; s9p4; s10p1 (2); s11p1 (4); s13p1; s14p2; s15p1 (2); s18p8; s20p4; s21p2; s21p3 (2); s21p4 (3); s21p5 (2); s21p6 (2); s21p7 (2); s21p8 (3); s21p9 (2); s23p3; s23p4; s23p6; s24p4

PROCESSED....29
HUD-50058Instr: p11;
7420.10G Gbk: 10-48 Ex 10-10; 11-7; 11-9 (2); 11-16 Ex 11-1; 12-5; 20-15; 21-7 (2); 21-11; 22-10; 22-18;
PIH Notices: 02-27; 02-21 (3); 02-14; 01-20; 00-27 (3);
Admin Plan: s8p5; s11p1 (3); s11p2; s16p3; s25p6

PROCESSES....27
24 CFR 982: .102 (2);
7420.10G Gbk: 4-1; 4-18; 5-23; 5-24; 8-1 (2); 8-4; 10-22; 10-23; 10-30; 10-35; 20-9; 20-11; 22-9;
PIH Notices: 02-27; 01-41; 00-11 (4); 00-11A (4); 00-09

PROCESSING....162
24 CFR 5: .214 (2); .216 (16); .218 (3); .230; .232; .234 (2);
24 CFR 982: .102;
HUD-903: p3;
HUD-903-1: p6;
7420.10G Gbk: 2-6; 2-9 (2); 4-4; 4-11; 4-14 (3); 4-15; 5-23; 8-2; 8-9; 8-15; 9-5; 10-26; 10-34; 11-1; 11-7; 11-8 (6); 11-9 (8); 12-9 (2); 12-10; 13-4; 13-5; 13-7 (2); 13-11 Ex 13-1; 19-6 (4); 19-11; 20-3; 21-4 (5); 21-7; 21-8; 21-9; 21-11 (4); 21-13 (2); 22-2; 22-6 (3); 22-7 (3); 22-18 (2); 24-7 (3); 24-14;
PIH Notices: 03-11 (10); 02-27 (4); 02-21 (4); 02-20; 02-14 (2); 02-06; 02-01; 01-41 (7); 01-20 (4); 01-10; 00-46; 00-27 (3); 00-09 (8); 99-52; 95-48 (2); 95-48 Tech Asst (2);
Admin Plan: s6p9; s9p1; s11p1 (2); s11p2 (3); s19p1; s24p7

PROCESSING ENTITY....24
24 CFR 5: .214 (2); .216 (16); .218 (3); .230; .232; .234

PROCESSOR....2
PIH Notices: 95-48; 95-48 Tech Asst

PROCURE....2
PIH Notices: 03-11; 03-11

PROCUREMENT....28
PIH Notices: 03-11 (5); 02-27 (22); 02-27

PROCUREMENTS....7
PIH Notices: 02-27 (6); 02-27

PRODUCT....7
24 CFR 5: .520;
HUD-50058: p ix;
HUD-50058Instr: p32;
7420.10G Gbk: 3-6; 20-7;
PIH Notices: 01-15 Impr Integ Hbk;
Admin Plan: s20p4

PRODUCTION....7
24 CFR 982: .553 (2);
7420.10G Gbk: 1-1; 1-3; 15-6; 21-5;
PIH Notices: 00-53

PRODUCTIVE....3
7420.10G Gbk: 9-9; 19-12;
Admin Plan: s1p1

PRODUCTIVITY....5
7420.10G Gbk: 4-6; 21-3; 21-5 (2); 21-6

PRODUCTS....7
24 CFR 982: .503;
7420.10G Gbk: 10-24;
PIH Notices: 02-20; 01-41; 01-15; 00-46; 00-09

PROFESSION....15
24 CFR 5: .609 (3);
7420.10G Gbk: 5-14 Ex 5-2 (3); 5-19 (2); 23-12;
PIH Notices: 01-15 Impr Integ Hbk (5); 01-15 Impr Integ Hbk

PROFESSIONAL....26
24 CFR 5: .661 (2);
24 CFR 35 SubM: .1225;

24 CFR 982: .631;
HUD-50058Instr: p25 (3); p74 (4); p75;
7420.10G Gbk: 2-13 Ex 2-1;
PIH Notices: 01-15; 95-48 (2); 95-48 Tech Asst (2);
Admin Plan: s1p5; s2p3; s5p2; s7p7; s11p2; s16p1; s18p6; s22p3

PROFESSIONALISM 4
24 CFR 982: .102;
PIH Notices: 95-48; 95-48 Tech Asst;
Admin Plan: s1p1; s20p4

PROFESSIONALLY 2
7420.10G Gbk: 2-6; 22-3

PROFESSIONALS 3
7420.10G Gbk: 5-31;
PIH Notices: 02-01; 99-52

PROFICIENCY 3
24 CFR 5: .603;
HUD-50058Instr: p71;
Admin Plan: s6p3

PROFICIENT 4
24 CFR 5: .502;
7420.10G Gbk: 5-11;
PIH Notices: 95-48; 95-48 Tech Asst

PROFICIENT IN ENGLISH 2
24 CFR 5: .502;
7420.10G Gbk: 5-11

PROFITMAKING 1
24 CFR 982: .551

PROFIT-MAKING 2
7420.10G Gbk: 1-15;
Admin Plan: s15p6

PROGRAM ABUSE 21
7420.10G Gbk: 20-6; 22-9 (2); 22-10 (5); 22-11; 22-15; 22-17; 22-18 (2);
PIH Notices: 02-07; 00-28;
Admin Plan: s7p7; s20p1; s20p2 (3); s20p2

PROGRAM ABUSES 1
7420.10G Gbk: 22-4

PROGRAM ACCESSIBILITY 68
24 CFR 5: .403;
HUD-50058Instr: p74;
7420.10G Gbk: 5-44;
PIH Notices: 95-48 (33); 95-48 Tech Asst (31);
Admin Plan: s1p3

PROGRAM BRIEFING 4
7420.10G Gbk: 8-1;
Admin Plan: s8p1; s13p2; s20p2

PROGRAM BRIEFINGS 1
Admin Plan: s8p2

PROGRAM EFFICIENCY 2
24 CFR 982: .102;
7420.10G Gbk: 22-3

PROGRAM ELIGIBILITY 5
7420.10G Gbk: 5-2; 5-13;
PIH Notices: 00-11A (2);
Admin Plan: s7p3

PROGRAM FRAUD 6
24 CFR 982: .163;
Admin Plan: s17p1; s17p2 (3); s17p2

PROGRAM FUNDED 4
HUD-50058Instr: p17 (2);
PIH Notices: 00-11A; 00-11A

PROGRAM FUNDING 16
24 CFR 982: .52; .103; .203 (2); .204; .206; .601 (3);
HUD-52641: p3;
7420.10G Gbk: 1-14; 4-22; 11-5;
PIH Notices: 03-23;
Admin Plan: s4p1; s19p1

PROGRAM FUNDING INCREMENT 1
24 CFR 982: .102

PROGRAM FUNDS 5
7420.10G Gbk: 5-34; 17-1; 20-1 (2); 22-16

PROGRAM FUNDS 15
24 CFR 35 SubM: .1200;
24 CFR 982: Intro; .156; .515;
7420.10G Gbk: 5-34; 17-1; 20-1 (2); 22-16;
PIH Notices: 00-24B;
Admin Plan: s4p1; s8p1; s11p2 (2); s17p2

PROGRAM INTEGRITY 9
7420.10G Gbk: 1-1; 1-10; 22-1; 22-9; 22-18 (2);
Admin Plan: s7p1; s20p1; s20p1

PROGRAM MANUAL 1
Admin Plan: s20p2

PROGRAM MOVE 14
Admin Plan: s8p3; s10p4; s13p1 (7); s14p1; s14p2; s15p5 (2); s15p5

PROGRAM MOVE IN 1
Admin Plan: s7p1

PROGRAM MOVES 4
Admin Plan: s8p3; s13p1 (2); s25p7

PROGRAM RECEIPTS 5
7420.10G Gbk: 10-31; 11-7; 20-1; 23-18; 23-18

PROGRAM RECEIPTS 16
24 CFR 982: .4; .156 (2); .157 (4); .352; .451 (2);
7420.10G Gbk: 10-31; 11-7; 20-1; 23-18 (2);
PIH Notices: 02-21

PROGRAM REQUIREMENT 2
7420.10G Gbk: 20-22; 22-9

PROGRAM REQUIREMENTS......96
24 CFR 5: 24 CFR 5; .508; .615;
24 CFR 982: .1; .2; .305 (2); .308; .501; .601; .637 (2); .643;
HUD-50058Instr: p62;
HUD-52641: p5; p10;
HUD-52641-A: p3;
HUD-52646: p2;
7420.10G Gbk: 1-1; 1-13; 2-2; 5-1; 5-11; 5-12; 5-21; 8-1 (3); 8-9; 8-10 (2); 8-14; 8-15; 9-1; 9-17 Ex 9-3; 9-19 Ex 9-4; 10-23 (2); 10-25; 10-32; 10-33; 11-1; 11-4; 11-11; 11-13; 11-14; 13-2 (2); 16-4; 18-1; 19-5; 21-2; 21-3; 21-5; 22-1 (4); 22-5; 22-7; 22-8; 22-9 (3); 22-10; 23-1; 23-10; 24-14;
PIH Notices: 01-41 (3); 01-15 Impr Integ Hbk; 01-06; 00-41; 00-24B; 00-23; 00-11; 00-11A; 00-09 (3);
Admin Plan: s1p2; s6p12 (2); s8p1; s9p2; s9p3; s11p1; s11p2; s11p3; s13p2; s17p2; s20p6; s22p2; s24p2; s24p5

PROGRAM RESERVE 41
7420.10G Gbk: 8-11; 20-13 (10); 20-14 (6); 20-15 (11); 20-16 (7); 20-17; 20-18; 20-27; 20-28; 20-29; 24-8
PIH Notices: 03-23

PROGRAM RESERVE ACCOUNT20
7420.10G Gbk: 8-11; 20-13 (2); 20-14 (3); 20-15 (10); 20-16 (2); 20-18; 24-8

PROGRAM RESERVE ACCOUNTS1
7420.10G Gbk: 20-13

PROGRAM RESERVES 17
7420.10G Gbk: 20-13 (2); 20-14 (6); 20-15; 20-16 (2); 20-19 Ex 20-3 (3); 20-22;
PIH Notices: 02-06; 00-49

PROGRAM RULE 6
24 CFR 982: .352;
HUD-50058Instr: p63;
PIH Notices: 02-20; 01-06; 00-46;
Admin Plan: s20p6

PROGRAM RULES 32
HUD-50058Instr: p47;
HUD-52665: p1;
7420.10G Gbk: 1-5; 2-6; 8-1; 10-42 Ex 10-5; 16-5 (2); 19-10; 21-7; 22-1; 22-2; 22-7; 23-10;
PIH Notices: 01-41 (3); 01-06; 00-41; 00-11A; 00-09 (4);
Admin Plan: s9p1; s17p1; s18p1; s20p1 (2); s20p2 (2); s20p2

PROGRAM UTILIZATION REPORT2
PIH Notices: 00-14; 00-14

PROGRAM VIOLATION 5
24 CFR 982: .551;
HUD-50058: p17;
HUD-50058Instr: p63;
Admin Plan: s20p5; s20p5

PROGRAM VIOLATIONS 1
7420.10G Gbk: 5-35

PROGRAM-DEFINED 1
7420.10G Gbk: 21-2

PROGRAM-HOMEOWNERSHIP ... 1
PIH Notices: 03-20

PROGRAMMATIC 10
PIH Notices: 03-20; 02-27 (2); 01-41 (2); 00-09 (4); 00-09

PROGRAMMED..............................5
7420.10G Gbk: 4-22; 10-25;
PIH Notices: 01-06 (2); 01-06

PROGRAMMER 1
PIH Notices: 02-27

PROGRAMMERS............................1
PIH Notices: 01-06

PROGRAMMING............................7
7420.10G Gbk: 4-13; 10-25;
PIH Notices: 00-24; 95-48 (2); 95-48 Tech Asst; 95-48 Tech Asst

PROGRAM-RELATED..................14
PIH Notices: 02-20 (7); 00-46 (6); 00-46

PROGRAMS 2
24 CFR 5: .520; .520

PROGRAM-SPECIFIC 2
PIH Notices: 02-20; 00-46

PROGRESS REPORT 8
24 CFR 982: .303;
HUD-50058Instr: p11; p59 (2);
7420.10G Gbk: 8-13 (2); 8-24 Ex 8-1; 23-19

PROGRESS REPORTS 9
7420.10G Gbk: 23-19 (7); Admin Plan: s21p9; s21p9

PROHIBIT 39
24 CFR 5: .309;
24 CFR 982: .53; .155 (2); .313; .314 (2); .553 (5); .637;
HUD-52641: p10;
HUD-52641-A: p2;
HUD-52646: p1;
7420.10G Gbk: 3-6; 6-10 Ex 6-2; 11-14; 12-9;
PIH Notices: 03-11; 02-01; 01-02 (2); 99-52; 95-48 (6); 95-48 Tech Asst (6);
Admin Plan: s16p1; s16p1

PROHIBITED 31
24 CFR 5: .236; .655 (2);
24 CFR 982: .202; .207 (2); .352;
HUD-50058Instr: p33;
HUD-52641: p6;
HUD-903: p2;
7420.10G Gbk: 1-7; 10-19; 10-22; 11-2; 14-4;
PIH Notices: 01-41; 01-15 Impr Integ Hbk; 01-02; 95-48 (5); 95-48 Tech Asst (5);
Admin Plan: s6p11; s16p2; s22p3

PROHIBITED INTEREST 2
HUD-52641: p6; p6

PROHIBITED INTEREST 2
HUD-52641: p6; p6

PROHIBITING 8
24 CFR 5: .321;
24 CFR 982: .553 (3); .626;
7420.10G Gbk: 11-11;
PIH Notices: 03-11; 01-02

PROHIBITION 41
24 CFR 5: .309; .522 (3);
24 CFR 982: .161; .352; .353; .521; .553; .625; .627; .632 (2); .633 (2); .641;
HUD-52641: p1; p5; p6; p10;
HUD-52641-A: p3;
7420.10G Gbk: 5-21; 11-11; 11-13; 11-14; 14-4 (2); 22-9;
PIH Notices: 02-15; 01-02; 95-48 (4); 95-48 Tech Asst (4);
Admin Plan: s9p3; s16p2; s24p2

PROHIBITIONS 12
24 CFR 5: .105 (2);
24 CFR 982: .553;
7420.10G Gbk: 22-9;
PIH Notices: 95-48 (3); 95-48 Tech Asst (3);
Admin Plan: s16p1; s20p6

PROHIBITIVE 1
7420.10G Gbk: 22-13

PROHIBITS 41
24 CFR 5: .327; .500;
HUD-50058Instr: p29;
HUD-52641: p1;
HUD-903: p2;
7420.10G Gbk: 5-11 (2); 5-42 (3); 5-44; 8-3; 14-4; 24-12;
PIH Notices: 03-23; 02-01 (2); 99-52 (2); 95-48 (12); 95-48 Tech Asst (9); 95-48 Tech Asst

PROJECT 459
24 CFR 5: .100 (2); .303 (5); .306 (14); .309 (2); .312 (3); .315 (8); .318 (32); .321 (2); .324 (2); .327 (4); .350 (15); .353 (25); .359 (7); .360 (15); .363 (5); .500; .504 (2); .516 (4); .518 (2); .601; .603 (2); .653 (5); .655 (8); .661 (16); .703;
24 CFR 982: 24 CFR 982 (2); .201 (2); .203 (6); .207; .504 (3); .521 (7);
HUD-50058: p2; p ii (2); p6; p viii; p10; p x; p xii (2);
HUD-50058Instr: p ii; p1; p7 (11); p9 (2); p10; p13 (3); p19 (3); p22 (2); p28; p37 (2); p42 (3); p47 (3); p50 (10); p74 (2); p75 (2);
HUD-52580-A: p1;
7420.10G Gbk: 1-8 (2); 1-9; 4-21 (2); 4-22 (3); 5-35; 5-48 Ex 5-5; 8-23; 20-5; 20-7; 20-13 (2); 20-27 (2); 23-2 (2); 23-13; 23-15;
PIH Notices: 03-23; 03-12; 02-22 (4); 02-21 (2); 02-20; 02-01 (6); 01-41 (60); 01-27 (3); 01-20; 01-15 Impr Integ Hbk; 01-10 (5); 01-02; 00-46; 00-27; 00-09 (39); 99-52 (6); 95-48 (3); 95-48 Tech Asst (3);
Admin Plan: s2p4 (2); s4p1 (3); s4p2; s7p5 (2); s15p2; s23p1; s23p3; s23p4; s23p5; s24p1 (7); s24p2;

s24p3 (7); s24p4 (6); s24p5; s24p6;

PROJECT ACCOUNT........................1
7420.10G Gbk: 20-13

PROJECT BASED.............................2
7420.10G Gbk: 24-15; 24-15

PROJECT BASED...........................23
HUD-50058: p10; p x;
HUD-50058Instr: p ii; p42;
7420.10G Gbk: 24-15 (2);
PIH Notices: 02-01 (2); 01-27; 99-52 (2);
Admin Plan: s4p1; s23p1; s23p4; s24p1 (5); s24p4; s24p5; s24p6; s24p7

PROJECT ELIGIBILITY 3
PIH Notices: 01-41 (2); 00-09

PROJECT OWNER.........................73
24 CFR 5: .100; .303; .306; .309; .312 (2); .315 (5); .318 (6); .321; .327; .350 (9); .353 (21); .359; .360 (12); .363 (5); .504; .516 (2);
HUD-50058Instr: p42; p74;
PIH Notices: 01-27

PROJECT OWNERS.......................21
24 CFR 5: .303 (4); .306 (2); .315 .318 (11); .321; .350 .353 (2); .359; .516; .516

PROJECT OWNER'S 3
24 CFR 5:

PROJECT RESERVE 1
7420.10G Gbk: 20-13

PROJECT WAITING LIST 1
24 CFR 5: .359

PROJECTBASED 6
HUD-50058Instr: p42;
7420.10G Gbk: 1-8; 1-9 (2); 20-8 Ex 20-1; 21-16 Ex 21-6

PROJECT-BASED.........................210
24 CFR 5: .100; .214 (2); .240; .514; .528; .601 (2); .634; .653 (8); .655 (2); .657 (2); .659; .661 (2); .801 (6);
24 CFR 982: .1; .102 (2); .203; .205 (3); .306; .352; .504 (3); .643;
HUD-50058: p10 (2); p x (2);
HUD-50058Instr: p38; p42 (7); p74; p78;
HUD-52641: p6;
HUD-52648: p2;
7420.10G Gbk: 1-1; 1-3; 1-6 (2); 1-8 (3); 1-9 (5); 2-6; 4-8 (2); 4-9; 4-22; 8-16; 10-15; 11-3; 11-18; 17-1; 21-11; 23-2;
PIH Notices: 02-22 (8); 02-07; 02-01; 01-41 (51); 01-27 (2); 01-10 (20); 01-06 (2); 00-14; 00-09 (31); 99-52; 99-11;
Admin Plan: s4p1; s23p5; s23p6; s24p1 (2); s24p2 (2); s24p6

PROJECT-BASING...........................1
Admin Plan: s24p1

PROJECTED 45
24 CFR 5: .318;
HUD-50058: p2 (2); p ii (2);
HUD-50058Instr: p12 (3);
7420.10G Gbk: 5-17; 5-46 Ex 5-5; 5-48 Ex 5-5; 20-6; 20-8; 20-13; 20-16; 20-20;
PIH Notices: 03-23 (13); 02-20; 02-06 (7); 02-01 (2); 01-10; 00-46; 99-52 (2); 95-48; 95-48 Tech Asst

PROJECTING 1
7420.10G Gbk: 20-22

PROJECTION 3
7420.10G Gbk: 20-7; 24-8;
PIH Notices: 02-27

PROJECTIONS 3
7420.10G Gbk: 24-3;
PIH Notices: 02-01; 99-52

PROJECTS 98
24 CFR 5: .300 (2); .303 (2); .306 (2); .312; .315 (2); .318 (2); .321 (2); .353; .360; .380; .653; .801 (5);
24 CFR 982: .310; .352; .453;
HUD-50058Instr: p13;
HUD-52641: p5;
HUD-52667: p ii (2);
7420.10G Gbk: 1-3; 8-16; 11-18; 15-4; 17-1; 20-20; 21-13; 23-3;
PIH Notices: 02-22 (3); 02-21 (3); 02-20; 02-06 (2); 02-01; 01-41 (16); 01-20; 01-15; 01-10 (2); 01-02; 00-46; 00-27; 00-11A; 00-09 (15); 99-52; 99-11;
Admin Plan: s4p1 (2); s16p2; s23p3; s24p4 (3); s24p5 (2)

PROMISE 5
7420.10G Gbk: 2-6; 2-11; 24-14;
PIH Notices: 95-48; 95-48 Tech Asst

PROMISES 1
7420.10G Gbk: 11-14

PROMISSORY NOTE......................1
Admin Plan: s17p1
PROMPT...27
24 CFR 5: .508;
24 CFR 982: .201; .404 (2); .554; .555; .619;
HUD-52648: p1;
7420.10G Gbk: 2-6 (2); 5-6; 10-33; 10-34; 10-35; 16-1; 19-2; 19-7; 19-11;
PIH Notices: 03-20 (2); 00-24B; 95-48; 95-48 Tech Asst;
Admin Plan: s16p1; s18p3; s21p5; s21p5
PROMPTED 2
PIH Notices: 01-06; 01-06
PROMPTLY....................................81
24 CFR 5: .236; .240; .514; .630 (2);
24 CFR 982: .152; .156; .305; .312; .313; .355 (6); .451; .551 (4); .555 (2); .636;
HUD-50058Instr: p38;
HUD-52641: p4 (2); p6; 8; p10;
HUD-52641-A: p1; p3;
HUD-52646: p2 (3);
HUD-52665: p1; p2;
7420.10G Gbk: 1-15 (2); 6-8; 8-4; 8-18; 10-33; 10-34 (2); 11-6; 13-6; 13-9; 16-5; 22-4;
PIH Notices: 02-27; 02-21 (4); 01-41; 01-20 (3); 01-15 Impr Integ Hbk (2); 01-06 (2); 00-27 (3); 00-09; 96-65 (6); 95-48 (2); 95-48 Tech Asst (2);
Admin Plan: s7p2; s18p1; s23p3; s24p6
PROMULGATE................................8
24 CFR 5: .312; .315 (4); .353; .380;
PIH Notices: 00-09
PROMULGATED.............................4
24 CFR 5: .312; .318; .321;
7420.10G Gbk: 10-15
PROMULGATION 1
24 CFR 5: .380
PROOF...38
24 CFR 5: .508; .514;
24 CFR 982: .310;
7420.10G Gbk: 5-9 Ex 5-1; 5-47 Ex 5-5; 10-8; 23-8 Ex 23-1 (2);
PIH Notices: 01-15; 01-15 Impr Integ Hbk (13);
Admin Plan: s3p1; s6p4; s6p7 (2); s7p3 (3); s7p7; s7p8; s9p4 (2); s16p2; s16p3 (2); s17p3; s18p7
PROOF OF AGE 2
24 CFR 5: .508;
7420.10G Gbk: 5-9 Ex 5-1
PROOF OF INCOME........................3
7420.10G Gbk: 5-47 Ex 5-5;
PIH Notices: 01-15 Impr Integ Hbk; 01-15 Impr Integ Hbk
PROPANE..1
24 CFR 5: .703
PROPER OPERATING CONDITION30
24 CFR 5: .703;
24 CFR 982: .401 (11); .605 (3); .614 (2);
HUD-52580-A: p6;
7420.10G Gbk: 10-3 (4); 10-5 (2); 10-7; 10-8 (3); 10-14; 17-2
PROPERTIES 80
24 CFR 982: .401;
HUD-52648: p2 (2);
7420.10G Gbk: 1-6; 2-3 (2); 3-4; 5-25 Ex 5-3; 9-3 (2); 9-6; 9-8; 9-11; 10-12; 10-42 Ex 10-5; 11-4;
PIH Notices: 03-12; 02-22 (3); 02-01; 01-41 (2); 01-10 (2); 01-02 (3); 00-41; 00-09 (2); 99-52; 99-11 (14); 95-48 (9); 95-48 Tech Asst (9);
Admin Plan: s11p1; s11p2 (3); s21p6 (2); s23p2 (3); s23p3 (2); s24p1; s24p2 (3); s24p4
PROPERTY 285
24 CFR 5: .100 (2); .214; .306 (4); .350; .603 (2); .609 (3); .661; .801 (2);
24 CFR 982: .157 (2); .307; .310 (3); .315; .520; .553; .623; .628 (3); .631; .633; .635;
HUD-50058Instr: p22 (2); p31 (2); p74 (2);
HUD-52517: p2;
HUD-52580: p5;
HUD-52580-A: p17 (2); p18;
HUD-52641: p9;
HUD-52641-A: p2 (2);
HUD-52667: p i;
HUD-903: p1 (3);
HUD-903-1: p2 (2);
7420.10G Gbk: 1-8 (2); 1-9 (4); 2-5; 3-3; 3-4; 4-26 Ex 4-2 (2); 5-14 Ex 5-

2; 5-15 Ex 5-2 (2); 5-23; 5-25 Ex 5-3 (3); 5-26 (6); 5-27; 5-38 (2); 5-39; 5-48 Ex 5-5; 5-49 Ex 5-5 (2); 8-16; 8-20; 9-3; 9-6; 9-11; 10-12; 10-16 (3); 10-30; 10-37 Ex 10-2 (5); 10-38 Ex 10-3; 10-39 Ex 10-4; 10-43 Ex 10-6; 10-44 Ex 10-7a; 10-45 Ex 10-7b; 12-2; 12-13 Ex 12-1; 12-16 Ex 12-4; 15-3; 18-4; 20-2; 20-3; 20-23 (2); 21-4; 24-12 (3); 24-14 (2);
PIH Notices: 03-11 (3); 02-27; 02-21; 02-14; 02-07; 01-41 (41); 01-20; 01-15 Impr Integ Hbk (9); 01-10 (9); 01-06; 00-28; 00-09 (39); 99-11 (8); 95-48 (5); 95-48 Tech Asst (5);
Admin Plan: s1p4; s1p6 (2); s1p7; s2p7; s6p10; s6p13; s7p5; s7p6 (3); s8p2; s8p3; s8p4; s8p5; s9p3 (2); s10p1 (4); s10p2 (4); s11p1 (2); s15p3 (2); s16p1; s16p3 (2); s19p1 (3); s22p1 (2); s22p4; s23p6; s24p3; s25p8

PROPERTY DAMAGE.....................2
24 CFR 5: .100;
Admin Plan: s15p3

PROPERTY DISPOSITION............... 14
24 CFR 5: .801 (2);
7420.10G Gbk: 1-9; 8-16; 20-3;
PIH Notices: 02-07; 01-41 (3); 01-10; 00-28; 00-09 (2); 00-09

PROPERTY LEDGER.......................2
7420.10G Gbk: 20-23; 20-23

PROPERTY LOSSES........................6
24 CFR 5: .609;
HUD-50058Instr: p31;
7420.10G Gbk: 5-15 Ex 5-2;
PIH Notices: 01-15 Impr Integ Hbk (2);
Admin Plan: s6p10

PROPERTY MANAGEMENT..........7
24 CFR 982: .310; .553;
HUD-52667: p i;
7420.10G Gbk: 18-4;
PIH Notices: 02-21; 01-20; 99-11

PROPERTY MANAGEMENT STAFF 5
24 CFR 982: .310; .553;
HUD-52641: p9;
HUD-52641-A: p2;
7420.10G Gbk: 15-2

PROPERTY MANAGERS................1
Admin Plan: s8p2

PROPERTY TAX..............................1
PIH Notices: 01-15 Impr Integ Hbk

PROPERTY TAXES..........................6
24 CFR 5: .609;
24 CFR 982: .520;
HUD-50058Instr: p31;
7420.10G Gbk: 5-15 Ex 5-2;
PIH Notices: 01-15 Impr Integ Hbk; 01-15 Impr Integ Hbk

PROPORTION..................................5
7420.10G Gbk: 20-17;
PIH Notices: 95-48 (2); 95-48 Tech Asst; 95-48 Tech Asst

PROPORTIONATELY.......................2
PIH Notices: 02-20; 00-46

PROPOSED ACTION.....................10
24 CFR 982: .553;
PIH Notices: 03-11;
Admin Plan: s18p3 (2); s18p4; s18p5; s20p7 (3); s20p7

PROPOSED HOUSEHOLD MEMBER 1
PIH Notices: 03-11

PROPOSED RENT..........................14
HUD-52517: p1;
7420.10G Gbk: 8-15; 8-18; 9-1; 9-10 (2); 14-4;
PIH Notices: 01-41 (4); 00-09 (2); 00-09

PROPOSED RULE...........................2
24 CFR 5: .312;
PIH Notices: 02-01

PROPOSED RULES 7
24 CFR 5: .353 (6); .353

PRORATA..1
7420.10G Gbk: 17-5

PRO-RATA 37
24 CFR 982: .613 (4); .617 (4);
7420.10G Gbk: 17-5; 17-6 (5); 17-7 (4); 17-8 (6); 17-9 (5);
Admin Plan: s19p1 (7); s19p1

PRO-RATA PORTION 18
24 CFR 982: .613 (4); .617 (4);
7420.10G Gbk: 17-7; 17-9;
Admin Plan: s19p1 (7); s19p1

PRORATE......................................16
24 CFR 5: .508; .520 (3);
24 CFR 982: .102 (2);

HUD-50058: p10; p11;
HUD-50058Instr: p42; p43 (2); p46; p47 (2);
7420.10G Gbk: 5-30;
Admin Plan: s18p7

PRO-RATE 1
7420.10G Gbk: 5-52 Ex 5-5

PRORATED 171
24 CFR 5: .508; .514; .516 (5); .518 (3); .520 (8); .522;
HUD-50058: p i; p5; p v (2); p9 (4); p ix; p10 (4); p x (3); p11 (4); p xi (2); p12 (4); p xii (3); p13 (3); p xiii (3); p14 (3); p xiv (2);
HUD-50058Instr: p17; p18 (2); p40 (2); p43 (6); p44 (9); p45 (2); p47 (8); p48 (7); p49 (4); p51 (5); p52 (4); p54 (5); p55 (3); p57 (6); p62; p68; p69 (4); p73 (2);
HUD-52665: p3;
7420.10G Gbk: 5-5 (8); 5-6 (2); 5-8 (2); 5-52 Ex 5-5; 6-6; 6-7 (6); 20-6; 20-7 (6); 20-9; 23-14;
PIH Notices: 03-23 (2); 02-21; 01-27 (3);
Admin Plan: s2p5; s6p11 (2); s14p1

PRO-RATED 4
HUD-50058Instr: p3;
HUD-52641: p4;
7420.10G Gbk: 11-5;
Admin Plan: s18p8

PRORATED ASSISTANCE 26
24 CFR 5: .516 (5); .518 (3); .520 (2); .522;
HUD-50058: p5; p v;
HUD-50058Instr: p17; p18 (2); p43; p48;
7420.10G Gbk: 5-5 (3); 5-6; 5-8; 6-6; 6-7;
PIH Notices: 01-27

PRO-RATED RENT 1
HUD-50058Instr: p3

PRORATING 5
24 CFR 5: .520 (3);
7420.10G Gbk: 20-7; 23-14

PRORATION 56
24 CFR 5: .514 (2); .518 (3); .520 (7);
24 CFR 982: .102;
HUD-50058: p ix; p10; p x (2); p11; p xi (2); p12; p xii; p13; p xiii (2); p14; p xiv (2);
HUD-50058Instr: p40; p44 (4); p48 (4); p51 (3); p54 (3); p55; p57 (4); p68;
7420.10G Gbk: 5-5; 5-8; 6-7 (4);
PIH Notices: 01-27

PROSECUTE 1
HUD-52648: p3

PROSECUTION 17
24 CFR 5: .514; .528;
24 CFR 982: .310;
HUD-52641: p9;
HUD-52641-A: p2;
HUD-903: p3;
HUD-903-1: p6;
7420.10G Gbk: 15-2; 15-6; 22-16 (4);
PIH Notices: 03-11;
Admin Plan: s17p2; s20p7; s20p7

PROSECUTORS 1
HUD-9886: p2

PROSPECTIVE 56
24 CFR 5: .303; .315 (2); .350; .359; .609 (2);
24 CFR 982: .54; .161; .301;
HUD-50058Instr: p29 (2);
HUD-52580-A: p4;
7420.10G Gbk: 2-4 (2); 2-5; 2-6; 2-7; 3-4 (2); 5-15 Ex 5-2; 5-39; 5-40 (3); 8-4; 8-6; 8-20 (3); 8-21; 9-5; 10-17 (2); 10-26 (2); 10-42 Ex 10-5; 10-43 Ex 10-6 (2); 11-14; 18-1; 24-9;
PIH Notices: 03-12; 01-15 Impr Integ Hbk (4); 01-02; 00-09;
Admin Plan: s6p9; s8p2; s8p3; s9p3 (3); s20p2

PROSPECTIVELY 2
Admin Plan: s6p9; s6p9

PROSPECTS 1
7420.10G Gbk: 22-10

PROTECTED CLASS 3
7420.10G Gbk: 5-11;
PIH Notices: 02-01; 99-52

PROVE 9
7420.10G Gbk: 8-7; 9-9; 20-26;
PIH Notices: 01-15 Impr Integ Hbk (3); 95-48; 95-48 Tech Asst;
Admin Plan: s15p4

PROVED 1
Admin Plan: s15p4

PROVEN 3

7420.10G Gbk: 8-14;
PIH Notices: 95-48; 95-48 Tech Asst

PROVING....................................1
PIH Notices: 01-15 Impr Integ Hbk

PROVISION..................................92
24 CFR 5: .110; .230 (3); .360 (4); .363; .514; .609;
24 CFR 982: .104; .312; .456; .553; .625;
HUD-50058Instr: p17; p75;
HUD-52641: p4; p5;
7420.10G Gbk: 2-1; 3-3; 3-4; 5-8; 5-10 Ex 5-1 (2); 5-11; 5-15 Ex 5-2; 5-16 Ex 5-2; 5-43; 9-1 (2); 9-2; 11-2 (2); 11-11; 11-12; 11-13; 20-27; 20-29;
PIH Notices: 03-23; 02-21; 02-20 (2); 02-01 (2); 01-41; 01-27 (4); 01-15; 01-15 Impr Integ Hbk (2); 01-06 (2); 00-46 (2); 00-11 (2); 00-11A (2); 00-09 (5); 99-52 (3); 95-48 (8); 95-48 Tech Asst (8);
Admin Plan: s2p2; s16p2; s23p2; s24p2; s25p7; s25p7

PROVISIONAL................................2
PIH Notices: 01-41; 00-09

PROVISIONS..................................225
24 CFR 5: .212; .214; .218 (3); .232; .236 (2); .238; .315 (5); .321 (5); .324 (3); .327; .353; .360 (2); .500 (2); .506; .508 (3); .514 (2); .522;
24 CFR 982: .158; .160; .308 (4); .310 (2); .352; .451; .452 (2); .521; .552 (3); .554; .555; .601; .625 (4); .632; .633; .641 (12); .642;
HUD-50058Instr: p32;
HUD-52517: p2;
HUD-52641: p3 (2); p4; 8 (3); p10 (4);
HUD-52641-A: p1 (3); p3 (4);
HUD-52646: p1 (4);
7420.10G Gbk: 3-2; 5-11; 5-16 Ex 5-2; 5-44 (2); 8-3; 8-21 (2); 8-22; 11-1; 11-5; 11-7; 11-12 (2); 11-14 (3); 11-15 (2); 11-17; 13-3; 15-1; 17-2; 17-10; 18-1; 22-4;
PIH Notices: 03-23 (5); 03-20; 03-11 (2); 02-21; 02-20; 02-01 (7); 01-41 (5); 01-27 (2); 01-20; 01-15 (3); 01-15 Impr Integ Hbk (3); 00-46; 00-41; 00-27; 00-24B; 00-11 (3); 00-11A (2); 00-09 (6); 99-52 (8); 99-11 (2); 95-48 (13); 95-48 Tech Asst (11);
Admin Plan: s1p4; s2p3; s2p4; s4p2; s5p3; s6p6; s8p5; s9p3; s10p4; s11p3; s13p1; s17p1; s18p7; s20p1; s22p1; s22p3; s23p2; s23p7; s24p1; s24p4; s24p6; s25p1; s25p7

PROXIMITY..................................7
24 CFR 5: .359 (2);
HUD-52580-A: p15; p17;
7420.10G Gbk: 2-7; 13-6; 21-6

PSYCHIATRIC................................9
24 CFR 5: .318 (2);
24 CFR 982: .352;
7420.10G Gbk: 8-16;
PIH Notices: 00-41; 95-48; 95-48 Tech Asst;
Admin Plan: s24p2; s25p2

PSYCHIATRIST...............................1
Admin Plan: s7p8

PSYCHOACTIVE...............................2
PIH Notices: 95-48; 95-48 Tech Asst

PSYCHOLOGICAL..............................4
PIH Notices: 95-48 (2); 95-48 Tech Asst; 95-48 Tech Asst

PSYCHOLOGIST...............................1
Admin Plan: s7p8

PUBLIC ASSESSMENTS.........................3
24 CFR 982: .635 (2);
HUD-50058Instr: p56

PUBLIC ASSISTANCE..........................18
24 CFR 5: .613; .615;
24 CFR 982: .202;
HUD-50058Instr: p5; p71;
7420.10G Gbk: 4-19; 4-26 Ex 4-2; 5-20 (5); 5-21; 23-1;
PIH Notices: 00-11A (3);
Admin Plan: s25p6

PUBLIC ASSISTANCE PAYMENTS1
7420.10G Gbk: 11-8

PUBLIC BENEFIT.............................1
HUD-50058Instr: p70

PUBLIC BENEFITS............................2
24 CFR 5: .630;
7420.10G Gbk: 6-8

PUBLIC COMMENT.............................5

24 CFR 982: .207;
7420.10G Gbk: 3-7; 4-16 (2); 4-16

PUBLIC ENTITIES....................... 119
PIH Notices: 02-01; 99-52 (2); 95-48 (58); 95-48 Tech Asst (57); 95-48 Tech Asst

PUBLIC ENTITY.......................... 253
24 CFR 5: .214;
PIH Notices: 02-01 (4); 99-52 (4); 95-48 (122); 95-48 Tech Asst (121); 95-48 Tech Asst

PUBLIC ENTITY'S 52
PIH Notices: 95-48 (26); 95-48 Tech Asst (25); 95-48 Tech Asst

PUBLIC HEALTH............................. 5
7420.10G Gbk: 10-22;
PIH Notices: 95-48 (2); 95-48 Tech Asst; 95-48 Tech Asst

PUBLIC HEALTH DEPARTMENT 26
24 CFR 35 SubM: .1225 (13);
7420.10G Gbk: 10-20 (6); 10-21; 10-22 (3);
PIH Notices: 02-07; 00-49; 00-49

PUBLIC HEALTH DEPARTMENTS 1
7420.10G Gbk: 10-22

PUBLIC HOUSING ASSESSMENT SYSTEM.. 1
PIH Notices: 99-11

PUBLIC MEETING 3
7420.10G Gbk: 4-16;
PIH Notices: 95-48; 95-48 Tech Asst

PUBLIC MEETINGS 3
7420.10G Gbk: 10-26;
PIH Notices: 95-48; 95-48 Tech Asst

PUBLIC NOTICE............................ 10
24 CFR 982: Intro; .201; .206 (7);
7420.10G Gbk: 4-1

PUBLIC NOTICES 1
7420.10G Gbk: 4-2

PUBLIC OFFICIAL 5
24 CFR 982: .161;
HUD-52641: p6;
7420.10G Gbk: 8-19; 11-2; 11-3

PUBLIC RECORD 3
PIH Notices: 01-15;
Admin Plan: s20p1; s20p3

PUBLIC RECORDS.......................... 3
Admin Plan: s20p4 (2); s20p4

PUBLIC SERVICE 7
HUD-52667: p i;
7420.10G Gbk: 2-5;
PIH Notices: 95-48 (2); 95-48 Tech Asst (2);
Admin Plan: s3p1

PUBLIC SERVICE ANNOUNCEMENTS........................ 3
PIH Notices: 95-48; 95-48 Tech Asst;
Admin Plan: s3p1

PUBLIC SERVICES.......................... 1
7420.10G Gbk: 22-10

PUBLIC TRANSPORTATION........ 20
7420.10G Gbk: 2-8; 8-7; 9-14 Ex 9-1; 9-16 Ex 9-2; 9-17 Ex 9-3; 21-6;
PIH Notices: 95-48 (7); 95-48 Tech Asst (6); 95-48 Tech Asst

PUBLICATION 19
24 CFR 982: .206;
7420.10G Gbk: 5-2;
PIH Notices: 03-12; 02-21; 02-07; 01-20 (2); 01-06; 01-01 (2); 00-49; 00-28; 00-27; 99-11; 95-48 (3); 95-48 Tech Asst;
Admin Plan: s6p11

PUBLICATIONS 8
24 CFR 982: .4;
7420.10G Gbk: 7-5;
PIH Notices: 02-27; 02-20; 02-01; 00-46; 99-11; 99-11

PUBLICITY...................................... 2
PIH Notices: 02-01; 99-52

PUBLICIZE...................................... 1
Admin Plan: s1p6

PUBLICIZED 4
PIH Notices: 02-27 (2); 95-48; 95-48 Tech Asst

PUBLICIZING 1
7420.10G Gbk: 20-3

PUBLICLY 10
24 CFR 5: .609;
HUD-50058Instr: p72 (2);
7420.10G Gbk: 5-15 Ex 5-2;
PIH Notices: 02-01; 01-15; 01-15 Impr Integ Hbk (2); 99-52;
Admin Plan: s23p2

PUBLISH... 8
24 CFR 982: .102;
7420.10G Gbk: 3-7; 9-4;

PIH Notices: 02-01; 01-01; 99-52; 95-48; 95-48 Tech Asst

PUBLISHED 164
24 CFR 5: .100; .609 (2);
24 CFR 35 SubM: .1200;
24 CFR 982: .102 (2); .401; .503 (5); .507; .519; .623;
HUD-50058Instr: p5;
HUD-52580-A: p8;
HUD-52648: p1;
7420.10G Gbk: 1-4 (3); 1-6 Ex 1-1; 3-5; 3-9; 4-14; 5-2; 5-10 Ex 5-1; 5-13; 5-16 Ex 5-2; 5-28; 7-1 (2); 7-2; 7-3 (3); 7-4 (2); 7-5 (2); 7-6; 7-9 (2); 7-10; 9-1; 9-19 Ex 9-4; 13-9; 17-12; 20-4; 20-5; 20-6; 20-9; 20-24; 23-7; 23-12;
PIH Notices: 03-23 (6); 02-27; 02-22 (2); 02-20 (32); 02-14; 02-07 (4); 02-01 (2); 01-20; 01-15; 01-15 Impr Integ Hbk (3); 01-06 (4); 01-01 (3); 00-49; 00-46 (26); 00-28 (3); 00-24A; 00-24B (2); 00-23; 00-11; 99-52 (2);
Admin Plan: s3p1; s11p2; s11p3 (4); s19p1 (3); s21p3 (2); s23p6

PUBLISHES 11
24 CFR 982: .102; .503; .643;
7420.10G Gbk: 1-5; 1-8; 5-3;
PIH Notices: 02-20; 01-06 (2); 01-01; 00-46

PUBLISHING 1
24 CFR 982: .101

PURGE 13
7420.10G Gbk: 4-6 (10); 4-7 (2);
Admin Plan: s4p2

PURGED 1
Admin Plan: s4p2

PURGING 13
7420.10G Gbk: 4-5 (4); 4-6 (5); 4-7 (3);
Admin Plan: s4p2

QC 2
PIH Notices: 02-27; 02-27

QHWRA 3
HUD-50058Instr: p1;
7420.10G Gbk: 1-4;
PIH Notices: 03-11

QUALIFICATION 11
24 CFR 5: .359; .518;
24 CFR 982: .204; .631; .632;
7420.10G Gbk: 4-8; 4-15;
PIH Notices: 01-15 Impr Integ Hbk; 95-48; 95-48 Tech Asst;
Admin Plan: s22p2

QUALIFICATIONS 16
24 CFR 5: .661 (2);
24 CFR 982: .4; .627; .632 (2);
7420.10G Gbk: 4-8; 4-14; 19-10; 22-10;
PIH Notices: 02-27; 95-48; 95-48 Tech Asst;
Admin Plan: s4p2; s24p3; s24p4

QUALIFIED 154
24 CFR 5: .214; .617 (5); .661;
24 CFR 982: .205; .626; .627; .631;
HUD-50058: p5 (2); p v (2);
HUD-50058Instr: p3; p17 (3); p18 (3); p19; p75 (2);
HUD-52648: p1;
7420.10G Gbk: 3-2; 4-9; 4-16; 5-20 (2); 10-32; 22-11;
PIH Notices: 03-11; 02-27; 02-22 (10); 02-01 (5); 01-15; 01-15 Impr Integ Hbk (9); 01-01 (4); 99-52 (5); 95-48 (36); 95-48 Tech Asst (36);
Admin Plan: s1p2; s1p3; s1p5; s4p1; s6p2 (2); s6p3 (3); s21p4; s24p4; s25p3; s25p4

QUALIFIED FAMILIES 1
Admin Plan: s25p4

QUALIFIED FAMILY 18
24 CFR 5: .617 (5);
PIH Notices: 01-15; 01-15 Impr Integ Hbk (9);
Admin Plan: s6p3 (2); s6p3

QUALIFIED INDIVIDUAL 11
HUD-50058Instr: p3;
PIH Notices: 95-48 (5); 95-48 Tech Asst (4); 95-48 Tech Asst

QUALIFY 61
24 CFR 5: .303; .518; .520; .609 (2); .655;
24 CFR 982: .4; .54; .207; .631; .634; .636;
HUD-50058: p5; p8; p viii; p11;
HUD-50058Instr: p19 (3); p36 (2); p38 (2); p46 (4); p47; p65 (2);

HUD-52580-A: p2;
HUD-52648: p4;
7420.10G Gbk: 3-2; 4-2; 4-16; 4-17; 4-18; 5-3; 5-16 Ex 5-2 (2); 5-43; 7-3; 18-6; 19-9; 19-10; 20-6; 23-6; 24-10;
PIH Notices: 01-41 (3); 01-20; 01-15 Impr Integ Hbk; 01-01 (2); 00-27; 00-09;
Admin Plan: s2p1; s18p7; s23p2; s24p6

QUALITY....................................222
24 CFR 5: .609; .703;
24 CFR 35 SubM: .1225;
24 CFR 982: 24 CFR 982 (7); .1; .4 (2); .355; .401 (4); .402; .405; .503; .507; .517; .605 (2); .609; .614 (2); .618 (2); .621;
HUD-50058: p i; p v (2); p xiv;
HUD-50058Instr: p1 (2); p3; p5; p21; p25; p56; p70; p72 (2); p73 (3);
HUD-52580: p1; p5; p6 (4);
HUD-52580-A: p1 (4); p17 (2); p18; p19 (4);
HUD-52641: p4; p10;
HUD-52641-A: p3;
HUD-52648: p1 (7);
7420.10G Gbk: 1-4; 4-10; 5-15 Ex 5-2; 7-7 (3); 8-4 (2); 9-2; 9-9 (2); 9-12; 9-14 Ex 9-1; 9-16 Ex 9-2; 9-17 Ex 9-3; 9-19 Ex 9-4; 10-1; 10-4; 10-10; 10-33; 10-47 Ex 10-9; 17-9; 19-5; 19-6; 19-12 (3); 21-5 (2); 21-9 (2); 21-16 Ex 21-6; 21-17; 22-5; 22-6 (2); 22-8 (2);
PIH Notices: 03-12 (3); 03-11 (2); 02-27 (12); 02-21; 02-20 (2); 02-07; 01-43; 01-41 (8); 01-20; 01-15 (4); 01-15 Impr Integ Hbk (6); 01-11; 01-06; 00-53; 00-49; 00-46 (2); 00-41; 00-28; 00-27; 00-24B (10); 00-23; 00-11; 00-11A; 00-09 (7);
Admin Plan: s4p2; s5p1; s5p3 (2); s6p13; s9p3; s9p4; s10p1 (4); s10p2; s10p3; s10p4; s15p6; s19p1 (7); s20p1; s20p2; s21p1; s21p2; s21p3; s21p4 (3); s21p5 (2); s22p3; s23p5 (2); s24p1; s24p5; s25p6

QUALITY CONTROL....................58
7420.10G Gbk: 1-10; 1-11; 4-18; 9-11 (3); 9-12; 10-23 (2); 10-24; 10-30 (3); 10-31 (5); 10-32 (3); 10-33 (8); 10-34; 10-47 Ex 10-9; 12-8; 12-11 (2); 18-10; 19-5; 19-12 (2); 19-13; 21-11; 21-13; 21-15 Ex 21-5; 21-16 Ex 21-6; 22-5 (8); 22-6 (6); 22-7

QUALITY CONTROL..................101
24 CFR 982: .405;
HUD-52648: p1 (6);
7420.10G Gbk: 1-10; 1-11; 4-18; 9-11 (3); 9-12; 10-23 (2); 10-24; 10-30 (3); 10-31 (5); 10-32 (3); 10-33 (9); 10-34; 10-47 Ex 10-9 (2); 12-8; 12-11 (2); 18-10; 19-5; 19-12 (4); 19-13; 21-11; 21-13; 21-15 Ex 21-5; 21-16 Ex 21-6 (2); 22-5 (8); 22-6 (7); 22-7;
PIH Notices: 02-27 (9); 01-15 (4); 01-15 Impr Integ Hbk (2); 01-06; 00-24B (5);
Admin Plan: s10p1; s20p1; s20p2; s21p1; s21p2; s21p4 (2); s21p5; s21p5

QUALITY CONTROL-ASSURING... 1
7420.10G Gbk: 19-6

QUALITY CONTROLS....................1
HUD-50058Instr: p1

QUALITY OF LIFE 6
24 CFR 5: .609;
HUD-50058Instr: p25; p70;
7420.10G Gbk: 5-15 Ex 5-2;
PIH Notices: 01-15 Impr Integ Hbk; 01-15 Impr Integ Hbk

QUARTERLY..................................26
24 CFR 5: .214 (2);
24 CFR 35 SubM: .1225 (2);
HUD-50058Instr: p2;
7420.10G Gbk: 4-15; 4-21; 5-46 Ex 5-5; 5-48 Ex 5-5; 9-7; 10-22 (2); 11-8 (2); 22-5; 22-7;
PIH Notices: 03-23 (2); 02-27 (4); 96-65;
Admin Plan: s1p6; s6p8; s8p3

QUESTION.....................................42
24 CFR 5: .100;
24 CFR 982: .555;
HUD-50058Instr: p5; p16 (2);

p20; p37; p42; p46; p56;
HUD-52580-A: p1; p15 (4);
HUD-903: p1 (2);
HUD-903-1: p3;
7420.10G Gbk: 3-6; 4-25 Ex 4-2; 5-7; 9-2; 11-4; 16-5; 22-7; 22-8; 24-13 (2);
PIH Notices: 01-41 (3); 01-10; 00-09 (8);
Admin Plan: s6p7; s15p3

QUESTIONABLE............................1
Admin Plan: s7p7

QUESTIONNAIRE..........................6
7420.10G Gbk: 2-3; 21-17;
PIH Notices: 95-48 (2); 95-48 Tech Asst; 95-48 Tech Asst

QUESTIONS..................................78
24 CFR 982: .312;
HUD-50058: p i;
HUD-50058Instr: p3 (3); p4 (2);
HUD-52580: p6;
HUD-52580-A: p17; p19;
HUD-903: p1; p3 (2);
7420.10G Gbk: 2-5; 3-7; 3-8; 4-13; 4-25 Ex 4-2; 4-26 Ex 4-2; 8-1; 8-9 (3); 8-22; 10-22; 10-40 Ex 10-4a; 10-41 Ex 10-4b; 10-42 Ex 10-5; 10-43 Ex 10-6; 10-46 Ex 10-8; 12-12 Ex 12-1; 12-13 Ex 12-1; 12-14 Ex 12-2; 12-15 Ex 12-3; 15-9 Ex 15-1; 19-2; 19-5 (2); 22-8 (2);
PIH Notices: 03-23 (2); 03-20 (2); 03-11; 02-27; 02-20 (2); 02-14; 02-06; 02-01 (3); 01-43; 01-41 (2); 01-33; 01-11; 01-10 (2); 01-06; 01-02; 01-01; 00-53; 00-46 (2); 00-41; 00-09 (2); 00-01; 99-52 (3); 98-66; 95-48; 95-48 Tech Asst;
Admin Plan: s7p4; s18p5

QUOTES..3
7420.10G Gbk: 5-49 Ex 5-5; 18-9;
Admin Plan: s7p6

RABBIT...1
24 CFR 5: .306

RACE...60
24 CFR 5: .655;
24 CFR 982: .202; .207; .304;
HUD-50058: p3 (7); p iii; p4 (7); p iv;
HUD-50058Instr: p15 (3); p73;
HUD-52641: p5; p10;
HUD-52641-A: p3;
HUD-52646: p2;
HUD-903: p1 (2); p2 (4); p4 (2);
7420.10G Gbk: 4-15; 4-19; 4-23 Ex 4-1; 4-25 Ex 4-2; 5-10 Ex 5-1; 5-11; 5-42 (3); 8-14; 11-13; 19-3; 19-6 (2); 19-7 (3);
PIH Notices: 02-21; 01-15; 01-02; 95-48; 95-48 Tech Asst;
Admin Plan: s1p2; s23p2

RACIAL...13
24 CFR 982: .158; .204;
HUD-50058Instr: p73 (2);
HUD-903: p2 (2);
7420.10G Gbk: 2-13 Ex 2-1; 4-8; 4-9; 4-14; 23-4;
Admin Plan: s4p1; s15p2

RADIO..5
7420.10G Gbk: 2-5; 4-3;
PIH Notices: 95-48; 95-48 Tech Asst;
Admin Plan: s3p1

RAILROAD.....................................1
HUD-50058Instr: p29

RAISE THE RENT...........................4
HUD-52641: 8;
HUD-52641-A: p1;
7420.10G Gbk: 8-22;
PIH Notices: 00-09

RAMP..12
PIH Notices: 02-01; 99-52; 95-48 (5); 95-48 Tech Asst (4); 95-48 Tech Asst

RAMPS..23
7420.10G Gbk: 5-30;
PIH Notices: 95-48 (11); 95-48 Tech Asst (10); 95-48 Tech Asst

RANDOM.......................................21
24 CFR 982: .207;
7420.10G Gbk: 3-2; 4-11; 4-12; 4-13; 4-14; 4-16; 4-18; 4-22; 7-5; 9-12;
PIH Notices: 02-27; 02-20; 00-46;
Admin Plan: s21p2; s21p3 (2); s21p4 (2); s21p5; s21p7

RANDOMLY...................................3
7420.10G Gbk: 4-13 (2); 4-13

RANGE..164
24 CFR 5: .653 (3);
24 CFR 982: .401 (4); .503 (11); .505; .517 (2); .614;
HUD-50058Instr: p60;
HUD-52517: p1;
HUD-52580: p2; p6 (2);

HUD-52580-A: p4 (8); p5 (4); p19 (2);
HUD-52641: p2;
HUD-52667: p1 (2);
7420.10G Gbk: 1-4; 2-1; 2-3 (3); 4-9; 6-7; 7-1 (2); 7-2 (6); 7-3; 7-6 (2); 7-7; 7-9 (2); 7-10; 8-5; 9-4; 9-5; 9-9 (2); 9-10; 10-4 (3); 10-5 (3); 10-6 (2); 13-10; 17-5; 18-2; 18-8; 20-18; 21-1; 21-3 (3); 22-5; 24-11 (5);
PIH Notices: 02-20 (22); 02-01 (2); 01-06 (5); 01-01 (4); 00-46 (21); 00-11 (2); 00-01; 99-52 (2); 98-66; 95-48 (2); 95-48 Tech Asst (2);
Admin Plan: s1p3; s1p7; s6p13; s9p3; s21p5

RANGED....1
7420.10G Gbk: 21-19

RANGES....16
24 CFR 982: .517;
HUD-52580-A: p4; p15;
HUD-52667: p i (2);
7420.10G Gbk: 7-2; 9-4; 9-9; 10-5; 18-1; 18-7 (3); 19-3; 19-6; 21-3

RANKED....2
Admin Plan: s24p4; s24p4

RANKING....2
7420.10G Gbk: 1-5; 1-5

RANKINGS....1
7420.10G Gbk: 3-2

RAPIDLY....3
7420.10G Gbk: 1-3; 9-7; 19-11

RAPIDS-MUSKEGON-HOLLAND.1
PIH Notices: 01-01

RAT....4
HUD-52580-A: p17 (3);
7420.10G Gbk: 10-14

RATABLE....3
7420.10G Gbk: 5-47 Ex 5-5 (2); 5-47 Ex 5-5

RATABLY....7
24 CFR 5: .609; .628 (2);
7420.10G Gbk: 5-14 Ex 5-2; 5-21;
PIH Notices: 01-15 Impr Integ Hbk; 01-15 Impr Integ Hbk

RATE....327
24 CFR 5: .100; .518 (2); .520 (2); .609;
24 CFR 982: .503 (8); .517; .521;
HUD-50058: p6 (5);
HUD-50058Instr: p2 (2); p22 (10); p23 (3); p43;
HUD-52580-A: p2; p6; p8; p13;
HUD-52648: p1 (2); p4 (4);
HUD-52667: p i (5);
7420.10G Gbk: 2-10; 4-1; 4-5; 4-11; 5-14 Ex 5-2; 5-24; 5-26 (2); 5-28; 5-48 Ex 5-5 (2); 7-2; 7-3 (3); 7-4 (2); 7-6; 7-9 (2); 7-10 (2); 8-1; 8-11 (4); 8-22; 9-8 (2); 9-9 (3); 12-13 Ex 12-1; 13-4; 13-6 (4); 18-4; 18-6 (7); 18-9; 18-10; 19-2 (5); 19-3 (4); 19-8 (6); 19-9 (2); 19-11 (4); 20-5 (3); 20-9; 20-10 (5); 20-11 (6); 20-17; 20-27 (2); 21-8; 21-17; 21-19; 24-2 (4); 24-3 (3); 24-4 (4); 24-5; 24-6 (5); 24-8 (4); 24-10 (2); 24-11; 24-16 (3);
PIH Notices: 03-23 (6); 02-27 (2); 02-22; 02-21 (15); 02-20 (10); 02-07 (2); 02-06 (2); 01-41 (3); 01-20 (6); 01-15; 01-15 Impr Integ Hbk (7); 01-06 (29); 01-01 (37); 00-46 (2); 00-28 (4); 00-27; 00-24; 00-24A (2); 00-24B (8); 00-09 (3); 95-48 (2); 95-48 Tech Asst (2);
Admin Plan: s6p11; s6p13 (2); s7p6; s8p1; s13p2; s21p3; s21p4 (2); s22p3; s24p4

RATES....99
24 CFR 982: .517; .520 (2);
HUD-50058Instr: p2;
HUD-52667: p i (5);
7420.10G Gbk: 2-1 (2); 2-11; 4-6; 7-4; 8-7; 8-11 (2); 8-14; 8-22; 10-24 (2); 11-4; 11-8; 12-16 Ex 12-4; 13-6 (3); 18-4; 18-6 (3); 18-9 (5); 19-8 (2); 19-9; 19-10; 19-11 (2); 19-12; 20-3; 20-4; 20-10; 20-17; 21-5; 21-7; 21-8; 21-9 (2); 21-10 (2); 21-11; 22-5 (2); 24-3; 24-4 (5); 24-5; 24-6 (3); 24-8; 24-9 (2); 24-10 (2); 24-12;
PIH Notices: 02-21 (3); 02-06 (6); 01-20; 01-06 (2); 01-01 (7); 00-53 (3); 00-

24B;
Admin Plan: s8p1 (2); s24p1

RATING 142
24 CFR 982: .503 (2);
HUD-52580: p7 (2);
HUD-52580-A: p1; p6; p8; p20 (2);
HUD-52648: p1;
7420.10G Gbk: 1-5 (2); 1-11 (9); 9-16 Ex 9-2; 10-27 (2); 10-32; 10-33; 19-2; 23-6;
PIH Notices: 02-27 (18); 02-20 (2); 01-06 (81); 01-01 (3); 00-34 (3); 00-24 (4); 00-24A (2);
Admin Plan: s21p9

RATS 3
24 CFR 5: .703;
HUD-52580-A: p17; p18

RAW 4
7420.10G Gbk: 19-3; 19-4 (2); 19-5

REAC 4
7420.10G Gbk: 20-29 (3);
PIH Notices: 01-15

READ 23
24 CFR 5: .350;
HUD-903: p1 (2);
HUD-903-1: p3;
7420.10G Gbk: 5-30; 19-3; 22-8;
PIH Notices: 01-06 (2); 00-45; 95-48 (7); 95-48 Tech Asst (5);
Admin Plan: s1p6

READABILITY 2
PIH Notices: 95-48; 95-48 Tech Asst

READABLE 2
Admin Plan: s1p3; s3p2

READER 1
7420.10G Gbk: 21-1

READERS 8
PIH Notices: 95-48 (4); 95-48 Tech Asst (3); 95-48 Tech Asst

READMITTED 1
HUD-50058Instr: p9

REAL ESTATE 55
24 CFR 982: .306; .630; .635 (2);
HUD-50058Instr: p56;
HUD-52667: p i;
HUD-903: p2;
HUD-903-1: p5;
7420.10G Gbk: 4-26 Ex 4-2; 5-12; 5-25 Ex 5-3; 5-26; 5-27; 5-28 (2); 5-49 Ex 5-5 (2); 8-12; 9-6; 18-4; 20-29; 22-4; 24-9; 24-11; 24-14 (2);
PIH Notices: 02-21; 02-20 (2); 02-07 (2); 01-33; 01-20; 01-15 Impr Integ Hbk (2); 01-10; 01-06; 01-02; 01-01 (2); 00-49; 00-46 (2); 00-41; 00-28 (2);
Admin Plan: s1p6 (2); s7p6 (3); s11p2; s16p2; s16p3; s20p4

REAL ESTATE AGENT 1
HUD-903-1: p5

REAL ESTATE AGENTS 3
7420.10G Gbk: 5-49 Ex 5-5 (2); 8-6

REAL ESTATE ASSESSMENT CENTER 3
7420.10G Gbk: 20-29; 22-4;
Admin Plan: s11p2

REAL ESTATE BROKER 2
7420.10G Gbk: 5-49 Ex 5-5;
Admin Plan: s7p6

REAL ESTATE SETTLEMENT PROCEDURES ACT 1
24 CFR 982: .630

REAL ESTATE TAX 2
7420.10G Gbk: 5-49 Ex 5-5;
Admin Plan: s7p6

REAL ESTATE TAXES 8
24 CFR 982: .306; .635 (2);
HUD-50058Instr: p56;
HUD-52641: p7;
7420.10G Gbk: 8-20; 11-4;
Admin Plan: s16p2

REALISTIC 4
7420.10G Gbk: 2-7; 5-27; 5-28;
PIH Notices: 00-09

REALLOCATE 2
24 CFR 982: .102; .102

REALLOCATED 3
24 CFR 982: .102;
7420.10G Gbk: 20-11;
PIH Notices: 02-14

REALTY AGENT 1
Admin Plan: s7p6

REASONABLE 472
24 CFR 5: .315 (2); .318 (10); .360 (3); .363; .403; .514 (2); .518 (2); .603 (4); .611 (2); .630 (2); .657;
24 CFR 982: Intro; .1; .4 (2); .54; .102 (2); .152 (2); .158; .201; .204; .303;

.305 (2); .306; .308 (2); .310; .316; .317; .353; .503; .504; .505 (2); .507 (6); .510; .516; .517 (2); .519; .520 (3); .551 (3); .552; .553 (5); .601; .606; .610; .613 (4); .615; .617 (3); .619 (2); .620; .622 (5); .624; .625 (7); .627 (2); .635 (2); .641; .643 (2);
HUD-50058Instr: p34; p36; p70; p71; p74 (2); p75; p76;
HUD-52580-A: p4; p5; p15;
HUD-52641: p1; p4;
HUD-52646: p2 (3);
HUD-52648: p1 (6);
HUD-52667: p i;
7420.10G Gbk: 1-15 (2); 2-7; 2-10; 3-5 (2); 3-8; 3-9 (5); 4-4 (3); 4-6; 4-13; 4-19; 5-25 Ex 5-3; 5-29; 5-30 (5); 5-38; 5-40; 5-43; 5-47 Ex 5-5; 5-49 Ex 5-5 (2); 5-50 Ex 5-5; 5-52 Ex 5-5; 6-6; 6-8; 7-1; 7-9; 8-12 (2); 8-16; 8-17; 9-1 (3); 9-12 (4); 9-17 Ex 9-3; 9-19 Ex 9-4; 10-18; 10-25; 10-26 (2); 10-27; 10-40 Ex 10-4a; 11-1; 11-16 Ex 11-1; 12-2; 12-6 (2); 12-10; 13-7; 14-3; 14-4; 16-1; 17-10; 17-11; 17-12; 18-1 (2); 19-8 (2); 19-11; 19-12; 20-3; 20-13; 21-4; 21-9; 22-2; 22-6; 22-12 (5); 22-13 (2); 22-15 (2); 22-17 (2); 23-2;
PIH Notices: 03-12 (2); 03-11 (4); 03-05 (2); 02-27; 02-22; 02-21 (2); 02-20; 02-07; 02-01 (29); 01-41 (21); 01-40 (2); 01-15 (2); 01-15 Impr Integ Hbk (9); 01-10; 01-06; 00-46; 00-28; 00-24B (12); 00-23; 00-09 (21); 99-52 (28); 95-48 (19); 95-48 Tech Asst (19);
Admin Plan: s1p3 (2); s1p4 (6); s1p5 (2); s3p2; s3p3; s6p2; s6p11; s7p6; s7p7; s8p1; s8p2; s8p5; s9p1; s10p2 (2); s10p3 (2); s11p1 (2); s11p2 (5); s11p3 (2); s11p1; s13p1; s14p2; s15p3; s15p4; s16p2 (2); s19p1 (12); s21p3 (5); s23p7 (2); s24p4; s24p5; s24p5

REASONABLE BELIEF..................3
24 CFR 982: .553;
PIH Notices: 95-48; 95-48 Tech Asst

REASONABLE CAUSE..................4
24 CFR 982: .553 (2);
PIH Notices: 03-11;
Admin Plan: s15p3

REASONABLE CHARGES 2
24 CFR 5: .603;
HUD-50058Instr: p70

REASONABLE CONSUMPTION...2
24 CFR 5: .603;
HUD-50058Instr: p76

REASONABLE COSTS...................6
24 CFR 5: .603;
HUD-50058Instr: p74;
7420.10G Gbk: 5-25 Ex 5-3; 5-30; 5-49 Ex 5-5; 5-49 Ex 5-5

REASONABLE EFFORT 1
Admin Plan: s15p4

REASONABLE EFFORTS 5
24 CFR 5: .363; .518 (2);
7420.10G Gbk: 5-47 Ex 5-5;
Admin Plan: s16p2

REASONABLE EXPENSES 5
24 CFR 5: .318; .603;
HUD-50058Instr: p34; p71;
PIH Notices: 02-21

REASONABLE FEE........................1
PIH Notices: 03-11

REASONABLE FEES......................1
PIH Notices: 03-11

REASONABLE HOURS 2
24 CFR 5: .360;
Admin Plan: s10p3

REASONABLE MODIFICATION...4
PIH Notices: 02-01; 99-52; 95-48; 95-48 Tech Asst

REASONABLE MODIFICATIONS18
7420.10G Gbk: 5-43;
PIH Notices: 02-01; 99-52; 95-48 (7); 95-48 Tech Asst (7);
Admin Plan: s1p4

REASONABLE PERIOD...............13
24 CFR 982: .553;
HUD-52580-A: p4; p5;
7420.10G Gbk: 4-4; 4-6; 4-13; 10-26; 22-12; 22-15;
PIH Notices: 03-05 (2); 01-40; 01-40

REASONABLE PERIOD OF TIME11
HUD-52580-A: p4; p5;
7420.10G Gbk: 4-4; 4-13; 10-26; 22-12; 22-15;
PIH Notices: 03-05 (2); 01-40; 01-40
REASONABLE RENT....................92
24 CFR 982: Intro; .4; .54; .158; .308; .353; .504; .507 (6); .510; .519; .520 (3); .613 (4); .617 (3); .619; .622 (5); .641;
HUD-50058Instr: p75;
HUD-52641: p4 (4); 8; p10;
HUD-52641-A: p1; p3;
HUD-52648: p1 (3);
7420.10G Gbk: 3-9; 9-2 (3); 9-12 (2); 9-16 Ex 9-2; 11-11; 11-12 (4); 12-8; 17-7 (3); 17-9 (5);
PIH Notices: 03-12; 02-27; 01-41 (4); 01-06; 00-24B (7); 00-09 (4);
Admin Plan: s11p2; s19p1 (7); s21p3
REASONABLE RENT BURDEN 1
24 CFR 982: .102
REASONABLE RENTAL INFORMATION................................1
7420.10G Gbk: 11-12
REASONABLE RENTS 1
7420.10G Gbk: 7-1
REASONABLE SYSTEM 3
PIH Notices: 01-15 Impr Integ Hbk (2);
Admin Plan: s21p3
REASONABLE TIME 20
24 CFR 5: .318; .514; .657;
24 CFR 982: .102; .201; .305; .516; .553;
7420.10G Gbk: 4-19; 8-17; 10-18; 10-25; 10-26; 10-27; 19-11; 22-15;
PIH Notices: 01-15 Impr Integ Hbk (2); 00-23;
Admin Plan: s1p5
REASONABLE TIME PERIOD.......2
7420.10G Gbk: 4-4; 10-40 Ex 10-4a
REASONABLE TIMEFRAMES 1
7420.10G Gbk: 16-1
REASONABLE TIMES 5
24 CFR 982: .551;
HUD-52646: p2;
7420.10G Gbk: 1-15;
Admin Plan: s10p2; s23p7
REBATES 6
24 CFR 5: .609;
HUD-50058Instr: p31;
7420.10G Gbk: 5-15 Ex 5-2;
PIH Notices: 01-15 Impr Integ Hbk (2); 01-15 Impr Integ Hbk
RECEIPT 88
24 CFR 5: .514 (4);
24 CFR 982: .102; .205; .451; .631; .634; .643;
HUD-50058Instr: p75;
HUD-52580: p5;
HUD-52580-A: p17;
HUD-52641: p1;
7420.10G Gbk: 4-1; 4-12; 5-10 Ex 5-1 (2); 5-21; 5-50 Ex 5-5 (2); 10-20; 10-21 (2); 10-23; 10-34; 11-7 (2); 11-11; 13-5; 16-3; 19-11 (2); 20-11; 20-24; 22-4;
PIH Notices: 03-11; 02-27 (5); 02-21 (4); 01-20 (4); 01-15 Impr Integ Hbk; 01-06 (11); 00-27 (4); 00-24A; 00-14; 96-65; 95-48 (2); 95-48 Tech Asst (2);
Admin Plan: s3p2; s6p9; s7p7; s7p8; s11p2; s13p1; s14p2; s18p7 (4); s23p6 (2); s25p1; s25p3
RECEIPTS 39
24 CFR 5: .609;
24 CFR 982: .4; .156 (2); .157 (4); .352; .451 (2);
7420.10G Gbk: 5-14 Ex 5-2; 5-25 Ex 5-3; 5-48 Ex 5-5; 5-51 Ex 5-5 (3); 5-52 Ex 5-5 (2); 12-13 Ex 12-1; 20-23; 20-27 (2);
PIH Notices: 02-21; 01-15 (4); 01-15 Impr Integ Hbk (7);
Admin Plan: s6p9; s7p5; s7p6; s7p7
RECEIVABLE 4
7420.10G Gbk: 20-24; 20-25 (2); 20-26
RECEIVABLE-OTHER 2
7420.10G Gbk: 20-26; 20-26
RECEIVERS....................................2
PIH Notices: 95-48; 95-48 Tech Asst
RECEIVING PHA 198
24 CFR 982: Intro; .4 (4); .152; .201 (2); .353 (2); .355 (53); .636 (5); .641;
HUD-50058: p x; p xi; p xiii;

p xiv;
HUD-50058Instr: p7 (3); p9 (2); p10 (2); p13 (2); p42 (3); p46 (3); p53 (3); p56 (2); p70 (3); p75 (2);
7420.10G Gbk: 2-9 (2); 4-20; 13-1; 13-2; 13-3 (9); 13-4 (4); 13-5 (10); 13-6 (8); 13-7 (7); 13-8 (12); 13-9 (12); 13-10 (2); 13-11 Ex 13-1; 20-24 (9); 20-25 (7); 21-8 (2); 23-18 (7);
PIH Notices: 01-06; 01-01 (2);
Admin Plan: s13p2; s13p2

RECEIVING PHAS........................6
7420.10G Gbk: 13-1; 13-4 (2); 13-9; 21-8;
PIH Notices: 01-01

RECEIVING PHA'S........................19
HUD-50058Instr: p7;
7420.10G Gbk: 4-20 (2); 13-4; 13-5 (4); 13-6; 13-7 (5); 13-8; 23-18 (2);
PIH Notices: 01-01; 01-01

RECEPTACLE........................1
HUD-52580-A: p2

RECEPTIONIST........................1
7420.10G Gbk: 21-14 Ex 21-4

RECEPTIVELY........................2
PIH Notices: 95-48; 95-48 Tech Asst

RECIPIENT........................17
24 CFR 35 SubM: .1200 (2);
HUD-50058Instr: p16 (2);
7420.10G Gbk: 5-9 Ex 5-1;
PIH Notices: 02-01 (6); 99-52 (5); 99-52

RECIPIENTS........................55
24 CFR 982: .202;
HUD-50058Instr: p28; p72;
7420.10G Gbk: 1-7; 4-19; 5-20 (2); 5-44 (7); 7-6;
PIH Notices: 02-21; 02-01 (13); 00-11 (4); 00-11A (2); 99-52 (13); 95-48 (3); 95-48 Tech Asst (3);
Admin Plan: s7p4

RECIPIENT'S........................5
HUD-50058Instr: p16;
PIH Notices: 02-01 (2); 99-52; 99-52

RECIPIENTS OF FEDERAL FINANCIAL ASSISTANCE........................8
PIH Notices: 02-01 (3); 99-52 (3); 95-48; 95-48 Tech Asst

RECOMPUTE........................2
7420.10G Gbk: 6-6; 21-7

RECONCILE........................2
7420.10G Gbk: 20-2;
PIH Notices: 00-09

RECONCILED........................1
7420.10G Gbk: 20-23

RECONCILES........................3
7420.10G Gbk: 20-27; 20-29;
PIH Notices: 00-09

RECONCILIATION........................8
HUD-9886: p1;
7420.10G Gbk: 20-27 (3); 20-29;
PIH Notices: 01-02; 00-11;
Admin Plan: s11p1

RECONSTRUCTION........................3
PIH Notices: 02-21; 01-20; 00-27

RECORD........................150
24 CFR 5: .214;
24 CFR 35 SubM: .1225;
24 CFR 982: .553 (10);
HUD-50058: p ii (3);
HUD-50058Instr: p11 (6); p12; p16 (3); p75;
HUD-52580-A: p1 (6); p2; p8 (2); p13;
HUD-52667: p i;
7420.10G Gbk: 4-4; 4-7; 4-8; 4-10; 5-10 Ex 5-1 (2); 5-37; 5-43; 5-44; 5-50 Ex 5-5 (2); 9-5; 9-8; 10-16; 10-22; 10-25; 10-28; 10-30; 10-33 (2); 10-34; 11-19; 12-3 (2); 12-4; 15-7 (3); 19-2; 19-8; 19-11; 20-1; 20-23 (4); 20-26; 22-3; 22-6; 22-13 (3); 22-14;
PIH Notices: 03-11 (23); 02-20; 01-41 (2); 01-15 (6); 01-06; 00-46; 00-24B (4); 00-09; 99-11; 95-48 (4); 95-48 Tech Asst (4);
Admin Plan: s1p4; s2p6; s7p4; s8p2; s8p3; s8p5; s11p1; s15p4; s15p5; s16p2; s16p3 (2); s18p2 (3); s18p3 (3); s20p1; s20p3 (2); s20p3

RECORDED........................26
24 CFR 5: .514 (2);
HUD-50058Instr: p7 (4); p10; p21;
HUD-52665: p3;
7420.10G Gbk: 4-10; 5-46 Ex 5-5; 8-15; 8-20; 8-23; 9-13 Ex 9-1; 10-24; 10-26; 11-16 Ex 11-1; 19-6; 20-25;
PIH Notices: 01-06; 95-48;

95-48 Tech Asst;
Admin Plan: s7p1; s11p2; s16p3

RECORDING 11
HUD-52580-A: p13;
7420.10G Gbk: 5-47 Ex 5-5; 9-10; 11-16 Ex 11-1; 19-1; 19-6; 21-3; 22-8;
PIH Notices: 02-27; 02-20; 00-46

RECORDINGS 4
PIH Notices: 95-48 (2); 95-48 Tech Asst; 95-48 Tech Asst

RECORDKEEPING 1
24 CFR 5: .661

RECORD-KEEPING 2
24 CFR 982: .158;
7420.10G Gbk: 11-19

RECORDS 147
24 CFR 5: .214; .234 (2); .510; .512 (2); .514;
24 CFR 982: Intro; .158 (15); .203; .307; .310; .553 (3); .555;
HUD-50058Instr: p11 (2);
HUD-52641: p5 (5);
HUD-52665: p1 (2); p2;
HUD-903-1: p3;
7420.10G Gbk: 2-5; 3-8; 4-22; 5-7; 5-12 (2); 5-39; 5-40; 5-47 Ex 5-5; 5-50 Ex 5-5 (4); 5-53 Ex 5-5; 10-22; 10-26; 10-31; 10-33; 10-36 Ex 10-1 (3); 11-11; 11-13 (4); 11-19; 12-3; 13-2 (2); 14-5; 20-1; 20-23 (3); 20-24; 20-25 (3); 21-4 (2); 22-7 (2); 22-17; 23-13;
PIH Notices: 03-11 (22); 02-01; 01-43; 01-41; 01-15 (5); 01-15 Impr Integ Hbk (5); 01-06; 00-28 (2); 00-24B (2); 99-52; 99-11;
Admin Plan: s4p1; s7p1; s7p5; s7p7; s15p4 (2); s18p6; s20p4 (7); s21p2 (3); s23p7; s25p5

RECORDS MANAGEMENT 2
PIH Notices: 03-11; 03-11

RECOVER 13
7420.10G Gbk: 10-29; 11-18; 22-16 (2);
PIH Notices: 95-48 (3); 95-48 Tech Asst (3);
Admin Plan: s17p1; s20p6; s20p8

RECOVERED 6
7420.10G Gbk: 5-37; 22-3; 22-17;
PIH Notices: 95-48; 95-48 Tech Asst;
Admin Plan: s6p10

RECOVERIES 10
24 CFR 982: Intro; .163;
7420.10G Gbk: 20-25 (3); 20-26; 22-16 (2); 22-17; 22-17

RECOVERING 4
HUD-903-1: p2;
7420.10G Gbk: 5-37; 11-12; 20-26

RECOVERS 2
24 CFR 982: .163;
7420.10G Gbk: 22-16

RECOVERY 43
24 CFR 5: .300;
24 CFR 982: .453; .619;
HUD-52641: p3; p4; p5;
7420.10G Gbk: 20-14; 20-25 (2); 20-26 (2); 22-16; 22-17 (3);
PIH Notices: 02-27 (4); 02-01; 01-43; 01-20 (2); 01-11 (2); 01-06 (3); 01-01; 00-53 (3); 00-45; 00-34; 00-27; 00-24 (2); 99-52; 99-11; 95-48; 95-48 Tech Asst;
Admin Plan: s6p10; s17p1

RECOVERY'S 3
PIH Notices: 02-27 (2); 02-27

RECREATION 15
7420.10G Gbk: 5-17;
PIH Notices: 95-48 (7); 95-48 Tech Asst (6); 95-48 Tech Asst

RECREATIONAL 8
24 CFR 982: .614;
7420.10G Gbk: 17-4; 17-5;
PIH Notices: 02-01; 99-52; 95-48; 95-48 Tech Asst;
Admin Plan: s1p1

RECURRENCE 1
7420.10G Gbk: 22-5

RECURRENT 1
HUD-50058Instr: p28

RECURRING 4
7420.10G Gbk: 5-47 Ex 5-5; 22-6;
PIH Notices: 99-11;
Admin Plan: s7p5

REDECORATION 2
HUD-52641: 8;
HUD-52641-A: p1

REDETERMINATION 8
24 CFR 5: .236; .609; .657;

24 CFR 982: .516;
HUD-52665: p1;
PIH Notices: 01-41; 01-15 Impr Integ Hbk; 00-09

REDETERMINATIONS....................1
24 CFR 982: .54

REDETERMINE...............................7
24 CFR 982: .355; .507 (2); .622;
HUD-52641: p4 (2);
7420.10G Gbk: 11-12

REDETERMINED 9
24 CFR 982: .353; .507; .519;
HUD-52641: p4; 8; p10;
HUD-52641-A: p1; p3;
7420.10G Gbk: 9-2

REDEVELOPMENT.........................2
PIH Notices: 01-15; 01-15

REDRESS..1
24 CFR 5: .514

REDUCTION 158
24 CFR 5: .236 (5); .514 (5); .520; .615 (20); .703;
24 CFR 35 SubM: .1225 (7);
24 CFR 982: .352; .401; .404; .453; .552; .619;
HUD-50058Instr: p28; p71; p73; p75 (2);
HUD-52641: p3; p4; p5;
7420.10G Gbk: 5-21 (3); 5-47 Ex 5-5 (3); 9-1; 9-7; 10-11; 10-12; 10-15; 10-17 (2); 10-19; 10-21 (11); 10-37 Ex 10-2 (2); 10-38 Ex 10-3 (5); 11-18; 12-9 (2); 14-2 (2); 19-2; 19-3 (2); 21-3; 21-7; 23-2;
PIH Notices: 03-23 (5); 03-20 (2); 03-12 (2); 03-11 (3); 02-21 (5); 02-14 (15); 02-07; 02-06; 01-41; 01-20 (3); 01-15; 01-15 Impr Integ Hbk (2); 01-10; 00-28 (3); 00-11 (2); 00-11A (2); 96-65 (2);
Admin Plan: s6p12 (2); s6p13 (4); s7p3 (2); s8p6 (2); s24p6

REDUCTION OF ASSISTANCE......4
24 CFR 5: .236 (3); .236

REDUCTIONS.................................7
7420.10G Gbk: 5-21;
PIH Notices: 03-23; 02-20; 02-14; 00-46; 00-09;
Admin Plan: s17p1

REEXAM..3
HUD-50058Instr: p77 (2); p77

REEXAMINATION 318
24 CFR 5: .214; .216 (3); .230 (2); .324; .350; .508 (3); .514; .601; .603; .609; .615; .657 (6); .659 (3);
24 CFR 982: .355; .502 (4); .505 (9); .516 (7); .517; .551 (2); .635;
HUD-50058: p2 (4); p ii (3); p ix (2); p x (2); p xi (2); p xii (2); p xiii (2); p xiv (2); p xv (2);
HUD-50058Instr: p1; p2 (2); p9 (10); p10 (8); p11 (5); p12 (15); p17; p33 (2); p37; p39 (2); p42 (2); p46 (2); p48 (2); p50 (2); p53 (2); p56 (3); p58 (2); p65; p70;
HUD-52646: p2;
HUD-52648: p1; p2;
HUD-52665: p1;
7420.10G Gbk: 1-5; 1-16 Ex 1-3; 2-9; 5-6; 5-13 (2); 5-21; 5-22 (2); 5-27; 5-31; 5-50 Ex 5-5; 7-7; 7-8 (4); 11-15; 12-1 (12); 12-2 (15); 12-3 (6); 12-4 (2); 12-5 (6); 12-6 (6); 12-7 (5); 12-8 (5); 12-9; 12-10 (2); 12-12 Ex 12-1 (3); 12-13 Ex 12-1; 12-14 Ex 12-2 (2); 13-7; 13-8; 14-2 (2); 14-3 (6); 15-5; 15-10 Ex 15-2; 18-8; 18-9; 19-2; 19-13 (3); 20-19 Ex 20-3; 20-24; 21-4 (2); 21-5 (3); 21-6 (2); 21-7; 21-14 Ex 21-4; 22-12; 23-7 (2); 23-13; 23-17 Ex 23-2; 24-13;
PIH Notices: 01-41 (2); 01-33; 01-15 (9); 01-15 Impr Integ Hbk (23); 01-10 (8); 00-24B (2); 00-09 (8);
Admin Plan: s6p8; s6p10; s11p2 (3); s21p4; s21p6

REEXAMINATIONS......................67
24 CFR 5: .657;
24 CFR 982: .355; .641;
HUD-50058Instr: p12 (3);
HUD-52648: p2;
7420.10G Gbk: 1-1; 1-10; 3-5; 8-2; 10-23; 12-1 (4); 12-2 (6); 12-3; 12-8 (3); 12-10 (3); 12-11; 13-8; 14-2; 19-4 (5); 19-13 (4); 21-2; 21-4; 21-6 Ex 21-1; 21-7 (2); 21-14 Ex 21-4;

PIH Notices: 01-33; 01-15 (5); 01-15 Impr Integ Hbk (5); 01-06; 00-53; 00-24A;
Admin Plan: s21p1; s21p2; s21p7 (3); s21p7

REEXAMINE....................................4
7420.10G Gbk: 9-1; 12-1;
PIH Notices: 00-24B;
Admin Plan: s11p1

REEXAMINED................................2
7420.10G Gbk: 22-10;
PIH Notices: 01-15

REEXAMINING...............................1
7420.10G Gbk: 1-13

REFER..42
24 CFR 5: .500; .528;
HUD-50058: p i;
HUD-50058Instr: p24; p28; p33 (2); p40; p68; p70;
7420.10G Gbk: 2-2; 2-5; 3-7; 5-6; 5-16 Ex 5-2; 8-3; 8-13; 8-21; 10-3; 21-13; 22-15; 22-16; 24-15;
PIH Notices: 01-15; 01-10; 01-06; 00-09; 95-48 (3); 95-48 Tech Asst (3);
Admin Plan: s2p6; s17p2; s23p3 (2); s23p4; s24p6 (2); s24p7; s24p7

REFERRAL.. 17
HUD-50058Instr: p28;
HUD-903: p1 (2);
7420.10G Gbk: 4-13; 21-11;
PIH Notices: 01-06 (2); 00-11 (2); 00-11A (2); 95-48; 95-48 Tech Asst;
Admin Plan: s4p2; s8p3; s8p4; s20p1

REFERRALS..................................34
24 CFR 5: .518;
7420.10G Gbk: 2-6 (2); 2-11 (3); 4-3; 21-11; 22-16; 23-6;
PIH Notices: 01-41; 00-11A; 00-09;
Admin Plan: s1p4; s2p7; s4p2 (2); s18p1; s20p1 (2); s20p3 (2); s23p2; s23p3 (2); s25p1 (3); s25p2; s25p3 (4); s25p3

REFRIGERATION...........................3
HUD-52667: p i;
7420.10G Gbk: 18-5; 18-6

REFRIGERATOR...........................38
24 CFR 982: .401; .517 (2); .609; .614;
HUD-52517: p1;
HUD-52580: p2; p6 (2);
HUD-52580-A: p4 (4); p5 (2); p19 (2);
HUD-52641: p2;
HUD-52667: p1 (2); p ii;
7420.10G Gbk: 9-14 Ex 9-1; 9-15 Ex 9-2; 10-4; 10-5 (5); 17-3; 17-5; 18-2; 18-7; 18-8;
Admin Plan: s6p13; s9p3; s10p1; s10p1

REFRIGERATORS...........................7
24 CFR 982: .517;
HUD-52667: p i (2);
7420.10G Gbk: 18-1; 18-7 (2); 18-7

REFUGEE...5
24 CFR 5: .518 (3);
7420.10G Gbk: 5-10 Ex 5-1; 5-10 Ex 5-1

REFUND 13
24 CFR 5: .318;
24 CFR 982: .313; .633;
HUD-50058Instr: p32;
HUD-52641: p10;
HUD-52641-A: p3;
7420.10G Gbk: 5-16 Ex 5-2; 5-24; 8-4; 22-12;
PIH Notices: 01-15 Impr Integ Hbk; 95-48; 95-48 Tech Asst

REFUNDABLE................................3
24 CFR 5: .318;
HUD-50058Instr: p28;
7420.10G Gbk: 23-15

REFUNDS 6
24 CFR 5: .609;
HUD-50058Instr: p31;
7420.10G Gbk: 5-15 Ex 5-2;
PIH Notices: 01-15 Impr Integ Hbk (2); 01-15 Impr Integ Hbk

REFUSAL.......................................12
24 CFR 5: .350;
24 CFR 982: .205;
HUD-903: p2;
7420.10G Gbk: 5-35 (2); 5-46 Ex 5-5; 16-2 (3);
PIH Notices: 01-41;
Admin Plan: s7p2; s18p2

REFUSAL TO COOPERATE............1
Admin Plan: s7p2

REFUSE...61
24 CFR 5: .318; .350 (2); .703;
24 CFR 982: .205; .316; .401 (4); .517 (2); .605; .609 (3); .614 (2); .618;
HUD-52580: p5;

HUD-52580-A: p17 (2); p18;
HUD-903: p1;
HUD-903-1: p2 (3);
7420.10G Gbk: 3-4; 4-8; 10-1; 10-4; 10-5 (2); 17-3; 17-7;
PIH Notices: 02-01 (2); 01-02; 00-09; 99-52 (2); 95-48 (9); 95-48 Tech Asst (9);
Admin Plan: s2p3; s23p6

REFUSE DISPOSAL....................... 14
24 CFR 5: .703;
24 CFR 982: .401; .605; .609 (2); .614; .618;
HUD-52580: p5;
HUD-52580-A: p17; p18;
7420.10G Gbk: 10-1; 10-4; 17-3; 17-7

REFUSE TO APPROVE 2
24 CFR 982: .316;
Admin Plan: s2p3

REFUSED... 6
24 CFR 982: .205;
HUD-903-1: p4;
7420.10G Gbk: 4-8;
PIH Notices: 01-02; 95-48; 95-48 Tech Asst

REFUSES 11
24 CFR 5: .350; .360;
7420.10G Gbk: 5-35; 8-10; 22-12;
PIH Notices: 01-41; 95-48 (2); 95-48 Tech Asst (2);
Admin Plan: s23p4

REFUSING..................................... 14
24 CFR 982: .552 (4);
7420.10G Gbk: 3-4; 8-19; 11-3; 15-5 (2);
PIH Notices: 01-02;
Admin Plan: s15p1 (3); s15p1

REGARDED AS HAVING................ 5
7420.10G Gbk: 5-37; 5-44;
PIH Notices: 95-48; 95-48 Tech Asst;
Admin Plan: s1p4

REGISTER 123
24 CFR 5: .100; .350 (6); .609;
24 CFR 982: .4 (2); .52; .101; .102 (12); .519; .643;
HUD-50058Instr: p5 (2); p30 (2); p32 (2);
HUD-52580-A: p15;
HUD-52641: p10;
HUD-52641-A: p3;
7420.10G Gbk: 5-10 Ex 5-1; 5-13; 5-16 Ex 5-2; 10-38 Ex 10-3; 10-39 Ex 10-4; 11-16 Ex 11-1; 11-19 (2); 13-9; 20-4; 20-5; 20-6; 20-9; 20-11; 20-20 (2); 20-23 (3); 20-24 (2); 22-6;
PIH Notices: 03-23 (5); 03-12; 02-21; 02-20 (3); 02-14 (2); 02-07 (3); 02-06 (2); 02-01 (3); 01-20; 01-15; 01-15 Impr Integ Hbk (4); 01-06 (2); 01-01; 00-49 (2); 00-46 (2); 00-34; 00-28 (3); 00-27; 00-24 (2); 00-24A (4); 00-24B; 00-11; 99-52 (3); 95-48 (6); 95-48 Tech Asst (6);
Admin Plan: s11p1

REGISTERED 2
7420.10G Gbk: 10-28; 10-30

REGISTERS 6
24 CFR 5: .324;
7420.10G Gbk: 20-23 (2);
PIH Notices: 00-24A; 95-48; 95-48 Tech Asst

REGISTRATION............................ 45
24 CFR 5: .350 (5); .363;
24 CFR 982: .553 (3);
HUD-50058: p3 (6); p iii; p4 (6); p iv;
HUD-50058Instr: p15 (3); p16 (11);
7420.10G Gbk: 5-4; 5-10 Ex 5-1; 13-2;
PIH Notices: 03-11; 00-53;
Admin Plan: s15p2 (2); s20p4

REGULAR CONTRIBUTIONS 12
24 CFR 5: .609;
HUD-50058Instr: p30;
7420.10G Gbk: 4-26 Ex 4-2; 5-14 Ex 5-2; 5-18 (2); 5-19;
PIH Notices: 01-15 Impr Integ Hbk (2);
Admin Plan: s6p8; s6p9; s6p9

REGULATORY AGREEMENT 8
24 CFR 5: .306;
24 CFR 982: .453;
HUD-52641: p5;
7420.10G Gbk: 1-9; 11-18;
PIH Notices: 01-41; 00-09;
Admin Plan: s16p2

REGULATORY REQUIREMENTS 13
24 CFR 982: .4;
PIH Notices: 02-27; 02-01 (5); 00-23; 99-52 (4); 99-52

REHAB 36
HUD-50058: p2; p12 (3); p xii (2);
HUD-50058Instr: p ii; p1 (2); p7; p50 (4); p78;

7420.10G Gbk: 9-14 Ex 9-1; 9-15 Ex 9-2; 21-16 Ex 21-6;
PIH Notices: 02-14 (3); 01-10;
Admin Plan: s7p8; s23p1; s23p2 (3); s23p3 (3); s23p4; s23p5; s23p6; s23p7; s23p8; s23p8

REHABILITATE 1
HUD-50058Instr: p61

REHABILITATED 12
24 CFR 982: .310 (2); .552 (2);
7420.10G Gbk: 1-3 (2); 15-7;
PIH Notices: 02-22; 95-48; 95-48 Tech Asst;
Admin Plan: s1p5; s23p4

REHABILITATED SUCCESSFULLY6
24 CFR 982: .310 (2); .552 (2);
PIH Notices: 95-48; 95-48 Tech Asst

REHABILITATES 1
Admin Plan: s24p4

REHABILITATION....................... 206
24 CFR 5: .100; .105; .504; .514 (3); .524; .630; .632; .653; .655; .657; .659; .801 (5);
24 CFR 982: .53; .205 (3); .310 (3); .552 (2); .553;
HUD-50058: p12 (2); p xii (4);
HUD-50058Instr: p ii; p3; p7; p9; p50 (6); p73 (4); p74;
7420.10G Gbk: 1-1; 1-8 (2); 3-7; 3-8; 4-8 (2); 4-9; 5-11; 5-37; 5-42; 5-44; 5-51 Ex 5-5; 5-52 Ex 5-5; 8-3; 8-16 (2); 10-15; 15-7 (2); 19-3; 20-5; 20-13 (3); 20-23; 21-13; 21-17; 21-19; 21-20; 23-3 (2);
PIH Notices: 03-23 (3); 03-11; 03-05; 02-14; 02-07; 02-01 (9); 01-41 (5); 01-40; 01-27 (2); 01-15 (2); 01-10 (5); 00-45; 00-28; 00-14 (3); 00-09 (5); 99-52 (9); 99-11; 95-48 (20); 95-48 Tech Asst (18);
Admin Plan: s2p4; s2p6; s6p5; s23p1 (11); s23p2; s23p3 (2); s23p4; s23p5 (5); s23p6; s24p1 (3); s24p2; s24p3 (2); s24p5 (3); s25p7 (2); s25p7

REHABILITATION ACT................ 40
24 CFR 5: .105; .524;
24 CFR 982: .53;
HUD-50058Instr: p3;
7420.10G Gbk: 3-8; 5-11; 5-42; 5-44; 8-3;
PIH Notices: 02-01; 00-45; 99-52; 95-48 (15); 95-48 Tech Asst (12); 95-48 Tech Asst

REHABILITATION ACTIVITY 1
Admin Plan: s2p4

REHABILITATION CENTER 1
Admin Plan: s6p5

REHABILITATION PROGRAM.... 11
24 CFR 982: .553;
7420.10G Gbk: 15-7;
PIH Notices: 03-11; 95-48 (2); 95-48 Tech Asst (2);
Admin Plan: s2p6; s25p7 (2); s25p7

REHABILITATION PROGRAMS.... 2
PIH Notices: 95-48; 95-48 Tech Asst

REHABILITATIONS 1
Admin Plan: s23p1

REHABILITATIVE 1
Admin Plan: s23p1

REIMBURSABLE............................. 2
PIH Notices: 01-15;
Admin Plan: s6p11

REIMBURSE......................................
31
24 CFR 982: .152; .155; .312; .313; .355 (2);
HUD-50058: p vii;
HUD-50058Instr: p25; p30; p35;
HUD-52641: p10;
HUD-52641-A: p3;
HUD-52665: p1;
7420.10G Gbk: 11-5; 13-9; 20-4 (2); 22-12;
PIH Notices: 03-11; 01-15 Impr Integ Hbk (2); 00-49 (4); 00-28; 96-65 (4); 96-65

REIMBURSED................................ 15
24 CFR 5: .603 (2);
24 CFR 982: .552;
HUD-50058Instr: p34 (2); p70; p71;
7420.10G Gbk: 5-29; 5-37; 15-5;
PIH Notices: 01-15; 96-65 (2);
Admin Plan: s7p7; s15p2

REIMBURSEMENT 101
24 CFR 5: .528; .603; .609 (4); .632 (5);
24 CFR 982: .4 (2); .313; .355; .514;

HUD-50058: p6; p x; p11; p xi (2); p xiii; p xiv;
HUD-50058Instr: p25; p27; p30 (2); p32; p39 (2); p41 (2); p42; p43 (2); p45 (2); p46; p48 (2); p49 (2); p51 (2); p52 (2); p53; p56; p76 (2);
HUD-52641: p10;
HUD-52641-A: p3 (2);
7420.10G Gbk: 5-14 Ex 5-2 (2); 5-15 Ex 5-2 (2); 5-16 Ex 5-2 (2); 5-19; 8-4; 14-5; 20-4; 20-6; 20-22 Ex 20-5; 22-6; 22-12;
PIH Notices: 03-11; 02-27 (2); 02-07; 01-41; 01-15 Impr Integ Hbk (13); 00-28 (2); 00-24B (2); 00-09 (2); 96-65 (6);
Admin Plan: s6p11; s6p13 (2); s7p7; s7p7

REIMBURSEMENTS 8
24 CFR 5: .601; .632;
PIH Notices: 01-15 (2); 01-15 Impr Integ Hbk; 96-65 (2); 96-65

REIMBURSES 1
PIH Notices: 96-65

REIMBURSING 4
24 CFR 5: .528;
PIH Notices: 00-28; 96-65; 96-65

REINFORCE 4
7420.10G Gbk: 8-14; 8-22; 22-9;
Admin Plan: s20p2

REINFORCEMENTS 2
PIH Notices: 02-01; 99-52

REINFORCES 1
PIH Notices: 00-11

REINSPECT 1
7420.10G Gbk: 10-32

RE-INSPECT 2
HUD-50058Instr: p21;
Admin Plan: s10p1

REINSPECTED 3
HUD-50058Instr: p21;
HUD-52648: p1; p1

REINSPECTING 1
HUD-50058Instr: p21

REINSPECTION 24
24 CFR 982: .405;
HUD-52580: p1; p7;
HUD-52580-A: p1; p20;
7420.10G Gbk: 2-9; 10-24; 10-26; 10-28 (2); 10-29 (2); 10-32; 10-33; 10-34 (5); 10-43 Ex 10-6; 10-48 Ex 10-10 (2); 21-9; 21-9

RE-INSPECTION 26
HUD-52580: p5;
HUD-52580-A: p17;
7420.10G Gbk: 10-29 (2); 10-44 Ex 10-7a (4); 10-45 Ex 10-7b (4); 10-46 Ex 10-8;
Admin Plan: s10p1 (2); s10p2 (7); s10p3 (3); s10p4

REINSPECTIONS 15
7420.10G Gbk: 10-23 (3); 10-32; 10-33; 10-34 (3); 19-12; 21-4;
PIH Notices: 00-24B (4); 00-24B

RE-INSPECTIONS 4
PIH Notices: 02-27 (2);
Admin Plan: s10p3; s10p3

RE-INSPECTS 1
Admin Plan: s21p4

REINSTATE 6
24 CFR 5: .630 (3);
24 CFR 982: .204;
7420.10G Gbk: 4-6; 10-29

RE-INSTATE 1
Admin Plan: s10p2

REINSTATED 2
HUD-50058Instr: p37;
7420.10G Gbk: 6-8

RE-INSTATED 2
7420.10G Gbk: 10-29;
Admin Plan: s10p4

REINSTATEMENT 4
PIH Notices: 02-15; 02-03; 01-43; 99-30

RE-INSTATEMENT 1
Admin Plan: s10p2

REINSTATES 4
7420.10G Gbk: 12-6;
PIH Notices: 02-15; 02-03; 99-30

REJECT 6
24 CFR 5: .216; .359;
7420.10G Gbk: 10-5;
PIH Notices: 00-53;
Admin Plan: s23p3; s24p5

REJECTED 6
7420.10G Gbk: 19-11; 24-12;
PIH Notices: 03-11 (2); 00-53;
Admin Plan: s23p4

REJECTION 13
24 CFR 5: .216; .359 (2);
HUD-9886: p2;

PIH Notices: 02-21; 02-01; 01-20; 00-27; 99-52;
Admin Plan: s3p3; s23p3; s24p6; s24p6

REJECTION LETTER 3
PIH Notices: 02-21; 02-01; 99-52

REJECTIONS 1
7420.10G Gbk: 24-12

REJECTS 3
PIH Notices: 01-41;
Admin Plan: s24p6; s24p6

RELATED BY BLOOD.................... 5
24 CFR 982: .516; .615;
7420.10G Gbk: 17-7;
Admin Plan: s2p2; s19p1

RELEASE 64
24 CFR 5: .230; .508 (3); .659 (6);
24 CFR 982: .516 (5); .551;
HUD-50058Instr: p2 (2); p3;
HUD-9886: p1 (2);
7420.10G Gbk: 4-3; 5-9 Ex 5-1; 5-12; 5-46 Ex 5-5; 5-47 Ex 5-5; 5-48 Ex 5-5; 5-49 Ex 5-5 (2); 15-1;
PIH Notices: 02-21 (2); 01-20 (2); 01-15 (2); 01-15 Impr Integ Hbk (6); 01-11; 00-53; 00-34; 00-27 (2); 00-24; 00-24B (2); 00-11A;
Admin Plan: s1p6 (3); s3p3 (2); s6p7; s7p2 (2); s7p4; s9p3; s20p4; s25p5; s25p6

RELEASE OF INFORMATION 4
7420.10G Gbk: 5-13 (2); 5-35; 12-3

RELEASE OF INFORMATION 15
HUD-50058Instr: p2 (2); p3;
HUD-9886: p1;
7420.10G Gbk: 5-13 (2); 5-35; 12-3;
Admin Plan: s1p6; s3p3; s7p2 (2); s7p4; s9p3; s20p4

RELEASED 12
24 CFR 5: .508 (2);
HUD-9886: p2 (2);
7420.10G Gbk: 5-9 Ex 5-1 (2);
PIH Notices: 01-15; 01-06; 00-53; 00-24 (2); 00-24A

RELEASES 1
PIH Notices: 00-24B

RELEVANCE 5
24 CFR 982: .553 (2);
HUD-52580-A: p6;
7420.10G Gbk: 15-7;
PIH Notices: 03-11

RELEVANT 46
24 CFR 5: .504; .514; .518; .603; .703;
24 CFR 982: .207; .310; .552; .555 (2);
HUD-52641: p5;
HUD-9886: p2;
7420.10G Gbk: 7-6; 8-7; 9-7; 11-13; 13-2; 13-4; 15-7; 16-4 (4); 16-5;
PIH Notices: 03-23; 02-27 (2); 02-20 (2); 02-01; 01-06; 01-02; 00-46 (2); 00-11A (2); 99-52; 95-48; 95-48 Tech Asst;
Admin Plan: s3p1; s16p2; s18p5 (2); s20p4; s22p4; s24p3

RELEVANT CIRCUMSTANCES 1
24 CFR 982: .552

RELEVANT FACTORS 2
24 CFR 5: .518;
Admin Plan: s16p2

RELIABILITATION 1
7420.10G Gbk: 5-40

RELIABILITY 3
PIH Notices: 02-27; 95-48; 95-48 Tech Asst

RELIABLE 16
7420.10G Gbk: 5-40; 5-50 Ex 5-5; 5-53 Ex 5-5; 8-21; 12-4; 18-6; 22-3;
PIH Notices: 00-24A; 95-48 (2); 95-48 Tech Asst (2);
Admin Plan: s2p3; s6p6; s6p11; s7p7

RELIGION...................................... 27
24 CFR 5: .655;
24 CFR 982: .202; .207; .304;
HUD-52641: p5; p10;
HUD-52641-A: p3;
HUD-52646: p2;
HUD-903: p1 (2); p2 (3); p4 (2);
7420.10G Gbk: 4-19; 5-10 Ex 5-1; 5-11; 5-42 (3); 8-14; 11-13;
PIH Notices: 02-21; 01-15;
Admin Plan: s1p2; s23p2

RELINQUISHING 2
PIH Notices: 01-41; 00-09

RELOCATE 11
7420.10G Gbk: 13-1 (2); 23-18;
PIH Notices: 02-21; 01-41; 00-09 (2); 95-48 (2); 95-48 Tech Asst; 95-48 Tech Asst

RELOCATED 4
7420.10G Gbk: 3-3;

PIH Notices: 02-21; 00-49;
Admin Plan: s24p3

RELOCATES....................................3
24 CFR 982: .623;
PIH Notices: 95-48; 95-48 Tech Asst

RELOCATING 10
7420.10G Gbk: 3-2; 4-13; 23-18 (2);
PIH Notices: 02-21 (2); 01-20 (2); 95-48; 95-48 Tech Asst

RELOCATION 90
24 CFR 5: .100;
HUD-50058Instr: p13;
7420.10G Gbk: 2-1; 2-2; 2-7; 21-5; 21-13; 21-16 Ex 21-6 (3); 24-16;
PIH Notices: 02-21 (24); 02-01 (3); 01-20 (25); 01-06; 00-27 (17); 99-52 (4);
Admin Plan: s24p3 (2); s25p7 (2); s25p7

RELOCATION BENEFITS..............1
PIH Notices: 02-21

REMAIN..78
24 CFR 982: .315; .355; .504;
HUD-50058: p v;
HUD-50058Instr: p18; p42; p56;
HUD-52641: p4;
HUD-52665: p3;
7420.10G Gbk: 1-9; 3-4; 7-2; 7-6; 7-8; 8-21; 9-11; 14-1; 14-4; 15-4; 15-9 Ex 15-1; 15-10 Ex 15-2; 24-12;
PIH Notices: 03-05; 02-27; 02-21; 02-20; 02-14; 01-41 (20); 01-40; 01-20; 01-01; 00-53 (2); 00-46; 00-41; 00-09 (13); 95-48; 95-48 Tech Asst;
Admin Plan: s5p2; s8p5; s23p1; s23p3; s23p7; s24p6; s25p1; s25p3; s25p5

REMAINDER...................................3
HUD-52665: p2 (2);
7420.10G Gbk: 1-15

REMAINED 4
7420.10G Gbk: 14-5;
PIH Notices: 01-10 (2); 00-09

REMAINING.................................64
24 CFR 5: .403 (2); .655;
24 CFR 982: .309; .315; .402; .605; .633;
HUD-50058Instr: p46; p72 (2); p75;
HUD-52665: p3;
7420.10G Gbk: 3-4; 5-2 (2); 5-22; 5-41; 8-4; 8-22; 10-38 Ex 10-3; 11-15; 13-6; 14-3; 15-7; 19-5; 20-7; 20-10; 20-11; 22-17; 23-7; 23-18; 24-10;
PIH Notices: 03-23 (3); 02-01 (2); 01-41; 01-20 (2); 01-10; 00-45; 00-09 (2); 99-52 (2);
Admin Plan: s2p2 (4); s2p3; s5p2; s6p10; s8p5 (3); s8p6 (2); s9p2; s10p3; s11p2; s13p2; s24p6

REMAINING MEMBER 13
24 CFR 5: .403 (2); .655;
HUD-50058Instr: p72 (2); p75;
7420.10G Gbk: 5-2 (2);
Admin Plan: s2p3; s8p5 (2); s8p6; s8p6

REMAINING MEMBER OF THE FAMILY 1
Admin Plan: s8p6

REMAINING MEMBERS 1
7420.10G Gbk: 15-7

REMAINS 46
24 CFR 982: .54; .315;
HUD-50058Instr: p42; p47;
7420.10G Gbk: 5-2; 7-8; 10-29; 11-6; 12-6; 13-7; 14-3 (2); 14-4; 15-4 (2); 23-3;
PIH Notices: 03-23 (3); 03-12; 01-41 (10); 01-20; 01-10 (2); 01-06; 00-09 (5); 95-48; 95-48 Tech Asst;
Admin Plan: s4p2; s5p2; s8p4; s23p5; s23p7

REMEDIAL.......................................5
PIH Notices: 02-27 (3); 95-48; 95-48 Tech Asst

REMEDIED.......................................2
HUD-52646: p2;
PIH Notices: 01-15 Impr Integ Hbk

REMEDIES.....................................32
24 CFR 982: Intro; .404 (2); .453; .456; .552; .619 (2); .641;
HUD-52641: p3 (3); p4 (2); p5 (4);
7420.10G Gbk: 11-18; 22-14 (2); 22-15 (2); 22-16 (2);
PIH Notices: 02-21; 95-48; 95-48 Tech Asst;
Admin Plan: s17p1; s18p4; s20p7; s24p6

REMEDY..21

24 CFR 982: .456 (2); .555;
HUD-52641: p4; p5 (3); p6;
7420.10G Gbk: 8-22; 16-2; 22-1; 22-11; 22-14;
PIH Notices: 02-27; 01-41; 95-48 (2); 95-48 Tech Asst (2);
Admin Plan: s18p4; s20p5

REMINDER....................................2
PIH Notices: 02-01; 99-52

REMOVABLE.................................3
24 CFR 5: .350;
PIH Notices: 95-48; 95-48 Tech Asst

REMOVAL....................................56
24 CFR 5: .318 (4); .321; .327; .353 (3); .360 (3); .363;
HUD-52580-A: p2 (2); p13 (2); p17 (3);
7420.10G Gbk: 4-7; 10-18;
PIH Notices: 02-21 (3); 02-01; 01-20 (3); 00-27 (3); 99-52; 99-11 (2); 95-48 (10); 95-48 Tech Asst (8);
Admin Plan: s4p2; s6p6; s18p2

REMOVAL FROM WAITING..........1
Admin Plan: s4p2

REMOVE.......................................35
24 CFR 5: .318; .350 (2); .353 (6); .360 (5); .363 (2);
24 CFR 982: .204; .205;
HUD-50058Instr: p11 (2); p26;
7420.10G Gbk: 4-5 (3); 4-6; 4-9;
PIH Notices: 02-01; 01-06; 99-52; 95-48 (2); 95-48 Tech Asst (2);
Admin Plan: s18p5; s18p7

REMOVED....................................19
24 CFR 5: .318;
24 CFR 982: .102; .204;
7420.10G Gbk: 3-2; 4-5; 4-7; 10-5; 10-16; 10-37 Ex 10-2;
PIH Notices: 01-06; 99-11; 95-48 (2); 95-48 Tech Asst (2);
Admin Plan: s4p2; s4p3; s6p6; s23p5

REMOVES......................................2
PIH Notices: 95-48; 95-48 Tech Asst

REMOVING..................................11
24 CFR 982: .54; .204; .516;
7420.10G Gbk: 4-7 (2); 20-7; 21-4;
PIH Notices: 99-11; 95-48; 95-48 Tech Asst;
Admin Plan: s7p8

RENEWAL...................................125
24 CFR 5: .324; .801;
24 CFR 982: Intro; .4 (3); .101; .102 (23); .308;
HUD-50058Instr: p13; p76;
HUD-52648: p2;
7420.10G Gbk: 8-21; 8-22; 20-7 (5); 20-8; 20-9 (6); 20-11 (2); 20-12 Ex 20-2 (2); 20-13 (5); 20-14; 20-15; 20-16; 20-18 (4); 20-19 Ex 20-3; 23-1; 23-13; 24-2; 24-13;
PIH Notices: 03-23 (35); 02-22; 02-20 (3); 02-14 (2); 02-06 (4); 01-41 (3); 01-06; 00-46 (3); 00-31; 00-09 (2); 99-30

RENEWAL FUNDING....................52
24 CFR 982: .102 (7);
HUD-52648: p2;
7420.10G Gbk: 20-7 (4); 20-8; 20-9 (5); 20-11 (2); 20-12 Ex 20-2 (2); 20-13 (3); 20-14; 20-15; 20-16; 20-18 (4); 20-19 Ex 20-3; 23-1;
PIH Notices: 03-23 (16); 02-14; 02-06

RENEWAL UNITS.............................12
24 CFR 982: .4; .102 (9);
7420.10G Gbk: 20-8 Ex 20-1;
PIH Notices: 03-23

RENOVATION.................................9
24 CFR 982: .310;
HUD-52641: p9;
HUD-52641-A: p2;
7420.10G Gbk: 9-14 Ex 9-1; 15-3;
PIH Notices: 02-01; 99-52; 95-48; 95-48 Tech Asst

RENOVATION OF THE UNIT.........3
24 CFR 982: .310;
HUD-52641: p9;
HUD-52641-A: p2

RENOVATIONS...............................1
7420.10G Gbk: 9-16 Ex 9-2

RENT BURDEN.............................34
24 CFR 982: .503;
HUD-50058: p v;
7420.10G Gbk: 6-2 (5); 6-3 (2); 6-5 (3); 6-6 (3); 7-5; 8-5; 8-6; 8-16 (2); 14-4 (3); 19-4; 24-11; 24-12 (3);
PIH Notices: 02-20 (3); 00-46 (2); 00-46

RENT BURDENS 10
24 CFR 982: .503;
7420.10G Gbk: 7-6 (2);
PIH Notices: 02-20 (3); 01-10; 00-46 (2); 00-46

RENT CALCULATION 33
HUD-50058: p v; p9 (2); p10 (2); p11 (2); p12 (2); p13 (2);
HUD-50058Instr: p39; p40; p43 (2); p48 (2); p51 (2); p54 (2); p77; p78;
7420.10G Gbk: 8-5; 12-3 (2); 24-7;
PIH Notices: 01-15 (3); 01-15 Impr Integ Hbk;
Admin Plan: s3p3; s6p13

RENT CALCULATION ERRORS.... 1
7420.10G Gbk: 19-4

RENT CALCULATIONS 4
HUD-50058Instr: p15;
7420.10G Gbk: 14-2;
PIH Notices: 01-15; 01-15

RENT CHANGE 1
7420.10G Gbk: 12-1

RENT CHANGES 2
7420.10G Gbk: 9-8;
Admin Plan: s23p6

RENT COLLECTION 1
7420.10G Gbk: 1-2

RENT COMPUTATION.................... 1
Admin Plan: s1p3

RENT CONTROL 7
24 CFR 982: Intro; .509 (2);
7420.10G Gbk: 9-2 (3); 9-2

RENT CONTROLLED 1
7420.10G Gbk: 9-2

RENT EQUATIONS......................... 1
PIH Notices: 01-15 Impr Integ Hbk

RENT FORMULA............................ 5
7420.10G Gbk: 14-2; 14-3; 14-5;
PIH Notices: 01-41; 00-09

RENT FORMULAS 1
7420.10G Gbk: 14-2

RENT INCREASE........................... 35
HUD-52665: p2;
7420.10G Gbk: 5-23; 6-6; 9-1 (2); 9-8; 9-12; 12-8; 12-9; 14-3; 14-4; 21-4 (2);
PIH Notices: 01-41 (7); 01-10 (3); 00-11A; 00-09 (7);
Admin Plan: s11p3; s11p1; s21p3; s24p5

RENT INCREASES 16
7420.10G Gbk: 1-6 Ex 1-1 (3); 3-5; 9-11; 12-5; 14-3 (2);
PIH Notices: 01-41; 01-10 (2); 00-09 (3);
Admin Plan: s11p1; s23p6

RENT PAYMENT.............................. 6
24 CFR 982: .451;
HUD-50058: p i;
HUD-50058Instr: p14;
7420.10G Gbk: 11-6;
PIH Notices: 00-24B;
Admin Plan: s9p3

RENT PAYMENTS 4
Admin Plan: s1p1; s6p9; s7p6; s13p1

RENT POLICIES.............................. 3
PIH Notices: 01-15 Impr Integ Hbk (2); 01-15 Impr Integ Hbk

RENT REASONABLENESS 152
24 CFR 982: .102; .308; .317; .352 (2); .509;
7420.10G Gbk: 1-1; 1-4; 1-10; 1-11; 1-16 Ex 1-3 (2); 2-9 (4); 2-10; 3-5 (2); 3-9; 7-6; 8-6; 8-7 (2); 8-18 (3); 9-1 (6); 9-2 (6); 9-3 (4); 9-4 (5); 9-5 (3); 9-6; 9-8 (4); 9-9 (2); 9-10 (2); 9-11 (9); 9-12 (4); 9-19 Ex 9-4; 10-25; 10-31; 10-32 (4); 11-11; 11-17; 14-4; 17-7 (2); 17-9 (2); 19-11; 20-3; 21-4 (6); 21-8; 21-11; 21-16 Ex 21-6; 22-2; 22-5; 22-6 (3); 24-11 (5);
PIH Notices: 03-12 (12); 02-27 (4); 01-41 (8); 01-10; 00-41; 00-09 (7);
Admin Plan: s8p2; s11p2 (4); s11p3; s11p1; s21p1; s21p2; s21p3; s21p3

RENT SUPPLEMENT 37
24 CFR 5: .236; .500; .504 (2); .520 (6); .601; .603;
PIH Notices: 01-41 (13); 01-27 (2); 00-09 (9); 00-09

RENT SUPPLEMENTS 2
24 CFR 982: .352;
7420.10G Gbk: 8-16

RENT TO OWNER 255
24 CFR 5: .520 (3); .632;
24 CFR 982: 24 CFR 982 (7); .4 (11); .54; .158; .305; .308 (3); .310; .317; .352; .353;

.451 (6); .452; .501; .504; .506 (3); .507 (6); .509 (2); .510; .514 (2); .515 (3); .519 (8); .520 (4); .521 (6); .613 (2); .617 (2); .619 (4); .622 (8); .623 (3); .641;
HUD-50058: p10; p x (5); p11 (3); p xi (7); p12; p xii (5); p13; p xiii (4);
HUD-50058Instr: p43 (7); p45 (2); p47 (4); p48 (3); p49 (7); p50; p51 (4); p52 (2); p54 (5); p55; p72 (4); p75 (3); p76;
HUD-52641: p1 (2); p4 (6); p5 (2); 8 (10); p10 (4);
HUD-52641-A: p1 (10); p3 (4);
HUD-52648: p1 (3); p2;
PIH Notices: 03-12; 02-27; 02-22; 01-41 (5); 01-10 (3); 00-41; 00-24B; 00-09 (6);
Admin Plan: s9p1; s11p1 (2); s11p2 (3); s11p3 (3); s19p1 (12); s21p3; s21p5; s21p7 (3); s21p7

RENTAL HISTORIES 2
7420.10G Gbk: 5-40; 5-40

RENTAL HISTORY 1
7420.10G Gbk: 5-40

RENTAL INFORMATION 2
7420.10G Gbk: 9-5;
PIH Notices: 02-27

RENTAL PROPERTIES 4
7420.10G Gbk: 5-25 Ex 5-3; 9-3; 9-8;
Admin Plan: s11p2

RENTAL PROPERTY 7
7420.10G Gbk: 2-5; 4-26 Ex 4-2; 5-48 Ex 5-5; 9-3; 9-6;
Admin Plan: s7p5; s8p4

RENTAL UNIT 12
24 CFR 982: .310 (2);
HUD-52641: p9;
HUD-52641-A: p2;
HUD-903-1: p5;
7420.10G Gbk: 8-15; 8-17; 9-9;
PIH Notices: 01-02; 00-24B;
Admin Plan: s2p2; s22p2

REPARATION 5
24 CFR 5: .609;
HUD-50058Instr: p31;
PIH Notices: 01-15 Impr Integ Hbk (2); 01-15 Impr Integ Hbk

REPARATION PAYMENTS 5
24 CFR 5: .609;
HUD-50058Instr: p31;
PIH Notices: 01-15 Impr Integ Hbk (2); 01-15 Impr Integ Hbk

REPARATIONS 1
7420.10G Gbk: 5-15 Ex 5-2

REPAYMENT 22
24 CFR 5: .630 (2);
24 CFR 982: .163;
HUD-50058: p2 (2); p ii (2);
HUD-50058Instr: p12 (4);
7420.10G Gbk: 12-10; 20-25; 22-4; 22-12; 22-15; 22-18;
PIH Notices: 01-41; 00-09;
Admin Plan: s17p1; s20p7; s20p7

REPAYMENT AGREEMENT 27
24 CFR 5: .630 (2);
24 CFR 982: .163;
HUD-50058: p2; p ii (2);
HUD-50058Instr: p12 (3);
7420.10G Gbk: 6-8; 15-5; 20-25; 22-12; 22-13 (4); 22-17 (6);
PIH Notices: 01-41; 00-09;
Admin Plan: s17p1; s20p7

REPAYMENT AGREEMENTS 3
7420.10G Gbk: 3-5; 22-4; 22-18

REPAYMENT POLICY 1
Admin Plan: s20p7

REPEAT 1
PIH Notices: 00-49

REPEATED 25
24 CFR 982: .310; .551;
HUD-52641: p9;
HUD-52641-A: p2 (2);
7420.10G Gbk: 1-15; 10-30; 10-42 Ex 10-5 (2); 15-1 (2); 15-5; 15-7;
PIH Notices: 01-41; 95-48; 95-48 Tech Asst;
Admin Plan: s10p5; s14p1 (2); s14p2; s15p5 (3); s20p5; s23p6

REPEATEDLY 2
7420.10G Gbk: 11-4;
Admin Plan: s20p6

REPLACE 16
HUD-50058Instr: p2; p34; p73;
7420.10G Gbk: 1-1; 5-40; 8-10; 24-6;
PIH Notices: 02-21; 02-01 (2); 01-41; 01-20; 00-27; 99-52 (2); 99-11

REPLACED....................................6
7420.10G Gbk: 1-2; 1-3;
PIH Notices: 02-01; 01-06; 99-52; 99-11
REPLACEMENT 91
HUD-50058: p14;
HUD-50058Instr: p13; p56;
HUD-52641: 8;
HUD-52641-A: p1;
HUD-52648: p2;
7420.10G Gbk: 5-10 Ex 5-1; 20-13; 23-2;
PIH Notices: 03-23 (2); 02-21 (27); 02-14; 02-01; 01-41 (3); 01-20 (26); 01-06; 00-27 (19); 00-09; 99-52
REPLACEMENTS 10
24 CFR 5: .318;
24 CFR 982: .635 (4);
HUD-50058: p xiv;
HUD-50058Instr: p56 (2);
PIH Notices: 02-07; 01-41
REPLACES 1
PIH Notices: 01-15
REPLENISHING..............................1
7420.10G Gbk: 20-15
REPORT FORM 3
HUD-50058: p1;
HUD-50058Instr: p i;
7420.10G Gbk: 19-2
REPRESENTATION 8
24 CFR 5: .514;
24 CFR 982: .555;
7420.10G Gbk: 3-9 (2); 9-11; 16-5 (2);
Admin Plan: s18p5
REPRESENTATIONS 2
Admin Plan: s20p1; s20p7
REPRESENTATIVE........................47
24 CFR 5: .363;
24 CFR 982: .4; .503 (2); .555; .633;
HUD-50058: p ii;
HUD-50058Instr: p4; p6;
HUD-52646: p1 (2);
7420.10G Gbk: 2-5; 4-9; 4-27 Ex 4-2; 7-5; 9-3 (2); 11-11; 21-16 Ex 21-6; 22-7; 23-8 Ex 23-1; 24-11;
PIH Notices: 03-11; 02-27 (3); 02-20 (4); 02-01; 00-46 (4); 99-52; 95-48 (4); 95-48 Tech Asst (2);
Admin Plan: s8p2; s18p3; s20p2; s20p7; s23p4
REPRESENTATIVES.....................34
24 CFR 5: .353 (4);
7420.10G Gbk: 16-4; 22-11; 23-3; 23-4 (2); 24-14;
PIH Notices: 02-03; 01-43; 01-40; 01-27; 01-15 (2); 01-11; 01-02; 00-53; 00-49; 00-45; 00-41; 00-31; 00-28; 00-23; 00-14; 99-52; 99-30; 99-11;
Admin Plan: s18p5; s20p2; s20p4; s25p4; s25p4
REPTILES 1
24 CFR 5: .306
REQUEST FOR TENANCY APPROVAL....................................54
HUD-50058: p v;
HUD-50058Instr: p21;
HUD-52517: p1 (4); p2;
7420.10G Gbk: 1-16 Ex 1-3; 3-2; 5-40; 8-11; 8-13 (4); 8-14 (2); 8-15 (5); 8-17 (2); 8-18; 9-8; 10-25 (3); 10-26; 11-19; 13-4; 13-7 (2); 18-1; 18-7 (4); 19-6 (2); 19-7 (2); 19-12; 21-4; 21-9; 24-13;
PIH Notices: 03-12; 01-41; 00-09;
Admin Plan: s8p2; s8p3; s8p5; s9p1
RESCHEDULE.................................... 9
7420.10G Gbk: 8-8; 10-40 Ex 10-4a; 10-41 Ex 10-4b; 24-7;
Admin Plan: s3p3 (2); s7p3; s18p5; s18p5
RE-SCHEDULE 4
7420.10G Gbk: 10-40 Ex 10-4a; 10-41 Ex 10-4b (2);
Admin Plan: s9p4
RESCHEDULED..............................5
7420.10G Gbk: 10-35;
Admin Plan: s11p1 (2); s15p6; s18p5
RE-SCHEDULED 1
Admin Plan: s8p2
RESCHEDULES 1
Admin Plan: s1p4
RESCHEDULING............................1
7420.10G Gbk: 10-30
RESERVE.....................................110
24 CFR 982: 24 CFR 982 (2); .4 (2); .54; .101; .102; .151; .152; .154 (7); .155 (10); .451; .515; .619;
HUD-50058Instr: p26;
7420.10G Gbk: 9-8; 17-10; 20-2; 20-13 (2); 20-14; 20-

29;
PIH Notices: 03-23 (37); 02-27; 02-21; 02-07 (2); 02-06 (21); 01-41; 01-20; 00-28 (2); 00-27; 96-65;
Admin Plan: s4p2; s19p1; s22p2; s22p3; s22p3

RESERVE ACCOUNT 15
24 CFR 982: Intro; .151; .154 (5);
7420.10G Gbk: 20-14;
PIH Notices: 03-23 (2); 02-06 (4);
Admin Plan: s22p3

RESERVED 194
24 CFR 5: .306;
24 CFR 982: .3; .4; .102 (5);
HUD-50058: p i (2); p4; p iv; p6 (2); p7 (2); p vii (2); p8; p viii; p9 (5); p ix (5); p10 (7); p x (5); p11 (3); p xi (3); p12 (2); p xii (2); p13 (6); p xiii (6); p14 (2); p xiv (2);
HUD-50058Instr: p3 (2); p17 (2); p33 (2); p36 (4); p37 (2); p39 (2); p40 (4); p41 (4); p42 (2); p43 (4); p44 (6); p45 (2); p47 (2); p48 (2); p49 (2); p51 (2); p52 (2); p53 (6); p54 (4); p55 (2); p57 (4);
7420.10G Gbk: 20-8 Ex 20-1 (12); 20-10 (3); 20-11 (2); 20-14 (2); 20-15 (7); 20-16; 20-18; 23-1 (2);
PIH Notices: 03-23 (8); 02-21 (2); 02-14; 02-06 (21); 01-15 Impr Integ Hbk;
Admin Plan: s21p9

RESERVED NUMBER OF UNITS 17
7420.10G Gbk: 20-8 Ex 20-1 (2); 20-10; 20-11; 20-14; 20-15 (6); 20-16; 20-18;
PIH Notices: 02-06 (3); 02-06

RESERVES 51
24 CFR 5: .653;
24 CFR 982: .102 (2); .151;
7420.10G Gbk: 10-44 Ex 10-7a; 10-45 Ex 10-7b; 20-13; 20-14 (2); 20-15;
PIH Notices: 03-23 (15); 02-07; 02-06 (16); 02-01 (2); 01-41; 01-10; 00-49; 00-28; 00-09; 99-52;
Admin Plan: s25p6

RESIDE.. 116
24 CFR 5: .240; .303; .508; .514; .611; .615; .655; .661 (2);
24 CFR 982: 24 CFR 982 (3); .4 (5); .207; .310; .311; .316; .402; .551 (2); .552; .602 (2); .605; .606 (3); .610 (6); .614; .615 (4); .618; .619; .620 (2);
HUD-50058: p v;
HUD-50058Instr: p17; p18; p39; p43; p46; p47 (2); p59; p68; p70; p71;
HUD-52641: p1; p2; p3; p5; 8; p10 (2);
HUD-52641-A: p1; p3 (2);
7420.10G Gbk: 1-8; 2-4; 4-17; 5-18; 5-28; 5-37; 5-38; 5-41; 7-3; 7-10 (2); 10-16; 10-44 Ex 10-7a; 15-6; 15-7; 17-4; 17-7 (2); 17-9; 22-14;
PIH Notices: 02-01; 01-41 (4); 01-27; 01-15 Impr Integ Hbk; 01-10; 00-23; 00-11A; 00-09 (3); 99-52;
Admin Plan: s2p3; s13p2; s14p2; s19p1 (10); s19p1

RESIDED.. 19
24 CFR 5: .655;
24 CFR 982: .4; .207; .553;
HUD-52648: p3 (3);
7420.10G Gbk: 2-4 (2);
PIH Notices: 02-07; 01-41 (2); 01-10; 01-06 (3); 00-49; 00-09; 00-09

RESIDENCE................................... 55
24 CFR 5: .630; .661 (2);
24 CFR 982: .4 (7); .353; .551 (4); .627; .633;
HUD-50058Instr: p46; p72 (3); p73;
HUD-52580: p1 (2);
HUD-52641: 8 (2);
HUD-52641-A: p1 (2);
HUD-52646: p2;
7420.10G Gbk: 1-15 (2); 3-3; 5-5; 5-9 Ex 5-1 (3); 5-10 Ex 5-1; 6-8; 11-4; 17-10;
PIH Notices: 01-27 (2); 01-15;
Admin Plan: s6p7 (3); s19p1; s22p4; s23p2 (3); s25p3 (3); s25p3

RESIDENCES 8
24 CFR 5: .703;
24 CFR 982: .306; .310;
HUD-52641: p9;
HUD-52641-A: p2;
7420.10G Gbk: 8-20; 10-1;
Admin Plan: s16p2

RESIDENCY 41
24 CFR 5: .318; .655 (15);
24 CFR 982: .4 (3); .202 (2); .207 (15);
7420.10G Gbk: 4-18; 13-2; 15-6;
PIH Notices: 01-15 Impr Integ Hbk;
Admin Plan: s2p2

RESIDENCY PREFERENCE 33
24 CFR 5: .655 (12);
24 CFR 982: .4 (3); .202 (2); .207 (11);
7420.10G Gbk: 4-17 (4); 4-17

RESIDENCY PREFERENCE AREA15
24 CFR 5: .655 (7);
24 CFR 982: .4; .207 (6); .207

RESIDENCY PREFERENCES.........4
24 CFR 5: .655;
24 CFR 982: .207 (2);
7420.10G Gbk: 4-17

RESIDENT 180
24 CFR 5: .303; .506; .609 (6); .615; .655; .661 (2);
24 CFR 35 SubM: .1200;
24 CFR 982: .201; .203; .605 (2); .614 (2); .615 (3); .620;
HUD-50058Instr: p13 (2); p17; p19; p25 (3); p28; p62; p70 (2); p72; p75 (3);
HUD-52641: p6;
7420.10G Gbk: 2-9; 3-3; 3-8 (4); 3-9 (4); 4-22; 5-4; 5-7; 5-9 Ex 5-1; 5-10 Ex 5-1 (2); 5-15 Ex 5-2 (5); 5-20; 5-51 Ex 5-5; 10-12; 10-16; 12-5; 13-2 (3); 17-3; 17-7; 19-3; 19-8;
PIH Notices: 03-11 (7); 03-05; 02-21; 02-01 (4); 01-41 (11); 01-40; 01-27 (2); 01-20; 01-15 (7); 01-15 Impr Integ Hbk (29); 01-06 (2); 00-45; 00-41; 00-27; 00-23; 00-11 (6); 00-09 (11); 00-01 (2); 99-52 (5); 99-11 (4); 98-66 (2);
Admin Plan: s2p4; s3p1; s6p12; s10p2; s19p1 (3); s20p2

RESIDENT ADVISORY BOARD 4
7420.10G Gbk: 3-8 (3); 3-9

RESIDENT ADVISORY BOARDS..2
7420.10G Gbk: 3-8; 3-9

RESIDENT COUNCIL......................1
Admin Plan: s3p1

RESIDENT COUNCILS 5
7420.10G Gbk: 3-9 (2);
PIH Notices: 01-15; 00-01; 98-66

RESIDENT EMPLOYMENT............1
PIH Notices: 00-11

RESIDENT INITIATIVES 4
24 CFR 5: .609;
7420.10G Gbk: 5-15 Ex 5-2;
PIH Notices: 01-15 Impr Integ Hbk; 01-15 Impr Integ Hbk

RESIDENT MANAGEMENT 18
24 CFR 5: .609;
7420.10G Gbk: 5-15 Ex 5-2; 5-20;
PIH Notices: 03-11; 03-05; 02-01 (2); 01-40; 01-27; 01-15; 01-15 Impr Integ Hbk (2); 00-01; 99-52 (3); 99-11; 98-66

RESIDENT MANAGEMENT CORPORATIONS 11
PIH Notices: 03-11; 03-05; 02-01 (2); 01-40; 01-27; 01-15; 99-52 (3); 99-11

RESIDENT ORGANIZATIONS......... 1
PIH Notices: 00-11

RESIDENT SERVICE STIPEND ... 11
24 CFR 5: .609 (2);
HUD-50058Instr: p25 (2);
7420.10G Gbk: 5-15 Ex 5-2;
PIH Notices: 01-15 Impr Integ Hbk (5); 01-15 Impr Integ Hbk

RESIDENT TRAINING 1
PIH Notices: 99-52

RESIDENTIAL................................41
24 CFR 5: .318;
24 CFR 982: .4; .310 (2); .401; .614; .633;
HUD-50058Instr: p72;
HUD-52641: p9;
HUD-52641-A: p2;
HUD-903: p1;
7420.10G Gbk: 2-13 Ex 2-1 (2); 5-11; 10-11; 17-5;
PIH Notices: 02-01 (3); 00-41 (2); 00-23 (2); 99-52 (3); 99-11 (2); 95-48 (6); 95-48 Tech Asst (6);
Admin Plan: s19p1

RESIDENTS 239
24 CFR 5: .655 (3); .661 (3);
24 CFR 35 SubM: .1200; .1210;

.1225;
24 CFR 982: .207 (2); .306 (2); .307; .310 (3); .551 (2); .552; .553 (5); .609 (5); .610 (2); .613; .614 (6); .615; .618 (3);
HUD-50058Instr: p2; p5; p25; p75 (3);
HUD-52580-A: p17; p18;
HUD-52641: p7;
7420.10G Gbk: 1-9 (2); 2-1; 2-13 Ex 2-1; 3-1; 3-6; 3-9 (2); 4-17; 8-20; 10-9; 10-12; 10-13 (2); 10-16; 10-17 (2); 10-21 (2); 11-3; 15-2; 17-3 (4); 17-4 (2); 17-5 (4); 17-7; 17-8; 20-3; 22-18; 23-3 (2);
PIH Notices: 03-11 (7); 02-27; 02-21 (2); 02-07; 02-01 (7); 01-41 (20); 01-20; 01-15 (13); 01-15 Impr Integ Hbk (17); 01-10; 00-41; 00-27; 00-11 (10); 00-11A (2); 00-09 (28); 00-01 (4); 99-52 (8); 99-11 (10); 98-66 (4);
Admin Plan: s1p4; s2p7; s9p3; s15p2 (2); s15p3; s16p2 (2); s19p1 (3); s19p1

RESIDENT'S..................................10
HUD-50058Instr: p17;
7420.10G Gbk: 17-4;
PIH Notices: 03-11; 01-15 (3); 01-15 Impr Integ Hbk (2); 00-11;
Admin Plan: s19p1

RESIDENTS'....................................8
7420.10G Gbk: 3-1; 3-6; 17-4 (2);
PIH Notices: 02-01; 00-11; 00-01; 98-66

RESIDES 34
24 CFR 5: .403;
24 CFR 982: .207; .402; .551; .613; .617;
HUD-50058Instr: p19 (2); p34; p42; p43; p46; p47 (2); p56; p59 (2); p72; p73;
HUD-52641: p10;
HUD-52641-A: p3;
7420.10G Gbk: 4-16; 5-41; 10-16; 11-13; 17-11; 23-15;
PIH Notices: 00-49;
Admin Plan: s19p1 (5); s22p4

RESIDING....................................123
24 CFR 5: .506; .508 (2); .609; .611; .617; .661 (3);
24 CFR 982: .201 (3); .203 (4); .207; .306; .310 (2); .311; .312 (2); .403; .551 (3); .553; .555; .604 (3); .605; .608 (3); .610; .613 (2); .617; .619; .625; .633; .635; .642 (2);
HUD-50058Instr: p70;
HUD-52641: p4; p7; p9 (2);
HUD-52641-A: p2 (5);
HUD-52648: p4 (3);
7420.10G Gbk: 1-7; 3-4; 4-17; 4-19; 4-21; 4-22 (3); 5-9 Ex 5-1 (2); 5-14 Ex 5-2 (2); 5-28; 8-17; 8-20; 10-2; 11-5; 15-2; 17-2; 17-7; 20-4;
PIH Notices: 03-11 (2); 02-20 (2); 02-01; 01-41 (6); 01-15; 01-15 Impr Integ Hbk (4); 01-10; 00-46 (2); 00-41; 00-24B (2); 00-23; 00-11A; 00-09 (5); 99-52;
Admin Plan: s2p4 (2); s5p2; s6p6; s16p2; s19p1 (6); s20p2; s24p6

RESOURCE.....................................18
24 CFR 982: .626;
HUD-50058Instr: p4;
7420.10G Gbk: 2-4; 2-6; 2-8; 8-7; 19-4; 20-24; 21-16 Ex 21-6; 22-17; 24-8;
PIH Notices: 01-15; 01-15 Impr Integ Hbk; 00-53; 00-11; 00-11A (2); 00-11A

RESOURCES 113
24 CFR 982: .612; .625; .632;
HUD-50058Instr: p3 (2); p5; p29; p72;
7420.10G Gbk: 1-8; 2-11; 3-1; 3-7 (2); 4-3; 4-6; 4-7; 4-9; 4-12; 8-2; 8-4 (2); 9-5; 11-8; 11-9; 12-8; 19-4; 20-1 (2); 20-17; 21-2; 21-7; 21-19; 22-4 (2); 22-10; 22-17 (2); 22-18; 23-1; 23-3; 23-4 (3); 23-5; 23-19; 24-1; 24-15;
PIH Notices: 03-12; 03-05; 02-27 (7); 02-01 (2); 01-40; 01-15 (6); 01-15 Impr Integ Hbk (2); 00-53 (2); 00-11 (9); 00-11A (6); 99-52; 99-11 (2); 95-48 (4); 95-48 Tech Asst (4);
Admin Plan: s1p5; s2p2; s6p8 (2); s9p1; s11p3; s20p1 (2); s24p2;

s25p1; s25p3 (3); s25p4; s25p5 (2); s25p6; s25p6

RESPA..1

24 CFR 982: .630

RESPONSE 63

HUD-50058Instr: p12;
HUD-52580: p1 (11); p2 (13); p3 (2);
HUD-52665: p1;
HUD-52667: p i;
HUD-903: p1;
7420.10G Gbk: 1-6; 4-7 (3); 4-13; 5-38; 10-30; 12-2; 12-4; 19-11 (2); 21-17; 23-7; 24-3 (3); 24-4 (2); 24-6 (3); 24-12;
PIH Notices: 03-11; 99-11; 96-65; 95-48; 95-48 Tech Asst;
Admin Plan: s4p2; s7p1; s20p1; s20p6; s21p5; s23p1

RESPONSIBILITIES 112

24 CFR 5: .214; .661;
24 CFR 35 SubM: .1200; .1225;
24 CFR 982: 24 CFR 982 (2); .152 (2); .153; .161; .301; .308; .310; .452 (2); .636 (2);
HUD-52641: p6; p10;
HUD-52641-A: p3;
HUD-52667: p i;
7420.10G Gbk: 1-1; 1-2; 1-7; 1-11 (2); 1-12; 1-13; 1-14 (4); 8-1; 8-2; 8-3; 8-19; 10-12; 10-14; 10-15; 10-17; 10-22; 10-29; 11-2; 11-3 (2); 11-7; 11-11; 11-15 (2); 11-17 (3); 13-1; 13-3; 13-5; 15-1; 19-1; 20-24 (3); 22-2; 22-7; 22-8; 22-9; 22-18; 23-18; 24-9;
PIH Notices: 03-11 (3); 02-27 (3); 02-20 (2); 01-41 (2); 01-15; 01-15 Impr Integ Hbk (4); 01-06; 00-46 (2); 00-31; 00-11A (5); 00-09 (3); 99-30; 95-48; 95-48 Tech Asst;
Admin Plan: s1p1; s8p1; s8p2; s8p3; s8p4; s10p1; s14p1; s15p6; s23p7; s25p1 (2); s25p3 (2); s25p7; s25p8

RESPONSIBILITY........................155

24 CFR 5: .318; .363; .508; .603; .615; .630; .659; .801 (2);
24 CFR 982: 24 CFR 982 (3); .3; .307 (3); .309; .310; .404; .406; .515 (2); .516; .553; .625; .641 (2);
HUD-50058Instr: p1; p5; p14; p71; p76;
HUD-52517: p2;
HUD-52580-A: p17;
HUD-52641: p3; p4; p6;
7420.10G Gbk: 1-4; 1-13; 3-3; 4-1; 4-7; 4-18; 5-9 Ex 5-1; 5-36 Ex 5-4; 5-39; 5-40 (2); 6-8; 8-20 (2); 9-11; 10-1; 10-15; 10-23 (2); 10-26; 10-28; 10-29; 10-33 (2); 10-34 (2); 10-36 Ex 10-1; 10-40 Ex 10-4a; 11-3; 11-6; 11-9; 11-12; 11-15; 12-8; 18-1 (3); 20-16; 20-18; 21-2; 21-3 (3); 21-4 (2); 22-2; 22-9; 22-18; 24-1;
PIH Notices: 03-20; 03-11 (2); 02-27 (5); 02-21; 02-14; 02-06; 02-01 (2); 01-41 (4); 01-20; 01-15 Impr Integ Hbk (4); 01-06 (3); 00-53; 00-27; 00-11 (2); 00-11A; 00-09 (2); 99-52 (2); 95-48 (5); 95-48 Tech Asst (5);
Admin Plan: s2p3; s2p6; s4p2; s6p5; s6p13; s9p3; s10p3 (3); s10p4 (2); s10p5 (3); s11p1; s20p1; s20p7; s23p4 (4); s23p7 (2); s25p4

RESPONSIBLE 304

24 CFR 5: .100 (3); .214; .230 (2); .236; .240 (3); .350 (2); .363 (3); .380 (2); .502 (3); .504 (3); .508 (20); .510 (2); .512 (8); .514 (32); .516; .518 (8); .524; .526 (3); .528 (2); .603 (2); .611 (3); .615 (2); .617 (3); .630 (15); .632; .705;
24 CFR 982: .307 (2); .310; .404 (3); .451; .452 (2); .551; .619 (4); .626;
HUD-50058: p i;
HUD-50058Instr: p10; p14 (2); p59; p70;
HUD-52580-A: p1; p4 (2); p15;
HUD-52641: p1; p3; p4; p6;
HUD-52648: p1 (2); p2;
7420.10G Gbk: 2-1; 3-1 (2); 4-1; 4-4; 5-2; 5-9 Ex 5-1 (2); 5-47 Ex 5-5; 6-6; 8-4; 8-23; 9-11; 10-7;

10-16; 10-17; 10-19; 10-21; 10-22; 10-26; 10-28 (2); 10-33; 10-34; 10-35; 11-9; 11-12 (2); 11-14; 11-17; 13-8; 13-9; 15-9 Ex 15-1; 15-10 Ex 15-2; 18-1; 18-7; 21-2; 21-3 (3); 21-4; 22-3; 22-4; 22-5 (3); 22-7; 22-9; 22-18 (2); 23-8 Ex 23-1 (3);
PIH Notices: 03-23; 03-11 (3); 02-27 (2); 02-20 (2); 02-14; 02-01 (3); 01-41 (10); 01-15 Impr Integ Hbk (2); 01-06; 01-02; 00-49 (2); 00-46 (2); 00-24B (2); 00-23 (2); 00-09 (6); 99-52 (3); 99-11 (3); 95-48 (5); 95-48 Tech Asst (5);
Admin Plan: s1p2; s2p2 (2); s2p6; s6p9; s7p5; s8p3; s8p4; s10p1 (4); s10p3; s10p4; s10p5 (3); s11p1; s13p2; s14p1; s20p3 (3); s20p6; s22p3 (2); s23p2; s23p3 (3); s24p3; s24p5 (3); s24p6; s24p7

RESPONSIBLE ENTITIES..............4
24 CFR 5: .508; .526 (2); .526

RESPONSIBLE ENTITY.................. 101
24 CFR 5: .100 (3); .236; .240 (3); .502 (3); .504; .508 (13); .510 (2); .512 (8); .514 (30); .516; .518 (7); .524; .528; .603 (2); .611 (3); .617 (3); .630 (14); .632;
HUD-50058Instr: p70;
PIH Notices: 03-11; 01-15 Impr Integ Hbk; 01-15 Impr Integ Hbk

RESPONSIBLE ENTITY'S.............7
24 CFR 5: .508 (3); .514 (2); .518; .630

RESPONSIBLE PARTIES 4
24 CFR 5: .350;
7420.10G Gbk: 23-8 Ex 23-1 (2); 23-8 Ex 23-1

RESPONSIBLE PARTY...................6
24 CFR 5: .363 (3);
7420.10G Gbk: 10-16; 10-33;
Admin Plan: s24p3

RESTITUTION.................................1
7420.10G Gbk: 22-17

RESTRAINED.................................1
24 CFR 5: .350

RESTRAINING...............................1
Admin Plan: s7p8

RESTRAINING ORDER 1
Admin Plan: s7p8

RESTRAINT.....................................1
24 CFR 5: .350

RESTRAINTS 2
PIH Notices: 95-48; 95-48 Tech Asst

RESTRICT.....................................15
24 CFR 5: .309;
24 CFR 982: .353; .401; .601;
7420.10G Gbk: 9-8; 10-2; 10-13; 21-7; 22-15;
PIH Notices: 96-65;
Admin Plan: s1p3; s10p1; s16p1; s16p2; s17p2

RESTRICTED 17
24 CFR 5: .236; .506;
HUD-50058Instr: p30;
HUD-9886: p2;
7420.10G Gbk: 1-8; 5-16 Ex 5-2 (2); 9-1; 10-2; 12-3;
PIH Notices: 01-27; 01-15 Impr Integ Hbk; 95-48 (2); 95-48 Tech Asst (2);
Admin Plan: s22p3

RESTRICTING..................................5
24 CFR 982: .632;
7420.10G Gbk: 5-6; 11-4; 21-9; 21-9

RESTRICTION...............................12
24 CFR 982: .306;
HUD-52641: p10;
HUD-52641-A: p2;
7420.10G Gbk: 8-19; 11-2;
PIH Notices: 01-41 (2); 00-09 (2);
Admin Plan: s2p4; s13p1; s16p2

RESTRICTIONS 39
24 CFR 5: .210; .234 (5); .315; .504 (3); .506; .514 (3); .524;
24 CFR 982: .54 (2); .554; .555; .632;
HUD-50058Instr: p40; p68;
7420.10G Gbk: 8-5; 16-1 (2); 17-9; 17-10; 17-11; 21-7;
PIH Notices: 95-48 (3); 95-48 Tech Asst (3);
Admin Plan: s13p1; s16p1; s16p2; s18p7

RESTRICTIVE................................2
7420.10G Gbk: 11-4; 16-5

RESTRICTS 1
Admin Plan: s6p7

RESTROOMS 7
24 CFR 5: .703;

PIH Notices: 95-48 (3); 95-48 Tech Asst (2); 95-48 Tech Asst
RESTRUCTURED PROJECT 1
24 CFR 982: .504
RESTRUCTURED PROJECTS 1
PIH Notices: 01-41
RESUME 3
7420.10G Gbk: 10-46 Ex 10-8; 23-8 Ex 23-1;
Admin Plan: s23p7
RESUMED 3
HUD-52665: p3;
7420.10G Gbk: 11-6;
Admin Plan: s6p3
RESUMES 1
PIH Notices: 02-27
RESUMPTION OF ASSISTANCE ... 3
24 CFR 982: .312 (2);
7420.10G Gbk: 3-4
RETAIN 41
24 CFR 5: .216; .510; .514;
24 CFR 982: .163;
HUD-50058Instr: p61;
7420.10G Gbk: 1-7; 2-5; 2-11; 4-10; 5-9 Ex 5-1; 7-7; 8-10; 9-8; 10-26; 18-10; 20-25; 22-16 (2); 22-17 (5);
PIH Notices: 02-20 (2); 02-14; 01-15 Impr Integ Hbk; 01-06; 00-46 (2); 95-48 (4); 95-48 Tech Asst (4);
Admin Plan: s6p13; s14p1; s20p6
RETAINED 17
24 CFR 982: .101;
7420.10G Gbk: 1-2; 4-10 (2); 12-4; 20-25; 20-26 (2); 20-27; 22-17;
PIH Notices: 03-23; 01-41; 01-15;
Admin Plan: s17p2; s18p3; s18p7; s20p1
RETAINING 4
24 CFR 5: .703;
7420.10G Gbk: 2-5; 11-9;
PIH Notices: 01-41
RETAINS 11
7420.10G Gbk: 13-9;
PIH Notices: 03-23 (4); 01-41 (2); 00-09 (2);
Admin Plan: s2p3; s8p5
RETALIATE 2
PIH Notices: 95-48; 95-48 Tech Asst
RETALIATED 2
PIH Notices: 95-48; 95-48 Tech Asst
RETALIATION 11
PIH Notices: 01-15; 95-48 (5); 95-48 Tech Asst (4); 95-48 Tech Asst
RETENTION 9
24 CFR 5: .514;
HUD-50058: p16;
HUD-50058Instr: p28; p61;
7420.10G Gbk: 20-26; 21-6; 22-17;
PIH Notices: 00-11;
Admin Plan: s8p5
RETENTION OF DOCUMENTS 1
24 CFR 5: .514
RETENTION OF PROCEEDS 1
7420.10G Gbk: 22-17
RETIREMENT 39
24 CFR 5: .210; .214 (2); .609;
HUD-50058: p16;
HUD-50058Instr: p5; p29 (5); p60 (3); p71;
HUD-9886: p1;
7420.10G Gbk: 5-12; 5-14 Ex 5-2; 5-25 Ex 5-3 (2); 5-26 (7); 5-28 (2); 12-16 Ex 12-4;
PIH Notices: 01-15 Impr Integ Hbk (6);
Admin Plan: s6p10 (2); s6p10
RETIREMENT BENEFIT 2
7420.10G Gbk: 5-12;
PIH Notices: 01-15 Impr Integ Hbk
RETIREMENT BENEFITS 2
HUD-50058Instr: p29;
7420.10G Gbk: 5-26
RETIREMENT FUND 1
PIH Notices: 01-15 Impr Integ Hbk
RETIREMENT FUNDS 6
24 CFR 5: .609;
7420.10G Gbk: 5-14 Ex 5-2;
PIH Notices: 01-15 Impr Integ Hbk (3);
Admin Plan: s6p10
RETIREMENT INCOME 5
24 CFR 5: .210; .214 (2);
HUD-50058Instr: p71;
HUD-9886: p1
RETROACTIVE 22
7420.10G Gbk: 5-24; 20-6;
PIH Notices: 01-41; 01-27; 01-10 (7); 00-28; 00-09 (4);
Admin Plan: s6p9; s6p10; s7p2; s9p4; s11p2; s20p5

RETROACTIVE RENT 1
Admin Plan: s7p2
RETROACTIVELY 9
7420.10G Gbk: 6-8; 12-10; 22-12;
PIH Notices: 02-27; 01-41; 01-10; 00-09;
Admin Plan: s6p5; s6p9
RETURN ADDRESS 1
24 CFR 5: .353
RETURN RECEIPT 1
Admin Plan: s23p6
RE-VERIFICATION.......................... 1
PIH Notices: 01-15
RE-VERIFY...................................... 1
7420.10G Gbk: 8-10
REVISE... 11
24 CFR 982: .54; .517 (2);
7420.10G Gbk: 3-1; 4-24 Ex 4-1; 4-25 Ex 4-2; 14-2; 18-4; 18-9 (2);
PIH Notices: 01-41
REVISED....................................... 77
24 CFR 5: .107;
24 CFR 982: .517;
HUD-50058Instr: p1 (5);
7420.10G Gbk: 12-7; 14-1; 14-2 (2); 14-5; 18-9 (3); 20-4; 20-13 (3); 20-28 (3);
PIH Notices: 03-23; 03-12 (3); 02-06; 01-41; 01-15; 01-11 (9); 01-06 (4); 01-01; 00-53 (17); 00-49 (2); 00-27; 00-24; 00-24A (3); 00-24B (4); 95-48 (2);
Admin Plan: s6p13 (2); s21p4; s25p7
REVISES 3
PIH Notices: 03-23; 01-41; 01-06
REVISING....................................... 9
24 CFR 982: .54;
7420.10G Gbk: 3-5 (2); 7-1; 7-6; 18-9; 22-8;
PIH Notices: 02-01; 99-52
REVISION..................................... 24
24 CFR 982: .310 (2);
HUD-52641: p9;
HUD-52641-A: p2;
7420.10G Gbk: 15-2; 15-3; 18-9 (3); 18-10; 20-14 (2);
PIH Notices: 03-23; 03-12; 02-06 (5); 01-41 (2); 00-09 (2);
Admin Plan: s6p13
REVISIONS................................... 21
24 CFR 982: .54; .517 (2);
HUD-52641: p5; 8;
HUD-52641-A: p1;
HUD-52667: p i; p ii;
7420.10G Gbk: 3-1; 3-4 (2); 14-3; 18-4 (2); 18-10 (2);
PIH Notices: 02-27 (2); 95-48 (2);
Admin Plan: s25p5
REVITALIZATION 8
HUD-50058Instr: p72;
PIH Notices: 02-21 (2); 02-01; 01-20 (2); 00-27; 00-27
REVITALIZE 1
Admin Plan: s23p1
REVITALIZED................................. 2
7420.10G Gbk: 2-13 Ex 2-1; 2-13 Ex 2-1
REVOCABLE.................................. 2
24 CFR 5: .603;
HUD-50058Instr: p22
RFLA 5
HUD-50058: p17; p xvii;
HUD-50058Instr: p63 (2); p63
RIGI 2
7420.10G Gbk: 22-16; 22-16
RISK ASSESSMENT 36
24 CFR 35 SubM: .1225 (7);
7420.10G Gbk: 10-12 (2); 10-20 (5); 10-21 (4); 10-39 Ex 10-4 (5); 20-4 (3);
PIH Notices: 02-07 (3); 00-49 (6);
Admin Plan: s21p1
RISK ASSESSMENTS................... 11
7420.10G Gbk: 10-20 (2); 10-22 (2); 20-4 (2);
PIH Notices: 00-49 (4); 00-23
RISK ASSESSOR............................ 3
HUD-52580: p5;
HUD-52580-A: p17;
7420.10G Gbk: 10-20
RISK ASSESSORS.......................... 1
7420.10G Gbk: 10-22
RIVER... 5
HUD-50058Instr: p30;
7420.10G Gbk: 2-12 Ex 2-1; 5-16 Ex 5-2;
PIH Notices: 01-15 Impr Integ Hbk;
Admin Plan: s25p7
ROAD 3
7420.10G Gbk: 15-10 Ex 15-2; 23-19;
PIH Notices: 03-11
ROADS 7
24 CFR 5: .703;
PIH Notices: 95-48 (3); 95-

48 Tech Asst (2); 95-48 Tech Asst

RODENT 9
24 CFR 5: .306; .703;
24 CFR 982: .401 (2); .614;
7420.10G Gbk: 10-13 (2); 10-14; 17-5

RODENT INFESTATION 7
24 CFR 5: .703;
24 CFR 982: .401 (2); .614;
7420.10G Gbk: 10-13 (2); 17-5

RODENTS 3
HUD-52580-A: p17;
7420.10G Gbk: 10-13; 10-14

ROOF 11
24 CFR 982: .401; .614 (2);
HUD-52580: p5;
HUD-52580-A: p13 (4); p14 (2);
7420.10G Gbk: 10-9

ROOFING 2
24 CFR 982: .631;
Admin Plan: s22p3

ROOFS 1
24 CFR 5: .703

ROTATE 1
7420.10G Gbk: 22-10

ROTATING 2
7420.10G Gbk: 22-10; 22-10

ROTATION 1
7420.10G Gbk: 10-34

ROUND 4
HUD-50058: p i;
HUD-50058Instr: p3; p14;
7420.10G Gbk: 24-4

ROUNDING 2
HUD-50058: p i;
HUD-50058Instr: p3

ROW HOUSE 3
HUD-52517: p1 (2);
HUD-52580-A: p1

ROW HOUSES 1
7420.10G Gbk: 18-2

ROW-HOUSE 1
24 CFR 982: .517

RULES OF EVIDENCE 5
24 CFR 5: .514;
24 CFR 982: .555;
7420.10G Gbk: 16-5;
Admin Plan: s15p4; s18p6

RUNNING WATER 19
24 CFR 5: .703;
24 CFR 982: .401 (3); .605; .614 (3);
HUD-52580-A: p5; p6; p7 (2);
7420.10G Gbk: 10-3 (2); 10-5 (2); 17-4 (2); 17-5

RURAL 13
24 CFR 5: .100; .300;
24 CFR 982: .352; .521;
HUD-50058Instr: p43;
HUD-52517: p1;
HUD-52580-A: p15;
7420.10G Gbk: 8-16 (2); 9-11;
PIH Notices: 01-02; 95-48; 95-48 Tech Asst

SAFE 65
24 CFR 5: .100; .315; .603; .703 (3);
24 CFR 982: .1; .4; .401 (3); .605; .614;
HUD-50058Instr: p70; p73 (2); p76;
HUD-52580-A: p2; p13; p16; p17; p18;
HUD-52646: p1;
7420.10G Gbk: 1-10; 5-49 Ex 5-5; 7-1; 8-17; 10-1; 10-7; 10-17; 10-22; 10-23; 11-9; 17-2;
PIH Notices: 02-22; 02-01 (2); 01-41 (4); 01-15 Impr Integ Hbk (3); 00-49 (2); 00-24B; 00-23; 00-11; 99-52 (2); 95-48 (6); 95-48 Tech Asst (6);
Admin Plan: s1p1; s1p1

SAFE DEPOSIT 1
7420.10G Gbk: 5-49 Ex 5-5

SAFE DEPOSIT BOX 1
7420.10G Gbk: 5-49 Ex 5-5

SAFEGUARD 1
HUD-52580-A: p15

SAFEGUARDS 3
24 CFR 5: .234;
HUD-52665: p1;
PIH Notices: 00-23

SAFELY 10
7420.10G Gbk: 10-7; 10-8; 10-9; 10-11;
PIH Notices: 95-48 (3); 95-48 Tech Asst (2); 95-48 Tech Asst

SAFER 2
PIH Notices: 02-01; 99-52

SAFEST 2
PIH Notices: 95-48; 95-48 Tech Asst

SAFETY 157
24 CFR 5: .318; .327 (2); .360 (2); .363; .703 (9);
24 CFR 982: .306 (2); .307; .310 (3); .401 (5); .551 (2); .553 (6);

.605 (2); .614 (2);
HUD-52580: p5 (2);
HUD-52580-A: p1; p2 (2); p8; p15 (11); p16; p17 (3); p18 (2);
HUD-52641: p7 (2); p9 (3);
HUD-52641-A: p2 (5);
7420.10G Gbk: 2-7; 5-39; 8-20 (3); 10-1; 10-2 (2); 10-7 (2); 10-8 (4); 10-9; 10-11 (4); 10-13 (2); 10-19; 11-3; 11-4 (2); 15-2 (3); 15-7; 17-2 (4); 17-5 (2);
PIH Notices: 03-11; 02-01 (4); 99-52 (4); 99-11 (11); 95-48 (11); 95-48 Tech Asst (11);
Admin Plan: s2p7; s9p3; s10p3; s15p2 (2); s15p3; s16p2 (2); s18p5

SAFETY HAZARDS.......................11
24 CFR 5: .703 (7);
HUD-52580-A: p15;
7420.10G Gbk: 10-2; 10-11; 10-11

SALARIES.....................................11
24 CFR 5: .609;
HUD-50058Instr: p71;
7420.10G Gbk: 5-14 Ex 5-2; 5-46 Ex 5-5; 20-22 Ex 20-5; 20-26; 21-2; 23-12;
PIH Notices: 01-15 Impr Integ Hbk (2); 01-15 Impr Integ Hbk

SALARY..11
HUD-50058Instr: p27;
HUD-9886: p1 (2);
7420.10G Gbk: 23-8 Ex 23-1; 23-16 Ex 23-2;
PIH Notices: 01-15 Impr Integ Hbk (5);
Admin Plan: s7p4

SALE OF THE PROPERTY.............7
24 CFR 982: .310;
HUD-52641: p9;
HUD-52641-A: p2;
7420.10G Gbk: 5-26; 15-3;
PIH Notices: 01-41; 00-09

SALESPERSON...............................1
HUD-903: p1

SALESPERSON'S...........................1
PIH Notices: 01-15 Impr Integ Hbk

SAME BUILDING...........................9
24 CFR 982: .308;
HUD-52641: p10;
HUD-52641-A: p3;
7420.10G Gbk: 10-4; 11-17;
PIH Notices: 95-48 (2); 95-48 Tech Asst; 95-48 Tech Asst

SAMPLE.......................................138
HUD-52580-A: p15;
HUD-52648: p1 (6);
7420.10G Gbk: 1-1; 2-4; 2-6; 4-7; 4-15 (2); 4-22 (2); 4-23 Ex 4-1; 4-25 Ex 4-2; 5-40; 6-3 (3); 6-9 Ex 6-1; 6-10 Ex 6-2; 8-6; 8-13; 9-3 (2); 9-5; 9-8 (2); 9-10 (2); 9-12 (2); 9-13 Ex 9-1; 9-15 Ex 9-2; 9-17 Ex 9-3; 10-17; 10-19; 10-23; 10-25; 10-26; 10-28; 10-29 (4); 10-30; 10-31 (3); 10-32 (6); 10-34; 10-36 Ex 10-1; 10-37 Ex 10-2; 10-38 Ex 10-3; 10-40 Ex 10-4a; 10-41 Ex 10-4b; 10-42 Ex 10-5; 10-43 Ex 10-6; 10-44 Ex 10-7a; 10-45 Ex 10-7b (2); 10-46 Ex 10-8; 11-15; 12-3 (2); 12-7 (3); 12-12 Ex 12-1; 12-13 Ex 12-1; 12-14 Ex 12-2; 12-15 Ex 12-3; 15-9 Ex 15-1; 15-10 Ex 15-2; 19-10 (3); 19-12 (3); 20-21; 20-27; 21-1; 21-6 Ex 21-1; 21-11; 22-6; 22-7 (8); 23-7;
PIH Notices: 03-20; 02-27 (8); 02-20; 01-41; 01-15; 01-01 (2); 00-46; 00-24B (6); 00-09;
Admin Plan: s21p2; s21p3 (3); s21p4 (3); s21p5 (5); s21p7; s21p7

SAMPLE FORM..............................4
7420.10G Gbk: 9-8 (2); 9-13 Ex 9-1; 9-15 Ex 9-2

SAMPLE NOTICE.........................13
7420.10G Gbk: 10-25; 10-26; 10-28; 10-29 (4); 10-30; 10-45 Ex 10-7b; 12-12 Ex 12-1; 12-13 Ex 12-1; 15-9 Ex 15-1; 15-10 Ex 15-2

SAMPLED.....................................24
24 CFR 35 SubM: .1225 (2);
HUD-52648: p1 (9);
7420.10G Gbk: 10-20 (2); 10-31; 19-10; 22-7;
PIH Notices: 02-27; 02-07 (2); 00-49; 00-28;
Admin Plan: s21p3 (2); s21p4

SAMPLES.....................................10
HUD-52648: p1 (2);
7420.10G Gbk: 12-3; 19-10; 22-7 (2);
PIH Notices: 02-27 (2); 00-23; 00-23

SAMPLE'S 1
7420.10G Gbk: 12-7

SANCTION 16
24 CFR 5: .615 (3);
HUD-50058Instr: p28; p75;
7420.10G Gbk: 5-21; 5-22 (3); 10-29;
PIH Notices: 00-11; 96-65 (3);
Admin Plan: s6p12; s6p12

SANCTIONED 1
PIH Notices: 00-11

SANCTIONING 1
PIH Notices: 00-11A

SANCTIONS 22
HUD-50058Instr: p2 (2);
7420.10G Gbk: 5-22; 10-23; 13-9; 19-2; 20-28; 22-16;
PIH Notices: 02-07; 01-15 Impr Integ Hbk; 01-06 (2); 00-53 (2); 00-28; 00-11; 96-65 (5); 96-65

SANITARY 91
24 CFR 5: .100; .315; .350 (2); .603; .703 (5);
24 CFR 982: .1; .4 (2); .401 (12); .605 (5); .608; .609 (2); .613; .614 (6); .618;
HUD-50058Instr: p42; p46; p70; p73 (2); p75; p76;
HUD-52580-A: p16;
HUD-52646: p1;
7420.10G Gbk: 1-10; 7-1; 8-17; 10-1 (3); 10-3 (4); 10-4 (3); 10-5; 10-11; 10-13 (2); 10-14; 10-23; 11-9; 17-1; 17-2 (3); 17-4; 17-7 (2); 17-9;
PIH Notices: 02-22; 02-01; 01-41 (4); 01-15 Impr Integ Hbk; 00-24B; 00-23; 99-52;
Admin Plan: s1p1; s19p1; s19p1

SANITARY STANDARDS 2
24 CFR 5: .350; .350

SASH LOCKS 1
24 CFR 982: .401

SASH PINS.......................................1
24 CFR 982: .401

SATELLITE 4
24 CFR 982: .517;
7420.10G Gbk: 18-1;
PIH Notices: 00-11;
Admin Plan: s6p13

SATELLITE TELEVISION..............2
24 CFR 982: .517;
Admin Plan: s6p13

SATURDAY......................................1
7420.10G Gbk: 10-34

SATURDAYS 1
Admin Plan: s25p8

SAVE...15
24 CFR 5: .512 (3);
7420.10G Gbk: 5-7 (4); 5-9 Ex 5-1;
PIH Notices: 01-06 (4); 95-48; 95-48 Tech Asst;
Admin Plan: s18p7

SAVING 3
7420.10G Gbk: 5-49 Ex 5-5; 12-13 Ex 12-1;
PIH Notices: 00-11

SAVINGS..40
24 CFR 5: .603; .609;
HUD-50058: p i; p6 (2);
HUD-50058Instr: p22 (4); p61; p74;
HUD-903: p2;
7420.10G Gbk: 4-26 Ex 4-2 (2); 5-14 Ex 5-2; 5-24; 5-25 Ex 5-3 (3); 5-48 Ex 5-5; 5-49 Ex 5-5; 12-9; 12-16 Ex 12-4; 22-3 (2);
PIH Notices: 01-15 Impr Integ Hbk (11); 00-11;
Admin Plan: s7p5; s22p3; s25p5

SAVINGS ACCOUNT.....................13
HUD-50058: p i; p6;
HUD-50058Instr: p22 (2);
7420.10G Gbk: 5-48 Ex 5-5; 5-49 Ex 5-5;
PIH Notices: 01-15 Impr Integ Hbk (4);
Admin Plan: s7p5; s22p3; s25p5

SAVINGS ACCOUNTS 10
HUD-50058: p6;
HUD-50058Instr: p22 (2); p61;
7420.10G Gbk: 4-26 Ex 4-2 (2); 5-25 Ex 5-3;
PIH Notices: 01-15 Impr Integ Hbk (2); 00-11

SCARCE HOUSING DOLLARS 1
PIH Notices: 01-15 Impr Integ Hbk

SCHEDULE...................................272
24 CFR 5: .353;
24 CFR 982: 24 CFR 982 (3); .503 (6); .505; .517 (20); .555 (2); .604; .608; .613 (2); .617 (2); .624; .635; .641 (2);
HUD-50058: p xv (2);
HUD-50058Instr: p12 (2); p58 (2);

HUD-52648: p1 (4);
HUD-52665: p2;
HUD-52667: p i (5); p ii;
7420.10G Gbk: 1-10; 4-12; 5-47 Ex 5-5 (6); 5-48 Ex 5-5 (2); 5-49 Ex 5-5 (2); 5-51 Ex 5-5; 6-3 (3); 6-9 Ex 6-1; 7-1 (3); 7-6 (5); 7-7 (2); 7-9; 8-6; 8-10; 8-15; 8-22 (2); 10-23; 10-26; 10-28; 10-30 (2); 10-44 Ex 10-7a (2); 10-45 Ex 10-7b; 11-1; 12-5; 12-8; 13-9; 16-2 (2); 17-3; 17-10; 17-11; 18-1 (6); 18-2 (3); 18-4 (6); 18-6; 18-7 (5); 18-8 (2); 18-9 (4); 18-10 (2); 19-5; 19-9; 20-3; 20-16; 20-28; 20-29 (3); 21-4; 23-5; 23-16 Ex 23-2; 24-7 (2); 24-13 (2); 24-16;
PIH Notices: 03-23 (3); 02-27 (6); 02-21; 02-20 (11); 02-06 (3); 01-20; 01-15 Impr Integ Hbk; 01-06 (28); 00-53 (2); 00-49 (2); 00-46 (8); 00-27 (2); 00-24B (10); 99-11; 96-65; 95-48 (3); 95-48 Tech Asst (3);
Admin Plan: s6p13 (4); s7p5 (3); s7p6 (2); s8p2; s9p4; s10p2 (4); s11p1; s18p3; s18p4 (2); s19p1 (3); s21p2; s21p4 (4); s23p3; s23p4; s25p5; s25p5

SCHEDULE C 2
7420.10G Gbk: 5-48 Ex 5-5;
Admin Plan: s7p5

SCHEDULE E 4
7420.10G Gbk: 5-48 Ex 5-5;
PIH Notices: 01-15 Impr Integ Hbk;
Admin Plan: s7p5; s7p6

SCHEDULE F 1
Admin Plan: s7p5

SCHEDULED 80
24 CFR 5: .216 (3); .230 (2); .659;
24 CFR 982: .551;
HUD-50058Instr: p9 (3); p10; p12 (4); p21;
HUD-52646: p2;
7420.10G Gbk: 5-21; 8-9 (2); 10-23 (3); 10-24 (2); 10-35 (2); 10-40 Ex 10-4a (2); 10-41 Ex 10-4b; 11-9; 12-12 Ex 12-1; 12-14 Ex 12-2; 13-7; 18-6; 19-9 (2); 23-4; 23-5; 24-4; 24-6;
PIH Notices: 02-21 (4); 01-20 (4); 01-15; 01-15 Impr Integ Hbk; 95-48; 95-48 Tech Asst;
Admin Plan: s3p3 (2); s8p2 (2); s9p4; s10p2; s10p3; s11p3; s11p1 (3); s11p2 (3); s13p1 (3); s15p6; s18p2; s18p4; s18p5 (2); s20p7; s23p4 (3); s25p8

SCHEDULE-ONCE 1
7420.10G Gbk: 16-4

SCHEDULERS 3
7420.10G Gbk: 21-4; 21-16 Ex 21-6; 21-16 Ex 21-6

SCHEDULES 34
24 CFR 982: .503;
HUD-52667: p i (4);
7420.10G Gbk: 7-1; 8-9; 10-31; 18-4; 18-6 (2); 18-9 (2); 21-4 (3); 24-7;
PIH Notices: 02-27; 02-20; 01-06 (3); 01-01 (2); 00-46; 00-24B; 95-48; 95-48 Tech Asst;
Admin Plan: s1p4; s7p4; s7p5; s7p6; s11p1; s15p6

SCHEDULING 27
24 CFR 982: .405;
7420.10G Gbk: 4-13; 8-8; 10-23 (6); 10-26; 10-27; 10-35 (2); 12-2 (2); 12-14 Ex 12-2; 19-12; 21-4; 21-11; 21-15 Ex 21-5 (2); 21-16 Ex 21-6;
PIH Notices: 02-27 (4);
Admin Plan: s20p4

SCHOLARSHIPS 5
7420.10G Gbk: 5-16 Ex 5-2; 5-20;
PIH Notices: 01-15 Impr Integ Hbk (2);
Admin Plan: s7p5

SCHOLARSHIP'S 1
PIH Notices: 01-15 Impr Integ Hbk

SCHOLARSIPS 1
HUD-50058Instr: p32

SCHOOL 68
24 CFR 5: .603;
24 CFR 982: .352;
HUD-50058: p7; p16 (2);
HUD-50058Instr: p15; p36 (2); p60 (6); p61 (5); p72;
7420.10G Gbk: 2-1; 5-17 (2); 5-30; 5-50 Ex 5-5; 5-53 Ex 5-5; 8-16; 13-1; 13-2; 21-5; 23-1; 23-9;

23-15; 23-16 Ex 23-2;
PIH Notices: 01-15; 95-48 (9); 95-48 Tech Asst (9);
Admin Plan: s3p2; s5p1 (2); s6p2; s6p6 (2); s6p7; s6p10; s6p11 (3); s7p3; s7p5 (2); s7p6

SCHOOL RECESSES 2
Admin Plan: s5p1; s6p6

SCHOOL RECORDS 4
7420.10G Gbk: 5-50 Ex 5-5; 5-53 Ex 5-5; 13-2;
Admin Plan: s7p5

SCHOOL-EQUIVALENCY 1
HUD-50058Instr: p60

SCHOOLING 8
HUD-50058: p16; p xvi (2);
HUD-50058Instr: p60 (4); p61

SCHOOLS 23
24 CFR 982: .630;
HUD-52648: p2;
7420.10G Gbk: 2-3; 2-6; 2-7; 4-3; 7-5; 8-4; 8-7;
PIH Notices: 95-48 (7); 95-48 Tech Asst (6); 95-48 Tech Asst

SCOPE 6
PIH Notices: 02-27 (4); 01-02;
Admin Plan: s10p1

SCRATCH 2
HUD-50058: p i;
HUD-50058Instr: p3

SCRATCHED 4
HUD-52580-A: p4 (3); p4

SCRATCHES 2
HUD-52580-A: p2;
7420.10G Gbk: 10-4

SCREEN 31
24 CFR 982: .307;
HUD-52580: p6;
HUD-52580-A: p19;
7420.10G Gbk: 1-14; 3-3 (2); 4-14; 5-39; 5-40; 8-21; 10-6; 10-25; 11-12; 23-6 (2); 24-14;
PIH Notices: 03-11 (3); 01-41; 00-09; 95-48 (4); 95-48 Tech Asst (4);
Admin Plan: s2p6; s9p3

SCREENED 2
HUD-52517: p2;
7420.10G Gbk: 4-14

SCREENING 73
24 CFR 982: Intro; .54; .307 (5); .552 (2); .553; .641;
HUD-52517: p2;
HUD-52641: p3 (2);
7420.10G Gbk: 1-14; 2-5; 2-8; 2-10; 3-3; 3-4; 3-7; 4-15; 4-16; 5-38 (2); 5-39 (4); 5-40 (8); 8-20 (2); 8-21; 11-12; 23-6; 24-14 (3);
PIH Notices: 03-11 (5); 02-01 (4); 01-41 (6); 01-15; 00-09; 99-52 (4);
Admin Plan: s1p3; s2p6 (3); s2p7; s23p4; s24p6

SCREENING CRITERIA..................2
7420.10G Gbk: 4-16;
Admin Plan: s2p7

SCREENING OF APPLICANTS 5
24 CFR 982: .54; .307; .552; .553;
PIH Notices: 01-41

SCREENS 3
7420.10G Gbk: 4-14; 4-15; 10-11

SEARCH TIME 32
24 CFR 982: .4; .503;
HUD-50058Instr: p76;
7420.10G Gbk: 3-3 (2); 3-7; 7-4; 8-11; 8-12 (3); 8-13; 8-22; 19-7; 19-8; 19-9 (3); 21-9 (2); 24-5 (2); 24-10 (7);
PIH Notices: 02-20; 01-41; 00-09

SEARCH TIMES 4
7420.10G Gbk: 24-5; 24-10 (2); 24-10

SEASONAL......................................6
24 CFR 5: .609;
7420.10G Gbk: 8-22; 12-1; 21-5;
PIH Notices: 01-15 Impr Integ Hbk; 01-15 Impr Integ Hbk

SEASONAL EMPLOYMENT 1
PIH Notices: 01-15 Impr Integ Hbk

SEASONALLY.................................1
7420.10G Gbk: 4-26 Ex 4-2

SECOND APPOINTMENT...............1
7420.10G Gbk: 12-14 Ex 12-2

SECOND LETTER............................2
Admin Plan: s7p2; s7p2

SECOND MEETING.........................1
Admin Plan: s7p3

SECOND NOTICE 9
7420.10G Gbk: 4-7; 10-23; 10-41 Ex 10-4b; 12-2; 12-3 (4); 12-14 Ex 12-2

SECOND NOTICES..........................1

7420.10G Gbk: 21-10

SECONDARY 39
24 CFR 5: .512 (8); .514 (5);
24 CFR 982: .625;
HUD-50058: p16;
HUD-50058Instr: p61 (3);
HUD-52580: p4;
HUD-52580-A: p1; p8; p13 (5); p14;
7420.10G Gbk: 5-7 (3); 5-8 (3); 5-9 Ex 5-1; 5-11 (2);
PIH Notices: 95-48; 95-48 Tech Asst;
Admin Plan: s20p7

SECONDARY MORTGAGE 1
24 CFR 982: .625

SECONDARY PURPOSE 1
Admin Plan: s20p7

SECONDARY VERIFICATION 20
24 CFR 5: .512 (7); .514 (5);
7420.10G Gbk: 5-7 (3); 5-8 (3); 5-11; 5-11

SECRETARIES 1
7420.10G Gbk: 10-15

SECRETARY 105
24 CFR 5: .100 (4); .110; .214; .300; .306; .504 (2); .801;
24 CFR 982: .160; .503 (2);
HUD-50058Instr: p30; p75;
HUD-903: p2 (2);
7420.10G Gbk: 7-4; 21-11; 21-12 Ex 21-3; 21-16 Ex 21-6 (5);
PIH Notices: 03-23; 03-20; 03-12; 03-11; 03-05; 02-27 (5); 02-22 (2); 02-21 (3); 02-20 (6); 02-15; 02-14; 02-07; 02-06; 02-03; 02-01; 01-43; 01-41 (2); 01-40; 01-33; 01-27 (2); 01-20 (3); 01-15; 01-15 Impr Integ Hbk; 01-11; 01-10; 01-06; 01-02; 01-01; 00-53; 00-49; 00-46 (6); 00-45; 00-41; 00-34; 00-31; 00-28; 00-27 (2); 00-24; 00-23; 00-14; 00-11; 00-09 (2); 00-01; 99-52; 99-30; 99-11; 98-66; 96-65; 95-48 (5); 95-48 Tech Asst (2); 95-48 Tech Asst

SECRETARY'S 19
PIH Notices: 02-20; 02-03; 01-40; 01-27; 01-15; 01-02; 00-49; 00-46; 00-45; 00-41; 00-31; 00-28; 00-23; 00-14; 99-52; 99-30; 99-11; 95-48; 95-48

SECTION 101 11
24 CFR 5: .500; .504;
24 CFR 982: .352;
PIH Notices: 01-41 (3); 01-27; 01-10; 00-09 (2); 00-09

SECTION 162 1
24 CFR 982: .352

SECTION 202 17
24 CFR 5: .100 (2); .240; .504; .601 (2); .603 (2); .801 (2);
24 CFR 982: .352 (2); .521;
HUD-50058Instr: p43;
HUD-52517: p1;
7420.10G Gbk: 8-16; 9-11

SECTION 207 6
24 CFR 5: .518 (3); .801;
7420.10G Gbk: 5-10 Ex 5-1; 5-10 Ex 5-1

SECTION 208 5
24 CFR 5: .518 (3);
7420.10G Gbk: 5-10 Ex 5-1; 5-10 Ex 5-1

SECTION 213 7
24 CFR 5: .801;
24 CFR 982: .101 (5); .101

SECTION 214 22
24 CFR 5: .500 (2); .504 (5); .506 (2); .508 (6); .512; .516; .518; .522; .526;
HUD-50058Instr: p17;
PIH Notices: 01-27

SECTION 220 1
24 CFR 5: .801

SECTION 221 21
24 CFR 5: .100 (2); .236; .801 (2);
24 CFR 982: .521;
HUD-50058Instr: p43;
HUD-52517: p1;
HUD-52648: p2;
7420.10G Gbk: 5-10 Ex 5-1 (2); 9-11;
PIH Notices: 01-41 (4); 01-06; 00-09 (3); 00-09

SECTION 23 9
24 CFR 982: .352;
HUD-52648: p2;
PIH Notices: 01-06; 00-09 (4);
Admin Plan: s22p5; s23p1

SECTION 231 1
24 CFR 5: .801

SECTION 232 1
24 CFR 5: .801

SECTION 234 1
24 CFR 5: .801

SECTION 235 16
24 CFR 5: .236; .500 (3); .504 (3); .508 (5); .520 (2);
PIH Notices: 01-27; 01-27

SECTION 236 40
24 CFR 5: .100; .236; .500 (2); .504 (3); .520 (4); .603; .801;
24 CFR 982: .352; .521;
HUD-50058Instr: p43; p47;
HUD-52517: p1;
HUD-52648: p2;
PIH Notices: 01-41 (9); 01-27 (2); 01-06; 00-09 (8); 00-09

SECTION 241 1
24 CFR 5: .801

SECTION 3 12
24 CFR 5: .105;
HUD-50058Instr: p ii; p14; p17; p71;
HUD-52641: p1;
7420.10G Gbk: 5-42;
PIH Notices: 01-27 (2); 01-15 Impr Integ Hbk;
Admin Plan: s2p7; s3p1

SECTION 3003 1
HUD-9886: p1

SECTION 302 2
24 CFR 982: .642;
7420.10G Gbk: 10-15

SECTION 33 9
PIH Notices: 02-21 (3); 01-20 (3); 00-27 (2); 00-27

SECTION 504 142
24 CFR 5: .105; .524;
24 CFR 982: .53;
HUD-50058Instr: p3 (2);
7420.10G Gbk: 5-44;
PIH Notices: 02-21; 02-01 (25); 01-20; 00-45 (3); 99-52 (22); 95-48 (44); 95-48 Tech Asst (39);
Admin Plan: s1p3

SECTION 504'S 4
PIH Notices: 95-48 (2); 95-48 Tech Asst; 95-48 Tech Asst

SECTION 515 7
24 CFR 5: .100;
24 CFR 982: .521;
HUD-50058Instr: p43;
HUD-52517: p1;
7420.10G Gbk: 9-11;
PIH Notices: 01-41; 01-41

SECTION 521 1
24 CFR 982: .352

SECTION 801 1
24 CFR 5: .100

SECTION 808 1
PIH Notices: 02-21

SECTION 811 6
24 CFR 5: .100; .240; .601; .603; .801;
24 CFR 982: .352

SECTION 8-ASSISTED HOUSING 1
24 CFR 5: .504

SECTION 8-FUP 2
HUD-50058Instr: p72; p72

SECURITY 278
24 CFR 5: .110; .210; .214 (10); .216 (2); .218; .318; .603; .609 (4); .617; .659; .661 (31);
24 CFR 982: Intro; .313 (6); .352; .401 (2); .452; .551; .605 (3); .614 (3); .618 (3); .627; .641;
HUD-50058: p i (4); p ii (2); p3 (6); p iii (2); p4 (6); p iv (2); p v; p6; p x; p xi; p xii; p xiii;
HUD-50058Instr: p3 (3); p5 (3); p6 (2); p15; p16 (6); p17 (2); p18; p29 (4); p43; p47; p50 (2); p53; p71; p74 (3); p75 (8); p76;
HUD-52580: p1; p2 (2); p3 (3); p4 (3);
HUD-52580-A: p1; p2; p3; p5; p7; p9; p10; p11; p12; p13; p14;
HUD-52665: p1 (3); p2;
HUD-9886: p1 (2); p2 (4);
7420.10G Gbk: 5-15 Ex 5-2 (2); 5-46 Ex 5-5; 9-14 Ex 9-1; 9-16 Ex 9-2; 9-17 Ex 9-3 (2); 10-1; 10-6 (2); 12-4; 12-16 Ex 12-4; 17-2 (2); 17-5; 17-8 (2); 24-9;
PIH Notices: 03-11; 01-15 (13); 01-15 Impr Integ Hbk (22); 01-06; 00-41 (2); 00-24B; 00-11; 00-11A (4);
Admin Plan: s2p1; s2p5 (7); s6p10; s7p3 (2); s7p4 (2); s7p7; s7p8 (12); s8p3; s8p4 (5); s9p1; s10p5 (2); s20p2; s20p6; s23p5 (2); s25p2

SECURITY DEPOSIT 52
24 CFR 982: Intro; .313 (5); .452; .641;
HUD-52517: p1 (2); p10 (6);

HUD-52641-A: p2 (3); p3 (3);
7420.10G Gbk: 8-4 (11); 8-5 (4); 8-7; 11-11; 11-14; 11-15; 11-17; 14-5 (2);
Admin Plan: s8p4 (4); s10p5 (2); s23p5; s23p5

SECURITY DEPOSITS 11
24 CFR 5: .318;
24 CFR 982: .313;
7420.10G Gbk: 2-7; 2-8; 2-11; 8-4 (2); 8-15;
PIH Notices: 00-11;
Admin Plan: s8p3; s8p4

SECURITY PERSONNEL 23
24 CFR 5: .661 (20);
HUD-50058Instr: p50; p74; p75

SECURITY PROFESSIONAL 2
24 CFR 5: .661;
HUD-50058Instr: p75

SECURITY SERVICES 5
24 CFR 5: .661 (3);
HUD-50058Instr: p74; p75

SEGREGATION 3
PIH Notices: 95-48; 95-48 Tech Asst;
Admin Plan: s1p3

SELECTION 170
24 CFR 5: .306 (2); .359; .601; .655 (9);
24 CFR 982: .54; .104; .205 (2); .207 (5); .307 (2); .353; .355;
HUD-50058: p17; p xvii;
HUD-50058Instr: p62 (2);
HUD-52648: p1 (3);
7420.10G Gbk: 1-2; 1-3; 1-4; 1-7; 1-10; 1-11; 1-16 Ex 1-3; 3-2 (2); 3-7 (2); 3-8; 3-9; 4-1 (4); 4-5; 4-8; 4-9 (2); 4-11; 4-12; 4-13; 4-14; 4-16 (5); 4-18 (3); 4-19; 4-21 (3); 4-22 (7); 5-38; 6-1; 6-4; 6-6; 7-1; 8-20; 8-21; 9-10; 12-3; 13-4 (2); 19-4 (2); 19-6; 19-10; 21-8 (3); 21-10; 23-5 (2); 23-6 (4); 23-19; 23-20 (5);
PIH Notices: 02-27 (18); 02-01 (2); 01-06; 00-24B (7); 99-52 (2); 95-48 (3); 95-48 Tech Asst (3);
Admin Plan: s2p6; s3p2 (2); s4p1; s21p1; s21p2; s21p3 (3); s23p3 (6); s24p1; s24p2; s24p3 (3); s24p4; s24p6 (4); s24p7

SELECTION CRITERIA................. 26
24 CFR 982: .104;
HUD-52648: p1;
7420.10G Gbk: 1-7; 3-2; 4-5; 4-21; 4-22; 23-20 (5);
PIH Notices: 02-27; 95-48 (3); 95-48 Tech Asst (3);
Admin Plan: s21p3; s23p3 (2); s24p3; s24p4; s24p6; s24p6

SELECTION PREFERENCE.......... 11
HUD-50058: p17; p xvii;
HUD-50058Instr: p62 (2);
7420.10G Gbk: 4-19; 12-3; 23-5; 23-6 (3); 23-19

SELECTION PREFERENCES 6
24 CFR 5: .601;
24 CFR 982: .207;
7420.10G Gbk: 3-7; 3-8; 4-16; 4-16

SELECTIONS.................................. 3
7420.10G Gbk: 4-22; 22-7;
PIH Notices: 02-27

SELECTIVE 1
7420.10G Gbk: 22-10

SELECTS....................................... 22
24 CFR 982: .1; .301;
7420.10G Gbk: 4-13; 4-18; 6-2; 6-3; 6-4 (2); 6-5 (3); 6-6; 8-1; 8-10; 8-17; 10-6; 10-13; 21-4;
PIH Notices: 00-24B;
Admin Plan: s5p1; s5p2; s5p3

SELF EMPLOYED 1
PIH Notices: 01-15 Impr Integ Hbk

SELF EMPLOYMENT 2
HUD-9886: p1;
PIH Notices: 01-15 Impr Integ Hbk

SELF EVALUATION 2
PIH Notices: 95-48; 95-48

SELF SUFFICIENCY..................... 12
HUD-50058: p17;
HUD-50058Instr: p13; p59; p61; p75;
PIH Notices: 02-27; 02-01 (3); 99-52 (2); 99-52

SELF-EMPLOYED 3
7420.10G Gbk: 5-19;
PIH Notices: 01-15; 01-15

SELF-EMPLOYMENT 9
24 CFR 5: .210; .214 (2);
24 CFR 982: .627;
HUD-50058Instr: p71 (2);
7420.10G Gbk: 5-19;
PIH Notices: 01-15 Impr Integ Hbk;
Admin Plan: s7p4

SELF-EVALUATION 38

PIH Notices: 02-01 (2); 99-52 (2); 95-48 (17); 95-48 Tech Asst (16); 95-48 Tech Asst

SELF-EVALUATIONS....................12
PIH Notices: 02-01 (4); 99-52 (4); 95-48 (2); 95-48 Tech Asst; 95-48 Tech Asst

SELF-HELP.......................................2
PIH Notices: 02-01; 99-52

SELF-SUFFICIENCY...................139
24 CFR 5: .603; .609; .613; .615 (3); .617 (2);
24 CFR 982: .4; .152;
HUD-50058: p i; p ii; p3 (7); p iii; p4 (7); p iv; p16; p xvi (3); p xvii;
HUD-50058Instr: p ii; p2; p3; p4; p10; p13; p16; p17; p29; p59; p70; p71 (2); p72 (2); p75 (3);
HUD-52648: p2; p3;
7420.10G Gbk: 3-8 (2); 5-14 Ex 5-2; 5-15 Ex 5-2; 5-21 (2); 5-22; 12-9; 23-1 (2); 23-3; 23-4; 23-6; 23-10; 23-13; 23-19;
PIH Notices: 01-15 Impr Integ Hbk (6); 01-06 (4); 00-24A; 00-24B; 00-11 (27); 00-11A (9);
Admin Plan: s1p1 (2); s6p2; s6p3 (2); s6p12 (2); s6p13; s8p3; s11p3 (2); s21p9; s22p2 (5); s25p3 (3); s25p4; s25p4

SELF-SUFFICIENCY INCENTIVES2
24 CFR 5: .617;
PIH Notices: 01-15 Impr Integ Hbk

SELF-SUFFICIENT........................10
HUD-50058Instr: p75;
7420.10G Gbk: 23-1; 23-3;
PIH Notices: 01-15 Impr Integ Hbk; 00-11 (2); 00-11A (3);
Admin Plan: s25p5

SEMAP..561
24 CFR 982: .503 (3);
HUD-52648: p1 (2); p3 (2); p4;
7420.10G Gbk: 1-1; 1-9 (2); 1-10 (5); 1-11 (3); 2-2 (3); 2-3 (2); 2-4; 3-9 (2); 4-18; 4-22 (4); 7-3; 7-4; 7-7; 7-9 (4); 7-10 (2); 8-1; 8-7; 8-11; 9-12 (5); 10-23 (2); 10-25; 10-27 (2); 10-29; 10-30; 10-31 (4); 10-32 (5); 10-33 (3); 10-34 (3); 10-35; 11-19 (2); 12-8; 12-10 (4); 12-11 (4); 13-6; 13-10 (3); 18-9 (2); 18-10 (2); 19-1 (3); 19-2; 19-4 (2); 19-5 (9); 19-10 (4); 19-12 (3); 19-13 (3); 20-14 (2); 22-7; 23-2; 23-19 (3); 24-1; 24-2 (2); 24-15 (2);
PIH Notices: 03-12; 02-27 (107); 02-21 (4); 02-20 (3); 02-06; 01-06 (202); 01-01 (17); 00-34 (31); 00-24 (27); 00-24A (18); 00-24B (7);
Admin Plan: s1p2; s21p1 (2); s21p2 (3); s21p3 (2); s21p4 (2); s21p5 (2); s21p6 (2); s21p9

SEMI-DETACHED............................4
HUD-50058: p5;
HUD-50058Instr: p21;
HUD-52517: p1;
7420.10G Gbk: 18-2

SEPARATE....................................160
24 CFR 5: .100; .318; .350; .508;
24 CFR 982: .4; .151; .204; .401; .503 (2); .505; .602; .607; .611; .616; .622; .623;
HUD-50058: p ii (2); p iii; p iv; p6;
HUD-50058Instr: p1 (2); p6 (2); p10; p14; p22; p24; p50; p75;
HUD-52580: p6 (2);
HUD-52580-A: p3; p4; p5; p6 (3); p7; p9; p10; p11; p12; p14; p16; p18; p19 (2); p20;
HUD-52648: p2; p4;
HUD-52665: p2;
HUD-52667: p i;
HUD-903: p1;
7420.10G Gbk: 3-2; 4-8 (2); 5-41; 7-6; 8-2; 9-5; 10-3; 10-29; 12-7; 15-8; 16-4; 17-1; 17-7; 17-11; 18-2 (2); 20-9; 20-23; 20-24 (2); 21-4 (2); 21-13 (3);
PIH Notices: 03-23 (3); 02-27; 02-21; 02-20 (2); 01-41 (4); 01-20 (2); 01-06 (7); 00-46 (2); 00-27 (3); 00-24; 00-09 (2); 95-48 (17); 95-48 Tech Asst (17);
Admin Plan: s4p1; s5p1 (2);

s9p3 (5); s11p1; s19p1 (6); s20p4

SEPARATED 6
HUD-52580-A: p2; p17;
7420.10G Gbk: 4-10; 10-18; 21-14 Ex 21-4;
Admin Plan: s25p1

SEPARATELY 18
24 CFR 5: .603;
24 CFR 982: .517;
HUD-50058Instr: p17; p59 (2); p76;
HUD-52648: p4;
7420.10G Gbk: 4-10; 8-23; 18-2; 18-6; 20-8 Ex 20-1; 24-11;
PIH Notices: 03-23; 03-12; 02-20; 01-06; 00-46

SEPARATES......................................1
PIH Notices: 03-23

SEPARATION 17
24 CFR 5: .603;
24 CFR 982: .315;
HUD-50058Instr: p72 (3);
7420.10G Gbk: 5-23; 5-27; 5-47 Ex 5-5;
Admin Plan: s2p3; s6p10; s7p4; s7p5; s7p7; s7p8; s8p5; s25p1; s25p1

SEPARATION AGREEMENT..........1
7420.10G Gbk: 5-23

SEPTEMBER.................................69
24 CFR 5: .508; .801 (8);
24 CFR 35 SubM: .1200 (5);
HUD-50058: p xiii;
HUD-50058Instr: p53; p78 (2);
7420.10G Gbk: 10-15; 10-22; 14-1; 20-4; 20-22;
PIH Notices: 03-23 (4); 02-27 (3); 02-21 (2); 02-20 (3); 02-03; 01-33 (2); 01-20; 01-10; 01-06; 00-53; 00-49; 00-46 (2); 00-45; 00-41 (2); 00-34 (7); 00-27 (3); 00-24A; 00-23 (5); 00-09; 99-11; 96-65;
Admin Plan: s21p2

SEPTIC..13
24 CFR 5: .703;
24 CFR 982: .401 (2); .614; .624;
HUD-52580-A: p15 (2);
7420.10G Gbk: 10-3; 10-13; 17-5; 17-12; 18-7;
Admin Plan: s19p1

SEPTIC TANK 6
24 CFR 5: .703;
24 CFR 982: .401; .614;
7420.10G Gbk: 10-13; 17-5; 18-7

SEQUENCE....................................16
HUD-50058: p xii (2);
HUD-50058Instr: p14; p50 (7);
7420.10G Gbk: 1-1; 4-18; 20-23;
PIH Notices: 01-41; 01-06; 00-09

SEQUENTIAL..................................1
7420.10G Gbk: 8-23

SERIOUS..61
24 CFR 5: .100;
24 CFR 982: .310; .401 (5); .551; .552; .614 (5);
HUD-52580-A: p2 (3); p6 (2); p13 (4); p15; p16; p17 (2);
HUD-52641: p9;
HUD-52641-A: p2 (2);
7420.10G Gbk: 1-15; 5-7; 8-12; 10-9 (4); 10-13; 15-1 (2); 15-5; 15-7; 17-5; 22-15; 23-7;
PIH Notices: 01-41; 01-01; 99-11; 96-65;
Admin Plan: s10p5; s14p1; s14p2; s15p2; s15p3; s15p5 (4); s16p2; s20p7; s23p6

SERVICE AGENCY............................ 2
Admin Plan: s4p2; s6p7

SERVICE OF NOTICE 2
24 CFR 5: .312; .353

SERVICE OF NOTICE TO TENANTS 1
24 CFR 5: .353

SERVICE PROVIDER 7
HUD-50058: p16 (2); p xvi;
HUD-50058Instr: p61 (2); p75; p75

SERVICE PROVIDERS....................6
7420.10G Gbk: 2-10; 19-3; 23-4;
PIH Notices: 00-11 (2); 00-11

SET ASIDE.....................................10
24 CFR 5: .609;
24 CFR 982: .601;
HUD-50058Instr: p29;
7420.10G Gbk: 5-15 Ex 5-2; 17-1;
PIH Notices: 01-15 Impr Integ Hbk;
Admin Plan: s19p1 (2); s22p1; s25p1

SET-ASIDE.......................................6

24 CFR 5: .801 (2);
PIH Notices: 02-27;
Admin Plan: s22p1; s24p1; s24p2

SET-OFF 1
Admin Plan: s17p1

SETTING 34
24 CFR 982: .614;
HUD-52580-A: p17 (2);
7420.10G Gbk: 2-9; 3-5 (2); 4-15; 5-44; 7-2; 7-9; 8-8; 10-15; 17-5; 18-1; 20-3; 22-8;
PIH Notices: 01-41 (2); 01-06 (2); 01-01; 00-09; 95-48 (6); 95-48 Tech Asst (5); 95-48 Tech Asst

SETTINGS 3
HUD-52580-A: p17;
PIH Notices: 95-48; 95-48 Tech Asst

SETTLEMENT 95
24 CFR 5: .603; .609;
24 CFR 982: .315; .630; .633;
HUD-50058Instr: p30 (2); p31; p32 (2);
HUD-52580-A: p17;
7420.10G Gbk: 5-15 Ex 5-2; 5-16 Ex 5-2 (4); 5-27 (2); 5-28 (2); 5-49 Ex 5-5; 20-2; 20-3 (2); 20-4; 20-5 (2); 20-7; 20-9 (2); 20-12 Ex 20-2; 20-18 (2); 20-27 (3); 20-28; 20-29; 22-16; 24-2; 24-15;
PIH Notices: 03-23 (9); 02-21 (4); 02-07 (10); 01-20; 01-15 Impr Integ Hbk (6); 00-49 (2); 00-28 (8); 00-09 (4); 96-65; 95-48 (2); 95-48 Tech Asst (2);
Admin Plan: s6p10; s7p4; s7p5; s18p4; s25p5

SETTLEMENT COSTS 4
7420.10G Gbk: 5-27 (2); 5-28; 5-49 Ex 5-5

SETTLEMENT REPORT 2
7420.10G Gbk: 20-2; 20-28

SETTLEMENTS 5
7420.10G Gbk: 5-23; 5-25 Ex 5-3; 12-13 Ex 12-1;
PIH Notices: 03-23; 01-15 Impr Integ Hbk

SEVENTY-FIVE PERCENT 3
7420.10G Gbk: 4-21 (2);
Admin Plan: s4p2

SEVERANCE PAY 5
24 CFR 5: .609;
HUD-50058Instr: p27;
7420.10G Gbk: 5-14 Ex 5-2;
PIH Notices: 01-15 Impr Integ Hbk; 01-15 Impr Integ Hbk

SEVERE 34
24 CFR 5: .360;
24 CFR 982: .401 (2); .614 (2);
HUD-52580-A: p2 (4); p3; p6 (2); p9; p10; p11; p12; p13 (4); p17; p18;
7420.10G Gbk: 10-3; 10-9 (2);
PIH Notices: 00-09; 95-48 (2); 95-48 Tech Asst (2);
Admin Plan: s1p5; s18p4; s25p2; s25p3

SEVERE ILLNESS 1
24 CFR 5: .360

SEVERELY 6
24 CFR 982: .401;
HUD-50058Instr: p72 (2);
7420.10G Gbk: 10-2;
PIH Notices: 95-48; 95-48 Tech Asst

SEWER 33
24 CFR 5: .703;
24 CFR 982: .401; .517;
HUD-52517: p1;
HUD-52580: p5;
HUD-52580-A: p6 (4); p15 (4); p16 (2); p18;
HUD-52641: p2;
HUD-52667: p1 (2); p i;
7420.10G Gbk: 9-14 Ex 9-1; 9-15 Ex 9-2; 10-3 (2); 10-4; 10-5; 10-10; 10-11; 10-13; 18-2 (2); 18-4; 18-8

SEWER GAS 5
24 CFR 982: .401;
HUD-52580-A: p15; p18;
7420.10G Gbk: 10-10; 10-11

SEWERS 1
7420.10G Gbk: 18-7

SEX 52
24 CFR 982: .202; .304; .401; .402; .553 (2);
HUD-50058: p3 (6); p4 (6);
HUD-50058Instr: p14;
HUD-52641: p5; p10;
HUD-52641-A: p3;
HUD-52646: p2;
HUD-903: p1 (2); p2 (3); p4;
7420.10G Gbk: 4-19; 4-25 Ex 4-2; 5-11; 5-41; 5-42 (3); 8-14; 10-6; 11-13; 12-7 (2); 12-16 Ex 12-4;
PIH Notices: 03-11; 02-21; 01-15; 95-48; 95-48 Tech Asst;

Admin Plan: s1p2; s5p1 (2); s15p2; s23p2

SEX OFFENDER 3
24 CFR 982: .553 (2);
Admin Plan: s15p2

SEX OFFENDERS 1
PIH Notices: 03-11

SEXUAL 5
PIH Notices: 95-48 (2); 95-48 Tech Asst (2);
Admin Plan: s1p2

SEXUAL ORIENTATION................. 3
PIH Notices: 95-48; 95-48 Tech Asst;
Admin Plan: s1p2

SHARE 137
24 CFR 982: 24 CFR 982 (2); .1; .4 (2); .101 (2); .305; .503 (2); .508 (2); .515 (4); .615; .619; .627;
HUD-50058: p11; p14 (2);
HUD-50058Instr: p20 (2); p48; p57 (3); p72; p73 (2);
HUD-52641: p6;
7420.10G Gbk: 1-2; 1-4; 1-5 (2); 2-10; 5-19; 5-27; 5-32; 6-1 (2); 6-2; 6-5; 7-1 (2); 8-1; 8-5; 8-9; 9-4; 12-6; 12-7 (2); 12-8; 12-9; 14-3; 17-1; 17-4; 17-5 (2); 17-6 (5); 17-7 (4); 17-8 (6); 17-9 (5); 17-10; 19-6;
PIH Notices: 02-20 (3); 02-01; 01-41 (8); 01-15 (4); 01-10 (19); 00-46 (3); 00-09 (5); 99-52; 95-48 (2); 95-48 Tech Asst (2);
Admin Plan: s19p1 (3); s21p7 (3); s21p7

SHARED HOUSING 87
24 CFR 982: 24 CFR 982 (5); .4 (4); .54; .601 (2); .614; .615 (5); .616 (2); .617 (7); .618 (5);
HUD-50058Instr: p20; p43 (2); p44 (2); p47 (5); p49 (2); p74; p75;
HUD-52580: p1 (3);
7420.10G Gbk: 3-5; 8-17; 10-1; 11-10; 17-7 (3); 17-8 (9); 17-9 (4);
Admin Plan: s9p2; s19p1 (16); s24p2

SHELTER 52
24 CFR 5: .360 (2); .363; .601; .603; .609 (4);
24 CFR 35 SubM: .1200 (2);
HUD-50058: p viii (2);
HUD-50058Instr: p15; p28; p37 (2); p72;
7420.10G Gbk: 3-3 (2); 5-14 Ex 5-2 (4); 5-20 (4); 5-21 (6); 5-47 Ex 5-5 (3); 17-4;
PIH Notices: 01-15 Impr Integ Hbk (8); 95-48; 95-48 Tech Asst;
Admin Plan: s9p2; s23p2 (2); s25p3

SHELTERS 7
HUD-50058Instr: p72;
PIH Notices: 95-48 (2); 95-48 Tech Asst (2);
Admin Plan: s23p2; s25p3

SHOPPER... 1
7420.10G Gbk: 9-6

SHOPPING 19
HUD-52667: p i;
7420.10G Gbk: 2-6; 2-13 Ex 2-1; 8-7; 9-17 Ex 9-3; 10-13; 13-8; 14-1 (4);
PIH Notices: 01-10 (6); 95-48; 95-48 Tech Asst

SHOPPING INCENTIVE................ 10
7420.10G Gbk: 14-1 (4);
PIH Notices: 01-10 (5); 01-10

SHORT TERM.................................. 1
7420.10G Gbk: 20-15

SHORTER TERM 10
24 CFR 982: .309 (2);
HUD-52641: p1 (2);
7420.10G Gbk: 8-22;
PIH Notices: 01-41 (2); 00-09 (2);
Admin Plan: s9p2

SHORTFALL 8
24 CFR 982: .102;
PIH Notices: 02-21; 02-06 (3); 01-20; 01-10; 00-09

SHORTFALL IN FUNDING............ 2
24 CFR 982: .102;
PIH Notices: 02-06

SHORTFALLS.................................. 1
PIH Notices: 02-06

SHORT-TERM.................................. 6
HUD-50058Instr: p28;
7420.10G Gbk: 4-11; 23-15;
PIH Notices: 02-01; 01-41; 00-09

SHOWER.. 27
24 CFR 982: .401; .605 (2); .614;
HUD-52580: p2; p6 (8); p7 (2); p19 (2);
7420.10G Gbk: 10-3 (4); 10-

4 (2); 17-2; 17-4;
PIH Notices: 95-48; 95-48 Tech Asst

SHOWERS 2
PIH Notices: 95-48; 95-48 Tech Asst

SHOWING 39
24 CFR 982: .203;
HUD-52580-A: p13;
7420.10G Gbk: 2-4; 2-8; 4-22; 5-46 Ex 5-5 (2); 5-48 Ex 5-5; 8-7; 11-8 (2); 13-8; 13-10; 19-3; 22-10; 24-3;
PIH Notices: 02-20 (3); 01-15 Impr Integ Hbk (6); 01-06 (2); 00-46 (3);
Admin Plan: s7p5; s7p6 (3); s7p8 (2); s16p3; s18p5; s21p7

SICK DAYS 1
7420.10G Gbk: 10-24

SIDEWALK 2
PIH Notices: 95-48; 95-48 Tech Asst

SIDEWALKS 6
PIH Notices: 95-48 (3); 95-48 Tech Asst (2); 95-48 Tech Asst

SIGHT IMPAIRMENTS 2
PIH Notices: 95-48; 95-48 Tech Asst

SIGN 108
24 CFR 5: .230 (3); .232 (2); .350; .508;
24 CFR 982: .551; .552;
HUD-50058Instr: p2 (4); p14;
HUD-52580-A: p6; p13;
HUD-52646: p2 (2);
HUD-9886: p1 (5);
7420.10G Gbk: 1-5; 1-7; 1-16 Ex 1-3; 3-5; 4-11; 4-14; 5-4; 5-9 Ex 5-1 (3); 5-13; 5-35; 8-10; 8-21; 8-24 Ex 8-1; 11-4; 11-14; 11-16 Ex 11-1; 12-3; 12-12 Ex 12-1; 14-2; 15-5; 20-13; 20-21; 22-4; 22-8; 22-12; 24-12; 24-13;
PIH Notices: 02-01; 01-15; 00-24B; 99-52; 95-48 (16); 95-48 Tech Asst (16);
Admin Plan: s1p3; s1p6; s2p5 (2); s3p2; s3p3 (3); s7p2 (3); s7p3 (2); s7p4; s7p8 (2); s15p1; s20p2 (2); s22p4

SIGN LANGUAGE 27
PIH Notices: 02-01; 99-52; 95-48 (12); 95-48 Tech Asst (12);
Admin Plan: s1p3

SIGNALED 1
7420.10G Gbk: 1-3

SIGNALS 5
7420.10G Gbk: 10-21;
PIH Notices: 95-48 (2); 95-48 Tech Asst; 95-48 Tech Asst

SIGNATORY 2
HUD-52641: p2; p2

SIGNATURE 26
24 CFR 5: .502;
HUD-52641: p2 (2);
HUD-52646: p1 (2);
HUD-52648: p3 (2);
HUD-52665: p1; p2;
HUD-903: p1 (2);
HUD-903-1: p5;
7420.10G Gbk: 4-23 Ex 4-1; 4-27 Ex 4-2 (2); 5-50 Ex 5-5; 9-16 Ex 9-2; 10-37 Ex 10-2; 10-38 Ex 10-3; 10-39 Ex 10-4; 12-3;
PIH Notices: 02-20; 00-46; 00-09;
Admin Plan: s20p2; s20p6

SIGNATURE 2
7420.10G Gbk: 9-18 Ex 9-3; 9-19 Ex 9-4

SIGNATURES 14
HUD-50058Instr: p2 (2);
HUD-9886: p1;
7420.10G Gbk: 5-12; 5-36 Ex 5-4; 11-11; 11-15; 12-3; 22-8; 24-13 (2);
PIH Notices: 02-21; 00-09;
Admin Plan: s20p2

SIGNED 115
24 CFR 5: .214; .230 (2); .234; .350; .360; .508 (9); .514;
24 CFR 982: .53;
HUD-50058Instr: p2; p9 (2); p12; p71; p72; p73;
HUD-52580: p5;
HUD-52580-A: p17;
HUD-52646: p1 (4);
HUD-903-1: p3;
HUD-9886: p2;
7420.10G Gbk: 1-14; 5-4 (3); 5-9 Ex 5-1 (4); 5-13 (2); 5-46 Ex 5-5 (4); 5-47 Ex 5-5 (5); 5-48 Ex 5-5; 5-49 Ex 5-5 (3); 5-50 Ex 5-5 (2); 5-51 Ex 5-5 (2); 11-2; 11-4; 11-15; 11-16 Ex 11-1 (2); 12-3; 12-4; 14-4; 19-12 (2); 20-

25; 21-4; 22-9 (2); 22-13; 22-17;
PIH Notices: 03-23; 03-11 (4); 02-21; 02-14; 02-06; 01-15 (3); 01-15 Impr Integ Hbk (3); 01-01; 00-11 (2); 95-48 (6); 95-48 Tech Asst (6);
Admin Plan: s7p1; s7p4 (2); s7p7; s8p2; s8p3; s9p1; s13p1; s16p3; s20p2; s20p2

SIGNER 1
7420.10G Gbk: 5-9 Ex 5-1

SIGNIFICANCE 8
PIH Notices: 95-48 (4); 95-48 Tech Asst (3); 95-48 Tech Asst

SIGNIFICANT 76
24 CFR 982: .614;
HUD-50058Instr: p38;
HUD-52580-A: p2; p13 (4);
7420.10G Gbk: 1-3; 4-6; 5-34; 8-4; 9-1; 11-15; 12-5; 13-8; 19-8; 19-9; 20-1; 20-2; 20-6; 20-17 (2); 20-28 (3); 21-2; 21-3; 21-6; 21-7; 21-8; 21-10; 22-4; 24-7; 24-13;
PIH Notices: 03-23; 02-27 (2); 02-07; 01-41 (7); 01-15; 01-10 (5); 01-01; 00-28; 00-11; 00-11A; 00-09 (8); 95-48 (7); 95-48 Tech Asst (5);
Admin Plan: s5p1

SIGNIFICANT OTHER 1
Admin Plan: s5p1

SIGNIFICANTLY 18
24 CFR 982: .401;
HUD-50058Instr: p38;
7420.10G Gbk: 16-4; 19-8; 21-17; 21-19; 22-7;
PIH Notices: 03-23; 02-20; 01-41 (3); 00-46; 00-09 (2); 96-65; 95-48; 95-48 Tech Asst

SIGNIFIES 3
HUD-52580: p5;
HUD-52580-A: p17;
7420.10G Gbk: 11-1

SIGNING 16
24 CFR 5: .230;
HUD-9886: p1;
7420.10G Gbk: 8-3; 8-8; 10-35; 14-4; 22-8; 23-13;
PIH Notices: 95-48 (2); 95-48 Tech Asst (2);
Admin Plan: s9p4 (3); s9p4

SIGNS 48
24 CFR 5: .508; .703;
HUD-50058: p i;
HUD-50058Instr: p3;
HUD-52580-A: p2 (2); p3; p5; p7; p9; p10; p11; p12;
7420.10G Gbk: 6-2; 8-12; 9-6; 9-8; 11-16 Ex 11-1; 14-4; 24-12;
PIH Notices: 00-24B; 95-48 (12); 95-48 Tech Asst (12);
Admin Plan: s9p4; s20p2; s20p2

SIMPLE 26
HUD-52580-A: p15;
7420.10G Gbk: 4-3; 4-4; 4-9; 4-10 (2); 5-26; 9-9; 19-9; 24-3; 24-5;
PIH Notices: 03-12; 03-11; 01-15; 01-15 Impr Integ Hbk; 95-48 (5); 95-48 Tech Asst (5);
Admin Plan: s22p3

SIMPLER 2
PIH Notices: 95-48; 95-48 Tech Asst

SIMPLEST 1
7420.10G Gbk: 24-3

SIMPLICITY 3
7420.10G Gbk: 22-10;
PIH Notices: 01-41; 00-09

SIMPLIFICATION 1
7420.10G Gbk: 21-3

SIMPLIFIED 2
HUD-50058Instr: p29;
7420.10G Gbk: 22-8

SIMPLIFIES 3
PIH Notices: 02-20; 00-46; 00-09

SIMPLIFY 2
7420.10G Gbk: 4-18;
PIH Notices: 03-12

SIMPLIFYING 2
PIH Notices: 95-48; 95-48 Tech Asst

SIMPLY 18
7420.10G Gbk: 4-16; 5-28; 8-1; 8-5; 9-7; 20-21; 21-9; 22-8;
PIH Notices: 01-41 (2); 01-06 (2); 00-09 (2); 96-65; 95-48; 95-48 Tech Asst;
Admin Plan: s25p4

SINGLE 129
24 CFR 5: .403; .653;

.655 (6); .703 (2); .801 (3);
24 CFR 982: Intro; .1; .4 (4); .151; .154; .155; .201 (5); .204 (2); .207 (3); .402 (2); .503 (2); .601 (5); .602; .625; .628; .643;
HUD-50058: p i; p5;
HUD-50058Instr: p3; p20 (2); p42 (3); p46 (3); p71; p72; p73; p75 (2);
HUD-52580: p1 (4); p2; p13;
HUD-903: p2;
HUD-903-1: p5;
7420.10G Gbk: 2-6; 4-8; 4-17; 4-20; 5-1; 5-2; 5-41 (3); 10-1; 10-18; 10-20; 17-7; 21-1; 21-5; 21-6; 22-1; 23-13;
PIH Notices: 03-23 (3); 02-27; 02-20 (4); 02-01 (3); 01-41; 01-06 (2); 00-53; 00-46 (4); 00-34; 00-09; 99-52 (3);
Admin Plan: s2p2 (2); s2p4; s4p1; s5p1 (2); s9p2 (2); s11p1; s16p3; s17p2; s19p1 (4); s23p1; s23p5; s24p6

SINGLE ACT.......................................
2
7420.10G Gbk: 22-1;
Admin Plan: s17p2

SINGLE FAMILY............................16
HUD-50058: p5;
HUD-52517: p1 (3);
HUD-903-1: p5;
7420.10G Gbk: 9-5; 9-6 (2); 9-8; 9-9; 9-10 (5);
Admin Plan: s9p2

SINGLE FAMILY DETACHED........3
HUD-50058: p5;
HUD-52580: p1;
HUD-52580-A: p1

SINGLE FAMILY HOUSE 3
HUD-903: p2;
7420.10G Gbk: 9-13 Ex 9-1; 9-15 Ex 9-2

SINGLE FAMILY UNIT 1
Admin Plan: s2p4

SINGLE PARENT 1
24 CFR 982: .4

SINGLE PERSON...........................19
24 CFR 5: .403; .655;
24 CFR 982: .201 (3); .402 (2); .602;
HUD-50058Instr: p72; p75;
7420.10G Gbk: 5-1; 5-2; 5-41 (3);
Admin Plan: s2p2 (2); s5p1; s19p1

SINGLE PERSONS.........................10
24 CFR 5: .653; .655 (5);
24 CFR 982: .207 (3);
7420.10G Gbk: 4-17

SINGLE ROOM OCCUPANCY.....29
24 CFR 5: .703 (2); .801 (2);
24 CFR 982: Intro; .4; .601 (3);
HUD-50058: p i;
HUD-50058Instr: p3; p20 (2); p42; p46; p73; p75;
HUD-52580: p1 (3);
7420.10G Gbk: 3-5; 10-1; 11-10; 17-1 (2);
Admin Plan: s9p2; s19p1 (2); s23p1

SINGLE-FAMILY 4
24 CFR 982: .517;
HUD-903: p1;
7420.10G Gbk: 2-13 Ex 2-1;
Admin Plan: s10p5

SINK 34
24 CFR 982: .401 (4); .614 (2);
HUD-52580: p2; p6 (2);
HUD-52580-A: p2; p4 (5); p5 (2); p6; p8; p9; p10; p11; p12; p17; p19 (2);
7420.10G Gbk: 10-3; 10-5 (5); 17-5; 17-5

SINK TRAP 9
24 CFR 982: .401 (2);
HUD-52580-A: p8; p9; p10; p11; p12;
7420.10G Gbk: 10-3; 10-5

SISTER 12
24 CFR 982: .306;
HUD-52517: p2;
HUD-52641: p5; p6 (2);
HUD-52646: p2;
7420.10G Gbk: 8-15; 8-19; 11-2;
PIH Notices: 95-48; 95-48 Tech Asst;
Admin Plan: s16p2

SITE 115
24 CFR 5: .703 (5);
24 CFR 982: .401 (4); .614 (4); .621; .628;
HUD-50058: p1; p i; p ii; p x; p xi; p xiii; p xiv; p xvi;
HUD-50058Instr: p1; p3; p4; p5 (3); p7 (8); p42; p46; p53; p56; p59;
HUD-52580: p5; p6;

HUD-52580-A: p13; p17; p18 (2); p19;
7420.10G Gbk: 1-3; 4-11 (2); 8-3 (2); 8-9 (2); 9-6; 9-7 (2); 10-1; 10-13 (3); 10-33; 10-34; 13-3; 17-5 (2); 17-10; 17-11; 19-2 (2); 24-14;
PIH Notices: 02-27 (8); 02-22; 02-20; 02-01 (3); 01-15; 01-15 Impr Integ Hbk; 01-06 (3); 01-02; 01-01; 00-53 (7); 00-46; 00-24; 00-23; 99-52 (3); 95-48 (2); 95-48 Tech Asst (2);
Admin Plan: s19p1; s24p1; s24p3 (2); s24p3

SITUATION....................................33
HUD-50058Instr: p21; p28; p59;
7420.10G Gbk: 4-16; 4-17; 5-21; 5-38; 8-4; 22-1 (2); 22-5; 22-10; 22-11; 22-14;
PIH Notices: 03-05; 01-41; 01-40; 01-11; 00-09; 95-48 (4); 95-48 Tech Asst (4);
Admin Plan: s6p11; s6p12 (2); s10p1; s11p3; s23p7

SITUATIONS 46
24 CFR 5: .630;
HUD-50058Instr: p3;
7420.10G Gbk: 1-9 (2); 3-2; 4-15; 9-4; 11-4 (2); 11-5; 11-6; 13-6; 16-5; 20-4 (2); 20-25; 22-1; 24-13;
PIH Notices: 03-05; 01-41; 01-40; 01-15; 01-15 Impr Integ Hbk (2); 00-09 (2); 99-11 (3); 96-65; 95-48 (6); 95-48 Tech Asst (6);
Admin Plan: s1p4; s4p2; s6p6; s6p7

SIX MONTH 8
7420.10G Gbk: 12-6;
PIH Notices: 01-01 (6); 00-28

SIX MONTHS.................................35
24 CFR 5: .518 (2); .617;
24 CFR 982: .503;
HUD-50058Instr: p9; p10;
HUD-52665: p1;
7420.10G Gbk: 7-4 (3); 12-6 (2); 13-4; 13-7; 13-9; 19-3 (2); 20-9; 24-2; 24-9;
PIH Notices: 03-05; 02-20; 01-41; 01-40; 01-15 Impr Integ Hbk; 01-01; 00-46; 00-11A; 00-09;
Admin Plan: s6p2; s6p7; s7p5 (2); s22p2; s25p5

SIX MONTHS' 2
PIH Notices: 03-23; 03-23

SIX PERSONS 2
24 CFR 982: .605;
7420.10G Gbk: 17-2

SIX YEAR 1
PIH Notices: 00-23

SIX YEARS....................................14
24 CFR 5: .216 (6);
HUD-9886: p2 (2);
7420.10G Gbk: 10-11; 10-12 (2);
PIH Notices: 01-15; 01-15 Impr Integ Hbk; 00-23

SIXTY..7
24 CFR 982: .308; .519 (2);
PIH Notices: 03-11; 96-65 (2);
Admin Plan: s8p4

SIXTY DAYS 8
24 CFR 982: .308; .519 (2);
HUD-52641: p10;
HUD-52641-A: p3;
HUD-52646: p1;
PIH Notices: 96-65; 96-65

SIZE 511
24 CFR 5: .315; .318 (2); .403; .518 (5);
24 CFR 982: .4; .201; .204 (6); .316; .355 (2); .401; .402 (18); .403 (5); .503 (10); .504; .505 (6); .507 (2); .516; .517 (4); .554 (2); .555 (3); .608; .609 (2); .613 (7); .614; .617 (2); .618; .619; .620; .622; .635 (2);
HUD-50058: p iii; p iv; p ix (3); p x; p xi; p xiii; p xiv (2); p xvii;
HUD-50058Instr: p14; p39 (2); p40; p42; p46; p47 (6); p53; p57 (2); p59; p62; p68 (2); p72 (4); p76 (2);
HUD-52580: p6 (4);
HUD-52580-A: p1; p4 (2); p15; p19 (4);
HUD-52641: p4 (2);
HUD-52646: p1 (4); p2;
HUD-52665: p1 (2); p2;
HUD-52667: p i (4); p ii;
HUD-9886: p2;
7420.10G Gbk: 2-1 (2); 2-13 Ex 2-1; 3-5; 3-8 (2); 4-1; 4-7; 4-9; 4-10; 4-11; 4-15; 4-18 (2); 5-2; 5-21 (2); 5-35; 5-41 (3); 5-42 (3); 5-47 Ex 5-5; 6-3 (2); 6-6 (2); 7-2; 7-

5; 7-6; 7-7 (4); 7-8 (4); 8-8 (2); 8-10 (2); 8-13; 8-17 (4); 8-23; 9-1; 9-2; 9-3; 9-5; 9-8; 9-11; 9-12; 9-13 Ex 9-1; 9-16 Ex 9-2; 10-4 (2); 10-5 (2); 10-6 (2); 10-18; 10-23; 10-24; 10-31 (3); 10-32; 11-5; 11-6; 11-19; 12-5; 12-7 (7); 13-5 (2); 13-7; 15-4; 16-1; 16-2 (2); 16-3; 17-2; 17-3; 17-5 (3); 17-6 (2); 17-8 (2); 17-11; 17-12; 18-1; 18-2 (3); 18-4; 18-5 (6); 19-3 (3); 19-4; 19-10; 20-15 (2); 20-17; 20-23; 20-28 (3); 21-1; 21-3; 21-5 (2); 21-8; 21-11 (2); 21-13; 21-17 (5); 21-18 (8); 21-19 (4); 22-5; 22-6; 22-7 (2); 22-12 (3); 22-13; 23-1 (2); 23-2 (7); 23-3 (4); 23-4 (2);

PIH Notices: 03-23; 03-12 (2); 02-27 (4); 02-22; 02-20 (13); 02-01 (3); 01-41 (27); 01-15; 01-15 Impr Integ Hbk (2); 01-06 (3); 00-46 (13); 00-24B (4); 00-11A; 00-09 (25); 99-52 (3); 99-11 (2); 95-48 (5); 95-48 Tech Asst (5);

Admin Plan: s2p4; s3p2; s4p1; s5p1 (9); s5p2 (13); s5p3 (10); s6p6 (3); s6p13; s8p6 (2); s9p1; s18p2 (2); s18p3; s18p4; s19p1 (8); s21p3; s21p5; s22p2; s23p3 (2); s23p4 (3); s23p7 (2); s24p3; s25p4 (2); s25p4

SIZE OF UNIT 3

24 CFR 982: .402;
HUD-50058Instr: p76;
HUD-52667: p i

SIZED 4

HUD-52667: p i;
PIH Notices: 01-41 (2); 00-09

SIZE-MAXIMUM 1

24 CFR 982: .402

SIZES 40

24 CFR 5: .100;
24 CFR 982: .4 (2); .402; .503 (5);
HUD-50058Instr: p75;
7420.10G Gbk: 3-4; 5-41; 7-4; 7-5; 7-6; 9-13 Ex 9-1; 10-7; 10-25; 18-2; 21-1; 21-17;
PIH Notices: 02-27; 02-22; 02-20 (7); 02-01; 01-01 (3); 00-46 (2); 00-27 (2); 00-24B; 99-52

SKILLED 4

7420.10G Gbk: 21-3 (2);
PIH Notices: 95-48; 95-48 Tech Asst

SKILLS 33

24 CFR 5: .603;
HUD-50058Instr: p61; p71;
7420.10G Gbk: 5-20; 8-1; 8-2; 10-18; 21-16 Ex 21-6; 23-6; 23-9;
PIH Notices: 01-15 Impr Integ Hbk; 00-11 (2); 95-48 (7); 95-48 Tech Asst (7);
Admin Plan: s6p3; s8p3 (2); s25p4 (2); s25p7

SKIP 43

24 CFR 982: .204;
HUD-50058: p5 (2); p7 (3); p vii; p9 (2); p10 (3); p11 (2); p12; p13 (2); p14 (2); p17;
HUD-50058Instr: p2; p20 (3); p34 (4); p42; p43; p44; p46; p48; p51; p53; p54; p56; p57; p61; p68;
7420.10G Gbk: 4-15; 4-18;
PIH Notices: 03-20

SLEEPING 43

24 CFR 5: .703;
24 CFR 982: .401 (4);
HUD-50058Instr: p72;
HUD-52580: p1 (4); p8 (4); p9; p10; p11; p12;
7420.10G Gbk: 5-42; 8-17; 10-6 (3); 10-8 (2); 10-10; 17-1;
PIH Notices: 02-01 (2); 99-52 (2); 95-48 (2); 95-48 Tech Asst (2);
Admin Plan: s5p1; s5p3 (3); s15p6; s19p1; s23p2; s25p3

SLEEPING ACCOMMODATION.... 3

HUD-50058Instr: p72;
Admin Plan: s23p2; s25p3

SLEEPING ACCOMMODATIONS.. 2

PIH Notices: 95-48; 95-48 Tech Asst

SLEEPING AREA 2

7420.10G Gbk: 5-42;
Admin Plan: s5p3

SLEEPING AREAS 3

24 CFR 5: .703;
PIH Notices: 02-01; 99-52

SLEEPING ROOM..........................10
24 CFR 982: .401 (3);
7420.10G Gbk: 8-17; 10-6 (2); 10-8; 10-10;
Admin Plan: s5p1; s5p3

SLEEPING ROOMS.........................5
HUD-52580: p1 (2); p8;
PIH Notices: 95-48; 95-48 Tech Asst

SLOT...2
7420.10G Gbk: 23-2; 23-2

SLOTS...37
24 CFR 982: .201; .206; .601;
HUD-50058Instr: p72;
HUD-52648: p2 (2); p3;
7420.10G Gbk: 4-1; 4-20; 23-5; 23-6 (2); 23-19 (6);
PIH Notices: 02-27 (3); 01-06 (12); 00-24A (2);
Admin Plan: s21p9; s21p9

SMALL BUSINESS........................10
7420.10G Gbk: 23-15;
PIH Notices: 02-27 (5); 02-22; 95-48; 95-48 Tech Asst;
Admin Plan: s7p5

SMALL CHILD..................................1
Admin Plan: s6p11

SMALL CHILDREN.........................2
7420.10G Gbk: 10-2; 10-2

SMALLER UNIT.............................5
7420.10G Gbk: 12-5; 22-12; 22-13;
PIH Notices: 00-27;
Admin Plan: s5p2

SMELL...1
HUD-52580-A: p15

SMELLS..1
HUD-52580-A: p4

SMOKE...57
24 CFR 5: .703 (3);
24 CFR 982: .401 (10); .605; .614;
HUD-52580: p3 (3); p4 (2);
HUD-52580-A: p8 (8); p9 (4); p10 (4); p11 (4); p12 (4); p17;
7420.10G Gbk: 10-13; 17-5;
PIH Notices: 99-11 (9);
Admin Plan: s10p4

SMOKE DETECTOR.......................4
7420.10G Gbk: 10-14 (3); 10-15

SMOKE DETECTOR.....................21
24 CFR 5: .703;
24 CFR 982: .401 (3);
HUD-52580-A: p8 (3); p9 (2); p10 (2); p11 (2); p12 (2);
7420.10G Gbk: 10-14 (3); 10-15;
PIH Notices: 99-11;
Admin Plan: s10p4

SMOKE DETECTORS..................10
7420.10G Gbk: 10-1; 10-14 (8); 17-2

SMOKE DETECTORS..................45
24 CFR 5: .703 (2);
24 CFR 982: .401 (6); .605;
HUD-52580: p3 (3); p4 (2);
HUD-52580-A: p8 (5); p9 (2); p10 (2); p11 (2); p12 (2);
7420.10G Gbk: 10-1; 10-14 (8); 17-2;
PIH Notices: 99-11 (7); 99-11

SMOKING.......................................8
PIH Notices: 95-48 (4); 95-48 Tech Asst (3); 95-48 Tech Asst

SOCIAL.......................................185
24 CFR 5: .110; .210; .214 (9); .216 (2); .218; .318; .603; .609 (2); .617; .659;
24 CFR 982: .352; .551; .553; .612; .614;
HUD-50058: p i (3); p ii (2); p3 (6); p iii (2); p4 (6); p iv (2); p v; p6; p x; p xi; p xii; p xiii;
HUD-50058Instr: p3 (2); p5 (2); p6 (2); p15; p16 (6); p17 (2); p18; p29 (3); p43; p47; p50; p53; p71; p72; p75 (4);
HUD-52665: p1; p2;
HUD-9886: p1 (2); p2 (4);
7420.10G Gbk: 1-2; 4-9; 8-8; 9-6; 17-4; 17-5; 21-5; 23-9;
PIH Notices: 03-11; 02-01 (2); 01-15 (12); 01-15 Impr Integ Hbk (18); 00-41; 00-24B; 00-11A (4); 99-52 (2); 95-48 (5); 95-48 Tech Asst (5);
Admin Plan: s2p1; s2p3; s2p5 (7); s3p1; s6p10; s7p3 (2); s7p4; s7p7; s7p8 (13); s9p1; s11p3; s20p2; s20p3; s20p6; s25p2; s25p4 (2); s25p4

SOCIAL ROOMS.............................1
24 CFR 5: .318

SOCIAL SECURITY.......................40
HUD-52646: p2;
7420.10G Gbk: 1-14; 4-23 Ex 4-1 (3); 4-25 Ex 4-2; 4-

26 Ex 4-2; 5-4; 5-12 (5); 5-13 (2); 5-14 Ex 5-2; 5-15 Ex 5-2; 5-17; 5-23; 5-36 Ex 5-4; 5-46 Ex 5-5 (3); 5-50 Ex 5-5; 12-4; 12-5; 12-9 (3); 12-13 Ex 12-1 (4); 12-16 Ex 12-4 (2); 19-1; 22-4 (2); 23-8 Ex 23-1; 23-15

SOCIAL SECURITY.....................190
24 CFR 5: .110; .210; .214 (9); .216 (2); .218; .603; .609 (2); .617; .659;
24 CFR 982: .352; .551;
HUD-50058: p i (3); p ii (2); p3 (6); p iii (2); p4 (6); p iv (2); p v; p6; p x; p xi; p xii; p xiii;
HUD-50058Instr: p3 (2); p5 (2); p6 (2); p15; p16 (6); p17 (2); p18; p29 (3); p43; p47; p50; p53; p71; p75 (4);
HUD-52646: p2;
HUD-52665: p1; p2;
HUD-9886: p1 (2); p2 (4);
7420.10G Gbk: 1-14; 4-23 Ex 4-1 (3); 4-25 Ex 4-2; 4-26 Ex 4-2; 5-4; 5-12 (5); 5-13 (2); 5-14 Ex 5-2; 5-15 Ex 5-2; 5-17; 5-23; 5-36 Ex 5-4; 5-46 Ex 5-5 (3); 5-50 Ex 5-5; 12-4; 12-5; 12-9 (3); 12-13 Ex 12-1 (4); 12-16 Ex 12-4 (2); 19-1; 22-4 (2); 23-8 Ex 23-1; 23-15;
PIH Notices: 03-11; 01-15 (12); 01-15 Impr Integ Hbk (18); 00-41; 00-24B; 00-11A (4);
Admin Plan: s2p1; s2p5 (7); s6p10; s7p3 (2); s7p4; s7p7; s7p8 (12); s9p1; s20p2; s20p6; s25p2

SOCIAL SERVICE...........................6
7420.10G Gbk: 9-6;
PIH Notices: 95-48 (2); 95-48 Tech Asst (2);
Admin Plan: s25p4

SOCIAL SERVICE AGENCIES 6
7420.10G Gbk: 8-8; 21-5;
PIH Notices: 02-01; 99-52;
Admin Plan: s3p1; s25p4

SOCIAL SERVICE AGENCIES 6
7420.10G Gbk: 8-8; 21-5;
PIH Notices: 02-01; 99-52;
Admin Plan: s3p1; s25p4

SOCIAL SERVICE AGENCY..........2
24 CFR 982: .553;
7420.10G Gbk: 23-9

SOCIAL SERVICE AGENCY...........2
24 CFR 982: .553;
7420.10G Gbk: 23-9

SOCIAL SERVICE PROVIDERS.....2
PIH Notices: 95-48; 95-48 Tech Asst

SOCIAL SERVICES..........................7
24 CFR 982: .612;
PIH Notices: 02-01; 99-52; 95-48; 95-48 Tech Asst;
Admin Plan: s11p3; s20p3

SOCIAL WORKER...........................2
Admin Plan: s2p3; s7p8

SOCIALLY 2
PIH Notices: 02-27; 02-27

SOCIO-ECONOMIC.........................1
Admin Plan: s1p1

SOFTWARE 50
7420.10G Gbk: 2-6 (5); 4-13; 4-22 (2); 11-7 (2); 12-2 (3); 12-8; 14-5 (2); 19-2 (3); 19-4; 19-8; 19-12 (2); 24-4;
PIH Notices: 03-20 (10); 02-20; 01-11 (2); 01-06; 00-53 (11); 00-46

SOIL...7
7420.10G Gbk: 10-20; 10-21; 10-38 Ex 10-3 (3); 10-39 Ex 10-4;
PIH Notices: 00-23

SOILED 3
HUD-52580-A: p2 (2); p2

SOLE MEMBER............................23
24 CFR 5: .403 (4); .655 (2);
24 CFR 982: .207 (2);
HUD-50058Instr: p71 (2);
7420.10G Gbk: 4-16 (2); 4-17 (2); 5-2 (3); 5-29;
Admin Plan: s6p6 (3); s8p5; s25p2

SOLICIT 6
7420.10G Gbk: 4-3;
PIH Notices: 02-27 (2);
Admin Plan: s2p3; s23p3; s24p7

SOLICITATION 5
PIH Notices: 03-11; 02-27 (3); 02-27

SOLICITED......................................2
HUD-52667: p i;
PIH Notices: 02-27

SOLICITS...1
24 CFR 982: .101

SOLUTION.......................................1

7420.10G Gbk: 21-10

SOLUTIONS 3
7420.10G Gbk: 21-8; 24-3;
PIH Notices: 01-15

SOLVE 1
7420.10G Gbk: 24-13

SON 6
7420.10G Gbk: 5-27; 5-30 (3); 5-31; 5-31

SOUND..43
24 CFR 5: .703 (3);
24 CFR 982: .401 (2); .614;
HUD-52580-A: p2 (3); p3 (3); p5 (3); p7 (3); p9 (3); p10 (3); p11 (3); p12 (3); p14 (5);
7420.10G Gbk: 9-12; 10-2; 10-9 (3); 17-5;
PIH Notices: 02-27; 02-27

SOUNDNESS...................................1
7420.10G Gbk: 23-5

SOURCE......................................125
24 CFR 5: .210; .236 (3); .400; .601; .603; .609; .659 (2); .701; .703;
24 CFR 35 SubM: .1225;
24 CFR 982: 24 CFR 982 (2); .5; .54; .104; .207; .317; .355; .406; .456; .516 (2); .521; .555; .624;
HUD-50058: p6 (3); p vii;
HUD-50058Instr: p5 (3); p22 (3); p24 (2); p31; p33 (2); p34; p35; p70; p71;
HUD-52580-A: p15 (6);
HUD-52641: p5; 8;
HUD-52641-A: p1;
7420.10G Gbk: 1-2; 4-23 Ex 4-1; 4-26 Ex 4-2; 5-13; 5-31; 5-35; 5-46 Ex 5-5 (2); 5-47 Ex 5-5 (5); 5-49 Ex 5-5; 5-50 Ex 5-5 (2); 5-51 Ex 5-5 (2); 5-52 Ex 5-5; 5-53 Ex 5-5; 7-6; 8-21; 9-8; 9-14 Ex 9-1; 9-15 Ex 9-2; 10-7 (3); 10-20 (2); 12-4 (2); 12-16 Ex 12-4 (2); 19-6; 21-17; 21-18 (2); 21-20; 22-2 (2); 22-3; 22-16;
PIH Notices: 02-27 (10); 01-15 (2); 01-15 Impr Integ Hbk (4); 00-24B;
Admin Plan: s6p6; s6p9; s6p11 (2); s7p1 (3); s7p5; s20p4

SOURCE OF INCOME.................. 11
24 CFR 5: .659;
24 CFR 982: .516;
HUD-50058: p6;
HUD-50058Instr: p22;
7420.10G Gbk: 4-26 Ex 4-2; 5-35; 5-46 Ex 5-5; 22-2;
PIH Notices: 01-15; 01-15 Impr Integ Hbk; 01-15 Impr Integ Hbk

SOURCES 116
24 CFR 5: .214; .615;
24 CFR 982: .207; .401; .451; .553;
HUD-50058: p6 (3);
HUD-50058Instr: p24 (2); p27; p30; p31 (2); p32 (2); p34;
HUD-52580: p1 (4);
HUD-52667: p i (5);
HUD-903: p1 (5); p2;
7420.10G Gbk: 2-6; 2-11; 3-7; 4-15; 4-16; 5-16 Ex 5-2; 5-17 (4); 5-20; 5-22; 5-34; 5-35; 5-46 Ex 5-5; 5-47 Ex 5-5; 5-48 Ex 5-5; 5-49 Ex 5-5; 5-50 Ex 5-5; 5-51 Ex 5-5 (2); 5-52 Ex 5-5 (3); 5-53 Ex 5-5 (3); 9-5 (3); 9-6 (2); 10-8; 10-20; 10-30; 12-11; 12-13 Ex 12-1; 12-16 Ex 12-4; 16-5; 18-4 (3); 19-5; 21-3; 22-11; 23-2 (2); 23-3; 23-15; 24-9; 24-11; 24-14;
PIH Notices: 03-23 (2); 02-27 (5); 02-20 (4); 02-01; 01-15; 01-15 Impr Integ Hbk (2); 00-46 (4); 00-41; 00-23; 99-52;
Admin Plan: s6p8; s7p1 (2); s7p2 (2); s7p6; s20p3; s20p4; s21p2

SOURCES OF INCOME..................4
HUD-50058Instr: p24;
7420.10G Gbk: 4-15; 5-17;
Admin Plan: s6p8

SPACE HEATER 1
HUD-52580-A: p15

SPACE HEATERS............................2
HUD-52580-A: p15; p16

SPACE HEATING 12
24 CFR 982: .517;
HUD-52667: p i; p ii (5);
7420.10G Gbk: 18-2; 18-5 (3); 18-6

SPANISH 4

HUD-50058Instr: p73;
HUD-903: p2;
Admin Plan: s1p5; s1p5

SPAYED....1
24 CFR 5: .318

SPECIAL ACCESSIBILITY FEATURES....1
24 CFR 5: .655

SPECIAL ADJUSTMENT....11
24 CFR 982: Intro; .520 (9); .521

SPECIAL ADJUSTMENTS....2
24 CFR 982: .519; .619

SPECIAL ADMISSION....20
24 CFR 982: Intro; .4; .202; .203;
HUD-50058Instr: p19; p75;
7420.10G Gbk: 8-10; 13-2 (2);
PIH Notices: 01-41 (4); 00-24B; 00-09 (5);
Admin Plan: s4p1

SPECIAL ADMISSIONS....10
24 CFR 982: .202; .204;
7420.10G Gbk: 1-7 (2); 4-18; 4-21;
Admin Plan: s4p1 (3); s4p1

SPECIAL CIRCUMSTANCES....7
24 CFR 982: .102 (2);
7420.10G Gbk: 1-11; 8-12; 22-1; 22-14; 23-2

SPECIAL CLAIM....3
Admin Plan: s10p2; s23p8; s23p8

SPECIAL CLAIMS....1
Admin Plan: s8p4

SPECIAL EQUIPMENT....6
24 CFR 5: .609;
7420.10G Gbk: 5-15 Ex 5-2; 5-30;
PIH Notices: 01-15; 01-15 Impr Integ Hbk; 01-15 Impr Integ Hbk

SPECIAL FEATURE....2
HUD-52580: p6;
HUD-52580-A: p19

SPECIAL FEATURES....3
7420.10G Gbk: 9-14 Ex 9-1; 9-16 Ex 9-2;
PIH Notices: 02-01

SPECIAL FEE....35
7420.10G Gbk: 20-5;
PIH Notices: 02-07; 01-41 (12); 01-10; 00-28 (3); 00-09 (16); 00-09

SPECIAL FEES....13
7420.10G Gbk: 20-3 (2); 20-4 (2); 20-6; 20-20; 20-21 Ex 20-4; 20-27 (2); 20-28; 20-29;
PIH Notices: 00-49; 00-28

SPECIAL HOUSING TYPE....23
24 CFR 982: .4 (6); .601 (9); .619;
HUD-52641: p1 (4);
7420.10G Gbk: 17-1 (2);
Admin Plan: s19p1

SPECIAL HOUSING TYPES....37
24 CFR 982: .4; .54; .601 (12);
HUD-52641: p1 (3);
7420.10G Gbk: 1-4; 3-5 (4); 10-1 (2); 11-10 (2); 17-1 (8); 19-4;
Admin Plan: s19p1; s19p1

SPECIAL INSPECTION....2
7420.10G Gbk: 10-30; 10-30

SPECIAL INSPECTIONS....8
7420.10G Gbk: 10-23 (2); 10-30 (3); 10-44 Ex 10-7a; 10-45 Ex 10-7b;
PIH Notices: 00-49

SPECIAL NEEDS....4
HUD-52641: p1;
7420.10G Gbk: 8-9; 21-8;
PIH Notices: 02-01

SPECIAL PAY....14
24 CFR 5: .609 (2);
HUD-50058Instr: p26 (2);
7420.10G Gbk: 5-14 Ex 5-2; 5-15 Ex 5-2; 23-12 (2);
PIH Notices: 03-05; 01-40; 01-15 Impr Integ Hbk (3); 01-15 Impr Integ Hbk

SPECIAL POLICIES....1
24 CFR 982: .54

SPECIAL PROGRAM....20
HUD-50058: p2; p ii;
HUD-50058Instr: p13; p61; p78;
7420.10G Gbk: 21-5; 21-11 (3); 21-13;
PIH Notices: 95-48 (3); 95-48 Tech Asst (3);
Admin Plan: s4p2; s19p1; s25p7; s25p8

SPECIAL PROGRAM ACCESSIBILITY....2
PIH Notices: 95-48; 95-48 Tech Asst

SPECIAL PROGRAM FUNDING....1
7420.10G Gbk: 4-21

SPECIAL PROGRAM REQUIREMENTS....1

24 CFR 982: .101

SPECIAL PROGRAMS 30
HUD-50058: p2 (5); p ii; p16;
HUD-50058Instr: p13; p59; p78;
7420.10G Gbk: 2-8; 8-8; 8-23; 21-13 (2); 21-15 Ex 21-5; 21-16 Ex 21-6; 21-17; 21-19; 21-20 (2);
PIH Notices: 95-48 (2); 95-48 Tech Asst (2);
Admin Plan: s4p2; s25p1 (3); s25p8

SPECIALIST 37
HUD-50058Instr: p4;
7420.10G Gbk: 4-13; 12-12 Ex 12-1 (3); 12-13 Ex 12-1; 12-14 Ex 12-2; 15-9 Ex 15-1; 15-10 Ex 15-2; 21-2; 21-3; 21-4 (10); 21-5 (2); 21-11; 21-12 Ex 21-3; 21-13; 21-15 Ex 21-5 (4); 21-16 Ex 21-6 (4); 22-10; 23-8 Ex 23-1;
Admin Plan: s7p8

SPECIALISTS................................15
7420.10G Gbk: 9-11; 21-3; 21-5 (2); 21-14 Ex 21-4 (2); 21-15 Ex 21-5; 21-16 Ex 21-6 (5);
PIH Notices: 01-15 (2); 01-15

SPECIALIZATION..........................17
7420.10G Gbk: 21-2 (2); 21-3 (8); 21-4 (2); 21-13 (4); 21-13

SPECIALIZED 15
7420.10G Gbk: 9-11; 17-1 (3); 21-3 (7); 23-1;
PIH Notices: 95-48; 95-48 Tech Asst;
Admin Plan: s25p2

SPECIALIZES..................................2
PIH Notices: 95-48; 95-48 Tech Asst

SPECIALIZING 1
7420.10G Gbk: 21-13

SPECIALLY 3
HUD-52580-A: p2;
7420.10G Gbk: 4-12;
PIH Notices: 00-53

SPECIALLY-DESIGNATED............1
7420.10G Gbk: 4-12

SPECIAL-PURPOSE 1
7420.10G Gbk: 3-7

SPECIFIC 208
24 CFR 5: .303; .306 (2); .380; .510; .609; .655;
24 CFR 982: .1 (2); .155; .207; .601 (4); .625;
HUD-50058Instr: p2; p12; p28; p61;
HUD-52580-A: p15;
HUD-903: p2;
7420.10G Gbk: 1-3; 1-6 (3); 1-7 (2); 1-8; 2-4; 2-6; 3-2; 3-4; 3-6; 4-2 (3); 4-3 (2); 4-4 (2); 4-7; 4-17; 4-19; 5-6; 5-15 Ex 5-2; 5-38; 5-39; 5-40; 6-2; 7-4; 7-6; 8-10; 8-18; 8-19; 8-22; 9-9; 9-10; 9-16 Ex 9-2; 10-1; 10-2; 10-5; 10-6; 10-15; 10-35; 11-1 (2); 11-2; 11-3; 12-4; 15-9 Ex 15-1; 17-1; 18-5; 19-2; 19-4; 19-7; 20-2; 20-5; 21-1; 21-2; 21-7; 21-11; 21-13; 22-4; 22-6; 22-8; 22-13; 23-6; 23-7; 23-15; 24-2; 24-3; 24-6; 24-10; 24-14;
PIH Notices: 03-23 (2); 03-11; 03-05; 02-27 (10); 02-21 (2); 02-20 (3); 02-07; 02-01 (5); 01-41 (9); 01-40; 01-15 (2); 01-15 Impr Integ Hbk (2); 01-10 (2); 01-02; 00-46 (3); 00-28; 00-11 (5); 00-11A (3); 00-09 (9); 99-52 (5); 99-11 (3); 95-48 (14); 95-48 Tech Asst (14);
Admin Plan: s1p4; s1p5; s3p3; s6p1; s7p2; s8p3; s15p4; s23p2 (2); s23p8; s24p4; s25p4 (2); s25p6

SPECIFIC DISABILITY...................7
24 CFR 5: .303; .655;
24 CFR 982: .207;
7420.10G Gbk: 4-17; 4-19;
PIH Notices: 02-01; 99-52

SPECIFIC PERFORMANCE...........2
HUD-52641: p5;
7420.10G Gbk: 11-18

SPECIFIC PERFORMANCE...........2
HUD-52641: p5;
7420.10G Gbk: 11-18

SPECIFICALLY 87
24 CFR 5: .309; .318; .518; .609 (6); .628;
24 CFR 982: .2; .3; .501; .504; .625;
HUD-50058: p viii;
HUD-50058Instr: p3; p26; p30; p31; p33; p37 (2); p70; p73;
HUD-52580-A: p18;

7420.10G Gbk: 1-7; 5-13; 5-14 Ex 5-2 (3); 5-15 Ex 5-2 (2); 5-16 Ex 5-2; 5-20 (2); 5-30; 5-43; 8-21; 10-2 (2); 10-28; 11-6; 13-10; 15-9 Ex 15-1; 15-10 Ex 15-2; 20-3; 22-3; 23-2; 24-14;
PIH Notices: 03-23; 03-12; 03-05; 02-27 (3); 02-20; 01-40; 01-15; 01-15 Impr Integ Hbk (11); 01-06 (2); 00-46; 00-11; 00-09; 95-48 (3); 95-48 Tech Asst (3);
Admin Plan: s1p6; s6p1; s6p12; s7p3; s23p1; s23p1

SPECIFICATION 5
24 CFR 5: .653;
24 CFR 982: .301; .308;
7420.10G Gbk: 8-21; 21-10

SPECIFICATIONS 2
Admin Plan: s24p5; s24p5

SPECIFICITY 2
24 CFR 5: .315;
Admin Plan: s23p6

SPECULATION 2
PIH Notices: 95-48; 95-48 Tech Asst

SPECULATORS 1
7420.10G Gbk: 9-1

SPEECH IMPAIRMENT 2
PIH Notices: 95-48; 95-48 Tech Asst

SPEECH IMPAIRMENTS 4
PIH Notices: 95-48 (2); 95-48 Tech Asst; 95-48 Tech Asst

SPEED 4
7420.10G Gbk: 5-35; 15-6; 24-13;
PIH Notices: 01-41

SPLIT 2
Admin Plan: s2p3; s8p5

SPLIT HOUSEHOLDS 2
Admin Plan: s2p3; s8p5

SPORADIC 11
24 CFR 5: .609;
HUD-50058Instr: p31;
7420.10G Gbk: 5-15 Ex 5-2; 5-19; 5-47 Ex 5-5;
PIH Notices: 01-15; 01-15 Impr Integ Hbk (3); 00-01; 98-66

SPORADIC INCOME 10
24 CFR 5: .609;
HUD-50058Instr: p31;
7420.10G Gbk: 5-15 Ex 5-2; 5-19;
PIH Notices: 01-15; 01-15 Impr Integ Hbk (3); 00-01; 98-66

SPOUSE 125
24 CFR 5: .230; .403 (3); .504; .518 (4); .522 (3); .603; .609 (2); .655 (2);
24 CFR 982: .4 (3); .207 (2); .315; .353; .634;
HUD-50058: p3; p4; p7 (6); p vii (6);
HUD-50058Instr: p2; p14 (5); p15 (2); p17 (3); p25 (2); p26 (3); p27; p33; p34; p35 (11); p36 (2); p61; p70 (2); p71 (3);
HUD-52641: p6;
7420.10G Gbk: 4-16 (2); 4-17 (2); 4-23 Ex 4-1; 4-25 Ex 4-2 (2); 4-27 Ex 4-2; 5-2 (2); 5-4 (2); 5-13; 5-14 Ex 5-2; 5-15 Ex 5-2; 5-18 (3); 5-29 (3); 5-31 (2); 5-32; 5-53 Ex 5-5; 12-13 Ex 12-1; 12-16 Ex 12-4; 13-2;
PIH Notices: 01-15 Impr Integ Hbk (5);
Admin Plan: s2p1; s2p2 (2); s5p1; s6p1 (2); s6p5 (2); s6p6; s7p3; s7p5; s11p1; s22p1; s25p2

SPOUSES 1
7420.10G Gbk: 5-4

SPOUSE'S 4
HUD-50058Instr: p26; p29 (2); p29

SPREADSHEET 5
7420.10G Gbk: 19-8 (2); 19-12;
PIH Notices: 02-20; 00-46

SPREADSHEETS 1
7420.10G Gbk: 12-8

SPRING 1
PIH Notices: 01-15 Impr Integ Hbk

SPRINKLER 13
24 CFR 982: .605 (2);
7420.10G Gbk: 17-2;
PIH Notices: 99-11 (8); 95-48; 95-48 Tech Asst

SRO 102
24 CFR 982: 24 CFR 982 (6); .4 (2); .601 (3); .602 (5); .604 (4); .605 (21);
HUD-50058: p i; p10; p11; p12 (2); p xii (4);
HUD-50058Instr: p3; p20 (2); p42 (2); p46 (2); p50 (6); p75;

HUD-52641: p1;
7420.10G Gbk: 3-5; 10-16; 11-10; 17-1 (3); 17-2 (14); 17-3 (4);
Admin Plan: s19p1 (8); s23p1 (2); s23p2 (2); s23p3

SSA 21
24 CFR 5: .214; .216 (3); .230; .234; .236;
HUD-50058: p i; p iii; p iv;
HUD-50058Instr: p3; p16 (2); p75;
7420.10G Gbk: 5-13 (2); 5-46 Ex 5-5 (2); 19-1;
PIH Notices: 01-15;
Admin Plan: s7p8

SSDI..1
7420.10G Gbk: 23-15

SSI...33
24 CFR 982: .627;
HUD-50058: p i; p6 (2);
HUD-50058Instr: p3; p29 (7); p75; p76;
7420.10G Gbk: 4-23 Ex 4-1; 5-23; 5-46 Ex 5-5 (2); 5-50 Ex 5-5 (2); 12-4; 12-13 Ex 12-1; 12-16 Ex 12-4; 23-15;
PIH Notices: 01-15 (5);
Admin Plan: s6p10; s7p4; s7p5; s7p8

SSN 81
24 CFR 5: .214; .216 (27); .218 (3);
HUD-50058: p i; p iii (3); p iv (2); p5; p v; p10; p x; p11; p xi; p12; p xii; p13; p xiii;
HUD-50058Instr: p3; p11; p16 (10); p18 (3); p42; p43; p47 (2); p50 (2); p53 (2); p75;
7420.10G Gbk: 5-12 (6); 12-5 (3); 12-5

STABILITY 1
7420.10G Gbk: 24-8

STABILIZATION 36
24 CFR 35 SubM: .1210; .1215 (2);
HUD-52580-A: p2 (3); p13 (3); p17 (3);
7420.10G Gbk: 10-17; 10-18 (9); 10-19 (5); 10-21 (3); 10-37 Ex 10-2; 20-4;
PIH Notices: 02-07 (2); 00-49; 00-49

STABILIZE...2
24 CFR 35 SubM: .1215;
7420.10G Gbk: 10-12

STABILIZED......................................4
HUD-52580-A: p2; p13; p17;
7420.10G Gbk: 10-18

STABLE RELATIONSHIP................2
Admin Plan: s2p2; s2p2

STAFF..486
24 CFR 5: .609;
24 CFR 982: .310; .553;
HUD-50058Instr: p5;
7420.10G Gbk: 2-4; 2-5 (4); 2-6; 3-1; 4-4 (2); 4-6 (4); 4-10 (2); 4-11 (2); 4-12 (6); 4-13 (6); 4-14 (2); 4-16; 4-18 (2); 4-22 (4); 5-15 Ex 5-2; 5-20; 5-31; 5-35; 5-38 (3); 5-45; 8-1 (2); 8-2 (4); 8-8; 8-9 (4); 8-11; 8-14; 8-23; 9-8 (4); 9-9; 9-10 (2); 9-11 (2); 9-12; 9-14 Ex 9-1 (2); 9-16 Ex 9-2 (2); 9-17 Ex 9-3; 10-1; 10-2 (3); 10-19; 10-22 (3); 10-24; 10-28 (2); 10-30 (2); 10-32 (2); 10-33; 10-35; 10-40 Ex 10-4a; 10-41 Ex 10-4b (2); 10-42 Ex 10-5; 10-43 Ex 10-6; 10-44 Ex 10-7a (2); 10-45 Ex 10-7b; 10-46 Ex 10-8 (2); 11-7 (2); 11-8; 11-10 (2); 11-15 (4); 11-19; 12-2; 12-3; 12-4 (3); 12-8 (5); 12-10; 13-4 (4); 13-6; 13-7; 13-9; 16-4 (7); 16-5; 19-1; 19-5 (4); 19-6 (2); 19-9 (2); 19-10 (5); 19-12 (5); 19-13 (5); 21-1 (2); 21-2 (11); 21-3 (8); 21-4 (2); 21-5 (5); 21-6; 21-7 (3); 21-8 (4); 21-9 (5); 21-10 (5); 21-11 (2); 21-13 (7); 21-17 (6); 21-18 (7); 21-19 (9); 21-20 (9); 22-1 (3); 22-3; 22-5 (5); 22-6; 22-7 (15); 22-8 (9); 22-9 (2); 22-10 (4); 22-11 (3); 22-17 (2); 22-18 (2); 23-16 Ex 23-2 (2); 24-2; 24-3; 24-6 (2); 24-7 (12); 24-8 (2); 24-9 (2); 24-10; 24-12; 24-13 (2); 24-15 (3);
PIH Notices: 03-23; 03-20 (2); 03-12; 03-11; 02-27 (16); 02-21; 02-20 (5); 02-07 (3); 02-01 (2); 01-41 (18); 01-20; 01-15 (6); 01-15 Impr Integ Hbk (2); 01-

06 (2); 00-53 (2); 00-49 (4); 00-46 (5); 00-41; 00-28 (3); 00-24B; 00-23; 00-11 (4); 00-11A (2); 00-09 (15); 99-52 (2); 99-11 (4); 95-48 (3); 95-48 Tech Asst (3);
Admin Plan: s1p1; s1p3 (3); s1p4 (2); s1p5 (2); s1p6 (3); s1p7; s2p1; s3p3; s7p1 (4); s8p1; s9p1; s17p3 (2); s18p1 (2); s18p5; s18p6; s20p1 (2); s20p2 (5); s20p3 (2); s20p4 (3); s20p6 (2); s20p7; s22p2; s25p1; s25p3 (2); s25p7; s25p8

STAFF PERSON 20
7420.10G Gbk: 2-6; 8-1; 10-35; 11-15; 19-5; 21-18; 21-19 (3); 22-8; 22-9;
PIH Notices: 01-41; 00-09;
Admin Plan: s3p3; s18p1; s20p4 (2); s20p6 (2); s20p7

STAFF PERSONS 2
7420.10G Gbk: 8-1;
Admin Plan: s18p6

STAFFING....................53
7420.10G Gbk: 1-1; 4-7; 4-12; 8-8; 9-11; 19-12; 21-1 (7); 21-2; 21-7 (2); 21-8; 21-9 (3); 21-10 (2); 21-13; 21-17 (5); 21-18 (4); 21-19 (5); 21-20 (2); 22-17 (2); 22-18; 24-6 (4); 24-7 (3);
PIH Notices: 02-27 (3); 02-27

STAFFING LEVEL 5
7420.10G Gbk: 21-1 (2); 24-6 (2); 24-7

STAFFING LEVELS....................12
7420.10G Gbk: 8-8; 21-1 (2); 21-17 (4); 21-18; 21-19 (2); 24-6; 24-7

STAFF'S 2
7420.10G Gbk: 19-12; 22-5

STAIR 1
HUD-52580-A: p8

STAIRCASES....................8
HUD-52580: p1;
HUD-52580-A: p8 (3); p9; p10; p11; p12

STAIRS....................24
24 CFR 5: .703 (3);
24 CFR 982: .401 (2);
HUD-52580: p5 (2);
HUD-52580-A: p13 (3); p14 (2); p17 (3); p18 (2);
7420.10G Gbk: 7-9; 10-9; 10-12 (2);
PIH Notices: 00-23; 95-48; 95-48 Tech Asst

STAIRWAY....................4
HUD-52580-A: p8; p17;
PIH Notices: 95-48; 95-48 Tech Asst

STAIRWAYS....................2
24 CFR 982: .614;
HUD-52580-A: p18

STAIRWELLS 1
HUD-52580-A: p17

STANDARD 756
24 CFR 5: .609; .628;
24 CFR 982: 24 CFR 982 (2); .1 (2); .4 (3); .301; .305; .308 (6); .310; .401; .402 (5); .502 (3); .503 (54); .504 (5); .505 (42); .508; .604 (5); .608 (7); .613 (6); .617 (6); .623 (2); .627 (3); .635 (13); .641; .643;
HUD-50058: p i; p vii (3); p11; p xi (2); p14; p xiv (3); p17;
HUD-50058Instr: p ii; p3 (2); p7 (2); p34; p35; p36 (2); p47 (9); p57 (4); p63 (2); p64; p74;
HUD-52580: p1 (4); p8;
HUD-52648: p2 (3);
7420.10G Gbk: 1-6 Ex 1-1; 1-11 (2); 5-7; 5-14 Ex 5-2; 7-1; 7-7; 8-21 (2); 9-9 (2); 10-1; 10-2 (4); 19-2; 19-12; 20-15; 20-26; 22-6; 24-2; 24-13;
PIH Notices: 03-23; 02-27 (4); 02-22 (9); 02-20 (119); 02-06; 02-01 (3); 01-41 (34); 01-15 Impr Integ Hbk (2); 01-10 (20); 01-06 (44); 01-01 (41); 00-46 (96); 00-41; 00-24A (4); 00-24B (3); 00-09 (51); 99-52 (3); 99-11; 95-48 (18); 95-48 Tech Asst (18);
Admin Plan: s5p3 (3); s6p4; s8p2; s9p1; s9p2; s11p1; s11p3 (4); s15p3; s19p1 (21); s20p4; s21p1; s21p6; s21p9; s22p2; s23p3; s24p4

STANDARD AMOUNTS 4
PIH Notices: 02-20 (2); 00-46; 00-46

STANDARD FORM.........................7
HUD-52641: p3;
7420.10G Gbk: 8-21 (4); 9-8; 11-12
STANDARD FORM.........................11
24 CFR 982: .308 (3);
HUD-52641: p3;
7420.10G Gbk: 8-21 (4); 9-8; 11-12;
Admin Plan: s9p2
STANDARD FORMAT.....................2
HUD-50058: p i;
HUD-50058Instr: p3
STANDARD FORMS 2
7420.10G Gbk: 12-3; 22-8
STANDARD FORMS 2
7420.10G Gbk: 12-3; 22-8
STANDARD HOUSING...................2
7420.10G Gbk: 10-1;
PIH Notices: 01-41
STANDARD OF PROOF 1
24 CFR 982: .310
STANDARD PRACTICE..................2
HUD-52641: 8;
HUD-52641-A: p1
STANDARD PRACTICE..................2
HUD-52641: 8;
HUD-52641-A: p1
STANDARDIZATION 2
7420.10G Gbk: 22-7;
PIH Notices: 96-65
STANDARDIZE..............................1
HUD-52665: p1
STANDARDIZED..........................11
7420.10G Gbk: 1-4; 4-7; 4-13; 19-1; 19-3 (2); 19-4; 22-6 (2); 22-11; 22-11
STANDARDIZING..........................1
PIH Notices: 00-09
STANDARDS...............................470
24 CFR 5: .318 (2); .350 (2); .514; .516; .661; .703 (5); .705; .801 (2);
24 CFR 35 SubM: .1225;
24 CFR 982: 24 CFR 982 (9); .1; .4 (5); .54 (4); .204; .301 (2); .306; .310; .355 (3); .401 (5); .402 (14); .403 (5); .517 (2); .553 (7); .554; .555 (3); .605 (7); .609 (3); .614 (4); .618 (4); .621; .625; .631; .635;
HUD-50058: p i; p v (2); p xiv;
HUD-50058Instr: p3; p15; p21; p47; p56; p63; p72 (3); p73 (7); p75 (2);
HUD-52580: p1; p6;
HUD-52580-A: p1 (3); p8 (3); p19;
HUD-52641: p6; p10;
HUD-52641-A: p3;
HUD-52648: p2 (4);
7420.10G Gbk: 3-1 (2); 3-4; 3-6 (2); 4-8; 5-41; 5-42 (2); 8-6; 8-17 (2); 8-19; 9-5; 9-11 (2); 9-16 Ex 9-2; 10-1; 10-2 (6); 10-3 (2); 10-4; 10-5; 10-8; 10-9; 10-14 (4); 10-15; 10-26; 10-32; 11-3; 15-6; 17-1; 17-2 (2); 17-7; 17-9; 19-1; 19-12 (3); 20-17; 21-1; 22-2; 24-2; 24-13 (2);
PIH Notices: 03-12; 03-11 (6); 02-27 (3); 02-20 (11); 02-07; 02-01 (7); 01-41 (19); 01-06 (8); 01-01 (11); 00-49; 00-46 (12); 00-41; 00-28; 00-24B (4); 00-23 (3); 00-09 (17); 99-52 (6); 99-11 (5); 95-48 (42); 95-48 Tech Asst (38);
Admin Plan: s1p1; s5p1 (9); s5p2 (7); s5p3 (7); s6p1; s6p6; s6p13; s7p1; s8p2 (2); s8p3; s9p3; s9p4; s10p1 (7); s10p3 (5); s10p4 (2); s11p1 (3); s11p3 (2); s11p1; s15p6; s18p1; s18p2; s18p3; s19p1 (8); s21p1; s21p2; s21p4; s21p6; s21p7; s22p3; s23p5 (3); s24p1 (2); s24p2; s24p5; s24p7
STATE AGENCY.............................18
24 CFR 5: .214; .609;
HUD-50058Instr: p28;
HUD-9886: p1;
7420.10G Gbk: 5-15 Ex 5-2; 22-16;
PIH Notices: 01-41; 01-15 Impr Integ Hbk (2); 01-06 (7); 00-23; 00-09
STATE HOUSING AGENCY...........1
24 CFR 5: .518
STATE HOUSING FINANCE AGENCY 2
24 CFR 5: .214; .653
STATE IDENTIFICATION 1
PIH Notices: 03-11

STATE LAW 28
24 CFR 5: .210 (2);
24 CFR 982: .310; .503;
HUD-50058Instr: p72; p73 (2);
HUD-52641: p9;
HUD-52641-A: p2;
7420.10G Gbk: 2-9; 4-27 Ex 4-2; 8-4; 15-2; 15-6;
PIH Notices: 02-20 (2); 01-41; 01-06 (2); 00-46 (2); 00-24B; 00-09; 95-48 (2);
Admin Plan: s10p5; s15p2; s23p3

STATE LAW ENFORCEMENT........ 1
PIH Notices: 03-11

STATE LAWS 10
7420.10G Gbk: 12-16 Ex 12-4;
PIH Notices: 00-23; 95-48 (4); 95-48 Tech Asst (3); 95-48 Tech Asst

STATEMENT 205
24 CFR 5: .230; .234; .350; .353 (2);
24 CFR 982: .2; .4; .102 (7); .201; .207; .301; .307 (2); .552; .554 (2); .555; .633 (3);
HUD-52517: p2 (2);
HUD-52641: p5;
HUD-52665: p1; p2 (2);
HUD-52667: p1 (2);
7420.10G Gbk: 3-1 (2); 3-7 (4); 3-8 (2); 4-9; 5-8; 5-39 (2); 5-40; 5-46 Ex 5-5 (2); 5-47 Ex 5-5 (6); 5-48 Ex 5-5 (2); 5-49 Ex 5-5; 5-50 Ex 5-5 (2); 5-51 Ex 5-5 (2); 5-52 Ex 5-5; 8-15; 10-36 Ex 10-1; 11-2 (3); 11-3; 12-4 (2); 12-13 Ex 12-1 (3); 12-15 Ex 12-3; 12-16 Ex 12-4 (2); 13-3; 16-1 (2); 16-3; 20-3; 20-4 (2); 20-5 (3); 20-9 (3); 20-10 (2); 20-12 Ex 20-2; 20-13; 20-15; 20-18 (2); 20-26; 20-27 (3); 20-29 (3); 22-1; 22-4; 23-5; 24-1; 24-2; 24-15;
PIH Notices: 03-12; 03-11; 02-27 (13); 02-21 (5); 02-07 (10); 02-06; 02-01 (4); 01-20; 01-15 Impr Integ Hbk (5); 01-06 (5); 00-53 (2); 00-49 (2); 00-28 (8); 00-24B; 99-52 (4); 95-48 (2); 95-48 Tech Asst (2);
Admin Plan: s1p1 (2); s1p4; s1p6; s6p8; s7p4; s7p5 (5); s7p6; s7p7; s8p2; s9p3; s11p1; s17p2; s18p8; s21p8; s22p4; s23p4 (4); s23p7 (2); s24p3; s25p5

STATEMENTS 67
24 CFR 5: .353; .514; .528; .801 (4);
24 CFR 982: .158;
HUD-52648: p3;
7420.10G Gbk: 2-3; 4-27 Ex 4-2 (2); 5-12 (2); 5-46 Ex 5-5 (3); 5-48 Ex 5-5 (2); 5-49 Ex 5-5 (3); 5-53 Ex 5-5; 11-18; 12-11 (3); 12-13 Ex 12-1; 12-16 Ex 12-4 (2); 20-9;
PIH Notices: 02-27; 02-01; 01-15 (3); 01-15 Impr Integ Hbk (6); 01-06 (5); 99-52;
Admin Plan: s6p7; s7p4 (2); s7p5 (3); s7p6 (6); s7p8; s20p1; s20p4 (2); s20p6; s20p7; s20p7

STATISTICAL 17
24 CFR 5: .100;
24 CFR 982: .201; .503;
HUD-50058Instr: p74;
7420.10G Gbk: 4-15; 4-19; 4-23 Ex 4-1; 4-25 Ex 4-2; 20-2;
PIH Notices: 02-20 (3); 01-06; 00-46 (3);
Admin Plan: s8p1

STATISTICAL COUNTERPART...... 5
24 CFR 982: .503;
PIH Notices: 02-20 (2); 00-46; 00-46

STATISTICALLY 11
24 CFR 982: .503 (2);
7420.10G Gbk: 7-5;
PIH Notices: 02-20 (4); 00-46 (3); 00-46

STATISTICS 2
7420.10G Gbk: 24-3; 24-3

STATUS 273
24 CFR 5: .318; .500 (2); .504 (6); .506 (2); .508 (34); .510 (6); .512 (11); .514 (14); .516; .518 (4); .520 (7); .524; .528; .659;
24 CFR 982: .51 (2); .53; .158; .201; .202 (2); .207; .304; .551; .552 (2); .554; .555;
HUD-50058: p iii; p iv; p5 (2); p v (3); p16 (2);

p xvi;
HUD-50058Instr: p9; p15 (6); p17 (6); p18 (7); p20; p21 (4); p59 (2); p60 (3); p68; p71 (2); p73 (2);
HUD-52665: p2 (2);
HUD-903: p1; p2 (3); p3; p4;
7420.10G Gbk: 1-7; 4-5 (2); 4-7 (2); 4-10; 4-14; 4-15; 4-16; 5-1; 5-3; 5-4 (2); 5-5 (2); 5-6 (5); 5-7; 5-8 (2); 5-9 Ex 5-1 (5); 5-10 Ex 5-1 (3); 5-35; 5-50 Ex 5-5 (8); 5-51 Ex 5-5; 5-53 Ex 5-5; 6-7; 8-14; 10-34; 12-3; 12-5; 12-13 Ex 12-1; 13-4; 15-5 (2); 16-3 (2); 19-3; 19-5; 19-6; 19-13; 20-11; 21-3; 22-3 (3); 23-6; 23-12 (2);
PIH Notices: 03-11; 02-27 (5); 02-21; 01-27 (2); 01-15 (2); 01-15 Impr Integ Hbk (2); 01-06 (3); 01-02; 00-24B; 95-48 (2);
Admin Plan: s1p2; s1p5; s2p1 (2); s2p2; s2p5 (4); s2p7; s3p2; s3p3 (2); s6p6; s6p7; s7p1; s7p3 (3); s7p4; s7p5 (3); s7p7 (2); s8p6; s18p1; s18p7 (2); s18p8

STATUTE 11
24 CFR 5: .236; .609; .653;
HUD-50058Instr: p31;
7420.10G Gbk: 5-16 Ex 5-2; 22-4;
PIH Notices: 03-11; 01-41; 01-15 Impr Integ Hbk;
Admin Plan: s6p5; s6p5

STATUTE OF LIMITATIONS 1
PIH Notices: 03-11

STATUTES 11
HUD-52641: p5; p10;
HUD-52641-A: p3;
PIH Notices: 02-21; 02-01; 01-20; 01-15; 01-02; 99-52; 95-48; 95-48 Tech Asst

STATUTORY 44
24 CFR 5: .110; .306; .516 (3);
24 CFR 982: .202;
HUD-50058Instr: p37;
7420.10G Gbk: 1-4; 6-1; 6-7;
PIH Notices: 02-22; 02-01 (9); 01-41; 01-15 Impr Integ Hbk; 01-10 (2); 00-53; 00-11; 00-09 (6); 99-52 (9); 95-48; 95-48 Tech Asst

STATUTORY FORMS 2
24 CFR 5: .516 (2)

STATUTORY FORMS OF ASSISTANCE 2
24 CFR 5: .516; .516

STATUTORY FORMULA 2
7420.10G Gbk: 6-1;
PIH Notices: 02-22

STATUTORY REQUIREMENT 3
24 CFR 982: .202;
PIH Notices: 01-15 Impr Integ Hbk; 00-11

STATUTORY REQUIREMENTS 4
7420.10G Gbk: 1-4;
PIH Notices: 02-01; 00-09; 99-52

STEPBROTHER 1
HUD-52641: p6

STEPCHILD 1
HUD-52641: p6

STEPPARENT 1
HUD-52641: p6

STEPS 93
24 CFR 5: .520; .703;
24 CFR 982: .301; .310; .401 (2); .614;
HUD-52580-A: p13 (3); p17; p18;
HUD-52667: p i (2);
HUD-903: p2;
7420.10G Gbk: 1-1; 2-2; 2-8; 2-9; 3-5 (2); 3-8; 4-20; 5-5 (2); 5-7; 5-11; 6-7; 9-10; 10-10; 10-13; 17-5; 19-2; 19-13; 20-8; 20-10; 20-11; 20-14; 20-15; 20-19 Ex 20-3; 21-8; 22-6; 22-13; 24-3;
PIH Notices: 03-23 (3); 02-21; 02-01; 01-41 (8); 01-10; 00-09 (9); 99-52; 95-48 (10); 95-48 Tech Asst (10);
Admin Plan: s20p1; s20p2 (2); s20p4; s25p7

STEPSISTER 1
HUD-52641: p6

STEREO 1
7420.10G Gbk: 10-9

STEREOTYPES 4
PIH Notices: 95-48 (2); 95-48 Tech Asst; 95-48 Tech Asst

STIPEND 16
24 CFR 5: .609 (3);
HUD-50058Instr: p25 (2);

7420.10G Gbk: 5-15 Ex 5-2 (2);
PIH Notices: 01-15 Impr Integ Hbk (8); 01-15 Impr Integ Hbk

STIPENDS 3
HUD-50058Instr: p25;
PIH Notices: 01-15 Impr Integ Hbk; 01-15 Impr Integ Hbk

STOCKHOLDER 1
24 CFR 5: .216

STOCKS 14
24 CFR 5: .603;
HUD-50058Instr: p22; p74;
7420.10G Gbk: 4-26 Ex 4-2; 4-27 Ex 4-2; 5-25 Ex 5-3; 5-27 (2); 5-28; 5-48 Ex 5-5; 12-13 Ex 12-1; 12-16 Ex 12-4;
PIH Notices: 01-15 Impr Integ Hbk;
Admin Plan: s7p5

STOPPING THE CLOCK 5
24 CFR 982: .4; .54;
HUD-50058Instr: p75;
7420.10G Gbk: 3-2; 8-13

STORAGE SPACE 1
7420.10G Gbk: 10-6

STORM DRAINAGE 1
24 CFR 5: .703

STOVE.. 34
24 CFR 982: .401 (4); .614;
HUD-52580: p2; p6 (2);
HUD-52580-A: p4 (8); p5 (4); p19 (2);
7420.10G Gbk: 9-14 Ex 9-1; 9-15 Ex 9-2; 10-4 (3); 10-5 (3); 10-6 (2);
Admin Plan: s10p1; s10p1

STOVES 4
HUD-52580-A: p4; p15;
7420.10G Gbk: 10-5; 10-7

STRAIGHT LINE DEPRECIATION 5
24 CFR 5: .609;
HUD-50058Instr: p25;
7420.10G Gbk: 5-14 Ex 5-2;
PIH Notices: 01-15 Impr Integ Hbk; 01-15 Impr Integ Hbk

STRAIGHT-LINE 3
7420.10G Gbk: 5-19; 5-48 Ex 5-5;
Admin Plan: s7p5

STRICTLY LIABLE 1
24 CFR 5: .318

STRUCTURAL 60
HUD-52580-A: p2 (4); p13 (5); p17;
PIH Notices: 02-01 (6); 99-52 (6); 95-48 (21); 95-48 Tech Asst (16); 95-48 Tech Asst

STRUCTURAL CHANGES 12
PIH Notices: 02-01; 99-52; 95-48 (5); 95-48 Tech Asst (4); 95-48 Tech Asst

STRUCTURAL MODIFICATIONS 14
PIH Notices: 02-01; 99-52; 95-48 (8); 95-48 Tech Asst (3); 95-48 Tech Asst

STRUCTURALLY 12
24 CFR 5: .703 (3);
24 CFR 982: .401 (2); .614;
7420.10G Gbk: 10-9 (3); 17-5;
PIH Notices: 95-48; 95-48 Tech Asst

STRUCTURALLY SOUND 10
24 CFR 5: .703 (3);
24 CFR 982: .401 (2); .614;
7420.10G Gbk: 10-9 (3); 17-5

STRUCTURE 53
24 CFR 5: .353;
24 CFR 35 SubM: .1200;
24 CFR 982: Intro; .1; .4; .401 (4); .614 (4); .631;
HUD-50058: p5; p v;
HUD-50058Instr: p11; p21 (2); p73;
HUD-52580-A: p13; p15 (6);
7420.10G Gbk: 3-7; 8-15; 10-1; 10-9 (3); 10-38 Ex 10-3; 17-5; 17-10; 20-1; 21-1 (2); 21-11; 21-13;
PIH Notices: 02-01; 00-24B; 99-52; 99-11; 95-48; 95-48 Tech Asst;
Admin Plan: s9p2; s10p5; s11p2; s19p1; s22p3; s22p3

STRUCTURED 1
Admin Plan: s21p1

STRUCTURES 13
HUD-50058Instr: p21;
HUD-52667: p i;
7420.10G Gbk: 10-39 Ex 10-4; 21-11;
PIH Notices: 02-01 (3); 00-09; 99-52 (3); 99-11; 99-11

STUDENT 63
24 CFR 5: .522 (9); .603 (2); .609 (3);
HUD-50058: p3; p4; p7;
HUD-50058Instr: p14 (2); p15; p25 (2); p26; p27; p31 (2); p32; p36 (2); p71; p72;
7420.10G Gbk: 5-4 (2); 5-5 (2);

5-15 Ex 5-2 (2); 5-16 Ex 5-2; 5-20 (3); 12-3;
PIH Notices: 01-15 Impr Integ Hbk (9); 95-48 (2); 95-48 Tech Asst (2);
Admin Plan: s3p3; s6p6 (2); s7p3; s7p5 (3); s25p5

STUDENT FINANCIAL ASSISTANCE 8
24 CFR 5: .609;
HUD-50058Instr: p31;
7420.10G Gbk: 5-15 Ex 5-2; 5-20 (2);
PIH Notices: 01-15 Impr Integ Hbk (2); 01-15 Impr Integ Hbk

STUDENT STATUS 1
Admin Plan: s7p5

STUDENTS 31
24 CFR 5: .522 (2);
HUD-50058: p vii;
HUD-50058Instr: p15; p36;
7420.10G Gbk: 5-4; 12-13 Ex 12-1;
PIH Notices: 01-15 Impr Integ Hbk (2); 95-48 (8); 95-48 Tech Asst (8);
Admin Plan: s3p2; s6p1; s6p7; s7p3; s7p5; s7p5

STUDENTS-....................................... 1
Admin Plan: s2p5

SUBCONTRACTOR........................ 7
24 CFR 982: .161; .553;
HUD-50058Instr: p13;
HUD-52641: p6;
7420.10G Gbk: 8-19; 11-2; 11-3

SUBCONTRACTORS 4
24 CFR 982: .157; .161;
HUD-52641: p6;
7420.10G Gbk: 11-14

SUBJECT TO CHANGE.................. 3
24 CFR 982: .451;
HUD-52641: p2; p4

SUBLEASE 5
24 CFR 982: .4; .551;
HUD-52641: 8;
HUD-52641-A: p1;
HUD-52646: p2

SUBLET 2
7420.10G Gbk: 1-2; 5-36 Ex 5-4

SUBLETTING................................. 1
7420.10G Gbk: 1-15

SUBMISSION 94
24 CFR 5: .508 (3); .514; .659 (2); .801 (4);
24 CFR 982: .157; .551;
HUD-52648: p1 (2); p2; p3 (2);
7420.10G Gbk: 1-5; 3-6 (2); 4-12; 4-23 Ex 4-1; 5-6 (3); 5-36 Ex 5-4; 7-10 (3); 8-13; 12-5; 13-4; 14-5; 20-2; 20-7; 20-29; 21-4; 24-2;
PIH Notices: 03-23; 03-20 (2); 03-11 (4); 02-27 (5); 02-21 (7); 02-20; 02-14 (2); 02-01; 01-20 (3); 01-15; 01-15 Impr Integ Hbk (2); 01-06 (7); 00-53 (3); 00-46; 00-34 (2); 00-27 (3); 00-24 (2); 00-24A; 00-24B; 99-52; 96-65;
Admin Plan: s3p1; s21p8 (2); s22p2; s24p2

SUBMISSIONS 13
PIH Notices: 03-20; 03-11 (6); 02-27; 01-15; 01-06 (2); 00-34; 00-24

SUBMIT 253
24 CFR 5: .210; .216 (9); .230 (3); .232; .353 (2); .508 (11); .514; .661; .801 (6);
24 CFR 982: .51; .53; .103; .157; .302 (3); .305 (2); .310; .355 (2); .551; .552 (3);
HUD-50058: p i;
HUD-50058Instr: p1; p2 (3); p9; p13 (2); p37; p59;
HUD-52646: p1; p2;
HUD-52648: p1;
HUD-52665: p2 (4);
7420.10G Gbk: 1-10; 1-11 (2); 2-3; 2-4; 3-7; 4-3 (2); 4-16; 5-6 (3); 5-7; 5-11; 5-35; 5-37; 8-11; 8-15 (4); 8-17 (2); 10-25; 11-2; 11-18; 11-19; 12-4; 12-5; 14-5 (2); 15-5; 15-7; 16-1; 19-1; 19-2 (6); 19-3 (2); 20-6; 20-14; 20-22; 20-28 (9); 20-29 (4); 23-3; 23-8 Ex 23-1; 23-14; 24-4; 24-6;
PIH Notices: 03-23 (7); 03-20; 03-11 (9); 02-27 (17); 02-21 (6); 02-20; 02-14 (3); 02-07; 01-43; 01-41 (3); 01-20 (4); 01-15 (3); 01-11; 01-06 (16); 01-01; 00-53 (5); 00-49; 00-46; 00-34 (7); 00-28 (2); 00-27 (4); 00-24; 00-24B (3); 00-14 (2); 00-09 (7); 96-

65; 95-48; 95-48 Tech Asst;
Admin Plan: s1p7; s3p1; s8p4; s8p5; s9p1 (2); s9p2; s15p1; s21p2; s24p3; s25p6

SUBORDINATE................................7
24 CFR 5: .514;
24 CFR 982: .554; .555;
7420.10G Gbk: 16-3; 16-4;
Admin Plan: s18p2; s18p6

SUBSIDIARY....................................8
7420.10G Gbk: 20-7; 20-23 (6); 23-13

SUBSIDIARY LEDGER...................1
7420.10G Gbk: 23-13

SUBSIDIARY LEDGERS.................2
7420.10G Gbk: 20-23; 20-23

SUBSIDIES 20
24 CFR 5: .617;
24 CFR 982: .1;
HUD-50058: p iii; p iv;
HUD-50058Instr: p14; p28; p72; p75;
7420.10G Gbk: 1-2; 1-3; 8-16; 9-1; 13-1; 23-15;
PIH Notices: 01-15; 01-15 Impr Integ Hbk (2); 00-24B (2);
Admin Plan: s6p3

SUBSIDIZE.. 7
24 CFR 982: .1; .204;
HUD-50058Instr: p42;
7420.10G Gbk: 4-18; 8-10; 24-8; 24-8

SUBSIDIZED.................................45
24 CFR 5: .318 (2);
24 CFR 982: 24 CFR 982 (2); .310; .401; .504; .521 (4);
HUD-50058: p viii; p10; p x;
HUD-50058Instr: p1 (2); p19; p38; p42; p43 (3); p47;
HUD-52517: p1;
HUD-52580-A: p4;
7420.10G Gbk: 2-13 Ex 2-1; 4-25 Ex 4-2; 5-27; 8-22; 9-11 (2); 9-13 Ex 9-1; 9-14 Ex 9-1; 10-4; 10-6; 23-6; 23-10; 23-16 Ex 23-2;
PIH Notices: 02-01; 01-02; 99-52;
Admin Plan: s8p4; s9p2;
:
24 CFR 982: Intro; .521 (2); .521

SUBSIDY......................................357
24 CFR 5: .520 (7);
24 CFR 982: 24 CFR 982 (2); .1 (6); .4 (3); .54; .205 (3); .301; .311; .317; .352 (5); .355 (2); .402 (12); .403 (3); .505; .517; .551; .554; .555 (2); .635;
HUD-50058: p5; p9 (2); p ix (5); p10; p x (2); p xi (2); p xii (2); p xiii (2); p14 (2); p xiv (2); p17 (3);
HUD-50058Instr: p13; p17; p39; p40 (11); p42; p43 (4); p44 (5); p47; p48 (6); p51 (5); p54 (6); p57 (6); p63 (3); p68 (6); p69 (11); p72; p74; p75 (2);
HUD-52517: p1 (3);
HUD-52641: p10;
HUD-52641-A: p3 (2);
HUD-52646: p2;
7420.10G Gbk: 1-1; 1-2; 1-3 (2); 1-4; 1-5 (2); 1-6 Ex 1-1 (3); 1-9; 1-10; 1-15; 1-16 Ex 1-3; 5-3; 5-5 (2); 5-38; 6-1; 6-2 (7); 6-3 (2); 6-4 (4); 6-6 (2); 6-7; 6-10 Ex 6-2 (4); 7-1; 8-2; 8-5 (4); 8-6; 8-22; 9-11; 11-3; 11-5; 12-6; 12-7 (3); 12-9; 13-5 (2); 13-7; 13-8; 13-9 (2); 14-1 (2); 14-2; 19-8; 19-10 (4); 20-3; 20-24; 20-26; 20-27; 20-29; 22-1 (2); 22-2; 22-3; 22-6 (2); 22-11 (2); 22-12 (5); 22-13 (2); 22-14; 23-13 (2);
PIH Notices: 02-22; 02-21; 01-41 (35); 01-15; 01-10 (5); 00-41; 00-24B (2); 00-09 (35);
Admin Plan: s2p2; s5p1 (7); s5p2 (5); s5p3 (2); s6p6; s8p2; s14p1; s18p2; s18p3; s22p2; s22p3; s22p4; s23p3; s23p4; s24p4; s24p7

SUBSIDY STANDARD....................9
24 CFR 982: .402;
7420.10G Gbk: 12-7 (5); 14-2; 17-5;
Admin Plan: s23p3

SUBSIDY STANDARDS................82
24 CFR 982: 24 CFR 982 (2); .4 (2); .54; .301; .355 (2); .402 (9); .403 (3); .517; .554;

.555 (2); .635;
HUD-50058Instr: p47; p72; p75;
7420.10G Gbk: 2-10; 3-4 (3); 5-41 (6); 8-6; 12-7 (3); 13-4; 13-7; 16-1; 16-2; 18-2; 23-7; 23-12;
PIH Notices: 01-41 (9); 00-09 (9);
Admin Plan: s5p1 (5); s5p2 (5); s5p3; s6p6; s18p2; s18p3; s24p7

SUBSISTENCE 1
HUD-50058Instr: p26

SUBSISTENCE ALLOWANCES 1
HUD-50058Instr: p26

SUBSTANCE 23
24 CFR 5: .100; .603; .801;
HUD-50058Instr: p71;
HUD-52580-A: p15;
HUD-903-1: p2;
7420.10G Gbk: 4-25 Ex 4-2; 5-37 (2); 5-43;
PIH Notices: 95-48 (2); 95-48 Tech Asst (2);
Admin Plan: s6p3; s15p2; s15p3 (2); s23p1; s23p2; s25p2; s25p3; s25p3

SUBSTANCE ABUSE 9
24 CFR 5: .603;
HUD-50058Instr: p71;
HUD-903-1: p2;
Admin Plan: s6p3; s23p1; s23p2; s25p2; s25p3; s25p3

SUBSTANDARD 6
24 CFR 5: .518;
HUD-50058Instr: p72;
7420.10G Gbk: 22-2; 22-6;
Admin Plan: s21p9; s21p9

SUBSTANDARD HOUSING 2
HUD-50058Instr: p72;
7420.10G Gbk: 4-17

SUBSTANDARD UNIT 1
7420.10G Gbk: 22-2

SUBSTANTIAL 48
24 CFR 5: .100; .528; .801 (2);
24 CFR 982: .520 (2);
HUD-52580-A: p2;
HUD-52665: p1;
7420.10G Gbk: 7-7; 8-8; 8-12; 8-16; 19-3; 21-13; 21-19; 22-15 (2);
PIH Notices: 03-23; 02-01 (5); 01-41; 01-15 Impr Integ Hbk; 01-10; 00-11; 00-09; 99-52 (5); 95-48 (6); 95-48 Tech Asst (6);
Admin Plan: s15p3; s23p1; s24p3

SUBSTANTIAL ADMINISTRATIVE 1
7420.10G Gbk: 22-15

SUBSTANTIAL IMPAIRMENT....... 2
PIH Notices: 95-48; 95-48 Tech Asst

SUBSTANTIAL REHABILITATION 9
24 CFR 5: .801 (2);
7420.10G Gbk: 8-16; 21-13;
PIH Notices: 02-01 (2); 99-52 (2);
Admin Plan: s23p1

SUBSTANTIATE 1
7420.10G Gbk: 20-14

SUBTRACT 52
24 CFR 5: .520;
24 CFR 982: .102;
HUD-50058: p vii (2); p ix; p x (2); p xi (3); p xii (4); p xiii (3); p xiv (3);
HUD-50058Instr: p22; p34; p36; p40; p44; p45; p48 (3); p49; p51 (2); p52 (2); p54; p55 (2); p57 (2);
HUD-52648: p2;
7420.10G Gbk: 6-7; 20-8 Ex 20-1; 20-10 (2); 20-11; 23-17 Ex 23-2 (6);
PIH Notices: 03-23

SUBTRACTED 11
24 CFR 982: .605;
HUD-50058: p xiii;
HUD-50058Instr: p54;
7420.10G Gbk: 5-22 (2); 20-11; 24-4;
PIH Notices: 02-21; 02-14; 01-15 Impr Integ Hbk;
Admin Plan: s6p1

SUBTRACTING 12
24 CFR 5: .520;
24 CFR 982: .515 (2); .605;
HUD-50058: p xi;
HUD-50058Instr: p49;
7420.10G Gbk: 5-28; 6-6; 8-5; 20-27;
PIH Notices: 01-15; 01-15 Impr Integ Hbk

SUBTRACTION 1
PIH Notices: 01-15 Impr Integ Hbk

SUCCESS 162
24 CFR 982: .503 (8);
HUD-50058Instr: p1;
7420.10G Gbk: 2-5; 2-8; 2-10; 2-11 (2); 3-7; 7-2; 7-3 (3); 7-4 (3); 7-

9 (2); 7-10 (3); 8-1; 8-11 (2); 8-14 (2); 8-22 (2); 8-23; 11-4; 12-8; 19-6; 19-8 (5); 19-9; 19-11 (6); 19-12; 20-17; 21-5; 21-7; 21-8; 21-9 (2); 21-11; 23-1; 24-4 (9); 24-5 (3); 24-6 (8); 24-8 (3); 24-9 (3); 24-10 (7); 24-11; 24-12 (2); 24-14;
PIH Notices: 02-20 (9); 02-06 (3); 01-06; 01-01 (46); 00-46; 00-11 (4);
Admin Plan: s8p1; s8p1

SUCCESS RATE 86
24 CFR 982: .503 (8);
7420.10G Gbk: 2-10; 7-2; 7-3 (3); 7-4 (2); 7-9 (2); 7-10 (2); 8-1; 8-11; 19-8 (3); 19-9; 24-4 (4); 24-5; 24-6 (5); 24-8 (2); 24-10 (2); 24-11;
PIH Notices: 02-20 (9); 01-06; 01-01 (35); 00-46

SUCCESS RATES 42
7420.10G Gbk: 2-11; 7-4; 8-11; 8-14; 8-22; 11-4; 19-8 (2); 19-11 (2); 19-12; 20-17; 21-5; 21-7; 21-8; 21-9 (2); 21-11; 24-4 (5); 24-5; 24-6 (3); 24-8; 24-9 (2); 24-10 (2);
PIH Notices: 02-06; 01-01 (7);
Admin Plan: s8p1; s8p1

SUCCESSFUL...............................70
24 CFR 982: .310; .552; .625;
7420.10G Gbk: 2-6; 2-7; 2-8; 4-4 (2); 4-14; 5-37; 5-40; 7-3; 7-9; 7-10; 8-9; 8-22; 9-12; 12-4; 15-7 (2); 19-9; 19-11; 20-15; 20-17; 21-9; 21-10; 21-19 (2); 23-7 (2); 24-4; 24-5 (9); 24-6; 24-10; 24-12; 24-15;
PIH Notices: 02-27 (3); 02-21; 02-06; 01-41; 01-01 (9); 00-09 (2); 95-48; 95-48 Tech Asst;
Admin Plan: s1p2; s2p6; s8p3; s22p2; s25p1; s25p5; s25p8

SUCCESSFUL COMPLETION...... 11
24 CFR 982: .310; .552;
7420.10G Gbk: 5-37; 15-7; 23-7 (2);
PIH Notices: 02-27 (2);
Admin Plan: s2p6; s22p2; s25p5

SUCCESSFULLY..........................40
24 CFR 982: .310 (3); .552 (3); .553; .625;
HUD-50058Instr: p11;
HUD-52648: p2;
7420.10G Gbk: 2-4; 2-7; 7-3; 7-4; 7-10; 8-8; 15-7 (2); 19-9;
PIH Notices: 03-11; 02-27 (2); 01-06 (4); 01-01 (2); 00-53; 00-28; 00-11; 95-48 (4); 95-48 Tech Asst (4);
Admin Plan: s22p2

SUCCESSIVE 2
24 CFR 982: .627;
PIH Notices: 01-10

SUCCESSOR...................................5
24 CFR 982: .401 (2);
HUD-52580-A: p8 (2);
7420.10G Gbk: 10-14

SUFFER..2
PIH Notices: 01-41; 00-09

SUFFERED 2
PIH Notices: 01-41; 00-09

SUFFERING....................................4
HUD-50058Instr: p32;
7420.10G Gbk: 5-16 Ex 5-2;
PIH Notices: 01-15 Impr Integ Hbk;
Admin Plan: s25p3

SUFFERS...8
PIH Notices: 01-41 (3); 01-10 (2); 00-09 (2); 00-09

SUFFICIENT 83
24 CFR 5: .350; .353; .508; .518; .661;
24 CFR 982: .102; .204 (2); .313; .314; .401; .553; .609; .614; .627; .637;
HUD-50058Instr: p60;
HUD-52580-A: p2;
HUD-52667: p ii;
7420.10G Gbk: 1-8; 4-1; 4-5 (2); 4-8; 4-9; 4-18 (2); 5-49 Ex 5-5; 5-50 Ex 5-5; 5-53 Ex 5-5; 8-9 (2); 8-10; 9-4; 9-10; 10-6; 10-8; 15-7; 18-8; 19-9 (2); 20-13; 22-14; 22-17; 22-18;
PIH Notices: 03-23 (3); 02-27 (5); 02-06 (2); 02-01; 01-43; 01-41 (2); 01-20; 01-15 Impr Integ Hbk; 01-10 (2); 01-06; 00-53; 00-27; 00-09; 99-52; 99-11; 95-48 (2); 95-48 Tech Asst (2);
Admin Plan: s5p2; s7p5; s7p6; s7p7; s8p1; s11p1; s16p3;

s23p3; s25p1; s25p3
SUFFICIENT EVIDENCE................3
24 CFR 982: .553;
7420.10G Gbk: 22-14;
Admin Plan: s16p3
SUFFICIENT FUNDING..................4
24 CFR 982: .314; .637;
PIH Notices: 01-20; 01-10
SUFFICIENTLY................................4
PIH Notices: 01-20; 00-53; 00-27;
Admin Plan: s7p7
SUGGEST...1
7420.10G Gbk: 21-1
SUGGESTED.................................12
24 CFR 982: .630;
7420.10G Gbk: 9-10; 9-19 Ex 9-4; 13-4; 22-13;
PIH Notices: 01-15; 00-24B (5); 99-11
SUGGESTING.................................3
7420.10G Gbk: 7-3; 14-4; 17-1
SUGGESTION.................................2
7420.10G Gbk: 8-8; 24-15
SUGGESTIONS...............................7
HUD-50058Instr: p3;
7420.10G Gbk: 4-3; 4-10; 7-5; 9-4;
PIH Notices: 02-27;
Admin Plan: s1p5
SUGGESTS.......................................5
7420.10G Gbk: 5-38; 7-7; 19-7; 22-4; 24-11
SUITABILITY...............................19
24 CFR 982: .54; .307 (2); .552;
HUD-52517: p2;
HUD-52641: p3;
HUD-9886: p1;
7420.10G Gbk: 1-14; 3-3; 5-38; 5-39; 5-40 (2); 8-21; 11-12;
Admin Plan: s2p6; s9p3; s23p3; s23p4
SUITABILITY FOR TENANCY....10
24 CFR 982: .54; .307 (2); .552;
HUD-52517: p2;
HUD-52641: p3;
7420.10G Gbk: 1-14; 5-40; 8-21; 11-12
SUITABLE....................................69
24 CFR 5: .100; .403;
24 CFR 982: .1; .4; .54 (2); .205; .206; .304; .401; .452; .503; .609;
HUD-50058: p i;
HUD-50058Instr: p15; p74;
HUD-52646: p1; p2;
HUD-52667: p i;
7420.10G Gbk: 1-7; 2-2; 3-3; 4-1; 4-3; 4-8; 4-12; 4-13; 7-4; 7-6; 8-1; 8-3; 8-12 (2); 8-15; 10-4; 10-43 Ex 10-6; 11-17; 15-4; 17-1; 23-7; 24-4; 24-8; 24-10;
PIH Notices: 03-05; 02-22; 02-21 (2); 02-20; 02-07 (2); 02-01 (2); 01-40; 01-20 (2); 00-28 (2); 00-24B; 99-52 (2);
Admin Plan: s1p3; s1p6; s5p3; s16p2; s23p4 (2); s25p2; s25p4; s25p4
SUMMARIZATION..........................1
PIH Notices: 01-06
SUMMARIZE..................................7
HUD-903: p1;
7420.10G Gbk: 9-9; 19-1; 22-6; 22-11;
PIH Notices: 02-20; 00-46
SUMMARIZED................................4
24 CFR 5: .353;
7420.10G Gbk: 19-13; 20-7;
PIH Notices: 01-06
SUMMARIZES.................................16
HUD-50058Instr: p5;
7420.10G Gbk: 1-15; 12-8; 19-2; 20-11; 20-23 (2); 21-17 (2);
PIH Notices: 02-27 (2); 02-20; 02-01; 00-53; 00-46; 99-52
SUMMARIZING..............................2
PIH Notices: 02-20; 00-46
SUMMER.......................................14
HUD-52580-A: p8; p15 (2);
7420.10G Gbk: 5-17;
PIH Notices: 01-15; 01-15 Impr Integ Hbk; 00-24 (2); 95-48 (3); 95-48 Tech Asst (2); 95-48 Tech Asst
SUMMER MONTHS........................6
HUD-52580-A: p8; p15 (2);
7420.10G Gbk: 5-17; 5-52 Ex 5-5; 10-24
SUPERMARKET.............................1
PIH Notices: 01-15 Impr Integ Hbk
SUPERMARKETS...........................1
7420.10G Gbk: 4-3
SUPERVISE....................................1
7420.10G Gbk: 21-13

SUPERVISED....18
24 CFR 982: .310 (2); .552 (2); .553;
HUD-50058Instr: p72;
7420.10G Gbk: 10-37 Ex 10-2; 15-7 (2); 21-14 Ex 21-4;
PIH Notices: 95-48 (3); 95-48 Tech Asst (3);
Admin Plan: s23p2; s25p3

SUPERVISED DRUG....8
24 CFR 982: .310 (2); .552 (2); .553;
7420.10G Gbk: 15-7;
PIH Notices: 95-48; 95-48 Tech Asst

SUPERVISED DRUG REHABILITATION....3
24 CFR 982: .553;
PIH Notices: 95-48; 95-48 Tech Asst

SUPERVISING....2
7420.10G Gbk: 12-8; 21-13

SUPERVISION....11
24 CFR 5: .318 (2); .653;
HUD-50058Instr: p28;
7420.10G Gbk: 21-3; 21-10; 21-13 (2); 21-15 Ex 21-5; 21-19; 23-15

SUPERVISOR....27
HUD-52580-A: p13;
HUD-52648: p1;
7420.10G Gbk: 9-10; 9-11 (2); 10-32; 10-37 Ex 10-2 (2); 13-7 (2); 19-5; 21-13; 21-20; 22-6 (2); 24-13;
PIH Notices: 01-15 (2);
Admin Plan: s10p2; s18p1 (4); s18p2; s20p2; s20p3; s21p4

SUPERVISORS....4
7420.10G Gbk: 19-13; 21-13 (2);
Admin Plan: s20p3

SUPERVISOR'S....1
HUD-52648: p1

SUPERVISORY....13
24 CFR 982: .405;
7420.10G Gbk: 12-2; 18-10; 21-2; 21-13 (3);
PIH Notices: 02-20 (2); 01-15; 00-46 (2); 00-24B

SUPERVISORY QUALITY CONTROL....2
24 CFR 982: .405;
PIH Notices: 00-24B

SUPPLEMENT....47
24 CFR 5: .236; .500; .504 (2); .520 (6); .601; .603;
PIH Notices: 02-01; 01-41 (13); 01-27 (2); 00-41; 00-24 (4); 00-24A (2); 00-09 (10); 99-52;
Admin Plan: s23p1

SUPPLEMENTAL....33
24 CFR 5: .214; .609 (2); .801;
24 CFR 982: .627;
HUD-50058: p i;
HUD-50058Instr: p3; p5; p29; p75; p76;
HUD-52580-A: p10; p11; p12;
7420.10G Gbk: 5-15 Ex 5-2 (2); 5-46 Ex 5-5; 8-7 (2); 9-8; 12-4; 12-16 Ex 12-4; 20-4;
PIH Notices: 02-01; 01-41 (2); 01-15 (2); 01-15 Impr Integ Hbk (3); 99-52;
Admin Plan: s11p2

SUPPLEMENTARY....8
24 CFR 5: .801;
24 CFR 982: .628;
7420.10G Gbk: 20-29;
PIH Notices: 01-15; 01-15 Impr Integ Hbk; 95-48; 95-48 Tech Asst;
Admin Plan: s7p4

SUPPLEMENTED....2
PIH Notices: 02-01; 99-52

SUPPLEMENTS....3
24 CFR 982: .352;
HUD-50058Instr: p29;
7420.10G Gbk: 8-16

SUPPLIED....60
24 CFR 5: .659;
24 CFR 982: .308 (2); .401; .551; .605 (2);
HUD-50058: p ix (2); p x (2); p xi (2); p xii (2); p xiii; p xv;
HUD-50058Instr: p39; p40; p43; p44; p47; p49; p50; p52; p54; p58;
HUD-52580-A: p4; p15;
HUD-52641: p1 (4);
7420.10G Gbk: 5-7; 10-5; 10-6; 11-11; 18-8;
PIH Notices: 03-20 (2); 03-12; 01-15 (4); 01-15 Impr Integ Hbk (3); 01-06 (9);
Admin Plan: s3p3; s9p2; s9p2

SUPPLIER....12
24 CFR 5: .632 (4);
24 CFR 982: .514 (3);
7420.10G Gbk: 11-6; 18-2;

PIH Notices: 01-15 Impr Integ Hbk (2); 01-15 Impr Integ Hbk

SUPPLIERS....................................13
HUD-52641: p6;
HUD-52667: p i (4);
7420.10G Gbk: 11-13; 18-2 (2); 18-4 (4); 18-9

SUPPLIERS'....................................1
7420.10G Gbk: 18-6

SUPPLIES 6
HUD-52646: p2;
7420.10G Gbk: 2-3;
PIH Notices: 03-12; 02-27; 01-01;
Admin Plan: s21p5

SUPPLY 67
24 CFR 5: .518; .659 (3);
24 CFR 982: .312; .401 (3); .551 (3); .633 (2);
HUD-52580: p5;
HUD-52580-A: p6; p15 (3); p16 (2);
HUD-52641: p6;
HUD-52646: p2 (2);
HUD-52667: p ii;
7420.10G Gbk: 3-3; 4-9; 7-6; 8-12; 8-21 (2); 10-1; 10-11 (4); 10-28; 11-12; 11-18; 18-4; 24-15 (3);
PIH Notices: 03-11 (2); 02-20; 02-14; 01-15; 01-15 Impr Integ Hbk (4); 01-06; 01-01 (2); 00-46; 99-11 (3);
Admin Plan: s1p2; s2p3; s3p3; s7p2; s8p2; s15p6 (2); s16p1; s22p4

SUPPLYING....................................8
24 CFR 982: .551; .633;
HUD-52580-A: p4 (2);
7420.10G Gbk: 1-14; 5-36 Ex 5-4 (2);
Admin Plan: s10p1

SUPPORT 139
24 CFR 5: .403; .508; .514 (4); .609;
24 CFR 982: .401; .454;
HUD-50058: p6;
HUD-50058Instr: p5; p15; p27; p28 (2); p30 (2); p73;
HUD-52580-A: p2; p6;
HUD-52641: p3;
7420.10G Gbk: 1-8; 1-11; 2-1; 2-4; 4-1; 4-4; 4-26 Ex 4-2 (2); 5-11; 5-14 Ex 5-2; 5-19; 5-23 (3); 5-29; 5-47 Ex 5-5 (2); 5-50 Ex 5-5; 7-1; 7-5 (2); 7-7; 8-11 (2); 8-12; 10-6; 10-8; 11-5; 12-11 (2); 12-13 Ex 12-1; 12-16 Ex 12-4; 16-5; 19-1; 20-11; 20-13 (3); 20-15 (6); 20-16; 20-21 Ex 20-4; 21-2; 21-5; 21-19; 22-17; 23-5 (2); 23-15; 23-19; 24-9;
PIH Notices: 03-23 (4); 03-20 (3); 03-11; 03-05 (3); 02-27 (2); 02-21; 02-06 (4); 02-01; 01-41; 01-40 (3); 01-20; 01-15 (2); 01-15 Impr Integ Hbk (5); 01-11; 00-53 (3); 00-11; 00-11A (3); 99-52; 95-48 (2); 95-48 Tech Asst (2);
Admin Plan: s1p1 (2); s2p3; s6p9 (5); s7p4 (3); s7p5; s11p3; s17p1; s21p2; s23p1; s23p2; s24p3; s25p1

SUPPORTING RECORDS................1
7420.10G Gbk: 20-1

SUPPORTIVE.................................52
24 CFR 5: .318 (2); .403; .601 (4); .603 (3); .617; .801 (2);
24 CFR 982: .4; .152; .316; .352 (2); .510 (3);
HUD-50058Instr: p13; p15; p27; p28 (2); p72; p73 (2); p75 (3);
PIH Notices: 02-01 (2); 00-41 (2); 00-11; 00-11A (3); 99-52 (2);
Admin Plan: s4p2 (2); s18p4; s23p2 (2); s24p4; s25p2 (2); s25p3; s25p4

SUPPORTIVE HOUSING.................6
24 CFR 5: .601; .801 (2);
24 CFR 982: .352 (2);
Admin Plan: s4p2

SUPPORTIVE SERVICE 3
7420.10G Gbk: 4-3; 23-4;
Admin Plan: s4p2

SUPPORTIVE SERVICES.............50
24 CFR 5: .318 (2); .403;
24 CFR 982: .4; .152; .316; .510 (3);
HUD-50058Instr: p13; p15; p27; p28 (2); p72; p73 (2); p75 (3);
HUD-52641: p1; 8 (2); p10;
HUD-52641-A: p1 (2); p3;
7420.10G Gbk: 23-2 (2); 23-5 (3); 23-9; 23-15;
PIH Notices: 02-01 (2); 00-41 (2); 00-11; 00-11A (3); 99-52 (2);

Admin Plan: s18p4; s23p2 (2); s24p4; s25p3; s25p4
SURCHARGE 4
PIH Notices: 95-48 (2); 95-48 Tech Asst; 95-48 Tech Asst
SURCHARGES 4
PIH Notices: 95-48 (2); 95-48 Tech Asst; 95-48 Tech Asst
SURRENDERING..............................1
PIH Notices: 01-15 Impr Integ Hbk
SURROUNDING 7
24 CFR 5: .661;
7420.10G Gbk: 2-13 Ex 2-1 (2); 22-14;
PIH Notices: 95-48; 95-48 Tech Asst;
Admin Plan: s10p5
SURROUNDING AREAS 1
Admin Plan: s10p5
SURROUNDING COMMUNITY 1
24 CFR 5: .661
SURVEY 61
24 CFR 982: .503 (2);
7420.10G Gbk: 2-4 (2); 2-5; 7-5 (2); 9-3 (3); 9-4 (2); 9-7; 9-13 Ex 9-1; 21-17 (5); 21-18 (6);
PIH Notices: 03-20; 03-11; 02-20 (16); 00-46 (16);
Admin Plan: s6p11; s11p2
SURVEYS.......................................19
7420.10G Gbk: 2-4 (2); 2-7; 7-5 (2); 9-3; 9-4 (4); 21-17; 21-18 (2);
PIH Notices: 02-20 (2); 00-46 (2);
Admin Plan: s21p2; s21p2
SUSPEND.......................................12
24 CFR 5: .630 (2);
HUD-52665: p3;
7420.10G Gbk: 4-21 (2); 6-8; 8-13; 11-18; 16-2 (2);
Admin Plan: s4p2; s18p2
SUSPENDED 23
24 CFR 5: .105 (2);
24 CFR 982: .305; .306; .628; .631;
HUD-50058Instr: p37;
HUD-52641: p6;
7420.10G Gbk: 6-8; 8-17; 8-18; 10-25; 11-1;
PIH Notices: 03-23; 01-41 (2); 00-09; 95-48; 95-48 Tech Asst;
Admin Plan: s6p5; s9p2; s11p1; s16p1
SUSPENDING.................................3
7420.10G Gbk: 8-13; 11-12;
PIH Notices: 01-11
SUSPENSION 42
24 CFR 5: .236 (5); .630 (4);
24 CFR 982: .4; .54; .303 (4); .404; .552; .554; .555;
HUD-50058Instr: p75;
HUD-52641: p3; p4; p5;
7420.10G Gbk: 3-2 (3); 6-8 (2); 8-13 (3); 13-4; 21-9;
Admin Plan: s6p4; s6p5 (5); s8p5; s18p4; s24p6
SUSPENSIONS 7
24 CFR 982: .54 (3); .301;
7420.10G Gbk: 8-5;
PIH Notices: 01-41; 00-09
SWICA...13
24 CFR 5: .214; .234 (4); .236 (6);
PIH Notices: 01-15; 01-15
SWICAS 17
24 CFR 5: .210 (2); .214; .230; .234 (2); .659;
HUD-50058Instr: p71;
7420.10G Gbk: 5-13 (2);
PIH Notices: 01-15 (6); 01-15 Impr Integ Hbk
SWITCH 6
HUD-52580-A: p6;
PIH Notices: 01-15 Impr Integ Hbk (3); 01-11; 00-53
SWITCHES.......................................6
24 CFR 5: .703 (2);
HUD-52580-A: p2;
7420.10G Gbk: 10-9;
PIH Notices: 02-01; 99-52
SWITCHING 3
7420.10G Gbk: 11-7; 11-8;
PIH Notices: 01-15 Impr Integ Hbk
SYNCHRONIZATION.....................2
7420.10G Gbk: 20-9; 20-9
SYNCHRONIZE 4
24 CFR 982: .102 (2);
7420.10G Gbk: 20-9; 20-9
SYNONYMOUS 1
HUD-50058Instr: p70
SYSTEM.......................................306
24 CFR 5: .214; .512 (6); .526; .703 (2);
24 CFR 982: .157; .202 (2); .207 (3); .401 (8); .605 (3); .614 (2); .624; .626;
HUD-50058: p i; p iii;
HUD-50058Instr: p1 (2); p2; p3; p5; p11; p16; p74;
HUD-52580-A: p6 (4); p7;

p8; p9; p10; p11; p12; p15 (24); p16 (2);
HUD-52667: p ii;
7420.10G Gbk: 1-11; 4-9 (2); 4-13 (4); 4-16 (6); 4-18 (6); 4-19; 4-21; 5-7 (2); 5-9 Ex 5-1; 5-20; 5-44; 8-7; 8-22 (2); 8-23 (6); 9-2; 9-9 (2); 9-12 (2); 9-17 Ex 9-3; 10-3 (2); 10-5 (2); 10-7 (5); 10-8 (5); 10-9; 10-14; 10-22 (2); 10-25 (4); 10-26 (2); 10-30; 10-31; 10-33 (2); 10-34 (5); 10-35 (2); 11-7 (4); 11-8 (4); 11-9 (2); 11-10 (2); 12-3; 12-8; 13-8; 17-2; 17-5; 17-12; 19-1 (4); 19-9; 19-12; 20-13; 21-3 (2); 21-4; 21-8 (3); 21-9; 22-5 (6); 22-6 (2); 23-6; 23-19; 24-5; 24-12;
PIH Notices: 03-20 (4); 03-11 (3); 02-27 (7); 02-21; 02-20; 01-43; 01-15 (2); 01-15 Impr Integ Hbk (4); 01-11 (2); 01-06 (28); 00-53 (4); 00-46; 00-34 (6); 00-28; 00-24; 00-14 (2); 00-11 (3); 99-11 (3); 95-48 (11); 95-48 Tech Asst (11);
Admin Plan: s6p4 (2); s7p2; s11p1; s17p2; s18p7; s19p1; s21p1; s21p2 (3); s21p3

SYSTEMATIC ALIEN VERIFICATION 2
24 CFR 5: .512;
7420.10G Gbk: 5-7

TANF 76
24 CFR 5: .603; .609 (2); .617 (2);
HUD-50058: p i; p6; p16 (2); p xvi; p17;
HUD-50058Instr: p3; p28 (8); p60; p61 (2); p63 (3);
7420.10G Gbk: 1-7; 2-11 (3); 4-23 Ex 4-1; 12-4; 23-3; 23-8 Ex 23-1; 23-15; 23-16 Ex 23-2 (5); 23-20 (4); 24-9;
PIH Notices: 01-15 (3); 01-15 Impr Integ Hbk (7); 00-11 (17); 00-11A;
Admin Plan: s6p2; s6p3; s7p5

TANK 7
24 CFR 5: .703;
24 CFR 982: .401; .614;
HUD-52580-A: p15;
7420.10G Gbk: 10-13; 17-5; 18-7

TANKS 1
7420.10G Gbk: 10-7

TARC 31
HUD-50058Instr: p2;
7420.10G Gbk: 20-14 (3);
PIH Notices: 02-27 (8); 01-43; 01-11; 01-06 (13); 00-53 (3); 00-24

TARGET 62
24 CFR 5: .613;
24 CFR 982: .202;
HUD-50058Instr: p1;
7420.10G Gbk: 1-10; 4-1; 4-2 (2); 4-19 (3); 5-2; 5-22; 19-1; 19-8; 20-20; 20-21 Ex 20-4; 20-21; 21-8; 22-10;
PIH Notices: 02-27; 01-41 (20); 00-11 (4); 00-11A (4); 00-09 (12);
Admin Plan: s22p2; s24p4

TARGETED 42
24 CFR 982: Intro; .203 (3);
7420.10G Gbk: 1-6 (2); 1-8 (2); 3-2 (4); 3-7 (2); 4-2; 4-4 (2); 4-21 (2); 4-22; 7-6; 17-1; 19-2; 21-8; 21-11;
PIH Notices: 02-27 (2); 02-01; 01-41 (3); 01-01; 00-11A; 00-09 (2); 99-52;
Admin Plan: s1p7; s4p1; s4p2 (3); s4p2

TARGETING 56
24 CFR 5: .617; .653 (2); .655;
24 CFR 982: Intro; .102; .201 (9);
HUD-50058: p5; p v;
HUD-50058Instr: p19 (5);
7420.10G Gbk: 4-5 (2); 4-8; 4-19 (2); 4-20; 4-21 (2); 5-3; 13-7 (2); 20-17; 21-8; 24-4;
PIH Notices: 02-01; 01-41 (3); 01-15 Impr Integ Hbk; 00-11 (3); 00-11A (3); 00-09 (3); 99-52;
Admin Plan: s3p2; s4p1; s4p2 (2); s11p3

TARGETS 2
PIH Notices: 02-27; 02-27

TASS 4
PIH Notices: 01-15 (3); 01-15

TAX CREDIT 28
24 CFR 982: .352;

HUD-50058: p16; p xvi;
HUD-50058Instr: p32; p60;
HUD-52517: p1;
7420.10G Gbk: 5-16 Ex 5-2;
PIH Notices: 02-22 (11); 02-15; 01-15 Impr Integ Hbk; 01-02 (7);
Admin Plan: s24p4

TAX CREDITS 5
HUD-50058Instr: p28;
7420.10G Gbk: 23-15; 24-15;
PIH Notices: 02-22; 01-15 Impr Integ Hbk

TAX DATA 4
7420.10G Gbk: 22-4;
Admin Plan: s7p3 (2); s7p3

TAX RETURN.................................11
HUD-9886: p1 (2);
7420.10G Gbk: 5-13; 5-48 Ex 5-5; 22-4 (3);
Admin Plan: s2p2; s7p2; s7p4; s7p5

TAX RETURNS 3
7420.10G Gbk: 5-50 Ex 5-5;
PIH Notices: 01-15 Impr Integ Hbk;
Admin Plan: s7p4

TDD 23
HUD-903: p3;
7420.10G Gbk: 5-44; 8-3;
PIH Notices: 95-48 (11); 95-48 Tech Asst (8); 95-48 Tech Asst

TECHNICAL ASSISTANCE 59
HUD-50058Instr: p3;
7420.10G Gbk: 1-10; 1-13; 11-7; 19-4; 19-5;
PIH Notices: 02-27 (25); 02-01 (4); 01-41 (2); 01-06; 00-09 (2); 99-52 (4); 99-11; 95-48 (8); 95-48 Tech Asst (5); 95-48 Tech Asst

TEENAGER 1
7420.10G Gbk: 5-38

TELECOMMUNICATION 6
PIH Notices: 95-48 (3); 95-48 Tech Asst (2); 95-48 Tech Asst

TELECOMMUNICATIONS 4
PIH Notices: 95-48 (2); 95-48 Tech Asst; 95-48 Tech Asst

TELEPHONE 163
24 CFR 5: .100; .214; .603;
24 CFR 982: .4; .517;
HUD-50058Instr: p76;
HUD-52580-A: p1 (2);
HUD-52646: p2 (6); p3 (9);
7420.10G Gbk: 2-3; 4-10; 4-13 (2); 4-23 Ex 4-1 (2); 4-27 Ex 4-2 (2); 5-35; 5-46 Ex 5-5 (2); 5-47 Ex 5-5 (4); 5-48 Ex 5-5; 5-49 Ex 5-5 (2); 5-50 Ex 5-5; 5-51 Ex 5-5 (2); 5-52 Ex 5-5 (2); 5-53 Ex 5-5 (2); 8-7; 9-8; 10-26; 10-34; 10-40 Ex 10-4a; 10-44 Ex 10-7a; 10-45 Ex 10-7b; 10-46 Ex 10-8; 10-48 Ex 10-10 (2); 12-13 Ex 12-1; 12-16 Ex 12-4 (2); 13-1; 13-3; 13-4; 13-8; 13-10; 13-11 Ex 13-1; 18-1; 21-9; 24-9; 24-12; 24-13;
PIH Notices: 03-20; 03-11 (2); 02-27 (4); 02-22; 01-41 (3); 01-06; 00-09; 00-01 (3); 99-11 (3); 98-66 (2); 95-48 (30); 95-48 Tech Asst (30);
Admin Plan: s3p1; s6p6; s6p13; s7p1; s7p6; s10p3; s18p1; s18p3; s20p1; s21p6

TELEPHONE CALLS.........................1
7420.10G Gbk: 24-9

TELEPHONES 15
7420.10G Gbk: 21-9;
PIH Notices: 95-48 (7); 95-48 Tech Asst (6); 95-48 Tech Asst

TELEVISION 11
24 CFR 982: .517;
7420.10G Gbk: 2-5; 4-3;
PIH Notices: 95-48 (3); 95-48 Tech Asst (3);
Admin Plan: s3p1; s6p13

TEMPERAMENT..............................1
24 CFR 5: .350

TEMPORARILY.............................48
24 CFR 5: .100 (2); .318 (2); .508; .609;
24 CFR 982: .201; .402;
HUD-50058: p v;
HUD-50058Instr: p10; p17; p19; p33; p36; p70;
HUD-52580-A: p2; p17;
HUD-52665: p3;
7420.10G Gbk: 3-3; 5-1; 5-5; 5-6; 5-13; 5-18 (2); 5-41; 20-18 (2);
PIH Notices: 03-23; 03-05 (3); 01-40 (3); 01-15 Impr Integ Hbk; 99-11;
Admin Plan: s2p2; s6p5 (5);

s6p6 (2); s15p3 (2); s24p3

TEMPORARILY ABSENT 18
24 CFR 5: .609;
HUD-50058: p v;
HUD-50058Instr: p17; p33; p36; p70;
7420.10G Gbk: 5-13; 5-18 (2);
PIH Notices: 03-05 (2); 01-40 (2); 01-15 Impr Integ Hbk;
Admin Plan: s6p5 (3); s6p5

TEMPORARILY AWAY.................... 5
24 CFR 982: .201; .402;
7420.10G Gbk: 5-1; 5-41;
Admin Plan: s2p2

TEMPORARY 122
24 CFR 5: .403; .506; .508; .516 (7); .518 (6); .520; .522; .603; .609 (2); .617 (2); .630 (6);
24 CFR 982: .401 (2); .520 (2); .609; .614;
HUD-50058: p i;
HUD-50058Instr: p3; p18 (3); p25; p28; p31; p37; p72 (3);
HUD-52580-A: p15; p18;
7420.10G Gbk: 3-3; 4-14; 5-8; 5-9 Ex 5-1; 5-10 Ex 5-1 (2); 5-15 Ex 5-2 (2); 5-19 (2); 6-8 (3); 10-5; 20-15; 21-6; 24-9;
PIH Notices: 03-05; 02-27; 02-06 (2); 01-41; 01-40; 01-15 Impr Integ Hbk (7); 01-06 (2); 00-11 (2); 00-11A; 00-09 (2); 00-01 (5); 98-66 (5); 95-48 (6); 95-48 Tech Asst (6);
Admin Plan: s2p2; s2p4; s6p5 (5); s6p7 (2); s18p8; s23p2 (2); s25p3; s25p3

TEMPORARY ABSENCE 3
24 CFR 5: .403;
HUD-50058Instr: p72;
Admin Plan: s2p2

TEMPORARY ASSISTANCE......... 13
24 CFR 5: .603; .609; .617 (2);
HUD-50058: p i;
HUD-50058Instr: p3; p28;
7420.10G Gbk: 24-9;
PIH Notices: 01-15 Impr Integ Hbk (2); 00-11 (2); 00-11A

TEMPORARY ASSISTANCE TO NEEDY FAMILIES.......................... 2
HUD-50058Instr: p28;
PIH Notices: 00-11

TEMPORARY DEFERRAL........... 21
24 CFR 5: .506; .508; .516 (7); .518 (6); .520; .522;
HUD-50058Instr: p18 (2);
7420.10G Gbk: 5-8;
Admin Plan: s18p8

TEMPORARY DEFERRAL OF TERMINATION 18
24 CFR 5: .506; .508; .516 (6); .518 (6); .520; .522;
HUD-50058Instr: p18; p18

TEMPORARY INCOME 1
7420.10G Gbk: 5-19

TEMPORARY RESIDENCE 4
HUD-50058Instr: p72;
7420.10G Gbk: 3-3;
Admin Plan: s23p2; s25p3

TEMPORARY RESIDENT 2
7420.10G Gbk: 5-9 Ex 5-1; 5-10 Ex 5-1

TEN 19
24 CFR 982: .605 (2); .634;
7420.10G Gbk: 5-27; 20-19 Ex 20-3; 24-3 (2); 24-4;
PIH Notices: 02-20; 01-41; 00-09; 95-48; 95-48 Tech Asst;
Admin Plan: s3p3 (2); s11p1; s18p7; s20p6; s22p4

TEN DAY.. 1
Admin Plan: s20p6

TEN DAYS 3
7420.10G Gbk: 13-8 (2);
Admin Plan: s18p7

TEN PERCENT 2
7420.10G Gbk: 20-19 Ex 20-3;
PIH Notices: 02-20

TEN YEARS..................................... 3
24 CFR 982: .634;
7420.10G Gbk: 24-15;
Admin Plan: s22p4

TENANCIES 11
24 CFR 982: .501 (2);
7420.10G Gbk: 1-5 (2); 5-40 (2); 11-10; 14-2;
PIH Notices: 01-33 (2); 00-09

TENANCY.................................... 379
24 CFR 5: .218 (2); .232; .309; .312; .318 (2); .321; .353 (5); .359 (3); .360; .514 (2); .520 (8);
24 CFR 982: 24 CFR 982 (11); .1 (3); .4 (2); .54 (2); .162; .301; .302 (6); .303 (2); .305 (10); .306 (5); .307 (7);

.308 (11); .309; .310 (20); .355 (2); .401; .402 (2); .452; .456; .501 (4); .502 (13); .503; .504 (2); .505; .507; .508; .510; .516 (2); .518; .519; .520; .521 (2); .552; .554; .555; .619; .622 (2); .623 (3); .636; .641 (8);
HUD-50058: p v;
HUD-50058Instr: p2; p21; p75;
HUD-52517: p2;
HUD-52580-A: p1;
HUD-52641: p3 (2); p4 (2); p6; 8 (3); p9 (7); p10 (3);
HUD-52641-A: p1 (3); p2 (7); p3 (3);
HUD-52646: p1 (2);
7420.10G Gbk: 1-14; 1-16 Ex 1-3; 3-4 (3); 5-38; 5-39 (4); 5-40 (5); 8-1 (3); 8-4; 8-6; 8-13; 8-15 (5); 8-16; 8-17 (2); 8-18 (7); 8-19 (2); 8-20 (3); 8-21 (4); 8-22 (2); 9-2; 9-7; 10-1; 10-18; 10-19; 10-24; 10-25 (2); 10-26 (5); 10-27 (2); 11-1 (2); 11-2; 11-12 (2); 11-13; 11-14 (4); 11-16 Ex 11-1 (2); 11-17; 11-18 (2); 11-19; 13-5; 14-1; 14-2; 15-1 (4); 15-2 (5); 15-3 (4); 15-5; 16-2 (2); 21-4; 21-10; 24-7; 24-9; 24-11; 24-12; 24-14;
PIH Notices: 03-12 (2); 03-05; 02-20; 02-01 (3); 01-41 (12); 01-40; 01-33; 01-10 (2); 00-49; 00-46; 00-09 (6); 99-52 (3);
Admin Plan: s2p6 (4); s2p7; s8p2 (2); s8p3; s8p4; s8p5; s9p1 (4); s9p2 (3); s9p3 (3); s11p2; s14p1 (3); s15p1 (2); s15p5 (3); s16p2 (2); s18p2; s19p1 (3); s23p6; s23p6

TENANCY ADDENDUM 82
24 CFR 982: .162; .302; .305 (2); .308 (6); .456; .636;
HUD-52517: p2;
HUD-52641: p1; p2; p3 (2); p5; p6 (2); 8 (4); p10 (5);
HUD-52641-A: p1 (4); p3 (6);
HUD-52646: p1 (5); p2;
7420.10G Gbk: 1-14; 8-6; 8-15 (2); 8-16; 8-21 (6); 11-1; 11-10; 11-12 (2); 11-13 (2); 11-14 (6); 11-15 (2); 11-19 (3); 12-6; 15-2;
PIH Notices: 01-41; 00-09 (2);
Admin Plan: s8p2; s9p2; s9p3; s9p3

TENANCY--RENT 1
24 CFR 982: .521

TENANT ASSESSMENT SUB-SYSTEM...1
PIH Notices: 01-15

TENANT CERTIFICATIONS...........1
7420.10G Gbk: 10-34

TENANT CONTRIBUTION.............1
24 CFR 982: .452

TENANT CONTRIBUTIONS 1
7420.10G Gbk: 6-1

TENANT COUNCILS.......................1
24 CFR 5: .380

TENANT DAMAGE 2
HUD-52580-A: p1;
PIH Notices: 00-24B

TENANT DAMAGES.......................1
7420.10G Gbk: 14-5

TENANT FILE 17
24 CFR 982: .516 (2);
7420.10G Gbk: 5-34; 5-39; 5-40; 9-10; 10-17; 12-4 (4); 12-5; 15-10 Ex 15-2; 22-6;
PIH Notices: 00-24B (2);
Admin Plan: s23p5

TENANT FILES.............................10
HUD-52648: p1 (2);
7420.10G Gbk: 12-11 (3); 22-7;
PIH Notices: 01-15;
Admin Plan: s7p1; s21p3; s21p4

TENANT INFORMATION 1
PIH Notices: 01-41

TENANT OPPORTUNITIES 2
PIH Notices: 02-01; 99-52

TENANT OPPORTUNITIES PROGRAM.......................................2
PIH Notices: 02-01; 99-52

TENANT PARTICIPATION.............1
7420.10G Gbk: 3-9

TENANT RENT 110
24 CFR 5: .240; .603 (2); .615; .634 (3);
24 CFR 982: .4;
HUD-50058: p9 (4); p10 (4); p x (2); p11 (3); p xi (2);

p12 (4); p xii (4); p13 (2); p17;
HUD-50058Instr: p9; p39 (3); p40 (2); p41; p43 (3); p44 (2); p45 (3); p48; p49 (5); p51 (6); p52 (5); p54; p55; p63; p69; p75; p76;
HUD-52648: p2;
7420.10G Gbk: 3-5; 11-19; 22-5;
PIH Notices: 01-40; 01-15 Impr Integ Hbk (9); 00-24B;
Admin Plan: s2p6; s6p1; s6p9 (2); s6p10 (2); s7p1; s7p3; s11p2 (5); s11p3; s17p1; s18p8; s21p7 (4); s22p3; s22p4; s23p4

TENANT RENT CALCULATIONS10
HUD-52648: p2;
7420.10G Gbk: 1-10;
PIH Notices: 02-27 (3); 01-06; 00-24A;
Admin Plan: s21p1; s21p2; s21p7

TENANT RENT CHANGES 2
HUD-50058Instr: p11; p11

TENANT RENT INCREASE............ 1
Admin Plan: s11p2

TENANT RENTS.............................. 1
PIH Notices: 01-15 Impr Integ Hbk

TENANT RESPONSIBILITIES 1
Admin Plan: s25p8

TENANT SELECTION................... 16
24 CFR 5: .306 (2);
7420.10G Gbk: 1-2; 4-1;
PIH Notices: 02-01; 00-24B (4); 99-52;
Admin Plan: s23p3 (4); s24p2; s24p6

TENANT SELECTION PLAN 2
24 CFR 5: .655; .655

TENANT-INSTALLED..................... 2
24 CFR 982: .517;
7420.10G Gbk: 18-1

TENANT-PAID UTILITIES............ 17
24 CFR 5: .632;
24 CFR 982: .504; .517; .555; .623;
7420.10G Gbk: 8-3; 17-11; 17-12; 18-1 (3); 18-7;
PIH Notices: 02-20; 01-41; 01-15 Impr Integ Hbk; 00-46;
Admin Plan: s10p5

TENANT-SUPPLIED...................... 12
24 CFR 982: .401; .517 (3);
HUD-52580-A: p4;
7420.10G Gbk: 10-4; 10-28;
PIH Notices: 01-41 (2); 00-09 (2); 00-09

TENANT-SUPPLIED UTILITIES 6
7420.10G Gbk: 10-28;
PIH Notices: 01-41 (2); 00-09 (2); 00-09

TERM 470
24 CFR 5: .214 (7); .306 (4); .318 (2); .500; .504 (3); .518; .603 (4); .615 (5); .630 (5); .661; .701;
24 CFR 982: 24 CFR 982 (3); .4 (9); .54 (5); .151 (4); .158 (2); .203; .301 (2); .302; .303 (15); .305 (6); .308 (3); .309 (12); .310 (4); .311 (2); .312; .314; .355 (4); .405; .451 (3); .502; .503 (2); .504; .505 (6); .520 (2); .521; .554; .555 (2); .605; .613; .617; .619; .623; .624; .625; .627; .634 (9); .641 (3);
HUD-50058: p xvii (2);
HUD-50058Instr: p11; p28; p47; p61; p62 (2); p70; p73; p74; p75 (3); p76;
HUD-52641: p1 (8); p2 (8); p3 (7); p4 (7); p5 (2); p6; 8 (5); p9 (10); p10;
HUD-52641-A: p1 (5); p2 (10); p3;
HUD-52646: p1; p2;
7420.10G Gbk: 1-8; 1-9 (4); 1-14; 1-16 Ex 1-3; 3-2 (3); 3-6; 4-13; 4-22; 5-44; 5-47 Ex 5-5; 6-8; 7-3; 7-4; 7-8 (2); 8-4; 8-5 (2); 8-11; 8-12 (2); 8-13 (8); 8-14; 8-16; 8-21 (2); 8-22 (8); 10-1 (2); 11-1 (2); 11-4 (4); 11-5 (4); 11-6 (2); 11-11 (2); 11-12 (3); 11-13; 11-15 (4); 11-17; 11-19 (2); 13-2; 13-4; 13-5 (3); 13-7; 15-1 (4); 15-2 (5); 15-3 (2); 15-6; 16-2 (2); 16-4; 17-12; 20-2; 20-3; 20-7 (2); 20-9 (2); 20-11; 20-15 (2); 20-16; 20-22 (4); 20-23; 21-9; 21-10; 22-1; 23-1; 23-7 (3); 23-9 (2); 23-10; 23-12; 23-18; 24-4;
PIH Notices: 03-23; 02-27 (2); 02-21 (4); 02-20 (5); 02-06; 01-41 (13); 01-27; 01-20; 01-15 Impr Integ Hbk;

01-10; 01-06; 01-01 (5); 00-46 (5); 00-27; 00-24B (5); 00-11; 00-11A; 00-09 (22); 00-01; 99-52; 98-66; 95-48 (3); 95-48 Tech Asst (3);
Admin Plan: s4p1; s6p5 (2); s6p13 (2); s8p2; s8p3; s8p4; s8p5 (6); s9p1; s9p2 (5); s9p3 (2); s10p1; s14p1 (3); s18p4; s19p1 (4); s23p3; s24p5; s25p2 (2); s25p4

TERMED 1
PIH Notices: 03-23

TERMINAL 2
7420.10G Gbk: 2-6;
PIH Notices: 03-11

TERMINALS 2
PIH Notices: 95-48; 95-48 Tech Asst

TERMINATE 201
24 CFR 5: .218; .240; .353 (5); .508; .514 (2);
24 CFR 982: .306; .310 (10); .311 (2); .312 (2); .314; .355 (2); .403 (2); .404 (2); .454; .502; .552 (10); .553 (6); .555 (3); .619; .638 (4);
HUD-52641: p3 (2); p4 (3); p6; p9 (7);
HUD-52641-A: p2 (8);
7420.10G Gbk: 5-7; 5-8 (2); 5-38; 8-6; 10-27 (4); 10-29 (2); 11-4; 11-5; 11-18 (2); 12-6; 12-15 Ex 12-3 (2); 13-8; 15-1 (4); 15-2 (2); 15-3 (4); 15-4 (2); 15-5 (5); 15-6 (3); 15-7 (4); 15-8; 15-9 Ex 15-1; 15-10 Ex 15-2; 16-3 (2); 16-5; 21-4; 22-9; 22-12 (3); 22-13; 22-14 (6); 22-15 (3); 23-10 (4); 23-13; 23-18; 24-3;
PIH Notices: 01-41 (6); 01-33; 01-10; 00-24B; 00-09 (6);
Admin Plan: s6p7 (2); s7p2; s9p2 (2); s10p5 (2); s14p1 (3); s14p2 (2); s15p1 (4); s15p2; s15p3; s15p4 (2); s16p2 (2); s17p2; s18p3; s18p4 (2); s18p7 (2); s20p7 (2); s20p8; s23p5 (2); s23p6 (2); s23p7

TERMINATED 92
24 CFR 5: .232; .508; .514 (8);
24 CFR 982: .309; .311; .314 (3); .552;
HUD-50058: p17 (2);
HUD-50058Instr: p13 (2); p16; p18; p62 (2); p63 (2);
HUD-52641: p3;
HUD-52648: p2;
HUD-52665: p3;
7420.10G Gbk: 3-4; 5-6; 5-8 (2); 5-10 Ex 5-1; 5-11; 5-37; 5-38 (3); 11-8; 12-3; 12-12 Ex 12-1; 12-14 Ex 12-2; 13-8; 14-4; 15-4; 15-6; 15-7; 15-10 Ex 15-2; 22-1; 22-6; 23-5; 23-9 (3); 23-10 (2); 23-18;
PIH Notices: 01-41 (3); 01-10 (2); 01-06; 00-49; 00-24B; 00-11A; 00-09 (2);
Admin Plan: s6p6; s6p7; s7p8 (2); s10p2; s10p4; s10p5; s13p1; s14p1 (4); s14p2; s15p5; s17p2; s18p7 (2); s18p8 (2); s21p5; s22p5; s23p4; s23p5

TERMINATES 69
24 CFR 982: .1; .309 (4); .311 (4); .314; .403 (2); .455; .502; .504 (2); .551; .555; .635;
HUD-50058Instr: p11 (2); p47;
HUD-52641: p3 (7); p9 (4);
HUD-52641-A: p2 (4);
7420.10G Gbk: 8-22 (2); 11-4 (2); 11-5; 15-3 (3); 15-4 (2); 15-8 (2); 21-11;
PIH Notices: 01-41 (7); 00-24B; 00-09 (9);
Admin Plan: s14p2; s15p5

TERMINATING 56
24 CFR 5: .514;
24 CFR 982: Intro; .54; .310; .403; .552; .553 (4); .641;
HUD-52646: p2;
HUD-52665: p3;
7420.10G Gbk: 1-9; 1-15; 3-2 (2); 5-26; 5-36 Ex 5-4; 10-29; 11-12; 12-1; 15-2; 15-5; 15-6; 15-8; 16-3; 21-2; 22-1 (2); 22-15; 23-5; 23-10 (3); 23-18;
PIH Notices: 01-41 (8); 00-09 (8);
Admin Plan: s6p10; s15p1; s18p3; s18p8

TERMINATION 354
24 CFR 5: .218; .232;

.236 (5); .321; .506; .508; .514 (16); .516 (6); .518 (8); .520; .522; .615;
24 CFR 982: 24 CFR 982 (7); .201; .203; .301; .309; .310 (11); .311 (3); .312; .314 (3); .403 (2); .404 (2); .453 (2); .454; .455; .502 (2); .510; .521; .551; .552 (9); .553 (3); .619 (2); .625; .635 (2); .637; .638 (3); .641;
HUD-50058Instr: p2; p11; p18 (3); p19; p27; p38;
HUD-52641: p3 (2); p4 (2); p5 (2); p9 (2);
HUD-52641-A: p2 (2);
HUD-52665: p3 (2);
HUD-9886: p1 (2);
7420.10G Gbk: 1-1; 2-9; 3-2; 3-5; 4-20; 4-22; 5-3; 5-7; 5-8; 5-26; 5-38; 10-19; 10-27; 10-28; 10-29 (2); 10-30 (4); 10-34 (2); 10-40 Ex 10-4a; 10-41 Ex 10-4b; 10-44 Ex 10-7a; 10-45 Ex 10-7b; 10-46 Ex 10-8 (2); 10-48 Ex 10-10; 11-4; 11-5; 11-14; 11-18 (2); 12-2; 12-3 (5); 12-6; 12-10; 13-3 (2); 13-8 (2); 15-1 (2); 15-2; 15-3 (2); 15-4 (3); 15-5 (3); 15-6 (4); 15-7 (6); 15-8; 15-9 Ex 15-1 (3); 15-10 Ex 15-2 (4); 16-2; 16-3; 18-1 (2); 19-13; 22-14; 23-2 (2); 23-9 (2); 23-10;
PIH Notices: 03-11; 01-41 (25); 01-33; 01-10 (11); 00-41; 00-11A (2); 00-09 (20); 95-48; 95-48 Tech Asst;
Admin Plan: s2p1; s2p4; s2p5; s6p7; s6p10 (2); s7p2 (2); s7p3 (2); s10p2; s10p3; s10p4 (5); s11p1 (2); s14p1 (4); s14p2 (3); s15p1 (7); s15p2 (4); s15p3; s15p4 (9); s15p5 (3); s15p6 (3); s16p2; s18p3; s18p7; s18p8 (2); s20p6; s21p5; s22p5 (2); s23p5 (2); s23p6 (7); s23p7; s23p8; s25p2; s25p3; s25p5

TERMINATION OF TENANCY 20
24 CFR 982: Intro; .310 (4); .641;
HUD-52641: p9 (3);
HUD-52641-A: p2 (3);
7420.10G Gbk: 4-27 Ex 4-2; 10-34; 11-14; 15-1 (3);
Admin Plan: s14p1; s15p5

TERMINATION WARNING 1
Admin Plan: s7p3

TERMINATIONS 34
HUD-52648: p2;
7420.10G Gbk: 1-6; 5-40; 8-23; 10-30; 11-5; 15-1 (5); 15-2 (2); 15-3; 15-4; 15-7;
PIH Notices: 02-27; 01-10 (9); 01-06 (2); 00-09 (2);
Admin Plan: s14p1 (2); s18p8; s23p6

TERMINOLOGY 2
PIH Notices: 95-48; 95-48 Tech Asst

TERMS 147
24 CFR 5: .107; .315; .353; .514; .603 (6); .630 (3); .661 (2);
24 CFR 982: .4 (6); .305; .308 (3); .310; .311; .403 (2); .503; .552; .619; .627 (3); .630; .631; .632 (4); .633; .634;
HUD-50058Instr: p25; p70; p71;
HUD-52641: 8; p10;
HUD-52641-A: p1; p3;
HUD-903: p1; p2 (2);
7420.10G Gbk: 1-9; 4-3; 5-15 Ex 5-2; 7-4; 8-5 (2); 8-21 (3); 8-22 (2); 10-29 (2); 10-41 Ex 10-4b; 10-42 Ex 10-5; 10-46 Ex 10-8; 11-1; 11-5; 11-14; 12-3; 12-8; 13-2; 14-1; 14-2; 15-1 (2); 20-9; 20-23; 22-1; 22-8; 22-13 (2); 23-9; 23-10 (2); 23-18; 24-7;
PIH Notices: 03-23 (3); 03-12; 03-11; 02-21; 02-20 (3); 02-01; 01-41 (3); 01-20; 01-15 (3); 01-15 Impr Integ Hbk; 01-10 (2); 01-01 (3); 00-46 (2); 00-27; 00-11A; 00-09 (5); 00-01; 98-66; 95-48 (3); 95-48 Tech Asst (3);
Admin Plan: s2p2; s6p1; s6p8; s9p2 (4); s13p1 (2); s14p1; s17p1 (2); s22p4; s23p6; s23p8 (2); s25p4

TESTIMONY...................................5
24 CFR 5: .514;

PIH Notices: 95-48; 95-48 Tech Asst;
Admin Plan: s15p4; s18p6

THERAPEUTIC 1
24 CFR 5: .350

THERAPEUTIC VALUE 1
24 CFR 5: .350

THERAPIST 1
Admin Plan: s7p8

THERMAL 6
24 CFR 982: .401 (3);
7420.10G Gbk: 10-1; 10-7; 10-7

THIRD PARTIES............................ 11
24 CFR 982: Intro; .456;
HUD-50058Instr: p28;
7420.10G Gbk: 12-3 (2); 12-8; 22-11; 23-15;
PIH Notices: 00-24B; 95-48; 95-48 Tech Asst

THIRD PARTY 75
24 CFR 5: .659 (2);
24 CFR 982: .456 (2); .516 (2);
HUD-52641: p5 (2);
HUD-52648: p1 (2);
7420.10G Gbk: 5-34 (2); 5-35 (8); 5-46 Ex 5-5 (2); 5-47 Ex 5-5; 5-48 Ex 5-5; 5-49 Ex 5-5; 5-50 Ex 5-5; 5-51 Ex 5-5; 5-52 Ex 5-5; 5-53 Ex 5-5; 9-3; 11-11; 11-13 (2); 12-4 (5); 12-11 (2); 22-2; 22-3 (4); 22-13;
PIH Notices: 02-27; 02-01; 01-15 (5); 01-15 Impr Integ Hbk (2); 00-41; 00-24B (4); 99-52; 95-48 (2); 95-48 Tech Asst (2);
Admin Plan: s1p5; s7p1 (5); s7p3; s7p6; s15p5; s21p4

THIRD PARTY VERIFICATION ... 19
24 CFR 5: .659 (2);
24 CFR 982: .516 (2);
HUD-52648: p1 (2);
PIH Notices: 01-15 (5); 01-15 Impr Integ Hbk (2); 00-24B (2);
Admin Plan: s7p1; s7p3; s7p6; s21p4

THIRD PARTY VERIFICATIONS ... 5
PIH Notices: 02-27; 00-24B (2);
Admin Plan: s7p1; s7p1

THIRD-PARTY 6
7420.10G Gbk: 18-6;
PIH Notices: 01-15 (2);
Admin Plan: s7p1 (2); s7p1

THIRD-PARTY VERIFICATION 1
PIH Notices: 01-15

THIRD-PARTY VERIFICATIONS ... 1
Admin Plan: s7p1

THIRTY 17
24 CFR 5: .508 (2);
HUD-50058Instr: p65;
7420.10G Gbk: 10-10; 10-18; 12-14 Ex 12-2; 12-15 Ex 12-3;
PIH Notices: 03-11;
Admin Plan: s5p2; s7p8; s11p2 (2); s18p7; s22p3; s23p3; s23p6; s23p7

THIRTY DAY 1
Admin Plan: s11p2

THIRTY DAYS................................. 5
Admin Plan: s11p2; s18p7; s23p3; s23p6; s23p7

THIRTY PERCENT.......................... 3
HUD-50058Instr: p65;
7420.10G Gbk: 11-6; 23-17 Ex 23-2

THOROUGH 9
7420.10G Gbk: 10-24; 10-25; 19-4; 21-3; 21-10; 22-4; 22-6;
PIH Notices: 02-27;
Admin Plan: s24p4

THOROUGHLY 2
7420.10G Gbk: 10-22;
Admin Plan: s20p3

THOROUGHNESS 3
7420.10G Gbk: 19-10; 22-5; 22-8

THREAT 33
24 CFR 5: .327 (2); .360 (2); .661 (2);
24 CFR 982: .307; .310; .401; .614;
7420.10G Gbk: 5-10 Ex 5-1; 5-39; 10-4; 10-8; 10-9; 17-5;
PIH Notices: 95-48 (7); 95-48 Tech Asst (7);
Admin Plan: s2p7; s9p3; s25p1

THREATEN 16
24 CFR 982: .102; .401; .552; .553 (5);
7420.10G Gbk: 10-10;
PIH Notices: 95-48 (3); 95-48 Tech Asst (3);
Admin Plan: s15p2

THREATENED............................... 11
24 CFR 5: .100; .363;
24 CFR 982: .315; .552;
HUD-52580-A: p2;
7420.10G Gbk: 15-6;
Admin Plan: s2p6; s15p2; s15p3 (2); s15p5

THREATENING................................9
24 CFR 982: .404 (2);
PIH Notices: 00-24B (2); 95-48;
95-48 Tech Asst;
Admin Plan: s15p2; s21p5;
s21p5

THREATENS..................................33
24 CFR 982: .306 (3); .310 (2);
.551 (2);
HUD-52641: p6; p7 (2);
p9 (3);
HUD-52641-A: p2 (5);
7420.10G Gbk: 8-20 (4); 11-
3 (2); 11-4; 15-2 (3);
15-7;
PIH Notices: 03-11;
Admin Plan: s16p2 (2); s16p2

THREATS..9
HUD-52580-A: p2; p15;
HUD-52665: p1;
HUD-903: p2;
7420.10G Gbk: 10-7; 10-11;
PIH Notices: 95-48; 95-
48 Tech Asst;
Admin Plan: s15p2

THREE MONTHS..........................12
7420.10G Gbk: 10-32; 19-12;
22-7;
PIH Notices: 03-23 (5); 00-53;
00-01; 98-66;
Admin Plan: s6p9

THREE PERCENT..........................14
24 CFR 5: .611;
7420.10G Gbk: 5-30; 5-32 (2);
5-33 (7); 5-34 (2);
PIH Notices: 01-15 Impr Integ Hbk

THREE WEEKS...............................2
HUD-903-1: p3;
7420.10G Gbk: 13-7

THREE YEAR.................................2
PIH Notices: 01-15 Impr Integ Hbk;
Admin Plan: s2p6

THREE YEARS.............................38
24 CFR 982: .4; .158 (2);
.503; .553;
HUD-50058Instr: p9; p10;
p12 (2);
7420.10G Gbk: 4-7 (2); 4-
10 (2); 5-1; 11-19; 18-9;
23-3;
PIH Notices: 03-11; 02-
20; 01-41; 01-15; 01-
15 Impr Integ Hbk (4); 01-
01; 95-48 (2); 95-
48 Tech Asst (2);
Admin Plan: s2p6 (5); s11p2;
s22p1; s22p1

THRESHOLD................................31
HUD-50058: p7; p vii (5);
HUD-50058Instr: p34 (3);
p35 (5);
7420.10G Gbk: 5-27 (3); 20-
10 (6); 21-7; 22-18;
PIH Notices: 02-07; 02-01;
01-06; 00-28; 99-52;
Admin Plan: s24p3

THURSDAY 2
:
PIH Notices: 02-22

TIME FRAME................................14
HUD-52648: p1;
7420.10G Gbk: 10-26; 10-34 (2);
10-35; 22-13; 24-5;
PIH Notices: 01-
15 Impr Integ Hbk; 01-06;
00-24B (2);
Admin Plan: s3p2; s10p3;
s21p5

TIME FRAMES..............................12
7420.10G Gbk: 10-26; 10-30;
10-33 (2); 10-34; 10-35;
10-44 Ex 10-7a; 10-45 Ex 10-
7b; 19-6 (3); 19-12

TIME LIMIT....................................9
24 CFR 5: .518; .615;
PIH Notices: 00-11A;
Admin Plan: s6p12 (2); s11p1;
s11p3; s18p2; s18p3

TIME LIMITATIONS.......................1
PIH Notices: 00-11

TIME LIMITS 2
7420.10G Gbk: 11-14;
PIH Notices: 00-11

TIME PERIOD 36
24 CFR 5: .216 (3); .508 (2);
.514; .518;
24 CFR 982: .102;
HUD-52580: p5;
HUD-52580-A: p15; p17;
HUD-52665: p2;
7420.10G Gbk: 5-6; 10-27; 10-
28; 10-29; 15-10 Ex 15-2;
22-13;
PIH Notices: 01-
15 Impr Integ Hbk (2); 00-11;
00-11A (2); 95-48 (3); 95-
48 Tech Asst (3);
Admin Plan: s3p3; s6p6;
s10p4 (2); s10p5; s18p7;
s22p2

TIME PERIODS 7
24 CFR 5: .353; .518;
7420.10G Gbk: 24-5;
PIH Notices: 95-48 (2); 95-
48 Tech Asst; 95-48 Tech Asst

TIME REQUIREMENTS.................1

Admin Plan: s15p6

TIME-CONSUMING........................1
7420.10G Gbk: 4-18

TIMEFRAME.................................7
7420.10G Gbk: 10-34; 11-12; 19-7 (2); 22-4;
Admin Plan: s23p5; s24p5

TIMEFRAMES...............................3
7420.10G Gbk: 15-5; 16-1;
Admin Plan: s10p2

TIME-FRAMES 2
PIH Notices: 00-09; 00-09

TIMELINE....................................15
7420.10G Gbk: 19-6;
PIH Notices: 02-27 (3); 02-06; 01-41 (5); 00-09 (4); 00-09

TIMELINES 3
PIH Notices: 01-41; 00-09;
Admin Plan: s24p3

TIMELINESS 7
7420.10G Gbk: 19-13; 24-12;
PIH Notices: 02-27 (3);
Admin Plan: s10p1; s11p1

TIMELY...56
24 CFR 5: .214; .353; .508; .514 (2);
HUD-50058Instr: p1; p10;
7420.10G Gbk: 2-6; 2-9 (6); 4-15; 5-7; 10-22; 10-26; 10-40 Ex 10-4a; 11-9; 11-15; 11-16 Ex 11-1; 12-1; 12-2; 12-4; 12-8; 19-13; 24-12;
PIH Notices: 03-23; 03-20; 03-11; 02-27 (5); 01-41; 01-15; 01-06; 00-49; 00-11A (3); 00-09; 96-65 (3);
Admin Plan: s3p1; s4p1; s6p9; s6p10; s9p1; s11p1; s22p3; s25p1; s25p3

TIMELY REPORTING......................1
Admin Plan: s11p1

TIMES-PICAYUNE 2
Admin Plan: s3p1; s3p1

TIMETABLE...................................1
7420.10G Gbk: 23-5

TIMING..14
24 CFR 5: .508;
24 CFR 982: .405;
7420.10G Gbk: 2-10; 4-12; 5-38; 16-3; 20-18; 21-5;
PIH Notices: 02-14; 01-41; 01-10; 00-09;
Admin Plan: s6p6; s10p2

TIP...5
PIH Notices: 01-15 (4); 01-15

TIPS 30
24 CFR 5: .609;
HUD-50058Instr: p3; p27; p71;
7420.10G Gbk: 5-14 Ex 5-2; 5-46 Ex 5-5 (2); 5-47 Ex 5-5; 5-48 Ex 5-5; 5-49 Ex 5-5; 5-50 Ex 5-5; 5-51 Ex 5-5; 5-52 Ex 5-5; 5-53 Ex 5-5; 8-3 (2); 12-8; 23-12;
PIH Notices: 01-15 (5); 01-15 Impr Integ Hbk (3);
Admin Plan: s7p4 (2); s20p1; s20p3

TITLE I..24
24 CFR 5: .306; .504; .801;
HUD-50058Instr: p75;
PIH Notices: 95-48 (10); 95-48 Tech Asst (9); 95-48 Tech Asst

TITLE II.......................................189
24 CFR 5: .105; .214; .306; .504; .801;
24 CFR 982: .53 (2);
7420.10G Gbk: 3-8; 5-42;
PIH Notices: 02-01 (4); 99-52 (4); 95-48 (95); 95-48 Tech Asst (76); 95-48 Tech Asst

TITLE III 35
PIH Notices: 02-01; 01-27; 99-52; 95-48 (18); 95-48 Tech Asst (13); 95-48 Tech Asst

TITLE II'S 14
PIH Notices: 95-48 (7); 95-48 Tech Asst (6); 95-48 Tech Asst

TITLE IL..2
PIH Notices: 95-48; 95-48 Tech Asst

TITLE IL'S 2
PIH Notices: 95-48; 95-48 Tech Asst

TITLE IV 14
24 CFR 5: .617; .630;
HUD-50058Instr: p17 (2); p32;
7420.10G Gbk: 5-16 Ex 5-2; 6-8;
PIH Notices: 01-15 Impr Integ Hbk (2); 00-11A (3); 95-48; 95-48 Tech Asst

TITLE V...12
HUD-50058Instr: p32;
7420.10G Gbk: 5-16 Ex 5-2;
PIH Notices: 01-15 Impr Integ Hbk; 01-10; 00-09 (4); 95-48 (2); 95-48 Tech Asst; 95-48 Tech Asst

TITLE VI 8

24 CFR 5: .105; .524;
24 CFR 982: .53;
HUD-50058: p i;
7420.10G Gbk: 3-8; 5-42;
PIH Notices: 02-21; 01-20

TITLE VIII..4
24 CFR 5: .100;
HUD-903: p3;
7420.10G Gbk: 5-42; 22-15

TO WORK....................................109
24 CFR 5: .611; .655;
24 CFR 982: .4; .207;
HUD-50058: p i; p2; p ii; p v (2); p7; p16 (2); p xvi (3); p17 (2); p xvii (2);
HUD-50058Instr: p ii; p1; p2 (2); p3; p4; p10; p11; p13 (3); p17 (2); p19 (2); p36 (2); p59 (3); p62 (2); p63 (2);
7420.10G Gbk: 1-7 (3); 2-11; 3-2; 4-12 (2); 4-17 (2); 4-26 Ex 4-2; 4-27 Ex 4-2; 5-29 (4); 5-30 (5); 5-33 (2); 5-34 (2); 5-52 Ex 5-5; 7-6; 20-17; 23-15; 23-16 Ex 23-2; 23-20; 24-10; 24-12;
PIH Notices: 03-23 (4); 02-27 (2); 02-21; 02-14; 02-01; 01-20; 01-15; 01-15 Impr Integ Hbk (2); 01-06 (2); 00-53 (2); 00-11 (6); 00-11A; 99-52; 95-48; 95-48 Tech Asst;
Admin Plan: s6p2 (2); s6p3; s6p10; s6p11 (2); s6p11

TOILET...31
24 CFR 982: .401; .605 (2); .614;
HUD-52580: p2;
HUD-52580-A: p6 (8); p7 (2); p8; p9; p10; p11; p12;
7420.10G Gbk: 10-3 (3); 10-4; 17-2; 17-4;
PIH Notices: 95-48 (2); 95-48 Tech Asst (2);
Admin Plan: s10p4

TOILETING 2
PIH Notices: 95-48; 95-48 Tech Asst

TOILETS 4
24 CFR 982: .605;
7420.10G Gbk: 17-2;
PIH Notices: 95-48; 95-48 Tech Asst

TOLERATE 1
Admin Plan: s20p4

TOLL...1
PIH Notices: 00-53

TOLLED 1
Admin Plan: s9p2

TOLL-FREE 7
HUD-903: p3;
7420.10G Gbk: 4-27 Ex 4-2; 22-18;
PIH Notices: 03-23; 01-15; 00-53; 00-53

TOLLING 10
7420.10G Gbk: 8-13 (2); 8-14 (2); 21-9 (4);
Admin Plan: s8p5; s8p5

TOO SMALL 5
24 CFR 5: .236;
24 CFR 982: Intro; .403; .641;
7420.10G Gbk: 10-2

TOOL 16
7420.10G Gbk: 1-9; 1-10; 2-11; 5-40; 8-11; 12-3; 20-20 (2); 20-22; 24-8;
PIH Notices: 01-43; 01-41; 01-15; 00-11; 00-09;
Admin Plan: s21p1

TOOLS...14
7420.10G Gbk: 7-2; 10-2; 13-9; 19-1; 19-4; 19-5; 20-1;
PIH Notices: 02-27; 01-15 (2); 00-11;
Admin Plan: s8p1; s8p3; s17p1

TOP FAMILY....................................2
24 CFR 982: .204;
7420.10G Gbk: 4-18

TOP OF THE WAITING LIST..........5
24 CFR 982: .204 (2);
HUD-52648: p1;
PIH Notices: 00-24B; 00-24B

TOTAL ASSETS...............................2
HUD-50058Instr: p23;
Admin Plan: s6p10

TOTAL ASSISTANCE PAYMENT...2
24 CFR 982: .4;
HUD-50058Instr: p72

TOTAL TENANT PAYMENT.......166
24 CFR 5: .240; .318; .520 (3); .603 (2); .628 (3); .630; .632; .634;
24 CFR 982: .4 (2); .301; .505 (2); .518; .623 (3); .627; .635 (2); .643;
HUD-50058: p i; p8; p viii (6); p ix (5); p x (5); p xi (2); p xii (5); p xiii (4); p xiv (2);

HUD-50058Instr: p ii; p3; p37 (3); p38 (2); p39; p40 (4); p43 (2); p44 (4); p48 (2); p50; p51 (3); p52 (3); p54 (3); p57 (2); p74; p76;
7420.10G Gbk: 1-6 Ex 1-1; 4-25 Ex 4-2; 5-13; 5-23; 5-24; 6-1 (4); 6-2; 6-5 (2); 6-10 Ex 6-2; 8-5; 8-6; 12-5 (2); 16-2; 16-3; 16-5; 22-2; 23-7 (2); 23-10; 23-11; 23-12; 23-13 (2); 23-16 Ex 23-2 (4);
PIH Notices: 02-20 (3); 01-41 (4); 01-15 Impr Integ Hbk (3); 01-10 (3); 00-46 (3); 00-41 (2); 00-24B (3); 00-09 (3);
Admin Plan: s6p1 (4); s6p4; s6p9 (2); s6p10; s7p1; s7p3; s11p1; s18p8; s19p1 (2); s22p3; s22p4; s23p3; s23p5; s23p7

TOTAL TENANT PAYMENTS 1
HUD-50058: p ix

TOTAL UNIT MONTHS..................3
24 CFR 982: .102;
PIH Notices: 03-23; 03-23

TOTAL UNIT MONTHS AVAILABLE 1
PIH Notices: 03-23

TOWN...29
24 CFR 982: .517;
HUD-52580: p1 (2); p15 (3); p17 (2);
7420.10G Gbk: 2-13 Ex 2-1; 18-2;
PIH Notices: 95-48 (9); 95-48 Tech Asst (9);
Admin Plan: s22p3

TOWN HOMES................................1
Admin Plan: s22p3

TOWN HOUSE 3
24 CFR 982: .517;
HUD-52580: p1;
HUD-52580-A: p1

TOWN HOUSES 1
7420.10G Gbk: 18-2

TOWNHOUSE 9
HUD-50058: p5;
7420.10G Gbk: 9-13 Ex 9-1; 9-15 Ex 9-2;
PIH Notices: 02-01 (3); 99-52 (2); 99-52

TOWNHOUSES 3
HUD-52667: p i;
PIH Notices: 02-01; 99-52

TOWNS 5
24 CFR 982: .503;
PIH Notices: 02-20 (2); 00-46; 00-46

TRACK 38
HUD-50058Instr: p1 (2); p59;
7420.10G Gbk: 1-10; 2-9; 8-11; 8-22; 8-23 (3); 10-22; 10-25; 10-26; 10-30; 10-33; 10-35; 10-48 Ex 10-10; 13-5; 13-7; 19-3; 19-6; 19-8 (2); 19-9 (3); 19-11; 19-12 (3); 19-13 (2); 24-5;
PIH Notices: 02-27 (2); 01-15 Impr Integ Hbk; 01-01;
Admin Plan: s21p2

TRACKED...7
7420.10G Gbk: 8-23; 12-2; 20-9; 24-6;
PIH Notices: 03-11; 01-06;
Admin Plan: s8p3

TRACKING.. 39
HUD-50058Instr: p3;
7420.10G Gbk: 4-15; 4-22; 8-22 (2); 8-23 (2); 10-22; 10-26; 10-30 (2); 10-33; 10-34 (2); 10-35; 11-19; 12-1; 12-8; 13-4; 19-1; 19-5; 19-6 (3); 19-8; 19-9;
PIH Notices: 02-27 (5); 01-15 (2); 01-06 (2);
Admin Plan: s6p4 (2); s11p1; s21p2

TRACKING SYSTEM 10
7420.10G Gbk: 8-23; 10-26; 10-30; 10-33; 10-34; 19-9;
PIH Notices: 01-06;
Admin Plan: s6p4 (2); s11p1

TRACKING SYSTEMS....................4
7420.10G Gbk: 8-23; 10-30; 10-35; 12-8

TRACKING-KNOWING 1
7420.10G Gbk: 19-5

TRACKS...5
7420.10G Gbk: 8-23; 13-7; 19-13; 22-4;
PIH Notices: 02-27

TRACS...2
PIH Notices: 01-15; 01-15

TRAFFICKING 2
7420.10G Gbk: 3-4; 8-20

TRAIN 7
24 CFR 5: .603;

HUD-50058Instr: p71;
7420.10G Gbk: 2-13 Ex 2-1; 12-8; 21-3;
PIH Notices: 01-15;
Admin Plan: s6p3

TRAINED....................................19
24 CFR 5: .303;
24 CFR 35 SubM: .1215;
7420.10G Gbk: 4-22; 10-18; 10-19; 10-20; 10-22; 10-32; 10-37 Ex 10-2; 22-5; 22-8;
PIH Notices: 03-11; 00-53; 00-49; 95-48 (2); 95-48 Tech Asst (2);
Admin Plan: s1p3

TRAINERS....................................1
PIH Notices: 03-12

TRAINING..................................183
24 CFR 5: .603 (3); .609 (6); .617; .655 (2); .661;
24 CFR 982: .207 (2);
HUD-50058: p16 (2); p xvi; p17; p xvii;
HUD-50058Instr: p27 (4); p28; p60 (3); p61 (4); p62 (2); p71 (3); p72; p73 (3); p75;
7420.10G Gbk: 1-13; 2-5; 2-10; 2-11 (3); 4-17; 4-18; 5-15 Ex 5-2 (6); 5-20 (7); 9-11; 10-2; 10-18; 10-19; 10-24; 10-33; 11-7; 12-8; 19-10 (2); 21-3; 22-7 (8); 22-9; 23-1 (2); 23-4; 23-5; 23-6; 23-7 (6); 23-8 Ex 23-1; 23-9 (3); 23-15; 24-9;
PIH Notices: 03-20; 02-27 (7); 02-01 (7); 01-15 (7); 01-15 Impr Integ Hbk (15); 00-24 (4); 00-11 (4); 00-11A (4); 99-52 (9); 99-11 (5); 95-48 (2); 95-48 Tech Asst (2);
Admin Plan: s6p2; s6p3 (5); s8p2; s8p3; s21p4; s25p4 (3); s25p7 (2); s25p8; s25p8

TRAINING DAYS..........................1
7420.10G Gbk: 10-24

TRAINING PROGRAM 6
24 CFR 5: .655;
24 CFR 982: .207;
HUD-50058Instr: p27;
7420.10G Gbk: 4-17; 5-20;
PIH Notices: 01-15 Impr Integ Hbk

TRAINING PROGRAMS 12
24 CFR 5: .609 (2); .655;
24 CFR 982: .207;
7420.10G Gbk: 2-11; 5-15 Ex 5-2 (2); 12-8;
PIH Notices: 01-15; 01-15 Impr Integ Hbk (2); 01-15 Impr Integ Hbk

TRANSCRIPT..................................1
24 CFR 5: .514

TRANSCRIPTION...........................6
PIH Notices: 95-48 (3); 95-48 Tech Asst (2); 95-48 Tech Asst

TRANSCRIPTS................................2
PIH Notices: 95-48; 95-48 Tech Asst

TRANSFER....................................29
24 CFR 982: .355; .551; .633 (3);
HUD-50058Instr: p9 (2); p71;
HUD-52641: 8;
HUD-52641-A: p1;
HUD-52646: p2;
7420.10G Gbk: 2-9; 5-27; 11-7; 20-11; 23-18;
PIH Notices: 02-27; 02-01 (2); 99-52 (2); 95-48; 95-48 Tech Asst;
Admin Plan: s6p7; s8p5; s16p3 (2); s19p1; s22p4

TRANSFERRED..............................9
24 CFR 982: .355;
7420.10G Gbk: 9-7; 20-8 Ex 20-1 (3);
Admin Plan: s6p7; s8p5 (2); s22p3

TRANSFERRING............................3
7420.10G Gbk: 11-3; 20-8 Ex 20-1;
PIH Notices: 00-11

TRANSFERS..................................11
24 CFR 982: .621;
HUD-52580-A: p13;
7420.10G Gbk: 10-24; 17-11; 17-12; 21-4;
PIH Notices: 02-06; 02-01; 99-52;
Admin Plan: s19p1; s23p6

TRANSIENT...................................4
PIH Notices: 95-48 (2); 95-48 Tech Asst; 95-48 Tech Asst

TRANSITION................................89
24 CFR 5: .518 (2);
24 CFR 982: .503;
7420.10G Gbk: 1-5; 1-7; 14-1 (3); 14-3 (2); 14-4;
PIH Notices: 02-20; 02-01 (7); 01-43; 01-41 (3); 01-11 (2); 01-06 (2); 00-46;

00-11 (2); 00-09 (4); 99-52 (7); 95-48 (30); 95-48 Tech Asst (17); 95-48 Tech Asst

TRANSITION PLAN 46
PIH Notices: 02-01 (4); 99-52 (4); 95-48 (24); 95-48 Tech Asst (13); 95-48 Tech Asst

TRANSITION PLANS 6
PIH Notices: 02-01 (3); 99-52 (2); 99-52

TRANSITIONAL 6
HUD-50058Instr: p28; p72; p76;
7420.10G Gbk: 12-4;
Admin Plan: s23p2; s25p3

TRANSITIONAL HOUSING 3
HUD-50058Instr: p72;
Admin Plan: s23p2; s25p3

TRANSLATE.................................... 2
7420.10G Gbk: 9-9; 22-3

TRANSLATED 2
7420.10G Gbk: 4-3; 8-2

TRANSLATES ....
1
Admin Plan: s1p5

TRANSLATING 1
7420.10G Gbk: 8-2

TRANSLATION 3
Admin Plan: s1p5 (2); s1p5

TRANSMISSION 18
24 CFR 5: .508 (2);
24 CFR 982: .158;
HUD-50058Instr: p1 (2); p3; p5;
7420.10G Gbk: 2-9; 5-4; 5-9 Ex 5-1; 14-5; 19-2 (3); 19-5;
PIH Notices: 01-06 (2); 00-53

TRANSMISSIONS 4
PIH Notices: 00-53 (3); 00-53

TRANSPORT 1
7420.10G Gbk: 8-4

TRANSPORTABLE 1
7420.10G Gbk: 17-10

TRANSPORTATION....................... 95
24 CFR 5: .609; .617;
24 CFR 982: .630;
HUD-50058: p16; p17;
HUD-50058Instr: p28 (3); p61 (2); p63 (2);
7420.10G Gbk: 2-3; 2-7; 2-8 (2); 2-10; 2-13 Ex 2-1; 4-12; 4-13; 5-15 Ex 5-2; 5-32; 5-51 Ex 5-5 (2); 8-7; 8-8; 8-14; 9-14 Ex 9-1; 9-16 Ex 9-2; 9-17 Ex 9-3; 21-6 (2); 23-5; 23-15 (3); 24-9;
PIH Notices: 02-27 (3); 02-21; 02-01 (4); 01-20; 01-15; 01-15 Impr Integ Hbk (4); 00-41; 00-11 (3); 00-11A; 00-09; 99-52 (4); 95-48 (17); 95-48 Tech Asst (15);
Admin Plan: s6p3; s25p6

TRANSPORTATION COSTS 1
PIH Notices: 02-27

TRANSPORTATION'S 2
PIH Notices: 95-48; 95-48 Tech Asst

TRASH 20
24 CFR 5: .703 (2);
24 CFR 982: .401; .517 (2); .614; .622 (2);
HUD-52580-A: p17 (3);
HUD-52667: p1 (2);
7420.10G Gbk: 10-5; 10-13 (2); 17-5;
Admin Plan: s10p5; s19p1; s19p1

TRASH COLLECTION 15
24 CFR 5: .703;
24 CFR 982: .517 (2); .622 (2);
HUD-52517: p1;
HUD-52641: p2;
HUD-52667: p1 (2);
7420.10G Gbk: 17-11; 18-1; 18-2; 18-8;
Admin Plan: s19p1; s19p1

TRAVEL TIME.................................. 7
7420.10G Gbk: 10-24; 21-6 (5);
Admin Plan: s6p11

TREASURY BILLS........................... 1
PIH Notices: 01-15 Impr Integ Hbk

TREATMENT 34
24 CFR 5: .603;
HUD-50058Instr: p71;
7420.10G Gbk: 4-1; 5-21; 5-23; 5-24; 5-32; 5-34; 5-37; 5-51 Ex 5-5; 10-15; 22-1; 22-10; 22-11;
PIH Notices: 01-15; 00-23 (7); 95-48 (5); 95-48 Tech Asst (5);
Admin Plan: s1p3; s6p3

TREATMENT PROGRAM 7
24 CFR 5: .603;
HUD-50058Instr: p71;
7420.10G Gbk: 5-37;
PIH Notices: 95-48 (2); 95-48 Tech Asst; 95-48 Tech Asst

TRIAL 1

7420.10G Gbk: 20-20

TRIBAL 6
24 CFR 5: .214;
HUD-50058Instr: p73;
HUD-903: p2;
PIH Notices: 01-11; 00-53; 00-53

TRIBE 9
HUD-50058Instr: p28 (2); p30 (2); p73;
7420.10G Gbk: 5-16 Ex 5-2;
PIH Notices: 01-15 Impr Integ Hbk (2); 00-01

TRIBES 30
HUD-50058Instr: p30 (2);
7420.10G Gbk: 5-16 Ex 5-2 (2);
PIH Notices: 02-01 (6); 01-15 Impr Integ Hbk (2); 01-11 (2); 00-53 (3); 00-45; 00-01 (3); 99-52 (6); 99-11; 98-66; 98-66

TRIGGER 3
PIH Notices: 01-15 Impr Integ Hbk; 95-48; 95-48 Tech Asst

TRIGGERED 4
PIH Notices: 95-48 (2); 95-48 Tech Asst; 95-48 Tech Asst

TRIGGERING 6
PIH Notices: 95-48 (3); 95-48 Tech Asst (2); 95-48 Tech Asst

TRIGGERS 2
7420.10G Gbk: 10-25; 14-5

TROUBLED 109
7420.10G Gbk: 1-11 (2); 20-14 (6);
PIH Notices: 02-27 (54); 02-21 (2); 02-20; 02-01; 01-43; 01-20 (4); 01-11 (2); 01-06 (20); 01-01 (2); 00-53 (3); 00-45; 00-34; 00-27 (2); 00-24 (3); 00-24A; 99-52; 99-11;
Admin Plan: s21p1

TROUBLED AGENCY RECOVERY CENTER 13
7420.10G Gbk: 20-14;
PIH Notices: 02-27; 02-01; 01-20 (2); 01-06 (2); 01-01; 00-53; 00-34; 00-24 (2); 99-52

TRUST 30
24 CFR 5: .214; .603 (7);
HUD-50058: p6;
HUD-50058Instr: p22 (4); p30 (4); p74;
7420.10G Gbk: 5-16 Ex 5-2 (3); 5-25 Ex 5-3; 12-13 Ex 12-1;
PIH Notices: 01-15 Impr Integ Hbk (4); 01-11; 00-53;
Admin Plan: s20p2

TRUSTEE 1
Admin Plan: s7p4

TRUSTS 2
7420.10G Gbk: 4-27 Ex 4-2; 5-25 Ex 5-3

TTP 271
24 CFR 5: .628 (2);
HUD-50058: p i; p8 (5); p viii (6); p9 (3); p ix (8); p10 (2); p x (5); p11; p xi (2); p12 (2); p xii (5); p13 (3); p xiii (4); p14; p xiv (3);
HUD-50058Instr: p ii; p3; p37 (4); p38 (4); p39 (6); p40 (6); p43 (3); p44 (5); p45 (2); p48 (4); p50 (2); p51 (6); p52 (5); p54 (6); p55 (2); p57 (4); p66 (6); p68 (2); p77;
7420.10G Gbk: 1-6 Ex 1-1 (6); 1-16 Ex 1-3; 3-5; 5-23; 5-24 (5); 6-1 (5); 6-2 (2); 6-3; 6-4 (7); 6-5 (5); 6-6; 6-7 (6); 6-8; 7-1 (2); 7-8 (4); 8-5 (2); 8-16; 11-8; 12-5; 12-6; 12-7 (3); 12-9; 13-3; 17-3 (2); 17-4 (2); 17-6 (5); 17-8 (2); 17-9 (3); 17-10 (2); 17-11 (2); 17-12 (2); 23-11 (15); 23-12 (4); 23-13 (4); 23-17 Ex 23-2 (6);
PIH Notices: 01-41 (2); 01-10 (32); 00-09 (2);
Admin Plan: s6p1 (3); s6p1

TUB 19
24 CFR 982: .401;
HUD-52580: p2; p6 (8); p7 (2); p19;
7420.10G Gbk: 10-3 (4); 10-4; 10-4

TUBERCULOSIS 4
PIH Notices: 95-48 (2); 95-48 Tech Asst; 95-48 Tech Asst

TURNOVER 35
7420.10G Gbk: 2-6; 3-2 (3); 4-1; 9-7; 10-21; 19-8 (5); 20-4; 20-15; 20-17; 21-3; 21-5; 24-3 (9); 24-6;
PIH Notices: 02-06 (5);
Admin Plan: s8p1; s25p2; s25p3

TURNOVERS 1

7420.10G Gbk: 4-5

TURTLE 1
24 CFR 5: .306

TURTLES 1
24 CFR 5: .306

TUTOR 2
PIH Notices: 95-48; 95-48 Tech Asst

TUTORIAL 1
Admin Plan: s25p5

TWELVE 38
24 CFR 5: .617 (7);
24 CFR 982: .4; .624; .627; .643;
HUD-50058Instr: p72; p74;
7420.10G Gbk: 12-1; 24-1;
PIH Notices: 01-41 (2); 01-15 Impr Integ Hbk (14); 00-09 (2);
Admin Plan: s6p8 (2); s19p1 (2); s19p1

TWELVE MONTH 16
24 CFR 5: .617 (4);
7420.10G Gbk: 5-16 Ex 5-2 (2); 18-4;
PIH Notices: 01-41; 01-15 Impr Integ Hbk (7); 01-15 Impr Integ Hbk

TWELVE MONTH EXCLUSION 6
24 CFR 5: .617 (2);
PIH Notices: 01-15 Impr Integ Hbk (3); 01-15 Impr Integ Hbk

TWELVE MONTHS 21
24 CFR 5: .617 (3);
24 CFR 982: .624;
HUD-50058Instr: p74;
7420.10G Gbk: 4-27 Ex 4-2; 10-27; 10-35; 20-9;
PIH Notices: 01-41; 01-15 Impr Integ Hbk (6); 00-09 (2);
Admin Plan: s6p8 (2); s19p1

TWICE 8
24 CFR 5: .350;
7420.10G Gbk: 4-14; 5-17; 21-19; 22-13; 24-3; 24-6;
PIH Notices: 00-53

TWO CALENDAR MONTHS 2
HUD-52641: p4;
7420.10G Gbk: 11-6

TWO MONTH 2
PIH Notices: 02-06; 02-06

TWO MONTHS 12
7420.10G Gbk: 5-24; 12-10 (4); 20-29;
PIH Notices: 02-06 (2); 01-10;
Admin Plan: s21p8 (2); s21p8

TWO PEOPLE 3
7420.10G Gbk: 12-7; 17-4; 17-5

TWO PERCENT 2
PIH Notices: 95-48; 95-48 Tech Asst

TWO PERCENTAGE 8
HUD-52648: p3 (2); p4 (2);
7420.10G Gbk: 2-4 (2);
PIH Notices: 01-06; 01-06

TWO STEP 1
7420.10G Gbk: 6-1

TWO WEEKS 2
PIH Notices: 02-14;
Admin Plan: s7p2

TWO YEAR 1
7420.10G Gbk: 5-50 Ex 5-5

TWO YEARS 20
24 CFR 5: .603;
HUD-50058Instr: p62;
7420.10G Gbk: 1-7; 4-26 Ex 4-2; 4-27 Ex 4-2; 5-25 Ex 5-3; 5-27; 5-46 Ex 5-5; 9-4; 9-7; 10-8; 20-14; 20-18; 23-7; 23-9; 23-20;
PIH Notices: 01-15 Impr Integ Hbk;
Admin Plan: s6p10; s7p3; s7p6

TWO-BEDROOM 13
24 CFR 982: .623;
7420.10G Gbk: 2-13 Ex 2-1; 5-3; 7-2; 12-7 (7);
PIH Notices: 02-20;
Admin Plan: s19p1

TWO-PERSON 3
24 CFR 982: .402;
7420.10G Gbk: 5-41;
Admin Plan: s5p1

TYPE 274
24 CFR 5: .315; .318 (2); .508; .518; .655;
24 CFR 982: .4 (6); .507; .517; .601 (11); .619;
HUD-50058: p2; p ii; p5; p v (2); p6 (3); p7; p vii; p9 (2); p ix (2); p10; p x (3); p11; p xi (3); p xii (2); p xiii (2); p xiv (2); p xv (2); p xvi;
HUD-50058Instr: p9 (2); p11; p12; p21 (2); p22; p24 (2); p28; p34 (2); p39 (2); p41 (2); p42 (4); p46 (4); p50 (2); p53 (2); p56 (2); p58 (2); p59 (2); p60; p75; p77 (4); p78 (3);

HUD-52517: p1 (6); p7;
HUD-52580-A: p1 (2); p2; p8; p9; p10; p11; p12; p15; p17 (3); p20;
HUD-52641: p2 (5);
HUD-52648: p1 (2); p2;
HUD-52667: p1; p i (4);
HUD-903: p1;
HUD-903-1: p3;
7420.10G Gbk: 1-7 (2); 2-13 Ex 2-1; 4-2 (2); 4-7; 4-9; 4-15; 4-16; 4-26 Ex 4-2 (2); 5-30 (3); 5-39; 5-47 Ex 5-5; 5-50 Ex 5-5; 8-15; 9-3 (3); 9-8; 9-9 (2); 9-10 (3); 9-12; 9-13 Ex 9-1; 9-15 Ex 9-2; 10-2; 10-5; 10-6 (3); 10-7; 10-13 (2); 10-14; 10-24; 10-28; 10-30; 10-37 Ex 10-2; 10-38 Ex 10-3; 10-39 Ex 10-4; 12-9 (2); 14-1; 17-1 (2); 18-1; 18-2 (8); 18-5; 18-8; 19-3; 20-2; 21-5; 21-9; 23-3; 24-11;
PIH Notices: 03-20 (2); 03-12 (2); 03-11; 02-27 (2); 02-20; 02-01 (3); 01-41 (2); 01-15 (3); 01-15 Impr Integ Hbk (9); 00-49; 00-46; 00-24B (3); 00-11; 00-11A; 99-52 (3); 95-48 (10); 95-48 Tech Asst (10);
Admin Plan: s1p3; s4p2 (2); s6p13; s7p4; s7p5; s9p1; s10p2; s10p3 (2); s11p2; s18p8; s19p1 (2); s20p5 (2); s21p3

TYPE OF UNIT................................4
24 CFR 5: .655;
HUD-52667: p i;
7420.10G Gbk: 9-9; 10-24

UFAS..137
PIH Notices: 02-01 (16); 99-52 (16); 95-48 (52); 95-48 Tech Asst (52);
Admin Plan: s24p2

UFAS STANDARDS.........................2
PIH Notices: 95-48; 95-48 Tech Asst

UMAS...4
PIH Notices: 03-23 (3); 03-23

UNASSISTED................................98
24 CFR 5: .518;
24 CFR 982: .4 (2); .308 (4); .313; .451; .507 (2); .610 (2); .613; .618; .622;
HUD-50058Instr: p43; p44; p47 (2); p75 (2);
HUD-52517: p2;
HUD-52648: p1 (2);
7420.10G Gbk: 2-11; 9-13 Ex 9-1; 10-2; 10-13; 15-8; 17-4; 17-5; 17-7; 17-8; 17-12; 24-12;
PIH Notices: 03-12 (6); 02-27 (2); 02-22 (3); 01-41 (13); 01-15 Impr Integ Hbk (2); 00-24B (2); 00-09 (14); 95-48 (2); 95-48 Tech Asst (2);
Admin Plan: s8p4; s9p1; s9p2; s9p3 (2); s11p1 (2); s11p2 (2); s19p1 (3); s21p3; s24p4 (2); s24p5

UNASSISTED RENTAL...................4
24 CFR 982: .622;
PIH Notices: 01-15 Impr Integ Hbk (2);
Admin Plan: s19p1

UNASSISTED RENTAL UNITS........1
7420.10G Gbk: 9-13 Ex 9-1

UNASSISTED TENANTS.............18
24 CFR 982: .308 (4); .313; .451;
HUD-52641: p1; p3; p10;
HUD-52641-A: p2;
7420.10G Gbk: 8-5; 8-21 (3); 9-1; 11-7; 11-11;
Admin Plan: s9p2

UNASSISTED UNIT........................1
7420.10G Gbk: 21-4

UNASSISTED UNITS....................52
24 CFR 982: .4; .507 (2);
HUD-50058Instr: p75;
HUD-52517: p2;
HUD-52641: p1; p4 (2); p5; 8;
HUD-52641-A: p1 (3);
7420.10G Gbk: 8-18 (2); 9-1; 9-2; 9-3 (4); 9-4; 9-6; 9-8; 9-12; 11-12; 11-13; 14-4; 17-10; 17-11;
PIH Notices: 03-12 (5); 02-27; 01-41 (6); 00-24B; 00-09 (4);
Admin Plan: s11p1; s11p2 (2); s21p3; s24p5

UNATTENDED...............................1
24 CFR 5: .318

UNAUDITED FINANCIAL STATEMENT....................................1
Admin Plan: s7p5

UNAUDITED FINANCIAL

STATEMENTS 1
24 CFR 5: .801
UNAUTHORIZED 10
24 CFR 982: .401;
HUD-9886: p1; p2 (2);
7420.10G Gbk: 10-12 (2);
Admin Plan: s6p7 (2); s6p8; s20p2
UNAUTHORIZED HOUSEHOLD MEMBER 2
Admin Plan: s6p7; s6p8
UNDELIVERABLE 1
7420.10G Gbk: 4-5
UNDER 18 12
HUD-50058: p3; p4; p7;
HUD-50058Instr: p14; p15; p29; p36 (2);
HUD-903: p1 (2);
HUD-903-1: p4;
PIH Notices: 01-15 Impr Integ Hbk
UNDER HOUSING 3
24 CFR 5: .514 (2); .514
UNDER SEVEN YEARS OF AGE... 1
Admin Plan: s23p4
UNDER THE CONTROL 8
24 CFR 5: .350; .603;
24 CFR 982: .306;
HUD-50058Instr: p22;
HUD-52641: p6;
7420.10G Gbk: 8-19; 11-3;
Admin Plan: s16p2
UNDER UTILIZATION 1
7420.10G Gbk: 20-10
UNDER-REPORTING 3
7420.10G Gbk: 19-10; 20-25;
PIH Notices: 01-15 Impr Integ Hbk
UNDER-SERVED 1
7420.10G Gbk: 4-12
UNDERSTAND 39
HUD-50058Instr: p1 (2); p2;
7420.10G Gbk: 4-18; 4-23 Ex 4-1; 4-27 Ex 4-2 (2); 6-3 (3); 6-5; 8-1; 8-22; 8-23; 9-4; 9-9; 9-10; 11-15; 12-16 Ex 12-4 (2); 19-1; 21-2 (2); 21-7; 22-7; 22-8; 24-7; 24-9; 24-11;
PIH Notices: 02-01; 01-15 (2); 00-11A; 99-52; 95-48; 95-48 Tech Asst;
Admin Plan: s1p3; s8p4; s20p7
UNDERSTANDING 31
7420.10G Gbk: 1-7 (2); 2-5; 8-1; 8-5; 8-23; 9-3; 16-5; 19-11; 22-2; 22-8 (2); 24-10; 24-13;
PIH Notices: 03-20; 03-11; 01-41; 01-15 (3); 01-06 (4); 00-09; 95-48 (2); 95-48 Tech Asst (2);
Admin Plan: s25p1; s25p7
UNDERSTANDS 4
7420.10G Gbk: 5-11; 11-15; 13-8; 21-3
UNDERUTILIZATION 8
7420.10G Gbk: 20-17;
PIH Notices: 02-21 (4); 01-20 (2); 01-20
UNDER-UTILIZATION 1
7420.10G Gbk: 20-9
UNDERUTILIZED 2
7420.10G Gbk: 20-16; 24-1
UNDER-UTILIZED 1
7420.10G Gbk: 20-17
UNDERWRITING 2
24 CFR 982: .625; .625
UNDISCLOSED 3
24 CFR 5: .216; .236;
Admin Plan: s20p4
UNDUE 54
7420.10G Gbk: 4-11; 5-44; 8-3;
PIH Notices: 02-01 (9); 01-41; 00-09; 99-52 (9); 95-48 (13); 95-48 Tech Asst (13);
Admin Plan: s1p3; s1p5 (3); s1p5
UNDUE ADMINISTRATIVE BURDEN 1
Admin Plan: s1p5
UNDUE BURDEN 5
PIH Notices: 02-01; 99-52; 95-48; 95-48 Tech Asst;
Admin Plan: s1p5
UNDUE BURDENS 2
PIH Notices: 95-48; 95-48 Tech Asst
UNDUE FINANCIAL 33
7420.10G Gbk: 4-11; 5-44; 8-3;
PIH Notices: 02-01 (8); 99-52 (8); 95-48 (6); 95-48 Tech Asst (6);
Admin Plan: s1p3; s1p5
UNDUE FINANCIAL BURDEN...... 3
PIH Notices: 95-48; 95-48 Tech Asst;
Admin Plan: s1p5
UNDUE HARDSHIP 12
PIH Notices: 01-41; 00-09; 95-48 (5); 95-48 Tech Asst (4); 95-48 Tech Asst
UNDULY 2

7420.10G Gbk: 10-2; 13-7

UNEARNED....................................7
24 CFR 5: .210; .214 (2);
HUD-50058Instr: p71;
HUD-9886: p1 (2);
PIH Notices: 01-15

UNEARNED INCOME.....................6
24 CFR 5: .210; .214;
HUD-50058Instr: p71;
HUD-9886: p1 (2);
PIH Notices: 01-15

UNEMPLOYED..............................11
24 CFR 5: .617 (2);
HUD-50058Instr: p74;
7420.10G Gbk: 12-9; 23-1;
PIH Notices: 01-15 Impr Integ Hbk (2); 00-11; 00-11A;
Admin Plan: s6p2; s6p2

UNEMPLOYMENT........................33
24 CFR 5: .214 (5); .609;
HUD-50058: p6;
HUD-50058Instr: p32 (2);
HUD-9886: p1 (2);
7420.10G Gbk: 4-26 Ex 4-2; 5-14 Ex 5-2; 5-23 (3); 5-24; 12-13 Ex 12-1;
PIH Notices: 01-15 (5); 01-15 Impr Integ Hbk (4);
Admin Plan: s6p9; s7p4 (3); s7p5; s20p3

UNEMPLOYMENT BENEFITS 9
HUD-50058: p6;
HUD-50058Instr: p32;
7420.10G Gbk: 4-26 Ex 4-2; 5-23 (2); 5-24;
PIH Notices: 01-15 (2);
Admin Plan: s7p5

UNEMPLOYMENT COMPENSATION 3
7420.10G Gbk: 5-47 Ex 5-5; 12-13 Ex 12-1; 12-16 Ex 12-4

UNEMPLOYMENT OFFICE 1
Admin Plan: s7p4

UNFINISHED ATTIC 1
HUD-52580-A: p8

UNFINISHED ATTICS 2
24 CFR 982: .401;
7420.10G Gbk: 10-14

UNIFORM COMMERCIAL CODE . 1
Admin Plan: s20p4

UNIFORM FEDERAL 7
PIH Notices: 02-01; 99-52; 95-48 (3); 95-48 Tech Asst;
Admin Plan: s24p2

UNIFORM FEDERAL ACCESSIBILITY STANDARDS 7
PIH Notices: 02-01; 99-52; 95-48 (3); 95-48 Tech Asst;
Admin Plan: s24p2

UNIFORM RELOCATION ASSISTANCE....................................1
24 CFR 5: .100

UNINTENTIONAL...........................8
7420.10G Gbk: 20-6; 22-1 (2); 22-9;
PIH Notices: 02-07; 00-28;
Admin Plan: s20p1; s20p5

UNINTENTIONAL VIOLATIONS .. 1
Admin Plan: s20p1

UNINTENTIONALLY 4
7420.10G Gbk: 22-2 (3); 22-10

UNIT CONDITION...........................1
7420.10G Gbk: 8-3

UNIT INSPECTION........................19
24 CFR 982: Intro; .158 (2); .405; .641;
HUD-52665: p2;
7420.10G Gbk: 8-15; 9-15 Ex 9-2; 10-25; 10-26 (2); 10-27; 10-28; 10-30 (2);
PIH Notices: 00-24B (3); 00-23

UNIT INSPECTIONS 8
24 CFR 982: .633;
7420.10G Gbk: 10-24; 10-30; 10-35; 20-3; 21-4; 21-6;
PIH Notices: 00-09

UNIT MONTH 5
24 CFR 982: .355;
7420.10G Gbk: 20-19 Ex 20-3; 20-20; 24-1;
PIH Notices: 96-65

UNIT MONTHS 56
24 CFR 982: .102 (2);
7420.10G Gbk: 20-5 (3); 20-10; 24-1 (7); 24-2 (4); 24-15 (2);
PIH Notices: 03-23 (33); 02-21 (2); 02-14; 01-10

UNIT OFFERED 1
24 CFR 5: .359

UNIT SIZE....................................124
24 CFR 982: .402 (2); .403; .503 (9); .507; .517; .613;
HUD-50058: p iii; p iv; p ix (2); p x; p xi; p xiii; p xiv (2); p xvii;
HUD-50058Instr: p14; p39 (2); p42; p46; p47; p53; p57; p62; p68; p72; p76;
HUD-52580-A: p1 (3);
HUD-52648: p2;

HUD-52667: p i (2);
7420.10G Gbk: 3-5; 4-18; 5-41 (2); 5-42 (2); 6-3 (2); 6-6; 7-2; 7-5; 7-6; 8-10 (2); 8-17 (2); 9-1; 9-5; 11-19; 12-7 (3); 13-5 (2); 16-1; 16-2; 16-3; 17-5; 17-8 (2); 18-2 (2); 18-5 (6); 19-4; 22-6;
PIH Notices: 02-27; 02-22; 02-20 (9); 02-01; 01-41 (2); 01-06 (2); 00-46 (9); 00-24B (2); 00-09 (2); 99-52;
Admin Plan: s5p1 (4); s5p3 (3); s19p1 (2); s23p3; s23p4

UNIT SIZES....................................21
24 CFR 982: .503 (5);
7420.10G Gbk: 7-4; 7-6; 9-13 Ex 9-1; 18-2;
PIH Notices: 02-27; 02-20 (6); 01-01 (3); 00-46; 00-24B

UNIT TRANSFERS..........................1
7420.10G Gbk: 21-4

UNIT TYPE....................................15
24 CFR 982: .507;
HUD-52580: p7;
HUD-52580-A: p20;
HUD-52641: p4;
HUD-52667: p1;
7420.10G Gbk: 9-2; 9-3; 9-4; 9-5; 9-12; 9-17 Ex 9-3; 9-19 Ex 9-4;
PIH Notices: 03-12; 01-15 Impr Integ Hbk; 00-24B

UNIT TYPES....................................4
24 CFR 982: .517;
HUD-52667: p i;
7420.10G Gbk: 18-2; 18-2

UNIT-MONTHS...............................7
7420.10G Gbk: 20-3; 20-9; 20-12 Ex 20-2 (2); 20-20 (2);
Admin Plan: s21p8

UNITS MONTHS.............................4
7420.10G Gbk: 20-10 (2); 24-2;
PIH Notices: 03-23

UNPAID..10
24 CFR 982: .313;
7420.10G Gbk: 5-25 Ex 5-3;
PIH Notices: 02-27 (2); 95-48; 95-48 Tech Asst;
Admin Plan: s8p4; s9p3; s23p8; s23p8

UNPAID BALANCE........................1
7420.10G Gbk: 5-25 Ex 5-3

UNPAID RENT..............................10
24 CFR 982: .313;
HUD-52641: p10;
HUD-52641-A: p3;
7420.10G Gbk: 8-4; 14-5 (2); 23-14;
Admin Plan: s8p4; s23p8; s23p8

UNPROFESSIONAL.........................1
Admin Plan: s20p4

UNREIMBURSED MEDICAL EXPENSES.......................................9
24 CFR 5: .611;
24 CFR 982: .632;
HUD-50058: p7; p vii;
HUD-50058Instr: p35 (2);
PIH Notices: 01-15; 01-15 Impr Integ Hbk; 01-15 Impr Integ Hbk

UNRELATED ADULTS....................1
Admin Plan: s5p1

UNREPORTED...............................12
PIH Notices: 03-23; 01-15 (2);
Admin Plan: s6p8; s7p2 (2); s7p5; s20p2; s20p3 (2); s20p4; s20p4

UNREPORTED INCOME.................6
Admin Plan: s6p8; s7p2; s7p5; s20p3; s20p4; s20p4

UNRESOLVED................................1
7420.10G Gbk: 3-8

UNSANITARY.................................1
7420.10G Gbk: 10-4

UNSANITARY CONDITIONS.........1
7420.10G Gbk: 10-4

UNSCHEDULED.............................3
7420.10G Gbk: 21-9 (2); 21-11

UNSUBSIDIZED.............................5
24 CFR 982: .401; .510;
HUD-52580-A: p4;
7420.10G Gbk: 9-13 Ex 9-1; 10-6

UNSUBSIDIZED TENANTS...........6
24 CFR 982: .401; .510;
HUD-52580-A: p4;
HUD-52641: 8;
HUD-52641-A: p1;
7420.10G Gbk: 10-4

UNSUCCESSFUL...........................10
24 CFR 5: .518;
7420.10G Gbk: 5-35; 12-4; 21-9 (3);
PIH Notices: 02-27 (2);
Admin Plan: s16p2; s25p6

UNUSED BALANCE.......................3
24 CFR 982: .313;
HUD-52641: p10;
HUD-52641-A: p3

UNUSUAL..3
7420.10G Gbk: 9-7; 21-13;

PIH Notices: 03-12

UNUSUALLY....................................6
24 CFR 5: .603 (3);
HUD-50058Instr: p71; p73; p76

UNUSUALLY HIGH.........................6
24 CFR 5: .603 (3);
HUD-50058Instr: p71; p73; p76

UNVENTED ROOM HEATERS......2
24 CFR 982: .401;
7420.10G Gbk: 10-7

UPDATE..54
24 CFR 5: .350 (3);
24 CFR 982: .517;
HUD-50058: p2 (2); p ii;
HUD-50058Instr: p10 (7); p11 (3); p12 (10); p59; p77;
7420.10G Gbk: 4-5; 4-7; 8-13; 9-7 (5); 11-10; 12-8; 18-4; 18-8;
PIH Notices: 02-27; 01-15; 01-06; 00-53 (4); 00-24 (2);
Admin Plan: s1p6 (3); s3p2

UPDATED.....................................20
24 CFR 35 SubM: .1225;
7420.10G Gbk: 3-2; 9-7 (2); 12-3; 12-5; 19-9; 20-21; 24-3;
PIH Notices: 03-05; 02-20; 02-01; 01-40; 01-15 Impr Integ Hbk (2); 00-53; 00-46; 00-24; 99-52;
Admin Plan: s25p4

UPDATES......................................12
24 CFR 5: .609;
24 CFR 982: .204 (2);
7420.10G Gbk: 4-7; 5-16 Ex 5-2; 9-7; 19-5 (2);
PIH Notices: 02-01; 01-15 Impr Integ Hbk; 95-48; 95-48 Tech Asst

UPDATING....................................15
7420.10G Gbk: 2-4; 3-1; 4-4; 4-5; 4-7; 9-7 (6); 9-8; 21-4;
PIH Notices: 02-27; 01-06

UP-FRONT....................................10
PIH Notices: 02-27; 01-15 (8); 01-15

UP-FRONT INCOME VERIFICATION 1
PIH Notices: 01-15

UPKEEP...4
HUD-50058Instr: p30;
HUD-52580: p6;
HUD-52580-A: p19;
7420.10G Gbk: 2-11

UP-TO-DATE.................................13
HUD-52648: p1;
7420.10G Gbk: 4-1 (2); 4-5; 4-15; 4-22; 8-7; 22-7; 24-3; 24-8;
PIH Notices: 01-15 Impr Integ Hbk; 00-24B;
Admin Plan: s21p4

UPWARD MOBILITY.....................1
Admin Plan: s1p1

URA..1
24 CFR 5: .100

URBAN.......................................123
24 CFR 5: 24 CFR 5; .100 (2); .105 (2); .110; .500; .504;
HUD-50058: p1; p i (2); p3; p5; p71;
HUD-52580: p1 (3); 8; p10;
HUD-52641-A: p1; p3;
HUD-52648: p1 (4); p2 (3); p3 (8);
HUD-903-1: p1;
7420.10G Gbk: 5-42; 8-7;
PIH Notices: 03-23; 03-20; 03-12; 03-11; 03-05; 02-27 (3); 02-22 (2); 02-21; 02-20; 02-15; 02-14; 02-07; 02-06; 02-03; 02-01; 01-43; 01-41 (4); 01-40; 01-33; 01-27 (2); 01-20; 01-15 (2); 01-15 Impr Integ Hbk; 01-11; 01-10 (3); 01-06; 01-02; 01-01; 00-53; 00-49; 00-46; 00-45; 00-41 (2); 00-34; 00-31; 00-28; 00-27; 00-24; 00-24B; 00-23; 00-14; 00-11; 00-09 (7); 00-01; 99-52; 99-30; 99-11; 98-66; 96-65 (2); 95-48 (4); 95-48 Tech Asst (2);
Admin Plan: s1p1; s20p1; s21p1; s22p1; s24p1; s25p1 (2); s25p2 (2); s25p6; s25p7

URINALS...2
24 CFR 982: .605;
7420.10G Gbk: 17-2

USEABLE...4
24 CFR 982: .625;
HUD-52580-A: p17;
PIH Notices: 02-01; 99-52

USEFUL...24
HUD-50058Instr: p3;
7420.10G Gbk: 1-1; 4-12; 8-7 (3); 8-11 (2); 9-3; 9-4; 9-7; 11-8; 13-4; 18-1; 19-12; 20-22; 24-10;

24-12;
PIH Notices: 02-20; 01-15 Impr Integ Hbk; 00-53; 00-46; 95-48; 95-48 Tech Asst

USEFULNESS..................................1
7420.10G Gbk: 24-10

USER..17
7420.10G Gbk: 5-7; 10-1;
PIH Notices: 01-15; 01-11; 01-06 (3); 01-01; 00-53; 00-34; 99-11 (2); 95-48 (2); 95-48 Tech Asst (2);
Admin Plan: s1p5

USER-FRIENDLY............................2
7420.10G Gbk: 8-7; 24-12

USERS...22
HUD-50058Instr: p1;
7420.10G Gbk: 9-4; 19-5 (3);
PIH Notices: 03-20 (2); 01-06 (4); 95-48 (5); 95-48 Tech Asst (5);
Admin Plan: s1p5

UTILITIES...311
24 CFR 5: .100; .518; .520; .603 (2); .609 (4); .632;
24 CFR 982: .4 (3); .308 (3); .404; .452; .504; .507; .517 (4); .520; .555; .619; .622 (2); .623;
HUD-50058: p viii (2); p ix (6); p x (6); p xi (6); p xii (6); p xiii (2); p xv (2);
HUD-50058Instr: p28; p37 (2); p39 (3); p40 (3); p43 (3); p44 (3); p47 (2); p48; p49 (4); p50 (2); p51; p52 (3); p54 (2); p58 (2); p72; p75; p76 (2);
HUD-52517: p1 (8); p2 (4); p3 (3); p4 (4); 8 (2); p9 (3); p10;
HUD-52641-A: p1 (4); p2; p3;
HUD-52648: p1 (3); p i (9); p ii (2);
HUD-9886: p2;
7420.10G Gbk: 1-14; 4-17; 5-14 Ex 5-2 (4); 5-20 (4); 5-21 (6); 6-1; 6-3 (4); 6-4 (2); 6-6 (4); 6-7; 6-9 Ex 6-1; 6-10 Ex 6-2 (2); 8-3; 8-5 (4); 8-6; 8-15; 8-18; 8-20; 8-21 (2); 9-2; 9-4 (4); 9-5; 9-7 (2); 9-8; 9-12; 10-8; 10-28 (2); 11-6 (2); 11-11 (3); 11-12 (5); 11-14; 11-17 (2); 12-10; 14-1; 17-4; 17-11 (3); 17-12; 18-1 (11); 18-2 (3); 18-3 Ex 18-1; 18-4 (2); 18-6; 18-7 (5); 18-8 (6); 22-2; 22-11; 23-15;
PIH Notices: 03-12 (2); 02-27; 02-22; 02-20 (4); 01-41 (4); 01-15 Impr Integ Hbk (10); 01-10; 00-46 (3); 00-41; 00-24B (7); 00-09 (5);
Admin Plan: s6p4; s6p6; s6p8; s6p13 (5); s7p6; s9p1; s9p2 (2); s10p4; s10p5; s11p1; s11p2; s19p1 (3); s21p3; s23p4; s24p3; s24p3

UTILITY.......................................393
24 CFR 5: .601; .603 (3); .632 (13); .634; .703;
24 CFR 982: 24 CFR 982 (2); .4 (3); .307; .403; .504; .514 (4); .517 (28); .520; .555 (3); .604 (2); .613 (3); .617 (3); .619; .623 (2); .624 (5); .635 (2); .641;
HUD-50058: p9 (2); p ix (4); p10 (2); p x (3); p11 (3); p xi (5); p12 (2); p xii (3); p13; p xiii (3); p14; p xiv (2); p15; p xv (2);
HUD-50058Instr: p39 (8); p40 (6); p41 (3); p42; p43 (10); p44 (8); p45 (3); p46; p47 (8); p48 (3); p49 (10); p50 (3); p51 (7); p52 (9); p53; p54 (5); p56 (3); p58 (5); p72; p76 (5);
HUD-52580-A: p1; p8;
HUD-52648: p1 (7);
HUD-52665: p3;
HUD-52667: p1 (2); p i (9); p ii (2);
7420.10G Gbk: 2-11; 5-18; 5-20; 6-3 (4); 6-6; 8-7; 8-8; 8-15; 9-14 Ex 9-1 (2); 9-15 Ex 9-2 (2); 11-6; 12-5; 17-12; 18-1 (4); 18-2 (7); 18-4 (9); 18-5 (4); 18-6 (7); 18-9 (3); 18-10; 20-9; 22-2; 24-9;
PIH Notices: 02-27 (2); 02-20 (4); 01-41 (4); 01-15 Impr Integ Hbk (10); 01-10; 01-06; 00-46; 00-41; 00-24B (21); 00-09 (5);
Admin Plan: s2p6; s5p3 (2);

s6p7; s6p9; s6p13 (13); s8p2; s8p3; s9p3; s11p1; s16p3; s18p3; s18p4; s19p1 (13); s20p4; s21p1; s21p2; s21p4 (6); s21p4

UTILITY ALLOWANCE 296

24 CFR 5: .603 (2); .632; .634;
24 CFR 982: 24 CFR 982 (2); .4 (2); .403; .504; .517 (21); .555 (2); .604 (2); .613 (3); .617 (3); .619; .623 (2); .624; .635 (2); .641;
HUD-50058: p9 (2); p ix (4); p10 (2); p x (2); p11 (2); p xi (3); p12 (2); p xii (3); p13; p xiii; p14; p xiv; p15; p xv (2);
HUD-50058Instr: p39 (6); p40 (6); p41; p43 (8); p44 (8); p45; p47 (8); p48; p49 (8); p50 (3); p51 (5); p52 (7); p54 (4); p56 (2); p58 (5); p72; p76 (3);
HUD-52648: p1 (4);
HUD-52667: p i (3); p ii;
7420.10G Gbk: 1-10; 5-5 (2); 6-3 (4); 6-4 (2); 6-6; 6-8; 6-9 Ex 6-1 (2); 8-6; 9-17 Ex 9-3; 9-19 Ex 9-4; 11-8; 12-5; 16-2 (3); 17-1; 17-3 (2); 17-6 (5); 17-8 (2); 17-9 (5); 17-10; 17-11; 17-12; 18-1 (9); 18-2 (3); 18-4 (4); 18-6; 18-7 (7); 18-8 (6); 18-9 (7); 18-10 (3); 19-5; 22-6;
PIH Notices: 02-27; 02-20 (3); 01-41 (4); 01-15 Impr Integ Hbk (3); 01-10; 01-06; 00-46; 00-41; 00-24B (10); 00-09 (5);
Admin Plan: s5p3 (2); s6p13 (6); s8p2; s11p1; s18p3; s19p1 (7); s21p1; s21p2; s21p4 (4); s21p4

UTILITY ALLOWANCE SCHEDULE 52

24 CFR 982: 24 CFR 982 (2); .517 (15); .555; .624; .641;
HUD-52648: p1 (4);
HUD-52667: p i (2); p ii;
PIH Notices: 02-27; 02-20 (3); 01-06; 00-46; 00-24B (9);
Admin Plan: s6p13 (3); s8p2; s11p1; s21p2; s21p4 (3); s21p4

UTILITY ALLOWANCE SCHEDULES 2

HUD-52667: p i;
PIH Notices: 00-24B

UTILITY ALLOWANCES 32

24 CFR 982: .517 (2); .555; .624 (2);
HUD-52648: p1;
HUD-52667: p i;
7420.10G Gbk: 1-13; 6-9 Ex 6-1; 12-10; 12-11 (2); 17-12 (2); 18-2; 18-6 (2); 18-9 (4); 18-10 (3);
PIH Notices: 02-27; 00-24B;
Admin Plan: s6p13; s8p3; s18p4; s19p1 (2); s19p1

UTILITY BILL 5

24 CFR 5: .632 (2);
24 CFR 982: .514;
7420.10G Gbk: 11-6;
PIH Notices: 01-15 Impr Integ Hbk

UTILITY BILLS 8

24 CFR 982: .307;
HUD-52646: p2;
7420.10G Gbk: 5-39; 18-1;
Admin Plan: s2p6; s6p7; s9p3; s16p3

UTILITY CONSUMPTION 4

7420.10G Gbk: 6-3; 18-4; 18-5;
PIH Notices: 00-24B

UTILITY HOOK-UP 4

24 CFR 982: .624;
7420.10G Gbk: 17-12;
Admin Plan: s19p1; s19p1

UTILITY REIMBURSEMENT.......53

24 CFR 5: .603; .632 (5);
24 CFR 982: .4;
HUD-50058: p x; p11; p xi (2); p xiii; p xiv;
HUD-50058Instr: p39 (2); p41 (2); p42; p43 (2); p45 (2); p46; p48 (2); p49 (2); p51 (2); p52 (2); p53; p56; p76 (2);
HUD-52665: p3;
7420.10G Gbk: 6-6 (6); 6-7; 6-8 (3); 11-6; 11-14;
PIH Notices: 01-15 Impr Integ Hbk (3);
Admin Plan: s6p13; s6p13

UTILITY REIMBURSEMENTS 2

24 CFR 5: .601; .632

UTILITY ROOM 2

HUD-52580-A: p1; p8

UTILITY SUPPLIER 11

24 CFR 5: .632 (4);

24 CFR 982: .514 (3);
7420.10G Gbk: 11-6;
PIH Notices: 01-15 Impr Integ Hbk (2); 01-15 Impr Integ Hbk

UTILITY SUPPLIERS 4
HUD-52667: p i (2);
7420.10G Gbk: 18-4; 18-4

UTILITY SUPPLIERS' 1
7420.10G Gbk: 18-6

UTILIZATION...............................123
7420.10G Gbk: 4-9; 7-10; 8-23; 13-4; 13-6 (4); 20-2; 20-7; 20-9; 20-10 (4); 20-11 (3); 20-13; 20-16 (7); 20-17 (4); 20-18; 20-19 Ex 20-3; 20-20 (4); 20-22; 20-30; 21-2; 24-1 (3); 24-2 (11); 24-3; 24-6 (2); 24-8 (4); 24-12; 24-15; 24-16 (3);
PIH Notices: 03-23 (2); 02-21 (22); 02-14; 02-06 (11); 02-01; 01-20 (8); 00-27; 00-14 (4); 99-52;
Admin Plan: s1p6; s3p1; s3p2; s4p2; s8p1 (2); s11p1

UTILIZE 18
24 CFR 982: .401; .605; .614;
7420.10G Gbk: 10-3; 20-16;
PIH Notices: 03-11 (3); 02-14 (2); 95-48; 95-48 Tech Asst;
Admin Plan: s1p4; s3p1; s8p1; s8p2; s9p1; s20p2

UTILIZED 15
7420.10G Gbk: 20-2; 20-16; 24-1;
PIH Notices: 02-27 (2); 02-14; 00-27; 95-48; 95-48 Tech Asst;
Admin Plan: s4p2; s7p2; s10p1; s15p6; s17p1; s20p1

UTILIZES...3
7420.10G Gbk: 20-15; 20-18;
Admin Plan: s3p2

UTTERED 1
Admin Plan: s20p6

VACANCIES 10
7420.10G Gbk: 9-5 (3); 9-7 (2); 24-12;
Admin Plan: s23p8 (2); s24p5; s24p7

VACANCY 32
24 CFR 5: .518 (2); .661;
HUD-52665: p3 (2);
7420.10G Gbk: 1-8 (2); 7-6; 8-7; 9-5; 9-6; 9-7; 14-5 (2); 19-11; 21-11; 24-15;
PIH Notices: 02-21; 01-41 (3); 01-20; 00-27; 00-09 (3);
Admin Plan: s8p4; s23p3; s23p4; s24p5 (2); s24p7

VACANCY LOSS.............................5
HUD-52665: p3 (2);
7420.10G Gbk: 14-5 (2);
Admin Plan: s8p4

VACANT 43
HUD-52580-A: p4; p8 (2); p17;
HUD-903: p1;
7420.10G Gbk: 2-6; 7-6 (2); 8-7; 8-15; 9-4; 9-5 (3); 9-6; 9-7 (3); 9-13 Ex 9-1; 10-21; 11-19; 19-11; 20-23; 24-9 (2); 24-15;
PIH Notices: 02-21; 02-01 (3); 01-41 (2); 01-20; 00-27; 00-24B; 00-09 (3); 99-52 (3);
Admin Plan: s23p3; s23p3

VACANT UNIT.................................4
7420.10G Gbk: 8-7; 9-7;
PIH Notices: 02-01; 99-52

VACANT UNITS............................16
7420.10G Gbk: 2-6; 7-6 (2); 9-4; 9-5 (3); 9-6; 24-9 (2); 24-15;
PIH Notices: 01-41; 00-09 (2);
Admin Plan: s23p3; s23p3

VACATE 11
24 CFR 982: .310; .314;
7420.10G Gbk: 13-3; 15-3;
Admin Plan: s8p3; s10p2; s13p1; s14p1; s23p5; s23p7; s23p8

VACATED 13
7420.10G Gbk: 11-19; 13-1; 14-5; 17-1; 20-23; 22-2; 22-13; 23-2;
Admin Plan: s13p2; s14p1 (2); s14p2; s23p8

VACATES..5
PIH Notices: 00-24B;
Admin Plan: s14p1; s14p2; s23p6; s24p6

VACATING.......................................2
7420.10G Gbk: 14-5;
Admin Plan: s10p5

VACATION.......................................3
24 CFR 982: .312;
7420.10G Gbk: 10-24;
Admin Plan: s7p6

VACATIONS 1
7420.10G Gbk: 21-3

VAGUE 1
Admin Plan: s20p3
VALIDATED 1
7420.10G Gbk: 5-46 Ex 5-5
VALIDATES 1
7420.10G Gbk: 19-2
VALIDATIONS 1
PIH Notices: 00-53
VALUABLE 9
7420.10G Gbk: 2-6; 9-5; 19-4; 19-9; 20-22; 21-10;
PIH Notices: 01-41; 00-11; 00-09
VALUATION 1
PIH Notices: 03-12
VALUE 124
24 CFR 5: .350; .603 (7); .609; .659;
24 CFR 982: .317 (2); .510; .516;
HUD-50058: p6 (5);
HUD-50058Instr: p22 (11); p23 (2); p74 (2);
7420.10G Gbk: 1-11; 4-27 Ex 4-2 (2); 5-14 Ex 5-2; 5-16 Ex 5-2 (2); 5-19 (2); 5-24; 5-25 Ex 5-3 (3); 5-26 (6); 5-27 (10); 5-28 (5); 5-34; 5-47 Ex 5-5 (2); 5-48 Ex 5-5 (2); 5-49 Ex 5-5 (5); 5-50 Ex 5-5; 9-8; 9-9 (2); 9-11; 12-4; 12-16 Ex 12-4; 17-11; 22-3; 22-7; 24-14;
PIH Notices: 02-27; 02-01; 01-15; 01-15 Impr I nteg Hbk (10); 00-24B (2); 99-52; 95-48 (2); 95-48 Tech Asst (2);
Admin Plan: s6p10 (6); s7p3; s7p5 (2); s7p6 (6); s21p4
VALUED... 1
7420.10G Gbk: 5-27
VALUES 7
HUD-50058: p6 (2);
HUD-50058Instr: p22 (2);
PIH Notices: 03-12; 02-27;
Admin Plan: s24p4
VALUING.. 2
7420.10G Gbk: 5-28;
PIH Notices: 03-12
VALUING ASSETS.......................... 1
7420.10G Gbk: 5-28
VAN 15
HUD-50058Instr: p35 (2);
7420.10G Gbk: 2-12 Ex 2-1;
PIH Notices: 95-48 (6); 95-48 Tech Asst (5); 95-48 Tech Asst
VARIATION 8
24 CFR 982: .401 (2);
HUD-52580-A: p13;
7420.10G Gbk: 9-9; 10-2; 18-9; 21-1;
PIH Notices: 03-20
VARIATIONS 22
24 CFR 5: .603 (3);
24 CFR 982: .401 (7);
HUD-50058Instr: p71; p73; p76;
7420.10G Gbk: 5-20; 9-10; 10-2 (4); 18-4; 21-1;
PIH Notices: 03-20
VASH 5
Admin Plan: s25p2 (2); s25p3 (2); s25p3
VEHICLE 31
HUD-50058Instr: p3;
PIH Notices: 02-27 (17); 95-48 (5); 95-48 Tech Asst (5);
Admin Plan: s3p2; s25p6; s25p6
VEHICLES 9
24 CFR 5: .703;
7420.10G Gbk: 5-25 Ex 5-3; 5-30; 22-7;
PIH Notices: 02-27 (4);
Admin Plan: s10p5
VENDOR....................................... 23
PIH Notices: 03-20 (5); 02-27 (12); 00-53;
Admin Plan: s10p1 (4); s25p6
VENDORS....................................... 6
HUD-50058Instr: p3;
PIH Notices: 00-53 (4); 00-53
VENDOR'S 2
PIH Notices: 02-27; 02-27
VENTILATED................................. 1
7420.10G Gbk: 10-19
VENTILATING 1
7420.10G Gbk: 10-10
VENTILATION 21
24 CFR 5: .703;
24 CFR 982: .401 (2);
HUD-52580: p2; p5;
HUD-52580-A: p2; p6 (4); p7; p15 (3); p16 (2);
7420.10G Gbk: 10-6; 10-8; 10-10 (2); 10-11
VERIFIABLE 3
Admin Plan: s20p1; s20p3; s20p3
VERIFICATION 427
24 CFR 5: .110; .214;

.216 (4); .218 (4); .236 (5); .240 (2); .508 (9); .512 (23); .514 (12); .526; .613; .659 (5);
24 CFR 35 SubM: .1225 (2);
24 CFR 982: .207; .355; .508; .516 (3);
HUD-50058: p3; p4; p5;
HUD-50058Instr: p15 (2); p17; p18 (2); p40; p44; p48; p51; p54; p57; p68;
HUD-52580-A: p1; p4 (3); p6 (3); p15 (4); p17;
HUD-52648: p1 (5);
7420.10G Gbk: 4-7; 4-13; 4-15; 4-17; 5-4 (3); 5-6 (2); 5-7 (10); 5-8 (3); 5-9 Ex 5-1 (6); 5-11 (3); 5-12; 5-17 (2); 5-21; 5-28; 5-34 (6); 5-35 (12); 5-36 Ex 5-4; 5-46 Ex 5-5 (6); 5-47 Ex 5-5 (4); 5-48 Ex 5-5 (4); 5-49 Ex 5-5 (6); 5-50 Ex 5-5 (2); 5-51 Ex 5-5 (5); 5-52 Ex 5-5 (4); 5-53 Ex 5-5 (4); 8-10; 10-20; 10-23; 10-28; 12-1 (3); 12-3; 12-4 (10); 12-5 (4); 12-8 (2); 12-10; 12-11 (3); 12-12 Ex 12-1 (2); 12-13 Ex 12-1 (3); 12-14 Ex 12-2; 13-3; 13-7; 19-1; 19-10 (3); 21-8; 21-10; 22-3 (8); 22-4 (3); 22-13; 24-7;
PIH Notices: 02-27; 02-01; 01-41 (3); 01-15 (27); 01-15 Impr Integ Hbk (12); 01-06; 01-01; 00-24B (3); 00-11 (2); 00-11A (10); 00-09 (3); 99-52;
Admin Plan: s1p5; s2p3 (3); s2p5 (5); s3p2 (2); s3p3 (5); s6p4; s6p6 (2); s6p9 (2); s6p13; s7p1 (12); s7p2 (3); s7p3 (6); s7p4 (10); s7p5 (7); s7p6 (8); s7p7 (9); s7p8 (8); s15p6; s20p1 (2); s20p2; s20p4 (2); s21p3 (2); s21p4 (4); s21p5 (2); s21p6 (2); s21p7 (2); s21p8 (3); s21p9 (2); s23p4

VERIFICATION FORM 12
7420.10G Gbk: 5-9 Ex 5-1 (2); 5-46 Ex 5-5; 5-47 Ex 5-5 (2); 5-48 Ex 5-5; 5-49 Ex 5-5; 12-4;
Admin Plan: s7p4 (3); s7p4

VERIFICATION FORMAT 1
Admin Plan: s7p8

VERIFICATION FORMS 10
7420.10G Gbk: 5-17; 5-49 Ex 5-5; 12-3;
PIH Notices: 01-15;
Admin Plan: s3p3; s7p1; s7p3; s7p5 (2); s7p6

VERIFICATION REQUEST FORM. 3
24 CFR 5: .512; .514;
7420.10G Gbk: 5-11

VERIFICATION SOURCES 1
Admin Plan: s7p2

VERIFICATIONS 24
7420.10G Gbk: 12-2; 12-4; 13-3; 13-8; 13-9; 19-10 (2); 19-13;
PIH Notices: 02-27; 01-15; 00-24B (2);
Admin Plan: s3p2; s3p3; s7p1 (7); s7p6; s23p3; s23p3

VERIFIED 70
24 CFR 5: .216; .236 (3);
24 CFR 982: .201; .553;
HUD-50058Instr: p15; p18;
HUD-52641: p5;
HUD-52648: p1;
7420.10G Gbk: 4-15; 4-18; 4-19; 5-3; 5-6; 5-10 Ex 5-1; 5-17; 5-46 Ex 5-5; 5-47 Ex 5-5 (2); 5-48 Ex 5-5; 5-49 Ex 5-5; 5-50 Ex 5-5 (4); 5-51 Ex 5-5 (2); 5-52 Ex 5-5; 5-53 Ex 5-5; 10-16; 10-31; 12-1; 12-10; 12-11; 16-5; 19-2; 21-8; 22-6;
PIH Notices: 02-01; 01-27; 01-15 (2); 01-15 Impr Integ Hbk (2); 01-01; 99-52;
Admin Plan: s2p1; s3p3 (2); s6p11; s7p1 (2); s7p2; s7p3 (2); s7p7; s7p8; s15p5; s20p6; s21p4; s21p6 (2); s21p7 (2); s21p8 (4); s21p9

VERIFIES 16
24 CFR 5: .512;
24 CFR 35 SubM: .1225;
24 CFR 982: .201; .404; .619;
HUD-52641: p3;
7420.10G Gbk: 1-11; 5-17; 5-23; 11-12; 12-10;
PIH Notices: 01-41; 01-15; 00-24B; 00-09;
Admin Plan: s7p1

VERIFY 113
24 CFR 5: .210 (2); .216 (10);

.218; .230 (2); .236; .240; .512; .514;
24 CFR 35 SubM: .1225;
24 CFR 982: .207; .312 (2); .551 (2);
HUD-50058: p i;
HUD-50058Instr: p2; p15; p16;
HUD-52580-A: p2; p4; p15;
HUD-52646: p2 (2);
HUD-9886: p1 (4); p2;
7420.10G Gbk: 4-17 (2); 4-18; 4-22 (2); 5-8 (2); 5-9 Ex 5-1; 5-12; 5-13 (3); 5-28; 5-40; 5-46 Ex 5-5; 5-48 Ex 5-5; 5-51 Ex 5-5 (2); 10-20; 10-32; 12-3; 12-12 Ex 12-1; 12-14 Ex 12-2; 15-6; 18-10; 22-3; 22-10; 23-3; 23-14;
PIH Notices: 03-11; 02-27; 02-06; 02-01 (2); 01-15 (4); 01-15 Impr Integ Hbk (3); 01-06 (2); 01-01; 00-24A; 00-24B (8); 00-11A (3); 99-52 (2);
Admin Plan: s1p4; s2p2; s5p2; s6p1; s6p4; s6p6; s6p9; s7p2 (2); s7p3; s7p5; s11p1; s18p7; s18p8; s20p4; s21p9

VERIFYING....................................22
24 CFR 5: .230;
24 CFR 982: .201;
HUD-9886: p2 (2);
7420.10G Gbk: 1-14; 4-17; 5-49 Ex 5-5 (2); 12-4; 13-2; 20-3; 21-4;
PIH Notices: 02-27; 02-06; 01-15 (2); 01-15 Impr Integ Hbk (3);
Admin Plan: s7p4; s7p6; s7p7

VERMIN...17
24 CFR 5: .703 (2);
24 CFR 982: .401 (3); .614;
HUD-52580-A: p17; p18;
7420.10G Gbk: 10-9 (2); 10-13 (4); 10-14; 17-5;
Admin Plan: s10p5

VERY LOW INCOME....................15
24 CFR 5: .603; .653 (6);
24 CFR 982: .201 (2);
HUD-50058Instr: p19; p76;
PIH Notices: 01-41; 00-24B; 00-09;
Admin Plan: s1p1

VERY LOW-INCOME....................17
7420.10G Gbk: 1-12; 2-1 (2); 2-8 (2); 3-3; 3-7; 4-8; 4-20; 23-10 (2); 23-11; 23-17 Ex 23-2;
PIH Notices: 03-20; 02-01; 99-52;
Admin Plan: s23p3

VERY YOUNG CHILDREN 2
24 CFR 982: .401;
7420.10G Gbk: 10-6

VERY-LOW INCOME......................1
Admin Plan: s23p3

VETERAN..6
HUD-50058Instr: p32;
7420.10G Gbk: 5-16 Ex 5-2;
PIH Notices: 01-15 Impr Integ Hbk;
Admin Plan: s25p2; s25p3; s25p3

VETERANS......................................8
7420.10G Gbk: 5-50 Ex 5-5;
PIH Notices: 00-41;
Admin Plan: s4p2; s25p2 (3); s25p3; s25p3

VETERAN'S 1
Admin Plan: s25p3

VETERINARIAN.............................1
24 CFR 5: .350

VIABILITY 2
24 CFR 5: .653;
Admin Plan: s24p4

VIABLE...9
PIH Notices: 02-27 (7); 99-11;
Admin Plan: s1p1

VICINITY..6
24 CFR 982: .306; .310; .551 (2); .553;
Admin Plan: s16p2

VICIOUS 1
24 CFR 5: .360

VICTIM 7
HUD-50058Instr: p32 (2);
HUD-903-1: p1;
7420.10G Gbk: 5-16 Ex 5-2 (2);
PIH Notices: 01-15 Impr Integ Hbk; 01-15 Impr Integ Hbk

VICTIM COMPENSATION 3
HUD-50058Instr: p32;
7420.10G Gbk: 5-16 Ex 5-2;
PIH Notices: 01-15 Impr Integ Hbk

VICTIMS 18
24 CFR 5: .655 (2);
24 CFR 982: .207 (3);
HUD-50058Instr: p32 (2);
7420.10G Gbk: 4-16; 4-17 (2); 5-16 Ex 5-2 (3);
PIH Notices: 01-15 Impr Integ Hbk (2); 95-48;

95-48 Tech Asst;
Admin Plan: s1p2

VICTIMS OF DOMESTIC VIOLENCE 6
24 CFR 5: .655 (2);
24 CFR 982: .207 (2);
7420.10G Gbk: 4-16; 4-17

VIETNAM 3
HUD-50058Instr: p32;
7420.10G Gbk: 5-16 Ex 5-2;
PIH Notices: 01-15 Impr Integ Hbk

VIETNAM VETERAN 3
HUD-50058Instr: p32;
7420.10G Gbk: 5-16 Ex 5-2;
PIH Notices: 01-15 Impr Integ Hbk

VIGOROUS.......................................9
24 CFR 982: .404 (2); .619;
HUD-52648: p1;
7420.10G Gbk: 10-33; 10-34;
PIH Notices: 00-24B;
Admin Plan: s21p5; s21p5

VILLAGE 1
7420.10G Gbk: 2-13 Ex 2-1

VILLAGES.......................................5
24 CFR 982: .503;
PIH Notices: 02-20 (2); 00-46; 00-46

VIOLATE...11
24 CFR 5: .238; .318; .350;
7420.10G Gbk: 8-20;
PIH Notices: 95-48 (3); 95-48 Tech Asst (3);
Admin Plan: s9p3

VIOLATED.....................................48
24 CFR 5: .353 (3);
24 CFR 982: .306 (2); .453 (2); .553 (2);
HUD-50058Instr: p63 (2);
HUD-52641: p5 (2); p6 (2);
HUD-903: p1;
HUD-903-1: p3;
7420.10G Gbk: 5-36; 8-18; 11-2; 11-4 (2);
PIH Notices: 01-41 (2); 00-09; 95-48 (6); 95-48 Tech Asst (6);
Admin Plan: s2p6; s15p4; s15p5; s16p1 (2); s20p5; s20p6 (4); s25p5

VIOLATES 5
24 CFR 982: .552;
7420.10G Gbk: 15-5 (2);
Admin Plan: s2p7; s15p2

VIOLATING.....................................7
24 CFR 982: .310;
HUD-52641: p9;
HUD-52641-A: p2;
7420.10G Gbk: 15-6; 24-13;
Admin Plan: s18p1; s20p1

VIOLATION 138
24 CFR 5: .321; .350; .353 (19);
24 CFR 35 SubM: .1225;
24 CFR 982: .202; .306; .310 (4); .353; .403; .551 (3); .552; .619; .638; .641;
HUD-50058: p17 (2);
HUD-50058Instr: p63 (2);
HUD-52580: p5;
HUD-52580-A: p17;
HUD-52641: p6; p9;
HUD-52641-A: p2;
HUD-903-1: p4;
7420.10G Gbk: 5-7; 5-36 Ex 5-4; 8-18; 8-19; 10-19; 10-21; 10-27 (3); 10-28; 10-29 (4); 10-33 (2); 10-34 (3); 10-46 Ex 10-8; 10-48 Ex 10-10; 11-1; 11-3; 11-12; 11-17; 11-18; 15-1; 15-2; 16-5; 18-1; 22-1; 22-9; 22-16;
PIH Notices: 02-21; 02-07; 01-41 (2); 01-20; 00-28 (2); 00-09; 99-11 (2); 96-65; 95-48 (6); 95-48 Tech Asst (6);
Admin Plan: s2p5; s5p3; s7p2; s10p3; s10p5; s13p2 (2); s14p1; s14p2; s15p1; s15p2; s15p3; s15p4 (2); s15p5 (5); s15p6; s16p1; s17p2; s20p5 (9); s20p7; s20p8; s23p6; s23p6

VIOLATION OF THE LEASE........20
24 CFR 982: .310; .353; .551; .552;
HUD-52641: 8; p9;
HUD-52641-A: p1; p2 (2);
7420.10G Gbk: 1-15; 13-2; 15-1; 15-5;
PIH Notices: 99-11;
Admin Plan: s13p2; s14p2; s15p2; s15p5 (2); s15p5

VIOLATIONS.................................56
HUD-903: p2 (2);
7420.10G Gbk: 1-9; 5-35; 5-40; 8-8; 10-28 (2); 10-29 (2); 10-30; 10-33 (2); 10-34 (3); 10-42 Ex 10-5 (2); 10-44 Ex 10-7a; 10-45 Ex 10-7b; 11-4; 15-1 (2); 15-4; 15-7 (3); 20-6; 21-4; 22-2; 22-15;
PIH Notices: 02-07; 02-01; 00-09; 99-52; 99-11 (2); 95-48 (2); 95-

48 Tech Asst (2);
Admin Plan: s10p5 (2); s14p1; s15p5 (2); s16p1; s16p2 (2); s18p1; s20p1; s20p2; s20p5 (2); s20p7; s23p3

VIOLATIONS OF THE LEASE 1
Admin Plan: s14p1

VIOLATOR 1
24 CFR 982: .310

VIOLATORS 1
PIH Notices: 03-11

VIOLENCE 20
24 CFR 5: .655 (2);
24 CFR 982: .207 (3); .315;
HUD-903: p3;
HUD-903-1: p6;
7420.10G Gbk: 2-11; 4-16; 4-17 (2);
PIH Notices: 02-01 (3); 99-52 (2);
Admin Plan: s15p2 (2); s15p2

VIOLENT 47
24 CFR 5: .100;
24 CFR 982: .4; .306 (2); .310; .316; .453; .551; .552; .553 (2);
HUD-52641: p5; p6; p7; p9;
HUD-52641-A: p2 (2);
7420.10G Gbk: 1-15; 4-15; 5-36 Ex 5-4; 5-37 (2); 8-19; 8-20; 11-3; 11-4; 15-2; 15-4; 15-6 (2); 21-4; 24-14;
Admin Plan: s2p3; s2p6 (3); s6p6; s15p2 (3); s15p3 (2); s15p5 (2); s16p1; s16p2; s23p7

VIOLENT CRIMINAL ACTIVITY 20
24 CFR 5: .100;
24 CFR 982: .4; .306 (2); .310; .316; .453; .551; .553 (2);
Admin Plan: s2p3; s2p6; s6p6; s15p2; s15p3 (2); s15p5; s16p1; s16p2; s23p7

VISIT 11
24 CFR 5: .303;
7420.10G Gbk: 8-14; 20-29; 24-13;
PIH Notices: 02-27 (3); 02-22 (2); 99-11;
Admin Plan: s6p7

VISITABILITY 25
PIH Notices: 02-01 (13); 99-52 (11); 99-52

VISITABLE 2
PIH Notices: 02-01; 99-52

VISITED 3
PIH Notices: 01-41; 00-09;
Admin Plan: s8p5

VISITING 4
24 CFR 5: .318;
PIH Notices: 02-21; 01-20; 99-11

VISITOR 3
Admin Plan: s6p7 (2); s6p8

VISITORS 3
PIH Notices: 95-48; 95-48 Tech Asst;
Admin Plan: s6p7

VISITOR'S 1
Admin Plan: s6p7

VISITS 12
24 CFR 982: .312;
7420.10G Gbk: 4-11; 4-13 (2); 12-13 Ex 12-1; 15-6;
PIH Notices: 99-11 (4); 95-48; 95-48 Tech Asst

VISUAL IMPAIRMENTS 3
7420.10G Gbk: 4-11;
PIH Notices: 95-48; 95-48 Tech Asst

VISUALLY IMPAIRED 2
7420.10G Gbk: 5-44; 8-3

VOCAL CORDS 3
24 CFR 5: .318;
PIH Notices: 95-48; 95-48 Tech Asst

VOCATIONAL 11
24 CFR 5: .603;
HUD-50058: p16;
HUD-50058Instr: p15; p60; p61 (2); p72;
7420.10G Gbk: 5-29;
PIH Notices: 95-48; 95-48 Tech Asst;
Admin Plan: s25p7

VOCATIONAL SCHOOL 1
HUD-50058Instr: p15

VOCATIONAL TRAINING 3
24 CFR 5: .603;
HUD-50058Instr: p72;
Admin Plan: s25p7

VOICE 31
7420.10G Gbk: 4-13 (2); 10-34;
PIH Notices: 95-48 (14); 95-48 Tech Asst (13); 95-48 Tech Asst

VOLATILE 1
7420.10G Gbk: 10-19

VOLUNTARY 61
24 CFR 982: .201; .203;
HUD-50058: p16;

HUD-50058Instr: p19; p38; p61 (2); p70;
HUD-903: p3;
7420.10G Gbk: 4-11; 4-20; 4-22; 5-3; 23-1; 23-2 (3); 23-4;
PIH Notices: 02-14 (6); 01-41 (13); 01-10; 00-53; 00-09 (12); 95-48 (2); 95-48 Tech Asst (2);
Admin Plan: s2p4; s8p4; s13p1; s25p2; s25p3; s25p5

VOLUNTARY CONVERSIONS 1
7420.10G Gbk: 23-2

VOLUNTARY WORK 1
HUD-50058Instr: p70

VOLUNTEER.................................... 6
HUD-50058Instr: p27;
7420.10G Gbk: 2-7; 5-16 Ex 5-2;
PIH Notices: 01-15 Impr Integ Hbk; 95-48; 95-48 Tech Asst

VOLUNTEER SERVICES................ 3
HUD-50058Instr: p27;
7420.10G Gbk: 5-16 Ex 5-2;
PIH Notices: 01-15 Impr Integ Hbk

VOLUNTEERS 3
HUD-50058Instr: p27;
7420.10G Gbk: 5-16 Ex 5-2;
PIH Notices: 01-15 Impr Integ Hbk

VOTE.. 1
7420.10G Gbk: 24-1

VOTER REGISTRATION................. 2
7420.10G Gbk: 13-2;
Admin Plan: s20p4

VOUCHER HOLDER..................... 27
24 CFR 982: .4;
HUD-50058Instr: p76;
7420.10G Gbk: 7-4; 8-8 (2); 11-17; 13-2; 13-7; 20-24 (4);
PIH Notices: 02-06 (2); 01-01 (8);
Admin Plan: s8p4; s9p1; s9p2 (2); s10p3

VOUCHER HOLDERS.................. 31
7420.10G Gbk: 5-38; 5-40; 7-3 (2); 7-4 (2); 7-5; 7-6; 7-7 (4); 7-9 (2); 8-7; 8-12 (2); 8-14; 9-9; 16-3; 17-1; 19-8; 19-11; 20-15; 20-17; 23-18; 23-20; 24-8; 24-9; 24-10; 24-15

VOUCHER ISSUANCE................. 21
HUD-50058Instr: p10;
7420.10G Gbk: 4-18; 8-10 (3); 13-4; 19-2; 19-6; 19-7 (4); 19-8; 19-11;
PIH Notices: 01-01 (2);
Admin Plan: s2p3; s2p4; s8p1; s8p5; s15p6

VOUCHER PROGRAM 430
24 CFR 5: .520 (3); .601; .603 (2); .617; .632 (2); .634; .653; .801;
24 CFR 35 SubM: .1200 (2);
24 CFR 982: Intro; .1 (5); .2; .4 (7); .201 (10); .205 (4); .353 (2); .355 (4); .402 (3); .501; .502 (5); .503 (3); .504; .552; .627; .631; .635; .636 (2); .638; .643;
HUD-50058: p xi; p16; p xvi; p17 (2);
HUD-50058Instr: p1; p2 (2); p9 (4); p10 (5); p12; p13; p19 (4); p42 (3); p47; p59 (2); p60; p62 (4); p63 (7); p71; p72; p73; p74; p75; p76 (3);
HUD-52580: p1 (7); p3 (4); p4 (2); 8 (5); p10 (3);
HUD-52641-A: p1 (5); p3 (3);
HUD-52648: p2 (3);
HUD-52665: p1; p2;
7420.10G Gbk: 1-4 (4); 1-5 (2); 1-7; 1-9; 3-1; 4-9; 4-20 (3); 4-25 Ex 4-2; 5-3; 5-37; 5-38; 7-9; 8-5; 8-6; 9-2; 11-14; 13-2; 13-4; 14-1; 15-6; 19-1; 19-10 (2); 20-2; 20-4; 20-8 Ex 20-1; 20-16; 20-22; 20-22 Ex 20-5; 20-23; 20-24 (2); 21-3; 21-11; 23-3; 23-19; 23-20 (3); 24-3; 24-6; 24-8; 24-9; 24-12; 24-13 (3); 24-15;
PIH Notices: 03-23 (5); 03-20 (7); 03-12 (3); 03-05 (3); 02-27 (14); 02-22 (7); 02-21 (7); 02-20 (12); 02-14 (2); 02-07 (7); 02-06 (3); 02-01 (8); 01-41 (18); 01-40 (3); 01-33 (4); 01-27 (3); 01-20 (4); 01-15; 01-10 (9); 01-06 (6); 01-02 (2); 01-01 (4); 00-49 (6); 00-46 (12); 00-41; 00-28 (6); 00-27 (2); 00-24B (4); 00-23 (2); 00-14; 00-11 (2); 00-09 (20); 99-52 (2);
Admin Plan: s3p1; s3p2; s4p2; s5p3; s6p2; s8p2 (3);

s8p4; s9p2 (2); s10p3; s11p3; s15p2; s16p1; s19p1 (2); s21p7 (2); s22p2; s22p3; s22p4; s22p5; s23p1; s23p8; s24p1 (2); s24p5; s24p6; s24p7; s25p1; s25p2; s25p4; s25p5

VOUCHER PROGRAMS 15
7420.10G Gbk: 1-1; 1-4 (6); 1-5; 20-8 Ex 20-1; 21-17; 21-18 (3); 21-19; 23-19

VOUCHER-HOLDER....................... 3
24 CFR 982: .53; .353; .452

VOUCHER-HOLDERS 2
PIH Notices: 01-02; 01-02

W-2.. 4
7420.10G Gbk: 5-46 Ex 5-5;
PIH Notices: 95-48 (2);
Admin Plan: s7p4

W-9.. 4
7420.10G Gbk: 11-18; 11-19 (2); 11-19

WAGE 45
24 CFR 5: .210; .214 (3); .617 (2); .659 (2);
24 CFR 982: .627;
HUD-50058: p6 (3);
HUD-50058Instr: p25 (2); p27; p71; p74;
HUD-9886: p1 (3);
7420.10G Gbk: 5-13; 16-5;
PIH Notices: 01-15 (12); 01-15 Impr Integ Hbk (4);
Admin Plan: s6p2 (3); s6p3; s20p3 (2); s20p4

WAGE DATA.................................... 2
PIH Notices: 01-15;
Admin Plan: s20p3

WAGE REPORTS.............................. 1
24 CFR 5: .214

WAGE SUBSIDIES........................... 3
24 CFR 5: .617;
PIH Notices: 01-15 Impr Integ Hbk;
Admin Plan: s6p3

WAGES.. 41
24 CFR 5: .210; .214 (5); .609;
HUD-50058: p6;
HUD-50058Instr: p25 (3); p26; p27 (3); p28; p71 (2);
HUD-9886: p1 (3);
7420.10G Gbk: 4-23 Ex 4-1; 5-14 Ex 5-2; 5-17 (6); 5-46 Ex 5-5 (2); 23-12; 23-15;
PIH Notices: 01-15 (2); 01-15 Impr Integ Hbk (4);
Admin Plan: s20p3; s20p4

WAIT... 18
7420.10G Gbk: 4-1; 4-4; 4-5; 4-15; 8-8; 8-9 (2); 8-10; 8-12 (2); 13-6; 13-7; 24-8;
PIH Notices: 01-06; 00-34 (2); 00-24;
Admin Plan: s23p1

WAIT LIST 1
Admin Plan: s23p1

WAITED 1
7420.10G Gbk: 21-8

WAITER'S.. 1
PIH Notices: 01-15 Impr Integ Hbk

WAITING 194
24 CFR 5: .216; .359; .655;
24 CFR 982: 24 CFR 982 (5); .4 (4); .54 (3); .201 (4); .202 (6); .203 (2); .204 (20); .205 (17); .206 (5); .207 (3); .355; .552; .629;
HUD-50058: p5; p v;
HUD-50058Instr: p18; p19 (4); p75 (2); p76 (2);
HUD-52648: p1 (5);
7420.10G Gbk: 4-12; 8-12; 19-6; 22-10;
PIH Notices: 02-27 (4); 02-06; 02-01 (3); 01-41 (6); 01-27 (3); 01-06; 00-24B (11); 00-09 (5); 99-52 (3); 95-48; 95-48 Tech Asst;
Admin Plan: s1p6; s2p1 (5); s2p3 (3); s2p5; s3p1 (3); s3p2 (5); s4p1 (10); s4p2 (5); s5p1; s15p1; s18p2; s18p8; s21p1; s21p2; s21p3 (4); s23p1 (2); s23p3 (3); s23p5; s24p6 (5); s24p7; s25p1 (2); s25p3 (2); s25p3

WAITING LIST 422
24 CFR 5: .216; .359; .655;
24 CFR 982: 24 CFR 982 (5); .4 (4); .54 (3); .201 (3); .202 (6); .203 (2); .204 (19); .205 (17); .206 (5); .207 (3); .355; .552; .629;
HUD-50058: p5; p v;
HUD-50058Instr: p19 (4); p75 (2); p76 (2);
HUD-52648: p1 (5);
7420.10G Gbk: 1-6; 1-7 (5); 1-8 (3); 1-10; 1-11; 1-13; 1-16 Ex 1-3; 3-2 (5);

3-7; 3-9 (2); 4-1 (12); 4-2 (3); 4-3; 4-4 (11); 4-5 (14); 4-6 (14); 4-7 (9); 4-8 (14); 4-9 (13); 4-10 (5); 4-11 (2); 4-12 (3); 4-13 (5); 4-14 (5); 4-15 (3); 4-16 (2); 4-17; 4-18 (13); 4-19 (2); 4-20 (3); 4-21 (2); 4-22 (9); 4-23 Ex 4-1; 5-35; 8-1; 8-10 (2); 8-12; 8-13; 8-23; 13-6 (2); 19-6; 19-7 (4); 19-8 (5); 19-9 (6); 19-10 (3); 20-4; 20-15; 21-2; 21-3 (4); 21-4 (2); 21-5 (2); 21-8 (7); 21-11; 21-13; 21-16 Ex 21-6 (2); 21-19 (2); 22-2; 22-7; 23-6; 23-10; 23-20 (2); 24-3 (6); 24-4 (2); 24-6 (2); 24-8;
PIH Notices: 02-27 (4); 02-06; 02-01 (3); 01-41 (6); 01-27 (3); 01-06; 00-24B (11); 00-09 (5); 99-52 (3);
Admin Plan: s1p6; s2p1 (5); s2p3 (3); s2p5; s3p1 (3); s3p2 (5); s4p1 (10); s4p2 (5); s5p1; s15p1; s18p2; s18p8; s21p1; s21p2; s21p3 (4); s23p1 (2); s23p3 (3); s23p5; s24p6 (5); s24p7; s25p1 (2); s25p3 (2); s25p3

WAITING LISTS............................14
24 CFR 982: .201; .204;
7420.10G Gbk: 1-6; 1-7; 3-7; 4-2; 4-6 (2); 4-8 (2); 4-18; 4-19; 21-8; 21-8

WAITS 1
7420.10G Gbk: 24-8

WAIVE..4
24 CFR 5: .110;
7420.10G Gbk: 8-19; 11-2; 15-10 Ex 15-2

WAIVED...7
24 CFR 982: .161;
HUD-50058: p8; p viii;
HUD-50058Instr: p37;
HUD-52641: p6;
7420.10G Gbk: 11-2;
Admin Plan: s16p2

WAIVER...11
HUD-52641: p5;
7420.10G Gbk: 4-20; 11-2 (4); 11-3; 15-10 Ex 15-2;
PIH Notices: 01-15; 00-41;
Admin Plan: s25p4

WAIVERS...4
24 CFR 5: 24 CFR 5; .110;
PIH Notices: 01-15 Impr Integ Hbk; 00-41

WAIVERS--TABLE 1
24 CFR 5

WALK...5
7420.10G Gbk: 21-9;
PIH Notices: 95-48 (2); 95-48 Tech Asst; 95-48 Tech Asst

WALKED..1
HUD-52580-A: p8

WALK-IN..6
7420.10G Gbk: 4-12 (4); 4-13; 21-9

WALKING..6
24 CFR 982: .614;
HUD-52580-A: p2;
PIH Notices: 95-48 (2); 95-48 Tech Asst; 95-48 Tech Asst

WALKS...5
24 CFR 5: .703;
24 CFR 982: .401; .614;
7420.10G Gbk: 10-13; 17-5

WALKUP..1
HUD-52517: p1

WALKWAYS...................................18
24 CFR 5: .703;
24 CFR 982: .401; .614;
7420.10G Gbk: 10-9;
PIH Notices: 95-48 (7); 95-48 Tech Asst (6); 95-48 Tech Asst

WALL..32
24 CFR 982: .401 (2); .614 (2);
HUD-52580: p1; p2 (2); p3 (3); p4 (2); p6 (2);
HUD-52580-A: p2 (3); p3; p5; p6 (2); p7; p8; p9; p10; p11; p12; p19 (2);
7420.10G Gbk: 10-9 (2);
PIH Notices: 99-11

WALLS 23
24 CFR 5: .703 (4);
24 CFR 982: .401; .614;
HUD-52580-A: p2 (2); p3; p5; p7; p9; p10; p11; p12; p13 (2); p17;
7420.10G Gbk: 10-9; 18-2;
PIH Notices: 02-01; 00-23; 99-52

WARM-BLOODED...........................1
24 CFR 5: .318

WARN...1
Admin Plan: s20p2

WARNING.......................................21
HUD-52648: p3;
7420.10G Gbk: 10-36 Ex 10-1;

15-7 (2); 20-10 (5); 20-11 (3); 24-2 (3);
PIH Notices: 95-48; 95-48 Tech Asst;
Admin Plan: s7p2; s7p3 (2); s20p5

WARNINGS 13
PIH Notices: 95-48 (6); 95-48 Tech Asst (6);
Admin Plan: s20p2

WASHER 5
HUD-52580-A: p8;
7420.10G Gbk: 9-13 Ex 9-1; 9-15 Ex 9-2; 9-17 Ex 9-3; 9-17 Ex 9-3

WASTE 32
24 CFR 5: .210; .318 (5); .350 (7); .703;
24 CFR 982: .401 (2); .517 (2); .605; .609; .614 (2);
7420.10G Gbk: 10-3 (2); 10-5 (2); 10-11; 19-9;
PIH Notices: 01-15 Impr Integ Hbk; 95-48; 95-48 Tech Asst;
Admin Plan: s20p1

WASTE REMOVAL 3
24 CFR 5: .318 (2); .318

WASTED 1
7420.10G Gbk: 9-1

WASTES 2
24 CFR 982: .401;
HUD-52580-A: p18

WATER 146
24 CFR 5: .703 (5);
24 CFR 982: .401 (7); .517 (2); .605; .614 (3);
HUD-52517: p1;
HUD-52580: p5 (2);
HUD-52580-A: p2 (3); p4 (4); p5; p6 (12); p7 (2); p13 (5); p15 (22); p16 (5);
HUD-52641: p2;
HUD-52667: p1 (4); p i (4); p ii (7);
7420.10G Gbk: 6-3; 6-9 Ex 6-1; 9-14 Ex 9-1 (2); 9-15 Ex 9-2 (2); 10-1; 10-3 (5); 10-4; 10-5 (4); 10-9 (2); 10-11 (6); 17-4 (2); 17-5; 18-2 (2); 18-4 (3); 18-5 (4); 18-6 (4); 18-8;
PIH Notices: 02-01; 99-52; 99-11 (2); 95-48 (4); 95-48 Tech Asst (4);
Admin Plan: s10p4

WATER HEATER 13
HUD-52580: p5;
HUD-52580-A: p15 (6); p16 (2);
7420.10G Gbk: 10-2 (2); 10-7; 10-11

WATER HEATERS 6
HUD-52580-A: p15 (4);
7420.10G Gbk: 10-11; 10-11

WATER HEATING 12
24 CFR 982: .517;
HUD-52517: p1;
HUD-52641: p2;
HUD-52667: p1 (2); p i (2);
7420.10G Gbk: 18-2 (2); 18-6; 18-7; 18-8

WATER HEATING SYSTEM 2
HUD-52580-A: p15; p15

WEATHER 8
HUD-52580: p6;
HUD-52580-A: p19;
7420.10G Gbk: 10-5; 10-10; 10-18; 10-24; 18-4;
PIH Notices: 00-23

WEATHERTIGHT 2
24 CFR 982: .401; .614

WEDLOCK 2
24 CFR 982: .202;
7420.10G Gbk: 4-19

WEEKEND 4
7420.10G Gbk: 4-12; 8-9;
PIH Notices: 01-01;
Admin Plan: s17p1

WEEKENDS 3
7420.10G Gbk: 9-6; 10-33;
Admin Plan: s18p5

WEIGHED 1
7420.10G Gbk: 4-12

WEIGHING 1
7420.10G Gbk: 8-8

WEIGHT 6
24 CFR 5: .318;
PIH Notices: 02-20; 01-06; 00-46;
Admin Plan: s15p4; s15p4

WEIGHTED 4
HUD-52648: p4;
PIH Notices: 02-20; 01-06; 00-46

WEIGHTS 2
7420.10G Gbk: 3-2; 10-25

WELFARE 413
24 CFR 5: .603 (3); .609 (7); .613 (3); .615 (61); .628 (3);
24 CFR 982: .352; .401; .614; .627 (3);
HUD-50058: p i; p2; p ii; p v (2); p6 (2); p8; p viii (4); p16 (2); p xvi (3); p17 (2);

p xvii (2);
HUD-50058Instr: p ii; p1; p2 (2); p3; p4; p5; p10; p11; p13 (3); p17 (4); p19 (2); p28 (4); p30; p37 (7); p59 (3); p62 (3); p63 (2); p66; p71 (4); p72 (2); p73 (2); p75 (8); p76 (5);
7420.10G Gbk: 1-6 Ex 1-1 (2); 1-7 (6); 2-11; 3-2; 4-3; 4-5; 4-23 Ex 4-1; 4-26 Ex 4-2; 5-14 Ex 5-2 (2); 5-18; 5-20 (4); 5-21 (13); 5-22 (12); 5-46 Ex 5-5 (2); 5-47 Ex 5-5 (3); 6-1 (2); 6-5; 6-10 Ex 6-2; 7-6; 8-5; 8-8; 10-13; 12-9; 17-5; 20-17; 22-11; 23-3; 23-4; 23-7 (2); 23-14 (2); 23-17 Ex 23-2; 23-18; 23-20;
PIH Notices: 02-14; 01-41; 01-15; 01-15 Impr Integ Hbk (16); 01-10 (3); 00-11 (50); 00-11A (66); 95-48 (3); 95-48 Tech Asst (3);
Admin Plan: s6p9; s6p12 (12); s6p13 (5); s7p3; s7p4 (2); s11p2 (3); s11p3 (3); s18p5; s22p1; s23p2; s25p1; s25p3; s25p4

WELFARE AGENCIES 18
24 CFR 5: .613; .615;
7420.10G Gbk: 5-18; 5-22; 23-4;
PIH Notices: 00-11 (11); 00-11A; 00-11A

WELFARE AGENCY....................100
24 CFR 5: .613; .615 (21);
HUD-50058Instr: p30; p37; p71; p72; p75 (4);
7420.10G Gbk: 1-7 (4); 5-20; 5-21 (2); 22-11;
PIH Notices: 01-15; 01-15 Impr Integ Hbk; 00-11 (9); 00-11A (42); 95-48; 95-48 Tech Asst;
Admin Plan: s6p12 (2); s6p13 (2); s7p3; s11p3; s25p1

WELFARE AGENCY'S...................2
24 CFR 5: .615; .615

WELFARE ASSISTANCE 69
24 CFR 5: .603; .609 (4); .615; .628 (3);
24 CFR 982: .627 (3);
HUD-50058: p viii (3);
HUD-50058Instr: p37 (4); p62; p71; p75; p76 (3);
7420.10G Gbk: 5-14 Ex 5-2 (5); 5-21; 5-23; 12-16 Ex 12-4; 23-1; 23-6; 23-7; 23-9 (2); 23-10; 23-14 (5);
PIH Notices: 01-15 Impr Integ Hbk (9); 00-11 (6); 00-11A (4);
Admin Plan: s6p9; s6p12 (2); s11p2; s11p3; s25p4

WELFARE ASSISTANCE PAYMENT 4
24 CFR 5: .609;
7420.10G Gbk: 5-14 Ex 5-2;
PIH Notices: 01-15 Impr Integ Hbk; 01-15 Impr Integ Hbk

WELFARE ASSISTANCE PAYMENTS..2
24 CFR 5: .609; .609

WELFARE BENEFIT......................15
24 CFR 5: .615 (6);
HUD-50058Instr: p28; p71; p73; p75;
7420.10G Gbk: 4-5; 5-21; 5-47 Ex 5-5;
Admin Plan: s6p12; s6p13

WELFARE BENEFIT REDUCTION 11
24 CFR 5: .615 (5);
HUD-50058Instr: p28; p71; p73; p75;
Admin Plan: s6p12; s6p13

WELFARE BENEFITS 26
24 CFR 5: .613; .615 (12);
HUD-50058Instr: p28; p71; p75;
7420.10G Gbk: 5-21; 12-9;
PIH Notices: 01-15 Impr Integ Hbk; 00-11A (3); 95-48; 95-48 Tech Asst;
Admin Plan: s6p12; s11p2

WELFARE BENEFITS REDUCTION..8
24 CFR 5: .615 (7); .615

WELFARE HOTELS.........................3
HUD-50058Instr: p72;
Admin Plan: s23p2; s25p3

WELFARE INCOME 38
24 CFR 5: .603; .615 (16);
HUD-50058: p6;
HUD-50058Instr: p28; p73;
7420.10G Gbk: 5-14 Ex 5-2 (2); 5-21 (2); 5-22 (8);
PIH Notices: 00-11;
Admin Plan: s6p12 (3); s6p13; s6p13

WELFARE OFFICES 1
7420.10G Gbk: 4-3

WELFARE RENT............................22
HUD-50058: p8; p viii;
HUD-50058Instr: p37 (2); p66;
7420.10G Gbk: 1-6 Ex 1-1 (2); 5-20 (2); 5-21 (2); 6-1 (2); 6-5; 6-10 Ex 6-2; 8-5; 23-17 Ex 23-2;
PIH Notices: 01-41; 01-15 Impr Integ Hbk; 01-10 (2); 01-10

WELFARE SANCTIONS 2
7420.10G Gbk: 5-22;
PIH Notices: 01-15 Impr Integ Hbk

WELFARE TO WORK....................39
HUD-50058: p i; p2; p ii; p v (2); p16 (2); p xvi (3); p17 (2); p xvii (2);
HUD-50058Instr: p ii; p1; p2 (2); p3; p4; p10; p11; p13 (3); p17 (2); p19 (2); p59 (3); p62 (2); p63 (2);
PIH Notices: 02-14; 00-11; 00-11A

WELFARE-TO-WORK...................42
24 CFR 5: .617;
24 CFR 982: .4 (2); .201 (2); .301 (3); .552 (2);
HUD-50058Instr: p13; p19 (2); p76;
7420.10G Gbk: 1-7; 4-20; 8-6; 15-6 (2); 21-5; 21-8; 21-11; 23-19 (7); 23-20 (8);
PIH Notices: 01-15 Impr Integ Hbk (2); 00-11; 00-11A;
Admin Plan: s15p2

WHEELCHAIR 27
HUD-50058Instr: p35;
7420.10G Gbk: 5-30 (2); 7-9; 9-16 Ex 9-2; 9-17 Ex 9-3;
PIH Notices: 02-01; 99-52; 95-48 (9); 95-48 Tech Asst (9);
Admin Plan: s1p3

WHEELCHAIRS............................25
7420.10G Gbk: 5-30;
PIH Notices: 02-01 (2); 99-52 (2); 95-48 (10); 95-48 Tech Asst (9); 95-48 Tech Asst

WIDOW..3
HUD-50058Instr: p29 (2); p29

WIDOW'S 1
PIH Notices: 01-15 Impr Integ Hbk

WILLFUL VIOLATIONS 1
Admin Plan: s20p2

WILLING 33
24 CFR 982: .160; .301; .302;
HUD-52646: p1;
HUD-52648: p2;
7420.10G Gbk: 2-3 (2); 2-7; 2-8 (2); 8-15; 9-4; 9-6; 9-7 (2); 10-2; 16-4; 21-2; 23-3;
PIH Notices: 02-21 (2); 02-01; 01-41; 01-20 (2); 00-09; 99-52;
Admin Plan: s1p7; s9p1; s9p2; s21p5; s21p6; s23p3

WILLINGNESS................................4
7420.10G Gbk: 21-9; 23-6; 24-12;
Admin Plan: s20p7

WIND..10
24 CFR 982: .621 (2);
HUD-52580-A: p2; p13 (2);
7420.10G Gbk: 10-10; 17-10; 17-11;
Admin Plan: s19p1; s19p1

WIND DAMAGE 5
24 CFR 982: .621;
HUD-52580-A: p13;
7420.10G Gbk: 17-10; 17-11;
Admin Plan: s19p1

WINDOW.......................................76
24 CFR 982: .401 (6);
HUD-52580: p1; p2 (2); p3 (3); p4 (2);
HUD-52580-A: p2 (13); p3 (2); p4 (3); p5; p6 (5); p7; p8 (7); p9 (2); p10 (2); p11 (2); p12 (2); p13; p17 (3);
7420.10G Gbk: 9-13 Ex 9-1; 9-15 Ex 9-2; 9-17 Ex 9-3; 10-6 (4); 10-7; 10-8; 10-10 (3); 10-11; 10-18;
PIH Notices: 01-41; 00-49; 00-09;
Admin Plan: s10p2

WINDOWS.....................................70
24 CFR 5: .703 (3);
24 CFR 982: .401 (6); .605; .614;
HUD-52580: p6 (4);
HUD-52580-A: p2 (11); p3 (2); p5 (2); p7 (3); p8; p9 (2); p10 (2); p11 (2); p12 (2); p13 (2); p14; p15 (2); p16; p17; p19 (4);
7420.10G Gbk: 9-6; 10-6 (5); 10-8 (2); 10-10 (2); 10-12 (3); 17-2;
PIH Notices: 00-23; 95-48;

95-48 Tech Asst

WINDOWS-BASED 1
7420.10G Gbk: 10-25

WIRING 14
24 CFR 982: .401; .517;
HUD-52580-A: p2 (5);
HUD-52667: p i;
7420.10G Gbk: 10-8; 10-9; 18-1;
PIH Notices: 99-11; 95-48; 95-48 Tech Asst

WITHDRAW 21
24 CFR 5: .653;
24 CFR 982: .156; .204; .316; .503; .520;
HUD-50058Instr: p62;
7420.10G Gbk: 4-6; 5-26;
PIH Notices: 03-11; 02-20 (5); 00-46 (5);
Admin Plan: s2p3

WITHDRAWAL 27
24 CFR 5: .609 (4);
24 CFR 982: .156; .503;
HUD-50058Instr: p25;
7420.10G Gbk: 4-10; 5-14 Ex 5-2 (4); 5-19 (2); 5-25 Ex 5-3; 5-28; 5-35;
PIH Notices: 02-20; 01-15 Impr Integ Hbk (8); 00-46

WITHDRAWALS 4
24 CFR 982: .156;
HUD-50058Instr: p25 (2);
7420.10G Gbk: 20-23

WITHDRAWING 4
24 CFR 982: .552;
7420.10G Gbk: 9-12; 23-10;
Admin Plan: s15p1

WITHDRAWN 8
24 CFR 5: .661;
7420.10G Gbk: 4-10; 5-25 Ex 5-3; 5-28; 19-7; 19-9;
PIH Notices: 01-15 Impr Integ Hbk;
Admin Plan: s15p5

WITHHOLD 8
7420.10G Gbk: 10-29; 23-10;
PIH Notices: 02-27 (2); 01-06; 95-48; 95-48 Tech Asst;
Admin Plan: s18p4

WITHHOLDING 6
7420.10G Gbk: 5-10 Ex 5-1 (2); 22-13; 23-5;
PIH Notices: 02-27; 02-27

WITNESS 4
PIH Notices: 00-11A; 95-48; 95-48 Tech Asst;
Admin Plan: s9p3

WITNESS PROTECTION 1
Admin Plan: s9p3

WITNESSES 15
24 CFR 5: .514;
24 CFR 982: .555;
HUD-903: p2;
7420.10G Gbk: 16-5; 22-11; 22-16;
PIH Notices: 95-48; 95-48 Tech Asst;
Admin Plan: s15p4; s18p3; s18p5 (2); s18p6; s20p4; s20p4

WOMAN 4
24 CFR 982: .402;
7420.10G Gbk: 5-19; 5-41;
Admin Plan: s5p1

WOMEN 2
7420.10G Gbk: 5-42; 10-36 Ex 10-1

WORD-FOR-WORD 6
24 CFR 982: .162; .308;
HUD-52517: p2;
HUD-52646: p1;
7420.10G Gbk: 11-12;
PIH Notices: 00-24B

WORK 336
24 CFR 5: .603 (5); .611; .615; .617; .630; .655;
24 CFR 982: .4; .207; .401;
HUD-50058: p i; p2; p ii; p v (2); p7; p16 (2); p xvi (3); p17 (2); p xvii (2);
HUD-50058Instr: p ii; p1 (2); p2 (2); p3; p4; p5; p10; p11; p13 (3); p17 (3); p19 (2); p25; p28 (3); p32; p36 (2); p59 (3); p62 (2); p63 (2); p70; p71 (4); p73 (2); p74;
HUD-52580: p5;
HUD-52580-A: p2; p5; p13; p17 (2);
HUD-52648: p1;
7420.10G Gbk: 1-4; 1-7 (4); 2-9 (2); 2-11; 3-2; 4-6; 4-12 (3); 4-17 (2); 4-25 Ex 4-2 (2); 4-26 Ex 4-2 (4); 4-27 Ex 4-2; 5-14 Ex 5-2; 5-17; 5-20; 5-21; 5-29 (5); 5-30 (5); 5-32; 5-33 (3); 5-34 (2); 5-43; 5-52 Ex 5-5; 6-8; 7-6; 8-15; 8-23; 9-7; 10-5; 10-17 (2); 10-18 (2); 10-22; 10-26; 10-33; 10-37 Ex 10-2 (3); 12-8; 12-9; 19-5; 19-12; 20-17; 21-1 (3); 21-2 (7); 21-3 (2);

21-5; 21-7 (2); 21-8 (2); 21-10; 22-6 (2); 22-7 (4); 23-1; 23-10; 23-15 (2); 23-16 Ex 23-2 (2); 23-20 (2); 24-10 (2); 24-12; 24-15 (2);
PIH Notices: 03-23 (4); 03-11 (2); 02-27 (45); 02-21 (2); 02-14; 02-01 (3); 01-41; 01-20 (2); 01-15 (10); 01-15 Impr Integ Hbk (6); 01-06 (4); 00-53 (2); 00-49 (2); 00-27; 00-11 (17); 00-11A (7); 00-09; 00-01; 99-52 (3); 99-11 (2); 98-66; 95-48 (10); 95-48 Tech Asst (10);
Admin Plan: s1p6; s4p2; s6p2 (2); s6p3 (3); s6p10; s6p11 (3); s6p12 (2); s6p13; s11p3; s20p4 (3); s24p5 (3)

WORK ACTIVITY............................5
HUD-50058Instr: p28;
7420.10G Gbk: 12-9;
PIH Notices: 00-11A (2); 00-11A

WORK NUMBER............................7
PIH Notices: 01-15 (6); 01-15

WORK PLACEMENT......................3
24 CFR 5: .603;
HUD-50058Instr: p71;
Admin Plan: s6p3

WORK PRODUCT...........................1
Admin Plan: s20p4

WORK STUDY................................3
HUD-50058Instr: p32;
7420.10G Gbk: 5-20;
PIH Notices: 01-15 Impr Integ Hbk

WORKABILITY..............................1
HUD-52580-A: p2

WORKED..9
24 CFR 5: .655;
24 CFR 982: .207;
7420.10G Gbk: 3-8; 4-17; 5-17; 12-16 Ex 12-4; 13-6; 24-15;
PIH Notices: 00-11A

WORKER..3
7420.10G Gbk: 12-16 Ex 12-4;
Admin Plan: s2p3; s7p8

WORKERS......................................5
24 CFR 982: .553;
7420.10G Gbk: 5-9 Ex 5-1; 21-19 (2);
PIH Notices: 01-15 Impr Integ Hbk

WORKERS'.....................................2
HUD-50058Instr: p27; p29

WORKER'S......................................8
24 CFR 5: .609 (2);
HUD-50058Instr: p31;
PIH Notices: 01-15 Impr Integ Hbk (4);
Admin Plan: s6p10

WORKER'S COMPENSATION.....10
24 CFR 5: .609 (2);
HUD-50058Instr: p31;
7420.10G Gbk: 5-14 Ex 5-2; 5-15 Ex 5-2;
PIH Notices: 01-15 Impr Integ Hbk (4);
Admin Plan: s6p10

WORKFARE 5
24 CFR 5: .603;
HUD-50058Instr: p71;
PIH Notices: 00-11A (2);
Admin Plan: s6p3

WORKFORCE...............................13
HUD-50058Instr: p27;
7420.10G Gbk: 5-16 Ex 5-2 (2);
PIH Notices: 01-15 (2); 00-11 (4); 00-01; 98-66; 95-48; 95-48 Tech Asst

WORKFORCE INVESTMENT........6
HUD-50058Instr: p27;
7420.10G Gbk: 5-16 Ex 5-2 (2);
PIH Notices: 00-11 (2); 00-11

WORKING..................................147
24 CFR 5: .655 (5); .703;
24 CFR 35 SubM: .1225;
24 CFR 982: .207 (4); .401;
HUD-50058Instr: p29;
HUD-52580: p6 (2);
HUD-52580-A: p2 (3); p3 (3); p4 (14); p5 (3); p6 (10); p7 (4); p8; p9 (4); p10 (4); p11 (4); p12 (4); p15 (3); p16; p18; p19 (2);
HUD-52665: p2;
7420.10G Gbk: 4-2; 4-3; 4-12; 4-16 (2); 4-17 (4); 4-18 (2); 8-9; 9-5; 10-5 (2); 10-8; 10-9; 10-10 (3); 10-20; 10-22; 12-16 Ex 12-4; 15-10 Ex 15-2; 16-5; 17-2; 19-11; 21-11; 23-10;
PIH Notices: 02-27 (14); 02-01 (2); 01-15 Impr Integ Hbk; 01-06; 00-11 (2); 99-52 (2); 95-48 (5); 95-48 Tech Asst (5);
Admin Plan: s2p6; s6p2; s6p11; s10p1; s11p1; s11p3; s23p6; s24p5; s25p8

WORKING FAMILIES 11
24 CFR 5: .655 (3);
24 CFR 982: .207 (2);
7420.10G Gbk: 4-12; 4-16 (2); 4-17; 8-9;
Admin Plan: s25p8

WORKING FAMILY 4
24 CFR 5: .655;
24 CFR 982: .207;
7420.10G Gbk: 4-17; 4-18

WORKING FAMILY PREFERENCE3
24 CFR 5: .655;
24 CFR 982: .207;
7420.10G Gbk: 4-17

WORKING RELATIONSHIP 2
7420.10G Gbk: 10-22;
Admin Plan: s11p3

WORKLOAD 20
7420.10G Gbk: 4-11; 8-9 (2); 10-23; 10-35; 11-15; 12-1; 19-10; 19-12; 21-1 (2); 21-2; 21-3; 21-5; 21-7 (4); 21-9;
PIH Notices: 01-06

WORK-LOAD 2
PIH Notices: 01-41; 00-09

WORKLOADS 4
7420.10G Gbk: 21-5; 21-8; 21-10; 21-17

WORKMANLIKE 1
7420.10G Gbk: 5-43

WORKPLACE 4
24 CFR 5: .105 (2);
PIH Notices: 95-48; 95-48 Tech Asst

WORKS 38
24 CFR 982: .4; .301 (3);
HUD-50058Instr: p60 (2);
HUD-52580-A: p4; p5 (2); p6 (2); p15 (2);
HUD-52648: p2;
7420.10G Gbk: 2-2; 2-3; 2-8; 2-9; 4-13 (2); 4-15; 5-17 (2); 5-29; 5-30 (2); 6-1; 8-1; 8-3; 8-10; 16-4; 21-3;
PIH Notices: 01-15 Impr Integ Hbk; 96-65;
Admin Plan: s8p1; s8p2 (2); s21p6

WORKSHEET 59
HUD-50058Instr: p ii (2); p64; p65 (3); p66; p67; p68 (4); p69;
7420.10G Gbk: 8-6; 20-20 (4); 20-21 Ex 20-4; 20-21 (2); 20-22; 23-14; 23-16 Ex 23-2 (2); 23-17 Ex 23-2;
PIH Notices: 02-20 (5); 01-41 (10); 00-46 (5); 00-27 (4); 00-09 (8); 00-09

WORKSHEETS 11
HUD-52667: p ii;
7420.10G Gbk: 18-4;
PIH Notices: 02-20 (2); 01-41 (3); 01-15; 00-46 (2); 00-09

WORKSHOP 5
7420.10G Gbk: 21-16 Ex 21-6;
Admin Plan: s8p3 (2); s8p4; s24p2

WORKSHOPS 9
7420.10G Gbk: 10-22; 10-26; 22-7; 22-9;
PIH Notices: 02-01; 00-11A (2); 99-52;
Admin Plan: s25p7

WORKSITE 1
7420.10G Gbk: 10-37 Ex 10-2

WORK-STUDY 1
7420.10G Gbk: 5-16 Ex 5-2

WORST CASE 1
24 CFR 982: .201

WRITTEN 267
24 CFR 5: .216; .312 (2); .353 (8); .360; .403; .508 (3); .514 (4); .611; .613; .615 (3); .630; .655; .661;
24 CFR 982: .4 (2); .54; .151; .156 (2); .201; .305; .308; .310; .313; .502; .552; .554; .555 (2);
HUD-50058: p6;
HUD-50058Instr: p22; p34; p38; p70 (2); p73 (3);
HUD-52641: p7; p10;
HUD-52641-A: p3;
HUD-52646: p2 (2);
HUD-52648: p1 (3); p2 (2);
7420.10G Gbk: 2-2; 2-3 (2); 2-8; 2-9; 3-1; 3-9 (3); 4-4; 4-5 (2); 4-10; 4-14; 4-16; 4-17; 4-22 (3); 5-8; 5-11; 5-21; 5-35 (2); 5-40; 5-46 Ex 5-5; 5-47 Ex 5-5 (3); 5-48 Ex 5-5; 5-49 Ex 5-5; 5-50 Ex 5-5 (2); 5-51 Ex 5-5 (3); 5-52 Ex 5-5 (4); 5-53 Ex 5-5; 8-2; 8-4; 8-7; 8-12; 8-15; 8-21; 9-11; 9-12; 10-2 (2); 10-15; 10-17; 10-21; 10-28; 10-29; 10-48 Ex 10-10; 11-1; 11-11;

11-14; 11-18 (2); 12-4 (2); 12-8; 12-10; 12-11; 12-15 Ex 12-3 (2); 13-3 (2); 14-3; 15-3; 15-4; 15-7 (2); 15-8; 16-1; 16-3 (2); 16-5; 19-2; 19-10; 20-6; 21-3; 21-7; 22-3 (2); 22-7 (2); 22-9; 22-11; 23-7;
PIH Notices: 03-11 (2); 02-27 (13); 02-07; 01-33; 01-15; 01-15 Impr Integ Hbk (6); 01-06 (7); 00-28; 00-24B; 00-11 (3); 00-11A; 95-48 (10); 95-48 Tech Asst (10);
Admin Plan: s1p3; s1p4; s1p5 (3); s2p3; s4p2; s6p8 (3); s6p13; s7p1 (6); s7p3; s7p4; s7p5 (2); s7p6 (2); s7p7 (5); s8p5 (2); s9p3; s14p1; s15p1; s15p2 (2); s15p4 (2); s16p3; s17p1; s17p3; s18p3; s18p5; s20p4; s21p3 (3); s21p5; s21p6; s23p3; s23p6; s23p7; s24p6 (2); s25p1

WRITTEN AGREEMENT 9
24 CFR 982: .4 (2);
HUD-50058Instr: p70; p73 (2);
HUD-52641: p10;
HUD-52641-A: p3;
7420.10G Gbk: 11-1;
Admin Plan: s25p1

WRITTEN COMMENT 1
7420.10G Gbk: 4-16

WRITTEN COMMENTS 3
24 CFR 5: .353 (2); .353

WRITTEN COMMUNICATION 2
24 CFR 5: .216;
7420.10G Gbk: 22-9

WRITTEN COMMUNICATIONS 2
PIH Notices: 95-48; 95-48 Tech Asst

WRITTEN DECISION 3
24 CFR 982: .555;
7420.10G Gbk: 16-5;
Admin Plan: s1p5

WRITTEN DECLARATION............. 2
24 CFR 5: .508; .508

WRITTEN LIST 2
24 CFR 982: .313;
7420.10G Gbk: 8-4

WRITTEN SUMMARIES................. 1
24 CFR 5: .353

WRITTEN SUMMARY 1
7420.10G Gbk: 8-7

WRITTEN VERIFICATION 18
24 CFR 5: .613;
7420.10G Gbk: 5-21; 5-35; 5-51 Ex 5-5; 5-52 Ex 5-5 (2); 12-11; 22-3;
PIH Notices: 01-15; 00-11;
Admin Plan: s1p5; s2p3; s6p13; s7p1 (2); s7p3; s7p5; s7p7

WRITTEN VERIFICATION FORM. 2
PIH Notices: 01-15 Impr Integ Hbk; 00-11A

WRITTEN VERIFICATIONS 1
Admin Plan: s7p1

WRONG-DOING 1
Admin Plan: s20p6

WTW... 101
24 CFR 5: .617;
24 CFR 982: .4 (2); .201 (3); .552;
HUD-50058: p i; p2; p16 (6); p xvi (5); p17 (7); p xvii (3);
HUD-50058Instr: p ii; p1; p2 (8); p3; p9 (4); p10; p11 (2); p13 (4); p17 (2); p19 (3); p59 (12); p60 (5); p62 (4); p63 (12); p76 (2); p77 (2);
7420.10G Gbk: 4-20 (4); 21-16 Ex 21-6;
PIH Notices: 01-15 Impr Integ Hbk; 00-11

X-RAY 1
PIH Notices: 00-23

YARD.. 4
HUD-52580: p6;
HUD-52580-A: p19;
7420.10G Gbk: 9-13 Ex 9-1; 9-15 Ex 9-2

YEAR CONSTRUCTED 4
HUD-52517: p1 (3);
7420.10G Gbk: 8-15

YEAR END 23
24 CFR 982: .102 (7);
7420.10G Gbk: 20-4; 20-5; 20-9; 20-27; 24-1;
PIH Notices: 02-21 (4); 02-06; 01-20; 01-06 (2); 00-49 (2); 00-28

YEAR END STATEMENT 10
24 CFR 982: .102 (7);
7420.10G Gbk: 20-27;
PIH Notices: 02-06; 01-06

YEAR TO DATE 4
PIH Notices: 03-23 (2);
Admin Plan: s7p4; s7p4

YEAR-END 63
7420.10G Gbk: 20-2; 20-3 (2); 20-4; 20-5; 20-7; 20-8 Ex 20-1; 20-9 (3); 20-10 (2); 20-12 Ex 20-2; 20-13; 20-15; 20-18 (2); 20-22; 20-26 (2); 20-27 (4); 20-28; 20-29; 24-1; 24-2; 24-15;
PIH Notices: 03-23 (10); 02-07 (9); 01-06 (2); 00-28 (7); 00-09 (4); 96-65;
Admin Plan: s21p8

YEAR-END STATEMENT 8
7420.10G Gbk: 20-9 (2); 20-10 (2); 20-13; 20-15; 24-1;
PIH Notices: 01-06

YOUNG CHILDREN........................4
24 CFR 982: .401;
7420.10G Gbk: 10-6; 10-15; 10-36 Ex 10-1

YOUTH...10
HUD-50058: p3; p4;
HUD-50058Instr: p14; p15; p36;
PIH Notices: 02-01 (3); 99-52; 99-52

YOUTHBUILD 3
PIH Notices: 02-01; 01-15 Impr Integ Hbk; 99-52

ZERO 110
24 CFR 5: .615;
24 CFR 982: .402; .604; .613; .618;
HUD-50058: p iii (2); p iv (2); p7 (2); p vii;
HUD-50058Instr: p3; p16 (2); p20; p34; p35 (4); p36; p37 (2); p39 (4); p40 (2); p42; p43 (3); p44 (2); p46; p47; p48 (2); p49 (3); p50 (2); p51; p52 (2); p53 (2); p54 (2); p58 (2); p62 (3); p69 (2);
7420.10G Gbk: 2-3; 5-23; 5-24; 5-41 (2); 10-11; 10-16; 12-6; 12-10; 12-11; 19-2;
PIH Notices: 03-23 (2); 02-27 (3); 01-06 (18); 00-24; 00-24A;
Admin Plan: s6p8; s6p13; s7p5; s11p2; s19p1 (3); s21p3; s21p4; s21p7 (3); s21p8; s23p7; s25p5

ZERO INCOME 4
7420.10G Gbk: 5-23;
Admin Plan: s6p8; s7p5; s11p2

ZERO-BEDROOM............................5
24 CFR 982: .503; .604; .608 (2);
Admin Plan: s19p1

ZEROS..6
HUD-50058: p iii; p iv;
HUD-50058Instr: p7 (3); p16

ZONE...2
PIH Notices: 95-48; 95-48 Tech Asst

ZONES...4
24 CFR 982: .626 (2);
PIH Notices: 95-48; 95-48 Tech Asst

ZONING 6
PIH Notices: 95-48 (2); 95-48 Tech Asst (2); s24p5

Friday, October 17, 2003

En español | Text only | Search/index

HUD news
Newsroom
Priorities
About HUD

Homes
Buying
Owning
Selling
Renting
Homeless
Home improvements
HUD homes
Fair housing
FHA refunds
Foreclosure
Consumer info

Communities
About communities
Volunteering
Organizing
Economic development

Working with HUD
Grants
Programs
Contracts
Work online
HUD jobs
Complaints

Resources
Library
Handbooks/ forms
Common questions

Tools
Let's talk
Webcasts
Mailing lists
Contact us
Help

October is Healthy Homes Month!

HUD is working with our Nation's communities to make sure our homes are protected from safety and health hazards, such as lead poisoning. Read how you can keep your home healthy, and learn how HUD is helping your community.

- Healthy Homes Month
- Help yourself to a healthy home
- Lead paint safety guide
- Martinez announces $147 million for healthy homes

HUD Highlights

- Secretary Martinez testifies on Government Sponsored Enterprises
- HUD introduces predatory lending brochure to help consumers avoid loan fraud
- Community Renewal Workshops – $26 Billion in Tax Savings is Available to Businesses
- HUD awards $29.4 million in grants to help local communities redevelop Brownfields and create jobs
- HUD settles case against national lender accused of inflating cost of credit reports
- Martinez applauds House passage of American Dream Downpayment Act
- Administration announces $75 million to provide services to chronically homeless
- Web Clinics for HUD Partners
- National calendar of events
- Daily message

At Your Service

- Learn how to use HUD's website
- Learn how to buy a HUD home
- Learn how to apply for public housing and Section 8
- See if HUD owes you a refund on your FHA loan
- Find a HUD-approved lender in your area
- Talk to a housing counselor
- File a housing discrimination complaint
- Submit Freedom of Information Act (FOIA) request
- Busque información en español
- Learn about the President's agenda to expand homeownership
- More services

Let's Talk

Talk with us and others about issues important to you:

- Current discussions
- Suggest your own topic

Local Information

Find information about homes and communities, organized by state.

Select a State 

Homes for Sale

Find homes fo sale from HUD other federal agencies.

Information For...

Citizens
- Homebuyers
- Senior citizens
- Veterans/Military
- Kids
- Students
- People with disabilities
- Researchers
- Landlords
- Tenants
- Colonias/farmworkers
- Native Americans
- Victims of Discrimination

Housing Industry
- Lenders
- Brokers
- Housing agencies/tribes
- Multifamily industry
- Appraisers
- Health care facilities provide

Other Partners
- Grantees/ non-profits
- Congress/ elected officials
- Small businesses
- Fair housing
- Faith-based Organizations
- Investors
- Auditors/ investigators

Now Playing

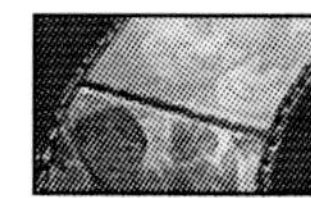

Be a Smart Consumer: Avc Predatory Lenc

Content updated October 14, 2003

 Back to

U.S. Department of Housing and Urban Development
451 7th Street S.W., Washington, DC 20410
Telephone: (202) 708-1112 TTY: (202) 708-1455
Find the address of a HUD office near you

Privacy Statem

HUD HOME WHAT'S NEW SHORT CUTS SEARCH FORMS E-MAIL PRIVACY STATEMENT

about HUDCLIPS

General information about HUDCLIPS. Sign our guest book and tell us what you think . (No user names or passwords are needed!!)

what's new!

List new documents that have been added to HUDCLIPS.
Read through a list of new features, hints, and answers to frequently asked questions.

short cuts

Access HUD Letters and Notices from past years.

Links to more recent information:
Most Recent Two Weeks of FR Notices
Current NOFAs
Super NOFAs
FR Notices Seeking Public Comment
HOC Reference Guide
2003 Mortgagee Letters
2003 PIH Notices
2003 Housing Notices
2003 Fair Housing and Equal Opportunity Notices
2003 CPD Notices
2002 Administrative, CIO, and GNMA Notices
HUD Monitoring Desk Guide--Training Edition (pdf file)
OMB Circulars
Code of Federal Regulations
Catalog of Federal Domestic Assistance (CFDA)
LDP and Debarment Lists
Section 8 Renewal Policy Guide
The Rent and Income Determination Quality Control Guide
Income Limits and Fair Market Rents

library

Directory for all of HUD's official policies and directives including notices, letters, handbooks, Code of Federal Regulations Title 24, US Codes Titles 12 and 42, and more!

forms

Search or browse the **forms** database to locate official forms in PDF and other formats.

Access the most frequently downloaded forms from last month

need assistance?

Send suggestions, ideas, and questions specifically related to HUDCLIPS WWW to HUDCLIPS staff at hudclips@aspensys.com.

Order hard copy of handbooks and guidebooks from HUDs Direct Distribution System.

Send questions to HUD staff

Look up HUD telephone numbers

Learn more about HUD Programs

Important information on third party tracers

Homeownership Center

NAHRO
building communities together

The National Association of Housing and Redevelopment Officials

2003 National Conference and Exhibition
October 19-22, 2003 Dallas, TX
Building a Stronger America
Through Housing, Economic & Community Development

SITE M.

RULES a

About NAHRO
Awards
Calendar
Conferences
HDLI
HOME Program
Join NAHRO
Legislative
Library - Links
Marketplace
Press Room
Professional Development
Programs and Policies
Publications
Regions / Chapters
Seminars
Software

Programs and Policies:

Select area...

Latest News

What's New

Salary and Benefits Information Survey
List of 2003 National Conference Exhibitors

Federal
Latest 1
2003 PI
Latest P
2
Issued:
2003 CP
Latest C
Iss
6/18/
Lat
Docu
post
HUD
HUD

E-mail Member Services

Looking for private capital to build affordable housing, turn around a neighborhood, revitalize your downtown or just need information on how to do it? Click on the NAHRO Access Alliance logo

The NAHRO M
and Suppliers
agency men
supply goods
to the H/C

Click for Info
NAHRO
Access Alliance

MEMBERS

Committees
DirectNews
Federal Register
Jobs
News
Network Central
Member Kiosk
Monitor Online
Presidents Kiosk
Programs and Policies
Small Agencies
Solutions Database

NAHRO Intr
Newest Joi
Part
ONE E
CORP

National Roll of Achievers

Certificates of recognition for public housing, section 8 residents, or other community beneficiaries of HUD programs

NAHRO's Housing Production Program Proposal

Our set of principles for increasing the affordable housing inventory and building partnerships among key local housing providers.

Congressional District Data

Assisted Housing and Community Development Data

Impact of the Loss of the PHDEP on Local Housing Agencies and Low Income Families

The Mill
Hous
Commissio
to Con
Read th

Members
Restructu

For a comprehensive description of current housing conditions and needs in the United States, please see **The**

Conferences on Tape

Audio tapes from our conferences

PHADA

The Public Housing Authorities Directors Association

information representation education participation

Friday, Oct. 17, 2003

2004 Commissioner's Conference, Orlando, FL

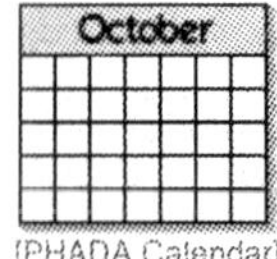

[PHADA Calendar]

E-Mail Alert

Disclaimer

MEMBERSHIP DIRECTORY

JOIN PHADA NOW!

HUD FY '04 BUDGET

Quick Reference

FY 2004 BUDGET
PHADA gives testimony before House subcommittee

The HUD Budget (PDF)
HUD's budget web page

OPERATING FUND
Harvard Public Housing Operating Cost Study

GAO REPORTS
GAO report examines receiverships at HAs (PDF)
GAO Report on HUD Multifamily Housing

QHWRA
Implementation Update, 4/6/01 (PDF)
Title V of H.R. 4194

2003 LEGISLATIVE FORUM
Session presentations from Washington

Housing News from PHADA

may require username and password register here

OCTOBER 17 UPDATE
Representative Nadler (D-NY) calls for additional Section 8 funding

OCTOBER 16 UPDATE
PHADA and other industry groups to hold briefing on Harvard Cost Study

OCTOBER 9 UPDATE
Congressional action on HUD Approp. bill will occur later this month

SEPTEMBER 29 UPDATE
PHADA notifies HUD that problems still remain with PHAS

▸ View all of October's breaking news stories

PHADA Position Paper on FY 2004 HUD Appropriations bill

▸ VIEW FILE (PDF)

HUD Notice implements 2003 Section 8 funding changes

▸ VIEW ARTICLE

Congress passes CR to keep funds flowing into new fiscal year

▸ VIEW ARTICLE

HUD proposes expanded HA discretion in eviction policies

▸ VIEW ARTICLE

To view the Advocate in PDF, you'll need the Acrobat Reader.

▸ View past Advocate issues ...

Rules & Notices

2003 Notices	9/26
Proposed Rules	9/16
Interim Rules	10/1
Final Rules	9/29
NOFAs	4/23
NOFA Awards	1/30
Nat. American	4/10

Red text indicates date of last update

UPDATED 10/15

Jobs in Housing

Public Housing Assessment System

The Advocate

Resource Library

PHADA Comments

select one

PHADA Testimony

select one

PHADA Alliances

Click on the logos below to read about PHADA's alliances.

The Public Housing Technical Resource Center

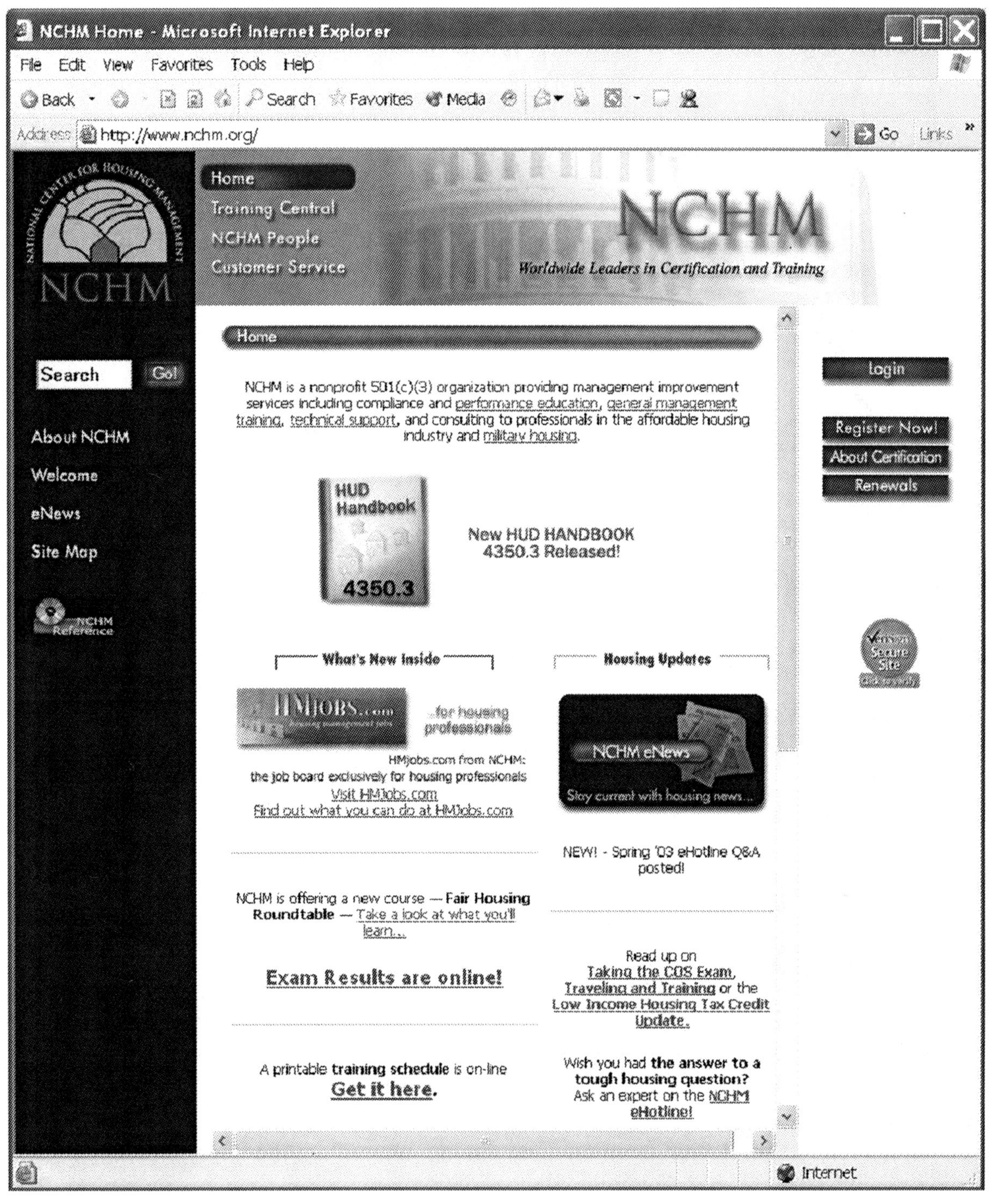
NCHM Home - Microsoft Internet Explorer
File Edit View Favorites Tools Help
Back Search Favorites Media
Address http://www.nchm.org/
Go Links
NATIONAL CENTER FOR HOUSING MANAGEMENT
NCHM
Home
Training Central
NCHM People
Customer Service
NCHM
Worldwide Leaders in Certification and Training
Search Go!
About NCHM
Welcome
eNews
Site Map
NCHM Reference
Home
NCHM is a nonprofit 501(c)(3) organization providing management improvement services including compliance and performance education, general management training, technical support, and consulting to professionals in the affordable housing industry and military housing.
HUD Handbook 4350.3
New HUD HANDBOOK 4350.3 Released!
What's New Inside
HMJOBS.com
...for housing professionals
HMjobs.com from NCHM: the job board exclusively for housing professionals
Visit HMJobs.com
Find out what you can do at HMJobs.com
NCHM is offering a new course — Fair Housing Roundtable — Take a look at what you'll learn...
Exam Results are online!
A printable training schedule is on-line
Get it here.
Housing Updates
NCHM eNews
Stay current with housing news...
NEW! - Spring '03 eHotline Q&A posted!
Read up on Taking the COS Exam, Traveling and Training or the Low Income Housing Tax Credit Update.
Wish you had the answer to a tough housing question? Ask an expert on the NCHM eHotline!
login
Register Now!
About Certification
Renewals
Internet

Breinigsville, PA USA
05 December 2010

250676BV00001B/49/A

9 781593 301286